ENVIRONMENTAL PROTECTION AND HUMAN RIGHTS

With unique scholarly analysis and practical discussion, this book provides a comprehensive introduction to the relationship between environmental protection and human rights that is being formalized into law in many legal systems. By illuminating human rights theory and the institutions that can be employed to meet environmental goals, this book instructs on environmental techniques and procedures that assist in the protection of human rights. The text provides cogent guidance on a growing international jurisprudence on the promotion and protection of human rights in relation to the environment that has been developed by international and regional human rights bodies and tribunals. It explores a rich body of case law that continues to develop within states on the environmental dimension of the rights to life, to health, and to public participation and access to information. Five compelling contemporary case studies are included online that implicate human rights and the environment, ranging from large dam projects to the creation of a new human right to a clean environment.

Donald K. Anton has been practicing and teaching international law and environmental law since 1988. Since 2000, he has been a member of the faculty of the Australian National University College of Law, where he teaches international environmental law, international law, marine and coastal law, international climate law, and environmental law. He is the author or coauthor of *International Environmental Law: Cases, Materials, and Problems* (2007); *International Law: Cases and Materials* (2005); *International Law: Politics, Values, and Functions* (1998); and *A Question of Justice Challenge: Global Environmental Protection* (1996).

Dinah L. Shelton is the Manatt/Ahn Professor of International Law at the George Washington University Law School and a member of the Inter-American Commission on Human Rights of the Organization of American States. Shelton is the author or editor of three prize-winning books, *Protecting Human Rights in the Americas* (coauthored with Thomas Buergenthal, 1982), *Remedies in International Human Rights Law* (2006), and the three-volume *Encyclopedia of Genocide and Crimes Against Humanity* (2004) as well as author of *International Environmental Law* (2004) and other publications in the fields of human rights and environmental law. She was awarded the Elisabeth Haub Prize for Environmental Law.

Environmental Protection and Human Rights

Donald K. Anton
Australia National University
College of Law

Dinah L. Shelton
George Washington University
School of Law

CAMBRIDGE
UNIVERSITY PRESS

CAMBRIDGE UNIVERSITY PRESS
Cambridge, New York, Melbourne, Madrid, Cape Town,
Singapore, São Paulo, Delhi, Mexico City

Cambridge University Press
32 Avenue of the Americas, New York, NY 10013-2473, USA

www.cambridge.org
Information on this title: www.cambridge.org/9780521747103

First published 2011
Reprinted 2012

A catalog record for this publication is available from the British Library.

Library of Congress Cataloging in Publication Data

Anton, Donald K.
Environmental protection and human rights / Donald K. Anton, Dinah Shelton.
  p. cm.
Includes bibliographical references and index.
ISBN 978-0-521-76638-8 (hardback) – ISBN 978-0-521-74710-3 (pbk.) 1. Environmental law,
International. 2. Human rights. I. Shelton, Dinah. II. Title.
K3585.A58 2011
344.04´6–dc22   2010037108

ISBN 978-0-521-76638-8 Hardback
ISBN 978-0-521-74710-3 Paperback

To Louis Henkin, teacher, colleague, and friend; and to Joseph Sax, who generously supported my first attempt at international environmental advocacy. They have led the struggle to defend human rights and protect the environment.

– DKA

To Connor Dillon, Nikolas Leith, and Claire Jillian Robinson, whose right to enjoy the wonders of the earth and transmit the same to their descendants must be preserved.

– DLS

Brief Contents

Contents

Acknowledgments

As with all publications, this text could not have been produced without the assistance and support of many individuals and institutions. It rests on the shoulders of our students, our colleagues, our able research assistants, and the law schools that are our place of work and in which we have taught these materials in preparing the text. Most important in the later stages of preparing the manuscript, we must thank Nick Bryner, George Washington University class of 2012, for his invaluable assistance in copyediting, obtaining permissions, and chasing down citations. His work was exemplary in promptness and quality, for which we are boundlessly grateful.

The materials herein have been used in teaching courses involving human rights and the environment at the University of Alabama School of Law, the Australian National University College of Law (ANU), the George Washington University Law School, the University of Auckland Faculty of Law, the University of Michigan Law School, the United Nations Institute for Training and Research, and the Vermont Law School. We are grateful to all these institutions for the opportunity to teach the subject matter and to our students in all of the courses for lessons about the material and sound feedback.

Don Anton is deeply grateful to the following colleagues for invaluable input and feedback: John Bonine, Hilary Charlesworth, Eileen Gauana, Svitlana Kravchenko, Bob Kuehn, Penelope Mathew, Cliff Rechtschaffen, and Matthew Zagor. Don particularly benefited from extensive collaboration with John Bonine and Svitlana Kravchenko on many of the issues raised by this text and the experience of coteaching a course on environmental justice and human rights with Bob Kuehn at the University of Alabama and the ANU, in which many of these materials were employed. Over many years, Pena Mathew has generously provided Don with important human rights insights.

Dinah Shelton is extremely grateful to Klaus Bosselmann and Prue Taylor for their hospitality and always-helpful discussions during her visit to the University of Auckland. She would also like to express deep appreciation to Daniel Taillant, Stephen Humphreys, Astrid Puentes, Dan Magraw, and other colleagues for their questions, comments, and contributions during this work in progress, especially on the issue of climate change and human rights. Special thanks to Günther Handl and Alan Boyle for their stimulating and insightful skepticism of some of the issues raised in these materials. She also derived great benefits from talks and seminars on the environment and human rights given at the University of Chicago, Harvard Law School, Universidad Nacional Autónoma de México, and Northwestern University.

We are grateful for the institutional support we have received from our home law schools, the Australian National University College of Law and the George Washington University Law School. Don Anton thanks Evan Caminker, dean of the University of Michigan, for generously supporting this project and for providing the resources to employ three impressive and able research assistants: Thomas Carter Seabaugh, Cara Wulf, and Ashley Tan. All three performed at a very high professional level. Don Anton is also thankful to his friends and colleagues at his home institution, the ANU College of Law, for their generous support and for the collegial, intellectual atmosphere that is always present.

Finally, we express our gratitude to our families. Don would like to thank his parents, Don and Aurora Anton, for being first and best teachers, and his family, Pene Mathew and Tom Anton, for their support and understanding. Dinah would like to thank her mother for providing the early freedom to roam outdoors and her children and grandchildren for ensuring that she still gets outside every so often.

We are grateful to the following authors and publishers for permission to reprint the extracts found herein. Any errors that may appear in the extracts are the responsibility of the editors of the present volume.

Philip Alston, "Reconceiving the U.N. Human Rights Regime: Challenges Confronting the New U.N. Human Rights Council," 7 *Melb. J. Int'l L.* 185, 186–88, 191–93 (2006), reprinted with permission of the author and *Melbourne Journal of International Law.*

Michael R. Anderson, "Human Rights Approaches to Environmental Protection: An Overview," in *Human Rights Approaches to Environmental Protection* 3–10 (A. Boyle & M. Anderson eds., 1996), reprinted with permission of Koninklijke BRILL NV.

Bank Information Center, "Multilateral Development Banks and Burma" 1–7 (October 2004), reprinted with permission of the Bank Information Center.

Bank Information Center, "Rebuked by Internal Investigation, World Bank Plans to Do More in DRC Forest Sector, but Will It Do Better?" (Jan. 16, 2008), reprinted with permission of the Bank Information Center.

Upendra Baxi, "Voices of Suffering, Fragmented Universality, and the Future of Human Rights," in *The Future of International Human Rights* 172–89 (Burns Weston & Stephen P. Marks eds., 1999), reprinted with permission of Koninklijke BRILL NV.

Nathalie Bernasconi-Osterwalder & David Hunter, "Democratizing Multilateral Development Banks," in *The New "Public": The Globalization of Public Participation* 161–62 (Carl Bruch ed., 2002), Copyright © 2002 Environmental Law Institute®, Washington, DC, reprinted with permission of ELI®.

Francoise Bouchet-Saulnier, "Myanmar – Responsibility to Protect?," Doctors Without Borders, May 21, 2008, available at http://www.doctorswithoutborders.org/publications/article.cfm?id=2740&cat=ideas-opinions, reprinted with permission of Doctors Without Borders/Médicins Sans Frontières.

Antoine Bouvier, "Protection of the Natural Environment in Time of Armed Conflict," 285 *Int'l Rev. Red Cross* 567–78 (1991), reprinted with permission of *International Review of the Red Cross.*

Thomas Buergenthal, "The Evolving International Human Rights System," 100 *Am. J. Int'l L.* 783, 792–801 (2006), reprinted with permission of *American Society of International Law.*

Paolo G. Carozza, "Human Dignity and Judicial Interpretation of Human Rights: A Reply," 19 *Eur. J. Int'l L.* 931–44 (2008), reprinted with permission of the author and *European Journal of International Law.*

Deborah Z. Cass, "Navigating the Newstream: Recent Critical Scholarship in International Law," 65 *Nordic J. Int'l L.* 341–45 (1996), reprinted with permission of *Nordic Journal of International Law.*

Hilary Charlesworth, "Feminist Ambivalence About International Law," 11 *Int'l Legal Theory* 1, 1–8 (2005), reprinted with permission of the author and the ASIL Interest Group on the Theories of International Law.

Coalition for an Effective African Court on Human and Peoples Rights, "About the African Court," reprinted with permission of the African Court Coalition/La Coalition pour une Cour Africaine des Droits de l'Homme et des Peuples/Coligação para um Tribunal Africano Eficaz na Defesa dos Direitos Humanos e dos Povos (also available in Arabic), reprinted with permission of the Coalition for an Effective African Court on Human and Peoples Rights.

Roberta Cohen, "Reconciling R2P with IDP Protection," vol. 2 *Global Responsibility to Protect* 15 (2010), reprinted with permission of CCC.

*Peter Coles, "Large Dams – The End of an Era?," *UNESCO Courier*, April 2000, at 10–11.

*Peter Coles & Lyla Bavadam, "A Barrage of Protest," *UNESCO Courier*, April 2000, at 11–13.

Matthew Craven, *The International Covenant on Economic, Social, and Cultural Rights: A Perspective on Its Development* 8–16 (1995), reprinted with permission of the author.

Matthew Craven, "The Protection of Economic, Social, and Cultural Rights Under the Inter-American System of Human Rights," in *The Inter-American System of Human Rights* 300–06 (D.J. Harris & S. Livingstone eds., 1998), reprinted with permission of the author and Oxford University Press.

Jack Donnelly, "Cultural Relativism and Universal Human Rights." 6 *Human Rights Quarterly* 400, 401, 410 (1984). © 1984 The Johns Hopkins University Press. Reprinted with permission of The Johns Hopkins University Press.

Michael Ewing-Chow, "First Do No Harm: Myanmar Trade Sanctions and Human Rights," 5 *Nw. Univ. J. Int'l Hum. Rts.* 153, 154–58 (2007). Reprinted by special permission of Northwestern University School of Law, *Journal of International Human Rights*, and the author.

Elizabeth Ferris, "Natural Disaster- and Conflict-Induced Displacement: Similarities, Differences, and Inter-Connections" (Mar. 27, 2008, Brookings Institution), *available at* http://www.brookings.edu/speeches/2008/0327_displacement_ferris.aspx. Reprinted with permission of the author.

Friends of the Earth International, "REDD Myths: A Critical Review of Proposed Mechanisms to Reduce Emissions from Deforestation and Degradation in Developing Countries," *Friends of the Earth*, December 2008, at 5–8, reprinted with permission of Friends of the Earth International, www.foei.org.

Emanuela-Chiara Gillard, ICRC Legal Advisor, International Association of Refugee Law Judges, World Conference Stockholm, 21–23 April 2005, in *The Asylum Process and the Rule of Law* 199–203, reprinted with permission of the International Association of Refugee Law Judges.

Ethan Goffman, "Environmental Refugees: How Many, How Bad?," ProQuest – Discovery Guide Series (June 2006), reprinted with permission of ProQuest.

Anita Margrethe Halvorssen, "Book Review, *Changing Course: A Global Business Perspective on Development and the Environment*," by Stephen Schmidheiny, with the Business Council for Sustainable Development (MIT Press, 1992), 4 *Colo. J. Int'l Envtl. L. & Pol'y* 241, 243–47 (1993), reprinted with permission of the author and *Colorado Journal of International Environmental Law and Policy*.

Günther Handl, "Human Rights and the Protection of the Environment," in *Economic, Social, and Cultural Rights: A Textbook* 303–15 (A. Eide, C. Krause, & A. Rosas eds., 2d ed., 2001), reprinted with permission of the publisher Koninklijke BRILL NV.

Laurence R. Helfer & Anne-Marie Slaughter, "Toward a Theory of Effective International Adjudication," 107 *Yale L.J.* 273, 338–43 (1997), reprinted with permission of *Yale Law Journal*.

Louis Henkin, *The Age of Rights* (1990), reprinted with permission of Columbia University Press.

Richard L. Herz, "Litigating Environmental Abuses Under the Alien Tort Claims Act: A Practical Assessment," 40 *Va. J. Int'l L.* 545, 547–50 (2000), reprinted with permission of the author and *Virginia Journal of International Law*.

Stephen Hodgson, *Modern Water Rights: Theory and Practice*, FAO Legislative Study No. 92 (2006), at 9–18, 37–41, 43–48, 88–89, 93–102, reprinted with permission of the Food and Agriculture Organization of the United Nations.

Rhoda E. Howard, "Dignity, Community, and Human Rights," in *Human Rights in Cross-Cultural Perspectives: A Quest for Consensus* 81–84, 86–87, 91 (A. An-Na'im ed., 1991), reprinted with permission of the University of Pennsylvania Press.

*Sources used in the online case studies.

Kevin Huyser, "Sustainable Development: Rhetoric and Reform at the World Bank," 4 *Transnat'l L. & Contemp. Probs.* 253, 255–70 (1994), reprinted with permission of *Transnational Law and Contemporary Problems*.

International Labour Organization, "Tripartite Declaration of Principles Concerning Multinational Enterprises and Social Responsibility (as amended in 2000)," *ILO Official Bulletin*, Vol. LXXXIII, 2000, Ser. A, No. 3, at 1–3, 6–7. Copyright © 2006 International Labour Organization, reprinted with permission.

Eugene Kamenka, "Human Rights, Peoples' Rights," in *The Rights of Peoples* 127–28 (James Crawford ed., 1988).

Benedict Kingsbury, "Reconciling Five Competing Conceptual Structures of Indigenous Peoples' Claims in International and Comparative Law," in *Peoples' Rights* (Philip Alston ed., 2001), reprinted with permission of the editor and Oxford University Press.

Karl Klare, "Legal Theory and Democratic Reconstruction," 25 *U. Brit. Colum. L. Rev.* 69, 97–98, 100–01 (1991), reprinted with permission of the author and *University of British Columbia Law Review*.

*John H. Knox, "Linking Human Rights and Climate Change at the United Nations," 33 *Harv. Envtl. L. Rev.* 477, 477–79, 484–95 (2009), reprinted with permission of *Harvard Environmental Law Review*.

Harold Hongju Koh, "Transnational Public Law Litigation," 100 *Yale L.J.* 2347–71 (1991), reprinted with permission of the author and *Yale Law Journal*.

Linda A. Malone, "The Responsibility to Protect Haiti," *ASIL Insight*, Mar. 10, 2010 (No. 7) (footnotes omitted), *available at* http://www.asil.org/files/insight100310pdf, reprinted with permission of the American Society of International Law.

Millennium Ecosystem Assessment, *Ecosystems and Human Well-Being: Synthesis* v, 1–2, 4–6, 9–15, 17–18, 20–24 (World Resources Institute 2005), reprinted with permission of World Resources Institute.

*Narmada River Map, reprinted with permission of Eureka Cartography.

Roderick Frazier Nash, *The Rights of Nature*. © 1989 by the Board of Regents of the University of Wisconsin System, reprinted with permission of The University of Wisconsin Press.

Eric W. Orts, "The Legitimacy of Multinational Corporations," in *Progressive Corporate Law* 247–59, 265–66 (Lawrence E. Mitchell ed., 1995), reprinted with permission of the Perseus Books Group.

Hari M. Osofsky, "Learning from Environmental Justice: A New Model for International Environmental Rights," 24 *Stan. Envtl. L.J.* 71, 78–87 (2005), reprinted with permission of the author and *Stanford Environmental Law Journal*.

Stephanie Peatling, "People First, River Second . . . ," *Sydney Morning Herald*, November 8, 2006, at 1, reprinted with permission of the author and *Sydney Morning Herald*.

Ole W. Pedersen, "European Environmental Human Rights and Environmental Rights: A Long Time Coming?," 21 *Geo. Int'l Envtl. L. Rev.* 73, 108–11 (2008), reprinted with permission of the author.

A.H. Robertson & J.G. Merrills, *Human Rights in the World: An Introduction to the Study of the International Protection of Human Rights* 257–59 (3d ed., Manchester University Press, 1989), reprinted with permission of the publisher.

Luis E. Rodriguez-Rivera, "Is the Human Right to Environment Recognized Under International Law? It Depends on the Source," 12 *Colo. J. Int'l Envtl. L. & Pol'y* 1, 31–37 (2001), reprinted with permission of the author and *Colorado Journal of International Environmental Law and Policy*.

Philippe Sands, *Principles of International Environmental Law* 294–97 (2003), ISBN 0521817943, reprinted with permission of the author.

John Scanlon, Angela Cassar, & Noémi Nemes, *Water as a Human Right?* 9–10 (IUCN Policy and Law Paper No. 51, 2004), reprinted with permission of International Union for Conservation of Nature.

*Sources used in the online case studies.

Oscar Schachter, "Human Dignity as a Normative Concept," 77 *Am. J. Int'l L.* 848, 848–50 (1983), reprinted with permission of the American Society of International Law.

Christopher H. Schroeder, "Lost in Translation: What Environmental Regulation Does That Tort Cannot Duplicate," 41 *Washburn L.J.* 583 (2002), reprinted with permission of the author.

Dinah Shelton, "Environmental Rights," *in Peoples' Rights* 187–94 (P. Alston ed., 2001), reprinted with permission of the author, editor, and Oxford University Press.

Dinah Shelton, "The Promise of Regional Human Rights Systems," in *The Future of International Human Rights* 353–61, 365–69 (Burns Weston & Stephen P. Marks eds., 1999), reprinted with permission of Koninklijke BRILL NV.

Jerome J. Shestack, "The Philosophical Foundations of Human Rights," *in Human Rights: Concepts and Standards* 33–35 (Janusz Symonides ed., 2000), Ashgate, Gower, & Lund Humphries Publishing. Reprinted with permission of the publisher.

Henry Steiner, "The Youth of Rights," 104 *Harv. L. Rev.* 917, 929–31 (1991) (Book Review of Louis Henkin, *The Age of Rights* (1990)), reprinted with permission of the author and the *Harvard Law Review.*

Ralph Steinhardt, "Laying One Bankrupt Critique to Rest: *Sosa v. Alvarez Machain* and the Future of Human Rights Litigation in U.S. Courts," 57 *Vand. L. Rev.* 2241, 2283–87 (2004), reprinted with permission of the author.

Christopher Stone, "Should Trees Have Standing? Towards Legal Rights for Natural Objects," 45 *S. Cal. L. Rev.* 450, 464–74 (1972), reprinted with permission of the author.

Cass Sunstein, "Rights and Their Critics," 70 *Notre Dame L. Rev.* 727, 730–48 (1995), reprinted with permission © by *Notre Dame Law Review*, University of Notre Dame.

Imre Szabo, "Historical Foundations of Human Rights and Subsequent Developments," in 1 *The International Dimensions of Human Rights* 11–16 (Karel Vasak ed., © Greenwood Press 1982), reprinted with permission of ABC-CLIO LLC.

Ruti Teitel, "Human Rights Genealogy," 66 *Fordham L. Rev.* 309–10 (1997), reprinted with permission of the author and *Fordham Law Review.*

J. Shand Watson, *Theory and Reality in the International Protection of Human Rights* 273–78, 286 (1999), reprinted with permission of Koninklijke BRILL NV.

United Nations Development Program, *Beyond Scarcity: Power, Poverty, and the Global Water Crisis, Human Development Report 2006*, at v–vi, 3, 7, 14–17, 19–20. © 2006 by the United Nations Development Program, Palgrave Macmillan, publishers. Reproduced with permission of Palgrave Macmillan.

United Nations Environment Programme, *From Conflict to Peacebuilding: The Role of Natural Resources and the Environment*, UNEP, Consultation Draft, September 2008, reprinted with permission of the United Nations Environment Programme.

United Nations Environment Programme, *Desk Study on the Environment in Iraq* (2003) extracts reprinted with permission of the United Nations Environment Programme.

United Nations Environment Programme, "Managing the Kosovo Refugee Crisis: Environmental Consequences," in UNEP, *Post-Conflict Environmental Assessment – Albania* 38–45, reprinted with permission of the United Nations Environment Programme.

David Weissbrodt & Muria Kruger, "Norms on the Responsibilities of Transnational Corporations and Other Business Enterprises with Regard to Human Rights," 97 *Am. J. Int'l L.* 901, 907, 912–13, 921 (2003), reprinted with permission of the American Society of International Law.

*World Commission on Dams, *Dams and Development: A New Framework for Decision-Making*, The Report of the World Commission on Dams: An Overview (Nov. 16, 2000), http://www.dams .org.

*World Wildlife Fund, Dams – Blessing and Curse?

*Sources used in the online case studies.

Abbreviations

ACWC	ASEAN Commission on the Promotion and Protection of the Rights of Women and Children
ASEAN	Association of South East Asian Nations
ATS/ATCA	Alien Tort Statute/Alien Tort Claims Act
AU	African Union
BIT	Bilateral investment treaty
BP	Bank Procedure (World Bank)
CAO	Compliance adviser ombudsman (World Bank Group)
CAT	Convention Against Torture and Other Forms of Cruel, Inhuman, or Degrading Treatment or Punishment
CBD	Convention on Biological Diversity
CCPR	U.N. Human Right Committee
CED	Committee on Enforced Disappearances
CEDAW	Convention on the Elimination of All Forms of Discrimination Against Women
CERD/UNCERD	International Convention on the Elimination of All Forms of Racial Discrimination
CESCR	Committee on Economic, Social, and Cultural Rights
CHR	Commission on Human Rights (replaced by the Human Rights Council)
CITES	Convention on International Trade in Endangered Species of Wild Fauna and Flora
CMW	Convention on the Protection of the Rights of All Migrant Workers and Members of Their Families
CPED	Convention on the Protection of All Persons from Enforced Disappearance
CRC	Convention on the Rights of the Child
CRPD	Convention on the Rights of Persons with Disabilities
CSD	Commission on Sustainable Development
CTRPD	Committee on the Rights of Persons with Disabilities
EBRD	European Bank for Reconstruction and Development
ECHR	European Convention for the Protection of Human Rights and Fundamental Freedoms
ECHR	European Court of Human Rights
ECOSOC	U.N. Economic and Social Council
EIA	environmental impact assessment

EIB	European Investment Bank
ENMOD	Convention on Military or Any Other Hostile Use of Environmental Modification Techniques
ESA	Endangered Species Act (U.S.)
ESC	European Social Charter
ESC Committee	U.N. Committee on Economic, Social, and Cultural Rights
EU	European Union
FAO	Food and Agriculture Organization
GA	U.N. General Assembly
GMOs	genetically modified organisms
HRC	U.N. Human Rights Council
IACHR	Inter-American Commission on Human Rights
IAEA	International Atomic Energy Agency
IBRD	International Bank for Reconstruction and Development
ICCPR	International Covenant on Civil and Political Rights
ICESCR	International Covenant on Economic, Social, and Cultural Rights
ICISS	International Commission on Intervention and State Sovereignty
ICJ	International Court of Justice
ICRC	International Committee of the Red Cross
ICSID	International Centre for Settlement of Investment Disputes
IDA	International Development Association
IDPs	Internally Displaced Persons
IFC	International Finance Corporation
ILC	International Law Commission
ILO	International Labour Organization
IMF	International Monetary Fund
IPCC	Intergovernmental Panel on Climate Change
IUCN	International Union for Conservation of Nature
NGO	nongovernmental organization
MA	Millennium Ecosystem Assessment
MDBs	Multilateral Development Banks
MDGs	Millennium Development Goals
MEA	Multilateral Environmental Agreement
MIGA	Multilateral Investment Guarantee Agency
MWC	Committee on the Protection of the Rights of All Migrant Workers and Members of Their Families
NAAEC	North American Agreement on Environmental Cooperation
NAFTA	North American Free Trade Agreement
OAS	Organization of American States
OECD	Organisation for Economic Co-operation and Development
OHCHR	Office of the U.N. High Commissioner for Human Rights
OP	Operational Policy (World Bank)
OSCE	Organization for Security and Co-operation in Europe
PIC	Prior Informed Consent
REDD	Reducing Emissions from Deforestation and Forest Degradation
SC	U.N. Security Council
SG	U.N. Secretary-General
UDHR	Universal Declaration of Human Rights

UNCC	U.N. Compensation Commission
UNCED	U.N. Conference on Environment and Development
UNCLOS	U.N. Convention on the Law of the Sea
UNECE	U.N. Economic Commission for Europe
UNEP	U.N. Environment Programme
UNESCO	U.N. Education, Scientific, and Cultural Organization
UNFCCC	U.N. Framework Convention on Climate Change
UNFF	U.N. Forum on Forests
UNIOSIL	U.N. Integrated Office in Sierra Leone
USTDA	United States Trade and Development Agency
VCLT	Vienna Convention on the Law of Treaties
WBG	World Bank Group
WHO	World Health Organization
WSSD	World Summit on Sustainable Development

Table of Cases

Cases

Treaties, Declarations, and Resolutions

Statutes and Constitutions

1 Law and the Environment

I. Introduction

Environmental protection emerged as a general public concern in the 1960s, although laws to counter specific local problems like urban air pollution can be found as early as the fourteenth century, when Edward I prohibited the burning of coal in open furnaces in London. More recently, as knowledge has spread about transboundary and global environmental problems, the public has begun seeking widespread preventive and remedial action to ensure that natural conditions remain conducive to life and to human well-being.

Policy makers responding to these demands increasingly understand that environmental protection must be addressed in a holistic and expansive manner. Local problems cannot be separated from national, regional, or even global conditions. As a result, the interface of domestic (both national and local) and international environmental law has rapidly expanded. Such an evolution corresponds to the physical reality of a biosphere composed of interdependent elements that do not recognize political boundaries and the increasingly transnational character of the human activities that harm nature and its processes. Internationalization of markets and the emergence of a global civil society present new opportunities as well as new challenges. Communication networks make possible more rapid knowledge of the existence and scope of environmental problems, but the widespread movement of persons and products may also contribute to those problems, for example, through the introduction of alien species and the spread of pollutants. Overconsumption threatens to exhaust living and nonliving resources, whereas rising greenhouse gas emissions detrimentally modify the global climate. Population concentrations strain resources and create levels of pollution beyond the earth's assimilative capacity. New problems resulting from technology and changes in the nature or scope of human activities are constantly being identified, such as the introduction of unprocessed endocrine-disrupting pharmaceuticals into fresh water. As a consequence, there is a constant need to develop and revise the national and international legal framework.

The geographic scope of environmental law is global, but so are its interdisciplinary requirements. Beyond such obvious topics as water law and endangered species legislation, laws and policies concerning energy, trade, investment, transportation, and consumer protection also affect environmental conditions. At the center of the problems, impacts, and solutions are individuals with rights guaranteed by national and international law. The interface between human rights and the environment is the focus of this book.

The first chapter introduces the problems posed, that is, the environmental stresses that threaten present and future populations throughout the world and the anthropogenic origins of those stresses. The chapter then turns to the various legal approaches that are often used to prevent and remedy environmental degradation, from property law concepts of nuisance and public trust to rights-based approaches. The chapter also provides a brief introduction to international environmental law and its sources.

A. *Defining the Environment and Its Characteristics*

A legal definition of the environment serves to delineate the scope of the subject, to determine the application of legal rules, and to establish the extent of liability when harm occurs. The word *environment* is borrowed from the French word *environner*, which means "to encircle." It applies broadly to all that surrounds a central point; thus, *environment* can include the aggregate of natural, social, and cultural conditions that influence the life of an individual or community. As such, environmental problems can be deemed to include such problems as traffic congestion, crime, noise, and poverty. Geographically, *environment* can refer to a limited area or encompass the entire planet, including the atmosphere and stratosphere. Consider the scope of the following definitions:

> "Environment": a complex of natural and anthropogenic factors and elements that are mutually interrelated and affect the ecological equilibrium and the quality of life, human health, the cultural and historical heritage and the landscape.
>
> Sec. 1(1) Environmental Protection Act (Supp.) (1991), Bulgaria

> "Environment": that part of nature which is or could be influenced by human activity.
>
> Art. 5(1) (1), Environmental Protection Act of June 1993, Slovenia

> "Environment" includes
>
> - natural resources both biotic and abiotic, such as air, water, soil, fauna and flora and the interactions between the same factors;
> - property which forms part of the cultural heritage;
> - the characteristics aspects of landscape.
>
> Art. 2(1), Convention on Civil Liability for Damage Resulting from Activities Dangerous to the Environment (Lugano, June 21, 1993)

> The sum of all external conditions affecting the life, development and survival of an organism.
>
> U.S. Environmental Protection Agency, www.epa.gov/OCEPAterm,
> *CERCLA, 42 U.S. Code ch. 103, § 101(8)*

The definitions encompass and reflect realities that shape environmental policy and law. First, environmental protection measures must take into account the laws of nature. The science of ecology recognizes that all environmental milieu (air, water, soil) and all species are interdependent. Harm to one aspect of the environment is thus likely to have broad and unforeseen consequences on other dimensions of nature, including human well-being. A toxic chemical spill at a gold mine, for example, not only will pollute the nearby soil but also can enter streams and rivers, be transported to the sea, and enter the food chain through absorption by plants and animals. Another reality is that many degraded or exploited resources are nonrenewable and thus exhaustible; even living resources may become extinct. Substances that in isolation may be benign can combine with others to produce new and unforeseen harms.

Planning and regulation is made more difficult by scientific uncertainty about many aspects of the physical world. Although there is an unprecedented amount of knowledge today, no one knows the ecological processes over the 5-billion-year history of the earth with sufficient detail and understanding to be able to predict all the consequences and causal relationships of various human activities. Scientific uncertainty thus often attends issues of the nature and scope of adverse environmental impacts of human activities. Exacerbating the uncertainty, damage often is perceived only years after the causative actions occur. It becomes difficult to determine future risk and to develop appropriate policies to avoid long-term harm. Debate centers on whether to adopt policies that assume that harmful consequences will occur unless activities are proven safe or whether to take a less cautious approach, knowing that some environmental consequences will be irreversible and may be life threatening.

All human activities have an impact on the environment. Each individual has an "ecological footprint" that represents the sum of that person's resource use and contributions to pollution. The ecological footprints of individuals vary considerably both within states and from one region of the world to another. Taken together, however, these impacts mean that environmental degradation generally stems from one of two main causes:

1. Use of resources at unsustainable levels
2. Contamination of the environment through pollution and waste at levels beyond the capacity of the environment to absorb them or render them harmless

These realities make it difficult to establish the limits of environmental law as an independent legal field; indeed, they imply the integration of environmental protection into all areas of law and policy.

Questions and Discussion

1. Under each of the foregoing definitions, what range of consequences would a proponent have to evaluate in a legally required environmental impact assessment prior to damming a river for hydroelectric power or creating a public park?
2. Do the definitions reflect an emphasis on human well-being, or are they seeking to protect nature independently of its utility to humans? Would environmental law include human rights issues under these definitions?

B. State of the Planet

Millennium Ecosystem Assessment
Ecosystems and Human Well-Being: Synthesis
1, 9–15, 17–18, 20–22, 23–24 (World Resources Inst., 2005)
(footnotes, figures and tables omitted)

[The U.N. secretary-general Kofi Annan called for preparation of the Millennium Ecosystem Assessment (MA) in 2000 in his report to the U.N. General Assembly, *We the Peoples: The Role of the United Nations in the 21st Century*. With the support of member states, the United Nations initiated the MA in 2001, with the secretariat coordinated by the United Nations Environment Programme. A governing board included representatives of international institutions, governments, business, nongovernmental organizations (NGOs), and indigenous peoples; the work ultimately involved more than 1,360 experts worldwide. The objective of the MA was to assess the consequences of ecosystem change for human well-being and to establish the scientific basis for actions needed to enhance the conservation and sustainable use of ecosystems and their contributions to human well-being. The MA findings are contained in five technical volumes and six synthesis reports on the world's ecosystems and the services they provide. The following extract is from one of the synthesis reports. – Eds.]

...An *ecosystem* is a dynamic complex of plant, animal, and microorganism communities and the nonliving environment interacting as a functional unit.... *Ecosystem services* are the benefits people obtain from ecosystems. These include *provisioning services* such as food, water, timber, and fiber; *regulating services* that affect climate, floods, disease, wastes, and water quality; *cultural services* that provide recreational, aesthetic, and spiritual benefits; and *supporting services* such as soil formation, photosynthesis, and nutrient cycling.... Although the MA emphasizes the linkages between ecosystems and human well-being, it recognizes that the actions people take that influence ecosystems result not just from concern about human well-being but also from considerations of the intrinsic value of species and ecosystems. Intrinsic value is the value of something in and for itself, irrespective of its utility for someone else.

Everyone in the world depends completely on Earth's ecosystems and the services they provide, such as food, water, disease management, climate regulation, spiritual fulfillment, and aesthetic enjoyment. Over the past 50 years, humans have changed these ecosystems more rapidly and extensively than in any comparable period of time in human history, largely to meet rapidly growing demands for food, fresh water, timber, fiber, and fuel. This transformation of the planet has contributed to substantial net gains in human well-being and economic development. But not all regions and groups of people have benefited from this process – in fact, many have been harmed. Moreover, the full costs associated with these gains are only now becoming apparent....

Finding #1: [Ecosystem Change in the Last 50 Years]

The structure and functioning of the world's ecosystems changed more rapidly in the second half of the twentieth century than at any time in human history.

- More land was converted to cropland in the 30 years after 1950 than in the 150 years between 1700 and 1850. Cultivated systems (areas where at least 30% of the landscape is in croplands, shifting cultivation, confined livestock production, or freshwater aquaculture) now cover one quarter of Earth's terrestrial surface.
- Approximately 20% of the world's coral reefs were lost and an additional 20% degraded in the last several decades of the twentieth century, and approximately 35% of mangrove area was lost during this time (in countries for which sufficient data exist, which encompass about half of the area of mangroves).
- The amount of water impounded behind dams quadrupled since 1960, and three to six times as much water is held in reservoirs as in natural rivers. Water withdrawals from rivers and lakes doubled since 1960; most water use (70% worldwide) is for agriculture.
- Since 1960, flows of reactive (biologically available) nitrogen in terrestrial ecosystems have doubled, and flows of phosphorus have tripled. More than half of all the synthetic nitrogen fertilizer, which was first manufactured in 1913, ever used on the planet has been used since 1985.
- Since 1750, the atmospheric concentration of carbon dioxide has increased by about 32% (from about 280 to 376 parts per million in 2003), primarily due to the combustion of fossil fuels and land use changes. Approximately 60% of that increase (60 parts per million) has taken place since 1959.

Humans are fundamentally, and to a significant extent irreversibly, changing the diversity of life on Earth, and most of these changes represent a loss of biodiversity.

- More than two thirds of the area of 2 of the world's 14 major terrestrial biomes and more than half of the area of 4 other biomes had been converted by 1990, primarily to agriculture.[1]
- Across a range of taxonomic groups, either the population size or range or both of the majority of species is currently declining.
- The distribution of species on Earth is becoming more homogenous; in other words, the set of species in any one region of the world is becoming more similar to the set in other regions primarily as a result of introductions of species, both intentionally and inadvertently in association with increased travel and shipping.
- The number of species on the planet is declining. Over the past few hundred years, humans have increased the species extinction rate by as much as 1,000 times over background rates typical over the planet's history (*medium certainty*). Some 10–30% of mammal, bird, and amphibian species are currently threatened with extinction (*medium to high certainty*). Freshwater ecosystems tend to have the highest proportion of species threatened with extinction.
- Genetic diversity has declined globally, particularly among cultivated species.

Most changes to ecosystems have been made to meet a dramatic growth in the demand for food, water, timber, fiber, and fuel.

Some ecosystem changes have been the inadvertent result of activities unrelated to the use of ecosystem services, such as the construction of roads, ports, and cities and the discharge of pollutants. But most ecosystem changes were the direct or indirect result of changes made to meet growing demands for ecosystem services, and in particular growing demands for food, water, timber, fiber, and fuel (fuelwood and hydropower).

Between 1960 and 2000, the demand for ecosystem services grew significantly as world population doubled to 6 billion people and the global economy increased more than sixfold. To meet this demand, food production increased by roughly two and a half times, water use doubled, wood harvests for pulp and paper production tripled, installed hydropower capacity doubled, and timber production increased by more than half.

The growing demand for these ecosystem services was met both by consuming an increasing fraction of the available supply (for example, diverting more water for irrigation or capturing more fish from the sea) and by raising the production of some services, such as crops and livestock. The latter has been accomplished through the use of new technologies (such as new crop varieties, fertilization, and irrigation) as well as through increasing the area managed for the services in the case of crop and livestock production and aquaculture.

Finding #2: [Gains and Losses from Ecosystem Change]

Degradation and Unsustainable Use of Ecosystem Services

Approximately 60% (15 out of 24) of the ecosystem services evaluated in this assessment (including 70% of regulating and cultural services) are being degraded or used unsustainably.... Ecosystem services that have been degraded over the past 50 years include capture fisheries, water supply, waste treatment and detoxification, water purification, natural hazard

---

[1] [A biome is the largest unit of ecological classification recognized below the level of the entire globe. It includes such groupings as deserts, tundra, temperate broadleaf forests, and flooded grasslands and savannas. Considerable ecological data have been reported and modeling undertaken using this categorization, making it a convenient basis for assessment. – Eds.]

protection, regulation of air quality, regulation of regional and local climate, regulation of erosion, spiritual fulfillment, and aesthetic enjoyment. The use of two ecosystem services – capture
fisheries and fresh water – is now well beyond levels that can be sustained even at current demands,
much less future ones. At least one quarter of important commercial fish stocks are overharvested
(high certainty). From 5% to possibly 25% of global freshwater use exceeds long-term accessible
supplies and is now met either through engineered water transfers or overdraft of groundwater
supplies (low to medium certainty).... Some 15–35% of irrigation withdrawals exceed supply rates
and are therefore unsustainable (low to medium certainty). While 15 services have been degraded,
only 4 have been enhanced in the past 50 years, three of which involve food production: crops,
livestock, and aquaculture. Terrestrial ecosystems were on average a net source of CO_2 emissions
during the nineteenth and early twentieth centuries, but became a net sink around the middle of
the last century, and thus in the last 50 years the role of ecosystems in regulating global climate
through carbon sequestration has also been enhanced.

Actions to increase one ecosystem service often cause the degradation of other services. For
example, because actions to increase food production typically involve increased use of water
and fertilizers or expansion of the area of cultivated land, these same actions often degrade other
ecosystem services, including reducing the availability of water for other uses, degrading water
quality, reducing biodiversity, and decreasing forest cover (which in turn may lead to the loss
of forest products and the release of greenhouse gasses). Similarly, the conversion of forest to
agriculture can significantly change the frequency and magnitude of floods, although the nature
of this impact depends on the characteristics of the local ecosystem and the type of land cover
change....

- *Most resource management decisions are most strongly influenced by ecosystem services entering
  markets; as a result, the nonmarketed benefits are often lost or degraded.* These nonmarketed
  benefits are often high and sometimes more valuable than the marketed ones. For example, one
  of the most comprehensive studies to date, which examined the marketed and nonmarketed
  economic values associated with forests in eight Mediterranean countries, found that timber
  and fuelwood generally accounted for less than a third of total economic value of forests in
  each country. Values associated with non-wood forest products, recreation, hunting, watershed
  protection, carbon sequestration, and passive use (values independent of direct uses) accounted
  for between 25% and 96% of the total economic value of the forests.
- *The total economic value associated with managing ecosystems more sustainably is often higher
  than the value associated with the conversion of the ecosystem through farming, clear-cut logging,
  or other intensive uses.* Relatively few studies have compared the total economic value (including
  values of both marketed and nonmarketed ecosystem services) of ecosystems under alternate
  management regimes, but some of the studies that do exist have found that the benefit of
  managing the ecosystem more sustainably exceeded that of converting the ecosystem.
- *The economic and public health costs associated with damage to ecosystem services can be
  substantial.*
  - The early 1990s collapse of the Newfoundland cod fishery due to overfishing resulted in the
    loss of tens of thousands of jobs and cost at least $2 billion in income support and retraining.
  - In 1996, the cost of U.K. agriculture resulting from the damage that agricultural practices
    cause to water (pollution and eutrophication, a process whereby excessive plant growth
    depletes oxygen in the water), air (emissions of greenhouse gases), soil (off-site erosion dam-
    age, emissions of greenhouse gases), and biodiversity was $2.6 billion, or 9% of average
    yearly gross farm receipts for the 1990s. Similarly, the damage costs of freshwater eutrophi-
    cation alone in England and Wales (involving factors including reduced value of waterfront
    dwellings, water treatment costs, reduced recreational value of water bodies, and tourism

losses) was estimated to be $105 [million]–$160 million per year in the 1990s, with an additional $77 million a year being spent to address those damages.

- The incidence of diseases of marine organisms and the emergence of new pathogens is increasing, and some of these, such as ciguatera, harm human health. Episodes of harmful (including toxic) algal blooms in coastal waters are increasing in frequency and intensity, harming other marine resources such as fisheries as well as human health. In a particularly severe outbreak in Italy in 1989, harmful algal blooms cost the coastal aquaculture industry $10 million and the Italian tourism industry $11.4 million.
- The frequency and impact of floods and fires has increased significantly in the past 50 years, in part due to ecosystem changes. Examples are the increased susceptibility of coastal populations to tropical storms when mangrove forests are cleared and the increase in downstream flooding that followed land use changes in the upper Yangtze River. Annual economic losses from extreme events increased tenfold from the 1950s to approximately $70 billion in 2003, of which natural catastrophes (floods, fires, storms, drought, earthquakes) accounted for 84% of insured losses.
- *The impact of the loss of cultural services is particularly difficult to measure, but it is especially important for many people. Human cultures, knowledge systems, religions, and social interactions have been strongly influenced by ecosystems.* A number of the MA sub-global assessments found that spiritual and cultural values of ecosystems were as important as other services for many local communities, both in developing countries (the importance of sacred groves of forest in India, for example) and industrial ones (the importance of urban parks, for instance).

The degradation of ecosystem services represents loss of a capital asset. Both renewable resources such as ecosystem services and nonrenewable resources such as mineral deposits, some soil nutrients, and fossil fuels are capital assets. Yet traditional national accounts do not include measures of resource depletion or of the degradation of these resources. As a result, a country could cut its forests and deplete its fisheries, and this would show only as a positive gain in [gross domestic product (GDP)] (a measure of current economic well-being) without registering the corresponding decline in assets (wealth) that is the more appropriate measure of future economic wellbeing. Moreover, many ecosystem services (such as fresh water in aquifers and the use of the atmosphere as a sink for pollutants) are available freely to those who use them, and so again their degradation is not reflected in standard economic measures.

When estimates of the economic losses associated with the depletion of natural assets are factored into measurements of the total wealth of nations, they significantly change the balance sheet of countries with economies significantly dependent on natural resources. For example, countries such as Ecuador, Ethiopia, Kazakhstan, Democratic Republic of Congo, Trinidad and Tobago, Uzbekistan, and Venezuela that had positive growth in net savings in 2001, reflecting a growth in the net wealth of the country, actually experienced a loss in net savings when depletion of natural resources (energy and forests) and estimated damages from carbon emissions (associated with contributions to climate change) were factored into the accounts.

While degradation of some services may sometimes be warranted to produce a greater gain in other services, often more degradation of ecosystem services takes place than is in society's interests because many of the services degraded are "public goods." Although people benefit from ecosystem services such as the regulation of air and water quality or the presence of an aesthetically pleasing landscape, there is no market for these services and no one person has an incentive to pay to maintain the good. And when an action results in the degradation of a service that harms other individuals, no market mechanism exists (nor, in many cases, could it exist) to ensure that the individuals harmed are compensated for the damages they suffer.

Wealthy populations cannot be insulated from the degradation of ecosystem services. Agriculture, fisheries, and forestry once formed the bulk of national economies, and the control of natural resources dominated policy agendas. But while these natural resource industries are often still important, the relative economic and political significance of other industries in industrial countries has grown over the past century as a result of the ongoing transition from agricultural to industrial and service economies, urbanization, and the development of new technologies to increase the production of some services and provide substitutes for others. Nevertheless, the degradation of ecosystem services influences human well-being in industrial regions and among wealthy populations in developing countries in many ways:

- The physical, economic, or social impacts of ecosystem service degradation may cross boundaries. . . . For example, land degradation and associated dust storms or fires in one country can degrade air quality in other countries nearby.
- Degradation of ecosystem services exacerbates poverty in developing countries, which can affect neighboring industrial countries by slowing regional economic growth and contributing to the outbreak of conflicts or the migration of refugees.
- Changes in ecosystems that contribute to greenhouse gas emissions contribute to global climate changes that affect all countries.
- Many industries still depend directly on ecosystem services. The collapse of fisheries, for example, has harmed many communities in industrial countries. Prospects for the forest, agriculture, fishing, and ecotourism industries are all directly tied to ecosystem services, while other sectors such as insurance, banking, and health are strongly, if less directly, influenced by changes in ecosystem services.
- Wealthy populations of people are insulated from the harmful effects of some aspects of ecosystem degradation, but not all. For example, substitutes are typically not available when cultural services are lost.
- Even though the relative economic importance of agriculture, fisheries, and forestry is declining in industrial countries, the importance of other ecosystem services such as aesthetic enjoyment and recreational options is growing.

It is difficult to assess the implications of ecosystem changes and to manage ecosystems effectively because many of the effects are slow to become apparent, because they may be expressed primarily at some distance from where the ecosystem was changed, and because the costs and benefits of changes often accrue to different sets of stakeholders. Substantial inertia (delay in the response of a system to a disturbance) exists in ecological systems. As a result, long time lags often occur between a change in a driver and the time when the full consequences of that change become apparent. For example, phosphorus is accumulating in large quantities in many agricultural soils, threatening rivers, lakes, and coastal oceans with increased eutrophication. But it may take years or decades for the full impact of the phosphorus to become apparent through erosion and other processes. Similarly, it will take centuries for global temperatures to reach equilibrium with changed concentrations of greenhouse gases in the atmosphere and even more time for biological systems to respond to the changes in climate.

Moreover, some of the impacts of ecosystem changes may be experienced only at some distance from where the change occurred. For example, changes in upstream catchments affect water flow and water quality in downstream regions; similarly, the loss of an important fish nursery area in a coastal wetland may diminish fish catch some distance away. Both the inertia in ecological systems and the temporal and spatial separation of costs and benefits of ecosystem changes often result in situations where the individuals experiencing harm from ecosystem changes (future generations, say, or downstream landowners) are not the same as the individuals gaining the benefits. These temporal and spatial patterns make it extremely difficult to fully assess costs and benefits associated with ecosystem changes or to attribute costs and benefits to different stakeholders. Moreover, the institutional arrangements now in place to manage ecosystems are poorly designed to cope with these challenges.

INCREASED LIKELIHOOD OF NONLINEAR (STEPPED) AND POTENTIALLY ABRUPT CHANGES IN ECOSYSTEMS

... Changes in ecosystems generally take place gradually. Some changes are nonlinear, however: once a threshold is crossed, the system changes to a very different state. And these nonlinear changes are sometimes abrupt; they can also be large in magnitude and difficult, expensive, or impossible to reverse. Capabilities for predicting some nonlinear changes are improving, but for most ecosystems and for most potential nonlinear changes, while science can often warn of increased risks of change[,] it cannot predict the thresholds at which the change will be encountered. Examples of large magnitude nonlinear changes include:

- *Disease emergence.* If, on average, each infected person infects at least one other person, then an epidemic spreads, while if the infection is transferred on average to less than one person, the epidemic dies out. During the 1997–98 El Niño, excessive flooding caused cholera epidemics in Djibouti, Somalia, Kenya, Tanzania, and Mozambique. Warming of the African Great Lakes due to climate change may create conditions that increase the risk of cholera transmission in the surrounding countries.
- *Eutrophication and hypoxia.* Once a threshold of nutrient loading is achieved, changes in freshwater and coastal ecosystems can be abrupt and extensive, creating harmful algal blooms (including blooms of toxic species) and sometimes leading to the formation of oxygen-depleted zones, killing most animal life.
- *Fisheries collapse.* For example, the Atlantic cod stocks off the east coast of Newfoundland collapsed in 1992, forcing the closure of the fishery after hundreds of years of exploitation. Most important, depleted stocks may take years to recover, or not recover at all, even if harvesting is significantly reduced or eliminated entirely.
- *Species introductions and losses.* The introduction of the zebra mussel into aquatic systems in the United States, for instance, resulted in the extirpation of native clams in Lake St. Clair and annual costs of $100 million to the power industry and other users.
- *Regional climate change.* Deforestation generally leads to decreased rainfall. Since forest existence crucially depends on rainfall, the relationship between forest loss and precipitation decrease can form a positive feedback, which, under certain conditions, can lead to a nonlinear change in forest cover.

The growing bushmeat trade poses particularly significant threats associated with nonlinear changes, in this case accelerating rates of change. Growth in the use and trade of bushmeat is placing increasing pressure on many species, especially in Africa and Asia. While the population size of harvested species may decline gradually with increasing harvest for some time, once the harvest exceeds sustainable levels, the rate of decline of populations of the harvested species will tend to accelerate. This could place them at risk of extinction and also reduce the food supply of people dependent on these resources in the longer term. At the same time, the bushmeat trade involves relatively high levels of interaction between humans and some relatively closely related wild animals that are eaten. Again, this increases the risk of a nonlinear change, in this case the emergence of new and serious pathogens. Given the speed and magnitude of international travel today, new pathogens could spread rapidly around the world.

The increased likelihood of these nonlinear changes stems from the loss of biodiversity and growing pressures from multiple direct drivers of ecosystem change. The loss of species and genetic diversity decreases the resilience of ecosystems, which is the level of disturbance that an ecosystem can undergo without crossing a threshold to a different structure or functioning. In addition, growing pressures from drivers such as overharvesting, climate change, invasive species, and nutrient loading push ecosystems toward thresholds that they might otherwise not encounter.

EXACERBATION OF POVERTY FOR SOME INDIVIDUALS AND GROUPS OF PEOPLE AND CONTRIBUTION TO GROWING INEQUITIES AND DISPARITIES ACROSS GROUPS OF PEOPLE

Despite the progress achieved in increasing the production and use of some ecosystem services, levels of poverty remain high, inequities are growing, and many people still do not have a sufficient supply of or access to ecosystem services.

- In 2001, 1.1 billion people survived on less than $1 per day of income, with roughly 70% of them in rural areas where they are highly dependent on agriculture, grazing, and hunting for subsistence.
- Inequality in income and other measures of human wellbeing has increased over the past decade. A child born in sub-Saharan Africa is 20 times more likely to die before age 5 than a child born in an industrial country, and this disparity is higher than it was a decade ago. During the 1990s, 21 countries experienced declines in their rankings in the Human Development Index (an aggregate measure of economic well-being, health, and education); 14 of them were in sub-Saharan Africa.
- Despite the growth in per capita food production in the past four decades, an estimated 852 million people were undernourished in 2000–2, up 37 million from the period 1997–99. South Asia and sub-Saharan Africa, the regions with the largest numbers of undernourished people, are also the regions where growth in per capita food production has lagged the most. Most notably, per capita food production has declined in sub-Saharan Africa.
- Some 1.1 billion people still lack access to improved water supply, and more than 2.6 billion lack access to improved sanitation. Water scarcity affects roughly 1–2 billion people worldwide. Since 1960, the ratio of water use to accessible supply has grown by 20% per decade.

The degradation of ecosystem services is harming many of the world's poorest people and is sometimes the principal factor causing poverty.

- Half the urban population in Africa, Asia, Latin America, and the Caribbean suffers from one or more diseases associated with inadequate water and sanitation. Worldwide, approximately 1.7 million people die annually as a result of inadequate water, sanitation, and hygiene.
- The declining state of capture fisheries is reducing an inexpensive source of protein in developing countries. Per capita fish consumption in developing countries, excluding China, declined between 1985 and 1997.
- Desertification affects the livelihoods of millions of people, including a large portion of the poor in drylands.

The pattern of "winners" and "losers" associated with ecosystem changes – and in particular the impact of ecosystem changes on poor people, women, and indigenous peoples – has not been adequately taken into account in management decisions. Changes in ecosystems typically yield benefits for some people and exact costs on others who may either lose access to resources or livelihoods or be affected by externalities associated with the change. For several reasons, groups such as the poor, women, and indigenous communities have tended to be harmed by these changes.

- Many changes in ecosystem management have involved the privatization of what were formerly common pool resources. Individuals who depended on those resources (such as indigenous peoples, forest-dependent communities, and other groups relatively marginalized from political and economic sources of power) have often lost rights to the resources.

- Some of the people and places affected by changes in ecosystems and ecosystem services are highly vulnerable and poorly equipped to cope with the major changes in ecosystems that may occur. Highly vulnerable groups include those whose needs for ecosystem services already exceed the supply, such as people lacking adequate clean water supplies, and people living in areas with declining per capita agricultural production.
- Significant differences between the roles and rights of men and women in many societies lead to increased vulnerability of women to changes in ecosystem services.
- The reliance of the rural poor on ecosystem services is rarely measured and thus typically overlooked in national statistics and poverty assessments, resulting in inappropriate strategies that do not take into account the role of the environment in poverty reduction. For example, a recent study that synthesized data from 17 countries found that 22% of household income for rural communities in forested regions comes from sources typically not included in national statistics, such as harvesting wild food, fuelwood, fodder, medicinal plants, and timber. These activities generated a much higher proportion of poorer families' total income than of wealthy families', and this income was of particular significance in periods of both predictable and unpredictable shortfalls in other livelihood sources.

Development prospects in dryland regions of developing countries are especially dependent on actions to avoid the degradation of ecosystems and slow or reverse degradation where it is occurring. Dryland systems cover about 41% of Earth's land surface and more than 2 billion people inhabit them, more than 90% of whom are in developing countries. Dryland ecosystems (encompassing both rural and urban regions of drylands) experienced the highest population growth rate in the 1990s of any of the systems examined in the [Millennium Assessment].... Although drylands are home to about one third of the human population, they have only 8% of the world's renewable water supply. Given the low and variable rainfall, high temperatures, low soil organic matter, high costs of delivering services such as electricity or piped water, and limited investment in infrastructure due to the low population density, people living in drylands face many challenges. They also tend to have the lowest levels of human well-being, including the lowest per capita GDP and the highest infant mortality rates.

The combination of high variability in environmental conditions and relatively high levels of poverty leads to situations where people can be highly vulnerable to changes in ecosystems, although the presence of these conditions has led to the development of very resilient land management strategies. Pressures on dryland ecosystems already exceed sustainable levels for some ecosystem services, such as soil formation and water supply, and are growing. Per capita water availability is currently only two thirds of the level required for minimum levels of human well-being. Approximately 10–20% of the world's drylands are degraded (*medium certainty*) directly harming the people living in these areas and indirectly harming a larger population through biophysical impacts (dust storms, greenhouse gas emissions, and regional climate change) and through socioeconomic impacts (human migration and deepening poverty sometimes contributing to conflict and instability). Despite these tremendous challenges, people living in drylands and their land management systems have a proven resilience and the capability of preventing land degradation, although this can be either undermined or enhanced by public policies and development strategies.

Finding #3: [Ecosystem Prospects for the Next 50 Years]

... The most important direct drivers of change in ecosystems are habitat change (land use change and physical modification of rivers or water withdrawal from rivers), overexploitation, invasive alien species, pollution, and climate change. These direct drivers are often synergistic. For example, in some locations land use change can result in greater nutrient loading (if the land is converted to high-intensity agriculture), increased emissions of greenhouse gases (if forest is cleared), and increased numbers of invasive species (due to the disturbed habitat).

- *Habitat transformation, particularly from conversion to agriculture:* Under the MA scenarios, a further 10–20% of grassland and forestland is projected to be converted between 2000 and 2050 (primarily to agriculture). The projected land conversion is concentrated in low-income countries and dryland regions. Forest cover is projected to continue to increase within industrial countries.
- *Overexploitation, especially overfishing:* Over much of the world, the biomass of fish targeted in fisheries (including that of both the target species and those caught incidentally) has been reduced by 90% relative to levels prior to the onset of industrial fishing, and the fish being harvested are increasingly coming from the less valuable lower trophic levels as populations of higher trophic level species are depleted.... These pressures continue to grow in all the MA scenarios.
- *Invasive alien species:* The spread of invasive alien species and disease organisms continues to increase because of both deliberate translocations and accidental introductions related to growing trade and travel, with significant harmful consequences to native species and many ecosystem services.
- *Pollution, particularly nutrient loading:* Humans have already doubled the flow of reactive nitrogen on the continents, and some projections suggest that this may increase by roughly a further two thirds by 2050. Three out of four MA scenarios project that the global flux of nitrogen to coastal ecosystems will increase by a further 10–20% by 2030 (*medium certainty*), with almost all of this increase occurring in developing countries. Excessive flows of nitrogen contribute to eutrophication of freshwater and coastal marine ecosystems and acidification of freshwater and terrestrial ecosystems (with implications for biodiversity in these ecosystems). To some degree, nitrogen also plays a role in creation of ground-level ozone (which leads to loss of agricultural and forest productivity), destruction of ozone in the stratosphere (which leads to depletion of the ozone layer and increased UVB radiation on Earth, causing increased incidence of skin cancer), and climate change. The resulting health effects include the consequences of ozone pollution on asthma and respiratory function, increased allergies and asthma due to increased pollen production, the risk of blue-baby syndrome, increased risk of cancer and other chronic diseases from nitrates in drinking water, and increased risk of a variety of pulmonary and cardiac diseases from the production of fine particles in the atmosphere.
- *Anthropogenic climate change:* Observed recent changes in climate, especially warmer regional temperatures, have already had significant impacts on biodiversity and ecosystems, including causing changes in species distributions, population sizes, the timing of reproduction or migration events, and an increase in the frequency of pest and disease outbreaks. Many coral reefs have undergone major, although often partially reversible, bleaching episodes when local sea surface temperatures have increased during one month by 0.5–1° Celsius above the average of the hottest months.

By the end of the century, climate change and its impacts may be the dominant direct driver of biodiversity loss and changes in ecosystem services globally. The scenarios developed by the Intergovernmental Panel on Climate Change project an increase in global mean surface temperature of 2.0–6.4° Celsius above preindustrial levels by 2100, increased incidence of floods and droughts, and a rise in sea level of an additional 8–88 centimeters between 1990 and 2100. Harm to biodiversity will grow worldwide with increasing rates of change in climate and increasing absolute amounts of change. In contrast, some ecosystem services in some regions may initially be enhanced by projected changes in climate (such as increases in temperature or precipitation), and thus these regions may experience net benefits at low levels of climate change. As climate change becomes more severe, however, the harmful impacts on ecosystem services outweigh the benefits in most regions of the world. The balance of scientific evidence suggests that there will be a significant net harmful impact on ecosystem services worldwide if global mean surface temperature increases more than 2° Celsius above preindustrial levels or at rates greater than 0.2° Celsius per decade (*medium certainty*). There is a wide band of uncertainty in the amount of warming that would result from any stabilized greenhouse gas concentration, but based on IPCC projections[,] this would require an eventual CO_2 stabilization level of less than 450 parts per million carbon dioxide (*medium certainty*).

. . .

The degradation of ecosystem services poses a significant barrier to the achievement of the Millennium Development Goals[2] and the MDG targets for 2015. The eight Millennium Development Goals [MDGs] adopted by the United Nations in 2000 aim to improve human well-being by reducing poverty, hunger, child and maternal mortality, by ensuring education for all, by controlling and managing diseases, by tackling gender disparity, by ensuring environmental sustainability, and by pursuing global partnerships. Under each of the MDGs, countries have agreed to targets to be achieved by 2015. Many of the regions facing the greatest challenges in achieving these targets coincide with regions facing the greatest problems of ecosystem degradation. Although socioeconomic policy changes will play a primary role in achieving most of the MDGs, many of the targets (and goals) are unlikely to be achieved without significant improvement in management of ecosystems. The role of ecosystem changes in exacerbating poverty (Goal 1, Target 1) for some groups of people has been described already, and the goal of environmental sustainability, including access to safe drinking water (Goal 7, Targets 9, 10, and 11), cannot be achieved as long as most ecosystem services are being degraded. Progress toward three other MDGs is particularly dependent on sound ecosystem management. . . .

Finding #4: [Reversing Ecosystem Degradation]

. . .

An effective set of responses to ensure the sustainable management of ecosystems must address the indirect and drivers just described and must overcome barriers related to:

- Inappropriate institutional and governance arrangements, including the presence of corruption and weak systems of regulation and accountability.
- Market failures and the misalignment of economic incentives.
- Social and behavioral factors, including the lack of political and economic power of some groups (such as poor people, women, and indigenous peoples) that are particularly dependent on ecosystem services or harmed by their degradation.
- Underinvestment in the development and diffusion of technologies that could increase the efficiency of use of ecosystem services and could reduce the harmful impacts of various drivers of ecosystem change.
- Insufficient knowledge (as well as the poor use of existing knowledge) concerning ecosystem services and management, policy, technological, behavioral, and institutional responses that could enhance benefits from these services while conserving resources.

---

[2] [In 2000, U.N. member states met to address the problem of extreme poverty throughout the world. The Millennial Development Goals they adopted, to be achieved by 2015, include addressing environmental conditions as they relate to poverty. Halfway through the commitment period, the United Nations issued a somewhat gloomy report on the progress being made towards achieving these goals. *See* Millennium Progress Report (2008). – *Eds.*]

All these barriers are further compounded by weak human and institutional capacity related to the assessment and management of ecosystem services, underinvestment in the regulation and management of their use, lack of public awareness, and lack of awareness among decision-makers of both the threats posed by the degradation of ecosystem services and the opportunities that more sustainable management of ecosystems could provide. . . .

INSTITUTIONS AND GOVERNANCE

. . . Many existing institutions at both the global and the national level have the mandate to address the degradation of ecosystem services but face a variety of challenges in doing so related in part to the need for greater cooperation across sectors and the need for coordinated responses at multiple scales. However, since a number of the issues identified in this assessment are recent concerns and were not specifically taken into account in the design of today's institutions, changes in existing institutions and the development of new ones may sometimes be needed, particularly at the national scale.

In particular, existing national and global institutions are not well designed to deal with the management of common pool resources, a characteristic of many ecosystem services. Issues of ownership and access to resources, rights to participation in decision-making, and regulation of particular types of resource use or discharge of wastes can strongly influence the sustainability of ecosystem management and are fundamental determinants of who wins and loses from changes in ecosystems. Corruption, a major obstacle to effective management of ecosystems, also stems from weak systems of regulation and accountability.

. . .

Economic and financial interventions provide powerful instruments to regulate the use of ecosystem goods and services. Because many ecosystem services are not traded in markets, markets fail to provide appropriate signals that might otherwise contribute to the efficient allocation and sustainable use of the services. A wide range of opportunities exists to influence human behavior to address this challenge in the form of economic and financial instruments. However, market mechanisms and most economic instruments can only work effectively if supporting institutions are in place, and thus there is a need to build institutional capacity to enable more widespread use of these mechanisms.

Promising interventions include:

- *Elimination of subsidies that promote excessive use of ecosystem services (and, where possible, transfer of these subsidies to payments for non-marketed ecosystem services).* Government subsidies paid to the agricultural sectors of [Organisation of Economic Co-operation and Development (OECD)] countries between 2001 and 2003 averaged over $324 billion annually, or one third the global value of agricultural products in 2000. A significant proportion of this total involved production subsidies that led to greater food production in industrial countries than the global market conditions warranted, promoted overuse of fertilizers and pesticides in those countries, and reduced the profitability of agriculture in developing countries. Many countries outside the OECD also have inappropriate input and production subsidies, and inappropriate subsidies are common in other sectors such as water, fisheries, and forestry. Although removal of perverse subsidies will produce net benefits, it will not be without costs. Compensatory mechanisms may be needed for poor people who are adversely affected by the removal of subsidies, and removal of agricultural subsidies within the OECD would need to be accompanied by actions designed to minimize adverse impacts on ecosystem services in developing countries.

- *Greater use of economic instruments and market-based approaches in the management of ecosystem services.* These include:

- Taxes or user fees for activities with "external" costs (tradeoffs not accounted for in the market). Examples include taxes on excessive application of nutrients or ecotourism user fees.
- Creation of markets, including through cap-and-trade systems. One of the most rapidly growing markets related to ecosystem services is the carbon market. Approximately 64 million tons of carbon dioxide equivalent were exchanged through projects from January to May 2004, nearly as much as during all of 2003. The value of carbon trades in 2003 was approximately $300 million. About one quarter of the trades involved investment in ecosystem services (hydropower or biomass). It is *speculated* that this market may grow to $10 billion to $44 billion by 2010. The creation of a market in the form of a nutrient trading system may also be a low-cost way to reduce excessive nutrient loading in the United States.
- Payment for ecosystem services. For example, in 1996 Costa Rica established a nationwide system of conservation payments to induce landowners to provide ecosystem services. Under this program, Costa Rica brokers contracts between international and domestic "buyers" and local "sellers" of sequestered carbon, biodiversity, watershed services, and scenic beauty. Another innovative conservation financing mechanism is "biodiversity offsets," whereby developers pay for conservation activities as compensation for unavoidable harm that a project causes to biodiversity.
- Mechanisms to enable consumer preferences to be expressed through markets. For example, current certification schemes for sustainable fisheries and forest practices provide people with the opportunity to promote sustainability through their consumer choices.

. . .

KNOWLEDGE RESPONSES

Effective management of ecosystems is constrained both by the lack of knowledge and information about different aspects of ecosystems and by the failure to use adequately the information that does exist in support of management decisions. In most regions, for example, relatively limited information exists about the status and economic value of most ecosystem services, and their depletion is rarely tracked in national economic accounts. Basic global data on the extent and trend in different types of ecosystems and land use are surprisingly scarce. Models used to project future environmental and economic conditions have limited capability of incorporating ecological "feedbacks," including nonlinear changes in ecosystems, as well as behavioral feedbacks such as learning that may take place through adaptive management of ecosystems. At the same time, decision-makers do not use all of the relevant information that is available. This is due in part to institutional failures that prevent existing policy-relevant scientific information from being made available to decision-makers and in part to the failure to incorporate other forms of knowledge and information (such as traditional knowledge and practitioners' knowledge) that are often of considerable value for ecosystem management.

Promising interventions include:

- *Incorporation of nonmarket values of ecosystems in resource management and investment decisions.* Most resource management and investment decisions are strongly influenced by considerations of the monetary costs and benefits of alternative policy choices. Decisions can be improved if they are informed by the total economic value of alternative management options and involve deliberative mechanisms that bring to bear noneconomic considerations as well. . . .
- *Enhancing and sustaining human and institutional capacity for assessing the consequences of ecosystem change for human well-being and acting on such assessments.* Greater technical capacity is needed for agriculture, forest, and fisheries management. But the capacity that exists

for these sectors, as limited as it is in many countries, is still vastly greater than the capacity for effective management of other ecosystem services.

Questions and Discussion

1. What is the underlying rationale for environmental protection? Is it concern for nature or concern for humans? Can the two be separated? *See* Klaus Bosselmann, When Two Worlds Collide: Society And Ecology (1995); Christopher D. Stone, The Gnat Is Older Than Man: Global Environment and the Human Agenda (1993); Roderick Frazier Nash, The Rights of Nature: A History of Environmental Ethics (1989).

2. To the extent environmental protection is about human well-being, does the concern expressed extend to humans presently alive or also to future generations? Why should present generations care about the future? If they do, how should the needs and interests of the future be determined and protected in the present? See the discussion of intergenerational equity, *infra* at section 5(a).

3. How can common-pool resources be managed? Garrett Hardin described a "tragedy of the commons" in 1968, positing a common pasture in which everyone in a village has unlimited grazing rights for cattle. It is to each person's advantage in the short run to maximize the grazing of her or his own cattle. Over time, the pasture is destroyed through overgrazing. Garrett Hardin, *Tragedy of the Commons*, 168 Science 243 (Dec. 13, 1968). The crashing fisheries in oceans around the world demonstrate the continued validity of Hardin's analysis. What legal solutions can address the tragedy of the commons in a state or in international commons areas like the high seas? Do rights have any role to play?

4. Are those persons and states who contribute the most to environmental degradation bearing their fair share of the resulting burdens? If not, should environmental law try to allocate more equitably the benefits and burdens of human activities that impact the environment?

5. To what extent does the Millennium Assessment suggest the need for environmental law as opposed to education, ethics, or other approaches to prevent further loss of ecosystem services?

6. What is the role of economic analysis and accounting revealed by the MA? Does GDP take into account ecological services? Can it? How can the value of honeybees in pollinating plants be measured? *See, e.g.,* Nature's Services: Societal Dependence on Natural Ecosystems (Gretchen C. Daily ed., 1997); Dana Clark & David Downes, What Price Biodiversity? (1995); Robert Costanza et al., An Introduction to Ecological Economics (1997); Herman E. Daly & Joshua Farley, Ecological Economics: Principles and Applications (2003); Michael Common & Sigrid Stagl, Ecological Economics: An Introduction (2005).

II. Approaches to Environmental Protection

Deep and growing concern for the environment and the ability of future generations to meet their needs has been a driver of profound changes in the law (both municipal and international) over the past fifty years. Today, a vast system of public environmental law in many countries forms one of the linchpins of the modern regulatory state. Alongside this public law edifice, other complementary legal and policy mechanisms promote environmental protection. In general, laws concerning the environment can be grouped into four broad categories: private law, especially tort and property law; public regulation (including criminal law); market mechanisms; and constitutional or human rights law. As you study these categories, consider how environmental law and policy (including the market) address the problems identified by the Millennium Assessment.

A. *Private Actions*

1. Nuisance, Strict Liability, and Negligence

Property and tort laws in many legal systems contain concepts that help protect individuals and their property from environmental harm. Laws relating to nuisance and trespass have been invoked in civil litigation, whereas the doctrine of public trust is more often found in constitutional and statutory provisions. Nuisance is an equitable doctrine that imposes liability when, after examining and balancing the benefits and burdens accruing to litigating parties, one party's use of property or resources is found to be an unreasonable or unjust interference with the other party's property or other interests.

The following two cases, one national and one international, illustrate how the law of nuisance and other private law concepts may be used to address certain environmental injury. Recall that although we are concerned with private actions, the tort of nuisance does have both a private law and a public law side.

Indian Council for Enviro-Legal Action v. Union of India,
1996 AIR 1446, 1448–69, [1996] INSC 244 (Feb. 13, 1996), 1996 SCC (3)

B.P. Jeevan Reddy, J.: – Writ Petition (C) No. 967 of 1989):

[1.] This writ petition filed by an environmentalist organization brings to light the woes of people living in the vicinity of chemical industrial plants in India. It highlights the disregard, nay, contempt for law and lawful authorities on the part of some among the emerging breed of entrepreneurs, taking advantage, as they do, of the country's need for industrialization and export earnings. Pursuit of profit has absolutely drained them of any feeling for fellow human beings – for that matter, for anything else. And the law seems to have been helpless. . . . It is such instances which have led many people in this country to believe that disregard of law pays and that the consequences of such disregard will never be visited upon them – particularly, if they are men with means. Strong words indeed – but nothing less would reflect the deep sense of hurt, the hearing of this case has instilled in us. The facts of the case will bear out these opening remarks.

2. Bichhri is a small village in Udaipur district of Rajasthan. To its north is a major industrial establishment, Hindustan Zinc Limited, a public sector concern. That did not affect Bichhri. Its woes began somewhere in 1987 when the fourth respondent herein, Hindustan Agro Chemicals Limited[,] started producing certain chemicals like Oleum (said to be the concentrated form of sulfuric acid) and Single Super Phosphate. The real calamity occurred when a sister concern, Silver Chemicals (Respondent No. 5), commenced production of "H" acid in a plant located within the same complex. "H" acid was meant for export exclusively. Its manufacture gives rise to enormous quantities of highly toxic effluents – in particular, iron-based and gypsum-based sludge – which if not properly treated, pose grave threat to mother Earth. It poisons the earth, the water and everything that comes in contact with it. Jyoti Chemicals (Respondent No. 8) is another unit established to produce "H" acid, besides some other chemicals. Respondents Nos. 6 and 7 were established to produce fertilizers and a few other products.

. . .

4. Because of the pernicious wastes emerging from the production of "H" acid, its manufacture is stated to have been banned in the western countries. But the need of "H" acid continues in the West. That need is catered to by the industries like the Silver Chemicals and Jyoti Chemicals in

this part of the world.... [The production of "H" acid in this case] has given birth to about 2400–2500 MT of highly toxic sludge.... Since the toxic untreated waste waters were allowed to flow out freely and because the untreated toxic sludge was thrown in the open[,]...the toxic substances have percolated deep into the bowels of the earth polluting the aquifers and the sub-terranean supply of water[,]...rendering it unfit for human consumption. It has become unfit for cattle to drink and for irrigating the land.... It spread disease, death and disaster in the village and the surrounding areas....

5. The present social action litigation was initiated in August 1989[,] complaining precisely of the above situation and requesting...appropriate remedial action.

. . .

49. Before we proceed to deal with the submissions of the learned counsel, it would be appropriate to notice the relevant provisions of law.

RELEVANT STATUTORY PROVISIONS:

50. Article 48A is one of the Directive Principles of State Policy. It says that the State shall endeavor to protect and improve the environment and to safeguard the forests and wildlife of the country. Article 51A sets out the fundamental duties of the citizens. One of them is "(g) to protect and improve the natural environment including forests, lakes, rivers and wild life and to have compassion for living creatures...."

CONSIDERATION OF THE SUBMISSIONS:

55.... This writ petition is not really for issuance of appropriate writ, order or directions against the respondents but is directed against the Union of India, Government of Rajasthan and R.P.C.B. to compel them to perform their statutory duties enjoined by the Acts aforementioned on the ground that their failure to carry out their statutory duties is seriously undermining the right to life (of the residents of Bichhri and the affected area) guaranteed by Article 21 of the Constitution. If this Court finds that the said authorities have not taken the action required of them by law and that their inaction is jeopardizing the right to life of the citizens of this country or of any section thereof, it is the duty of this Court to intervene. If it is found that the respondents are flouting the provisions of law and the directions and orders issued by the lawful authorities, this Court can certainly make appropriate directions to ensure compliance with law and lawful directions made thereunder. This is a social action litigation on behalf of the villagers of Bichhri whose right to life, as elucidated by this Court in several decisions, is invaded and seriously infringed by the respondents as is established by the various Reports of the experts called for, and filed before, this Court. If an industry is established without obtaining the requisite permission and clearances and if the industry is continued to be run in blatant disregard of law to the detriment of life and liberty of the citizens living in the vicinity, can it be suggested with any modicum of reasonableness that this Court has no power to intervene and protect the fundamental right to life and liberty of the citizens of this country?

. . .

57. So far as the responsibility of the respondents for causing the pollution in the wells, soil and the aquifers is concerned, it is clearly established by the analysis Report referred to in the Report of the Central experts team dated November 1, 1993. Indeed, a number of Orders passed by this Court, referred to hereinbefore, are premised upon the finding that the respondents are responsible for the said pollution. It is only because of the said reason that they were asked to defray the cost of removal and storage of sludge. It is precisely for this reason that, at one stage, the respondents had also undertaken the de-watering of polluted wells. Disclaiming the responsibility for the pollution in and around Bichhri village, at this stage of proceedings, is clearly an afterthought. We accordingly hold and affirm that the respondents alone are responsible for all the damage to the soil, to the

underground water and to the village Bichhri in general, damage which is eloquently portrayed in the several Reports of the experts mentioned hereinabove.... [I]t may perhaps be appropriate to clarify that so far as removal of remaining sludge and/or the stoppage of discharge of further toxic wastes are concerned, it is the absolute responsibility of the respondents to store the sludge in a proper manner [in the same manner in which 720 MT of sludge has already been stored] and to stop the discharge of any other or further toxic wastes from its plants including Sulphuric Acid Plant and to ensure that the wastes discharged do not flow into or through the sludge.

. . .

61. Sri K.N. Bhat submitted that the rule of absolute liability is not accepted in England or other Commonwealth countries and that the rule evolved by the House of Lords in *Rylands v. Fletcher* [1866 (3) H.L.330] is the correct rule to be applied in such matters. Firstly, in view of the binding decision of this Court in *Oleum Gas Leak Case* (AIR 1987 SC 1086), this contention is untenable, for the said decision expressly refers to the rule in *Rylands* but refuses to apply it saying that it is not suited to the conditions in India.

. . .

65.... We are convinced that the law stated by this Court in *Oleum Gas Leak Case* is by far the more appropriate one – apart from the fact that it is binding upon us.... According to this rule, once the activity carried on is hazardous or inherently dangerous, the person carrying on such activity is liable to make good the loss caused to any other person by his activity irrespective of the fact whether he took reasonable care while carrying on his activity. The rule is premised upon the very nature of the activity carried on. In the words of the Constitution Bench, such an activity "can be tolerated only on the condition that the enterprise engaged in such hazardous or inherently dangerous activity indemnifies all those who suffer on account of the carrying on of such hazardous or inherently dangerous activity regardless of whether it is carried on carefully or not." The Constitution Bench has also assigned the reason for stating the law in the said terms. It is that the enterprise (carrying on the hazardous or inherently dangerous activity) alone has the resource to discover and guard against hazards or dangers – and not the person affected and the practical difficulty (on the part of the affected person) in establishing the absence of reasonable care or that the damage to him was foreseeable by the enterprise.

66. Once the law in *Oleum Gas Leak Case*... is held to be the law applicable, it follows, in the light of our findings recorded hereinbefore, that Respondents Nos. 4 to 8 are absolutely liable to compensate for the harm caused by them to villagers in the affected area, to the soil and to the underground water and hence, they are bound to take all necessary measures to remove the sludge and other pollutants lying in the affected area... and also to defray the cost of the remedial measures required to restore the soil and the underground water spruces. Sections 3 and 4 of Environment (Protection) Act confers upon the Central Government the power to give directions of the above nature and to the above effect. Levy of costs required for carrying out remedial measures is implicit in Sections 3 and 4[,] which are couched in very wide and expansive language. Appropriate directions can be given by this Court to the Central Government to invoke and exercise those powers with such modulations as are called for in the facts and circumstances of this case.

67. The question of liability of the respondents to defray the costs of remedial measures can also be looked into from another angle, which has now come to be accepted universally as a sound principle, viz., the "Polluter Pays" Principle.

[...]The polluter pays principle demands that the financial costs of preventing or remedying damage caused by pollution should lie with the undertakings which cause the pollution, or produce the goods which cause the pollution. Under the principle it is not the role of government to meet the costs involved in either prevention of such damage, or in carrying out remedial action, because the effect of this would be to shift the financial burden of the pollution incident to the taxpayer. The "polluter pays" principle was promoted by the Organisation for Economic Co-operation and

Development (OECD) during the 1970s when there was great public interest in environmental issues. During this time there were demands on government and other institutions to introduce policies and mechanisms for the protection of the environment and the public from the threats posed by pollution in a modern industrialized society. Since then there has been considerable discussion of the nature of the polluter pays principle, but the precise scope of the principle and its implications for those involved in past, or potentially polluting activities have never been satisfactory agreed.

Despite the difficulties inherent in defining the principle, the European Community accepted it as a fundamental part of its strategy on environmental matters, and it has been one of the underlying principles of the four Community Action Programmes on the Environment....

Thus, according to this principle, the responsibility for repairing the damage is that of the offending industry. Sections 3 and 5 empower the Central Government to give directions and take measures for giving effect to this principle. In all the circumstances of the case, we think it appropriate that the task of determining the amount required for carrying out the remedial measures, its recovery/realisation and the task of undertaking the remedial measures is placed upon the Central Government in the light of the provisions of the Environment (Protection) Act, 1986. It is, of course, open to the Central Government to take the help and assistance of State Government, R.P.C.B. or such other agency or authority, as they think fit.

. . .

70. DIRECTIONS: Accordingly, the following directions are made:

1. The Central Government shall determine the amount required for carrying out the remedial measures including the removal of sludge lying in and around the complex of Respondents 4 to 8, in the area affected in village Bichhri and other adjacent villages, on account of the production of "H" acid and the discharges from the Sulphuric Acid Plant of Respondents 4 to 8.... Subject to the Orders, if any, passed by this Court, the said amount shall represent the amount which Respondents 4 to 8 are liable to pay to improve and restore the environment in the area.... In case of failure of the said respondents to pay the said amount, the same shall be recovered by the Central Government in accordance with law. The factories, plant, machinery and all other immovable assets of Respondents 4 to 8 are attached herewith. The amount so determined and recovered shall be utilised by the M.E.F. for carrying out all necessary remedial measures to restore the soil, water sources and the environment in general of the affected area to its former state.

2. On account of their continuous, persistent and insolent violations of law, their attempts to conceal the sludge, their discharge of toxic effluents from the Sulphuric Acid Plant which was allowed to flow through the sludge, and their non-implementation of the Orders of this Court – all of which are fully borne out by the expert committees' Reports and the findings recorded hereinabove – Respondents 4 to 8 have earned the dubious distinction of being characterised as "rogue industries." They have inflicted untold misery upon the poor, unsuspecting villagers, despoiling their land, their water sources and their entire environment – all in pursuance of their private profit. They have forfeited all claims for any consideration by this Court. Accordingly, we herewith order the closure of all the plants and factories of Respondents 4 to 8 located in Bichhri village. The R.P.C.B. is directed to seal all the factories/units/plants of the said respondents forthwith. So far as the Sulphuric Acid Plant is concerned, it will be closed at the end of one week from today, within which period Respondent No. 4 shall wind down its operations so as to avoid risk of any untoward consequences, as asserted by Respondent No. 4 in Writ Petition (C) No. 76 of 1994. It is the responsibility of Respondent No. 4 to take necessary steps in this behalf. The R.P.C.B. shall seal this unit too at the end of one week from today. The re-opening of these plants shall depend upon their compliance with the directions made and obtaining of all requisite permissions and consents from the relevant authorities. Respondents 4 to 8 can apply for directions in this behalf after such compliance.

3. So far as the claim for damages for the loss suffered by the villagers in the affected area is concerned, it is open to them or any organization on their behalf to institute suits in the appropriate civil court. If they file the suit or suits *in forma pauperis*, the State of Rajasthan shall not oppose their applications for leave to sue *in forma pauperis*.

4. The Central Government shall consider whether it would not be appropriate, in the light of the experience gained, that chemical industries are treated as a category apart.

Since the chemical industries are the main culprits in the matter of polluting the environment, there is every need for scrutinizing their establishment and functioning more rigorously. No distinction should be made in this behalf as between a large-scale industry and a small-scale industry or for that matter between a large-scale industry and a medium-scale industry. All chemical industries, whether big or small, should be allowed to be established only after taking into considerations all the environmental aspects and their functioning should be monitored closely to ensure that they do not pollute the environment around them. It appears that most of these industries are water-intensive industries. If so, the advisability of allowing the establishment of these industries in arid areas may also require examination. Even the existing chemical industries may be subjected to such a study and if it is found on such scrutiny that it is necessary to take any steps in the interests of environment, appropriate directions in that behalf may be issued under Sections 3 and 5 of the Environment Act. The Central Government shall ensure that the directions given by it are implemented forthwith.

5. The Central Government and the R.P.C.B. shall file quarterly Reports before this Court with respect to the progress in the implementation of Directions 1 to 4 aforesaid.

. . .

7. The Central Government may also consider the advisability of strengthening the environment protection machinery both at the Center and the States and provide them more teeth. The heads of several units and agencies should be made personally accountable for any lapses and/or negligence on the part of their units and agencies. The idea of an environmental audit by specialist bodies created on a permanent basis with power to inspect, check and take necessary action not only against erring industries but also against erring officers may be considered. The idea of an environmental audit conducted periodically and certified annually, by specialists in the field, duly recognised, can also be considered. The ultimate idea is to integrate and balance the concern for environment with the need for industrialisation and technological progress.

Respondents 4 to 8 shall pay a sum of Rupees fifty thousand by way of costs to the petitioner[,] which had to fight this litigation over a period of over six years with its own means. Voluntary bodies, like the petitioner, deserve encouragement wherever their actions are found to be in furtherance of public interest. The said sum shall be deposited in this Court within two weeks from today. It shall be paid over to the petitioner.

Questions and Discussion

1. Note that the Court rejects the rule in *Rylands v. Fletcher*, 1868 LR 3 HL 330, as inappropriate for India. The Court states:

    61. . . . [F]or the sake of completeness, we may discuss the rule in *Rylands* and indicate why that rule is inappropriate and unacceptable in this country. The rule was first stated by Blackburn, J. (Court of Exchequer Chamber) in the following words:

    We think that the true rule of law is, that the person who for his own purposes brings on his lands and collects and keeps there anything likely to do mischief if it escapes, must keep it in at his peril, and, if he does not do so, is *prima facie* answerable for all the damage which is the natural consequence of its escape. He can excuse himself by shewing that the escape was owing to the plaintiff's default; or perhaps that the escape was the consequence of *vis major*, or the act of God; . . . and it seems but reasonable and just that the neighbor, who has brought something on his own property which was not naturally there, harmless to others so long as it is confined to his own property, but which he knows to be mischievous if it gets on his neighbour's, should be obliged to make good the damage which ensues if he does not succeed in confining it to his own property.

62. The House of Lords, however, added a rider to the above statement, viz., that the user by the defendant should be a "non-natural" user to attract the rule. In other words, if the user by the defendant is a natural user of the land, he would not be liable for damages. Thus, the twin tests – apart from the proof of damage to the plaintiff by the act/negligence of the defendants – which must be satisfied to attract this rule are "foreseability" and "non-natural" user of the land.

63. The rule in *Rylands* . . . has been approved by the House of Lords in the recent decision in *Cambridge Water Company v. Eastern Counties Leather, PLC* (1994) (2) W.L.R.53. The plaintiff, Cambridge Water Company, was a statutory corporation engaged in providing public water supply within a certain area including the city of Cambridge. It was lifting water from a bore well situated at some distance from Sawstyn. The defendant-company, Eastern Leather, was having a tannery in Sawstyn. Tanning necessarily involves decreasing of pelts. For that purpose, the defendant was using an oregano chlorine called P.C.E. P.C.E. was stored in a tank in the premises of the defendant. The plaintiff's case was that on account of the P.C.E. percolating into the ground, the water in its well became contaminated and unfit for human consumption and that on that account it was obliged to find an alternative source at a substantial cost. It sued the defendant for the resulting damages. The plaintiff based his claim on three alternative grounds, viz., negligence, nuisance and the rule in *Rylands*. The Trial Judge (High Court) dismissed the action in negligence and nuisance holding that the defendant could not have reasonably foreseen that such damage could occur to the plaintiff. So far as the rule in *Rylands* was concerned, the Trial Judge held that the user by the defendant was not a non-natural user and hence, it was not liable for damages. On appeal, the Court of Appeal declined to decide the matter on the basis of the rule in Rylands. It relied strongly upon the ratio in *Ballard v. Tomlinson* (1885) 29 Ch.D.115 holding that no person having a right to use a common source is entitled to contaminate that source so as to prevent his neighbor from having a full value of his right of appropriation. The Court of Appeal also opined that the defendant's use of the land was not a natural use. On appeal by the defendant, the House of Lords allowed the appeal holding that foreseeability of the harm of the relevant type by the defendant was a pre-requisite to the right to recover damages both under the heads of nuisance and also under the rule in *Rylands* and since that was not established by the plaintiff, it has to fail. The House of Lords, no doubt, held that the defendant's use of the land was a non-natural use but dismissed the suit, as stated above, on the ground that the plaintiff has failed to establish that pollution of their water supply by the solvent used by the defendant in his premises was in the circumstances of the case foreseeable by the defendant.

64. The Australian High Court has, however, expressed its disinclination to treat the rule in *Rylands* as an independent head for claiming damages or as a rule rooted in the law governing the law of nuisance in *Burnie Port Authority v. General Jones Pty Ltd.* (1994) 68 Australian Law Journal 331. The respondent, General Jones Limited, has stored frozen vegetables in three cold storage rooms in the building owned by the appellant, Burnie Port Authority (Authority). The remaining building remained under the occupation of the Authority. The Authority wanted to extend the building. The extension work was partly done by the Authority itself and partly by an independent contractor (Wildridge and Sinclair Pty. Ltd.). For doing its work, the contractor used a certain insulating material called E.P.S., a highly inflammable substance. On account of negligent handling of E.P.S., there was a

fire which inter alia damaged the rooms in which General Jones had stored its vegetables. On an action by General Jones, the Australian High Court held by a majority that the rule in *Rylands* having attracted many difficulties, uncertainties, qualifications and exceptions, should now be seen, for the purposes of Australian Common Law, as absorbed by the principles of ordinary negligence. The Court held further that under the rules governing negligence, if a person in control of a premises, introduces a dangerous substance to carry on a dangerous activity, or allows another to do one of those things, owes a duty of reasonable care to avoid a reasonably foreseeable risk of injury or damage to the person or property of another. In a case where a person or the property of that other is lawfully in a place outside the premises, the duty of care varies in degree according to the magnitude of the risk involved and extends to ensuring that such care is taken. Applying the said principle, the Court held that the Authority allowed the independent contractor to introduce or retain a dangerous substance or to engage in a dangerous activity in its premises[,] which substance and activity caused a fire that destroyed the goods of General Jones. The evidence, the Court held, established that the independent contractor's work was a dangerous activity in that it involved real and foreseeable risk of a serious conflagration unless special precautions were taken. In the circumstances, it was held that the Authority owed a non-delegable duty of care to General Jones to ensure that its contractor took reasonable steps to prevent the occurrence of a fire and the breach of that duty attracted liability pursuant to the ordinary principles of negligence for the damage sustained by the respondent.

65. On a consideration of the two lines of thought [one adopted by the English Courts and the other by the Australian High Court], we are of the opinion that any principle evolved in this behalf should be simple, practical and suited to the conditions obtaining in this country.

AIR 1996 SC 1464–1465. The Court, thus, considers three different bases for liability for environmental harm: (1) nuisance; (2) strict liability, i.e. the rule in *Rylands v. Fletcher*; and (3) negligence. How do they differ? Which does the court apply? Is this appropriate? Why?

2. The Court refers to this action as social action litigation, also known as public interest litigation. Can you define these terms? What impact do traditional standing requirements have on such litigation? In India, the doctrines of representative standing and citizen standing have developed to allow entities such as the environmentalist organization plaintiff in this case to obtain standing without showing a direct interest or special injury as historically required. Representative standing confers standing on volunteers to advance claims on behalf of the poor and oppressed who would otherwise lack the ability, resources, or knowledge to pursue an action. Citizen standing allows a concerned citizen (or organization) to sue in her or his own right as a member of the public to whom a public duty is owed by government agencies. *See* Armin Rosencranz, Shyam Divan & Martha L. Noble, Environmental Law and Policy in India 118–27 (1991).

3. Justice Reddy, in paragraph 65 of the preceding opinion, refers to article 21 of the Indian Constitution. Article 21 provides: "No person shall be deprived of his life or personal liberty except according to procedure established by law." The Constitution of India (*as modified up to December 1, 2007*). *See generally* M.C. Jain Kagzi, 2 The Constitution of India 1003–26 (6th ed., 2004) In *Francis v. Union Territory of Delhi*, the Supreme Court held that the "right to life enshrined in Article 21 cannot be restricted to mere animal existence. It means something much more than just physical survival. The right to life includes the right to live with human dignity, and all that goes along with it, namely, the bare necessities of life, such as adequate nutrition, clothing and shelter overhead and facilities for reading, writing and expression in diverse forms, freely moving about and mixing and co-mingling with fellow human beings." AIR 1981 SC 746, 747. How is Article 21 relevant to the instant

case? The more direct environmental implications of Article 21 are considered herein in Chapter 7.II.C.

4. The Court also mentions article 51A(g) of the Indian Constitution, which sets forth fundamental duties of citizens, including the duty to "protect and improve the natural environment." Would an action in negligence lie for a breach of this duty?

5. Is it appropriate for the Court to order closure of the plant as a remedy?

Trail Smelter Case (U.S. v. Can.), III U.N. RIAA 1905, 1938–1966 (award of Mar. 11, 1941); Ann. Digest (1938–40), no. 104

[The interstate *Trail Smelter* arbitration is perhaps the best-known international environmental case. The Consolidated Mining and Smelting Company Limited of Canada (today known as Teck Resources Limited) operated a zinc and lead smelter along the Columbia River at Trail, British Columbia, about ten miles north of the international boundary with the state of Washington. In the period between 1925 and 1935, the U.S. government objected to the Canadian government that sulfur dioxide emissions from the operation were causing damage to the Columbia River valley. Eventually, the two countries agreed to submit the dispute to arbitration. The arbitral panel, which found no international treaties or precedents on point for transboundary air pollution, relied heavily on interstate cases from within federal systems, which in turn relied on private law doctrines of nuisance. – Eds.]

[By Jan Hostie, Charles Warren & R.A.E. Greenshields:] The Tribunal herewith reports its final decisions.

The controversy is between two Governments involving damage occurring, or having occurred, in the territory of one of them (the United States of America) and alleged to be due to an agency situated in the territory of the other (the Dominion of Canada). In this controversy, the Tribunal did not sit and is not sitting to pass upon claims presented by individuals or on behalf of one or more individuals by their Government, although individuals may come within the meaning of "parties concerned," in Article IV and of "interested parties,'" in Article VIII of the Convention and although the damage suffered by individuals did, in part, "afford a convenient scale for the calculation of the reparation due to the State" (see Judgment No. 13, Permanent Court of International Justice, Series A, No. 17, pp. 27, 28). (*Cf.* what was said by the Tribunal in the decision reported on April 16, 1938, as regards the problems arising out of abandonment of properties, Part Two, Clause (1).)

As between the two countries involved, each has an equal interest that if a nuisance is proved, the indemnity to damaged parties for proven damage shall be just and adequate and each has also an equal interest that unproven or unwarranted claims shall not be allowed. . . .

. . .

. . . On February 22, 1934, the Canadian Government declared (letter of the Secretary of State for External Affairs to the Minister of the United States at Ottawa) that it "would be entirely satisfied to refer the Tribunal to the principles of law as recognized and applied by the courts of the United States of America in such matters." Now, the matters referred to in that sentence are determined by the preceding sentences:

> The use of the word "injury" is likely to cause misunderstanding which should be removed when the actual terms of the issue are settled for inclusion in the Convention. In order to avoid such misunderstanding, it would seem to be desirable to use the word "damage" in place of "injury" and further, either to define the word actually used by a definition to be incorporated in the Convention or else by reference to the general principles of the law which are applied by the courts in the two countries in dealing with cognate matters.

This passage shows that the "cognate questions" parties had in mind in drafting the Convention were primarily those questions which in cases between private parties, find their answer in the law of nuisances.

. . .

PART THREE

The second question under Article III of the Convention is as follows:

> . . . [W]hether the Trail Smelter should be required to refrain from causing damage in the State of Washington in the future and, if so, to what extent?

. . .

The first problem which arises is whether the question should be answered on the basis of the law followed in the United States or on the basis of international law. The Tribunal, however, finds that this problem need not be solved here as the law followed in the United States in dealing with the quasi-sovereign rights of the States of the Union, in the matter of air pollution, whilst more definite, is in conformity with the general rules of international law.

Particularly in reaching its conclusions as regards this question as well as the next, the Tribunal has given consideration to the desire of the high contracting parties "to reach a solution just to all parties concerned."

As Professor Eagleton puts it (*Responsibility of States in International Law*, 1928, p. 80): "A State owes at all times a duty to protect other States against injurious acts by individuals from within its jurisdiction." A great number of such general pronouncements by leading authorities concerning the duty of a State to respect other States and their territory have been presented to the Tribunal. These and many others have been carefully examined. International decisions, in various matters, from the Alabama case onward, and also earlier ones, are based on the same general principle, and, indeed, this principle, as such, has not been questioned by Canada. But the real difficulty often arises rather when it comes to determine what, *pro subjecta materie*, is deemed to constitute an injurious act.

A case concerning, as the present one does, territorial relations, decided by the Federal Court of Switzerland between the Cantons of Soleure and Argovia, may serve to illustrate the relativity of the rule. Soleure brought a suit against her sister State to enjoin use of a shooting establishment which endangered her territory. The court, in granting the injunction, said: "This right (sovereignty) excludes . . . not only the usurpation and exercise of sovereign rights (of another State) . . . but also an actual encroachment which might prejudice the natural use of the territory and the free movement of its inhabitants." As a result of the decision, Argovia made plans for the improvement of the existing installations. These, however, were considered as insufficient protection by Soleure. The Canton of Argovia then moved the Federal Court to decree that the shooting be again permitted after completion of the projected improvements. This motion was granted. "The demand of the Government of Soleure," said the court, "that all endangerment be absolutely abolished apparently goes too far." The court found that all risk whatever had not been eliminated, as the region was flat and absolutely safe shooting ranges were only found in mountain valleys; that there was a federal duty for the communes to provide facilities for military target practice and that "no more precautions may be demanded for shooting ranges near the boundaries of two Cantons than are required for shooting ranges in the interior of a Canton." (R. O. 26 I, p. 450, 451; R. O. 41, I, p. 137; see D. Schindler, "The Administration of Justice in the Swiss Federal Court in Intercantonal Disputes," *American Journal of International Law*, Vol. 15 (1921), pp. 172–174.)

No case of air pollution dealt with by an international tribunal has been brought to the attention of the Tribunal nor does the Tribunal know of any such case. The nearest analogy is that of water pollution. But, here also, no decision of an international tribunal has been cited or has been found.

There are, however, as regards both air pollution and water pollution, certain decisions of the Supreme Court of the United States which may legitimately be taken as a guide in this field of international law. For it is reasonable to follow by analogy, in international cases, precedents established by that court in dealing with controversies between States of the Union or with other controversies concerning the quasi-sovereign rights of such States, where no contrary rule prevails in international law and no reason for rejecting such precedents can be adduced from the limitations of sovereignty inherent in the Constitution of the United States.

In the suit of the State of Missouri v. the State of Illinois (200 U.S. 496, 521) concerning the pollution, within the boundaries of Illinois, of the Illinois River, an affluent of the Mississippi flowing into the latter where it forms the boundary between that State and Missouri, an injunction was refused. "Before this court ought to intervene," said the court, "the case should be of serious magnitude, clearly and fully proved, and the principle to be applied should be one which the court is prepared deliberately to maintain against all considerations on the other side. (*See* Kansas v. Colorado, 185 U.S. 125.)" The court found that the practice complained of was general along the shores of the Mississippi River at that time, that it was followed by Missouri itself and that thus a standard was set up by the defendant which the claimant was entitled to invoke.

As the claims of public health became more exacting and methods for removing impurities from the water were perfected, complaints ceased. It is significant that Missouri sided with Illinois when the other riparians of the Great Lakes' system sought to enjoin it to desist from diverting the waters of that system into that of the Illinois and Mississippi for the very purpose of disposing of the Chicago sewage.

In the more recent suit of the State of New York against the State of New Jersey (256 U.S. 296, 309), concerning the pollution of New York Bay, the injunction was also refused for lack of proof, some experts believing that the plans which were in dispute would result in the presence of "offensive odors and unsightly deposits," other equally reliable experts testifying that they were confidently of the opinion that the waters would be sufficiently purified. The court, referring to Missouri v. Illinois, said: ." . . . the burden upon the State of New York of sustaining the allegations of its bill is much greater than that imposed upon a complainant in an ordinary suit between private parties. Before this court can be moved to exercise its extraordinary power under the Constitution to control the conduct of one State at the suit of another, the threatened invasion of rights must be of serious magnitude and it must be established by clear and convincing evidence."

What the Supreme Court says there of its power under the Constitution equally applies to the extraordinary power granted this Tribunal under the Convention. What is true between States of the Union is, at least, equally true concerning the relations between the United States and the Dominion of Canada.

In another recent case concerning water pollution (283 U.S. 473), the complainant was successful. The City of New York was enjoined, at the request of the State of New Jersey, to desist, within a reasonable time limit, from the practice of disposing of sewage by dumping it into the sea, a practice which was injurious to the coastal waters of New Jersey in the vicinity of her bathing resorts.

In the matter of air pollution itself, the leading decisions are those of the Supreme Court in the State of Georgia v. Tennessee Copper Company and Ducktown Sulphur, Copper and Iron Company, Limited. Although dealing with a suit against private companies, the decisions were on questions cognate to those here at issue. Georgia stated that it had in vain sought relief from the State of Tennessee, on whose territory the smelters were located, and the court defined the nature of the suit by saying: "This is a suit by a State for an injury to it in its capacity of quasi-sovereign. In that capacity, the State has an interest independent of and behind the titles of its citizens, in all the earth and air within its domain."

On the question whether an injunction should be granted or not, the court said (206 U.S. 230):

It [the State] has the last word as to whether its mountains shall be stripped of their forests and its inhabitants shall breathe pure air.... It is not lightly to be presumed to give up quasi-sovereign rights for pay and ... if that be its choice, it may insist that an infraction of them shall be stopped. This court has not quite the same freedom to balance the harm that will be done by an injunction against that of which the plaintiff complains, that it would have in deciding between two subjects of a single political power. Without excluding the considerations that equity always takes into account[,] ... it is a fair and reasonable demand on the part of a sovereign that the air over its territory should not be polluted on a great scale by sulphurous acid gas, that the forests on its mountains, be they better or worse, and whatever domestic destruction they may have suffered, should not be further destroyed or threatened by the act of persons beyond its control, that the crops and orchards on its hills should not be endangered from the same source.... Whether Georgia, by insisting upon this claim, is doing more harm than good to her own citizens, is for her to determine. The possible disaster to those outside the State must be accepted as a consequence of her standing upon her extreme rights.

Later on, however, when the court actually framed an injunction, in the case of the Ducktown Company (237 U.S. 474, 477) (an agreement on the basis of an annual compensation was reached with the most important of the two smelters, the Tennessee Copper Company), they did not go beyond a decree "adequate to diminish materially the present probability of damage to its (Georgia's) citizens."

Great progress in the control of fumes has been made by science in the last few years and this progress should be taken into account.

The Tribunal, therefore, finds that the above decisions, taken as a whole, constitute an adequate basis for its conclusions, namely, that, under the principles of international law, as well as of the law of the United States, no State has the right to use or permit the use of its territory in such a manner as to cause injury by fumes in or to the territory of another or the properties or persons therein, when the case is of serious consequence and the injury is established by clear and convincing evidence.

The decisions of the Supreme Court of the United States which are the basis of these conclusions are decisions in equity and a solution inspired by them, together with the régime hereinafter prescribed, will, in the opinion of the Tribunal, be "just to all parties concerned," as long, at least, as the present conditions in the Columbia River Valley continue to prevail.

Considering the circumstances of the case, the Tribunal holds that the Dominion of Canada is responsible in international law for the conduct of the Trail Smelter. Apart from the undertakings in the Convention, it is, therefore, the duty of the Government of the Dominion of Canada to see to it that this conduct should be in conformity with the obligation of the Dominion under international law as herein determined.

Questions and Discussion

1. What does the tribunal mean when it says that the state has an interest "independent of and behind the titles of its citizens, in all the earth and air within its domain"? Is the state anything more than its citizens? What is its independent interest?

2. How "serious" must the damage caused by an activity be before it gives rise to state responsibility? How would one establish a clear and convincing link between serious injury and the activity complained of in a case involving multiple parties or states?

3. In deciding whether to order cessation of an activity responsible for transboundary harm, should a tribunal consider the utility of the activity to the source state? Compare 2 RESTATEMENT (THIRD) OF THE FOREIGN RELATIONS LAW OF THE UNITED STATES § 601 cmt. c (1986),

with Günther Handl, *National Uses of Transboundary Air Resources: The International Entitlement Issue Reconsidered*, 26 Nat. Resources J. 405, 413–27 (1986). In fact, reparations in the form of money damages were deemed sufficient by the tribunal, and the smelter continued to discharge pollutants that carried across the U.S. border for decades. In 2003, the smelter was subject to a U.S. Environmental Protection Agency (EPA) Unilateral Administrative Order under section 106 of the Comprehensive Environmental Response, Compensation, and Liability Act, 42 U.S.C. §§ 9601–75. The smelter and Canadian government objected and the smelter refused to comply. Subsequently, Native Americans brought a citizen suit under the Act. *Pakootas v. Teck Cominco Metals Ltd.*, 452 F.3d 1066 (9th Cir. 2006) (affirming denial of defendant's motion to dismiss), *cert. denied*, 128 S. Ct. 858, 169 L. Ed. 2d 722 (2008). *See generally* Transboundary Harm in International Law: Lessons from the Trail Smelter Arbitration (Rebecca Bratspies & Russell A. Miller eds., 2006).

4. In the U.S. Supreme Court judgment on global climate change, *Massachusetts v. EPA*, 549 U.S. 497 (2007), the majority also relied on *Georgia v. Tennessee Copper Company and Ducktown Sulphur, Copper and Iron Company, Ltd.*, determining that states and local communities had standing to sue the federal EPA for its failure to regulate greenhouse gases. Does this suggest that interstate cases against major emitters of greenhouse gases could be filed in an international tribunal?

5. Several interstate cases filed at the International Court of Justice indicate the continued validity of nuisance or good neighborliness in combating environmental harm. For one such dispute, see Case Study I, Chapter 12 (online).

Note on the Pulp Mills Case

On April 20, 2010, the International Court of Justice (ICJ) delivered its judgment in the case concerning *Pulp Mills on the River Uruguay (Argentina v. Uruguay)*, available at www.icj-cij.org. The dispute between the parties concerned the planned construction, authorized by Uruguay, of two pulp mills on the Uruguay River. The river constitutes the boundary between Argentina and Uruguay, as defined by a bilateral treaty concluded at Montevideo on 7 April 1961 (635 U.N.T.S. 9074, p. 98). Article 7 of the treaty provides for the establishment by the parties of a "régime for the use of the river" covering various subjects, including the conservation of living resources and the prevention of water pollution of the river. The "régime for the use of the river" contemplated in Article 7 of the 1961 Treaty was established through the 1975 Statute of the River Uruguay (the "1975 Statute"). Article 1 of the 1975 Statute states that the parties adopted it "to establish the joint machinery necessary for the optimum and rational utilization of the [Uruguay River], in strict observance of the rights and obligations arising from treaties and other international agreements in force for each of the parties." To implement the 1975 Statute, the parties created CARU (Administrative Commission of the River Uruguay/Comision Administratif del Rio Uruguay) and established procedures in connection with it, so as to enable the parties to fulfill their substantive obligations.

Although the dispute was based on alleged breaches of the 1975 Statute, the references in the 1975 Statute to other treaties, as well as the backdrop of general international law in all disputes, led the ICJ to pronounce on the customary law nature of several norms at issue in the case. The Court first indicated that the 1975 Statute is perfectly in keeping with the requirements of international law on the implementation of treaties, since the mechanism for cooperation between states is governed by the principle of good faith.

The Court examined the nature and role of CARU and then considered whether Uruguay had complied with its obligations to inform CARU and to notify Argentina of its plans. The Court invoked the principle of prevention of environmental harm, which it called a customary rule, having its origins in the due diligence that is required of a state in its territory. It is "every State's obligation not to allow knowingly its territory to be used for acts contrary to the rights of other States" (*Corfu Channel (United Kingdom v. Albania)*), Merits, Judgment, I.C.J. Reports 1949, p. 22). According to the ICJ, a state is thus obliged to use all the means at its disposal to avoid activities that take place in its territory, or in any area under its jurisdiction, causing significant damage to the environment of another state. This obligation "is now part of the corpus of international law relating to the environment" (*Legality of the Threat or Use of Nuclear Weapons, Advisory Opinion*, I.C.J. Reports 1996 (I), p. 242, para. 29).

The Court observed that the obligation to inform CARU allowed for the initiation of cooperation between the parties that is necessary to fulfill the obligation of prevention. The duty to inform CARU arises as soon as one party is in possession of a plan which is sufficiently developed to enable CARU to make a preliminary assessment of whether the proposed works might cause significant damage to the other party. Uruguay did not so inform CARU, as required by article 7, despite the several requests to do so. The Court concluded that Uruguay had failed to comply with the obligation imposed on it by article 7, paragraph 1, of the 1975 Statute.

The Court turned to environmental impact assessment as a requirement of customary international law, noting that for the parties to comply properly with their obligations under article 41(a) and (b) of the 1975 Statute (to protect and preserve the aquatic environment) they must carry out an environmental impact assessment. Moreover, once operations have started and, where necessary, throughout the life of the project, continuous monitoring of its effects on the environment must be undertaken. The Court commented, however, that general international law does not specify the scope and content of an environmental impact assessment. It pointed out as well that Argentina and Uruguay are not parties to the Espoo Convention on Environmental Impact Assessment in a Transboundary Context and noted that the other instrument Argentina invoked, the UNEP Goals and Principles, was not binding on the parties. However, as guidelines issued by an international technical body, the UNEP text has to be taken into account by each party, in accordance with article 41(a) of the Statute, in adopting measures within its domestic regulatory framework. The UNEP instrument provides only that the "environmental effects in an EIA should be assessed with a degree of detail commensurate with their likely environmental significance" (Principle 5) without giving any indication of minimum core components of the assessment. Consequently, the Court concluded that it is for each state to determine in its domestic legislation or in the authorization process for the project, the specific content of the environmental impact assessment required in each case, having regard to the nature and magnitude of the proposed development and its likely adverse impact on the environment as well as to the need to exercise due diligence in conducting such an assessment.

In one of the more surprising findings, the Court expressed its view that the parties had no legal obligation to consult the affected populations; however, the Court added that this was based on the instruments invoked by Argentina. In fact, Argentina failed to argue any human rights obligation to consult or to otherwise emphasize this obligation as part of the duty of prevention. Further limiting the impact of the Court's statement, it also found that Uruguay had, in fact, held consultations.

Following a detailed examination of the parties' arguments, the Court ultimately found that there was no conclusive evidence in the record to show that Uruguay had not acted with the requisite degree of due diligence or that the discharges of effluent from the Orion (Botnia) mill had had deleterious effects or had caused harm to living resources or to the quality of the water or to the ecological balance of the river after it started its operations in November 2007. Consequently, on the basis of the evidence submitted to it, the Court concluded that Uruguay had not breached its obligations under article 41.

The Court held that the obligations of the parties include continuous monitoring the quality of the waters of the river and of assessing the impact of the operation of the Orion (Botnia) mill on the aquatic environment:

> [B]oth Parties have the obligation to enable CARU, as the joint machinery created by the 1975 Statute, to exercise on a continuous basis the powers conferred on it by the 1975 Statute, including its function of monitoring the quality of the waters of the river and of assessing the impact of the operation of the Orion (Botnia) mill on the aquatic environment.

Uruguay, for its part, "has the obligation to continue monitoring the operation of the plant in accordance with Article 41 of the Statute and to ensure compliance by Botnia with Uruguayan domestic regulations as well as the standards set by CARU." The Court concluded that, under the 1975 Statute, "[t]he Parties have a legal obligation . . . to continue their co-operation through CARU and to enable it to devise the necessary means to promote the equitable utilization of the river, while protecting its environment."

2. The Public Trust Doctrine

In addition to allowing private actions based in tort, some legal systems apply the long-established property doctrine of public trust to protect natural resources and lands. The doctrine of public trust, traced to Roman law, holds that navigable waters, the sea, and the land along the seashore are common property open to use by all. Many courts have adopted and applied the public trust doctrine to fishing rights, access to the shore, and navigable waters and the lands beneath them. After the publication of an influential law review article in 1970, courts began to expand the doctrine and apply it to wildlife and public lands. *See, e.g., Wade v. Kramer*, 459 N.E.2d 1025, 1027 (Ill. App. Ct. 1984); Joseph Sax, *The Public Trust Doctrine in Natural Resource Law: Effective Judicial Intervention*, 68 MICH. L. REV. 471 (1970); JOSEPH L. SAX, DEFENDING THE ENVIRONMENT: A STRATEGY FOR CITIZEN ACTION, ch. 7 (1970). *See also* Bernard Cohen, *The Constitution, the Public Trust Doctrine, and the Environment*, 1970 UTAH L. REV. 388. The public trust doctrine emphasizes the duties of the government as trustee, imposing on it an obligation to conserve the corpus of the trust and ensure common access to and use of it by present and future generations. As a Virginia court said in 1932: "The *jus publicum* and all rights of the people, which are by their nature inherent or inseparable incidents thereof, are incidents of the sovereignty of the State. Therefore by reason of the object and purposes for which it was ordained, the Constitution impliedly denies to the legislature to power to relinquish, surrender, or destroy, or substantially impair the jus publicum." *Commonwealth v. Newport News*, 158 Va. 521 at 546, 164 S.E. 689 at 697 (1932). *See also Payne v. Kassab*, 312 A.2d 86 (Pa. Commw. Ct. 1973), *aff'd* 361 A.2d 263 (Pa. 1976).

In the following case, the public trust doctrine is invoked to protect freshwater resources.

United Plainsmen Association v. North Dakota State Water Conservation Commission, 247 N.W. 2d 457, 458–464 (N.D. 1976)

PEDERSON, Justice.

This is an appeal by the United Plainsmen Association, a North Dakota non-profit corporation, from a decision of the district court of Burleigh County dismissing the complaint for failure to state a claim upon which relief could be granted.

The complaint sought an injunction against the North Dakota State Water Conservation Commission and Vernon Fahy, State Engineer.... We hold that the district court did err in dismissing the complaint, we deny a temporary restraining order, and remand the case for further proceedings.

. . .

The injunction sought by United Plainsmen would have prevented the State Engineer from issuing future water permits for coal-related power and energy production facilities until there is a comprehensive short and long-term plan for the conservation and development of the State's natural resources, which, United Plainsmen contends, is required by § 61-01-26, NDCC, and the common law Public Trust Doctrine existing in this State....

. . .

Although it is not mandatory, § 61–01-26, entitled "Declaration of state water resources policy," is a significant advisory policy statement. The last sentence therein clearly indicates that it is not to be construed to limit, impair or abrogate the rights, powers, duties or functions of any department or agency of the State. This statute provides but little support for United Plainsmen's contention that the State Engineer must complete short- and long-term planning as a condition precedent to the issuance of water permits.

. . .

The foregoing, however, does not relieve the Commission and State Engineer of mandatory planning responsibilities with respect to the issuance of water permits, and we note that counsel for the Commission emphasized in his argument that the State Engineer and the Commission do have plans and do not reject the concept of prior planning. We agree with United Plainsmen that the discretionary authority of state officials to allocate vital state resources is not without limit but is circumscribed by what has been called the Public Trust Doctrine.

This doctrine was first clearly defined in *Illinois Central Railroad v. Illinois*, 146 U.S. 387, 13 S. Ct. 110, 36 L. Ed. 1018 (1892), a case in which the United States Supreme Court was called upon to decide the competency of the State of Illinois to convey, by legislative grant, a portion of Chicago's harbor on Lake Michigan to the Illinois Central Railroad.

That the State holds the title to the lands under the navigable waters of Lake Michigan, within its limits, in the same manner that the State holds title to soils under tide water, by the common law, we have already shown, and that title necessarily carries with it control over the waters above them whenever the lands are subjected to use.... It is a title held in trust for the people of the State that they may enjoy the navigation of the waters, carry on commerce over them, and have liberty of fishing therein freed from the obstruction or interference of private parties." 146 U.S. at 452, 13 S. Ct. At 118.

The State can no more abdicate its trust over property in which the whole people are interested, like navigable waters and soils under them, so as to leave them entirely under the use and control of private parties, except in the instance of parcels mentioned for the improvement of the navigation and use of the waters, or when parcels can be disposed of without impairment of the public interest in what remains, than it can abdicate its police powers in the administration of government and the preservation of the peace. 146 U.S. at 453, 13 S. Ct. At 118.

We cannot, it is true, cite any authority where a grant of this kind has been held invalid, for we believe that no instance exists where the harbor of a great city and its commerce have been allowed to pass into the control of any private corporation. But the decisions are numerous which declare that such property is held by the State, by virtue of its sovereignty, in trust for the public. The ownership of the navigable waters of the harbor and of the lands under them is a subject of public concern to the whole people of the State. The trust with which they are held, therefore, is governmental and cannot be alienated, except in those instances mentioned of parcels used in the improvement of the interest thus held, or when parcels can be disposed of without detriment to the public interest in the lands and waters remaining. 146 U.S. at 455–56.

The Commission, the State Engineer, and the lower court, while acknowledging the existence of this doctrine in North Dakota interpret it in a narrow sense, limiting its applicability to conveyances of real property. We do not understand the doctrine to be so restricted. The State holds the navigable waters, as well as the lands beneath them, in trust for the public. North Dakota's Constitution, Article XVII, § 210, states:

All flowing streams and natural water courses shall forever remain the property of the state for mining, irrigating and manufacturing purposes.

Section 61–01–01, NDCC, further defines the public waters of this State:

All waters within the limits of the state from the following sources of water supply, namely:

1. Waters on the surface of the earth excluding diffused surface waters but including surface waters whether flowing in well defined channels or flowing through lakes, ponds, or marshes which constitute integral parts of a stream system, or waters in lakes; and
2. Waters under the surface of the earth whether such waters flow in defined subterranean channels or are diffused percolating underground waters; and
3. All residual waters resulting from beneficial use, and all waters artificially drained; and
4. All waters, excluding privately owned waters, in areas determined by the state engineer to be noncontributing drainage areas. A noncontributing drainage area is hereby defined to be any area which does not contribute natural flowing surface water to a natural stream or watercourse at an average frequency oftener than once in three years over the latest thirty year period;

belong to the public and are subject to appropriation for beneficial use and the right to the use of these waters for such use, shall be acquired pursuant to the provisions of chapter 61–04.

Sections 61-04-06 and 61-04-07, NDCC, provide:

61-04-06. *Approval of application – Endorsing approval – Contents.* – Upon the receipt of the proof of publication, the state engineer shall determine from the evidence presented by the parties interested, from such surveys of the water supply as may be available, and from the records, whether there is unappropriated water available for the benefit of the applicant. If so, he shall endorse his approval on the application, which thereupon shall become a conditional water permit allowing the applicant to appropriate water, and shall state in such approval the time within which the water shall be applied to a beneficial use.

61-04-07. *Rejection of applications–Appeal to district court.* – If, in the opinion of the state engineer, no unappropriated water is available, he shall reject an application made under the provisions of this chapter. He shall decline to order the publication of notice of any application which does not comply with the requirements of the law and the rules and regulations thereunder. He may refuse to consider or approve an application or to order the publication of notice thereof if, in his opinion, the approval thereof would be contrary to the public interest. In determining the public interest, the state engineer shall be limited to those considerations within his jurisdiction. Any applicant, within sixty days from the date of refusal to approve an application, may appeal to the district court of the county in which the proposed place of diversion or storage is situated, from any decision of the state engineer which denies a substantial right. In the absence of such appeal, the decision of the state engineer shall be final.

These statutes provide a means by which those who seek use of public waters can petition the State Engineer for water permits. In the performance of this duty of resource allocation consistent with the public interest, the Public Trust Doctrine requires, at a minimum, a determination of the potential effect of the allocation of water on the present water supply and future water needs of this State. This necessarily involves planning responsibility. The development and implementation of some short and long-term planning capability is essential to effective allocation of resources "without detriment to the public interest in the lands and waters remaining."

We believe that § 61-01-01, NDCC, expresses the Public Trust Doctrine.

The public trust concept has been acknowledged throughout the country in varying forms. Without using those specific terms, this court said, in *Baeth v. Hoisveen*, 157 N.W.2d 728, 733 (N.D.1968);

North Dakota is, in part, a semiarid State. Therefore, concern for the general welfare could well require that the water resources of the State be put to beneficial use to the fullest extent of which they are capable, and that the waste or unreasonable method of use of water be prevented, and that the conservation of such water be exercised with a view to the reasonable and beneficial use thereof in the interests of the people and the public welfare. We feel that the foregoing factors formed the basis for the legislative enactment of Section 61-01-01, N.D.C.C.

We said that section line right-of-way is a public trust in *Saetz v. Heiser*, 240 N.W.2d 67, 72 (N.D. 1976).

In *Payne v. Kassab*, 11 Pa. Cmwlth. 14, 312 A.2d 86, 93 (1973), the court stated that the following Pennsylvania constitutional provision affixed a public trust concept to the management of public natural resources of that State:

"The people have a right to clean air, pure water, and to the preservation of the natural, scenic, historic and esthetic values of the environment. Pennsylvania's public natural resources are the common property of all the people, including generations yet to come. As trustee of these resources, the Commonwealth shall conserve and maintain them for the benefit of all the people." [Constitution of Pennsylvania, Art. I, Section 27.]

In declaring the taking of one-half acre of land from a public park to widen a public street to be constitutionally permissible, that court said:

The result of our holding is a controlled development of resources rather than no development.

We must recognize, as a corollary of such a conclusion, that decision makers will be faced with the constant and difficult task of weighing conflicting environmental and social concerns in arriving at a course of action that will be expedient as well as reflective of the high priority which constitutionally has been placed on the conservation of our natural, scenic, esthetic and historical resources. 312 A.2d at 94.

In an action for damages for the destruction of fish caused by the introduction of a "deleterious substance" into a creek in violation of a statute, the New Jersey court, in *State, Dept. of Envir. Pro. v. Jersey Central P. & L. Co.*, 125 N.J. Super. 97, 308 A.2d 671, 674 (1973), discussed the Public Trust Doctrine in the following terms:

There can be little debate that the public trust has been diminished by the loss of these fish.

... The State has not only the right but also the affirmative fiduciary obligation to ensure that the rights of the public to a viable marine environment are protected, and to seek compensation for any diminution in that trust corpus.

It is evident that the Public Trust Doctrine is assuming an expanding role in environmental law. *See* 61 Am. Jur. 2d 950, Pollution Control, § 145. As one author has commented:

> It is clear that the historical scope of public trust law is quite narrow. Its coverage includes, with some variation among the states, that aspect of the public domain below the low-water mark on the margin of the sea and the great lakes, the waters over those lands, and the waters within rivers and streams of any consequence.…
>
> If any of the analysis in this Article makes sense, it is clear that the judicial techniques developed in public trust cases need not be limited either to these few conventional interests or to questions of disposition of public properties.… Thus, it seems that the delicate mixture of procedural and substantive protections which the courts have applied in conventional public trust cases would be equally applicable and equally appropriate in controversies involving air pollution, the dissemination of pesticides, the location of rights of way for utilities, and strip mining on wetland filling on private lands in a state where governmental permits are required." Sax, *The Public Trust Doctrine in Natural Resource Law: Effective Judicial Intervention*, 68 Mich. L. Rev. 471, 556–557 (1969–1970).

No one has suggested the need for such an expansive application of the Public Trust Doctrine here. Confined to traditional concepts, the Doctrine confirms the State's role as trustee of the public waters. It permits alienation and allocation of such precious state resources only after an analysis of present supply and future need.

The Legislature has indicated its desire to see such planning take place, although not in mandatory language. Until the Legislature speaks more forcefully, we think the Public Trust Doctrine requires, as a minimum, evidence of some planning by appropriate state agencies and officers in the allocation of public water resources, and that the Environmental Law Enforcement Act (Chapter 32-40, NDCC) requires more than a plenary dismissal of the action.

United Plainsmen has requested a temporary restraining order, enjoining the further issuance of water permits pending trial on the merits in the lower court. A temporary injunction or restraining order may be granted if it appears by the complaint that the plaintiffs are entitled to the relief requested, and that such relief consists of restraining acts which would, if continued, produce injury to the plaintiffs during the litigation. Section 32-06-02, NDCC. We are not convinced that a temporary restraining order is necessary or advisable in this instance.

During oral argument counsel for appellees stated that, of the total number of water permits considered each year, a very small percentage is in the industrial category relating to energy conversion. Of that small percentage of industrial water use applications considered, only a few are actually granted and some that are granted will never be used because of other causes which prevent the intended development.

We express no opinion about the ultimate outcome of the trial on the merits, should that point be reached in this case. We acknowledge, however, that there is merit in the argument that the extent of planning is somewhat related to the sums appropriate therefor by the Legislature, and that United Plainsmen action to defeat legislation, such as S.B. 2088 and S.B. 2253, Forty-fourth Legislative Assembly, designed to accomplish more refined scientific planning, militates against its argument. Quite obviously, too, the type of study and impact statement which would have been necessary under the North Dakota Environmental Policy Act of 1975 (H.B. 1058, Forty-fourth Legislative Assembly), had it become law, are not required. It may be that the planning being done by the Commission, according to the oral argument made in this Court, is sufficient.

We hold that the dismissal was premature and improvident under the circumstances. The amended complaint charges a failure to devise any water conservation plan, as well as a failure to consider injury to the public. For the purpose of the motion to dismiss, the trial court and this Court must consider all allegations of the complaint to be true. We hold, accordingly, that the complaint does state a claim upon which relief could be granted, if proved, and, therefore, must be reinstated.

Reversed and remanded for further proceedings.

Questions and Discussion

1. The Supreme Court of India also has relied upon the public trust doctrine in several cases. In *M.C. Mehta v. Kamal Nath et al.* (1997 (1) SCC 388), the court noted that the Indian legal system, based on English common law, includes the public trust doctrine as part of its jurisprudence. The doctrine makes the state "the trustee of all natural resources which are by nature meant for public use and enjoyment. As such, the public at large is the beneficiary of the seashore, running waters, air, forests, and ecologically fragile lands. The state as a trustee is under a legal duty to protect the natural resources. These resources meant for public use cannot be converted into private ownership. The aesthetic use and the pristine glory cannot be permitted to be eroded for private, commercial, or any other use unless the courts find it necessary, in good faith, for public good, and in public interest to encroach upon the said resources." Using this doctrine, the Court quashed a lease granted for a private motel and ordered the government to take over the area and restore it to its original condition. The Court called the lease of ecologically fragile land "a patent breach of the public trust."

2. Fishing rights, free access to the shore, and navigation are traditional public access rights that are reaffirmed in several U.S. state constitutions as well as in jurisprudence. *See, e.g.*, CAL. CONST. art. I, s. 25; R.I. CONST. art. I. s. 17; ALA. CONST. art. 1 s. 24. Other constitutional provisions that refer to trusteeship over environmental resources include HAW. CONST. art. XI; PA. CONST. art. I, § 27; VA. CONST. art. XI, § 3; ALA. CONST. art. VIII; CAL. CONST. art. X, § 2; FLA. CONST. art. II, § 7; LA. CONST. art. IX; MASS. CONST. § 179; MICH. CONST. art. IV, § 52; MONT. CONST. art. IX, § 1; N.M. CONST. art. XX, § 21; N.Y. CONST. art. XIV; N.C. CONST. art. XIV, § 5; R.I. CONST. art. 1, § 17; TEX. CONST. art. XVI, § 59.

3. Some courts have expanded the public trust doctrine to create the notion of public guardianship. *See, e.g., Bulankulame v. Secretary, Ministry of Industrial Development et al. (Eppawela Case)* (Sup. Ct. Sri Lanka, 2000). In Australia, the doctrine of public trust has been applied to challenge harmful activities in public areas. In *Willoughby City Council v. Minister*, 78 LGERA 19, 27 (1992), which concerned commercial activities in part of a national park, Justice Stein of the New South Wales Land and Environment Court said, "[N]ational parks are held by the State in trust for the enjoyment and benefit of its citizens, including future generations. In this instance the public trust is reposed in the Minister, the director and the service. These public officers have a duty to protect and preserve national parks and exercise their functions and powers within the law in order to achieve the objects of the National Parks and Wildlife Act." In contrast, the Australian Capital Territory Supreme Court has summarily dismissed the contention that a public trust in the Black Mountain Reserve arose out of the declaration of the Reserve as a public park and the trust obligated the government to maintain the environmental quality of the area. Without analysis, Justice Smithers curtly said, "I do not think there is any such trust or obligation upon the [government] arising out of the declaration of the reserve as a public park." *Kent v. Johnson*, 2 ACTR 1, 42 (1973).

4. Note that the public trust doctrine extends only to those natural resources that are viewed as part of the corpus of the trust and not to the environment as a whole. Is it appropriate and would it be useful to extend this doctrine to the air, ecological processes, biodiversity, and other components of the environment? Should the oceans as a whole be declared part of a

global public trust? The atmosphere and the climate? An expansive public trust is found in article XI, section 1, of Hawaii's Constitution:

> For the benefit of present and future generations, the State and its political subdivisions shall conserve and protect Hawaii's natural beauty and all natural resources, including land, water, air, minerals and energy sources, and shall promote the development and utilization of these resources in a manner consistent with their conservation and in furtherance of the self-sufficiency of the State. All public natural resources are held in trust by the State for the benefit of the people.

5. Several subsidiary rules of trust law could be important in fleshing out the application of justice principles, such as those that require the trustee to monitor and report on the status of the trust corpus. These rules should impose legal obligations on public officials to monitor the state of the environment and provide information periodically to the public in an accessible form and through an accessible medium. Monitoring and reporting requirements are already required of states parties to most major environmental agreements, including the Convention on International Trade in Endangered Species of Wild Fauna and Flora (article VII), the Convention on Biological Diversity (article 26), the U.N. Framework Convention on Climate Change (article 12), and the Montreal Protocol on Substances That Deplete the Ozone Layer (article 7).

6. For various approaches to the reach of the public trust doctrine, see Scott W. Reed, *The Public Trust Doctrine: Is It Amphibious?* 1 J. Envtl L. & Litig. 107, 107–08, 118 (1986); Charles F. Wilkinson, *The Public Trust Doctrine in Public Land Law*, 14 U.C. Davis L. Rev. 269, 316 (1980); Alison Rieser, *Ecological Preservation as a Public Property Right: An Emerging Doctrine in Search of a Theory*, 15 Harv. Envtl. L. Rev. 393, 398–99 (1991); Matthew Thor Kirsch, *Upholding the Public Trust in State Constitutions*, 46 Duke L.J. 1169–1210 (1997); Tim Bonyhady, *A Usable Past: The Public Trust in Australia*, 12 Envtl Planning L.J. 329 (1995).

B. *Public Regulation*

Public law is a second approach, and still the most prominent one, to environmental protection. Legislative texts often establish general environmental policy, supplemented by specific laws and administrative regulations. Broad or framework environmental statutes have been adopted in many countries, such as the *National Environmental Policy Act* (United States, 1969); *Environmental Law* (Bulgaria, (1991); *Law on the Protection of the Environment* (Russia, 2001); and *Environmental Management Act* (Trinidad and Tobago, 1995/2000).

These statutes use common regulatory techniques and procedures, including environmental impact and risk assessment, prior licensing, and emission standards. At the same time, they may respond to particular environmental concerns in a particular country, such as the safety and environmental consequences of nuclear power plants, large dams, or extractive industries like oil or coal. In most cases, environmental legislation is supplemented and given greater specificity in administrative regulations.

In addition to general framework laws, national laws often regulate a single environmental milieu, such as water, air, soil, or biological diversity, as a result of the particular environmental problems facing a given area, political or economic priorities, or the ease of achieving consensus on a specific environmental issue. One difficulty with sectoral regulation is that it can sometimes overlook the interrelated and interdependent nature of the environment.

A more comprehensive approach seeks integrated pollution prevention and control (i.e., protection against pollution of all natural systems necessary to support the biosphere). The focus of integrated pollution prevention and control is on eliminating or at least reducing the input of each polluting substance, noting its origin and geographic target. Integrated pollution prevention and control aspires to a cradle-to-grave approach that considers the whole life cycle of substances and products, anticipates the effects of substances and activities on all environmental media, minimizes the quantity and harmfulness of waste, uses a single method such as risk assessment for estimating and comparing environmental problems, and involves complementary use of objectives and limits.

Lost in Translation: What Environmental Regulation Does That Tort Cannot Duplicate, 41 Washburn L.J. 583, 585–86, 589–96, 598–602 (2002) (footnotes omitted or renumbered)

Christopher H. Schroeder

... The first ... basic difference [between regulation and tort law] relates to the processes through which desired levels of environmental quality are established. A regulatory regime establishes the amount of environmental degradation legally permitted through a collective or public decision-making process, whereas tort law establishes that amount through a private law process of judicial application of general principles to particular cases. Tort law still applies community or collective norms, often under a rubric of "unreasonableness." Those norms, though, are spelled out through an iterative process of individualized litigation, not through an intentional decision of some public entity.

The key to this distinction is the public versus private identification of environmental quality levels, not the fact that private actors sue each other in the private case instead of using administrative or legislative procedures in the public case. Private litigation might well be used to supplement or supplant a public enforcement scheme that operates through bureaucracies, inspectors, administrative compliance orders, administrative law judges and the like. The citizen suit provisions that can be found in almost all pollution related statutes are intended to do just this. Citizen suits, however, are limited to enforcing standards established by the regulatory process. Private litigation that uses statutory or regulatory violations as negligence *per se* can also supplement public enforcement. There are many things to be said in connection with the possibilities of private versus public enforcement of the public standards, but such forms of litigation do not set those standards.

... One might claim that the consequences of tort law will approximate the environmental quality levels that the collective desires or should appropriately be seeking. Decentralizing dispute resolution would in that case be justified as a means to a collectively congenial end. Tort law might have this pleasing consequence, furthermore, even if the underlying motivations and ends of tort law itself were in significant respects autonomous from influence by the collective selection of desired results.

... There are significant externalities involved in disputes over environmental quality, externalities that can be spatial, temporal or value-based. Spatial externalities arise when the actions of the parties involved in a private transaction have physical effects on the interests of persons remote from the site of the transaction. Temporal externalities involve the implications of actions affecting the environment on future generations. Value-based externalities involve the wide variety of interests implicated by non-anthropocentric ethical systems, such as those positing that animals and even ecosystems are entitled to respect in their own right. These values deserve a "place at the table" when actions that significantly affect them are taken. The internal structure of the tort system, however, requires only that the interests of the parties before the court be respected, thus leaving it up to the beneficence of the parties to raise the concerns of the unrepresented, assuming the court would permit them to do so. That beneficence will often substitute inadequately for more inclusive structures, such as public ones. Therefore, the structure of the tort system supplies an argument in favor of public mechanisms, not private ones, to deal with environmental issues that implicate many interests.

. . .

The goal of much modern environmental regulation is to prevent harm to the environment before it occurs, with an implementation structure that includes prior approvals, permits that embody standards to be met, and the monitoring of compliance, all with that goal in mind. Modern environmental regulation announces to risk takers the legally enforceable levels of risk or harm. Unlike tort, environmental regulation does not even contemplate compensation of victims, the remedy that is essential to tort's ex post operation, but its increasing reliance on criminal and civil liability for fines and jail time for responsible corporate officers and others can get the attention of risk takers better than tort can. Permit requirements translate rules and regulations into risk taker specific terms as they frequently do and administrative agencies exist to provide further guidance. Environmental regulation does not ask risk takers to appraise their own risks, thus reducing the problem of over-optimism. Because the regulation is ex ante, it does not depend on detection of harm caused (which might be years down the road), but instead depends on detection of present violations. While such detection also can be difficult, it will be less so than the detection tort requires. In sum, the compliance signal regulation sends to risk takers faces much less interference or static than does tort's deterrence signal, as the following discussion elucidates.

The deterrence theory of tort states its objective as the prevention of harm, just like environmental regulation. Unlike regulation, though, tort has an operational structure designed to function ex post, after harm has occurred. Its objective of preventing acts from occurring that can be judged to be inefficient or unreasonable is one that it must accomplish through implementation and enforcement structures that operate after the fact. For such a system to deter, it must be able to send a signal to parties regarding their future behavior, but to send that signal it must have a case of prior harm to decide.

There are some limited exceptions to tort's ex post operation, but they do not significantly change the ex post nature of that regime. Equity courts did and courts still do recognize a cause of action for anticipatory nuisance, brought prior to harm occurring. Plaintiffs have most frequently sought to bring this type of action, though, in efforts to enjoin conflicting land uses prior to the landowner commencing with the land use, where the extent of the harm that the land use would eventually cause is highly predictable. Where harm is more speculative, even though it might be more likely than not, courts are reluctant to intervene before the fact. The requirement that harm must be imminent and practically certain before an injunction will lie substantially impairs the usefulness of the anticipatory injunction.[3]

The limited circumstances in which injunctions will lie fail to cover many types of cases in which people today worry about environmental risks. Consequently, for many environmental risks the ability of tort to prevent harm will depend entirely on the success of its deterrent effect, which must inevitably be an indirect effect of the signal or message that the tort system sends. It is not enough that tort cases send a message, either. That message must be heard, understood and acted upon before deterrence succeeds. These downstream components to the mechanism of deterrence depend upon individuals, incentive structures and institutions that tort cannot affect directly.

. . .

---

[3] See, e.g., Rackleff v. Texaco Trading & Transp., Inc., 611 So. 2d 95 (Fla. Dist. Ct. App. 1992) (anticipatory nuisance is available only in limited circumstances to enjoin prospective harm that will necessarily result in the creation of a nuisance). Injunctive relief will also lie in cases of continuing tort, but these are cases in which harm has occurred and is ongoing or recurrent, so they fit the ex post model.

There is however, more to be said. Predicting the consequences of tort's deterrence signal–and hence its impact on environmental quality at the point in time that the public desires, before harm occurs–requires more precision than is provided by the blunt conclusion that people react ex ante to the prospect of liability. The question is do they react in a predictable and satisfactory way. The deterrence theory of tort aspires to eliminate only undesirable behavior, defined against a standard of efficiency or unreasonableness, and it predicts that this level of deterrence will be what is observed.

On whether or not this prediction is borne out in practice, the empirical evidence is also fairly compelling, and it is negative evidence. When it comes to achieving the level of risk reduction predicted by the deterrence models, tort law is "not as effective as economic models suggest."[4]

. . .

. . . Compound these real imperfections with the highly imperfect understanding of them by judges and juries, and the idea that the size of the signal could be modulated to compensate, so as to achieve the correct level of deterrence, becomes rather implausible.

In contrast to tort's ex post structure, the preventive, ex ante orientation toward environmental quality levels is a fundamental attribute of the modern environmental regulatory regime. The basic architecture of that regime came into being in a remarkably short period of time, between 1969 to 1976, when a broad environmental movement helped sweep our core environmental statutes onto the pages of the United States Code. Looking back on the history of that movement, we can locate reasons for why these laws have the ex ante orientation that they do.

Prior to the explosion of legislation around the time of the first Earth Day, American social and political expectations had begun to change, and it was change in the direction of insisting on the prevention of exposure to harm or the potential to harm through our common environment.

. . .

The preventive, or precautionary, nature of the early environmental legislation is one of that legislation's central organizing principles, and one that squarely clashes with common law tort. These clashing perspectives were fully ventilated, and their contrasting implications examined, in the landmark case of *Ethyl Corp. v. EPA*, 541 F.2d 1 (D.C. Cir. 1976). In *Ethyl*, Judge Skelly Wright championed an ex ante precautionary interpretation of a Clean Air Act provision authorizing the EPA to regulate additives to gasoline and diesel fuel, and Judge Malcolm Wilkey ably represented the ex post tort law opposition.

. . .

. . . To replace the enforcement of environmental regulation with tort law would require convincing people that the preventive, precautionary results that we want can actually be better achieved through a system that concerns itself with prevention only by using litigation to signal future risk takers. As we have already discussed, though, tort's deterrence message will in many cases only be faintly heard and imperfectly obeyed.

In sum, shifting from regulation to tort necessitates convincing the public to make a choice to relinquish the authority to choose levels of environmental quality through collective decision making mechanisms, exactly reversing one of the main ambitions of the environmental movement since its inception. Doing so would at the very least require a conviction that tort's mechanisms of deterrence could approximate the levels of environmental quality desired by the public. Instead, there are substantial reasons to believe that such satisfactory outcomes will not result from tort's weak deterrence signal as applied to environmental risks, even if the public could be convinced to abandon its preference for ex ante structures of environmental quality protection.

Besides the weaknesses in the claim that tort can provide the environmental results that the public desires, there is a significant point to be made about the structure of governance involved in the choice between private and public determination of levels of environmental quality. Public

4 Gary T. Schwartz, *Reality in the Economic Analysis of Law: Does Tort Law Really Deter?*, 42 UCLA L. Rev. 377, 443–44 (1994).

choices are in an important sense prior to private ones. By establishing the conditions and constraints within which private autonomy can be exercised, collective choices significantly shape the decision making environment within which private choices are made. Public choices, for example, can be made with a view to securing the sound functioning of markets through laws that protect private property, enforce contracts, impose liability for fraud and provide for recovery for losses. Such laws enable private choices to be made and markets to operate more efficiently.

Other public choices can restrict certain kinds of transactions, effectively imposing constraints on what can be traded in markets. Examples of such rules are those preventing discrimination on the basis of race, gender, religion or national origin, rules requiring employers to make reasonable accommodations for persons with disabilities and rules prohibiting child labor. These sorts of constraints have a long established pedigree. To a considerable degree, modern environmental legislation reflects the conviction that significant choices about environmental quality ought to operate as constraints on what can be traded in private markets, or resolved through private tort litigation, rather than choices that should be left entirely to those private transactions themselves. As Pete Andrews has expressed the point with respect to environmental and health related legislation:

> President Lincoln did not sign the Emancipation Proclamation on the basis of its economic efficiency . . . nor does society condone murder, theft, perjury, or many other forms of behavior even if their overall economic benefits exceed their costs. These forms of behavior are simply prohibited as unacceptable. Similarly, U.S. health legislation often has been based on the philosophy of protecting citizens as fully as possible from involuntary health hazards, within the constraints of what is technically feasible.
>
> In this conceptual framework, government is not simply a corrective instrument on the margins of economic markets but an equally central arena in which the members of society choose and legitimize – however imperfectly in practice – their collective value. . . . Such actions may or may not be directed toward economic efficiency.[5]

. . .

Now, even assuming that tort operated in exactly the way that an idealized law-and-economics analysis portrays, a tort regime would still produce enormously different results from the levels of environmental quality the current regulatory regime seeks to achieve. Environmental legislation regularly establishes standards different from those chosen by cost-benefit considerations, standards aimed at protecting public health as much as possible within the limits of technical and economic feasibility.

. . .

The regulation of criteria air pollutants under the Clean Air Act provides an . . . illustration of the difference between a standard enacted by public choice and a cost-benefit standard. In selecting a health-based standard for the control of the criteria air pollutants, Congress intentionally chose to preclude the consideration of compliance costs, and thus to make it a near certainty that standard-setting for these ubiquitous pollutants would not adhere to cost-benefit principles. If the calculations of industry petitioners are credible, it is very difficult to make a national cost-benefit case for the latest reduction in permissible levels of ozone. It would be quite impossible to make such a case on the more localized level at which tort litigation occurs, where every separate compliance measure could be the subject of litigation, even using the EPA's more favorable economic estimates. Under a tort regime, air quality standards would be different.

. . .

There are, then, three important and deep points of contrast between tort and regulation. Environmental regulation operates ex ante in an explicit and direct way. Tort operates ex post,

---

5 Richard N.L. Andrews, *Cost-Benefit Analysis as Regulatory Reform, in* COST-BENEFIT ANALYSIS AND ENVIRONMENTAL REGULATIONS: POLITICS, ETHICS, AND METHODS 107, 112 (Daniel Swartzman et al. eds., 1982).

and has ex ante effects indirectly and then only in an attenuated form. Environmental regulation makes choices about appropriate levels of environmental quality through public processes, and views those choices as constraints on private action. Tort makes choices about appropriate levels of environmental quality through private, individual decisions, and those decisions tend to treat environmental quality as an ordinary commodity whose level should coincide with a cost-benefit determination.

. . .

. . . There are certain types of environmental harms that are objects of public concern and yet largely evade the tort system because of the doctrinal restrictions of the tort regime. Tort will not be able to address these situations well. On the other hand, there is a paradigm case of harm that tort is relatively well equipped to address. The more the features of an environmental risk resemble the features of the paradigm case of harm or injury tort was originally developed to handle, the better tort is in addressing the environmental risk. Contrariwise, as the features of an environmental risk deviate from the paradigm, the harder it is for tort to address those risks absent wholesale restructuring of tort doctrine.

. . .

. . . The fundamental [problem] arises in situations where harm falls broadly on a large group and any individual harm does not rise above a threshold necessary to constitute an actionable injury. In that case, the sources of the harm may be causing harm that in the aggregate justifies intervention, but no one will be able to litigate. Even if this doctrinal threshold is passed, plaintiffs with small injuries face daunting and unattractive transaction costs of litigation. While class action devices can ameliorate some of the transaction costs problem, cases of only moderate individual injury remain difficult to bring.

. . . [C]oncentrated effects from diffuse origins, present different doctrinal problems, especially ones having to do with the cause-in-fact requirement. Joint and several liability can provide plaintiffs with one way around an individualized cause-in-fact showing; this has the practical effect of shifting the burden onto the defendants to figure out a way to apportion the plaintiff's loss among themselves, or for individual defendants to disprove a causal connection between their acts and the plaintiff's harm. The range of cases to which joint and several liability applies is under continual pressure from defendants claiming it to be unfair.

. . . [D]iffuse effects from diffuse origins, pose the greatest challenges for tort. Ozone, for example, is produced from precursors that themselves originate from numerous sources, including stationary and mobile sources, both local and remote. Plaintiffs having asthma attacks face insurmountable difficulties in identifying and bringing into court enough defendants sufficient even to capture a bare majority of the human origins of causes of asthma attacks, let alone the entire group of responsible sources. Sustaining the burden of showing that plaintiff's harm resulted from the actions of the defendants will thus prove quite difficult. Compounding the problem of absent defendants is the fact that asthma attacks can be caused by factors other than manmade elevated ozone. The manmade causes of asthma attacks may actually be a small enough fraction of total expected asthma attacks that the plaintiff could not prevail on cause-in-fact even if she had 100 percent of the human origins of ozone present as defendants.

Background rates of injury can make toxic cases instances of diffuse effects as well. Seeing how requires a little elaboration, because from the ex post perspective of tort, a suit for injury of the type expected from toxic exposure would wait until harm had occurred. At that point, the case would look like a case of concentrated effects, and hence one that tort might at least in some halting way handle. The difficulty is that in a case in which the effects caused by the manmade risks remain hidden within a slightly elevated background rate, we cannot tell whether a given case of harm originates in something done by the defendant(s) or in some other causes, including natural ones. Because the tort is non-signature, we cannot trace any harm back to any specific human origin, so the effects of defendants' risky behavior will remain spread out among the entire exposed population as risk exposure, rather than as identifiable concentrated harm. When the contribution of the defendant to the total expected incidence of harm is significant but small, it will be possible to say that the defendant more likely than not caused some harm, but impossible to say which harm. This concatenation of elements has led some commentators to urge a cause of action for having exposed people to risk. So far, however, the common law tort system has remained quite resistant to such an innovation[].

[These c]ases . . . , then, are likely to remain impervious to the doctrines of tort. Yet such risks–diffuse effects from diffuse origins–are among some of the most important objects of regulatory attention today. In cases such as these, shifting from regulation to tort would be tantamount to abandoning efforts to reduce the prevalence or magnitude of such risks.

Questions and Discussion

1. Does Professor Schroeder make a convincing argument about the need for regulation? Is there still a place for private litigation? Where do human rights lie, in the public or private realm?

2. Does human rights law, which often relies on litigation to enforce rights, have the same ex post problems as tort or property law?

3. For other comparisons of private and public law, see Peter Cane, *Rethinking the Relationship Between Tort Law and Environmental Regulation*, 41 WASHBURN L.J. 427, 447 (2002); D. DEWEES ET AL., EXPLORING THE DOMAIN OF ACCIDENT LAW: TAKING THE FACTS SERIOUSLY (1996); Troyen A. Brennan, *Environmental Torts*, 46 VAND. L. REV. 1, 6 (1993); Keith Hylton, *When Should We Prefer Tort Law to Environmental Regulation?*, 41 WASHBURN L.J. 515, 520, (2002); Kenneth S. Abraham, *The Relation Between Civil Liability and Environmental Regulation: An Analytical Overview*, 41 WASHBURN L.J. 379, 382 (2002).

4. The regulatory model has its own challenges: (1) determining at what level of governance – local, state, regional or international – regulations should be enacted; (2) taking into account scientific knowledge and uncertainty over the short and long term; (3) coordinating the various regulations across governance units to ensure compatibility and synergies; (4) ensuring that the legal measures adopted are scientifically sound and aim at a high level of protection; and (5) making sure that the measures are equitable and that the poor and vulnerable are not made worse of. The following section examines some of the most common regulatory techniques.

1. Standard Setting

Process standards often are used to regulate the operations of hazardous activities, such as waste treatment plants or chemical factories. They also may regulate or prohibit the use of certain substances, such as ozone-depleting chemicals, in the manufacturing process. Indonesia, for example, banned the use of chlorofluorocarbons (CFCs) in manufacturing processes as of July 2008, on the basis of Industry Ministry Regulation No. 33/2007.

Product standards, in contrast, are used for items that are created or manufactured for sale or distribution. Such standards often attempt to harmonize and may regulate the following:

- The physical or chemical composition of items, such as pharmaceuticals or detergents. Examples include regulations that control the sulfur content of fuels or list substances whose presence is forbidden in certain products, for instance, mercury in pesticides or lead in paint. An example from U.S. regulations is given herein.

- The technical performance of products, such as maximum levels of pollutant or noise emissions from motor vehicles, or specifications of required product components, such as catalytic converters.
- The handling, presentation, and packaging of products, particularly those that are toxic. Packaging regulations may focus on waste minimization and safety.

TITLE 16, PART 1303 – BAN OF LEAD-CONTAINING PAINT AND CERTAIN CONSUMER PRODUCTS BEARING LEAD-CONTAINING PAINT, 42 Fed. Reg. 44199, Sept. 1, 1977, as amended Dec. 19, 2008

§ 1303.1 Scope and application.

(a) In this part 1303, the Consumer Product Safety Commission declares that paint and similar surface-coating materials for consumer use that contain lead or lead compounds and in which the lead content (calculated as lead metal) is in excess of 0.06 percent of the weight of the total nonvolatile content of the paint or the weight of the dried paint film (which paint and similar surface-coating materials are referred to hereafter as "lead-containing paint") are banned hazardous products under sections 8 and 9 of the Consumer Product Safety Act (CPSA), 15 U.S.C. 2057, 2058. (See parts 1145.1 and 1145.2 for the Commission's finding under section 30(d) of the Consumer Product Safety Act (CPSA) that it is in the public interest to regulate lead-containing paint and certain consumer products bearing such paint under the CPSA.) The following consumer products are also declared to be banned hazardous products:

(1) Toys and other articles intended for use by children that bear "lead-containing paint."
(2) Furniture articles for consumer use that bear "lead-containing paint."

(b) This ban applies to the products in the categories described in paragraph (a) of this section that are manufactured after February 27, 1978, and which are "consumer products" as that term is defined in section 3(a) (1) of the Consumer Product Safety Act. Accordingly, those of the products described above that are customarily produced or distributed for sale to or for use, consumption, or enjoyment of consumers in or around a household, in schools, in recreation, or otherwise are covered by the regulation. Paints and coatings for motor vehicles and boats are not included within the scope of the ban because they are outside the statutory definition of "consumer product." In addition to those products which are sold directly to consumers, the ban applies to products which are used or enjoyed by consumers after sale, such as paints used in residences, schools, hospitals, parks, playgrounds, and public buildings or other areas where consumers will have direct access to the painted surface.

(c) The Commission has issued the ban because it has found (1) that there is an unreasonable risk of lead poisoning in children associated with lead content of over 0.06 percent in paints and coatings to which children have access and (2) that no feasible consumer product safety standard under the CPSA would adequately protect the public from this risk.

· · ·

For economic reasons, product standards usually are adopted for an entire industry. In general, standards for new products are drafted to reflect the best-available pollution-control technology, in some cases requiring a percentage reduction of pollutants emitted in comparison with older sources.

Emission standards apply to fixed installations, such as factories or homes; mobile sources of pollution are more often regulated by product standards. Emission standards establish obligations of result, leaving to the polluter the choice of means to conform to the norm. Often the environmental milieu of the discharge, such as groundwater, air, soil, is a variant factor. Emission standards may also change according to the number of polluters and the capacity of the sector to absorb pollutants. Different standards may be imposed in response to particular climatic conditions, such as persistent fog or inversion layers.

Emission standards are based on several assumptions: (1) that a certain level of some contaminants will not produce any undesirable effect; (2) that there is a finite capacity of each environment to accommodate substances without unacceptable consequences (the assimilative capacity); and (3) that the assimilative capacity can be quantified, apportioned to each actor, and utilized. Each of these assumptions has been questioned, because all chemicals discharged into the environment are likely to lead to statistically significant deterioration. Pollution occurs when the effects of the contamination can be measured. Emission standards most often reflect a political decision about the amount of pollution that is deemed acceptable.

Finally, quality standards fix the maximum allowable level of pollution in an environmental milieu or target during normal periods. A quality standard may set the level of mercury permissible in rivers, the level of sulfur dioxide in the air, or the noise level of airplanes in the proximity of residential areas. Quality standards often vary according to the particular use made of the environmental resource. For example, different water-quality standards may be set for drinking water and for waters used for bathing or fishing. Quality standards also can vary in geographic scope, covering national or regional zones, or a particular resource, such as a river or lake, but each quality standard establishes base norms against which compliance or deviance are measured.

2. Restrictions and Prohibitions

If an activity, product, or process threatens serious environmental harm, strict measures can be imposed in an effort to reduce or eliminate the harm. When the likelihood of harm is too great, the measure may call for a total ban. The numbers and types of restrictions are almost unlimited, but certain ones are commonly used. Many involve listing banned substances or protected species. The lists are not placed in the law itself, which would require amendment each time a change is needed; rather, the lists are annexed or placed in easily modified regulations. An example is the U.S. Endangered Species Act of 1973, which is partially reprinted here.

ENDANGERED SPECIES ACT OF 1973,
Public Law 93–205, Approved Dec. 28, 1973, 87 Stat. 884, as Amended through
Public Law 107–136, Jan. 24, 2002

SEC. 2. [16 U.S.C. 1531] (A) FINDINGS. – The Congress finds and declares that –

(1)   various species of fish, wildlife, and plants in the United States have been rendered extinct as a consequence of economic growth and development untempered by adequate concern and conservation;

(2)   other species of fish, wildlife, and plants have been so depleted in numbers that they are in danger of or threatened with extinction;

(3)   these species of fish, wildlife, and plants are of esthetic, ecological, educational, historical, recreational, and scientific value to the Nation and its people;

(4)   the United States has pledged itself as a sovereign state in the international community to conserve to the extent practicable the various species of fish or wildlife and plants facing extinction, pursuant to –

    (A) migratory bird treaties with Canada and Mexico;

    (B) the Migratory and Endangered Bird Treaty with Japan;

    (C) the Convention on Nature Protection and Wildlife Preservation in the Western Hemisphere;

(D) the International Convention for the Northwest Atlantic Fisheries;

(E) the International Convention for the High Seas Fisheries of the North Pacific Ocean;

(F) the Convention on International Trade in Endangered Species of Wild Fauna and Flora; and

(G) other international agreements; and

(5) encouraging the States and other interested parties, through Federal financial assistance and a system of incentives, to develop and maintain conservation programs which meet national and international standards is a key to meeting the Nation's international commitments and to better safeguarding, for the benefit of all citizens, the Nation's heritage in fish, wildlife, and plants.

(b) PURPOSES. – The purposes of this Act are to provide a means whereby the ecosystems upon which endangered species and threatened species depend may be conserved, to provide a program for the conservation of such endangered species and threatened species, and to take such steps as may be appropriate to achieve the purposes of the treaties and conventions set forth in subsection (a) of this section.

(c) POLICY. –

(1) It is further declared to be the policy of Congress that all Federal departments and agencies shall seek to conserve endangered species and threatened species and shall utilize their authorities in furtherance of the purposes of this Act.

(2) It is further declared to be the policy of Congress that Federal agencies shall cooperate with State and local agencies to resolve water resource issues in concert with conservation of endangered species.

DETERMINATION OF ENDANGERED SPECIES AND THREATENED SPECIES § 4. [16 U.S.C. 1533]

(a) GENERAL. –

(1) The Secretary shall by regulation promulgated in accordance with subsection (b) determine whether any species is an endangered species or a threatened species because of any of the following factors:

(A) the present or threatened destruction, modification, or curtailment of its habitat or range;

(B) overutilization for commercial, recreational, scientific, or educational purposes;

(C) disease or predation;

(D) the inadequacy of existing regulatory mechanisms; or

(E) other natural or manmade factors affecting its continued existence.

. . .

(3) The Secretary, by regulation promulgated in accordance with subsection (b) and to the maximum extent prudent and determinable –

(A) shall, concurrently with making a determination under paragraph (1) that a species is an endangered species or a threatened species, designate any habitat of such species which is then considered to be critical habitat; and

(B) may, from time-to-time thereafter as appropriate, revise such designation.

(b) BASIS FOR DETERMINATIONS. –

(1) (A) The Secretary shall make determinations required by subsection (a) (1) solely on the basis of the best scientific and commercial data available to him after conducting a review of the status of the species and after taking into account those efforts, if any, being made by any State or foreign nation, or any political subdivision of a State or foreign nation, to protect such species, whether by predator control, protection of habitat and food supply, or other conservation practices, within any area under its jurisdiction, or on the high seas.

(B) In carrying out this section, the Secretary shall give consideration to species which have been –
  (i) designated as requiring protection from unrestricted commerce by any foreign nation, or pursuant to any international agreement; or
  (ii) identified as in danger of extinction, or likely to become so within the foreseeable future, by any State agency or by any agency of a foreign nation that is responsible for the conservation of fish or wildlife or plants.

(2)   The Secretary shall designate critical habitat, and make revisions thereto, under subsection (a) (3) on the basis of the best scientific data available and after taking into consideration the economic impact, and any other relevant impact, of specifying any particular area as critical habitat. The Secretary may exclude any area from critical habitat if he determines that the benefits of such exclusion outweigh the benefits of specifying such area as part of the critical habitat, unless he determines, based on the best scientific and commercial data available, that the failure to designate such area as critical habitat will result in the extinction of the species concerned.

(3)   (A) To the maximum extent practicable, within 90 days after receiving the petition of an interested person under section 553(e) of title 5, United States Code, to add a species to, or to remove a species from, either of the lists published under subsection (c), the Secretary shall make a finding as to whether the petition presents substantial scientific or commercial information indicating that the petitioned action may be warranted. If such a petition is found to present such information, the Secretary shall promptly commence a review of the status of the species concerned. The Secretary shall promptly publish each finding made under this subparagraph in the Federal Register.

. . .

(d)   PROTECTIVE REGULATIONS. – Whenever any species is listed as a threatened species pursuant to subsection (c) of this section, the Secretary shall issue such regulations as he deems necessary and advisable to provide for the conservation of such species. The Secretary may by regulation prohibit with respect to any threatened species any act prohibited under section 9(a) (1), in the case of fish or wildlife, or section 9(a) (2) in the case of plants, with respect to endangered species; except that with respect to the taking of resident species of fish or wildlife, such, regulations shall apply in any State which has entered into a cooperative agreement pursuant to section 6(c) of this Act only to the extent that such regulations have also been adopted by such State.

. . .

(f)   (1) RECOVERY PLANS. – The Secretary shall develop and implement plans (hereinafter in this subsection referred to as "recovery plans") for the conservation and survival of endangered species and threatened species listed pursuant to this section, unless he finds that such a plan will not promote the conservation of the species. The Secretary, in development and implementing recovery plans, shall, to the maximum extent practicable –
A. give priority to those endangered species or threatened species, without regard to taxonomic classification, that are most likely to benefit from such plans, particularly those species that are, or may be, in conflict with construction or other development projects or other forms of economic activity;
B. incorporate in each plan –
  (i) a description of such site-specific management actions as may be necessary to achieve the plan's goal for the conservation and survival of the species;
  (ii) objective, measurable criteria which, when met, would result in a determination, in accordance with the provisions of this section, that the species be removed from the list; and

(iii) estimates of the time required and the cost to carry out those measures needed to achieve the plan's goal and to achieve intermediate steps toward that goal.

(2) The Secretary, in developing and implementing recovery plans, may procure the services of appropriate public and private agencies and institutions and other qualified persons. Recovery teams appointed pursuant to this subsection shall not be subject to the Federal Advisory Committee Act.

. . .

Critics of listing restricted or banned products claim that the utility of doing so is limited, because it is inherently responsive to previously identified problems, is often based on uncertain dose-response relationships, and is not specific or flexible enough to be truly protective. Several hundred new substances are introduced each year and may cause considerable harm before their environmental impacts are known, especially given the possibilities that pollutants are transformed after coming into contact with others on release. Setting legal limits for the concentration of substances requires a judgment on the amount of damage that is acceptable as a consequence of human activities and how much the population is willing to pay for reducing or lowering the risks of such damage.

The listing approach also raises practical problems in enforcement. A substance, such as mercury or cadmium, usually is discharged in the environment as a component of many different products rather than in its pure form.

Laws for the protection of biological diversity frequently require the imposition of limits on taking specimens of protected resources. General protective measures may restrict injury to and destruction or taking of some or all wild plants and animals. Hunting and collecting restrictions prohibit nonselective means of killing or capturing specimens of wildlife. Taking restrictions and prohibitions may apply to nonliving and living resources, although such measures are imposed more frequently for flora and fauna.

3. Licensing

Licenses represent a middle ground between unregulated practices and absolute prohibition. Most licensing systems operate on the basis of a list or an inventory of activities necessitating a license, because they pose foreseeable risks to the environment. The lists may constitute part of the basic laws or be contained in a supplementary legal instrument. Laws generally seek to ensure that concerned members of the public are given the opportunity to express an opinion before the project is approved, establishing the means to provide information and consultation. The particular characteristics of the projects or sites concerned may determine what sector of the public is affected, control the location where the information can be consulted, and establish the particular methods of information (e.g., posters, newspapers, displays). States also may determine the manner according to which the public should be consulted; whether by written submission, public inquiry, or other; and fix the appropriate time limits for the various stages of the procedure. Once the inquiry is closed, the authority may grant a license with appropriate conditions or give partial or temporary authorization or refuse a license entirely. If the license is refused, there may be grounds for appeal to a judicial body for review of the decision. In most cases, there are both time limits and restrictions on who may take the appeal.

Internationally, states parties to various treaties are required to license the movement of hazardous substances in international trade. The delivery of export licenses and permits is often subject to the prior authorization of the importing state. Such consent is required by the Basel Convention on the Control of Transboundary Movements of Hazardous Wastes. The 1998 Convention on Prior Informed Consent extends the system of double authorization to hazardous substances and products others than wastes. It also represents a step toward interstate recognition of national permits.

4. Environmental Impact Assessment Procedures

Prior assessment of the environmental impacts of proposed activities originated in the United States in the late 1960s. Throughout the 1970s and early 1980s, other states and international agreements began imposing environmental impact assessment (EIA) requirements that were increasingly broad in their scope and detailed in their requirements and provisions. At present, environmental impact assessment is singularly important in both domestic and international environmental law. The laws and regulations commonly provide that states should not undertake or authorize activities without prior consideration, at an early stage, of their environmental effects, and they sometimes also require risk assessment. Many domestic laws and multilateral environmental agreements (MEAs) include provisions requiring consultation and dissemination of information to the public. The World Bank, the International Finance Corporation (IFC), and the regional development banks all require environmental impact assessments of any bank-financed, assisted, and/or implemented project. The World Bank's Operational Policy 4.01 describes its procedure of environmental assessment during project preparation and before appraisal. The environmental assessment covers project-specific and other environmental impacts in the area influenced by the project.

OP 4.01 – Environmental Assessment, World Bank Operational Manual, January, 1999 (as amended in 2004 and 2007) (footnotes omitted)

1. The Bank requires environmental assessment (EA) of projects proposed for Bank financing to help ensure that they are environmentally sound and sustainable, and thus to improve decision making.

2. EA is a process whose breadth, depth, and type of analysis depend on the nature, scale, and potential environmental impact of the proposed project. EA evaluates a project's potential environmental risks and impacts in its area of influence; examines project alternatives; identifies ways of improving project selection, siting, planning, design, and implementation by preventing, minimizing, mitigating, or compensating for adverse environmental impacts and enhancing positive impacts; and includes the process of mitigating and managing adverse environmental impacts throughout project implementation. The Bank favors preventive measures over mitigatory or compensatory measures, whenever feasible.

3. EA takes into account the natural environment (air, water, and land); human health and safety; social aspects (involuntary resettlement, indigenous peoples, and physical cultural resources); and transboundary and global environmental aspects. EA considers natural and social aspects in an integrated way. It also takes into account the variations in project and country conditions; the findings of country environmental studies; national environmental action plans; the country's overall policy framework, national legislation, and institutional capabilities related to the environment and social aspects; and obligations of the country, pertaining to project activities, under relevant international environmental treaties and agreements. The Bank does not finance project activities that would contravene such country obligations, as identified during the EA. EA is initiated as

early as possible in project processing and is integrated closely with the economic, financial, institutional, social, and technical analyses of a proposed project.

4. The borrower is responsible for carrying out the EA. For Category A projects, the borrower retains independent EA experts not affiliated with the project to carry out the EA. For Category A projects that are highly risky or contentious or that involve serious and multidimensional environmental concerns, the borrower should normally also engage an advisory panel of independent, internationally recognized environmental specialists to advise on all aspects of the project relevant to the EA. The role of the advisory panel depends on the degree to which project preparation has progressed, and on the extent and quality of any EA work completed, at the time the Bank begins to consider the project.

5. The Bank advises the borrower on the Bank's EA requirements. The Bank reviews the findings and recommendations of the EA to determine whether they provide an adequate basis for processing the project for Bank financing. When the borrower has completed or partially completed EA work prior to the Bank's involvement in a project, the Bank reviews the EA to ensure its consistency with this policy. The Bank may, if appropriate, require additional EA work, including public consultation and disclosure.

6. The *Pollution Prevention and Abatement Handbook* describes pollution prevention and abatement measures and emission levels that are normally acceptable to the Bank. However, taking into account borrower country legislation and local conditions, the EA may recommend alternative emission levels and approaches to pollution prevention and abatement for the project. The EA report must provide full and detailed justification for the levels and approaches chosen for the particular project or site.

EA Instruments

7. Depending on the project, a range of instruments can be used to satisfy the Bank's EA requirement: environmental impact assessment (EIA), regional or sectoral EA, environmental audit, hazard or risk assessment, and environmental management plan (EMP). EA applies one or more of these instruments, or elements of them, as appropriate. When the project is likely to have sectoral or regional impacts, sectoral or regional EA is required.

Environmental Screening

8. The Bank undertakes environmental screening of each proposed project to determine the appropriate extent and type of EA. The Bank classifies the proposed project into one of four categories, depending on the type, location, sensitivity, and scale of the project and the nature and magnitude of its potential environmental impacts.

  (a) *Category A*: A proposed project is classified as Category A if it is likely to have significant adverse environmental impacts that are sensitive, diverse, or unprecedented. These impacts may affect an area broader than the sites or facilities subject to physical works. EA for a Category A project examines the project's potential negative and positive environmental impacts, compares them with those of feasible alternatives (including the "without project" situation), and recommends any measures needed to prevent, minimize, mitigate, or compensate for adverse impacts and improve environmental performance. For a Category A project, the borrower is responsible for preparing a report, normally an EIA (or a suitably comprehensive regional or sectoral EA) that includes, as necessary, elements of the other instruments referred to in para. 7.

  (b) *Category B*: A proposed project is classified as Category B if its potential adverse environmental impacts on human populations or environmentally important areas–including wetlands, forests, grasslands, and other natural habitats–are less adverse than those of

Category A projects. These impacts are site-specific; few if any of them are irreversible; and in most cases mitigatory measures can be designed more readily than for Category A projects. The scope of EA for a Category B project may vary from project to project, but it is narrower than that of Category A EA. Like Category A EA, it examines the project's potential negative and positive environmental impacts and recommends any measures needed to prevent, minimize, mitigate, or compensate for adverse impacts and improve environmental performance. The findings and results of Category B EA are described in the project documentation (Project Appraisal Document and Project Information Document).

(c) *Category C*: A proposed project is classified as Category C if it is likely to have minimal or no adverse environmental impacts. Beyond screening, no further EA action is required for a Category C project.

(d) *Category FI*: A proposed project is classified as Category FI if it involves investment of Bank funds through a financial intermediary, in subprojects that may result in adverse environmental impacts.

EA for Special Project Types

Sector Investment Lending

9. For sector investment loans (SILs), during the preparation of each proposed subproject, the project coordinating entity or implementing institution carries out appropriate EA according to country requirements and the requirements of this policy. The Bank appraises and, if necessary, includes in the SIL components to strengthen, the capabilities of the coordinating entity or the implementing institution to (a) screen subprojects, (b) obtain the necessary expertise to carry out EA, (c) review all findings and results of EA for individual subprojects, (d) ensure implementation of mitigation measures (including, where applicable, an EMP), and (e) monitor environmental conditions during project implementation. If the Bank is not satisfied that adequate capacity exists for carrying out EA, all Category A subprojects and, as appropriate, Category B subprojects–including any EA reports–are subject to prior review and approval by the Bank.

Financial Intermediary Lending

10. For a financial intermediary (FI) operation, the Bank requires that each FI screen proposed subprojects and ensure that subborrowers carry out appropriate EA for each subproject. Before approving a subproject, the FI verifies (through its own staff, outside experts, or existing environmental institutions) that the subproject meets the environmental requirements of appropriate national and local authorities and is consistent with this OP and other applicable environmental policies of the Bank.

11. In appraising a proposed FI operation, the Bank reviews the adequacy of country environmental requirements relevant to the project and the proposed EA arrangements for subprojects, including the mechanisms and responsibilities for environmental screening and review of EA results. When necessary, the Bank ensures that the project includes components to strengthen such EA arrangements. For FI operations expected to have Category A subprojects, prior to the Bank's appraisal each identified participating FI provides to the Bank a written assessment of the institutional mechanisms (including, as necessary, identification of measures to strengthen capacity) for its subproject EA work. If the Bank is not satisfied that adequate capacity exists for carrying out EA, all Category A subprojects and, as appropriate, Category B subprojects – including EA reports – are subject to prior review and approval by the Bank.

Emergency Operations Under OP 8.00

12. The policy set out in OP 4.01 normally applies to emergency operations processed under OP/ *Rapid Response to Crises and Emergencies*. However, when compliance with any requirement of

this policy would prevent the effective and timely achievement of the objectives of an emergency operation, the Bank may exempt the project from such a requirement. The justification for any such exemption is recorded in the loan documents. In all cases, however, the Bank requires at a minimum that (a) the extent to which the emergency was precipitated or exacerbated by inappropriate environmental practices be determined as part of the preparation of such projects, and (b) any necessary corrective measures be built into either the emergency operation or a future lending operation.

Institutional Capacity

13. When the borrower has inadequate legal or technical capacity to carry out key EA-related functions (such as review of EA, environmental monitoring, inspections, or management of mitigatory measures) for a proposed project, the project includes components to strengthen that capacity.

Public Consultation

14. For all Category A and B projects proposed for IBRD or IDA financing, during the EA process, the borrower consults project-affected groups and local nongovernmental organizations (NGOs) about the project's environmental aspects and takes their views into account. The borrower initiates such consultations as early as possible. For Category A projects, the borrower consults these groups at least twice: (a) shortly after environmental screening and before the terms of reference for the EA are finalized; and (b) once a draft EA report is prepared. In addition, the borrower consults with such groups throughout project implementation as necessary to address EA-related issues that affect them.

Disclosure

15. For meaningful consultations between the borrower and project-affected groups and local NGOs on all Category A and B projects proposed for IBRD or IDA financing, the borrower provides relevant material in a timely manner prior to consultation and in a form and language that are understandable and accessible to the groups being consulted.

16. For a Category A project, the borrower provides for the initial consultation a summary of the proposed project's objectives, description, and potential impacts; for consultation after the draft EA report is prepared, the borrower provides a summary of the EA's conclusions. In addition, for a Category A project, the borrower makes the draft EA report available at a public place accessible to project-affected groups and local NGOs. For SILs and FI operations, the borrower/FI ensures that EA reports for Category A subprojects are made available in a public place accessible to affected groups and local NGOs.

17. Any separate Category B report for a project proposed for IDA financing is made available to project-affected groups and local NGOs. Public availability in the borrowing country and official receipt by the Bank of Category A reports for projects proposed for IBRD or IDA financing, and of any Category B EA report for projects proposed for IDA funding, are prerequisites to Bank appraisal of these projects.

18. Once the borrower officially transmits the Category A EA report to the Bank, the Bank distributes the summary (in English) to the executive directors (EDs) and makes the report available through its InfoShop. Once the borrower officially transmits any separate Category B EA report to the Bank, the Bank makes it available through its InfoShop. If the borrower objects to the Bank's releasing an EA report through the World Bank InfoShop, Bank staff (a) do not continue processing an IDA project, or (b) for an IBRD project, submit the issue of further processing to the EDs.

Implementation

19. During project implementation, the borrower reports on (a) compliance with measures agreed with the Bank on the basis of the findings and results of the EA, including implementation of any EMP, as set out in the project documents; (b) the status of mitigatory measures; and (c) the findings of monitoring programs. The Bank bases supervision of the project's environmental aspects on the findings and recommendations of the EA, including measures set out in the legal agreements, any EMP, and other project documents.

5. Land Use Regulation

Land use controls play a major role in environmental law for both urban and rural areas, through zoning, physical planning, and creating protected areas. Zoning can help distribute equitably and appropriately activities harmful to the environment and it allows for application of different legal rules from zone to zone for more effective protection. Physical planning merges provisions for infrastructure and town and country planning to integrate conservation of the environment into social and economic development.

Several international environmental instruments require states parties to set aside areas for specific management or the in situ conservation of biological diversity. Other special areas are mandated by treaty to protect monuments and sites of outstanding importance for geological, physiographical, paleontological, or other scientific reasons, or for aesthetic purposes. Buffer zones surrounding protected areas help preserve them from harmful outside influences. Activities that do not have adverse effects on the protected area may be allowed to continue. Interconnected corridors, created through land use regulations or private contracts and other incentives, are necessary to allow genetic exchanges to occur between protected areas and may be international in scope.

6. Criminal Law

National law is increasingly imposing criminal liability on those who pollute or otherwise harm the environment. In the United States, almost all federal environmental laws provide criminal penalties for "knowing" or "willful" violations. *See, e.g.,* Clean Air Act §113(c); Clean Water Act §309(c). Some thirty lawyers at the U.S. Environmental Protection Authority focus exclusively on criminal enforcement. Martin Harrell, Joseph J. Lisa & Catherine L. Votaw, *Federal Environmental Crime: A Different Kind of "White Collar" Prosecution*, 23 NAT. RESOURCES & ENV'T 3 (2009). In many instances, a company, its directors, and other senior managers may be held responsible. Several existing international agreements call on states to enact and apply penalties adequate to deter violations.

Environmental offenses have characteristics that distinguish them from other crimes. Most criminal law is based on a direct individual relation between a perpetrator and a victim who has been harmed. In contrast, environmental protection can involve perpetrators and victims who can be identified only statistically, because harm results from long-term multiple causes. Two responses are possible. The first is to assume the existence of danger or harm to public interests that are traditionally protected by penal law, such as life, health, and property. The other is to develop new offenses against the environment, protecting independent natural elements without requiring an element of provable harm to specific victims. Both approaches can be found in existing provisions of penal law. Still, tensions exist at the crossroads of environmental law and criminal law and the divergent characteristics of each pose significant challenges to their integration. *See* Richard Lazarus, *Meeting the Demands of Integration in the Evolution of Environmental Law: Reforming Environmental Criminal Law*, 83 GEO. L.J. 2407 (1995).

C. Market Mechanisms

A third construct for environmental protection became popular beginning in the 1980s, with the advent of deregulation and privatization. Market-based approaches to changing human behavior emerged in preference to command-and-control measures. In part, this move constituted a reaction to dense regulatory networks that were deemed inefficient and a drain on competitiveness and investment. Economic instruments, however, largely remain within the regulatory framework because they require laws and institutions to oversee their operation. Purely market-based approaches such as voluntary agreements have been criticized as inequitable, ineffective, and unable to truly account for harm to public goods like air, water, and other parts of the commons. They do not and perhaps cannot, serve to protect long-term interests like future generations. *See generally* ENVIRONMENTAL JUSTICE AND MARKET MECHANISMS: KEY CHALLENGES FOR ENVIRONMENTAL LAW AND POLICY (Klaus Bosselmann & Benjamin Richardson eds., 1999).

Economic incentives include not only direct investment subsidies but also preferential loans, accelerated depreciation allowances, tax differentials, tax exemptions, credits, and other promotional measures. Often such measures aim to include the cost of environmental damage, as well as the cost of raw materials, production, marketing, and so on, in the price of a product. Environmental funds, which have been created in several countries, often directly finance environmental protection. Even the concept of product changes, as the consumption of fresh air and clean water becomes priced and polluters pay, through fees or taxes, for causing deterioration to these resources. In some countries, government financial assistance and incentives, taking the form of low-interest loans or grants, aid the construction and operation of more environmentally safe installations and recycling systems.

Subsidies to be legal under the General Agreement on Tariffs and Trade/World Trade Organization (GATT/WTO), should not create significant distortions in international trade and investment. Subsidies to new polluting installations are generally prohibited; however, public authorities may aid research and development for the purpose of stimulating experimentation with new pollution control technologies and development of new pollution abatement equipment. They also may subsidize antipollution investment in the framework of regional, industrial, social, agricultural, and scientific policies or whenever new environmental protection measures would create serious economic dislocations. Subsidies are a particular problem in respect to exploitation of living resources. Subsidies can allow the expansion of fishing fleets by, for example, supporting the building of new, larger ships or allowing purchase of new equipment; or they can hinder the reduction of fleets by supporting economically unsustainable capacity. In the latter instance, subsidies have the effect of slowing the exit of capital from the fishing industry even when it is in difficulty because of overcapacity and declining catches.

Product labels aim to influence consumer choices by providing information on the nutritional content of foods, the proper use and hazards of cleaning products, and the dangers of cigarettes. Eco-labels instruct on environmentally safe products and promote their purchase by the public. In some instances, a public or private body awards positive labels to products that are less destructive of the environment than similar competitive products, on the basis of a holistic, overall judgment of the product's environmental quality. Labeling programs are difficult to administer because of the need to comprehensively assess the entire life cycle of the product and to establish product categories and criteria.

As Professor Schroeder notes in the following extract, environmental law in recent years has adopted new market mechanisms including the techniques of tradable emissions, joint implementation, and bubbles. A system of negotiable permits fixes the total amount of pollution permissible in an area. Each polluting company is required to obtain an emission permit conforming to emission standards. Companies investing in processes that reduce pollution may exchange or sell their permits to other companies located in the same geographic area. The permits may be traded within emission limits determined by the authorities. Resource extraction concessions can also be issued and traded. Such tradeable permits leave allocation of polluting behavior to the market. The initial distribution of permits may be based on historical levels of emissions but they may need to be reduced if they present an unacceptable risk of harm to those in that area.

Joint implementation is related to the idea of negotiable permits. Many states and scholars favor joint implementation as a cost-effective means for addressing anthropogenic climate change, because reduction in carbon dioxide emissions anywhere in the world should produce a positive effect in mitigating climate change. The argument in favor of such trading is that it lowers the overall cost of reducing emissions and may increase the amount of abatement that can be achieved. Article 4(2) of the U.N. Framework Convention on Climate Change (UNFCCC) endorses the general concept of joint implementation. It provides that any developed country, to meet its commitments, may transfer to or acquire from any other party "emission reduction units" for projects aimed to reduce emissions or enhance anthropogenic removals by sinks that absorb greenhouse gases in any sector of the economy. On a theoretical level, it may be questioned whether joint implementation violates the polluter-pays principle by allowing polluters to continue their activities without paying full costs. Responding to this concern, the UNFCCC imposes the condition that any such project reduce emission by sources or enhance removal by sinks beyond the amount that would otherwise occur.

Like all forms of environmental regulation, each economic incentive must be studied to evaluate its effectiveness in protecting the environment. Effectiveness requires analysis of the changes of producer and/or consumer behavior and the costs of the measures taken. Some procedures may have only small effect while being administratively cumbersome and thus do not meet the requirements of efficiency or effectiveness. In contrast, incentives for environmental protection may contribute to economic growth and preserve natural resources.

Lost in Translation: What Environmental Regulation Does that Tort Cannot Duplicate, 41 WASHBURN L.J. 583, 602–05 (2002) (footnotes omitted)

Christopher H. Schroeder

The acid rain abatement program of the 1990 Amendments to the Clean Air Act provides an exemplary case study of [an] incentive-based approach[].... The program does not instruct any specific firm as to how much it must reduce individual emissions, or even whether it must reduce them at all. Instead, Title IV creates a system of marketable permits, or allowances, and mandates that once the program is initiated that it is unlawful to emit sulphur dioxide in excess of the number of allowances owned. Finally, by statute the program establishes the quantity of allowances necessary to permit the mandated levels to be met, but not exceeded, and it also makes the initial allocation of those allowances. Coal fired powerplants in the Midwest received the bulk of the allowances, based on a percentage of their historic emission levels. Other allowances were retained by the EPA to be sold at public auction, and still others were made available as incentives to facilities that undertook especially beneficial reduction programs.

The acid rain program creates a private property regime for the control of acid rain precursors. It retains a preventive structure and the public selection of environmental goals, while eliminating much of the normal regulatory superstructure and giving firms the flexibility to choose the least costly strategy available to them, given the constraint that they must own allowances to match their emissions. A utility facing steep costs of pollution abatement can go into the marketplace and purchase additional allowances, while one facing favorable costs can reduce emissions below the level of currently owned allowances and then sell the excess. Utilities can also reallocate allowances among their own powerplants according to the same least cost principle. It has been estimated that the cost savings achieved by this approach compared to the traditional command-and-control approach amount to several billion dollars per year.

Cap-and-trade techniques such as the acid rain program create property regimes that ought to be used more in situations where the environmental problem comes from many sources and has widely dispersed effects, such as is the case with acid rain itself. Interestingly, this is just the category of environmental problems which tort law is poorly equipped to address.

Strong environmentalists have historically opposed market creation devices for two principal reasons. First, by enabling polluting firms to acquire a "license to pollute," they sanction the amount of pollution that the firm continues to emit. Second, environmentalists have been skeptical of the efficacy of such devices, fearing that firms will find ways to avoid actual pollution reductions. While zealous environmentalists will remain skeptical of such devices on these grounds, these objections are diminishing in significance among the rest of the environmental community. The license to pollute objection rests on a view of the objectives of environmental quality that sees any amount of potentially harmful pollution to be contrary to the public's choice. It is becoming apparent, however, the public is not committed to such an absolutist goal. This does not mean that it wishes the choice of environmental goals to be abandoned to the market and to tort litigation, however. Rather, much as the right to free speech is strongly valued but at the same time understood not to condone shouting "fire" in a crowded theater, the public is currently struggling to articulate the limitations on its strong preference for environmental quality. As for the possibility that tradeable permits will not work, there are indeed pitfalls to be avoided in the structuring of such markets and there are situations in which they will not work well. Still, the success of the acid rain program, as well as other instances, has helped establish the efficacy of market creation devices in situations where they are appropriate and well designed.

As confidence increases that market or incentive based regimes can be designed so that desired levels of environmental quality will result, the use of such mechanisms will increase. The use of property regimes in this way can move forward to supplant or supplement traditional environmental regulation in ways that tort regimes cannot because property regimes can be designed so that the selection of the desired level of environmental quality can continue to be set through public means and because requirements to purchase necessary rights to the environment ex ante can be clearly articulated and understood by regulated parties. The structure of property regimes is thus compatible with the distinctive features of the regulatory system that we have seen separate tort from regulation and which the public continues to prefer.

D. *Rights-Based Approaches*

The fourth paradigm for environmental protection is rights-based. In addition to its focus on ensuring the enjoyment of all civil, political, economic, cultural, and social rights, it can emphasize the right to a certain quality of environment because that quality is linked to, indeed a prerequisite for, the enjoyment of internationally and domestically guaranteed rights. Rights-based approaches were initially thought to have the defect of being nonjusticiable, but courts are increasingly enforcing constitutional and international rights to environmental quality. Many courts have broadened standing to permit legal redress for violations of environmental rights, without requiring individualized injury to health or property, because one major motive for guaranteeing environmental rights is to prevent injury from occurring. *See, e.g., Montana Environmental Information Center v. Department of Environmental Quality*, 296 Mont. 207, 988 P.2d 1236 (1999) infra p. 523.

Rights-based approaches to environmental protection are closely linked to concepts of environmental justice. There are many meanings attached to this term. To some, justice is the fundamental source or rationale providing the moral underpinnings from which law emerges. Environmental justice can also be seen not a source of law but as its ultimate goal or outcome. Justice has also been presented as an alternative to law, with a meaning akin to fairness or equity. Narrower usages center on (1) legal institutions and procedures for accountability and dispute settlement and (2) the substantive content of norms regulating the use of power over persons and resources. To some extent, the different invocations of environmental justice correspond to classic distinctions between procedural, reparative, and distributive justice. The primary modalities for achieving environmental justice include allocation and management of scarce resources; restraints on the exercise of power; and enforcement of the rule of law, including the rights guaranteed by law. Chapters 6 and 7 focus on substantive and procedural environmental rights.

Questions and Discussion

1. Given the developed laws and policies to address environmental degradation and conserve natural resources, what is the value-added of a rights-based approach?
2. To what extent does environmental law and policy have to be concerned with extraterritorial sources and impacts of environmental harm?

III. International Environmental Law*

International law was long defined as the body of binding norms governing the relations between states. If states create international law, the reverse is also true, to some extent, because international law establishes the requisite characteristics of a state. International law confers on states unique rights and privileges denied other types of institutions and organizations, but international law can also govern other legal persons, and even individuals. In the *Restatement of the Foreign Relations Law of the United States*, international law is defined as the law that concerns "the conduct of states and of international organizations and with their relations *inter se*, as well as with some of their relations with persons, whether natural or juridical." ALI, Restatement of the Foreign Relations law of the United States (Third), § 101 (1987). The modern definition is particularly important in the field of environmental protection, because most environmental harm is caused by activities in the private sector and not those of governments. The ability of international law to reach nonstate conduct is thus essential to achieving effective environmental protection.

---

* This section relies on the authors' earlier published works, especially Alexandre Kiss & Dinah Shelton, A Guide to International Environmental Law 3–11, 32–44, 90–92, 104–09 (Martinus Nijhoff 2007) and Alexandre Kiss & Dinah Shelton, Judicial Handbook on Environmental Law 14–16 (UNEP 2005). The material has been adapted for purposes of this volume, and new sources and text added.

Although international law may regulate some of the actions of nonstate actors, that law remains a product of express or implicit agreement among states. Nonstate actors may contribute to the elaboration of international texts and influence state behavior in ways that may contribute to the development of international custom, but they do not as such make public international law. Instead, as discussed in the next section, international law regulates conduct through rules based on the consensual adoption of treaties and the development of customary international law based on state practice viewed as obligatory (*opinio juris*). Rules normally become binding on nonstate actors through their incorporation into the domestic law of states. Only rarely, and largely in the field of crimes, does international law impose direct obligations on purely private conduct.

A. *Sources: What Is International Law?*

International law is created and identified in reliance on lawmaking sources set forth in article 38(1) of the Statute of the International Court of Justice (ICJ), initially drafted in 1920 for its predecessor, the Permanent Court of International Justice. Although applying only to the ICJ, article 38 represents the authoritative listing of processes that states have identified and accepted as capable of creating rules binding on them; it remains, to date, the only such listing. It sets out, in order, general or specialized international conventions (treaties), international custom as evidence of a general practice accepted as law, and general principles of law recognized by civilized nations. Judicial decisions and doctrine are cited in article 38 as "subsidiary means to identify" or find international law, but neither constitutes a means by which such a law is created.

Article 38 does not explicitly set a hierarchy among the three lawmaking sources, and the relationships can be complex. In general, treaties are interpreted in conformity with customary law where possible, but it is accepted that states inter se can modify their customary international obligations by treaty, provided the customary obligations do not constitute peremptory or fundamental norms of international law. In such an instance, the treaty provisions would be considered against international public policy and invalid. *See* art. 53, Vienna Convention on the Law of Treaties (VCLT) (May 23, 1969), 1155 U.N.T.S. 331.

Current international practice also relies heavily on the diverse activities of international organizations, which can contribute to the development of a new rule of law, in particular, by adopting nonbinding texts in which member states may express approval for the emergence of new norms. Nonbinding norms play more than a nominal role in the formation of international law in general and environmental law in particular. The nonbinding normative texts are discussed herein under the heading by which they are commonly known: "soft law."

1. Treaties

The Vienna Convention on the Law of Treaties, 1155 U.N.T.S. 331 (May 23, 1969), sets forth the basic law of treaties and is generally accepted as a statement of customary rules. It defines a treaty as

> an international agreement concluded between States in written form and governed by international law, whether embodied in a single instrument or in two or more related instruments and whatever its particular designation.

VCLT, rt. 2.1(a). This definition omits all international agreements to which intergovernmental or nongovernmental organizations are parties, as well as agreements concluded by internal agencies not entitled to bind the state, for example, port authorities or customs offices. Yet all the entities mentioned enter into agreements intending to cooperate and apply agreed norms for environmental protection. In fact, a separate Vienna Convention, concluded in 1985, concerns treaties entered into by international organizations. It also should be noted that while the VCLT definition of treaties refers to agreements in writing, the Permanent Court of International Justice held that oral agreements may be legally binding. *Case Concerning the Legal Status of Eastern Greenland (Den. v. Nor.)*, 1933 P.C.I.J. (ser. A/B) No. 53. Most important, the definition indicates that the question of whether a given text is a treaty is determined by whether it is governed by international law, that is, is legally binding. This is a matter of the intent of the states concluding the agreement and concededly produces the somewhat circular notion that an instrument is a treaty if it is legally binding, and it is legally binding if it is a treaty. From state practice, however, it is clear that many international agreements are intended not to be legally binding but to express political commitments. Failure to abide by such nonbinding agreements may be considered unfriendly or a political affront, but the failure does not constitute a breach of international law.

Until the twentieth century, treaties were nearly all bilateral and most of them concerned boundaries, diplomatic relations, the high seas, shared fresh water, trade, and extradition. The governing principle was reciprocity of obligations. The principle of reciprocity established a legal equilibrium between the obligations accepted by one state and the advantages it obtained from the other contracting party.

Exceptions to reciprocal treaties have long existed and include bilateral and multilateral treaties to combat slavery and the slave trade, abolition of child labor, and other humanitarian topics. Typically, the agreements confer benefits on individuals and not on other states parties; for this reason, they are often referred to as creating unilateral obligations. Following World War II, nonreciprocal obligations enlarged still further to include the general international protection of human rights, regulations on the use of Antarctica and its surrounding seas, codes governing activities in outer space, and reaffirmation of freedom of the high seas with an obligation to safeguard the marine environment. Rules of international environmental law may be considered among the nonreciprocal obligations, as generally they do not bring immediate reciprocal advantages to contracting states when their objective is to protect species of wild plant and animal life, the oceans, the air, the soil, and the countryside. Sovereign equality is also implicated, because, for example, states upstream on an international river are not in the same situation as those downstream. For coastal states, similarly, the general direction of winds and ocean currents may cut against the equality of the parties and diminish reciprocity in legal benefits and burdens.

Today, multilateral regulatory treaties are common, the topics governed by international law have proliferated, and nonstate actors are increasingly part of the international legal system. Modern treaties often affect a state's internal laws and practices rather than directly regulating interstate relations, as was the case with earlier bilateral agreements. In describing these developments, some international jurists have posited the existence in international law of treaty-laws, distinguished from treaty-contracts. In its Advisory Opinion on *Reservations to the Convention on Genocide*, 1951 ICJ 15, the International Court of Justice provided support for this idea by distinguishing reciprocal treaties from conventions like the Genocide Convention in which states do not have any interests of their own; instead, "they merely have, one and all, a common interest, namely, the accomplishment of those high purposes which are the *raison d'être* of the convention." In a subsequent case, the Court said that agreements like the Genocide Convention created obligations *erga omnes*, duties owed to all states. If this is the case, it may imply that any and all states have standing to complain of violations by one of the parties, as no state is likely to suffer material injury, but all suffer legal injury because of the violation of law. In municipal law, a similar distinction is made between public law legislated in the general interest and contract law that allows parties to create private rights and duties by contract.

a. *Adoption of Treaties*

Treaties are normally negotiated by authorized representatives or the heads of state during negotiations that are convened by an international organization or at a diplomatic conference called for the purpose. A treaty text may be adopted by vote or by consensus and then opened for signature. Multilateral agreements rarely become binding on signature but usually require ratification according to procedures established by the internal law of a ratifying party. However, VCLT article 18 obliges a state to refrain from acts when:

(a) it has signed the treaty or has exchanged instruments constituting the treaty subject to ratification, acceptance or approval, until it shall have made its intention clear not to become a party to the treaty; or

(b) it has expressed its consent to be bound by the treaty, pending the entry into force of the treaty and provided that such entry into force is not unduly delayed.

Once the text has been approved by the negotiating body, most agreements specify the means by which states signal their acceptance, and this is usually by ratification of it. If ratification is required, the domestic approval of the treaty must be followed by deposit of an instrument of ratification with the authority designated as the depository, to inform other parties to the treaty that it has been accepted. A state that has not signed the treaty and wishes to join will usually file an instrument of accession rather than ratification; there is no legal significance to the different terminology. Multilateral treaties usually specify a minimum number of ratifying states for the treaty to enter into force and become legally binding on the states parties as of that date.

To maximize state participation in multilateral agreements, provisions may be included allowing reservations to be entered at the time of signing, ratification, or accession. A reservation is

a unilateral statement, however phrased or named, made by a State, when signing, ratifying, accepting, approving or acceding to a treaty, whereby it purports to exclude or to modify the legal effect of certain provisions of the treaty in their application to that State.

Art. 1(b). States sometimes file "reservations" which are not, because they do not modify their legal obligations, and sometimes states will label as an "understanding" a statement that is in fact a reservation. The test is whether or not the rights or duties under the treaty are changed in any way. The VCLT permits states to attach reservations as follows:

Article 19 – Formulation of reservations

A State may, when signing, ratifying, accepting, approving or acceding to a treaty, formulate a reservation unless:

(*a*) the reservation is prohibited by the treaty;

(*b*) the treaty provides that only specified reservations, which do not include the reservation in question, may be made; or

(c)   in cases not failing under subparagraphs (a) and (b), the reservation is incompatible with the object and purpose of the treaty.

Many modern environmental agreements bar reservations because of the complicated package of bargains made during the negotiations.

b. *Compliance with Treaty Obligations*

For treaties in force, the fundamental rules of treaty law are set forth in the VCLT as follows:

Article 26 – "Pacta sunt servanda"

Every treaty in force is binding upon the parties to it and must be performed by them in good faith.

Article 27 – Internal law and observance of treaties

A party may not invoke the provisions of its internal law as justification for its failure to perform a treaty. . . .

Neither the rupture of diplomatic relations nor a change of government affects the continuity of treaty obligations. As with contract law, there are nonetheless rules that govern the validity of treaties and provide legitimate excuses for nonperformance by a party, including such matters as duress, impossibility of performance, fundamental change of circumstances, or material breach by another party. Armed conflict may affect the continuity of some agreements, but not those aimed to protect the human person or the environment.

In general, treaties are not retroactive and only apply from the moment they enter into force for a particular state. Some treaties may allow denunciation after a specified notice period, but many others are of indefinite duration. Unless otherwise stated, treaties apply to all persons and territories over which the state has jurisdiction, including aircraft, ships, and space objects. Complex issues of jurisdiction may arise where sovereignty is divided as a result of occupation or where sovereignty is absent, as in Antarctica.

c. *Treaty Interpretation*

The interpretation of a treaty is governed primarily by its text. Article 31 of the VCLT is accepted as a statement of customary international law on the topic:

Article 31 – General rule of interpretation

1.   A treaty shall be interpreted in good faith in accordance with the ordinary meaning to be given to the terms of the treaty in their context and in the light of its object and purpose.
2.   The context for the purpose of the interpretation of a treaty shall comprise, in addition to the text, including its preamble and annexes:
     (a)   any agreement relating to the treaty which was made between all the parties in connection with the conclusion of the treaty;
     (b)   any instrument which was made by one or more parties in connection with the conclusion of the treaty and accepted by the other parties as an instrument related to the treaty.
3.   There shall be taken into account, together with the context:
     (a)   any subsequent agreement between the parties regarding the interpretation of the treaty or the application of its provisions;

(b) any subsequent practice in the application of the treaty which establishes the agreement of the parties regarding its interpretation;

(c) any relevant rules of international law applicable in the relations between the parties.

4. A special meaning shall be given to a term if it is established that the parties so intended.

Article 32 – Supplementary means of interpretation

Recourse may be had to supplementary means of interpretation, including the preparatory work of the treaty and the circumstances of its conclusion, in order to confirm the meaning resulting from the application of article 31, or to determine the meaning when the interpretation according to article 31:

(a) leaves the meaning ambiguous or obscure; or

(b) leads to a result which is manifestly absurd or unreasonable.

Other rules of international law and the subsequent practice of the states parties to the agreement have proved more important in multilateral treaty interpretation than the original intent of the drafters, which the VCLT relegates to a subsidiary role, to confirm meaning or resolve ambiguities arising through application of the primary rules of interpretation. The emphasis on the text and subsequent practice is particularly useful in giving effect to multilateral agreements, where the original intent of nearly two hundred states would be extremely difficult to ascertain independent of the agreed-on text. The intent of the parties can be more readily determined for bilateral treaties, where the drafting history found in the minutes and other documentation is less complex and contradictory.

d. *Enforcement*

The failure to observe a treaty is an international wrong, giving rise to state responsibility to cease the breach and make reparations for any injuries caused to another state. Domestic law, whether constitutional, statutory, or case law, is no defense to failure to perform treaty obligations. Treaty enforcement traditionally was done by the injured party, which could withhold benefits under the treaty, by applying the principle of reciprocity. Thus, the failure of one state to comply with the requirements of a bilateral extradition treaty could result in its treaty partner refusing to extradite in response. Trade agreements remain an area in which the threat of retaliatory action is a means of deterring violations and enforcing the treaties. Where consequential harm occurs that cannot be cured by reciprocal action, an injured state may assert a claim for reparations under the law of state responsibility, usually through diplomatic channels but increasingly in international tribunals. Since the creation of the United Nations, multilateral treaties rely less on retaliatory action in the case of breach and more on the creation of institutions and compliance mechanisms to review state compliance. Such procedures may result in publication of reports that identify failures, adoption of incentives, or other actions aimed to promote compliance.

e. *Common Environmental Treaty Techniques*

Environmental treaties differ from other kinds of treaties, having specific characteristics that respond to the needs of environmental protection. They share several main features. First, international environmental treaties frequently cross-referencing other international instruments. Recent marine environment treaties, for example, cite the rules of the U.N. Convention on the Law of the Sea or "generally accepted international standards," sometimes incorporating such rules by reference. The result is a complex network of regulation and the extension of treaties to a wide range of states.

Second, states use the technique of framework conventions, meaning that a convention of general scope is adopted, proclaiming basic principles on which consent can be achieved. The parties foresee the elaboration of additional protocols containing more detailed obligations. The protocols are separately ratified but usually interpreted and applied to carry out the aims of the main agreement.

Third, international environmental agreements adopted to respond to urgent problems must be implemented in the shortest possible time. Taking this into account, negotiating states have adopted the technique of approving interim application of the agreements pending their entry into force. This technique was used with the 1998 FAO Convention on Prior Informed Consent and the 1995 Agreement for the Implementation of the Provisions of UNCLOS relating to the Conservation and Management of Straddling Fish Stocks and Highly Migratory Fish Stocks, article 41.

Finally, states have developed an effective response to rapid advances in scientific knowledge and the emergence of new problems by drafting treaties that establish stable general obligations but also add flexible provisions, especially those prescribing technical norms. The latter may designate the specific products that cannot be dumped or discharged in a given area or may identify the endangered species needing additional protection. The general obligations are set forth in the treaty, which remains stable, whereas the detailed listing of products or species is reserved to legally-binding annexes that can be modified easily without amending the principal treaty.

2. Customary International Law

The content of customary international law is found in widespread and consistent state practices, followed because the states believe the practices are legally required. State practice must be general, although it need not be universal. State practice is identified through, for example, official government texts and statements, court decisions, laws, and diplomatic exchanges. *See Filartiga v. Pena-Irala*, 630 F.2d 876 (2d Cir. 1980). Conduct in violation of such official acts is treated as a violation of the law, not as extinguishing the custom. If a significant number of states adopt laws and official policies that lead them to act contrary to the purported rule, a new norm may emerge.

Not all state practice forms customary international law. State acts engaged in because they are convenient or polite do not give rise to custom, because the sense of legal obligation is absent. Instead, states must have a conviction that the rule is obligatory, referred to as *opinio juris*. Such *opinio juris* may be implied if state practice is general and consistent over a lengthy time.

3. General Principles of Law

General principles of law are those concepts and rules found in the major legal systems of the world and appropriate for application in international relations. Because such rules have been adopted in national law, consent to their application in international law is inferred. Thus, the International Court of Justice recognized the existence of corporations as legal persons in the *Barcelona Traction* case because of wide recognition of the personality of such business entities in modern law. *Barcelona Traction, Light and Power Company, Ltd. (Belg. v. Spain)* 1970 ICJ 3 (Feb. 5). General principles have often been used to fill in gaps in international law during interstate litigation.

4. "Soft Law"

States now often place normative statements and agreements in non-legally-binding or political instruments, such as declarations, resolutions, and programs of action. These instruments, often referred to as "soft law", may make it easier to press dissenters into conforming behavior, because states are free to use political pressure to induce others to alter their policies, although generally they cannot demand that others conform to legal norms the latter have not accepted. Nonbinding commitments may be entered into precisely to reflect the will of the international community to resolve a pressing global problem over the objections of one or a few states causing the problem while avoiding the doctrinal barrier of their lack of consent to be bound by the norm. New problems also may require innovative means of rule making when nonstate actors are the source of the harm and target of the regulations; they generally cannot negotiate or be parties to treaties, and they are not involved in the creation of customary international law, but they have a direct interest in any legal regulation adopted. Their participation may thus be crucial to effectiveness of the law. The emergence of codes of conduct and other "soft law" in part reflects the desire to bring them into the lawmaking process.

Several other reasons may be adduced for the increasing use of non-legally-binding instruments:

1. The statutes of most international intergovernmental organizations do not invest organs of the institution with the right to adopt binding decisions, so that they can express their will – or rather the will of their member states on specific matters – only through recommendations or other declarative acts. The recommendations may contain normative statements, but they are not binding. International conferences of states, like the Stockholm Conference on the Human Environment, often similarly result in declarations that express the conclusions of the meeting and agreed principles for future action, including statements of law. Some recommendations, such as the resolutions of the U.N. General Assembly concerning the prohibition of large-scale pelagic drift-net fishing or the recommendations of the Organisation for Economic Co-operation and Development concerning transboundary pollution, can became binding rules at the end of an evolution of state practice (customary law) or by repetition and incorporation in binding national and international legal instruments.

2. Multilateral conventions relating to environmental protection have created specific organs such as the Conferences of Parties, assisted by secretariats and, in some cases, by specialized bodies. The power of such organs to adopt decisions and norms that are binding for the states parties varies and is often uncertain. Legal counsels may issue opinions that have an impact but are not legally binding.

3. Nonbinding texts are typically easier than treaties to negotiate quickly and amend in the light of new problems. Scientific knowledge and public awareness can be the major factors pressing for international action.

4. States may decide to forgo the often lengthy treaty-making process to avoid domestic constitutional or political barriers. Recommendations, joint declarations, guidelines, or other common rules of conduct express their commitments but do not necessitate formal ratification. Texts that are not subject to national ratification can take instant effect. This is the case, for instance, with the safety regulations drafted by the International Atomic Energy Agency.

5. In some circumstances, the subject matter under consideration may make non-legally-binding instruments more appropriate than formal agreements. The best examples are Action Plans, such as Agenda 21, adopted by the 1972 Rio Conference on Environment and Development, and the Arctic Environmental Protection Strategy. The contents set out general policy goals and guiding principles rather than specific legal obligations capable of immediate implementation.

6. The drafting and implementation of soft law instruments more easily allows the participation of international institutions and nonstate actors than does the process of treaty negotiating, which is usually formal and restricted to delegates from states. The International Union for Conservation of Nature prepared the first draft of the World Charter of Nature, which was sent out by the U.N. General Assembly to the member states for comments, after which the Assembly adopted it on October 28, 1982. Nongovernmental organizations also can participate in the adoption and the monitoring of special agreements that are formally not binding, such as memoranda of understanding (MOUs). The Convention on the Conservation of Migratory Species of Wild Animals (Bonn, Sept. 19, 1979), for example, was complemented by several MOUs or administrative arrangements signed not only by states but also by so-called cooperating organizations, including intergovernmental and nongovernmental bodies.

7. Some nongovernmental industrial, environmental, and consumer protection associations adopt norms that can be implemented as legal rules. The International Standard Organization (ISO), a nongovernmental body founded in 1946 to promote voluntary international standards and to facilitate global trade, has adopted a number of worldwide technical standards related to the environment. The ISO is composed of more than one hundred national standardization bodies, one from each represented country. Although ISO is an NGO, most national bodies participating in it are public agencies, giving it a mixed character.

In summary, nonbinding rules have the necessary flexibility to enable the international community to approach problems requiring international cooperation, such as the protection of migratory species, or to address new matters, like promoting sustainable energy sources. Parallel to this evolution, it may be noted that national authorities also make use of nonbinding or voluntary agreements with private parties, such as industrial associations, forest or other landowners, indigenous groups, or scientific institutions. These nonbinding instruments can involve scientific research, land use, or reduction of pollution.

Although nonbinding international agreements sometimes are criticized as ineffective, compliance with such instruments may reach high rates. Different factors affect compliance with nonbinding norms, just as they affect compliance with binding ones. Compliance may be enhanced by the presence of a legally binding text that provides the legal foundation for the nonbinding instrument. The content or substance of the nonbinding norm can assist compliance if it is sufficiently precise to allow for immediate implementation and enable the appropriate bodies to monitor compliance and to take sanctions against those who do not respect it. The involvement of regional and local authorities in compliance procedures also can be a positive factor. National authorities may foster awareness of such norms through media coverage, at all levels, involving regional and local authorities as well as civil society.

B. *Relationship of International Law and Domestic Legal Systems*

The relationship between national law and international law varies considerably from one legal system to another. International law is considered the supreme body of law by international tribunals and in international relations among states. Thus, a state may not invoke a provision of its national law to excuse its violation of international law. The law of state responsibility provides that each breach of an international obligation attributable to a state automatically gives rise to a duty to cease the breach and make reparation for any injury caused, irrespective of national law.

Within states, international law may be legally binding and applied by courts as a result of one or more means that are usually specified in the constitution. Legal doctrine has developed two theories, known as monism and dualism, in an attempt to explain and classify national practice, but the reality is more complex than the theory. Monism posits a unified body of rules, and because international law is law, it automatically forms part of this body of rules and is hierarchically superior to other law. Dualism sees separate legal orders and looks to each jurisdiction to determine the sources of law and their hierarchy.

In general, the theory of monism and dualism applies only to customary (or unwritten) international law and even then in limited fashion. Some legal systems require that customary international law be incorporated into national law through legislation or executive order before it becomes the law of the land. Other legal systems view international law as automatically part of the legal order and enforceable by judges without legislative action. The constitutions of Italy, Germany, and the Netherlands all have constitutional provisions expressly stipulating that rules of general (or customary) international law are part of the municipal law of the state and enjoy precedence over domestic legislation. Most common law countries consider customary international law to be part of the common law and automatically binding as national law, following Blackstone's precept ("the law of nations (wherever any problem arises which is properly the object of its jurisdiction) is here adopted in its full extent by the common law and is held to be part of the law of the land," WILLIAM BLACKSTONE, IV COMMENTARIES *67).

Precedent exists in several jurisdictions finding particular environmental norms to constitute customary international law. *See, e.g., Vellore Citizens Welfare Forum v. Union of India*, [1996] AIR SC 2715 (finding the principles of sustainable development, polluter pays, and precaution to be part of customary international law). A number of states – including Australia, Canada, Malaysia, and New Zealand – have asserted in international legal pleadings and memorials before international tribunals that the precautionary principle is now customary international law. *See, e.g.,* ITLOS, Malaysian Request for Provisional Measures, *Dispute Concerning Land Reclamation Activities by Singapore Impinging Upon Malaysia's Rights in and Around the Straits of Johor Inclusive of the Areas Around Point 20 (Malaysia v. Singapore)* (Sept. 4, 2003), p. 8, para. 18; ICJ, New Zealand Request for an Examination of the Situation, *Request for an Examination of the Situation in Accordance with Paragraph 63 of the Court's Judgment of 20 December 1974 (New Zealand v. France)* (Aug. 21, 1995), pp. 53–55, *available at* http://www.icj-cij.org/docket/files/97/7187.pdf.

The position of treaties in national law varies even more; some constitutions specify that ratified treaties are automatically the law of the land and must be applied by judges in cases where an issue concerning them arises. Other states, like the United Kingdom and Australia, require that a treaty be incorporated by legislation before the judiciary may apply the agreement. English courts have consistently held that a treaty concluded by the United Kingdom does not become part of the municipal law except and insofar as it is made so by Parliament. Yet a third group of states, like the United States, distinguishes self-executing treaties, which judges may apply, from non-self-executing treaties, which require legislative action before judges may enforce them.

Like other treaties, environmental agreements may contain obligations capable of immediate judicial application and other obligations that require action by the political branches.
Non-self-executing provisions of treaties encompass an obligation on the part of states to
enact the necessary legislation or regulations. The 1979 Bonn Convention on the Conservation of Migratory Species of Wild Animals, for example, requires states parties along the
migratory range of animals listed in Convention Annex I to forbid the taking of any of those
animals. States also may be called on to designate or create organs to be entrusted with certain
functions, such as maintaining contacts with the authorities of other states parties or issuing
licenses or authorizations for regulated activities. Of particular interest are treaty provisions
that oblige states parties to enact and enforce penal sanctions against persons who violate their
terms. Without implementing legislation, judicial powers to enforce non-self-executing treaty
obligations may be limited. *See, e.g., Talisman (Trinidad) Petroleum Ltd. v. Environmental
Authority* (Trinidad & Tobago Environmental Commission, 2003) (reversing denial of a oil
drilling lease in a wetland because the legal framework had not been enacted to protect the
area under the Ramsar Convention).

When international law has been incorporated and made binding, it may rank at the
level of constitutional law or be superior, equal to, or inferior to legislation, according to the
hierarchy of legal sources, generally stipulated in the constitution. Where international law
is not binding as part of domestic law, it may still be considered persuasive in interpreting
constitutional or statutory provisions, and in common law states, it may aid in the development
of the common law. The jurisprudence of international tribunals also can be considered in
these contexts. *See, e.g.,* Anthony Mason, *International Law as a Source of Domestic Law, in*
INTERNATIONAL LAW AND AUSTRALIAN FEDERALISM 210, 220–22 (Donald R. Rothwell & Brian
Opeskin eds., 1997); Gerald L. Neuman, *The Uses of International Law in Constitutional
Interpretation*, 98 AM. J. INT'L L. 82 (2004).

Judges may also find persuasive the law of other nations, especially those whose legal
systems are similar to theirs. *See* ANNE-MARIE SLAUGHTER, A NEW WORLD ORDER ch. 2
(2004). In *Roper v. Simmons*, 543 U.S. 551, 125 S. Ct. 1183, 161 L. Ed. 2d 1 (2005) and
Lawrence v. Texas, 539 U.S. 558, 123 S. Ct. 2472, 156 L. Ed. 2d 508 (2003), the U.S. Supreme
Court examined international human rights law and foreign law to support its decisions to
abolish the death penalty for offenders younger than eighteen years old (*Roper*) and to strike
down a statute criminalizing sodomy between consenting homosexual adults (*Lawrence*).
In *Andhra Pradesh Pollution Control Board-II v. Prof. M.V. Nayudu & Others* [2001] 4 LRI
657, Sup. Ct. India, the Court referred to the Declaration of the U.N. Water Conference;
the International Covenants on Civil and Political and Economic, Social, and Cultural
Rights; and the Rio Declaration on Environment and Development as persuasive authority in
implying a right of access to drinking water as part of the right to life in the Indian Constitution.
The Court also made reference to jurisprudence of the European Court of Justice, the
European Court of Human Rights, and the Inter-American Commission on Human Rights,
as well as decisions of national courts of the Philippines, Colombia, and South Africa. Some
constitutions require that judges consider international or foreign law in interpreting domestic
law.

On occasion, courts have looked to treaties for the meaning of undefined terms in national
law. In *Ramiah and Autard v. Minister of the Environment and Quality of Life*, Cases 4/95
and 5/95 (Mar. 7, 1997), the Mauritius Environment Appeal Tribunal looked to the Ramsar
Convention for a definition of wetlands, although the Convention had not yet been ratified
by Mauritius. The Ministry of Environment agreed that the Convention provided guidance
on the issue.

A court may also take judicial notice of studies done by international organizations as evidence of environmental damage. In *Pedro Flores et al. v. Corporación del Cobre (CODELCO)*, a Chilean court of appeals referred to a UNEP study in finding that the coastline in question was one of the most seriously polluted around the Pacific Ocean. *Pedro Flores et al. v. Corporación del Cobre (CODELCO)*, Corte de Appelaciones (June 23, 1988), Rol 12.753.FS641, *aff'd* Sup. Ct. Chile (ordering disclosure of information, an expert report on the coastline, and an injunction to prevent further pollution).

C. *The Development of International Environmental Law*

1. Beginnings to Stockholm

The first international environmental agreements dealt with shared living resources and appeared only in the nineteenth century, with the conclusion of international fishing treaties and agreements to protect various plant species. The primary purpose of the agreements was to sustain the harvesting of economically valuable species. The aim required international action, because many of the species were migratory or located in areas outside national boundaries, such as on the high seas.

Several early boundary-waters treaties contained measures to reduce and prevent water pollution, as neither state could protect water quality without the other state's cooperation. The agreement respecting boundary waters between the United States and Canada (Washington, Jan. 11, 1909) is still considered a model. It remains in force and was strengthened during the 1970s by other agreements – U.S.-Canada Agreement Relating to the Establishment of Joint Pollution Contingency Plans for Oil and Other Noxious Substances (June 19, 1974), 25 U.S.T. 1280, T.I.A.S. 7861; U.S.-Canada Agreement on Great Lakes Water Quality with Annexes (Nov. 22, 1978), 30 U.S.T. 1383, T.I.A.S. No. 9257, amended Oct. 16, 1983, T.I.A.S. No. 10798. This original agreement instituted a mixed commission that continues to play a role in pollution control.

Some genuinely ecological approaches emerged in the 1930s, with the adoption of two regional instruments that can be seen as precursors to present-day approaches to environmental protection. First, the Convention Relative to the Preservation of Fauna and Flora in their Natural State (London, Nov. 8, 1933) applied to an Africa then largely colonized. The London Convention and the other instrument, the Convention on Nature Protection and Wildlife Preservation in the Western Hemisphere (Washington, Oct. 12, 1940), envisaged the establishment of reserves and the protection of wild animals and plants, especially migratory birds.

After World War II, the international community responded to specific environmental threats caused by technological change and expanded economic activities. The growing use of supertankers to transport oil by sea led to the first efforts to combat marine pollution during the 1950s. The utilization of nuclear energy led to other international regulation. A 1963 treaty, for example, restricted some military uses of radioactive materials. *See* Treaty Banning Nuclear Weapons in the Atmosphere, in Outer Space, and Underwater (Moscow, Aug. 5, 1963), 480 U.N.T.S. 43, 14 U.S.T. 1313. During this period, environmental concerns also increasingly appeared in general international legal texts.

The 1967 black tides off the coasts of France, England, and Belgium, caused by the grounding of the oil tanker *Torrey Canyon*, sharply emphasized the growing threats to the environment. The United Nations took action in 1968, shortly after the *Torrey Canyon* incident, when the General Assembly convened the World Conference on the Human

Environment, held in Stockholm in 1972. G.A. Res. 2398 (XXIII), Dec. 3, 1968. This decision gave rise to intense and diverse activity, particularly in intergovernmental organizations whose mandate could be interpreted to extend to environmental problems. Numerous national and international nongovernmental environmental organizations and governments also engaged in preparatory work.

Even before the Stockholm Conference, international cooperation sought to counter marine oil pollution through adopting preventive measures and establishing liability rules. Several steps also were taken to conserve wild animals and their habitats, notably the conclusion of the Convention on Wetlands of International Importance (Ramsar, Feb. 2, 1971) and the Convention for the Conservation of Antarctic Seals (London, June 1, 1972).

Although these actions responded to some of the urgent environmental problems, ambitious preparations for the Stockholm Conference continued. When the Stockholm meeting took place June 5–16, 1972, it brought together some 6,000 persons, including delegations from 113 states, representatives of every major intergovernmental organization, 700 observers sent by 400 nongovernmental organizations, invited individuals, and some 1,500 journalists.

The inclusiveness helped the Conference achieve an internationally recognized significance, particularly in bringing together the developed and developing countries. In Stockholm, developing countries voiced fears that wealthy nations would condition foreign economic assistance on environmental protection or divert those funds previously dedicated to development towards environmental deterioration.

The Conference adopted notable texts during a closing plenary session, including the Stockholm Declaration on the Human Environment, adopted on June 16, 1972; an "Action Plan" containing 109 recommendations; and a long resolution proposing institutional and financial commitments by the United Nations. The Action Plan also contains sections dedicated to economic and social development as a condition for environmental protection. Various principles promote transfer of financial and technical aid, stability of prices, and adequate remuneration for basic commodities and raw materials, enhancement of the potential for progress of developing countries, and international assistance to aid developing countries to face costs that can delay incorporation of environmental safeguards in development planning. These were the first comprehensive statements of international concern with environmental protection.

Stockholm Declaration on the Human Environment,
U.N. Doc. A/CONF.48/14/Rev.1, *reprinted in* 11 I.L.M. 1416 (1972)

Principle 1

Man has the fundamental right to freedom, equality and adequate conditions of life, in an environment of a quality that permits a life of dignity and well-being, and he bears a solemn responsibility to protect and improve the environment for present and future generations. In this respect, policies promoting or perpetuating apartheid, racial segregation, discrimination, colonial and other forms of oppression and foreign domination stand condemned and must be eliminated.

Principle 2

The natural resources of the earth, including the air, water, land, flora and fauna and especially representative samples of natural ecosystems, must be safeguarded for the benefit of present and future generations through careful planning or management, as appropriate.

Principle 3

The capacity of the earth to produce vital renewable resources must be maintained and, wherever practicable, restored or improved.

Principle 4

Man has a special responsibility to safeguard and wisely manage the heritage of wildlife and its habitat, which are now gravely imperilled by a combination of adverse factors. Nature conservation, including wildlife, must therefore receive importance in planning for economic development.

Principle 5

The non-renewable resources of the earth must be employed in such a way as to guard against the danger of their future exhaustion and to ensure that benefits from such employment are shared by all mankind.

Principle 6

The discharge of toxic substances or of other substances and the release of heat, in such quantities or concentrations as to exceed the capacity of the environment to render them harmless, must be halted in order to ensure that serious or irreversible damage is not inflicted upon ecosystems. The just struggle of the peoples of all countries against pollution should be supported.

Principle 7

States shall take all possible steps to prevent pollution of the seas by substances that are liable to create hazards to human health, to harm living resources and marine life, to damage amenities or to interfere with other legitimate uses of the sea.

Principle 8

Economic and social development is essential for ensuring a favorable living and working environment for man and for creating conditions on earth that are necessary for the improvement of the quality of life.

Principle 9

Environmental deficiencies generated by the conditions of under-development and natural disasters pose grave problems and can best be remedied by accelerated development through the transfer of substantial quantities of financial and technological assistance as a supplement to the domestic effort of the developing countries and such timely assistance as may be required.

Principle 10

For the developing countries, stability of prices and adequate earnings for primary commodities and raw materials are essential to environmental management, since economic factors as well as ecological processes must be taken into account.

Principle 11

The environmental policies of all States should enhance and not adversely affect the present or future development potential of developing countries, nor should they hamper the attainment of better living conditions for all, and appropriate steps should be taken by States and international organizations with a view to reaching agreement on meeting the possible national and international economic consequences resulting from the application of environmental measures.

Principle 12

Resources should be made available to preserve and improve the environment, taking into account the circumstances and particular requirements of developing countries and any costs which may emanate- from their incorporating environmental safeguards into their development planning and the need for making available to them, upon their request, additional international technical and financial assistance for this purpose.

Principle 13

In order to achieve a more rational management of resources and thus to improve the environment, States should adopt an integrated and coordinated approach to their development planning so as to ensure that development is compatible with the need to protect and improve the human environment for the benefit of their population.

Principle 14

Rational planning constitutes an essential tool for reconciling any conflict between the needs of development and the need to protect and improve the environment.

Principle 15

Planning must be applied to human settlements and urbanization with a view to avoiding adverse effects on the environment and obtaining maximum social, economic and environmental benefits for all. In this respect projects which arc designed for colonialist and racist domination must be abandoned.

Principle 16

Demographic policies which are without prejudice to basic human rights and which are deemed appropriate by Governments concerned should be applied in those regions where the rate of population growth or excessive population concentrations are likely to have adverse effects on the environment or development, or where low population density may prevent improvement of the human environment and impede development.

Principle 17

Appropriate national institutions must be entrusted with the task of planning, managing or controlling the environmental resources of States with a view to enhancing environmental quality.

Principle 18

Science and technology, as part of their contribution to economic and social development, must be applied to the identification, avoidance and control of environmental risks and the solution of environmental problems and for the common good of mankind.

Principle 19

Education in environmental matters, for the younger generation as well as adults, giving due consideration to the underprivileged, is essential in order to broaden the basis for an enlightened opinion and responsible conduct by individuals, enterprises and communities in protecting and improving the environment in its full human dimension. It is also essential that mass media of communications avoid contributing to the deterioration of the environment, but, on the contrary, disseminates information of an educational nature on the need to protect and improve the environment in order to enable man to develop in every respect.

Principle 20

Scientific research and development in the context of environmental problems, both national and multinational, must be promoted in all countries, especially the developing countries. In this connection, the free flow of up-to-date scientific information and transfer of experience must be supported and assisted, to facilitate the solution of environmental problems; environmental technologies should be made available to developing countries on terms which would encourage their wide dissemination without constituting an economic burden on the developing countries.

Principle 21

States have, in accordance with the Charter of the United Nations and the principles of international law, the sovereign right to exploit their own resources pursuant to their own environmental policies, and the responsibility to ensure that activities within their jurisdiction or control do not cause damage to the environment of other States or of areas beyond the limits of national jurisdiction.

Principle 22

States shall cooperate to develop further the international law regarding liability and compensation for the victims of pollution and other environmental damage caused by activities within the jurisdiction or control of such States to areas beyond their jurisdiction.

Principle 23

Without prejudice to such criteria as may be agreed upon by the international community, or to standards which will have to be determined nationally, it will be essential in all cases to consider the systems of values prevailing in each country, and the extent of the applicability of standards which are valid for the most advanced countries but which may be inappropriate and of unwarranted social cost for the developing countries.

Principle 24

International matters concerning the protection and improvement of the environment should be handled in a cooperative spirit by all countries, big and small, on an equal footing. Cooperation through multilateral or bilateral arrangements or other appropriate means is essential to effectively control, prevent, reduce and eliminate adverse environmental effects resulting from activities conducted in all spheres, in such a way that due account is taken of the sovereignty and interests of all States.

Principle 25

States shall ensure that international organizations play a coordinated, efficient and dynamic role for the protection and improvement of the environment.

Principle 26

Man and his environment must be spared the effects of nuclear weapons and all other means of mass destruction. States must strive to reach prompt agreement, in the relevant international organs, on the elimination and complete destruction of such weapons.

. . .

The Stockholm Conference had immense value in drawing attention to the problem of environmental deterioration and methods to prevent or remedy it. The Conference was global both in its planetary conception of the environment and in its view of institutional structures and world policies. It was also global in addressing all the major environmental themes of the time.

Questions and Discussion

1. One of the most important principles in the Stockholm Declaration is Principle 1. It has had an important influence on the development of a human rights approach to environmental protection. Does Principle 1 clearly establish a human right to a clean or healthy environment?

2. Principle 21 of the Declaration is probably the most famous. What does Principle 21 require? How does it relate to the *Trail Smelter* arbitration? Although often observed in the breach, Principle 21 is viewed by most international environmental lawyers as a statement of customary international law. *See, e.g.,* Alexandre Kiss, *The International Protection of the Environment, in* THE STRUCTURE AND PROCESS OF INTERNATIONAL LAW: ESSAYS IN LEGAL PHILOSOPHY, DOCTRINE AND THEORY 1074–75 (Ronald St. J. Macdonald & Douglas M. Johnston eds., 1986). *But see* OSCAR SCHACTER, INTERNATIONAL LAW IN THEORY AND PRACTICE 364–65 (1991). In 1996, eleven of the fourteen judges of the International Court of Justice, in a case involving the issue of whether the threat or use of nuclear weapons is prohibited by international law, recognized that the " existence of the general obligation of States to ensure that activities within their jurisdiction and control respect the environment of other States or of areas beyond national control is now part of the corpus of international law relating to the environment." *Legality of the Threat of Use of Nuclear Weapons,* [1996(I)] I.C.J. Reports 226, 241–42. What is the practical effect in the difference in the formulation of the obligation not to cause harm in Principle 21 and by the International Court of Justice? Consider that article 3 of the Convention on Biological Diversity restates in binding legal fashion the exact wording used in Principle 21 of the Stockholm Declaration; consider also that as of February 2009 every state in the world except three (including the United States, which initiated the *Trail Smelter* arbitration) were parties to the Convention. As a practical matter does it really matter whether Principle 21 has become customary international law?

3. Principle 24 of the Declaration requires states to cooperate in addressing environmental problems. The duty to cooperate (also known as good-neighborliness) is premised on the fact that "safeguarding the ecological balance" of the planet is "an 'essential interest' of all states." *Case Concerning the Gabčíkovo-Nagymaros Project* (Hungary v. Slovakia) [1997] I.C.J. Reports 7, 41 (quoting 2 Y.B. INT'L L. COMM'N pt. 2, at 39, para. 14 (1980)). The duty to cooperate has important environmental application, but it also applies across the entire range of international relations between states. *See* art. 74 of the U.N. Charter; 1970 Declaration of Principles on International Law Concerning Friendly Relations and Cooperation Among States in Accordance with the Charter of the United Nations, G.A. Res. 2625, 25 U.N. GOAR Supp. (No. 28), Annex at 123, U.N. Doc. A/80289 (1970); the *MOX Plant Case* (United Kingdom v. Ireland) (provisional measures), Order of 3 December 2001 (duty to cooperate is a fundamental principle of the law of the sea and general international law); *Case Concerning the Kasiliki/Sedudu Island* (Botswana v. Namibia) [1999] I.C.J. 1045 (cooperation entails establishing suitable common regimes). *See also Lac Lanoux* arbitration (Spain v. France), 12 U.N.R.I.A.A. 285.

2. From Stockholm to Rio

International environmental law substantially increased after the Stockholm Conference. The dominant approach of the 1970s concentrated on protecting specific sectors of the environment: marine and fresh waters, atmosphere, outer space, wild plants, and animals. During the 1980s, it became increasingly evident that this sectoral or end-of-the-pipeline approach was insufficient to address environmental deterioration. Thus, a new approach emerged, which aimed to regulate sources and risks of harm, especially those that could affect more than one sector. This eventually led to common management of shared resources and holistic ecosystem protection.

In the 1980s, new problems emerged that had not been perceived earlier, such as long-range air pollution and depletion of the ozone layer. The global Convention for the Protection of the Ozone Layer (Vienna, Mar. 22, 1985) and its Protocol (Montreal, Sept. 16, 1987) created an effective international system to reduce levels of ozone-depleting substances. The unprecedented nuclear catastrophe at Chernobyl, on April 26, 1986, raised awareness of the risks of nuclear power plants and led to the almost-immediate adoption of two conventions, the first requiring rapid notification of nuclear accidents, the second covering assistance in the case of a nuclear accident or radioactive emergency. *See* Convention on Early Notification of a Nuclear Accident and Convention on Assistance in the Case of a Nuclear Accident or Radiological Emergency (Vienna, Sept. 26, 1986).

As environmental laws evolved, it became clear that substances and processes that threaten to cause environmental harm must be regulated during their entire lifetime, including waste disposal. The issue became an international one when waste generators, seeking to dispose of their wastes at the least possible expense, began extensive dumping of toxic and hazardous wastes in developing countries. The Convention on the Control of Transboundary Movements of Hazardous Wastes and their Disposal (Basel, Mar. 22, 1989) and regional treaties on the topic concluded for Africa (Bamako, Jan. 29, 1991), Central America (Panama, Dec. 11, 1991), and the South Pacific (Waigani, Sept. 16, 1995) established a legal regime to address the problem.

In 1983, the General Assembly voted to create the World Commission on Environment and Development, an independent body linked to but outside the U.N. system and later more commonly known as the Brundtland Commission. Its mandate was to take up the critical relationship between environmental protection and economic development and to formulate realistic proposals for reconciling or balancing the two subjects; to propose new forms of international cooperation on these issues to influence policies in the direction of needed changes; and to raise the levels of understanding and commitment to action of individuals, organizations, businesses, and governments. The conclusions of the Brundtland Report stressed the need for an integrated approach to development policies and projects that, if environmentally sound, should lead to sustainable economic development in both developed and developing countries. The Report emphasized the need to give higher priority to anticipating and preventing problems. It defined *sustainable development* as development that meets present and future environment and development objectives and concluded that without an equitable sharing of the costs and benefits of environmental protection within and between countries, neither social justice nor sustainable development can be achieved.

The Brundtland Report led the United Nations to convene a second global conference on the environment in 1992 in Rio de Janeiro, Brazil, under the title U.N. Conference on Environment and Development (UNCED). The very name of the conference reflected a change of approach from that of the Stockholm Conference on the Human Environment. The UNCED met in Rio de Janeiro from June 3–14, 1992. One hundred seventy-two states (all but six members of the United Nations) were represented by close to 10,000 participants, including 116 heads of state and government; Japan alone sent 300 delegates. One thousand four hundred nongovernmental organizations were accredited as well as nearly nine thousand journalists.

Five texts emerged from the meeting. Two important conventions, drafted and adopted before the Conference, were opened for signature at Rio: the U.N. Framework Convention on Climate Change and the Convention on Biological Diversity. The Conference also adopted a declaration whose title reflects the difficulties of reaching agreement on it: "Non-legally binding authoritative statement of principles for a global consensus on the management, conservation and sustainable development of all types of forests."

Two texts adopted at UNCED have a general scope: the Declaration on Environment and Development and an action program called Agenda 21. The Declaration, a short statement of twenty-seven principles, has a composite character that its legislative history can explain. It reaffirms the Stockholm Declaration of 1972 on which it seeks to build, but its approach and philosophy are different. The central concept is sustainable development, as defined by the Brundtland Report, which integrates development and environmental protection.

The Rio Declaration on Environment and Development,
Report of the United Nations Conference on Environment and Development
A/CONF.151/26/Rev.1 (Vol. 1)
(3–14 June 1992), Annex I, pp. 3–8, *reprinted in* 31 I.L.M. 874 (1992)

Principle 1

Human beings are at the centre of concerns for sustainable development. They are entitled to a healthy and productive life in harmony with nature.

Principle 2

States have, in accordance with the Charter of the United Nations and the principles of international law, the sovereign right to exploit their own resources pursuant to their own environmental and developmental policies, and the responsibility to ensure that activities within their jurisdiction or control do not cause damage to the environment of other States or of areas beyond the limits of national jurisdiction.

Principle 3

The right to development must be fulfilled so as to equitably meet developmental and environmental needs of present and future generations.

Principle 4

In order to achieve sustainable development, environmental protection shall constitute an integral part of the development process and cannot be considered in isolation from it.

Principle 5

All States and all people shall cooperate in the essential task of eradicating poverty as an indispensable requirement for sustainable development, in order to decrease the disparities in standards of living and better meet the needs of the majority of the people of the world.

Principle 6

The special situation and needs of developing countries, particularly the least developed and those most environmentally vulnerable, shall be given special priority. International actions in the field of environment and development should also address the interests and needs of all countries.

Principle 7

States shall cooperate in a spirit of global partnership to conserve, protect and restore the health and integrity of the Earth's ecosystem. In view of the different contributions to global environmental degradation, States have common but differentiated responsibilities. The developed countries acknowledge the responsibility that they bear in the international pursuit to sustainable development in view of the pressures their societies place on the global environment and of the technologies and financial resources they command.

Principle 8

To achieve sustainable development and a higher quality of life for all people, States should reduce and eliminate unsustainable patterns of production and consumption and promote appropriate demographic policies.

Principle 9

States should cooperate to strengthen endogenous capacity-building for sustainable development by improving scientific understanding through exchanges of scientific and technological knowledge, and by enhancing the development, adaptation, diffusion and transfer of technologies, including new and innovative technologies.

Principle 10

Environmental issues are best handled with participation of all concerned citizens, at the relevant level. At the national level, each individual shall have appropriate access to information concerning the environment that is held by public authorities, including information on hazardous materials and activities in their communities, and the opportunity to participate in decision-making processes. States shall facilitate and encourage public awareness and participation by making information widely available. Effective access to judicial and administrative proceedings, including redress and remedy, shall be provided.

Principle 11

States shall enact effective environmental legislation. Environmental standards, management objectives and priorities should reflect the environmental and development context to which they apply. Standards applied by some countries may be inappropriate and of unwarranted economic and social cost to other countries, in particular developing countries.

Principle 12

States should cooperate to promote a supportive and open international economic system that would lead to economic growth and sustainable development in all countries, to better address the problems of environmental degradation. Trade policy measures for environmental purposes should not constitute a means of arbitrary or unjustifiable discrimination or a disguised restriction on international trade. Unilateral actions to deal with environmental challenges outside the jurisdiction of the importing country should be avoided. Environmental measures addressing transboundary or global environmental problems should, as far as possible, be based on an international consensus.

Principle 13

States shall develop national law regarding liability and compensation for the victims of pollution and other environmental damage. States shall also cooperate in an expeditious and more determined manner to develop further international law regarding liability and compensation for adverse effects of environmental damage caused by activities within their jurisdiction or control to areas beyond their jurisdiction.

Principle 14

States should effectively cooperate to discourage or prevent the relocation and transfer to other States of any activities and substances that cause severe environmental degradation or are found to be harmful to human health.

Principle 15

In order to protect the environment, the precautionary approach shall be widely applied by States according to their capabilities. Where there are threats of serious or irreversible damage, lack of full scientific certainty shall not be used as a reason for postponing cost-effective measures to prevent environmental degradation.

Principle 16

National authorities should endeavour to promote the internalization of environmental costs and the use of economic instruments, taking into account the approach that the polluter should, in principle, bear the cost of pollution, with due regard to the public interest and without distorting international trade and investment.

Principle 17

Environmental impact assessment, as a national instrument, shall be undertaken for proposed activities that are likely to have a significant adverse impact on the environment and are subject to a decision of a competent national authority.

Principle 18

States shall immediately notify other States of any natural disasters or other emergencies that are likely to produce sudden harmful effects on the environment of those States. Every effort shall be made by the international community to help States so afflicted.

Principle 19

States shall provide prior and timely notification and relevant information to potentially affected States on activities that may have a significant adverse transboundary environmental effect and shall consult with those States at an early stage and in good faith.

Principle 20

Women have a vital role in environmental management and development. Their full participation is therefore essential to achieve sustainable development.

Principle 21

The creativity, ideals and courage of the youth of the world should be mobilized to forge a global partnership in order to achieve sustainable development and ensure a better future for all.

Principle 22

Indigenous people and their communities and other local communities have a vital role in environmental management and development because of their knowledge and traditional practices. States should recognize and duly support their identity, culture and interests and enable their effective participation in the achievement of sustainable development.

Principle 23

The environment and natural resources of people under oppression, domination and occupation shall be protected.

Principle 24

Warfare is inherently destructive of sustainable development. States shall therefore respect international law providing protection for the environment in times of armed conflict and cooperate in its further development, as necessary.

Principle 25

Peace, development and environmental protection are interdependent and indivisible.

Principle 26

States shall resolve all their environmental disputes peacefully and by appropriate means in accordance with the Charter of the United Nations.

Principle 27

States and people shall cooperate in good faith and in a spirit of partnership in the fulfilment of the principles embodied in this Declaration and in the further development of international law in the field of sustainable development.

Questions and Discussion

1. How do the provisions of the Rio Declaration differ from those of the Stockholm Declaration? Which principles in either or both texts can be considered legal principles from which obligations may emerge?
2. A second general document adopted by the Rio Conference is Agenda 21, a program of action consisting of forty chapters with 115 specific topics contained in eight hundred pages. There are four main parts:
   - socioeconomic dimensions (e.g., habitats, health, demography, consumption, and production patterns);
   - conservation and resource management (e.g., atmosphere, forest, water, waste, chemical products);
   - strengthening the role of nongovernmental organizations and other social groups, such as trade unions, women, youths; and
   - measures of implementation (e.g., financing, institutions).

The chapters concerning the atmosphere (ch. 9), biological diversity (ch. 15), the oceans (ch. 17), and freshwater resources (ch. 18), as well as discussion of specific problems such as biotechnology (ch. 15), toxic chemicals (ch. 19), and waste (chs. 20–22) have been influential in the development of national and international environmental law. Agenda 21 pays particular attention to national legislation. It makes frequent reference to national laws, measures, plans, programs, and standards. Chapter 8, "Integrating Environment and Development in Decision-Making," advocates the use of legal and economic instruments for planning and management, with incorporation of efficiency criteria in decisions. It recognizes the importance of country-specific laws and regulations for transforming environment and development policies into action, adding that not only "command-and-control" methods should be used but also a normative framework for economic planning and market instruments. Such methods can also be useful for the implementation of international treaty obligations.

3. From Rio to Johannesburg

The Rio documents joined environmental protection and economic development in the concept of sustainable development. This emphasis is understandable, because the current economic system presents numerous challenges to environmental protection. The north-south disparity in wealth and capacity creates difficulties in imposing uniform norms and standards through international agreements. The desire for free trade in goods and services in the international economic system generates opposition to trade barriers adopted to protect the environment. A related issue is competitive disadvantage: a state taking measures to protect the environment must count the increased costs that are borne by its economy. Preoccupation with conditions of competition is evident in the work of the Organisation of Economic Co-operation and Development (OECD) and the environmental side agreement to the North American Free Trade Agreement (NAFTA). The latter calls for cooperation to better conserve, protect, and enhance the environment while avoiding the creation of trade distortions or new trade barriers. Other regional free trade agreements mention environmental cooperation as an aim, including the Treaty Establishing the South African Development Community (Windhoek, Aug. 17, 1992); Treaty Establishing a Common Market for Eastern and Southern Africa (Kampala, Nov. 5, 1993); Agreement on the North American Free Trade Area (Washington, Ottawa, Mexico City, Dec. 17, 1992); Tropical Timber Agreement (Jan. 26, 1994) and European Energy Charter (Dec. 17, 1994).

In the aftermath of Rio, virtually every major international convention concerning multilateral cooperation added environmental protection as one of the goals of the states parties. Areas of international law that developed during earlier periods began evolving in new directions because of insistence that they take into account environmental considerations. The result was an infusion of environmental norms into nearly every branch of international law.

New issues have emerged as a result of the continual necessity to anticipate or respond to the consequences of technological change. Advances in biotechnology have led to the need to promote biosafety, centered on two related issues: first, the handling of living modified organisms (LMOs) in the laboratory to protect workers and prevent the accidental liberation of such organisms into the surrounding ecosystem (i.e., contained use); second, the need for regulatory systems to govern the deliberate release of LMOs into the environment for testing or commercial purposes. States parties to the Convention on Biological Diversity adopted a protocol on biosafety on January 29, 2000, to address those issues.

Ecosystem protection has broadened and deepened as well. The earlier sectoral aim of protecting wild fauna and flora is now incorporated in the comprehensive goal of maintaining biological diversity in situ. This expanded and integrated vision includes efforts to reverse the trend toward monocultural agriculture and stockbreeding, as well as to combat the abuse of pesticides and fertilizers. An integrated or holistic approach to environmental protection appears in particular in recent instruments concerning environmental protection in large ecosystems: Antarctica (Madrid Protocol of 1991), the Alps (Salzburg Convention of 1991 and Chambéry Protocols of 1994), the Arctic region (1996 Declaration), and the Carpathian Mountain Convention (Kiev, 2003).

The same trend can be seen in the shift toward protecting freshwater resources as hydrographic units rather than individual watercourses. The unity of water resources in a hydrographic basin and a consequent ecosystem approach to regulating such resources is now generally accepted. The U.N. Convention on the Non-Navigational Uses of International Watercourses (New York, May 21, 1997), which unified the international legal status of surface and subsurface water, hastened recognition of the need to regulate fresh waters in the entire catchment basin, mainly a regional task. The problem ahead is to organize the shared management of water resources by all riparian states.

Most states now accept that global efforts are required to solve many aspects of environmental deterioration, such as ocean pollution, depletion of stratospheric ozone, the greenhouse effect, and threats to biodiversity. The required cooperation necessitates adjustments between industrialized and developing countries. The International Convention to Combat Desertification in Those Countries Experiencing Serious Drought and/or Desertification, particularly in Africa (June 17, 1994) is one of the most significant results of such cooperation, strongly reflecting the concept of common but differentiated responsibilities. In addition, it takes the principle of cooperation and melds it with the right of public participation, thus emphasizing the need for all levels of governance and civil society to be involved in actions to combat desertification.

4. The World Summit on Sustainable Development

In the decade after the Rio Conference, environmental concerns encountered increasing competition on the international agenda from economic globalization, deregulation, and privatization, an emphasis on free trade, and the development crises of countries with high levels of poverty. The United Nations convened a conference to mark the tenth anniversary of the Rio meeting but failed to mention the environment in its name. Instead, it was convened as the World Summit on Sustainable Development.

Between August 26 and September 4, 2002, the representatives of more than 190 countries met in Johannesburg, South Africa, to "reaffirm commitment to the Rio Principles, the full implementation of Agenda 21 and the Programme for the Further Implementation of Agenda 21." At the end of the Conference, the participating governments adopted the Declaration on Sustainable Development affirming their will to "assume a collective responsibility to advance and strengthen the interdependent and mutually reinforcing pillars of sustainable development – economic development, social development and environmental protection – at local, national, regional and global levels." Para. 5. While recognizing that "the global environment continues to suffer," and acknowledging the loss of biodiversity; the depletion of fish stocks; the progress of desertification; the evident adverse effects of climate change; and the pollution of the air, of water and of the sea (para. 13), the Declaration mainly focused on development and poverty eradication, especially in the poorest countries.

There is no comprehensive international environmental agreement addressing these matters in a holistic manner, nor is there a single agency addressing the problems. The lack of coordination among different agencies and treaty bodies has had some negative effect on the success of environmental laws and policies and is a priority issue for the future.

Environmental law and policy also must grapple with the lack of scientific certainty about many aspects of the physical world. Scientific uncertainty often attends issues of the nature and scope of the adverse environmental impacts of human activities. Exacerbating the uncertainty, damage often is measurable only years after the causative actions have occurred. Given this situation, questions arise over how to develop environmental policy and how to allocate risk between the present and the future. Many decisions cannot await scientific certainty, assuming that something approaching certainty can ever be achieved. Therefore, debate centers on whether a policy should be adopted to assume that harmful consequences will occur unless activities or products are proven safe or whether to take a less cautious approach, knowing that many environmental processes and changes may be irreversible and ultimately life threatening.

In addition to uncertainty and irreversibility, environmental law must recognize the fact that the environment is dynamic and constantly evolving. This characteristic requires flexible laws and policies that are capable of rapid alteration in response to new circumstances. At the same time, and perhaps paradoxically, the legal framework must look to the long term in its efforts to maintain life and the ecological balance in an unseeable future.

5. UNCSD 2012

On December 24, 2009, the General Assembly of the United Nations passed a resolution deciding "to organize, in 2012, the United Nations Conference on Sustainable Development at the highest possible level . . . and . . . accept[ed] with gratitude the generous offer of the Government of Brazel to host the Conference." G.A. Res. 64/236 (31 March 2010). The General Assembly agreed that the Conference will result in a focused political document that should ensure the balanced integration of economic development, social development and environmental protection, "as these are interdependent and mutually reinforcing components of sustainable development." Id.

D. *Principles of International Environmental Law*

The complexity of many environmental issues makes specific regulation difficult at the international level. Instead, principles play an important role in setting forth the general approach or bases for the development of national law and policy.

1. Prevention of Harm

Originating in the *Trail Smelter* arbitration, the duty to prevent extraterritorial environmental harm was most famously stated in the 1972 Stockholm Declaration, Principle 21. The principle has been repeated in MEAs like the Convention on Biological Diversity (art. 3) and the U.N. Climate Change Convention. The U.S. *Restatement of Foreign Relations Law (Third)*, section 601, similarly refers to the obligation of states "to conform to generally accepted international rules and standards for the prevention, reduction, and control of injury to the environment of another state or of areas beyond the limits of national jurisdiction." The International Court of Justice has called the duty to prevent extraterritorial environmental harm part of customary international law.

The duty to avoid transfrontier pollution requires each state to exercise due diligence, which means to act reasonably and in good faith to regulate public and private activities subject to its jurisdiction or control that are potentially harmful to any part of the environment. The principle does not impose an absolute duty to prevent all harm but instead requires each state to prohibit those activities known to cause significant harm to the environment and to mitigate harm from lawful activities that may harm the environment.

The general duty of prevention emerges from the international responsibility not to cause significant damage to the environment extraterritorially, but the preventive principle seeks to avoid harm irrespective of whether or not there are transboundary impacts. The rationale derives from the interdependence of all parts of the environment and the fact that some environmental injury, such as the extinction of a species of fauna or flora, is irreversible. Even when harm is remediable, the costs of rehabilitation may be prohibitive. Article 192 of the U.N. Convention on the Law of the Sea first expressed the general requirement of prevention by affirming that "[s]tates have the general obligation to protect and preserve the marine environment." Subsequently, article 20 of the 1997 U.N. Convention on the Non-Navigational Uses of International Watercourses (New York, May 21, 1997) affirmed the same duty for international fresh water. The 1992 Convention on Biological Diversity lists the measures that should be taken to ensure conservation and sustainable use of biological resources within states parties.

The requirement to prevent harm is complex owing to the number and diversity of the legal instruments in which it appears. It can perhaps better be considered an overarching aim that gives rise to a multitude of legal mechanisms, including prior assessment of environmental harm and procedures to license or authorize hazardous activities, including setting the conditions for operation and the consequences of violations. Emission limits and other product or process standards, the use of best-available techniques (BAT), and similar techniques can all be considered applications of the principle of prevention. Prevention also can involve the elaboration and adoption of overarching strategies and policies. Prior assessment of activities, monitoring, notification, and exchange of information are general obligations contained in nearly all environmental agreements. The failure to comply with any of these requirements can indicate the absence of due diligence.

2. Precaution

The proclamation of the precautionary principle, which the U.S. government prefers to call the precautionary approach, can be considered one of the most important provisions in the Rio Declaration. Principle 15 provides:

> In order to protect the environment, the precautionary principle shall be widely applied by States according to their capabilities. Where there are threats of serious or irreversible damage, lack of full scientific certainty shall not be used as a reason for postponing cost effective measures to prevent environmental degradation.

Formulations of the precautionary principle are relatively recent, but since 1992, the precautionary principle has appeared in almost all international instruments related to environmental protection. It has also been applied in national laws and jurisprudence. The Indian Supreme Court has said the following:

> Duty is cast upon the Government under Article 21 of the Constitution of India to protect the environment and the two salutary principles which govern the law of environment are: (i) the principles of sustainable development and (ii) the precautionary principle. It needs to be highlighted that the Convention on Biological Diversity has been acceded to by our country and,

therefore, it has to implement the same. As was observed by this Court in *Vishaka and Ors. v. State of Rajasthan and Ors.* (1997 (6) SCC 241), in the absence of any inconsistency between the domestic law and the international conventions, the rule of judicial construction is that regard must be had to international convention and norms even in construing the domestic law. It is, therefore, necessary for the Government to keep in view the international obligations while exercising discretionary powers under the Conservation Act unless there are compelling reasons to depart therefrom.

The United Nations Conference on Human Environment held in Stockholm during June 1972 brought into focus several alarming situations and highlighted the immediate need to take steps to control the menace of pollution to the Mother Earth, air and of space failing which, the Conference cautioned mankind, it should be ready to face the disastrous consequences. The suggestions noted in this Conference were reaffirmed in successive Conferences followed by Earth Summit held at Rio-de Janeiro (Brazil) in 1992.

K.M. Chinnappa, T.N. Godavarman Thirumalpad v. Union of India et al., [2002] INSC 453 (2002). The Canadian Supreme Court applied the precautionary principle in the following case.

Canada Ltée (Spraytech, Société d'arrosage) and Services des espaces verts Ltée/Chemlawn v. Hudson (Town), No. 114957
Judgment of the Supreme Court
200 D.L.R. (4th) 419, 425–40, (2001)2 SCR 241; ILDC 185 (CA 2001)

[1] L'Heureux-Dubé J. (Gonthier, Bastarache and Arbour JJ. concur[r]ing): – The context of this appeal includes the realization that our common future, that of every Canadian community, depends on a healthy environment. In the words of the Superior Court judge: "Twenty years ago, there was very little concern over the effect of chemicals such as pesticides on the population. Today, we are more conscious of what type of an environment we wish to live in, and what quality of life we wish to expose our children [to]" ((1993), 19 M.P.L.R. (2d) 224, at p. 230). This Court has recognized that "[e]veryone is aware that individually and collectively, we are responsible for preserving the natural environment . . . environmental protection [has] emerged as a fundamental value in Canadian society": *Ontario v. Canadian Pacific Ltd.*, 1995 CanLII 112 (S.C.C.), [1995] 2 S.C.R. 1031, at para. 55. *See also Friends of the Oldman River Society v. Canada (Minister of Transport)*, 1992 CanLII 110 (S.C.C.), [1992] 1 S.C.R. 3, at pp. 16–17.

[2] Regardless of whether pesticides are in fact an environmental threat, the Court is asked to decide the legal question of whether the Town of Hudson, Quebec, acted within its authority in enacting a by-law regulating and restricting pesticide use.

. . .

I. Facts

[5] The appellants are landscaping and lawn care companies operating mostly in the region of greater Montreal, with both commercial and residential clients. They make regular use of pesticides approved by the federal *Pest Control Products Act*, R.S.C. 1985, c. P-9, in the course of their business activities and hold the requisite licences under Quebec's *Pesticides Act*, R.S.Q., c. P-9.3.

[6] The respondent, the Town of Hudson ("the Town"), is a municipal corporation governed by the *Cities and Towns Act*, R.S.Q., c. C-19 ("C.T.A."). It is located about 40 kilometres west of Montreal and has a population of approximately 5,400 people, some of whom are clients of the appellants. In 1991, the Town adopted By-law 270, restricting the use of pesticides within its perimeter to specified locations and for enumerated activities. The by-law responded to residents'

concerns, repeatedly expressed since 1985. The residents submitted numerous letters and comments to the Town's Council. The definition of pesticides in By-law 270 replicates that of the *Pesticides Act*.

[7] In November 1992, the appellants were served with a summons by the Town to appear before the Municipal Court and respond to charges of having used pesticides in violation of By-law 270. The appellants pled not guilty and obtained a suspension of proceedings in order to bring a motion for declaratory judgment before the Superior Court (under art. 453 of Quebec's *Code of Civil Procedure*, R.S.Q., c. C-25). They asked that the court declare By-law 270 (as well as By-law 248, which is not part of this appeal) to be inoperative and *ultra vires* the Town's authority.

[8] The Superior Court denied the motion for declaratory judgment, finding that the by-laws fell within the scope of the Town's powers under the C.T.A. This ruling was affirmed by a unanimous Quebec Court of Appeal.

. . .

V. Analysis

A. Did the Town Have the Statutory Authority to Enact By-law 270?

[18] In *R. v. Sharma*, 1993 CanLII 165 (S.C.C.), [1993] 1 S.C.R. 650, at p. 668, this Court recognized "the principle that, as statutory bodies, municipalities 'may exercise only those powers expressly conferred by statute, those powers necessarily or fairly implied by the expressed power in the statute, and those indispensable powers essential and not merely convenient to the effectuation of the purposes of the corporation' (Makuch, *Canadian Municipal and Planning Law* (1983), at p. 115)." Included in this authority are "general welfare" powers, conferred by provisions in provincial enabling legislation, on which municipalities can draw. . . .

. . .

[20] While enabling provisions that allow municipalities to regulate for the "general welfare" within their territory authorize the enactment of by-laws genuinely aimed at furthering goals such as public health and safety, it is important to keep in mind that such open-ended provisions do not confer an unlimited power. Rather, courts faced with an impugned by-law enacted under an "omnibus" provision such as s. 410 C.T.A. must be vigilant in scrutinizing the true purpose of the by-law. In this way, a municipality will not be permitted to invoke the implicit power granted under a "general welfare" provision as a basis for enacting by-laws that are in fact related to ulterior objectives, whether mischievous or not. . . .

. . .

[23] Section 410(1) C.T.A. provides that councils may make by-laws:

410(1) To secure peace, order, good government, health and general welfare in the territory of the municipality, provided such by-laws are not contrary to the laws of Canada, or of Québec, nor inconsistent with any special provision of this Act or of the charter.

. . .

[24] The appellants argue that By-law 270 imposes an impermissible absolute ban on pesticide use. They focus on s. 2 of the by-law, which states that: "The spreading and use of a pesticide is prohibited throughout the territory of the Town." In my view, the by-law read as a whole does not impose such a prohibition. By-law 270's ss. 3 to 6 state locations and situations for pesticide use. . . .

. . .

[26] In *Shell, supra*, at pp. 276–77, Sopinka J. for the majority quoted the following with approval from Rogers, *supra*, § 64.1 at p. 387:

In approaching a problem of construing a municipal enactment a court should endeavour firstly to interpret it so that the powers sought to be exercised are in consonance with the purposes of the corporation. The provision at hand should be construed with reference to the object of the municipality: to render services to a group of persons in a locality with a view to advancing their health, welfare, safety and good government.

In that case, Sopinka J. enunciated the test of whether the municipal enactment was "passed for a municipal purpose." Provisions such as s. 410(1) C.T.A. . . . must have a reasonable connection to the municipality's permissible objectives. As stated in *Greenbaum, supra,* at p. 689: "municipal by-laws are to be read to fit within the parameters of the empowering provincial statute where the by-laws are susceptible to more than one interpretation. However, courts must be vigilant in ensuring that municipalities do not impinge upon the civil or common law rights of citizens in passing *ultra vires* by-laws."

[27] . . . Based on the distinction between essential and non-essential uses of pesticides, it is reasonable to conclude that the Town by-law's purpose is to minimize the use of allegedly harmful pesticides in order to promote the health of its inhabitants. This purpose falls squarely within the "health" component of s. 410(1). . . .

[28] The appellants claim that By-law 270 is discriminatory and therefore *ultra vires* because of what they identify as impermissible distinctions that affect their commercial activities. There is no specific authority in the C.T.A. for these distinctions. . . .

[29] Without drawing distinctions, By-law 270 could not achieve its permissible goal of aiming to improve the health of the Town's inhabitants by banning non-essential pesticide use. If all pesticide uses and users were treated alike, the protection of health and welfare would be sub-optimal. For example, withdrawing the special status given to farmers under the by-law's s. 4 would work at cross-purposes with its salubrious intent. Section 4 thus justifiably furthers the objective of By-law 270. Having held that the Town can regulate the use of pesticides, I conclude that the distinctions impugned by the appellants for restricting their businesses are necessary incidents to the power delegated by the province under s. 410(1) C.T.A. They are "so absolutely necessary to the exercise of those powers that [authorization has] to be found in the enabling provisions, by necessary inference or implicit delegation"; *Arcade Amusements, supra,* at p. 414, quoted in *Greenbaum, supra,* at p. 695.

[30] To conclude this section on statutory authority, I note that reading s. 410(1) to permit the Town to regulate pesticide use is consistent with principles of international law and policy. My reasons for the Court in *Baker v. Canada (Minister of Citizenship and Immigration),* [1999] 2 S.C.R. 817, at p. 861, 174 D.L.R. (4th), observed that "the values reflected in international human rights law may help inform the contextual approach to statutory interpretation and judicial review." As stated in *Driedger on the Construction of Statutes, supra,* at p. 330:

> [T]he legislature is presumed to respect the values and principles enshrined in international law, both customary and conventional. These constitute a part of the legal context in which legislation is enacted and read. *In so far as possible, therefore, interpretations that reflect these values and principles are preferred.* [Emphasis added.]

[31] The interpretation of By-law 270 contained in these reasons respects international law's "precautionary principle," which is defined as follows at para. 7 of the *Bergen Ministerial Declaration on Sustainable Development* (1990):

> In order to achieve sustainable development, policies must be based on the precautionary principle. Environmental measures must anticipate, prevent and attack the causes of environmental degradation. Where there are threats of serious or irreversible damage, lack of full scientific certainty should not be used as a reason for postponing measures to prevent environmental degradation.

Canada "advocated inclusion of the precautionary principle" during the Bergen Conference nego-tiations (D. VanderZwaag, CEPA Issue Elaboration Paper No. 18, *CEPA and the Precautionary Principle/Approach* (1995), at p. 8). The principle is codified in several items of domestic legisla-tion: see for example the *Oceans Act*, S.C. 1996, c. 31, Preamble (para. 6); *Canadian Environmental Protection Act*, 1999, S.C. 1999, c. 33, s. 2(1) (*a*); *Endangered Species Act*, S.N.S. 1998, c. 11, ss. 2(1) (*h*) and 11(1).

[32] Scholars have documented the precautionary principle's inclusion "in virtually every recently adopted treaty and policy document related to the protection and preservation of the environment" (D. Freestone and E. Hey, "Origins and Development of the Precautionary Princi-ple," in D. Freestone and E. Hey, eds., *The Precautionary Principle and International Law* (1996), at p. 41. As a result, there may be "currently sufficient state practice to allow a good argument that the precautionary principle is a principle of customary international law" (J. Cameron and J. Abouchar, "The Status of the Precautionary Principle in International Law," in *ibid.*, at p. 52). *See also* O. McIntyre and T. Mosedale, "The Precautionary Principle as a Norm of Customary International Law" (1997), 9 *J. Env. L.* 221, at p. 241 ("the precautionary principle has indeed crystallised into a norm of customary international law"). The Supreme Court of India consid-ers the precautionary principle to be "part of the Customary International Law" (A.P. *Pollution Control Board v. Nayudu*, 1999 S.O.L. Case No. 53, at para. 27). *See also Vellore Citizens Wel-fare Forum v. Union of India*, [1996] Supp. 5 S.C.R. 241. In the context of the precautionary principle's tenets, the Town's concerns about pesticides fit well under their rubric of preventive action.

Questions and Discussion

1. In its judgment in the *Affaire Tătar c. Roumanie* (App. No. 67021/01, in French only), delivered March 17, 2009, the European Court of Human Rights quoted extensively from the Stockholm and Rio Declarations, among other international sources, and cited to developments in the European Union to conclude that, in Europe, the precautionary principle has evolved from being a philosophical concept to becoming a legal norm. The court held Romania liable for failing to take measures to protect individuals from the hazards of a gold-mining operation, recalling to the government the importance of the precautionary principle (para. 120).

2. In general, the precautionary principle can be considered the most developed form of prevention. Precaution means preparing for potential, uncertain, or even hypothetical threats, when there is no irrefutable proof that damage will occur. It is prevention based on probabilities or contingencies, but it cannot eliminate all conjectural or speculative risks that lack any scientific basis, such as those based on astrological predictions or psychic visions. Precaution particularly applies when the consequences of nonaction could be serious or irreversible. Policy makers must consider the circumstances of a given situation and decide whether scientific opinion is based on credible evidence and reliable scientific methodology. Such a development expands the important role of scientists in the protection of the environment: decision makers must adopt measures based on a general knowledge of the environment and the problems its protection raises.

3. A number of commentators maintain that the precautionary principle requires a reversal of the ordinary burden of proof on those seeking to prohibit an activity because of threats to the environment or human health. These scholars claim that, under the precautionary principle, those seeking to engage in a potentially harmful activity must bear the burden of proving that such an activity will be harmless or within an acceptable level of risk, taking into account any risk management plans. *See, e.g.*, Charmain Barton, *The Status of the*

Precautionary Principle in Australia, 22 Harv. Envtl. L. Rev. 509, 519–21 (1998). *See also* the discussion in Tim O'Riordan & James Cameron, *The History and Contemporary Significance of the Precautionary Principle, in* Interpreting the Precautionary Principle 12, 13–26 (Tim O'Riordan & James Cameron eds., 1994). Does Principle 15 of the Rio Declaration support this view?

4. *See also Fuel Retailers Association of Southern Africa v. Director-General Environmental Management, Department of Agriculture, Conservation and Environment, Mpumalanga Province, et al.*, Case No. CCT 67/06; ILDC 783 (ZA 2007) (South Africa), excerpted in Chapter 7.

3. The Polluter-Pays Principle

The polluter-pays principle seeks to impose the costs of environmental harm on the party responsible for the pollution. This principle was set out by the OECD as an economic principle and as the most efficient way to allocate costs of pollution prevention and control measures introduced by the public authorities in member countries. It is intended to encourage the internalization of environmental costs and the rational use of scarce environmental resources and to avoid distortions in international trade and investment. This can be interpreted in different ways: compensation for damage may or may not be included; the concept of the polluter can vary, from the producer of merchandise to the consumer who uses it. International practice thus far seems to aim to eliminate public subsidies for pollution abatement by companies.

In fact, pollution control costs can be borne by the community, by those who pollute, or by consumers. Using the example of an industry that discharges pollutants into a river, there are at least five possible allocations of the economic consequences:

1. The river can remain polluted, as a public good common resource, and rendered unsuitable for certain downstream activities, causing the downstream community to suffer an economic loss;
2. The downstream community can build an adequate water treatment plant at its own cost;
3. The polluter may receive public subsidies for controlling the pollution;
4. The polluter bears the costs of pollution control in application of the polluter-pays principles;
5. The enterprise incorporates the costs of pollution abatement in the price of the products and passes them on to the consumer.

Disincentives, such as penalties and civil liability, can also be considered applications of the polluter-pays principle. They aim to induce actors to take greater care in their behavior to avoid the increased costs represented by the penalties. Little empirical work has been done, but there is some evidence for the deterrent effect of a liability regime. As a matter of economic analysis, in a perfect market those responsible for harm would be expected to invest in prevention when the cost of prevention is likely to avoid damage that would be more costly to restore than to prevent. The market is not perfect, however, in part because of regulatory intervention. For example, prevention may require new equipment that tax regulations demand be capitalized and depreciated over time, whereas the costs of restoration can be deducted immediately as expenses, making the latter preferable to the former as an economic matter. Permit requirements may make changes to installations more difficult and costly, even if the result is greater prevention. The uncertainty of harm, its scale, or likelihood may also contribute to a decision that the costs of prevention are greater than the potential costs of liability.

4. Sustainable Development

Since the end of the 1980s, the principle of sustainable development has dominated international activities in the field of environmental protection. It was defined in the 1987 Report of the World Commission on Environment and Development as "development that meets the needs of the present without compromising the ability of future generations to meet their own needs." World Commission on Environment and Development, U.N. Doc. A/42/47 (11 Dec. 1987), *reprinted in* OUR COMMON FUTURE 43 (1987) (also known as the "Bruntland Commission Report" after the Commission's chair, former Norwegian Prime Minister Gro Harlem Brundtland). The Report identified the critical objectives of sustainable development:

- reviving growth but changing its quality;
- meeting essential needs for jobs, food, energy, water, and sanitation;
- ensuring a sustainable level of populations;
- conserving and enhancing the resource base;
- reorienting technology and managing risk; and
- merging environment and economics in decision making.

Principle 4 of the Rio Declaration states that, "in order to achieve sustainable development, environmental protection shall constitute an integral part of the development process and cannot be considered in isolation from it." Approaches that take into account long-term strategies and that include the use of environmental and social impact assessment, risk analysis, cost-benefit analysis, and natural resources accounting are necessary. The integration of environmental, social, and economic policies also requires transparency and broad public participation in governmental decision making.

As its title shows, the Johannesburg World Summit on Sustainable Development focused on this concept with particular emphasis on eradicating poverty. During the same year, the first attempt to define sustainable development in a binding text appeared in article 3(1)(a) of the Convention for Cooperation in the Protection and Sustainable Development of the Marine and Coastal Environment of the Northeast Pacific (Antigua, Feb. 18, 2002):

> For the purpose of this Convention sustainable development means the process of progressive change in the quality of life of human beings, which places it as the center and primordial subject of development, by means of economic growth with social equity and the transformation of methods of production and consumption patterns, and which is sustained in the ecological balance and vital support of the region. This process implies respect for regional, national and local ethnic and cultural diversity, and full participation of people in peaceful coexistence and in harmony with nature, without prejudice to and ensuring the quality of life of future generations.

In the same treaty, the concept of maintaining environmental services is considered essential to sustainable development. According to the Convention, it means the services provided by the functions of nature itself, such as the protection of soil by trees, the natural filtration and purification of water, and the protection of habitat for biodiversity. Art. 3(1)(c).

Case Concerning the Gabčíkovo-Nagymaros Project (Hungary v. Slovakia),
1997 I.C.J. 7, 77–78

[In this case, the International Court of Justice had occasion to directly consider how to balance the need for economic development with environmental protection. In a 1977 bilateral treaty, Hungary and Slovakia agreed to build and operate a dam and system of locks on the Danube River, intended to significantly contribute to the economies of both states by increasing shipping access and by powering two large hydroelectric power plants. The parties recognized that the project also could threaten the surrounding environment and included treaty provisions "for the protection of nature" and obligating the parties to ensure that water quality was not diminished.

In 1989, Hungary suspended work on the project because new evidence had come to light about greater adverse environmental consequences than originally anticipated and there was growing domestic public opposition to the project. In 1992, Hungary notified Slovakia that it was terminating the treaty. Slovakia proceeded unilaterally to construct a modified system of locks known as Variant C and put it into operation, dramatically reducing the flow of the Danube River downstream into Hungary. Hungary demanded that Slovakia restore the Danube to its pre-Variant C status. Slovakia refused.

In 1993, the parties agreed to submit this dispute to the ICJ. The Court ruled that Hungary had breached the 1977 treaty by suspending work on the project and that the breach could not be excused on the ground of ecological necessity. The Court also held that Slovakia was responsible for the interference with Hungary's interests in the Danube through the operation of Variant C. The ICJ concluded that the 1977 treaty was still in force and directed the parties to enter into good faith negotiations to reach a workable solution. In the course of its judgment the Court acknowledged the existence of international environmental norms and directed the parties to consider the principle of sustainable development in trying to reconcile the competing environmental and development aspects of the situation. – *Eds.*]

140. It is clear that the Project's impact upon, and its implications for, the environment are of necessity a key issue. The numerous scientific reports which have been presented to the Court by the Parties – even if their conclusions are often contradictory – provide abundant evidence that this impact and these implications are considerable.

In order to evaluate the environmental risks, current standards must be taken into consideration. This is not only allowed by the wording of Articles 15 and 19, but even prescribed, to the extent that these articles impose a continuing – and thus necessarily evolving – obligation on the parties to maintain the quality of the water of the Danube and to protect nature.

The Court is mindful that, in the field of environmental protection, vigilance and prevention are required on account of the often irreversible character of damage to the environment and of the limitations inherent in the very mechanism of reparation of this type of damage.

Throughout the ages, mankind has, for economic and other reasons, constantly interfered with nature. In the past, this was often done without consideration of the effects upon the environment. Owing to new scientific insights and to a growing awareness of the risks for mankind – for present and future generations – of pursuit of such interventions at an unconsidered and unabated pace, new norms and standards have been developed, set forth in a great number of instruments during the last two decades. Such new norms have to be taken into consideration, and such new standards given proper weight, not only when States contemplate new activities but also when continuing with activities begun in the past. This need to reconcile economic development with protection of the environment is aptly expressed in the concept of sustainable development.

For the purposes of the present case, this means that the Parties together should look afresh at the effects on the environment of the operation of the Gabčíkovo power plant. In particular they must find a satisfactory solution for the volume of water to be released into the old bed of the Danube and into the side-arms on both sides of the river.

Jayal and Others v. India and Others, (2004) 9 SCC 362, 2003(7) SCALE54

[This case concerned a challenge to the construction of the Terhi Dam. The petitioners alleged that further study and tests were necessary to ensure the safety of the dam and that conditions imposed by an environmental clearance issued for the project had not been complied with. As a result, the petitioners claimed that the project had to be halted until the further tests were completed and the conditions complied with. The Court refused to order the additional tests because the "decision-making agency took a well informed decision... there is no need to interfere." It stated, "This Court cannot sit in judgment over the cutting edge of scientific analysis relating to the safety of any project.... When the Government or the concerned authorities after due consideration of all viewpoints and full application of mind took a decision, then it is not appropriate for the Court to interfere." The Court also ruled that the conditions imposed by the environmental clearance had been complied with, even if there had been occasional lapses that had to be enforced by the supervising agencies. In the course of addressing the conditions issue, the Court made the following observations about the connection between environment and development and the imposition of environmental conditions. – *Eds.*]

RAJENDRA BABU, J., Writ Petition No. 295 of 1992:

. . .

21. Before adverting to other issues, certain aspects pertaining to the preservation of ecology and development have to be noticed. In... *M.C Mehta v. Union of India*, 2002 (4) SCC 353, it was observed that the balance between environmental protection and developmental activities could only be maintained by strictly following the principle of "sustainable development." This is a development strategy that caters the needs of the present without negotiating the ability of upcoming generations to satisfy their needs. The strict observance of sustainable development will put us on a path that ensures development while protecting the environment, a path that works for all peoples and for all generations. It is a guarantee to the present and a bequeath to the future. All environmental related developmental activities should benefit more people while maintaining the environmental balance. This could be ensured only by the strict adherence of sustainable development without which life of coming generations will be in jeopardy.

23. ...The right to development includes the whole spectrum of civil, cultural, economic, political and social process, for the improvement of peoples' well being and realization of their full potential. It is an integral part of human rights. Of course, construction of a dam or a mega project is definitely an attempt to achieve the goal of wholesome development. Such works could very well be treated as integral component for development.

24. ...[A]dherence [to the] sustainable development principle is a *sine qua non* for the maintenance of the symbiotic balance between the rights to environment and development. Right to environment is a fundamental right. On the other hand right to development is also one. Here the right to "sustainable development" cannot be singled out. Therefore, the concept of "sustainable development" is to be treated as an integral part of "life" under Article 21 [of the Indian Constitution]. The weighty concepts like inter-generational equity..., public trust doctrine..., and precautionary principle..., which we declared as inseparable ingredients of our environmental jurisprudence, could only be nurtured by ensuring sustainable development.

25. To ensure sustainable development is one of the goals of Environmental Protection Act, 1986 (for short "the Act") and this is quite necessary to guarantee "right to life" under Article 21. If the Act is not armed with the powers to ensure sustainable development, it will become a barren shell. In other words, sustainable development is one of the means to achieve the object and purpose of the Act as well as the protection of "life" under Article 21. Acknowledgment of this principle will breathe new life into our environmental jurisprudence and constitutional resolve.

Sustainable development could be achieved only by strict compliance of the directions under the Act. The object and purpose of the Act – "to provide for the protection and improvement of environment" [–] could only be achieved by ensuring the strict compliance of its directions. The concerned authorities by exercising [their] powers under the Act will have to ensure the acquiescence of sustainable development. Therefore, the directions or conditions put forward by the Act need to be strictly complied with. Thus the power under the Act cannot be treated as a power simpliciter, but it is a power coupled with duty. It is the duty of the State to make sure the fulfillment of conditions or direction under the Act. Without strict compliance, right to environment under Article 21 could not be guaranteed and the purpose of the Act will also be defeated. The commitment to the conditions thereof is an obligation both under Article 21 and under the Act. The conditions glued to the environmental clearance for the Tehri Dam Project given by the Ministry of Environment vide its Order dated July 19, 1990 has to be viewed from this perspective.

Questions and Discussion

1. Can environmental protection and economic development be reconciled? Is that what sustainable development attempts to achieve? At least part of the reason that the Brundtland Commission met such a favorable reception from the vast majority of states is because it posits that "only growth can eliminate poverty. Only growth can create the capacity to solve environmental problems. But growth cannot be based on overexploitation of resources. . . . It must be managed to enhance the resource base on which all countries depend." Gro Harlem Brundland, *Global Change and Our Common Future, in* ONE EARTH, ONE FUTURE: OUR CHANGING GLOBAL ENVIRONMENT 150 (Cheryl Simon Silver with Ruth S. DeFries eds., 1990). Why would such a formulation be attractive to a broad spectrum of states very differently situated economically, environmentally, politically, socially, and so on?

2. Does the principle of sustainable development imply limits? Is it the same as sustainable growth implied in note 1 here? Does integrating environment and development somehow subordinate environmental concerns to development? On these and other issues, see Marc Pallemaerts, *International Environmental Law from Stockholm to Rio: Back to the Future?*, 1 REVUE. EUR. COMM. & INT'L ENVTL L. 254–66.

3. To what extent should the needs of poor nations for economic development override environmental concerns? Consider the principle of common but differentiated responsibilities discussed in the following section.

5. Equitable Principles

In most national legal systems, equity has played a major part in determining the distribution of rights and responsibilities in conditions of scarcity and inequality. The general value of equity is largely accepted in this context, but debate exists on the appropriate principles to determine equitable allocation, such as whether decisions should be based on need, capacity, prior entitlement, just deserts, the greatest good for the greatest number, or strict equality of treatment. In addition, a single factor, such as need, may be asserted by more than one actor or group of actors. Equity also may provide a basis for decision in the absence of law or when it is necessary to fill in gaps in existing norms, such as when new issues emerge that give rise to disputes. International tribunals have applied equity in this way, but usually on the basis that the equitable principle being invoked is a general principle of law recognized by Article 38(1)(c) of the Statute of the International Court of Justice. Thus, international courts have applied notions, such as equitable estoppel. *See Diversion of the Waters of the Meuse*, P.C.I.J. (ser. A/B) No. 70, at 25, where the Permanent Court of International Justice held that it was inequitable for the applicant state to complain of a harmful act that the applicant itself had committed in the past.

In international environmental law, some developing countries have argued for exemptions from legal norms or for preferential treatment on the basis that international legal rules impose on them a disproportionate environmental burden because of the export of pollution from wealthier countries while they are unable to share in the benefits derived from activities producing the pollution. Trade preferences that accord differential and more favorable treatment to developing countries, as an exception to article I of GATT, reflect such equitable adjustments to the law. Developing countries have successfully pressed the issue of equitable allocation of resources and burden sharing for several reasons. First, they hold the major part of the earth's biological resources and need or want to use them for economic development, whereas developed states have an interest in the conservation and sustainable utilization of these resources, many of which are the source of desired products, as well as a foundation of ecological processes (e.g., tropical forests as carbon sinks). Second, developing countries have been able to focus on fairness in pointing out the predominant responsibility of wealthier states for pollution. Third, developing states can legitimately plead their inability to participate or comply in environmental protection agreements as a result of poverty and weak institutions.

Equity has been used most often in environmental agreements to fairly allocate and regulate scarce resources and to ensure that the benefits of environmental resources, the costs associated with protecting them, and any degradation that occurs (i.e., all the benefits and burdens) are fairly shared by all members of society. In this respect, equity is an application of the principles of distributive justice, which seek to reconcile competing social and economic policies to obtain the fair sharing of resources. It does this by incorporating equitable principles in legal instruments to mandate just procedures and results.

Concern about the equitable distribution of the burdens of environmental protection has led to the creation of a series of financial mechanisms, exemptions, provisions for the transfer of technology, and flexibility in the time required for compliance with international obligations. Capacity building through the provision of financial resources and the transfer of technology is widely included in global multilateral environmental agreements and often becomes a condition for compliance by developing countries. Explicitly stating that economic and social development and poverty eradication are the first and overriding priorities of developing-country parties, the Convention on Biological Diversity (CBD) and the U.N. Framework Convention on Climate Change (UNFCCC) make the provision of financial resources and the transfer of technology from developed country parties a condition for the implementation of treaty obligations by developing country parties. Other conventions, such as the Convention to Combat Desertification in Those Countries Experiencing Serious Drought and/or Desertification, Particularly in Africa, express a concern for the special needs and circumstances of developing countries, particularly the least developed, in combating environmental degradation.

a. *Intergenerational Equity*

Intergenerational equity as a principle of international justice is based on the recognition of three key facts: (1) human life emerged from, and is dependent on, Earth's natural resource base, including its ecological processes, and is thus inseparable from environmental conditions; (2) human beings have a unique capacity to alter the environment on which life depends; and (3) no generation has a superior claim to Earth's resources, because humans did not create them but inherited them. From these facts the notion emerges that humans who are alive today have a special obligation as custodians or trustees of the planet to maintain its integrity to ensure the survival of the human species. Those living have received a heritage from their ancestors in which they have beneficial rights of use that are limited by the interests and needs of future generations. This limitation requires each generation to maintain the corpus of the trust and pass it on in no worse condition than it was received. Another way to consider the issue is to view current environmental goods, wealth, and technology as owing to the progress of prior generations. This debt cannot be discharged backward so it is projected forward and discharged in the present on behalf of the future.

The equitable concept of trust places obligations on the trustees, such as conserving and maintaining the trust resources. The trustees, also the present generation of beneficiaries, are thus constrained in their use of resources. Meeting the obligation calls for minimizing or avoiding long-term and irreversible damage to the environment. Three implications emerge from the principle of intergenerational equity: first, that each generation is required to conserve the diversity of the natural and cultural resource base so that it does not unduly restrict the options available to future generations to satisfy their own values and needs. Second, the quality of ecological processes passed on should be comparable to that enjoyed by the present generation. Third, the past and present cultural and natural heritage should be conserved so that future generations will have access to it. These rights and obligations derive from a notion of human society that extends beyond the totality of the current planetary population, giving it a temporal dimension. Although it may be objected that there are no rights holders present to correspond to the obligations imposed, the Philippines Supreme Court has found that present generations have standing to represent future generations in the following case.

Minors Oposa v. Secretary of the Department of Environment and Natural Resources, Supreme Court of the Philippines, [1993] PHSC 577 (en banc), reprinted in 33 I.L.M. 168 (1994)

DAVIDE, JR., J.:

... [T]his petition bears upon the right of Filipinos to a balanced and healthful ecology which the petitioners dramatically associate with the twin concepts of "inter-generational responsibility" and "inter-generational justice." Specifically, it touches on the issue of whether the said petitioners have a cause of action to "prevent the misappropriation or impairment" of Philippine rainforests and "arrest the unabated hemorrhage of the country's vital life-support systems and continued rape of Mother Earth."

... The principal plaintiffs ... are all minors duly represented and joined by their respective parents. ... The complaint was instituted as a taxpayers' class suit and alleges that the plaintiffs "are all citizens of the Republic of the Philippines, taxpayers, and entitled to the full benefit, use and enjoyment of the natural resource treasure that is the country's virgin tropical rainforests." The same was filed for themselves and others who are equally concerned about the preservation of said resource but are "so numerous that it is impracticable to bring them all before the Court." The minors further asseverate that they "represent their generation as well as generations yet unborn."

. . .

Petitioners contend that the complaint clearly and unmistakably states a cause of action as it contains sufficient allegations concerning their right to a sound environment based on Articles

19, 20 and 21 of the Civil Code (Human Relations), Section 4 of Executive Order (E.O.) No. 192 creating the DENR, Section 3 of Presidential Decree (P.D.) No. 1151 (Philippine Environmental Policy), Section 16, Article II of the 1987 Constitution recognizing the right of the people to a balanced and healthful ecology, the concept of generational genocide in Criminal Law and the concept of man's inalienable right to self-preservation and self-perpetuation embodied in natural law. Petitioners likewise rely on the respondent's correlative obligation, per Section 4 of E.O. No. 192, to safeguard the people's right to a healthful environment.

. . .

Before going any further, [w]e must first focus on some procedural matters. . . .

This case . . . has a special and novel element. Petitioners minors assert that they represent their generation as well as generations yet unborn. We find no difficulty in ruling that they can, for themselves, for others of their generation and for the succeeding generations, file a class suit. Their personality to sue in behalf of the succeeding generations can only be based on the concept of intergenerational responsibility insofar as the right to a balanced and healthful ecology is concerned. Such a right, as hereinafter expounded, considers the "rhythm and harmony of nature." Nature means the created world in its entirety. Such rhythm and harmony indispensably include, inter alia, the judicious disposition, utilization, management, renewal and conservation of the country's forest, mineral, land, waters, fisheries, wildlife, off-shore areas and other natural resources to the end that their exploration, development and utilization be equitably accessible to the present as well as future generations. Needless to say, every generation has a responsibility to the next to preserve that rhythm and harmony for the full enjoyment of a balanced and healthful ecology. Put a little differently, the minors' assertion of their right to a sound environment constitutes, at the same time, the performance of their obligation to ensure the protection of that right for the generations to come.

The *locus standi* of the petitioners having thus been addressed, We shall now proceed to the merits of the petition.

After a careful perusal of the complaint in question and a meticulous consideration and evaluation of the issues raised and arguments adduced by the parties, We do not hesitate to find for the petitioners and rule against the respondent Judge's challenged order for having been issued with grave abuse of discretion amounting to lack of jurisdiction.

. . .

The complaint focuses on one specific fundamental legal right – the right to a balanced and healthful ecology which, for the first time in our nation's constitutional history, is solemnly incorporated in the fundamental law. Section 16, Article II of the 1987 Constitution explicitly provides:

SEC. 16. The State shall protect and advance the right of the people to a balanced and healthful ecology in accord with the rhythm and harmony of nature.

This right unites with the right to health which is provided for in the preceding section of the same article:

SEC. 15. The State shall protect and promote the right to health of the people and instill health consciousness among them.

While the right to a balanced and healthful ecology is to be found under the Declaration of Principles and State Policies and not under the Bill of Rights, it does not follow that it is less important than any of the civil and political rights enumerated in the latter. Such a right belongs to a different category of rights altogether for it concerns nothing less than self-preservation and self-perpetuation – aptly and fittingly stressed by the petitioners – the advancement of which may even be said to predate all governments and constitutions. As a matter of fact, these basic rights need not even be written in the Constitution for they are assumed to exist from the inception of humankind. If they are now explicitly mentioned in the fundamental charter, it is because of the well-founded fear of its framers that unless the rights to a balanced and healthful ecology and to health are mandated as state policies by the Constitution itself, thereby highlighting their continuing importance and imposing upon the state a solemn obligation to preserve the first and protect and advance the second, the day would not be too far when all else would be lost not only for the present generation, but also for those to come – generations which stand to inherit nothing but parched earth incapable of sustaining life.

The right to a balanced and healthful ecology carries with it the correlative duty to refrain from impairing the environment.

. . .

Thus, the right of the petitioners (and all those they represent) to a balanced and healthful ecology is as clear as the DENR's duty – under its mandate and by virtue of its powers and functions under E.O. No. 192 and the Administrative Code of 1987 – to protect and advance the said right.

A denial or violation of that right by the other who has the correlative duty or obligation to respect or protect the same gives rise to a cause of action. Petitioners maintain that the granting of the TLAs, which they claim was done with grave abuse of discretion, violated their right to a balanced and healthful ecology; hence, the full protection thereof requires that no further TLAs should be renewed or granted.

A cause of action is defined as:

> . . . an act or omission of one party in violation of the legal right or rights of the other; and its essential elements are legal right of the plaintiff, correlative obligation of the defendant, and act or omission of the defendant in violation of said legal right.

. . .

After a careful examination of the petitioners' complaint, we find the statements under the introductory affirmative allegations, as well as the specific averments under the sub-heading CAUSE OF ACTION, to be adequate enough to show, *prima facie*, the claimed violation of their rights. On the basis thereof, they may thus be granted, wholly or partly, the reliefs prayed for. It bears stressing, however, that insofar as the cancellation of the TLAs is concerned, there is the need to implead, as party defendants, the grantees thereof for they are indispensable parties.

. . .

The last ground invoked by the trial court in dismissing the complaint is the non-impairment of contracts clause found in the Constitution. . . . In the first place, the respondent Secretary did not, for obvious reasons, even invoke in his motion to dismiss the non-impairment clause. If he had done so, he would have acted with utmost infidelity to the Government by providing undue and unwarranted benefits and advantages to the timber license holders because he would have forever bound the Government to strictly respect the said licenses according to their terms and conditions regardless of changes in policy and the demands of public interest and welfare. He was aware that as correctly pointed out by the petitioners, into every timber license must be read Section 20 of the Forestry Reform Code (P.D. No. 705) which provides:

> . . . Provided, That when the national interest so requires, the President may amend, modify, replace or rescind any contract, concession, permit, licenses or any other form of privilege granted herein. . . .

Needless to say, all licenses may thus be revoked or rescinded by executive action. It is not a contract, property or a property right protected by the due process clause of the Constitution. In *Tan vs. Director of Forestry*, 125 SCRA 302, 325 [1983], this Court held:

...A timber license is an instrument by which the State regulates the utilization and disposition of forest resources to the end that public welfare is promoted. A timber license is not a contract within the purview of the due process clause; it is only a license or privilege, which can be validly withdrawn whenever dictated by public interest or public welfare as in this case.

A license is merely a permit or privilege to do what otherwise would be unlawful, and is not a contract between the authority, federal, state, or municipal, granting it and the person to whom it is granted; neither is it property or a property right, nor does it create a vested right; nor is it taxation' (37 C.J. 168). Thus, this Court held that the granting of license does not create irrevocable rights, neither is it property or property rights (*People vs. Ong Tin*, 54 O.G. 7576)....

Since timber licenses are not contracts, the non-impairment clause ... cannot be invoked.
                                                . . .
Finally, it is difficult to imagine, as the trial court did, how the non-impairment clause could apply with respect to the prayer to enjoin the respondent Secretary from receiving, accepting, processing, renewing or approving new timber licenses for, save in cases of renewal, no contract would have as of yet existed in the other instances. Moreover, with respect to renewal, the holder is not entitled to it as a matter of right.

WHEREFORE, . . . petitioners may . . . amend their complaint to implead as defendants the holders or grantees of the questioned timber license agreements.

Questions and Discussion

1. Can future generations have rights?
2. What difference would it have made to the *Minors Oposa* case if future generations had not been mentioned?
3. For some of the voluminous literature on intergenerational equity, see RESPONSIBILITIES TO FUTURE GENERATIONS (Ernest Partridge ed., 1981); Shorge Sato, *Sustainable Development and the Selfish Gene: A Rational Paradigm for Achieving Intergenerational Equity*, 11 N.Y.U. ENVTL. L.J. 503 (2003); Paul Barresi, *Beyond Fairness to Future Generations: An Intragenerational Alternative to Intergenerational Equity in the International Environmental Arena*, 11 TUL. ENVTL L.J. 59 (1997–98); Dinah Shelton, *Intergenerational Equity, in* SOLIDARITY: A STRUCTURAL PRINCIPLE OF INTERNATIONAL LAW 123 (Rüdiger Wolfrum & Chie Kojima eds., 2010); Bryan Norton, *Ecology and Opportunity: Intergenerational Equity and Sustainable Options, in* FAIRNESS AND FUTURITY: ESSAYS ON ENVIRONMENTAL SUSTAINABILITY AND SOCIAL JUSTICE ch. 5 (Andrew Dobson ed., 1999); EDITH BROWN WEISS, IN FAIRNESS TO FUTURE GENERATIONS: INTERNATIONAL LAW, COMMON PATRIMONY, AND INTERGENERATIONAL EQUITY (1989); James C. Wood, *Intergenerational Equity and Climate Change*, 8 GEO. INT'L ENVTL. L. REV. 293 (1996); Lawrence B. Solum, *To Our Children's Children's Children: The Problems of Intergenerational Ethics*, 35 LOY. L.A. L. REV. 163, 169–71 (2001).
4. What about intragenerational equities? Is this what is meant by environmental justice? Or is intragenerational equity in fact the concept of human rights? Is intragenerational equity reflected in the following two principles?

b. *Common but Differentiated Responsibilities*

The principle of common but differentiated responsibilities is now widely incorporated in environmental treaties. It calls broadly for developed countries to take the lead in solving existing global environmental problems. Thus, even though the responsibility for protecting the environment is to be shared among all nations, countries should contribute differently to international environmental initiatives depending on their capabilities and responsibilities.

The broader version of the principle would oblige the developed world to pay for past harms, as a form of corrective justice, as well as present and future harms. For both climate change and depletion of stratospheric ozone, the global community finds itself at the tipping point because of the conduct of the developed world. It is precisely because of this conduct that the marginal environmental costs of developing-nation industrialization today are high. Developed nations thus should pay for any reductions or modifications the developing world has to make in the process of industrialization, because developed-world industrialization has unfairly circumscribed the ability of the developing world to pass off the negative externalities of development on the environment. The true social and environmental costs of developed-nation industrialization were never accounted for in the past, so the unfairly obtained windfall should now be redistributed.

Developing nations thus argue that they are entitled to the resources and technology from developed nations and that developed nations should have to internalize the environmental costs of ongoing and future developing-nation industrialization. Some treaty provisions reflect this view. Article 5(5) of the amended Montreal Protocol on Substances that Deplete the Ozone Layer, for example, provides that developing countries' capacity to fulfill the obligations and implement the control measures specified in the Montreal Protocol will depend on the effective implementation by developed nations of financial cooperation and transfer of technology as set out in the Protocol. Similar statements are contained in article 4(7) of the U.N. Framework Convention on Climate Change and article 20(4) of the Convention on Biological Diversity.

An even broader justification calls for adjustments on the basis of restitution. It suggests that developed nations are not entitled to preserve the wealth they have accrued through industrial development, because those entitlements were obtained in a manner that does not justify their retention. If entitlements are perceived as transcending the area of environmental harms and extending into the externalities of the North's industrial development generally, including colonialism, mercantilism, and labor exploitation, then this could become a considerably more ambitious program.

c. *Equitable Utilization of Shared Resources*

Equitable utilization is a widely accepted principle applied in apportioning shared resources, such as watercourses and fish and other exploited species. It finds expression in article 2 of the 1997 U.N. Convention on the Law of Non-Navigational Uses of International Watercourses, which calls on the parties to take all appropriate measures to ensure that international watercourses are used in a reasonable and equitable way.

The status of equitable utilization as a fundamental norm in the field of shared natural resources was affirmed by the ICJ in the *Case Concerning the Gabčíkovo-Nagymaros Project (Hung./Slov.)*, Judgment of Sept. 5, 1997, 1997 ICJ 7. In the earlier *Fisheries Jurisdiction Cases (U.K. v. Iceland; FRG v. Iceland)*, the ICJ stressed the obligation of reasonable use and good-faith negotiations aimed at an equitable result, taking into account the needs of conservation and the interests of all exploiters of the fishing resource. *Fisheries Jurisdiction Cases (U.K. v. Iceland; FRG v. Iceland)*, Judgment of July 25, 1974, 1974 ICJ 3; and 1974 ICJ 175. Thus, the notion of equitable utilization is one that attempts to make a "reasonable" allocation or reach a fair result in distribution of a scarce resource, based on what are deemed to be relevant factors, such as need, prior use or entitlement, and other interests. On a substantive level, each party is held to have an equal right to use the resource, but because one party's use can affect the beneficial uses of others and not all uses can be satisfied, some limitations are necessary. The Watercourses Convention states that equitable and reasonable uses are to be "consistent with adequate protection of the watercourse." Art. 5. The phrase suggests that uses that would substantially harm the watercourse could be inherently inequitable and indicates how positive rules may restrict the scope and application of equitable principles.

Notions of entitlement stemming from prior uses, strict equality, proportional use based on population, and priority accorded to certain uses all have been asserted at one time or another as a basis for determining what is an equitable allocation. In some instances, the parties agree in advance on certain divisions or priorities. The 1909 Boundary Waters Treaty between the United States and Canada relies on equality of use for the generation of power (each country being entitled to use half the waters along the boundary) and equitable sharing of water for irrigation. In contrast, the 1959 Nile Agreement between the Sudan and Egypt for Full Utilization of Nile Waters confirmed the "established rights" of each party, without identifying them, and additional amounts were allocated on other equitable bases. Although the Nile agreement seems to view established rights as guaranteed by law, most other instruments take the better view and include prior entitlements as one factor in determining equitable allocation.

The idea of equitable utilization in the past had as a corollary that no use had inherent priority over any other. Today, there appears to be a move toward recognizing that some resource uses have priority over others. In the use of fresh water, for example, emphasis is being placed on the satisfaction of basic human needs – that is, the provision of safe drinking water and sanitation. The Watercourses Convention provides that in the event of a conflict between the uses of an international watercourse, special regard is to be given to the requirements of vital human needs (art. 10), whereas the U.N. Committee on Economic, Social, and Cultural Rights, in its General Comment 12 on the Right to Water, insists that priority be given to safe drinking water and sanitation, with a guaranteed minimum amount to be provided to every person. Thus, substantive human rights considerations help determine appropriate allocation.

E. *Major International Environmental Agreements*

Although there are hundreds of international environmental agreements – some six hundred relating to international watercourses – there are a few major treaties, similar to the core human rights instruments, that address broad issues of concern. These are summarized here, with some of their key provisions.

1. Biological Diversity and Species Agreements

The Convention on Biological Diversity was concluded on June 2, 1992, and entered into force on December 29, 1993. It is the only global comprehensive instrument on Earth's biological resources, and its preamble begins with a reference to the "intrinsic value of biological diversity." The CBD establishes ecological norms for conduct toward all life on the planet, norms that are to be implemented through national conservation strategies and plans of action, taking into account the regulations contained in other international agreements. Biological diversity, or biodiversity, has thus become a unifying concept denoting all living organisms and ecosystems and their intricate interdependence. It has replaced nature conservation as the primary term used in regulating human actions towards other components of the living world. Its aims and scope are described in the opening provisions:

Article 1. Objectives

The objectives of this Convention, to be pursued in accordance with its relevant provisions, are the conservation of biological diversity, the sustainable use of its components and the fair and equitable sharing of the benefits arising out of the utilization of genetic resources, including by appropriate access to genetic resources and by appropriate transfer of relevant technologies, taking into account all rights over those resources and to technologies, and by appropriate funding.

Article 2. Use of Terms

For the purposes of this Convention:

"Biological diversity" means the variability among living organisms from all sources including, inter alia, terrestrial, marine and other aquatic ecosystems and the ecological complexes of which they are part; this includes diversity within species, between species and of ecosystems.

"Biological resources" includes genetic resources, organisms or parts thereof, populations, or any other biotic component of ecosystems with actual or potential use or value for humanity.

Article 3. Principle

States have, in accordance with the Charter of the United Nations and the principles of international law, the sovereign right to exploit their own resources pursuant to their own environmental policies, and the responsibility to ensure that activities within their jurisdiction or control do not cause damage to the environment of other States or of areas beyond the limits of national jurisdiction.

The Convention primarily concerns the rights and responsibilities of states at the national level. Their general obligation is to take effective national action to halt the destruction of species, habitats, and ecosystems, including the adoption of regulations on conservation of biological resources, legal responsibility, regulation of biotechnology, and norms on access to and compensation for use of genetic materials. The states parties are to apply the Convention requirements inside their territorial limits, as well as to processes and activities under their jurisdiction or control wherever located.

The Convention contains several innovative features. Biological diversity is recognized as a "common concern of humankind,". It makes clear that "the authority to determine access to genetic resources rests with the national governments and is subject to national legislation." Developing countries insisted on this extension of the norm of permanent sovereign over natural resources and the correlative requirement of prior informed consent by the party providing the genetic resource (art. 15.5). It may be viewed as the counterpart to developed country efforts to ensure intellectual property rights over industrial development of products derived from biological resources, including living material itself. The Convention reflects a compromise, taking a positive stance on the flow of genetic resources by calling on states parties to facilitate access for environmentally sound uses and not to impose restrictions that are counter to the objectives of the Convention. Balanced with this access, other states parties must take measures to share "in a fair and equitable way" the results of research and development of uses of genetic resources and economic benefits on a mutually agreed basis with the state providing those resources.

The emphasis on national sovereignty is balanced by enunciating broad state duties. The preamble indicates that states "are responsible for conserving their biological diversity and for using their biological resources in a sustainable manner." The body of the Convention details several specific obligations, including a requirement that states parties identify important components of biological diversity that may need special conservation measures, and identify and monitor processes and activities that may have significant adverse effects on biological diversity. Art. 7. With this information, they must develop national strategies and plans integrating conservation of biological diversity into relevant sectoral plans and programs and decision making. Art. 6. The planning requirement is reinforced by the requirement in article 10(a) that parties integrate consideration of the conservation and sustainable use of biological resources into national decision making. Annex I contains indicative lists for the identification and monitoring of (1) ecosystems and habitats; (2) species and communities; and (3) genomes and genes of social, scientific, and economic importance.

After long debate among the negotiators, the Convention established a preference for in situ conservation, with ex situ conservation used to complement in situ measures. In situ conservation is defined as "conservation of ecosystems and natural habitats and the maintenance and recovery of viable populations of species in their natural surroundings and, in the case of domesticated or cultivated species, in the surroundings where they have developed their distinctive properties." Art. 2. Conservation measures range from establishment of protected areas to rehabilitation of degraded ecosystems and protection of natural habitats, including through the enactment of municipal legislation. Art. 8. The Convention also contains a provision intended to counter the widespread destruction of native species that can occur through the introduction of exotic species. Most important, states parties are to protect ecosystems and to regulate or manage biological resources important for the conservation of biological diversity whether they are within or without protected areas.

Sustainable use is a major theme of the Convention and is defined as "the use of components of biological diversity in a way and at a rate that does not lead to the long-term decline of biological diversity, thereby maintaining its potential to meet the needs and aspirations of present and future generations." Art. 2. Parties agree to regulate or manage harvested biological resources by developing sustainable methods and minimizing adverse impacts on biological diversity. States must initiate research, training, and public education, as well as techniques like environmental impact assessment. Special emphasis is given to protecting and encouraging traditional cultural practices if compatible with sustainable use and to the adoption of incentives for the conservation and sustainable use of components of biological diversity.

The Convention reiterates the general principles of international environmental law, including responsibility for and redress of transfrontier damage (arts. 3, 14), cooperation (art. 5), access to information (arts. 14, 17), and prevention. The development agenda of UNCED is also reflected in the articles that prescribe specific rules of identification and monitoring, access to genetic resources (art. 15), access to and transfer of technology (art. 16), and technical and scientific cooperation (art. 18).

As with the 1987 Montreal Protocol and later amendments to it, the CBD establishes a legal relationship between the conservation obligations of developing countries and the financial obligations of developed countries. The latter group of countries is required to provide "new and additional financial resources" to a financial mechanism for the use of developing countries. There is explicit recognition that the implementation of obligations under the Convention is linked to and dependent on adequate funding being supplied. In addition, implementation must take into account "the fact that economic and social development and eradication of poverty are the first and overriding priorities of the developing country Parties."

Nearly all states adhere to the Convention except, notably, the United States. The Conference of the Parties has held regular sessions at which it has adopted important decisions and recommendations on environmental impact assessment, introduction of alien species, transboundary cooperation, and the involvement of local and indigenous communities in protecting biodiversity. The question of access to biological resources has been particularly contested. The CBD asserts the rights of states over plant and animal genetic resources under their jurisdiction, creating a complex relationship of rights and duties. On the one hand, authority to determine access to genetic resources rests with the national governments and is subject to national legislation. Art. 15.1. On the other hand, each state party must endeavor to create conditions to facilitate access to genetic resources for environmentally sound uses by other parties and should not impose restrictions that run counter to the Convention's objectives. When access is granted, it shall be on mutually agreed terms and be subject to prior informed consent by the party providing the genetic resource, unless that party determines otherwise. The treaty requirements have been further elaborated in the Bonn Guidelines on Access to Genetic Resources, adopted by Decision VI/24 of the Sixth Conference of the Parties in April 2002.

After extensive negotiations, the CBD states parties adopted the Protocol on Biosafety (Jan. 29, 2000). The objective of the Protocol is to contribute to ensuring an adequate level of protection in the safe transfer, handling, and use of living biotechnology modified organisms that may have adverse effects on the conservation and sustainable use of biological diversity, taking into account risks to human health and specifically focusing on transboundary movements. Preamble, arts. 1 and 4. The Protocol does not apply to the transboundary movement of living modified organisms that are pharmaceuticals for human use and that are addressed by relevant international agreements or organizations, nor to the transit and contained use of living modified organisms. These exceptions do not preclude a party from subjecting such actions to prior risk assessment. Arts. 5 and 6. The Protocol institutes an "advance informed agreement" procedure that mirrors prior-informed-consent procedures contained in other international treaties.

Numerous other international agreements protect migratory species, from birds to fish; habitats; and endangered and threatened species. Migratory species are subject to special protection by treaties, such as the 1972 Convention for the Protection of World Cultural and Natural Heritage, which requires states to identify, protect, conserve, present, and transmit natural heritage in their territory, and the 1979 Bonn Convention on the Conservation of Migratory Species of Wild Animals, which is aimed at all range states, that is, those through which such species transit and in which they spend part of their lives. States parties to the Bonn Convention are obliged to ban or regulate the taking of these animals in cases where the conservation status of such animals – the sum of influences on their long-term distribution and abundance – is unfavorable.

Questions and Discussion

1. What are the aims of the Convention? Are they compatible?
2. Does article 3 contradict the very aims of the Convention in affirming state sovereignty over natural resources? Where have you seen the language of article 3 before? Does it deny or override private property rights and the rights of indigenous peoples?
3. What is the legal status of biological diversity? Do all people and all states have an interest in maintaining the existence of elephants and whales? Is it a legal interest?

2. U.N. Framework Convention on Climate Change and the Kyoto Protocol

The first signs of international concern over climate change emerged in a series of international conferences on carbon dioxide between 1985 and 1987. On December 6, 1988, the

U.N. General Assembly adopted Resolution 43/53 on the conservation of the global climate for present and future generations of mankind. It stated that climate change is a "common concern of mankind" and that it was necessary to adopt promptly the necessary measures to deal with it within a global framework. On December 21, 1990, the U.N. General Assembly adopted another resolution on the protection of the world climate for present and future generations. The Resolution reflected a desire for an Intergovernmental Negotiating Committee to prepare a general and effective convention on climate change.

The U.N. Framework Convention on Climate Change, adopted May 8, 1992 in New York, and opened for signature during the Rio de Janeiro Conference, defines climate change as a modification of the climate that is attributed directly or indirectly to human activity, which alters the composition of the global atmosphere, and that is in addition to natural climate variability observed over comparable time periods. (art. 1(2)). The objective of the Convention is as follows:

> The ultimate objective of this Convention and any related legal instruments that the Conference of the Parties may adopt is to achieve, in accordance with the relevant provisions of the Convention, stabilization of greenhouse gas concentrations in the atmosphere at a level that would prevent dangerous anthropogenic interference with the climate system. Such a level should be achieved within a time-frame sufficient to allow ecosystems to adapt naturally to climate change, to ensure that food production is not threatened and to enable economic development to proceed in a sustainable manner.

UNFCCC, Art. 3. The major obligations of all parties, and the differentiated obligations of developing states, are mainly contained in article 4:

1. All Parties, taking into account their common but differentiated responsibilities and their specific national and regional development priorities, objectives and circumstances, shall:
   (a) Develop, periodically update, publish and make available to the Conference of the Parties, in accordance with Article 12, national inventories of anthropogenic emissions by sources and removals by sinks of all greenhouse gases not controlled by the Montreal Protocol, using comparable methodologies to be agreed upon by the Conference of the Parties;
   (b) Formulate, implement, publish and regularly update national and, where appropriate, regional programmes containing measures to mitigate climate change by addressing anthropogenic emissions by sources and removals by sinks of all greenhouse gases not controlled by the Montreal Protocol, and measures to facilitate adequate adaptation to climate change;
   (c) Promote and cooperate in the development, application and diffusion, including transfer, of technologies, practices and processes that control, reduce or prevent anthropogenic emissions of greenhouse gases not controlled by the Montreal Protocol in all relevant sectors, including the energy, transport, industry, agriculture, forestry and waste management sectors;
   (d) Promote sustainable management, and promote and cooperate in the conservation and enhancement, as appropriate, of sinks and reservoirs of all greenhouse gases not controlled by the Montreal Protocol, including biomass, forests and oceans as well as other terrestrial, coastal and marine ecosystems;
   (e) Cooperate in preparing for adaptation to the impacts of climate change; develop and elaborate appropriate and integrated plans for coastal zone management, water resources and agriculture, and for the protection and rehabilitation of areas, particularly in Africa, affected by drought and desertification, as well as floods;

(f) Take climate change considerations into account, to the extent feasible, in their relevant social, economic and environmental policies and actions, and employ appropriate methods, for example impact assessments, formulated and determined nationally, with a view to minimizing adverse effects on the economy, on public health and on the quality of the environment, of projects or measures undertaken by them to mitigate or adapt to climate change;

(g) Promote and cooperate in scientific, technological, technical, socio-economic and other research, systematic observation and development of data archives related to the climate system and intended to further the understanding and to reduce or eliminate the remaining uncertainties regarding the causes, effects, magnitude and timing of climate change and the economic and social consequences of various response strategies;

(h) Promote and cooperate in the full, open and prompt exchange of relevant scientific, technological, technical, socio-economic and legal information related to the climate system and climate change, and to the economic and social consequences of various response strategies;

(i) Promote and cooperate in education, training and public awareness related to climate change and encourage the widest participation in this process, including that of non-governmental organizations; and

(j) Communicate to the Conference of the Parties information related to implementation, in accordance with Article 12

UNFCCC, Art. 4.

Applying the principle of common but differentiated responsibilities and capabilities, the treaty provides that its developed-country parties should take the lead in combating climate change and its adverse effects (art. 3(1)). Annex I to the Convention lists as developed thirty-six countries and the European Community; they pledge to adopt national and regional policies and take corresponding measures to mitigate climate change by limiting their emissions of greenhouse gases and protecting and enhancing their greenhouse sinks and reservoirs. They recognize the need for equitable and appropriate contributions to the global effort. To this end, each is obliged to communicate, within six months of the entry into force of the Convention for it, and periodically thereafter, detailed information on its policies and measures. This information is reviewed by the Conference of the Parties. The UNFCCC also calls for application of the principles of precaution and sustainable development (art. 3).

The parties to the UNFCCC can choose from a range of policy options to counter anthropogenic climate change, some of the policies having important impacts on national economies. Measures could include improving energy efficiency, forest management, air-pollution control, fuel switching, and the restructuring of transportation. Many environmental economists support carbon taxes as a way to establish appropriate incentives away from polluting fuels. Reforestation and other measures to expand carbon sinks are also possible.

A Conference of the Parties (COP), held December 1–10, 1997, adopted the Kyoto Protocol, moving toward the development of precise rules to mitigate anthropogenic climate change. The Protocol specifies different goals and commitments for developed and developing countries concerning future emission of greenhouse gases. The main features of the Protocol are the reduction targets accepted by the industrialized countries, without corresponding obligations for developing countries; acknowledgment of the role of sinks (seas, forests) of greenhouse gases and their inclusion in the targets; the possible creation of "bubbles" and trading emissions as means for reducing their aggregate emissions and joint implementation agreements with countries that only emit small amounts of greenhouse gases, in principle developing countries. The Protocol adopts a "big bubble approach": developed countries are allowed to join together and thereby attain their emission reduction commitments jointly by aggregating their anthropogenic carbon dioxide equivalent emissions of greenhouse gases listed in Annex A by at least 5 percent (averaging 5.2 percent) less than 1990 levels by the first commitment period of 2008–2012. These reductions cover six greenhouse gases: carbon dioxide, methane, nitrous oxide, hydrofluorocarbons (HFCs), perfluorocarbons (PFCs), and sulfur hexafluoride (SF_6), the last three of which are substitutes for ozone depleting substances regulated under the Montreal Protocol.

Article 2 lists methods that may be used to achieve quantified emission limitation and reduction: enhancement of energy efficiency, protection and enhancement of sinks and reservoirs of greenhouse gases, promotion of sustainable forms of agriculture, increased use of new and renewable forms of energy and of environmentally sound technologies, reduction or phasing out of market imperfections, use of economic instruments, limitation and reduction of emissions of greenhouse gases in the transport sector, and limitation and/or reduction of methane through recovery and use in waste management.

Another specific form of cooperation in the reduction of greenhouse gases is emission trading. According to article 6(1), any developed country, for the purpose of meeting its commitments, may transfer to or acquire from, any other party emission reduction units resulting from projects aimed at reducing emissions. It also can enhance removals of greenhouse gases in any sector of the economy. The condition is that any such project provides a reduction in emission by sources or an enhancement of removal by sinks, which is additional to any that would otherwise occur. The acquisition of emission reduction units thus shall be supplemental to domestic actions for the purposes of meeting commitments under article 3. A developed country may also authorize legal entities to participate, under its responsibility, in actions leading to the generation, transfer, or acquisition of emission reduction units (art. 6(3)). The COP continues to work on relevant principles, modalities, rules, and guidelines, in particular for verification, reporting, and accountability for emission trading (art. 16bis).

In addition to bubbles and trading, article 12 outlines a "clean development mechanism," the task of which is to assist developing countries in achieving sustainable development and in contributing to the ultimate objective of the convention. It also may assist developed countries in achieving compliance with their quantified emission limitation and reduction commitments. On a voluntary basis, emission reductions resulting from each project activity shall be certified by operational entities to be designated by the COP and approved by each party involved (art. 12(5)). Developing countries will benefit from project activities resulting in certified emission reductions (CERs), whereas developed countries may use the CERs accruing from such project activities to contribute to compliance with their quantified emission limitation and reduction commitments (art. 12(3)(b)). The Clean Development Mechanism (CDM) will assist in arranging funding of certified project activities as necessary. Any CERs obtained during the period 2000–08 can be used by developed countries to assist in achieving compliance in the commitment period 2008–12.

Monitoring of greenhouse gases plays an important role in the Kyoto Protocol. Developed countries must establish national systems to estimate anthropocentric emissions by sources and removals by sinks (art. 5), as well as annual inventories to incorporate the supplementary information necessary to demonstrate compliance with the commitments accepted under the Protocol (art. 7). Such information will be reviewed by teams composed of experts nominated by parties to the Framework Convention and, as appropriate, by intergovernmental organizations and coordinated by the Secretariat. The information submitted by the parties and the reports of the expert reviews shall be submitted to the COP, which can take decisions on any matter required for the implementation of the Protocol (art. 8).

Articles 10 and 11 of the Protocol concern developing countries. Their emissions are not limited, but they should formulate, where relevant, cost effective national and, where appropriate, regional programs to improve the quality of local emission factors, formulate, implement, publish, and regularly update national or regional programs to mitigate climate change, taking into account all relevant economic activities. Developed party cooperation with developing countries shall include the transfer of, or access to, environmentally sound technologies, know-how, practices, and processes pertinent to climate change, as well as capacity building. New and additional financial resources should be provided to meet the agreed full costs incurred by developing country parties in advancing the implementation of existing commitments.

The COP of the UNFCCC serves as the Meeting of the Parties to the Kyoto Protocol. It keeps under regular review the implementation of the Protocol and makes the decisions necessary to promote its effective implementation. It assesses, on the basis of the information made available to it, the overall effects of the measures taken and makes recommendations on any matters necessary for the implementation of the Protocol. Art. 13. The COP meets every year to review the implementation of the Convention and adopts decisions and resolutions, published in reports. Successive decisions taken by the COP make up a detailed set of rules for practical and effective implementation of the Convention. The Parties agreed that an ambitious climate change deal would be reached at COP15 in Copenhagen in December 2009 to follow on the first phase of the U.N.'s Kyoto Protocol, which expires in 2012. The agreement was a mere political declaration, however, and a binding agreement for a second commitment period remains necessary.

3. U.N. Convention on the Law of the Sea

The year of the Stockholm Conference also saw the beginning of the Third U.N. Conference on the Law of the Sea, whose work resulted in the U.N. Convention on the Law of the Sea (UNCLOS) (Montego Bay, Dec. 10, 1982). In general, UNCLOS reflects customary international law and provides the overall legal framework for ocean activities. Its comprehensive regulation addresses the protection and preservation of the marine environment in part XII. In addition, article 145 specifically aims to prevent pollution resulting from exploration and exploitation of the deep seabed. The Convention recognizes the competence of the coastal state to combat pollution in the territorial sea (art. 21) and proclaims its competence in the UNCLOS-created exclusive economic zone (art. 56). However, UNCLOS contains no new substantive rules to combat pollution of the high seas, although there are new rules protecting marine living resources.

The provisions of UNCLOS affirm coastal state authority and duty to conserve biological resources in the zones over which it exercises jurisdiction (i.e., the territorial sea, the exclusive economic zone (EEZ), and the continental shelf). In the EEZ, the coastal state has the duty to ensure that the maintenance of the living resources is not endangered by overexploitation. Article 61 of UNCLOS requires coastal states to cooperate in appropriate cases with international organizations to achieve the goal of maintaining or restoring populations of harvested species at levels that can produce the maximum sustainable yield. In addition, all states have the obligation to take measures applicable to their nationals that may be necessary for the conservation of the living resources of the high seas and to cooperate with one another in this regard. Since UNCLOS, fisheries regimes have been created with increasing frequency to address the growing crisis in depletion of marine living resources. In 1995, the global Agreement on Straddling Fish Stocks and Highly Migratory Fish Stocks, 34 I.L.M. 1542 (1995), was concluded to provide further protection for marine living resources.

The law of marine environmental protection has also developed regionally, following the main directions of UNCLOS. First, states of different maritime regions of the Northern Hemisphere (i.e., the Baltic Sea, Northeast Atlantic, and Black Sea) concluded general treaties on these waters. Second, the U.N. Environment Programme (UNEP) initiated a regional seas program that resulted in treaty systems, each consisting of a main convention, additional protocols, and often Action Plans for the development of the region. The regional seas program aims to create a comprehensive system of treaties and protocols for each targeted area. The earliest of these treaty systems concerns the Protection of the Mediterranean Sea Against Pollution (Barcelona, Feb. 16, 1976). The main treaty is accompanied by two protocols, the Protocol for the Prevention of Pollution of the Mediterranean Sea by Dumping from Ships and Aircraft and the Protocol Concerning Cooperation in Combating Pollution of the Mediterranean Sea by Oil and Other Harmful Substances in Cases of Emergency. Five additional protocols, subsequently concluded, relate to Pollution from Land-Based Sources (Athens, May 17, 1980), Mediterranean Specially Protected Areas (Apr. 3, 1982, replaced by a new protocol on the topic June 10, 1995), Pollution Resulting from Exploration and Exploitation of the Continental Shelf and the Seabed and Its Subsoil (Madrid, Oct. 14, 1994), and Pollution of the Mediterranean Sea by Transboundary Movements of Hazardous Wastes and Their Disposal (Izmir, Oct. 1, 1996). Taken together, more than 130 states today cooperate in the UNEP's regional seas program.

The environmental provisions of UNCLOS cover the three major sources of marine pollution: land-based sources, vessel source pollution, and atmospheric pollution. The provisions apply to all ocean surfaces, not only the high seas but also to areas under the jurisdiction of coastal states. They also seek to combat marine pollution by various preventive measures, including the duty to notify states of any imminent danger of pollution, to develop contingency plans for responding to incidents, to monitor the risks of pollution, and to assess potential effects of planned activities that may cause substantial pollution or significant changes in the marine environment and communicate such assessments. Article 192 of UNCLOS proclaims that states have a general obligation to protect and preserve the marine environment. Clauses relating to the preservation of marine biological resources are contained in the sections of the Convention regulating each of the established marine zones.

International cooperation, both regionally and globally, is presented as an obligation, explicitly with the aim of formulating and elaborating international rules and standards and "recommended practices and procedures" (art. 197). Specific provisions govern cooperation in emergencies (arts. 198–99). States also are required to monitor continuously the risks or effects of pollution. In particular, they must "keep under surveillance" the effects of any activities that they permit or in which they engage, to determine whether those activities are likely to pollute the marine environment. Art. 204. The results obtained from such surveillance must be communicated to international organizations, which should make them available to all states (art. 205). In addition, states should assess the potential effects of any activities that may cause substantial pollution and communicate the results of such assessments (art. 206). As a final element in the framework of international cooperation, the Convention foresees assistance to developing states in the fields of science and technology and preferential treatment for these states by international organizations (arts. 202–03).

The Convention identifies three states competent to exercise jurisdiction over matters of marine pollution: flag states, port states, and coastal states. One aspect common to the jurisdiction of all three is the obligation to take into account or enact and enforce internationally agreed rules and standards. States "shall adopt laws and regulations and take other measures necessary to implement applicable international rules and standards established through competent international organizations or diplomatic conference to prevent and control pollution of the marine environment" from various sources (arts. 213–14, 216–20, 222).

4. The Ozone Agreements

In 1974, scientists hypothesized that the emission of chlorine-based ozone-depleting substances into the atmosphere might result in the destruction of the upper stratospheric ozone layer. By the 1980s, their hypothesis was proved beyond doubt.

Ozone is a form of oxygen, containing one more atom than the oxygen breathed in the atmosphere. Although ground-level ozone in the form of smog produces harmful environmental consequences, stratospheric ozone, whose strongest concentrations are found between twenty and twenty-five kilometers above Earth, filters a part of the sun's ultraviolet radiation, which otherwise would injure life on Earth. The absorption of ultraviolet rays by stratospheric ozone is also a source of climatic energy. According to a study prepared under the aegis of the UNEP, a reduction in ozone not only risks an increase in the number of human skin cancers and harm to the eyes but also has unforeseen biological effects, because all living beings have evolved under the protection of the ozone layer.

The anthropogenic source of ozone depletion was clear by the late 1970s. The utilization of chlorofluorocarbons (CFCs), contained in aerosol sprays and to a lesser extent in solvents and refrigeration, was identified as a major contributing cause. When first developed, CFCs were viewed favorably, because they are nontoxic, nonflammable, noncorrosive, inexpensive, and stable. The very stability of CFCs is the source of the problem, because they migrate over long distances and survive for many years. When they reach the stratosphere intact, solar radiation breaks the molecules apart to free reactive chlorine atoms, catalyzing chain reactions that destroy ozone; even if production and use of ozone-depleting substances are phased out, the problem will remain for some time because of the substances already released. By 1985, it was understood that most depletion of the ozone layer occurs on a seasonal basis above Antarctica and, increasingly, over the Arctic region. The Antarctic ozone hole has expanded to a size greater than North America, and scientists expect it to begin shrinking only in thirty to fifty years as ozone-depleting substances are removed from the atmosphere.

The discovery that widely used chemical substances were destroying stratospheric ozone induced a number of countries in the early 1980s to unilaterally ban the use of CFCs for aerosol sprays. At the same time, their general use made it obvious that the problem could not be solved unilaterally or even regionally. Thus, the UNEP made protection of stratospheric ozone a priority item in its legal Action Plan and after several years of effort, succeeded in advancing the negotiation of the Convention for the Protection of the Ozone Layer (Vienna, Mar. 22, 1985).

The treaty is a framework convention, providing the basis for systematic cooperation among the states parties to ensure the continued existence of stratospheric ozone. The general obligation of states parties, however, is directed more at the consequences of the depletion – to take appropriate measures to protect human health and the environment against adverse effects resulting or likely to result from human activities that modify or are likely to modify the ozone layer (art. 2). The Convention details the duty to cooperate in research and scientific assessments. It also requires cooperation in the legal, scientific, and technical fields, including the exchange of information. States parties generally are to make known their laws, their national administrative measures, and legal research relevant to protection of the ozone layer, as well as relevant methods and terms of licensing and availability of patents.

Article 8 of the Vienna Convention anticipates that the Conference of the Parties (COP) may adopt protocols to the Convention. The COP adopted the Montreal Protocol on Substances that Deplete the Ozone Layer (Montreal, Sept. 16, 1987) at a time when scientific uncertainty remained about global ozone loss and increases in ultraviolet radiation reaching the earth. The action taken in adopting the Protocol thus represented the first significant application of the precautionary principle in international environmental law.

The Montreal Protocol foresees the control of various forms of chlorofluorocarbons and halons and their progressive elimination. Industrial countries agreed to cut production and use of CFCs in half by 1998 and to freeze production and use of halons by 1992. Countries with an annual consumption of CFCs under 0.3 kilograms per capita, which were mainly developing countries, were given a ten-year period to comply. The Protocol also restricted trade between states parties and nonparties to discourage defections and provide states with an incentive to join the treaty, thus addressing the free-rider problem.

The Montreal Protocol came into force on January 1, 1989. New information indicated that ozone losses were two to three times more severe than had been predicted. Participating states then adopted a declaration of adjustment calling for accelerated phaseout of substances that destroy stratospheric ozone, in light of scientific findings. The parties agreed on new and shorter deadlines for the complete phaseout of substances. Later amendments to the Montreal Protocol endorsed a financial mechanism and an interim international fund consisting of voluntary contributions from the industrialized nations to assist developing countries in meeting the costs of compliance with the Convention and Protocols. For the first time, an international environmental treaty called for financial transfers from industrialized to developing countries and conditioned compliance by developing states on those transfers. With this amendment, both China and India ratified the Protocol.

The Fourth Meeting of the parties (Copenhagen, Nov. 1992) advanced the phaseout dates for industrial countries to 1994 for halons and to 1996 for CFCs, methyl chloroform, and carbon tetrachloride. It also took up the question of hydrochlorofluorocarbons (HCFCs), a proposed substitute for CFCs that is still ozone depleting but less so than CFCs. The agreement called for their complete phaseout by 2030. A 1995 meeting in Vienna added a phaseout for methyl bromide by the year 2010 for industrial countries. The meeting also strengthened requirements for industrialized-country use of HCFCs and added a complete phaseout by 2040 for developing countries. Subsequently, the states parties adopted new reduction schedules for a number of ozone-depleting substances, as well as decisions on illegal trade in such substances and on financial issues.

With the various actions taken by the states parties, the 1985 Vienna Convention for the Protection of the Ozone Layer has grown into an international treaty system composed of the Convention itself, the Montreal Protocol, and its amendments. It is managed by the Conference of the Parties to the Vienna Convention, the Meeting of the Parties to the Montreal Protocol, a Financial Mechanism, and a secretariat. Nearly one hundred chemicals are controlled by the ozone treaty regime as of the beginning of 2011.

International efforts to protect the ozone layer have had substantial impact. By 2006, global production of the most significant ozone-depleting substances, CFCs, was down 95 percent from the peak year of 1988. Several countries and regions advanced beyond the agreements. The European Union announced a phaseout of HCFCs by 2015, five years before it is legally required to do so. The U.S. Clean Air Act mandates the phaseout of methyl bromide nine years ahead of the Protocol requirements. Other countries similarly have accelerated their compliance. Although the task is not complete, the international community clearly responded to the issue. What may be important for the future is to ensure compatibility between the ozone and climate change regimes, as several substitutes for ozone-depleting substances are greenhouse gases.

5. Hazardous Substances and Waste

The problem of toxic or dangerous wastes is becoming increasingly serious. Growing numbers of dump sites have been found to contain toxic products. The transport of toxic or dangerous substances from one country to another to eliminate, recycle, or dispose of them is one of the most common forms of exporting pollution. Transboundary movements increased substantially during the 1980s because of the economic advantages involved in shipping wastes for disposal to poorer countries where the costs are much lower and regulation may be less strict or the monitoring of compliance less effective. The most targeted countries have been those that offer protection against claims and import wastes without always being concerned about the dangers they pose. The resulting problems have led at least thirty-nine states to adopt and implement national legislation entirely prohibiting the importation into or transshipment through their territories of all foreign wastes. In addition, by the end of the 1980s, a general opposition to transboundary movements of hazardous wastes led to international regulation, first at a global level, then regionally.

There is general agreement that the best means to control wastes is to reduce the quantity of wastes produced. Those that are produced can be eliminated by different methods: discharge into surface dumps, burial in the earth, submersion into the oceans or lakes, and incineration. More ecological methods consider wastes, as much as possible, as primary derived material that should be reutilized or recycled.

At the global level, the Convention on the Control of Transboundary Movements of Hazardous Wastes and their Disposal (Basel, Mar. 22, 1989) established a global framework for international regulation, although it has been criticized as not going far enough. The Convention defines wastes as substances or objects that are disposed of or are intended to be disposed of or are required to be disposed of by the provisions of national law. The hazardous character of wastes is defined by combined approaches of Annexes I, II, and III. Annex I lists categories of wastes to be controlled (e.g., chemical wastes from medical care in hospitals, and waste from different products, such as pharmaceuticals, or production of specified substances, such as biocides or organic solvents). Annex II contains two categories of wastes that require special consideration: wastes collected from households and residues arising from the incineration of household wastes. Annex III adds a list of hazardous characteristics of wastes, such as explosive, flammable, oxidizing, poisonous, infectious, corrosive, toxic, and eco-toxic. This combined method is increasingly used in international regulation, as the simple listing of polluting substances is inadequate.

Some of the important provisions in the Basel Convention are the following:

- The generation of hazardous wastes and other wastes and their transboundary movement should be reduced to a minimum consistent with the environmentally sound and efficient management of such wastes (arts. 4(2)(a) and (d));
- A signatory state cannot send hazardous waste to another signatory state that bans importation of it (art. 4(1)(b)), to another signatory state if the importing country does not have the facilities

to dispose of the waste in an environmentally sound manner (arts. 4(2)(b)(e)–(g)), or to any nonparty state (art. 4(5));

- Every country has the sovereign right to refuse to accept a shipment of hazardous wastes (arts. 4(1)(a) and (12));
- Before an exporting country can start a shipment on its way, it must have the importing country's consent in writing (art. 4(1)(c));
- When an importing country proves unable to dispose of legally imported waste in an environmentally sound way, then the exporting state has a duty either to take it back or to find some other way of disposing of it in an environmentally sound manner (art. 8);
- The parties consider that "illegal traffic in hazardous wastes is criminal" (art. 4(3));
- Shipments of hazardous waste must be packaged, labeled, and transported in conformity with generally accepted and recognized international rules and standards (art. 4(7)(b)) and accompanied by a movement document from the point at which a transboundary movement commences to the point of disposal (art. 4(7));
- Bilateral agreements may be made, but they must conform to the terms of the Basel Convention and be no less environmentally sound (art. 11);
- Parties should cooperate in the training of technicians, exchange of information, and transfer of technology (arts. 10 and 13).

At the Second Meeting of the Conference of the Parties (COP-2) in March 1994, parties agreed to an immediate ban on the export from OECD to non-OECD countries of hazardous wastes intended for final disposal. In 1995, the parties agreed to formally incorporate the ban in the Basel Convention as an amendment (Decision III/1).

Finally, in 1998, parties to the Basel Convention turned their attention to elaborating a liability protocol, which was concluded December 10, 1999, and to drafting guidelines on environmentally sound management of particular categories of hazardous wastes (e.g., lead-acid batteries, plastic wastes, decommissioned ships to be dismantled). These guidelines may include technical specifications for recycling and reclamation and specific strategies for implementation.

As for hazardous non-waste substances in international trade, in 1998, the Food and Agricultural Organization (FAO) sponsored adoption of the Rotterdam Convention on the Prior Informed Consent Procedure for Certain Hazardous Chemicals and Pesticides in International Trade (PIC Convention) (Sept. 10, 1998). The PIC Convention relies in large part on private actors to ensure that information on chemical and pesticide hazards is made available to the public. Each party is to regulate the labeling of exported Annex III chemicals, as well as chemicals banned or severely restricted in its territory, to ensure the provision of information about risks and/or hazards to human health or the environment, taking into account relevant international standards. A further major step in the control of hazardous chemicals occurred when 154 states and the European Union adopted the Stockholm Convention on Persistent Organic Pollutants (POPs, May 22, 2001). Persistent organic pollutants possess toxic properties; resist decay; bioaccumulate; and are transported through air, water, and with migratory species across international boundaries, where they accumulate in terrestrial and aquatic ecosystems. They create risks to health, especially in developing countries and in the polar ecosystems. Using the precautionary approach and advocating the polluter-pays principle, the Convention insists on the responsibility of POP manufacturers to reduce adverse effects caused by their products and to provide information to users, governments, and the public at large on the hazardous properties of these chemicals.

F. *Compliance and Enforcement*

Ensuring compliance with international treaties and custom is one of the main issues in international law. In a society composed of sovereign states that have exclusive jurisdiction over their territory, including maritime areas and airspace, compliance with obligations which the states have accepted raises specific problems that increase when environmental matters are in question. First, most environmental problems initially arise in the limits of national jurisdiction and do not immediately and directly harm other states, so the latter cannot file claims for reparations unless the obligations are designated as ones owed *erga omnes*. One may think of the prohibited use of CFCs, the emission of excessive greenhouse gases, or the destruction of biological diversity. In such instances, the normal sanction in treaty law, which consists in other states withholding equivalent treaty benefits from the breaching party, does not make sense and other types of noncompliance consequences must be foreseen.

Second, violations of MEAs are most often committed by nonstate actors, from individuals to large-scale industries. Governments are responsible, because they have accepted the treaty obligations, but, in practice, compliance may be difficult, because the state must commit scarce political and economic resources to ensure the required result. In many instances, the political costs of enforcing national and international law on the private sector may be greater than when the state regulates its own activities. States have various direct sanctions available to control the behavior of state agents, from disciplinary measures to dismissal. The regulation of nonstate behavior, however, is likely to require legislation that may be difficult to adopt when the nonstate actors play a powerful role in the domestic political arena. This is a key factor in the environmental field. Where there are costs imposed on industries that have a high degree of political representation, the state may find it difficult to ensure compliance. Both the will and capacity of the state to comply can become compromised.

1. State Responsibility

In international law, the law of state responsibility determines the consequences of a state's failure to comply with its international obligations. In general, it requires a state that breaches an international obligation to cease the violation and to provide reparations for any harm caused to another state. This responsibility based on fault may be distinguished from imposition of liability for environmentally deleterious effects of lawful acts, that is, liability without fault. In environmental law, the latter concept can be considered an application of the polluter-pays principle, which requires that the operator or actor who benefits from a lawful activity bear the risk of loss when harm is done to others. Such imposition of strict liability is rare.

According to international law, states are responsible for international law violations that can be attributed to them. In August 2001, the International Law Commission completed the Draft Articles on the Responsibility of States for Internationally Wrongful Acts, which the U.N. General Assembly "took note of" in Resolution 56/83 (Dec. 2001). According to article 2 of the Draft Articles, a state commits an international wrong when an act or omission attributable to it constitutes a breach of an international obligation of the state. Article 3 adds that the characterization of an act of a state as internationally wrongful is governed by international law. In other words, the primary rules of conduct for states (i.e., their rights and duties) establish whether an act or omission constitutes a wrongful act. At present, as discussed in the following section, only a handful of treaties make states strictly liable for any harm that occurs in another state's territory as a result of specific activities, even if the state has otherwise complied with its legal obligations. The large majority of multilateral environmental treaties focus not on the harm to the injured state but on the conduct of the acting state, by imposing duties of comportment and of result.

Although traditional norms of state responsibility most frequently concern the treatment of aliens and their property, the *Trail Smelter* arbitration of 1941 recognized that principles of state responsibility are applicable in the field of transboundary pollution; consequently, states may be held liable to private parties or other states for pollution that causes significant damage to persons or property.

The principle of state responsibility for transboundary environmental harm is contained in numerous international texts and has been recognized by the International Court of Justice. See: *Legality of the Threat or Use of Nuclear Weapons*, Advisory Opinion, 1996 ICJ 241–42, para. 29 and *Case Concerning the Gabčíkovo Nagymaros Project (Hung. v. Slovakia)*, 1997 ICJ 7, para. 53 (Sept. 25).

The law of state responsibility requires establishing a link of causality between a culpable act and the damage suffered, and the damage must not be too remote or too speculative. Pollution poses specific problems for several reasons. First, the distance separating the source from the place of damage may be dozens or even hundreds of miles, creating doubts about the causal link even where polluting activities can be identified.

Second, the noxious effects of a pollutant may not be felt until years or decades after the act. Increase in the rate of cancers as a consequence of radioactive fallout, for example, can be substantially removed in time from the polluting incident. This problem was highlighted by the 1986 Chernobyl accident, which immediately caused twenty-nine deaths but that directly or indirectly may have produced thousands of cases of cancer over the long term. Intervening factors may play a role as well.

Third, some types of damage occur only if the pollution continues over time. This is true of the deterioration of buildings and monuments, for example, or, in certain circumstances, of vegetation. Proof of causation also is made difficult by the fact that some substances cause little harm in isolation but are toxic in combination. Imputing responsibility to one source rather than another is difficult.

Fourth, the same pollutant does not always produce the same detrimental effects because of important variations in physical circumstances. Thus, dumping polluting substances in a river will not cause the same damage during times of drought as it will during periods when water levels are high. Similarly, wind or the lack of it, fog, or sunlight can modify the impact of air pollution or even the nature of pollution. Urban smog, for example, is exacerbated by atmospheric inversions (layers of warm, still air held below a cold-air mass) that block elimination of the air pollutants. The latter derive from multiple sources, including industry, domestic heating, and motor vehicles. In such a situation, it appears impossible to impute injury to a single precise cause to impose responsibility. Long-distance pollution, especially long-range air pollution, poses unique problems in identifying the author of the harm and precludes relying on traditional rules of state responsibility. Even at a short distance, proving the identity of the polluter can pose problems. For example, gas emissions from motor vehicles are harmful, including the fumes of each individual automobile. Yet it is difficult to apply rules of responsibility and demand reparations from each driver, because the numbers are too great and the effects produced by each unit are relatively limited. Nonetheless the cumulative effects are significant because of the part played by nitrous oxide (NO_2) and burned hydrocarbons (HCs) in the formation of ozone at medium altitudes during sunny periods; they are also factors in the depletion of forests. One answer being suggested is pollution or carbon taxes.

Another issue of state responsibility concerns the extent to which states are accountable for the actions of private parties under their jurisdiction or control. As a general rule, it can be said that the state whose territory serves to support the activities causing environmental damage elsewhere or under whose control it occurs is responsible for the resulting harm. The necessary element of an act or omission by a state agent is generally present, because the large majority of domestic activities capable of causing serious environmental harm outside the country requires prior approval or licensing under domestic legislation, thus making attribution possible. Such approval normally will suffice to engage the responsibility of the competent territorial authority.

2. Compliance Procedures

The traditional practice whereby each state party to a treaty monitors whether other states parties comply with the requirements of the agreement remains basic to environmental agreements. According to the Basel Convention on Transboundary Movement of Hazardous Wastes, for example, each party suspecting a breach is to inform the Secretariat and the offending party. The Secretariat, in turn, informs other parties. Also, MEAs frequently establish their own international supervisory mechanisms or designate specific states as having supervisory functions. Article 218 of UNCLOS provides, for example, that when a ship voluntarily enters a port or offshore installation, the port state can investigate and, where the evidence warrants, institute proceedings regarding any maritime discharge violation of applicable international rules and standards.

Some noncompliance procedures instituted by international environmental agreements aim to provide assistance to the defaulting state. The Montreal Protocol to the Ozone Convention, for example, establishes a procedure whereby a party that cannot meet its obligations may report its compliance problems to the Implementation Committee. The Implementation Committee consists of ten parties elected by the Meeting of the Parties for two years on the basis of equitable geographical distribution. In addition, any party that has concerns about another party's implementation of its obligations under the Protocol can communicate the concerns in writing, supported by corroborating information, to the Secretariat. The Implementation Committee can request further information or, on the invitation of the party concerned, can undertake information gathering on site.

At the end of the procedure, the Committee reports to the Meeting of the Parties. Any recommendation it considers appropriate can be included in the report, which is made available to the parties six weeks before the meeting. The Meeting of the Parties may decide on steps to bring about full compliance with the Protocol. Any state involved in a matter under consideration by the Implementation Committee cannot take part in the elaboration and adoption of recommendations concerning it. The parties subject to the procedure must subsequently inform the Meeting of the Parties of the measures they have taken in response to the report. Annex V of Decision IV/18 contains an indicative list of measures that might be taken by the Meeting of the Parties in respect of noncompliance with the Protocol. The first consists in providing assistance, for, for example, the collection and reporting of data, technology transfer, financing, information transfer, and training. At the second level, cautions, or warnings, are issued. The third level involves the suspension of specific rights and privileges under the Protocol. Such rights and privileges can concern industrial rationalization, production, consumption, trade, transfer of technology, financial mechanisms, and industrial arrangements.

3. Periodic State Reporting

The compliance procedures for MEAs are most often informational. The MEAs routinely contain an obligation for the parties to report on their measures of implementation and compliance. The procedure requires states parties to a treaty to address periodic reports to an organ established or designated by the treaty, indicating the implementing measures they have taken. Most global MEAS and many regional ones use this technique, but only in a few cases is state reporting part of a comprehensive system to promote compliance or ultimately to result in enforcement measures.

Reporting must be distinguished from mere exchange of information or occasional communication of factual or scientific information not necessarily related to the implementation of environmental agreements. Reports on the implementation of MEAs usually include two categories of information. First, they summarize or transmit the legal and administrative instruments that states parties adopted or intend to adopt to implement the agreement. Second, they transmit factual information, mostly scientific data, on the status of a given component of the environment, on its deterioration or threats to it, and in some instances on the proposed remedies.

In addition to periodic reports required by treaty provision, a contracting party or, often, the MEA secretariat may request information from a party, mainly concerning facts or measures taken and planned to be taken on matters included in the MEA. *See, e.g.,* arts. 10 and 12 of the Convention on Cooperation for the Protection and Sustainable Use of the Danube River (Sofia, June 29, 1994). Such information may be protected when it is related to industrial and commercial secrets or other confidential pieces of information. *Id.* at art. 13. Public information also may complement state reports.

State reporting on the implementation of MEA obligations gradually emerged. One of the earliest treaties, the Ramsar Convention on Wetlands of International Importance (Feb. 2, 1971), did not foresee a reporting procedure, but it was created by COP Recommendation 2.1, adopted in 1984. The UNESCO Convention for the Protection of the World Cultural and Natural Heritage (Paris, Nov. 16, 1972) was one of the first MEAs to include a reporting obligation. Article 29 provides that the states parties to the Convention shall submit reports to the General Conference of UNESCO, in which they give information on the legislative and administrative provisions that they have adopted and any other action, which they have taken for the application of the Convention, together with details of the experience they have acquired in this field. Most of the MEAs adopted since 1972, whether global or regional, provide for reporting by states parties on their implementation.

The content of the periodic reports can be specified by the MEA itself or, more frequently, detailed by a treaty body. The COPs or secretariats often prepare models for national reports, including questionnaires and directives for the presentation of information. One of the first MEAs to prescribe precise rules on reporting was the Convention on International Trade in Endangered Species. Annual reports should contain a summary of the number and type of permits and certificates of export and import granted; the states with which such trade occurred; the numbers or quantities and types of specimens; the names of species included in one of the appendixes; and where appropriate, the size and sex of the specimens in question. Moreover, a biennial report must be prepared on legislative, regulatory, and administrative measures taken to enforce the provisions of the Convention. Such information shall be available to the public where this is not inconsistent with the law of the party concerned.

The obligation to address reports to an organ designated by an international instrument would be of little utility if the reports were not subject to review and critique. Thus, the mandates of treaty bodies typically include review of state reports.

A U.N. study undertaken in the context of human rights reporting sets forth the objectives of international reporting procedures. *Report of the 3d Session of the U.N. Committee on Economic, Social and Cultural Rights*, U.N. Doc. E/1989/22 (24 Feb, 1989), Annex III. It is equally relevant to MEA reporting. It says that the reporting procedure should ensure that states parties undertake a comprehensive initial review of national legislation, administrative rules, and procedures and practices, either before or soon after ratification, and regularly monitor the actual situation with respect to each of the obligations, to become aware of the extent to which the various duties are or are not being fulfilled. It also should facilitate public scrutiny of relevant government policies, encouraging the involvement of various sectors of society in the formulation, implementation, and review of national policies. On the international level, the procedure should provide a basis for the state party, as well as the supervisory body, to evaluate effectively the progress made in the realization of the obligations contained in the treaty. The procedure can facilitate the exchange of information among state parties and develop a better understanding of the common problems faced.

Questions remain about the effectiveness of reporting systems. States tend to be less than forthcoming about problems and defects in the implementation of their treaty obligations. In response, it may be noted that even the fact of having to write a report may exercise a positive influence on state behavior, because many government officials become involved in assessing state performance against international obligations. Internationally, state reports are often discussed in the supervisory organs, and during the process independent experts or representatives of other states can question delegates from the state authoring the report. The strength of the system is both psychological and political. States may not always protect the environment as they should, but they seek to maintain a good reputation in this field where the public opinion is particularly sensitive. Thus, they normally make efforts to avoid or mitigate damage that could result in condemnation or criticism during review of their reports. The presence of NGO observers and the press at the meetings of treaty bodies can play a major role in this regard.

4. Civil Society Petitions

Only two environmental agreements have established a complaints procedure open to civil society to denounce noncompliance by states parties with their international obligations. One, the Aarhus Convention on Information, Public Participation and Access to Justice is discussed in Chapter 6. The other agreement is the North American Agreement on Environmental Cooperation, known informally as the NAFTA Side Agreement. North American Agreement on Environmental Cooperation, Sept. 14, 1993, 32 I.L.M. 1480 (1993). Its procedure enables the public to complain when one of the three governments (Canada, Mexico, and the United States) appears to be failing to enforce its environmental laws effectively. Members of the public trigger the process by submitting to the Commission for Environmental Cooperation (CEC) a claim alleging such a failure on the part of any of the NAFTA partners. Any nongovernmental organization or person established or residing in the territory of a party to the Agreement may make a submission in writing on enforcement matters for consideration by the Secretariat of the CEC. Following a review of the submission, the CEC may investigate the matter and publish a factual record of its findings, subject to approval by the CEC Council. The procedure is explained by the CEC Guidelines.

Questions and Discussion

1. Is a petition worth it? Since 1995, the CEC has received sixty-six complaints and prepared fifteen factual records. Seven of the factual records were on petitions against Mexico, seven concerned Canada, and only one against the United States.

2. For evaluations and critiques of the CEC complaints procedure, see Tseming Yang, *The Effectiveness of the NAFTA Environmental Side Agreement's Citizen Submission Process: A Case Study of the Metales y Derivados Matter*, 76 UNIV. COLO. L. REV. 443 (2005); Mark R. Goldschmidt, *The Role of Transparency and Public Participation in International Environmental Agreements: The North American Agreement on Environmental Cooperation*, 29 B.C. ENVTL. AFF. L. REV. (2002); John Knox, *A New Approach to Compliance with International Environmental Law: The Submission Procedure of the NAFTA Environmental Commission*, 28 ECOLOGY L.Q. 1, 88 (2001); David L. Markell, *The Commission for Environmental Cooperation's Citizen Submission Process*, 12 GEO. INT'L ENVTL. L. REV. 545 (2000); Christopher N. Bolinger, *Assessing the CEC on Its Record to Date*, 28 L. & POL'Y IN INT'L BUSINESS (1997); GREENING NAFTA: THE NORTH AMERICAN COMMISSION FOR ENVIRONMENTAL COOPERATION (John Knox & David Markell eds. 2003).

3. Linda Malone and Scott Pasternack outline three strategies for civil society to pursue in holding states to their environmental commitments. As you read the following extract, consider how you might specifically use the strategies:

> First, NGOs can submit petitions to MEA treaty secretariats calling on those bodies to take steps to resolve a particular environmental and public health harm that is not receiving adequate attention but is occurring within a member nation-state. Second, NGOs can encourage nation-states to initiate state-to-state dispute resolution under these MEAs to help resolve an environmental or public health problem. Detailed below, these strategies may help to strengthen the effectiveness of MEAs and better protect the environment and public health. Third, where the MEA allows, NGOs can participate at MEA Conferences of the Parties or appropriate bodies of charter-based institutions and lobby member states to take particular environmental action.
>
> Using these strategies may compensate for the weak enforcement mechanisms found in MEAs. Such weak enforcement mechanisms have undermined the ability of MEAs to protect the environment and public health as effectively as perhaps intended, especially in the wake of competing political demands. Although the International Court of Justice ("ICJ") may provide effective secondary enforcement of MEA dispute resolution decisions, the voluntary nature of nation-state personal jurisdiction before the ICJ makes this enforcement avenue unappealing at best, and, more often, unavailable.
>
> . . .
>
> II. STRATEGY NO. 1: PETITIONING MEA SECRETARIATS
>
> A. Strategy Summary
>
> If the action or omission of a nation-state party to a particular MEA results in an environmental or public health harm that undermines the MEA, then an NGO can often informally submit a petition to the secretariat of that relevant MEA and call upon that secretariat to pressure the nation-state to change its behavior.
>
> One of several different outcomes may result from such a petition. First, the state party may take action to resolve the environmental or public health problem. Second, the MEA secretariat may work with a state party to resolve the problem. Third, the petition may raise public awareness of a previously unknown concern.
>
> Remember that because this strategy is new and innovative, concerns may exist among the NGO community that if a petition is not prepared properly, then MEA secretariats

may decide never to consider petitions from any non-state actors in the future. Therefore, seeking assistance . . . can help strengthen your petition or lead to alternative strategies to resolve your issue.

. . .

III. STRATEGY NO. 2: LOBBYING STATE PARTIES TO INITIATE DISPUTE RESOLUTION PROCEEDINGS

MEA dispute resolution processes are available only for nation-states to bring claims against nation-states concerning matters within the scope of the given MEA. Therefore, non-state actors, such as NGOs, can and ought to request and encourage sympathetic governments – not necessarily their own – to file claims on behalf of such NGOs against nation-states that maintain a law or practice that harms the protection of the environment within the scope of that MEA.

Such a dispute could result in several different outcomes, similar to what may result from NGOs petitioning secretariats. First, the state party may take action to resolve the environmental or public health problem. Second, the MEA secretariat may pressure a state party to resolve the problem. Third, the petition may raise public awareness of a previously unknown concern.

An NGO wanting to pursue this strategy should determine which entity within the government of the nation-state represents that nation-state at such dispute resolution proceedings. Once determine[d], the NGO should submit a written request or schedule an in-person meeting with that office.

. . .

IV. STRATEGY NO. 3: PARTICIPATING AT MEA CONFERENCES OF THE PARTIES OR IN APPROPRIATE BODIES OF CHARTER-BASED INSTITUTIONS

Most MEAs allow non-state actors to participate as observers at periodic meetings among the MBA members states known as the Conference of the Parties ("COPs") in the case of conventions and Meetings of the Parties ("MOPs") in the case of Protocols. These mandatory gatherings require member states to report on the status of the MBA and focus on how to improve it. Member state attendees of COPs include the key government employees within a given member state and the staff of the MBA secretariat who are often the most knowledgeable about that MBA, who are experts in the field related to the MBA, and who may be responsible for making important decisions for the given member state and/or the MBA secretariat with respect to the development to that MBA. Consequently, attending the COP affords an NGO tremendous access to those who may be able to improve the enforcement of a given MBA with respect to a particular environmental or public health issue of concern to the NGO. Moreover, observer NGOs can often lobby generally on an issue among an audience intimately involved and familiar with the MBA, even if the observer NGO cannot vote.

In addition to participating at MBA COPs, civil society also can obtain similar consultative status with charter-based international governmental organizations such as the United Nations or the Organization of American States. Generally speaking, such status enables NGOs to attend legislative sessions, submit written statements, and make oral statements on a periodic basis.

Undertaking the strategy of participating at MBA conferences involves a few straightforward steps. First, one must again determine the MBA most relevant to one's environmental or public health issue of concern. Second, one must assess whether one has expertise in the field related to the MEA as such expertise is often a prerequisite for obtaining observer status. Third, one must consult the text of the MBA to confirm that it allows NGOs to attend the COP and/or MOP as an observer. Most do. . . . Fourth, one should consult the internet site for the MBA's secretariat to locate the procedures for applying for observer status. Such status may be available permanently for all COPs and/or MOPs or only temporarily for one particular COP and/or MOP Often applications must be submitted far in advance of the date of the COP and/or MOP Fifth, once one obtains observer status, one should locate other NGOs with observer status and build a coalition of groups interested in one's issue prior to attending the COP and/or MOP Most MBA internet sites list entities with observer status. Sixth, one should prepare to lobby just as one prepares to lobby in other arenas.

Apart from COP and MOP participation, civil society can also obtain consultative or observer status with charter-based international or regional organizations. Such status may vary with each institution.

Linda A. Malone & Scott Pasternack, Defending the Environment: Civil Society Strategies to Enforce International Environmental Law 153–59 (2004).

2 The Environment as a Human Rights Issue

The Environment Is Man's First Right[1]

I. Introduction

Over the past sixty years, international human rights law and then international environmental law developed as distinct domains of international law. Almost from the emergence of contemporary international environmental law in the late 1960s, a relationship between the two areas was strongly perceived. In 1972, the governments participating in the first major multilateral conference on the environment, held in Stockholm, proclaimed in the concluding Stockholm Declaration that "[t]he protection and improvement of the human environment is a major issue which affects the well-being of peoples." *Report of the U.N. Conference on the Human Environment, Declaration of the U.N. Conference on the Human Environment,* U.N. Doc. A/CONF.48/14/Rev.1, p. 3 (June 5–16, 1972). As we saw in Chapter 1, the Stockholm Declaration also solemnly declared, in the language of human rights, that "[m]an has the fundamental right to freedom, equality and adequate conditions of life, in an environment of a quality that permits a life of dignity and well-being, and he bears a solemn responsibility to protect and improve the environment for present and future generations." *Id.* at p. 4 (Principle 1).

During the preparations for the Stockholm Conference and increasingly thereafter, states began adopting constitutional provisions concerning the environment, often using rights language. In the 1980s, the linkage between human rights and the environment recognized in the Stockholm Declaration was enshrined in binding international agreements. The African Charter on Human Rights, adopted in Nairobi, Kenya, on June 27, 1981, proclaimed, "All peoples shall have the right to a general satisfactory environment favorable to their development." Article 24, African Charter on Human and Peoples Rights, AFRICAN CHARTER ON HUMAN AND PEOPLES RIGHTS, O.A.U. Doc. CAB/LEG/67/3 Rev. 5,

---

[1] Ken Saro-Wiwa, *Stand by Me and the Ogoni People*, 10 Earth Island Journal 35 (No. 3, 1995). Saro-Wiwa was hanged, along with eight others, in Nigeria on November 10, 1995, ostensibly for incitement to murder. However, most believe that the defendants were put to death for raising environmental concerns about oil exploitation by Royal Dutch Petroleum in their ancestral Ogoni lands. For a compelling account of the events, see IKE OKONTA & ORONTO DOUGLAS, WHERE VULTURES FEAST: SHELL HUMAN RIGHTS AND OIL IN THE NIGER DELTA (2003). Several human rights cases resulted. The African Commission delivered the landmark *SERAC v. Nigeria* decision, reprinted in Chapter 6, while Shell Oil had to pay for its alleged complicity in an Alien Tort Statute case in the United States. In June 2009, after ten years in the courts and on the eve of trial, the parties agreed to settle three related law suits for $15.5 million. See also *International Pen, Constitutional Rights Project, Interights on behalf of Ken Saro-Wiwa Jr. and Civil Liberties Organization v. Nigeria*, Comms. 137/94, 139/94, 154/96 and 161/97, 12ᵗʰ Ann. Act. Rep. Annex V (1998), 7 IHRR 274 (2000).

reprinted in 21 I.L.M. 58 (1982). A more detailed formulation of the right was included in the Additional Protocol to the American Human Rights Convention on Economic and Social Rights, adopted in San Salvador, El Salvador, on November 17, 1988 (hence the Protocol of San Salvador). It proclaimed both the rights of individuals and the duty of states in this field:

1. Everyone shall have the right to live in a healthy environment and to have access to basic public services.
2. The States Parties shall promote the protection, preservation, and improvement of the environment.

Article 11, ADDITIONAL PROTOCOL TO THE AMERICAN CONVENTION ON HUMAN RIGHTS IN THE AREA OF ECONOMIC, SOCIAL, AND CULTURAL RIGHTS, O.A.S.T.S. 69, reprinted in 28 I.L.M. 156 (1989).

A. *Tension or Complementarity?*

The assertions in the Stockholm Declaration sparked an early academic search for jurisprudential bases for linking rights and the environment. A number of texts and articles appeared in which the international legal case was made for "the human rights of individuals to be guaranteed a pure, healthful, and decent environment." W. PAUL GORMLEY, HUMAN RIGHTS AND ENVIRONMENT: THE NEED FOR INTERNATIONAL COOPERATION 1, 233 (1976). Today, the protection of the environment and the promotion of human rights are increasingly seen by many as intertwined, complementary goals. For Christopher Weeramantry, a former vice president of the International Court of Justice, this is self-evident. In his separate opinion in *Case Concerning the Gabčíkovo-Nagymaros Project*, Judge Weeramantry wrote:

> The protection of the environment is . . . a vital part of contemporary human rights doctrine, for it is a *sine qua non* for numerous human rights such as the right to health and the right to life itself. It is scarcely necessary to elaborate on this, as damage to the environment can impair and undermine all the human rights spoken of in the Universal Declaration and other human rights instruments.

Case Concerning the Gabčíkovo-Nagymaros Project, [1997] I.C.J. Rep. 7, 91–92.

Yet other scholars reject the connection between human rights and the environment, seeing incompatibility or even danger in their coupling. In their view, human rights and environmental protection are based on fundamentally different and ultimately irreconcilable value systems; as such, they are much more likely to conflict with each other than to be complementary or mutually reinforcing. The arguments proceed, on the one hand, with some environmental lawyers maintaining that a human rights focus for environmental law ultimately reduces all other environmental values to an instrumental use for humanity so that the quality of human life can be enhanced. This human-centered, utilitarian view reduces the nonhuman and nonliving aspects of ecosystems to their economic value to humans and promotes unsustainable resource exploitation and environmental degradation as a human good. On the other hand, some human rights lawyers believe that linking human rights and the environment diminishes the importance and focus on protection of more immediate human rights concerns, such as ending genocide, extrajudicial killings, torture, and arbitrary detention.

Professor Shelton posits a third view that she says seems to best reflect the current state of play in law and policy:

> [This view] sees human rights and environmental protection as each representing different, but overlapping, societal values. The two fields share a core of common interests and objectives, although obviously not all human rights violations are necessarily linked to environmental degradation. Likewise, environmental issues cannot always be addressed effectively within the human rights framework, and any attempt to force all such issues into a human rights rubric may fundamentally distort the concept of human rights. This approach [thus] recognizes the potential conflicts between environmental protection and human rights, but also the contribution each field can make to achieving their common objectives.

Dinah Shelton, HUMAN RIGHTS, ENVIRONMENTAL RIGHTS, AND THE RIGHT TO ENVIRONMENT, 28 Stan. J. Int'l L. 103, 105 (1991).

Perhaps these conflicting or different views help explain why the relationship between human rights and the environment has had a slow, ad hoc, and uneven development. Disputes continue about how best to ensure that human rights and environmental protection are mutually supportive. For instance, some favor approaches that deploy or reinterpret existing human rights in the cause of environmental protection. Others insist that the development of new substantive rights for and to the environment per se is necessary.

Questions and Discussion

1. Throughout this chapter, bear in mind a distinction between two potential rights holders and what they mean for the environment. First, human rights, possessed by the human being, may provide certain protection for the environment derivatively when enforced. Second, the environment itself might be accorded rights that can be invoked by an appropriate party in cases of violation. For the most part, the environmental rights that we will study here are not rights for the environment per se. Instead, we will be concerned the deployment of traditional human rights, such as the right to life and health as a proxy for environmental protection. We will also examine the emergence of a new human right (or more accurately, a collection of rights) brought to bear on environmental protection for the benefit of the inherent dignity of all human beings. Are these two views incompatible? Does Shelton's third view assist in reconciliation?

2. A few environmental rights proposals surfaced even before the beginning of the modern environmental movement. Italy's post–World War II constitution of 1948 was the first to include a provision on the topic. Most countries took up the issue, however, only as concern about environmental harm and its consequences increased. Frits W. Hondius, *Environment and Human Rights*, 41 Y.B. ASS'N ATTENDERS & ALUMNI HAGUE ACAD. INT'L L. 68 (1971); E.F. Roberts, *The Right to a Decent Environment: A Premature Construct*, 1 ENVTL. POL'Y & L. 185, 188 (and articles cited at * [on page 188]). *See generally* David W. Orr, *Constitutional Divide: Bridging U.S. Law and the Ecological Necessities of Life and Liberty*, 23 ORION 19, 22–23 (2004).

B. A Primer on Rights

When we claim that humans have rights or that the environment itself has rights, it is important to be clear what we mean by the term *rights*. As Pound observed, "There is no more ambiguous word in legal and juristic literature than the word right." Roscoe Pound,

IV JURISPRUDENCE 56 (1959). A more detailed treatment will follow in Chapter 3, but an exposure now is important and will set the stage.

Ordinarily, the idea of rights connotes a substantial interest recognized and bounded by the law. A right is conferred as a mechanism to protect those substantial interests recognized in law. But a right can be more or less. A legal right might be absolute (at least in theory) or might need to be balanced when it comes in to conflict with other rights. A right can also exist in a prelegal or extralegal state as a moral claim outside the law.

The nature and creation of rights are products of direct human experience with wrongs. *See* MORRIS R. COHEN, LAW AND THE SOCIAL ORDER 148 (1933); Paul Vinogradoff, *Foundation of a Theory of Rights*, 34 YALE L.J. 60, 66–67 (1924). So, for instance, the Universal Declaration of Human Rights (UDHR), like the U.N. Charter, is a result of the traumatic historical experience of World War II and the atrocities and suffering it caused. The UDHR gives specificity to the general references to human rights scattered throughout the U.N. Charter, whose Preamble makes clear the concerns of its drafters: "We the peoples of the United Nations determined to save succeeding generations from the scourge of war, which twice in our lifetime has brought untold sorrow to mankind, and to reaffirm faith in fundamental human rights, in the dignity and worth of the human person, in the equal rights of men and women." *See* CASS R. SUNSTEIN, THE SECOND BILL OF RIGHTS: FDR's UNFINISHED REVOLUTION AND WHY WE NEED IT MORE THAN EVER 35–36 (2004).

1. Human Rights and Universal Aspirations

For the purpose of this book, the term *rights* is not necessarily limited to those rights that have been legally conferred by virtue of a judicial decision, statute, constitution, treaty, or customary law. Human rights are often said to resemble fundamental or natural rights in the natural law tradition – that is, they are rights that do not owe their existence to a legal source and do not depend on legal sanction. Instead, human rights are claimed to transcend legal systems not in accord with those rights and to obtain in all places and at all times regardless of what the positive law provides. Legal systems should embody rights. If one does not, it is deficient. From the start of the contemporary human rights movement following World War II, human rights have had universal aspirations, the foundation document being called the Universal Declaration of Human Rights (UDHR). The "relativity" of rights, though, has sometimes challenged universal claims through counterclaims of particularity or cultural specificity. Compare, for instance, the following accounts of the universality of the UDHR.

A WORLD MADE NEW: ELEANOR ROOSEVELT AND THE UNIVERSAL DECLARATION OF HUMAN RIGHTS 221–22 (2001)
Mary Ann Glendon

The problem of what universality might mean in a multicultural world haunted the United Nations human rights project from the beginning. In June 1947, when word of a proposed human rights declaration reached the American Anthropological Association, that group's executive board sent a letter to the Human Rights Commission warning that the document could not be "a statement of rights conceived only in terms of the values prevalent in the countries of Western Europe and America." . . . Earlier that year some of the world's best-known philosophers had been asked to ponder the question, "How is an agreement conceivable among men who come from the four corners of the earth and who belong not only to different cultures and civilizations, but to different spiritual families and antagonistic schools of thought?"

No one has yet improved on the answer of the... philosophers: Where basic human values are concerned, cultural diversity has been exaggerated. The group found, after consulting with Confucian, Hindu, Muslim, and European thinkers, that a core of fundamental principles was widely shared in countries that had not yet adopted rights instruments and in cultures that had not embraced the language of rights. Their survey persuaded them that basic human rights rest on "common convictions," even though those convictions "are stated in terms of different philosophic terms." The philosophers concluded that even people who seem to be far apart in theory can agree that certain things are so terrible in practice that no one will publicly approve them and that certain things are so good in practice that no one will publicly oppose them.

The Complexity of Universalism in Human Rights,
in HUMAN RIGHTS WITH MODESTY: THE PROBLEM OF UNIVERSALISM 61
(A. Sajó ed., 2004)
Makau Mutua

... Sanctimonious to a fault, the UDHR underscored its arrogance by proclaiming itself the common standard of achievement for all peoples and nations. The fact that a half-century later human rights have become a central norm of global civilization does not vindicate their universality.... Non-Western philosophies and traditions particularly on the nature of man and the purposes for political society were either unrepresented or marginalized during the early formation of human rights....

There is no doubt that the current human rights corpus is well meaning. But that is beside the point.... International human rights fall within the historical continuum of the European colonial project in which whites pose as the saviors of a benighted and savage non-European world. The white human rights zealot joins the unbroken chain that connects her to the colonial administrator, the Bible-wielding missionary, and the merchant of free enterprise....

Thus human rights reject the cross-fertilization of cultures and instead seek the transformation of non-Western cultures by Western cultures.

Questions and Discussion

1. Does it matter that authorship of the UDHR included representatives from Lebanon, China, and Latin America as well as from Europe and North America? Even if the membership of the United Nations was largely Western in 1948, does the subsequent development of regional human rights systems in every region of the world, all based on and referring to the UDHR, support claims of universality?

2. How does one tell whether or not a right is universal? If a human right to environmental quality exists, is it universal? Why?

3. Human rights are of special value because they are premised on the inherent dignity and value of all persons who are deemed to possess equal worth. They require, in Immanuel Kant's phrase, for individuals to be treated as ends and not as means. KANT, POLITICAL WRITINGS 24 (H.S. Reiss ed., 1991). In addition, the importance of human rights is that they serve as constraints on other incompatible individual and collective goals. So, to have the right to do W (or the right to require X to do Y or to forbear from doing Z) puts the holder of the right in a strong position in relation to others without a countervailing right. *See generally* THEORIES OF RIGHTS (Jeremy Waldron ed., 1984).

2. Rights of the Environment

Just as the inherent value of human beings serve as a predicate for human rights, so, too, it has been argued that all other nonhuman living beings (and even nonliving components of ecosystems) possess an intrinsic worth that justifies according rights to nonhumans and their environments. It is not difficult to find statements about the inherent value of the environment. Almost every state in the world – one hundred ninety-three states, not including the United States – is party to the Convention on Biological Diversity (the most widely ratified environmental treaty today). In the preamble to the Convention, states parties recognize "the intrinsic value of biological diversity and of the ecological, genetic, social, economic, scientific, educational, cultural, recreational and aesthetic values of biological diversity and its components." UN Doc. UNEP/Bio.Div/CONF/L.2 (May 22, 1992), 1760 U.N.T.S. 142 (1993). Biological diversity includes diversity with and between species, as well as the ecological complexes of which they are part.

Aldo Leopold, writing in 1949, argued that the time had come to establish at least moral rights for the environment. Leopold famously wrote:

> There is yet no ethic dealing with man's relation to land and to the animals and plants which grow upon it. . . . The land-relation is still strictly economic, entailing privileges but not obligations.
>
> The extension of ethics to [the] environment is, if I read the evidence correctly, an evolutionary possibility and an ecological necessity. . . .
>
> The land ethic simply enlarges the boundaries of the community to include soils, waters, plants, and animals, or collectively: the land.
>
> . . . A land ethic of course cannot prevent the alteration, management, and use of these "resources," but it does affirm their right to continued existence and, at least in spots, their continued existence in a natural state.
>
> In short, a land ethic changes the role of *Homo sapiens* from conqueror of the land-community to plain member and citizen of it. It implies respect for his fellow-members, and also respect for the community as such.

Aldo Leopold, A SAND COUNTY ALMANAC AND SKETCHES HERE AND THERE 203–04 (1949).

Questions and Discussion

1. It is difficult to find legal examples that translate the recognition of intrinsic value into enforceable rights on behalf of the environment. Why? Are there problems with coherency? Enforceability? Skeptics are easy to find. In their view, a right for nonhumans or nonliving things is nonsense. *See* P.S. Elder, *Legal Rights for Nature: The Wrong Answer to the Right(s) Question*, 22 OSGOOD HALL L.J. 285, 288–89 (1984). Moreover, it is argued that courts should not provide environmental protection through a so-called right because it involves political choices over the use of scarce resources. Finally, it is claimed that a right of the environment itself is impossibly vague and incapable of judicial application because there is no way to discern what the environment itself would prefer. *See* Mark Sagoff, *On Preserving the Natural Environment*, 84 YALE L.J. 205 (1974).

   Another explanation for the difficulty in establishing rights of the environment might be found in the fact that very often it takes considerable time to move from moral claim to law. The slow process by which an extralegal fundamental right is harnessed to create a legal obligation can be seen in the evolution in ethical understanding about slavery, which finally resulted in legal prohibition. The necessary constellation of political, economic, and moral conditions took centuries to develop before the fundamental right to be free from slavery became a legal right. In the United States, slavery was not abolished until after a bloody civil war.

Yet another explanation may lie in the way environmental law itself has developed. Professor Dan Tarlock suggests that "environmental law has failed to develop a substantive theory of environmental quality entitlement. The western tradition of expanding the concept of human dignity left no room for the protection of non-human values." A. Dan Tarlock, *Environmental Law, but Not Environmental Protection*, in NATURAL RESOURCES POLICY AND LAW: TRENDS AND DIRECTIONS 162, 171 (L.J. MacDonnell & S.F. Bates eds., 1993). This suggestion seems to be supported by Justice William O. Douglas, who wrote about a wilderness "bill of rights" in 1965:

> The Bill of Rights, which makes up the first ten Amendments to our Constitution, contains in the main guarantees to minorities. These are guarantees of things that government cannot do to the individual because of his conviction of belief or other idiosyncrasies. When it comes to wilderness we need a similar Bill of Rights to protect *those whose* spiritual values extend to the rivers and lakes, the valleys and the ridges, and *who* find life in a mechanized society worth living only because those splendid resources are not despoiled.

William O. Douglas, A WILDERNESS BILL OF RIGHTS 86 (1965) (emphasis added).

Under the Douglas theory, it appears that wilderness is deserving of protection because of its importance to "idiosyncratic" nature lovers. It is this "minority" that is to be accorded rights in line with the Western tradition of increasing protection of human values or dignity. This is not to say that wilderness does not receive surrogate protection through the enforcement of the legal rights of humans to wilderness, or that the law does not exhibit a concern for (or even legal recognition of) wilderness through the protection of the human holder of the legal right. It is rather that the nonhuman values of wilderness, outside of those important to human rights holders, are left unprotected.

Douglas significantly expanded his view in the context of legal standing seven years later in his famous dissent in *Sierra Club v. Morton*, 405 U.S. 727, 741–55 (1972) ("Contemporary public concern for protecting nature's ecological equilibrium should lead to the conferral of standing upon environmental objects to sue for their own preservation." *Id.* at 741–42). For important eco-centric approaches to rights, see PRUE TAYLOR, AN ECOLOGICAL APPROACH TO INTERNATIONAL LAW: RESPONDING TO CHALLENGES OF CLIMATE CHANGE, ch. 5 (1998); KLAUS BOSSELMANN, WHEN TWO WORLDS COLLIDE: SOCIETY AND ECOLOGY (1995).

2. Legal measures and efforts to protect all or part of the natural world have been undertaken in several countries. In the German Land of Thüringen, a constitutional provision protects animals against cruel treatment. Article 32 of the Constitution of the German Land of Thüringen provides: "Animals are to be respected as living beings and fellow creatures. They will be protected from treatment inappropriate to the species and from avoidable suffering." In Austria, various groups mounted litigation to have a chimpanzee declared a person with rights. The most ambitious change has taken place in Ecuador, where a constitutional amendment in 2008 declared nature to be a legal person. It now provides the following:

> *Title II, Chapter Six, Article 66 –*
>
> It is recognized and guaranteed to persons:
>
> . . .
>
> 27. The Right to live in a healthy, ecologically balanced, pollution free environment and in harmony with nature.

Title II, Chapter Seven, Article 71 –

Nature[,] or Pacha Mama, where life plays and performs, is entitled to full respect, existence, and the maintenance and regeneration of its vital cycles, structure, functions and evolutionary processes. Any person, community, nation or nationality may require the public authority to comply with the rights of nature. The principles enshrined in the Constitution, will be used to apply and interpret these rights, as appropriate. The State will encourage individuals, legal persons, and collective entities to protect nature and promote respect for all the elements that form an ecosystem.

Title II. Chapter Seven, Article 72 –

Nature is entitled to restoration. This restoration is independent of the obligation of the State and persons or companies to compensate individuals and groups that depend on affected natural systems. In cases of severe or permanent environmental impact, including those linked to the exploitation of nonrenewable natural resources, the State shall establish the most effective mechanisms to achieve the restoration, and take appropriate measures to eliminate or mitigate adverse environmental consequences.

Title II, Chapter Seven, Article 73 –

The State will apply precautionary and restrictive measures to activities that could lead to species extinction, destruction of ecosystems, or the permanent alteration of natural cycles. The import of organisms and organic and inorganic material that may ultimately alter the national genetic heritage is prohibited.

Title II, Chapter Seven, Article 74 –

Individuals, communities, peoples and nations are entitled to benefit from the environment and natural resources that allow them to live well. Environmental services are not subject to appropriation; their production, delivery, use and development are regulated by the state.

For an analysis of international efforts respecting one aspect of this issue, see Anthony D'Amato & Sudhir Chopra, *Whales: Their Emerging Right to Life*, 85 AM. J. INT'L L. 21 (1991).

3. Academic literature on the subject of human rights and the environment continues to grow. Major texts include the following: HUMAN RIGHTS APPROACHES TO ENVIRONMENTAL PROTECTION (Alan Boyle & Michael Anderson eds., 1996); ENVIRONMENTAL RIGHTS: LAW, LITIGATION & ACCESS TO JUSTICE (Sven Deimann & Bernard Dyssli eds., 1995); THE RIGHT OF THE CHILD TO A CLEAN ENVIRONMENT (Agata Fijalkowski & Malgosia Fitzmaurice eds., 2000); ELI LOUKA, BIODIVERSITY AND HUMAN RIGHTS (2002); LINKING HUMAN RIGHTS AND THE ENVIRONMENT (Romina Picolotti & Jorge Daniel Taillant eds., 2003); HUMAN RIGHTS, SUSTAINABLE DEVELOPMENT AND THE ENVIRONMENT (Antonio Augusto Cançado Trindade ed., 1995); LAURA WESTRA, ENVIRONMENTAL JUSTICE AND THE RIGHTS OF UNBORN AND FUTURE GENERATIONS (2006); HUMAN RIGHTS IN NATURAL RESOURCE DEVELOPMENT (Donald Zillman, Alastair Lucas & George (Rock) Pring eds., 2002). *See also* LINDA A. MALONE & SCOTT PASTERNACK, DEFENDING THE ENVIRONMENT: CIVIL SOCIETY STRATEGIES TO ENFORCE INTERNATIONAL ENVIRONMENTAL LAW, ch. 1 (2004).

Four important pamphlets are also worth noting: Boston Research Center, *Human Rights, Environmental Law and the Earth Charter* (1998); Council of Europe, *Manual on Human Rights and the Environment: Principles Emerging from the Case-Law of the European Court of Human Rights* (2006); Council of Europe, *Environmental Protection and the European Convention on Human Rights* (2005); Aaron Sachs, *Eco-Justice: Linking Human Rights and the Environment* (Worldwatch Paper 127, 1995).

A collection of international and regional decisions and cases exists in 3 INTERNATIONAL ENVIRONMENTAL LAW REPORTS: HUMAN RIGHTS AND ENVIRONMENT (Cairo A.R. Robb ed., 2001).

For early treatments of the synergies between the legal corpus of human rights and the environment see *Earthcare: The Human Right to a Sound Environment*, 1 EARTH L.J. 187 (1975); James L. Elsman, *Proposed First Amendment to the United Nations Charter: Right to a Natural Environment*, 12 CODICILLUS 42 (1971); W. Paul Gormley, *The Right to a Safe and Decent Environment*, 28 INDIAN J. OF INT'L L. 90 (1974); Gregory Ho, *United Nations Recognition of the Human Right to Environmental Protection*, 2 EARTH L.J. 225 (1976); Frits Hondius, *Environment and Human Rights*, 41 Y.B. ASS'N ATTENDERS & ALUMNI HAGUE ACAD. INT'L L. 68 (1971).

For an extensive early bibliography, see Donald K. Anton, *International Environmental Law Bibliography*, in ENVTL. L. REP. ch. 3 (1992), *available at* http://www.elr.info/International/ielpre92/CHAP03.pdf.

For a collection of international instruments, see MAGUELONNE DÉJEANT-PONS, HUMAN RIGHTS AND THE ENVIRONMENT: COMPENDIUM OF INSTRUMENTS AND OTHER INTERNATIONAL TEXTS ON INDIVIDUAL AND COLLECTIVE RIGHTS RELATING TO THE ENVIRONMENT IN THE INTERNATIONAL AND EUROPEAN FRAMEWORK (2002).

C. When Rights Conflict

People First, River Second...
Sydney Morning Herald, Nov. 8, 2006, at 1
Stephanie Peatling

Draining wetlands and cutting environmental flows to the Murray-Darling river system will be considered by a team of public servants ordered by state and territory leaders to find ways to guarantee towns, farmers, and irrigators do not run out of water.

A meeting between the Prime Minister, John Howard, and four state leaders yesterday heard the drought was much worse than a one-in-100-year event; it was more like one in 1,000 years.

But scientists and environmentalists say the needs of the river system must be considered alongside those of the people relying on its water.

Professor Gary Jones, the head of the Co-operative Research Centre for Freshwater Ecology, said: "Whilst I recognise these are tough times for everyone concerned, we have to be careful because it won't do any good to damage the river system in the long term."

The executive director of the Australian Conservation Foundation, Don Henry, said any decision to forgo water for environmental purposes would be a "total admission of failure despite years and years of warning."

"We have to look after farmers that are suffering but the really crucial thing is we have to speed up work to bring the Murray-Darling back to health," he said.

After yesterday's summit, permanent water trading between [New South Wales], Victoria, and South Australia will begin on January 1 next year. The leaders said this would free up water by dealing with the problem of overallocation of water licences. They agreed to work out how to secure water supplies for 2007–08. A group of state and federal public servants was asked to draw up plans for how this will be done. It will report back by the middle of December.

Mr. Howard said he would not direct them to consider specific proposals but "it will be apparent what some of the options are, including the draining of wetlands and allowing some of the dams to dry up. They will be considered. The purpose is to get a warts-and-all action plan. It's serious and we all understand that."

Water efficiency measures and alternative water source projects, such as desalination, will be prioritised when the Federal Government hands out funds from its $2 billion National Water Initiative. . . .

A scientific report, commissioned by a similar group of ministers in 2002, found 1,500 gigalitres of water – enough to fill Sydney Harbour three times – was needed to address the decline of the whole Murray-Darling system. A meeting of ministers the following year agreed to find a third of that water to sustain five key environmental sites along the river system, but none of that water has yet been returned to the river. . . .

The human need for fresh water demonstrates that, when push comes to shove, rights for the environment per se may become untenable, at least when protection of the environment qua environment impinges on provision of basic human needs. The next reading, a keystone in the literature on rights for the environment, takes a more environmentally accommodating approach.

Should Trees Have Standing? Towards Legal Rights for Natural Objects, 45 S. Cal. L. Rev. 450, 464, 466, 473–74 (1972) Christopher Stone

It is not inevitable, nor is it *wise*, that natural objects should have no rights to seek redress in their own behalf. It is no answer to say that streams and forests cannot have standing because streams and forests cannot speak. Corporations cannot speak either; nor can states, estates, infants, incompetents, municipalities or universities. Lawyers speak for them, as they customarily do for the ordinary citizen with legal problems. One ought, I think, to handle the legal problems of natural objects as one does the problems of legal incompetents – human beings who have become vegetable. If a human being shows signs of becoming senile and has affairs that he is *de jure* incompetent to manage, those concerned with his well being make such a showing to the court, and someone is designated by the court with the authority to manage the incompetent's affairs. . . .

On a parity of reasoning, we should have a system in which, when a friend of a natural object perceives it to be endangered, he can apply to a court for the creation of a guardianship. . . .

. . . If, for example, the Environmental Defense Fund should have reason to believe that some company's strip mining operations might be irreparably destroying the ecological balance of large tracts of land, it could, under this procedure, apply to the court in which the lands were situated to be appointed guardian. As guardian, it might be given rights of inspection (or visitation) to determine and bring to the court's attention a fuller finding on the land's condition. If there were indications that under the substantive law some redress might be available on the land's behalf, then the guardian would be entitled to raise the land's rights in the land's name, *i.e.*, without having to make the roundabout and often unavailing demonstration . . . that the "rights" of the club's members were being invaded. Guardians would also be looked to for a host of other protective tasks, e.g., monitoring effluents (and/or monitoring the monitors), and representing their "wards" at legislative and administrative hearings on such matters as the setting of state water quality standards. . . .

As far as adjudicating the merits of a controversy is concerned, there is also a good case to be made for taking into account harm to the environment – in its own right. As indicated above, the traditional way of deciding whether to issue injunctions in law suits affecting the environment, at least where communal property is involved, has been to strike some sort of balance regarding the economic hardships *on human beings*. . . .

The argument for "personifying" the environment, from the point of damage calculations, can best be demonstrated from the welfare economics position. Every well-working legal-economic system should be so structured as to confront each of us with the full costs that our activities are imposing on society. Ideally, a paper-mill, in deciding what to produce – and where, and by what methods – ought to be forced to take into account not only the lumber, acid and labor that its production "takes" from other uses in the society, but also what costs alternative production plans will impose on society through pollution. . . .

Questions and Discussion

1. Christopher Stone, like Justice William O. Douglas, who followed Stone's reasoning in dissent in *Sierra Club v. Morton*, 405 U.S. 727, 741–55 (1972), generally has been in the legal minority when it comes to rights for the environment itself. Is it just that Stone and Douglas were too far ahead of the thinking of the majority? Consider the following from Thomas Merton, a Trappist monk influential during the development of the early environmental movement:

> Some beavers, in Connecticut, have built a dam and are flooding a lot of roads. The highway department of the county where this disaster is taking place has brought the matter to court, asking for the power to remove these audacious beavers.
>
> The Attorney General, in Hartford, hands down a decision making this possible, by saying that the rights of rational animals are inferior to those of the state, and therefore the rights of beavers are just that much more inferior to the rights of the state. Therefore, the beavers have to get out.
>
> On the other hand, the beavers also have rights, therefore "these little animals should be compensated." They will be removed to another home, where they will be "able to perform and exercise their natural skill and ability." . . .
>
> This hierarchy, *beavers: rational animals: state*, is just abstract enough to make me feel disturbed by the whole story. I wish they had kicked out the beavers without such a lot of talk: because obviously no court is going to bother with the rights of beavers anyway, not really. How can a court make itself responsible for dealing out justice to beavers? . . .
>
> I have no doubt the beavers have certain natural "rights," but I have every doubt whether those rights can be protected by a human court of law as if they were the rights of human beings. And what are the rights of these beavers? Life, liberty, and the pursuit of happiness? The court said they had a right to perform and exercise their natural skill and ability. . . .
>
> I don't suppose even a State supreme court could go so far as to puzzle over the rights of rabbits in relation to foxes. Let us take it for granted that irrational animals have rights before men who are capable of making judgments, but not before other animals.
>
> Even if beavers have rights (which I don't doubt), it doesn't do you any good to talk about them, or to guarantee them, or anything of the sort. On the contrary, to make a big argument over the rights of beavers is a suspicious enough joke to cast doubt on the validity of the rights of men.
>
> There is one very simple way of dealing with beavers: not according to rights, but according to love. . . .
>
> But admittedly a law court is not designed to take care of questions insofar as they can be decided by love: that is the difference between a court and a confessional. So let it pass.

THOMAS MERTON, THE SECULAR JOURNAL OF THOMAS MERTON 11–13 (1959). Who has the better argument, Stone or Merton?

2. As you will learn in greater detail in Chapters 5 and 7, the Committee on Economic, Social, and Cultural Rights established under the International Covenant on Economic, Social, and Cultural Rights (ICESCR) has issued the General Comment on the Human Right to

Water. General Comment No. 15 (2002), U.N. Doc. E/C.12/2002/11 (Jan. 20, 2003) on the Right to Water under articles 11 and 12 of the ICESCR states: "The human right to water is indispensable for leading a life in human dignity. It is a prerequisite for the realization of other human rights.... The human right to water entitles everyone to sufficient, safe, acceptable, physically accessible, and affordable water for personal and domestic uses. An adequate amount of safe water is necessary to prevent death from dehydration, to reduce the risk of water-related disease and to provide for consumption, cooking, personal, and domestic hygienic requirements." *Id.* at ¶¶ 1–2.

3. The foregoing reading highlights the tension that can arise when human needs and environmental protection come into conflict in the context of access to water and the protection of watercourses and drainage basins by ensuring adequate environmental flows. These tensions raise difficult questions about the purpose and function of linking human rights with the environment. For instance, when environmental human rights and other human rights come into conflict, which is to prevail? On what basis?

THE RIGHTS OF NATURE: A HISTORY OF ENVIRONMENTAL ETHICS 131–133 (1989)
Roderick Frazier Nash

After Stone and Douglas located the conceptual door to the rights of nature in 1972, philosophers and legal theorists were quick to push it open. One indication of their growing interest was the application of John Rawls's *Theory of Justice* (1971) to environmental issues.... [Lawyers] who read Rawls in the 1970s seized on his theories to make a case for nature. The more conservative simply contended that Rawls could be understood as supporting a moral obligation to resist environmental degradation in the interests of future generations of humans.

Others extended Rawls more radically. In 1974, Laurence H. Tribe, a Harvard law professor, proposed adding nature to the contractual arrangements between people that Rawls presumed occurred at the beginning of any society.... Noting Christopher Stone's work, Tribe pointed to the recent growth of the idea that "persons are not the only entities in the world that can be thought to possess rights." Although it was possible to understand this concept as a "legal fiction," Tribe preferred to see it as evidence of the capacity of humans to develop "new possibilities for respect and new grounds for community."... Tribe wrote about a "spirit of moral evolution" that had recently spread to include blacks and women and was beginning to incorporate animals, plants, and might, in the ... future include "canyons ... a mountain or a seashore."...

The same idea surfaced in an even more specific form in David F. Favre's 1979 proposal in the journal *Environmental Law* to enact a new constitutional amendment on behalf of wildlife. Favre, a professor at the Detroit College of Law, correctly questioned the widespread use of the phrase "animal rights." As a lawyer Favre knew that the interests of non-human creatures might be defended as a category of human rights, but in existing legal systems they as yet possessed no rights [of their own]. Favre sought to correct this with an addition to the document that provided the basis for rights in the American political system. His suggested amendment to the Constitution state that "all wildlife ... shall have the right to a natural life." Humans must not "deprive any wildlife of life, liberty or habitat without due process of law." Favre explained that human survival interests could override wildlife rights, and he knew enough about ecology to recognize that in the absence of natural predation people might need to check excessive wildlife populations in the interests of those creatures. Thus his system tended to focus on the rights of species and habitats rather than individual organisms. Like Stone, he understood that humans would be the actual defenders of inarticulate wildlife in courts....

Questions and Discussion

1. How do Tribe and Favre advance Stone's argument? Is the protection of the environment (or aspects of the environment) to be preferred when conflicting human interests, needs, or rights come into conflict with such protection? If such a preference is not automatic, what sort of balancing test would be appropriate to employ? Under what circumstances would environmental interests prevail over human interests, if ever?

2. How would the theories presented herein apply in the context of the diminishing water in the Murray-Darling Basin in Australia, discussed in the newspaper excerpt? Would they protect environmental flows of the river? If so, on what basis? Do you need more facts? If so, what would you want to know?

II. Human Rights Approaches to Environmental Protection

A. *Mobilizing Human Rights for the Environment*

Environmental Rights,
in PEOPLES' RIGHTS 187–194
(Philip Alston ed., 2001)
Dinah Shelton

Human rights law and environmental protection interrelate at present in four different ways. First, those primarily interested in the environment utilize or emphasize relevant human rights guarantees in drafting international environmental instruments. They select from among the catalogue of human rights those rights that can serve the aims of environmental protection, independent of the utility of such protection for the enjoyment of other human rights. Recognizing the broad goals of environmental protection, the emphasis is placed on rights such as freedom of association for members of non-governmental environmental organizations and the right to information about potential threats to the environment, which may be used for nature protection nor necessarily related to human health and well-being. The weakness of compliance mechanisms in nearly all international environmental agreements raises questions about the short-term effectiveness of this method in achieving the goals of environmental protection, at least when compared with recourse to the more developed human rights supervisory machinery.

A second approach invokes existing human rights law and institutions, recasting or applying human rights guarantees when their enjoyment is threatened by environmental harm. This method is unreservedly anthropocentric. It seeks to ensure that the environment does not deteriorate to the point where the human right to life, the right to health, the right to a family and private life, the right to culture, the right to safe drinking water, or other human rights are seriously impaired. Environmental protection is thus instrumental, not an end in itself. . . . With a focus on the consequences of environmental harm to existing human rights, this approach can serve to address most serious cases of actual or imminently-threatened pollution. The primary advantage it offers, compared to pursuing the environmental route, is that existing human rights complaint machinery may be invoked against those states whose level of environmental protection falls below that necessary to maintain any of the guaranteed human rights. From the perspective of environmental protection, however, this human rights approach is deficient because it generally does not address threats to non-human species or to ecological processes. . . .

The third approach aims to incorporate the environmental agenda fully into human rights by formulating a new human right to an environment that is not defined in purely anthropocentric terms, an environment that is not only safe for humans, but one that is ecologically-balanced and sustainable in the long term. Various international efforts have been undertaken in this direction . . . and some have proved successful. Nonetheless, despite the inclusion of ecological concerns in various formulations of the right, strict environmentalists continue to object to the anthropocentrism inherent in taking a human rights approach to environmental protection. In addition, the notion of a right to environment has met resistance from others who claim that the concept cannot be given content, who assert that the inherent variability of environmental conditions and qualities means no justiciable standards can be developed.

Finally, a fourth approach questions claims of rights in regard to environmental protection, preferring to address the issue as a matter of human responsibilities. Several projects to draft declarations of human responsibilities are underway and most have a strong environmental focus. Even some human rights texts that proclaim environmental rights balance these with a statement of human duties. . . .

The interrelationship of human rights and environmental protection is undeniable. First, the enjoyment of internationally recognized human rights depends upon environmental protection. Without diverse and sustained living and non-living resources, human beings cannot survive. The problem can be demonstrated by the example of freshwater. Only 2 per cent of the water of the earth is accessible for human use. Any loss of water resources, especially pollution of underground aquifers poses dangers for generations to come. According to the U.N. Water Council between 5 million and 10 million people die each year as a result of polluted drinking water, most of them women and children in poverty. Severe water shortages exist in 26 countries and by 2050, two-thirds of the world's population could face water shortages. Sixty per cent of the world's drinking water is located in just 10 countries and much of it is polluted. Freshwater shortages are already raising tensions and threaten to be a cause of future interstate conflicts. Air pollution, contaminated soil and loss of food sources add to the problems of health and survival. Maintenance of the earth's cultural diversity, in particular the preservation of indigenous peoples and local communities, requires conserving the areas in which they live.

In turn, environmental protection is enhanced by the exercise of certain human rights, such as the right to information and the right to political participation. Unlike the field of human rights, where most violations are committed by state agents, environmental harm largely stems from actions of the private sector. Effective compliance necessitates knowledge of environmental conditions and norms. In addition, local communities play a vital role in preserving the resources upon which they depend. Allowing those potentially affected to participate in decision-making processes concerning harmful activities may prevent or mitigate the threatened harm and contribute to public support for environmental action, as well as lead to better decisions. In the event the activity goes forward and harm is suffered, remedies can provide for restoration or remediation of the damaged environment.

Despite a common core of interest, the two topics remain distinct. Environmental protection cannot be wholly incorporated into the human rights agenda without deforming the concept of human rights and distorting its programme. Ecologists are concerned with the preservation of biological diversity, including species not useful or even harmful to humans, as well as with ecological processes whose full significance may not be fully known or understood. The central concern is the protection of nature because of its intrinsic value, not because its protection will provide immediate benefits to humans.

Further, not all human rights are immediately relevant to environmental protection, e.g., the right to a name and the right to marry are not crucial to achieving the environmental agenda. From the human rights perspective, neither does it appear that the enjoyment of these rights is negatively affected by environmental harm.

The view that mankind is part of a global ecosystem may reconcile the aims of human rights and environmental protection, because both ultimately seek to achieve the highest quality of sustainable life for humanity within existing natural conditions. Potentially conflicting differences of emphasis still exist, however, because the essential concern of human rights law is to protect individuals and groups alive today within a given society, an aim that might be referred to as intragenerational equity. Environmental law adds to the goal of human rights the additional purpose of sustaining life globally by balancing the needs and capacities of present generations of all species with those of the future; it is thus also concerned with intergenerational equity and inter-species equity. Together, the three aims can be seen to comprise the concept of environmental justice. Clearly, the broad protection of nature at times may conflict with preservation of individual rights, such as the right to property. It is not surprising, then, that international environmental law and international human rights law have at times placed emphasis on different components of environmental protection and human rights.

The proposal to guarantee a right internationally to an environment of a specified quality raises additional considerations. Some argue that it is unlikely that environmental protection will be accepted as a human right and efforts in this direction divert attention from other more worthy causes. Yet, laws often respond to perceived social problems by restraining the exercise of power and establishing agreed norms of public conduct. Viewed from this perspective, laws protecting human rights respond to threats to human dignity and existence by upholding the immutable foundations of human rights as recognized in international instruments. Formulations of rights reflect emerging social values. Thus, as environmental protection comes to be perceived as fundamental to human dignity and well-being, it moves towards the requisite acceptance. The growing awareness of the breadth and depth of the environmental crisis can be seen in increasing recourse to rights language.

An immediate, practical objective of international human rights law is to gain international recognition of specific human rights. Successfully placing personal entitlements within the cat-egory of human rights preserves them from the ordinary political process. Rights may thus sig-nificantly limit the political will of a democratic majority, as well as a dictatorial minority. The limitation on domestic political decisions is an important consequence of elaborating a right. In the environmental field, the high short-term costs involved in many environmental protection measures often make environmental decisions unpopular with economically affected communi-ties. The recognition that environmental protection is a core value and right can be particularly valuable in countering this disapproval and ensuring that the long-term needs of humanity are not sacrificed to short-term interests. . . .

Ultimately, the definition of a right to environment must refer to substantive environmental standards that quantitatively regulate harmful air pollution and other types of emissions. Some see this as undermining any claim that environmental protection can be considered a human right. In their view, it cannot be considered inalienable, defined as the impermissibility of derogations, because the constant reordering of socio-economic priorities involved in setting environmental policies precludes its having a fixed character. However, this same evolution and reordering of priorities and values is seen in respect to other internationally recognized human rights: edu-cation, equality and non-discrimination – especially in regard to what constitutes impermissible distinctions and therefore who benefits from the right – and in defining what constitutes cruel, inhuman or degrading treatment or punishment. Few if any rights are absolute or fixed in content and most are subject to limitations and even suspensions or derogations. Recognizing a particular interest or claim as a human right is one means of establishing an order or priority, in setting the right above other competing interests and claims not deemed rights.

To say that environmental entitlements have been and will continue to be susceptible to restric-tions for the sake of other, socio-economic objectives, such as ensuring continued "development" or "saving jobs[,]" is to establish the conclusion as a criterion. If there is no right to a safe and healthy environment, environmental considerations will be balanced against other social interests on an equal basis. Alternatively, if there is both a right to development and a right to environment, the same balancing of juridically equal interests is required. Only if one of the interests is designated a right does it have what [Ronald Dworkin refers to as a "trumping" effect requiring that the balance be presumptively resolved in its favour.

Although establishing emission or quality standards requires extensive international regulation of environmental sectors based upon impact studies, such regulation is by no means impossible. Adoption of quality standards demands extensive research and debate involving public participation, but substantive minima are a necessary complement to the procedural rights leading to informed consent. Otherwise, a human rights approach to environmental protection would be ineffective in preventing serious environmental harm.

Establishing the content of a right through reference to independent and variable standards is often used in human rights, especially with regard to economic entitlements, and need not be a barrier to recognition of the right to a specific environmental quality. Rights to an adequate standard of living and working conditions and to social security are sometimes further defined in international accords such as the European Social Charter or Conventions and Recommendations of the International Labour Organization. States implement these often flexible obligations according to changing economic indicators, needs and resources. The "framework" of the human rights treaty contains the basic guarantee to be supplemented by further international, national and local regulations, laws and policies.

A similar approach could be utilized to give meaning to a right to environment. Both the threats to humanity and the resulting necessary measures are subject to constant change based on advances in scientific knowledge and conditions of the environment. Thus, it is impossible for a human rights instrument to specify precisely what measures should be taken, i.e., the products that should not be manufactured or the precise balance of land uses. These technical details can be negotiated and regulated through international environmental norms and standards, where the necessary measures to implement the right to environment can be determined by reference to independent environmental findings and regulations capable of rapid amendment. The variability of implementing demands imposed by the right to environment in response to different threats over time and place does not undermine the concept of the right, but merely takes into consideration its dynamic character.

Finally, it is claimed that there are political risks to recognizing a right to environment because different conditions require different solutions and it "might turn into an extremely effective legal platform for internationalizing national decision-making in areas that represent the core of traditional state sovereignty." This is true, but all international human rights law involves an invasion of "the core" of traditional state sovereignty. The law exists precisely for that reason and reflects the fact that the content of the reserved domain of states is constantly evolving. The sovereignty or domestic jurisdiction objection was raised by Mexico when the Inter-American Human Rights Commission considered a complaint regarding alleged election fraud; by the former Soviet Union when the United Nations began to discuss its failure to permit the emigration of Soviet Jews; by South Africa in response to criticisms of apartheid. States have always been reluctant to adopt and implement international human rights norms. They have done so in response to public pressure, especially from non-governmental organizations, which became convinced that decisions about how governments treat human beings should not be exempt from international scrutiny and accountability.

Questions and Discussion

1. The four interrelationships between human rights law and environmental protection are explicitly recognized in a landmark document, and accompanying report, prepared by Fatma Zohra Ksentini, special rapporteur of what was known as the Sub-Commission for the Promotion and Protection of Human Rights (it was abolished in 2007 when the U.N.

Human Rights Commission was replaced by the Council). The Document is known as the Declaration of Principles on Human Rights and the Environment and is considered more fully in Case Study V in the online Case Studies that accompany this text.

2. Like the readings in the introductory section, Professor Shelton highlights tensions raised by linking human rights and the environment. She suggests that the tensions might be reconciled by recognizing that both fields "ultimately seek to achieve the highest quality of sustainable life for humanity within existing natural conditions." Is this reasoning persuasive? What if existing conditions are insufficient?

Human Rights Approaches to Environmental Protection: An Overview, *in* HUMAN RIGHTS APPROACHES TO ENVIRONMENTAL PROTECTION 2–10 (A. Boyle & M. Anderson eds., 1996) Michael R. Anderson

1. Relationship between Human Rights and the Environment

Upon . . . inspection, the precise relationship between human rights and environmental protection is far from clear. The relationship may be conceived in two main ways. First, environmental protection may be cast as a means to the end of fulfilling human rights standards. Since degraded physical environments contribute directly to infringements of the human rights to life, health, and livelihood, acts leading to environmental degradation may constitute an immediate violation of internationally recognized human rights. The creation of a reliable and effective system of environmental protection would help ensure the well-being of future generations as well as the survival of those persons, often including indigenous or economically marginalized groups, who depend immediately upon natural resources for their livelihoods.

In the second approach, the legal protection of human rights is an effective means to achieving the ends of conservation and environmental protection. Thus the full realization of a broad spectrum of first and second generation rights would constitute a society and a political order in which claims for environmental protection are more likely to be respected. A more ambitious variant of this view provides that there is and should be an inalienable human right to a satisfactory environment, and that legal means should exist to enforce this right in a consistent and effective manner. Put in these terms, it is no longer the impact of the environment on other human rights which is the law's focus, but the quality of the environment itself. Expressed in this qualitative way, a right to a decent environment has much in common with other claims, such as sustainable development or intergenerational equity, and suffers comparable problems of subjectivity, definition, and relativity[,] which make it inherently problematic for any notion of universal human rights.

2. Human Rights Approaches to Environmental Protection

. . . If we accept that the concept of human rights is viable (some reject the idea altogether), and that rights may be extended to human goods beyond the core liberties (some argue that this dilutes the impact of human rights), then it remains to be seen how human rights approaches add anything to existing arrangements for environmental protection. . . . [T]here appear three main approaches: first, mobilizing existing rights to achieve environmental ends; secondly, reinterpreting existing rights to include environmental concerns; and thirdly, creating new rights of an explicitly environmental character. . . .

(a) Mobilizing Existing Rights

. . . [H]uman rights norms which are already protected under international instruments and domestic constitutions play an important role in environmental protection. It may even be argued that existing rights, if fully realized, are so robust in themselves that proposals for new environmental rights are at best superfluous and at worst counter-productive. The body of existing rights at the international level is detailed and comprehensive. An argument may be made out that if activists devoted their attentions to securing additional ratifications and campaigning for effective implementation of existing international instruments, rather than dreaming up and promoting new standards, then environmental protection will follow automatically. Whether this argument stands or falls depends upon the scope of existing rights, and these may be considered in their entirety, including: first, civil and political rights; secondly, economic, social and cultural rights; and thirdly, the right to self-determination.

(i) Civil and Political Rights

... [T]he importance of civil and political rights lies in their ability to foster an environmentally-friendly political order. The realization of such rights – including the rights to life, association, expression, political participation, personal liberty, equality, and legal redress – goes a long way toward enabling concerned groups to voice their objection to environmental damage. These guarantees are necessary preconditions for mobilizing around environmental issues and making effective claims to environmental protection. The converse is also true, for serious damage to the physical environment is frequently accompanied by repression of activists and denial of access to information....

(ii) Economic, Social and Cultural Rights

While civil and political rights may contribute to environmental protection principally through guarantees of process and participation, the second generation rights contribute mainly through substantive standards of human well-being. Existing human rights treaties ... already contain provisions on the right to health, the right to decent living conditions, and the right to a decent working environment – all of which may bear directly upon environmental conditions. The right to health, for instance, if approached rigorously, requires the state to take steps to protect its citizens from a poisonous environment and to provide environmental goods conducive to physical and mental well-being. In many cases, this will require policies to prevent environmental degradation. The right to health may be linked to environmental protection in another way, too.... [P]olicies designed to protect humans may also protect flora, fauna, and ecological processes as a consequence. For example, measures designed to guard against the radiological exposure of humans will also protect non-human species from exposure.

In addition to the right to health, other second generation rights may also be used to environmental ends. The right to education may help to raise environs mental awareness, and equip disadvantaged groups with the skills required to combat ecological damage in political fora.... [I]lliteracy can leave the marginalized unable to work the levers of the existing political system.... [Violation of] cultural rights can [also] accompany environmental degradation. So the right to participate in cultural life, if properly protected, may require the state to preserve the physical environments upon which certain cultures depend.

Like civil and political rights, the second generation rights offer considerable promise, particularly since international supervision of economic, social, and cultural rights involves the monitoring of general policies with regard to human welfare. Also, because such rights are related directly to human well-being and capacity building, rather than simply the character of the political order, they are conceptually closer to environmental matters than first generation rights....

(iii) Right to Self-Determination

At another level, the collective right to self-determination ... may contribute to environmental protection in two ways. Where local environments were subjected to imperial priorities under colonialism, the acquisition of statehood has liberated peoples to manage their own resources.

The concept of permanent sovereignty over natural resources, which emerged from the post-war drive for self-determination, aimed to assert a degree of economic self-determination which might provide states with the legal space in which environmentally degrading foreign investment could be restrained. Efforts in this area largely failed, however, and even in those areas where they did succeed through nationalization of foreign property, it is hardly clear that post-colonial governments exercised greater environmental sensitivity than the private firms they supplanted.

There is a second approach to self-determination which does not assert that absolute sovereignty should be granted, but rather that ethnically distinct groups should be accorded a degree of political and economic autonomy within existing state boundaries. This is one of the justifications for recognizing the rights of indigenous peoples. . . . [I]ndigenous or tribal peoples [may be] particularly vulnerable to environmental degradation. . . . Existing international law, including the [International Labour Organization's] Indigenous and Tribal Peoples Convention of 1989, may apply in such circumstances. . . . [T]he Convention requires party States to safeguard the environment in co-operation with the peoples concerned, but does little to afford actual rights to indigenous groups. There is a tendency in international law to treat indigenous groups as objects of protection rather than legal subjects capable of exercising rights. However, it is only with effective rights that such groups may act to protect their immediate environments from outside depredation. The key to mobilizing the right to self-determination for indigenous peoples or other distinct populations is finding an effective procedural remedy under existing legal regimes. . . .

(b) Reinterpretation of Existing Rights

While existing human rights standards do provide some weapons which can be used in environmental protection, there is an argument that they are inadequate so long as conventional means of interpreting and applying such rights are followed. On this argument, the mere mobilization of existing rights norms will not satisfy environmental needs. Instead, existing rights must be reinterpreted with imagination and rigour in the context of environmental concerns which were not prevalent at the time existing rights were first formulated.

Established human rights standards which do not directly touch upon environmental issues may house an implicit relevance capable of juridical development. The right to life, for example, may be deemed to be infringed where the state fails to abate the emission of highly toxic products into supplies of drinking water. If enforcement bodies explicitly recognize such links, then environmental criteria may be incorporated overtly into the monitoring and enforcement of the right to life. This approach has been developed probably most fully by the Indian judiciary, which . . . has been active for more than a decade in fashioning environmental rights out of a more conventional catalogue of constitutional rights. The expansion has been explicit, so rather than the courts simply examining environmental matters in the course of enforcing the right to life, the judges have stated directly that the right to life includes the right to live in a healthy environment, a pollution-free environment, and an environment in which ecological balance is protected by the state. . . .

. . . Apart from the rights to life and health, which other settled rights might lead to direct environmental protection? Several candidates emerge. First, the right to equality may be read widely to include the right to equal access to, and protection of, environmental resources. . . . [A] profound inequality of exposure to environmental degradation is a consequence of economic and political inequalities. Affluence and poverty create different environmental problems, and it is sometimes the case that only the problems of affluence are addressed in state policy. An effective right to procedural equality would help in such circumstances, but some judicial enforcement of a right to substantive equality, as has occurred in India, holds far greater potential. Secondly, the right to freedom of speech may easily be extended to encompass the right to voice objections to environmental damage. . . . Thirdly, although the right to property has conventionally been conceived mainly in terms of political and economic protection, it is amenable to a thoroughgoing environmental reinterpretation. [B]ut . . . the right to property may be a two-edged sword since, although it may be used to protect customary land rights and the environmental quality of land in general, it may also be used by private developers to inhibit the creation of national parks and conservation areas. It is precisely for this reason that a full reinterpretation of the right, rather than a mere mobilization of it, is necessary for environmental protection. Fourthly, religious rights may have an environmental dimension. . . . [T]he right to religious practice and profession [may also serve] as a possible vehicle [for environmental protection].

(c) New Human Rights [for] Environmental Protection

Although existing human rights, if fully mobilized, may offer a great deal to global and local environmental protection, there are good reasons to suspect that they will fall short of meeting desired ends. Established human rights standards approach environmental questions obliquely, and lacking precision, provide clumsy tools for urgent environmental tasks. It may be argued that a comprehensive norm, which relates directly to environmental goods, is required. . . . [Scholars] are divided on whether new environmental rights, if desirable, should be mainly procedural or substantive in character.

(i) Procedural rights

. . . [There are] a range of procedural rights at both the international and domestic levels which are relevant to environmental protection. These include: the right to information, including the right to be informed in advance of environmental risks; the right to participate in decision-making on environmental issues at both the domestic and international level; the right to environmental impact assessment; the right to legal redress, including expanded *locus standi* to facilitate public interest litigation; and the right to effective remedies in case of environmental damage.

A procedural or participatory approach promises environmental protection essentially by way of democracy and informed debate. The enthymeme in this argument is that democratic decision-making will lead to environmentally friendly policies. The point remains to be demonstrated, but one argument in its favour is that in creating legal gateways for participation, it is possible to redress the unequal distribution of environmental costs and benefits. Thus marginalized groups who currently suffer the most deleterious effects of environmental degradation – including women, the dispossessed, and communities closely dependent upon natural resources for their livelihood – can be included in the social determination of environmental change. If the people who make the decisions are the same as those who pay for and live by the consequences of the decisions, then we go a long way toward protecting the environment.

There is another argument in favour of a procedural right, rather than a substantive right, which is this: because the desired quality of the environment is a value judgment which is difficult to codify in legal language, and which will vary across cultures and communities, it is very difficult to arrive at a single precise formulation of a substantive right to a decent environment. Therefore, the more flexible, honest, and context-sensitive approach is to endow people with robust procedural rights which will foster open and thoroughgoing debate on the matter. Much the same argument applies to the pursuit of sustainable development.

(ii) Substantive rights

Yet even if the virtues of procedural rights are acknowledged, they may not provide adequate protection of environmental goods. If we take this view, then an argument for a substantive right to a satisfactory environment may emerge. . . . [A] substantive right can provide more effective protection, and may play a role in defining and mobilizing support for environmental issues.

Advocates of substantive environmental rights may not trust procedural rights alone for the simple reason that even if procedural or participatory rights are fully realized, and perfectly distributed throughout civil society, it is entirely possible that a participatory and accountable polity may opt for short-term affluence rather than long-term environmental protection. Democracies are entirely capable of environmental destruction, and may even be structurally predisposed to unfettered consumption. Indeed, the industrial democracies of the North, with their liberal rights-based legal systems, are disproportionately responsible for much environmental damage, including the consumption of finite resources and the emission of greenhouse gases. The point is that procedures alone cannot guarantee environmental protection. But if substantive rights are contemplated, then urgent questions of definition and application arise. . . .

Questions and Discussion

1. In January 2002, the U.N. High Commissioner for Human Rights and the Executive Director of the U.N. Environment Programme jointly convened an expert group to review and assess progress that had been achieved since the 1992 U.N. Conference on Environment and Development (UNCED) in promoting and protecting human rights in relation to environmental questions and in the framework of Agenda 21. The expert group made a number of recommendations in connection with both substantive and procedural rights outlined by Anderson herein. *See Meeting of Experts on Human Rights and the Environment, Final Text* (Jan. 16, 2002), *available at* http://www2.ohchr.org/english/issues/environment/environ/conclusions.htm.

2. Professor Anderson mentions that economic, social, and cultural rights are second-generation human rights. Some scholars have described the evolution and development of human rights in terms of three generations, although other scholars reject the classification system as inaccurate and overly simplistic. The first generation of human rights is said to constitute long-standing civil and political rights opposable against the state and includes rights such as the right to life. The second generation of rights emerged more recently and is concerned with economic, social, and cultural welfare. The so-called third generation of human rights (also called solidarity rights or people's rights, on account of their group nature) involves collective claims and is imperfectly recognized. As we will further explore, the substantive right to live and work in an environment of a certain minimum quality can fall into either the second or the third category. The African Charter treats it as a collective people's right, whereas the Protocol of San Salvador includes it as one of the economic and social rights guaranteed by the treaty. For an examination of the controversy surrounding the terminology of third generation rights, see Philip Alston, *A Third Generation of Solidarity Rights: Progressive Development or Obfuscations of International Human Rights Law?*, 29 NETHERLANDS INT'L L. REV. 307 (1982).

3. Professor Anderson notes that one value of a human right is "that it is available as a moral trump card precisely when legal arrangements fail." Do you agree? Is a moral trump card a sufficient substitute for binding legal norms requiring or prohibiting state action? Are there any moral trump cards available in environmental law?

B. *Critiques and Responses*

In addition to the problems outlined herein, Professor Günther Handl has made one of the most fulsome critiques of the wisdom of developing and promoting a human right to the environment.

Human Rights and the Protection of the Environment, *in* Economic, Social & Cultural Rights: A Textbook 303–15 (A. Eide, C. Krause & A. Rosas eds., 2d ed., 2001)
Günther Handl

[The] relationship between protection of the environment and protection and promotion of human rights . . . is a complex one that is often misunderstood. . . . [C]ontrary to frequently voiced opinion, it is far from clear that the objectives underlying human rights and environmental protection norms are either fully complementary or truly indivisible. . . .

. . . [A]scription of specific human rights characteristics to a given environmental claim and recourse to established human rights processes for vindication of such a claim would, it is suggested, make a difference in outcome. However, . . . the underlying assumption that such a right provides a "complementary alternative to traditional international environmental law" is not self-evidently correct.

. . . In short, the core controversy in the long-standing debate over human rights and the environment relates to the existence and utility of environmental human rights proper. . . .

2. Is There a Substantive Environmental Human Right in Contemporary International Law

. . . [E]vidence of actual supportive state practice . . . remains an essential element of any argument that a given human rights claim is recognized by general [i.e., customary] international law. When analysed from this perspective, the case for a substantive environmental human right at the international level is a weak one.

At a global level, neither the Universal Declaration of Human Rights (1948) nor the 1966 International Covenant on Economic, Social and Cultural Rights (CESCR) readily lends support to the idea of an existing substantive human right to a clean environment. . . . Article 25 of the Declaration is not generally deemed to have come to reflect today customary international law [and] merely refers to everybody's "right to a standard of living adequate for the health and well-being of himself and of his family." Article 12, paragraph 2(b) of the CESCR commits States Parties to improve "all aspects of environmental and industrial hygiene." But this reference is . . . "so narrow that it scarcely addresses environmental protection at all."

One of the earliest characterizations of an entitlement that truly sounds like an environmental human rights can be found instead in Principle 1 of the 1972 Stockholm Declaration on the Human Environment. . . . However, at the time of its adoption, Principle 1 . . . was understood not to reflect customary law. . . .

. . . The issue of [a human right to the environment] was brought into sharp focus again in 1994 [with the Ksentini Report]. With the aim of facilitating consolidation at United Nations level of "the right of a satisfactory environment," the report included a set of draft Principles on Human Rights and the Environment that postulated the existence of a generic human right to a "secure, healthy, and ecologically sound environment." While the draft Principles have since been the subject of various procedural resolutions by the United Nations Commission on Human Rights, . . . the fact remains that the Commission has thus far taken no substantive action on them. Today, the outlook for its formal adoption remains cloudy.

At the regional level, the European human rights system does not recognize – either expressly or implicitly – a substantive environmental human right. Proposals of such an entitlement have yet to find acceptance as an operational normative concept. There are, however, other regional human rights treaties that do endorse the concept of a substantive environmental human right [(i.e., The African Charter on Human and Peoples' Rights and the American Convention on Human Rights). The African] formulation . . . has been criticized for latent ambiguities concerning the entitlement's meaning and scope, one of them stemming from the inherent potential for conflict between its environmental protection and development objectives. Operationally, the right is conceptualized not as a programmatic entitlement, but as one that would be effective immediately.... Given the socio-economic realities of Africa, this stipulation is clearly an implausible one ...

The other regional regime of interest in the inter-American system.... It is by no means certain ... that the institutions involved in supervising domestic implementation and international protection of [San Salvador Protocol Article 11's right to live in a healthy environment] might be willing or able to use Article 11 effectively as a vehicle for pushing an environmental protection agenda....

Notwithstanding an exceedingly slim evidentiary basis in international practice ... for a general acceptance of a substantive right to a clean, healthy or satisfactory environment, in her final report, Special Rapporteur Ksentini optimistically concludes that "[a]t the regional and universal level, recognition of the right to a satisfactory environment as a human right is reflected ... in the related normative developments." ... In the final analysis, what is required is evidence of unequivocal support by states. Such evidence, however, is lacking. Evidence of this kind is also unlikely to be forthcoming in the near future.... A summary of the key arguments militating against the postulation of a substantive environmental human right [follows].

The credibility of the claim that a generic, substantive – as against procedural – environmental human right could be an effective vehicle for the protection of the environment is based on two premises. One, it assumes that because they would be couched in human rights terms, environmental protection objectives would be accorded priority over other competing socio-economic objectives. Two, it assumes that, if necessary, such human rights-based objectives could also be vindicated through recourse to established human rights processes and institutions. Tested against these implicit assumptions, it is difficult to see how a substantive environmental human right, if viewed as a third-generation ... right, could be an effective tool in the above sense. Such a "right" would commonly be understood to imply a corresponding commitment of states, international organizations and others to work cooperatively towards the realization of the environmental objectives concerned. By definition[,] such a "right" hardly evinces the quality of a truly normative concept that would determine priorities among competing social, economic or political goals. For the same reason, namely its inherently defective normative quality, and quite apart from the problem that such an environmental entitlement's contents is non-specific, it would not be routinely invo[c]able in any international human rights *fora*....

If, on the other hand, the proposed substantive environmental human right is understood to represent aspects of a first generation, a second generation right, or to represent a mix thereof, its application in practice would be intrinsically problematical because of the notion's latent ambiguity, that is, indeterminacy of its contents.... [A]ny ad hoc attempt at establishing criteria for the evaluation of states' compliance with their obligations flowing from the generic environmental human right would be fraught with political and technical difficulties. It would raise questions about the proper division of labour between human rights and environmental institutions, as well as the appropriate *locus* of decision-making, at the international as against the national level. In other words, such an entitlement, if recognized, could lead to a redrawing of traditional demarcation lines between domestic and international jurisdiction by turning the right into a platform for "internationalizing" national decision-making in sensitive core areas of traditional state sovereignty. By the same token, such a generic right offers a powerful tool for socio-economic engineering by human rights decision-making bodies, thus raising justified concerns about the technical adequacy and, indeed, democratic legitimacy of a human rights-based approach to vindicating collective environmental interests.

It is true, of course, that indeterminacy is not a feature intrinsically incompatible with the notion of human rights, either of civil and political or economic, social and cultural rights. Thus, to redress the problem of normative ambiguity that could serve as a subterfuge for states' inaction in realizing the entitlement concerned, the idea of a "core content" of economic, social and cultural rights was first advanced in the 1980s. It was endorsed in 1990 by the Committee on Economic, Social and Cultural Rights as "a minimum core obligation to ensure the satisfaction of, at the very least, minimum essential levels of each of the rights incumbent upon every State party." Similarly, the notion of a "minimum threshold" approach to assessing states' compliance with their obligations has gained support as a means of implementing economic, social or cultural human rights of a vague or ill-defined nature. Drawing on these developments, it has been suggested that a generic environmental human right could be accorded normative specificity in similar fashion by reference to pertinent international environmental quality standards. However, this method of filling the definitional gaps in some of the established economic, social and cultural rights does not readily work also for a new environmental human right. Unlike the former established rights, most of which are, to begin with, more narrowly circumscribed, any definitional refinement of the latter holds exceedingly broad social, economic and political implications, in short, has true cross-sectoral ramifications. . . .

These and other concerns over a generic international environmental human right – such as over its anthropocentric bias, its possible application in the form of differential local standards inconsistent with the presumed universality of human rights, its preventive function, as well as its possible redundancy – all illustrate the concepts problematical nature. Rejection of the present-day utility of a generic, substantive environmental human right does not, however, imply a denial of the fact that human rights instruments have significant operational implications for environmental protection purposes. The opposite is true, of course. Environmental concerns are routinely being redressed incidentally – *par ricochet*, so to speak – by application of established human rights norms. . . .

Questions and Discussion

1. In addition to the problems mentioned by Professor Handl, a human right to the environment has also been seen to have the following disadvantages: (1) a right to environment will not guarantee that disadvantaged groups benefit from this strategy, as it does not include economic and political reform; (2) a right to environment can displace other forms of legal remedy that are better suited to environmental issues, such as national tort and administrative laws; and (3) a right to environment will likely attract overt opposition from polluters and national governments. Michael R. Anderson, *Human Rights Approaches to Environmental Protection: An Overview, in* Human Rights Approaches to Environmental Protection 22–23 (Alan Boyle & Michael R. Anderson eds., 1996). How would you respond to these critiques? Recall Professor Schroeder's discussion of the advantages and disadvantages of the tort and regulatory approaches in Chapter 1. The following extract provides other counterarguments.

Is the Human Right to Environment Recognized under International Law? It Depends on the Source,
12 Colo. J. Int'l Envtl. L. & Pol'y 1, 31–37 (2001)
(footnotes omitted)
Luis E. Rodriguez-Rivera

Criticisms regarding the elaboration of the human right to environment have paralleled those received by other new or emerging rights. The most thorough critique of the *right to environment* (substantive component of the *expansive right of environment*) was made by Günther Handl, who concluded that the proposition of a generic international environmental entitlement was highly questionable.... A human rights approach to environmental protection, including the articulation of a substantive *right to environment*, has been tagged with the following disadvantages: (1) a simple *right to environment* may not address the complex and technical issues present in the environmental *problématique*; (2) a *right to environment* merely addresses the social symptoms and does not solve the structural causes of environmental degradation, such as the relationships of political economy; (3) a *right to environment* does not guarantee that disadvantaged groups will benefit from this strategy as it does not include economic and political reform; (4) a *right to environment* may displace other forms of legal remedy which are better suited to environmental issues, such as national tort and administrative laws; and (5) a *right to environment* may attract overt opposition from polluters and national governments.

These criticisms are flawed.... [A] human rights approach to environmental protection and the elaboration of the substantive *right to environment* does not imply that it is the *only* or *best* approach for global environmental protection.... Efforts should be made in all relevant areas. An obvious gap exists today in the protection of human life and dignity from threats associated with environmental degradation, especially when such threats are a consequence of actions or inactions taken by an individual's own national government. This is where a human rights approach to environmental protection is the most effective strategy to achieve such protection....

A second objection to the substantive component of the *expansive right to environment* that Handl raised relates to the intrinsic relativity or uncertainty due to its lack of definition. In this context, cultural relativism has been identified as a problem in implementing the substantive component of the *expansive right to environment*, but, as stated before, this is the same objection that has been raised with other economic, social, and cultural rights (e.g., right to an adequate standard of living, right to health, right to education). Nonetheless, the problem of ambiguity is not fatal since tribunals are today in a position to effectively expand the content of the *right to environment*. A problem related to the uncertainty surrounding the definition of the substantive component of the *expansive right to environment* is that this right would be non-justiciable. However, this criticism is meritless. In addition to the fact that the *right to environment* is justiciable in tribunals, international human rights law recognizes that an international system for the implementation and supervision of states' compliance with human rights obligations is sufficient to satisfy the requirement of enforceability....

Another criticism expressed by Handl was that the substantive *right to environment* would be difficult to conceptualize as an inalienable or non-derogable human right since environmental protection involves a complex balancing and ordering of socio-economic priorities. Thus, Handl argued that "[e]nvironmental entitlements have been and will continue to be susceptible to restrictions for the sake of other, socio-economic objectives, such as ensuring continued 'development' or 'saving jobs.'" Shelton accurately responds to this criticism by stating that it merely establishes "the conclusion as a criterion." Since the establishment of the *expansive right to environment* would have the "trumping" effect referred to above, the susceptibility that Handl perceives exists against environmental protection policies would be effectively curtailed. Furthermore, it is inaccurate to rely on hierarchical terms when discussing the existence of human rights since the "international community as a whole has neither established a uniform list of non-derogable rights nor ranked non-derogable rights ahead of derogable rights ... unless, of course, its status as a peremptory norm of general international law is recognized."

Handl expressed three more objections to the establishment of the substantive component of the *expansive right to environment*: the anthropocentric nature of human rights, the redundancy in this approach with international environmental law, and the inevitable debasing of the human rights currency.... This article earlier concluded that by incorporating the intrinsic value of the environment into the definition of the *expansive right to environment*, the criticisms that the *right to environment* is inherently flawed because of its anthropocentric approach are answered. But, this response only relates to the substantive level of the anthropocentricity objection. Alan Boyle has suggested that the implications of the argument for anthropocentricity are also structural in nature:

> They point to a need for integration of human claims to a decent environment within a broader decision-making process, capable also of taking account of the competing interests of future generations, other states and the common interest in common spaces and wildlife preservation; in other words, for a balancing of polycentric interests through international co-operation and supervisory institutions.

Although Boyle is hesitant to conclude that the integration and balancing of environmental concerns within human rights supervisory and judicial institutions is an achievable exercise, there is not a persuasive enough reason to conclude otherwise. Of course, the structural or decision-making process related to the anthropocentricity argument necessitates a different focus and expertise in those integrating and balancing human and ecological interests; however, this is true of any technical area of international law, such as international trade, among others.

Regarding the redundancy between the human right to environment and international environmental law, Handl explained that:

> [T]he proposal of a generic environmental human right, to the extent that it is driven by a desire to "open up" the international environmental decision-making process, or to ensure better monitoring and supervision of states' environmentally sensitive activities at home, diverts attention from the task of building upon already existing structures and mechanisms or institutionalizing a cross-sectional global environmental review mechanism; it would result in duplicative efforts without ever coming close to bringing about the same environmental benefits as would, for example, efforts spent on enhancing the formal status of NGOs within existing fora and processes, or on establishing a global environmental review process.

In agreeing with Handl's redundancy argument, Boyle elaborated that "given the now extensive scope of international law and policy, and [its] intrusion into all aspects of environmental protection, including the reserved domain of domestic sovereignty, what is left for a substantive human right to a decent environment to do that has not already been done?" Again, the *expansive right to environment* must be seen as complimentary to international environmental law and not as a parallel or alternative scheme. The establishment of the human right to environment would fill a gap still open in international environmental law. That is, the protection of human life and dignity from threats associated with environmental degradation, especially when such threats result as a consequence of actions or inactions taken by an individual's own national government. The implementation of the *expansive right to environment* would inevitably benefit from human rights and international environmental law's supervisory mechanisms, but this does not necessarily mean that duplicative efforts or institutions would result from the human rights approach to environmental protection.

Moreover, to argue that environmental protection is best served by efforts to develop procedures and access to these procedures ignores that the implementation of the procedural approach (*environmental rights*) would be ineffective without the existence of a substantive *right to environment*. The procedural approach by itself may serve as an enforcement mechanism for the implementation of the *expansive right to environment*. However, *environmental rights* do not, and cannot, by themselves protect human life and dignity from threats associated with environmental degradation. In elaborating that substantive international environmental norms must limit the discretion of those national political bodies whose final decisions on projects and actions affect the environment, Shelton accurately noted:

> Procedural guarantees of information and participation can prove insufficient to protect the environment if a fully informed society decides to sacrifice environmental quality in order to advance economic or cultural considerations. Such decisions can have harmful consequences for other states or the international commons. . . . In sum, environmental rights, understood as procedural guarantees of information and political participation which have been reformulated and extended specifically to cover environmental decisions, can effectively protect the environment only if coupled with substantive international regulation. However, such a linking of procedural rights to substantive environmental norms may go farther by leading to the creation of a new human right: the right to environment.

Related to the normative relativity objection previously discussed, Handl argued that the ambiguity in the definition of the *right to environment* would undermine the notion of human rights by devaluing the "symbolic value of the traditional human rights label," thus resulting in the "debasing of the human rights 'currency.'" Although most writers agree that a dynamic approach should be adopted in the development of human rights concepts, there is a fear that to draw up "international shopping lists" of rights would threaten the integrity and enduring significance of the human rights tradition. It is difficult to disagree with this general proposition. However, this proposition should not be used to curtail *a priori* any discussions regarding the establishment or existence of new human rights. New rights must measure to certain minimum standards in order to gain international recognition. The *expansive right to environment* has been found to qualify as a human right under these minimum standards.

The strongest objection raised by Handl, as well as traditionalist legal scholars in general, is that the proponents of the human right to environment have failed to support their claims by producing solid positive evidence. More specifically, Handl concluded:

> In sum, international practice does not support the claim of an existing generic human right to a healthy environment. The evidentiary basis that proponents of such a right relie [*sic*] upon is simply too narrow or normatively too weak to lend itself to that major normative extrapolation that a human right to a healthy environment would undoubtedly represent.
>
> This evidentiary objection is built on the following assumptions: (1) the *expansive right to environment* has not found any express affirmation in any binding or effective international legal instrument; (2) the *expansive right to environment* finds its support in *indirect, normatively "soft," or limited in scope* evidence; (3) the incorporation of the *expansive right to environment* in national constitutions and legislation is irrelevant absent evidence of actual domestic practice consistent with the same; and (4) current state practice does not support the *expansive right to environment*. These assumptions are consistent with the traditionalist proposition that international norms are required to evince state consent, be it through binding treaties or state practice. However, as discussed before, the sources of international norms are the object of debate among international legal scholars. Thus, in order to respond to Handl's evidentiary objection, the sources which should be considered in evaluating the existence of new human rights, particularly that of the human right to environment, must be examined.

This casebook considers in detail the legal existence of a number of environmental rights – both international and national – including the general human right to a healthy environment. Throughout your study of these materials, ask yourself whether you agree with Professor Handl or whether the sources of positive law might support Rodriguez-Rivera.

III. The Environmental Justice Dimension

Learning from Environmental Justice: A New Model
for International Environmental Rights,
24 STAN. ENVTL. L.J. 71, 78–87 (2005)
Hari M. Osofsky

Advocates seeking to address environmental harm to humans at an international level must contend with the inherently multifaceted nature of such harms. Although the various negative impacts implicate several areas of law, they do not fit neatly into any one of those areas. No matter how the problems are characterized – as violations of international environmental law, human rights law, or anti-discrimination law – the description of them will be incomplete.

International environmental law primarily focuses on environmental damage, rather than on its impact on human beings. Its ultimate end is certainly to serve human purposes; both treaty and customary international environmental law aim to solve problems that matter to people, and our species' survival may depend on our ability to find more sustainable approaches. But the focus of environmental treaties is primarily on constraining environmentally deleterious behavior, rather than on preventing injuries to people. The Montreal Protocol, for instance, creates a structure for limiting ozone depleting emissions, rather than for minimizing the injuries that might result from the pollution. Similarly, the principles of international environmental law primarily address prevention of environmental damage and responsibility for remediation; even the obligation not to cause environmental harm centers on a state's broad obligation not to use its territory in a way that causes damage in another state – as encapsulated in the *Trail Smelter* arbitration – rather than on a more specific duty to avoid human impact.

In contrast, international human rights law focuses entirely upon human impacts, with little concern for the environmental dimension of the problem. Only two binding human rights treaties contain a right to a healthy environment – the African Charter on Human and Peoples' Rights and the San Salvador Protocol – so most human rights litigation brought to address environmental harm involves an application of general rights, such as rights to life and health, to the environmental harm. In fifteen of the sixteen case studies, for example, the claimed rights violations included the environment as part of the factual situation causing the harm; the rights themselves had no specific connection to the environment.

The international law preventing discrimination, which can be viewed as a subset of the human rights regime, has a similarly limited focus. Environmental harm is relevant to a claim under the International Convention on the Elimination of All Forms of Racial Discrimination, the anti-discrimination provisions of other binding international agreements, or the customary international law prohibiting racial discrimination only to the extent that the harm constitutes discrimination. Nondiscriminatory harm falls outside of the parameters of concern, and thus a large portion of environmental harm to humans is not within the ambit of this area of law. . . .

States' sovereignty and equality serve as foundations for international law. These principles emerged from the classical Westphalian conception of the state's absolute authority over its people and territory. Although both international environmental and human rights law provide exceptions to the Westphalian concept of sovereignty, they differ fundamentally in the extent to which they interfere with state sovereignty when acts have no direct transnational consequences. The human rights regime allows greater intrusion upon states' internal affairs and thus reaches situations that international environmental law cannot.

1. International Environmental Law

The international community began to put limits on environmental sovereignty well before the modern treaty regime emerged following the Stockholm Conference in 1972. In addition to the early conventions on migratory wildlife and shared watercourses, the 1941 *Trail Smelter* arbitration reinforced the notion that compensation must accompany state behavior that produces environmental damage beyond its borders. The international environmental treaty regime that exploded following the 1972 conference at Stockholm addresses problems ranging from regulating the use of Antarctica and outer space to controlling marine, river, and air pollution to protecting endangered species. By the 1980s a "second generation" of environmental treaties had emerged to address more complex global issues such as ozone depletion, climate change, shared use of the ocean, movement and disposal of hazardous waste, and biodiversity. Additional declarations reinforced the principles that undergird these agreements and the customary international law that emerged from them. The limitations created by these agreements attempt to address not only transboundary but also global commons harms.

Despite these incursions upon traditional sovereignty, international environmental law constrains international intervention when behavior lacks transboundary or global commons impacts. This principle has been enunciated in both the Stockholm and Rio Declarations and throughout the scholarly literature. Although the international community certainly would prefer that states follow good internal environmental practices, international environmental law provides no basis for external intervention when the harm is purely domestic.

2. *International Human Rights Law*

International human rights law, including its protections against discrimination, challenges traditional notions of sovereignty by viewing a state's treatment of its citizens as of international rather than merely domestic concern. Universal jurisdiction provides the formal legal basis for intervention into another state's serious human rights violations when other jurisdictional ties, such as territoriality or nationality, do not exist, on the theory that some behaviors are so unacceptable that they are every nation's concern regardless of where they occur or who they involve.

In the aftermath of World War II's genocidal atrocities, a number of states recognized genocide, war crimes, crimes against peace, and crimes against humanity as crimes of an international nature and created a structure for international and national prosecutions of such violations. Following these trials and the creation of the United Nations, whose charter explicitly promotes human rights, members of the international community adopted numerous human rights documents and treaties covering an ever-widening range of rights.

Some of these human rights treaties have created international and regional tribunals to hear claims of human rights abuses suffered within state parties' borders. In addition, treaties addressing violations of slavery, apartheid, terrorism, and torture have contained increasingly explicit international criminalization and universal jurisdiction provisions. Some nations' courts – particularly those of the United States and other common law countries, have adjudicated human rights claims – based mainly on customary international law, on universal jurisdictional grounds.

These various mechanisms have not provided certain redress for victims of human rights violations. Only states – and not individuals – have standing to bring claims before the International Court of Justice. The existing international and regional human rights tribunals do accept petitions from private parties, but have limited enforcement mechanisms. Similarly, United States courts have had difficulty collecting the large judgments awarded for human rights violations abroad.

Moreover, prior to the establishment of the International Criminal Court, international prosecutions of human rights violations were entirely ad hoc, arising out of a desire to address the atrocities committed during the conflicts of World War II, the former Yugoslavia, and Rwanda. These ad hoc tribunals, like the fledgling International Criminal Court, have focused primarily on the prosecution of international criminals rather than on the redress of victims' grievances. That prosecutorial focus has limited their utility as forums in which victims can address environmental harms.

Despite these limitations, international human rights law provides a potential avenue of redress for victims of environmental damage.... [V]ictims of environmental abuse have been able to obtain positive judgments from international and regional human rights tribunals. Nations retain permanent sovereignty over their natural resources, but face checks on how they treat the people who are affected by resource use. If environmental damage constitutes a human rights violation, grounds exist for a claim under international law, even when the harm occurs solely within a state's territorial jurisdiction. The international human rights regime thus provides a mechanism for limiting state sovereignty when environmental harm impacts human beings....

Advocates have used human rights law to bring actions before various tribunals on behalf of victims of environmental harm when other legal options would have led to sovereignty roadblocks. Their efforts and the resultant decisions have been inconsistent, however, with different claims made on similar facts. For instance, in United States federal courts, when plaintiffs brought claims for severe environmental harm caused by resource-extractive industries, grounds ranged from the right to life and health in some cases to international environmental law, cultural genocide, and genocide in another.

Although a combination of opportunism and litigation strategy may at least partially explain the lack of coordinated approaches, these inconsistencies may also result from the lack of a coherent legal regime. Because of the dearth of treaties that contain a binding right to a healthy environment, most claims of environmental rights violations apply general rights – those with no specific connection to the environment – to the particular factual contexts. Moreover, the range of arguments made in the regional and international forums, which reflect differences in the treaties upon which they depend, present an unclear path for future claimants.

These divergent approaches are not only confusing but also potentially damaging to plaintiffs. In the United States Alien Tort Statute context, for example, the Second Circuit used the Fifth Circuit's rejection of genocide and cultural genocide claims in *Beanal v. Freeport-McMoran* as persuasive authority to undermine claims based on the rights to life and health in *Flores v. Southern Peru Copper Corporation*.

Questions and Discussion

1. Linkages between human rights and the environment are restricted neither to international law nor to developing countries. Environmental burdens in the United States, for example, have in many instances been disproportionately borne by minority, disadvantaged, or impoverished communities that have little political or economic power. Indeed, in many countries, not all are guaranteed an environment of equal quality or equal protection under environmental law. This failure of the law has led to the growth of the environmental justice movement and efforts to apply municipal civil and political rights to environmental discrimination. *See* CLIFFORD RECHTSCHAFFEN & EILEEN GAUNA, ENVIRONMENTAL JUSTICE: LAW, POLICY & REGULATION (2d ed., 2009); ENVIRONMENTAL LAW AND JUSTICE IN CONTEXT (Jonas Ebbesson & Phoebe Okowa eds., 2009).

2. Professor Shelton comments that environmental justice might be thought of comprising three distributive justice aims: intragenerational equity, intergenerational equity, and interspecies equity. She makes an explicit link between environmental justice and human rights. She writes:

   Recently, the concept of environmental justice has come to play an important role in international environmental law and policy as a means of integrating human rights and environmental law, even as the content and scope of the term remains under discussion. It is increasingly recognized that favorable natural conditions are essential to the fulfillment of human desires and goals. Preservation of these conditions is a basic need of individuals and societies. Environmental justice encompasses preserving environmental quality, sustaining the ecological well-being of present and future generations, and reconciling competing interests. There is also an element of distributional justice, as it has become clear that the poor and marginalized of societies, including the global society, disproportionately suffer from environmental harm.

Environmental justice emphasizes the environment as a social good rather than a commodity or purely economic asset. The focus is on the proper allocation of social benefits and burdens, both in the present and in the future. Thus, it requires the equitable distribution of environmental amenities and environmental risks, the redress and sanctioning of environmental abuses, the restoration and conservation of nature and the fair allocation of resource benefits. The "polluter-pays" principle itself is based on the concept of environmental justice, as it encompasses the notion that those who engage in and profit from activities that damage the environment should be liable for the harm caused. On the most fundamental level, environmental justice can be seen as a term that encompasses the twin aims of environmental protection and international protection of human rights.

Dinah Shelton, *The Environmental Jurisprudence of International Human Rights Tribunals, in* Linking Human Rights and the Environment 23 (Romina Picolotti & Jorge D. Taillant eds., 2003).

3.   International environmental law includes several equitable concepts in addition to that of polluter pays. The principle of common but differentiated responsibilities, enunciated in the 1992 Rio Declaration and incorporated into major Multilateral Environmental Agreements (MEAs) such as the U.N. Framework Convention on Climate Change and the Convention on Biological Diversity, is based on recognition of the varying responsibilities of states for contributing to present-day environmental problems as well as differential capacity to mitigate the resulting harm. *See* Dinah Shelton, *Equity, in* Oxford Handbook of International Environmental Law (Dan Bodansky, Jutta Brunnee & Ellen Hay eds., 2007). Agreements such as the International Whaling Convention also refer to the interests of future generations.

IV. Recognition of the Rights Related to the Environment in Law

Principles of International Environmental Law 294–297 (2003)
Philippe Sands

. . . [S]ome non-binding and widely accepted declarations supporting the individual right to a clean environment have been adopted. Although the 1982 World Charter for Nature does not expressly provide for the individual's right to a clean environment, it was one of the first instruments to recognise the right of individuals to participate in decision-making and have access to means of redress when their environment has suffered damage or degradation. The 1989 Declaration of [T]he Hague on the Environment recognised "the fundamental duty to preserve, the ecosystem" and "the right to live in dignity in a viable global environment," and the consequent duty of the community of nations vis-à-vis present and future generations to do all that can be done to preserve the quality of the environment. The U.N. General Assembly has declared that "all individuals are entitled to live in an environment adequate for their health and well-being"; and the U.N. Commission on Human Rights has affirmed the relationship between the preservation of the environment and the promotion of human rights. More specifically, the Sub-Commission on Prevention of Discrimination and Protection of Minorities has considered the relationship between human rights and the movement and dumping of toxic and dangerous products and wastes, supported further study, and considered the relationship between the environment and human rights in the context of chemical weapons. The Sub-Commission has also received reports on "Human Rights and the Environment" which analyse many of the key concepts and provide information on decisions of international bodies. More specifically, the U.N. Commission on Human Rights has declared that the movement and dumping of toxic and dangerous products endanger basic human rights such as "the right to the highest standard of health, including its environmental aspects." Efforts to further develop language on environmental rights continues under the auspices of several international institutions including the Council of Europe and the U.N. Economic Commission for Europe. Other efforts include the [International Union for the Conservation of Nature's (IUCN)] draft International Covenant on Environment and Development prepared by the IUCN's Commission on Environmental Law.

Many states have adopted national measures linking the environment and individual rights. The constitutions of about 100 states now expressly recognise the right to a clean environment. These constitutional provisions vary in their approach: they provide for a state duty to protect and preserve the environment; or declare the duty to be the responsibility of the state and citizens; or declare that the duty is imposed only upon citizens; or declare that the individual has a substantive right in relation to the environment; or provide for an individual right together with the individual or collective duty of citizens to safeguard the environment; or provide for a combination of various state and citizen duties together with an individual right.

What are the practical consequences of recognising the link between international human rights law and the protection of the environment? The question may be addressed in the context of the distinction which has been drawn in international human rights law between economic and social rights, and civil and political rights. The nature and extent of economic and social rights determines the substantive rights to which individuals are entitled, including in particular the level below which environmental standards (for example, in relation to pollution) must not fall if they are to be lawful. Civil and political rights, which are also substantive in nature and sometimes referred to as "due process" rights, determine procedural and institutional rights (such as the right to information or access to judicial or administrative remedies). International environmental law has progressed considerably in building upon existing civil and political rights and developing important new obligations, most notably in the 1998 Aarhus Convention which provides for rights of access to information, to participation in decision-making, and to access to justice. While economic and social rights have traditionally been less well developed in practice, recent judicial decisions indicate that international courts and tribunals are increasingly willing to find violations of substantive environmental rights.

Questions and Discussion

1. Are references to environmental protection or the right to a safe and healthy environment sufficiently widespread in constitutional law to call either one a "general principle of law recognized by civilized nations" in the wording of article 38(1)(c) of the Statute of the International Court of Justice? Would it help to have a further breakdown of the more than one hundred constitutions to which Sands refers?

2. Every year the public interest environmental law firm, Earthjustice, produces a report on human rights and the environment for what is now the U.N. Human Rights Council (until 2006, the Commission on Human Rights); see further Chapter 3. These reports elaborate developments and trends at the international and municipal levels, including case studies. The reports can be viewed at http://www.earthjustice.org/our_work/issues/international/human_rights/human-rights-report/international_human_rights_full_report.html.

3. A collection of environmental constitutional provisions from around the world are found on a Web site maintained by the Environmental Law Alliance Worldwide, a group of public

interest environmental lawyers and scientists working across borders to protect the environment. See Environmental Law Alliance Worldwide, Australia – Comparative Constitutional Language for Environmental Amendments to the Australian Constitution, *available at* http://www.elaw.org/node/1512. A collection of U.S. state environmental constitutional provisions are found in Barry E. Hill, Steve Wolfson, & Nicholas Targ, *Human Rights and the Environment: A Synopsis and Some Predictions*, 16 GEO. INT'L ENVTL. L. REV. 359, app. A (2003).

3 An Introduction to Human Rights Origins and Theory

I. The Development of Human Rights

To appreciate the role of human rights in the cause of environmental protection, it is essential to understand the historical development and debates over human rights. The following readings highlight the essential features of human rights to prepare the way for more detailed consideration in subsequent chapters of how they relate to the environment.

A. *Introduction*

Historical Foundations of Human Rights and Subsequent Developments,
in 1 The International Dimensions of Human Rights 11–16
(Karel Vasak ed., 1982) (footnotes omitted)
Imre Szabo

For some authors, the origins of human rights go back to Greek antiquity[; for some, even further]. They consider that human rights should come under natural law. The classic example, taken from Greek literature, is that of Antigone: according to Sophocles, when Creon reproaches Antigone for having buried her brother despite her having been forbidden to do so, Antigone replies that she has acted in accordance with the unwritten and unchanging laws of heaven. In philosophy the general tendency is to view the problem of human rights – or more precisely that of man's natural rights (and it is to be noted that equating the one with the other obscures the problem at the level of theory) – in terms of the doctrine of stoicism.

It is more difficult to seek the origins of human rights in Roman law, although an attempt has been made to discover in Cicero's work certain ideas relating to this subject. On the one hand, Roman law postulated the existence of a natural law, that is to say, of man's natural rights: according to Ulpian, natural law is that which nature teaches to all living beings. But, on the other hand, this natural law is linked to the *jus gentium*, which has at least two meanings. It signifies first of all the rights of those who are not Roman citizens, and thus refers to those rights to which men are entitled wherever they go; it also represents international law at the same time.

It should not be forgotten, particularly when speaking of the present significance of human rights, that all that derives from the Graeco-Roman world relates to a system in which Aristotle recognized the legitimacy of slavery. In that world it was considered to be perfectly natural (and therefore in conformity with natural law) that there should exist radical social differences which exclude *ab ovo* the central idea of human rights: that of the equality of men.

It would be a grave mistake to attempt to trace back the origins of human rights to social systems which were not familiar with its basic condition governing the existence of human rights, namely, the idea of freedom and equality. It is not possible to project a new institution upon social relations which have been superseded, and to which it does not correspond. In order for human rights to appear as the general rule in society and for them to be felt both as a need and as a reality, it was indispensable for there to be basic social changes in the relations of production (and, more precisely, in the relations of ownership) within the previous social system – feudalism. Everyone's rights had to be recognized as being, in principle, equal with regard to ownership and the acquisition and enjoyment of property. True, the right to property had previously been regarded as a natural right, or in other words, as a fundamental and inalienable right of man, first by Aquinas, then later, more explicitly, by Grotius, who set this right outside the universe of natural rights. Grotius had asserted that the right to property had been "introduced by human will" and, so that we should not be offended, he invited us to understand and to consider our property as corresponding to natural law.

Two major ideas emerged from this line of reasoning, but both subsequently splintered off from their origins: these were the ideas of freedom and equality. The idea of freedom was that of free ownership, of the free possession of property, and to this was later added the idea of free enterprise, with all the other corollaries of freedom. But its origins should never be forgotten, for they account for its appearance and for its development.

As for the idea of equality, it too owes its origin, at least in part, to the appearance of a new type of ownership. It signified equality for all as regards the right to acquire property, but considering it more closely, its true origin turns out to be connected with the political idea of the State in the modern sense of the term. It also concerned equality in respect of participation in political life. Consequently, equality was, so to speak, a political idea and a political right, whereas freedom possessed an economic character, at least so far as its origins were concerned. According to modern political philosophy, every individual should possess equal rights in the life of the State. Subsequently, the notion of equality was made to apply to the whole of man, to all of man's abilities and all of his rights.

However, an important difference was to remain between freedom and equality: bound up with ownership, freedom was considered to be a right which the State could not restrict because it was an absolute right. This was not true of equality as it was regarded as a political right and, as such, it could be restricted by the State.

· · ·

By and large, the origins of human rights, in respect of positive law, are traced back to documents which appeared in recent centuries. According to this point of view – the upholders of which are few in number since the majority of authors consider human rights to be natural rights – human rights are contracts concluded by the State with the population and, first of all, with the nobility. These contracts are seen as preserving certain rights for men while preventing the State from interfering in the exercise of those rights. The legal force of these rights is seen as being founded (contrary to the conception of the theory of the contract founded on natural law) on the will of the State, or better still, in the circumstances of the period, on their recognition by the King.

· · ·

According to the most traditional conception of human rights, at the time that men passed from the primitive state to the social state they concluded a contract between themselves (the idea of which was first posited long before Rousseau), and by this contract they renounced part of their natural rights, which they had enjoyed in their free state, while preserving certain basic rights: the right to life, freedom and equality. The rights thus preserved constituted eternal and inalienable rights that every social and State system was obliged to respect. As for the origin of these rights, however, there are various differences to be found in the way in which the conception founded on natural law is set forth. The theory of the social contract is the product of the school of natural law which made its appearance in the [fifteenth and sixteenth] cent[u]ries. According to this school, human rights are bound up with man's basic nature from which they derive, and for which reason they constitute human rights.

According to another conception, which goes back to [John] Locke and his *Letters on Tolerance*, the starting point was tolerance in respect of other religions or, in other words, the right to profess any religion. Again, what is involved is a conception referring to natural law. Furthermore, this idea set the scene for the creation of the United States of America, considering that freedom of religion played an important part in this connection.

There do of course exist other conceptions of human rights, for instance that according to which human rights originated in human understanding. Conceptions of this kind were already subscribed to in the Middle Ages. Virtually all the feudal varieties of the natural law theory (which consider the omnipotence of the absolute monarch to be a matter of natural law) belong to this type of thinking, and the same is true of the Kantian theory of law, founded on reason. This theory, like all the others, is forced to start off from certain premises established *a priori* and from which it is possible to deduce human rights. We find these premises in the metaphysical character of the rights.

. . .

The French Declaration of the Rights of Man and of the Citizen of 1789 and other documents, which appeared subsequently, make a distinction between, on the one hand, the rights of man and, on the other, the rights of the citizen. Man in these texts appears as a being who is imagined to exist outside society, who is assumed to exist prior to society. As for the citizen, he is subject to the State's authority. On this account, the rights of man are natural and inalienable rights, while the rights of the citizen are positive rights, rights granted by positive law. Human rights are fundamental rights for the very same reason that they existed before the State, whereas the rights of the citizen are subordinate to and depend upon them.

Human Rights Genealogy, 66 FORDHAM L. REV. 301, 309–10 (1997)
Ruti Teitel

The international human rights founding story is one that is said to be *sua sponte*, a radical birthing, a discontinuous affair with only an ambivalent relation to preexisting rights theory. Nevertheless, consider the meaning of the idea of rights as being "born" in the mid-twentieth century, seemingly without preexisting rights for[e]bears? This representation as an immaculate conception preserves the natural law claims. Telling the story this way, as an extraordinary narrative that begins in the war's aftermath, represents international human rights in atomistic fashion, as somehow insulated from preexisting rights theory. The account also plays a role in distorting international human rights theory, generating tension and incoherence.

To some degree, the theoretical framework of international human rights rests awkwardly on preexisting theory. Historically, theories of consensus and the social contractarian tradition, predicated on assumptions about the relationship of the individual to the state, justified rights theory. Specifically, the political predicate of the state's role as protector and guarantor of individual rights provided justification for the theory. Indeed, this view drew from the social contract theory underlying the liberal state.

Postwar revelations tragically challenged these theoretic bedrock assumptions rendering them inappropriate for responding to the central Auschwitz problem of the twentieth century. The contractarian foundations of previous rights theory appeared inapt for comprehending the strange shift in recognition of the position of the modern state – from rights protector to rights violator. The shift could not help but have normative implications for understanding the political regimes as well as for related constitutional and other rights principles. With the move away from social contract as the source of rights authority, new questions arose regarding alternative sources of authority for international human rights and their constraints.

Questions and Discussion

1. The precursors to modern human rights discussed in the foregoing selections often appear based more on political or economic consideration than on humanitarian concern. Do you think the moral objections to inhumane practices and action can move to legal prohibitions without such political or economic predicates?

2. Many scholars perceive a gap between human rights theory and the ongoing violations of established human rights in practice. If certain actions are always prohibited no matter the surrounding circumstances, such as genocide, is it possible for human rights theory to explain the difference between the uniform support for the Genocide Convention and apparent violations in Rwanda and elsewhere? Is a concession to the role of politics and consent in the international legal system sufficient?

3. Professor Szabo wrote during the Communist rule and Soviet occupation of Hungary. Does this have any bearing on his views about the right to property and feudalism? Does the Cold War explain in part why there is no right to property in the U.N. covenants on human rights? As you will see, postwar divisions had a significant impact on the development of human rights law at the United Nations.

B. *Religious, Cultural, and National Legal Antecedents*

The extensive legal protection for human rights that currently exists in national, regional, and international law is the product of millennia of struggle by individuals concerned with human justice and well-being. *See* MICHELINE R. ISHAY, THE HISTORY OF HUMAN RIGHTS: FROM ANCIENT TIMES TO THE GLOBALIZATION ERA (2d ed., 2008). These visionaries have provided inspiration and guidance, some of them acting out of religious belief and duty, others out of compassion or a sense of responsibility. Perhaps holding sentiments attributed to Edmund Burke, they believed that "[a]ll that is necessary for the triumph of evil is that good men [and women] do nothing." THE YALE BOOK OF QUOTATIONS 116 (Fred R. Shapiro ed., 2006). Or, like Margaret Mead, they "never doubt[ed] that a small group of thoughtful, committed individuals can change the world, indeed it is the only thing that ever has." Robert B. Textor, *Introduction, in* MARGARET MEAD: THE WORLD AHEAD: AN ANTHROPOLOGIST ANTICIPATES THE FUTURE 12 (Robert B. Textor ed., 2005).

1. Religious Traditions

Religious scholars have often emphasized in one way or another that "all of the major religions of the world seek in one way or another to speak to the issue of human responsibility to others." PAUL GORDON LAUREN, THE EVOLUTION OF HUMAN RIGHTS: VISIONS SEEN 5 (1998). If one accepts a central tenet of most, if not all, religions – that every human being is sacred – then divine authority establishes the inherent value of every person. This common humanity means that every person has a high moral standing that requires appropriate consideration. *See generally* LEONARD SWINDLER, RELIGIOUS LIBERTY AND HUMAN RIGHTS: IN NATIONS AND IN RELIGIONS (1986). Of course, the theological doctrines of major religions do not speak of human rights per se but instead address ethical obligations and responsibilities toward others. At the same time, the rationales underlying these duties – equality, human dignity, and the sacredness of life – provide a foundation for the concept of human rights. *See generally* ROBERT TRAER, FAITH IN HUMAN RIGHTS: SUPPORT IN RELIGIOUS TRADITIONS FOR A GLOBAL STRUGGLE (1991).

For instance, the Hindi texts of the four Vedas, the Agamas, and Upanishads address the necessity for moral behavior, the importance of duty (dharma), and good conduct toward others suffering and in need. The Vedas in particular stress that all life is sacred, to be loved and respected. One is to strive for noninjury (ahimsa) – not causing pain to any living being at any time through the actions of one's mind, speech, or body. *See generally* Kana Mitra, *Human Rights in Hinduism, in* HUMAN RIGHTS IN RELIGIOUS TRADITIONS (Arlene Swidler ed., 1982).

In Judaism, the sacredness of the individual, endowed with equal worth and value, is important. Isaiah 58:6–7 teaches this: "undo the tongs of the yoke, let the oppressed go free[,] . . . share your bread with the hungry, and bring the homeless poor into your house." The Talmud can be read as addressing privacy and property rights, including the right to protection against property damage caused by pollution. (Bava Bathra Mishnah 2:4, 9; Babylonian Talmud, 2b and 6b). The ethics of the Torah contain "the principle that in the eyes of the law all people are equal (Leviticus 19:15) and that every person can demand his rights and that justice must be extended to all alike." SAMUEL BELKIN, IN HIS IMAGE: THE JEWISH PHILOSOPHY OF MAN EXPRESSED IN RABBINIC TRADITION 87 (1960).

Buddhism contains the injunction to respect all life and duties of understanding and charity. Achieving a sense of selflessness (anatman) is supposed to trigger feelings of universal compassion. Buddhism urges the renunciation of differences of caste and rank in favor of universal brotherhood and equality. Indeed, for Buddhists, nature is no more subordinate to human beings than human beings are to nature. Moral considerateness extends beyond humans and Buddhism might be seen as offering a kind of ecological view of life: "Under the commandment 'Not to destroy any life,' the rights of animals and plants are as equally recognized as are human rights." Masao Abe, *Religious Tolerance and Human Rights: A Buddhist Perspective, in* RELIGIOUS LIBERTY AND HUMAN RIGHTS IN NATIONS AND IN RELIGIONS 202 (Leonard Swidler ed., 1986).

Two pillars of belief in Islam are charity to others and lifting the burdens of those less fortunate. The Qur'an speaks to justice, the sanctity of life, freedom, mercy, compassion, and respect for all human beings. Islam teaches that all races are equal and that religious toleration should be guaranteed. Jews and Christians, for instance, should be protected from all insults and vexations; they should have equal rights and practice their religion as freely as Muslims do. *See generally* Rashid Ahmad Jullundhri, *Human Rights and Islam, in* UNDERSTANDING HUMAN RIGHTS: AN INTERDISCIPLINARY AND INTERFAITH STUDY (Alan D. Falconer ed., 1980).

A number of Confucian texts, including *Analects of Confucius, Doctrine of the Mean,* and *Great Learning*, stress that harmony and cooperation exist when duty and responsibility toward others leads to treating all human beings as having equal worth and to recognizing that, "within the four seas, all men are brothers." *Analects of Confucius*, bk. 12, 5, 113. A fundamental teaching, akin to the golden rule, is "do not impose on others what you yourself do not desire." *Analects*, bk. 15, 23. Individual self-actualization involves the pursuit of an altruistic path. "If there is righteousness in the heart, there will be beauty in the character. If there is beauty in the character, there will be harmony in the home. If there is harmony in the home, there will be order in the nation. If there be order in the nation, there will be peace in the world." *Great Learning*, cited in HUSTON SMITH, THE RELIGIONS OF MAN 181 (1958).

Human dignity, based on the idea that each person is a child of God, provides a Christian foundation for human rights. *See* JOHN WARWICK MONTGOMERY, HUMAN RIGHTS AND HUMAN DIGNITY: AN APOLOGETIC FOR THE TRANSCENDENT PERSPECTIVE (1986). Christianity holds a number of ethical imperatives that can be considered human rights predicates: A message of equality – "there is neither Greek nor Jew, nor slave nor free, nor man nor woman, but we are all one in Christ" (Galatians 3:28); respect for others – "whatever you would that men should do to you, do you even so to them" (Matthew 7:12); charity – "If there is a poor man among your brothers . . . do not be hardhearted or tightfisted toward your poor brother. Rather be openhanded and freely lend him whatever he needs" (Deuteronomy 15:7–8); toleration – "But love your enemies, do good to them, and lend to them without expecting to get anything back" (Luke 6:35).

Questions and Discussion

1. Robert Traer served as the executive director of the International Association for Religious Freedom (IARF) from 1990 to 2000, and in that capacity, he represented the work of the IARF on religious freedom at the United Nations. Traer notes that, in practice, religious commitment to human rights has not always been readily apparent:

    > Religious support for human rights may seem commonplace today, but this was not always the case. The growing consensus about human rights among religious leaders is a new development that has yet to be widely recognized and understood. This revolution in religious thought is exemplified by religious leaders' current support for the Universal Declaration of Human Rights, which was drafted by the U.N. Commission on Human Rights. . . .
    >
    > When the United Nations approved the declaration, only a few representatives of religious institutions were among the advocates of this historic statement. In particular, Lutheran theologian O. Frederick Nolde, who represented the Federal Council of Churches and was the first director of the Commission of the Churches on International Affairs (CCIA), lobbied very effectively for inclusion of human rights in the U.N. Charter and for specific provisions in the Universal Declaration.
    >
    > However, many religious communities expressed substantial opposition to the Universal Declaration. Islamic Saudi Arabia abstained from voting for the declaration because it did not explicitly acknowledge that all rights come from God. Many Protestants were also concerned that the declaration did not refer directly to God as the creator of rights. And while the papal nuncio in Paris, Monsignor Roncalli – later to become Pope John XXIII – aided René Cassin in drafting the declaration, the Vatican newspaper *Osservatore Romano* attacked it for failing to recognize the sovereignty of God.

    Robert Traer, *Religious Communities in the Struggle for Human Rights*, 105 CHRISTIAN CENTURY 835, 836 (1988). Why was there religious reluctance about human rights in the mid-twentieth century? Why does it appear today that all major religious traditions claim to have had a hand in the creation of contemporary human rights norms?

2. Some scholars believe that the exclusive moral foundation for human rights comes from religious ethics. Michael Perry, for instance, supposes that nothing outside of religious precepts can support the ethical platform of the human rights enterprise:

    > If, as I suspect, there exists no plausible nonreligious ground for the morality of human rights, then the growing marginalization of religious belief in many societies that have taken human rights seriously – in particular, in many liberal democracies – has a profoundly worrisome consequence: it may leave those societies bereft of the intellectual resources to sustain the morality of human rights.

    Michael J. Perry, *The Morality of Human Rights: A Problem for Nonbelievers?*, 133 COM-MONWEAL, July 14, 2006, at 16. Do you agree? Can you think of other wellsprings of moral authority for human rights? Consider the discussion of the cultural and philosophical roots of human rights below. Can reliance on these meet Perry's supposition of the need for a religious predicate?

3. Just as religion provides a moral backdrop to human rights, it has also been seen as providing (or, alternatively, as undermining) an ethical underpinning for shaping our attitude toward the natural world. Lynn White, for example, drew on the biblical injunction of human dominion over the earth (Genesis 1:28) and took the view that religion – at least as observed in the West – was inimical to environment. Writing in 1967, White argued that the Judeo-Christian and Islamist traditions "not only established a dualism of man and nature but also insisted that it is God's will that man exploit nature for his proper ends." Lynn White Jr., *The Historical Roots of Our Ecological Crisis*, 155 SCIENCE 1203, 1205 (1967). White's thesis set off an extensive debate about the role of religion as ethical guide to the environment. For a good bibliography on the debates, see Timothy C. Weiskel, *The Environmental Crisis and Western Civilization: The Lynn White Controversy* (1997), http://ecoethics.net/bib/1997/enca-001. htm. Since White wrote, most, if not all, religions have pointed to doctrine and teachings supportive of environmental protection. *See* ROGER S. GOTTLIEB, THE SACRED EARTH: RELIGION, NATURE, ENVIRONMENT pts. III–VII (2d ed., 2004). For a pathfinder, see JOHN NOYCE, RELIGION AND THE ENVIRONMENT: A BIBLIOGRAPHY (1998).

2. Philosophical and Cultural Roots

Germs of the idea of human rights seem to be contained in the historical development of many, if not all, major cultures and the philosophers they have produced. Of course, the manner in which the rights are conceptualized varies over time and across cultures. For instance, the Chinese philosopher Hsün-tzu (Hsuntzu), writing circa 300 B.C., believed that a root cause of human difficulty was bound up in unrestrained human selfishness. He observed that "demand far exceeds supply, so that struggles will inevitably result: – The consequence of individual life without mutual aid is poverty; the consequence of corporate life without recognizing individual rights is strife. . . . In order to relieve anxiety and eradicate strife, nothing is as effective as the institution of corporate life based on a clear recognition of individual rights." HSUNTZE, ENRICHING A COUNTRY, *qtd.* in LIANG CHI-CHAO, HISTORY OF CHINESE THOUGHT DURING THE EARLY TSIN PERIOD 64 (1930).

Some traditional, precolonial African societies contained democratic foundations, allowing for all members of the group to participate in the decision-making process. John Beattie, *Checks on the Abuse of Political Power in Some African States: A Preliminary Framework for Analysis*, 9 SOCIOLOGUS 97 (1959), *reprinted in* COMPARATIVE POLITICAL SYSTEMS 355, 361–73 (R. Cohen & J. Middleton eds., 1967). The rights to life and personal security were often paramount. S.B.K. Asante, *Nation Building and Human Rights in Emergent African Nations*, 2 CORNELL INT'L L.J. 72, 73–74 (1969). In many traditional African societies, the concept of rights had a group aspect so that egalitarian aspirations and economic benefit sharing was the norm. F.O. AWOGU, POLITICAL INSTITUTIONS AND THOUGHT IN AFRICA 83 (1975). In some regions of Africa, certain communities "took pride in according respect and human rights to women, children and old persons." EMMANUEL G. BELLO, AFRICAN CUSTOMARY HUMANITARIAN LAW 29 (1980).

In Greek philosophy we see the antecedents to the development of a core human rights idea contained in natural law – the idea of transcendent norms applicable in all times and places. The classic example, used by Szabo earlier in this chapter, is Sophocles' *Antigone*. Sophocles writes in his tragedy of *Antigone* (circa 442 B.C.) of how Antigone buries her brother Polynice's body, despite being forbidden to do so by an edict of Creon, the ruler of Thebes.

Creon is furious and has Antigone brought before him. Antigone defends the morality of her own actions by asserting that she has acted in accordance with the unwritten and unchanging laws of heaven. MICHAEL BERTRAM CROWE, THE CHANGING PROFILE OF THE NATURAL LAW 6 (1977). Greek philosophy envisioned for "citizens" equal respect, equality before the law, equality in political power and suffrage, and equality of civil rights. *See* J.M. KELLY, A SHORT HISTORY OF WESTERN LEGAL THEORY 26–31 (1992). Query the nature of this "equality," however, because even for Aristotle, the institution of slavery and the exclusion of women and children was part of the "natural" order and none was considered a citizen. Aristotle, *Politics* (350 B.C.), bk. 1.

In Roman philosophy, Cicero, in his treatise *De Legibus* ("On the Laws") (circa 43 B.C.), advances the idea of the natural law in a vocabulary akin to a more modern secularized natural law theory. He argues that natural law and universal justice bind all human society together and apply to all without distinction. Each person has unique dignity, which imposes on all the responsibility to look after others. This natural law is eternal and unchangeable and valid for all nations and for all times. In one of Cicero's most famous passages, he writes:

> True law is right reason in agreement with nature, diffused among all men; constant and unchanging, it should call men to their duty by its precepts, and deter them from wrongdoing by its prohibitions; and it never commands or forbids upright men in vain, while its rules and restraints are lost upon the wicked. To curtail this law is unholy, to amend it illicit, to repeal it impossible; nor can we be dispensed from it by the order either of senate or of popular assembly; nor need we look for anyone to clarify or interpret it; nor will it be one law at Rome and a different one at Athens, nor otherwise tomorrow than it is today; but one and the same law, eternal and unchangeable, will bind all peoples and all ages; and God, its designer, expounder and enactor, will be as it were the sole and universal ruler and governor of all things; and whoever disobeys it, because by this act he will have turned his back on himself and on man's very nature, will pay the heaviest penalty, even if he avoids the punishments which are adjudged fit for his conduct.

Marcus Tullius Cicero, *De Republica* 2, 22 (c. 51 B.C.), *qtd. in* GEORGE MOUSOURAKIS, THE HISTORICAL AND INSTITUTIONAL CONTEXT OF ROMAN LAW 25 n.70 (2003).

The Age of Enlightenment sees the concept of natural law and individual rights formally linked together. In England, John Locke's *Second Treatise of Government* (1690) argued for "natural rights" and claimed that every individual possesses certain fundamental and equal rights, including over property, before the existence of any organized society and the establishment of government. People are born in a state of perfect equality and enjoy all rights equally. Societies and governments are formed to preserve those rights, not to usurp or deny them. In France, Jean-Jacques Rousseau, in his *Discourse on Inequality* (1754), advances the idea of natural rights and the theory of the natural man. Rousseau looked to the hypothetical state of nature, as did other philosophers of the day, including Locke and [Thomas] Hobbes (although Hobbes goes in the other direction), as a moral guide. In his most important work, *The Social Contract* (1762), Rousseau asserts that man is born free with intrinsic worth. Man is also born with inalienable, natural rights. These rights are independent of positive law and cannot be surrendered to a sovereign in any sort of implicit social contract designed to protect their natural rights from abuse.

During this period, women thinkers also begin to assert natural rights of women. In 1791, Olympe de Gouges (nom de plume of Marie Gouze) drafted the Declaration of the Rights of Woman and Citizen (France). Article 1 of the Declaration proclaims that "woman is born free and remains equal to man in her rights." In 1793, de Gouges was beheaded for treason on account of her work for women's rights. In 1792, Mary Wollstonecraft published *A Vindication of the Rights of Women*. Wollstonecraft had a generally conservative worldview, but many view her text as the first great feminist treatise. The first chapter takes up the idea of natural rights and questions who it is that possesses those rights and on what grounds. Wollstonecraft argues that, because natural rights arise by virtue of human reason and human reason is given by God to both men and women, it is a wrong for men to deny natural rights to women. *See* BARBARA TAYLOR, MARY WOLLSTONECRAFT AND THE FEMINIST IMAGINATION 105–106 (2003).

It should be noted that the idea of natural rights had detractors, the most famous perhaps being Jeremy Bentham and Edmund Burke. In *Anarchical Fallacies* (written 1791–95, published 1816), Bentham asserts that the phrase "natural rights" is a "perversion of language." Bentham argues that the only real rights are "legal rights" created by positive law; that there can be no rights anterior to government, which is not the product of a fictitious social contract but arises by force or custom; that natural rights are ambiguous because they implicate general rights over no specific object, leading to the result that one might have a claim over anything; and that natural rights anterior to law would mean anarchy because they could not be limited by law or enforced by law. Bentham concludes that the phrase "natural rights" is "simple nonsense: natural and imprescriptible rights, rhetorical nonsense, – nonsense upon stilts."

In arguing that the French Revolution was a mistake, Burke, similarly, took issue with natural rights. In *Reflections on the Revolution in France* (1790), published less than two years after the storming of the Bastille, Burke argued against abrupt breaks with the past and existing institutions (even those hostile to natural rights). For Burke, natural rights are perfect in the abstract, but "their abstract perfection is their practical defect. By having a right to every thing they want every thing." He maintained that the collective wisdom of ancestors had constructed effective modes of governance – for Burke, a hereditary monarchy – to provide for human wants over many generations. Striking out in any new, untested direction would be risky and would likely result in the anarchy that Burke saw after the French Revolution. In response to Burke, Thomas Paine published his best seller *The Rights of Man* (1791). In it, he made early use of the expression "human rights."[1] After highlighting defects in a hereditary system of government, including the exclusion of the will of the people governed, Paine wrote: "The hereditary system, therefore, is as repugnant to human wisdom as to human rights; and is as absurd as it is unjust." Paine ascribed inspiration for the text to all religious traditions that observe the unity of humankind and the equality of all individuals.

Questions and Discussion

1. As the select, potted history here demonstrates, the ideas that have inspired and guided the development of human rights are common to all humankind, and human rights have benefited from all major trends of thought. One particular good demonstration of this fact is contained in a text prepared by the U.N. Educational, Scientific, and Cultural Organization

---

[1] Earlier uses of the phrase, albeit not ordinarily in a contemporary sense, can be found in Anonymous, *A Poem, Occasion'd by the Late Discontents and Disturbances in the State*, 1691, *in* 4 POEMS ON AFFAIRS OF STATE 285, 299 (1707) ("And Human Rights t'assert, is to rebel"); Anonymous, *On the Five Bustoes in Her Majesty's Hermitage, in* 3 THE GENTLEMAN'S MAGAZINE; OR, MONTHLY INTELLIGENCER FOR THE YEAR 1733 167, at 208 (No. 28, Apr. 1733) ("check lawless power, and human rights maintain"); FRANCIS HUTCHESON, A SHORT INTRODUCTION TO MORAL PHILOSOPHY IN THREE BOOKS; CONTAINING ELEMENTS OF ETHICKS AND THE LAW OF NATURE 180 (1753); *Political Sketches, Inscribed to His Excellency John Adams*, 64 CRITICAL REVIEW 46, 47 (1788) ("The author speaks . . . on the original foundations of human rights, revealed by the study of the law of nature"); 3 THE PARLIAMENTARY REGISTER; OR, HISTORY OF THE PROCEEDINGS AND DEBATES OF THE HOUSE OF COMMONS 262 (1776) (Dec. 7, 1775, speech by Mr. Hartley) ("reason and justice are above all human rights").

(UNESCO) under the direction of Jeanne Hirsch, the first director of UNESCO's Division of Philosophy. Entitled BIRTHRIGHT OF MAN (1968), it collects an enormous variety of thought important to human rights from all the world's cultural traditions.

2. There has been, and still is, a tension between human rights in theory and in practice. In a contemporary context, Michael Freeman observes:

> The concept of human rights raises problems that are, on the one hand, practical and urgent, and, on the other hand, theoretical and abstract. For human rights proponents and academics whose work is oriented towards activism, the concept connotes the prevention of political murders, "disappearances," torture, and unjust imprisonment. The concept of human rights also raises theoretical issues about the requirements of legitimate government and the nature of the good life. It is widely recognized that these two dimensions of human rights work exist and should, in principle, be integrated with one another. This integration, however, can prove difficult in practice. For activists, the pressure of rescuing fellow human-beings from actual and imminent injustice relegates theoretical questions to a low priority. Those who look to philosophers and political theorists for assistance may be disappointed, for the theoretical disputation is inconclusive. Thus, there is a gap between human rights activism and theory.

Michael Freeman, *The Philosophical Foundations of Human Rights*, 16 HUM. RTS. Q. 491 (1994). An attempt to point toward ways to reconcile this tension is beyond this text, but awareness of the tension is important, especially in an environmental context, because as Chapter 2 indicates, using human rights to protect the environment is counterintuitive to some.

3. Historical Laws of Local Nature

The international protection of human rights is closely tied to the local or national protection of human rights. Over a long period, human rights developed in nations and states as a limiting force on unbridled state power. This development was slow and uneven, but before international human rights could take root, human rights had to be viewed by the international community as a whole as a necessary part of national constitutional orders. This general need was perceived only after World War I, with the establishment of international obligations, discussed in this chapter in Section D, to respect certain basic individual rights. This set the stage for the wholesale development of international human rights following World War II. *See* CHRISTIAN TOMUSCHAT, HUMAN RIGHTS: BETWEEN IDEALISM AND REALISM 9 (2003). Here, we trace the national development of human rights antecedents from their first known appearance through the U.S. Bill of Rights.

The Egyptian legal system is the oldest known legal system, dating back to beyond 4000 B.C. JOHN HENRY WIGMORE, 1 A PANORAMA OF THE WORLD'S LEGAL SYSTEMS 11 (1928). In Egyptian cosmology, Maat (meaning "straight" or "true") was the goddess of justice. A text ordered produced by Ramses III, akin to the *Domesday Book* of William the Conqueror, records at least part of the Pharaoh's philosophy on justice: "I planted the whole land with trees and green things, and made the people to dwell in their shade. . . . I rescued the humble from their oppressors. I made every man safe in his home. I preserved the lives of those who sought my court of justice." JAMES HENRY BREASTED, 4 ANCIENT RECORDS OF EGYPT § 210 (1907). In the twelfth dynasty, Khnem-hotep writes: "His majesty [King Amenemhet] came that he might abolish wrong, . . . set right abuses . . . ; allotting the water-course rights according to the recorded titles of former times, that he might do justice." *Id.* One of the first international treaties we have record of, a treaty of peace between Ramses II and the chief of the invading Hittites (c. 1300 B.C.), recorded on a wall at Karnak, establishes significant protection for deserters. "Articles" 16 and 17 provide on the basis of reciprocity that "any man who may . . . abscond and be delivered back to the great [ruler of Egypt or chief of Kheta] shall not be prosecuted for his offense; his property shall not be seized nor his wives nor children, nor himself be put to death nor mutilated." *Id.* 3, at 163. Contemporary scholars have also discovered that the laws of the Pharaohs required judges to "[m]ake sure that all is done according to the law, that custom is observed and the right of each man respected." PAUL GORDON LAUREN, THE EVOLUTION OF HUMAN RIGHTS 10 (1998).

The Babylonian Code of Hammurabi (1760 B.C.) is the oldest legal code known today. It was based on earlier texts that are now lost and represented a codification and development of the customary law of the region. Although many aspects of the Code today are incompatible with human rights (in particular, the punishments imposed), other portions established basic principles that are familiar to modern conceptions of human rights, such as equal protection of the law, justice to the poor, rights for the weak against the strong, and remedies for mistreatment of prisoners. For women, it bestowed separate rights in property, rights of inheritance, and protection in connection with divorce and maintenance. *See* Leon R. Yankwich, *The Cultural Background and Some of the Social Phases of the Code of Hammurabi*, 4 S. CAL. L. REV. 20 (1930); Frank L. Fetzer, *The Code of Hammurabi: The Oldest Known Legal Code*, 35 COM. L.J. 726 (1930). In the Prologue to the Code, Hammurabi expresses the fundamental purposes behind the establishment of his kingdom: "to cause justice to prevail in the land, to destroy the wicked and the evil, to prevent the strong from oppressing the weak . . . and [to] enlighten the land and to further the welfare of the People." ROBERT FRANCIS HARPER, THE CODE OF HAMMURABI KING OF BABYLON 3 (1904).

In 539 B.C., more than a thousand years after the Code of Hammurabi, Babylonia was conquered by Cyrus the Great. In establishing his new kingdom of Persia, Cyrus issued a charter or proclamation in which he explains why he conquered Babylon and the measures to be instituted in the new era. In the charter, it is possible to locate forerunners of human rights concepts of liberty and security, freedom of movement and religious belief, the right to property, and some other economic and social rights. *See* Hirad Abtahi, *Reflections on the Ambiguous Universality of Human Rights: Cyrus the Great's Proclamation as a Challenge to the Athenian Democracy's Perceived Monopoly on Human Rights*, 36 DENV. J. INT'L L. & POL'Y 55, 64–74 (2007).

In India, before the ascendency of the Brahman branch of the Hindu legal system, the Buddhist branch held sway. Propagated by the Edicts of King Asoka (300 B.C.), the Hindu legal system guaranteed freedom of religion. *See* Arcot Krishnaswami, *Study of Discrimination in the Matter of Religious Rights and Practices*, U.N. Doc. E/CN.4/Sub.2/200/Rev.1 (U.N. Sales No. 60.XIV.2) (1960). Other Indian customary law developed humanitarian laws of war, protecting all places of religious worship, civilian houses, and property against attack. The wartime principle of discrimination between combatants and noncombatants is found in the Law of Manu: no killing is permitted of one who is sleeping, who is without his armor, who is naked, who is deprived of his weapons, who is only looking on and not fighting, or is engaged in fighting with another person. Prisoners of war, the sick, and the wounded were to be well treated. *See* ZAKONY MANU, LAWS OF MANU 134–35 (1992), *qtd. in* Olga Butkevych, *The History of Ancient International Law: Challenges and Prospects*, 5 J. HIST. INT'L L. 189, 207 (2003).

In 1188, demands for and the granting of individual rights from various European monarchs began. *See generally* LYNN HUNT, INVENTING HUMAN RIGHTS: A HISTORY 112–204 (2007). In the Spanish kingdom of León in 1188, the Cortes, a feudal assembly, obtained a series of particular rights from King Alfonso IX. These included the rights of an accused to a trial and the inviolability of life, honor, home, and property. At Runnymede in England, the barons forced King John to sign the Magna Carta in 1215, thus establishing a rule of law and granting freemen of the realm broadly applicable civil rights: "no freeman shall be arrested, or detained in prison or deprived of his Freehold, or Liberties, . . . but by the lawful judgment of his peers, or by the law of the land." 25 Edw. 1 (1297), cap. 29, *reprinted in* 1 STATUTES AT LARGE 1, 7 (Owen Ruffhead ed., 1763). There followed in England the Petition of Right (1628) and Habeas Corpus Act (1679) and the Bill of Rights (1689). Similarly, in 1222 Hungary, King András was persuaded by nobles to sign the Golden Bull, which recognized the "Hungarian Nation" and created the framework for an annual meeting of the diet. The text ends with a "resistance clause" that ensures the right of individuals to disobey royal acts not conforming to the law, in effect creating a constitutional monarchy. Any noble arrested was entitled to a fair trial. Antal Visegrady, *Transition to Democracy in Central and Eastern Europe: Experiences of a Model Country – Hungary*, 1 WILL. & MARY BILL OF RTS J. 245, 260 (1992).

In the colonial origins of the United States we find the emergence of governance structures, based on popular consent, that begin to entail rights. The oldest surviving compact based on popular consent – The Plymouth Combination of 1620 (popularly known as the Mayflower Compact) – contains a provision for the application of "equal Laws." In 1638, Maryland passed one of the earliest U.S. statements on religious freedom in An Act for Church Liberties. The 1640 Massachusetts Body of Liberties, a sort of constitutional code adopted by the Massachusetts General Court, contained seven of the twenty-six specific rights contained in the U.S. Bill of Rights, including due process, equality before the law, freedom of assembly, and freedom of expression. The Connecticut Code of Laws of 1650 contains due process rights, including the right to trial by jury. Even more rights are contained in the 1682 Charter of Liberties and Frame of Government of the Province of Pennsylvania and the New York Charter of Liberties and Privileges of 1683. All the documents referred to in this paragraph are collected and reprinted in COLONIAL ORIGINS OF THE AMERICAN CONSTITUTION: A DOCUMENTARY HISTORY (Donald S. Lutz ed., 1998).

The ideas of freedom and liberty – along with all the connotations of rights they entail – played a central part in the American War of Independence, and later in the French Revolution. It is in the lead-up to these conflicts that the age of the declaration of rights begins. In Virginia, the 1776 Virginia Declaration of Rights, largely drafted by George Mason, provides that "all men are by nature equally free and independent, and have certain inherent rights." *See* Donald S. Lutz, *The Virginia Declaration of Rights and Constitution*, in ROOTS OF THE REPUBLIC: AMERICAN FOUNDING DOCUMENTS INTERPRETED 150 (Stephen L. Schechter ed., 1990). The U.S. Declaration of Independence, drafted by Thomas Jefferson, is true to its natural law roots. It famously proclaims: "We hold these truths to be self-evident, that all men are created equal, that they are endowed by their Creator with certain unalienable rights, that among these are life, liberty and the pursuit of happiness. That to secure these rights, governments are instituted among men, deriving their just powers from the consent of the governed. That whenever any form of government becomes destructive of those ends, it is the right of the people to alter or to abolish it, and to institute new government." *See* Donald S. Lutz, *The United States Constitution*, in ROOTS OF THE REPUBLIC: AMERICAN FOUNDING DOCUMENTS INTERPRETED 266 (Stephen L. Schechter ed., 1990). A more detailed elaboration of rights would wait until 1791, when the Bill of Rights to the U.S. Constitution (Amendments I–X) was approved by the United States. *See* John P. Kaminski & Richard B. Bernstein,

The Bill of Rights, in ROOTS OF THE REPUBLIC: AMERICAN FOUNDING DOCUMENTS INTER-
PRETED 423 (Stephen L. Schechter ed., 1990).

In the meantime, in France, the Declaration of the Rights of Man and Citizen (1789)
proclaimed, "All are born and remain free and equal in rights." These rights are "natural
and imprescriptible." Political rights include the right to vote and to participate in politics.
Civil rights include the right to equality before the law, the right to be protected against
arbitrary arrest or punishment, the right to be presumed innocent until proven guilty, the
right to hold personal opinions and religious beliefs, the right of freedom of expression, and
the right to possess property. JOHN HALL STEWART, A DOCUMENTARY SURVEY OF THE FRENCH
REVOLUTION 431 (1951).

Questions and Discussion

1. For each person favoring human rights throughout the world there were powerful opponents
   who sought to retain privilege, hierarchy, hereditary rule, property, continuity, and caste.
   Human rights proponents were challenging and in turn were challenged by vested interests:
   Thomas Paine was hung in effigy in English cities; Voltaire's writings were banned. As we
   have seen, conservative authors like Burke referred to the "monstrous fiction" of human
   equality. Bentham rejected the idea of natural law, calling it "simple nonsense" and labeling
   human rights "nonsense on stilts." People should know "their proper place."

2. Even with limited religious, cultural, and national nods to human rights, much remained
   to be done to improve the situation for the vast majority of the global population. The
   notion of divine right of rule continued in many countries. Ruling elites aimed to maintain
   power and cultural practices that subordinated women, children, racial minorities, and
   workers. Slavery was widespread, and torture was a prevalent method of investigation and
   punishment. Executions were held in public places, and capital punishment was imposed
   for a wide variety of offenses. Educational opportunities were limited to the very rich; a few
   landholders dominated the numerous and landless poor. Some human rights abuses gave
   problems even to rulers because they led to long and impoverishing wars. In particular,
   religious persecution, forced conversions, and massacres of religious minorities provoked
   conflicts throughout the world. After repeated and prolonged wars in Europe, peace treaties
   began to include the first human rights provisions that guaranteed freedom of religion.

C. *International Law on Specific Issues Before the Twentieth Century*

Although the concept of internationally protected human rights in general did not appear until
the twentieth century, specific human rights issues emerged and were matters of international
concern as early as the seventeenth century.

1. Religious Liberty

On October 24, 1648, the Articles of the Treaties of Peace signed at Münster (Austria, Spain,
and France) and Osnabrück (Austria and Sweden), in Westphalia, ended the Thirty Years'
War between Protestant and Catholic areas of Europe. Although the Treaty of Westphalia
is often cited as the beginning of the nation-state system and modern international law,
the Treaty is also significant in that it contains various provisions that today are part of
human rights law. First, the Westphalian treaty signed at Münster declares an amnesty for all
offenses committed during the "troubles" (Art. 2) and provides for restitution of property and

ecclesiastical or lay status (Art. 6–34). Second, freedom of contract is indicated by annulling those contracts procured under duress and threats. Freedom of movement, of commerce, and the right to legal protection are included. Most important, article 28 provides

> [t]hat those of the Confession of Augsburg, and particularly the Inhabitants of Oppenheim, shall be put in possession again of their Churches, and Ecclesiastical Estates, as they were in the Year 1624, as also that all others of the said Confession of Augsburg, who shall demand it, shall have the free Exercise of their Religion, as well in public Churches at the appointed Hours, as in private in their own Houses, or in others chosen for this purpose by their Ministers, or by those of their Neighbours, preaching the Word of God.

Treaty of Westphalia, in 1 MAJOR PEACE TREATIES OF MODERN HISTORY 7 (Fred L. Israel ed., 1967). The Westphalian Treaty of Osnabrück with Sweden contained a similar provision. Pope Innocent X promptly declared null and void the articles in the treaties of Westphalia relating to religious matters, but the principle of religious liberty was established, as was the link between peace and respect for human rights.

The protection of religious liberty continued to be a matter of concern in Europe through the Congress of Vienna (1814–15), which acknowledged that religious intolerance could jeopardize international peace and security. Thus, the participating states pledged to maintain religious equality and assure equal protection and favor to every sect. They specifically agreed to effect "an amelioration in the civil state of those who profess the Jewish religion in Germany," paying "particular attention to the measures by which the enjoyment of civil rights shall be secured and guaranteed to them." *See General Treaty Signed in Congress*, at Vienna, June 9, 1815, Act No. IX Federative Constitution of Germany, Art. 16, T.C. HANSARD, 32 PARLIAMENTARY DEBATES (Parliamentary Papers) 71, 174 (1816). Similarly, in 1839, the Ottoman Sultan Abdülmecid promulgated the Hatti-i Sherif, a decree that guaranteed legal, social and political rights "to all our subjects, of whatever religion or sect they may be" and "they shall enjoy them without exception." (Hatti-i Sherif, 3 Nov. 1839; a second decree, the Islahat Fermani, followed in 1856 and similarly guaranteed nondiscrimination on the basis of religion, language, or race). *See* PAUL GORDON LAUREN, THE EVOLUTION OF HUMAN RIGHTS: VISIONS SEEN 65 (1998).

2. Abolition of Slavery and the Slave Trade

Among the first widespread efforts of the nineteenth century to protect humanity against injustice were those aimed at the institution of slavery. Slavery had existed throughout history and across the world, but it changed fundamentally in the sixteenth century with the transatlantic slave trade from Africa. The numbers alone exceeded those of any past practice. Moreover, slavery came to focus on Africa and to lead to the emergence of ideologies of racism, apartheid, and segregation. From the sixteenth to the nineteenth century, the international slave trade flourished and slavery was legally practiced in most countries of the world.

Yet almost from the beginning, a small but vocal minority expressed its determined opposition to slavery. These individuals began to organize the world's first nongovernmental organizations devoted to a human rights issue. They published articles and pamphlets, they preached against slavery, and they organized active campaigns of protest. Slaves themselves engaged in uprisings in Saint-Domingue, Haiti, and elsewhere. Many of those most outspoken against the abuse were themselves former and reformed slave traders or slave owners. They saw and used the gap between the proclamations of rights, especially in the United

Kingdom, United States, and France, as well as the high ideals of religion and philosophy, and the practice of slavery. They were thus able to draw intellectual and moral strength from the general proclamations of human rights. New economic interests that did not rely on slavery joined the movement.

Throughout the first part of the nineteenth century, public pressure grew. In Britain, public agitation forced members of Parliament to confront the issue. As early as 1807, public opinion forced votes in the U.S. Congress and British Parliament to end the participation of both countries in slave trading. The U.S. Act to Prohibit the Importation of Slaves was matched by the British Act for the Abolition of the Slave Trade. Both made it illegal to trade in, purchase, sell, barter, or transport any human cargo for the purpose of slavery.

Neither law could be effective, however, without international measures of enforcement and the agreement of other nations. The focus turned to the Congress of Vienna in 1814–15, where antislavery activists, who viewed the issue as one of fundamental moral and religious obligation, pressed for action. About this time, Thomas Clarkson's highly influential tract *Essay on the Impolicy of the African Slave Trade in Two Parts* (1788), was translated from English into French, German, Spanish, and Italian. The British delegate at the Congress of Vienna complained about the public pressure being mounted, but its force could not be denied. The Congress of Vienna established a special committee on the international slave trade and finally agreed to sign the Eight Power Declaration, which acknowledged that the international slave trade was "repugnant to the principles of humanity and universal morality" and that "the public voice in all civilized countries calls aloud for its prompt suppression." Yet the declaration did not make slave trading a crime, sanction the arrest of slavers, or provide machinery for enforcement.

Treaty language soon followed, however. During the Congress itself, the Second Peace of Paris treaty, signed November 20, 1815, by Britain, Russia, Austria, Prussia, and France, included a pledge to consider measures "for the entire and definitive abolition of a Commerce so odious and so strongly condemned by the laws of religion and nature." *See* William L. Chew III, *The Second Peace of Paris, in* 2 THE HISTORICAL ENCYCLOPEDIA OF WORLD SLAVERY 570 (Junius P. Rodriguez ed., 1997). The Treaty of Ghent signed by the United States and Britain the same year declared traffic in slaves "irreconcilable with the principles of humanity and justice." *Treaty of Peace and Amity*, Feb. 18, 1815, 12 T.I.A.S. 47.

Antislavery societies continued their pressure, led by William Wilberforce in the United Kingdom. In addition, the pope issued instructions to all Catholics to abstain from the slave trade. In 1840, the first World Anti-Slavery Conference was organized. Eventually governments responded. By 1882, a network of more than fifty bilateral agreements permitted the search of suspected slave ships on the high seas, without regard to flag. Internally, states slowly emancipated their slaves in response to public pressure. Britain did so in 1833; France, in 1848; and most Latin American countries, as they became independent. Simón Bolívar, who was instrumental in Latin America's struggle for independence, was a leading opponent of the slave trade and proclaimed the emancipation of slaves in 1816. The issue of slavery became a major motivation for the U.S. Civil War, and President Lincoln issued the Emancipation Proclamation in 1863. Cuba and Brazil were the last countries in the Western Hemisphere to abolish slavery, in the late 1880s.

By 1890, governments were prepared to take effective international action. They negotiated the 1890 General Act for the Repression of the African Slave Trade, which referred to the "crimes and devastations engendered" by trafficking in humans. The Act required actions be taken to suppress the slave trade at sea and along inland caravan routes, to prosecute and punish slave traders, and to liberate captured slaves. The agreement thus reflected the principle of shared international responsibility to respond to gross human rights violations and marked the first general agreement on a common standard of behavior for all states. (Further agreements on abolition of slavery and repression of the slave trade were concluded in 1919, 1926, and 1956).

3. The Emergence of Humanitarian Law

As early as the fourth century B.C., the Chinese military theorist Sun Tzu wrote in *The Art of War* that an obligation exists to care for the wounded and prisoners of war. Yet, for the most part, warfare was not governed by any mutually acceptable rules limiting the actions of soldiers. The Industrial Revolution had a military side to it, and weaponry began an ongoing evolution of increased destructiveness. Armies became more professional and larger, as conscription spread during following the Napoleonic Wars. At the same time, the emergence of the press and increased literacy brought home the horrors and atrocities of conflict. The confluence of all these factors led to growing concern with the conditions of war, the treatment of wounded and sick, and the protection of civilians.

The U.S. Civil War and the Crimean War in Europe brought public attention forcefully to bear on wartime conditions. Francis Lieber produced *Instructions for the Government Armies of the United States in the Field*, which was issued by the War Department (as revised) as General Orders No. 100. *Reprinted in* RICHARD SHELLY HARTIGAN, LIEBER'S CODE AND THE LAW OF WAR 45–71 (1983). This was the first Western written regulation of armed conflict. In Europe in 1859, Henry Dunant witnessed the Battle of Solferino, where three hundred thousand troops battled for fifteen hours, leaving thousands of wounded among the dead. Dunant's account of the battle aroused public opinion, and others offered to support Dunant in an effort to create an international relief society to care for the wounded as individual human beings without regard to nationality, class, or race. An organizing committee invited governments to send representatives to Geneva to translate this dream into reality. The Geneva International Conference met in 1863 and attracted thirty delegates from fourteen countries, as well as four funding agencies. They left the meeting having created a Geneva-based private international organization, the International Committee of the Red Cross (ICRC).

Within a year, the ICRC, led by Dunant, organized a second conference of government representatives. They negotiated the 1864 Geneva Convention for the Amelioration of the Condition of the Wounded in Armies in the Field, the first international agreement to protect individuals in times of war. The treaty required all signatories to acknowledge and respect the neutrality or immunity of military hospitals and their staffs, and to protect them from attack. Red Cross societies and volunteers quickly emerged and became visible in every subsequent conflict.

By 1899, the Hague Peace Conference could conclude the broad Convention on the Laws and Customs of War on Land, which explicitly spoke of the "rights" of the wounded to receive medical treatment, of prisoners of war to be given food and clothing and protection under the law, of individuals to be considered inviolable when surrendering, and of civilians to be protected from unlimited warfare. In 1907, the Hague Peace Conference extended humanitarian law by concluding new agreements on land and marine warfare. In the agreements, the Marten's Clause expressed the consensus of participants that the means and methods of warfare are not unlimited. Convention Respecting the Laws and Customs of War on Land, Hague IV, 18 Oct. 1907; Convention for the Adaptation to Maritime Warfare of the Principles of the Geneva Convention, Hague X, 18 Oct. 1907. The Marten's Clause reads: "Until a more complete code of the laws of war has been issued, the High Contracting Parties deem it expedient to declare that, in cases not included in the Regulations adopted by them, the inhabitants and the belligerents remain under the protection and the rule of the principles of the law of nations, as they result from the usages established among civilized peoples, from the laws of humanity, and the dictates of the public conscience."

4. Injury to Aliens

International travel has always been hazardous. Throughout history, merchants, diplomats, and others traveling abroad have been vulnerable to robbery, murder, enslavement, or impressment. Ships at sea were frequently looted by privateers or pirates. The loss of a national was and still is seen as the loss of a valuable asset belonging to the sovereign, whether prince or state. Those who caused harm to foreign nationals diminished the wealth of the sovereign to whom such nationals were deemed to belong. Through protests, reprisals, interventions, and other state practice the rule emerged that a state was responsible for acts committed against foreign nationals in its territory and by its nationals on the high seas. The ruler of the acting party and the state itself were deemed to be collectively responsible for the damage caused to the foreign citizen. The victim's ruler could authorize the victim, his family, or commercial partners to use self-help against the other country and its citizens. These letters of marque and reprisal authorized the capture of vessels or cargoes belonging to the state whose nationals were responsible for the wrong, but over time, several procedural prerequisites developed. Most important, it emerged that those wronged had to first seek to obtain justice from the government of the country in which the damage occurred or whose citizens inflicted the injury. Only after a denial of justice were reprisals authorized. Second, reprisals had to be proportional to the wrong done; some countries required strict accounting to the government for the execution of reprisals. By the nineteenth century, reprisals for injuries to aliens were removed from private hands and became the prerogative of the state, and by the middle of that century, the concept arose of peaceful, third-party settlement of disputes by arbitration or claims commission. In presenting such claims, the petitioning state was deemed to be asserting its own right to ensure that its subjects were not mistreated in violation of international law.

In rare instances, a state would claim the right to intervene not only for the protection of its own nationals but also on behalf of oppressed minorities. In 1860, the major European powers authorized France to intervene to protect the Christian population in Lebanon against massacres by the Druses. Russia similarly intervened in Bulgaria in the 1870s for humanitarian purposes. Weaker states rightly objected to the selectivity and self-interest that motivated many so-called humanitarian interventions.

Questions and Discussion

1. Although these specific topics became matters of international concern, the general issue of human rights was still felt to be within the domestic jurisdiction of states. Oppenheim's Treatise on International Law, written at the beginning of the twentieth century, opined that "the so-called rights of man" cannot enjoy protection under international law because that law is concerned solely with the relations between states and cannot confer rights on individuals. L. OPPENHEIM, 1 INTERNATIONAL LAW: A TREATISE § 212 (2d ed., 1912). Yet the very exceptions that had been created demonstrated that there was nothing inherently domestic about matters of human rights. Human rights specifically or generally became subjects of international concern when states agreed to make them so.

2. Contemporary human rights tend to focus predominately on the individual and his or her relationship with the state. Do any of the situations addressed above take account of the relationship between a state and its citizens? If not, what is the focus?

D. *The Early Twentieth Century*

The turn of the century saw a wave of globalization with technological advances in communications (e.g., telephone, telegraph) and transportation (e.g., rail networks, steamships) accompanied by increasing mobility of wealth through movements of capital and labor. The world became smaller and international awareness increased. Nongovernmental organizations (NGOs) increased in number and variety. The first intergovernmental organizations were formed, starting with the International Telegraph Union (1865), the International Postal Union (1874), and the International Meteorological Organization (1878). Among the NGOs, the Ligue des Droits de l'Homme, which published its first information in 1901, sought to ensure liberty, justice, equality, and fraternity to all humanity. It organized conferences and pressured governments on human rights throughout the world. In Iran and China, authors published works promoting the rights of individuals. *See, e.g.*, MIRZĀ ABDUL'RAHIM TĀLIBOV NAJJĀR TABRIZI, ĪZĀHĀT DAR KHOSUS-E AZĀDI (Explanations Concerning Freedom) (1906); KANG YOUWEI, DA TONGSHU (The Book of Great Unity) (1884–1900, published 1935). The International Office of Public Health, created in 1907, advocated a global right to health.

On the regional level, the effort to create a confederation of Latin American states in 1826 led to a series of regional meetings to discuss mutual defense and other forms of cooperation. Before 1890, these meetings or congresses were convoked in response to specific problems or needs. They became institutionalized with the holding of the First International American Conference in Washington, D.C., in 1889–90. The Conference created the International Union of American Republics, later changed to the Pan-American Union, which met in regular sessions until 1938 and then emerged after World War II as the Organization of American States. The Union took up human rights issues very early; it adopted a convention relative to the rights of aliens in 1902, supplemented in 1928, conventions on asylum in 1928 and 1933, and a convention on nationality in 1933 (other conventions on the rights of women are mentioned later in this chapter).

Humanitarian efforts on behalf of persecuted minorities took the form of diplomatic protests, formal complaints, and in some cases military action. The actions were often very selective, and human rights too frequently were invoked as a pretext for intervention. Nonetheless, shining the spotlight on human rights violations made it more difficult for governments to ignore their own internal problems. Various groups subjected to discrimination and other deprivations of rights pressed for change, from the formation of the National Association for the Advancement of Colored People in the United States to the public protests of Mohandas Gandhi in South Africa.

World War I and events surrounding it proved the dangers of nationalism and ethnic conflict; many ethnic and religious minorities suffered great loss of life. The carnage led to international efforts to ensure minority rights. The revolutions of the early twentieth century drew the attention of all governments to the dangers of denying economic, social, and cultural rights.

1. Economic and Social Rights: Capitalism, Industrialization, and the Formation of the International Labour Organization

In the nineteenth century, serfdom was abolished in many countries, but the emergence and development of the Industrial Revolution led to a rapid expansion in the numbers of exploited workers, including young children, in urban centers, primarily in Europe and North America. The average factory workweek in Europe in the mid-nineteenth century was eight-four hours. Poverty, starvation, epidemics, and crime were rampant. The obvious social injustices provoked reform movements within countries and eventually on the international level.

Workers fought to create the first trade unions and to take action against abuses. Socialism and Communism emerged as forces. The Catholic Church took up the issue of social justice, most famously in the 1891 encyclical *Rerum Novarum*, of Pope Leo XIII, on the working classes, which focused on "the natural rights of mankind." The encyclical affirms the right of everyone to procure for themselves and their families the basic needs of life: "Rights must be religiously respected wherever they exist, and it is the duty of the public authority to prevent and punish injury and to protect each one in the possession of his own. Still, when there is question of protecting the rights of individuals, the poor and helpless have a claim to special consideration. The richer class have many ways of protecting themselves." Encyclical Letter, *Rerum Novarum* (May 15, 1891): Leonis XIII, P.M. Acta XI, Rome 1892. *See further* Rerum Novarum: A Symposium Celebrating 100 Years of Catholic Social Thought (Ronald F. Duska ed., 1992).

The dangers of denying a decent living were apparent in the years before and after World War I. Revolution came to Mexico, Russia, and Ireland. Riots and strikes occurred in Germany, Russia, Austria, and Italy. The 1910 Mexican Revolution resulted in the first constitution in the world, in 1917, containing guarantees of economic, social, and cultural rights. During the same year, a Chilean jurist, Alejandro Álvarez, drafted the International Rights of the Individual, arguing the need for internationally protected human rights for all. Lenin's Declaration of the Rights of the Peoples of Russia called for abolishing all privileges and disabilities based on nationality or religion.

Even before the revolutions and World War I, governments under pressure to reform realized the necessity of international action to avoid distortions in competition coming from low labor standards. Some of them met to form the International Association for the Protection of Labor, with an International Labor Office. In 1906, they concluded two conventions – one on night work for women and the other prohibiting phosphorus in the manufacture of matches – for the protection of specific economic and social rights, for the first time obliging governments to respect certain rights of their own citizens. Following the end of the war, pressed by labor unions, governments created the Commission on International Labor Legislation, comprising labor representatives. The Commission produced a draft convention for the establishment of a permanent organization for international labor law, to promote "lasting peace through social justice." The proposal envisaged a membership of states represented by a unique tripartite structure of government, labor, and business. The Commission also produced a second text, a statement of general principles that declared that "labor should not be regarded merely as a commodity or article of commerce" and that human beings are entitled to "a reasonable standard of life." Other principles called for adoption of an eight-hour workday, abolition of child labor, rights of association, and equal pay for men and women for equal work.

Many of the general principles were combined with the draft convention to become the Constitution of the International Labor Organization (ILO). It was an organization founded on human rights principles and its subsequent work has elaborated on and detailed aspects of economic and social rights. The mandate of the ILO was echoed in the Covenant of the League of Nations, in which all members pledged themselves "to secure and maintain fair and humane conditions of labor for men, women and children, both in their own countries and in all countries to which their commercial and industrial relations extend." They agreed to support enforcement of agreements to combat traffic in women and children, as well as drugs, and to take steps to prevent and control disease.

By 1933, the ILO had adopted forty conventions, covering hours of work, maternity leave, unemployment, conditions of labor at night for women and children, equality of pay, minimum age at sea, forced labor, and freedom of association.

2. The League of Nations and Minorities Treaties

President Woodrow Wilson's Fourteen Points promised to support liberty, the right of self-determination, and equality of rights across borders. According to Wilson, "self-determination is not a mere phrase. It is an imperative principle of action, which statesmen will henceforth ignore at their peril." Address by President Wilson to Congress, Feb. 11, 1918, *quoted in* HAROLD S. JOHNSON, SELF-DETERMINATION WITHIN THE COMMUNITY OF NATIONS 33 (1967). Negotiations at the Paris Peace Conference proved contentious but ultimately redrew borders throughout Europe, thereby ending large multinational empires but creating a host of new minorities in new states. To protect those minorities, a series of minorities treaties provided human rights guarantees. Poland, Czechoslovakia, Yugoslavia, Romania, and Greece, as a condition of their creation or expansion, had "to assure full and complete protection of life and liberty" to all of their inhabitants "without distinction of birth, nationality, language, race, or religion." The treaties specified equal protection of the law, equal civil and political rights, language rights, and the rights of minorities to establish their own schools and cultural institutions. Specific protection was afforded Jewish and Muslim minorities. To reinforce the treaties, each one contained a provision stating that "the stipulations in the foregoing articles, as far as they affect persons belonging to racial, religious, or linguistic minorities, constitute obligations of international concern and shall be placed under the guarantee of the League of Nations." Societé des Nations/League of Nations, Doc. C.L. 110, 1928.

As for the Covenant of the League of Nations, although there were some references to economic rights, other proposals, such as one recognizing "religious persecution and intolerance as fertile sources of war" and promising that member states "make no law prohibiting or interfering with the free exercise of religion and that they will in no way discriminate, either in law or in fact, against those who practice any particular creed, religion or belief," failed to be adopted. Most controversial of all at the Paris Peace Conference was the issue of race, because of the millions of people who at that time were subjected to colonial exploitation and victimized by the legacy of slavery. Japan and China, the two Asian countries at the conference, sought to include a reference to racial equality but ran into profound opposition from colonial powers. When a vote was taken and the majority favored including the reference, the chairman suddenly discovered a "rule" requiring unanimity. Despite challenge and protest, the chair's decision against including the provision remained. Public opinion expressed outrage over the West's hypocrisy and demonstrations broke out throughout the world. The unwillingness of the great powers to accept the same rules for themselves that they were imposing on others did not go unnoticed.

In practice, the League came to use respect for minority rights as a condition of membership. The League also encouraged states to sign bilateral agreements protecting minority rights. The organization further expressed its desire "that the States which are not bound by any legal obligations to the League with respect to Minorities will nevertheless observe in the treatment of their own racial, religious, or linguistic minorities at least as high a standard of justice and toleration as is required by any of the Treaties and by the regular action of the Council." Res. adopted 21 Sept. 1922.

The League moved beyond substantive norms to create supervisory machinery and procedures to monitor compliance with the minority treaty obligations. Petitions could be brought to the League of Nations, and some nine hundred were during the time the procedure was operational. If the secretary-general of the League considered a claim meritorious, he could recommend to the Council that it appoint an ad hoc minorities committee to investigate the matter and try to reach a mutually acceptable settlement. If this friendly settlement effort failed, the complaint could be sent to the council as a whole or to the Permanent Court of International Justice (PCIJ). It was through this means that the PCIJ received two requests for advisory opinions. The first case, the *Rights of Minorities in Upper Silesia (Minority Schools)*, 1928 P.C.I.J. (ser. A) No. 15, concerned the application of racial, linguistic, or religious criteria for admission to school. The court held any such criteria for admission unacceptable. In its advisory opinion in *Minority Schools in Albania*, 1935 P.C.I.J. (ser. A/B) No. 64, the court insisted on the necessity of maintaining equality in fact as well as in law in educational institutions. In this respect, the closing of minority schools was deemed incompatible with equal protection because it would destroy the means of preserving cultural uniqueness.

Although the League of Nations' system of minorities protection functioned well for fifteen years, it ultimately failed. Those subject to it objected that they were bound by laws that did not apply to the major powers. Further, the United States' refusal to join the League of Nations undermined its effectiveness, as did the requirement of unanimity before the Council could act.

3. Civil and Political Rights for Women

Many of the women who became leaders in the struggle for women's rights began as abolitionists in the antislavery campaigns of the nineteenth century. They learned effective techniques of organizing and protesting. They also learned the importance of the moral claim of equality. Through their efforts, changes began in national law, with women obtaining the right to vote in Finland and Australia in 1906, and in Norway in 1913. (Even earlier, in what were then U.S. territories, women achieved suffrage in 1869 in Wyoming and in 1870 in Utah). In China, the revolutionary feminist Qui Jin organized the first women's association in China and advocated equal rights for women. Japanese and Filipina women also associated and published works on women's rights. Similar organizations and efforts appeared in Egypt, Iran, India, Sri Lanka, Indonesia, Vietnam, Turkey, and Korea. *See* KUMARI JAYAWARDENA, FEMINISM AND NATIONALISM IN THE THIRD WORLD (1986). They soon moved to cooperate internationally by forming NGOs and international federations of trade unions, such as the International Ladies' Garment Workers' Union.

Many of the international efforts to guarantee rights for women took place in the regional meetings of the Pan-American Union. The 1933 Convention on the Nationality of Women was the first to provide binding guarantees. It was followed by the Inter-American Convention on the Granting of Political Rights to Women (1948) and the Inter-American Convention on the Granting of Civil Rights to Women (1948), both preceding U.N. treaty action by more than thirty years. In addition to the treaties, the Conferences adopted resolutions on the rights of women, the first in 1923. The 1928 Conference recommended states adopt legislation on maternity leave and nondiscrimination in employment.

Questions and Discussion

1. As you can see, the first movement toward international protection of human rights was partial and incomplete. In addition to labor, minorities, and women, following World War

I, the League of Nations established the mandate system. The mandated territories were the former colonies of the defeated powers, placed under the administration of various victorious powers. To prevent overreach and abuse by administering powers, the peoples in the mandated territories became a "sacred trust of civilization" and international minimum standards were established (art. 22(1)). The Covenant of the League was silent about human rights in respect to parties to the Covenant, but it did require that "freedom of conscience and religion" be provided in the mandated territories and that "abuses such as the slave trade" be prohibited (art. 22(5)). No mention was made of political freedom for mandates, however. Also, no provision was made for the receipt of petitions from the peoples placed under the new mandate system. However, petitions were made, and as a result, procedural rules for petitions were established. *See* D. Rauschning, *Mandates, in* 3 ENCYCLOPEDIA OF PUBLIC INTERNATIONAL LAW 280, 285 (1997).

2. The first half of the twentieth century thus saw the list of international human rights concerns grow, to encompass economic rights, social and cultural rights, and the rights of minorities. Global and regional institutions not only engaged in standard setting but also created the first international petition procedures. The transboundary dimensions of economic issues perhaps made it easier for states to accept international regulation of workers' rights. The issue of national minorities was so closely linked to the onset of World War I that the link between peace and human rights appeared undeniable.

E. *Generalizing Human Rights in Global and Regional Systems of Protection*

On January 6, 1941, President Franklin Roosevelt enunciated his famous Four Freedoms in his eighth Annual Message to Congress. The Four Freedoms expressed were freedom of speech and expression, freedom of religion, freedom from fear, and freedom from want. According to Roosevelt, "the social and economic problems . . . are the root cause of the social revolution which is today a supreme factor in the world." *The Annual Message to Congress*, in [1940] THE PUBLIC PAPERS AND ADDRESSES OF FRANKLIN D. ROOSEVELT 663, 672 (President Roosevelt ed., 1941).

Drawing on these Four Freedoms, on August 14, 1941, the United States and United Kingdom issued a bilateral declaration known as the Atlantic Charter. The Charter also proclaimed the right of self-determination. Atlantic Charter, [1941] THE PUBLIC PAPERS AND ADDRESSES OF FRANKLIN D. ROOSEVELT 314 (Samuel I. Rosenman ed., 1950). These principles were reaffirmed by the twenty-six Allies in the Joint Declaration of the U.N. Pledging Cooperation for Victory on January 1, 1942. [1941] THE PUBLIC PAPERS AND ADDRESSES OF FRANKLIN D. ROOSEVELT 3 (Samuel I. Rosenman ed., 1950). Conferences of the Latin American states became increasingly vocal about human rights before and during World War II, expressing their concern through resolutions: 1936, Humanization of War; 1938, Defense of Human Rights and Persecution for Racial or Religious Motives; 1945, International Protection of the Essential Rights of Man. *See* Mary Ann Glendon, *The Forgotten Crucible: The Latin American Influence on the Idea of Universal Human Rights*, 16 HARV. HUM. RTS. L.J. 27 (2003).

As is now well known, the U.N. Charter contains more than a dozen references to human rights, from the Preamble to the end. The very purposes of the United Nations include cooperation in the promotion of respect for human rights and fundamental freedoms for all. Many of the provisions were included because of pressure from NGOs and smaller states, especially those of Latin America. The original Dumbarton Oaks proposals for the United Nations prepared by the great powers contained only one general provision about human rights. Even with the amendments, many governments felt the provisions were too weak, and thus it was agreed that an international bill of rights should be concluded as soon as possible after the Charter. In his closing speech to the San Francisco Conference, U.S. President Harry Truman referred to the "framing of an international bill of rights" and observance of human rights and fundamental freedoms. He added: "Unless we can attain those objectives for all men and women everywhere – without regard to race, language or religion – we cannot have permanent peace and security." The first step was to list and define human rights. Even before that, the provisions of the U.N. Charter made clear that henceforth respect for human rights within the member states of the United Nations would be a matter of international concern.

While the United Nations was emerging as a global institution, two regional bodies took up the human rights challenge. Given the widespread movement for human rights, it should not be surprising that regional organizations being created or reformed after the war should have added human rights to their agendas. All of them drew inspiration from the human rights provisions of the U.N. Charter and the Universal Declaration of Human Rights.

Europe had been the theater of the greatest atrocities of World War II and felt compelled to press for international human rights guarantees as part of European reconstruction. Faith in Western European traditions of democracy, the rule of law, and individual rights inspired belief that a regional system could be successful in avoiding future conflict and in stemming postwar revolutionary impulses supported by the Soviet Union. The Congress of Europe meeting at The Hague in May 1948 announced its desire for a united Europe with free movement of persons, ideas, and goods. It also expressed desire for "a Charter of Human Rights guaranteeing liberty of thought, assembly and expression as well as the right to form a political opposition" and "a Court of Justice with adequate sanctions for the implementation of this Charter." COUNCIL OF EUROPE, HUMAN RIGHTS TODAY: EUROPEAN LEGAL TEXTS 41 (1999).

The Americas had a tradition of regional approaches to international issues, including human rights, which grew out of regional solidarity developed during the movements for independence. Pan-American conferences had taken action on several human rights matters well before the creation of the United Nations. This history of concern led the Organization of American States to refer to human rights in the Charter of the Organization of American States, Apr. 30, 1948, 2 U.S.T. 2394, U.N.T.S. 48, and to adopt the American Declaration of the Rights and Duties of Man (1948), in OAS, Basic Documents Pertaining to Human Rights in the Inter-American System, OEA/Ser.L/VII.92, doc. 31, rev. 3 (1996) at 17. It later adopted the American Convention of Human Rights (1969), in OAS, Basic Documents Pertaining to Human Rights in the Inter-American System, OEA/Ser.L/VII.92, Doc. 31, rev. 3 (1996), at 23.

1. Standard Setting (1948–1969)

The purpose of the United Nations to promote respect for and observance of human rights could be achieved only once agreement was reached on the meaning of the term *human rights*. From 1948 until the late 1960s, the United Nations focused its attention on listing those rights whose protection should be guaranteed by all states under international supervision. Regional organizations similarly drafted agreements listing internationally guaranteed human rights.

The first general human rights text adopted internationally was the Declaration of the Rights and Duties of Man, adopted by resolution of the Organization of American States in Bogotá, at the same meeting that concluded the Charter of the Organization. The

American Declaration preceded by some six months the Universal Declaration of Human Rights, which was adopted December 10, 1948, by the U.N. General Assembly in Resolution 217 (III). The Declaration called itself "a common standard of achievement for all peoples and all nations." Eleanor Roosevelt said it might well become "the Magna Carta of all mankind." Tom J. Farer, *The United Nations and Human Rights: More Than a Wimper, Less Than a Roar* 229, in HUMAN RIGHTS IN THE WORLD COMMUNITY: ISSUES AND ACTION (Richard Pierre Claude and Burns H. Weston, eds., 1992) The Declaration has become this and more, as it today represents an agreed statement of the definition of *human rights*, as that term is used in the U.N. Charter. It has been reaffirmed in global and regional treaties and in the U.N. Conferences on Human Rights (Teheran, Vienna). The importance of this early agreement on the content of human rights cannot be overemphasized. The recasting of human rights policy as international law made it more difficult for states to ignore human rights claims.

The same resolution that approved the Universal Declaration also mandated work on a binding treaty on human rights. Although the initial work of the Commission devoted attention to civil and political rights, the General Assembly in 1950 decided in favor of including economic, social, and cultural rights as well. In 1952, on the basis of a proposal of India and Lebanon, supported by Belgium and the United States, the General Assembly decided that there should be two separate covenants with as many similar provisions as possible and that both should include a right of peoples and nations to self-determination.

During the drafting of the covenants, several ambitious proposals emerged. Australia proposed creating an international court of human rights; Uruguay supported appointment of a high commissioner for human rights; the French sought an international investigation commission headed by an attorney general. India wanted all issues of human rights violations to be investigated and remedies enforced by the Security Council. Britain, the United States, and the Soviet Union were cautious. The Soviet Union, in particular, opposed all enforcement machinery by invoking article 2(7) of the Charter. Despite this opposition, the Commission on Human Rights completed its work on the draft covenants in 1954 and submitted them to the Economic and Social Council (ECOSOC). From there, the covenants went to the Third Committee of the U.N. General Assembly, where they were debated for more than ten years. It was only in 1966 that the General Assembly voted and approved the covenants, one year after the adoption of the International Convention for the Elimination of All Forms of Racial Discrimination (in force, 1969). Another ten years passed before the covenants entered into force, with provision for a mandatory periodic reporting system and an optional interstate complaint process. Individual communications were left to a separate protocol.

As noted, it took nearly two decades to finalize and adopt the two U.N. covenants. During the process, it became clear that the compliance mechanisms at the global level would not be strong and that any judicial procedures to enforce human rights would have to be on the regional level. As a result, beginning with Europe, regional systems focused on the creation of procedures of redress, thus establishing control machinery to supervise the implementation and enforcement of the guaranteed rights.

The European system, the first to be fully operational, began with the creation of the Council of Europe by ten Western European states in 1949. Statute of the Council of Europe, May 5, 1949. ETS No. 1, Gr. Brit. T.S. No. 51 (Cmnd. 8969). It has since expanded to include Central and Eastern European countries, bringing the total membership to forty-seven states in 2010. Article 3 of the Council's Statute provides that every member state must accept the principles of the rule of law and of the enjoyment by all persons in its jurisdiction of human rights and fundamental freedoms. Membership in the Council is de facto conditioned on adherence to the European Convention on Human Rights (ECHR) and its protocols. See Committee of Ministers, Declaration on Compliance with Commitments Accepted by Member States of the Council of Europe, adopted on 10 Nov. 1994, reprinted in Council of Europe, Information Sheet No. 35 (July–December 1994, 1995), App. 1, 146.

As the first human rights system, the ECHR began with a short list of civil and political rights, to which additional guarantees have been added over time. In addition, the jurisprudence of the European Court of Human Rights has been relatively conservative compared to that of other systems, which reflects an early concern for maintaining state support in light of the innovations of the European system and the then-optional nature of the court's jurisdiction. The European system was the first to create an international court for the protection of human rights and to create a procedure for individual denunciations of human rights violations. An earlier, more limited effort was made in 1907 with the creation of the Central American Court of Justice. The court was designed to "represent the national conscience of Central America." MANLEY O. HUDSON, INTERNATIONAL TRIBUNALS 173 (1944). Accordingly, it was given jurisdiction over interstate cases as well as between states and individuals. *Id.* at 68.) The role of the victim was initially very limited and admissibility requirements were stringent. As the system has matured, however, the institutional structures and normative guarantees have been considerably strengthened. Although most of the changes result from efforts to improve the effectiveness of the system and add to its guarantees, some of the evolution has been responsive to the activities of other regional organizations within and outside Europe. Others have resulted from the impact of expanding membership in the Council of Europe.

The European system is in fact characterized by its evolution through the adoption of treaties and protocols. Through its Parliamentary Assembly, the Council has drafted a series of human rights instruments. The most significant texts are the 1950 European Convention on Human Rights and Fundamental Freedoms (ECHR) and its fifteen protocols,[2] the 1961 European Social Charter (ESC) with its protocols,[3] the European Convention for the Prevention of Torture and its protocols,[4] the European Charter for Regional or Minority

---

[2] Convention for the Protection of Human Rights and Fundamental Freedoms, ETS No. 5, as completed by Protocol No. 2, ETS No. 44, and amended by Protocol No. 3, ETS No. 45, Protocol No. 5, ETS No. 55, and Protocol No. 8, ETS No. 118. In addition, the following protocols have been adopted:

- Protocol to the Convention, ETS No. 9
- Protocol No. 4, ETS No. 46, Securing Certain Rights and Freedoms
- Protocol No. 6, ETS No. 114, Concerning the Abolition of the Death Penalty
- Protocol No. 7, ETS No. 117
- Protocol No. 9, ETS No. 140
- Protocol No. 10, ETS No. 146
- Protocol No. 11, ETS No. 155, Restructuring the Control Machinery. Art. 34 allows for individual applications to the European Court of Human Rights.
- Protocol No. 12, ETS No. 177
- Protocol No. 13, ETS No. 187, Concerning Abolition of the Death Penalty in All Circumstances
- Protocol No. 14, ETS No. 194, amending the Control System of the Convention
- Protocol No. 14bis, ETS No. 204.

[3] *European Social Charter*, ETS No. 35. The Charter entered into force on February 26, 1965, and was revised in 1996. The Charter and revised Charter have forty-three contracting parties as of March 30, 2010. A Protocol to the Charter, adopted in 1988, imposes legal obligations in regard to additional economic and social rights. It entered into force on September 4, 1992. ETS No. 128. The 1991 Turin Protocol (ETS No. 142) is not yet in force as it requires the ratification of all parties to the Charter. A further Protocol, adopted November 9, 1995 (ETS No. 158), to provide for a system of collective complaints is in force. Finally, as of May 11, 2010, thirty states have accepted the revised Charter (ETS No. 163).

[4] European Convention for the Prevention of Torture, ETS No. 126. Protocol 1 widens the geographical scope of the Convention by enabling states not members of the Council of Europe to accede to it by invitation. ETS No. 151. Protocol 2 makes technical

Languages,[5] and the 1995 Framework Convention for the Protection of National Minorities. An additional protocol to the Convention on Cybercrime entered into force in 2006,[6] which criminalizes acts of a racist or xenophobic nature through computer systems. And the Convention on Action Against Trafficking in Human Beings[7] entered into force in 2009; the Convention on Access to Official Documents[8] was adopted that year but has yet to receive the requisite number of ratifications to come into force. Together these instruments form a network of mutually reinforcing human rights protections in Europe.

The European Union (EU) – to be distinguished from the Council of Europe, which is often seen as a path to EU membership – also addresses human rights in Europe. Article 6 of the Treaty on the European Union establishes as a principle that that the Union is "found on . . . respect for human rights" and under Article 6 all states that seek to join the EU must adhere to this principle. The EU has the Charter of Fundamental Rights, which was adopted in 2000 and proclaimed a second time in 2007 to give it binding legal effect. The Charter has been repeatedly cited in the opinions of the advocates-general and has on several occasions influenced the conclusions of the European Court of Justice (ECJ). The ECJ also regularly applies international human rights law in its decisions, particularly when seeking common human rights standards. In 2007, Council Regulation (EC) No 168/2007 (15 Feb. 2007) established the European Fundamental Rights Agency. The Agency provides EU institutions and member states with assistance and expertise in the implementation of the Charter.

The inter-American system as it exists today began with the transformation of the Pan-American Union into the Organization of American States (OAS). The OAS Charter proclaims the "fundamental rights of the individual" as one of the Organization's basic principles. The 1948 American Declaration on the Rights and Duties of Man gives definition to the Charter's general commitment to human rights. *Interpretation of the American Declaration of the Rights and Duties of Man within the Framework of article 64 of the American Convention on Human Rights*, Advisory Opinion OC-10/89, July 14, 1989, Series A No. 10. More than a decade later, in 1959, the OAS created the seven member Inter-American Commission of Human Rights with a mandate of furthering respect for human rights among member states. In 1965, the Commission's competence was expanded to accept communications, to request information from governments, and to make recommendations to bring about more effective observance of human rights. The American Convention of Human Rights, signed in 1969, conferred additional competence on the Commission to oversee compliance with the Convention. American Convention on Human Rights, Nov. 22, 1969 *reprinted in* 9 I.L.M. 673 (1970). The Convention, which entered into force in 1978, also created the Inter-American Court of Human Rights. The Court has jurisdiction over contentious cases submitted against states that accept its jurisdiction, and the Court may issue advisory opinions.

The Commission's jurisdiction extends to all thirty-five OAS member states. The twenty-five states that have ratified the Convention are bound by its provisions, whereas other member states are held to the standards of the American Declaration. Communications may be filed

---

changes to the arrangements for elections of the members of the European Committee for the Prevention of Torture and Inhuman and Degrading Treatment or Punishment. ETS No. 152. Both Protocols entered into force in 2001. See A. Cassese, *A New Approach to Human Rights: The European Convention for the Prevention of Torture*, 83 AM. J. INT'L. L. 128 (1989); M. Evans & R. Morgan, *The European Convention for the Prevention of Torture: Operational Practice*, 41 INT'L L. & COMP. L. Q. 590 (1992).

[5] *European Charter for Regional or Minority Languages*, ETS No. 148, entry into force March 1, 1998.

[6] Additional Protocol to the Convention on Cybercrime, concerning the Criminalisation of Acts of a Racist and Xenophobic Nature Committed through Computer Systems, ETS No. 189.

[7] Council of Europe Convention on Action Against Trafficking in Human Beings, ETS No. 197.

[8] Council of Europe Convention on Access to Official Documents, ETS No. 205.

against any state; the optional clause applies only to interstate cases. Standing for nonstate actors to file communications is broad. The Commission may also prepare country reports and conduct on-site visits to individual countries, examining the human rights situation in the particular country and making recommendations to the government. Country reports have been prepared on the Commission's own initiative and at the request of the country concerned. The Commission may also appoint special rapporteurs to prepare studies on hemisphere-wide problems.

As with the European system, the inter-American system has expanded its protections over time through the adoption of additional human rights norms. The major instruments are the Inter-American Convention for the Prevention and Punishment of Torture;[9] the Additional Protocol to the American Convention on Human Rights in the Area of Economic, Social and Cultural Rights;[10] the Second Additional Protocol to the American Convention on Human Rights to Abolish the Death Penalty;[11] the Inter-American Convention on the Prevention, Punishment, and Eradication of Violence Against Women;[12] the Inter-American Convention on Forced Disappearance of Persons;[13] the Inter-American Convention on the Elimination of All Forms of Discrimination Against Persons with Disabilities,[14] the Inter-American Declaration of Principles on Freedom of Expression,[15] the Inter-American Democratic Charter,[16] and the still-incomplete Draft American Declaration on the Rights of Indigenous Peoples.[17]

2. Development of Compliance Mechanisms (1967–1998)

Many people throughout the world viewed the founding of the United Nations as the creation of an institution to redress human rights violations. Thousands of petitions began to flow to the United Nations. The Commission on Human Rights asked the U.N. legal counsel what to do about the petitions. The legal counsel responded that the Commission had no power to take any action in regard to any complaints concerning human rights. The Commission accepted this opinion, which was approved by the Economic and Social Council in 1947 in Res. 75(V) and reaffirmed in 1959 in Res. 728(F). By the mid-1960s, however, the influx of newly independent states led to a reexamination of the question. In 1966, the General Assembly, in Res. 2144(XXI), invited the Economic and Social Council (ECOSOC) and the Commission to "give urgent consideration to ways and means of improving the capacity of the United Nations to put a stop to violations of human rights wherever they might occur." The

---

[9] Inter-American Convention to Prevent and Punish Torture, 1985 OAS T.S. No. 67, *reprinted in* 25 I.L.M. 519 (1986), entry into force February 28, 1987.

[10] Additional Protocol to the American Convention on Human Rights in the Area of Economic, Social and Cultural Rights (Protocol of San Salvador), OAS T.S. No. 69, OAS Doc. OEA/Ser.A/42 (SEPF), *reprinted in* 28 I.L.M. 161 (1989), entry into force Nov. 16, 1999.

[11] Protocol to the American Convention on Human Rights to Abolish the Death Penalty. OAS T.S. No. 73, *reprinted in* 29 I.L.M. 1447 (1990), entry into force Aug. 28, 1991.

[12] Inter-American Convention on the Prevention, Punishment and Eradication of Violence against Women, OAS Treaties Register A.61 (June 9, 1994), 27 U.S.T. 3301, 1438 U.N.T.S. 63, *reprinted in* 33 I.L.M. 1534 (1994), entry into force Mar. 5, 1995.

[13] Inter-American Convention on Forced Disappearance of Persons, OAS Doc. OAE/Ser.P/AG/Doc.3114/94 (1994), *reprinted in* 33 I.L.M. 1529 (1994), entry into force Mar. 28, 1996.

[14] Inter-American Convention on the Elimination of All Forms of Discrimination Against Persons with Disabilities, OAS Doc. AG/RES. 1608 (XXIX-O/99) (June 7, 1999), OAS Treaties Register A.65, entry into force Sept. 14, 1991.

[15] Inter-American Declaration of Principles on Freedom of Expression, *reprinted in* Basic Documents Pertaining to Human Rights in the Inter-American System, OAS Doc. OAS/Ser.L/V/I.4 rev.12 (Jan. 31, 2007).

[16] Inter-American Democratic Charter (adopted by acclamation, Sept. 11, 2001), OAS Doc. OEA/Ser.P/AG/Res.1 (2001), *reprinted in* Basic Documents Pertaining to Human Rights in the Inter-American System, OAS Doc. OAS/Ser.L/V/I.4 rev.12 (Jan. 31, 2007).

[17] Working Group to Prepare the Draft American Declaration on the Rights of Indigenous Peoples, Twelfth Meeting of Negotiations in the Quest of Points of Consensus, *Record of the Current Status of the Draft American Declaration on the Rights of Indigenous Peoples*, OAS Doc. OAE/Ser.K/XVIGT/DADIN/doc.334/08 rev.5 (Dec. 3, 2009).

Council responded by adopting ECOSOC Res. 1235, approving the Commission's decision to give annual public consideration to a new agenda item entitled "Question of the violation of human rights and fundamental freedoms, including policies of racial discrimination and segregation and of apartheid, in all countries, with particular reference to colonial and other dependent countries and territories." In this context, the Council approved the Commission's intention to make a thorough study of situations that reveal a consistent pattern of gross violations of human rights.

Three years later, the Commission approved another procedure whereby it would examine "communications, together with replies of governments, if any, which appear to reveal a consistent pattern of gross violations of human rights." In Res. 1503, ECOSOC approved the Commission's decision. Subsequently, the Sub-Commission and Commission of the United Nations examined communications to find those situations of gross and systematic violations. The U.N. bodies also developed innovative mechanisms such as thematic rapporteurs and working groups to enhance compliance by states with human rights obligations. Treaty-monitoring bodies also have moved toward more effective compliance mechanisms, with optional protocols either adopted or negotiated for several major human rights instruments to allow for the filing of individual petitions. Other mechanisms involve early warning and on-site inspections.

Standard setting did not cease, of course. The U.N. efforts focused on elaborating on and giving further detail to rights already proclaimed and to further protection for groups historically disfavored. Thus, a number of universal conventions continue to be adopted, including the Convention on the Elimination of All Forms of Discrimination Against Women (1979), the U.N. Convention Against Torture (1984), the Convention on the Rights of the Child (1989), the Convention on the Protection of the Rights of All Migrant Workers and Members of Their Families (1990), the Convention on the Rights of Persons with Disabilities (2006), and the International Convention for the Protection of All Persons from Enforced Disappearance (2006).

On the regional level, since 1998, the European system has included the European Court of Human Rights, with compulsory jurisdiction over interstate and individual cases against parties to the European Convention on Human Rights. The American Convention on Human Rights inaugurated the Inter-American Court of Human Rights once the Convention entered into force in 1978. The functioning European and inter-American courts are one of the great contributions to human rights by regional systems.

In Africa, the regional promotion and protection of human rights is established by the African Charter on Human and Peoples' Rights (African Charter). The Assembly of Heads of State and Government of the Organization of African Unity (OAU) adopted the African Charter on June 27, 1981. African Charter on Human and Peoples' Rights, OAU Doc. CAB/LEG./67/3/Rev. 5, *reprinted in* 21 I.L.M. 59 (1982), entry into force Oct. 21, 1986.

In 2002, the OAU became the African Union (AU). Articles 3 and 4 of the Constitutive Act of the African Union, AU Doc. CAB/LEG/23.15 (May 26, 2001), establishes an important place for human rights on the African agenda. One notable program, started by the OAU in 2001 and continued under AU auspices, is the New Partnership for Africa's Development (NEPAD). The linkages of human rights, the environment, and sustainable development are explicitly acknowledge in paragraph 9 of the *NEPAD Declaration on Democracy, Political, Economic and Corporate Governance*, AU Doc. AHG/235 (XXXVIII) Annex I (July 8, 2002). Part of the institutional architecture of NEPAD is the African Peer Review Mechanism (APRM). Participation in APRM is voluntary. It is a self-monitoring system and its mandate is to ensure that the policies and practices of participating states conform to agreed standards in four thematic areas: democracy and political governance; economic governance and management; corporate governance; and socio-economic development. Its purpose is to foster the adoption of policies that lead to, inter alia, sustainable development. *African Peer Review Base Document*, AU Doc. AGH/235 (XXXVIII) Annex 2 (July 8, 2002). In conducting peer reviews that involve human rights issues, the APRM involves existing AU human rights institutions with the assessments. APRM, *Organisation and Processes*, NEPAD/HGSIC-3–2003/APRM/Guideline/O&P (Mar. 9, 2003).

The African Charter has been ratified by all fifty-three AU member states. The African Charter differs from other regional treaties in its inclusion of "peoples' rights." It also includes economic, social, and cultural rights to a greater extent than either the European Convention or the American Convention. *See generally* THE AFRICAN CHARTER ON HUMAN AND PEOPLES' RIGHTS (2d ed., Malcolm Evans & Rachel Murray eds., 2008). The African Charter establishes the African Commission on Human and Peoples' Rights of eleven independent members elected for a renewable period of six years. The African Charter confers four functions on the Commission: promotion of human and peoples' rights, protection of those rights, interpretation of the Charter, and the performance of other tasks that may be entrusted to it by the Assembly of Heads of State and Government. The Commission may undertake studies, conduct training and teaching, convene conferences, initiate publication programs, disseminate information, and collaborate with national and local institutions concerned with human and peoples' rights. Unlike the other systems, the African system envisages not only interstate and individual communications procedures but also a special procedure for situations of gross and systematic violations. The African system includes the Protocol on the Establishment of an African Court on Human and Peoples' Rights[18] and the Protocol the Rights of Women in Africa.[19] In addition, specific conventions for refugees[20] and children[21] have been adopted.

Looking at the African Court of Human Rights, which opened its doors in 2004, unlike its European and American counterparts, it is empowered to apply *any* human rights instrument that is ratified by all states involved in a case, including universal treaties. As does the European Court, the African Court has jurisdiction to hear cases brought directly by individuals and NGOs, but only if they have been granted AU observer status.

Virtually all the legal instruments creating the various regional systems refer to the Universal Declaration of Human Rights (UDHR) and the U.N. Charter, providing a measure of uniformity in the fundamental guarantees and a reinforcement of the universal character of the Declaration. The rights contained in the treaties also reflect the human rights norms set forth in other global human rights declarations and conventions, in particular the U.N. Covenants on Civil and Political Rights (CCPR) and Economic, Social and Cultural Rights (CESCR). In addition, as each successive system has been created it has looked to normative instruments and the jurisprudence of those systems founded earlier.

The European system, "considering the Universal Declaration of Human Rights," provides that the "like-minded" governments of Europe have resolved "to take the first steps for

---

[18] Protocol to the African Charter on Human and Peoples' Rights on the Establishment of an African Court on Human and Peoples' Rights, AU Doc. OAU/LEG/EXP/AFCHPR/PROT(III) (June 9, 1998), entry into force Jan. 25, 2004 (this protocol will be superseded and the Court supplanted for parties to the Protocol on the Statute of the African Court of Justice and Human Rights when it comes into force).

[19] Protocol to the African Charter on Human and Peoples' Rights on the Rights of Women in Africa, AU Doc. Assembly/AU/Dec.14 (II) (July 11, 2003), entry into force Nov. 25, 2005.

[20] Convention Governing Specific Aspects of the Refugee Problems in Africa, 1001 U.N.T.S. 45, entry into force June 20, 1974.

[21] African Charter on the Rights and Welfare of the Child, OAU Doc. CAB/LEG/TSG/Rev.1 (July 11, 1990), entry into force Nov. 29, 1999.

the collective enforcement of certain of the rights stated in the Universal Declaration." The Preamble to the American Convention also cites the UDHR, as well as referring to the OAS Charter, the American Declaration of the Rights and Duties of Man, and other international and regional instruments not referred to by name. The drafting history of the American Convention shows that the states involved used the European Convention, the UDHR, and the Covenants in deciding on the Convention's guarantees and institutional structure.

The African Charter mentions the U.N. Charter and the Universal Declaration of Human Rights in connection with the pledge made by the African states to promote international cooperation. In the Charter's Preamble, the African states also reaffirm in sweeping fashion "their adherence to the principles of human and peoples' rights and freedoms contained in the declarations, conventions and other international instruments adopted by the Organization of African Unity, the Movement of Non-Aligned Countries and the United Nations."

Yet there are clear differences in the regional instruments in the framework of the universal norms. The differences may be less pronounced than appears at first reading, however, because of provisions regarding choice of law and canons of interpretation contained in the regional instruments. The application of these provisions has led to a cross-referencing and mutual influence in jurisprudence that is producing some convergence in fundamental human rights principles.

3. Individual Complaints Procedures

One of the greatest contributions of the regional systems is the establishment of individual complaint mechanisms for judicial or quasi-judicial redress of human rights violations. Europe was the first to create a commission and court that could hear complaints, followed by the Americas and now Africa. The Inter-American Commission on Human Rights, from its creation in 1960, interpreted its powers broadly to include the ability "to make general recommendations to each individual state as well as to all of them." Inter-American Commission on Human Rights, First Report 1960, OAS Doc. OEA/Ser.L/V/II.1, Doc. 32 (1961). This was deemed to include the power to take cognizance of individual petitions and use them to assess the human rights situation in a particular country, based on the American Convention for Human Rights for states parties and on the normative standards of the American Declaration for states not party to the Convention. The inter-American system was thus the first to make the complaints procedure mandatory against all member states.

The regional commissions and courts have gradually strengthened their procedures for handling complaints. In the European system, a slow evolution toward individual standing first allowed individuals to appear before the court in the guise of assistants to the Commission. A protocol later permitted them to appear by right. Under Protocol 11 to the European Convention on Human Rights, individual complainants have had sole standing since 1998.

The European Social Charter has also been strengthened through amendment and through practice. For a general review of the evolution of the European Social Charter, see David Harris, *The Council of Europe (II): The European Social Charter, in* An Introduction to the International Protection of Human Rights: A Textbook 243 (Raija Hanski & Markku Hanski eds., 1999).

Additional rights were added by the 1988 Protocol, and a second protocol in 1991 radically revised the system of supervision, although this protocol is not yet in force. An even greater change occurred with the 1995 Additional Protocol, which provides for a system of collective complaints from trade unions and employers' organizations and from NGOs.[22] In 1996, the European Social Charter was revised to expand the number of substantive rights covered again and incorporate provisions of the subsequent protocols.[23]

In the inter-American system, the Commission has consistently taken steps to improve the processing of cases, most recently with the reform of its Rules of Procedure in 2009. It now determines admissibility before evaluating the merits of the claim and holds hearings on admissibility or the merits at the request of either party or on the Commission's initiative. The restructuring of the case system in the inter-American system involves greater use of provisional measures, registration of petitions, the creation of chambers for hearings, and more on-site visits to gather evidence. In addition, the Commission has developed a structured friendly settlement procedure and stronger means to protect confidentiality. The Commission has consistently appointed petitioners or their legal representatives as Commission legal advisers when bringing a matter before the Inter-American Court of Human Rights, a practice first developed in the European system. *See Rules of Procedure of the Inter-American Commission on Human Rights* (approved as amended by the Commission at its 137th regular period of sessions, 13 Nov. 2009).

The African system has evolved quickly through the African Commission's interpretation of its powers and revision of its rules of procedure. The African Commission, like the Inter-American Commission, may "give its views or make recommendations to Governments." The African Commission has read this to include the formulation of principles and rules for the resolution of human rights problems in specific states. As do the other commissions, the African Commission negotiates friendly settlements. Unlike the Inter-American and European Commissions, it is developing its own follow-up actions. In various Nigerian cases, for instance, the Commission recommended the release of persons whom it decided were wrongfully detained and decided "to bring the file to Nigeria for the planned mission in order to verify that . . . [the victims] had been released." Case 60/91 8th p. 4. Also Case 87/93, The Constitutional Rights Project (in re Zamani Lakwot et al.) v. Nigeria, at 7–9.

In its procedures on communications, the African Commission has benefitted from the experience of the other systems. It follows the usual two-stage process of considering a communication for admissibility and on the merits. It set a three-month time limit in which states must reply to requests for information and make observations regarding the admissibility of communications. If the Commission determines a petition is admissible, it again gives the state three months to submit explanations or statements regarding the case. The Commission is empowered under the African Charter to issue what amounts to advisory opinions when a state, an institution of the AU, or an African Organization recognized by the AU requests an interpretation of any provision of the Charter. The Commission has adopted and strengthened rules on conflict of interest and has agreed on the possibility of requesting provisional measures, despite a lack of specific reference to such measures in the Charter. The African Commission's rule on provisional measures is almost identical to article 63(2) of the American Convention. With the advent of the African Court, the Commission can submit cases of alleged human rights violations to the Court, and likewise, the Court can request the opinion of or transfer cases to the Commission. Under Rule 33 of the Interim Rules of Court and articles 5(3) and 34(6) of the Protocol on the Establishment of an African

---

[22] Additional Protocol to the European Social Charter Providing for a System of Collective Complaints, ETS No. 158, entry into force July 1, 1998.

[23] European Social Charter (revised), ETS No. 163, entry into force July 1, 1999.

Court on Human and Peoples' Rights, individuals and NGOs can petition the Court directly when a state party recognizes the competence of the Court to receive such petitions.

In general, all the systems have enhanced their complaints procedures by providing means for greater participation of victims and their representatives. In most cases, these changes have occurred through action by the supervisory bodies rather than through amending the basic texts.

4. From State to Individual Responsibility (1998–present)

As early as 1948, the United Nations adopted the Convention on the Prevention and Punishment of the Crime of Genocide. It was the first convention (and remains one of only two) to declare the acts referred to as "crimes under international law." The other convention to use such terminology is the Convention Against Apartheid. Neither convention establishes an international compliance system but leaves punishment of offenders to national courts. Nuremburg provided a precedent for international criminal prosecution of the most serious violations of human rights, but it was a precedent not followed until 1993, when the U.N. Security Council created an ad hoc tribunal for the former Yugoslavia, followed one year later by a similar tribunal to consider genocide in Rwanda. It was in 1998 that the principle of individual responsibility for the most serious violations of human rights and humanitarian law became generalized at the international level, with the adoption of the Rome Statute of the International Criminal Court. Many issues remain open, however, such as the relationship between criminal responsibility and customary immunities for diplomats and heads of state. Also to be developed are issues of corporate responsibility, whether civil or criminal. Remedies, including rehabilitation and compensation for victims, are also on the agenda for the coming years.

F. *Normative and Institutional Evolution*

Human rights systems have evolved through a complex interplay of environmental pressures, institutional changes, and intersystem contacts. Perhaps most important, the dynamic reading given human rights guarantees by the global and regional supervisory organs has prevented a rigid formalism from reducing the relevance of human rights bodies as circumstances change and new problems arise. Judicial power in the regional systems is very significant, created in large part by the character of human rights conventions. They are written in general terms, leaving ample scope for judges and commissioners to apply and creatively interpret their provisions. The European Court of Human Rights has confirmed that "the Convention is a living instrument which . . . must be interpreted in the light of present-day conditions." Tyrer v. United Kingdom, 26 Eur. Ct. H.R. (ser. A) at 10 (1978). The Organization of American States has similarly emphasized the notion of "evolving American law." See Donald T. Fox, *Inter-American Commission on Human Rights Finds United States in Violation*, 82 Am. J. Int'l L. 601, 602 (1988).

All of the systems have a growing case law detailing the rights and duties enunciated in the basic instruments. The jurisprudence of the regional human rights bodies has thus become a major source of human rights law. In many instances, this case law reflects a convergence of the different substantive protections in favor of broad human rights protections. In other instances, differences in treaty terms or approach have resulted in a rejection of precedent from other systems. For example, the European and Inter-American courts take very different approaches to their remedial powers on the basis of the different language of their respective treaties. In case law, the Inter-American Court has also rejected the European doctrine of margin of appreciation. In general, the judges and the commissioners have been willing to substantiate or give greater authority to their interpretations of the rights guaranteed by referencing not only their own prior case law but also the decisions of other global and regional bodies.

Some decisions cross-reference specific articles of other instruments. The European Court of Human Rights has used article 19(2) of the International Covenant on Civil and Political Rights (ICCPR) to extend the application of article 10 of the European Convention to cover freedom of artistic expression. Muller et al., 133 Eur. Ct. H.R. (ser. A) at para. 27 (1988). It has referred to the U.N. Convention on the Rights of the Child in regard to education, Costello-Roberts v. UK, 247C Eur. Ct. H.R. (ser. A) at para. 27 (1993), and both the ICCPR and American Convention in regard to the right to a name as part of European Convention art. 8. Burghartz v. Switzerland, 280B Eur. Ct. H.R. (ser. A) at para. 24 (1994). Best known is the *Soering* case, in which the Court found implicit in article 3 of the European Convention the obligation of article 3 of the U.N. Torture Convention not to extradite someone who might face torture. Soering v. UK, 161 Eur. Ct. H.R. (ser. A) at para. 88 (1989).

The Inter-American Court frequently uses other international court decisions and international human rights instruments to interpret and apply inter-American norms. It has referred to the European Convention, *Compulsory Membership in an Association Prescribed by Law for the Practice of Journalism*, 5 Inter-Am. Ct. H.R. (ser. A) (1985) at para. 43–46; the CCPR and other U.N. treaties, *Enforceability of the Right to Reply or Correction*, 7 Inter-Am. Ct. H.R. (ser. A) (1986) at para. 25; and decisions of the European Human Rights Commission and the Court, *Proposed Amendments to the Naturalization Provisions of the Constitution of Costa Rica*, Advisory Opinion OC-4/84, January 19, 1984, Inter-Am. Ct. H.R. (Ser. A) No. 4 (1984), paras. 50–51. It has explicitly stated that it will use cases decided by the European Court, *Compulsory Membership in an Association Prescribed by Law for the Practice of Journalism*, 5 Inter-Am. Ct. H.R. (ser. A) (1985) para. 52, and the Human Rights Committee when their value is to augment rights protection and has indicated a commitment to the nonincorporation of restrictions from other systems. *Id.* at para. 51. Inter-American Commission and Court decisions in turn provide extensive jurisprudence on due process, conditions of detention and treatment of detainees, legality of amnesty laws, rape as torture, disappearances, obligations to ensure respect for rights, direct applicability of norms, exhaustion of local remedies, burden and standard of proof, admissibility of evidence, and general doctrine of interpretation of human rights treaties.

The decisions of the African Commission also show the influence of other regional systems. The Commission has adopted several doctrines established in European and inter-American case law: presumption of the truth of the allegations from the silence of government (*see, e.g.,* the Commission's decisions in communications 59/91, 60/91, 87/93, 101/93 and 74/92); the notion of continuing violations (Communication 142/94 Muthuthurin Njoka v. Kenya, at 13; Case 39/90), continuity of obligations in spite of a change of government, (Joined cases 83/92, 88/93, 91/93 Jean Yaovi Degli, Union Interafricaine des Droits de l'Homme, Commission International de Juristes v. Togo); state responsibility for failure to act (Communication 74/92, *Commission Nationale des Droits de l'Homme et des Libertés v. Chad*), and the presumption that the state is responsible for custodial injuries (Tomasi v France, 241 Eur. Ct. H.R. (ser A) at para. 40–41 (1993).

In regard to admissibility of communications, the African Commission, like other regional bodies, has found that some so-called remedies are "not of a nature that requires exhaustion" because they are discretionary and nonjudicial. The African Commission and the

Inter-American Court emphasize the need for independence of the judiciary and the guarantees of a fair trial. The African Commission has called attacks on the judiciary "especially invidious, because while [they are] a violation of human rights in itself, [they permit] other violations of rights to go unredressed." *See* 60/91 Constitutional Rights Project v. Nigeria, Communications Annex, 8th Annual Report of the African Commission on Human Rights, p. 3.

Although the mutual influence of the systems is clear, there are regional differences in the nature of cases filed that have limited the relevance of precedents from other systems. In Europe, historically, virtually all cases raised questions of law on agreed-on facts. In addition, a large percentage concerned procedural guarantees in civil and criminal proceedings. With changes in the European system, the jurisprudence has become more expansive, but contrasts remain with the inter-American system. Nearly all the inter-American cases have concerned the factual determination of state responsibility for the death, disappearance, or other mistreatment of individuals. The result has been an inter-American focus on issues of standard of proof and burden of proof that rarely arise in the European system. For this reason, most of the references to European jurisprudence are found in the Inter-American Court's advisory opinions on questions of law. The Inter-American Commission has also had to be concerned with the widespread armed conflicts in the region. As a result, it has had to document human rights violations by nonstate actors, thereby making an important contribution to international human rights law. International Responsibility for the Promulgation and Enforcement of Laws in Violation of the Convention, 14 Inter-Am. Ct. H.R. (ser. A) (1994).

The matters submitted in Africa have involved varied issues, including trade union freedoms, arbitrary detention, killings, and the right to health. *See, e.g.,* 64/92 Krischna Achutan (on behalf of Aleke Banda), 68/92 Amnesty International on behalf of Orton and Vera Chirwa; and 78/92 Amnesty International on Behalf of Orton and Vera Chirwa v. Malawi. Although it has adopted established doctrines from the other systems, the African Commission has also used some of the unique provisions of the African Charter to progressively apply its guarantees. The Commission has held, for example, that the absence of a derogation clause in the African Charter means the Charter as a whole remains in force even during periods of armed conflict. *See* Communication 74/92, *Commission Nationale des Droits de l'Homme et des Libertes v. Chad*, AHG/207(XXXII) Annex VIII at 12, 16

To the extent that there is a progressive convergence of human rights norms, it is in large part stimulated by victims and their lawyers. They submit memorials that draw attention to the relevant case law of other systems and help to expand human rights protections by obtaining a progressive ruling in one system, then invoking it in another. This tendency is enhanced by the liberal standing rules of the inter-American and African systems. Many complaints are filed by NGOs familiar with and operating in more than one system. Most of the communications submitted to the African system thus far, for example, have come from groups such as Amnesty International, the International Commission of Jurists, and the Lawyers Committee for Human Rights. In the European system, briefs submitted amicus curiae by NGOs similarly draw attention to regional and global norms and jurisprudence. The epistemic community of NGOs has its parallel in the regular meetings of the commissioners and judges of the regional systems. The resulting progressive development of regional human rights law strongly suggests that no human rights lawyer should rely solely on the jurisprudence of a single system in pleading a case.

Normative evolution has been matched by institutional developments. The United Nations now has a high commissioner for human rights, field offices, and widespread use of special rapporteurs on thematic and country studies. Regional human rights procedures and institutions have evolved perhaps to an even greater extent. Although some changes result from amendments to the basic legal instruments, at least as much change is due to regional bodies developing their own implied powers. A serious commitment to giving effect to regional protections is evident in the evolution of the functions and procedures of regional human rights bodies.

Questions and Discussion

1. Despite continuing controversy over the aims, normative content, and powers of global and regional institutions, human rights law can be said to have restrained many dictatorial powers and established the criteria for transition to democracy and the rule of law. It also succeeded in challenging many totalitarian and authoritarian governments, although it cannot claim sole credit for democratization over the past two decades. What factors underlie the successes in human rights? Does the ethical and moral aspect figure in? What about the involvement of nonstate actors? Can the lessons taught by these successes be used to protect the environment?

2. Unfortunately, there have been and continue to be too many human rights abuses in the world, including failures to prevent or halt many situations of massive abuses, including genocide. Can you identify reasons for these deficiencies? Is the sovereignty barrier still a problem? What about the fact that states are at one and the same time both protectors and violators of human rights? What about the turnaround principle – a reluctance by states to protest against abuses stems from concern about reciprocal complaints? Could broader diplomatic concerns pose problems?

3. Human rights governance is limited by its own design, which had in mind restraining powerful government agents. It has not succeeded in addressing the massive violations that occur in weak or failed states where anarchy and civil conflict prevail. Violations by nonstate actors that cannot be controlled by a state generally fall outside the scope of most human rights law (aside from international criminal law covering crimes against humanity and war crimes). What challenges does this gap raise for the deployment of human rights in aid of environmental protection?

G. *The Challenge of Human Rights in the Realm of the* Domaine Réservé

In Lassa Oppenheim's classic treatise published at the beginning of the twentieth century, international law was defined as a law exclusively governing the relations among states. L. OPPENHEIM, INTERNATIONAL LAW 3–14 (1st ed., 1905). Defining international law in this manner meant that by definition individuals and other nonstate actors, such as corporations and international organizations, could not be subjects of international law. Instead, Oppenheim classified individuals as potential objects of international law, like territory, natural resources, and other state assets over which each government had exclusive jurisdiction. In summary, individuals had no rights, duties, or standing in international law. As a corollary, how each state treated its nationals was considered an internal matter and not a topic of international concern. As shown earlier, only if a government, through an act or omission, caused injury to a foreign national and failed to afford redress did an international issue arise. An unredressed injury was considered an affront to the state of nationality, which could take up the matter through an interstate claim against the injuring state.

Until the middle of the twentieth century, it remained exceptional for international law to confer direct rights and duties on individuals, but a continual expansion of such norms finally led to a change in the definition of international law to include other actors, especially from the end of World War II, when human rights law became a major topic of international regulation. By 1948, Judge Jessup could write that "international law or the law of nations must be defined as law applicable to states in their mutual relations and to individuals in their relations with states.... [It] may also be applicable to certain interrelationships of individuals themselves, where such interrelationships involve matters of international concern." P. JESSUP, A MODERN LAW OF NATIONS 17 (1948). As late as 1963, however, Brierly defined international law as "the body of rules and principals of action which are binding upon civilized states in their relation with one another." J.L. BRIERLY, THE LAW OF NATIONS (6th ed., 1963). Today, the Restatement (Third) of Foreign Relations Law expresses the general understanding that international law can govern the relations among states and other actors in the international arena:

> "International law"... consists of rules and principles of general application dealing with the conduct of states and of international organizations and with their relations inter se, as well as with some of their relations with persons, whether natural or juridical.

Sec. 101, RESTATEMENT (THIRD) OF THE FOREIGN RELATIONS LAW OF THE UNITED STATES (1987).

The changing status of the individual can be seen in enhanced procedural standing and in the elaboration of substantive rights and obligations imposed by international law. Direct access of individuals to national and international fora is a marked departure from traditional rules of diplomatic protection, whereby only the state of nationality could pursue a claim on behalf of an injured individual against the wrongdoing state. Tribunals created to enforce human rights and settle economic disputes now often have jurisdiction over claims brought by individuals injured by state action. The state of nationality or the state allegedly at fault may disagree with "internationalizing" the dispute, but the injured individual, regardless of nationality, can nonetheless assert rights directly against the responsible state.

The internationalization of human rights most clearly indicates the changing status of the individual. Classic international law, reflected in the *Nottebohm* judgment of the International Court of Justice, emphasized the bond of nationality and the rights and duties conferred on the individual by the state. In contrast, human rights texts and tribunals today emphasize that human rights are not derived from the state but are inherent attributes of the human person guaranteed by international law. The U.N. Human Rights Committee in its General Comment No. 26 (Continuity of Obligations) emphasized the objective nature of human rights guarantees:

> The rights enshrined in the Covenant belong to the people living in the territory of the State party.... [O]nce the people are accorded the protection of the rights under the Covenant, such protection devolves with territory and continues to belong to them, notwithstanding change in government of the State party, including dismemberment in more than one State or State succession or any subsequent action of the State party designed to divest them of the rights guaranteed by the Covenant.

ICCPR, *General Comment No. 26 (Continuity of Obligations)*, UN Doc. CCPR/C/21/ Rev.1/Add.8/Rev.1 (8 December 1997).

Charter of the United Nations, 1 U.N.T.S. XVI (June 26, 1945) Article 2(7)

Nothing contained in the present Charter shall authorize the United Nations to intervene in matters which are essentially within the domestic jurisdiction of any state or shall require the Members to submit such matters to settlement under the present Charter; but this principle shall not prejudice the application of enforcement measures [by the Security Council] under Chapter VII.

The Youth of Rights, 104 HARV. L. REV. 917, 929–931 (1991) (reviewing LOUIS HENKIN, THE AGE OF RIGHTS (1990))
Henry Steiner

... Unlike many components of classical international law, the human rights movement was not meant to work out matters of reciprocal convenience among states – for example, sovereign or diplomatic immunities – or to aim only at regulating areas of historical conflicts among states – for example, use of the sea or air space, or treatment by a state of its alien population. Rather it reached broad areas of everyday life within states that are vital to the internal rather than international distribution of political power. As international law's aspirations grew, as that law became more critical of and hence more distanced from states' behavior, the potential for conflict between human rights advocates within a state and that state's controlling elites escalated.

Even the most consensual of rights, the right not to be tortured, has a subversive potential. If, as [an] Amnesty International report suggests, torture amounts to the price of dissent because it is "most often used as an integral part of a government's security strategy," abolishing torture lowers that price. Oppressive regimes prefer to keep the price high.

Other rights included in the Universal Declaration and the *Civil-Political Rights Covenant* influence the structure of government more directly. Abolishing discrimination on grounds of race, ethnicity, religion, or gender can radically alter economic and social arrangements and redirect political power. Protecting rights of speech, expression, and association will give citizens not only security against arbitrary state action, but also the chance to develop a diverse and vibrant civil society that can influence the directions of the state as effectively as governmental policies influence it....

The stakes for power rise as we move further along the spectrum of human rights. The major human rights instruments empower citizens to "take part" in government and to vote in secrecy in genuine, periodic, and non-discriminatory elections. In given circumstances, an authoritarian government can stop torturing and arresting without surrendering its monopoly of power.... [H]owever, such a government cannot grant the right to political participation without signing its death warrant. "Throw out the rascals" speaks the more dramatically after decades of unchosen and oppressive regimes....

Particular clusters of civil-political rights thus challenge many of the world's governments in unavoidable, implacable ways....

But the aspirations of the human rights movement... also has a "utopian" dimension that envisions a vibrant and broadly based political community. Such a vision underscores the potential of the human rights movement for conflict with regimes all over the world. A society honoring the full range of contemporary human rights would be hospitable to many types of pluralism [and resist imposing] one final truth, at least to the point of allowing and protecting difference.

Questions and Discussion

1. Revisit this excerpt from Steiner after studying the critique of human rights by so-called new stream scholars later in this chapter, at pp. 211–14. Do human rights really undermine the internal authority of the state?

2. The internal challenge posed by human rights is also similarly posed by international environmental norms. Professor Schachter points out in connection with the slow, partial, and uneven development of international law to regulate environmental problems that "[m]ost governments hesitate to give up sovereign rights over activities within their jurisdictions, while uncertainties as to causes and effects impede action. Most serious, perhaps, is the resistance to restraints that might reduce economic growth and well-being." Oscar Schachter, *The Emergence of International Environmental Law*, 44 J. INT'L AFFAIRS 457 (1991). It is no doubt because international environmental law challenges many fundamental concepts of traditional international law that its development is recent and has been halting. In many ways, international environmental law seeks to limit state sovereignty, attempts to interlope in the domestic jurisdiction of states, proposes to create greater state responsibility and liability, and promotes the involvement of nonstate actors in the process of formulating and implementing environmental norms. An additional consideration is the potentially limitless scope of obligation in time and distance. Most human rights obligations are drafted to extend to a state's territory and jurisdiction on the assumption that states lack the power to deprive those in other states or future generations of their rights. Given the extent and long-term consequences of transfrontier pollution and greenhouse gas emissions, such an assumption cannot be made with respect to activities affecting the environment.

    As in the field of human rights, the development of far-reaching international norms concerning the environment has been controversial and hotly contested. Yet the pace of international industrialization, urbanization and population growth, the increase in all forms of transportation, and the use of hazardous and nuclear materials have forced states to act in nontraditional ways to prevent and mitigate resulting environmental harm that cannot be contained by imaginary boundaries between states and cannot be handled or avoided by any one state acting alone. Just as the atrocities associated with World War II prompted international action on human rights, the complex and potentially life-threatening problems of ozone depletion, climate change, marine pollution, and so on, are compelling states to join in common cause for global environmental protection. *See generally* Donald K. Anton (reporter), *The Internationalization of Domestic Law: The Shrinking* Domaine Réservé, 87 PROC. AM. SOC'Y INT'L L. 553, 574 (1993).

II. The Idea of Human Rights

Recall in the previous chapter that we distinguished between fundamental or moral rights and legal rights. It is the legally normative version of human rights that we will mainly treat in this text and with which contemporary human rights practice is mainly concerned. As Professor Henkin explains:

> The idea of human rights that has received currency and universal (if nominal) acceptance in our day . . . does not ground or justify itself in natural law, in social contract, or in any other political theory. In international instruments representatives of states declare and recognize human rights, define their content, and ordain their [legal] consequences within political societies and in the system of nation-states. The justification of human rights is rhetorical, not philosophical. Human

rights are self-evident, implied in other ideas that are commonly intuited and accepted. Human rights are derived from accepted principles, or are required by accepted ends – societal ends such as peace and justice; individual ends such as human dignity, happiness, fulfillment.

Louis Henkin, The Age of Rights 2 (1990).

Nevertheless, to fully appreciate human rights and its discourse, we do consider in this chapter the distinctions between the legal and nonlegal, the prescriptive and philosophical. Such distinctions become especially important when we consider that what constitutes a legally protected human right today may not have been recognized as such at earlier points in history. Because the position of a right to the environment is in doubt, looking at the precursors of legality can illuminate the situation. As Merrills observes:

> If we take . . . the suggestion that individuals may be said to enjoy certain moral rights with regard to environmental matters, it is not difficult to see how such things as a right to compensation for harm, a right to be consulted and to make representations on issues of concern, and a right of access to environmental information can all be accommodated within . . . the idea that rights demarcate a sacrosanct area of life in order to promote self-realization and development. *Whether or not there are legal rights to give these entitlements effective expression*, it is not unreasonable to see the moral rights of the individual as engaged when what is at stake is bound up with life, property, and the ability to run one's affairs, as the matters just referred to unquestionably are. We can therefore conclude that though the notion of environmental rights would probably have appeared strange to the philosophers who pioneered the concept of human rights, there is nothing in the concept or its rationale which is incompatible with their thinking.

J.G. Merrills, *Environmental Protection and Human Rights: Conceptual Aspects*, in Human Rights Approaches to Environmental Protection 25, 28 (Alan Boyle & Michael Anderson eds., 1996) (emphasis added).

Of course, this is not the same thing as demonstrating that a right to environment should be recognized, but it does show that such a right is compatible with the theoretical foundations of human rights. As you study the following tracts, consider whether, and if so how, human rights ought to be deployed on an eco-centric basis.

A. *The Nature of Human Rights*

The Philosophical Foundations of Human Rights,
in Human Rights: Concepts and Standards 31, 33–35 (Janusz Symonides ed., 2000)
Jerome J. Shestack

We turn first to the question, what do we mean by human "rights"? Let us focus initially on the word "human." To speak of "human" rights requires a conception of what rights one possesses by virtue of being human. Of course, we are not speaking here of human rights in the self-evident sense that those who have them are human, but in the sense that, in order to have them, one need only be human. Put another way, are there rights that human beings have simply because they are human beings and independent of their varying social circumstances and degrees of merit? The answers which individuals and states provide to this question have great bearing on their attitudes and their vigour with respect to protecting human rights.

Some scholars identify human rights as those which are "important," "moral" and "universal." It is comforting to adorn human rights with those characteristics, but such attributes themselves contain ambiguities. For example, when we say a right is "important" enough to be a "human" right, we may be speaking of one or more of the following qualities: (1) intrinsic value, (2) instrumental value, (3) value in a scheme of rights, (4) importance in not being outweighed by other considerations, or (5) importance as structural support for the system of the good life. "Universal" and "moral" are perhaps even more complicated words. What makes certain rights universal, moral and important, and who decides? This is another way, perhaps, of getting at the question of what is the source or authority for human rights, or how they can be established or justified.

Approaches to these questions vary widely. Intuitive moral philosophers claim that definitions of human rights are futile because they involve moral judgments which must be self-evident and are not further explicable. Other moral philosophers, faced with the instability of meaning, focus on the consequences of human rights, or what they are for. A refinement on this process, advanced by the prescriptivist school says that we should not be concerned with what is sought to be achieved by issuing a moral (human rights) utterance but with what is actually done in issuing it: that is what act is accomplished, what facts are brought into existence....

The definitional process does not become easier when we examine the second word in the term human "rights." Certainly, "rights" is a chameleon-like term which can describe a variety of legal relationships. Sometimes, "right" is used in its strict sense of the right-holder being entitled to something with a correlative duty in another. Sometimes, "right" is used to indicate an immunity from having a legal status altered, Sometimes it indicates a privilege to do something. Sometimes, it refers to a power to create a legal relationship. Although all of these terms have been identified as rights, each invokes different protections and produces variant results.

For example, when we speak of an inalienable right, do we mean a right on which no expectations or limitations are valid? Or do we mean a prima facie right with a special burden on the proponent of any limitation? Or do we mean a principle which must be followed unless some other moral principle weighty enough to allow abridgment arises?

If we classify a right as a claim against a government to refrain from certain acts, such as not to torture its citizens or deny them freedom of speech, religion or emigration, then other complexities arise. If a particular claim stems from a metaphysical concept such as the nature of humanity, or from a religious concept such as the divine will, or from some other a priori concept, then the claim may really be an immunity to which normative judgments should not apply. If, however, the claim is based on certain interests such as the common good, other problems arise, such as the need to determine the common good, or the need to balance other societal interests, which may allow a wide variety of interpretations not supportive of individual human rights demands.

If we speak of the "rights" in the International Covenant on Economic, Social and Cultural Rights, such as the right to favourable conditions of work, social security, health, education, fair wages, a decent standard of living, and even holidays with pay, what do we intend? Are these rights which individuals can assert? Or are they only aspirational goals? If they are rights, on whom are the correlative duties?

If we speak of privileges, there are other concerns. If the privileges are granted by the state, then presumably the state is entitled to condition them. Does the right of a state to derogate from rights in an international covenant mean that the rights are only privileges? Here, too, the answer is connected to the moral strength and inviolability of the "right" or "privilege" that is involved.

The definitional answers to these many questions are complex. And part of the complexity is that in defining we must confront the conflicts between utilitarian and anti-utilitarian philosophy, between values of equality and liberty between absolute and relativist conceptions of rights, all issues of moral justification.

To summarize..., even where international law has established a conventional system of human rights, a philosophical understanding of the nature of rights is not just an academic exercise. Understanding the nature of the "right" involved can help clarify our consideration of the degree of protection available, the nature of derogations or exceptions, the priorities to be afforded to various rights, the question of the hierarchical relationships in a series of rights, the question of whether rights "trump" competing claims based on cultural rooting, and similar problems. To be sure, the answer to these questions may evolve over time through legal rulings, interpretations, decisions and pragmatic compromises. But how those answers emerge will be influenced, if not driven, by the moral justifications of the human rights in issue.

Human Rights, Peoples' Rights, in THE RIGHTS OF PEOPLES 127–28
(James Crawford ed., 1988)
Eugene Kamenka

Rights are claims that have achieved a special kind of endorsement or success: legal rights by a legal system; human rights by widespread sentiment or an international order. All rights arise in specific historical circumstances. They are claims made, conceded or granted by people who are themselves historically and socially shaped. They are asserted by people on their own behalf or as perceived and endorsed implications of specific historical traditions, institutions, and arrangements or of a historically conditioned theory of human needs and human aspirations, or of a human conception of a Divine plan and purpose. In objective fact as opposed to (some) subjective feeling, they are neither eternal nor inalienable; neither prior to society or societies nor independent of them. Some such rights can be singled out, and they often are singled out, as social ideals, as goals to strive toward. But even as such, they cannot be divorced from social content and context.

Claims presented as rights are claims that are often, perhaps usually, presented as having a special kind of importance, urgency, universality, or endorsement that makes them more than disparate or simply subjective demands. Their success is dependent on such endorsement – by a government or a legal system that has power to grant and protect such rights by a tradition or institution whose authority is accepted in those circles that recognize these claims as rights, by widespread social sentiment, regionally, nationally, or internationally.

Claims, whether presented as rights or not, conflict. So do the traditions, institutions and authorities that endorse the claim as a right. They conflict both with each other and, often, in their internal structure, implications, and working out. It is a feature of rights propaganda, for this very reason, to emphasize and elevate one right at a time or seriatim, but not to examine their relationship to each other too closely. Bringing rights claims in relation with each other at the practical level is the distinctive and central task of the law, a task the importance of which is matched only by its complexity. . . .

The concept of human rights is no longer tied to belief in God or natural law in its classical sense. But it still seeks or claims a form of endorsement that transcends or pretends to transcend specific historical institutions and traditions, legal systems, governments, or national and even regional communities. Like moral claims more generally, it asserts in its own behalf moral and sometimes even logical priority – connection with the very concept (treated as morally loaded) of what it means to be a human being or a person, or of what it means to behave morally. These are questions on which moral philosophers do have a certain expertise, at least in seeing where the difficulties lie, and on which they, like ordinary people throughout the world, have long disagreed and continue to disagree.

For the international lawyer, however, and increasingly for the lawyer in general, human rights are no longer simply moral or political claims, statements of the law that ought to be which have no base as such in the law that is. . . .

Questions and Discussion

1.   What would you say are the special characteristics, strengths, and weaknesses of a movement based on rights generally? In particular, how does the contemporary influence of the theory of natural rights bear on environmental protection through human rights?

2.   Kamenka states that the success of a human right, including a right to environment, depends on a special kind of endorsement. What does he mean? Is this endorsement different from the political victory of competing ideas of the good? How would you tell whether the right to environment had received such an endorsement?

B. *A Case for Human Rights*

THE AGE OF RIGHTS 2–5 (1990)
Louis Henkin

Human rights are rights of individuals in society. Every human being has, or is entitled to have, "rights" – legitimate, valid, justified claims – upon his or her society; claims to various "goods" and benefits. Human rights are not some abstract, inchoate "good"; they are defined, particular claims listed in international instruments such as the Universal Declaration of Human Rights and the major covenants and conventions. They are those benefits deemed essential for individual well-being, dignity, and fulfillment, and that reflect a common sense of justice, fairness, and decency. In the constitutional jurisprudence of the United States . . . individual rights have long been thought of as consisting only of "immunities," as limitations on what government might do *to* the individual. Human rights, on the other hand, include not only these negative "immunity claims" but also positive "resource claims," claims to what society is deemed required to do *for* the individual. They include liberties – freedom *from* (for example, detention, torture), and freedom *to* (speak, assemble); they include also the right to food, housing, and other basic human needs.

Human rights are universal: they belong to every human being in every human society. They do not differ with geography or history, culture or ideology, political, or economic system, or stage of societal development. To call them "human" implies that all human beings have them, equally and in equal measure, by virtue of their humanity – regardless of sex, race, age; regardless of high or low "birth," social class, national origin, ethnic, or tribal affiliation; regardless of wealth or poverty, occupation, talent, merit, religion, ideology, or other commitment. Implied in one's humanity, human rights are inalienable and imprescriptible: they cannot be transferred, forfeited, or waived; they cannot be lost by having been usurped, or by one's failure to exercise or assert them.

Human rights are *rights*; they are not merely aspirations, or assertions of the good. To call them rights is not to assert, merely, that the benefits indicated are desirable or necessary; or, merely, that it is "right" that the individual shall enjoy these goods; or even, merely, that it is the duty of society to respect the immunity or provide the benefits. To call them "rights" implies that they are claims "as of right," not by appeal to grace, or charity, or brotherhood, or love; they need not be earned or deserved. The idea of rights implies entitlement on the part of the holder in some order under some applicable norm; the idea of human rights implies entitlement in a moral order under a moral law, to be translated into and confirmed as legal entitlement in the legal order of a political society. When a society recognizes that a person has a right, it affirms, legitimates, and justifies that entitlement, and incorporates and establishes it in the society's system of values, giving it important weight in competition with other societal values.

Human rights imply the obligation of society to satisfy those claims. The state must develop institutions and procedures, must plan, must mobilize resources as necessary to meet those claims. Political and civil rights require laws, institutions, procedures, and other safeguards against tyranny, against corrupt, immoral, and inefficient agencies or officials. Economic and social rights in modern society require taxation and spending and a network of agencies for social welfare. The idea of human rights implies also that society must provide some system of remedies to which individuals may resort to obtain the benefits to which they are entitled (or be compensated for their loss). Together, the affirmation of entitlement, the recognition by society of an obligation to mobilize itself to discharge it, and the implication of remedy, all enhance the likelihood that the right will be realized, that individuals will actually enjoy the benefits to which they are entitled.

Human rights are claims upon society. These claims may derive from moral principles governing relations between persons, but it is society that bears the obligation to satisfy the claims. Of course, the official representatives of society must themselves respect individual freedoms and immunities; political society must also act to protect the individual's rights against private invasion. As regards claims to economic and social benefits, society must act as insurer to provide them if individuals cannot provide them for themselves. Thus, government must protect me from assault by my neighbor, or from wolves, and must ensure that I have bread or hospitalization; in human rights terms my rights are against the state, not against the neighbor or the wolves, the baker, or the hospital. The state may arrange to satisfy my claims by maintaining domestic laws and institutions that give me, say, rights and remedies in tort against my neighbor, or administrative remedies against a corrupt, misguided, or inefficient bureaucrat, or access to public schools or health services. Those legal rights and remedies against individuals or agencies within society give effect to my human rights claims upon society.

The idea of human rights has implications for the relation of the individual's rights to other public goods. It is commonly said that human rights are "fundamental." That means that they are important, that life, dignity, and other important human values depend on them; it does not mean that they are "absolute," that they may never be abridged for any purpose in any circumstances. Human rights enjoy a *prima facie*, presumptive inviolability, and will often "trump" other public goods. Government may not do some things, and must do others, even though the authorities are persuaded that it is in the society's interest (and perhaps even in the individual's own interest) to do otherwise; individual human rights cannot be lightly sacrificed even for the good of the greatest number, even for the general good of all. But if human rights do not bow lightly to public concerns, they may be sacrificed if countervailing societal interests are important enough, in particular circumstances, for limited times and purposes, to the extent strictly necessary. The Universal Declaration recognizes that rights are subject to limitations determined by law "for the purpose of securing due recognition and respect for the rights and freedoms of others and of meeting the just requirements of morality, public order, and the general welfare in a democratic society." . . .

The idea of rights accepts that some limitations on rights are permissible but the limitations are themselves strictly limited. Public emergency, national security, public order are weighty terms, bespeaking important societal interests, but they are not to be lightly or loosely invoked, and the conception of national security or public order cannot be so large as to swallow the right. Derogations are permitted only in time of a public emergency that threatens the life of the nation, not as a response to fears (warranted or paranoid) for other values, or for the security of a particular regime. Even in an authentic emergency, a society may derogate from rights only to the extent strictly required by the exigencies of the situation, and even such necessary derogations must not involve invidious inequalities, and may not derogate from basic rights: they must not invade the right to life, or involve torture or cruel, inhuman punishment, slavery or servitude, conviction of crime under *ex post facto* laws, denial of rights as a person before the law, or violate freedom of thought, conscience, or religion. Moreover, considerations of public emergency permitting derogations, or of national security or public order permitting limitations on certain rights, refer to a universal standard, monitored by external scrutiny and judgment.

In sum, the idea of human rights is that the individual counts – independent of and in addition to his or her part in the common good. Autonomy and liberty must be respected, and the individual's basic economic-social needs realized, as a matter of entitlement, not of grace or discretion (even by wise and benevolent authority, or even by "the people"). The individual has obligations to others and to the community, and society may ask all individuals to give up some of their rights for the rights of others and for the common good, but there is a core of individuality that cannot be invaded or sacrificed. And all individuals count equally. An individual's right can be sacrificed to another's right only when choice is inevitable, and only according to some principle of choice reflecting the comparative value of each right. No particular individual can be singled out for particular sacrifice, except at random or by some other "neutral principle," consistent with the spirit of equal protection of the laws.

. . .

Human rights, as conceived by and specified in the Universal Declaration and other international instruments, are the rights of individuals. . . .

Groups may have rights in domestic legal systems but, at least at its origin, the human rights movement did not address them. Later, the principal international human rights covenants declared the rights of "peoples" to self-determination and to sovereignty over their natural resources, but those provisions were an exceptional addition to the general conception in the covenants that human rights are claims of a person upon his or her own society. There has been a movement to recognize other "generations of rights" – a right to peace, to development, to a healthy environment – but none of these has been incorporated into any legally binding human rights agreement.

Questions and Discussion

1. Professor Henkin states the case for human rights forcefully. Yet there is recognition that rights are limitable. In human rights terms, there may be derogation from rights in defined circumstances and for broader social purposes. Reference is made to article 29(2) of the Universal Declaration and the ability of a state to derogate from rights for the purpose of "meeting the just requirements of morality, public order, and the general welfare in a democratic society." In an environmental context, what might this mean?

    For example, many scientists believe that the increasing global human population is a major contributing factor in creating environmental stress. There is, however, a human right to found a family and to determine the number, timing, and spacing of one's children. Art. 16, Universal Declaration of Human Rights, G.A. Res. 217A, U.N. Doc. A/810 (1948); Art. 16(1)(e), Convention on the Elimination of all Forms of Discrimination Against Women, G.A. Res. 34/180 (Dec. 18, 1979); Art. 23(2), International Covenant on Civil and Political Rights, G.A. Res. 2200A (XXI) (Dec. 16, 1966). Could a state rely on article 29 of the Universal Declaration to enact a law controlling population? Are you persuaded that prescribing the number of children people may have is a "just requirement" of public order and general welfare dictated by the unsustainable carrying capacity of the earth in relation to population?

2. At the start of the Henkin excerpt, he asserts that human rights belong to *individuals* in a society. At the end of the piece, Henkin mentions that other "generations" of rights, including the right to environment, have been pushed for inclusion in the corpus of human rights but have yet to find acceptance. As noted in Chapters 2 and 4, the right to environment is often categorized as a third-generation right, as well as a solidarity or group right, on account of both the recent vintage and the wide nature of the right when observed. However, as you should glean from the excerpt, tensions do exist between individual human rights and group rights. Some argue that all human rights belong to the individual as the name – *human rights* – indicates. Human rights are viewed as opposed to the group in all its forms. Just as important, an emphasis on group rights is viewed as a threat to human rights because of their potential to justify infringements of individual rights in the name of protecting the rights of the larger group. The other side rejects these criticisms as

without foundation, particularly because, as the other side sees it, the individual is first and foremost a member of society, to which he owes duties. Consider Merrills's treatment of the problem:

> What about the suggestion that the right to a clean, healthy, or otherwise appropriate environment should be regarded as a collective right? Here what is posited is that groups or communities, defined in some way, should be the beneficiaries of a right which could be argued to be vital to their existence or survival. The right would be classified as an economic, social, and cultural right and as such would constitute a claim on the resources of the wider community, also to be defined, rather than a protection from interference. . . . [T]here would appear to be no obvious reason why groups, as well as individuals, should not enjoy rights of this kind. As regards environmental rights specifically, it is easy to imagine a situation in which environmental conditions may be so bound up with the life of communities as to justify placing groups in a moral position analogous to that of individuals. . . . [I]f the question is whether as a matter of principle we could find justification for treating the right to a clean environment as a collective moral right, the answer appears to be yes.

J.G. Merrills, *Environmental Protection and Human Rights: Conceptual Aspects, in* HUMAN RIGHTS APPROACHES TO ENVIRONMENTAL PROTECTION 25, 28 (Alan Boyle & Michael Anderson eds., 1996). A final note: in thinking about group rights and collective rights, it is important to recognize that while generally collective in application, it is perfectly possible that they might be invoked by individuals.

C. *Critiques of Human Rights and Responses Thereto*

We now turn to consider criticisms that have been advanced against the idea and use of human rights. Recall the stark, early rejection of natural rights by Jeremy Bentham ("nonsense on stilts") and Edmund Burke ("gross and stupid absurdity") discussed previously.

**Rights and Their Critics, 70 NOTRE DAME L. REV. 727,
730–48 (1995) (footnotes omitted)
Cass Sunstein**

I. THE CHARGES

Numerous charges have been made against rights, and it will be useful to begin by separating distinct claims that tend to be run together. We might disaggregate the charges into six different categories.

A. *The Social Foundations of Rights*

Some people suggest, as part of their critique of rights, that rights are essentially social and collective in character and that the rhetoric of rights obscures this point. For example, rights come from the state in the sense that they depend for their existence on collective institutions. Without the law of property, set out by the collectivity, property rights cannot be secure. Without the law of contract, saying that agreements are enforceable under certain conditions, contracts could not exist in the way that we understand them. In the critics' view, many claims based on rights, and especially claims for individual rights, tend to disguise the social character of rights and in particular the need for collective and communal support. The result, it is said, is confusion and an inability to draw lines between rights that are desirable from the social point of view and rights that are not.

B. *The Rigidity of Rights*

... [C]ritics charge that rights have a "strident and absolutist character, and that for this reason they impoverish political discourse. Rights do not admit of compromise. They do not allow room for competing considerations. For this reason, they impair and even foreclose deliberation over complex issues not" realistically soluble by simple formulas. ...

Rooted in nineteenth-century ideas of absolute sovereignty over property, rights are said to be ill-adapted to what we usually need, that is, a careful discussion of trade-offs and competing concerns. If rights are (in Ronald Dworkin's suggestive and influential phrase, criticized below) "trumps," they are for that very reason harmful to the difficult process of accommodating different goals and considerations in resolving such thorny problems as abortion, the environment, and plant closings.

C. *Indeterminacy*

In one of his greatest aphorisms, Justice Holmes wrote that "general propositions do not decide concrete cases." Rights, of course, take the form of general propositions. For this reason they are said to be indeterminate and thus unhelpful.

If we know that there is a right to private property, we do not know whether an occupational safety and health law or a law requiring beach access is permissible. In fact, we know relatively little. Standing by itself, the constitutional protection against government "takings" tells us very little about how to handle particular problems. This is true of rights generally. To say that there is a right to equal protection of the law is not to say, for example, that affirmative action programs are acceptable, mandatory, or prohibited. In fact, the right to equal protection of the law requires a great deal of supplemental work to decide cases. The right must be specified in order to have concrete meaning. The specification will depend on premises not contained within the announcement of the right itself. Rights purport to solve problems, but when stated abstractly – it is claimed – they are at most the beginning of a discussion.

Perhaps the area of free speech is the most vivid illustration. Everyone agrees that such a right exists; but without supplemental work, we cannot know how to handle the hard questions raised by commercial speech, libel, obscenity, or campaign finance restrictions. A serious problem with modern free speech discussions is that the term "free speech" tends to be used as if it handled the hard questions by itself.

D. *Excessive Individualism*

A different objection is that rights are unduly individualistic and associated with highly undesirable characteristics, including selfishness and indifference to others. Rights miss the "dimension of sociality;" they posit selfish, isolated individuals who assert what is theirs, rather than participating in communal life. Rights, it is said, neglect the moral and social dimensions of important problems.

The important and contested right of privacy, for example, is said to have emerged as an unduly individual right, rooted in the "properly paradigm" and loosened from connections to others. Critics urge that this conception of the issues involved in the so-called privacy cases misses crucial aspects of the relevant problems – abortion, family living arrangements, and the asserted right to die. Such issues do not involve simple privacy; they call up a range of issues about networks of relationships, between individuals and the state, between individuals and families, between individuals and localities. Perhaps the abortion issue is especially problematic when conceived in terms of a "right to privacy." Many people, on both sides of the abortion controversy, are uncomfortable with the "privacy" rhetoric. Inattentive to the unborn or to the situation of mothers, American law has been said to have, perversely, left the pregnant woman genuinely alone, without people "willing to help her either to have the abortion she desired, or to keep and raise the child who was eventually born." ...

E. Protection of Existing Distributions and Practices

To some critics, a key problem with rights is that they tend to be used for what the critics see as pernicious ends. Partly because rights are indeterminate in the abstract, they can be used as an excessively conservative and antidemocratic force, protecting existing distributions from scrutiny and change. Some people think that the historical function of rights has been to insulate current practice from legitimate democratic oversight. ...

F. Rights Versus Responsibilities

A final and especially prominent objection is that the emphasis on rights tends to crowd out the issue of responsibility. In American law and in American public discourse, some critics complain, it is too rare to find the idea that people owe duties to each other, or that civic virtue is to be cultivated, prized, and lived. Rights, and especially new protections of rights since the 1960s, are said to be a major problem here.

In a simple formulation: People who insist on their rights too infrequently explore what it is right to do. Or they become dependent on the official institutions charged with safeguarding rights, rather than doing things for themselves. The controversy over whether rights turn women or blacks into a "dependent class" is in part about this issue. People who insist that their status as victims entitles them to enforce their legal rights may not conceive of themselves in ways that engender equality and equal citizenship. ...

II. Concepts and Partial Truths

. . .

The conception of rights as interests that operate as "trumps" against the collectivity raises more difficulty, largely because it is not clear that this conception is really helpful. The first problem is that almost every right is defeasible at some point, and defeasible just because the collective interest is very strong. ... [N]o right is absolute. If, for example, the rest of the human race will be eliminated because of the protection of a right, the right will certainly be redefined or legitimately infringed, probably under some version of the "compelling interest" test. The real question then becomes when rights are defeasible because of collective justifications – under what conditions and for what reasons. The formula of "trumps" is misleading for this reason. We need to know what sorts of reasons are admissible and how weighty they must be; these are the key questions in the exploration of rights.

Rights characteristically limit the kinds of arguments that can be used by way of justification, and they characteristically require justifications of special weight. Above all, rights exclude certain otherwise admissible reasons for action. But ideas of this kind do not support the "trumps" metaphor and indeed lead in quite different directions.

[Another] problem is that many conceptual puzzles are raised by the understanding of rights as interests operating "against" the collectivity. Often rights are something that the collectivity recognizes and protects in order to protect its interests. If this is so, there is no easy opposition between rights and the collectivity. . . . Rights are collectively conferred and designed to promote collective interests. They are protected by social institutions for social reasons. In such cases, rights may in a sense operate against the collectivity once they are conferred; government may not take property just because it wants to do so. But even in such cases, rights are guaranteed in the first instance both by and for the collectivity (which of course has no existence apart from the individuals who compose it).

. . .

As they operate in law, rights generally *are* specified. Hence the rights protected by the Constitution and the common law are far from indeterminate, however hard it is to know what they are when stated abstractly. The claim of indeterminacy is for this reason far too broad. The problem, to which the critics have correctly drawn attention, lies in the use of general claims of right to resolve cases in which the specification has not yet occurred.

It is also true that efforts to think about many social and economic problems in terms of rights can obscure those problems. A claimed right to clean air and water or to safe products and workplaces makes little sense in light of the need for close assessment, in particular cases, of the advantages of greater environmental protection or more safety, as compared with the possible accompanying disadvantages – higher prices, lower wages, less employment, and more poverty. Perhaps the legal system will create rights of a kind after it has undertaken this assessment. But to the extent that the regulatory programs of the 1970s were billed as simple vindications of "rights," they severely impaired political deliberation about their content and about the necessity for tradeoffs.

. . .

Despite the various partial truths in the attack on rights, there is a pervasive problem in that attack: rights need not have the functions or consequences that they are alleged to have. The challenge to rights is properly directed against certain kinds of rights, not against rights in general. At most, the challenge to rights creates a contingent, partial warning about the appropriate content of rights and about the possibly harmful role of certain social institutions safeguarding rights. It is not what it purports to be, that is, a general claim about rights as a social institution. More specifically, the current devaluation of rights suffers from two serious problems. Both of these problems are products of some pervasive confusions.

Many critics of rights complain about what they see as a cultural shift from the 1960s, in which rights have crowded out responsibilities? Simply as a matter of cultural description, the claim is far too crude. In some areas, including for example sexuality, it is plausible to say that a belief in private autonomy has prevailed at the expense of a commitment to responsible behavior. But in other areas, the last few decades have witnessed an increase in social and legal responsibilities and a decreased commitment to rights. Consider, for example, cigarette smoking; corporate misconduct; air and water pollution; sexual harassment; and racist and sexist speech. In all of these areas, people who were formerly autonomous, and free to act in accordance with their own claims of right, are now subject to socially and sometimes legally enforced responsibilities. We have seen, in the last few decades, a redefinition of areas of right and a redefinition of areas of responsibility. I do not intend to celebrate these redefinitions, but only to suggest that purely as a matter of description, there has been no general shift from responsibility to rights.

. . .

[Another] problem is that the critics seem to think that the explosion of "rights talk" accounts for certain social failures, including failures of social responsibility. This is far too simple a claim. In fact, the opposite is as likely true – failures of social responsibility give rise to assertions of rights. . . .

[These] problems can be brought together if we attend to a familiar conceptual confusion. Often critics write as if rights and responsibilities are opposed, or as if those who favor the former are completely different from those who favor the latter. As they see it, rights are individual, atomistic, selfish, crude, licentious, antisocial, and associated with the Warren Court. Responsibilities, on the other hand, are seen as collective, social, altruistic, nuanced, and associated with appropriate or traditional values. But this understanding is quite inadequate, for some rights lack the characteristics claimed for them, and other rights have the features associated with responsibilities.

For example, the right to freedom of speech may be owned by individuals, but it is a precondition for a highly social process, that of democratic deliberation. That right keeps open the channels of communication; it is emphatically communal in character. It ensures a *sine qua non* of sociality, an opportunity for people to speak with one other. Indeed, everyone who owns a speech right does so partly so as to contribute to the collectivity; it is this fact that explains the government's inability to "buy" speech rights even when a speaker would like to sell. So too, the right to associational freedom is hardly individualistic. It is meant precisely to protect collective action and sociality.

. . .

The claimed opposition between rights and responsibilities faces some additional difficulties as well. Rights of the most traditional sort, including property, may be the necessary condition for enabling a sense of collective responsibility to flourish. People without rights to their property may be so dependent on official will that they cannot exercise their responsibilities as citizens. Moreover, a principal characteristic of totalitarian states is the endless cataloguing of responsibilities owed by citizens to the state. The Soviet Constitution was an ignoble example. For example, that Constitution created a duty "to make thrifty use of the people's wealth," "to preserve and protect socialist property," to "work conscientiously," and "to concern themselves with the upbringing of children." The Soviet Constitution offers a cautionary note against enthusiasm for responsibilities, at least if these are to be treated as an explicit, legally codified concern of the state (putting the Hohfeldian point to one side).

Voices of Suffering, Fragmented Universality, and the Future of Human Rights, in THE FUTURE OF INTERNATIONAL HUMAN RIGHTS 172–89 (Burns Weston & Stephen P. Marks ed., 1999) (footnotes and section numbers omitted) Upendra Baxi

Many critiques of human rights have gained wide currency. Unmitigated skepticism about the possibility and/or desirability of human rights is frequently promoted. Unsurprising when stemming from autocratic or dictatorial leaders or regimes who criticize human rights norms and standards on the grounds of their origin, scope, and relevance (almost always reeking of expediency and bad faith), [but] such critiques, when they emanate from the foremost social thinkers, require response.

. . . [R]esponsible critiques of human rights are concerned with: (a) the modes of production of human rights; (b) the problems posed by the politics of universality of human rights and the politics of identity/difference; and (c) the arguments from relativism and multiculturalism.

Too Many Rights or Too Few?

Is it the case that the late Christian twentieth century "suffers" from an overproduction of human rights standards and norms, entailing a policy and resource overload that no government or regime, however conscientious, can bear? Should every human need find an embodiment in a human rights norm? Does overproduction entail a belief that each and every major human/social problem is best defined and solved in terms of human rights, in terms of the talismanic property of human rights enunciations? Should concentrations of economic power be allowed to harness these talismanic properties?

I address here only the issue of overproduction. The important question concerns, perhaps not the quantity but the quality of human rights norms and standards since the UDHR, with insistence on their universality and interdependence. . . .

The astonishing quantity of human rights production generates various experiences of skepticism and faith. Some complain of exhaustion (what I call "rights-weariness"). Some suspect sinister imperialism in diplomatic maneuvers animating each and every human rights enunciation (what I call "rights-wariness"). Some celebrate human rights as a new global civic religion which, given a community of faith, will address and solve all major human problems (what I call "human rights evangelism"). Their fervor is often matched by those NGOs that tirelessly pursue the removal of brackets in pre-final diplomatic negotiating texts of various United Nations' summits as triumphs in human solidarity (what I call "human rights romanticism"). Some other activists believe that viable human rights standards can best be produced by exploiting contingencies of international diplomacy (what I call "bureaucratization of human rights"). And still others insist that the real birthplaces of human rights are far removed from the ornate rooms of diplomatic conferences and are found, rather, in the actual sites (acts and feats) of resistance and struggle (what I call "critical human rights realism").

. . .

Politics of Identity/Difference

Informed by post-modernist mood, method, and message, critics of "contemporary" human rights, which champions the universality of human rights, remain anxious at the re-emergence of the idea of "universal reason;" a legacy of the Age of Enlightenment that helped to perfect justifications for classical colonialism and racism and for universal patriarchy. The notion of universality invokes not merely new versions of essentialism about human nature but also the notion of meta-narratives: global stories about power and struggles against power. In both of these tropes, do we return to "totalization" modes of thought and practice?

Critics of essentialism remind us that the notion "human" is not pre-given (if, indeed, anything is) but constructed, often with profound rights-denying impacts. Post-modernist critiques now lead us to consider that the idiom of the universality of human rights may have a similar impact. For example, the motto "Women's Rights [A]re Human Rights" masks, often with grave costs, the heterogeneity of women in their civilizational and class positions. So does the appellation "indigenous" in the search for a commonly agreed declaration of indigenous people's rights. Similarly, the human rights instruments on child rights ignore the diversity of children's circumstances. In many societies, the passage between the first and second childhood or the distinction between "child" and "adult" is brutally cut short, as with child labor, the girl child, or children conscripted into insurrectionist-armed warfare.

Are then identities, universalized all over again in positing a universal bearer of human rights, obscuring the fact that identities may themselves be vehicles of power, all too often inscribed or imposed? And do the benign intentions that underlie such performative acts of power advance the cause of human rights as well as they serve the ends of power?

. . .

The post-modernist critique of human rights further maintains that the telling of large global stories ("meta-narratives") is less a function of emancipation than an aspect of the politics of intergovernmental desire that ingests the politics of resistance. Put another way, meta-narratives serve to co-opt into mechanisms and processes of governance the languages of human rights such that bills of rights may, with impunity, adorn many a military constitutionalism and that so-called human rights commissions may thrive upon state/regime sponsored violations. Not surprisingly, the more severe the human rights violation, the more the power elites declare their loyalty to the regime of human rights. . . .

. . .

Arguments from Relativism

. . .

"Contemporary" human rights paradigms constantly invite interrogation when they stress the universality of human rights. It is maintained by many, and in various ways, that universal human rights are simply impossible because what counts as "human" and as "rights" belonging to humans are context-bound and tradition-dependent. There is no transcultural fact or being that may be called "human" to which universal human rights may be attached. . . .

. . .

. . . The American Anthropological Association, in its 1947 critique of the draft declaration of the UDHR, stated, memorably, that doctrines of "the white man's burden."[24]

> have been employed to implement economic exploitation and to deny the right to control their own affairs to millions of peoples over the world, where the expansion of Europe and America has not meant . . . the literal extermination of the whole populations. Rationalized in terms of ascribing cultural inferiority to these peoples, or in conceptions of backwardness in development of their "primitive mentality," that justified their being held in the tutelage of their superiors, the history of the expansion of the western world has been marked by demoralization of human personality and the disintegration of human rights among the people over whom hegemony has been established.

This was stated with elegant clarity in the pre-post-modern era! And even today critiques of the universality of human rights enact only variations on this theme.

Questions and Discussion

1. Sunstein claims that the right to clean air or water makes little sense without context, in particular the need to balance competing needs by employing a sort of utilitarian calculus in weighing advantages and disadvantages to see what scenario entails most benefits. Is this your understanding of how human rights come into being? Should it be?
2. Of the types of human rights criticism outlined by Sunstein and Baxi, which one(s) are the most persuasive? Why? What responses would you make to meet the criticism?
3. Toward the end of the Sunstein excerpt, he considers the relationship between rights and responsibilities. Many of the constitutions around the world that contain explicit environmental rights also contain duties, either on individuals or the state (or both), to protect the environment. Can you have one without the other? For greater treatment of the idea of social ordering on the basis of responsibility, as opposed or in addition to rights, see *infra* this Chapter at pp. 220–23.
4. Sunstein writes that if "the rest of the human race will be eliminated because of the protection of a right, the right will certainly be redefined or legitimately infringed." This seems reasonable, but consider that on July 8, 1996, the International Court of Justice handed down the advisory opinion *Legality of the Threat or Use of Nuclear Weapons*,

---

[24] A reference to a poem by Rudyard Kipling, which was used to romanticize colonial empires as noble enterprises. Rudyard Kipling, *White Man's Burden*, McClure's Magazine, Feb. 1899, at 290.

1996 I.C.J. 226 (July 8). In what has been called a nonholding, by a vote of 7–7, with the president's casting vote, the Court determined in *dispositif* paragraph 105(2)E that, "in view of the current state of international law, and of the elements of fact at its disposal," it could not "conclude definitively whether the threat or use of nuclear weapons would be lawful or unlawful in an extreme circumstance of self-defence, in which the very survival of a State would be at stake." Does this mean that the right of survival entitles a state to blow up the world in an act of self-defense? Did the Court miss other rights that should "trump" such an antisocial result?

Legal Theory and Democratic Reconstruction,
25 U. BRIT. COLUM. L. REV. 69, 97–98, 100–01 (1991)
Karl Klare

... [R]ights skepticism concerns the efficacy and limitations of the rights tradition in relationship to social change. There is much discussion of the gap between "rights on the books" and "rights in the real world." Additionally, the skeptics call attention to certain self-imposed limitations internal to rights discourse stemming from its embrace of the public/private distinction....

... [H]uman freedom can ... be invaded or denied by nongovernmental forms of power, by domination in the so-called "private sphere." Human dignity is denied by *de jure* racial segregation, but it is also denied by employers who discriminate on the basis of race. Laws barring adult homosexuals from privately and consensually expressing their sexuality deny freedom and autonomy, but so, too, do homophobic social practices such as housing discrimination and gay bashing. The expression of dissent can be inhibited by the cost of media access as well as by abuses of state power. Rights charters almost invariably concern restrictions on state power and therefore leave intact many forms of "private" domination, including hierarchies of class, race, gender and sexual preference. The skeptics argue that the vision of freedom embodied in the rights tradition is for this reason partial and incomplete.

... A strong version of rights skepticism suggests that the fixation on the individual/state relationship in the rights tradition actually diverts intellectual and political resources from other, needed approaches to social justice.

... [I]t is conceivable that rights discourse can be transformed to accommodate these criticisms; that we can articulate a panoply of self-determination rights in social and economic life....

... [R]ights concepts are sufficiently elastic so that they can mean different things to different people. People who seek to reinforce hierarchy and perpetuate domination can speak the language of rights, often with sincerity. But there is an even deeper problem. Even those who would consistently invoke rights in the service of self-determination, autonomy and equality find that rights concepts are internally contradictory. That is because, like all of legal discourse, rights theory is an arena of conflicting conceptions of justice and human freedom. ... Human rights discourse holds that its claims are universal yet also embodies a belief in the right of all peoples to cultural autonomy and self-determination.

Thus, choices must be made in elaborating any structure of human rights guarantees, just as in the course of specifying market structures, and the choices bear socially and politically significant consequences. The problem is that rights discourse itself does not provide neutral decision procedures with which to make such choices.

... My point here is that, by itself, rights discourse does not and probably cannot provide us with the criteria for deciding between conflicting claims of right. In order to resolve rights conflicts, it is necessary to step outside the discourse. One must appeal to more concrete and therefore more controversial analyses of the relevant social and institutional contexts than rights discourse offers; and one must develop and elaborate conceptions of and intuitions about human freedom and self-determination by reference to which one seeks to assess rights claims and resolve rights conflicts.

Questions and Discussion

1. How do the discussions and understandings above relate to an enforceable human right to a healthy environment? Are there public and/or private issues involved? If individual choices about consumption are viewed as private and generally beyond the law, does that bear on environmental rights?

2. The following excerpt will give you a taste of the definitional issues connected with the debate associated with the creation of such a right. A more detailed treatment of this rights candidate is contained in Case Study V in the online Case Studies that accompany this text.

HUMAN RIGHTS IN THE WORLD: AN INTRODUCTION TO THE STUDY OF THE INTERNATIONAL PROTECTION OF HUMAN RIGHTS 257–59 (3d ed., 1989) A.H. Robertson & J.G. Merrills

This brings us back to the so-called "new rights": the right to development, the right to the environment, the right to share in the common heritage of mankind, the right to peace, and so on. Are these concepts human rights in any meaningful sense of that term? In trying to answer this question, there are several factors to be borne in mind.

In the first place, the word "human" in the expression "human rights" has a specific meaning. It indicates that the rights under consideration are rights pertaining to human beings by virtue of their humanity. As stated in both the U.N. Covenants, "these rights derive from the inherent dignity of the human person." In our view this means that the rights which can properly be called "human rights" are rights of individual human beings stemming from their nature as human beings, and not rights of groups, associations, or other collectives. This is borne out of the wording repeatedly used in the Universal Declaration and in the Covenant on Civil and Political Rights, "Everyone has the right . . ."; while the Covenant on Economic, Social, and Cultural Rights repeatedly stipulates that "the States Parties . . . recognize the right of everyone, to . . . the different rights protected." It is quite clear from this language that what the Universal Declaration and the Covenants are concerned with is the rights of individual human beings. True, there is an exception in Article 1 of both Covenants, which states, "All peoples have the right of self-determination." But it is clear from the *travaux* that this was regarded as a special provision, and its exceptional character is under lined by the fact that [it] is placed in a distinct chapter of each Covenant, and separated from the articles relating to individual human rights.

This being so, is it accurate to designate as "human-rights" so-called rights which pertain not to individuals but to groups or collectives? Usage, of course, is a matter of convention and there is room for more than one view as to what is appropriate here. . . . [H]owever, language and thinking will be clearer if we use the expression "human rights" to designate "individual" rights and "collective rights" to designate the rights of groups and collectives, a distinction which also has the advantage of being consistent with much generally accepted practice.

The second consideration relates to the use of the word "rights" in the expression "new human rights." Economic development, the protection of the environment, the common heritage of mankind and peace: are these concepts "rights" in any meaningful sense? They can, and should, be objectives of social policy. They may be items in a political programme. However, they are certainly not legally enforceable claims. Most people no doubt prefer peace. But if one's country is at war, it is certain that there is no legally enforceable "right to peace." Naturally, it would be possible to "define 'rights' in such a way as to include all" desirable objectives of social policy, and in that event, the "new human rights" would become "rights" by virtue of the definition. But this would be to distort the ordinary meaning given to the term "human rights" and, more seriously, would run together goals which enlightened humanity ought to pursue with claims which are already protected by international law. The trouble arises, then, because advocates of the "new human rights" are confusing objectives of social policy with rights "in the lawyers" sense. If one wishes to see some objective achieved – a clean and healthy environment, for example – it is tempting to say that this is a right to which we are all entitled. But it is not a good idea to take wishes for reality.

The last point to be borne in mind is that there is a crucial distinction between legal rights and moral rights. We may consider that we have a moral right to something – consideration from others, perhaps – when we have no legal right to it at all. Countless examples could be given. If advocates of the new human "rights" assert that we have a moral right to peace, to the environment, and so on, then many will be inclined to agree. But there is all the difference in the world between these and other' moral rights, on the one hand, and, on the other, rights, whether civil and political or economic and social, which have been incorporated in international treaties. While it is true that moral ideas provide both an incentive to create new law and a yardstick for its interpretation, until the process of law-making has taken place, "new human rights" must remain, in the realm of speculation.

Question and Discussion

1. How damaging to a rights-based international campaign, such as a human rights and environment campaign, are the criticisms about rights discourse and argument in the preceding articles? Are the responses to the criticisms persuasive? Can you think of other responses?

III. Perspectives on Human Rights Claims

As we saw previously, the international law of human rights has a number of philosophical forebears that support legal and political argument and discourse about the creation, nature, extent, validity, and exceptions to human rights norms. In brief compass, we set forth five perspectives in the sections that follow. As you read them, consider how Pierre Teilhard de Chardin, during the drafting of the Universal Declaration of Human Rights, observed that there would be agreement on the list of human rights as long as no agreement was required about why they should be included on the list.

A. Natural Law

As already discussed, many human rights that are secured by international law today were repeatedly asserted outside the law well before they became protected by treaties, international custom, or generally accepted international legal principles. A common feature of many of these prelaw claims is their reliance on religious doctrine and/or theories of justice independent of state lawmaking. Indeed, rather than invoking formal legal authority as a means to protect rights, these prelaw assertions were often intended to challenge entrenched legal arrangements based on a transcendent higher authority of the underlying religious doctrine or theory of justice.

The invocation of higher authority rests on the assumption that certain actions are always wrong, no matter what the circumstance, and this remains a central feature of modern human rights practice. It is also a foundation of the natural law tradition, for which early international law had a strong affinity. Indeed, early international lawyers such as Vitoria and Grotius employed natural law to develop the theories that launched modern international law in the fifteenth and sixteenth centuries. Vitoria, for instance, has been viewed as using natural law to assert the rights of indigenous peoples in the New World, especially as they related to territory. *See* Franciscus de Vitoria, *De Indus* (1532), *reprinted as* THE FIRST REFLECTION ON THE INDIANS LATELY DISCOVERED (John Pawley Bate trans.), *in* JAMES BROWN SCOTT, THE SPANISH ORIGIN OF INTERNATIONAL LAW: FRANCISCO DE VITORIA AND HIS LAW OF NATIONS, Appendix A, xxiv–xxv (1934). This view, however, has been criticized in contemporary scholarship as without objective foundation. *See* S. JAMES ANAYA, INDIGENOUS PEOPLES IN INTERNATIONAL LAW 16–19 (2d ed., 2004).

THEORY AND REALITY IN THE INTERNATIONAL PROTECTION OF HUMAN RIGHTS 273–78, 286 (1999)
J. Shand Watson

Some writers [accept] the simple assertion that international human rights norms must be valid on the basis of natural law.... [O]ne... finds reference to the idea that natural law was the precursor of modern human rights, and that natural law and international law are interrelated not only in a historic, but in a formal sense. This process is intermingled with a desire to make the works of certain writers highly authoritative, to raise them at least to the level of primary sources. First among these "fathers" of international law is Grotius whose views, in the opinion of some, are determinative of the truth or falsity of a proposition concerning international law....

For hundreds of years, there has been a desire by some to be able to review the validity of laws of a state not by its own terms, but by reference to an external legal system. In the past this was done almost routinely by appealing to natural law, but since about the turn of the [twentieth] century such an appeal is no longer made directly. This is due to the gradual collapse of natural law's authority resulting from the lack of any source of objective validity for its norms, and the concomitant susceptibility of such schemes to abuse for ulterior purposes.... Despite this, the need to make pronouncements on the validity of legal regimes is still felt by many, and some other system with an aura of authority has had to be found to fill that need. Very clearly, the choice that has been made to carry out that function is international law, and nowhere is this choice plainer and more obvious than in the literature on the internationalizing of human rights.

The proposed role of international law in this area is on all fours with the role of the former natural law. What the proponents of the system are asserting is that a rule of law, or even an entire domestic legal system, can be illegal because of its being inconsistent with the law as some higher level. In order to achieve this, an attempt is made to blend natural law philosophy with the theory of international law. It is a desire to review the validity of the positive law of states that is behind the constant attempt to change the decentralized, customary international legal system into a prescriptive, hierarchic one....

The use of international law as a substitute for natural law is a process that is already well under way. One more and more often encounters the view that a particular government is to be considered "illegitimate" and that it should therefore be removed from power. The test for this legitimacy is no longer to be found in the constitution of the state in questions, or in the acts of recognition by other states, but is rather to be found in what is required by "human rights."

Such higher review of states' legal systems is facilitated by commonly held beliefs about law which produce the impression that there are substantial similarities between international law and natural law. There is, for example, the fairly widespread belief that law is always good and that, therefore, any system of rules which is claimed to be carrying out a good purpose must somehow be legitimate. Since no one can deny the proper treatment of his or her fellow man is highly to be commended, it is easy to transfer the moral and ethical legitimacy therein to norms designed for that purpose. . . .

The similarities between [natural law and human rights] can also be quite specific. Some have pointed out there are strong ties between the substantive rights advocated by the revolutionary authors of eighteenth and nineteenth century Europe and the rights enumerated in the Universal Declaration. Indeed, the linguistic similarities between the Universal Declaration of 1948 and the French Declaration of 1787 . . . indicate the 1948 document is firmly rooted in the eighteenth century natural law philosophy of the latter. . . .

                                                         . . .

. . . [I]t is important to emphasize that there are two distinct techniques for eliciting the rules and principles of natural law. The first is the *a priori* method, whereby one establishes rules which comport with reason, divine will or any other presumptively valid source. The second is the a *posteriori* method whereby the rules are found by observing the antecedent social facts, and inducing rules therefrom. In the former method, the rules function in an unbounded prescriptive manner, making this approach compatible with the legislative technique associated with hierarchies. In the latter, the rules are primarily descriptive, being summaries of the participants' behaviour. . . . These two approaches to natural law are . . . about as far apart as one can get while staying within the general definition of "law." In one, the rule is completely independent of social reality, while in the other the rule is the product of social reality. . . .

. . . The advocates of human rights routinely make several assumptions derived from natural law that are not appropriate in analyzing international law. First, it is assumed that international law is "superior" to domestic law. . . . Second, it is assumed that international norms in the area should be universal. Third, it is assumed that it is appropriate to consider the individual human being as the subject of international rights, rather than states. All of these are product of the selection of the a priori version of natural law as a basis for international human rights.

Question and Discussion

1. As Watson states, for early writers on international law in its classic form, such as Bartolomé de Las Casas, Vitoria, and Grotius, the "natural law approach begins with the assumption that there are natural laws, both theological and metaphysical, which confer certain particular rights upon individual human beings. These rights find their authority either in divine will or in specified metaphysical absolutes." MYERS S. MCDOUGAL, HAROLD D. LASWELL, & LUNG-CHU CHEN, HUMAN RIGHTS AND WORLD PUBLIC ORDER 68 (1980). As you might surmise, the natural law tradition is often rejected because of the lack of objectivity behind what are asserted to be "higher principles," which lends it to capture by advocates of particular views. Can you see any way around this problem and the criticisms advanced by Watson? Is the response by Paul Seighart satisfactory? Seighart writes:

    [T]he need for standards founded on systems of divine or natural law has disappeared, and with it the need for the legal positivist to object to them. To judge whether a national law is good or bad, just or unjust, recourse is no longer necessary to the Creator or Nature, or to belief in either of them. Instead, one may refer to the rules of international human rights law, as defined in the relevant instruments which have been brought into existence since 1945.

PAUL SEIGHART, THE INTERNATIONAL LAW OF HUMAN RIGHTS 15 (1983).

B. *Legal Positivism*

Legal positivism arose, at least in part, as a response to the loss in faith of the ability of natural law to provide a normatively objective measure. Positivism contrasts, even today, with some analytical methods by which human rights proponents of diverse backgrounds converge on common fundamental human rights claims. Positivism locates the state as the exclusive source of authority and views legal rules as the positive enactments of states. Law can be "explained without reference to the extra-legal, the mysterious, the ideal or the moral." Instead, "[l]aw is made by an act of will, not found by an act of magic." PHILIP ALLOTT, THE HEALTH OF NATIONS: SOCIETY AND LAW BEYOND THE STATE 47 (2002). Legal positivism came to dominate international legal theory in the late nineteenth and twentieth centuries.

Positivism "crept into international law in the course of the nineteenth century. Two hundred years ago, international law was rooted in ethics. . . . One hundred years ago, law had become far more a matter of formal rules, de-linked from morality and rooted in sovereign will." David Kennedy, *Modern War and Modern Law*, 12 INT'L LEGAL THEORY 55, 67 (2006). An international legal positivist views the consent of states (ordinarily express, but sometimes tacit with custom) as the "rule of recognition . . . for the identification of primary rules of obligation." H.L.A. HART, THE CONCEPT OF LAW 97 (1961). In other words, for international legal positivists, it is the consent of states that provides the ultimate source of international law; either consent through ratification of a human rights treaty, for example, or consent to customary law through state practice. In the realm of human rights today, states have consented to a wide array of customary human rights norms and human rights treaties, which makes it possible to analyze and apply human rights from a purely positivist perspective.

Still, as a contemporary human rights text recognizes, "the modern scope of human rights engages not just states but also international institutions, nongovernmental organizations, individual claimants, and other actors; human rights practice involves much more than the straightforward application of existing legal texts or readily discernible custom. Human rights activists continue to propose new human rights norms, and the line between what the law *is* and what the law *ought* to be is often blurred. As a result, human rights discourse inevitably draws heavily on pre-positive notions of justice, very much in the natural law tradition." RICHARD B. LILLICH, HURST HANNUM, S. JAMES ANAYA & DINAH L. SHELTON, INTERNATIONAL HUMAN RIGHTS: PROBLEMS OF LAW, POLICY, AND PRACTICE 35 (2006).

Questions and Discussion

1. Can you identify difficulties posed by a purely positivistic outlook on human rights? What sort of prospects would human rights have in a legal system that does not enact rules to further human rights? What about a legal system that incorporates positive rules that are antithetical to human rights?
2. An important issue for those who approach human rights from a law-centered perspective is to consider is whether human rights can be influential and effective outside of positive law, or even whether a legal approach is best. Amartya Sen takes the view that "we need to

see human rights . . . over a much bigger arena, of which legal motivation, actual legislation and judicial enforcement form only one part." Amartya Sen, *Human Rights and the Limits of the Law*, 27 CARDOZO L. REV. 2913, 2916 (2006). As part of his argument, Sen distinguishes three sorts of human rights in terms of their status as "proto-legal," "post-legal," and "ideal-legal." For positivists, as explained already, the action lies almost exclusively with postlegal rights; those rights that have already embodied in legal rules. Sen, like many others, sees this as too limited. From a legal perspective, he points out that human rights can have effective impact before they become law. In protolegal form, ethical human rights claims not only provide fodder for new law but also can provide normative pull through high-level political recognition or civil society agitation. Do you agree? In considering ideal-legal forms of human rights, the question, for Sen, is whether legal transformation of ethical human rights claims into a specified legal rule is always best, or "ideal." Sen believes that, in some situations, it might be more desirable to deploy education or public discussion to effect change or to protect rights, rather than legislating coercive legal rules. Can you suggest when this might be so?

C. *Feminist Theory*

Contemporary international legal theory includes robust feminist analysis and critique of existing power structures supported by international law. Feminist legal scholars offer a critique of international law based on often-unrecognized gendered attitudes, which come out in the following extract.

Feminist Ambivalence About International Law, 11 INT'L LEGAL THEORY 1, 1–8 (2005) Hilary Charlesworth

Being a professional feminist means carrying a label wherever you go. We can be confident that no one at this conference[25] has been asked to present a masculinist perspective on questions of international law. Masculinity has so permeated the mainstream of international law that it has become the norm. The particular (the masculine) has become the general. As I grow older and more impatient, I look forward to the day when issues of sex and gender will become less relevant, and concerns of humanity will become more significant. This will mean that women will not be required to speak as women, simply because men are always speaking as men.

In the context of a grand establishment organization, such as the American Society of International Law, the feminist perspective carries a whiff of danger about it. Allowing a feminist to participate, suggests the broadmindedness of the Society and its tolerance of offbeat perspectives. While I believe that the Society is born of a genuine liberal tolerance, it is striking that the tolerance is passive and does not lead to any real engagement of ideas.

Looking at the major writings in international law and theory over the past decade, it is very hard to detect any real attempt to engage with feminist theories of international law, or indeed with any outsider perspectives. Feminist theories seem to remain in a scholarly ghetto, at most a brief footnote, in international legal scholarship. Fernando Tesón is an exception to this tendency and I welcome his interest (though it is highly critical) in feminist theories of international law.

Of course, the meaning of feminism is highly contentious. I have surveyed students in both the United States and in Australia and discovered that the most common definition of feminism is a refusal by women to shave their legs! What are the central concerns of feminist jurisprudence?

[25] Author refers to the 2005 Annual Meeting of the American Society of International Law, held in Washington, D.C.

The term "feminism" is an over-extended umbrella; we can readily find bitter theoretical disputes between scholars who identify themselves as feminists. Examples include the debate over pornography, or the trafficking of women.

An early search for points of commonality among women has fractured. Now it is common to find references to "feminisms" rather than "feminism." The Canadian academic Denise Réaume challenged the idea of feminist jurisprudence as a distinctive school of thought and has attempted to recognize the diversity within feminist scholarship. She proposed an account of feminist jurisprudence as "an analysis of the exclusion of (some) women's needs, interests, aspirations, or attributes from the design or application of the law." This account does not require a thick substantive conception of the aims of feminism. In other words, it assumes a broad commitment to the equality of women, without defining what equality actually is. Réaume's notion of feminist jurisprudence also builds on the sense that the injustice women face is structural and systemic; feminist jurisprudence is skeptical about the justice of traditional power structures.

I find this explanation of feminist jurisprudence (with the exclusion of women) attractive as an alternative to the radical feminism, associated most strongly with the writings of Catharine MacKinnon, because it does not depend on a notion of the universal victimization of women and the universal empowerment of men. It moves us away from the rather dispiriting and often paralyzing idea that women are eternally downtrodden at the hands of an international brotherhood of men.

I use the theme exclusion of women, in the design and application of law, as a response to why states should obey international law. I offer three reflections on this topic, but acknowledge that they do not all point in the same direction.

First, using the lens of the exclusion of women, it might be said that the reason states should obey international law is that it gives much greater attention to the position of women than almost any national legal system. Perhaps the most obvious example of this is in the area of human rights, where the 1979 Convention on the Elimination of All Forms of Discrimination Against Women (CEDAW) gives treaty status to the norm of nondiscrimination against women. This is why major women's groups support the ratification of CEDAW. In my country, Australia, national sex discrimination laws gain constitutional basis from Australia's ratification of CEDAW. Other responses in international law to the situation of women include the International Criminal Court statute's explicit recognition of rape as a war crime.

My first response is that, from the perspective of the exclusion of women, the normative values of international law are superior to those of national law. International law, at least, includes some recognition of the needs and aspirations of women. At the same time, we should acknowledge all the barriers that still prevent states from taking international law with respect to women seriously. Perhaps more than in any other area of international law, states have crafted many techniques to avoid implementing international norms relating to women in national legal systems. These techniques include extensive reservation toward CEDAW and the invocation of notions of "local culture" as a reason not to accept the principle of women's equality with men.

A longer look at international legal norms leads to a second observation: by and large, women remain excluded from the design of international law. The international legal principle of nondiscrimination on the basis of sex is primarily focused on discrimination in the public world, but even with this limitation, it is very hard to take it seriously. For example, the individuals currently debating over the norms related to the use of force in Iraq are almost entirely male. Women's voices have been comprehensively diverted. Of the major law-making institutions of the U.N. Charter, the International Court of Justice has one woman member, and the International Law Commission has two. Yet, this great imbalance is not seen to impinge on the legitimacy of these legal bodies.

The reform agenda in international law calls (at best) for equality in the participation of women. It does not deal at all with the gendered or male-centric bases of concepts such as peace, security, democracy and self-determination. We can see that international law implicitly excludes women by assuming a male norm. In other words, international law is built on the understanding that "whatever is true of men, or makes sense to them . . . automatically suffices for women." It might also be noted that international law pays only perfunctory attention to differences among women. For example, international humanitarian law is concerned with women chiefly in roles as mothers. In some contexts, the limits of international law with respect to women can constitute a restraint on the development of progressive national law. Thus, a constitutional challenge was made to Australian sexual harassment laws on the ground that CEDAW does not refer to sexual harassment. Although this challenge was unsuccessful, it illustrates the more general problem.

At a third level, whether states should obey international law when it conflicts with national law can, itself, be interrogated from a feminist perspective. The question assumes that international law and national legal systems are all command-and-control-type systems. What if we were to think of the relationship between international law and municipal law as less of a competition and more of a conversation or exchange? If one aim of this conversation is to reverse the exclusion of women, this could lead to a less competitive and more productive relationship between the two legal systems. This prescription might sound straightforward, but we must recognize that it goes against the values of all dominant cultures.

As things stand, neither international law nor most national legal systems respond adequately to the exclusion of women. Indeed, from a feminist perspective, it may be more accurate to say that the two legal systems are symbiotic: they work together to normalize the exclusion of women. In this sense, we should be more interested in alliances between the two legal systems, rather than their divergence. Both use complex and fluid disciplinary techniques to define truth and normality with respect to women's lives.

We must question the adequacy of theories in compliance with international law that do not take into account the exclusion of women from the design and application of all forms of law. For example, is it not relevant that the "iterative process of discourse" (celebrated in the Chayes' managerial model of compliance) is almost exclusively between men? Is Harold Koh's account of the transnational legal process (by which international norms are internalized) limited because it does not pay enough attention to the sexed identity of the players in the internalization process? Compliance is negotiated through a masculine grapevine, although occasionally women may be allowed to participate. And why is Fernando Tesón not interested in the absence of women in public decision-making in "democratic" states? When respected mainstream scholars begin to address these types of issues, we will be making significant progress.

Questions and Discussion

1.   Principle 20 of the Rio Declaration recognizes that "[w]omen have a vital role in environmental management and development. Their full participation is therefore essential to achieve sustainable development." U.N. DECLARATION ON ENVIRONMENT AND DEVELOPMENT, U.N. Doc. A/CONF.151/26 (June 13, 1992). Principle 20 is more fully elaborated in Chapter 24 of Agenda 21, the "road map" on sustainable development agreed to at Rio in 1992. See AGENDA 21: EARTH'S ACTION PLAN 493–500 (Nicolas Robinson ed., 1993).

2.   What aspects of environmental rights can you think of that might be gendered? Consider climate change. In September 2007, the Council of Women World Leaders (CWWL), Women's Environment and Development Organization (WEDO), and the Heinrich Böll Foundation North America held a discussion at the Permanent Mission of Germany to the United Nations on the ways climate change affects women. The roundtable was a precursor to the U.N. secretary-general's high-level climate change meeting. Participants included more than sixty governmental, U.N., and NGO representatives. Discussants noted that

while the U.N. Framework Convention on Climate Change (UNFCCC) lacks references to gender, climate change is not "gender neutral." Climate change and gender have a wider array of interstices including justice, human rights, and human security. Representatives from Honduras, Senegal, Suriname, Thailand, Uganda, and the United States (New Orleans) discussed their experiences demonstrating these connections. Participants at the roundtable called for gender equality to be incorporated into climate change planning and decision making, and for national and global policies to include gender components of climate change and be guided by international human rights treaties such as the Convention on the Elimination of all Discrimination against Women. The roundtable called for the UNFCCC to create a gender strategy, devote resources to gender-specific climate change research and develop reporting tools that nations could implement to provide data to the UNFCCC.

D. *New Stream Scholarship*

A fourth approach to international law and human rights is encompassed in a body of legal theory commonly known as new stream scholarship. While advancing a number of different critiques of the existing system and structures, a major tenet of new stream scholarship asserts that all law is essentially indeterminate and ultimately subject to politics rather than politically neutral in its conception and application. *See, e.g.*, Martii Koskenniemi, FROM APOLOGY TO UTOPIA: THE STRUCTURE OF INTERNATIONAL LEGAL ARGUMENT 40–50 (1989). From this position, analysis of new stream scholars often involves inquiry into dominant and subservient political context, existing power structures and imbalances, worldviews related to the articulation and invocation of legal norms, and extralegal impediments in the processes in which they function.

Navigating the Newstream: Recent Critical Scholarship in International Law,
65 NORDIC J. INT'L L. 341–45 (1996)
Deborah Z. Cass

Generations of legal scholars have reinvented their fields by a ritual overthrowing of their predecessors and one group within the current crop of international lawyers is no exception. These lawyers, who label themselves as Newstream, are presently involved in a theory battle with those the new scholars label, somewhat negatively, as Mainstream. This otherwise esoteric battle is interesting because it coincides with a changed perception about the role of international law in structuring and regulating international public order.... [For instance, w]hat is the role of the weakened nation state in the new regional arrangements of world order? How will human rights regimes overcome the chasms of cultural difference between societies? What is "culture" anyway? What is the nature of the relationship between international trade regulation and local governance? Can reconstituted units of failed federations accommodate disparate ethnic interests? It is in the service of answering these dilemmas that the new brand of legal scholarship has risen to prominence, claiming to challenge the certainties of the old....

. . .

There is little doubt that a large body of compelling work has now been written, associated with the rubric of Newstream, and that its continued neglect by the Mainstream risks stultifying the field and prevents the development of a more nuanced and responsive international legal theory. The Newstream critique's major strength, its sense of a mission to create a new international law, risks being blunted by the lack of dialogue between the two approaches. Moreover, as pedagogical tools, the Newstream writings are invaluable because they offer plausible explanations of international law making, interpretation and application, at a point in time in which traditional understandings about law have been questioned by (post)modern insights into cultural fragmentation, the making of history and the role of language in law. The work also echoes a widespread interdisciplinary interest in language and its effect on the structure of ideas.

Despite these strengths Newstream scholars do not exploit the critique's potential because they often fail to make explicit evaluative choices. If they perceive law as simply a variable set of argumentative possibilities, these possibilities are not being used to effect change. There are problems internal to the critique as well, for example it [is] often condescending and reductive tone, and its occasionally derivative and abstract theorizing.

. . .

The Newstream, positioning themselves in opposition to the Mainstream, have challenged the international law tradition at three levels. . . . I will briefly sketch the three challenges: *conceptual, methodological, and strategic.*

Newstream writers are making a *conceptual* claim about Mainstream scholarship which has three parts. First, the Newstream regard Mainstream international law as having adopted a complacent approach toward questions of how to define culture and differences between cultures. . . . This is exemplified in the arid debates over self-determination and cultural relativism. By contrast Newstream writers claim that the way in which culture is defined determines the legal rule which ensues, and that the meaning of what is culture is thus primary to the doctrines which have evolved. Second, they contend that Mainstream international law represents itself as an account of history as progress in which the doctrine of sovereignty develops from an uncertain principle of naked power distribution to a more formal, regulable legal mechanism. . . . Newstream accounts suggests that the story is more complex and that sovereignty can be re-interpreted in the light of different readings of the historical development of international law, in a manner which would inevitably unsettle interpretations of important doctrines such as acquisition, or territorial integrity. Third, they argue that Mainstream scholars have maintained a fiction that law-making can be reduced to either custom (a reflexive process of locating and amalgamating the practice and belief of states), or agreement and the drafting of new treaties, and so have failed to sufficiently take into account contemporary theoretical insights relating to language and representation. . . . If law is constituted by language rather than simply objective behavior and belief, then its foundations are less certain and its reconstitution is not only possible but obligatory. In short, the Newstream argues that Mainstream literature relies upon an untenable set of ideas about culture, sovereignty, and law-making.

In addition to these substantive, conceptual claims the Newstream argues that the Mainstream has a limited approach to method. So the second level of challenge is *methodological* provoking Newstream writers to experiment with different analytical devices. . . . First, new approaches method often locates and dissects twinned conceptual oppositions underlying history, sovereignty and culture, thereby revealing the unstable and contingent nature of the law which they support. . . . Second, Newstream writings represent international actors as being engaged on a highly personal quest, thereby undermining the notional objectivity and formality of international rules. . . . The device of the quest also produces an evocative descriptive framework, a personal and personally revealing account of law, and a mechanism to explore the internal contradiction between international law's idealism and its ordinariness. Finally, Newstream work uses language in ways which emphasize the conceptual and methodological themes just noted. . . .

Third, there is *a strategic* level to the challenge. . . . Here Newstream scholars reinvigorate pre-existing reform strategies, in an attempt to shift the emphasis of lawmaking from one of reform to radical reconceptualization. This is accomplished by incorporating perspectives foreign to the discipline and hitherto absent, and by situating legal problems more fully in their political and cultural context . . . ; by provocative rewritings of doctrinal history . . . ; and by integrating political considerations into legal analysis. . . .

. . . [W]hile these Newstream challenges could be transformative tools of changing law their potential is largely unrealized.

Questions and Discussion

1. Because international human rights depend on the state in creation and enforcement, some new stream students view international human rights law as severely limited by the state-centric international legal system. The question is posed: In an international system based on the overwhelming dominance of states, can there be any hope for international human rights to serve as a bulwark against abuses in most cases?

    > Although the human rights vocabulary expresses relentless suspicion of the state, by structuring emancipation as a relationship between an individual right holder and the state, human rights places the state at the center of the emancipatory promise. However much one may insist on the priority or pre-existence of rights, in the end rights are enforced, granted, recognized, implemented, their violations remedied, by the state. By consolidating human experience into the exercise of legal entitlements, human rights strengthens the national governmental structure and equates the structure of the state with the structure of freedom. To be free is . . . to have an appropriately organized state. We might say that the right-holder imagines and experiences freedom only as a citizen. This encourages autochthonous political tendencies and alienates the "citizen" from both his or her own experience as a person and from the possibility of alternative communal forms.

    David Kennedy, *The International Human Rights Movement: Part of the Problem?*, 15 Harv. Hum. Rts J. 101, 113 (2002).
    What is Kennedy's point? Is it different from the observation that international treaty regimes for implementing human rights are inherently weak because international law is predicated on consent and states cannot be forced to accept them or because even if accepted, enforcement is problematic? What alternative might there be to the protection of human rights by the state? For a rebuttal to Kennedy, see Hilary Charlesworth, *Author! Author! A Response to David Kennedy*, 15 Harv. Hum. Rts. J. 127 (2002).

2. In terms of environmental rights, how does the new stream scholarship apply? B.S. Chimni, a new stream Marxist thinker, writes about the underlying structural problem in evaluating the contributions of Professor Richard Falk (author of the pathbreaking text This Endangered Planet: Prospects and Proposals for Human Survival (1971)) to the discipline:

    > Central to the formulation of an ecological outlook is the perspective on man/nature relationship – structural considerations, the recorded past, the current basis, and the beliefs and principles on which the future should be organised. In the final analysis, individuals probe the man/nature relationship to better grasp the human situation and the conditions and prospects for human fulfilment. Therefore, . . . man dominates all ecological controversy, raising a whole host of questions concerning culture, consciousness and traditions. . . .
    >
    > The existential consciousness of man is shaped by dimensions of time and space in which he is located. Living in a society in which men believe that to have is to be, display utter apathy in the face of crises which afflict [the environment], view with cynicism any talk of human solidarity, and feel secure in a world of technological rationality, it is [important to] understand the reasons which have allowed such a state of affairs to come to pass, in order to envisage ways of changing it.

B.S. Chimni, International Law and World Order: A Critique of Contemporary
Approaches 171–72 (1993).

E. *Human Dignity*

Dignity, Community, and Human Rights, in Human Rights in Cross-Cultural Perspectives: A Quest for Consensus 81–84, 86–87, 91 (A. An-Na'im ed., 1991)
Rhoda E. Howard

. . . [Most] known human societies did not and do not have conceptions of human rights. Human rights are a moral good that one can accept – on an ethical basis – and that everyone ought to have in the modern state-centric world. To seek an anthropologically based consensus on rights by surveying all known human cultures, however, is to confuse the concepts of rights, dignity, and justice. One can find affinities, analogues, and precedents for the actual content of internationally accepted human rights in many religious and cultural (geographic and national) traditions; but the actual concept of human rights, as will be seen, is particular and modern, representing a radical rupture from the many status-based, nonegalitarian, and hierarchical societies of the past and Present. . . .

. . .

I define human dignity as the particular cultural understandings of the inner moral worth of the human person and his or her proper political relations with society. Dignity is not a claim that an individual asserts against a society; it is not, for example, the claim that one is worthy of respect merely because one is a human being. Rather, dignity is something that is granted at birth or on incorporation into the community as a concomitant of one's particular ascribed status, or that accumulates and is earned during the life of an adult who adheres to his or her society's values, customs, and norms: the adult, that is, who accepts normative cultural constraints on his or her particular behavior. . . .

Many indigenous groups (that is, the remnants of precapitalist societies destroyed – physically, culturally, or both – during the process of European conquest and/or settlement) now make claims for the recognition of their collective or communal rights. When they do so they are not primarily interested in the human rights of the individual members of their collectives. Rather, they are interested in the recognition of their *collective dignity*, in the acknowledgment of the value of their collective way of life as opposed to the way of life of the dominant society into which they are unequally "integrated." . . .

Thus in most known past or present societies, human dignity is not private, individual, or autonomous. It is public, collective, and prescribed by social norms. The idea that an individual can enhance his or her "dignity" by asserting his or her human rights violates many societies' most fundamental beliefs about the way social life should be ordered. Part of the dignity of a human being consists of the quiet endurance and acceptance of what a human rights approach to the world would consider injustice or inequality. . . .

. . .

What then is a human being? For many societies, the human being is the person who has learned and obeys the community's rules. A nonsocial atomized individual is not human; he or she is a species of "other" – perhaps equivalent to a (presocialized) child, a stranger, a slave, or even an animal. There is very little room in most societies for Mead's "I" – the individual, self-reflective being – to emerge over the "me," that part of a being that absorbs his or her community's culture and faithfully follows the rules and customs expected of a person of his or her station. The human group takes precedence over the human person. . . .

This does not mean that human rights are not relevant, in the late twentieth century, to those societies in the world that retain precapitalist, nonindividualist notions of human dignity, honor, and the social order. The rise of the centralized state makes human rights relevant the world over. It does mean that to look for universalistic "roots" of human rights in different social areas of the world . . . or in different religious traditions, is to abstract those societies and religions from culture and history. One can find, in Judaism and Christianity for example, strong moral analogues to the content – although not the concept – of contemporary human rights. But one can also find moral precepts justifying inequality and denial of what are now considered fundamental human rights. . . .

. . .

. . . All societies do have underlying conceptions of human dignity and social justice. These conceptions can be identified; and certain commonalities of belief, for example, in the social value of work, can also be located on a transcultural basis. But in most known human societies, dignity and justice are not based on any idea of the *inalienable right* of the *physical*, socially *equal* human being against the claims of family, community, or the state. They are based on just the opposite, that is, the *alienable privileges* of *socially unequal* beings, considered to embody gradations of humanness according to socially defined status categories entitled to different degrees of respect.

While all societies have underlying concepts of dignity and justice, few have concepts of rights. Human rights, then, are a particular expression of human dignity. In most societies, dignity does not imply human rights. There is very little cultural – let alone universal – foundation for the concept, as opposed to the content, of human rights. The society that actively protects rights both in law and in practice is a radical departure for most known human societies.

Human Dignity as a Normative Concept,
77 Am. J. Int'l L. 848, 848–50 (1983)
Oscar Schachter

The "dignity of the human person" and "human dignity" are phrases that have come to be used as an expression of a basic value accepted in a broad sense by all peoples.

Human dignity appears in the Preamble of the Charter of the United Nations as an ideal that "we the peoples of the United Nations" are "determined" to achieve. . . .

The term dignity is also included in Article 1 of the Universal Declaration of Human Rights. . . .

The Helsinki Accords in Principle VII affirm that the participating states will promote the effective exercise of human rights and freedoms, "all of which derive from the inherent dignity of the human Person."

References to human dignity are to be found in various resolutions and declarations of international bodies. National constitutions and proclamations, especially those recently adopted, include the ideal or goal of human dignity in their references to human rights. Political leaders, jurists and philosophers have increasingly alluded to the dignity of the human person. . . . No other ideal seems so clearly accepted as a universal social good.

We do not find an explicit definition of the expression "dignity of the human person" in international instruments or (as far as I know) in national law. Its intrinsic meaning has been left to intuitive understanding, conditioned in large measure by cultural factors. . . .

An analysis of dignity may begin with its etymological root, the Latin "dignitas" translated as worth (in French, "valeur"). One lexical meaning of dignity is "intrinsic worth." Thus, when the U.N. Charter refers to the "dignity and worth" of the human person, it uses two synonyms for the same concept. The other instruments speak of "inherent dignity," an expression that is close to "intrinsic worth."

What is meant by "respect" for "intrinsic worth" or "inherent dignity" of a person? "Respect" has several nuanced meanings: "esteem," "deference," "a proper regard for," "recognition of." These terms have both a subjective aspect (how one feels or thinks about another) and an objective aspect (how one treats another). Both are relevant to our question, but it seems more useful to focus on the latter aspect for purposes of practical measures.

One general answer to our question is suggested by the Kantian injunction to treat every human being as an end, not as a means. Respect for the intrinsic worth of every person should mean that individuals are not to be perceived or treated merely as instruments or objects of the will of others. This proposition will probably be generally acceptable as an ideal. There may be more questions about its implications. I shall suggest such implications as corollaries of the general proposition.

The first is that a high priority should be accorded in political, social and legal arrangements to individual choices in such matters as beliefs, way of life, attitudes and the conduct of public affairs. Note that this is stated as a "high priority," not an absolute rule. We may give it more specific content by applying it to political and psychological situations. In the political context, respect for the dignity and worth of all persons, and for their individual choices, leads, broadly speaking, to a strong emphasis on the will and consent of the governed. . . .

Human Dignity and Judicial Interpretation of Human Rights: A Reply
[to Christopher McCrudden], 19 Eur. J. Int'l L. 931, 932–42 (2008)
Paolo G. Carozza

. . . [H]uman rights is very far from merely an expression of the universality of human dignity. . . . The universal value of human dignity remains in a complex and concrete relationship with the particular positive law of any given, specific legal context, such that "it remains informal, flexible and pluralistic in its relationship to local law and culture." It is not sufficient, therefore, to regard the use of human dignity in human rights adjudication just as an exercise in the "universalistic naturalism." . . . Rather, it is a process of specification, of *determinatio* in the language of the classical natural law tradition – using human reason and freedom to give specific practical expression to more general abstract principles. Crucially, this means that the instantiation can be realized in a variety of different ways, each different from one another but each fully consistent with the general principle. That is the "working out of the practical implications of human dignity in varying concrete contexts." . . .

[According to Christopher McCrudden,] human dignity [contains] three important ideas: an ontological claim about the intrinsic worth of the human person; a relational claim about how others should treat human persons in view of their inherent value; and a claim regarding the proper role of the state vis-à-vis the individual (i.e., that the state exists for the good of persons and not vice-versa). It is worth noting, first, that there are in fact two different but interrelated concepts at work in this idea of human dignity as McCrudden describes it: (a) the ontological claim that all human beings equally have this status, this equal moral worth; and (b) combining the second and third elements of McCrudden's description, the normative principle that all human beings are entitled to have this status of equal moral worth respected by others and therefore also have a duty to respect it in all others. One might more precisely refer, therefore, to the "status and basic principle" of human dignity.

McCrudden at first acknowledges that this status and basic principle of human dignity are not merely fatuous or insignificant. Even stated at very high levels of generality and incompleteness, they have served to catalyse political action for human rights and their recognition in positive law. They are widely accepted and employed by judges in interpreting that law. And they are sufficiently robust in substance to challenge and undermine the legitimacy of a wide array of political and economic systems which at different times have wielded power in ways systematically contrary to the good of human persons. Nevertheless, despite this potency McCrudden thereafter seems relatively dismissive of the value of the minimum core content of the status and principle of dignity, referring to it as an "empty shell."

. . .

. . . McCrudden then proposes at least two possible conclusions, one more ambitious and the other relatively modest. The larger claim is that the gap between minimum core content and wide divergence at the margins exposes judicial dignity-talk as fundamentally a sham. The earlier "recognition of the fundamental worth of the human person as a fundamental principle to which the positive law should be accountable" is just "apparent." The appeal to dignity in fact "seems to camouflage" manipulability and indeterminacy with a superficially legitimizing (but in fact false and parasitic) claim of universality. . . . McCrudden . . . offers also the more restrained [conclusion]: that "in the judicial interpretation of human rights there is no common substantive conception of dignity, although there appears to be an acceptance of the concept of dignity." A corollary of his more modest conclusion is that "the concept of human dignity has contributed little to developing a consensus on the implications of any of the three basic elements of the minimum core." In other words, judicial use of "dignity" is not dishonest, perhaps, but it is not particularly helpful either (at least insofar as we do or should seek common understandings of the status and basic principle of human dignity).

. . .

In addition, perhaps one can go even a couple of steps further than McCrudden allows in describing the content of the minimum core. For instance, he lays out very synthetically and accurately the critical mediating function which the status and basic principle of human dignity played in the negotiation and adoption of the Universal Declaration of Human Rights. Given the agreement on dignity as the most significant pillar of the Universal Declaration's edifice, should we not regard the rest of the Universal Declaration as itself specifying to another degree the content of the more general recognition of the status and basic principle of human dignity? Its 30 Articles by themselves still do not give us the specificity necessary to make hard choices about how to balance, say, the right to education or freedom of association against other aspects of the common good (including the rights of others), so the greater detailing of the content of human dignity does not obviate the need for judicial interpretation which reaches beyond the minimum core of the concepts. But it does suggest that the minimum core may be a little thicker than McCrudden acknowledges, and accordingly more useful to judicial interpretation and protection of human rights.

Finally, we should not ignore the possibilities of bolstering our understanding of the minimum core of human dignity through serious philosophical reflection on human reality. McCrudden's emphasis on the existence or not of a consensus about its meaning is understandable – he rightly points out that such cross-cultural agreement has always been a part of the "holy grail" of human rights concepts. As a practical matter, we do and must seek consensus on fundamental principles in order to secure widespread acceptance and effective realization of human rights. That does not mean, however, that consensus is itself the basis for the truth of any assertion of the requirements of human dignity. In other words, even where there is not an international consensus on some aspect of the minimum requirements of human dignity, there may be good reason to affirm its validity; conversely, the existence of an international consensus regarding human dignity is not an infallible sign of its truth. If the "status" prong of the idea of dignity which McCrudden articulates – the ontological claim that each human being has inherent worth as an individual person – is true, then that dignity exists whether or not there is a consensus about its meaning and content. Where there is disagreement, then, it may well be the case that one of the positions is mistaken. Notwithstanding the mid-sixteenth century Spanish controversy over the rationality of the indigenous people of the New World, they nonetheless did have equal human dignity and natural rights; the lack of consensus on the question can hardly be said to have destroyed the objective fact of their human nature and the basic requirements of justice that their dignity demanded. . . .

Questions and Discussion

1. McDougal, Laswell, and Chen have written of "fundamental demands" associated with a "world public order of human dignity" that are now common across the globe. They opine:

> Different peoples located in different parts of the world, conditioned by varying cultural traditions and employing divergent modes of social organization, may of course assert these fundamental demands in many different modalities and nuances of international practice. There would appear, however, to be an overriding insistence, transcending all cultures and climes, upon the greater production and wider distribution of basic values, accompanied by increasing recognition that a world public order of human dignity can tolerate wide differences in specific practices by which values are shaped and shared, so long as all demands and practices are effectively appraised and accommodated in terms of common interest.

> MYRES MCDOUGAL, HAROLD D. LASWELL, & LUNG-CHU CHEN, HUMAN RIGHTS AND WORLD PUBLIC ORDER: THE BASIC POLICIES OF AN INTERNATIONAL LAW OF HUMAN DIGNITY 5–6 (1980).

2. As Professor Carroza's analysis of human dignity shows, the very idea that human rights norms can be of a universal nature has been resisted on the ground that it (the universal idea) is dominated by a particular cultural perspective – especially Western liberal traditions – to the exclusion or at the expense of others. Picking up on criticism of the universal natural law tradition, cultural relativists claim that one's cultural background necessarily dictates the moral values underlying the identification and promotion of human rights. The problem with universalism is the great diversity of cultures (and attendant diverse social, religious, political, and economic organization) in the world. This diversity is asserted to belie inherent universal human rights because of necessarily differing moral assessments about rights claims. The following excerpts outline the nature of relativist claims and responses thereto. It is important to be aware that relativism has been used by dictators and repressive governments as a shield against international scrutiny of gross human right violations. As a result, the legitimacy of cultural relativity in relation to human rights suffers.

Cultural Relativism and Universal Human Rights,
6 HUM. RTS. Q. 400, 400–01, 410 (1984) (footnotes and italics omitted)
Jack Donnelly

Cultural relativity is an undeniable fact; moral rules and social institutions evidence an astonishing cultural and historical variability. Cultural relativism is a doctrine that holds that (at least some) such variations are exempt from legitimate criticism by outsiders, a doctrine that is strongly supported by notions of communal autonomy and self-determination. . . .

. . .

Strong cultural relativism holds that culture is the principal source of the validity of a moral right or rule. In other words, the presumption is that rights (and other social practices, values, and moral rules) are culturally determined, but the universality of human nature and rights serves as a check on the potential excesses of relativism. At its furthest extreme, just short of radical relativism, strong cultural relativism would accept a few basic rights with virtually universal application, but allow such a wide range of variation for most rights that two entirely justifiable sets might overlap only slightly.

Weak cultural relativism holds that culture may be an important source of the validity of a moral right or rule. In other words, there is a weak presumption of universality, but the relativity of human nature, communities, and rights serves as a check on potential excesses of universalism. At its furthest extreme, just short of radical universalism, weak cultural relativism would recognize a comprehensive set of prima facie universal human rights and allow only relatively rare and strictly limited local variations and exceptions.

. . .

Across the continuum of strong and weak relativisms there are several levels or types of relativity. In a rough way, three hierarchical levels of variation can be distinguished, involving cultural relativity in the substance of lists of human rights, in the interpretation of individual rights, and in the form in which particular rights are implemented. The range of permissible variation at a given level is set by the next higher level. For example, "interpretations" of a right are logically, limited by the specification of the substance of a right The range of variation in substance is set by the notions of human nature and dignity, from which any list of human rights derives. In other words, as we move "down" the hierarchy we are in effect further specifying and interpreting, in a broad sense of that term, the higher level.

. . .

Standard arguments for cultural relativism rely on examples such as the precolonial African village, Native American tribes, and traditional Islamic social systems. Elsewhere I have argued that human rights – rights/titles held against society equally by all persons simply because they are human beings – are foreign to such communities, which instead employed other, often quite sophisticated, mechanisms for protecting and realizing defensible conceptions of human dignity. The claims of communal self-determination are particularly strong here, especially if we allow a certain moral autonomy to such communities and recognize the cultural variability of the social side of human nature. . . .

Where there is a thriving indigenous cultural tradition and community, arguments of cultural relativism based on the principle of the self-determination of peoples offer a strong defense against outside interference – including disruptions that might be caused by the introduction of "universal" human rights.

PROBLEMS AND PROCESS: INTERNATIONAL LAW AND HOW WE USE IT 96–97 (1994)
Rosalyn Higgins

It is sometimes suggested that there can be no fully universal concept of human rights, for it is necessary to take into account the diverse cultures and political systems of the world. In my view this is a point advanced mostly by states, and by liberal scholars anxious not to impose the Western view of things on others. It is rarely advanced by the oppressed, who are only too anxious to benefit from perceived universal standards. The non-universal, relativist view of human rights is in fact a very state-centred view and loses sight of the fact that human rights are human rights and not dependent on the fact that states, or groupings of states, may behave differently from each other so far as their politics, economic policy, and culture are concerned. I believe, profoundly, in the universality of the human spirit. Individuals everywhere want the same essential things: to have sufficient food and shelter; to be able to speak freely; to practise their own religion or to abstain from religious belief; to feel that their person is not threatened by the state; to know that they will not be tortured, or detained without charge, and that, if charged, they will have a fair trial. I believe there is nothing in these aspirations that is dependent upon culture, or religion, or stage of development. They are as keenly felt by the African tribesman as by the European city-dweller, by the inhabitant of a Latin American shanty-town as by the resident of a Manhattan apartment.

Questions and Discussion

1. Can the idea of human dignity help surmount the problem of cultural relativity? Why or why not?
2. How do you think cultural relativism might impact human rights important for environmental protection? What about rights for the environment?
3. For a recent treatment on the idea of human solidarity as a relativist bridge, see Karl Wellens, *Revisiting Solidarity as a (Re-)emerging Constitutional Principle: Some Further Reflections, in* SOLIDARITY: A STRUCTURAL PRINCIPLE OF INTERNATIONAL LAW 3 (Rüdiger Wolfrum & Chie Kojima eds., 2010).

IV. Individual Duties as a Means of Social Ordering

Social ordering on the basis of human rights is not the only possibility. Some thinkers prefer to address the issue of protecting human dignity on the bases of responsibilities rather than rights.

On March 25–28, 1997 the United Nations Educational, Scientific and Cultural Organization (UNESCO), headquartered in Paris, held the first meeting of a Committee of philosophers representing a wide range of religious, ethnic, ethical and philosophical traditions to produce a Draft Declaration providing a philosophical basis for a global ethic for universal Human Responsibilities. On September 1, 1997[,] the InterAction Council, comprised of about 25 former Heads of State and Government, adopted a more refined Draft Declaration of Human Responsibilities. The InterAction Council's text follows.

UNIVERSAL DECLARATION OF HUMAN RESPONSIBILITIES, *available at*
http://www.interactioncouncil.org/udhr/declaration/udhr.pdf
Proposed by InterAction Council

Fundamental Principles for Humanity

Article 1
Every person, regardless of gender, ethnic origin, social status, political opinion, language, age, nationality, or religion, has a responsibility to treat all people in a humane way.

Article 2
No person should lend support to any form of inhumane behavior, but all people have a responsibility to strive for the dignity and self-esteem of all others.

Article 3
No person, no group or organization, no state, no army or police stands above good and evil; all are subject to ethical standards. Everyone has a responsibility to promote good and to avoid evil in all things.

Article 4
All people, endowed with reason and conscience, must accept a responsibility to each and all, to families and communities, to races, nations, and religions in a spirit of solidarity: What you do not wish to be done to yourself, do not do to others.

Non-Violence and Respect for Life

Article 5
Every person has a responsibility to respect life. No one has the right to injure, to torture or to kill another human person. This does not exclude the right of justified self-defense of individuals or communities.

Article 6
Disputes between states, groups or individuals should be resolved without violence. No government should tolerate or participate in acts of genocide or terrorism, nor should it abuse women, children, or any other civilians as instruments of war. Every citizen and public official has a responsibility to act in a peaceful, non-violent way.

Article 7
Every person is infinitely precious and must be protected unconditionally. The animals and the natural environment also demand protection. All people have a responsibility to protect the air, water and soil of the earth for the sake of present inhabitants and future generations.

Justice and Solidarity

Article 8
Every person has a responsibility to behave with integrity, honesty and fairness. No person or group should rob or arbitrarily deprive any other person or group of their property.

Article 9
All people, given the necessary tools, have a responsibility to make serious efforts to overcome poverty, malnutrition, ignorance, and inequality. They should promote sustainable development all over the world in order to assure dignity, freedom, security and justice for all people.

Article 10
All people have a responsibility to develop their talents through diligent endeavor; they should have equal access to education and to meaningful work. Everyone should lend support to the needy, the disadvantaged, the disabled and to the victims of discrimination.

Article 11
All property and wealth must be used responsibly in accordance with justice and for the advancement of the human race. Economic and political power must not be handled as an instrument of domination, but in the service of economic justice and of the social order.

Truthfulness and Tolerance

Article 12
Every person has a responsibility to speak and act truthfully. No one, however high or mighty, should speak lies. The right to privacy and to personal and professional confidentiality is to be respected. No one is obliged to tell all the truth to everyone all the time.

Article 13
No politicians, public servants, business leaders, scientists, writers or artists are exempt from general ethical standards, nor are physicians, lawyers and other professionals who have special duties to clients. Professional and other codes of ethics should reflect the priority of general standards such as those of truthfulness and fairness.

Article 14
The freedom of the media to inform the public and to criticize institutions of society and governmental actions, which is essential for a just society, must be used with responsibility and discretion. Freedom of the media carries a special responsibility for accurate and truthful reporting. Sensational reporting that degrades the human person or dignity must at all times be avoided.

Article 15
While religious freedom must be guaranteed, the representatives of religions have a special responsibility to avoid expressions of prejudice and acts of discrimination toward those of different beliefs. They should not incite or legitimize hatred, fanaticism and religious wars, but should foster tolerance and mutual respect between all people.

Mutual Respect and Partnership

Article 16
All men and all women have a responsibility to show respect to one another and understanding in their partnership. No one should subject another person to sexual exploitation or dependence. Rather, sexual partners should accept the responsibility of caring for each other's well-being.

Article 17
In all its cultural and religious varieties, marriage requires love, loyalty and forgiveness and should aim at guaranteeing security and mutual support.

Article 18
Sensible family planning is the responsibility of every couple. The relationship between parents and children should reflect mutual love, respect, appreciation and concern. No parents or other adults should exploit, abuse or maltreat children.

Conclusion

Article 19
Nothing in this Declaration may be interpreted as implying for any state, group or person any right to engage in any activity or to perform any act aimed at the destruction of any of the responsibilities, rights and freedom set forth in this Declaration and in the Universal Declaration of Human Rights of 1948.

Questions and Discussion

1. Review the Universal Declaration on Human Rights (UDHR). Can the UDHR and the Declaration of Human Responsibilities comfortably exist together?
2. In terms of provision of environmental protection, which declaration does a better job? Why? Note that many constitutions around the world impose duties on citizens to protect or conserve the environment, including the constitutions of Argentina (art. 41), Azerbaijan

(art. 78), Belarus (art. 55), Benin (art. 27), Burkina Faso (art. 29), Cameroon (Preamble), Cape Verde (art. 82(f)), Ethiopia (art. 92(4)), Ghana (art. 41(k)), Guyana (art. 25), India (art. 51A), Iran (art. 50), Kyrgyz Republic (art. 35(2)), Madagascar (art. 39), Mongolia (art. 17(2)), Mozambique (art. 72), Poland (art. 71), Portugal (art. 66), Seychelles (art. 40), Spain (art. 45), Sri Lanka (art. 28), Thailand (sec. 57 (bis)), Turkey (art. 56), and Yugoslavia (art. 52(2)). *See* CONSTITUTIONS OF THE COUNTRIES OF THE WORLD (Albert P. Blaustein & Gisbert H. Flanz eds.) (multivolume loose-leaf).

3. Communitarian critics of the liberal conception of individual rights assert that it ignores how our social roles situate each of us and, indeed, how they help constitute us. For communitarians, full membership in the common life of society, whereby each person meaningfully contributes to public life, is most important. *See* Michael Sandel, *Morality and the Liberal Ideal*, NEW REPUBLIC, May 7, 1984, at 16, 17. Does a focus on duty satisfy communitarians? Are there other problems?

4. Is there any reason to insist on rights being enshrined in national and international law while leaving individual responsibilities and duties to be partly governed by law (civil and criminal) and partly left to the realm of morality and ethics?

4 The International Protection of Human Rights

I. Introduction

To appreciate the role of human rights in the cause of environmental protection, it is essential that you understand the nature and evolution of human rights law. In this dynamic field, the relationship between environmental protection and human rights is still very much a work in progress. Studying the growth in the corpus of human rights norms and institutions will aid in developing a sense of if and when asserted environmental rights can be brought to bear on various situations.

This chapter starts with the opening of the modern era of human rights following World War II and takes you through the development of what is called the International Bill of Rights and other so-called core global treaties. It then presents an overview of regional systems that complement and supplement the U.N. efforts. The chapter then considers several important and unique features of human rights treaties and the implication those features have for environmental protection. As in Chapter 3, the readings in this chapter continue to highlight the essential features of human rights generally to prepare the way for more detailed consideration in subsequent chapters of how they relate to the environment.

After the trauma of World War II, states sought to create global and regional organizations that would help ensure that war would be avoided and human rights respected. The United Nations attempts to do both. Article 2(4) of the U.N. Charter prohibits the unilateral use or threats of force to resolve disputes, subject to a circumscribed right of self-defense. Just as important, article 1(3) of the Charter establishes that "promoting and encouraging respect for human rights" is one of the major purposes of the United Nations. The Charter refers to human rights in a number of places (the Preamble, and arts. 1(3), 55, and 56), but nowhere are human rights defined or listed in the Charter. Proposals to include a Bill of Rights in the Charter itself, the majority coming from Latin America, were unsuccessful, largely because of time constraints at the San Francisco Conference. Instead, members of the U.N. created Commission on Human Rights in 1946. The Commission became the Human Rights Council in 2006. The Council is a high-level body reporting to the General Assembly; it is composed of forty-seven states responsible for promoting and protecting human rights in the world. The Commission, as it then was, drafted the first global instrument listing human rights – the Universal Declaration of Human Rights.

The Universal Declaration was followed by the Convention on the Elimination of All Forms of Racial Discrimination in 1965 and two treaties in 1966: the International Covenant on Civil and Political Rights, 999 U.N.T.S. 171, and the International Covenant on Economic, Social, and Cultural Rights, 993 U.N.T.S. 3. Both Covenants came into force in 1976. The Declaration and Covenants are often referred to as the International Bill of Rights.

II. The Universal Declaration of Human Rights

The Universal Declaration was, as its name suggests, intended to be universal. It was adopted by the international community in the United Nations and was intended to provide a common standard of achievement for all states and cultures. As you study the Declaration, bear three things in mind. First, at the time of adoption in 1949, environmental consciousness was barely existent and environmental rights did not enter the picture, even though almost from the outset the United Nations took the view that the "conservation of resources" had "to be regarded as an end itself." *See* U.N. SCIENTIFIC CONFERENCE ON THE CONSERVATION AND UTILIZATION OF RESOURCES, Aug. 17–Sept. 6, 1949, U.N. Doc. E/CONF.7/7, Foreword (1950). Accordingly, no mention of explicit environmental rights per se will be found in the document. Second, the Declaration makes no distinction between civil, political, economic, social, or cultural rights. All find equal voice. Third, the Declaration started its life as a political declaration with no legally binding content per se. It contains no provisions on state obligations or enforcement provisions. For the drafting history, see Louis B. Sohn, A *Short History of United Nations Documents on Human Rights*, in THE UNITED NATIONS AND HUMAN RIGHTS 101 (18th Report of the Commission to Study the Organization of Peace) (1968); JOHANNES MORSINK, THE UNIVERSAL DECLARATION ON HUMAN RIGHTS: ORIGINS, DRAFTING, AND INTENT (2000).

The idea of the Universal Declaration of Human Rights originated in 1945 at the San Francisco U.N. Conference on International Organization, convened to establish the U.N. Organization. It was suggested by some states that the U.N. Charter contain a "bill of rights." The issue was considered by Committee I/1 of the conference, but it ultimately decided that the issue was better addressed following the formation of the U.N. A article 68 of the Charter, however, did require the Economic and Social Council to establish a commission(s) for the promotion of human rights and little time was lost in acting on a more detailed rights document. On February 15, 1946, the Council created the germ of the Commission on Human Rights and on June 21, 1946, it adopted the terms of reference for the permanent Commission.

The Commission held its first regular session in Lake Success, New York, in 1947. It decided that the Drafting Committee consisting of the chair (Eleanor Roosevelt, United States), vice chair (Peng-chun Chang, China), and rapporteur (Charles Malik, Lebanon) should formulate a preliminary draft Bill of Rights. Some prickly personalities and intellectual rivalries made drafting difficult and the Economic and Social Council soon decided that the Drafting Committee be enlarged to include members from a variety of regions and legal traditions (Australia, Chile, China, France, Lebanon, Soviet Union, United Kingdom, and United States). The Commission requested "the Secretary-General to collect all possible information on the subject" of a bill of rights. Working from this and from submissions received at the San Francisco Conference, the Drafting Committee submitted the Declaration to the Commission in June 1948, which approved it by a vote of 12–4, with abstentions by Soviet bloc states. The Declaration was then adopted by the General Assembly on December 10, 1948, without dissent, although there were eight abstentions (six Soviet bloc states and Saudi Arabia and South Africa). *See further* [1946–47] U.N.Y.B. 524–25; [1948–49] U.N.Y.B. 524–37; John P. Humphrey, *The Universal Declaration of Human Rights: Its History, Impact and Juridical Character, in* HUMAN RIGHTS: THIRTY YEARS AFTER THE UNIVERSAL DECLARATION 21–28 (B.G. Ramcharan ed., 1979).

As you read the Declaration, reflect on the following questions: Are the rights contained in the UDHR truly universal? If so, what makes them so? Which of the rights have environmental importance? Why? If you were going to include explicit environmental rights in a similar declaration, how would you go about deciding what rights to include and the specific language to use? Would these rights be universal too? On what basis? How would these rights be enforced?

UNIVERSAL DECLARATION OF HUMAN RIGHTS,
G.A. Res. 217A (III) (Dec. 10, 1948),
reprinted in HUMAN RIGHTS: A COMPILATION OF INTERNATIONAL INSTRUMENTS,
U.N. Doc. ST/HR/Rev.4 (Vol. 1, Pt. 1) (1993)

Whereas recognition of the inherent dignity and of the equal and inalienable rights of all members of the human family is the foundation of freedom, justice and peace in the world,

Whereas disregard and contempt for human rights have resulted in barbarous acts which have outraged the conscience of mankind, and the advent of a world in which human beings shall enjoy freedom of speech and belief and freedom from fear and want has been proclaimed as the highest aspiration of the common people,

Whereas it is essential, if man is not to be compelled to have recourse, as a last resort, to rebellion against tyranny and oppression, that human rights should be protected by the rule of law,

Whereas it is essential to promote the development of friendly relations between nations,

Whereas the peoples of the United Nations have in the Charter reaffirmed their faith in fundamental human rights, in the dignity and worth of the human person and in the equal rights of men and women and have determined to promote social progress and better standards of life in larger freedom,

Whereas Member States have pledged themselves to achieve, in co-operation with the United Nations, the promotion of universal respect for and observance of human rights and fundamental freedoms,

Whereas a common understanding of these rights and freedoms is of the greatest importance for the full realization of this pledge,

Now, Therefore the General Assembly proclaims this Universal Declaration of Human Rights as a common standard of achievement for all peoples and all nations, to the end that every individual and every organ of society, keeping this Declaration constantly in mind, shall strive by teaching and education to promote respect for these rights and freedoms and by progressive measures, national and international, to secure their universal and effective recognition and observance, both among the peoples of Member States themselves and among the peoples of territories under their jurisdiction.

Article 1

All human beings are born free and equal in dignity and rights. They are endowed with reason and conscience and should act towards one another in a spirit of brotherhood.

Article 2

Everyone is entitled to all the rights and freedoms set forth in this Declaration, without distinction of any kind, such as race, colour, sex, language, religion, political or other opinion, national or social origin, property, birth or other status. Furthermore, no distinction shall be made on the basis of the political, jurisdictional or international status of the country or territory to which a person belongs, whether it be independent, trust, non-self-governing or under any other limitation of sovereignty.

Article 3

Everyone has the right to life, liberty and security of person. . . .

Article 5

No one shall be subjected to torture or to cruel, inhuman or degrading treatment or punishment.

Article 6

Everyone has the right to recognition everywhere as a person before the law.

Article 7

All are equal before the law and are entitled without any discrimination to equal protection of the law. All are entitled to equal protection against any discrimination in violation of this Declaration and against any incitement to such discrimination.

Article 8

Everyone has the right to an effective remedy by the competent national tribunals for acts violating the fundamental rights granted him by the constitution or by law.

Article 9

No one shall be subjected to arbitrary arrest, detention or exile.

Article 10

Everyone is entitled in full equality to a fair and public hearing by an independent and impartial tribunal, in the determination of his rights and obligations and of any criminal charge against him.

Article 11

(1) Everyone charged with a penal offence has the right to be presumed innocent until proved guilty according to law in a public trial at which he has had all the guarantees necessary for his defence.

(2) No one shall be held guilty of any penal offence on account of any act or omission which did not constitute a penal offence, under national or international law, at the time when it was committed. Nor shall a heavier penalty be imposed than the one that was applicable at the time the penal offence was committed.

Article 12

No one shall be subjected to arbitrary interference with his privacy, family, home or correspondence, nor to attacks upon his honour and reputation. Everyone has the right to the protection of the law against such interference or attacks.

Article 13

(1) Everyone has the right to freedom of movement and residence within the borders of each state.

(2) Everyone has the right to leave any country, including his own, and to return to his country. . . .

Article 16

(1) Men and women of full age, without any limitation due to race, nationality or religion, have the right to marry and to found a family. They are entitled to equal rights as to marriage, during marriage and at its dissolution.

(2) Marriage shall be entered into only with the free and full consent of the intending spouses.

(3) The family is the natural and fundamental group unit of society and is entitled to protection by society and the State.

Article 17

(1) Everyone has the right to own property alone as well as in association with others.

(2) No one shall be arbitrarily deprived of his property.

Article 18

Everyone has the right to freedom of thought, conscience and religion; this right includes freedom to change his religion or belief, and freedom, either alone or in community with others and in public or private, to manifest his religion or belief in teaching, practice, worship and observance.

Article 19

Everyone has the right to freedom of opinion and expression; this right includes freedom to hold opinions without interference and to seek, receive and impart information and ideas through any media and regardless of frontiers.

Article 20

(1) Everyone has the right to freedom of peaceful assembly and association.

(2) No one may be compelled to belong to an association.

Article 21

(1) Everyone has the right to take part in the government of his country, directly or through freely chosen representatives.

(2) Everyone has the right of equal access to public service in his country.

(3) The will of the people shall be the basis of the authority of government; this will shall be expressed in periodic and genuine elections which shall be by universal and equal suffrage and shall be held by secret vote or by equivalent free voting procedures.

Article 22

Everyone, as a member of society, has the right to social security and is entitled to realization, through national effort and international co-operation and in accordance with the organization and resources of each State, of the economic, social and cultural rights indispensable for his dignity and the free development of his personality.

Article 23

(1) Everyone has the right to work, to free choice of employment, to just and favourable conditions of work and to protection against unemployment. . . .

Article 24

Everyone has the right to rest and leisure, including reasonable limitation of working hours and periodic holidays with pay.

Article 25

(1) Everyone has the right to a standard of living adequate for the health and well-being of himself and of his family, including food, clothing, housing and medical care and necessary social services, and the right to security in the event of unemployment, sickness, disability, widowhood, old age or other lack of livelihood in circumstances beyond his control.

(2) Motherhood and childhood are entitled to special care and assistance. All children, whether born in or out of wedlock, shall enjoy the same social protection.

Article 26

(1) Everyone has the right to education. . . .

(2) Education shall be directed to the full development of the human personality and to the strengthening of respect for human rights and fundamental freedoms. It shall promote understanding, tolerance and friendship among all nations, racial or religious groups. . . .

Article 27

(1) Everyone has the right freely to participate in the cultural life of the community, to enjoy the arts and to share in scientific advancement and its benefits.

(2) Everyone has the right to the protection of the moral and material interests resulting from any scientific, literary or artistic production of which he is the author.

Article 28

Everyone is entitled to a social and international order in which the rights and freedoms set forth in this Declaration can be fully realized.

Article 29

(1) Everyone has duties to the community in which alone the free and full development of his personality is possible.

(2) In the exercise of his rights and freedoms, everyone shall be subject only to such limitations as are determined by law solely for the purpose of securing due recognition and respect for the rights and freedoms of others and of meeting the just requirements of morality, public order and the general welfare in a democratic society....

Questions and Discussion

1. "The Universal Declaration was not generally conceived as law but as 'a common standard of achievement' for all to aspire to; hence its approval without dissent." Louis Henkin, *Introduction, in* THE INTERNATIONAL BILL OF RIGHTS 9 (Louis Henkin ed., 1981). As Professor Falk writes:

   > [T]he original articulation of international human rights in the form of the Universal Declaration of Human Rights . . . was not *initially* perceived to be a significant development. . . . This enumeration of [human rights] standards was at most conceived as an admonishment to governments, and more relevantly, as a kind of heterogenous wish list. . . . In effect, at birth the Declaration amounted to a rather innocuous and syncretist statement of consensus about desirable social goals and future aspirations for humanity as a whole. . . . Also, it should be appreciated that by using the language of "declaration" and by avoiding all pretensions of implementation, a clear signal was given that the contents were not to be treated as . . . authoritative and binding.

   > Perhaps more damaging was the patent hypocrisy manifest in the issuance of the Universal Declaration. Many of the endorsing governments were at the time imposing control over their society in a manner that systematically ignored or repudiated the standards being affirmed by the Universal Declaration. . . . So from the outset . . . to make the observance of human rights a matter of international law, there were strong grounds for skepticism as to whether to regard the development as nominal rather than substantive. . . . Only the most naïve legalist could ignore the obvious rhetorical question: Why did oppressive governments agree to such an elaborate framework for human rights unless their leaders were convinced that the Universal Declaration was nothing more than a paper tiger?

   RICHARD A. FALK, HUMAN RIGHTS HORIZONS: THE PURSUIT OF JUSTICE IN A GLOBALIZING WORLD 37–38 (2000). Professor Falk recognizes, however, that the Universal Declaration has exerted a large normative influence of time, including by adding human rights discourse to international relations; promoting the development of important human rights treaties (including its own codification in the Covenant on Civil and Political Rights and the Covenant of Economic, Social, and Cultural Rights); enhancing the role of human rights within the United Nations, and engaging civil society in the international legal system. *Id.* at 53–56.

In addition to codification by the two covenants, some legal scholars maintain that all the justiciable rights in the Universal Declaration are "now part of the customary law of nations and therefore binding on all states." John Humphrey, *The International Bill of Rights and Implementation*, 17 WM. & MARY L. REV. 527, 529 (1976). *See also* MYRES MCDOUGAL, HAROLD D. LASSWELL, & LUNG-CHU CHENG, HUMAN RIGHTS AND WORLD PUBLIC ORDER 273–74, 325–27 (1980). Undoubtedly, this is so for a number, or even most, of the rights set out in the Universal Declaration. Still, it is important (at least in positivist terms) in making a claim such as this to ensure that evidence of state practice accompanied by the requisite *opinio juris* exists with respect to each right claimed to be custom. A more nuanced (and positivist) analysis is offered by Professor Schachter:

> [I]n time ... the Declaration [may] be treated as obligatory. However, for the present ... [n]either governments nor courts have accepted the Universal Declaration as an instrument with obligatory force....
>
> This conclusion, however, does not dispose of claims that some important human rights included in the Declaration have become customary law ... and therefore binding on all States. The evidence for this must, of course, focus on the specific rights in question. ... [O]ne must look for "practice" and *opinio juris* mainly in the international forums where human rights issues are actually discussed, debated and sometimes resolved by general consensus.... In those settings, governments take positions on a general and specific level: they censure, condemn, or condone particular conduct. An evaluation of those actions and their effects on State conduct provides a basis for judgements on whether a particular right ... has become customary international law. Such inquiries [will] include pronouncements by national leaders, legislative enactments, judicial opinions, and scholarly studies. No single event will provide the answer. One essential test is whether there is a general conviction that particular conduct is internationally unlawful. Occasional violations do not nullify a rule that is widely observed. The depth and intensity of condemnation are significant indicators of State practice in this context. Applying these indicators on a global scale is obviously not an easy task, nor is it a one time effort.... Nonetheless there is little doubt that some human rights [in the Universal Declaration] are recognized as mandatory for all countries, irrespective of treaty. The most obvious are the prohibitions against slavery, genocide, torture and other cruel, inhumane or degrading treatment. No government would contend that these prohibitions apply only to those parties to the treaties that outlaw them. The list does not stop there.

OSCAR SCHACHTER, INTERNATIONAL LAW IN THEORY AND PRACTICE 336–38 (1991). In considering the normativity of the UDHR, it is important to be aware that today all its provisions are considered by the Human Rights Council in its Universal Periodic Review of States. Given their experience with the Universal Declaration, do you see why some (many) states might be hesitant to commit to the Draft Declaration of Principles on Human Rights and the Environment discussed below? How might such resistance be met and overcome?

2. Do you understand the distinction between international legal obligations created by a treaty and obligations that arise because of customary international law? Perhaps some explanation is in order. The two great sources of international law are treaties (which can be called conventions, covenants, statutes, protocols, and so on, without altering the legal significance of the instrument) and customary international law – although general principles of law are also recognized as a source of international legal obligation. *See* GÉZA HERCZEGH, GENERAL PRINCIPLES OF LAW AND THE INTERNATIONAL LEGAL ORDER (1969).

   Treaties, which are today the predominant source of binding international law, become binding on states by virtue of the consent of the state through ratification of a treaty. Treaties have come to the fore because of the need to respond to rapidly changing situations; something customary law has trouble doing because of the slow way in which it ordinarily develops.

Most of the treaties involving human rights and the environment are multilateral treaties, treaties involving many parties. They also are known as lawmaking treaties in the sense that many of the norms they contain are new but also in the sense that they can promote the development of customary international law that binds states that are not party to a particular lawmaking treaty. The law relating to treaty making, entry into force, effect, interpretation, breach, and termination is itself largely customary international law, which has itself been included and expanded in the Vienna Convention on the Law of Treaties, 1155 U.N.T.S. 331 (1969), which also, in addition to custom, binds parties to the Vienna Convention.

Customary international law historically played a much greater role in international legal regulation than it does today. During the eighteenth and nineteenth centuries, states adopted in their mutual relations certain standard practices that evolved into binding rules. Through widespread adherence and repeated use, these practices by states were complied with because of the belief by states that compliance was obligatory. This subjective belief in the need for compliance is what is referred to by Schachter in the foregoing excerpt as *opinio juris* (*sive necessitatis*). At some point, usages will command a consensus of states and become a matter of normative custom (in the legal sense). In international law, then, certain patterns of behavior that are repeated over a significant period tend to be accepted as the proper way of doing things, giving rise to a norm of international law based on custom. Things, of course, are much more complex than this simple explanation, but these are the basics necessary to any course on environmental protection and human rights. *See further* Maurice H. Mendelson, *The Formation of Customary International Law*, 272 Recueil des Cours 155, and select bibliography at 403 (1998).

Do you see the importance of looking at these two separate and distinct sources of international law in all cases when you are analyzing whether or not a state is bound by a legal rule?

III. U.N. Treaties: The Core Agreements

As you have seen, the Universal Declaration contains and does not distinguish among civil, political, economic, social, and cultural rights. The mandate of the Commission, in drafting the Declaration, called on it to also draft binding legal norms. Objections to the negotiation of any treaty, based on notions of sovereignty and feasibility, were raised by a small number of states at the outset, but these were soon overcome. Initially, only one treaty was envisioned that would include political and civil rights, but economic, cultural, and social rights were quickly added to the draft instrument. Also included in the draft was the right of an individual to petition an international body for redress.

The United States and other Western states opposed the inclusion of economic, social, and cultural rights alongside civil and political rights in one treaty. They argued that economic, social, and cultural rights were, in essence, not rights at all but future goals dependent on the availability of resources. And they insisted that the well-established legal character of civil and political rights would be harmed by the inclusion of economic, social, and cultural aspirations. Further objections were made to the proposal for individual right of petition. A compromise was reached whereby not one, but two, treaties were adopted, whereas the right of individual petition would be contained in a separate instrument and would apply only to civil and political rights (at least until 2008, when the U.N. General Assembly adopted and opened for signature the Optional Protocol to the Covenant on Economic, Social, and Cultural Rights, A/RES/63/117 (Dec. 10, 2008), which provides for complaints). After many years of gestation and negotiation, two treaties were eventually adopted in 1966: the International Covenant on Civil and Political Rights (ICCPR) and the International Covenant on Economic, Social, and Cultural Rights (ICESCR). A year earlier, the United Nations adopted its first major human rights treaty, the Convention on the Elimination of All Forms of Racial Discrimination.

At this point, visit this casebook's online companion collection of case studies and materials and study the International Covenant on Civil and Political Rights, adopted and opened for signature, ratification, and accession by G.A. Res. 2200A (XXI) of Dec. 16, 1966, and the International Covenant on Economic, Social, and Cultural Rights, adopted and opened for signature, ratification, and accession by G.A. Res. 2200A (XXI) of Dec. 16, 1966.

Questions and Discussion

1. Note that several rights in the Civil and Political Covenant are absolute. Article 8(1), for instance, demands that "[n]o one shall be held in slavery." Other civil and political rights, however, are less demanding, raising the prospect of conflict. In situations where rights are not absolute, conflict can arise between the rights of two or more individuals. One right might be "trumped" or limited by another right. Or public interests might be implicated where a right impinges on social values.

2. Do you see a common pattern of rights limitation in the Civil and Political Covenant? *See* Alexandre C. Kiss, *Permissible Limitations on Rights, in* THE INTERNATIONAL BILL OF RIGHTS: THE COVENANT ON CIVIL AND POLITICAL RIGHTS (Louis Henkin ed., 1981). Can you distinguish between a limitation and a derogation?

3. Do you see any categorical rights (in the sense of absolute) in the Economic, Social, and Cultural Covenant? What about article 8? According to some scholars, the flexible phrasing of this Covenant indicates that it addresses a different quality of right. Ian Brownlie, for example, characterizes economic, social, and cultural rights as "programmatic and promotional." Their achievement involves effort over time. IAN BROWNLIE, PRINCIPLES OF PUBLIC INTERNATIONAL LAW 539 (6th ed., 2003).

4. The Universal Declaration made no distinction between categories of rights and the two Covenants were negotiated and opened for signature at the same time without distinction. However, the mere fact that political and civil rights were divorced from economic, social, and cultural rights in the two Covenants, augmented by the existence of the Optional Protocol to the Civil and Political Covenant, has propagated the idea that the nature and quality of the rights guaranteed by each Covenant are different in kind. What do you think? Consider how Matthew Craven deals with these arguments in the following excerpt.

THE INTERNATIONAL COVENANT ON ECONOMIC, SOCIAL, AND CULTURAL RIGHTS:
A PERSPECTIVE ON ITS DEVELOPMENT 8–16 (1998) (footnotes omitted)
Matthew Craven

That economic, social, and cultural rights have been identified as a discrete category of human rights is most usually explained in terms of their distinct historical origin. . . . In fact the reason for making a distinction . . . could be more accurately put down to the ideological conflict between East and West pursued in the arena of human rights during the drafting of the Covenants. The Soviet States, on the one hand, championed the cause of economic, social, and cultural rights, which they associated with the aims of the socialist society. Western States, on the other hand, asserted the priority of civil and political rights as being the foundation of liberty and democracy in the "free world." The conflict was such that during the drafting of the International Bill of Rights the intended treaty was divided into two separate instruments which were later to become the ICCPR and the ICESCR.

The fact of separation has since been used as evidence of the inherent opposition of the two categories of rights. In particular, it has led to a perpetuation of excessively monolithic views as to the nature, history, and philosophical conception of each group of rights and has contributed to the idea that economic, social, and cultural rights are in reality a distinct and separate group of human rights. Of greater concern, however, is that despite the clear intention not to imply any notion of relative value by the act of separating the Covenants it has nevertheless reinforced claims as to the hierarchical ascendance of civil and political rights. Although within the U.N. there is now almost universal acceptance of the theoretical "indivisible and interdependent" nature of the two sets of rights, the reality in practice is that economic, social, and cultural rights remain largely ignored. As the Committee on Economic, Social, and Cultural Rights has pointed out, the reality is that:

> the international community as a whole continue to tolerate all too often breaches of economic, social and cultural rights which, if they occurred in relation to civil and political rights, would provoke expressions of horror and outrage and would lead to concerted calls for immediate remedial action. In effect, despite the rhetoric, violations of civil and political rights continue to be treated as though they were far more serious, and more patently intolerable, than massive and direct denials of economic, social and cultural rights.

The picture is even less promising at the national level. In the majority of States, economic, social, and cultural rights are almost entirely absent from the common discourse on human rights. Even in those States where economic and social rights are constitutionally enacted or where the ICESCR forms part of domestic law, national courts have relied upon the oversimplified characterization of economic and social rights as "non-justiciable" rights, with the result that they have rarely given them full effect. In turn, the lack of national case law directly related to economic, social, and cultural rights has itself perpetuated the idea that those rights are not capable of judicial enforcement.

The scepticism with which economic and social rights are currently considered generally rests upon two basic assertions: first, that human rights derive from a "natural law" pedigree which is concerned with individual autonomy and freedom, and provides a justification for civil and political rights but not for economic, social, and cultural rights. The latter, being "second" rather than "first" generation rights are seen to derive from a distinct source and have a different, even conflicting, theoretical rationale. The second basic assertion is that economic, social, and cultural rights lack the essential characteristics of universality and absoluteness which are the hallmarks of human rights properly so-called and have therefore "debilitated, muddied, and obscured" the notion of human rights.

With respect to the first assertion, it is commonly held that human rights have their direct source in the natural rights philosophy of the eighteenth century and from there an indirect source to natural law dating back to the philosophy of the Greeks. One of the principal hallmarks of the natural rights theory was its individualism, and its emphasis on personal autonomy and freedom from State interference. Indeed it was the perceived "atomistic" or "egoistic" nature of the philosophy that so enraged its later critics. The philosophy of radical individualism, particularly as developed later by Nozick, conceives of rights in negative terms (as negative liberties), justifying principally a limited range of civil rights. Under this approach, economic, social, and cultural rights not only fall outside the scope of human rights but also, in so far as they require an element of wealth redistribution, they represent an unjustified interference in individual liberty.

There are a number of objections that might be made to this thesis. First, it is by no means universally agreed that the natural law tradition did in fact provide a coherent philosophical basis for the modern notion of human rights. To assert that the rights expressed in the Universal Declaration were inspired solely by the philosophy of Hobbes or Locke is little more than mere speculation and indeed might lend force to claims of cultural relativism. In reality, it is likely that the International Bill of Rights was drafted "not because ... [States] had agreed on a philosophy, but because they had agreed, despite philosophical differences, on the formulation of a solution to a series of moral and political problems." Human rights, in this sense, is a name given to "plural and divergent ideologies," such that a search for an immutable or universal foundation is bound to fail.

Secondly, even if one were to accept the basic assertion that human rights have their roots in the natural rights philosophies of the seventeenth and eighteenth centuries one is not left with a coherent picture of which rights might accordingly be justified. While the philosophies of Hobbes and Locke are often interpreted as providing the basis for only a limited range of civil rights, Locke does refer extensively to the right to private property which is, if anything, an economic or social right. Similarly, the later eighteenth century philosophies and texts do not confine themselves solely to civil rights. Recognition is given, for example, not only to political rights, but also to a number of social and economic rights.

Ultimately, one might concede that human rights are a species of natural right (as is implied by the terms of the UDHR), but that is only to say that they must be deduced from human nature rather than from custom or from law; it does not stipulate a particular historical pedigree or that they should be conditioned by the liberal overtones of eighteenth century doctrines of natural rights. Modern "natural rights" theories vary enormously and may be identified as such only in so far as they are all based upon some morally relevant characteristic of human nature or the human condition. For example, the notions of practical reasonableness, moral autonomy, human needs, human dignity, equality, equal respect, or human development have all been utilized as bases for rights theories. The range of rights to which each theory gives recognition depends entirely upon the theory of nature that has been adopted. As Donnelly points out, there is nothing inherently limited about the natural rights approach as, although it specifies the source and form of human rights, "the content is provided by the particular theory of human nature that one adopts."

Two general forms of justification for economic, social, and cultural rights may be identified. The first views them as being essential conditions for the full enjoyment of civil and political rights. It is argued that the ideals of freedom or moral autonomy can only be made meaningful if the individual also enjoys a certain degree of material security; freedom of expression, for example, has little importance to the starving or homeless. This is a limited form of justification as material security only has an instrumental value and is relevant only in so far as it contributes to individual freedom. The second, and fuller, form of justification views economic, social, and cultural rights as inherently valuable considerations irrespective of what they contribute to the enjoyment of civil and political rights. For example, such rights may be considered universal human rights in so far as they relate to fundamental elements of the individual's physical nature, whether that be their physical needs or their ability to enjoy social goods.

The second principal argument against economic, social, and cultural rights is that, unlike the traditional category of civil and political rights, they are neither universal nor categorical and therefore lack the essential characteristics of human rights. Human rights are said to be universal in so far as they are ascribed to every individual by virtue of their humanity rather than as a result of their position or role in society. Economic, social, and cultural rights, it is argued, fail the test of universality in that they only refer [to] classes of people. For example, the right to social security is a right that may be claimed only by people fulfilling the requisite criterion of need. The same criticism, however, may be directed towards a number of civil and political rights (like the right to a fair trial or the right to vote), which only apply to individuals in certain socially defined situations (when accused or when old enough). The point is that all such rights are universal in the sense that they apply (at least potentially) to everyone; it is just that the exercise of those rights is related to the particular circumstances in which individuals find themselves.

Another particular characteristic of human rights is that they are of such fundamental importance that no one may be deprived of them "without a grave affront to justice." Cranston argues, referring in particular to the right to holidays with pay, that economic and social rights lack that element of paramountcy. Rather, they are mere "liberality and kindness" embodied in "moral ideals" which cannot be immediately realized. The simple response is that even if it is conceded that the right to paid holidays is not ultimately fundamental, the same cannot be said with respect to other economic or social rights such as the rights to food or housing. Indeed those rights might in some circumstances be said to be more important than other civil and political rights such as the right to vote.

The thrust of Cranston's argument, however, goes to another more important point. Rights, he argues, are such important interests, they "must be respected here and now." Whereas that is the case with respect to civil and political rights which are "negative" and defined in terms of non-interference, economic and social rights are by their nature "positive" rights demanding the provision of resources, such as health, education, or welfare which cannot be realized immediately. As Fried commented:

> It is logically possible to treat negative rights as categorical entities. . . . Positive rights, by contrast, cannot as a logical matter be treated as categorical entities because of the scarcity limitation. It is not just that it is too costly to provide a subsistence diet to the whole Indian subcontinent in time of famine – it may simply be impossible.

This argument relies upon two assertions: first that economic and social rights, unlike civil and political rights, are not "absolute" in that they are dependant upon the existence of sufficient resources and can only be implemented progressively. Secondly, only those rights that are capable of immediate implementation qualify as human rights.

While it appears that certain economic and social rights are contingent for their implementation upon the existence of sufficient resources, it is not necessarily appropriate categorically to differentiate their implementation from that of civil and political rights. On the one hand, it is clear that several economic and social rights, such as the right to join and form trade unions, are primarily rights of non-interference. It is in fact possible to identify duties of forbearance with respect to most economic and social rights. On the other hand, it would be wrong to suggest that civil and political rights themselves are entirely negative or free of cost. The right to a fair trial, for example, assumes the existence and maintenance of a system of courts. Similarly, the protection of civil and political rights at an inter-individual level necessitates the operation of a police force and a penal system. As Shue notes, it would be "either fatuous or extraordinarily scholastic" to maintain that civil and political rights, such as freedom from torture, can be ensured merely through an increase in restraint. In fact, as Shue points out, most human rights can be seen to impose three core obligations upon States: the duty to avoid depriving, the duty to protect from deprivation, and the duty to aid the deprived. When viewed in such a light, differences between rights, or between groups of rights, become merely a matter of emphasis.

The second assertion which lies at the heart of Fried's approach is that one cannot speak of the individual possessing a "right" if they are not able to "claim" or "enforce" it as such. Stoljar explains:

> You cannot have a right unless it can be claimed or demanded or insisted upon. . . . Rights are thus performative-dependent, their operative reality being their claimability; a right one could not claim, demand, ask or enjoy or exercise would be vacuous attribute.

One response to this might be that in so far as economic and social rights have been given recognition in international law, the individual has a basis for making a strong moral or political claim against the State, especially where that State is party to the ICESCR. What appears to be suggested, however, is that rights are dependent upon the existence of specific legal remedies. While this might ring true in national legal systems, it is difficult to reconcile this approach with the theory of international human rights. It has to be accepted that an appeal to human rights is important principally when national law remedies are unavailable or inadequate; it is in fact an appeal to the adjustment of national law and practice. The appeal is not necessarily vitiated by the absence of specific international remedies open to the individual. Indeed the nature of international law is such that the question of enforceability has never been conclusive as to the existence of international rights or duties.

In the final analysis, there are no really convincing arguments either for denying economic, social, and cultural rights the status of human rights or for maintaining absolute distinctions between them and civil and political rights. Certainly differences between rights might be identified in terms of their historical recognition, philosophical justification, or emphasis in implementation but rarely in any coherent or categorical manner. Indeed it should be borne in mind that the identification of economic, social, and cultural rights as a discrete and separate group of rights was principally a result of the ideological rivalry between East and West during the drafting of the International Bill of Rights.

Questions and Discussion

1. Craven mentions that it at least appears that certain economic and social rights are contingent on sufficient resources for their implementation. Do you agree? How about environmental rights? Do they depend on sufficient resources? If so, what happens when those resources are lacking?

2. What rights in the two Covenants lend themselves to claims by which environmental harm can be prevented or stopped? How would the arguments run? Are civil and political rights, on the one hand, or economic, social, and cultural rights, on the other hand, more important for environmental protection? Why?

3. Do you agree that there is no real distinction between the various types of rights in the two Covenants? If you agree with this proposition generally, are there situations you can imagine where you would be reluctant to see courts adjudicating questions about economic, social, and cultural rights? What about questions tied to a right to the environment? What are these situations and why the reluctance?

A. The Obligations Imposed by the Covenants

Article 2 of the ICCPR obliges states "to respect and ensure to all individuals" the rights recognized in the Covenant. States must "ensure" that everyone who has suffered a violation of her or his rights has an "effective remedy." What does this require? Are duties to refrain from violation only borne by states since the ICCPR is concerned with state violations? Can others besides the state violate your right to political participation on environmental matters under article 25? Can your right to life be violated by a lethal toxic spill by private industry under article 6? Consider the observations below of the U.N. Human Rights Committee (CCPR), the body set up to superintend the ICCPR. The Committee provides guidance to states in its General Comments on the implementation of the Covenant. What follows is a General Comment on the nature of states' obligations and municipal implementation of the ICCPR.

General Comments were initially intended to be the official response of the CCPR to the periodic reports that concern states parties' implementation of the Covenant and that states parties are required to submit to the Committee. However, General Comments have come to reflect the Committee's experiences with both the reporting process and the process of individual communications by victims of human rights violations pursuant to the First Optional Protocol to the Covenant. General Comments have thus become collations of the Committee's "jurisprudence." However, it is important to note that neither the Human Rights Committee nor any of the other treaty bodies are courts. Even when making decisions concerning individual cases, they do not deliver binding decisions but their "views." As a result, states parties intent on adhering to their own interpretation have sometimes impugned the authority of the Committee's interpretations. The General Comments often focus on a particular article and seek to give an authoritative interpretation of the provision concerned.

The Nature of the General Legal Obligation Imposed on States Parties to the Covenant
Human Rights Committee, General Comment No. 31 [80], adopted on Mar. 29, 2004 (2187th mtg.), CCPR/C/21/Rev.1/Add.13 (May 26, 2004) (brackets in original)

. . .

2. While article 2 is couched in terms of the obligations of State Parties towards individuals as the right-holders under the Covenant, every State Party has a legal interest in the performance by every other State Party of its obligations. This follows from the fact that the "rules concerning the basic rights of the human person" are *erga omnes* obligations and that, as indicated in the fourth preambular paragraph of the Covenant, there is a United Nations Charter obligation to promote universal respect for, and observance of, human rights and fundamental freedoms. Furthermore, the contractual dimension of the treaty involves any State Party to a treaty being obligated to every other State Party to comply with its undertakings under the treaty. In this connection, the Committee reminds States Parties of the desirability of making the declaration contemplated in article 41. It further reminds those States Parties already having made the declaration of the potential value of availing themselves of the procedure under that article. However, the mere fact that a formal interstate mechanism for complaints to the Human Rights Committee exists in respect of States Parties that have made the declaration under article 41 does not mean that this procedure is the only method by which States Parties can assert their interest in the performance of other States Parties. On the contrary, the article 41 procedure should be seen as supplementary to, not diminishing of, States Parties' interest in each others' discharge of their obligations. Accordingly, the Committee commends to States Parties the view that violations of Covenant rights by any State Party deserve their attention. To draw attention to possible breaches of Covenant obligations by other States Parties and to call on them to comply with their Covenant obligations should, far from being regarded as an unfriendly act, be considered as a reflection of legitimate community interest.

3. Article 2 defines the scope of the legal obligations undertaken by States Parties to the Covenant. A general obligation is imposed on States Parties to respect the Covenant rights and to ensure them to all individuals in their territory and subject to their jurisdiction (see paragraph 10 below). Pursuant to the principle articulated in article 26 of the Vienna Convention on the Law of Treaties, States Parties are required to give effect to the obligations under the Covenant in good faith.

4. The obligations of the Covenant in general and article 2 in particular are binding on every State Party as a whole. All branches of government (executive, legislative and judicial), and other public or governmental authorities, at whatever level – national, regional or local – are in a position to engage the responsibility of the State Party. The executive branch that usually represents the State Party internationally, including before the Committee, may not point to the fact that an

action incompatible with the provisions of the Covenant was carried out by another branch of government as a means of seeking to relieve the State Party from responsibility for the action and consequent incompatibility. This understanding flows directly from the principle contained in article 27 of the Vienna Convention on the Law of Treaties, according to which a State Party "may not invoke the provisions of its internal law as justification for its failure to perform a treaty." Although article 2, paragraph 2, allows States Parties to give effect to Covenant rights in accordance with domestic constitutional processes, the same principle operates so as to prevent States parties from invoking provisions of the constitutional law or other aspects of domestic law to justify a failure to perform or give effect to obligations under the treaty. In this respect, the Committee reminds States Parties with a federal structure of the terms of article 50, according to which the Covenant's provisions "shall extend to all parts of federal states without any limitations or exceptions."

5. The article 2, paragraph 1, obligation to respect and ensure the rights recognized by in the Covenant has immediate effect for all States parties. Article 2, paragraph 2, provides the overarching framework within which the rights specified in the Covenant are to be promoted and protected. The Committee has as a consequence previously indicated in its General Comment 24 that reservations to article 2, would be incompatible with the Covenant when considered in the light of its objects and purposes.

6. The legal obligation under article 2, paragraph 1, is both negative and positive in nature. States Parties must refrain from violation of the rights recognized by the Covenant, and any restrictions on any of those rights must be permissible under the relevant provisions of the Covenant. Where such restrictions are made, States must demonstrate their necessity and only take such measures as are proportionate to the pursuance of legitimate aims in order to ensure continuous and effective protection of Covenant rights. In no case may the restrictions be applied or invoked in a manner that would impair the essence of a Covenant right.

7. Article 2 requires that States Parties adopt legislative, judicial, administrative, educative and other appropriate measures in order to fulfil their legal obligations. The Committee believes that it is important to raise levels of awareness about the Covenant not only among public officials and State agents but also among the population at large.

8. The article 2, paragraph 1, obligations are binding on States [Parties] and do not, as such, have direct horizontal effect as a matter of international law. The Covenant cannot be viewed as a substitute for domestic criminal or civil law. However the positive obligations on States Parties to ensure Covenant rights will only be fully discharged if individuals are protected by the State, not just against violations of Covenant rights by its agents, but also against acts committed by private persons or entities that would impair the enjoyment of Covenant rights in so far as they are amenable to application between private persons or entities. There may be circumstances in which a failure to ensure Covenant rights as required by article 2 would give rise to violations by States Parties of those rights, as a result of States Parties' permitting or failing to take appropriate measures or to exercise due diligence to prevent, punish, investigate or redress the harm caused by such acts by private persons or entities. States are reminded of the interrelationship between the positive obligations imposed under article 2 and the need to provide effective remedies in the event of breach under article 2, paragraph 3. The Covenant itself envisages in some articles certain areas where there are positive obligations on States Parties to address the activities of private persons or entities. For example, the privacy-related guarantees of article 17 must be protected by law. It is also implicit in article 7 that States Parties have to take positive measures to ensure that private persons or entities do not inflict torture or cruel, inhuman or degrading treatment or punishment on others within their power. In fields affecting basic aspects of ordinary life such as work or housing, individuals are to be protected from discrimination. . . .

9. The beneficiaries of the rights recognized by the Covenant are individuals. Although, with the exception of article 1, the Covenant does not mention he rights of legal persons or similar entities or collectivities, many of the rights recognized by the Covenant, such as the freedom to manifest one's religion or belief (article 18), the freedom of association (article 22) or the rights of members of minorities (article 27), may be enjoyed in community with others. The fact that the competence of the Committee to receive and consider communications is restricted to those submitted by or on behalf of individuals (article 1 of the Optional Protocol) does not prevent such individuals from claiming that actions or omissions that concern legal persons and similar entities amount to a violation of their own rights.

10. States Parties are required by article 2, paragraph 1, to respect and to ensure the Covenant rights to all persons who may be within their territory and to all persons subject to their jurisdiction. This means that a State party must respect and ensure the rights laid down in the Covenant to anyone within the power or effective control of that State Party, even if not situated within the territory of the State Party. As indicated in General Comment 15 adopted at the twenty-seventh session (1986), the enjoyment of Covenant rights is not limited to citizens of States Parties but must also be available to all individuals, regardless of nationality or statelessness, such as asylum seekers, refugees, migrant workers and other persons, who may find themselves in the territory or subject to the jurisdiction of the State Party. This principle also applies to those within the power or effective control of the forces of a State Party acting outside its territory, regardless of the circumstances in which such power or effective control was obtained, such as forces constituting a national contingent of a State Party assigned to an international peace-keeping or peace-enforcement operation.

11. . . . . [T]he Covenant applies also in situations of armed conflict to which the rules of international humanitarian law are applicable. While, in respect of certain Covenant rights, more specific rules of international humanitarian law may be specially relevant for the purposes of the interpretation of Covenant rights, both spheres of law are complementary, not mutually exclusive.

12. Moreover, the article 2 obligation requiring that States Parties respect and ensure the Covenant rights for all persons in their territory and all persons under their control entails an obligation not to extradite, deport, expel or otherwise remove a person from their territory, where there are substantial grounds for believing that there is a real risk of irreparable harm, such as that contemplated by articles 6 and 7 of the Covenant, either in the country to which removal is to be effected or in any country to which the person may subsequently be removed. The relevant judicial and administrative authorities should be made aware of the need to ensure compliance with the Covenant obligations in such matters.

13. Article 2, paragraph 2, requires that States Parties take the necessary steps to give effect to the Covenant rights in the domestic order. It follows that, unless Covenant rights are already protected by their domestic laws or practices, States Parties are required on ratification to make such changes to domestic laws and practices as are necessary to ensure their conformity with the Covenant. Where there are inconsistencies between domestic law and the Covenant, article 2 requires that the domestic law or practice be changed to meet the standards imposed by the Covenant's substantive guarantees. Article 2 allows a State Party to pursue this in accordance with its own domestic constitutional structure and accordingly does not require that the Covenant be directly applicable in the courts, by incorporation of the Covenant into national law. The Committee takes the view, however, that Covenant guarantees may receive enhanced protection in those States where the Covenant is automatically or through specific incorporation part of the domestic legal order. The Committee invites those States Parties in which the Covenant does not form part of the domestic legal order to consider incorporation of the Covenant to

render it part of domestic law to facilitate full realization of Covenant rights as required by article 2.

14. The requirement under article 2, paragraph 2, to take steps to give effect to the Covenant rights is unqualified and of immediate effect. A failure to comply with this obligation cannot be justified by reference to political, social, cultural or economic considerations within the State.

15. Article 2, paragraph 3, requires that in addition to effective protection of Covenant rights States Parties must ensure that individuals also have accessible and effective remedies to vindicate those rights. Such remedies should be appropriately adapted so as to take account of the special vulnerability of certain categories of person, including in particular children. The Committee attaches importance to States Parties' establishing appropriate judicial and administrative mechanisms for addressing claims of rights violations under domestic law. The Committee notes that the enjoyment of the rights recognized under the Covenant can be effectively assured by the judiciary in many different ways, including direct applicability of the Covenant, application of comparable constitutional or other provisions of law, or the interpretive effect of the Covenant in the application of national law. Administrative mechanisms are particularly required to give effect to the general obligation to investigate allegations of violations promptly, thoroughly and effectively through independent and impartial bodies. National human rights institutions, endowed with appropriate powers, can contribute to this end. A failure by a State Party to investigate allegations of violations could in and of itself give rise to a separate breach of the Covenant. Cessation of an ongoing violation is an essential element of the right to an effective remedy.

16. Article 2, paragraph 3, requires that States Parties make reparation to individuals whose Covenant rights have been violated. Without reparation to individuals whose Covenant rights have been violated, the obligation to provide an effective remedy, which is central to the efficacy of article 2, paragraph 3, is not discharged. In addition to the explicit reparation required by articles 9, paragraph 5, and 14, paragraph 6, the Committee considers that the Covenant generally entails appropriate compensation. The Committee notes that, where appropriate, reparation can involve restitution, rehabilitation and measures of satisfaction, such as public apologies, public memorials, guarantees of non-repetition and changes in relevant laws and practices, as well as bringing to justice the perpetrators of human rights violations.

17. In general, the purposes of the Covenant would be defeated without an obligation integral to article 2 to take measures to prevent a recurrence of a violation of the Covenant. Accordingly, it has been a frequent practice of the Committee in cases under the Optional Protocol to include in its Views the need for measures, beyond a victim-specific remedy, to be taken to avoid recurrence of the type of violation in question. Such measures may require changes in the State Party's laws or practices.

18. Where the investigations referred to in paragraph 15 reveal violations of certain Covenant rights, States Parties must ensure that those responsible are brought to justice. As with failure to investigate, failure to bring to justice perpetrators of such violations could in and of itself give rise to a separate breach of the Covenant. These obligations arise notably in respect of those violations recognized as criminal under either domestic or international law, such as torture and similar cruel, inhuman and degrading treatment (article 7), summary and arbitrary killing (article 6) and enforced disappearance (articles 7 and 9 and, frequently, 6). Indeed, the problem of impunity for these violations, a matter of sustained concern by the Committee, may well be an important contributing element in the recurrence of the violations. When committed as part of a widespread or systematic attack on a civilian population, these violations of the

Covenant are crimes against humanity (see Rome Statute of the International Criminal Court, article 7).

Accordingly, where public officials or State agents have committed violations of the Covenant rights referred to in this paragraph, the States Parties concerned may not relieve perpetrators from personal responsibility, as has occurred with certain amnesties (see General Comment 20 (44)) and prior legal immunities and indemnities. Furthermore, no official status justifies persons who may be accused of responsibility for such violations being held immune from legal responsibility. Other impediments to the establishment of legal responsibility should also be removed, such as the defence of obedience to superior orders or unreasonably short periods of statutory limitation in cases where such limitations are applicable. States parties should also assist each other to bring to justice persons suspected of having committed acts in violation of the Covenant that are punishable under domestic or international law.

19. The Committee further takes the view that the right to an effective remedy may in certain circumstances require States Parties to provide for and implement provisional or interim measures to avoid continuing violations and to endeavour to repair at the earliest possible opportunity any harm that may have been caused by such violations.

20. Even when the legal systems of States parties are formally endowed with the appropriate remedy, violations of Covenant rights still take place. This is presumably attributable to the failure of the remedies to function effectively in practice. Accordingly, States parties are requested to provide information on the obstacles to the effectiveness of existing remedies in their periodic reports.

Questions and Discussion

1. Consider whether the ICCPR article 2 obligations are more onerous than the obligations set out in article 2 of the International Covenant on Economic, Social, and Cultural Rights (ICESCR). What is the difference between "respect" and "ensure" and "take steps"? Does it make a difference that the ICCPR protects the rights of the individual and the ICESCR is drafted in terms of obligations of states?

2. The formulation of the obligation to respect and ensure also appears in article 1 of the American Convention on Human Rights. The scope of the obligation was held to include a duty to prevent, investigate, and punish violations of protected rights in the *Velásquez Rodríguez* Case, Inter-Am. Ct. H.R. (ser. C) No. 4 (July 29, 1988). What is the standard of care that this obligation imposes? According to the judgment, a state has an obligation to exercise due diligence in preventing the violation of human rights in the first instance, and if an individual or enterprise violates a human right protected by the Convention, the state has an obligation to investigate the violation and punish the perpetrator. Sonia Picado, a former judge of the Inter-American Court of Human Rights, has written that this case is the Court's "most important precedent to date." Sonia Picado, *The Evolution of Democracy and Human Rights in Latin America: A Ten Year Perspective*, 11 Hum. Rts Brief 28 (Spring 2004).

3. How do these general obligations apply in an environmental context? For instance, what obligations does a state have to ensure that industrial activities and waste disposal do not expose humans and the environment to harm? Is there a geographic or temporal limit to the obligations?

4. Under article 2(1) of the ICESCR, states undertake to realize the rights provided for "individually and through international assistance and cooperation, especially economic and technical." Does this provision impose on obligation on well-off states to provide assistance to struggling states so that they can realize the economic, social, and cultural rights of their inhabitants?

General Comment No. 3 [of the Committee on Economic, Social, and Cultural Rights], U.N. Doc. HRI/GEN/1/Rev.6 (May 12, 2003)

Article 2 is of particular importance to a full understanding of the Covenant and must be seen as having a dynamic relationship with all of the other provisions of the Covenant. It describes the nature of the general legal obligations undertaken by States parties to the Covenant. Those obligations include both what may be termed (following the work of the International Law Commission) obligations of conduct and obligations of result. While great emphasis has sometimes been placed on the difference between the formulations used in this provision and that contained in the equivalent article 2 of the International Covenant on Civil and Political Rights, it is not always recognized that there are also significant similarities. In particular, while the Covenant provides for progressive realization and acknowledges the constraints due to the limits of available resources, it also imposes various obligations which are of immediate effect. Of these, two are of particular importance in understanding the precise nature of States parties' obligations. One of these . . . is the "undertaking to guarantee" that relevant rights "will be exercised without discrimination." . . .

The other is the undertaking in article 2(1) "to take steps," which in itself, is not qualified or limited by other considerations. The full meaning of the phrase can also be gauged by noting some of the different language versions. In English the undertaking is "to take steps," in French it is "to act" ("s'engage . . . agir") and in Spanish it is "to adopt measures" ("a adoptar medidas"). Thus while the full realization of the relevant rights may be achieved progressively, steps towards that goal must be taken within a reasonably short time after the Covenant's entry into force for the States concerned. Such steps should be deliberate, concrete and targeted as clearly as possible towards meeting the obligations recognized in the Covenant.

The means which should be used in order to satisfy the obligation to take steps are stated in article 2(1) to be "all appropriate means, including particularly the adoption of legislative measures." The Committee recognizes that in many instances legislation is highly desirable and in some cases may even be indispensable. For example, it may be difficult to combat discrimination effectively in the absence of a sound legislative foundation for the necessary measures. In fields such as health, the protection of children and mothers, and education, as well as in respect of the matters dealt with in articles 6 to 9, legislation may also be an indispensable element for many purposes. . . .

Among the measures which might be considered appropriate, in addition to legislation, is the provision of judicial remedies with respect to rights which may, in accordance with the national legal system, be considered justiciable. The Committee notes, for example, that the enjoyment of the rights recognized, without discrimination, will often be appropriately promoted, in part, through the provision of judicial or other effective remedies. Indeed, those States parties which are also parties to the International Covenant on Civil and Political Rights are already obligated (by virtue of arts. 2 (paras. 1 and 3), 3 and 26) of that Covenant to ensure that any person whose rights or freedoms (including the right to equality and non-discrimination) recognized in that Covenant are violated, "shall have an effective remedy" (art. 2(3)(a)). In addition, there are a number of other provisions in the International Covenant on Economic, Social and Cultural Rights, including articles 3, 7(a)(i), 8, 10(3), 13(2)(a), (3) and (4) and 15(3) which would seem to be capable of immediate application by judicial and other organs in many national legal systems. Any suggestion that the provisions indicated are inherently non-self-executing would seem to be difficult to sustain. . . .

The principal obligation of result reflected in article 2(1) is to take steps "with a view to achieving progressively the full realization of the rights recognized" in the Covenant. The term "progressive realization" is often used to describe the intent of this phrase. The concept of progressive realization constitutes a recognition of the fact that full realization of all economic, social and cultural rights will generally not be able to be achieved in a short period of time. In this sense the obligation differs significantly from that contained in article 2 of the International Covenant on Civil and Political Rights which embodies an immediate obligation to respect and ensure all of the relevant rights. Nevertheless, the fact that realization over time, or in other words progressively, is foreseen under the Covenant should not be misinterpreted as depriving the obligation of all meaningful content. It is on the one hand a necessary flexibility device, reflecting the realities of the real world and the difficulties involved for any country in ensuring full realization of economic, social and cultural rights. On the other hand, the phrase must be read in the light of the overall objective, indeed the raison d'être, of the Covenant which is to establish clear obligations for States parties in respect of the full realization of the rights in question. It thus imposes an obligation to move as expeditiously and effectively as possible towards that goal. Moreover, any deliberately retrogressive measures in that regard would require the most careful consideration and would need to be fully justified by reference to the totality of the rights provided for in the Covenant and in the context of the full use of the maximum available resources.

On the basis of the extensive experience gained by the Committee, as well as by the body that preceded it, over a period of more than a decade of examining States parties' reports the Committee is of the view that a minimum core obligation to ensure the satisfaction of, at the very least, minimum essential levels of each of the rights is incumbent upon every State party. Thus, for example, a State party in which any significant number of individuals is deprived of essential foodstuffs, of essential primary health care, of basic shelter and housing, or of the most basic forms of education is, prima facie, failing to discharge its obligations under the Covenant. If the Covenant were to be read in such a way as not to establish such a minimum core obligation, it would be largely deprived of its raison d'être. By the same token, it must be noted that any assessment as to whether a State has discharged its minimum core obligation must also take account of resource constraints applying within the country concerned. Article 2(1) obligates each State party to take the necessary steps "to the maximum of its available resources." In order for a State party to be able to attribute its failure to meet at least its minimum core obligations to a lack of available resources it must demonstrate that every effort has been made to use all resources that are at its disposition in an effort to satisfy, as a matter of priority, those minimum obligations.

The Committee wishes to emphasize, however, that even where the available resources are demonstrably inadequate, the obligation remains for a State party to strive to ensure the widest possible enjoyment of the relevant rights under the prevailing circumstances. Moreover, the obligations to monitor the extent of the realization, or more especially of the non-realization, of economic, social and cultural rights, and to devise strategies and programmes for their promotion, are not in any way eliminated as a result of resource constraints. . . .

Similarly, the Committee underlines the fact that even in times of severe resources constraints whether caused by a process of adjustment, of economic recession, or by other factors the vulnerable members of society can and indeed must be protected by the adoption of relatively low-cost targeted programmes.

General Comment No. 9 [of the Committee on Economic, Social, and Cultural Rights], U.N. Doc. HRI/GEN/1/Rev.6 (May 12, 2003)

. . . [S]everal principles follow from the duty to give effect to the Covenant and must therefore be respected. First, the means of implementation chosen must be adequate to ensure fulfilment of the obligations under the Covenant. The need to ensure justiciability . . . is relevant when determining the best way to give domestic legal effect to the Covenant rights. Second, account should be taken of the means which have proved to be most effective in the country concerned in ensuring the protection of other human rights. Where the means used to give effect to the Covenant on

Economic, Social and Cultural Rights differ significantly from those used in relation to other human rights treaties, there should be a compelling justification for this, taking account of the fact that the formulations used in the Covenant are, to a considerable extent, comparable to those used in treaties dealing with civil and political rights.

Third, while the Covenant does not formally oblige States to incorporate its provisions in domestic law, such an approach is desirable. Direct incorporation avoids problems that might arise in the translation of treaty obligations into national law, and provides a basis for the direct invocation of the Covenant rights by individuals in national courts. For these reasons, the Committee strongly encourages formal adoption or incorporation of the Covenant in national law.

C. The Role of Legal Remedies

Legal or Judicial Remedies?

The right to an effective remedy need not be interpreted as always requiring a judicial remedy. Administrative remedies will, in many cases, be adequate and those living within the jurisdiction of a State party have a legitimate expectation, based on the principle of good faith, that all administrative authorities will take account of the requirements of the Covenant in their decision-making. Any such administrative remedies should be accessible, affordable, timely and effective. An ultimate right of judicial appeal from administrative procedures of this type would also often be appropriate. By the same token, there are some obligations, such as (but by no means limited to) those concerning non-discrimination, in relation to which the provision of some form of judicial remedy would seem indispensable in order to satisfy the requirements of the Covenant. In other words, whenever a Covenant right cannot be made fully effective without some role for the judiciary, judicial remedies are necessary.

Justiciability

In relation to civil and political rights, it is generally taken for granted that judicial remedies for violations are essential. Regrettably, the contrary assumption is too often made in relation to economic, social and cultural rights. This discrepancy is not warranted either by the nature of the rights or by the relevant Covenant provisions. It is important in this regard to distinguish between justiciability (which refers to those matters which are appropriately resolved by the courts) and norms which are self-executing (capable of being applied by courts without further elaboration). While the general approach of each legal system needs to be taken into account, there is no Covenant right which could not, in the great majority of systems, be considered to possess at least some significant justiciable dimensions. It is sometimes suggested that matters involving the allocation of resources should be left to the political authorities rather than the courts. While the respective competences of the various branches of government must be respected, it is appropriate to acknowledge that courts are generally already involved in a considerable range of matters which have important resource implications. The adoption of a rigid classification of economic, social and cultural rights which puts them, by definition, beyond the reach of the courts would thus be arbitrary and incompatible with the principle that the two sets of human rights are indivisible and interdependent. It would also drastically curtail the capacity of the courts to protect the rights of the most vulnerable and disadvantaged groups in society.

Self-Executing

The Covenant does not negate the possibility that the rights it contains may be considered self-executing in systems where that option is provided for. Indeed, when it was being drafted, attempts to include a specific provision in the Covenant to the effect that it be considered "non-self-executing" were strongly rejected. In most States, the determination of whether or not a treaty provision is self-executing will be a matter for the courts, not the executive or the legislature. In order to perform that function effectively, the relevant courts and tribunals must be made aware of the nature and implications of the Covenant and of the important role of judicial remedies in its implementation. Thus, for example, when Governments are involved in court proceedings, they should promote interpretations of domestic laws which give effect to their Covenant obligations. Similarly, judicial training should take full account of the justiciability of the Covenant. It is especially important to avoid any a priori assumption that the norms should be considered to be non-self-executing. In fact, many of them are stated in terms which are at least as clear and specific as those in other human rights treaties, the provisions of which are regularly deemed by courts to be self-executing.

D. The Treatment of the Covenant in Domestic Courts

In the Committee's guidelines for States' reports, States are requested to provide information as to whether the provisions of the Covenant "can be invoked before, and directly enforced by, the Courts, other tribunals or administrative authorities". Some States have provided such information, but greater importance should be attached to this element in future reports. In particular, the Committee requests that States parties provide details of any significant jurisprudence from their domestic courts that makes use of the provisions of the Covenant.

**General Comment No. 14 [of the Committee on Economic,
Social, and Cultural Rights],
U.N. Doc. HRI/GEN/1/Rev.6 (May 12, 2003)**

The right to health [in article 12], like all human rights, imposes three types or levels of obligations on States parties: the obligations to *respect, protect* and *fulfil*. In turn, the obligation to fulfil contains obligations to facilitate, provide and promote. The obligation to *respect* requires States to refrain from interfering directly or indirectly with the enjoyment of the right to health. The obligation to *protect* requires States to take measures that prevent third parties from interfering with article 12 guarantees. Finally, the obligation to *fulfil* requires States to adopt appropriate legislative, administrative, budgetary, judicial, promotional and other measures towards the full realization of the right to health.

Specific Legal Obligations

In particular, States are under the obligation to *respect* the right to health by, *inter alia*, refraining from denying or limiting equal access for all persons, including prisoners or detainees, minorities, asylum seekers and illegal immigrants, to preventive, curative and palliative health services; abstaining from enforcing discriminatory practices as a State policy; and abstaining from imposing discriminatory practices relating to women's health status and needs. Furthermore, obligations to respect include a State's obligation to refrain from prohibiting or impeding traditional preventive care, healing practices and medicines, from marketing unsafe drugs and from applying coercive medical treatments, unless on an exceptional basis for the treatment of mental illness or the prevention and control of communicable diseases. Such exceptional cases should be subject to specific and restrictive conditions, respecting best practices and applicable international standards, including the Principles for the Protection of Persons with Mental Illness and the Improvement of Mental Health Care.

In addition, States should refrain from limiting access to contraceptives and other means of maintaining sexual and reproductive health, from censoring, withholding or intentionally misrepresenting health-related information, including sexual education and information, as well as from preventing people's participation in health-related matters. States should also refrain from unlawfully polluting air, water and soil, e.g. through industrial waste from State-owned facilities, from using or testing nuclear, biological or chemical weapons if such testing results in the release of substances harmful to human health, and from limiting access to health services as a punitive measure, e.g. during armed conflicts in violation of international humanitarian law.

Obligations to *protect* include, *inter alia*, the duties of States to adopt legislation or to take other measures ensuring equal access to health care and health-related services provided by third parties; to ensure that privatization of the health sector does not constitute a threat to the availability, accessibility, acceptability and quality of health facilities, goods and services; to control the marketing of medical equipment and medicines by third parties; and to ensure that medical practitioners and other health professionals meet appropriate standards of education, skill and ethical codes of conduct. States are also obliged to ensure that harmful social or traditional practices do not interfere with access to pre- and post-natal care and family-planning; to prevent third parties from coercing women to undergo traditional practices, e.g. female genital mutilation; and to take measures to protect all vulnerable or marginalized groups of society, in particular women, children, adolescents and older persons, in the light of gender-based expressions of violence. States should also ensure that third parties do not limit people's access to health-related information and services.

The obligation to *fulfil* requires States parties, *inter alia*, to give sufficient recognition to the right to health in the national political and legal systems, preferably by way of legislative implementation, and to adopt a national health policy with a detailed plan for realizing the right to health. States must ensure provision of health care, including immunization programmes against the major infectious diseases, and ensure equal access for all to the underlying determinants of health, such as nutritiously safe food and potable drinking water, basic sanitation and adequate housing and living conditions. Public health infrastructures should provide for sexual and reproductive health services, including safe motherhood, particularly in rural areas. States have to ensure the appropriate training of doctors and other medical personnel, the provision of a sufficient number of hospitals, clinics and other health-related facilities, and the promotion and support of the establishment of institutions providing counselling and mental health services, with due regard to equitable distribution throughout the country. Further obligations include the provision of a public, private or mixed health insurance system which is affordable for all, the promotion of medical research and health education, as well as information campaigns, in particular with respect to HIV/AIDS, sexual and reproductive health, traditional practices, domestic violence, the abuse of alcohol and the use of cigarettes, drugs and other harmful substances. States are also required to adopt measures against environmental and occupational health hazards and against any other threat as demonstrated by epidemiological data. For this purpose they should formulate and implement national policies aimed at reducing and eliminating pollution of air, water and soil, including pollution by heavy metals such as lead from gasoline. Furthermore, States parties are required to formulate, implement and periodically review a coherent national policy to minimize the risk of occupational accidents and diseases, as well as to provide a coherent national policy on occupational safety and health services.

The obligation to *fulfil (facilitate)* requires States *inter alia* to take positive measures that enable and assist individuals and communities to enjoy the right to health. States parties are also obliged to *fulfil (provide)* a specific right contained in the Covenant when individuals or a group are unable, for reasons beyond their control, to realize that right themselves by the means at their disposal. The obligation to *fulfil (promote)* the right to health requires States to undertake actions that create, maintain and restore the health of the population. Such obligations include: (i) fostering recognition of factors favouring positive health results, e.g. research and provision of information; (ii) ensuring that health services are culturally appropriate and that health care staff are trained to recognize and respond to the specific needs of vulnerable or marginalized groups; (iii) ensuring that the State meets its obligations in the dissemination of appropriate information relating to healthy lifestyles and nutrition, harmful traditional practices and the availability of services; (iv) supporting people in making informed choices about their health. . . .

Core Obligations

In General Comment No. 3, the Committee confirms that States parties have a core obligation to ensure the satisfaction of, at the very least, minimum essential levels of each of the rights enunciated in the Covenant, including essential primary health care. Read in conjunction with more contemporary instruments, such as the Programme of Action of the International Conference on Population and Development, the Alma-Ata Declaration provides compelling guidance on the core obligations arising from article 12. Accordingly, in the Committee's view, these core obligations include at least the following obligations:

(a) To ensure the right of access to health facilities, goods and services on a non-discriminatory basis, especially for vulnerable or marginalized groups;

(b) To ensure access to the minimum essential food which is nutritionally adequate and safe, to ensure freedom from hunger to everyone;

(c) To ensure access to basic shelter, housing and sanitation, and an adequate supply of safe and potable water;

(d) To provide essential drugs, as from time to time defined under the WHO Action Programme on Essential Drugs;

(e) To ensure equitable distribution of all health facilities, goods and services;

(f) To adopt and implement a national public health strategy and plan of action, on the basis of epidemiological evidence, addressing the health concerns of the whole population; the strategy and plan of action shall be devised, and periodically reviewed, on the basis of a participatory and transparent process; they shall include methods, such as right to health indicators and benchmarks, by which progress can be closely monitored; the process by which the strategy and plan of action are devised, as well as their content, shall give particular attention to all vulnerable or marginalized groups.

The Committee also confirms that the following are obligations of comparable priority:

(a) To ensure reproductive, maternal (pre-natal as well as post-natal) and child health care;

(b) To provide immunization against the major infectious diseases occurring in the community;

(c) To take measures to prevent, treat and control epidemic and endemic diseases;

(d) To provide education and access to information concerning the main health problems in the community, including methods of preventing and controlling them;

(e) To provide appropriate training for health personnel, including education on health and human rights.

Questions and Discussion

1. How does one conclude that all human rights impose three basic kinds of obligations – obligations to respect, to protect, and to fulfill rights – if this is not expressly made clear in the provisions concerning the general obligations of states (e.g., art. 2 of the two Covenants)? Does this gloss over that all rights in the ICESCR are to be "progressively realized"?

2. Do you agree that the concept of minimum core content is a sustainable interpretation of the ICESCR given the weak language of article 2 of the Covenant? What of the list of required activities in General Comment No. 14? How, if at all, do they bear on the environment?

B. *Implementation of the Covenants by the Treaty Committees*

Both the ICCPR and the ICESCR establish Committees (the Human Rights Committee and the Committee on Economic, Social, and Cultural Rights, respectively) for the purpose of, inter alia, superintending the implementation of the obligations established by the Covenant. The following article illustrates how the Human Rights Committee engages with implementation issues by reviewing state party reports required to be periodically submitted under the ICCPR, as well as receiving individual complaints in appropriate circumstances. Implementation and compliance issues are examined more fully in Chapter 5.

Toward a Theory of Effective International Adjudication,
107 YALE L.J. 273, 338–43 (1997)
Laurence R. Helfer & Anne-Marie Slaughter

A. *An Overview of the [U.N. Human Rights] Committee*

The UNHRC engages in two principal activities in supervising states parties' compliance with the ICCPR: a reporting procedure and a petition procedure. Although both methods are broadly designed to ensure that states respect their treaty obligations, each procedure requires very different actions on the part of the Committee. These differences highlight the Committee's functions as both an investigative supervisory body and a quasi-judicial monitoring body.

1. The Reporting Process

Article 40 of the ICCPR requires all states parties to file reports with the Committee "on the measures they have adopted which give effect to the rights recognized herein and on the progress made in the enjoyment of those rights." Initial reports are due within one year of the treaty's entry into force with the subsequent reports due at five year intervals thereafter. In general, the Committee treats initial reports as a time to establish a constructive dialogue with state representatives and devotes more detailed attention to specific human rights practices in subsequent periodic reports.

Once a state party files its report, the Committee reviews its submission in a public session in New York or Geneva. Government representatives are invited to attend, make brief oral presentations, and respond to the Committee's substantive questions about the report. The scope of the Committee's inquiry is not limited by a state's submission and it is free to use any information available, including documents provided by nongovernmental organizations. After the public hearing, the Committee drafts written comments on the report and on the state party's responses to its questions; these comments are published in its annual report to the General Assembly.

The Committee has adopted guidelines to assist states parties in complying with their reporting obligations. Initial reports are to include two sections: an introduction describing the general legal framework of the state party, followed by an article-by-article presentation of information on (1) the legislative, administrative, or other measures in force in regard to each right; (2) restrictions or limitations imposed on the enjoyment of each right; (3) factors or difficulties affecting the enjoyment of each right; and (4) information on progress made in guaranteeing the right. For periodic reports, the Committee prepares a list of nonexhaustive issues that it intends to cover during the session and forwards them to the state representatives in advance of the meeting. Increasingly, these lists of issues have focused on "factors and difficulties that may be affecting implementation of the Covenant."

The Committee does not conceive of its role in the reporting process as "contentious or inquisitory." Instead, its function "is to assist State parties in fulfilling their obligations under the Covenant, to make available to them the experience the Committee has acquired in its examination of other reports and to discuss with them various issues relating to the enjoyment of the rights enshrined in the Covenant." Because the Committee seeks to understand the applicability of the

ICCPR to a very wide field of national laws and practices, and because many reports often contain inadequate information, the Committee has generally confined itself to questioning government representatives to obtain additional information or clarification about the implementation of the treaty. It has avoided openly criticizing individual states for failing to comply with their treaty obligations. The Committee, however, has repeatedly expressed its dissatisfaction with the failure of many states parties to submit initial and periodic reports in a timely fashion.

. . .

3. The Petition System

The Committee's other major jurisprudential function is the consideration of written "communications" from individuals under the First Optional Protocol to the ICCPR. The Committee has taken on quasi-judicial functions in interpreting the treaty in these cases. Specifically, it acts as an arbiter of contentious disputes between individuals and states, provides victims of human rights violations with an international forum for relief where domestic remedies are unavailable or insufficient, and generates a "specific problem-centred jurisprudence."

The Committee cannot perform these functions for all of the states party to the Covenant, however, since it is only authorized to consider complaints against states that have ratified the Optional Protocol. . . . This creates a "double standard of adherence to covenant rights" in which states that have ratified the Optional Protocol are subject to a far greater level of scrutiny of their compliance with the ICCPR than states that have refrained from ratification. For example, in contrast to its reluctance to criticize states parties during the reporting process, the Committee has not hesitated in expressing its displeasure with states that do not respond to an individual's allegations or otherwise decline to take an active role in resolving a case.

Even once a state has ratified the Optional Protocol, the ability to file a petition with the Committee is subject to several restrictions. First, only individuals can bring a complaint before the Committee; a group cannot file a claim on an individual's behalf. Second, if the laws of the state provide domestic remedies for the alleged violations of the ICCPR, those remedies must be exhausted prior to filing a communication with the Committee. Third, the communication must not be an abuse of the right of submission, anonymous, or otherwise "incompatible with the provisions of the Covenant." Fourth, the communication must not be under consideration by another international monitoring body. Finally, the individual must provide sufficient facts to substantiate his or her allegations.

Assuming an individual overcomes these hurdles, the Committee declares the communication admissible and then receives written submissions by both the aggrieved individual and the state party. The Committee cannot engage in factfinding and it does not take testimony or hear oral arguments from the parties. After reviewing the written submissions, the Committee determines in a private meeting whether the facts presented disclose a violation of the Covenant.

The Committee then authors an opinion, ambiguously referred to in the Optional Protocol as the "views" of the Committee. These views, which "follow a judicial pattern and are effectively decisions on the merits, set forth the allegations of the author, the responses of the state party, the decision on admissibility, and any interim measures, followed by the facts upon which the Committee bases its decision. The views also list certain "considerations" upon which the Committee has based its decision. These include a state party's degree of cooperation with the Committee in resolving the case, the burden of proof, a reference to one or more general comments or to prior case law, and an interpretation of the substantive requirements of the treaty. Finally, the decisions contain a statement of "the view of the [Committee] on the 'obligation' of the State party in light of [its] findings."

B. Toward an Increasingly Judicial Approach to the Petition System

Although the foregoing summary reveals the diverse functions that the Committee exercises in monitoring states parties' compliance with the Covenant, it is the consideration of communications under the Optional Protocol that has recently brought the most attention to the Committee and its work. In addition, the increasing number of states that have ratified the Optional Protocol over the last decade, together with the widening audience of litigants, attorneys, activists, and scholars who follow the Committee's activities, has made the petition system an ever more important part of its work. With greater visibility has come a concomitant rise in the number of communications filed with the Committee and an increase in their complexity.

The Committee's response to these developments reveals a trend of remarkable importance: In numerous and diverse ways, the Committee is behaving more and more like a judicial arbiter of human rights disputes, even when granted only limited powers by states parties. Although lacking many of the institutional characteristics possessed by supranational tribunals . . . the Committee has, within the limits of its authority and sometimes arguably beyond it, followed an increasingly court-like method of operation. Particularly striking, . . . are the Committee's efforts to improve compliance with its decisions.

Since 1990, the Committee has become quite outspoken in its view that defending states are under an obligation to comply with unfavorable decisions against them. Further, it has taken concrete steps to monitor compliance, appointing one of its members as a special rapporteur to record states responses. . . . [T]he Committee has taken steps to increase adherence to its decisions. Specifically, it has begun to publish the compliance information it collects and to identify publicly each state that refuses to implement its views.

. . .

Article 28 of the Covenant provides that the Committee "shall be composed of nationals of states party to the present Covenant who shall be of high moral character and recognized competence in the field of human rights, consideration being given to the usefulness of participation of some persons having legal experience." . . . [I]ts members need not be lawyers or jurists. In practice, however, "nearly all members of the Committee have completed a legal education and are or were employed in the legal field," a fact which commentators believe has resulted in the "high quality of decisions on individual communications."

Although all of the Committee members are acknowledged experts in human rights, the background and experience of individual members vary considerably. Most have worked as university professors specializing in public international law; others are judges, prosecutors, lawyers, diplomats, public officials, or politicians. Because the Committee works on a part-time basis generally taking up no more than two months of each year, its members often simultaneously work for regional tribunals such as the [European Court of Human Rights,] the European Commission of Human Rights, or the Inter-American Commission on Human Rights, or U.N. treaty or political bodies such as the Committee Against Torture, the United Nations Human Rights Commission, and the General Assembly. . . .

. . .

Unlike other supranational courts, the Committee has no authority to conduct independent factfinding or to require states parties to supply information concerning an alleged treaty violation. Nor may it compel the parties or their representatives to appear before it in person to assess their credibility, query their proof, or evaluate their legal arguments. Instead, the Committee must merely consider the communications it receives "in light of all written information made available to it by the individual and the State Party concerned."

Commentators have uniformly criticized the Committee's limited powers in this regard, noting that the current procedure is "unsatisfactory" and "has considerably restricted the possibilities for adequate taking of evidence" since the Committee is unable to verify "conflicting depictions of the facts," either by "oral examination of parties or witnesses or by on-site inspection." Accordingly, these commentators have urged the Committee, with the consent of the state party concerned, to hold oral hearings and conduct on-site investigations. Alternatively, the Committee may suggest, and states parties may seek, an amendment to the Optional Protocol to provide for such procedures.

Although hobbled by its limited textual mandate, the Committee has attempted to compensate for its limited powers by spelling out in detail what is expected of states parties when it brings a communication to their attention. In particular, the Committee has emphasized that a state "should make available to [it] all the information at its disposal," including "copies of the relevant decisions of the courts and findings of any investigations which have taken place into the validity of the complaints made." The state must also "investigate in good faith all the allegations of violations of the Covenant against it and its authorities and furnish the Committee with detailed information about the measures, if any, taken to remedy the situation."

Notwithstanding these procedural requirements, in numerous cases the Committee has received either insufficient or no cooperation from the state involved. To prevent the truculent attitude on the part of such states from vitiating the Optional Protocol procedures, the Committee has developed a default judgment jurisprudence under which the author's plausible and substantiated allegations form the basis for its findings of fact and legal conclusion that the Covenant has been violated. Although attractive to individuals seeking to hold such states accountable for human rights abuses, this body of decisions nevertheless may be seen as crediting factual assertions that have not been fully substantiated or skirting difficult legal issues for want of any meaningful adversarial process. . . .

Questions and Discussion

1. Do you think that a court rather than a body of experts would be more apropos to receive petitions about alleged violations? Why do you suppose states established the Human Rights Committee and the Committee on Economic, Social, and Cultural Rights instead? In the following section, we will see that judicial protection of human rights is one of the hallmarks of the regional human rights systems. Why do you suppose there is a difference?

2. It has been generally accepted that the views of the Human Rights Committee are not legally binding at international law. However, Helfer and Slaughter assert that parties are legally bound to act in accordance with the Committee's view. Helfer & Slaughter, *supra*, at n.362. Is there a distinction here? *See* Fausto Pocar, *La valeur juridique des constatations du Comité des Droits de l'Homme*, 1991–92 CAN. HUM. RTS. Y.B. 129.

IV. Regional Systems for the Protection of Human Rights

Regional systems for human rights protection were taken note of in the origins and development of human rights in Chapter 3. The institutions that have been established under these regional systems are also covered in more detail in Chapter 5. However, it is important now to gain a sense of the nature of these systems to appreciate the jurisprudence that follows.

The Promise of Regional Human Rights Systems, in
THE FUTURE OF INTERNATIONAL HUMAN RIGHTS 353–61, 365–69
(Burns H. Weston & Stephen P. Marks eds., 1999)
Dinah Shelton

The promise of regional systems can initially be understood by considering why regional systems exist. First, regional systems are a product of the global concern with human rights that emerged at the end of the Second World War. Given the widespread movement for human rights, it should not be surprising that regional organizations being created or reformed after the War should have added human rights to their agendas. All of them drew inspiration from the human rights provisions of the United Nations Charter and the Universal Declaration of Human Rights.

Second, historical and political factors encouraged each region to focus on human rights issues. The Americas had a tradition of regional approaches to international issues, including human rights, growing out of regional solidarity developed during the movements for independence. Pan American Conferences had taken action on several human rights matters well before the creation of the United Nations. This history of concern led the Organization of American States to refer to human rights in its Charter and to adopt the Inter-American Declaration on the Rights and Duties of Man some months before the United Nations completed the Universal Declaration of Human Rights.

Europe had been the theater of the greatest atrocities of the Second World War and felt compelled to press for international human rights guarantees as part of European reconstruction. Faith in western European traditions of democracy, the rule of law and individual rights inspired belief that a regional system could be successful in avoiding future conflict and in stemming post-war revolutionary impulses supported by the Soviet Union.

Somewhat later, African states emerged from colonization as self-determination became a recognized part of the human rights agenda; continued struggles for national cohesion as well as human rights abuses in South Africa encouraged regional action in Africa....

A third impulse to regionalism came from frustration at the long-stalled efforts of the United Nations to get a human rights treaty to complete the international bill of rights. Indeed, it took nearly two decades to finalize and adopt the two U.N. Covenants. During the process, it became clear that the compliance mechanisms at the global level would not be strong and any judicial procedures to enforce human rights would have to be on the regional level. As a result, beginning with Europe, regional systems focused on the creation of procedures of redress, establishing control machinery to supervise the implementation and enforcement of the guaranteed rights. The functioning European and Inter-American courts are one of the great contributions to human rights by regional systems. The June 8, 1998 protocol to the African Charter, ... create[d] a court in the African system....

Thus, regional systems have elements of uniformity and diversity in their origins. All of them began as the global human rights system was developing and they were inspired by the agreed universal norms. At the same time, each region had its own issues and concerns. As the systems have evolved, the universal framework within which they began and their own interactions have had surprisingly strong influence, leading to converging norms and procedures in an overarching interdependent and dynamic system. In many respects they are thinking globally and acting regionally. Each uses the jurisprudence of the other systems and amends and strengthens its procedures in reference to the experience of others. In general, the mutual influence of the regional systems is highly progressive, both in normative development and institutional reforms.

[Fully operational regional systems exist today in Europe, the America, and Africa. New systems are emerging through the Arab League, which adopted and revised an Arab Charter of Human Rights (1994, 2004), and the Association of South-East Asian States' establishment of an Inter-governmental Commission on Human Rights (2009) and a Commission on the Promotion and Protection of the Rights of Women and Children (2010). – Eds.]

The European System

The European system, the first to be fully operational, began with the creation of the Council of Europe by ten Western European states in 1949. Article 3 of the Council's Statute provides that every member state must accept the principles of the rule of law and of the enjoyment by all persons within its jurisdiction of human rights and fundamental freedoms. Membership in the Council is *de facto* conditioned upon adherence to the European Convention on Human Rights and its Protocols.

As the first human rights system, the ECHR began with a short list of civil and political rights, to which additional guarantees have been added over time. In addition, the jurisprudence of the European Court of Human Rights has been relatively conservative compared to that of other systems, reflecting an early concern for maintaining state support in light of the innovations of the European system and the then-optional nature of the court's jurisdiction. The European system was the first to create an international court for the protection of human rights and to create a procedure for individual denunciations of human rights violations. The role of the victim was initially very limited and admissibility requirements were stringent. As the system has matured, however, the institutional structures and normative guarantees have been considerably strengthened. Although most of the changes result from efforts to improve the effectiveness of the system and add to its guarantees, some of the evolution has been responsive to the activities of other regional organizations within and outside Europe. Others have resulted from the impact of expanding membership in the Council of Europe.

The European system is in fact characterized by its evolution through the adoption of treaties and protocols. Through its Parliamentary Assembly, the Council has drafted a series of human rights instruments. The most significant texts are the 1950 European Convention on Human Rights and Fundamental Freedoms (ECHR) and its eleven protocols, the 1961 European Social Charter (ESC) with its Protocols, the European Convention for the Prevention of Torture and its protocols, the European Charter for Regional or Minority Languages, and the 1995 Framework Convention for the Protection of National Minorities. Together these form a network of mutually reinforcing human rights protections in Europe.

The Inter-American System

The Inter-American system as it exists today began with the transformation of the Pan American Union into the Organization of American States (OAS). The OAS Charter proclaims the "fundamental rights of the individual" as one of the Organization's basic principles. The 1948 American Declaration on the Rights and Duties of Man gives definition to the Charter's general commitment to human rights. Over a decade later, in 1959, the OAS created a seven member Inter-American Commission of Human Rights with a mandate of furthering respect for human rights among member states. In 1965, the Commission's competence was expanded to accept communications, request information from governments, and make recommendations to bring about more effective observance of human rights. The American Convention of Human Rights, signed in 1969, conferred additional competence on the Commission to oversee compliance with the Convention. The Convention, which entered into force in 1978, also created the Inter-American Court of Human Rights. The Court has jurisdiction over contentious cases submitted against states that accept its jurisdiction and the Court may issue advisory opinions.

The Commission's jurisdiction extends to all 35 OAS member states. The twenty-five states which have ratified the Convention are bound by its provisions, while other member states are held to the standards of the American Declaration. Communications may be filed against any state; the optional clause applies only to inter-state cases. Standing for non-state actors to file communications is broad.

The Commission may also prepare country reports and conduct onsite visits to individual countries, examining the human rights situation in the particular country and making recommendations to the government. Country reports have been prepared on the Commission's own initiative and at the request of the country concerned. The Commission may also appoint special rapporteurs to prepare studies on hemisphere-wide problems.

Like the European system, the Inter-American system has expanded its protections over time through the adoption of additional human rights norms. The major instruments are: the Inter-American Convention for the Prevention and Punishment of Torture; the Additional Protocol to the American Convention on Human Rights in the Area of Economic, Social and Cultural Rights; the Second Additional Protocol to the American Convention on Human Rights to Abolish the Death Penalty; the Inter-American Convention on the Prevention, Punishment, and Eradication of Violence against Women; the Inter-American Convention on Forced Disappearance of Persons; and the Declaration of the Rights of Indigenous Peoples.

The African System

In Africa, the regional promotion and protection of human rights is established by the African Charter on Human and Peoples' Rights (African Charter), designed to function within the framework of the Organization for African Unity (OAU). The Assembly of Heads of State and Government adopted the African Charter on 27 June 1981.... [T]he African Charter had been ratified by [all of] the 53 OAU member states. The African Charter differs from other regional treaties in its inclusion of "peoples' rights." It also includes economic, social and cultural rights to a greater extent than either the European Convention or the American Convention.

The Charter establishes an African Commission on Human and Peoples' Rights of eleven independent members elected for a renewable period of six years. The African Charter confers four functions on the Commission: promotion of human and peoples' rights; protection of those rights; interpretation of the Charter; and the performance of other tasks which may be entrusted to it by the Assembly of Heads of State and Government. The Commission may undertake studies, conduct training and teaching, convene conferences, initiate publication programs, disseminate information and collaborate with national and local institutions concerned with human and peoples' rights. Unlike the other systems, the African system envisages not only inter-state and individual communications procedures, but a special procedure for situations of gross and systematic violations.

. . .

The seemingly endless debate over universality and diversity in human rights law is inescapable when evaluating regional systems. The issue of normative diversity is complex. Virtually all the legal instruments creating the various regional systems refer to the Universal Declaration of Human Rights (UDHR) and the Charter of the United Nations, providing a measure of uniformity in the fundamental guarantees and a reinforcement of the universal character of the Declaration. The rights contained in the treaties also reflect the human rights norms set forth in other global human rights declarations and conventions, in particular the United Nations Covenants on Civil and Political Rights (CCPR) and Economic, Social and Cultural Rights (CESCR). In addition, as each successive system has been created it has looked to normative instruments and the jurisprudence of those systems founded earlier. Yet, there are clear differences in the regional instruments within the framework of the universal norms. The differences may be less pronounced than appears at first reading, however, because of provisions regarding choice of law and canons of interpretation contained in the regional instruments. The application of these provisions has led to a cross-referencing and mutual influence in jurisprudence that is producing some convergence in fundamental human rights principles.

The European system, "considering the Universal Declaration of Human Rights," provides that the "like-minded" governments of Europe have resolved "to take the first steps for the collective enforcement of certain of the rights stated in the Universal Declaration." (Preamble) The Preamble to the American Convention also cites the UDHR, as well as referring to the OAS Charter, the American Declaration of the Rights and Duties of Man, and other international and regional instruments not referred to by name. The drafting history of the American Convention shows that the states involved utilized the European Convention, the UDHR and the Covenants in deciding upon the Convention guarantees and institutional structure. The African Charter mentions the Charter of the United Nations and the Universal Declaration of Human Rights in connection with the pledge made by the African States to promote international cooperation. In the Charter's Preamble, the African States also reaffirm in sweeping fashion "their adherence to the principles of human and peoples' rights and freedoms contained in the declarations, conventions and other international instruments adopted by the Organization of African Unity, the Movement of Non-Aligned Countries and the United Nations." The Preamble to the Arab Charter also explicitly reaffirms the principles of the United Nations Charter, the Universal Declaration of Human

Rights, and the provisions of the two United Nations International Covenants, on Civil and Political Rights and on Economic, Social and Cultural Rights.

While basing themselves on universal norms, regional instruments also contain different guarantees and emphases; indeed the preambles of all the regional instruments refer to their regional heritages. The European Convention focuses on civil rights, especially due process. The American system is strongly concerned with democracy and the rule of law, having experienced repeated military coups in the region. Its preamble begins with a reference to democratic institutions and its guarantees emphasize the right to participate in government and the right to judicial protection. . . . The African Charter focuses on economic development, calling it essential to pay particular attention to the right to development. It is also unique in including peoples' rights, but the preamble indicates that they are viewed as instrumental, as it recognizes "that the reality and respect of peoples' rights should necessarily guarantee human rights."

. . .

In other regions, rights have been added. In the European system, even before the signing of the Convention, the Assembly proposed the inclusion of additional rights, added by Protocol 1. The evolutionary character of the European system, reflected in its eleven protocols and related human rights treaties, is not unique. Regional systems seem to add new rights in a kind of feedback process of mutual inspiration, including such specific guarantees as abolition of the death penalty, action to combat violence against women, right to a satisfactory environment, and strengthened guarantees in regard to economic, social and cultural rights. The right to a satisfactory environment, for example, was first enunciated in the African Charter (art. 24). Subsequently, the American system added a similar guarantee to the Protocol of San Salvador on Economic, Social and Cultural Rights (art. 11). It is notable that in no case has a right been limited or withdrawn by a later instrument. The dynamic interplay of the systems is characteristic of the non-linear complexity and evolution of modern systems.

V. Economic, Social, and Cultural Rights: Justiciability[1]

As seen herein (particularly in General Comment No. 9), the question of justiciability, or judicial enforcement of rights, is inextricably linked with the nature of the obligations imposed by such rights. Many parties to the ICESCR have not implemented the Covenant in their municipal law. A common excuse has been that it is undesirable to legislate for rights entailed in the ICESCR because the judiciary is ill equipped to adjudicate on the broad social and economic policy issues involved. *See* Michael J. Dennis & David P. Stewart, *Justiciability of Economic, Social and Cultural Rights: Should There Be an International Complaints Mechanism to Adjudicate the Rights to Food, Water, Housing and Health?*, 98 AM. J. INT'L L. 462 (2004).

Despite protests about justiciability, on the sixtieth anniversary of the Universal Declaration, the General Assembly unanimously adopted the text of an Optional Protocol to the ICESCR that will allow for individuals and groups to petition the ESCR Committee. U.N. Doc. A/RES63/117 (Dec. 10, 2008). The new Optional Protocol largely follows the pattern established by other treaty individual complaint procedures. However, in recognition of the nature of the "progressive realization" and resource-dependent aspect of ICESCR rights, the Committee must "consider the reasonableness of the steps taken by the State Party," and it must recognize that there are "a range of possible policy measures" that might be appropriate (art. 8(4)). A margin of appreciation provision similar to that found in the European system

---

[1] This section draws on the work of Penelope Mathew, *in* DONALD K. ANTON, PENELOPE MATHEW & WAYNE MORGAN, INTERNATIONAL LAW 753–61 (2005).

was rejected as inappropriate for general international law. *See* Claire Mahon, *Progress at the Front: The Draft Optional Protocol to the International Covenant on Economic, Social and Cultural Rights*, 8 HUM. RTS. L. REV. 617, 631–38 (2008).

A number of countries have introduced economic, social, and cultural rights into their national constitutions in some form. In particular, the Constitution of South Africa contains economic, social, and cultural rights that the Constitutional Court of South Africa has held to be judicially enforceable. One such provision concerns the right to housing. Section 26 of the South African Constitution provides the following:

1) Everyone has the right to have access to adequate housing.
2) The State must take reasonable legislative and other measures, within its available resources, to achieve the progressive realization of this right.
3) No one may be evicted from their home, or have their home demolished, without an order of court made after considering all the relevant circumstances. No legislation may permit arbitrary evictions.

Housing is an endemic problem in South Africa; the lack of housing for the poorest (inevitably black) citizens has resulted in "land invasions" or squatting, frequently on land owned by white South Africans. *See, e.g.*, Sharon LaFraniere & Michael Wines, *Africa Puzzle: Landless Blacks and White Farms*, N.Y. TIMES, Jan. 6, 2004, at 1. In the *Grootboom* case, extracted below, a group of poor, black South Africans were squatting on land earmarked for low-cost housing. They had moved to the land because of the appalling conditions in their previous squatter settlement at Wallacedene. Their accommodation in Wallacedene, which was waterlogged and close to a major road, consisted of shacks without running water, sewers, or garbage removal services. A few of the shacks had electricity. Many of the group had been on the waiting list for low-cost housing for seven years. Members of the group were evicted from their new squatter settlement pursuant to a court order but a day earlier than envisaged: their possessions were burned, and no alternative housing was arranged.

In the *Grootboom* case, the Court had to consider the efforts of the state to provide new housing. Although the scheme to create new housing was laudable, the Court found that the absence of provision for those in a crisis situation, such as Ms. Irene Grootboom and other members of the group, meant that the state's measures were not reasonable.

Republic of South Africa v. Grootboom, Constitutional Court of South Africa, (1) SA 46 (CC) (2001)

YACOOB, J. (on behalf of the Court).

... [T]he concept of housing development as defined is central to the [Housing] Act. Housing development, as defined, seeks to provide citizens and permanent residents with access to permanent residential structures with secure tenure ensuring internal and external privacy and to provide adequate protection against the elements. What is more, it endeavours to ensure convenient access to economic opportunities and to health, educational and social amenities. All the policy documents before the Court are postulated on the need for housing development as defined. This is the central thrust of the housing development policy.

The definition of housing development as well as the general principles that are set out do not contemplate the provision of housing that falls short of the definition of housing development in the Act. In other words there is no express provision to facilitate access to temporary relief for people who have no access to land, no roof over their heads, for people who are living in intolerable conditions and for people who are in crisis because of natural disasters such as floods and fires, or because their homes are under threat of demolition. These are people in desperate need. Their immediate need can be met by relief short of housing which fulfils the requisite standards of durability, habitability and stability encompassed by the definition of housing development in the Act.

What has been done in execution of this programme is a major achievement. Large sums of money have been spent and a significant number of houses has been built. Considerable thought, energy, resources and expertise have been and continue to be devoted to the process of effective housing delivery. It is a programme that is aimed at achieving the progressive realisation of the right of access to adequate housing.

A question that nevertheless must be answered is whether the measures adopted are reasonable within the meaning of section 26 of the Constitution. Allocation of responsibilities and functions has been coherently and comprehensively addressed. The programme is not haphazard but represents a systematic response to a pressing social need. It takes account of the housing shortage in South Africa by seeking to build a large number of homes for those in need of better housing. The programme applies throughout South Africa and although there have been difficulties of implementation in some areas, the evidence suggests that the state is actively seeking to combat these difficulties....

The Cape Metro has realised that this desperate situation requires government action that is different in nature from that encompassed by the housing development policy described earlier in this judgment. It drafted a programme (the Cape Metro land programme) in June 1999, some months after the respondents had been evicted....

... [T]he programme is briefly described as follows:

The Accelerated Managed Land Settlement Programme (AMSLP) can ... be described as the rapid release of land for families in crisis, with the progressive provision of services. This programme should benefit those families in situations of crisis. The programme does not offer any benefits to queue jumpers, as it is the Metropolitan Local Council who determines when the progressive upgrading of services will be taken.

The Accelerated Managed Land Settlement Programme (AMSLP) includes the identification and purchase of land, planning, identification of the beneficiaries, township approval, pegging of the erven [A South African plot of land, ordinarily in an urban location. Eds.], construction of basic services, resettlement and the transfer of land to the beneficiaries.

We were informed by counsel during the hearing that although this programme was not in force at the time these proceedings were commenced, it has now been adopted and is being implemented.

The Cape Metro land programme was formulated by the Cape Metro specifically to assist the metropolitan local councils to manage the settlement of families in crisis." Important features of this programme are its recognition of (i) the absence of provision for people living in crisis conditions; (ii) the unacceptability of having families living in crisis conditions; (iii) the consequent risk of land invasions; and (iv) the gap between the supply and demand of housing resulting in a delivery crisis. Crucially, the programme acknowledges that its beneficiaries are families who are to be evicted, those who are in a crisis situation in an existing area such as in a flood-line, families located on strategic land and families from backyard shacks or on the waiting list who are in crisis situations. Its primary objective is the rapid release of land for these families in crisis, with services to be upgraded progressively....

Counsel for the appellants supported the nationwide housing programme and resisted the notion that provision of relief for people in desperate need was appropriate in it. Counsel also submitted that section 26 did not require the provision of this relief. Indeed, the contention was that provision for people in desperate need would detract significantly from integrated housing development as defined in the Act. . . .

The absence of this component may have been acceptable if the nationwide housing programme would result in affordable houses for most people within a reasonably short time. However the scale of the problem is such that this simply cannot happen. Each individual housing project could be expected to take years and the provision of houses for all in the area of the municipality and in the Cape Metro is likely to take a long time indeed. The desperate will be consigned to their fate for the foreseeable future unless some temporary measures exist as an integral part of the nationwide housing programme. Housing authorities are understandably unable to say when housing will become available to these desperate people. The result is that people in desperate need are left without any form of assistance[,] with no end in sight. Not only are the immediate crises not met. The consequent pressure on existing settlements inevitably results in land invasions by the desperate thereby frustrating the attainment of the medium and long-term objectives of the nationwide housing programme. That is one of the main reasons why the Cape Metro land programme was adopted.

The national government bears the overall responsibility for ensuring that the state complies with the obligations imposed upon it by section 26. The nationwide housing programme falls short of obligations imposed upon national government to the extent that it fails to recognise that the state must provide for relief for those in desperate need. They are not to be ignored in the interests of an overall programme focussed on medium and long-term objectives. It is essential that a reasonable part of the national housing budget be devoted to this, but the precise allocation is for national government to decide in the first instance.

This case is concerned with the Cape Metro and the municipality. The former has realised that this need has not been fulfilled and has put in place its land programme in an effort to fulfil it. This programme, on the face of it, meets the obligation which the state has towards people in the position of the respondents in the Cape Metro. Indeed, the amicus accepted that this programme "would cater precisely for the needs of people such as the respondents, and, in an appropriate and sustainable manner." However, as with legislative measures, the existence of the programme is a starting point only.

What remains is the implementation of the programme by taking all reasonable steps that are necessity to initiate and sustain it. And it must be implemented with due regard to the urgency of the situations it is intended to address.

Effective implementation requires at least adequate budgetary support by national government. This, in turn, requires recognition of the obligation to meet immediate needs in the nationwide housing programme. Recognition of such needs in the nationwide housing programme requires it to plan, budget and monitor the fulfilment of immediate needs and the management of crises: This must ensure that a significant number of desperate people in need are afforded relief, though not all of them need receive it immediately. Such planning too will require proper co-operation between the different spheres of government. . . .

Questions and Discussion

1. Note that the Court finds that the state must make provision for those in a crisis situation, but it does not direct the state as to how to do this, nor does it comment on the precise balance between this short-term aim and medium- to long-term goals. Would you agree with the assessment by Joan Fitzpatrick and Ron Slye that the Court has effectively determined that economic, social, and cultural rights in South Africa are generally to be thought of as group rights, whereby groups, particularly the disadvantaged, are to be properly taken into account as a matter of governmental policy rather than as individual claims on particular resources? *See* Joan Fitzpatrick and Ron C. Slye, *International Decisions: Republic of South Africa*

v. Grootboom. Case No. CCT 11/00. 2000 (11) BCLR 1169. Constitutional Court of South Africa, October 4, 2000; Minister of Health v. Treatment Action Campaign. Case No. CCT 8/02, http://www.concourt.gov.za. *Constitutional Court of South Africa, July 5, 2002,* 97 AM. J. INT'L L. 669–80 (2003). Does the emphasis on review of policy to ensure it is reasonable, rather than directives to the political arms of government concerning particular individuals, demonstrate that the courts can have a role in the adjudication of economic, social, and cultural rights that does not trespass greatly into the sphere of governmental policy decision making?

2. The Court does not rely on the concept of minimum core content as advocated by the Committee on Economic, Social, and Cultural Rights, although the Court does refer to the jurisprudence of the Committee with approval, particularly when the language of the South African constitutional provision mirrors that of the Covenant. Factors that led the Court not to adopt the same approach as the Committee included the lack of adequate data and the differences in wording between the Covenant and section 26 of the Constitution. Do you think that the concept of minimum core content would have been a preferable route to a decision than the Court's reliance on the term *reasonable* in section 26 of the South African Constitution? Note that the Court appears to have retreated even further from the concept of the minimum core content in *Minister of Health v. Treatment Action Campaign,* Case No. CCT 8/02. Constitutional Court of South Africa, July 5, 2002, 2002(5) SA 721 (CC); 2002 (10 BCLR 1033 (CC). In that decision, the Court again used the concept of reasonableness in governmental policy, this time determining that it was unconstitutional for government not to provide to those poor mothers and babies for whom it was medically indicated access to the anti-AIDS drug nevirapine, despite the presence in such hospitals of the necessary training and counseling services and when the drug was administered to some people from limited research and training sites.

3. As discussed earlier, the ICESCR complaints procedure allows for the ESC Committee to receive individual communications. The communications can be made "by or on behalf of individuals or groups of individuals, under the jurisdiction of a State Party, claiming to be victims of a violation of any of the economic, social, and cultural rights set forth in the Covenant by that State Party. Where a communication is submitted on behalf of individuals or groups of individuals, this shall be with their consent unless the author can justify acting on their behalf without such consent." Such complaints must be filed within one year of the exhaustion of local remedies and not be submitted to another complaints procedure. The Committee may issue interim measures in urgent cases of potentially irreparable harm, one of the few treaty bodies given this power. Unusually, article 4 adds a requirement of actual harm:

> The Committee may, if necessary, decline to consider a communication where it does not reveal that the author has suffered a clear disadvantage, unless the Committee considers that the communication raises a serious issue of general importance.

Does the Protocol settle the issue of justiciability?

VI. Human Rights and Environmental Harm

The decision by the African Commission on Human excerpted below illustrates the justiciability of economic, social, and cultural rights in an environmental context. It has been called a landmark in its integrative approach to all human rights (civil, political, economic, social, and cultural). It is also important for its extended analysis of the nature of human and peoples' rights obligations under the African Charter.

Social and Economic Rights Action Center and the Center for Economic and Social Rights v. Nigeria, Decision Regarding Communication 155/96 (Oct. 27, 2001), African Commission on Human and Peoples' Rights (footnotes and citations omitted)

Summary of Facts:

1. The Communication alleges that the military government of Nigeria has been directly involved in oil production through the State oil company, the Nigerian National Petroleum Company (NNPC), the majority shareholder in a consortium with Shell Petroleum Development Corporation (SPDC), and that these operations have caused environmental degradation and health problems resulting from the contamination of the environment among the Ogoni People.

2. The Communication alleges that the oil consortium has exploited oil reserves in Ogoniland with no regard for the health or environment of the local communities, disposing toxic wastes into the environment and local waterways in violation of applicable international environmental standards. The consortium also neglected and/or failed to maintain its facilities causing numerous avoidable spills in the proximity of villages. The resulting contamination of water, soil and air has had serious short and long-term health impacts, including skin infections, gastrointestinal and respiratory ailments, and increased risk of cancers, and neurological and reproductive problems.

3. The Communication alleges that the Nigerian Government has condoned and facilitated these violations by placing the legal and military powers of the State at the disposal of the oil companies. The Communication contains a memo from the Rivers State Internal Security Task Forte, calling for "ruthless military operations."

4. The Communication alleges that the Government has neither monitored operations of the oil companies nor required safety measures that are standard procedure within the industry The Government has withheld from Ogoni Communities information on the dangers created by oil activities. Ogoni Communities have not been involved in the decisions affecting the development of Ogoniland.

5. The Government has not required oil companies or its own agencies to produce basic health and environmental impact studies regarding hazardous operations and materials relating to oil production, despite the obvious health and environmental crisis in Ogoniland. The government has even refused to permit scientists and environmental organisations from entering Ogoniland to undertake such studies. The government has also ignored the concerns of Ogoni Communities regarding oil development, and has responded to protests with massive violence and executions of Ogoni leaders.

6. The Communication alleges that the Nigerian government does not require oil companies to consult communities before beginning operations, even if the operations pose direct threats to community or individual lands.

7. The Communication alleges that in the course of the last three years, Nigerian security fortes have attacked, burned and destroyed several Ogoni villages and homes under the pretext of dislodging officials and supporters of the Movement of the Survival of Ogoni People (MOSOP). These attacks have come in response to MOSOP's nonviolent campaign in opposition to the destruction of their environment by oil companies. Some of the attacks have involved uniformed combined forces of the police, the army, the air-forte, and the navy; armed with armoured tanks and

other sophisticated weapons. In other instances, the attacks have been conducted by unidentified gunmen, mostly at night. The military type methods and the calibre of weapons used in such attacks strongly suggest the involvement of the Nigerian security fortes. The complete failure of the Government of Nigeria to investigate these attacks, let alone punish the perpetrators, further implicates the Nigerian authorities.

8. The Nigerian Army has admitted its role in the ruthless operations which have left thousands of villagers homeless. The admission is recorded in several memos exchanged between officials of the SPDC and the Rivers State Internal Security Task Force, which has devoted itself to the suppression of the Ogoni campaign. One such memo calls for "ruthless military operations" and "wasting operations coupled with psychological tactics of displacement." At a public meeting recorded on video, Major Okuntimo, head of the Task Forte, described the repeated invasion of Ogoni villages by his troops, how unarmed villagers running from the troops were shot from behind, and the homes of suspected MOSOP activists were ransacked and destroyed. He stated his commitment to rid the communities of members and supporters of MOSOP.

9. The Communication alleges that the Nigerian government has destroyed and threatened Ogoni food sources through a variety of means. The government has participated in irresponsible oil development that has poisoned much of the soil and water upon which Ogoni fanning and fishing depended. In their raids on villages, Nigerian security forces have destroyed crops and killed farm animals. The security forces have created a state of terror and insecurity that has made it impossible for many Ogoni villagers to return to their fields and animals. The destruction of farmlands, rivers, crops and animals has created malnutrition and starvation among certain Ogoni Communities.

Complaint:

10. The communication alleges violations of Articles 2, 4, 14, 16, 18(1), 21, and 24 of the African Charter.

11. The communication was received by the Commission on 14th March 1996. The documents were sent with a video.

12. On 13th August 1996 letters acknowledging receipt of the Communication were sent to both Complainants.

13. On 13th August 1996, a copy of the Communication was sent to the Government of Nigeria.

14. At the 20th Ordinary Session held in Grand Bay, Mauritius in October 1996, the Commission declared the Communication admissible, and decided that it would be taken up with the relevant authorities by the planned mission to Nigeria.

15. On 10th December 1996, the Secretariat sent a Note Verbale and letters to this effect to the government and the Complainants respectively.

16. [– 29. From December 1996 – November 2000, the Commission was unable to obtain a response from the Nigerian Government to the allegations in the Communication].

30. At the 28th Ordinary Session of the Commission held in Cotonou, Benin from 26th October to 6th November 2000, the Commission deferred further consideration of the case to the next session. During that session, the Respondent State submitted a Note Verbale stating the actions taken by the Government of the Federal Republic of Nigeria in respect of all the communications filed against it, including the present one. In respect of the instant communication, the [N]ote [V]erbale admitted the gravamen of the complaints but went

on to state the remedial measures being taken by the new civilian administration and they included:

- Establishing for the first time in the history of Nigeria, a Federal Ministry of Environment with adequate resources to address environmental related issues prevalent in Nigeria and as a matter of priority in the Niger delta area
- Enacting into law the establishment of the Niger Delta Development Commission (NDDC) with adequate funding to address the environmental and social related problems of the Niger delta area and other oil producing areas of Nigeria
- Inaugurating the Judicial Commission of Inquiry to investigate the issues of human rights violations. In addition, the representatives of the Ogoni people have submitted petitions to the Commission of Inquiry on these issues and these are presently being reviewed in Nigeria as a top priority matter

31. The above decision was communicated to the parties on 14th November 2000.

. . .

34. At it 30th session held in Banjul, the Gambia from 13th to 27th October 2001, the African Commission reached a decision on the merits of this communication.

LAW
Admissibility

35. Article 56 of the African Charter governs admissibility. All of the conditions of this Article are met by the present communication. Only the exhaustion of local remedies requires close scrutiny.

36. Article 56(5) requires that local remedies, if any, be exhausted, unless these are unduly prolonged.

37. One purpose of the exhaustion of local remedies requirement is to give the domestic courts an opportunity to decide upon cases before they are brought to an international forum, thus avoiding contradictory judgements of law at the national and international levels. Where a right is not well provided for in domestic law such that no case is likely to be heard, potential conflict does not arise. Similarly, if the right is not well provided for, there cannot be effective remedies, or any remedies at all.

38. Another rationale for the exhaustion requirement is that a government should have notice of a human rights violation in order to have the opportunity to remedy such violation, before being called to account by an international tribunal. . . . The exhaustion of domestic remedies requirement should be properly understood as ensuring that the State concerned has ample opportunity to remedy the situation of which applicants complain. It is not necessary here to recount the international attention that Ogoniland has received to argue that the Nigerian government has had ample notice and, over the past several decades, more than sufficient opportunity to give domestic remedies.

39. Requiring the exhaustion of local remedies also ensures that the African Commission does not become a tribunal of first instance for cases for which an effective domestic remedy exists.

40. The present communication does not contain any information on domestic court actions brought by the Complainants to halt the violations alleged. However, the Commission on numerous occasions brought this complaint to the attention of the government at the time but no response was made to the Commission's requests. In such cases the Commission has held that in the absence of a substantive response from the Respondent State it must decide on the facts provided by the Complainants and treat them as given. . . .

41. The Commission takes cognisance of the fact that the Federal Republic of Nigeria has incorporated the African Charter on Human and Peoples' Rights into its domestic law with the result that all the rights contained therein can be invoked in Nigerian courts including those violations alleged by the Complainants. However, the Commission is aware that at the time of submitting this communication, the then Military government of Nigeria had enacted various decrees ousting the jurisdiction of the courts and thus depriving the people in Nigeria of the right to seek redress in the courts for acts of government that violate their fundamental human rights. In such instances, and as in the instant communication, the Commission is of the view that no adequate domestic remedies are existent. . . .

42. It should also be noted that the new government in their Note Verbale referenced 127/2000 submitted at the 28th session of the Commission held in Cotonou, Benin, admitted to the violations committed then by stating, "there is no denying the fact that a lot of atrocities were and are still being committed by the oil companies in Ogoni Land and indeed in the Niger Delta area."

The Commission therefore declared the communication admissible.

Merits

43. The present Communication alleges a concerted violation of a wide range of rights guaranteed under the African Charter for Human and Peoples' Rights. Before we venture into the inquiry whether the Government of Nigeria has violated the said rights as alleged in the Complaint, it would be proper to establish what is generally expected of governments under the Charter and more specifically vis-à-vis the rights themselves.

44. Internationally accepted ideas of the various obligations engendered by human rights indicate that all rights – both civil and political rights and social and economic – generate at least four levels of duties for a State that undertakes to adhere to a rights regime, namely the duty to respect, protect, promote, and fulfil these rights. These obligations universally apply to all rights and entail a combination of negative and positive duties. As a human rights instrument, the African Charter is not alien to these concepts and the order in which they are dealt with here is chosen as a matter of convenience and in no way should it imply the priority accorded to them. Each layer of obligation is equally relevant to the rights in question.

45. At a primary level, the obligation to respect entails that the State should refrain from interfering in the enjoyment of all fundamental rights; it should respect right-holders, their freedoms, autonomy, resources, and liberty of their action. With respect to socio economic rights, this means that the State is obliged to respect the free use of resources owned or at the disposal of the individual alone or in any form of association with others, including the household or the family, for the purpose of rights-related needs. And with regard to a collective group, the resources belonging to it should be respected, as it has to use the same resources to satisfy its needs.

46. At a secondary level, the State is obliged to protect right-holders against other subjects by legislation and provision of effective remedies. This obligation requires the State to take measures to protect beneficiaries of the protected rights against political, economic and social interferences. Protection generally entails the creation and maintenance of an atmosphere or framework by an effective interplay of laws and regulations so that individuals will be able to freely realize their rights and freedoms. This is very much intertwined with the tertiary obligation of the State to promote the enjoyment of all human rights. The State should make sure that individuals are able to exercise their rights and freedoms, for example, by promoting tolerance, raising awareness, and even building infrastructures.

47. The last layer of obligation requires the State to fulfil the rights and freedoms it freely undertook under the various human rights regimes. It is more of a positive expectation on the part of the

State to move its machinery towards the actual realisation of the rights. This is also very much intertwined with the duty to promote mentioned in the preceding paragraph. It could consist in the direct provision of basic needs such as food or resources that can be used for food (direct food aid or social security).

48. Thus States are generally burdened with the above set of duties when they commit themselves under human rights instruments. Emphasising the all embracing nature of their obligations, the International Covenant on Economic, Social, and Cultural Rights, for instance, under Article 2(1), stipulates exemplarily that States *"undertake to take steps . . . by all appropriate means, including particularly the adoption of legislative measures."* Depending on the type of rights under consideration, the level of emphasis in the application of these duties varies. But sometimes, the need to meaningfully enjoy some of the rights demands a concerted action from the State in terms of more than one of the said duties. Whether the government of Nigeria has, by its conduct, violated the provisions of the African Charter as claimed by the Complainants is examined here below.

49. In accordance with Articles 60 and 61 of the African Charter, this communication is examined in the light of the provisions of the African Charter and the relevant international and regional human rights instruments and principles. The Commission thanks the two human rights NGOs who brought the matter under its purview: the Social and Economic Rights Action Center (Nigeria) and the Center for Economic and Social Rights (USA). Such is a demonstration of the usefulness to the Commission and individuals of *actio popularis*, which is wisely allowed under the African Charter. It is a matter of regret that the only written response from the government of Nigeria is an admission of the gravamen of the complaints which is contained in a note verbale and which we have reproduced above at paragraph 30. In the circumstances, the Commission is compelled to proceed with the examination of the matter on the basis of the uncontested allegations of the Complainants, which are consequently accepted by the Commission.

50. The Complainants allege that the Nigerian government violated the right to health and the right to clean environment as recognized under Articles 16 and 24 of the African Charter by failing to fulfill the minimum duties required by these rights. This, the Complainants allege, the government has done by –:

- Directly participating in the contamination of air, water and soil and thereby harming the health of the Ogoni population,
- Failing to protect the Ogoni population from the harm caused by the NNPC Shell Consortium but instead using its security forces to facilitate the damage
- Failing to provide or permit studies of potential or actual environmental and health risks caused by the oil operations

Article 16 of the African Charter reads:

(1) Every individual shall have the right to enjoy the best attainable state of physical and mental health.
(2) States Parties to the present Charter shall take the necessary measures to protect the health of their people and to ensure that they receive medical attention when they are sick.

Article 24 of the African Charter reads:

All peoples shall have the right to a general satisfactory environment favourable to their development.

51. These rights recognise the importance of a clean and safe environment that is closely linked to economic and social rights in so far as the environment affects the quality of life and safety

of the individual. As has been rightly observed by Alexander Kiss, "an environment degraded by pollution and defaced by the destruction of all beauty and variety is as contrary to satisfactory living conditions and development as the breakdown of the fundamental ecologic equilibria is harmful to physical and moral health."

52. The right to a general satisfactory environment, as guaranteed under Article 24 of the African Charter or the right to a healthy environment, as it is widely known, therefore imposes clear obligations upon a government. It requires the State to take reasonable and other measures to prevent pollution and ecological degradation, to promote conservation, and to secure an ecologically sustainable development and use of natural resources. Article 12 of the International Covenant on Economic, Social and Cultural Rights (ICESCR), to which Nigeria is a party, requires governments to take necessary steps for the improvement of all aspects of environmental and industrial hygiene. The right to enjoy the best attainable state of physical and mental health enunciated in Article 16(1) of the African Charter and the right to a general satisfactory environment favourable to development (Article 16(3)) already noted obligate governments to desist from directly threatening the health and environment of their citizens. The State is under an obligation to respect the just noted rights and this entails largely non-interventionist conduct from the State, for example, not carrying out, sponsoring or tolerating any practice, policy or legal measures violating the integrity of the individual.

53. Government compliance with the spirit of Articles 16 and 24 of the African Charter must also include ordering or at least permitting independent scientific monitoring of threatened environments, requiring and publicising environmental and social impact studies prior to any major industrial development, undertaking appropriate monitoring and providing information to those communities exposed to hazardous materials and activities and providing meaningful opportunities for individuals to be heard and to participate in the development decisions affecting their communities.

54. We now examine the conduct of the government of Nigeria in relation to Articles 16 and 24 of the African Charter. Undoubtedly and admittedly, the government of Nigeria, through NNPC has the right to produce oil, the income from which will be used to fulfil the economic and social rights of Nigerians. But the care that should have been taken as outlined in the preceding paragraph and which would have protected the rights of the victims of the violations complained of was not taken. To exacerbate the situation, the security forces of the government engaged in conduct in violation of the rights of the Ogonis by attacking, burning and destroying several Ogoni villages and homes.

55. The Complainants also allege a violation of Article 21 of the African Charter by the government of Nigeria. The Complainants allege that the Military government of Nigeria was involved in oil production and thus did not monitor or regulate the operations of the oil companies and in so doing paved a way for the Oil Consortiums to exploit oil reserves in Ogoniland. Furthermore, in all their dealings with the Oil Consortiums, the government did not involve the Ogoni Communities in the decisions that affected the development of Ogoniland. The destructive and selfish role-played by oil development in Ogoniland, closely tied with repressive tactics of the Nigerian Government, and the lack of material benefits accruing to the local population, may well be said to constitute a violation of Article 21.

Article 21 provides
1. All peoples shall freely dispose of their wealth and natural resources. This right shall be exercised in the exclusive interest of the people. In no case shall a people be deprived of it.
2. In case of spoliation the dispossessed people shall have the right to the lawful recovery of its property as well as to an adequate compensation.

3. The free disposal of wealth and natural resources shall be exercised without prejudice to the obligation of promoting international economic co-operation based on mutual respect, equitable exchange and the principles of international law.

4. States parties to the present Charter shall individually and collectively exercise the right to free disposal of their wealth and natural resources with a view to strengthening African unity and solidarity.

5. States Parties to the present Charter shall undertake to eliminate all forms of foreign economic exploitation particularly that practised by international monopolies so as to enable their peoples to fully benefit from the advantages derived from their national resources.

56. The origin of this provision maybe traced to colonialism, during which the human and material resources of Africa were largely exploited for the benefit of outside powers, creating tragedy for Africans themselves, depriving them of their birthright and alienating them from the land. The aftermath of colonial exploitation has left Africa's precious resources and people still vulnerable to foreign misappropriation. The drafters of the Charter obviously wanted to remind African governments of the continent's painful legacy and restore co-operative economic development to its traditional place at the heart of African Society.

57. Governments have a duty to protect their citizens, not only through appropriate legislation and effective enforcement but also by protecting them from damaging acts that may be perpetrated by private parties. . . . This duty calls for positive action on part of governments in fulfilling their obligation under human rights instruments. The practice before other tribunals also enhances this requirement as is evidenced in the case *Velásquez Rodríguez v. Honduras*. In this landmark judgment, the Inter-American Court of Human Rights held that when a State allows private persons or groups to act freely and with impunity to the detriment of the rights recognised, it would be in clear violation of its obligations to protect the human rights of its citizens. Similarly this obligation of the State is further emphasised in the practice of the European Court of Human Rights, in *X and Y v. Netherlands*. In that case, the Court pronounced that there was an obligation on authorities to take steps to make sure that the enjoyment of the rights is not interfered with by any other private person.

58. The Commission notes that in the present case, despite its obligation to protect persons against interferences in the enjoyment of their rights, the Government of Nigeria facilitated the destruction of the Ogoniland. Contrary to its Charter obligations and despite such internationally established principles, the Nigerian Government has given the green light to private actors, and the oil Companies in particular, to devastatingly affect the well-being of the Ogonis. By any measure of standards, its practice falls short of the minimum conduct expected of governments, and therefore, is in violation of Article 21 of the African Charter.

59. The Complainants also assert that the Military government of Nigeria massively and systematically violated the right to adequate housing of members of the Ogoni community under Article 14 and implicitly recognised by Articles 16 and 18(1) of the African Charter.

Article 14 of the Charter reads:

The right to property shall be guaranteed. It may only be encroached upon in the interest of public need or in the general interest of the community and in accordance with the provisions of appropriate laws.

Article 18(1) provides:

The family shall be the natural unit and basis of society. It shall be protected by the State . . .

60. Although the right to housing or shelter is not explicitly provided for under the African Charter, the corollary of the combination of the provisions protecting the right to enjoy the best attainable state of mental and physical health, cited under Article 16 above, the right to property, and the protection accorded to the family forbids the wanton destruction of shelter because when housing is destroyed, property, health, and family life are adversely affected. It is thus noted that the combined effect of Articles 14, 16 and 18(1) reads into the Charter a right to shelter or housing which the Nigerian Government has apparently violated.

61. At a very minimum, the right to shelter obliges the Nigerian government not to destroy the housing of its citizens and not to obstruct efforts by individuals or communities to rebuild lost homes. The State's obligation to respect housing rights requires it, and thereby all of its organs and agents, to abstain from carrying out, sponsoring or tolerating any practice, policy or legal measure violating the integrity of the individual or infringing upon his or her freedom to use those material or other resources available to them in a way they find most appropriate to satisfy individual, family, household or community housing needs. Its obligations to protect obliges it to prevent the violation of any individual's right to housing by any other individual or non-state actors like landlords, property developers, and land owners, and where such infringements occur, it should act to preclude further deprivations as well as guaranteeing access to legal remedies. The right to shelter even goes further than a roof over ones head. It extends to embody the individual's right to be let alone and to live in peace- whether under a roof or not.

62. The protection of the rights guaranteed in Articles 14, 16, and 18(1) leads to the same conclusion. As regards the earlier right, and in the case of the Ogoni People, the Government of Nigeria has failed to fulfil these two minimum obligations. The government has destroyed Ogoni houses and villages and then, through its security forces, obstructed, harassed, beaten and, in some cases, shot and killed innocent citizens who have attempted to return to rebuild their ruined homes. These actions constitute massive violations of the right to shelter, in violation of Articles 14, 16, and 18(1) of the African Charter.

63. The particular violation by the Nigerian Government of the right to adequate housing as implicitly protected in the Charter also encompasses the right to protection against forced evictions. The African Commission draws inspiration from the definition of the term "forced evictions" by the Committee on Economic Social and Cultural Rights which defines this term as "the permanent removal against their will of individuals, families and/or communities from the homes and/or which they occupy, without the provision of, and access to, appropriate forms of legal or other protection." Wherever and whenever they occur, forced evictions are extremely traumatic. They cause physical, psychological and emotional distress; they entail losses of means of economic sustenance and increase impoverishment. They can also cause physical injury and in some cases sporadic deaths. . . . Evictions break up families and increase existing levels of homelessness. In this regard, General Comment No. 4 (1991) of the Committee on Economic, Social and Cultural Rights on the right to adequate housing states that "all persons should possess a degree of security of tenure which guarantees legal protection against forced eviction, harassment and other threats" (E/1992/23, annex III. Paragraph 8(a)). The conduct of the Nigerian government clearly demonstrates a violation of this right enjoyed by the Ogonis as a collective right.

64. The Communication argues that the right to food is implicit in the African Charter, in such provisions as the right to life (Art. 4), the right to health (Art. 16) and the right to economic, social and cultural development (Art. 22). By its violation of these rights, the Nigerian Government trampled upon not only the explicitly protected rights but also upon the right to food implicitly guaranteed.

65. The right to food is inseparably linked to the dignity of human beings and is therefore essential for the enjoyment and fulfilment of such other rights as health, education, work and political

participation. The African Charter and international law require and bind Nigeria to protect and improve existing food sources and to ensure access to adequate food for all citizens. Without touching on the duty to improve food production and to guarantee access, the minimum core of the right to food requires that the Nigerian Government should not destroy or contaminate food sources. It should not allow private parties to destroy or contaminate food sources, and prevent peoples' efforts to feed themselves.

66. The government's treatment of the Ogonis has violated all three minimum duties of the right to food. The government has destroyed food sources through its security forces and State Oil Company; has allowed private oil companies to destroy food sources; and, through terror, has created significant obstacles to Ogoni communities trying to feed themselves. The Nigerian government has again fallen short of what is expected of it as under the provisions of the African Charter and international human rights standards, and hence, is in violation of the right to food of the Ogonis.

67. The Complainants also allege that the Nigerian Government has violated Article 4 of the Charter which guarantees the inviolability of human beings and everyone's right to life and integrity of the person respected. Given the wide spread violations perpetrated by the Government of Nigeria and by private actors (be it following its clear blessing or not), the most fundamental of all human rights, the right to life has been violated. The Security forces were given the green light to decisively deal with the Ogonis, which was illustrated by the wide spread terrorisations and killings. The pollution and environmental degradation to a level humanly unacceptable has made it living in the Ogoni land a nightmare. The survival of the Ogonis depended on their land and farms that were destroyed by the direct involvement of the Government. These and similar brutalities not only persecuted individuals in Ogoniland but also the whole of the Ogoni Community. They affected the life of the Ogoni Society as a whole. The Commission conducted a mission to Nigeria from the 7th–14th March 1997 and witnessed first hand the deplorable situation in Ogoni land including the environmental degradation.

68. The uniqueness of the African situation and the special qualities of the African Charter on Human and Peoples' Rights imposes upon the African Commission an important task. International law and human rights must be responsive to African circumstances. Clearly, collective rights, environmental rights, and economic and social rights are essential elements of human rights in Africa. The African Commission will apply any of the diverse rights contained in the African Charter. It welcomes this opportunity to make clear that there is no right in the African Charter that cannot be made effective. As indicated in the preceding paragraphs, however, the Nigerian Government did not live up to the minimum expectations of the African Charter.

69. The Commission does not wish to fault governments that are labouring under difficult circumstances to improve the lives of their people. The situation of the people of Ogoniland, however, requires, in the view of the Commission, a reconsideration of the Government's attitude to the allegations contained in the instant communication. The intervention of multinational corporations may be a potentially positive force for development if the State and the people concerned are ever mindful of the common good and the sacred rights of individuals and communities. The Commission however takes note of the efforts of the present civilian administration to redress the atrocities that were committed by the previous military administration as illustrated in the Note Verbale referred to in paragraph 30 of this decision.

For the above reasons, the Commission,

Finds the Federal Republic of Nigeria in violation of Articles 2, 4, 14, 16, 18(1), 21 and 24 of the African Charter on Human and Peoples' Rights;

Appeals to the government of the Federal Republic of Nigeria to ensure protection of the environment, health and livelihood of the people of Ogoniland by:

- Stopping all attacks on Ogoni communities and leaders by the Rivers State Internal Securities Task Force and permitting citizens and independent investigators free access to the territory;
- Conducting an investigation into the human rights violations described above and prosecuting officials of the security forces, NNPC and relevant agencies involved in human rights violations;
- Ensuring adequate compensation to victims of the human rights violations, including relief and resettlement assistance to victims of government sponsored raids, and undertaking a comprehensive cleanup of lands and rivers damaged by oil operations;
- Ensuring that appropriate environmental and social impact assessments are prepared for any future oil development and that the safe operation of any further oil development is guaranteed through effective and independent oversight bodies for the petroleum industry; and
- Providing information on health and environmental risks and meaningful access to regulatory and decision-making bodies to communities likely to be affected by oil operations.

Urges the government of the Federal Republic of Nigeria to keep the African Commission informed of the outcome of the work of – :

- The Federal Ministry of Environment which was established to address environmental and environment related issues prevalent in Nigeria, and as a matter of priority, in the Niger Delta area including the Ogoni land;
- The Niger Delta Development Commission (NDDC) enacted into law to address the environmental and other social related problems in the Niger Delta area and other oil producing areas of Nigeria; and
- The Judicial Commission of Inquiry inaugurated to investigate the issues of human rights violations.

Questions and Discussion

1. The African Commission on Human and Peoples' Rights held that "Article 24 of the African Charter . . . requires the State to take reasonable and other measures to prevent pollution and ecological degradation, to promote conservation, and to secure an ecologically sustainable development and use of natural resources." What specific actions are required by the state to fulfill the obligations imposed by article 24?
2. Does the Commission's decision allow the enforcement of collective rights of the Ogoni people? Consider paragraph 45 of the decision.
3. How is it that the Commission is able to insist that the right to shelter and the right to food are inherent in the African Charter when they are not expressed? Is its reasoning persuasive?
4. Under what circumstances will violations of rights by private actors be attributable to a state? What does giving "the green light to private actors" in paragraph 58 entail?
5. Professor Shelton maintains that the decision on the *Ogoniland* case "offers a blueprint for merging environmental protection, economic development, and guarantees of human rights." Dinah Shelton, *Decision Regarding Communication 155/96 (Social and Economic Rights Action Center/Center for Economic and Social Rights v. Nigeria). Case No. ACHPR/COMM/A044/1*, 96 AM. J. INT'L L. 937, 942 (2002). Can you see how? Are there limits to the application of the case outside the African context because article 24 is unique and the rights created are not individual rights but peoples' rights? *See also* F. Coomins, *The Ogoni Case Before the African Commission on Human and Peoples' Rights*, 52 INT'L & COMP. L.Q. 749 (2003).

VII. Common Aspects of Human Rights Treaties

A. *Reservations*

VIENNA CONVENTION ON THE LAW OF TREATIES, 1155 U.N.T.S. 331
(May 23, 1969)

Section 2. Reservations

Article 19
Formulation of Reservations

A State may, when signing, ratifying, accepting, approving or acceding to a treaty, formulate a reservation unless:

(a) the reservation is prohibited by the treaty;

(b) the treaty provides that only specified reservations, which do not include the reservation in question, may be made; or

(c) in cases not falling under sub-paragraphs (a) and (b), the reservation is incompatible with the object and purpose of the treaty.

Article 20
Acceptance of and Objection to Reservations

1. A reservation expressly authorized by a treaty does not require any subsequent acceptance by the other contracting States unless the treaty so provides.

2. When it appears from the limited number of the negotiating States and the object and purpose of a treaty that the application of the treaty in its entirety between all the parties is an essential condition of the consent of each one to be bound by the treaty, a reservation requires acceptance by all the parties.

3. When a treaty is a constituent instrument of an international organization and unless it otherwise provides, a reservation requires the acceptance of the competent organ of that organization.

4. In cases not falling under the preceding paragraphs and unless the treaty otherwise provides:

(a) acceptance by another contracting State of a reservation constitutes the reserving State a party to the treaty in relation to that other State if or when the treaty is in force for those States;

(b) an objection by another contracting State to a reservation does not preclude the entry into force of the treaty as between the objecting and reserving States unless a contrary intention is definitely expressed by the objecting State;

(c) an act expressing a State's consent to be bound by the treaty and containing a reservation is effective as soon as at least one other contracting State has accepted the reservation.

5. For the purposes of paragraphs 2 and 4 and unless the treaty otherwise provides, a reservation is considered to have been accepted by a State if it shall have raised no objection to the reservation by the end of a period of twelve months after it was notified of the reservation or by the date on which it expressed its consent to be bound by the treaty, whichever is later.

Article 21
Legal Effects of Reservations and of Objections to Reservations

1. A reservation established with regard to another party in accordance with articles 19, 20 and 23:

(a) modifies for the reserving State in its relations with that other party the provisions of the treaty to which the reservation relates to the extent of the reservation; and

(b) modifies those provisions to the same extent for that other party in its relations with the reserving State.

2. The reservation does not modify the provisions of the treaty for the other parties to the treaty inter se.

3. When a State objecting to a reservation has not opposed the entry into force of the treaty between itself and the reserving State, the provisions to which the reservation relates do not apply as between the two States to the extent of the reservation.

. . .

A Note on Reservations

The Vienna Convention does not establish an objective, third-party arbiter of questions concerning reservations. In theory, the ICJ would fulfill this role, as noted by the Court in the *Reservations to the Convention and Punishment of the Crime of Genocide* (Advisory Opinion), [1951] I.C.J. 15. However, the jurisdiction of the ICJ is not compulsory. This is to be contrasted with the situation in the case of *Belilos v. Switzerland*, 10 E.H.R.R. 466. The *Belilos* case concerned the European Convention for the Protection of Human Rights and Fundamental Freedoms – a treaty that has always provided for adjudication in the form of the European Court of Human Rights (although acceptance of jurisdiction of the Court was originally optional).

The lack of compulsory jurisdiction means that problems could arise in relation to reservations prohibited by the terms of article 19(a), (b) and (c). It may be necessary to think of the fact and consequences of impermissible reservations as distinct, though related, issues. Despite the fact that one might think that reservations incompatible with the object and purpose of the treaty are simply invalid and therefore do not need to be the subject of objections, in practice, there is often no third party arbiter of the validity of the reservations. The other states parties determine whether the reservation is accepted, by their conduct.

This difficult issue exposes one of a number of gaps and ambiguities in the Vienna Convention regime. The International Law Commission is currently trying to resolve it, among other problems, by working on the adoption of a guide to state practice. In his first report on the question of reservations to treaties, the Commission's special rapporteur, Professor Alain Pellet, described two distinct schools of thought concerning the question of "impermissible" reservations – namely the permissibility school and the opposability school. As summarized in the Yearbook of the International Law Commission, Professor Pellet stated that,

> in the quarrel between the schools of permissibility and of opposability, the adherents of permissibility considered that a reservation contrary to the object and purpose of the treaty was in itself void, irrespective of the reactions of the co-contracting States. Conversely, the adherents of the opposability school, more marked by relativism, thought that the only test consisted of the objections of the other States.

1 Y.B. *Int'l L. Comm.* U.N. (1995), at 149, para. 13. The ILC Drafting Committee provisionally adopted the text of the draft guidelines on reservations to treaties in June 2010. *See* U.N. Doc. A/CN.4/L/760/Add.2 (June 4, 2010).

The issue has been particularly problematic in relation to treaties that are not governed by the normal considerations of reciprocity and that have monitoring bodies, such as human rights treaties. To do their work, these bodies must have an understanding of which obligations have been undertaken by particular states, and they have sometimes taken strong stands on reservations that appear to them to be incompatible with the object and purpose of the treaty. In the view of the human rights treaty bodies, and in the view of many commentators, states parties have failed to object to reservations that appear on an objective view to be against the object and purpose of the treaty.

The International Covenant on Civil and Political Rights has been subject to a number of reservations. The instrument of ratification by the United States contained a long list of reservations and declarations of understanding prompting the Human Rights Committee, which supervises the Covenant, to take a stance on reservations in a General Comment.

The Human Rights Committee's General Comment on reservations sets out the Committee's view as to the validity of particular kinds of reservations, along with the Committee's view as to its own authority to determine whether reservations are valid. Most controversially, perhaps, the Committee took the view that invalid reservations are severable and that the state seeking to enter invalid reservations will become party to the Covenant without the benefit of the reservation.

General Comment No. 24 (52) [of the Human Rights Committee], U.N. Doc. CCPR/C/21/Rev.1/Add.6 (November 4, 1994)

The absence [in the Covenant] of a prohibition on reservations does not mean that any reservation is permitted. The matter of reservations under the Covenant and the first Optional Protocol is governed by international law. Article 19(3) of the Vienna Convention on the Law of Treaties provides relevant guidance. It stipulates that where a reservation is not prohibited by the treaty or falls within the specified permitted categories, a State may make a reservation provided it is not incompatible with the object and purpose of the treaty. Even though, unlike some other human rights treaties, the Covenant does not incorporate a specific reference to the object and purpose test, that test governs the matter of interpretation and acceptability of reservations.

In an instrument which articulates very many civil and political rights, each of the many articles, and indeed their interplay, secures the objectives of the Covenant. The object and purpose of the Covenant is to create legally binding standards for human rights by defining certain civil and political rights and placing them in a framework of obligations which are legally binding for those States which ratify; and to provide efficacious supervisory machinery for the obligations undertaken.

Reservations that offend peremptory norms would not be compatible with the object and purpose of the Covenant. Although treaties that are mere exchanges of obligations between States allow them to reserve *inter se* application of rules of general international law, it is otherwise in human rights treaties, which are for the benefit of persons within their jurisdiction. Accordingly, provisions in the Covenant that represent customary international law (and *a fortiori* when they have the character of peremptory norms) may not be the subject of reservations. Accordingly, a State may not reserve the right to engage in slavery, to torture, to subject persons to cruel, inhuman or degrading treatment or punishment, to arbitrarily deprive persons of their lives, to arbitrarily arrest and detain persons, to deny freedom of thought, conscience and religion, to presume a person guilty unless he proves his innocence, to execute pregnant women or children, to permit the advocacy of national, racial or religious hatred, to deny to persons of marriageable age the right to marry, or to deny to minorities the right to enjoy their own culture, profess their own religion, or use their own language. And while reservations to particular clauses of article 14 may be acceptable, a general reservation to the right to a fair trial would not be.

Applying more generally the object and purpose test to the Covenant, the Committee notes that, for example, reservation to article 1 denying peoples the right to determine their own political status and to pursue their economic, social and cultural development, would be incompatible with the object and purpose of the Covenant. Equally, a reservation to the obligation to respect and ensure the rights, and to do so on a non-discriminatory basis (article 2(1)) would not be acceptable.

Nor may a State reserve an entitlement not to take the necessary steps at the domestic level to give effect to the rights of the Covenant (article 2(2)).

The Committee has further examined whether categories of reservations may offend the "object and purpose" test. In particular, it falls for consideration as to whether reservations to the non-derogable provisions of the Covenant are compatible with its object and purpose. While there is no hierarchy of importance of rights under the Covenant, the operation of certain rights may not be suspended, even in times of national emergency. This underlines the great importance of non-derogable rights. But not all rights of profound importance, such as articles 9 and 27 of the Covenant, have in fact been made non-derogable. One reason for certain rights being made non-derogable is because their suspension is irrelevant to the legitimate control of the state of national emergency (for example, no imprisonment for debt, in article 11). Another reason is that derogation may indeed be impossible (as, for example, freedom of conscience). At the same time, some provisions are non-derogable exactly because without them there would be no rule of law. A reservation to the provisions of article 4 itself, which precisely stipulates the balance to be struck between the interests of the State and the rights of the individual in times of emergency, would fall in this category. And some non-derogable rights, which in any event cannot be reserved because of their status as peremptory norms, are also of this character – the prohibition of torture and arbitrary deprivation of life are examples. While there is no automatic correlation between reservations to non-derogable provisions, and reservations which offend against the object and purpose of the Covenant, a State has a heavy onus to justify such a reservation.

The Covenant consists not just of the specified rights, but of important supportive guarantees. These guarantees provide the necessary framework for securing the rights in the Covenant and are thus essential to its object and purpose. Some operate at the national level and some at the international level. Reservations designed to remove these guarantees are thus not acceptable. Thus, a State could not make a reservation to article 2, paragraph 3, of the Covenant, indicating that it intends to provide no remedies for human rights violations. Guarantees such as these are an integral part of the structure of the Covenant and underpin its efficacy. The Covenant also envisages, for the better attainment of its stated objectives, a monitoring role for the Committee. Reservations that purport to evade that essential element in the design of the Covenant, which is also directed to securing the enjoyment of the rights, are also incompatible with its object and purpose. A State may not reserve the right not to present a report and have it considered by the Committee. The Committee's role under the Covenant, whether under article 40 or under the Optional Protocols, necessarily entails interpreting the provisions of the Covenant and the development of a jurisprudence. Accordingly, a reservation that rejects the Committee's competence to interpret the requirements of any provisions of the Covenant would also be contrary to the object and purpose of that treaty.

. . . Reservations often reveal a tendency of States not to want to change a particular law. And sometimes that tendency is elevated to a general policy. Of particular concern are widely formulated reservations which essentially render ineffective all Covenant rights which would require any change in national law to ensure compliance with Covenant obligations. No real international rights or obligations have thus been accepted. And when there is an absence of provisions to ensure that Covenant rights may be sued on in domestic courts, and, further, a failure to allow individual complaints to be brought to the Committee under the first Optional Protocol, all the essential elements of the Covenant guarantees have been removed.

The issue arises as to whether reservations are permissible under the first Optional Protocol and, if so, whether any such reservation might be contrary to the object and purpose of the Covenant or of the first Optional Protocol itself. . . . States accept the substantive rights of individuals by reference to the Covenant, and not the first Optional Protocol. The function of the first Optional Protocol is to allow claims in respect of those rights to be tested before the Committee. Accordingly, a reservation to an obligation of a State to respect and ensure a right contained in the Covenant, made under the first Optional Protocol when it has not previously been made in respect of the same rights under the Covenant, does not affect the State's duty to comply with its substantive obligation. A reservation cannot be made to the Covenant through the vehicle of the Optional Protocol but such a reservation would operate to ensure that the State's compliance with that obligation may not be tested by the Committee under the first Optional Protocol. And because the object and purpose of the first Optional Protocol is to allow the rights obligatory for a State under the Covenant to be tested before the Committee, a reservation that seeks to preclude this would be contrary to the object and purpose of the first Optional Protocol, even if not of the Covenant. A reservation to a substantive obligation made for the first time under the first Optional Protocol would seem to reflect an intention by the State concerned to prevent the Committee from expressing its views relating to a particular article of the Covenant in an individual case. . . .

The Committee finds it important to address which body has the legal authority to make determinations as to whether specific reservations are compatible with the object and purpose of the Covenant. . . .

. . . [I]t is the Vienna Convention on the Law of Treaties that provides the definition of reservations and also the application of the object and purpose test in the absence of other specific provisions. But the Committee believes that its provisions on the role of State objections in relation to reservations are inappropriate to address the problem of reservations to human rights treaties. Such treaties, and the Covenant specifically, are not a web of inter-State exchanges of mutual obligations. They concern the endowment of individuals with rights. The principle of inter-State reciprocity has no place, save perhaps in the limited context of reservations to declarations on the Committee's competence under article 41. And because the operation of the classic rules on reservations is so inadequate for the Covenant, States have often not seen any legal interest in or need to object to reservations. The absence of protest by States cannot imply that a reservation is either compatible or incompatible with the object and purpose of the Covenant. Objections have been occasional, made by some States but not others, and on grounds not always specified; when an objection is made, it often does not specify a legal consequence, or sometimes even indicates that the objecting party none the less does not regard the Covenant as not in effect as between the parties concerned. . . .

It necessarily falls to the Committee to determine whether a specific reservation is compatible with the object and purpose of the Covenant. . . . Because of the special character of a human rights treaty, the compatibility of a reservation with the object and purpose of the Covenant must be established objectively, by reference to legal principles, and the Committee is particularly well placed to perform this task. The normal consequence of an unacceptable reservation is not that the Covenant will not be in effect at all for a reserving party. Rather, such a reservation will generally be severable, in the sense that the Covenant will be operative for the reserving party without benefit of the reservation.

Reservations must be specific and transparent, so that the Committee, those under the jurisdiction of the reserving State and other States parties may be clear as to what obligations of human rights compliance have or have not been undertaken. Reservations may thus not be general, but must refer to a particular provision of the Covenant and indicate in precise terms its scope in relation thereto. When considering the compatibility of possible reservations with the object and purpose of the Covenant, States should also take into consideration the overall effect of a group of reservations, as well as the effect of each reservation on the integrity of the Covenant, which remains an essential consideration. States should not enter so many reservations that they are in effect accepting a limited number of human rights obligations, and not the Covenant as such. So that reservations do not lead to a perpetual non-attainment of international human rights standards, reservations should not systematically reduce the obligations undertaken only to those presently existing in less demanding standards of domestic law. Nor should interpretative declarations or reservations seek to remove an autonomous meaning to Covenant obligations, by pronouncing them to be identical, or to be accepted only in so far as they are identical, with existing provisions of domestic law. States should not seek through reservations or interpretative declarations to determine that the meaning of a provision of the Covenant is the same as that given by an organ of any other international treaty body.

Questions and Discussion

1. The most controversial aspect of the General Comment is probably the Committee's view that it may determine the validity of a reservation and that it may hold that the reservation is severed. The same approach was taken by the European Court of Human Rights in *Belilos v. Switzerland*, 10 E.H.R.R. 466, at para. 60. Given the importance of state consent to international legal obligations, do you think that it is possible to take the view that the state wished to become a party to a treaty without its reservation? Should an invalid reservation nullify the consent to become a party to the treaty? Should the state be told to consider withdrawing its reservation and, if so, who should be responsible for doing this – the other states parties, or a treaty body or other monitoring body. In *Belilos*, the Court dealt with this issue of consent as follows:

   > The declaration in question does not satisfy two of the requirements of [the Article of the European Convention on Human Rights that deals with reservations], with the result that it must be held to be invalid. At the same time, it is beyond doubt that Switzerland is, and regards itself as, bound by the Convention irrespective of the validity of the declaration. Moreover, the Swiss Government recognised the Court's competence to determine the latter issue, which it argued before it.

   Is this convincing? France, the United Kingdom, and the United States responded critically to General Comment no. 24. In relation to the question of severability, France stated that it considered the position that a reservation is severable to be "incompatible with the law of treaties." The United Kingdom argued that "severability would entail excising both the reservation and the parts of the treaty to which it applies. Any other solution they would find deeply contrary to principle." The United States said that it was "completely at odds with established legal practice and principles." *See* Observations of States Parties under art. 40, para. 5, of the Covenant, CCPR A/51/40, Annex VI.

2. There are other aspects of the General Comment that are questionable. For example, while it flows from the nature of *jus cogens* norms that any unilateral act (e.g., an act of recognition, a reservation to a treaty) that is incompatible with them is invalid, why should it not be possible to enter a reservation in respect of a norm of customary international law? Recall that there is nothing to prevent states from contracting out of provisions of customary international law inter se through a treaty. Only if the norm is *jus cogens* is this prohibited. Is a reservation to a norm of customary international law prohibited because human rights are inherent and the object and purpose of a human rights treaty must be to further rather than to diminish human rights? By contrast, there seems to be agreement that a reservation to the reporting obligation under the Covenant is incompatible with the object and purpose of the Covenant.

3. Though acknowledging that the existence of monitoring bodies for human rights treaties raises considerations that were not contemplated by the framers of these treaties, the

International Law Commission (ILC) has tended to support the application of the Vienna Convention regime and, in particular, in 1997 asserted the view that reservations may not simply be severed.

Report of the International Law Commission on the Work of Its Forty-Ninth Session, A/52/10, at ch. 5 (May 12–July 18, 1997).

The International Law Commission has considered, at its forty-ninth session, the question of the unity or diversity of the juridical regime for reservations. The Commission is aware of the discussion currently taking place in other forums on the subject of reservations to normative multilateral treaties, and particularly treaties concerning human rights, and wishes to contribute to this discussion in the framework of the consideration of the subject of reservations to treaties that has been before it since 1993 by drawing the following conclusions:

1. The Commission reiterates its view that articles 19 to 23 of the Vienna Conventions on the Law of Treaties of 1969 and 1986 govern the regime of reservations to treaties and that, in particular, the object and purpose of the treaty is the most important of the criteria for determining the admissibility of reservations;

2. The Commission considers that, because of its flexibility, this regime is suited to the requirements of all treaties, of whatever object or nature, and achieves a satisfactory balance between the objectives of preservation of the integrity of the text of the treaty and universality of participation in the treaty;

3. The Commission considers that these objectives apply equally in the case of reservations to normative multilateral treaties, including treaties in the area of human rights and that, consequently, the general rules enunciated in the above-mentioned Vienna Conventions govern reservations to such instruments;

4. The Commission nevertheless considers that the establishment of monitoring bodies by many human rights treaties gave rise to legal questions that were not envisaged at the time of the drafting of those treaties, connected with appreciation of the admissibility of reservations formulated by States;

5. The Commission also considers that where these treaties are silent on the subject, the monitoring bodies established thereby are competent to comment upon and express recommendations with regard, *inter alia*, to the admissibility of reservations by States, in order to carry out the functions assigned to them;

6. The Commission stresses that this competence of the monitoring bodies does not exclude or otherwise affect the traditional modalities of control by the contracting parties, on the one hand, in accordance with the above-mentioned provisions of the Vienna Conventions of 1969 and 1986 and, where appropriate by the organs for settling any dispute that may arise concerning the interpretation or application of the treaties;

7. The Commission suggests providing specific clauses in normative multilateral treaties, including in particular human rights treaties, or elaborating protocols to existing treaties if States seek to confer competence on the monitoring body to appreciate or determine the admissibility of a reservation;

8. The Commission notes that the legal force of the findings made by monitoring bodies in the exercise of their power to deal with reservations cannot exceed that resulting from the powers given to them for the performance of their general monitoring role;

9. The Commission calls upon States to cooperate with monitoring bodies and give due consideration to any recommendations that they may make or to comply with their determination if such bodies were to be granted competence to that effect in the future;

10. The Commission notes also that, in the event of inadmissibility of a reservation, it is the reserving State that has the responsibility for taking action. This action may consist, for example, in the State either modifying its reservation so as to eliminate the inadmissibility, or withdrawing its reservation, or forgoing becoming a party to the treaty;

11. The Commission expresses the hope that the above conclusions will help to clarify the reservations regime applicable to normative multilateral treaties, particularly in the area of human rights;

12. The Commission emphasizes that the above conclusions are without prejudice to the practices and rules developed by monitoring bodies within regional contexts.

Questions and Discussion

1. Which body holds the better view on reservations to human rights treaties, the Human Rights Committee or the International Law Commission? Why? Note that work on this issue has continued without any definitive conclusions. *See, e.g.*, Int'l Law Comm., *Fourteenth Report on Reservations to Treaties* (Alain Pellet, Special Rapporteur), U.N. Doc. A/CN.4/614 (Apr. 2, 2009); Comm'n on Hum. Rts., Sub-Comm'n on the Promotion & Protection of Hum. Rts., *Reservations to Human Rights Treaties*, U.N. Doc. E/CN.4/Sub.2/2004/42 (July 19, 2004).

2. Should reservations work any differently in the context of international environmental law? For example, in 1998, Cuba sought to enter a reservation to protect the hawksbill sea turtle by the Protocol Concerning Specially Protected Areas and Wildlife (SPAW), but only after Cuba had already ratified the SPAW. No fewer than three legal opinions emerged, each reaching different conclusions. Two opinions concluded for different reasons that the reservation was impermissible and the third opinion concluded that the reservation was permissible. Professor Wold analyzes the Cuban reservation and concludes that the weight of legal authority is against the validity of the reservation. Chris Wold, *Implementation of Reservations in International Environmental Law Treaties: The Cases of Cuba and Iceland*, 14 COLO. J. INT'L ENVTL. L. & POL'Y 53 (2003).

B. *Denouncing and Reacceding with a Reservation*

Another aspect of peculiar to human rights treaties is the question whether a state may denounce a treaty and then reaccede with a reservation that it had not entered before. One special example is that of Trinidad and Tobago's purported withdrawal from and reaccession to the First Optional Protocol to the International Covenant on Civil and Political Rights because too many death penalty cases were successfully challenged before the Human Rights Committee. The reservation provides, in part, that

> ... Trinidad and Tobago re-accedes to the Optional Protocol to the International Covenant on Civil and Political Rights with a Reservation to article 1 thereof to the effect that the Human Rights Committee shall not be competent to receive and consider communications relating to any prisoner who is under sentence of death in respect of any matter relating to his prosecution, his detention, his trial, his conviction, his sentence or the carrying out of the death sentence on him and any matter connected therewith.

In *Rawle Kennedy v. Trinidad and Tobago*, the Human Rights Committee declared the reservation invalid.

Rawle Kennedy v. Trinidad and Tobago,
Human Rights Committee, Communication No. 845/1999,
U.N. Doc. CCPR/C/67/D/845/1999 (Dec. 31, 1999)

In its General Comment No. 24, the Committee expressed the view that a reservation aimed at excluding the competence of the Committee under the Optional Protocol with regard to certain provisions of the Covenant could not be considered to meet [the test of compatibility with the object and purpose of the treaty]:

> The function of the first Optional Protocol is to allow claims in respect of [the Covenant's] rights to be tested before the Committee. Accordingly, a reservation to an obligation of a State to respect and ensure a right contained in the Covenant, made under the first Optional Protocol when it has not previously been made in respect of the same rights under the Covenant, does not affect the State's duty to comply with its substantive obligation. A reservation cannot be made to the Covenant through the vehicle of the Optional Protocol but such a reservation would operate to ensure that the State's compliance with that obligation may not be tested by the Committee under the first Optional Protocol. And because the object and purpose of the first Optional Protocol is to allow the rights obligatory for a State under the Covenant to be tested before the Committee, a reservation that seeks to preclude this would be contrary to object and purpose of the first Optional Protocol, even if not of the Covenant.

The present reservation, which was entered after the publication of General Comment No. 24, does not purport to exclude the competence of the Committee under the Optional Protocol with regard to any specific provision of the Covenant, but rather to the entire Covenant for one particular group of complainants, namely prisoners under sentence of death. This does not, however, make it compatible with the object and purpose of the Optional Protocol. On the contrary, the Committee cannot accept a reservation which singles out a certain group of individuals for lesser procedural protection than that which is enjoyed by the rest of the population. In the view of the Committee, this constitutes a discrimination which runs counter to some of the basic principles embodied in the Covenant and its Protocols, and for this reason the reservation cannot be deemed compatible with the object and purpose of the Optional Protocol. The consequence is that the Committee is not precluded from considering the present communication under the Optional Protocol.

Questions and Discussion

1. Does the reservation single out a particular class of persons? Does it really seek to single out a particular category of human rights violations? Is this distinction important?
2. Given that Trinidad and Tobago is still subject to reporting requirements with respect to death penalty cases and will be subject to communications from victims of human rights violations in cases other than those involving the death penalty, is it possible to argue that the reservation is compatible with the object and purpose of the Protocol?
3. Looking at the problem from the perspective of other states parties, in addition to the human beings the treaty is designed to protect, is there anything wrong with the tactic of denunciation and reaccession adopted by Trinidad and Tobago? Is it sufficient protection for other states that they may now object to the reservation? Or does the strategy of denunciation and reaccession raise suspicions that the principle of *pacta sunt servanda* ("treaties are to be observed in good faith") has been circumvented and that the other states parties have not been dealt with in good faith? This has been suggested by the responses to the reservation by the Netherlands, Germany, Sweden, Ireland, Spain, France, and Italy.

C. *Limitations and Derogations from Human Rights*

There are very few rights that may be considered absolute. It is common for human rights treaties to provide that rights may be derogated from in times of public emergency. Article 4 of the ICCPR is an example:

1. In time of public emergency which threatens the life of the nation and the existence of which is officially proclaimed, the States Parties to the present Covenant may take measures derogating from their obligations under the present Covenant to the extent strictly required by the exigencies of the situation, provided that such measures are not inconsistent with their other obligations under international law and do not involve discrimination solely on the ground of race, colour, sex, language, religion or social origin.

2. No derogation from articles 6, 7, 8 (paragraphs 1 and 2), 11, 15, 16 and 18 may be made under this provision.

3. Any State Party to the present Covenant availing itself of the right of derogation shall immediately inform the other States Parties to the present Covenant, through the intermediary of the Secretary-General of the United Nations, of the provisions from which it has derogated and of the reasons by which it was actuated. A further communication shall be made, through the same intermediary, on the date on which it terminates such derogation.

It is notable that some human rights treaties do not provide for derogation. For example, the International Covenant on Economic, Social, and Cultural Rights does not contain a derogation clause. The jurisprudence of the Committee on Economic, Social, and Cultural Rights indicates that the rights of the Covenant are such that they apply during times of emergency (as no purpose would be gained by derogating from them), whereas the flexibility provided for by article 2 (the general provision on obligation) and article 4 (which permits limitations to rights) is sufficient to deal with other exigencies, such as resource constraints imposed by a public emergency. In the case of some other treaties, it might be possible to argue for the application of the general treaty law concept of force majeure, although caution must be exercised when applying a concept more usually applied to treaties based on reciprocity than in the context of human rights. *See further* A.-L. SVENNSON-MCCARTHY, THE INTERNATIONAL LAW OF HUMAN RIGHTS AND STATES OF EXCEPTION WITH SPECIAL REFERENCE TO THE TRAVAUX PRÉPARATOIRES AND THE CASE-LAW OF THE INTERNATIONAL MONITORING ORGANS 198 (1998).

Those rights that are listed as nonderogable are not necessarily absolute. The prohibition on torture admits of no exceptions, but article 6 of the ICCPR – the right to life – permits limitations. In particular, imposition of the death penalty for the most serious crimes is tolerated by article 6 (although the Second Optional Protocol to the Covenant aims to abolish it). In addition, other rights such as the right to freedom of expression in article 19 have specific limitations clauses. Thus freedom of expression may be limited to protect the reputations of others, for example. The ICESCR contains a generally applicable clause on limitations in article 4, the terms of which are intended to confine the limitations that might be imposed by states.

Limitations are restrictions that may be imposed outside the context of a public emergency. They, too, attract conditions. Article 5 of both Covenants imposes the following conditions:

1. Nothing in the present Covenant may be interpreted as implying for any State, group or person any right to engage in any activity or perform any act aimed at the destruction of any of the rights and freedoms recognized herein or at their limitation to a greater extent than is provided for in the present Covenant.

2. There shall be no restriction upon or derogation from any of the fundamental human rights recognized or existing in any State Party to the present Covenant pursuant to law, conventions, regulations or custom on the pretext that the present Covenant does not recognize such rights or that it recognizes them to a lesser extent.

Other principles may be gleaned from particular limitations clauses and that contained in article 29(1) of the Universal Declaration on Human Rights. Article 29 of the UDHR is as follows:

> In the exercise of his rights and freedoms, everyone shall be subject only to such limitations as are determined by law solely for the purpose of securing due recognition and respect for the rights and freedoms of others and of meeting the just requirements of morality, public order and the general welfare in a democratic society.

Similar words are used in limitations clauses in the Covenants and in regional human rights treaties. From these provisions and the jurisprudence of the various human rights bodies, it is clear that limitations may only be imposed by law for purposes such as public morality, national security public order, and the rights of others and that they must be proportionate and nondiscriminatory.

5 International Human Rights Institutions and Procedures

I. Introduction

This chapter examines the international and regional systems for reporting, monitoring, and "enforcing" human rights obligations. When environmental destruction results in human injury that breaches applicable human rights provisions, it may be possible to invoke the jurisdiction of a human rights body under established procedures to remedy both the human rights violation and the underlying environmental degradation causing the violation. For lawyers concerned with environmental protection, the well-developed human rights committees, commissions, and other mechanisms empowered to investigate and act on alleged human rights abuses have provided a major attraction, despite the fact that the approach is retrospective, because bringing a human rights case implies that harm (sometimes irreparable) has already been done. It is thus important to keep in mind that most human rights institutions also have a proactive promotional function that allows inquiry, training, guidelines on best practices, and other actions to prevent harm from occurring.

Few international environmental treaties establish an independent treaty body to supervise treaty obligations. Reporting obligations sometimes exist, but without such an independent institutional structure, there can be no hope of monitoring or enforcement outside of the parties to the agreement. Even where an institutional body is established pursuant to an international environmental treaty, only the Aarhus Compliance Committee (see Chapter 6) has been charged with any significant independent monitoring and enforcement powers akin to those of human rights institutions. Accordingly, it often appears to environmental lawyers that by deploying international human rights law and procedures in environmental cases, they will be able to obtain the benefit (ordinarily absent) of the monitoring and enforcement power of human rights bodies. *See generally* Daniel Bodansky, *The Role of Reporting in International Environmental Treaties: Lessons for Human Rights Supervision*, in THE FUTURE OF U.N. HUMAN RIGHTS TREATY MONITORING 361 (Philip Alston & James Crawford eds. 2000).

Even though international enforcement is more robust in the human rights field than areas of environmental concern, it is important to be aware that problems still remain. At the most basic level, human rights obligations run from the state to individuals, rather than from state to state, as in much of international law. As a result, human rights violations almost always occur in a particular state's jurisdiction. This fact has at least three legal ramifications.

First, and unfortunately, some governments continue to resist international human rights supervision. They protest international interference in their domestic affairs when human rights abuses occur and political interests are at stake. As emphasized earlier, however, such resistance is wholly without foundation, because human rights violations are the legitimate concern of the entire international community because human rights establish – in the words of the Universal Declaration – "a common standard of achievement for all peoples and all nations." The Universal Declaration and subsequent human rights instruments clearly intend for human rights to be a subject of international relations and a matter properly monitored and discussed by the international community.

Second, aside from the 1948 Genocide Convention, the major human rights treaties do not contain compromissory clauses allowing resort to the International Court of Justice or other third-party judicial dispute settlement, although all the major treaties provide for the filing of interstate complaints before the treaty-monitoring body, a procedure that is rarely used. More important, though, because human rights obligations do not run from state to state but from state to individual, important incentives to comply with international law are largely absent. The sort of reciprocity envisioned and retaliation sanctioned by the Vienna Convention on the Law of Treaties (VCLT) for breaches of international obligations are non sequiturs with human rights. A threat by a state to suspend the operation of a human rights treaty in its borders as a response to the breach of human rights by another state, as allowed by article 60 of the VCLT, is counterproductive nonsense. As a result, international monitoring and enforcement mechanisms generally focus on reputational and retaliatory incentives to promote compliance and improve a state's human rights record. *See generally* ANDREW T. GUZMAN, HOW INTERNATIONAL LAW WORKS: A RATIONAL CHOICE THEORY ch. 3 (2008). As we will see, outside regional courts that issue binding judgments (and the Security Council, in extreme cases of massive human rights violations), very little can be done by international bodies addressing human rights to actually compel compliance outside of dialogue and shaming. For this reason, linking human rights to other issues like security or trade, as was done in the Conference on Security and Cooperation in Europe (also known as the Helsinki Accords), is sometimes used as a powerful means to induce positive changes in state behavior.

Third, like much of international law, the municipal sphere remains paramount in the enforcement of an individual's human rights; international tribunals largely view their role as subsidiary. Although there are well-recognized exceptions, in all cases, an aggrieved individual must exhaust local remedies before an approach to an international human rights body will lie. *See* C.F. AMERASINGHE, LOCAL REMEDIES IN INTERNATIONAL LAW 359 (1990). Of course, the effectiveness of enforcement by municipal legal systems is affected by myriad variables, including political leaders and their commitment to human rights, the system of government, the way in which international obligations are implemented internally, and the resources of a state.

International human rights monitoring and enforcement can take three different institutional tracks – although in some instances, more than one track might be available: (1) U.N. Charter bodies, (2) global treaty bodies, and (3) regional human rights systems. Note that all the organizations involved in each strand are part of or created by international governmental organizations (IGOs). Importantly, however, the individuals involved in human rights treaty body monitoring and enforcement act (or are supposed to act) independent of instructions from any government. This is not true of the Charter-based organs of the United Nations, excepting the Office of the High Commissioner, which is part of the secretariat whose independence is mandated by the Charter. Other Charter organs like the Security Council, General Assembly, and Human Rights Council are composed of state representatives taking instructions from their governments. Although nongovernmental organizations (NGOs) and individuals may have influential access to these organizations, they have no decision-making power.

In the United Nations, four organs established by the U.N. Charter address human rights issues: the Security Council; the General Assembly; the Economic and Social Council (ECOSOC); and, increasingly, the International Court of Justice. The Secretariat division having responsibility for human rights is the Office of the High Commissioner of Human Rights, located in Geneva. It is also important to keep in mind the specialized agencies of the United Nations, many of whose mandates involve human rights and environmental matters. The World Health Organization, for example, has taken up the issue of safe drinking water and other health-related issues on the basis of its constitution's reference to the right to health. The International Labour Organization, which dates back to the early twentieth century, has treaties and recommendations on the working environment and hazardous substances, including pesticides. The Food and Agriculture Organization has been occupied with the right to food, including matters related to fisheries and agriculture. All these organizations have considered aspects of the linkages between human rights and the environment, as has the U.N. Educational, Scientific, and Cultural Organization (UNESCO), which is responsible for the operation of the World Heritage Convention.

In 1946, the Economic and Social Council created what was called for nearly fifty years the U.N. Commission on Human Rights (CHR), which reported to ECOSOC. It was the CHR's Sub-Commission on the Promotion and Protection of Minorities (a body of independent human rights experts) that produced the Draft Declaration of Principles on Human Rights and the Environment discussed in Case Study V in the online Case Studies that accompany this text. In 2006, the General Assembly replaced the Commission with the U.N. Human Rights Council (HRC) – which now reports to the General Assembly – to promote needed reforms and raise the profile of human rights. The HRC carries on the work of the Commission in the area of "special procedures" – mechanisms established to examine the human right situation in specific states and thematic human rights issues. In addition, a new procedure called universal periodic review is in place that allows the HRC to review the human rights record of all 192 U.N. members every five years. There is a revised complaints procedure that allows individuals and NGOs to bring complaints about human rights abuses before the Council. An advisory committee that has been called the Council's think tank has some of the functions and many of the members of the former subcommission.

Nine core human rights treaties adopted under the auspices of the United Nations have used the institutional technique of a committee to review state party compliance with treaty terms. Committees have been established under the International Covenant on Civil and Political Rights (ICCPR; the Human Rights Committee, which is an independent body and not to be confused with the U.N. Human Rights Council) and the International Covenant of Economic, Social, and Cultural Rights (ICESCR; Committee on Economic, Social, and Cultural Rights), as well as the International Convention on the Elimination of All Forms of Racial Discrimination (CERD; Committee on the Elimination of All Forms of Racial Discrimination); the Convention on the Elimination of All Forms of Discrimination Against Women (CEDAW; Committee on the Elimination of Discrimination Against Women); the Convention Against Torture and Other Forms of Cruel, Inhuman, or Degrading Treatment or Punishment (CAT; (Committee Against Torture and Sub Committee on Prevention of Torture for the Optional Protocol to the Convention Against Torture); the Convention on the Rights of the Child (CRC; Committee on the Rights of the Child); the Convention on the Protection of the Rights of All Migrant Workers and Members of Their Families (CMW; Committee on Migrant Workers), the Convention on the Rights of Persons with Disabilities (CRPD; Committee on the Rights of Persons with Disabilities), and the International

Convention for the Protection of All Persons from Enforced Disappearance (CPED; Committee on Enforced Disappearances).

With mostly minor variations, the work of all treaty committees follows a similar pattern. As we have seen, treaty committees regularly issue "General Comments" on the nature of the guaranteed rights and on state obligations. Such comments enrich the substantive understanding of often sweeping provisions. However, review of state compliance and performance begins with the submission of periodic reports by states on the measures they have taken to implement the treaty and the difficulties they have encountered. Of course, self-reporting raises obvious problems related to the self-interest of states submitting these reports. Accordingly, under a number of these major treaties (or pursuant to an optional protocol) it is possible for an interstate complaint to be brought or for a state to consent to additional scrutiny by allowing the committee to receive communications from individuals alleging that their rights have been violated.

Regional human rights systems provide the third track of human rights monitoring and enforcement. Regional human rights systems, with courts, commissions, and other human rights bodies, have been created by the Council of Europe; the Organization of American States (OAS); the African Union (AU); and as of July 2009, the Association of South East Asian Nations (ASEAN). All of these are discussed in more detail later in Section III.

II. The U.N. Charter Bodies

Each of the principal organs of the United Nations may play a role in the protection of human rights by considering thematic issues and individual country situations. These activities can include consideration of human rights related to environmental harm. The five principal organs of the United Nations relevant to human rights and the environment are the Security Council (SC), the General Assembly (GA), the Secretary-General (SG), the Economic and Social Council (ECOSOC), and the International Court of Justice (ICJ). The Trusteeship Council is a sixth principal organ, but it became defunct with the independence of Palau in 1994. Malta proposed that the Trusteeship Council be assigned new responsibilities, including environmental stewardship and management of areas beyond national jurisdiction, but the proposal has received relatively little support. *See Review of the Role of the Trusteeship Council: Report of the Secretary General*, U.N. Doc. A/50/1011 (Aug. 1, 1996).

A. *Security Council*

The Security Council (SC) is principally charged with the maintenance of international peace and security. It comprises fifteen members, five of which are permanent members (China, France, Russia, United States, and United Kingdom). Members of the United Nations must carry out "decisions" of the Council under the U.N. Charter, and the Council can enforce the judgments of the International Court of Justice in contentious cases. U.N. Charter, articles 25 & 94(2). Decisions on all substantive matters considered by the Council require an affirmative vote of nine members, including all five permanent members. U.N. Charter, article 27. This, of course, gives the permanent members a veto power over decisions; abstention from voting is not considered a veto.

The SC was long silent about human rights for the most part, apart from decolonization and the situation of apartheid in South Africa. In more recent times, with the resolution of those issues and the proliferation of internal and international armed conflicts, it has ordered sanctions and the use of force in a few cases of massive human rights violations. Somalia,

Haiti, Iraq, and the former Yugoslavia are key examples. The failure of the Security Council to intervene in the face of the "killing fields" in Cambodia and genocide in Rwanda, which saw the slaughter of eight hundred thousand people in about one hundred days, disillusioned the United Nations, many of its members, and other actors. It led to extensive rethinking of the principle of intervention for humanitarian reasons. A U.N. inquiry condemned the failure by the United Nations to prevent the genocide in Rwanda and called on the "Security Council . . . to act to prevent acts of genocide or gross violations of human rights wherever they may take place." *Report of the Independent Inquiry into the Actions of the United Nations During the 1994 Genocide in Rwanda*, U.N. Doc. S/1999/1257 (Dec. 16, 1999). The shadow of the atrocities in the Darfur region of Sudan hangs heavily on the United Nations, even though the Security Council has had significant and continuing involvement in both situations.

The disquiet about Rwanda led the International Commission on Intervention and State Sovereignty (ICISS) to develop, in 2001, the concept of a responsibility to protect. ICISS, THE RESPONSIBILITY TO PROTECT (2001), *available at* http://www.iciss.ca/pdf/Commission-Report. pdf. The responsibility to protect involves two major aspects. First, and most important, it recasts and limits the common idea of state sovereignty as freedom, returning to the concept of functional sovereignty set forth by the arbitrator Judge Huber in the *Island of Palmas* case, 2 UNRIAA 831 (1928). Huber coupled sovereign rights with sovereign responsibilities, viewing the guarantees of the former as dependent on the exercise of the latter. *See also* H. LAUTERPACHT, THE FUNCTION OF LAW IN THE INTERNATIONAL COMMUNITY 97–100 (1933) (arguing in connection with the *Bering Sea* arbitration that "the freedom of the sea could not mean the absence of any legal regulation whatsoever," at 98). In the words of Philip Allott, the ICISS report further turns ideas about sovereignty "inside out like a glove" (or more accurately, turns it back outside in). PHILIP ALLOTT, EUNOMIA: NEW ORDER FOR A NEW WORLD 243 (1990). The responsibility to protect attempts to socialize states (in the sense of shared norms of cooperative behavior) in the international system by imposing responsibilities for the welfare of each other's populations.

Second, the responsibility to protect first makes each state primarily responsible for the welfare of its population. If a state is unable or unwilling to fulfill this primary responsibility in cases in which the population is suffering serious harm, it becomes the responsibility of other states, collectively (and ordinarily under the control of the Security Council), to take up that responsibility and end the suffering. ICISS, THE RESPONSIBILITY TO PROTECT 17 (2001). By limiting outsider responsibility to situations involving serious harm, the ICISS insists on a "just cause" before intervention is permissible. Intervention is thus limited to "conscience-shocking" situations involving, for example, large-scale loss of life produced by deliberate state action or a state's inability to prevent such loss. *Id.* at 32–33. Importantly for human rights and the environment, the collective responsibility of the international community to protect includes situations involving "environmental catastrophes, where the state concerned is either unwilling or unable to cope, or call for assistance, and significant loss of life is occurring or threatened." *Id.* at 33. This recalls earlier proposals, pressed by the French government among others, for a right of ecological intervention and for the creation of so-called Green Helmets. *See* Linda A. Malone, *"Green Helmets": A Conceptual Framework for Security Council Authority in Environmental Emergencies*, 17 MICH. J. INT'L L. 515 (1995).

The Security Council was also involved in the environmental harm and loss caused by Iraq in the 1991 Gulf War with Kuwait. In that case, the Security Council declared Iraq "liable under international law for any direct loss, damage, including environmental damage and the depletion of natural resources, or injury . . . as a result of Iraq's unlawful invasion and occupation of Kuwait." S.C. Res. 687, at ¶ 16 (Apr. 3, 1991). The Security Council shortly thereafter established the U.N. Compensation Fund, administered by the U.N. Compensation Commission, a temporary subsidiary body of the Security Council established for this purpose. S.C. Res. 692, at ¶ 3 (May 20, 1991). Eventually, more than 2.6 million claims were submitted to the Commission, including claims involving injury to the health of millions of individuals and ecological harm. *See, e.g., Report and Recommendations Made by the Panel of Commissioners Concerning the First Installment of "F4" Claims*, U.N. Doc. S/AC.26/2001/16, at ¶¶ 266–96, 494–532, 665–706, 762–68 (June 22, 2001). The Governing Council of the Commission was still following up environmental claims awards in 2010. *See Decision Concerning Follow-up Programme for Environmental Claims Awards Taken by the Governing Council of the United Nations Compensation Commission*, U.N. Doc. S/AC.26/Dec.258 (Dec. 8, 2005). *See also* Chapter 9.

Questions and Discussion

1. The responsibility to protect was endorsed by the General Assembly following the 2005 World Summit. 2005 *World Summit Outcome*, G.A. Res. 60/1, U.N. Doc. A/RES/60/1 (Oct. 24, 2005). The World Summit and General Assembly made clear, however, that collective action to protect populations was limited to that authorized by the Security Council. The idea of the responsibility to protect has also met some significant academic resistance because it reflects a political tool that is so vague that "it suits too many cross-purposes." José E. Alvarez, *The Schizophrenias of R2P*, 23 Am. Soc'y Int'l L. Newsl. 1, 11 (2007).

   In terms of human rights threatened by environmental disasters, how might the responsibility to protect come in to play in the case of climate change resulting in the complete inundation of a low-lying island state like Tuvalu? What about the case of dry-land degradation that displaces hundreds of thousands or millions of people, making a livelihood for those people impossible? *See further* Chapter 9.

2. The former leader of the Soviet Union, Mikhail Gorbachev, and others raised the issue of environmental conditions as a matter of national and international security as early as the 1990s. In particular, there were concerns about water shortages leading to water wars. The issue did not gain much traction at the time, but in 2007, the Security Council took up the issue of climate change as an issue of global security. Do you see the linkages?

3. The U.N. Environment Programme has been involved in fact-finding in the aftermath of many of the conflicts mentioned, including Kuwait, Iraq, and the former Yugoslavia, assessing environmental harm and its impact on the local population. Those results were recently compiled and published. *See* UNEP, Protecting the Environment During Armed Conflict: An Inventory and Analysis of International Law (2009).

B. *General Assembly*

The General Assembly (GA) consists of all U.N. state members – currently, 192 states. Its resolutions are not per se legally binding, but they often reflect the attitudes of the international community as a whole and can have an important impact on the development of customary international law. Much of the debate and drafting of various documents takes place in the GA's six main committees. Three of the committees have particular relevance for human rights: the Third Committee (Social, Humanitarian, and Cultural), the Fifth Committee (Administrative and Budgetary), and the Sixth Committee (Legal).

The preamble and articles 1, 55, and 56 of the U.N. Charter make clear that promoting respect for human rights is a central purpose of the United Nations and an obligation of member states. Under the U.N. Charter, the GA has the power to "discuss any questions or any matters within the scope of the Charter" and "to initiate studies and make recommendations for the purpose of... assisting in the realization of human rights." Articles 10 & 13. The GA has adopted many resolutions on human rights beginning with resolutions on apartheid and racial discrimination and, in more recent times, adopting resolutions on topics such as trafficking of women. *See* G.A. Res. 52/98 A/RES/52/98 (Feb. 6, 1998). It is responsible, along with the secretary-general, for overseeing the Office of the High Commissioner for Human Rights, which the GA created in 1993. The GA, as mentioned, replaced the old Commission on Human Rights with the Human Rights Council in 2006 and is responsible for superintending the Council.

1. The Former Commission and Subcommission

In 1946, with the atrocities of World War II fresh in mind, the Preparatory Commission of the United Nations recommended that the Economic and Social Council immediately establish the Commission on Human Rights and direct it to formulate an "international bill of rights" and to prepare studies and recommendations that "would encourage the acceptance of higher standards in this field and help to check and eliminate discrimination and other abuses." Louis Sohn, *A Short History of United Nations Documents on Human Rights*, in COMMISSION TO STUDY THE ORGANIZATION OF PEACE, THE UNITED NATIONS AND HUMAN RIGHTS (Eighteenth Report) 37, 56 (1968). The recommendation was approved by the General Assembly in resolution 7(I) on February 12, 1946, and four days later, ECOSOC created the Commission on Human Rights. Economic and Social Council, res. 5(I), Feb. 16, 1946, ECOSOC OR, 1st Sess. 163. A subsequent ECOSOC resolution conferred on the Commission the mandate to submit to the Council "proposals, recommendations and reports" regarding

(a) an international bill of rights;
(b) international declarations or conventions on civil liberties, the status of women, freedom of information and similar matters;
(c) the protection of minorities;
(d) the prevention of discrimination on grounds of race, sex, language or religion; and
(e) any other matter concerning human rights not covered by other items.

Economic and Social Council, Res. 9(II), June 21, 1946, ECOSOC OR, 2nd Sess. Standard setting, in particular, formulation of an international bill of rights, was thus to be the focus of the Commission's work. The Commission's functions were not limited to standard setting, however, and during its tenure, it had to determine its priorities among a number of different matters. Nonetheless, at least during its first twenty years, standard setting was its main role. Indeed, in 1948, the Commission's chairwoman, Eleanor Roosevelt, wrote that the work of the Commission should be directed "for years to come" to drafting "many conventions on special subjects." Mrs. Franklin D. Roosevelt, *The Promise of Human Rights*, 26 FOREIGN AFF. 470, 476–77 (1948). Philip Alston has likened this role to that of the International Law Commission but restricted to matters of human rights.

In 1990, the Secretary-General of the United Nations observed that the United Nations had "from its very inception... engaged itself in elaborating human rights instruments and establishing bench marks against which standards of behavior can be measured." Secretary-General, Rep. on the Work of the Organization U.N. GAOR, 45th Sess. At 15, U.N. Doc. A/45/1 (1990), at 10. In 2005, his successor claimed that "the body of international human rights norms developed to date by the Commission is, perhaps, its greatest legacy." *Explanatory Note by the Secretary-General to the President of the General Assembly*, U.N. Doc. A/59/2005/Add.1 (Apr. 13, 2005), para. 11 Some observers assert that the Commission's primary standard-setting activities were limited to a few years at the inception of the organization (1947–54), but others disagree, and the first view is not supported by an examination of the practice of the organization. In fact, the Commission could not avoid being continually engaged in standard setting from its creation until its demise.

Although the Human Rights Commission was an important locus of standard setting from its first session, it was not the exclusive body engaged in this process, nor was it the origin of most standard-setting projects. The Commission, instead, most often reviewed, debated, and adopted initiatives originating in the Sub-Commission or General Assembly, from NGOs and, occasionally, from the Secretariat. In addition, quite a few major human rights instruments were concluded without any input from the Commission. Topics falling under the mandate of a specialized agency, such as labor rights and education, understandably have been dealt with by the relevant agency, but it is also apparent that, in other instances, states or U.N. bodies chose to bypass the Commission and initiate the drafting and adoption of new standards in another U.N. body, including the General Assembly, ECOSOC, or the Commission on the Status of Women.

Even when the Human Rights Commission on rare occasions did initiate projects, article 62(3) of the U.N. Charter entrusts the final elaboration and adoption of instruments to the Economic and Social Council and the General Assembly. The General Assembly, especially in its Third Committee, often made substantial revisions before giving final approval to the completed texts, even after the Commission had engaged in lengthy substantive negotiations. If there was a silent partner in the process, it was ECOSOC, which usually sent through Commission texts without comment or change.

The process of elaborating standards involved numerous actors, including states taking leadership on an issue, the Sub-Commission, specialized agencies, NGOs, the General Assembly (especially in the Third and Sixth Committees), and the Secretariat. Original authorship normally cannot be attributed to a single entity and even less to an individual. The multiplicity of actors with different viewpoints participating in the drafting process had both a positive and a negative dimension. On the negative side, the desire for consensus sometimes led to vague, weakened, and (some claim) inconsistent obligations. On the positive side, the process invested states in the final product, often producing positive changes in national laws and practices even before the text was finalized.

The Commission can rightly claim most of the credit for the Universal Declaration of Human Rights (UDHR), as it completed the text during two sessions over less than eighteen months. The General Assembly proclaimed it some six months later. The Commission's work was aided by having more than a dozen drafts submitted by governments, NGOs, and individuals, many coming in even before its first session. The drafts were compiled into a single Secretariat text by the director of the human rights division, John Humphrey. In June 1947, the Commission's drafting committee (Eleanor Roosevelt, Charles Malik, and P.C. Chang, later augmented by the members representing the Soviet Union, the United Kingdom, France, Australia, and Chile) reviewed the detailed Secretariat outline. French representative René Cassin was given responsibility for revising the Secretariat outline and preparing a draft declaration. The full drafting committee spent two weeks debating the resulting text before adjourning. Before the following Commission session in December 1947, the Sub-Commission made its contribution to the UDHR, submitting proposals for two articles: a draft article on minority rights, which failed to be adopted, and a rather weak provision on the right to seek asylum, which was adopted.

During its two-week session of December 1947, the Commission completed the text of the Declaration and referred it to ECOSOC, member governments, and other U.N. bodies for review. The Commission's drafting committee reconvened in May 1948 to consider the replies from governments. On June 18, the Commission adopted the Declaration by a 12–0 vote, with four Eastern European members abstaining.

Political and ideological differences over rights were evident from the beginning of the drafting process. First, states were divided between those that wanted a declaration only and those that sought binding obligations in a treaty or covenant. Ultimately, the two sides agreed that both types of instrument should be prepared and submitted to the General Assembly. Other problems were less amenable to compromise: several delegations sought explicitly to guarantee the right to life "from the time of conception." Some Arab states objected to including the right to change religion. Soviet-bloc countries, along with Asian states and the few independent African states, supported self-determination and minority rights, proposals that clashed with the views of colonial powers. The East-West divide over civil and political rights and economic, social, and cultural rights affected the drafting of the Declaration, which came fully to the forefront when it came time to convert the Declaration into a binding treaty or treaties. Throughout the drafting process, governments devoted nearly as much time debating the legal status of the Declaration as they did to its contents.

The Commission's practice from the beginning was generally to adopt nonbinding declarations before negotiating a binding agreement. In addition, the Commission and Sub-Commission adopted numerous declarations, resolutions, guidelines and codes of conduct that have not been succeeded by treaties. The latter category mainly consists of new and sometimes controversial topics.

As the standard-setting work of the Commission moved beyond the rights expressly mentioned in the UDHR, a relatively consistent practice developed for addressing the new matters. Often a single government or a group of governments would make a specific proposal to pronounce a new right. If the Commission accepted the proposal, it would commonly request the Sub-Commission or Secretariat to study its dimensions, on the basis of which it would either draft or recommend that the Sub-Commission draft a set of principles, a declaration, or a convention. Most of these were negotiated in presession working groups of the Commission. Working groups were used to draft not only the declaration on the right to development but also draft declarations on minorities, the rights of human rights defenders, and the rights of mental patients. In 1992, a working group was established to draft a declaration on disappearances, which completed its work rapidly, sending for adoption by the General Assembly the Declaration on the Protection of All Persons from Enforced Disappearances.

Declarations became a normal precursor to a convention, but sometimes became the sole product, because of political disagreements over the topic. The Declaration on the Elimination of All Forms of Intolerance and of Discrimination Based on Religion or Belief, for example, was adopted by a divided vote in the Commission and passed by the General Assembly without a vote, after a compromise was negotiated on the right to change one's religion.

The process of adopting normative resolutions did not differ greatly from that used to conclude treaties, although fewer Commission resolutions have been subject to major modification after being submitted to the Third Committee. Indeed, the Committee often simply repeats the language of the Commission text. However, the Committee and the General Assembly have played important roles when the Commission has been unable to reach agreement on a text. The report of the Commission's Working Group on a Declaration on the Right to Development, for example, was sent to the General Assembly to break a political impasse in the group. The Assembly succeeded in resolving the major concerns and adopted the Declaration in 1986, with only the United States voting against the text.

Throughout its tenure, the Sub-Commission was a key part of the Commission's standard-setting process, especially for nonbinding instruments. Its working papers and studies provided the background for issues under consideration and often were the impetus for standard setting by the Commission. In some instances, the Sub-Commission prepared the first drafts of normative texts, although the Commission did not always accept the Sub-Commission's drafts and even sought to limit the latter's standard setting activities in recent years. Although there has been much attention focused on the process of standard setting, it is also important to consider the results. The Web site for the Office of the High Commissioner for Human Rights lists nine "core" treaties, some of which are supplemented by optional protocols. It also posts a listing of more than ninety other standard-setting instruments. There clearly is little reason to complain about the quantity of human rights standard setting by the United Nations as a whole, especially if one adds the specialized agencies to the list. Indeed, there is a risk of devaluing the currency if too many new rights are added. As early as 1986, the General Assembly adopted a resolution to exercise some degree of quality control over the production of new standards. G.A. Res. 41/120, U.N. Doc. A/RES/41/120 (Dec. 4, 1986), recommends principles to guide states in developing new international human rights instruments. They suggest that proposed new texts should (1) be consistent with existing norms; (2) be "of fundamental character," (c) be "sufficiently precise to give rise to identifiable and practicable rights and obligations"; and (d) provide "realistic and effective implementation machinery." *Id.* at para. 4. Commentators also have examined U.N. standard setting and proposed standards for standards. *See, e.g.*, Philip Alston, *Conjuring Up New Human Rights: A Proposal for Quality Control*, 78 Am. J. Int'l L. 607 (1984). In part, the concern stems from the link between quantity and quality, with a fear that an increase in the former inevitably results in a decline in the latter. Another concern is with the capacity of states to comply with the multitude of norms and standards now in place.

It is possible to suggest that the problem of normative proliferation is a consequence of too many standard-setting bodies. As noted earlier, the Commission itself was not responsible for or even involved in drafting many of the major human rights treaties and declarations. Instead, numerous other bodies throughout the UN system became a source of human rights instruments. Overlapping jurisdiction, with a plethora of bodies engaged in adopting human rights norms, can produce synergies, but can also mean overlapping of inconsistent norms.

Another critique of the standard-setting process concerns the length of time involved in concluding normative texts, despite a decision by the Commission that, "in most instances[,] the established time-frame should in principle not exceed five years." U.N. Commission on Human Rights, Decision 2000/109, Annex, para. 60 (April 26, 2000). Some instruments required a decade or more to negotiate, becoming less demanding in the process.

The lengthy process of negotiation may result in texts that are poorly drafted, inconsistent, or overlapping with other normative texts. The government of Spain linked this poor quality to problems of implementation, noting that "the legal inadequacies of many of the treaties adopted recently [is] a situation which in turn creates major problems in terms of the interpretation and application of such treaties." Review of the Multilateral Treaty-Making Process, U.N. Doc. ST/LEG/SER.B/21, at 43 (U.N. Sales No. E F.83.V.8 (1985)). Of course, a level of generality may be necessary to achieve consensus. It also allows normative instruments to evolve to respond to contemporary needs. With increasing numbers of human rights bodies hearing cases, interpretive jurisprudence can give guidance to states on the meaning of rights and the scope of their obligations, but it also shifts standard setting away from states to small quasi-judicial bodies.

The practices described also raise the question of whether nonaction is a form of action. Several normative texts drafted by the Commission or Sub-Commission or recommended for drafting have never been approved, for example a treaty on religious intolerance and a draft declaration on human rights and the environment.

Clearly, the Commission's position between the Sub-Commission and the Assembly led to variable practices in standard setting. Some drafting was done by each of the three bodies. The Assembly sometimes insisted on retaining exclusivity over the negotiations. When the Sub-Commission engaged in standard setting, it was often with considerably more input from NGOs than was the case at the Commission. Indeed, some resolutions and drafts were jointly written by one or more members of the Sub-Commission with NGO representatives. When the product became too progressive, the Commission or ECOSOC would circumscribe the Commission's activities.

Undoubtedly, standard setting by the Commission was a political activity. This should not come as a surprise or be taken as a criticism – lawmaking in every society is a political activity. One may disagree with the political choices made or question the disinterest and neutrality of the lawmaker, but it is impossible to view lawmaking as anything other than a political process. The replacement of the Commission by the Council will not change this fact, but unfortunately it may remove some of the checks and mitigating factors that most encouraged standard setting by the Commission. In particular, the presence of an independent expert body, the Sub-Commission, working closely with NGOs and civil society, was indispensable in revealing many of the serious human rights problems that needed attention and required the adoption of international standards. Without such an expert body, there is a risk that the Council will lack the expert advice or stimulus to act.

2. The Human Rights Council

Thomas Franck claimed two decades ago that "no indictment of the U.N. has been made more frequently or with greater vehemence than that it singles out Western and pro-Western states for obloquy, while ignoring far worse excesses committed by socialist and Third World nations." THOMAS FRANCK, NATION AGAINST NATION: WHAT HAPPENED TO THE U.N. DREAM AND WHAT THE U.S. CAN DO ABOUT IT 224 (1985). Third-world commentators maintain that the opposite is true, asserting that the United Nations has focused disproportionately on developing countries. Although these contradictory views may indicate that the United Nations is rather more even handed than is generally accepted, a perception of politicization and lack of standards eroded the credibility and legitimacy of the U.N. Human Rights Commission, leading to its replacement in 2006 by the Human Rights Council.

An optimist could see the increased politicization of human rights at the former Human Rights Commission and U.N. General Assembly as a backhanded tribute to the success of the human rights movement in the past fifty years. Human rights violators seek to manipulate the system because it has an impact and constitutes a threat to their abusive exercise of power. As Egon Schwelb noted in looking back over the first twenty-five years of the U.N. practice, "neither the vagueness and generality of the human rights clauses of the Charter nor the domestic jurisdiction clause have prevented the U.N. from considering, investigating, and judging concrete human rights situations, provided there was a majority strong enough and wishing strongly enough to attempt to influence the particular development." Egon Schwelb,

The International Court of Justice and the Human Rights Clauses of the Charter, 66 AM. J. INT'L L. 337, 341 (1972).

On March 15, 2006, the U.N General Assembly adopted Resolution 60/251 creating the Human Rights Council. The HRC replaced the sixty-year-old Commission on Human Rights (CHR), which many governments and observers felt was no longer effective. Professor Alston explains the Commission's fall from grace.

Reconceiving the U.N. Human Rights Regime: Challenges Confronting the New U.N. Human Rights Council,
7 MELB. J. INT'L L. 185, 186–88, 191–93 (2006)
Philip Alston

While the debates preceding the [2006] reforms were protracted and at times heated, there was a surprising degree of consensus on three propositions: that the 60-year-old Commission had brought discredit upon itself and had largely failed; that a new, higher-level body with a different composition had to be established; and that the institutional machinery of the U.N. in the human rights field needed to be strengthened. This consensus, however, masked deep disagreements about what exactly went wrong with the Commission and what key ingredients should be included in the formula for the new Council. As a result, the General Assembly resolution proclaiming the new order resolved only the most basic structural issues as to the Council's composition and election procedure, and only laid down rather broad guidelines governing the procedures and institutional arrangements which the Council should adopt in order to carry out the wide ranging tasks assigned to it.

The establishment of the Commission was mandated by the *Charter of the United Nations*. After its first session in 1946, its many achievements have included the drafting of the *Universal Declaration of Human Rights* ('UDHR') and a plethora of subsequent human rights treaties. Having grown in size, it eventually consisted of 53 governments, elected on a rotating basis for three-year terms by the Economic and Social Council ('ECOSOC'). It became the lynchpin of the institutional arrangements designed to promote and protect human rights – a status which defied the fact that it was institutionally inferior in the overall U.N. institutional hierarchy to both ECOSOC and the General Assembly....

Its tasks of fostering cooperation and building capacity were uncontroversial – at least in principle, although not always in practice. In contrast, its mandate to promote global respect for human rights and to respond to rights violations was intrinsically controversial because it required that it monitor and call to account many of the countries that sat as members of the Commission.

In its final few years, and especially since 1998, these controversies plagued the operations of the Commission and resulted in a rancorous debate among governments, often reflecting a North-South split. Accusations of politicisation, double standards and unprofessionalism led many commentators to conclude that the Commission had lost its credibility and prompted calls for far-reaching reforms of its operation. Unsurprisingly, however, the diagnosis that it had lost credibility was motivated by radically divergent perceptions of what it should have been doing and what it had done or failed to do. While many of the critics called for a conciliatory approach that would avoid confrontation with governments, others impugned its credibility precisely because it had failed to condemn governments that they considered to be responsible for egregious cases of human rights violations.

Much of the debate over the past few years revolved around the question of the composition of the Commission. The *Wall Street Journal Europe*, for example, accused the U.N. of conferring legitimacy on regimes with abysmal human rights records by allowing them to sit on the

Commission, asking "[h]ow can the U.N. claim any legitimacy if it still allows Sudan to sit on its Human Rights Commission?" At the Commission's 2004 session, the U.S. delegation took up this theme and insisted that "[t]his important body should not be allowed to become a protected sanctuary for human rights violators who aim to pervert and distort its work." It argued that only "real democracies" should enjoy the privilege of membership. There are many other examples of this type of discourse, which implied that the characterisation of countries as "democratic," "law abiding," "human rights respecting," and so on was a reasonably straightforward exercise, if only the political will were present.

The relevant resolutions governing the membership of the Commission never addressed the standards that needed to be met by countries seeking election. Indeed, the only criterion that has ever been important in determining the composition of the Commission was representation of different cultures and legal systems through a geographical balance. Criteria such as relative economic strength, the ability to contribute to the effective implementation of relevant resolutions, compliance with particular standards, or membership of specific treaty regimes have never been seriously contemplated, despite the fact that they are well known in other intergovernmental fora such as the Security Council, the World Bank, the International Monetary Fund and some environmental regimes.

For the purposes of this analysis, the controversy over the Commission's composition can be traced back to May 2001, when the U.S. presented its candidacy for re-election to the Commission on which it had served continuously since 1946. Its defeat, accompanied by the success of candidates perceived to be patently less worthy or qualified, provoked a harsh reaction within the US. Members of Congress talked of "withholding aid from countries that voted against the U.S., although the fact that the ballot was secret rendered that option infeasible. The then National Security Adviser, Condoleezza Rice, condemned the vote, saying that the "sad thing is that the country that has been the beacon for those fleeing tyranny for 200 years is not on this commission, and Sudan is. . . . It's very bad for those people who are suffering under tyranny around the world. And it is an outrage." A rather different approach was taken by China's official *Xinhua News Agency*, which said the U.S. lost because it had "undermined the atmosphere for dialogue" and had used "human rights . . . as a tool to pursue its power politics and hegemony in the world."

GENERAL ASSEMBLY RESOLUTION 60/251,
U.N. Doc. A/RES/60/251 (Apr. 3, 2006)

The General Assembly . . .

1. *Decides* to establish the Human Rights Council, based in Geneva, in replacement of the Commission on Human Rights, as a subsidiary organ of the General Assembly; the Assembly shall review the status of the Council within five years;

2. *Decides* that the Council shall be responsible for promoting universal respect for the protection of all human rights and fundamental freedoms for all, without distinction of any kind and in a fair and equal manner;

3. *Decides also* that the Council should address situations of violations of human rights, including gross and systematic violations, and make recommendations thereon. It should also promote the effective coordination and the mainstreaming of human rights within the United Nations system;

4. *Decides further* that the work of the Council shall be guided by the principles of universality, impartiality, objectivity and non-selectivity, constructive international dialogue and cooperation, with a view to enhancing the promotion and protection of all human rights, civil, political, economic, social and cultural rights, including the right to development;

5. *Decides* that the Council shall, *inter alia*:

(*a*) Promote human rights education and learning as well as advisory services, technical assistance and capacity-building, to be provided in consultation with and with the consent of Member States concerned;

(*b*) Serve as a forum for dialogue on thematic issues on all human rights;

(*c*) Make recommendations to the General Assembly for the further development of international law in the field of human rights;

(*d*) Promote the full implementation of human rights obligations undertaken by States and follow-up to the goals and commitments related to the promotion and protection of human rights emanating from United Nations conferences and summits;

(*e*) Undertake a universal periodic review, based on objective and reliable information, of the fulfillment by each State of its human rights obligations and commitments in a manner which ensures universality of coverage and equal treatment with respect to all States; the review shall be a cooperative mechanism, based on an interactive dialogue, with the full involvement of the country concerned and with consideration given to its capacity-building needs; such a mechanism shall complement and not duplicate the work of treaty bodies; the Council shall develop the modalities and necessary time allocation for the universal periodic review mechanism within one year after the holding of its first session;

(*f*) Contribute, through dialogue and cooperation, towards the prevention of human rights violations and respond promptly to human rights emergencies;

(*g*) Assume the role and responsibilities of the Commission on Human Rights relating to the work of the Office of the United Nations High Commissioner for Human Rights, as decided by the General Assembly in its resolution 48/141 of 20 December 1993;

(*h*) Work in close cooperation in the field of human rights with Governments, regional organizations, national human rights institutions and civil society;

(*i*) Make recommendations with regard to the promotion and protection of human rights;

(*j*) Submit an annual report to the General Assembly

6. *Decides also* that the Council shall assume, review and, where necessary, improve and rationalize all mandates, mechanisms, functions and responsibilities of the Commission on Human Rights in order to maintain a system of special procedures, expert advice and a complaint procedure; the Council shall complete this review within one year after the holding of its first session;

7. *Decides further* that the Council shall consist of forty-seven Member States, which shall be elected directly and individually by secret ballot by the majority of the members of the General Assembly; the membership shall be based on equitable geographical distribution, and seats shall be distributed as follows among regional groups: Group of African States, thirteen; Group of Asian States, thirteen; Group of Eastern European States, six; Group of Latin American and Caribbean States, eight; and Group of Western European and other States, seven; the members of the Council shall serve for a period of three years and shall not be eligible for immediate re-election after two consecutive terms; . . .

10. *Decides further* that the Council shall meet regularly throughout the year and schedule no fewer than three sessions per year, including a main session, for a total duration of no less than ten weeks, and shall be able to hold special sessions, when needed, at the request of a member of the Council with the support of one third of the membership of the Council; . . .

Questions and Discussion

1. It may be too soon to tell whether the Council will be able to overcome the criticisms of the Commission. *See* Gareth Sweeny & Yuri Saito, *An NGO Assessment of the New Mechanisms of the U.N. Human Rights Council*, 9 Hum. Rts. L. Rev. 203, 218–19 (2009). The Council was criticized early in an editorial for continuing to be too soft on human

rights violators. *See A Discredit to the United Nations*, N.Y. TIMES, Nov. 21, 2006, at A28. Other assessment was more positive. *See* Helen Upton, *The Human Rights Council: First Impressions and Future Challenges*, 7 HUM. RTS. L. REV. 29, 39 (2007).

2. The old Commission had fifty-three members, which met each year for six weeks at a single session in March and April. In addition, special sessions were sometimes called. The new Council has forty-seven members and meets regularly throughout the year, in at least three sessions, which together, run no less than ten weeks. It can also hold special sessions. As of March 2011, it had held sixteen such sessions, eight of them concerning Israel and the occupied territories. Members of the Council, like members of the Commission, are diplomats or other governmental representatives (as opposed to human rights experts). This caused the Commission's deliberations to become frequently politicized. It is difficult to see how this politicization will be avoided by the Council.

3. The former Sub-Commission for the Promotion and Protection of Human Rights (earlier titled the Sub-Commission on Prevention of Discrimination and Protection of Minorities) was a body of twenty-six independent experts. As independent experts, the Sub-Commission members often took more radical positions than the old Commission. In connection with human rights and the environment, as noted in Chapter 2, pp. 133–34 in August 1989, the Sub-Commission appointed Mrs. Fatma Zohra Ksentini as special rapporteur, to ultimately prepare a study of the problem of the environment and its relation to human rights. Following five years of work, the special rapporteur released a final report that included Draft Principles on Human Rights and the Environment, reprinted in the Online Case Studies and Material that accompany this text. The principles were passed on to the Human Rights Commission for its consideration. The Commission sought and received comments from governments and NGOs, but the Declaration was not approved before the demise of the Commission and has not been taken up by the Council. Instead, the issue has moved to the agenda of UNEP. Is this a better place for it?

The following excerpt gives you a glimpse at the rationale behind what Professors Birnie and Boyle have called "an extensive and sophisticated statement of environmental rights and obligations at the international level based on a survey of national and international human rights law and international environmental law." PATRICIA BIRNIE & ALAN BOYLE, INTERNATIONAL LAW AND THE ENVIRONMENT 255 (2d ed., 2002). It also refers to a number of human rights organizations that we will consider in this chapter.

> ### Review of Further Developments in Fields with Which the Sub-Commission Has Been Concerned: Human Rights and the Environment,
> U.N. Doc. E/CN.4/Sub.2/1994/9 (July 6, 1994)
> **Fatma Zohra Ksentini, Special Rapporteur**

For the particular purposes of this study of human rights and the environment, it is . . . important to establish the legal framework for pursuing what have become the essential demands of this century, in order to take up the legitimate concerns of our generation, to preserve the interests of future generations and mutually to agree upon the components of a right to a healthy and flourishing environment.

The Special Rapporteur remains convinced that providing the various agents and beneficiaries of this evolving right with the legal framework and means of expression, communication, participation and action will reinforce the channels for dialogue, discussion and cooperation nationally, regionally and internationally, thereby making it possible to define the mutually agreed component of this right as well as its harmonious application, in conformity with the universally recognized fundamental principles of human rights. Human rights would thereby gain a new dimension. In addition, they should make it possible to go beyond reductionist concepts of "mankind first" or "ecology first" and achieve a coalescence of the common objectives of development and environmental protection. This would signify a return to the principal objective that inspired the Universal Declaration of Human Rights, whose article 28 states: "Everyone is entitled to a social and international order in which the rights and freedoms set forth in this Declaration can be fully realized." . . .

The problems of the environment are no longer being viewed exclusively from the angle of the pollution affecting the industrialized countries but seen rather as a worldwide hazard threatening the planet and the whole of mankind, as well as future generations. There is now a universal awareness of the widespread, serious and complex character of environmental problems, which call for adequate action at the national, regional and international levels.

The realization of the global character of environmental problems is attested to by the progress made in understanding the phenomena that create hazards for the planet, threaten the living conditions of human beings and impair their fundamental rights. These phenomena concern not only the natural environment (the pollution of water, air and atmosphere, seas, oceans and rivers; depletion of the ozone layer; climatic changes) and natural resources (desertification, deforestation, soil erosion, disappearance of certain animal species; deterioration of flora and fauna; exhaustion of non-renewable resources, etc.) but also populations and human settlements (housing, town planning, demography, etc.), and the rights of human beings (the human environment, living, working and health conditions; conditions for the exercise and enjoyment of fundamental rights) . . . .

Environmental damage has direct effects on the enjoyment of a series of human rights, such as the right to life, to health, to a satisfactory standard of living, to sufficient food, to housing, to education, to work, to culture, to non-discrimination, to dignity and the harmonious development of one's personality, to security of person and family, to development, to peace, etc. . . .

Conversely, human rights violations in their turn damage the environment. This is true of the right of peoples to self-determination and their right to dispose of their wealth and natural resources, the right to development, to participation, to work and to information, the right of peaceful assembly, freedom of association, freedom of expression, etc.

In the light of the foregoing, the Special Rapporteur is of the view that effective implementation of the right to a satisfactory environment cannot be dissociated from the twinned efforts to preserve the environment and ensure the right to development. Nor can it be achieved without resolute action to ensure the enjoyment of all human rights.

In order to give practical expression to the right to a satisfactory environment, there is a need for development strategies that are directed towards the implementation of a substantive part of that right (the right to development, to life, to health, to work, etc.). These must go hand in hand with the promotion of the related procedural aspects (due process, right of association and of assembly, freedom of expression, right of recourse, etc.).

Implementation of the right to a satisfactory environment calls for commitment and participation on the part of everyone at all levels, beginning with the family unit, where environmental education starts. It depends on the existence of effective national legal remedies; local administrative or other courts, national institutions and ombudsmen provide guarantees of the protection of this right. The Special Rapporteur notes with satisfaction the development of such recourse guarantees in many countries.

The right to a satisfactory environment is also a right to prevention[,] which gives a new dimension to the right to information, education, and participation in decision-making. The right to restitution, indemnification, compensation, and rehabilitation for victims must also be seen from the angle of the special responsibility that would follow from the absence of preventive measures.

The right to a satisfactory environment is also a right to the "conservation" of nature for the benefit of future generations. This "futuristic" dimension restores to human rights their original purpose, as embodied in the Charter of the United Nations and the Universal Declaration of Human Rights of 1948. It foreshadows a "new public order" of human rights which would set acceptable limitations on those rights in the general interest while entailing corresponding duties on the part both of the public authorities and of individuals, associations and other components of civil society. . . .

Recommendations

The "human rights" component of the right to a satisfactory environment lends itself . . . to immediate implementation by various bodies, under existing mechanisms for following up regional and international human rights instruments. The practice being developed within those bodies is decisive and should bring into sharper focus the content of the right to a satisfactory environment, the ways and means of implementing it, and the related procedural aspects.

The Special Rapporteur recommends that the various human rights bodies should examine, in the various fields of concern to them, the environmental dimension of the human rights under their responsibility. . . .

In submitting the draft declaration of principles on human rights and the environment contained in the annex to this report to the Sub-Commission on Prevention of Discrimination and Protection of Minorities and the Commission on Human Rights, the Special Rapporteur expresses the hope that the draft will help the United Nations to adopt, in the course of the present United Nations Decade of International Law, a set of norms consolidating the right to a satisfactory environment – defined as an integral part of the world partnership for peace, development and progress for all.

C. *Human Rights Council Special Procedures*

Special Procedures of the Human Rights Council, *available at*
http://www2.ohchr.org/english/bodies/chr/special/index.htm
Office of the U.N. High Commissioner for Human Rights

"Special procedures" is the general name given to the mechanisms established by the Commission on Human Rights and assumed by the Human Rights Council to address either specific country situations or thematic issues in all parts of the world. Currently, there are 31 thematic and 8 country mandates. The Office of the High Commissioner for Human Rights provides these mechanisms with personnel, policy, research and logistical support for the discharge of their mandates.

Special procedures' mandates usually call on mandate holders to examine, monitor, advise and publicly report on human rights situations in specific countries or territories, known as country mandates, or on major phenomena of human rights violations worldwide, known as thematic mandates. Various activities are undertaken by special procedures, including responding to individual complaints, conducting studies, providing advice on technical cooperation at the country level, and engaging in general promotional activities.

Special procedures are either an individual (called "Special Rapporteur," "Special Representative of the Secretary-General" or "Independent Expert") or a working group usually composed of five members (one from each region). The mandates of the special procedures are established and defined by the resolution creating them. Mandate-holders of the special procedures serve in their personal capacity, and do not receive salaries or any other financial compensation for their work. The independent status of the mandate-holders is crucial in order to be able to fulfill their functions in all impartiality. . . .

Most Special Procedures receive information on specific allegations of human rights violations and send urgent appeals or letters of allegation to governments asking for clarification. In 2008, a total of 911 communications were sent to Governments in 118 countries. [Sixty-six percent] of these were joint communications of two or more mandate holders.

Mandate holders also carry out country visits to investigate the situation of human rights at the national level. They typically send a letter to the Government requesting to visit the country, and, if the Government agrees, an invitation to visit is extended. Some countries have issued "standing invitations," which means that they are, in principle, prepared to receive a visit from any special procedures mandate holder. As of 10 February 2010, 67 States had extended standing invitations to the special procedures. After their visits, special procedures' mandate-holders issue a mission report containing their findings and recommendations.

Starting June 2006, the Human Rights Council engaged in an institution building process, which included a review of the special procedures system. On 18 June 2007, at the conclusion of its fifth session, the Human Rights Council adopted a Resolution 5/1 entitled "Institution-building of the United Nations Human Rights Council," which included provisions on the selection of mandate holders and the review of all special procedures mandates. The review was conducted throughout 2007 and 2008. All thematic mandates were extended. New thematic mandates have also been established, namely on contemporary forms of slavery (2007), on access to safe drinking water and sanitation (2008) and on cultural rights (2009). Country mandates have been extended with the exception of Belarus, Cuba, the Democratic Republic of the Congo and Liberia. At its 11th session, the Human Right Council created the mandate of independent expert on the situation of human rights in the Sudan, which replaced a previous country mandate, for a period of one year. The independent expert was appointed at the 12th session of the Human Rights Council. A mandate-holder's tenure in a given function, whether it is a thematic or country mandate, will be no longer than six years (two terms of three years for thematic mandate-holders).

In June 2007, the Council also adopted Resolution 5/2, containing a Code of Conduct for special procedures mandate holders. At the Annual Meeting of special procedures in June 2008, special procedures mandate holders adopted their Manual, which provides guidelines on the working methods of special procedures. At the same meeting, they also adopted an Internal Advisory Procedure to review practices and working methods, by which the Code of Conduct and other relevant documents, including the Manual, are implemented to enhance the effectiveness and independence both of the special procedures system as a whole and of individual mandate-holders. At its 8th session, the Human Rights Council adopted a Presidential statement concerning the terms of special procedures mandate holders and their compliance with the Code of Conduct.

Questions and Discussion

1. The excerpt on Special Procedures of the Human Rights Council by the Office of the High Commissioner for Human Rights refers to thematic issues as a type of special procedures mechanism. These are in contrast to individual country studies. The thematic approach was developed in the 1980s by the Commission to address a specific human rights problem, such as forced disappearances, after a few countries objected to being singled out for violations that they claimed were widespread. Thus, thematic mechanisms look at a particular issue, such as the adverse effects of the illicit movement and dumping of toxic and dangerous products and wastes on the enjoyment of human rights. Special rapporteurs are regularly invited to make on-site visits by states. Why would these countries, or any country, open themselves to greater risk of exposure on human rights issues by extending a standing invitation?

2. Special procedures also often, but not always, allow special rapporteurs to receive information about human rights abuses in particular states and to communicate that information

to the government concerned. When a thematic rapporteur receives information that suggests the need for an urgent appeal, the rapporteur communicates with the government in question, seeking information and asking for preventive or investigatory action. A real benefit of the thematic mechanism in terms of individuals seeking to call environmental human rights issues to the fore is that the rapporteur may receive information from NGOs or environmental lawyers. *See* Linda A. Malone & Scott Pasternack, Defending the Environment: Civil Society Strategies to Enforce International Environmental Law 30–31 (2004). Depending on the political nature of the government, these communications are treated seriously or not. Sometimes a communication will prompt an internal investigation and follow-up in national courts if warranted. Other times the communication will be entirely ignored. Although the special rapporteur has no legal enforcement powers, the public exposure involved with an investigation may exert reputational pressure or unleash remedial political actions in the state where the abuse has taken place. In addition, if there are repeated communications against a state, it will create evidence of a pattern of abuse that can be used in other fora.

3. While many of the individuals involved in the U.N. Special Procedures (either country or thematic) display far more independence than the members of the Council, their effectiveness can be limited by political and funding problems. The countries being examined must consent to visits, for example, while the individuals serving as rapporteurs or on working groups are, like the treaty body members, part-time, and only their expenses are covered. In his report "Strengthening of the United Nations: An Agenda for Further Change," U.N. Doc. A/57/387 (Sept. 9, 2002), Secretary-General Kofi Annan stated that the quality of the work by the special procedures needed to be improved and that the U.N. had to better support the special procedures. How can this be done? How can the sovereignty barrier be hurdled?

4. Former Secretary-General Kofi Annan described the special procedures as the "crown jewel" of the U.N. human rights system. As the previous reading indicates, there are two general types of special procedures. First, there are country mandates in which mandate holders investigate situations in specific countries that appear to reveal a consistent pattern of gross human rights violations. Second, there are thematic procedures that are devoted to a human rights issue or theme that transcend any particular state and are likely to be global in scope. Regardless of the type of special procedure, all of them serve at least two basic functions: (1) a fact-finding function in individual cases and (2) a norm development function. How do you think these mechanisms can be employed to help protect the environment?

1. Fact-Finding

Regardless of the title employed (special rapporteur, special representative of the secretary-general, representative of the secretary-general, representative of the commission on human rights, independent expert), the special procedures of the Human Rights Council serve, in large measure, a fact-finding function. International human rights monitors involved in special procedures are charged with determining the accurate nature of a given situation and reporting on how human rights are implicated in the situation. Political objectivity and procedural fairness are essential for special procedures to have the desired impact. Accordingly, the individuals appointed as fact-finders have distinguished credentials and a Code of Conduct was approved for country mandate holders of special procedures on June 2007.

The in-country visits that fact-finding entails are a vital component of the special procedures. Amnesty International, a human rights NGO, observes that these special procedures
"are at the core of the U.N. human rights machinery. As independent and objective experts
who are able to monitor and rapidly respond to allegations of violations occurring anywhere
in the world, they play a critical and often unique role in promoting and protecting human
rights. They are among the most innovative, responsive and flexible tools of the human rights
machinery." The problem of state consent for a visit, however, raises obstacles for fact-finding.
For instance, the special rapporteur on torture recently listed thirty-one countries to which
requests for visits had been issued and remained pending.

A special procedures mandate holder can – instead of an in-country visit, or in addition –
employ the techniques of allegation letters and urgent actions. The allegation letter requests
a government to respond to allegations of human rights abuses. The urgent actions are used
to issue a request to a government to take or cease actions to prevent or mitigate human rights
violations.

The excerpt that follows illustrates the common approach of mandate holders. It contains
the rules by which fact-finding is conducted (whether by visit, allegation letter, or urgent
actions).

Manual of the United Nations Human Rights Special Procedures (August 2008), *available at*
http://www2.ohchr.org/english/bodies/chr/special/docs/Manual_English_23jan.pdf
Coordinating Committee of Special Procedures, Human Rights Council

Communications
Definition and Purpose

. . .

28. Most Special Procedures provide for the relevant mandate-holders to receive information
from different sources and to act on credible information by sending a communication to the
relevant Government(s). Such communications are sent through diplomatic channels, unless
agreed otherwise between individual Governments and the Office of the High Commissioner for
Human Rights, in relation to any actual or anticipated human rights violations which fall within
the scope of their mandate.

29. Communications may deal with cases concerning individuals, groups or communities,
with general trends and patterns of human rights violations in a particular country or more
generally, or with the content of existing or draft legislation considered to be a matter of concern.
Communications related to adopted or draft legislation may be formulated in various ways, as
required by the specificities of each mandate.

30. Communications do not imply any kind of value judgment on the part of the Special
Procedure concerned and are thus not per se accusatory. They are not intended as a substitute for
judicial or other proceedings at the national level. Their main purpose is to obtain clarification in
response to allegations of violations and to promote measures designed to protect human rights. . . .

35. In communications sent to Governments, the source is normally kept confidential in order
to protect against reprisals or retaliation. An information source may, however, request that its
identity be revealed.

36. In light of information received in response from the Government concerned, or of further
information from sources, the mandate-holder will determine how best to proceed. This might
include the initiation of further inquiries, the elaboration of recommendations or observations to
be published in the relevant report, or other appropriate steps designed to achieve the objectives
of the mandate.

37. The text of all communications sent and responses received thereon is confidential until such time as they are published in relevant reports of mandate-holders or mandate-holders determine that the specific circumstances require action to be taken before that time. Periodic reports issued by the Special Procedures should reflect the communications sent by mandate-holders and annex the governments' responses thereto. They may also contain observations of the mandate-holders in relation to the outcome of the dialogue with the Government. The names of alleged victims are normally reflected in the reports, although exceptions may be made in relation to children and other victims of violence in relation to whom publication of names would be problematic.

2. Criteria for taking action

38. Information submitted to the Special Procedures alleging violations should be in written, printed or electronic form and include full details of the sender's identity and address, and full details of the relevant incident or situation. Information may be sent by a person or a group of persons claiming to have suffered a human rights violation. NGOs and other groups or individuals claiming to have direct or reliable knowledge of human rights violations, substantiated by clear information, may also submit information so long as they are acting in good faith in accordance with the principles of human rights and the provisions of the UN Charter, free from politically motivated stands. Anonymous communications are not considered. Communications may not be exclusively based on reports disseminated by mass media.

39. Allegations should ideally contain clear and concise details regarding the name of individual victim(s) or other identifying information, such as date of birth, sex, passport number and place of residence; ethnic or religious group when appropriate; the name of any community or organization subject to alleged violations; information as to the circumstances, including available information as to the date and place of any incident(s); alleged perpetrators; suspected motives; contextual information; and any steps already taken at the national, regional or international level in relation to the case.

40. A decision to take action on a case or situation rests in the discretion of the mandate-holder. That discretion should be exercised in light of the mandate entrusted to him or her as well as the criteria laid out in the Code of Conduct. The criteria will generally relate to: the reliability of the source and the credibility of information received; the details provided; and the scope of the mandate.

41. Each mandate-holder may adopt criteria or guidelines governing the acceptance of information or the taking of action. A number of Special Procedures have developed standard requirements/questionnaires to facilitate the collection of relevant information. It is up to mandate-holders to seek additional information from the original source or from other appropriate sources in order to clarify the issues or verify the credibility of the information.

42. Unlike the requirements of communication procedures established under human rights treaties, communications may be sent by the mandate holder even if local remedies in the country concerned have not been exhausted. The Special Procedures are not quasi-judicial mechanisms. Rather, they are premised upon the need for rapid action, designed to protect victims and potential victims, and do not preclude in any way the taking of appropriate judicial measures at the national level.

3. Urgent Appeals

43. Urgent appeals are used to communicate information in cases where the alleged violations are time-sensitive in terms of involving loss of life, life-threatening situations or either imminent or ongoing damage of a very grave nature to victims that cannot be addressed in a timely manner by the procedure under letters of allegation. The intention is to ensure that the appropriate State

authorities are informed as quickly as possible of the circumstances so that they can intervene to end or prevent a human rights violation.

44. Urgent appeals are addressed to concerned Governments through diplomatic channels, unless agreed otherwise between individual Governments and the Office of the High Commissioner for Human Rights.

45. Urgent appeals also generally follow a standard format consisting of four parts: (i) a reference to the resolution creating the mandates concerned; (ii) a summary of the available facts, and when applicable an indication of previous action taken on the same case; (iii) an indication of the specific concerns of the mandate-holder in light of the provisions of relevant international instruments and case law; and (iv) a request to the Government to provide information on the substance of the allegations and to take urgent measures to prevent or stop the alleged violations. The content of the questions or requests addressed to the Government will vary significantly according to the situation in each case. Governments are generally requested to provide a substantive response within thirty days. In appropriate cases mandate-holders may decide to make such urgent appeals public by issuing press releases.

4. Letters of Allegation

46. Letters of allegation are used to communicate information about violations that are alleged to have already occurred and in situations where urgent appeals do not apply.

47. Letters of allegation generally follow a standard format consisting of four parts: (i) a reference to the resolution creating the mandate(s) concerned; (ii) a summary of the available facts, and when applicable an indication of previous action taken on the same case; (iii) an indication of the specific concerns of the mandate-holder in light of the provisions of relevant international instruments and case law; and (iv) a request to the Government to provide information on: (a) the substance of the allegations; (b) measures taken to investigate and punish alleged perpetrators; (c) compensation, protection, or assistance provided to the alleged victims; (d) legislative, administrative and other steps taken to avoid the recurrence of such violations in the future; and (e) other relevant information. The content of the specific questions or requests addressed to the Government may vary considerably according to the substance of the allegations.

48. Governments are usually requested to provide a substantive response to communication letters within two months. Some mandate-holders forward the substance of the replies received to the source for its comments.

. . .

C. Country Visits

1. Definition and Purpose

52. Country visits are an essential means to obtain direct and first-hand information on human rights violations. They allow for direct observation of the human rights situation and facilitate an intensive dialogue with all relevant state authorities, including those in the executive, legislative and judicial branches. They also allow for contact with and information gathering from victims, relatives of victims, witnesses, national human rights institutions, international and local NGOs and other members of civil society, the academic community, and officials of international agencies present in the country concerned.

53. Country visits generally last between one and two weeks but can be shorter or longer if the circumstances so require. The visit occurs at the invitation of a State. Its purpose is to assess the actual human rights situation in the country concerned, including an examination of the relevant

institutional, legal, judicial, and administrative aspects and to make recommendations thereon in relation to issues that arise under the relevant mandate.

54. Country visits by mandate-holders provide an opportunity to enhance awareness at the country, regional and international levels of the specific problems under consideration. This is done, *inter alia*, through meetings, briefings, press coverage of the visit and dissemination of the report.

2. Invitations and Requests for Visits

55. A Government may take the initiative to invite a mandate-holder to visit the country. Alternatively a mandate-holder may solicit an invitation by communicating with the Government concerned, by discussions with diplomats of the country concerned, including especially the Permanent Representative to the United Nations Office in Geneva or at Headquarters, or by other appropriate means. The GA, the HRC, or the High Commissioner for Human Rights might also suggest or request that a visit be undertaken.

56. When a State does not respond to requests for an invitation to visit, it is appropriate for a mandate-holder to remind the Government concerned, to draw the attention of the Council to the outstanding request, and to take other appropriate measures designed to promote respect for human rights. An updated table of the status of requests for country visits is maintained on the website of the OHCHR.

57. Considerations which might lead a mandate-holder to request to visit a country include, *inter alia*, human rights developments at the national level (whether positive or negative), the availability of reliable information regarding human rights violations falling within the mandate, or a wish to pursue a particular thematic interest. Other factors which might be taken into account in determining which visits to undertake at any particular time might include considerations of geographical balance, the expected impact of the visit and the willingness of national actors to cooperate with the mandate-holder, the likelihood of follow-up on any recommendations made, the recent adoption by one or more treaty bodies of relevant concluding observations, the upcoming examination of the situation by one or more treaty bodies, recent or proposed visits by other Special Procedure mandate-holders, the list of countries scheduled for consideration under the Council's Universal Periodic Review (UPR) mechanism, follow up to the recommendations and conclusions of the UPR mechanism, and the priorities reflected in OHCHR's country engagement strategy.

58. In 2004, the CHR on Human Rights strongly encouraged all States to extend a "standing invitation" to all thematic Special Procedures. By extending such an invitation States announce that they will automatically accept a request to visit by any of the Special Procedures. The extension of a standing invitation, and the overall cooperation afforded to Special Procedures, are appropriately taken into account by the GA in considering the "pledges and commitments" made by States seeking election to the HRC. Additionally, the Code of Conduct "urges all States to cooperate with, and assist, the special procedures in the performance of their tasks."

59. Where appropriate country visits might be undertaken by several mandate-holders acting together, or by mandate-holders in conjunction with other representatives of the international community.

Questions and Discussion

Working the Fact-Finding Special Procedures. If you were representing an individual or group whose human rights were being violated by environmental harm, would you seek to have the Human Rights Council create a new special procedure to investigate? Or would you use one of the existing mandates, such as the right to food or the right to housing? What would you expect to achieve?

You might also write directly to a country rapporteur if a mandate exists for the country of concern. Current country mandates can be viewed at http://www2.ohchr. org/english/bodies/chr/special/countries.htm. The decision to intervene is at the discretion of the country's mandate holder, but to improve the chance of intervention taking place, you need to address the following:

- Identification of the alleged victim(s)
- Identification of the alleged perpetrators of the violation
- Identification of the person(s) or organization(s) submitting the communication (this information will be kept confidential)
- Date and place of incident
- A detailed description of the circumstances of the incident in which the alleged violation occurred.

See http://www2.ohchr.org/english/bodies/chr/special/communications.htm.

The investigations of special rapporteurs are ordinarily made available to the public. As you read the following two excerpts, identify areas that a lawyer could draw on to press for more human rights protection.

Report of the Special Rapporteur on the Adverse Effects of the Illicit Movement and Dumping of Toxic and Dangerous Products and Wastes on the Enjoyment of Human Rights, U.N. Doc. A/HRC/7/21/Add.3 (Feb. 28, 2008) – Preliminary Note on the Mission to the United Republic of Tanzania (Jan. 21–30, 2008)

INTRODUCTION

1. The Special Rapporteur on the adverse effects of the illicit movement and dumping of toxic and dangerous products and wastes on the enjoyment of human rights carried out a fact-finding mission to the United Republic of Tanzania from 21 to 30 January 2008. This preliminary note provides the initial observations and recommendations of the Special Rapporteur. A full report, including his conclusions and recommendations will be submitted subsequently to the Human Rights Council.

2. The Special Rapporteur would like to thank the Government of the United Republic of Tanzania for extending an invitation to him. He would like to thank in particular the Ministry of Foreign Affairs and International Cooperation and the Ministry of Energy and Minerals for their contribution and efforts in organizing the mission while regretting that he did not have full opportunity to brief in person relevant officials at the end of his mission, as it was not possible to arrange suitable meetings. The Special Rapporteur further regrets that he was unable to meet relevant authorities and visit sites which deal with industrial toxic wastes and dangerous products such as Persistent Organic Pollutants (POPs) and Polychlorinated biphenyls (PCBs).

3. During the visit, the Special Rapporteur was able to have meetings with a variety of stakeholders including the Vice President's Office – Division of Environment, National Environment Management Council, Dar es Salaam City Council, the Ministry of Health and Social Welfare, the Tanzania Port Authority, Occupational Health and Safety Authority, and the Government Chemist Laboratory Agency. The Special Rapporteur also met with the Lake Victoria Environmental Management Project, academics, non-governmental organizations and a wide range of

civil society, mining consulting companies and individuals and villagers in the Lake Victoria area practicing small-scale mining.

4. The Special Rapporteur visited areas within and around Dar es Salaam including the Mtoni and Pugukinyamwezi dumpsites. He also visited the Lake Victoria Area including the cities and regions of Mwanza, Geita and Shinyanga. In Geita, he had the opportunity to visit the Geita Gold Mine and Nyaragusu areas where small-scale and medium-scale gold mining is taking place. In Shinyanga, he was able to see areas where small-scale diamond mining is taking place. Finally, the Special Rapporteur visited the Williamson Diamond Mine in Mwadui . . . .

6. The objective of the Special Rapporteur's mission to the United Republic of Tanzania was to enable him to gather first-hand information on the impact that mining activities are having on the human rights of the local population. The Special Rapporteur also looked at the use of chemicals and the waste management system for both industrial and domestic waste in the country.

GENERAL OBSERVATIONS

Adequate Legal Framework

7. The Special Rapporteur observed that the Government of the United Republic of Tanzania has a comprehensive range of laws and subsidiary instruments that deal with the particular issue of toxic and dangerous products and wastes. Some examples that he wishes to highlight include the Mining Act of 1998, the Industrial and Consumer Chemical (Management & Control) Act of 2003, the National Environmental Management Act of 2004 and the Land Act of 1999 amongst others. While the Special Rapporteur notes that such legal developments are relatively recent, he looks forward to monitoring implementation of these laws and their ability to limit the adverse effects of toxic and dangerous products and wastes on the environment and on the human rights of the people of the United Republic of Tanzania.

Right to Information

8. The Special Rapporteur notes that the Government does appear to have appropriate mechanisms in place to deal with issues of chemical management. The United Republic of Tanzania has legislation in place protecting the right to information and public participation concerning environmental matters as stipulated in Article 178 of the Environmental Management Act 2004. It appears, however, that there are constraints on the full enforcement of that legislation due to limited capacity of the State. The Special Rapporteur was informed by a variety of stakeholders that the public may not have received any or sufficient information on the different chemical substances and dangerous products that they are exposed to in their workplaces or their communities.

The Mining Sector

Small-scale mining

9. The Special Rapporteur notes with concern the large volume of unregulated small-scale mining that is taking place around the country. He had the opportunity to witness small-scale mining of both gold and diamonds using chemicals such as mercury and other dangerous products during the extraction process without the use of proper safety equipment. He is concerned that substantial amounts of mercury are obtained by small-scale miners from "unofficial" sources[,] which are outside the control of government.

10. In some cases, the miners do not have adequate information about the impact mercury can have on their health and the dangers of the improper disposal of tailings and their effect on their livelihood and the environment. In a number of areas, land, water, plants and livestock may be at

a high risk of contamination from mercury and other dangerous wastes. In other cases, the Special Rapporteur was informed of small-scale miners who have some awareness of the dangers of using mercury and other chemicals in the extraction process. However, due to poverty, inadequate information and the lack of a suitable alternative, the miners continue to use mercury and other dangerous products without appropriate safety measures, endangering both the environment and their own health.

Large-scale mining

11. The Special Rapporteur is concerned about the operations of large mining companies in the United Republic of Tanzania. He observed that there seems to be limited Government supervision of the operations of big mining corporations. He was informed about tensions that have been arising in different parts of the country due to the discontent of local communities affected by large scale mining operations.

12. The Special Rapporteur also notes with concern that large scale gold mining companies do not conduct adequate awareness campaigns to sensitize villagers in their areas of operation of the dangers posed by contact with wastes from their operations, particularly cyanide. The Special Rapporteur was informed of cases in which villagers and livestock have come in contact with such waste with serious consequences.

CONCLUSIONS AND RECOMMENDATIONS

13. The Special Rapporteur acknowledges and welcomes the sensitization efforts undertaken by the Government and other stakeholders for small-scale (artisanal) miners to raise awareness of the effects of mercury and other dangerous chemicals used during the extraction process for gold and diamonds. However, he urges the Government and other stakeholders, including the United Nations Country Team and civil society to step up efforts to inform the public of the risks posed by mining as well as by toxic chemicals used in the textile industries and tanneries. Different media and format should be used and disseminated throughout rural and urban areas in the local languages and dialects. Attention should be paid to isolated rural areas and illiterate populations in order for this effort to be effective.

14. The Government should monitor more closely the operations of large-scale mining companies particularly with regard to occupational health and safety standards and relations between the mining corporations and the surrounding communities.

15.The Special Rapporteur encourages the Government to increase the human and technical resources of the National Environmental Council (NEMC) in order to enable it to carry out its work in both rural and urban areas more effectively.

16. In order to improve regulation of the environmental and human rights impacts of mining activities, the Special Rapporteur urges the Government to develop a database of mining-related illnesses that have affected the communities that inhabit the mining areas.

17. While the Special Rapporteur welcomes the Government's initiative to ensure that environmental impact assessments are carried out before granting mining licenses, it should be noted that environmental impact assessments do not fully take into account the human rights impact of environmental degradation in mining areas. The Special Rapporteur urges the Government and mining corporations to also carry out social impact assessments to better protect and promote the human rights of the local population.

. . .

Press Release, *Toxic Waste: U.N. Expert Releases Report on "Probo Koala" Incident*, (Sept. 16, 2009)

United Nations

GENEVA – "We still don't know – and we may never know – the full effect of the dumping of 500 tons of toxic waste in Cote d'Ivoire," said U.N. expert Okechukwu Ibeanu, "but there seems to be strong prima facie evidence that the reported deaths and adverse health consequences are related to the dumping of the waste from the cargo ship 'Probo Koala.'"

The Special Rapporteur on the adverse effects of the movement and dumping of toxic and dangerous products and wastes on the enjoyment of human rights will present to the press his report to the Human Rights Council concerning the incident. The press conference will take place on Thursday 17 September 2009, at 11:00, in Press Room I at the Palais des Nations, Geneva.

In August 2006, the "Probo Koala" dumped 500 tons of toxic waste belonging to the Dutch commodity trading company Trafigura in various sites in the district of Abidjan, Cote d'Ivoire. According to official estimates, there were 15 deaths, 69 persons hospitalised and more than 108,000 medical consultations resulting from the incident. Prior to its journey to Côte d'Ivoire, the "Probo Koala" had inter alia docked in Amsterdam, the Netherlands.

The report contains the findings and recommendations of the Special Rapporteur concerning his official visits to Côte d'Ivoire and the Netherlands, undertaken as part of his efforts to examine the effects on the enjoyment of human rights of the movement and dumping of toxic and dangerous wastes arising from the incident.

Without prejudice to legal proceedings in the Netherlands and the United Kingdom concerning the exact composition and toxic nature of the waste in question, Ibeanu encouraged all actors involved to take all necessary measures "to address possible long-term human health and environmental effects of the incident."

"Further action should be taken to protect the right to life, the right to the enjoyment of the highest attainable standard of physical and mental health and the right to a healthy environment of all affected victims and their families," stressed the Special Rapporteur.

2. Norm Development

As with the report prepared by Fatma Zohra Ksentini, "Review of Further Developments in Fields with Which the Sub-Commission Has Been Concerned: Human Rights and the Environment," occasionally special rapporteurs contribute to norm development. These reports may provide a theoretical foundation for the progressive development of new human rights norms. They may extrapolate new applications for existing norms to enhance protection against human rights violations. They may indentify lacuna in the law. They may offer persuasive interpretations of custom or treaties. Continuing with the theme of adverse effects of the illicit movement and dumping of toxic and dangerous products and wastes on the enjoyment of human rights, consider the normative synergies present in the following report of the special rapporteur.

Report of the Special Rapporteur on the Adverse Effects of the Illicit Movement and Dumping of Toxic and Dangerous Products and Wastes on the Enjoyment of Human Rights, U.N. Doc. A/HRC/7/21 (Feb. 18, 2008) (footnotes omitted)

The present report contains a summary of the activities of the Special Rapporteur on the adverse effects of the illicit movement and dumping of toxic and dangerous products and wastes on the enjoyment of human rights. In view of the review of the special procedure mandates by the Human Rights Council, the Special Rapporteur outlines the main conclusions developed under the mandate concerning the challenges posed by the illicit movement and dumping of toxic and dangerous products and wastes to the enjoyment of human rights.

The report includes a section highlighting the importance of the right to information and participation. The Special Rapporteur notes that the rights to information and participation are both rights in themselves and essential tools for the exercise of other rights, such as the right to life, the right to the highest attainable standard of health, the right to adequate housing and others. The section includes a discussion of current legal frameworks on the rights to information and participation that exist at the international and regional levels. Reference is also made to the different forms of implementation and monitoring mechanisms that can be used at the national level.

. . .

I. INTRODUCTION

1. The present report is submitted in accordance with General Assembly resolution 60/251 and Human Rights Council resolution 5/1.

2. The Commission on Human Rights adopted its first resolution on the adverse effects of the illicit movement and dumping of toxic and dangerous products and wastes on the enjoyment of human rights in 1995. In its resolution 1995/81, the Commission affirmed that the illicit traffic and the dumping of toxic and dangerous products and wastes constituted a serious threat to the rights to life and health, and it established the mandate of the Special Rapporteur to analyse the adverse effects on human rights of such phenomena. . . .

3. In his first report as mandate-holder (E/CN.4/2005/45), the Special Rapporteur, Okechukwu Ibeanu, informed the Commission that he intended to adopt a thematic focus in his forthcoming reports. He identified criteria such as the extent and gravity of actual or potential human rights violations arising from a particular issue, and whether an analysis from the perspective of victims of human rights violations could add impetus to international efforts to address a particular issue, to be applied when choosing the thematic issues on which to focus his reports.

4. Previous reports submitted to the Commission pursuant to the Special Rapporteur's mandate have addressed a variety of issues, including the adverse effects on human rights resulting from exposure to hazardous chemicals, particularly pesticides. Other reports have included information about the elaborate, multilateral legal framework adopted or being developed in the sphere of international environmental law with a view to preventing adverse effects on humans and the environment from exposure to some of the most dangerous chemicals. In his previous report to the Council, the Special Rapporteur chose to focus on the impact of armed conflict on exposure to toxic and dangerous products and wastes. Although war has always had an adverse effect on the environment, the voluntary or incidental release of toxic and dangerous products in contemporary armed conflicts has an important adverse effect on the enjoyment of human rights.

5. In the present report, the Special Rapporteur has chosen to focus on the right to information and participation. Access to and communication of information about toxic and dangerous products and wastes and their effects on the environment are essential to guarantee certain other rights, such as the rights to life, to health and to adequate food.

. . .

III. ADVERSE EFFECTS ON HUMAN RIGHTS OF THE ILLICIT MOVEMENT AND DUMPING OF TOXIC AND DANGEROUS PRODUCTS AND WASTES

14. In order to facilitate the review of the mandate by the Human Rights Council, the Special Rapporteur wishes to recall some basic information about the illicit movement and dumping

of toxic and dangerous products and wastes, and highlight their impact on fundamental human rights.

15. In recent decades, the movement of hazardous wastes and products across the globe, and particularly from developed to developing countries, has continued to flourish, often without appropriate safeguards, despite international standards and norms which prohibit dumping or illicit movements. Disparities in domestic legal standards and the high costs of disposing of toxic waste effectively and safely have resulted in the regular movement of wastes across borders and frontiers, often illegally.

16. In 1980, 80 per cent of the trade in hazardous wastes was between developed countries. In 1988, between 2 and 2.5 million tons of waste were transported among the European members of the Organization for Economic Cooperation and Development (OECD). In 1987 and 1988, the existence of a number of contracts between Western companies and African countries was made public. The information on the contracts showed that transnational corporations based in developed countries were selling toxic wastes and hazardous products to States in the South, in particular in Africa, where small payments could secure ample land on which to dump such wastes. Transfers of waste were justified initially on the grounds that African countries had adequate land for safe disposal of such wastes and that the income generated could serve development needs. However, the limited technical capacity of such countries to dispose of it was ignored, as were the long-term consequences of burying and incinerating waste, which were the common disposal methods. Increasing global attention to this type of waste transfers led to greater regulation and the emergence of global norms. Unfortunately, regulation then led many companies to increasingly resort to illegal or illicit movement and dumping of wastes and dangerous products, with far-reaching consequences for human rights.

17. The Special Rapporteur notes that, apart from direct transfers of waste and dangerous products, there appears to have been an increase in indirect transfers through the relocation of polluting industries, industrial activities and/or technologies which generate hazardous wastes from OECD to non-OECD countries. High environmental and health standards coupled with strong opposition from local authorities or community and labour organizations in OECD countries have also fuelled such relocation.

18. Although the Special Rapporteur acknowledges that developing countries trade in hazardous products and toxic wastes owing to the poverty and the dire developmental situation of the countries concerned, the overall risks to life, health and the environment always outweigh short-term monetary benefits. The disposal of hazardous products and wastes requires technical knowledge for safe handling, technology which is often not available in destination countries. Advanced technology is needed for the safe disposal of waste, such as that generated by industrial chemicals, pesticides, poison, drugs, "e-wastes" (such as computers, refrigerators and cell phones) and for ship-breaking. Ironically, developed countries that have such technology are increasingly less likely to dispose of such wastes, but instead send them to developing countries that lack the necessary know-how.

19. Given the current scenario, the human rights of local populations in countries that are net receivers of toxic products and wastes are threatened by the dumping of hazardous wastes for disposal or storage and by the trade in hazardous waste for recycling or further use. Such risks are also involved in the selling of wastes to poor countries under the waste-to-energy plants that are often promoted to produce free energy. Other forms of exposure for the local population are generated by lead recycling factories, the export of plastic residues, the export of ships for recycling operations, and the export of waste-intensive industries such as asbestos-related industries, cyanide heap-leaching and chlorine-related facilities in the chlor-alkali industry and tanneries.

20. The Special Rapporteur notes that, because of structural conditions in many developing countries, women and the young are particularly at risk from transfers of toxic and dangerous products and wastes. Women, children and the young are often among the poorest and therefore likely to work in polluting industries and scavenge dumps of waste for reusable materials. They are also most likely to have limited access to information on waste products and to health facilities in the event of contamination. The Special Rapporteur calls for greater global attention to the gender and age dimensions of the illicit movement and dumping of toxic and dangerous products and wastes on the enjoyment of human rights.

21. The prevalence of low environmental standards, weak or no regulatory institutions and poor monitoring, poverty and development needs in developing countries continue to serve as pull factors for the dumping of hazardous products and wastes. The Special Rapporteur would also like to highlight that corruption, both in the developing and developed countries, is sadly a factor in the transboundary movement of hazardous wastes and products.

22. In spite of relevant international normative frameworks related to both the environment and human rights, the trade in hazardous wastes and products persists and is on the increase. The Special Rapporteur notes with disappointment that, where regional mechanisms such as the Bamako Convention exist, the norms and standards they have established are often observed only in the event of breach. Consequently, such regional mechanisms have become ineffective in curbing the illicit transboundary movement of wastes.

23. The impact of the illicit movement and dumping of toxic and dangerous products and wastes can be particularly severe on the enjoyment of the rights to life, health, food and work. The right to a remedy should also be seen as central to the relationship between toxic wastes and human rights.

A. Right to Life

24. The right to life, which is enshrined in article 3 of the Universal Declaration of Human Rights and article 6 of the International Covenant on Civil and Political Rights, is seen as a right which is "non-derogable" and the most important, since without it, all other rights would be devoid of meaning. The Human Rights Committee has said that it is a right that should not be interpreted narrowly and that States should take positive measures to guarantee, including measures to reduce infant mortality and to increase life expectancy.

25. The right to life involves, at the very least, a prohibition on the State not to take life intentionally or negligently. The right to life is one of the first rights to be affected by the production, use, trading and temporary or final disposal, including dumping, of toxic wastes and products. In extreme cases, where environmental disasters such as Chernobyl and Bhopal occur, this right can be invoked by individuals to obtain compensation from the State insofar as it is responsible for the disaster.

26. According to information gathered by the mandate over the years, many of the violations in various parts of the world involve violations of that right in the form of immediate death, life-threatening diseases such as cancer, infant mortality, sterility and other major handicaps and diseases. One such example of such a violation of this right is the Chernobyl incident, which has claimed many victims and displaced populations.

B. Right to the Highest Attainable Standard of Health

27. Every human being is entitled to the enjoyment of the highest attainable standard of health conducive to living in dignity. The Committee on Economic, Social and Cultural Rights noted that the right to health was closely related to and dependent upon the realization of other human rights,

including the rights to food, housing, work, education, human dignity, life, non-discrimination, equality, the prohibition of torture, privacy, access to information and the freedoms of association, assembly and movement. Furthermore, the Committee recognized that the highest attainable standard of physical and mental health was not confined to the right to health care, but embraced a wide range of socio-economic factors that promoted conditions in which people could lead a healthy life and extended to the underlying determinants of health, such as food and nutrition, housing, access to safe and potable water and adequate sanitation, safe and healthy working conditions and a healthy environment.

C. Right to Adequate Food

28. The right to adequate food is part of the broader right to an adequate standard of living, which also includes housing and clothing, and the distinct fundamental right to be free from hunger, which aims at preventing people from starving and is closely linked to the right to life. As is the case for other human rights, this right is indivisibly linked to the inherent dignity of the human person and is indispensable for the fulfilment of other universal guarantees enshrined in the International Bill of Human Rights. The Committee on Economic, Social and Cultural Rights considers that the core content of the right to adequate food implies the availability of food in a quantity and quality sufficient to satisfy the dietary needs of individuals, free from adverse substances, and acceptable within a given culture.

D. Right to Work

29. The right to work is enshrined in article 23 of the Universal Declaration of Human Rights and article 6 of the International Covenant on Economic, Social and Cultural Rights. Every individual has the right to be able to work, allowing the person to live in dignity. According to the Committee on Economic, Social and Cultural Rights, the right to work is a fundamental right which is essential for realizing other human rights and forms an inseparable and inherent part of human dignity. The right to work plays an important role in the survival of the individual as well as that of his or her family.

E. Right to Remedy

30. Where there is a right, there is a remedy. This principle is expressed in article 2, paragraph 3(a), of the International Covenant on Civil and Political Rights, which guarantees victims of human rights violations an effective remedy. There are two aspects to the right to a remedy: access to justice and substantive redress. They require the existence of independent and impartial bodies with the capacity to afford redress after a hearing which respects due process guarantees. More and more national administrative and judicial bodies throughout the world are giving effect to the right to a remedy in cases of alleged violations of constitutional rights to a sound environment, related in some cases to the right to life or to health. While the International Covenant on Economic, Social and Cultural Rights has no provision comparable to article 2(3) of the International Covenant on Civil and Political Rights, it has been argued that the rights it recognizes also require that remedies be available for victims of violations. The Committee on Economic, Social and Cultural Rights has noted, for example, that any person or group victim of a violation of the right to health should have access to effective judicial or other appropriate remedies at both the national and international levels and should be entitled to adequate reparation.

IV. RIGHT TO INFORMATION AND PARTICIPATION

31. The Special Rapporteur has decided to focus the present report on the importance of the right to information and participation in relation to his mandate. He continues to receive information and communications with regard to the violation of the right to information in environmental

matters. Trends show that States, corporations and other private entities generally do not share vital information about the potential effects of pollution and irreversible damage to the environment until an incident has occurred. In such cases and when an incident has occurred, the relevant authorities and/or actors are often reluctant to disclose information of vital importance to the victims and their defence. Such information is either withheld, falsified, provided after a delayed amount of time or given piecemeal in order to confuse or be deemed unusable. Governmental authorities often justify this behaviour on national security grounds, transnational corporations for considerations of trade secrecy.

32. The Special Rapporteur considers that the right to information and participation are both rights in themselves and also essential to the exercise of other rights, such as the right to life, the right to the highest attainable standard to health and the right to adequate food, among others. Lack of information denies people the opportunity to develop their potential to the fullest and realize the full range of their human rights.

33. The Special Rapporteur considers the right to information and participation highly relevant in the context of the adverse effects of the illicit movement and dumping of toxic and dangerous products on the environment and on the enjoyment of basic human rights. Public access to information when requested and the obligation of public authorities to disclose and inform, irrespective of requests, are imperative for the prevention of environmental human rights problems and the protection of the environment.

34. The Special Rapporteur notes that there are many cases that have been brought to his attention of disputes between citizens and Governments in developing countries and between developing countries and transnational corporations over the movement of toxic and dangerous products and wastes. Disputes often arise owing to a lack of information or the failure of the State or of corporations to ensure full disclosure of the potential dangers of activities carried out by those corporations to individuals, communities and the environment. He notes that, in many cases, even Governments claim not to have access to the necessary information on the potential dangers to human beings and the environment.

35. The Special Rapporteur would like to stress that the responsibility of States is particularly important when dealing with the issue of toxic waste, including the disposal of nuclear wastes, and the production or use of pesticides, chemical products and toxins because of the dangers to the health and well-being of human beings that they pose.

36. National security, "trade secrets," the principle of confidentiality of matters *sub judice*, or other grounds invoked against reasonable requests for information on toxic and dangerous products and wastes must be applied with caution. The Special Rapporteur stresses that Governments may only invoke such grounds insofar as they are in conformity with the relevant derogation or limitation clauses of international human rights instruments. The use of such concepts must be regularly reviewed to ensure that the public's right to information is not unduly restricted.

37. The Special Rapporteur considers it important that individuals, communities and neighbour-ing countries have information regarding hazardous materials and conditions at industrial facilities located in their vicinity in order to undertake disaster risk reduction and preparedness wherever there is a danger of large-scale industrial accidents, like those in Chernobyl and Bhopal. Individ-uals, communities and neighbouring countries must have information regarding the full extent of environmental impact of proposed development projects in their regions in order to participate meaningfully in decisions that could expose them to increased pollution, environmental degra-dation and other such effects. Individuals, communities and neighbouring countries must have information regarding pollutants and wastes associated with industrial and agricultural processes. The Special Rapporteur considers it a clear duty of the State to disclose such information.

38. In developing countries, the Special Rapporteur notes the frequent violation of the right to information regarding the transboundary movement of wastes and dangerous products. Among other things, the Special Rapporteur notes with great concern that toxic wastes and dangerous products are often not labelled in the local language, which further exposes the population to severe health and environmental risks. In addition, it must be mentioned that hazardous products and wastes in developing nations are frequently dumped in rural and isolated areas, where there is a high prevalence of illiteracy and inadequate information.

39. Widespread political instability in many developing countries means that vital information that is necessary to the health, environment and well-being of the population is often withheld from the public, apparently on the grounds that it is necessary to uphold national security, and prevent civil unrest. In his previous report to the Council (A/HRC/5/5), the Special Rapporteur stated that one of the consequences of armed conflicts was the trafficking of dangerous products and wastes and their illicit dumping. Armed conflicts can also have a negative impact on the right to information and participation, which in turn increases the likelihood that toxic wastes and products will be illicitly moved and dumped.

40. Although the media could play an indispensable role in information dissemination in communities, countries and regions, as well as both the rural and urban areas about the illegal movement of hazardous products and wastes, it is often the case in developing countries that the freedom of the press is severely curtailed or simply does not exist.

41. The rights to information and participation, and their particular importance for both human rights and environment matters, are, however, well reflected in the international legal framework, in both human rights law and environmental law. Some basic elements of that legal framework and the importance of monitoring mechanisms are described below. . . .

42. The right to information is frequently presented as an individual and group right that constitutes an essential feature of democratic processes and of the right to participation in public life. Article 19 of the Universal Declaration of Human Rights states that everyone has the right to freedom of opinion and expression; that right includes freedom to hold opinions without interference and to seek, receive, and impart information and ideas through any media and regardless of frontiers. Article 21 of the Declaration would be rendered meaningless unless individuals and groups have access to relevant information on which to base the exercise of the vote or otherwise express the will of the people.

43. The right as a legally binding treaty obligation is enshrined in article 19 of the International Covenant on Civil and Political Rights. Article 19(2) stipulates that everyone should have the right to freedom of expression; that right should include freedom to seek, receive and impart information and ideas of all kinds, regardless of frontiers, either orally, in writing or in print, in the form of art, or through any other media of his choice. Article 19(3) does allow certain restrictions, but they should only be such as are provided by law and are necessary (a) for the respect of the rights and reputations of others; (b) for the protection of national security or of public order, or of public health and morals. Article 25 of the Covenant in turn prescribes that every citizen should have the right and the opportunity to take part in the conduct of public affairs.

44. While there are no explicit references in the core international human rights treaties to the right to information and participation with regard to environmental matters, the Special Rapporteur would like to recall that the Rio Declaration on Environment and Development focused on the right to information, participation and remedies with regard to environmental conditions. Principle 10 of the Rio Declaration stipulates that participation of all concerned citizens should be practised when environmental issues are concerned. At the national level, it calls for each individual to have appropriate access to all appropriate information concerning the environment

held by public authorities, including information on hazardous materials and activities in their communities, and the opportunity to participate in decision-making processes. It further calls upon States to facilitate and encourage public awareness and participation by making information widely available. It further calls upon States to ensure that access to judicial and administrative proceedings, including redress and remedy, is provided.

45. Principle 18 of the Declaration calls upon States to immediately notify other States of any natural disasters or other emergencies that are likely to produce sudden harmful effects on the environment of those States. It reminds States that efforts should be made by the international community to help States that are afflicted by such calamities. Principles 20, 21 and 22 call for the wide participation of women, youth, indigenous peoples and other communities in protecting the environment and fostering development.

46. Article 15(2) of the Rotterdam Convention on the Prior Informed Consent Procedure for Certain Hazardous Chemicals and Pesticides in International Trade of 10 September 1998 requires each State party to ensure, to the extent practicable, that the public has appropriate access to information on chemical handling and accident management and on alternatives that are safer for human health or the environment than the chemicals listed in annex III to the Convention.

47. The Stockholm Convention on Persistent Organic Pollutants of 22 May 2001 aims at protecting human health and the environment from persistent organic pollutants. Article 10(i) provides that each party should, within its capabilities, promote and facilitate provision to the public of all available information on persistent organic pollutants and ensure that the public has access to public information and that the information is kept up to date. The Convention also calls for education and public awareness programmes to be developed, in particular for women, children and the poorly educated (art. 10(1)(c)). Parties to the Convention are also obligated to make accessible to the public, on a timely and regular basis, the results of their research, development and monitoring activities pertaining to persistent organic pollutants (art. 11(2)(e)). The Convention stipulates that, although parties that exchange information pursuant to the Convention should protect any confidential information, information on health and safety of humans and the environment should not be regarded as confidential (art. 9(5)).

48. The Basel Convention on the Control of Transboundary Movements of Hazardous Wastes and Their Disposal sets out obligations for the exchange of information for both the State concerned and interested parties. In article 4(2)(f), the Convention clearly requires that information about a proposed transboundary movement of hazardous wastes and other wastes be provided to the States concerned and that it clearly state the effects of the proposed movement on human health and the environment. In article 4(2)(h), it encourages cooperation through activities with other parties and/or interested organizations for the dissemination of information on transboundary movements in order to improve environmentally sound management and to work towards the prevention of illegal traffic. Article 13(1) provides that parties to the Convention should ensure that, should an accident occur during the transboundary movement of wastes and other wastes or their disposal and that is likely to present risks to human health and the environment in other States, those States are immediately informed.

49. The Convention on Access to Information, Public Participation in Decision-Making and Access to Justice in Environmental Matters, signed in Aarhus, Denmark, on 25 June 1998, takes a very comprehensive approach to the recognition of the importance of the right to information and public participation. As [of] 17 September 2007, there were 41 parties to the Convention. Although it was open for signature only to State members of the Economic Commission for Europe and those with consultative status with it (art. 17), article 19 of the Convention opens the door to accession by other States on the condition that they are members of the United Nations and that the accession is approved by the meeting of the parties to the Convention. In the preamble, it

states that "every person has the right to live in an environment adequate to his or her health and well-being, and the duty, both individually and in association with others, to protect and improve the environment for the benefit of present and future generations." In the following paragraph, it states that, in order to be able to assert that right and observe that duty, citizens must have access to information, be entitled to participate in decision-making and have access to justice in environmental matters, and, in that regard, citizens may need assistance in order to exercise their rights.

50. Articles 4 and 5 of the Convention obligates States parties to collect and publicly disseminate information, and to make such information available to the public in response to requests. Each party to the Convention is to publish a national report on the state of the environment every three to four years. In addition to the national report, the party is obliged to disseminate legislative and policy documents, treaties and other international instruments relating to the environment. Each party must ensure that public authorities, upon request, provide environmental information to a requesting person without the latter having to state an interest. Information should be made public within one month, or, in exceptional cases, in not more than two months (art. 4(2)). In addition to providing information on request, each State party must be proactive, ensuring that public authorities collect and update environmental information relevant to their functions. This requires States parties to establish mandatory systems to obtain information on proposed and existing activities which could significantly affect the environment. (art. 5(1)). The Convention does provide for a number of exceptions in article 4(4) to the duty to inform, in the light of other political, economic and legal considerations, but they are to be interpreted in a restrictive way and take into account the public interest served by disclosure.

51. Public participation is guaranteed by articles 6 to 8 of the Convention. Public participation is required in regard to all decisions on whether to permit or renew permission for industrial, agricultural and construction activities listed in annex I to the Convention, as well as other activities which may have a significant impact on the environment (art. 6(1)(a)–(b)). The public must be informed in detail about the proposed activity early in the decision-making process and be given time to prepare and participate in the decision-making (art. 6(2)–(3)). In addition to providing for public participation in decisions on specific projects, the Convention calls for public participation in the preparation of environmental plans, programmes, policies, laws and regulations (arts. 7 and 8).

. . .

63. The Special Rapporteur would like to appeal to States to implement the right to information by establishing specific legislation conforming to international norms and standards. Ensuring effective implementation of the right to information requires proper training in their responsibilities for persons involved in implementing the law in how to deal with requests for information and how to interpret the law.

64. The Special Rapporteur also encourages Governments to be proactive in promoting the right to information and to educate the public on how to claim it. He would like to remind States that right to information laws should not only require public authorities to provide information upon request but also impose a duty on public bodies to actively disclose, disseminate and publish information. One such example of facilitating proactive disclosure of information would include the creation of systems informing the public on right to information laws. The implementation of right to information laws would also entail the setting up of systematic records management, including managing, recording and archiving.

65. States should also set up information commissions as general oversight bodies to regulate the implementation and oversight of right to information laws, or ensure that such functions, together with the necessary capacity and resources, are entrusted to national human rights institutions. The

Special Rapporteur notes that, although many models of information commissions already exist in different regions, they usually have similar functions, acting as external independent authorities with a clear mandate to supervise the implementation of the right to information.

V. CONCLUSIONS AND RECOMMENDATIONS

66. The Special Rapporteur would like to stress that the right to participation in public life is linked very closely with the right to information (and to education). The right to popular participation in decision-making is enshrined in article 21 of the Universal Declaration of Human Rights and several other international instruments. The exercise of the right to participation would be meaningless if there was no access to relevant information on issues of concern.

67. The Special Rapporteur believes that the Human Rights Council may want to recognize explicitly the right to information as a precondition for good governance and the realization of all other human rights. States should move towards implementing the right to information enshrined in the Universal Declaration of Human Rights and the International Covenant on Civil and Political Rights. The Special Rapporteur notes that information held by the State should be considered to be held in trust for the public, not as belonging to the Government. Although the State can invoke national security or defence clauses, it is the view of the Special Rapporteur that this responsibility should not be abused by States or used to derogate from their duty to protect and promote the rights of their citizens in relation to the adverse effects of toxic and dangerous products and wastes.

68. The Special Rapporteur would like to appeal to both developed and developing States to adhere more strictly to international normative frameworks, such as the Basel Convention on the Control of Transboundary Movements of Hazardous Wastes and Their Disposal. The Special Rapporteur notes that there are currently 170 parties to the Convention and appeals to those States that have not already done so to consider ratifying it. The Special Rapporteur also urges States to take into account, and if possible become parties to, other legal instruments such as the Aarhus Convention, which are central to the full realization of the right to information with regard to environmental matters, which in turn would help combat the adverse effects of the illicit movement and dumping of toxic and dangerous products and wastes on the enjoyment of human rights.

69. While the Special Rapporteur acknowledges that developing countries are sometimes left with little choice owing to developmental needs and situations of poverty, both developing and developed States need to find alternative solutions to the trade of toxic wastes and dangerous products. Although the income generated by such trade is very attractive, States need to take into account the future costs and long-term consequences of environmental degradation, as well as their obligation to save future generations from a multitude of health problems. The Special Rapporteur is particularly concerned about the consequences of these health problems for women and young persons and appeals to States to put in place adequate means for their protection.

70. The Special Rapporteur would like to emphasize that developed countries must not see developing nations as "cheap dumping grounds" to get rid of unwanted and hazardous products and wastes. While the Special Rapporteur welcomes the high environmental and health standards that often prevail in developed States, at both the national and the regional level, it is his hope that developed countries will consider passing on key knowledge on the safe handling of toxic and dangerous products, and their experience in monitoring safety standards and the effective running of regulatory mechanisms, to developing countries.

Questions and Discussion

1.   The Council allocates approximately half an hour for each special rapporteur to present his or her annual report. Although the reports are supposed to be submitted well in advance, so they can be translated into the U.N. official languages, how likely is it that the members of the Council will read and study all of the reports, as well as the NGO submissions, and papers relating to other matters on the Council's agenda? How should the reports be used to maximize their impact? Would you cite to them in national or international litigation?

3. The 1503 Procedure

The confidential communication-petition procedure under ECOSOC Resolution 1503 (XLVII) (1970), established a "[p]rocedure for dealing with communications relating to violations of human rights and fundamental freedoms." Under the 1503 procedure, the former Commission had the mandate to examine a consistent pattern of gross and reliably attested violations of human rights and fundamental freedoms occurring in any country of the world. Any individual or group claiming to be the victim of such human rights violations could submit a complaint, as could any other person or group with direct and reliable knowledge of such violations. When an NGO submitted a complaint, it had to be acting in good faith and in accordance with recognized principles of human rights. The organization also had to have reliable direct evidence of the situation it is describing. The 1503 procedure permitted the investigation of individual communications establishing a consistent pattern of gross human rights violations.

The 1503 Procedure, as revised by ECOSOC Resolution 2000/3, was reestablished by the Human Rights Council in Resolution 2006/103, pursuant to General Assembly Resolution 60/251 (Mar. 15, 2006), in which the Council was requested to "review and, where necessary, improve and rationalize, within one year after the holding of its first session, all mandates, mechanisms, functions and responsibilities of the former Commission on Human Rights, including the 1503 procedure, in order to maintain a system of special procedures, expert advice and a complaint procedure."

One of the major problems with the procedure is its confidential nature. Names of states being investigated are announced, but no information concerning the investigation or its outcome is officially released to the public. Nonetheless, information is often publicized by NGOs when they submit their complaints, and sources within the United Nations or government delegations sometimes leaked material, perhaps in an effort to influence the direction the case would take.

Human Rights Council Complaints Procedure, available at
http://www2.ohchr.org/english/bodies/chr/complaints.htm
Office of the High Commissioner for Human Rights

. . .

How does the complaint procedure work?

Pursuant to Council resolution 5/1, the Complaint Procedure is being established to address consistent patterns of gross and reliably attested violations of all human rights and all fundamental freedoms occurring in any part of the world and under any circumstances.

It retains its confidential nature, with a view to enhancing cooperation with the State concerned. The procedure, *inter alia*, is to be victims-oriented and conducted in a timely manner.

Two distinct working groups – the Working Group on Communications and the Working Group on Situations – are established with the mandate to examine the communications and to bring to the attention of the Council consistent patterns of gross and reliably attested violations of human rights and fundamental freedoms.

Manifestly ill-founded and anonymous communications are screened out by the Chairperson of the Working Group on Communications, together with the Secretariat, based on the admissibility criteria. Communications not rejected in the initial screening are transmitted to the State concerned to obtain its views on the allegations of violations.

The Working Group on Communications (WGC) is designated by the Human Rights Council Advisory Committee from among its members for a period of three years (mandate renewable once). It consists of five independent and highly qualified experts and is geographically representative of the five regional groups. The Working Group meets twice a year for a period of five working days to assess the admissibility and the merits of a communication, including whether the communication alone or in combination with other communications, appears to reveal a consistent pattern of gross and reliably attested violations of human rights and fundamental freedoms. All admissible communications and recommendations thereon are transmitted to the Working Group on Situations.

The Working Group on Situations (WGS) comprises five members appointed by the regional groups from among the States member of the Council for the period of one year (mandate renewable once). It meets twice a year for a period of five working days in order to examine the communications transferred to it by the Working Group on Communications, including the replies of States thereon, as well as the situations which the Council is already seized of under the complaint procedure. The Working Group on Situations, on the basis of the information and recommendations provided by the Working Group on Communications, presents the Council with a report on consistent patterns of gross and reliably attested violations of human rights and fundamental freedoms and makes recommendations to the Council on the course of action to take.

Subsequently, it is the turn of the Council to take a decision concerning each situation thus brought to its attention.

What are the criteria for a communication to be accepted for examination?

A communication related to a violation of human rights and fundamental freedoms is admissible, unless:

- It has manifestly political motivations and its object is not consistent with the U.N. Charter, the Universal Declaration of Human Rights and other applicable instruments in the field of human rights law; or
- It does not contain a factual description of the alleged violations, including the rights which are alleged to be violated; or
- Its language is abusive. However, such communication may be considered if it meets the other criteria for admissibility after deletion of the abusive language; or
- It is not submitted by a person or a group of persons claiming to be the victim of violations of human rights and fundamental freedoms or by any person or group of persons, including NGOs acting in good faith in accordance with the principles of human rights, not resorting to politically motivated stands contrary to the provisions of the U.N. Charter and claiming to have direct and reliable knowledge of those violations. Nonetheless, reliably attested communications shall not

be inadmissible solely because the knowledge of the individual author is second hand, provided they are accompanied by clear evidence; or

- It is exclusively based on reports disseminated by mass media; or
- It refers to a case that appears to reveal a consistent pattern of gross and reliably attested violations of human rights already being dealt with by a special procedure, a treaty body or other United Nations or similar regional complaints procedure in the field of human rights; or
- The domestic remedies have not been exhausted, unless it appears that such remedies would be ineffective or unreasonably prolonged.

The National Human Rights Institutions (NHRIs), when they are established and work under the guidelines of the Principles Relating to Status of National Institutions (the Paris Principles) including in regard to quasi-judicial competence, can serve as effective means in addressing individual human rights violations.

Where to send communications?

Communications intended for handling under the Council Complaint Procedure may be addressed to:

Human Rights Council and Treaties Division
Complaint Procedure
OHCHR-UNOG 1211 Geneva 10, Switzerland
Fax: (41 22) 917 90 11
E-mail: CP@ohchr.org

Questions and Discussion

1. Although you must state your name when making a complaint, you may request that it be suppressed if the complaint is forwarded to the government concerned. All material provided by individuals and governments, as well as the decisions taken at the various stages of the procedure, remain confidential and are not made public. However, although these rules of confidentiality are binding on the U.N. bodies dealing with your complaint, they do not preclude you from disclosing the fact that you have submitted a complaint under the 1503 procedure.

2. As with all other human rights procedures, the 1503 procedure has advantages and disadvantages. The advantages are that you may submit a complaint against any country without needing to check whether it has ratified a particular treaty or limited its obligations under the instrument. Once you have submitted a complaint, you do not have to respond again at a later point with further information – the initial complaint is sufficient. With the 1503 procedure, it is possible for your complaint to reach the highest level of the U.N. human rights machinery, the Human Rights Council. It may thus result in pressure being brought to bear on a state to change laws, policies, or practices that infringe internationally guaranteed human rights. Drawbacks of the procedure include the fact that the submitter is never part of the process after the complaint is filed and is not informed of the decisions taken at the various stages of the process, the reasons for them, or the relevant government's responses to the complaint. It is also a political process handled by a political body, and the results of the procedure often have been meager. States do not like to condemn other states for human rights violations, and those states that are the targets of complaints lobby very hard to avoid any public consideration of cases brought under 1503. Note that the Council has discontinued several of the country studies that were authorized as a result of earlier

1503 complaints. Finally, the procedure is protracted and, unlike the thematic and country procedures, there is no provision for urgent measures of protection.

4. The 1235 Procedure

The Human Rights Council, at least in its first years, has assumed the main monitoring and enforcement mechanisms employed by its predecessor, the Human Rights Commission. The first is the 1503 Procedure discussed previously.

The second procedure inherited from the Commission is the annual debate on human rights, during which any grave human rights situation may be discussed based on ECOSOC Resolution 1235 (XLII) (1967). Under Resolution 1235, the Council may "examine information relevant to gross violations of human rights" and "may make a thorough study of situations which reveal a consistent pattern of violations of human rights." In so doing, the Council may establish a working group or rapporteur to examine the situation in a particular country.

Given the governmental nature of the Council, the discussion can be highly politicized, and some notorious situations have not resulted in Council resolutions. For example, the People's Republic of China has routinely escaped censure. With the former Commission, the situation in East Timor before the 1999 self-determination ballot only came to the fore after the 1991 Dili Massacre, resulting in two resolutions, including a highly critical one in 1997.

5. The Role of Nongovernmental Organizations

The U.N. human rights system is distinctive not only for the fact that individual human beings have a place alongside states but also for the role of nongovernmental organizations (NGOs). For example, NGOs play a significant role in the deliberations of the U.N. Human Rights Council and the treaty bodies. Also, NGOs may be given consultative status with the Council. Pursuant to Human Rights Council Resolution 5/1, the participation of NGOs in the Advisory Committee is based on the arrangements and practices observed by the Commission on Human Rights, including Economic and Social Council Resolution 1996/31 of July 25, 1996 (para. 83). As a result, accredited NGOs may request that items be included on the agendas, attend meetings, and make written and oral submissions. Often, NGOs provide materials to the treaty bodies that may be used during the reporting process as a counterweight to the sometimes-superficial material provided by states. However, there may be some problems with overreliance on NGO material. Some governments are highly skeptical of the role of NGOs as opposed to that of elected representatives.

C. *International Court of Justice*

The International Court of Justice (ICJ) has sometimes had the opportunity to rule on human rights issues. For example, it has examined the question of self-determination in the advisory opinions in the *Namibia* and *Western Sahara* advisory opinions (*Legal Consequences for States of the Continued Presence of South Africa in Namibia (South West Africa) notwithstanding Security Council Resolution 276 (1970)*, 1971 I.C.J. 16; *Western Sahara (Advisory Opinion)*, 1975 I.C.J. 12). In the *Legal Consequences of the Construction of a Wall in the Occupied Palestinian Territory* (Advisory Opinion), 2004 I.C.J. 136, the Court considered the rights of the Palestinians in the occupied territories.

In the *Legality of the Threat of Use of Nuclear Weapons* (Advisory Opinion), 1996 I.C.J. 226, the court considered, inter alia, the international law of human rights, especially humanitarian law, and environmental protection. In reliance on these and other international norms, the court opined that "the threat or use of nuclear weapons would generally by contrary to the rules of international law," even though it could not say that the use of nuclear weapons would be "definitively" prohibited if the very survival of a state is at stake. *Id.* at 241–42, 247–60, 266.

Among its contentious cases, the *Nuclear Tests Cases* (Australia v. France) (New Zealand v. France) (Interim Measures), 1973 I.C.J. 99 & 135; *Case Concerning the Gabčíkovo-Nagymaros Project* (Hungary/Slovakia), 1997 I.C.J. 7; *Case Concerning Armed Activities on the Territory of the Congo (New Application: 2002)* (Democratic Republic of the Congo v. Rwanda (Provisional Measures), 2002 I.C.J. 219; and *Case Concerning Pulp Mills on the River Uruguay* (Argentina v. Uruguay) (Apr. 20, 2010) all involve environment, and the latter two also raise human rights concerns.

Articles 26–29 of the ICJ Statute allow the Court to form chambers (a smaller bench consisting of three to five judges) to hear cases. In particular, article 26 allows the Court to create a chamber to hear a particular category of dispute. In 1993, the Court announced that it had formed a special chamber to hear environmental disputes, but to date, no environmental dispute the Court has considered has been referred to the chamber.

D. *The Secretariat*

The Secretariat, headed by the Secretary-General (SG), is the fourth formal organ of the United Nations. The SG is appointed for five-year terms by the GA on the recommendation of the SC (and subject to the veto of the five permanent SC members). Like the SC, for years the SG was reticent on human rights issues because of a fear that heavy involvement would offend governments and thereby raise barriers to the SG's wider responsibilities for peace and security. Indeed, the proposal that ultimately led to the creation of the post of high commissioner for human rights in December 1993 was strongly opposed by the SG at the time, Boutros Boutros-Ghali.

By contrast, Kofi Annan, and the current SG, Ban Ki-moon, have been much more proactive in the human rights area. For example, in 2005, Kofi Annan recommended the establishment of the U.N. Integrated Office in Sierra Leone (UNIOSIL) following the conclusion of a six-year peacekeeping mission. Annan envisioned that part of the mission of UNIOSIL would be to consolidate peace by addressing deficits in many areas, including human rights and sustainable development. *Twenty-fifth Report of the Secretary-General on the United Nations Mission in Sierra Leone*, U.N. Doc. S/2005/273/Add.2 (July 28, 2005). The recommendation was subsequently authorized by the Security Council. S.C. Res. 1620 (2005). In a more recent example, in July 2009, Ban Ki-moon called on the regime in Myanmar (formerly Burma) to work with the United Nations to promote, among other things, "respect for human rights and sustainable development." Secretary-General's Briefing to the Security Council on Myanmar, SC/9704, 6161st mtg., (July 13, 2009).

As noted earlier, in 1993, the General Assembly established the post of High Commissioner for Human Rights. The commissioner and the Office of the High Commissioner for Human Rights undertake various activities, including field presences in a number of countries. The Office, headed by the high commissioner, acts as the secretariat division responsible for supporting the treaty bodies and the Human Rights Council.

The Commissioner, who has a broad mandate for promoting and protecting human rights, is able to be relatively proactive by comparison with the treaty bodies and more independent than the members of the Human Rights Council. However, the preparedness to be outspoken on human rights issues has depended on the personality of the particular person occupying the office.

E. *Economic and Social Council*

Human rights fall perhaps most squarely within the mandate of the U.N. Economic and Social Council (ECOSOC). As discussed previously, ECOSOC created and oversaw the work of the Commission on Human Rights, the predecessor of the current Human Rights Council. Oversight of the Council has moved to the General Assembly. However, ECOSOC is still the parent body of one functional human rights commission, the U.N. Commission on the Status of Women.

In a manner similar to the 1503 procedure, any individual or NGO can submit a communication to the Commission on the Status of Women containing information relating to alleged violations of human rights that affect the status of women in any country in the world. The communications are then examined by a working group on communications, which prepares a report in which the most frequently submitted categories of communications are named. The Commission on the Status of Women considers the report and submits then on its part, if the Commission deems it necessary, an accompanied report to ECOSOC containing recommendations on the measures to be taken on the subject of tendencies and regularities that emerge from the communications.

In the environmental realm, ECOSOC is responsible for two functional commissions: the Commission on Sustainable Development (CSD) and the U.N. Forum on Forests (UNFF). Although neither of these "green" commissions has human rights in its mandate per se, the work of both includes areas highly relevant. For example, the CSD areas of work are based on Agenda 21, a forty-chapter road map on sustainable development, and include the topics of poverty, health, human settlements, environmental hazards, and capacity building. All of these have consequential bearing on human rights.

Similarly, the UNFF's Multi-Year Program of Work 2007–2015 emphasizes the theme of forests for people. This includes treatment of indigenous and forest-dependent communities and the forest land tenure (and associated rights) of those communities. In May 2009, at its eighth session, UNFF included discussion on forests and climate change recognizing the serious threat that climate change poses to millions of people whose lives and livelihoods depend on forests. An earlier forest dialogue that fed into the eighth session established five principles that should be considered polestars for post-2012 climate arrangements, including "processes to clarify and strengthen tenure, property and carbon rights, giving full recognition to Indigenous Peoples, small forest owners, the forest workplace and local communities." *See* Rep. of the Secretary-General, Forests and Climate Change, U.N. Doc. E/CN.18/2009/4, at 13 (Feb. 9, 2009).

Also notable, in 2000, ECOSOC decided to establish a second mechanism concerning indigenous peoples – the Permanent Forum on Indigenous Issues – as a subsidiary body of ECOSOC. Composed of independent experts, this institution also promises to be representative of the real concerns of indigenous peoples.

III. The Treaty Committees

A. *Introduction*[1]

The United Nations has generated many particularized treaties devoted to specific human rights issues. Some of them deal with particular groups of vulnerable people – such as the 1951

---

[1] This section draws on the work of Penelope E. Mathew in DONALD K. ANTON, PENELOPE MATHEW & WAYNE MORGAN, INTERNATIONAL LAW: CASES AND MATERIALS 779–785 (2005).

Convention Relating to the Status of Refugees and the 1989 Convention on the Rights of the Child. Others – for example, the 1948 Convention on the Prevention and Punishment of the Crime of Genocide and the 1984 Convention Against Torture and Other Cruel, Inhuman, or Degrading Treatment or Punishment – elaborate on particular rights or responsibilities. Ten treaties have committees responsible for their supervision. Table 3.1, prepared by Professor Penelope Mathew, gives details of these treaty bodies and their basic activities.

The Committees are made up of independent experts ranging in number from ten to twenty-three (CEDAW). They are expected to give opinions that are independent of any state, including that of their nationality. However, given that states parties nominate and elect committee members, it is inevitable that some committee members have views that are close, if not identical, to that of the government that nominates them.

The Committees are not judicial bodies, but in the majority of instances, the Committees have the authority to decide on the merits of individual complaints. In all cases, the jurisdiction of the Committee over individual complaints must be accepted by States: states parties either make a declaration under a particular provision of the treaty to the effect that the Committee may hear individual complaints or they become party to a separate instrument, as is the case with the ICCPR, ICESCR and CEDAW. The Committees render their views in relation to communications by individuals. The status of these views is debated. Some committees, and especially some of their individual members, argue that the views represent an authoritative interpretation of the treaty and must be given due deference by states in good faith. In contrast, some states, in particular Australia, have decided not to bring their practice into line with some committee decisions, citing the fact that the views are not binding. However, given that the Committees must have authority to interpret the treaty to state their views, most jurists agree with the Committees that their interpretations are more authoritative than the interpretation made by the particular state concerned and that states parties have a good faith obligation to respect them. A failure to comply with the Committees' decisions could thus be seen as a violation of the treaty. Joseph, Castan, and Schultz cautiously argue:

> [T]he HRC [Human Rights Committee] is the pre-eminent interpreter of the ICCPR which is itself legally binding. The HRC's decisions are therefore strong indicators of legal obligations, so rejection of those decisions is good evidence of a State's bad faith attitude towards its ICCPR obligations.

Sarah Joseph, Jenny Schultz & Melissa Castan, The International Covenant on Civil and Political Rights 14 (2000).

Some committees also have the power to hear complaints made by other states. CERD makes this jurisdiction compulsory, but in all other treaties, states must make a declaration under a particular provision of the treaty concerned (see Table 3.1), and only states that have made such a declaration can make complaints. The procedure is thus optional and reciprocal. These provisions have never been used.

All the Committees receive periodical reports from states parties to the relevant treaties. These reports are supposed to detail states' efforts to implement the treaty. The Committees invite the state to send representatives to the sessions at which the report will be considered. The immediate aim is to establish "constructive dialogue" between the state and committee members. As Professor Bayefsky notes, the long-term goals are more complex, requiring a focus that goes beyond the immediate task of reporting:

> The treaty standards, the associated production of reports and the periodic dialogue is intended to cultivate a progression largely at the national level from (a) understanding and awareness of the

Table 3.1. *The Functioning of Human Rights Treaty Bodies*

Treaty	Committee	Periodical Reports	State Complaints	Individual Complaints	Other
International Covenant on Civil and Political Rights (ICCPR)	Human Rights Committee	Every 5 years or more urgently as the Committee determines	Article 41 – optional and reciprocal	First Optional Protocol	
International Covenant of Economic, Social, and Cultural Rights (ICESCR)	Committee on Economic, Social, and Cultural Rights	Every 5 years – generally from the consideration of the last report rather than the date of the report's submission	No	Optional Protocol	
Convention for the Elimination of All Forms of Racial Discrimination (CERD)	Committee on the Elimination of Racial Discrimination	Every 2 years (but the Committee may consider several of one state's reports at one time)	Article 11 – compulsory	Article 14 – optional	
Convention for the Elimination of All Forms of Discrimination Against Women (CEDAW)	Committee on the Elimination of Discrimination Against Women	Every 4 years (but note the Committee's practice concerning consolidated overdue reports)	No	Optional Protocol	Inquiry procedure under the Optional Protocol
Convention against Torture and other Cruel, Inhuman or Degrading Treatment or Punishment (CAT)	Committee Against Torture	Every 4 years	Article 21 – optional and reciprocal	Article 22 – optional	Inquiry Procedure Under Optional Protocol, subcommittee on prevention may visit places of detention
Convention on the Rights of the Child (CRC)	Committee on the Rights of the Child	Every 5 years	No	No	
International Convention on the Rights of All Migrant Workers and Members of Their Families (CMW)	Committee on the Protection of the Rights of All Migrant Workers and Members of Their Families (MWC)	Every 5 years	Article 76 – optional and reciprocal	Article 77 – optional	
Convention on the Rights of Persons with Disabilities (CRPD)	Committee on the Rights of Persons with Disabilities (CRPD)	Every 4 years or at request of CRPD	Article 6 – Optional Protocol	Optional Protocol	
Convention on the Protection of All Persons from Enforced Disappearance (CPED)	Committee on Enforced Disappearances (CED)	Initial 2-year period	Article 32 – optional and reciprocal	Article 30 (relatives) – not optional Article 31 (individual) – optional	

standards, to (b) reviewing of laws, policies and practices against those standards, to (c) planning concrete actions to improve the shortfalls revealed, to (d) monitoring the implementation of those plans, to (e) reporting and feedback from a dialogue with the treaty bodies.

ANNE BAYEFSKY, THE U.N. HUMAN RIGHTS TREATY SYSTEM: UNIVERSALITY AT THE CROSS-ROADS 67 (2001). Both the immediate aim and the long-term goals are difficult to realize, as many reports are late, and others are simply not submitted. Often, too, the reports are lacking in the necessary detail and rather self-serving. Several of the committees have adopted procedures to address those concerns.

In particular, the committees have garnered information from other sources, especially NGOs, which may submit shadow or alternative reports to supplement the information provided by the state. (Shadow reports are prepared when there is access to the state report; alternative reports are prepared when there is no such access.) In some cases, committees – in particular the CERD Committee, the Human Rights Committee, and the Committee on Economic, Social, and Cultural Rights – have moved to consider the situation in a particular state in the absence of a state report.

The committees' end product is a set of concluding observations on the state's report. The concluding observations generally take the format of commenting first on the good points of the state's report and its human rights record and then on the areas of concern. Concluding observations are something of an innovation. The only upshot of reporting processes mentioned in the treaties are general comments (ICCPR, ICESCR, CAT, Convention on the Rights of the Child (CRoC)) or "general recommendations" (CERD and CEDAW). The Soviet bloc had wished to avoid states being singled out for adverse comments on their human rights records; thus, the comments were to be general. However, since 1992 – when the Soviet bloc disintegrated – the committees have taken the view that concluding observations in respect to individual reports may be adopted. *See* Yuji Iwasawa, *The Domestic Impact of International Human Rights Standards: The Japanese Experience*, in THE FUTURE OF U.N. HUMAN RIGHTS TREATY MONITORING 254, 257 (P. Alston & J. Crawford eds., 2000).

Two committees, the CAT and CEDAW Committees, have an inquiry procedure, and other committees, particularly the CERD Committee, have tried to develop urgent procedures to be proactive concerning human rights issues. As the committees' members are part-time members who are often remunerated only for expenses, or, at best, by a small honorarium, and the Committees meet for limited sessions each year (meetings may take place two to three times a year for two to three weeks – some committees having more meeting time than others), there is a backlog of reports and communications. This, among other factors, has led to calls for reform of the treaty body system. The United Nations itself commissioned a report from an independent expert – Professor Philip Alston, who is a former chair of the Committee on Economic, Social, and Cultural Rights. Professor Alston wrote three reports. In his final report, he recorded the backlogs occurring in the treaty body system and described how the situation would become worse as near universal ratification of the major treaties occurred and yet another treaty – the Migrant Workers Convention – entered into force. As he noted, the burdens on both states and the treaty committees would become untenable. *See particularly Final Report on Enhancing the Long-Term Effectiveness of the United Nations Human Rights Treaty System*, E/CN.4/1997/74, at paras. 81–84 (Mar. 27, 1997). Professor Alston's suggestions for reform include the following:

• Consolidated reports – that is, the submission of one report by a State which would satisfy the requirements of all treaty bodies to which the State is required to report;

- Elimination of comprehensive periodic reports and the submission in most cases in their stead of reports tailored to particular issues in particular states [this already occurs in some cases – *Eds.*]; and
- Consolidation of the treaty bodies so that one or two bodies replaced the 6 [now 9] bodies.

Discussion of these and other options – such as expansion and updating of the "core document," which provides background information about each state, concerning matters such as the governmental system – is ongoing. The secretary-general has reported on (the fairly sparse) responses to Professor Alston's reports. *See Report of the Secretary-General on the Consultations Conducted in Respect of the Report of the Independent Expert on Enhancing the Long-Term Effectiveness of the United Nations Human Rights Treaty System*, E/CN.4/19998/85 (Feb. 4, 1998) and *Report of the Secretary-General on the Consultations Conducted in Respect of the Report of the Independent Expert on Enhancing the Long-Term Effectiveness of the United Nations Human Rights Treaty System*, E/CN.4/2000/98 (Jan. 20, 2000). *See also* Office of the High Commissioner for Human Rights, *Plan of Action Submitted by the United Nations High Commissioner for Human Rights*, Annex to *In Larger Freedom: Towards Development, Security and Human Rights for All, Report of the Secretary-General*, U.N. Doc. A/59/2005/Add.3 (May 26, 2005).

Proposals for reform continue. In 2003, an independent meeting of experts met to discuss a background note on reform of treaty-monitoring bodies prepared by the Office of the High Commissioner for Human Rights. Several of the ideas of the independent expert (Professor Alston) were commented on and problems with the recommendation for a consolidated report were noted:

- The marginalization of specific issues,
- Unmanageable length,
- Diminished overall utility of the report, including for civil society,
- Different periodicities [i.e., the time-frames for reporting contained in each treaty differ, as may the dates of accession to particular treaties],
- The burden of preparation on States parties,
- Burden and complexity of consideration by treaty bodies,
- Complexity and cost for the secretariat,
- Usefulness of specific reports for building national constituencies around particular issues and identifying lacunae in domestic legislation, policies and programmes,
- Requirement of amendment of treaties,
- A single report would inevitably result in a summary, and
- A single report does not solve the issue of non-reporting.

Report of a Meeting on Reform of the Human Rights Treaty Body System, Malbun, Liechtenstein, 4–7 May 2003, annexed to letter dated June 13, 2003, from the Permanent Representative of Liechtenstein to the United Nations addressed to the Secretary-General, A/58/123, at para. 27. Points for and against focused reports, as opposed to comprehensive reports, included the following:

Advantages

- Framework for systematic follow-up to concluding observations or comments,
- Allow for shorter reports,
- Allow for more substantive and effective cross-referencing of reports,

- Reduce overall burden for States parties, treaty bodies and the secretariat,
- Improve quality of dialogue between States parties and treaty bodies,
- Allow for more in-depth analysis of issues and areas of concern,
- Provide framework for quality and focused concluding observations, and
- More effective use of secretariat resources.

Concerns

- Focused reports might not comply with overall reporting obligations,
- Neglect of areas for periods of time,
- Allow for a non-comprehensive approach to reporting on treaty obligations, as well as selective implementation,
- Marginalization of some issues and related constituencies at a national level,
- Such reports would not address non-reporting by States parties,
- Such reports might focus solely on issues receiving public attention,
- Narrowing of the basis of information for future reports,
- Focused reports might limit opportunities for States parties to highlight successes in implementation and best practices, and
- Lack of clarity as to the basis of the focused report.

Id. at paras. 43 and 44.

More recently, the high commissioner for human rights, building on the body of academic and diplomatic opinion favoring the consolidation and unification, proposed a consolidated treaty body to superintend all human rights conventions. *Concept Paper on the High Commissioner's Proposal for a Unified Standing Treaty Body, Report by the Secretariat, Fifth Inter-Committee Meeting of the Human Rights Bodies*, U.N. Doc. HRI/MC/2006/2 (March 26, 2006). *See also* Michael Bowman, *Towards a Unified Treaty Body for Monitoring Compliance with U.N. Human Rights Conventions? Legal Mechanisms for Treaty Reform*, 7 HUM. RTS. L. REV. 225 (2007); Michael O'Flaherty & Claire O'Brien, *Reform of U.N. Human Rights Treaty Monitoring Bodies: A Critique of the Concept Paper on the High Commissioner's Proposal for a Unified Standing Treaty Body*, 7 HUM. RTS. L. REV. 141 (2007).

Questions and Discussion

1. Which, if any, of the suggestions put forward by Professor Alston do you favor and why? Are there any benefits to the current fragmented system?
2. Starting in 1984, and annually since 1995, the chairs of human rights bodies meet to discuss how to enhance the work of the treaty bodies. Starting in 2002, the various human rights treaty committees have also met to consider effective procedures and to harmonize working methods. For an elaboration and comparison of the state reporting process and procedures of the Committees, see *Report on the Working Methods of the Human Rights Treaty Bodies Relating to the State Party Reporting Process*, U.N. Doc. HRI/MC/2008/4 (June 5, 2008). Since 2008, the intercommittee meeting has convened two times a year. It has continued to consider reform of the treaty-reporting system at its meetings.
3. As a lawyer, how would you make use of the treaty bodies to advance a client's case involving human rights violations caused by environmental harm? *See* LINDA A. MALONE & SCOTT PASTERNACK, DEFENDING THE ENVIRONMENT: CIVIL SOCIETY STRATEGIES TO ENFORCE INTERNATIONAL ENVIRONMENTAL LAW 14–30 (2004).

B. *Committee Complaints Procedures*

1. General Procedures

Fact Sheet No. 7/Rev. 1, Complaints Procedure, available at
http://www.ohchr.org/Documents/Publications/FactSheet7Rev.1en.pdf
Office of the High Commissioner for Human Rights

Introduction

Anyone may bring a human rights problem to the attention of the United Nations and thousands of people around the world do so every year. What kinds of complaints about alleged human rights violations does the United Nations receive and how does it deal with them? This Fact Sheet explains the procedures open to individuals and groups who want the United Nations to take action on a human rights situation of concern to them.

It is through individual complaints that human rights are given concrete meaning. In the adjudication of individual cases, international norms that may otherwise seem general and abstract are put into practical effect. When applied to a person's real-life situation, the standards contained in international human rights treaties find their most direct application. The resulting body of decisions may guide States, non-governmental organizations (NGOs) and individuals in interpreting the contemporary meaning of the texts concerned.

. . .

The complaint mechanisms under individual treaties are complemented by complaints procedure before the . . . Human Rights [Council] and the Commission on the Status of Women. These two procedures, involving political bodies composed of State representatives, are among the oldest in the United Nations system. They have a different focus from complaints under the international treaties, which provide individual redress through quasi-judicial mechanisms. Complaints to the [Council] focus on more systematic patterns and trends of human rights violations and may be brought against any country in the world. As with the procedures under the treaties, the [Council] mechanisms seek to avoid legal and technical terms and procedures and are open to everybody. The Fact Sheet is divided into two parts. The first examines complaints procedure under the individual treaties in greater detail and the second concentrates on the [Council]. You should be aware that these mechanisms operate on the basis of diverse mandates and procedures. As a result, each mechanism has a variety of advantages and disadvantages. You may wish to compare them before electing where your claim may be considered most fruitfully.

Part 1: Complaints Under the International Human Rights Treaties

Overview

This part of the Fact Sheet explains the complaint mechanisms that are currently available under [. . .] four international human rights treaties: the International Covenant on Civil and Political Rights, the Convention against Torture, the International Convention on the Elimination of Racial Discrimination and the Convention on the Elimination of All Forms of Discrimination against Women. A human rights treaty is a formal document negotiated by States, which imposes binding obligations to protect and promote rights and freedoms on States parties that officially accept it (commonly through "ratification"). The full texts of the treaties are accessible on the web site of the Office of the United Nations High Commissioner for Human Rights (OHCHR).

The basic concept is that anyone may bring a complaint alleging a violation of treaty rights to the body of experts set up by the treaty for quasi-judicial adjudication. These "treaty bodies," as they are often called, are committees composed of independent experts elected by States parties to the relevant treaty. They are tasked with monitoring implementation in States parties of the rights set forth in the treaties and with deciding on complaints brought against those States. While there are some procedural variations between the four mechanisms, their design and operation are very similar. Accordingly, what follows is a general description of the typical features of a complaint under any of the four treaties. Readers should then refer to the descriptions of the individual treaties, which identify aspects differing from the general norm.

Against whom can a complaint under a treaty be brought?

A complaint under one of the four treaties can be brought only against a State that satisfies two conditions. First, it must be a party to the treaty in question, having ratified or otherwise accepted it. (To check whether a State is a party to the treaty, consult the Treaty Body database on the OHCHR web site. To access the database, click on *Documents* on the home page followed by *Treaty body database, Ratifications and reservations* and *States parties*; then check the relevant country. Alternatively, you may contact the Petitions Team or the Division for the Advancement of Women, depending on the treaty, via the contact details listed at the end of this part of the Fact Sheet.)

Second, the State party must have recognized the competence of the committee established under the relevant treaty to consider complaints from individuals. In the case of the International Covenant on Civil and Political Rights and the Convention on the Elimination of All Forms of Discrimination against Women, a State recognizes the Committee's competence by becoming a party to a separate treaty: the First Optional Protocol to the Covenant or the Optional Protocol to the Convention. (To see the text of the Protocols and to check whether a State is a party to either or both, consult the OHCHR web site as described above.) In the case of the Convention against Torture and the International Convention on the Elimination of Racial Discrimination, States recognize the Committee's competence by making a declaration to that effect under a specific article of the Convention, articles 22 and 14 respectively. (To check whether a State has made either of these declarations, access the OHCHR web site as described above, clicking on *Declarations on procedural articles* once you have selected the relevant State.)

Who can bring a complaint?

Anyone can lodge a complaint with a committee against a State that satisfies these two conditions, claiming that his or her rights under the relevant treaty have been violated. It is not necessary to have a lawyer prepare your case, though legal advice usually improves the quality of the submissions. Be aware, however, that legal aid is not provided under the procedures. You may also bring a claim on behalf of another person on condition that you obtain his or her written consent. In certain cases, you may bring a case without such consent. For example, where parents bring cases on behalf of young children or guardians on behalf of persons unable to give formal consent, or where a person is in prison without access to the outside world, the relevant committee will not require formal authorization to lodge a complaint on another's behalf.

What information do you need to provide in your complaint?

A complaint to a committee, also called a "communication" or a "petition," need not take any particular form. While the model complaint form and guidelines appended to this Fact Sheet (as annexes 1 and 2) focus on specific information, any correspondence supplying the necessary particulars will suffice. Your claim should be in writing and signed. It should provide basic personal information – your name, nationality and date of birth – and specify the State party against which your complaint is directed. If you are bringing the claim on behalf of another person, you should provide proof of their consent, as noted above, or state clearly why such consent cannot be provided.

You should set out, in chronological order, all the facts on which your claim is based. A crucial requirement is that your account is as complete as possible and that the complaint contains all information relevant to your case. You should also detail the steps you have taken to exhaust the remedies available in your country, that is steps taken before your country's local courts and authorities. You should state whether you have submitted your case to another means of international investigation or settlement. On these two matters, see the section entitled "The admissibility of your case" below for further important details. Lastly, you should state why you consider that the facts you have outlined constitute a violation of the treaty in question. It is helpful, though not strictly necessary, for you to identify the articles of the treaty that have allegedly been violated. You should provide this information in one of the secretariat's working languages.

In addition, you should supply all documents of relevance to your claims and arguments, especially administrative or judicial decisions on your claim by national authorities. It is also helpful if you provide copies of relevant national laws. If they are not in an official language of the committee's secretariat, consideration of your complaint will be speeded up if you can arrange for a translation (either full or summary).

If your complaint lacks essential information, you will be contacted by the secretariat with a request for the additional details.

When can you make a complaint under the human rights treaties?

In general, there is no formal time limit after the date of the alleged violation for filing a complaint under the relevant treaties. It is usually appropriate, however, to submit your complaint as soon as possible after you have exhausted domestic remedies. Delay in submitting your case may also make it difficult for the State party to respond properly. In exceptional cases, submission after a protracted period may result in your case being considered inadmissible by the committee in question.

The Procedure

If your complaint contains the essential elements outlined above, your case is registered, that is to say formally listed as a case for consideration by the relevant committee. You will receive advice of registration.

At that point, the case is transmitted to the State party concerned to give it an opportunity to comment. The State is requested to submit its observations within a set time frame. The two major stages in any case are known as the "admissibility" stage and the "merits" stage. The "admissibility" of a case refers to the formal requirements that your complaint must satisfy before the relevant committee can consider its substance. The "merits" of the case are the substance, on the basis of which the committee decides whether or not your rights under a treaty have been violated. These stages are described in greater detail below. The time within which the State is required to respond to your complaint varies between procedures and is also specified below in the sections dealing with them individually.

Once the State replies to your submission, you are offered an opportunity to comment. Again, the time frames vary somewhat between procedures (see below for details). At that point, the case is ready for a decision by the relevant committee. If the State party fails to respond to your complaint, you are not disadvantaged. Reminders are sent to the State party and if there is still no response, the committee takes a decision on your case on the basis of your original complaint.

Special Circumstances of Urgency or Sensitivity

Each committee has the facility to take urgent action where irreparable harm would otherwise be suffered before the case is examined in the usual course. The basis for such interim action by individual committees is set out below for each procedure. The common feature is that the committee in question may, at any stage before the case is considered, issue a request to the State party for what are known as "interim measures" in order to prevent any irreparable harm. Typically, such requests are issued to prevent actions that cannot later be undone, for example the execution of a death sentence or the deportation of an individual facing a risk of torture. If you wish the committee to consider a request for interim measures, it is advisable to state this explicitly. In any case, you should identify as carefully and comprehensively as possible the reasons why you consider such action to be necessary.

If there are particularly sensitive matters of a private or personal nature that emerge in the complaint, you may request that the committee suppress identifying elements in its final decision so that your identity does not become public. The committee may also, of its own motion, suppress these or other matters in the course of consideration of the complaint.

The Admissibility of Your Case

Before the committee to which you have brought your case can consider its merits or substance, it must be satisfied that the claim meets the formal requirements of admissibility. When examining admissibility, the committee may consider one or several of the following factors:

- If you are acting on behalf of another person, have you obtained sufficient authorization or are you otherwise justified in doing so?
- Are you (or the person on whose behalf you are bringing the complaint) a victim of the alleged violation? You must show that you are personally and directly affected by the law, policy, practice, act or omission of the State party which you claim has violated or is violating your rights. It is not sufficient simply to challenge a law or State policy or practice in the abstract (a so-called *actio popularis*) without demonstrating how you are individually a victim of the law, policy or practice in question.
- Is your complaint compatible with the provisions of the treaty invoked? The alleged violation must relate to a right actually protected by the treaty. If [not,] . . . your claim would be, in legal terms, inadmissible *ratione materiae*.
- Is your complaint sufficiently substantiated? If the relevant committee considers, in the light of the information before it from all sides, that you have not sufficiently developed the facts of your complaint or the arguments for a violation of the Covenant, it may reject the claim as insufficiently substantiated for the purposes of admissibility. This ground is analogous to the rejection of a case by other courts, international and domestic, as "manifestly ill-founded."
- Does your complaint relate to events that occurred prior to the entry into force of the complaint mechanism for your State? As a rule, a committee does not examine complaints dating from a period prior to this date and your complaint is regarded, in legal terms, as inadmissible *ratione temporis*. There are, however, exceptions. In cases where the effects of the event in question have extended into the period covered by the complaint mechanism, a committee may consider the overall circumstances. . . .
- Have you exhausted all domestic remedies? A cardinal principle governing the admissibility of a complaint is that you must, in general, have exhausted all remedies in your own State before bringing a claim to a committee. This usually includes pursuing your claim through the local court system, and you should be aware that mere doubts about the effectiveness of such action do not, in the committees' view, dispense with this requirement. There are, however, limited exceptions to this rule. If the exhaustion of remedies would be unreasonably prolonged, or if they would plainly be ineffective (if, for example, the law in your State is quite clear on the

point at issue) or if the remedies are otherwise unavailable to you (owing, for example, to denial of legal aid in a criminal case), you may not be required to exhaust domestic remedies. . . .

- Is your claim an abuse of the complaints process? In rare cases, the committees may consider a case to be a frivolous, vexatious or otherwise inappropriate use of the complaints procedure and reject it as inadmissible, for example if you bring repeated claims to the committee on the same issue although they have already been dismissed.
- Is your complaint being examined under another mechanism of international settlement? If you have submitted the same claim to another treaty body or to a regional mechanism such as the Inter-American Commission on Human Rights, the European Court of Human Rights or the African Commission on Human and Peoples' Rights, the committees cannot examine your complaint, the aim being to avoid unnecessary duplication at the international level. . . .
- Is your complaint precluded by a reservation the State has made to the Optional Protocol? A State may have entered a procedural reservation to the complaint mechanism limiting the committee's competence to examine certain communications. For example, States may preclude a committee's consideration of claims that have in the past been considered by another international mechanism. In very rare cases, a committee may decide that a particular reservation is impermissible and consider the communication notwithstanding the purported reservation. . . .

If you think there is a risk that your claim may be considered inadmissible on one of these grounds, it is helpful to present your counterarguments in the initial complaint. In any event, the State party, when responding to your complaint, will probably argue that your case is inadmissible if it considers that one of these grounds may apply. You will then be able to present your view when commenting on the State party's submissions.

The Merits of Your Case

Once a committee decides your case is admissible, it proceeds to consider the merits of your complaint, stating its reasons for concluding that a violation has or has not occurred under the various articles it considers applicable. A number of States have also entered substantive reservations that may limit the scope of the human rights obligations they assume under the treaties. (The text of any reservations or declarations entered may be accessed in the Treaty Body database on the OHCHR web site as described above. Be sure to check that a reservation has not been subsequently withdrawn, as in such cases the State party will have accepted, in the meantime, the full obligation imposed by the relevant article.) In most cases, a committee will decline to consider complaints falling within areas covered by a reservation, though in exceptional circumstances, as noted above, it may find a reservation impermissible and consider the case despite the purported reservation.

To form an idea of what a committee considers to be the scope of the rights contained in the treaty for which it is responsible, you may look at its previous decisions, its so-called "General Comments" expanding on the meaning of various articles, and its concluding observations on reports submitted periodically by States parties to the treaty concerned. These documents are accessible on the OHCHR web site through the Treaty Body database. There are also numerous academic articles and textbooks on the jurisprudence of the various committees that may be of assistance.

Consideration of Your Case

The committees consider each case in closed session. Although some have provisions for oral components of proceedings in their rules of procedure, the practice has been to consider complaints on the basis of the written information supplied by the complainant and the State party.

Accordingly, it has not been the practice to receive oral submissions from the parties or audio or audio-visual evidence (such as audio cassettes or videotapes). Nor do the committees go beyond the information provided by the parties to seek independent verification of the facts. It follows that they do not consider briefs provided by third parties (often called *amicus* briefs).

Once the committee takes a decision on your case, it is transmitted to you and the State party simultaneously. One or more committee members may append a separate opinion to the decision if they come to a different conclusion from the majority or perhaps reach the same conclusion but for different reasons. The text of any final decision on the merits of your case or of a decision of inadmissibility will be posted on the OHCHR's web site as part of the committee's jurisprudence.

What happens once a committee decides your case?

It should be noted at the outset that there is no appeal against committee decisions and that, as a rule, the decisions are final. What happens to your case subsequently depends on the nature of the decision taken.

When the committee decides that you have been the victim of a violation by the State party of your rights under the treaty, it invites the State party to supply information within three months on the steps it has taken to give effect to its findings. See the descriptions of the specific procedures for further details.

When the committee decides that there has been no violation of the treaty in your case or that your complaint is inadmissible, the process is complete once the decision has been transmitted to you and the State party.

When the committee considers your case admissible, either in general or with reference to specific claims or articles, the general procedure set out above applies. That is to say, the State party is requested to make submissions on the merits within a specific time frame. You then have a period for comment on the submissions, following which the case is usually ready for consideration by the committee.

2. Human Rights Committee

Fact Sheet No. 7/Rev. 1, Complaints Procedures, available at
http://www.ohchr.org/Documents/Publications/FactSheet7Rev.1en.pdf
Office of the High Commissioner for Human Rights

Details of the Procedure

The following comments expand on the general description of procedures before the committees. Complaints under the Optional Protocol that contain the necessary elements are referred to the Committee's Special Rapporteur on New Communications. The Special Rapporteur decides whether your case should be registered under the Optional Protocol and issues any pertinent instructions.

If the case is registered, the [Human Rights] Committee's usual course of action, given the large number of complaints received under this procedure, is to consider the admissibility and merits of the case simultaneously. To this end, the State party against whom the complaint is directed has six months to present its submissions on the admissibility and merits of the case. When it does so, you have two months to comment, following which the case is ready for a decision by the Committee. As noted above, if the State party fails to respond to your complaint, you are not disadvantaged. In such a case, the State party receives two reminders after the six-month deadline has passed. If there is still no reply, the Committee considers the complaint on the basis of the information you initially supplied. On the other hand, if the State party presents submissions after a reminder, they are transmitted to you and you have the opportunity to comment.

Occasionally, the Committee adopts a different procedure to maximize the time at its disposal to consider communications and to spare both States parties and complainants needless effort. For example, if a State party, within two months of receiving a complaint, presents submissions relating only to admissibility and the Committee considers that there may indeed be serious doubts on that score, it may invite you to comment only on those submissions. The Committee will then take a preliminary decision on admissibility alone and proceed to the merits stage only if the case is declared admissible. If it is, the State party is given a further six months to present submissions on the merits of the communication and you are in turn requested to comment within two months. You will be informed of any such departure from the usual practice.

You should be aware that, given the large number of cases brought under the Optional Protocol, there may be a delay of several years between the initial submission and the Committee's final decision.

Special circumstances of urgency

For the Human Rights Committee, situations of urgency requiring immediate action fall under rule 86 of its rules of procedure. In such cases, the Committee's Special Rapporteur on New Communications may issue a request to the State party for interim measures with a view to averting irreparable harm before your complaint is considered. The Committee views compliance with such a request as inherent in a State party's obligations under the Optional Protocol and any failure to comply as a breach thereof.

Additional pointers on the admissibility of your case

There are two aspects of the admissibility of a case that require further comment. First, the Human Rights Committee has developed specific exceptions to the rule that the events complained of should have occurred after the entry into force of the Optional Protocol for your State. If, since the date of entry into force, the events have had continuing effects that violate the Covenant, for example if the State has failed to resolve the status of a person who "disappeared" prior to the date in question or if a person is serving a term of imprisonment following an unfair trial prior to that date, the Committee may decide to consider the whole circumstances of the complaint. Alternatively, it is usually a sufficient ground for the Committee to examine the whole complaint if, after the date of entry into force of the Optional Protocol, there has been a court decision or some other State act relating to an event preceding that date.

Two points may be made regarding the question of simultaneous examination of the same claim under another mechanism of international settlement. The Committee has decided that, for its purposes, the "1503 procedure" [discussed under the section dealing the U.N. Human Rights] and complaints to a special rapporteur of the [Council] do not constitute such a mechanism. Accordingly, your claim to the Human Rights Committee will not be declared inadmissible if you are concurrently pursuing options such as these. Second, the Committee has taken the view that, inasmuch as the Covenant provides greater protection in some respects than is available under other international instruments, facts that have already been submitted to another international mechanism can be brought before the Committee if broader protections in the Covenant are invoked. It should be added that, in the Committee's view, complaints dismissed by other international mechanisms on procedural grounds have not been substantively examined; the same facts may therefore be brought before the Committee.

Details about complaint procedures under the International Convention for the Elimination of All Forms of Racial Discrimination and the Optional Protocol to the Convention on the Elimination of All Forms of Discrimination Against Women can also be obtained from the Web site of the Office of the High Commissioner for Human Rights (http://www.hchr.org). In what human rights and environment contexts might these be important? In cases of environmental racism, could you turn to the CERD Committee? What about environmental problems with a disproportionate impact on women? Would you think about CEDAW as an option?

IV. Regional Systems

This section explores the three operational regional human rights systems in Europe, the Americas, and Africa. The nascent systems under the 2004 Arab Charter and the 2009 and 2010 ASEAN agreements establishing two commissions on human rights are noted but not be discussed in detail.

The European Convention on Human Rights established the first regional system for the protection of human rights. The inter-American and African systems followed in turn. All three of these operational systems strive to supplement and enhance the U.N. human rights activities. The regional systems are asserted to provide protective mechanisms suited to their regions. In addition to guaranteeing many of the universal rights in multilateral treaties, each regional system also establishes rights seen as particularly important to the region on account of its history, traditions and cultures.

Activities concerning human rights began early in the Americas and in Europe. The Organization of American States adopted the American Declaration on the Rights and Duties of Man months before the U.N. General Assembly approved the Universal Declaration on Human Rights (UDHR), and the American Declaration's provisions were consulted during the drafting process of the UDHR. The Council of Europe adopted the European Convention for the Protection of Human Rights and Fundamental Freedoms (hereafter, European Convention on Human Rights) in 1950 with the stated purpose of providing enforcement machinery for some of the rights contained in the UDHR. The Convention created a quasi-judicial commission and a court to enforce the Convention, and the Convention remains one of the most strongly enforced human rights instruments in the world. Nevertheless, many officials at the United Nations and some observers initially viewed the concept of regionalism in human rights with suspicion because they feared it would undermine the universal guarantees of human rights. However, during the three decades it took to draft the covenants and have them enter into force, regional treaties came to be seen as a positive development.

As with the U.N. human rights practices, the regional systems have evolved considerably through the adoption of additional human rights treaties and the creation of further institutions. For example, the European system has had a commissioner for human rights since 1999, and under the 1987 European Convention for the Prevention of Torture and Inhuman and Degrading Treatment and its two Protocols of 2002, a committee makes periodic visits to countries to investigate the conditions of detention facilities.

As noted previously, the Arab world has an embryonic human rights system. The Arab Charter on Human Rights was adopted (in 1994) and revised in 2004 to make it more compatible with global norms. It has entered into force and establishes a commission whose mandate is limited to reviewing state reports.

In Asia, on July 29, 2009, the Association of South East Asian Nations (ASEAN) adopted the Terms of Reference (TOR) for the ASEAN Inter-Governmental Commission on Human Rights. The Commission was inaugurated on October 23, 2009, at the fifteenth ASEAN summit by the Cha-Am Hua Hin Declaration on the Intergovernmental Commission on Human Rights. The ASEAN body has met with some criticism because of its weak mandate in the TOR. *See, e.g.,* ASEAN's "Human Rights" Council; Not

Off to a Great Start, WALL ST. J. ONLINE, Oct. 26, 2009, *available at* http://online.wsj. com/article/SB10001424052748704335904574494771231953200.html. At present, the Commission only has consultative status, cannot receive individual complaints, and is composed of officials appointed by their governments. Each appointing government has the power to remove its commissioner. Nonetheless, active NGOs working with friendly governments helped achieve the establishment of human rights obligations in the 2007 ASEAN Charter and continue to press for strengthening the Commission's mandate. Some argue that the ASEAN Charter contains provisions that may allow the Commission to develop into an effective body over time, as has happened in other regions. Michelle Staggs Kelsall, *The New ASEAN Intergovernmental Commission on Human Rights: Toothless Tiger or Tentative First Step?*, 90 ASIA PACIFIC ISSUES 1–8 (Sept. 2009).

Despite criticism, ASEAN members established another human rights related–commission in April 2010 at the sixteenth summit in Hanoi. Called the ASEAN Commission on the Promotion and Protection of the Rights of Women and Children (ACWC), its functions are to promote the implementation of international instruments, ASEAN instruments, and other instruments related to the rights of women and children and to develop policies, programs, and innovative strategies to promote and protect the rights of women and children to complement the building of the ASEAN Community. It will also promote public awareness and education of the rights of women and children in ASEAN. Each ASEAN member state is to appoint two representatives to the ACWC – one representative on women's rights and one representative on children's rights. When appointing their representatives to the ACWC, member states are to give due consideration to competence in the field of the rights of women and children, integrity, and gender equality.

A. *The European Human Rights System*

The Evolving International Human Rights System,
100 AM. J. INT'L L. 783, 792–94 (2006)
Thomas Buergenthal

. . .

The European Convention for the Protection of Human Rights and Fundamental Freedoms established what has become the most effective international system for the protection of individual human rights to date. It has also served as a model for the two other regional human rights systems. The Convention traces its origin to the late 1940s, when the states constituting the Council of Europe, then a grouping of Western European states only, concluded that U.N. efforts to produce a treaty transforming the lofty principles proclaimed in the Universal Declaration of Human Rights into a binding international bill of rights would take many years to come to fruition. Rather than wait, they decided that the Council of Europe should proceed on its own. The justification for not waiting was expressed in the preamble to the European Convention, which stated that the members of the Council of Europe were "resolved, as the Governments of European countries which are like-minded and have a common heritage of political traditions, ideals, freedom and the rule of law, to take the first steps for the collective enforcement of certain of the rights stated in the Universal Declaration."

By 1953, the ten ratifications necessary to bring the Convention into force had been deposited, and a total of forty-[seven] states are now parties to it. This dramatic increase in its membership is due in large measure to the geopolitical transformation of Europe that resulted from the demise of the Soviet Union and the end of the Cold War. Today most European states are members of the Council of Europe and states parties to the Convention, including Russia and some former Soviet Republics, as well as the United Kingdom, France, and Germany. In the meantime, the Convention itself and the system it established have also been significantly transformed.

When the European Convention entered into force, it guaranteed only a dozen basic civil and political rights. The list of these rights has grown significantly over the years with the adoption of additional protocols that have expanded the Convention's catalog of rights. In the meantime, these rights have been extensively interpreted by the Convention institutions and the national courts of the member states. In the process, the meaning and scope of these rights also have increasingly come to reflect the contemporary needs of European society. The result is a modern body of human rights law to which other international, regional, and national institutions frequently look when interpreting and applying their own human rights instruments.

In addition, the institutions of the European Convention have undergone extensive changes. The original Convention machinery consisted of a European Commission and Court of Human Rights. The main function of the Commission was to pass on the admissibility of all applications, both interstate and individual. Of the various admissibility requirements, the exhaustion of domestic remedies occupied much of the Commission's time. Because not all states parties to the Convention had been required to accept the jurisdiction of the Court when they ratified the Convention, the Commission also had to deal with cases that were not or could not be referred to the Court. At that time, only states and the Commission had standing to bring cases to the Court; individuals did not.

The institutional structure of the European system was substantially changed with the adoption of Protocol No. 11 to the Convention, which entered into force in 1998. It abolished the Commission and gave individuals direct access to the Court. The Convention thus became the first human rights treaty to give individuals standing to file cases directly with the appropriate tribunal. Today the European Court numbers forty-[seven] judges, that is, a judge for each member state of the Council of Europe. The Plenary Court, which consists of all judges, exercises mainly administrative functions. The judicial work of the Court is performed by three bodies of judges: Committees (three judges), Chambers (seven judges), and the Grand Chamber (seventeen judges). The Committees are authorized to reject, by unanimous vote, individual applications as inadmissible. Chambers deal with the remaining admissibility issues and the merits of most interstate and individual applications. The Grand Chamber has a dual function. Under certain circumstances, particularly when a Chamber is called upon to decide serious questions of interpretation of the Convention or its protocols, it may opt to relinquish its jurisdiction in favor of the Grand Chamber. In certain "exceptional cases," the Grand Chamber may also act as an appellate tribunal and hear cases already decided by a Chamber.

Over time, the European Court of Human Rights for all practical purposes has become Europe's constitutional court in matters of civil and political rights. Its judgments are routinely followed by the national courts of the states parties to the Convention, their legislatures, and their national governments. The Convention itself has acquired the status of domestic law in most of the states parties and can be invoked as such in their courts. While at times some of the newer states parties find it difficult to live up to their obligations under the Convention, a substantial majority of states applies the Convention faithfully and routinely.

The success of the European Convention system has brought with it a caseload for the Court that it has found more and more difficult to cope with. To address this problem, in 2004 the Council of Europe adopted Protocol No. 14 to the Convention . . . [T]he Protocol should enable the Court to reduce its caseload substantially by a variety of methods, some of which have not escaped criticism because they are likely to result, so it is claimed, in the automatic rejection of many meritorious cases. It cannot be doubted, however, that the current caseload has become unmanageable, seriously impeding the effective implementation of the Convention.

Questions and Discussion

1.   The European Convention has had a limited list of rights coupled by stronger enforcement mechanisms than is found in other regional systems. It is now supervised by a permanent court (the institution of a European Commission having been abolished) pursuant to Protocol 11 to the Convention. The court sits in Strasbourg, France. Both states parties and individuals, who have direct access to the court, may complain before the court, whose jurisdiction is compulsory. The secretary-general of the Council of Europe may request reports from states, although there is no periodic reporting procedure like that of U.N. treaty bodies. For a description of reports requested to 2002, see CLARE OVEY & ROBIN C.A. WHITE, JACOBS AND WHITE: EUROPEAN CONVENTION ON HUMAN RIGHTS 11–12 (3d ed., 2002).

2.   The European Convention contains only civil and political rights, although the First Protocol to the Convention contains provisions concerning property and education. The rationale for the focus on civil and political rights was similar to the reasons for the division of the rights enshrined in the Universal Declaration on Human Rights between the two Covenants. Nonetheless, the Court has addressed numerous economic and social issues through its enunciation of the positive obligations of states to secure the rights contained in the Convention. In particular, many environmental matters have come before the court.

3.   Economic, social, and cultural rights are generally protected by the European Social Charter. The Charter was adopted in 1961 and the Revised European Social Charter was adopted in 1996. The Charter is supervised primarily by the European Committee of Social Rights. In addition to reviewing state reports, the Committee has been able to hear collective complaints from certain organizations (including NGOs with consultative status with the Council of Europe and employers' groups and unions within states parties) relating to rights contained in the Social Charter, since the entry into force of an additional protocol.

4.   The European Court has made many important and innovative contributions to the corpus of international human rights law, including at the interface of human rights and the environment. Strikingly, the Court has consistently held that it is not bound by the framer's interpretation of the terms of the Convention. Indeed, all regional courts and commissions view their human rights instruments as "living instruments" that must be applied in light of current conditions. They also utilize the jurisprudence of other human rights bodies to ensure that the rule most favorable to the individual is applied. However, the European Court, more than others, applies a deferential standard in reviewing state practices. The Court's deferential doctrine is known as the margin of appreciation, which means that the Court exercises prudence in the face of divergent practices in Europe, particularly in relation to issues of public morality. *See Handyside v. United Kingdom*, 1 E.H.RR. 737 (1976). The Court has applied the margin-of-appreciation doctrine to emphasize its subsidiary role in the protection of human rights compared to that of national legal systems. Its rationale is based on the belief that governmental officials of a state are better placed than the Court to balance individual rights against broader societal interests when they come into conflict. Under the doctrine, the state is allowed legislative, administrative, and judicial discretion in reaching the right balance. The Court will intervene only when the balance that has been struck is an abuse of discretion. Unfortunately, the doctrine has not been applied consistently, and it is therefore difficult to predict outcomes from case to case. *See* HELEN FENWICK, CIVIL LIBERTIES AND HUMAN RIGHTS 36–39 (2007). Can you see how the

margin of appreciation might come into play in human rights and environment cases? *See* MALGOSIA FITZMAURICE, CONTEMPORARY ISSUES IN INTERNATIONAL ENVIRONMENTAL LAW 179–180 (2009). *See also* DANIEL GARCIA SAN JOSÉ, ENVIRONMENTAL PROTECTION AND THE EUROPEAN CONVENTION ON HUMAN RIGHTS ch. 3 (2005); Christian Schall, *Public Interest Litigation Concerning Environmental Matters Before Human Rights Courts: A Promising Future Concept?*, 20 J. ENVTL. L. 417 (2008).

B. *The American Human Rights System*

The Evolving International Human Rights System,
100 AM. J. INT'L L. 783, 794–97 (2006)
Thomas Buergenthal

When the Charter of the Organization of American States (OAS) was adopted in Bogota, Colombia, in 1948, it made only general references to human rights. But the same Bogota conference also proclaimed the American Declaration of the Rights and Duties of Man, though merely in the form of a nonbinding conference resolution. Before the American Convention on Human Rights entered into force in 1978, the human rights provisions of the OAS Charter, read together with the American Declaration, provided the sole, albeit rather weak, legal basis for the protection of human rights by the OAS.

Until 1960, the OAS made no serious effort to create a mechanism for the enforcement of these rights. That year the Inter-American Commission on Human Rights was established. Composed of seven independent experts elected by the General Assembly of the OAS, the Commission was charged with the promotion of the rights proclaimed in the American Declaration. It was to perform this task by preparing country studies and by adopting resolutions of a general character only. Six years later, the Commission was authorized to establish a limited petition system that allowed it to receive individual communications, charging large-scale violations of a selected number of basic rights set out in the American Declaration, including the right to life, equality before the law, freedom of religion, freedom from arbitrary arrest, and the right to due process of law. . . .

In the early years of its existence, both as autonomous entity and later as Charter organ, the Commission was kept busy preparing reports on human rights situations in various countries. These reports were grounded in on-site visits and information in petitions presented to it. The Commission adopted its first country reports in the early 1960s. These dealt with the human rights situations in Cuba, Haiti, and the Dominican Republic. Only the Dominican Republic granted permission for a visit to the country, making it the first OAS member state to host a so-called *in loco* or on-site investigation by the Commission. During that on-site visit, the Commission criss-crossed the country, held hearings, and met with different groups of claimants. This modus operandi was subsequently adopted for on-site visits generally. The Commission's most dramatic on-site investigation took place in Argentina. There it verified the allegations of the massive forced disappearances that had occurred in that country during its "dirty war." The publication of its report on the Argentine situation had a highly beneficial impact on conditions in that country. For many years, even after the entry into force of the American Convention on Human Rights, the Commission's *in loco* investigations occupied much of its time, primarily because in the 1960s, 1970s, and early 1980s many Latin American countries continued to be ruled by authoritarian regimes that engaged in widespread violations of human rights. Most of these states did not, of course, ratify the Convention until the installation of democratic regimes in their countries. The investigations and reports of the Commission provided the only means for pressuring these states to improve their human rights conditions.

The American Convention on Human Rights was concluded in San José, Costa Rica, in 1969 and came into force in 1978. Like the European Convention, the American Convention guarantees only civil and political rights. While the list of rights the European Convention guarantees has grown with the adoption of further protocols, the drafters of the American Convention opted for a comprehensive instrument that drew heavily on the much more extensive catalog of rights enumerated in the International Covenant on Civil and Political Rights. However, not all the rights guaranteed in the American Convention are derived from the Civil and Political Covenant. Some of them reflect the historical and cultural traditions of the Americas, such as the provision that guarantees the right to life. It provides, inter alia, that this right "shall be protected by law and, in general, from the moment of conception." Delegates from Latin America's overwhelmingly Catholic countries insisted on this provision during the drafting of the Convention.

The institutional structure of the American Convention is modeled on that of the European Convention as originally drafted, that is, before its Protocol No. 11 entered into force. The American Convention provides for a seven-member Inter-American Commission on Human Rights and an Inter-American Court of Human Rights of seven judges. Because the Commission established by the Convention retains the powers its predecessor exercised as an OAS Charter organ, all OAS member states have the right to nominate and elect the members of the Commission. But only the states parties to the Convention may nominate and elect the judges of the Court. Since to date not all OAS member states have ratified the Convention, the Commission continues to apply the human rights provisions of the Charter and the American Declaration of the Rights and Duties of Man to these states, besides acting as a Convention organ with regard to the states parties to that instrument. Importantly, this dual role of the Commission permits it to deal with massive violations of human rights that, though not within its jurisdiction as a Convention organ, it can address as a Charter organ regardless of whether or not the state in question is a party to the Convention. By contrast, the European Convention applies in principle only to individual human rights violations as such.

By ratifying the American Convention, states are automatically considered to have accepted the jurisdiction of the Commission to hear cases brought against them by individuals. Interstate complaints can be heard by the Commission only if the applicant and respondent states have each filed a separate declaration accepting the Commission's jurisdiction to receive such complaints. Until Protocol No. 11 to the European Convention on Human Rights entered into force, no other human rights instrument conferred on individuals the favorable status they enjoy under the American Convention. The Inter-American Commission passes on the admissibility of individual and interstate communications. If the matter is not referred to the Inter-American Court, the Commission examines the merits of the case, assists in efforts to work out a friendly settlement, and, failing that, makes findings on the merits. If the state party in question has accepted the jurisdiction of the Court, the Commission or an interested state may refer the case to the Court. Individuals have no standing to do so. Nevertheless, since 2001, once a case has been referred to the Court, individuals have been permitted to appear before it to plead their case. While in the early years of the Court's existence, the Commission tended to refer cases to it rarely, this situation changed in 2001 when it adopted new Rules of procedure, which provide, with some minor exceptions, for referral to the Court of all cases of noncompliance by states with the Commission's recommendations.

Today the Inter-American Court of Human Rights, which has both contentious and advisory jurisdiction, plays an ever more important role in the inter-American human rights system. Most of the states that have ratified the Convention to date have now also accepted the Court's contentious jurisdiction. The American Convention, moreover, allows OAS member states, whether or nor they have ratified the Convention, and all OAS organs to request advisory opinions from the Court, seeking the interpretation of the Convention or of other human rights treaties of the inter-American system. Advisory opinions may also be sought on the compatibility with the Convention of national legislation. Because the Court's case law has grown significantly since the adoption of the Commission's 2001 Rules of Procedure, states find it increasingly necessary to bring their national legislation and judicial practice into conformity with the Convention to avoid being held in violation of it.

Questions and Discussion

1. The American human rights system began with the American Declaration on the Rights and Duties of Man, adopted by the Organization of American States in 1948. Formally nonbinding, there were no implementation mechanisms for the Declaration. As explained previously, in 1960, the OAS General Assembly approved the creation of the seven-member independent Inter-American Commission on Human Rights. The Commission's mandate was elaborated in its statute, approved one year later, and the Commission began functioning as an organ of consultation and promotion of human rights. The Statute also gave the Commission the power to request information of states, conduct studies and inquiries, and to make recommendations. The Commission read its mandate from the beginning as allowing it to make specific recommendations to individual states, to conduct on-site inquiries and to consider complaints. These powers were confirmed in a revision to the Statute in 1965, and the Commission was elevated to a treaty organ when the OAS Charter was revised by the entry into force of the Protocol of Buenos Aires in 1970. These developments gave the Commission supervisory authority over the human rights performance of all thirty-five OAS member states, using the American Declaration as the normative standard.

2. In 1969, the OAS adopted the American Convention on Human Rights, which entered into force in 1978. It created a new institution, the American Court of Human Rights, and conferred a new role on the Commission, monitoring compliance with the Convention by states parties. The Commission, as a quasi-judicial body, may investigate allegation of rights violations in relation to the Convention or the Declaration, depending on whether the accused state has ratified the Convention. Individual victims or NGOs may complain to the Commission about human rights violations, and the Commission's jurisdiction is compulsory (art. 44). States may also complain, although the Commission's jurisdiction is optional in this respect (art. 45). The Court's contentious jurisdiction is also optional (art. 62). For those states that declare their acceptance, the Court may issue binding judicial decisions in cases referred by the Commission or the defending state party (art. 61); private parties have no standing to bring cases to the Court. The Court, which is composed of seven judges and located in San José, Costa Rica, also may issue advisory opinions at the request of any OAS member state or the Commission.

   The Commission was slow to refer cases to the Court, because the Convention is not retroactive. Once it entered into force in 1978, any violation that occurred thereafter had first to be considered through the exhaustion of local remedies then it had to be evaluated and decided by the Commission. The Commission could then refer the case to the Court, provided the state had accepted the Court's optional jurisdiction (which many states were initially reluctant to do). Thus, in its first years, the Court mainly handed down advisory opinions, one of which, Advisory Opinion No. 10, held that the American Declaration on the Rights and Duties of Man is indirectly legally binding as an authoritative interpretation of the references to human rights in the OAS Charter.

*Interpretation of the American Declaration of the Rights and Duties of Man Within
the Framework of Article 64 of the American Convention on Human Rights,*
Advisory Opinion OC-10/89, July 14, 1989, Inter-Am. Ct. H.R. (ser. A) No. 10 (1989)
Inter-American Court of Human Rights

The Charter of the Organization refers to the fundamental rights of man in its Preamble ((paragraph three) and in Arts. 3(j), 16, 43, 47, 51, 112 and 150; Preamble (paragraph four), Arts. 3(k), 16, 44, 48, 52, 111 and 150 of the Charter revised by the Protocol of Cartagena de Indias), but it does not list or define them. The member states of the Organization have, through its diverse organs, given specificity to the human rights mentioned in the Charter and to which the Declaration refers.

This is the case of Article 112 of the Charter (Art. 111 of the Charter as amended by the Protocol of Cartagena de Indias)[,] which reads as follows:

> There shall be an Inter-American Commission on Human Rights, whose principal function shall be to promote the observance and protection of human rights and to serve as a consultative organ of the Organization in these matters. An inter-American convention on human rights shall determine the structure, competence, and procedure of this Commission, as well as those of other organs responsible for these matters.

Article 150 of the Charter provides as follows:

> Until the inter-American convention on human rights, referred to in Chapter XVIII (Chapter XVI of the Charter as amended by the Protocol of Cartagena de Indias), enters into force, the present Inter-American Commission on Human Rights shall keep vigilance over the observance of human rights.

These norms authorize the Inter-American Commission to protect human rights. These rights are none other than those enunciated and defined in the American Declaration. That conclusion results from Article 1 of the Commission's Statute, which was approved by Resolution No. 447, adopted by the General Assembly of the OAS at its Ninth Regular Period of Sessions, held in La Paz, Bolivia, in October, 1979. That Article reads as follows:

1. The Inter-American Commission on Human Rights is an organ of the Organization of the American States, created to promote the observance and defense of human rights and to serve as consultative organ of the Organization in this matter.
2. For the purposes of the present Statute, human rights are understood to be:
    a. The rights set forth in the American Convention on Human Rights, in relation to the States Parties thereto;
    b. The rights set forth in the American Declaration of the Rights and Duties of Man, in relation to the other member states.

Articles 18, 19 and 20 of the Statute enumerate these functions.

The General Assembly of the Organization has also repeatedly recognized that the American Declaration is a source of international obligations for the member states of the OAS. For example, in Resolution 314 (VII-O/77) of June 22, 1977, it charged the Inter-American Commission with the preparation of a study to "set forth their obligation to carry out the commitments assumed in the American Declaration of the Rights and Duties of Man." In Resolution 371 (VIII-O/78) of July 1, 1978, the General Assembly reaffirmed "its commitment to promote the observance of the American Declaration of the Rights and Duties of Man," and in Resolution 370 (VIII-O/78) of July 1, 1978, it referred to the "international commitments" of a member state of the Organization to respect the rights of man "recognized in the American Declaration of the Rights and Duties of Man." The Preamble of the American Convention to Prevent and Punish Torture, adopted and signed at the Fifteenth Regular Session of the General Assembly in Cartagena de Indias (December, 1985), reads as follows:

Reaffirming that all acts of torture or any other cruel, inhuman, or degrading treatment or punishment constitute an offense against human dignity and a denial of the principles set forth in the Charter of the Organization of American States and in the Charter of the United Nations and are violations of the fundamental human rights and freedoms proclaimed in the American Declaration of the Rights and Duties of Man and the Universal Declaration of Human Rights.

Hence it may be said that by means of an authoritative interpretation, the member states of the Organization have signaled their agreement that the Declaration contains and defines the fundamental human rights referred to in the Charter. Thus the Charter of the Organization cannot be interpreted and applied as far as human rights are concerned without relating its norms, consistent with the practice of the organs of the OAS, to the corresponding provisions of the Declaration.

In view of the fact that the Charter of the Organization and the American Convention are treaties with respect to which the Court has advisory jurisdiction by virtue of Article 64(1), it follows that the Court is authorized, within the framework and limits of its competence, to interpret the American Declaration and to render an advisory opinion relating to it whenever it is necessary to do so in interpreting those instruments.

For the member states of the Organization, the Declaration is the text that defines the human rights referred to in the Charter. Moreover, Articles 1(2)(b) and 20 of the Commission's Statute define the competence of that body with respect to the human rights enunciated in the Declaration, with the result that to this extent the American Declaration is for these States a source of international obligations related to the Charter of the Organization.

For the States Parties to the Convention, the specific source of their obligations with respect to the protection of human rights is, in principle, the Convention itself. It must be remembered, however, that, given the provisions of Article 29(d), these States cannot escape the obligations they have as members of the OAS under the Declaration, notwithstanding the fact that the Convention is the governing instrument for the States Parties thereto.

Questions and Discussion

1. Advisory Opinion No. 10 confirms that the Commission may investigate violations of human rights on the part of those states that have not become party to the American Convention, such as the United States, by reference to the American Declaration. It has done so on a number of occasions. For example, the Commission issued precautionary measures against the United States in a case concerning detainees at Guantánamo Bay. Is Advisory Opinion No. 10 sound? Do you think the United States and other nonparties to the Convention anticipated such a result by approving the Declaration? How important is their original intent, given the legal developments in the system since 1948?

2. As with the United Nations and Europe, the inter-American system has adopted additional normative instruments, all of which are under the monitoring of the Inter-American Commission. They are published in the in Basic Documents Pertaining to Human Rights in the Inter-American System, OEA/Ser.L.V/II.82 doc.6 rev.1 at 67 (1992).

1. Economic and Social Rights (Including Environmental Rights) in the American Human Rights System: Applicable Norms

The American Declaration contains civil, political, economic, social, and cultural rights. However, the 1969 American Convention on Human Rights is generally concerned with civil and political rights. The Commission, which prepared one of the later drafts of the Convention, reasoned that member states would not agree to the inclusion of economic, social, and cultural rights – indeed, the limited reference to these rights drafted by the Commission provoked strong negative reactions from most OAS members, including the United States. Matthew Craven, *The Protection of Economic, Social and Cultural Rights under the Inter-American System of Human Rights, in The Inter-American System of Human Rights*, 289, 298 (D.J. Harris & S. Livingstone eds., 1998). Article 26 of the Convention, the final compromise reached on economic, social, and cultural rights is extremely limited.

Article 26 – Progressive Development,
American Convention on Human Rights, July 18, 1978,
O.A.S. Treaty Series No. 36, 1144 U.N.T.S. 123

The States Parties undertake to adopt measures, both internally and through international cooperation, especially those of an economic and technical nature, with a view to achieving progressively, by legislation or other appropriate means, the full realization of the rights implicit in the economic, social, educational, scientific, and cultural standards set forth in the Charter of the Organization of American States as amended by the Protocol of Buenos Aires.

Advisory Opinion No. 10, concerning the effect of the American Declaration is potentially relevant to Convention parties with respect to the enforcement of economic, social, and cultural rights, as Matthew Craven explains below.

The Protection of Economic, Social, and Cultural Rights Under the Inter-American System of Human Rights, in THE INTER-AMERICAN SYSTEM OF HUMAN RIGHTS 300–06
(D.J. Harris & S. Livingstone eds., 1998)
Matthew Craven

... The Commission's power to act upon petitions is governed initially by Article 41(f) of the Convention. Its competence in that regard is spelt out in more detail in Article 44 of the Convention, which specifies initially that persons, groups or Non-Governmental Organizations may lodge petitions with the Commission "concerning denunciations or complaints of violation of this Convention by a State party." This would appear to allow for the submission and receipt of complaints in relation to purported violations of Article 26 [on progressive realization of rights implicit in the OAS Charter], as, for example, when a State arbitrarily legislates against trade union membership or discriminates against a social group by refusing its members access to public educational facilities.

   Volio points out, however, that Article 45 provides that complaints may only be considered if they allege a violation of the rights "set forth" in the Convention. He concludes that as the economic, social, and cultural rights are not specifically "set forth" in the Convention, they may not be the subject of complaints. Whilst this is true of Article 45, which relates exclusively to the system of inter-State complaints and which is subject to special acceptance, different wording is used in Article 47[,] which governs admissibility in general. That article refers to the rights "guaranteed" by the Convention (Article 48, in addition, refers to the rights "protected' by the Convention)." This language, it is considered, does not necessitate the conclusion that petitions are excluded in relation to economic, social, and cultural rights. Nevertheless, that position has been the one adopted by the Commission. Article 31 of the Commission's Regulations, provides that the Commission shall take into account alleged violations by a State party of the "human rights *defined* in the American Convention" [emphasis added]. Only in a remote sense are any economic, social, and cultural rights actually "defined" in the American Convention.

Given the obvious limitations of both Articles 26 and 42, it would appear that economic, social and cultural rights are afforded greater protection under the terms of the American Declaration than under the Convention. This raises an interesting question as regards the precise relationship between these two instruments, particularly as to whether the Declaration obligations subsist even for States parties to the Convention. There are essentially two views on the question, each of which has certain distinct consequences in terms of the protection of economic, social and cultural rights. The first approach is to view the inter-American human rights system as one in the process of organic development in which the later instruments are taken to provide the most complete expression of the human rights to which they all refer. The Convention, as such, is taken to supersede the Declaration both chronologically and normatively, with the effect that once a State becomes party to the Convention, the Declaration no longer has legal significance. This view gains some support from the terms of Article 2(1) of the Commission's Statute, which provides that in the exercise of its functions the Commission is to treat "human rights" as being those contained in the Declaration for member states which are not yet party to the Convention, and those in the Convention for those States which have duly ratified that instrument.

The second approach would be to view the Convention, not as a replacement of the Declaration, but rather as a complementary instrument. Just as much as the Universal Declaration forms part of the International Bill of Rights alongside the U.N. Covenants, the Declaration would therefore retain its full effect and stand alongside the American Convention. This approach has some support in the terms of Article 29(d) of the Convention, which provides that: "No provision of this Convention shall be interpreted as: . . . (d) excluding or limiting the effect that the American Declaration of the Rights and Duties of Man and other international acts of the same nature may have." On this view, any obligations that might have been assumed in relation to the Declaration will therefore subsist for all States, even for those that have become party to the Convention. This would enable the Commission to continue its "Charter role" in supervising the implementation of the economic, social and cultural rights in the Declaration even in relation to States parties to the Convention on the basis of their Charter obligations concerning human rights.

. . .

The attitude of the Commission towards the application of the Declaration in relation to States parties to the Convention has been largely negative. In general, the Commission has interpreted the terms of Article 2(1) of the Statute in a strict manner, only having reference to the terms of the Declaration in relation to States which have yet to become parties to the Convention. In relation to the States parties themselves, it has either not received any communications relating to Article 26 or it has treated such communications as being beyond its competence to consider. An example of the latter approach is found in a case in which the Commission considered the petitioners' claim that the Convention had incorporated the rights in the Declaration into the Convention by way of Article 2(1) of the Statute. The Commission noted that to take this view was inconsistent with the terms of Article 31(2) of the Vienna Convention and ran counter to the structure of the Statute which distributed the competences of the Commission according to whether or not States were party to the Convention. It concluded that in relation to States party to the Convention, "the IACHR can only, in accordance with its own Regulations (Article 31), take into consideration the petitions on presumed violations of rights defined in the American Convention on Human Rights." It added that "[t]he right to work is still not incorporated into the Convention which does not include economic, social and cultural rights."

Even if these arguments were to be accepted as sound, which it is considered they are not, it appears that the Commission has subsequently modified its position. The Commission has now adopted the view that it can, in certain circumstances, consider petitions referring to rights in the Declaration even in relation to States parties to the Convention. This change of heart on the part of the Commission was undoubtedly brought about by, and certainly followed on from, an earlier opinion of the inter-American Court.... Having found that for States parties to the Convention "the specific source of their obligations with respect to the protection of human rights is, in principle, the Convention itself," it went on to note that "given the provisions of Article 29(d), these States cannot escape their obligations they have as members of the OAS under the Declaration." Although the Court was not altogether unambiguous in its comments, this wording does suggest at least that States retain their substantive obligations in relation to the Declaration, obligations which, in the scheme of the Charter arrangements, would carry with it supervision by the Commission.

The context in which the Commission came to reconsider the matter was one in which it was reviewing an application relating to events occurring prior to Argentina's ratification of the Convention. The question was raised whether, in light of Article 2(1) of its Statute, the Commission was competent to apply the Declaration in relation to Argentina despite the fact that it was now a State party to the Convention. In light of its previous practice, one might have assumed the question to have been answered in the negative. However, the Commission, taking note of the opinion of the Court in OC-10/89, took the view that "[r]atification of the Convention by Member states at least complemented, augmented or perfected the international protection of human rights in the inter-American system, but did not create them *ex novo*, nor did it extinguish the previous or subsequent validity of the American Declaration." It therefore concluded that Argentina remained bound by the terms of the Declaration and found it to have violated Articles I, XVIII, and XXVI of the Declaration. What is particularly surprising is that the Commission need not have gone as far as it did in order to come to this conclusion. It could quite easily have declared the American Declaration to be relevant only insofar as the case concerned events that had occurred prior to ratification of the Convention[,] which was inapplicable *ratione temporis*. To suggest, however, that the Convention did not extinguish the subsequent validity of the Declaration appears to be a distinct departure from the Commission's previous practice, and is potentially propitious for the protection of the economic, social and cultural rights.

... It is considered that even if the Statute of the Commission does appear to point in a different direction, it would be contrary to the object and purpose of the various human rights instruments and antithetical to the idea of the development of the system as a whole, to suggest that States have in fact dispensed with obligations in relation to the implementation of economic, social and cultural rights in the Charter merely in virtue of ratifying the Convention. Unless the Convention is seen as entirely superseding the Declaration in a legal sense, a point which has never been seriously contemplated, it must be concluded that the Declaration retains its normative force. The only conceivable argument then is that ratification of the Convention, whilst not changing States' existing obligations, does alter the competence of the Commission in relation to supervision. In other words, while States would retain their obligations in relation to the Declaration, the Commission would no longer exercise any supervisory role in that regard. This again would amount to a surrender of advances previously achieved in the inter-American system and for that reason should not be lightly presumed. It would also run counter to the general scheme of the Charter, which supposes that its human rights provisions fall within the remit of the Commission.

Question and Discussion

Which of the two positions concerning the relationship between the American Declaration and the American Convention, as described by Craven, do you find most persuasive? Note that the Commission has begun considering alleged violations of article 26. *See San Mateo de Huanchor*, Case 12/471, OEA/Ser/L/V/II.121 (Oct. 15, 2002). The Commission decided that the petition was admissible but found that there was insufficient evidence to make a finding on the allegation.

2. Environmental Rights

An Additional Protocol to the American Convention on Human Rights in the area of economic, social, and cultural rights (Protocol of San Salvador) contains twenty-two articles guaranteeing rights similar to those in the ICESCR. The Protocol's implementation mechanisms are limited, however. Only two rights – the freedom to join and form trade unions and the right to education – may be the subject of the petition procedure set out in the American Convention on Human Rights. In general, enforcement is left to a reporting system primarily supervised by the Inter-American Economic and Social Council and the Inter-American Council for Education, Science, and Culture, both of which are composed of governmental representatives. This has not precluded the Commission from addressing such issues as the land, territory, and resource rights of indigenous peoples and other economic matters.

Article 11 addresses the environment. Even before the entry into force of the Protocol in 1999, the Commission and Court had dealt with numerous environmental issues that affected the rights to health, religion, and property.

ARTICLE 11 – RIGHT TO A HEALTHY ENVIRONMENT, ADDITIONAL PROTOCOL TO THE AMERICAN CONVENTION ON HUMAN RIGHTS IN THE AREA OF ECONOMIC, SOCIAL, AND CULTURAL RIGHTS (Nov. 17, 1988), O.A.S. Treaty Series No. 69, *reprinted in Basic Documents Pertaining to Human Rights in the Inter-American System,* OEA/Ser.L.V/II.82 doc.6 rev.1 at 67 (1992)

1. Everyone shall have the right to live in a healthy environment and to have access to basic public services.

2. The States Parties shall promote the protection, preservation, and improvement of the environment.

Questions and Discussion

1. One commentator observes that article 11 "clearly grants an environmental right and specifies affirmative state obligations. The operative provisions require both international cooperation and the adoption of domestic legislation for the achievement of rights." Prudence E. Taylor, *From Environmental to Ecological Human Rights: A New Dynamic in International Law?*, 10 GEO. INT'L ENVTL. L. REV. 309, 346 (1998). Do you agree? How is compliance to be achieved? In what ways does article 11 provide meaningful environmental protection?

2. In reading article 11, it is also important to be aware of articles 1 and 2 of the San Salvador Protocol. Article 1 provides that parties "undertake to adopt the necessary measures, both domestically and through international cooperation, especially economic and technical, to the extent allowed by their available resources, and taking into account their degree of development, for the purpose of achieving progressively and pursuant to their internal legislations, the full observance of the rights recognized in this Protocol." Article 2 provides that, "[i]f the exercise of the rights set forth in this Protocol is not already guaranteed by legislative or other provisions, the States Parties undertake to adopt... such legislative or other measures as may be necessary for making those rights a reality." What is the effect of these provisions in relation to article 11? Article 2 appears to contemplate legislative or regulatory measures in relation to article 11. But does article 1 mean that if a state lacks resources, it can do nothing? If so, who makes that determination?

3. For a recent guide to filing environmental cases in the inter-American system, see Inter-American Association for Environmental Defense, Environmental Defense Guide: Building Strategies for Litigating Cases Before the Inter-American System of Human Rights (2010). For a review of the environmental jurisprudence of the Commission and Court, see Dinah Shelton, *Environmental Rights and Brazil's Obligations in the Inter-American Human Rights System*, 40 GWU Int'l L. Rev. 733 (2009).

C. *The African Human Rights System*

The Evolving International Human Rights System,
100 Am. J. Int'l L. 783, 797–801 (2006)
Thomas Buergenthal

The African human rights system evolved in two distinct stages in a manner somewhat similar to that of its inter-American counterpart. The first stage consisted of the adoption in 1981 by the Organization of African Unity, now the African Union, of the African Charter on Human and Peoples' Rights. It entered into force in 1986 and in the meantime has been ratified by all fifty-three-member states of the African Union. The Charter created an African Commission on Human and Peoples' Rights, but not a court. The African Court of Human and Peoples' Rights was established later by means of a separate protocol that came into force in 2004. The Court was formally inaugurated only in 2006.

The catalog of rights that the African Charter guarantees differs from its European and inter-American counterparts in several important respects. The Charter proclaims not only rights but also duties, and it guarantees both individual and peoples' rights. In addition to civil and political rights, the African Charter sets out a series of economic and social rights. The Charter permits the states parties to impose more extensive restrictions and limitations on the exercise of the rights it proclaims than the European and inter-American human rights instruments. It also does not contain a derogation clause, which leaves the question open whether all rights in the African Charter are derogable. The Charter's catalog of rights was heavily influenced by the rights proclaimed in the Universal Declaration of Human Rights and the two International Covenants on Human Rights. African historical traditions and customs are also reflected in some provisions of the Charter, particularly those dealing with duties of individuals and family matters.

The Commission's mandate is "to promote human and peoples' rights and ensure their protection in Africa." It is composed of eleven elected members who serve in their individual capacities. The Commission has promotional and quasi-judicial powers. It discharges its promotional functions by preparing studies, convening conferences and workshops, disseminating information, and collaborating with NGOs. The Commission has the power to make recommendations to governments, calling on them to address human rights problems that have come to its attention from its review of the periodic country reports the states parties are required to submit to it, as well as from other sources, including its own on-site visits and country studies.

The Commission is also empowered to render interpretive opinions and to deal with interstate and individual complaints. The states parties, the African Union, and intergovernmental African organizations recognized by the latter may request advisory opinions from the Commission regarding interpretation of the African Charter on Human and Peoples' Rights. These advisory powers acquire a special significance in light of two Charter provisions. One of these is Article 60, which reads as follows:

> The Commission shall draw inspiration from international law on human and peoples' rights, particularly from the provisions of various African instruments on human and peoples' rights, the Charter of the United Nations, the Charter of the [African Union], the Universal Declaration of

Human Rights, other instruments adopted by the United Nations and by African countries in the field of human and peoples' rights as well as from the provisions of various instruments adopted within the Specialized Agencies of the United Nations of which the parties to the present Charter are members.

The other provision is Article 61. It contains the following language:

The Commission shall also take into consideration, as subsidiary measures to determine the principles of law, other general or special international conventions, laying down rules expressly recognized by member states of the [African Union], African practices consistent with international norms on human and peoples' rights, customs generally accepted as law, general principles of law recognized by African states as well as legal precedents and doctrine.

These interesting and unique provisions provide the Commission with a valuable legislative tool capable of ensuring that its interpretations of the African Charter keep pace with developments in the international human rights field in general. Through the years, the Commission has increasingly relied on these provisions with a view to strengthening the normative contents of the African Charter.

The powers of the African Commission to deal with interstate and individual communications are much more limited than those conferred by the European and inter-American human rights treaties. The Commission is so constrained in part because its findings with regard to the communications it receives cannot be made public without the permission of the African Union's Assembly of Heads of State and Government, a political body that has traditionally not been inclined to take strong action against serious violators of human rights. The Commission's power to deal with individual petitions is limited, furthermore, to "cases which reveal the existence of a series of serious or massive violations of human and peoples' rights." Thus, what we have here is not really a mechanism for individual petitions as it exists in the two other regional human rights systems. It is, rather, a procedure that permits individuals to file petitions charging massive or persistent violations of human rights, but not individual violations of one or the other right guaranteed by the African Charter. It is worth noting, though, that in the past the African Commission found ways around this problem by hearing claims that on their face may nor have met the strict requirements of the above provision.

The new African Court of Human and Peoples' Rights, whose function it is to "complement the protective mandate" of the African Commission, has contentious and advisory jurisdiction. Its contentious jurisdiction is broader than that of the European and inter-American Courts; it extends to disputes arising not only under the Charter and the Protocol establishing the Court, but also "under any other relevant Human Rights instrument ratified by the States concerned." On its face, this broad language would permit the Court to adjudicate disputes between African states even with regard to non-African human rights instruments to which they are parties. The Court's contentious jurisdiction covers cases filed by the African Commission, states parties that are applicants and respondents in cases heard before the Commission, states parties whose citizens are victims of human rights violations, and African intergovernmental organizations. NGOs with observer status before the Commission and individuals as such may also institute proceedings before the Court, provided the state party against which the case is filed previously recognized that right in a separate declaration.

The Court also has extensive advisory jurisdiction powers. These are spelled out in Article 4(1) of the Protocol, which reads as follows:

At the request of a Member State of the [African Union], the [AU], any of its organs, or any African organization recognized by the [AU], the Court may provide an opinion on any legal matter relating to the Charter or any other relevant human rights instruments, provided that the subject matter of the opinion is not related to a matter being examined by the Commission.

It remains to be seen how the Court will interpret the phrase "any other relevant human rights instruments" in dealing with requests for advisory opinions. This open-ended language might be read to permit the Court to render advisory opinions relating to any human rights instruments whatsoever. It might also be argued that the reference to "relevant" instruments was intended to indicate that Article 4(1) referred only to human rights instruments relevant to the interpretation of the Charter.

. . . [T]he political, economic, and social problems Africa faces are much more severe than the comparable problems that plague the Americas or Europe. In addition to severe poverty and corruption, the African continent continues to be the victim of wars and internal armed conflicts that have killed millions of human beings, while AIDS is ravaging the entire populations of some countries. Africa has also not been able to rid itself of authoritarian regimes, some of which still hold power. It will therefore not be easy in the short term for the African Court and Commission to create an effective regional human rights system.

————————

The regional human rights system for Africa can be viewed as arising with the adoption of the Convention on Specific Aspects of the Refugee Problem in Africa in 1969. Julie Harrington, *The African Court on Human and People's Rights, in* THE AFRICAN CHARTER ON HUMAN AND PEOPLE'S RIGHTS: THE SYSTEM IN PRACTICE, 1986–2000, at 306 (M.D. Evans & R. Murray eds., 2002). That Convention is notable for its more generous definition of refugees as compared with the 1951 Convention on the Status of Refugees. It was more than a decade after the refugee convention, however, that the African states adopted a general regional human rights treaty and created a body to promote and protect the rights it enshrines. It is also important in connection with displacement caused by environmental disasters considered in Chapter 9.

1. The Banjul Charter

Both the American and the Universal Declaration set forth rights and duties. The Banjul Charter is distinctive among human rights treaties, however, in that it contains both rights and duties and people's rights alongside individual rights. In terms of environmental rights, article 24 establishes a "peoples'" right to environment. In terms of duties, articles 27 and 29 are far more particular than, for example, article 29 of the Universal Declaration of Human Rights.

African [Banjul] Charter on Human and Peoples' Rights, 1982 (June 27, 1981), OAU Doc. CAB/LEG/67/3 rev. 5; 21 I.L.M. 58 (1982)

Article 24

All peoples shall have the right to a general satisfactory environment favorable to their development. . . .

Article 27

1. Every individual shall have duties towards his family and society, the State and other legally recognized communities and the international community.

2. The rights and freedoms of each individual shall be exercised with due regard to the rights of others, collective security, morality and common interest.

Article 28

Every individual shall have the duty to respect and consider his fellow beings without discrimination, and to maintain relations aimed at promoting, safeguarding and reinforcing mutual respect and tolerance.

Article 29

The individual shall also have the duty:

1. to preserve the harmonious development of the family and to work for the cohesion and respect for the family, to respect his parents at all times, to maintain them in case of need;

2. to serve his national community by placing his physical and intellectual abilities at its service;

3. not to compromise the security of the State whose national or resident he is;

4. to preserve and strengthen social and national solidarity, particularly when the latter is threatened;

5. to preserve and strengthen the national independence and the territorial integrity of his country and to contribute to its defence in accordance with the law;

6. to work to the best of his abilities and competence, and to pay taxes imposed by law in the interest of the society;

7. to preserve and strengthen positive African cultural values in his relations with other members of the society, in the spirit of tolerance, dialogue and consultation and, in general, to contribute to the promotion of the moral well-being of society; and

8. to contribute to the best of his abilities, at all times and at all levels, to the promotion and achievement of African unity.

Questions and Discussion

1. Can you identify the rights holder under article 24? What is a "general satisfactory environment" he or she has a right to? Some scholars maintain that the people's rights are held in common by the entire population of a state rather than by an individual, ethnic minority, or other social grouping. Does that raise problems? For instance, does each individual in the population need to be deprived of a general satisfactory environment before there is a breach? Does it mean that the population (all members) must join in a claim rather than a representative being permitted to claim on a people's behalf?
2. Notice the link to development in article 24. Does this require provision of an environment that promotes economic and social development? Does the link to development mean that in the event of conflict between environmental and developmental priorities that one should be preferred to the other? That they must be balanced?

2. The Work of the African Commission on Human and Peoples' Rights and the Environment

The African Commission on Human and People's Rights has largely been required to invent its own monitoring mechanisms and procedures, as the Banjul Charter is sometimes vague or even silent. Article 62, for example, provides for periodic reports but does not mention the Commission or say what action should be taken on the reports. The Commission has, however, developed guidelines concerning the reporting process and has pursued an active dialogue with states parties. Articles 47–53 clearly deal with state communications, and this provision has been used on at least one occasion. By contrast, articles 55–59, which refer to "other communications," are far from clear as to what the Commission should do with such communications. Article 58 refers only to action on communications concerning a series of serious or massive violations of human and peoples' rights. This is in stark contrast to the detail concerning admissibility of such communications in article 56. However, the Commission has accepted communications concerning the violations of particular individuals' rights. The majority of the Commission's caseload (which has been small) has concerned violations of civil and political rights. *See generally* Christof Heyns, *Civil and Political Rights in the African Charter, in* THE AFRICAN CHARTER ON HUMAN AND PEOPLES' RIGHTS: THE SYSTEM IN PRACTICE, 1986–2000, 137 (Malcolm D. Evans & Rachel Murray, eds., 2002).

Review *Decision Regarding Communication 155/96, Social and Economic Rights Action Center/Center for Economic and Social Rights v. Nigeria*, in Chapter 4. Professor Shelton evaluated the Commission's approach to article 24 in positive terms:

> The Commission...assessed the claimed violations of the rights to health (Article 16) and to a general satisfactory environment (Article 24). In coupling the two rights, the Commission...recognized that a "clean and safe environment...is closely linked to economic and social rights in so far as the environment affects the quality of life and safety of the individual." It found that the right to a general satisfactory environment "imposes clear obligations upon a government," requiring the state "to take reasonable and other measures to prevent pollution and ecological degradation, to promote conservation, and to secure an ecologically sustainable development and use of natural resources." Moreover, government compliance with the spirit of Articles 16 and 24 of the African Charter must also include ordering or at least permitting independent scientific monitoring of threatened environments, requiring and publicizing environmental and social impact studies prior to any major industrial development, undertaking appropriate monitoring and providing information to those communities exposed to hazardous materials and activities and providing meaningful opportunities for individuals to be heard and to participate in the development decisions affecting their communities.
>
> Applying these obligations to the facts of the case, the Commission concluded that although Nigeria had the right to produce oil, it had not protected the Article 16 and Article 24 rights of those in the Ogoni region.

Dinah Shelton, *Decision Regarding Communication 155/96 (Social and Economic Rights Action Center/Center for Economic and Social Rights v. Nigeria)*. Case No. ACHPR/COMM/A044/1, *available at* http://www.umn.edu/humanrts/africa/comcases/allcases.html. *African Commission on Human and Peoples' Rights*, May 27, 2002, 96 AM. J. INT'L L. 937, 939 (2002).

3. The Relationship Between the New Court and the Commission

Until recently, another distinctive feature of the Banjul Charter was that its implementation was monitored by the Commission and there was no court of human rights, because at the establishment of the Charter, the Commission was viewed by many as more compatible with African traditions of conciliation. However, Harrington writes that some commentators saw the absence of a court as a political decision that would have to be reversed later, and that this view has proved correct. A Protocol to the African Charter on the Establishment of the African Court on Human and People's Rights was adopted in 1998 and entered into force on

January 25, 2005. A lengthy process of ratification and amendment followed, as revealed in this summary by the African Commission.

About the African Court,
available at http://www.africancourtcoalition.org/editorial.asp?page_id=16
Coalition for an Effective African Court on Human and Peoples Rights
. . .

The protocol establishing the African Court came into force on 25 January 2005 after receipt of the 15th instrument of ratification of the Comoros on 25 December 2004. The AU Commission called on States Parties to nominate candidates to serve on the African Court. By July 2004, nine States Parties had already submitted their nominations for judges. Three States, namely the Gambia, Lesotho and Senegal, which later withdrew, offered to host the African Court. At the January 2005 AU Summit, the Assembly of Heads of State and Government decided to postpone the election of judges to July 2005.

Decision to Integrate the African Court

Following a proposal by the Chairperson of the Assembly of the AU and head of the Federal Republic of Nigeria, President Olusegun Obasanjo, the AU decided to integrate the African Human Rights Court and the Court of Justice of the African Union. Underlying this decision was the concern at the growing number of AU institutions, which it could not afford to support. The AU Commission was requested to work out the modalities on the implementation of the decision to integrate the courts.

A panel of legal experts met in Addis Ababa, Ethiopia from 13–14 January 2005 to consider the decision and make recommendations. This panel drafted a protocol entitled, "Draft Protocol on the Integration of the African Court on Human and Peoples' Rights and the Court of Justice of the AU." This was presented to the Executive Council of the AU at the summit in Abuja, Nigeria, January 2005. The AU Commission recommended that the integrity of the jurisdiction of the two courts should be retained while at the same time making it possible to administer the protocols through the same court by way of special chambers, and the necessary amendments to both protocols be effected through the adoption of a new protocol by the AU Assembly of Heads of States and Governments.

At the January 2005 AU Summit, the Executive Council decided to refer the report of the Permanent Representatives Committee (these are ambassadors to the AU in Addis Ababa, Ethiopia) and the AU Commission's reports to a meeting of legal experts from governments for their recommendations, which would be presented at the next ordinary session of the AU in July 2005. Further and importantly, the Executive Council decided that the operationalisation of the African Court should continue without prejudice.

A meeting of government legal experts took place in Addis Ababa, Ethiopia from 29th March to 1st April 2005 to consider these documents. Acknowledging the complexities involved in creating an integrated judicial system, the meeting recommended that (1) the operationalisation of the African Court should continue, (2) the ratification of the protocol establishing the Court of Justice of the AU should continue until it comes into force, and (3) that only then should the process to integrate the two courts resume. The body of government experts further recommended that the AU should determine the seat of and elect judges to the African Court.

At the July AU Summit in Sirte, Libya, the Assembly of Heads of State and Government decided that the African Human Rights Court should be set up and the processes towards putting it in operation should begin. The Assembly further decided that the African Human Rights Court, and the merged court, will be headquartered in the East African region. Only states that have ratified the protocol establishing the African Human Rights Court can qualify to offer to host the Court.

From 21st to 25th November 2005, a working group on the draft single legal instrument relating to the merger of the African Court on Human and Peoples' Rights and the Court of Justice of the African Union met to examine the draft document.

Election of Judges

States Parties were requested to submit candidates to serve on the African Court by 30 November 2005. By December, there were fifteen candidates who include senior judges and academics. The election of judges finally took place at the mid-term AU Summit from 16–24 January 2006.

AFRICAN [BANJUL] CHARTER ON HUMAN AND PEOPLES' RIGHTS
(June 27, 1981), OAU Doc. CAB/LEG/67/3 rev. 5; 21 I.L.M. 58 (1982)

Article 55

1. Before each Session, the Secretary of the Commission shall make a list of the communications other than those of States parties to the present Charter and transmit them to the members of the Commission, who shall indicate which communications should be considered by the Commission.

2. A communication shall be considered by the Commission if a simple majority of its members so decide.

Protocol to the African Charter on Human and Peoples' Rights on the Establishment of the African Court on Human and Peoples' Rights (June 9, 1998), OAU/LEG/MIN/AFCHPR/PROT(III)

Article 5

1. The following are entitled to submit cases to the Court:

    (a) Commission
    (b) The State Party, which had lodged a complaint to the Commission
    (c) The State Party against which the complaint had been lodged at the Commission
    (d) The State Party whose citizen is a victim of human rights violation
    (e) African Intergovernmental Organizations

2. When a State Party has an interest in a case, it may submit a request to the Court to be permitted to join.

3. The Court may entitle relevant Non Governmental organizations (NGOs) with observer status before the Commission and individuals to institute cases directly before it, in accordance with article 34(6) of this Protocol.

Article 6

1. The Court, when deciding on the admissibility of a case instituted under article 5(3) of this Protocol, may request the opinion of the Commission[,] which shall give it as soon as possible.

2. The Court shall rule on the admissibility of cases taking into account the provisions of Article 56 of the Charter.

3. The Court may consider cases or transfer them to the Commission.

Article 34 . . .

6. At the time of the ratification of this Protocol or any time thereafter, the State shall make a declaration accepting the competence of the Court to receive cases under Article 5(3) of this Protocol. The Court shall not receive any petition under Article 5(3) involving a State Party which has not made such a declaration.

Questions and Discussion

1. Compare the provisions of the Protocol on standing with the provisions of the Banjul Charter with respect to individual communications. In what ways is standing limited, and what might be the reason for this? How do these limitations compare with other regional instruments and the U.N. human rights treaties?

2. Although the jurisdictional provisions relating to individuals are narrower for the Court than for the Commission, the Protocol is silent or ambiguous regarding many aspects of the relationship between the two organs.

6 Procedural Human Rights and the Environment

I. Introduction

At the 1972 Stockholm Conference on the Human Environment, the United States proposed including the right to a safe and healthy environment in the Stockholm Declaration. The lack of state support for such a right became evident and resulted in the somewhat ambiguous text of Principle 1, which nonetheless links environmental protection and human rights. After Stockholm, environmental scholars and activists began to consider human rights in a more instrumental fashion, identifying those rights whose enjoyment could be considered a prerequisite to effective environmental protection. They focused in particular on the procedural rights of access to environmental information, public participation in decision making, and access to justice and remedies in the event of environmental harm. *See, e.g.,* A.-Ch. Kiss, *Peut-on définir le droit de l'homme à l'environnement?*, 1976 REVUE JURIDIQUE DE L'ENVIRONNEMENT 15; Kiss, *Le droit à la conservation de l'environnement*, 2 REVUE UNIVERSELLE DES DROITS DE L'HOMME 445 (1990); Kiss, *An Introductory Note on a Human Right to Environment, in* ENVIRONMENTAL CHANGE AND INTERNATIONAL LAW 551 (E. Brown Weiss ed., 1992).

By the 1992 Rio Conference on Environment and Development, the need for public involvement in environmental protection was widely accepted. Chapter 23 of Agenda 21, on strengthening the role of major groups, proclaims that individuals, groups, and organizations should have access to information relevant to the environment and development, held by national authorities, including information on products and activities that have or are likely to have a significant impact on the environment, as well as information on environmental protection matters. The Rio Declaration on Environment and Development, A/CONF.151/26/Rev.1 (Vol. I) (3–14 June 1992), Annex I, pp. 3–8, calls for it on the ground of efficiency rather than as a matter of rights: "Environmental issues are best handled with the participation of all concerned citizens at the relevant level" (Principle 10). Principle 10 adds, however, a clear mandate that individuals

> shall have appropriate access to information concerning the environment that is held by public authorities, including information on hazardous materials and activities in their communities, and the opportunity to participate in decision-making processes. States shall facilitate and encourage public awareness and participation by making information widely available. Effective access to judicial and administrative proceedings, including redress and remedy, shall be provided.

Id, Principle 10. Numerous environmental instruments now contain the three procedural rights, which also form part of human rights guarantees. Each right is discussed in turn in the following sections.

II. Access to Environmental Information

Access to environmental information is a prerequisite to public participation in decision making and to monitoring governmental and private-sector activities. The nature of environmental deterioration, which often arises only long after a project is completed and can be irreversible, compels early and complete data to make informed choices. Transboundary impacts also produce significant demands for information across borders.

A right to information can mean, narrowly, freedom to seek information or, more broadly, a right to access to information or a right to receive it. Corresponding duties of the state can be limited to abstention from interfering with individual efforts to obtain information from public or private entities, or it can require the state to obtain and disseminate all relevant information concerning both public and private projects that might affect the environment. If the government duty is limited to abstention from interfering with the ability of individuals or associations to seek information from those willing to share it, then little may be obtained. A governmental obligation to release information about its own projects can increase public knowledge but fails to provide access to the numerous private-sector activities that can affect the environment. Information about the latter may be obtained by the government through licensing or environmental impact requirements. Imposing on the state a duty to disseminate this information in addition to details of its own projects provides the public with the broadest base for informed decision making.

A. *Environmental Instruments and Jurisprudence*

Informational rights, in weak and strong versions, are widely found in environmental treaties.[1] Article 6 of the U.N. Framework Convention on Climate Change exemplifies the weak approach. It provides that its parties "shall promote and facilitate at the national and, as appropriate, sub-regional and regional levels, and in accordance with national laws and regulations, and within their respective capacities, public access to information and public participation." The U.N. Convention on Biological Diversity similarly does not oblige states parties to provide information but refers in its preamble to the general lack of information and knowledge regarding biological diversity and affirms the need for the full participation of women at all levels of policy-making and implementation. Article 13 of the Convention calls for education to promote and encourage understanding of the importance of conservation of biological diversity. Article 14 provides that each contracting party, "as far as possible and as appropriate," shall introduce "appropriate" environmental impact assessment procedures and "where appropriate" allow for public participation in such procedures.

---

[1] *E.g.*, Convention for the Protection of the Marine Environment of the North-East Atlantic (Paris, Sept. 22, 1992), art. 9; Convention on Civil Liability for Damage Resulting from Activities Dangerous to the Environment (Lugano, June 21, 1993), arts. 13–16; North-American Agreement on Environmental Co-operation (Sept. 13, 1993), art. 2(1)(a); International Convention to Combat Desertification in Those Countries Experiencing Serious Drought and/or Desertification, Particularly in Africa (Paris, June 17, 1994), Preamble, arts. 10(2)(e), 13(1)(b), 14(2), 19, and 25; Convention on Co operation and Sustainable Use of the Danube River (Sofia, June 29, 1994), art. 14; Energy Charter Treaty, Lisbon (Dec. 17, 1994), art. 19(1)(i) and 20; Amendments to the 1976 Barcelona Convention for the Protection of the Mediterranean Sea against Pollution (Barcelona, June 10, 1995), arts. 15 and 17; Protocol Concerning Specially Protected Areas and Biological Diversity in the Mediterranean (Barcelona, June 10, 1995), art. 19; Rotterdam Convention on the Prior Informed Consent Procedure for Certain Hazardous Chemicals and Pesticides in International Trade (Sept. 10, 1998), art. 15(2); Protocol on Water and Health to the 1992 Convention on the Protection and Use of Transboundary Watercourses and International Lakes (London, June 17, 1999), art. 5(i); Cartagena Protocol on Biosafety to the Convention on Biological Diversity (Montreal, Jan. 29, 2000), art. 23; International Treaty on Plant Genetic Resources for Food and Agriculture (Nov. 3, 2001).

Broader guarantees of public information are found in regional agreements, such as the 1992 Paris Convention on the North-East Atlantic (art. 9), which requires the contracting parties to ensure that their competent authorities are required to make available relevant information to any natural or legal person, in response to any reasonable request, without the person having to prove an interest, without unreasonable charges, and within two months of the request. Other treaties require states parties to inform the public of specific environmental hazards. The International Atomic Energy Agency (IAEA) Joint Convention on the Safety of Spent Fuel Management and on the Safety of Radioactive Waste Management (Vienna, Sept. 5, 1997) is based, to a large extent, on the principles contained in the IAEA document "The Principles of Radioactive Waste Management." The Preamble of the treaty recognizes the importance of informing the public on issues regarding the safety of spent fuel and radioactive waste management. This is reinforced in articles 6 and 13, on the siting of proposed facilities, which require each state party to take the appropriate steps to ensure that procedures are established and implemented to make information available to members of the public on the safety of any proposed spent-fuel management facility or radioactive waste management facility. Similarly, article 10(1) of the global Convention on Persistent Organic Pollutants (Stockholm, May 22, 2001) specifies that each party shall, within its capabilities, promote and facilitate provision to the public of all available information on persistent organic pollutants and ensure that the public has access to public information and that the information is kept up to date (art.10 (1)(b) & (2)).

Some international organizations have issued nonbinding declarations proclaiming a right to environmental information. The World Health Organization's European Charter on the Environment and Health states that "every individual is entitled to information and consultation on the state of the environment." European Charter on Environment and Health, adopted Dec. 8, 1989, by the First Conference of Ministers of the Environment and of Health of the Member States of the European Region of the World Health Organization. The states participating in the Organization for Security and Cooperation in Europe (OSCE) have confirmed the right of individuals, groups, and organizations to obtain, publish, and distribute information on environmental issues. Conference on Security and Cooperation in Europe, Sofia Meeting on Protection of the Environment (Oct.–Nov. 1989) (CSCE/SEM.36, Nov. 2, 1989). The Bangkok Declaration, adopted October 16, 1990, affirms similar rights in Asia and the Pacific, and the Arab Declaration on Environment and Development and Future Perspectives of September 1991 speaks of the right of individuals and nongovernmental organizations to acquire information about environmental issues relevant to them. *See* Ministerial Declaration on Environmentally Sound and Sustainable Development in Asia and the Pacific (Bangkok, Oct. 16, 1990), A/CONF.151/PC/38 (affirming "the right of individuals and nongovernmental organizations to be informed of environmental problems relevant to them, to have the necessary access to information, and to participate in the formulation and implementation of decisions likely to affect their environment," at para. 27); Arab Declaration on Environment and Development and Future Perspectives, adopted by the Arab Ministerial Conference on Environment and Development (Cairo, Sept. 19–12, 1991), A/46/632, *cited in* U.N. Doc. E/CN.4/Sub.2/1992/7, at 20.

B. *Human Rights Texts and Jurisprudence*

Human rights texts generally contain a right to freedom of information or a corresponding state duty to inform. The right to information is included in the Universal Declaration of Human Rights (art. 19), the International Covenant on Civil and Political Rights (art. 19(2)), the American Declaration of the Rights and Duties of Man (art. 10), the American Convention on Human Rights (art. 13), and the African Charter on the Rights and Duties of Peoples (art. 9). European states are bound by article 10 of the European Convention on Human Rights, which guarantees "the freedom to receive information." In the case of *Leander v. Sweden*, 116 Eur. Ct. H.R. (ser. A) (1987), para. 74, the Court unanimously stated:

> the right to receive information basically prohibits a Government from restricting a person from receiving information that others wish or may be willing to impart to him. Article 10 does not, in circumstances such as those of the present case, confer on the individual a right of access to a register containing information on his personal position, nor does it embody an obligation on the Government to impart such information to the individual.

This narrow interpretation has been maintained in environmental cases. In *Anna Maria Guerra and 39 others against Italy*, Case 14967/89, 1998–1 E.C.H.R., Judgment of February 19, 1998, the applicants complained of pollution resulting from operation of a chemical factory situated near their town, the risk of major accidents at the plant, and the absence of regulation by the public authorities. Invoking article 10 (freedom of information), the applicants asserted in particular the government's failure to inform the public of the risks and the measures to be taken in case of a major accident, prescribed by the domestic law transposing the European Community's Seveso directive. EEC Directive on the Major Accident Hazards of Certain Industrial Activities, 82/501/EEC, 1982 O.J. 230, amended by 87/216/EEC (Mar. 19, 1987). A Grand Chamber of the European Court of Human Rights affirmed that article 10 generally only prohibits a government from interfering with a person's freedom to receive information that others are willing to impart. However, the Court recharacterized the claim and unanimously found a violation of article 8, the right to family, home, and private life. Its judgment observed that the individuals waited throughout the operation of fertilizer production at the company for essential information "that would have enabled them to assess the risks they and their families might run if they continued to live at Manfredonia, a town particularly exposed to danger in the event of an accident at the factory." Note that the Court's judgment in *Öneryildiz v. Turkey*, reprinted in Chapter 7, similarly found implicit in the right to life an obligation on government authorities to provide information about hazardous activities.

The Court has recently advanced toward a broader interpretation of the notion of "freedom to receive information," under article 10 of the European Convention, especially when the information in question is of interest to the public and sought by groups of individuals that serve a "watchdog" function essential in democracies. *Case of Társaság a Szabadságjogokért v. Hungary*, Application no. 37374/05, Eur. Ct. H.R., 2009–, (April 14, 2009), para. 26–29, 35. The Court has recognized that the public has a right to receive information of general interest. Its case law in this field has been developed mainly in relation to press freedom, which serves to impart information and ideas on such matters. The function of the press includes the creation of forums for public debate. See *Observer and Guardian v. the United Kingdom*, 216 Eur. Ct. H.R. (November 26, 1991) § 59 and *Thorgeir Thorgeirson v. Iceland*, 239 Eur. Ct. H.R. (June 25, 1992) § 63. However, the realization of public participation is not limited to the media or professional journalists and extends to nongovernmental organizations acting in the public interest.

The European Court has also applied article 10 in applications challenging prosecutions for defamation following the dissemination of environmental information.

Case of Bladet Tromsø & *Stensaas v. Norway*, Application No. 21980/93, 1999-III Eur. Ct. H.R. 289 (20 May 1999)

THE FACTS

I. THE CIRCUMSTANCES OF THE CASE

A. Background to the Case

... 6. The first applicant is a limited liability company, Bladet Tromsø A/S, which publishes the daily newspaper *Bladet Tromsø* in the town of Tromsø. The second applicant, Mr. Pål Stensaas, was its editor. He was born in 1952 and lives at Nesbrua, near Oslo.

Tromsø is a regional capital of the northern part of Norway. It is the centre of the Norwegian seal hunting industry and has a university which includes an international polar research centre....

7. Mr. Odd F. Lindberg had been on board the seal hunting vessel *M/S Harmoni* ("the *Harmoni*") during the 1987 season as a freelance journalist, author and photographer. Several of his articles pertaining to that season had been published by *Bladet Tromsø*. These had not been hostile to seal hunting. On 3 March 1988 Mr. Lindberg applied to the Ministry of Fisheries to be appointed seal hunting inspector for the 1988 season on board the *Harmoni*. Following his appointment on 9 March 1988 he served on board the *Harmoni* from 12 March to 11 April 1988, when the vessel returned to its port in Tromsø. Thereafter, and until 20 July 1988, *Bladet Tromsø* published twenty-six articles on Mr. Lindberg's inspection.

8. On 12 April 1988 *Bladet Tromsø* printed an interview with Mr. Lindberg in which he stated, *inter alia*, that certain seal hunters on the *Harmoni* had violated the 1972 Seal Hunting Regulations – as amended in 1980 – issued by the Ministry of Fisheries....

. . .

The article did not mention any seal hunter by name or provide any details of the allegedly illegal hunting methods.

9. In order to defend themselves against the accusations contained in the above article of 12 April 1988 the skipper on the *Harmoni* and three of its crew members gave interviews[,] which *Bladet Tromsø* published on 13 April....

. . .

10. Mr. Lindberg's official report on the hunting expedition was completed on 30 June 1988, two and a half months after the expedition. This was significantly later than the normal time allotted to the preparation of such reports and after the Ministry of Fisheries had enquired about it. The Ministry received it on 11 July 1988 and, because of the holiday period, did not review it immediately.

In his report, Mr. Lindberg alleged a series of violations of the seal hunting regulations and made allegations against five named crew members. He stated, *inter alia*:

> I have also noticed that [seals] which have been shot in such a manner that they appear to be dead have "awakened" during the flaying.... I experienced several times that animals which were being flayed "alive" showed signs that their brains' electric activity had not been terminated."

Mr. Lindberg recommended that there should be a seal hunting inspector on every vessel and that compulsory training should be organised for all first-time hunters. Their knowledge of the regulations should also be tested. Finally, Mr. Lindberg recommended an amendment to the regulations as regards the killing of mature seals in self-defence.

B. Order of Non-Disclosure of the Report

11. The Ministry of Fisheries decided temporarily to exempt Mr. Lindberg's report from public disclosure relying on section 6, item 5, of a 1970 Act relating to Access of the Public to Documents in the Sphere of the Public Administration (*lov om offentlighet i forvaltningen*, Law No. 69 of 19 June 1970). Under this provision, the Ministry was empowered to order that the report not be made accessible to the public, on the ground that it contained allegations of statutory offences. . . .

C. The Impugned Articles Published on 15 and 20 July 1988

12. In . . . [an] article of 15 July 1988 *Bladet Tromsø*, having received a copy of the report which Mr. Lindberg had transmitted to the Ministry of Fisheries, reproduced some of his statements concerning the alleged breaches of the seal hunting regulations by members of crew of the *Harmoni*. . . .

13. On 19 and 20 July 1988 *Bladet Tromsø* published the entire report in two parts. . . .

D. Related Publications by Bladet Tromsø During the Period from 15 to 20 July 1988

. . .

15. On 18 July 1988 *Bladet Tromsø* published a further interview with crew member Mr. Kvernmo, entitled "Severe criticism against the seal hunting inspector: The accusations are totally unfounded." The caption under a photograph on the front page stated:

"Sheer lies. 'Judging from what has transpired in the media regarding [Mr. Lindberg's] report, I would characterise his statements as sheer lies', says Mr. Kvernmo. [He] . . . demands that the report be handed over immediately [to the crew]. In this he is supported by two colleagues, Mr. [S.] and Mr. [M.]. . . ."

The interview with Mr. Kvernmo continued inside the newspaper and bore the headline "'Mr. Lindberg is lying.'" . . .

. . .

17. On 19 July 1988 *Bladet Tromsø* published an article entitled:

"The Sailors' Federation is furious and brands the seal report as:
'A work commissioned by Greenpeace!'" . . .

18. On the same date *Bladet Tromsø* published an interview with Mr. Lindberg, in which he stressed that his report had included positive statements concerning ten crew members, whom he named.

19. In an interview published by *Bladet Tromsø* on 20 July 1988 a representative of Greenpeace denied that it had been involved in any way in producing Mr. Lindberg's report.

E. Other Related Publications, Contemporaneous with or Post-Dating the Impugned Publications

. . .

25. On 15 July 1988 the Norwegian News Agency issued a news bulletin reiterating some of the information provided by *Bladet Tromsø* on the same date as to Mr. Lindberg's allegations. . . .

. . .

27. Mr. Lindberg's report continued to receive a wide coverage in other media as well. On 29 July and 3 August 1988 extensive excerpts from the report were published in *Fiskaren*, a bi-weekly for fishermen. . . .

. . .

29. Over the following months the debate about Mr. Lindberg's report died out until 9 February 1989, when he gave a press conference in Oslo. A film entitled "Seal Mourning" (containing footage shot by Mr. Lindberg from the *Harmoni*) showed certain breaches of the seal hunting regulations. Clips from the film were broadcast by the Norwegian Broadcasting Corporation later the same day and the entire film was broadcast by a Swedish television channel on 11 February 1989. During the next days scenes from the film were broadcast by up to twenty broadcasting companies worldwide, including CNN and the British Broadcasting Corporation.

[Crew members of the *Harmoni* successfully instituted defamation proceedings against the applicants, seeking compensation and requesting that certain statements appearing in Mr. Lindberg's report and reproduced by *Bladet Tromsø* on July 15 and 20 be declared null and void. The District Court unanimously found the statements defamatory. The applicants were denied leave to appeal because the Supreme Court found it obvious that the appeal would not succeed. – *Eds.*]

. . .

THE LAW

I. ALLEGED VIOLATION OF ARTICLE 10 OF THE CONVENTION

49. The applicants complained that the Nord-Troms District Court's judgment of 4 March 1992, against which the Supreme Court refused leave to appeal on 18 July 1992, had constituted an unjustified interference with their right to freedom of expression under Article 10 of the Convention.

. . .

> 2. The exercise of these freedoms, since it carries with it duties and responsibilities, may be subject to such formalities, conditions, restrictions or penalties as are prescribed by law and are necessary in a democratic society, in the interests of national security, territorial integrity or public safety, for the prevention of disorder or crime, for the protection of health or morals, for the protection of the reputation or rights of others, for preventing the disclosure of information received in confidence, or for maintaining the authority and impartiality of the judiciary."

50. It was common ground between those appearing before the Court that the impugned measures constituted an "interference by [a] public authority" with the applicants' right to freedom of expression as guaranteed under the first paragraph of Article 10. Furthermore, there was no dispute that the interference was "prescribed by law" and pursued a legitimate aim, namely "the protection of the reputation or rights of others" and thus fulfilled two of the conditions for regarding the interference as permissible under the second paragraph of this Article. The Court arrives at the same conclusion on these issues.

The dispute in the case under consideration relates to the third condition, that the interference be "necessary in a democratic society." The applicants and the Commission argued that this condition had not been complied with and that Article 10 had therefore been violated. The Government contested this contention.

. . .

B. The Court's Assessment

1.*General Principles*

58. According to the Court's well-established case-law, the test of "necessity in a democratic society" requires the Court to determine whether the "interference" complained of corresponded to a "pressing social need," whether it was proportionate to the legitimate aim pursued and whether the reasons given by the national authorities to justify it are relevant and sufficient (see the *Sunday Times* (no. 1) v. the United Kingdom judgment of 26 April 1979, Series A no. 30, p. 38, § 62). In assessing whether such a "need" exists and what measures should be adopted to deal with it, the national authorities are left a certain margin of appreciation. This power of appreciation is not, however, unlimited but goes hand in hand with a European supervision by the Court, whose task it is to give a final ruling on whether a restriction is reconcilable with freedom of expression as protected by Article 10.

59. One factor of particular importance for the Court's determination in the present case is the essential function the press fulfils in a democratic society. Although the press must not overstep certain bounds, in particular in respect of the reputation and rights of others and the need to prevent the disclosure of confidential information, its duty is nevertheless to impart – in a manner consistent with its obligations and responsibilities – information and ideas on all matters of public interest (see the *Jersild v. Denmark* judgment of 23 September 1994, Series A no. 298, p. 23, § 31; and the *De Haes and Gijsels v. Belgium* judgment of 24 February 1997, *Reports of Judgments and Decisions* 1997-I, pp. 233–34, § 37). In addition, the Court is mindful of the fact that journalistic freedom also covers possible recourse to a degree of exaggeration, or even provocation (see the *Prager and Oberschlick v. Austria* judgment of 26 April 1995, Series A no. 313, p. 19, § 38). In cases such as the present one the national margin of appreciation is circumscribed by the interest of democratic society in enabling the press to exercise its vital role of "public watchdog" in imparting information of serious public concern (see the *Goodwin v. the United Kingdom* judgment of 27 March 1996, *Reports* 1996-II, p. 500, § 39).

60. In sum, the Court's task in exercising its supervisory function is not to take the place of the national authorities but rather to review under Article 10, in the light of the case as a whole, the decisions they have taken pursuant to their power of appreciation (see, among many other authorities, *Fressoz and Roire v. France* [GC], no. 29183/95, § 45, ECHR 1999-I).

2. *Application of Those Principles to the Present Case*

61. In the instant case the Nord-Troms District Court found that two statements published by *Bladet Tromsø* on 15 July 1988 and four statements published on 20 July were defamatory, "unlawful" and not proved to be true. One statement – "Seals skinned alive" – was deemed to mean that the seal hunters had committed acts of cruelty to the animals. Another was understood to imply that seal hunters had committed criminal assault on and threat against the seal hunting inspector. The remaining statements were seen to suggest that some (unnamed) seal hunters had killed four harp seals, the hunting of which was illegal in 1988. The District Court declared the statements null and void and, considering that the newspaper had acted negligently, ordered the applicants to pay compensation to the seventeen plaintiffs.

The Court finds that the reasons relied on by the District Court were relevant to the legitimate aim of protecting the reputation or rights of the crew members.

62. As to the sufficiency of those reasons for the purposes of Article 10 of the Convention, the Court must take account of the overall background against which the statements in question were made. Thus, the contents of the impugned articles cannot be looked at in isolation of the controversy that seal hunting represented at the time in Norway and in Tromsø, the centre of the

trade in Norway. It should further be recalled that Article 10 is applicable not only to information or ideas that are favourably received or regarded as inoffensive or as a matter of indifference, but also to those that offend, shock or disturb the State or any sector of the population (see the *Handyside v. the United Kingdom* judgment of 7 December 1976, Series A no. 24, p. 23, § 49). Moreover, whilst the mass media must not overstep the bounds imposed in the interests of the protection of the reputation of private individuals, it is incumbent on them to impart information and ideas concerning matters of public interest. Not only does the press have the task of imparting such information and ideas: the public also has a right to receive them. Consequently, in order to determine whether the interference was based on sufficient reasons which rendered it "necessary," regard must be had to the public-interest aspect of the case.

63. In this connection the Court has noted the argument, relied on by the District Court that *Bladet Tromsø*'s manner of presentation, in particular in the article of 15 July 1988, suggested that the primary aim, rather than being the promotion of a serious debate, was to focus in a sensationalist fashion on specific allegations of crime and to be the first paper to print the story.

In the Court's view, however, the manner of reporting in question should not be considered solely by reference to the disputed articles in *Bladet Tromsø* on 15 and 20 July 1988 but in the wider context of the newspaper's coverage of the seal hunting issue. During the period from 15 to 23 July 1988 *Bladet Tromsø*, which was a local newspaper with – presumably – a relatively stable readership, published almost on a daily basis the different points of views, including the newspaper's own comments, those of the Ministry of Fisheries, the Norwegian Sailors' Federation, Greenpeace and, above all, the seal hunters. Although the latter were not published simultaneously with the contested articles, there was a high degree of proximity in time, giving an overall picture of balanced news reporting. This approach was not too different from that followed three months earlier in the first series of articles on Mr. Lindberg's initial accusations and no criticism appears to have been made against the newspaper in respect of those articles. As the Court observed in a previous judgment, the methods of objective and balanced reporting may vary considerably, depending among other things on the medium in question; it is not for the Court, any more than it is for the national courts, to substitute its own views for those of the press as to what techniques of reporting should be adopted by journalists (see the *Jersild* judgment cited above, p. 23, § 31).

Against this background, it appears that the thrust of the impugned articles was not primarily to accuse certain individuals of committing offences against the seal hunting regulations or of cruelty to animals. On the contrary, the call by the paper on 18 July 1988 for the fisheries authorities to make a "constructive use" of the findings in the Lindberg report in order to improve the reputation of seal hunting can reasonably be seen as an aim underlying the various articles published on the subject by *Bladet Tromsø*. The impugned articles were part of an ongoing debate of evident concern to the local, national and international public, in which the views of a wide selection of interested actors were reported.

64. The most careful scrutiny on the part of the Court is called for when, as in the present case, the measures taken or sanctions imposed by the national authority are capable of discouraging the participation of the press in debates over matters of legitimate public concern (see the *Jersild* judgment cited above, pp. 25–26, § 35).

65. Article 10 of the Convention does not, however, guarantee a wholly unrestricted freedom of expression even with respect to press coverage of matters of serious public concern. Under the terms of paragraph 2 of the Article the exercise of this freedom carries with it "duties and responsibilities," which also apply to the press. These "duties and responsibilities" are liable to assume significance when, as in the present case, there is question of attacking the reputation of private individuals and undermining the "rights of others." As pointed out by the Government, the seal hunters' right to protection of their honour and reputation is itself internationally recognised under Article 17 of the International Covenant on Civil and Political Rights. Also of relevance for the balancing of competing interests which the Court must carry out is the fact that under

Article 6 § 2 of the Convention the seal hunters had a right to be presumed innocent of any criminal offence until proved guilty. By reason of the "duties and responsibilities" inherent in the exercise of the freedom of expression, the safeguard afforded by Article 10 to journalists in relation to reporting on issues of general interest is subject to the proviso that they are acting in good faith in order to provide accurate and reliable information in accordance with the ethics of journalism (see the *Goodwin* judgment cited above, p. 500, § 39, and *Fressoz and Roire* cited above, § 54).

66. The Court notes that the expressions in question consisted of factual statements, not value-judgments (cf., for instance, the *Lingens v. Austria* judgment of 8 July 1986, Series A no. 103, p. 28, § 46). They did not emanate from the newspaper itself but were based on or were directly quoting from the Lindberg report, which the newspaper had not verified by independent research (see the *Jersild* judgment cited above, pp. 23 and 25–26, §§ 31 and 35). It must therefore be examined whether there were any special grounds in the present case for dispensing the newspaper from its ordinary obligation to verify factual statements that were defamatory of private individuals. In the Court's view, this depends in particular on the nature and degree of the defamation at hand and the extent to which the newspaper could reasonably regard the Lindberg report as reliable with respect to the allegations in question. The latter issue must be determined in the light of the situation as it presented itself to *Bladet Tromsø* at the material time, rather than with the benefit of hindsight, on the basis of the findings of fact made by the Commission of Inquiry a long time thereafter.

67. As regards the nature and degree of the defamation, the Court observes that the four statements to the effect that certain sealers had killed female harp seals were found defamatory, not because they implied that the hunters had committed acts of cruelty to the animals, but because the hunting of such seals was illegal in 1988, unlike the year before. According to the District Court, "the statements [did] not differ from allegations of illegal hunting in general." Whilst these allegations implied reprehensible conduct, they were not particularly serious.

The other two allegations – that seals had been skinned alive and that furious hunters had beaten up Mr. Lindberg and threatened to hit him with a gaff – were more serious but were expressed in rather broad terms and could be understood by readers as having been presented with a degree of exaggeration.

More importantly, while *Bladet Tromsø* publicised the names of the ten crew members whom Mr. Lindberg had exonerated, it named none of those accused of having committed the reprehensible acts. Before the District Court each plaintiff pleaded his case on the basis of the same facts and the District Court apparently considered each of them to have been exposed to the same degree of defamation, as is reflected in the fact that an equal award was made to each of them.

Thus, while some of the accusations were relatively serious, the potential adverse effect of the impugned statements on each individual seal hunter's reputation or rights was significantly attenuated by several factors. In particular, the criticism was not an attack against all the crew members or any specific crew member (see the *Thorgeir Thorgeirson v. Iceland* judgment of 25 June 1992, Series A no. 239, p. 28, § 66).

68. As regards the second issue, the trustworthiness of the Lindberg report, it should be observed that the report had been drawn up by Mr. Lindberg in an official capacity as an inspector appointed by the Ministry of Fisheries to monitor the seal hunt performed by the crew of the *Harmoni* during the 1988 season. In the view of the Court, the press should normally be entitled, when contributing to public debate on matters of legitimate concern, to rely on the contents of official reports without having to undertake independent research. Otherwise, the vital public-watchdog role of the press may be undermined (see, *mutatis mutandis*, the *Goodwin* judgment cited above, p. 500, § 39).

69. The Court does not attach significance to any discrepancies, pointed to by the Government, between the report and the publications made by Mr. Lindberg in *Bladet Tromsø* one year before in quite a different capacity, namely as a freelance journalist and an author.

70. The newspaper was, it is true, already aware from the reactions to Mr. Lindberg's statements in April 1988 that the crew disputed his competence and the truth of any allegations of "beastly killing methods." It must have been evident to the paper that the Lindberg report was liable to be controverted by the crew members. Taken on its own, this cannot be considered decisive for whether the newspaper had a duty to verify the truth of the critical factual statements contained in the report before it could exercise its freedom of expression under Article 10 of the Convention.

71. Far more material for this purpose was the attitude of the Ministry of Fisheries, which had appointed Mr. Lindberg to carry out the inspection and to report back. As at 15 July 1988 *Bladet Tromsø* was aware of the fact that the Ministry had decided to exempt the report from public disclosure with reference to the nature of the allegations – criminal conduct – and to the need to give the persons named in the report an opportunity to comment. It has not been suggested that, by publishing the relevant information, the newspaper was acting in breach of the law on confidentiality. Nor does it appear that, prior to the contested publication on 15 July 1988, the Ministry had publicly expressed a doubt as to the possible truth of the criticism or questioned Mr. Lindberg's competence. Rather, according to a bulletin of the same date by the Norwegian News Agency, the Ministry had stated that it was possible that illegal hunting had occurred.

On 18 July 1988 the Norwegian News Agency reported the Ministry as having stated that veterinary experts would consider the controversial Lindberg report and that the Ministry would issue information of the outcome and possibly also of the circumstances of Mr. Lindberg's recruitment as inspector; and, moreover, that the Ministry would not comment any further until it had collected more information. On 19 July the News Agency reported that the Ministry had believed, on the basis of information provided by Mr. Lindberg himself, that his research background was far more extensive than it was in reality. It was on 20 July, the same date as the last of the disputed publications, that the Ministry expressed doubts as to Mr. Lindberg's competence and the quality of the report.

In the Court's opinion, the attitude expressed by the Ministry before 20 July 1988 does not constitute a ground for considering that it was unreasonable for the newspaper to regard as reliable the information contained in the report, including the four statements published on 20 July to the effect that specific but unnamed seal hunters had killed female harp seals. In fact, the District Court later found that one such allegation had been proved true.

72. Having regard to the various factors limiting the likely harm to the individual seal hunters' reputation and to the situation as it presented itself to *Bladet Tromsø* at the relevant time, the Court considers that the paper could reasonably rely on the official Lindberg report, without being required to carry out its own research into the accuracy of the facts reported. It sees no reason to doubt that the newspaper acted in good faith in this respect.

73. On the facts of the present case, the Court cannot find that the crew members' undoubted interest in protecting their reputation was sufficient to outweigh the vital public interest in ensuring an informed public debate over a matter of local and national as well as international interest. In short, the reasons relied on by the respondent State, although relevant, are not sufficient to show that the interference complained of was "necessary in a democratic society." Notwithstanding the national authorities' margin of appreciation, the Court considers that there was no reasonable relationship of proportionality between the restrictions placed the applicants' right to freedom of expression and the legitimate aim pursued. Accordingly, the Court holds that there has been a violation of Article 10 of the Convention.

[The Court awarded damages for the full amount of pecuniary losses the applicants proved they had suffered, as well as costs and expenses. – *Eds.*]

. . .

JOINT DISSENTING OPINION OF JUDGES PALM, FUHRMANN AND BAKA

We disagree with the majority opinion that there has been a violation of Article 10 of the Convention on the facts of this case.

. . .

It is the right to the protection of reputation aspect of the present case which has been given insufficient attention in the Court's judgment and which motivates the present dissent. The crucial watchdog role of the press in a democratic society has been positively asserted and defended by this Court in the course of a large corpus of cases concerning freedom of expression which have stressed not only the right of the press to impart information but also the right of the public to receive it. In so doing the Court has played an important role in laying the foundations for the principles which govern a free press within the Convention community and beyond. However, for the first time the Court is confronted with the question of how to reconcile the role of newspapers to cover a story which is undoubtedly in the public interest with the right to reputation of a group of identifiable private individuals at the centre of the story. In our view the fact that a strong public interest is involved should not have the consequence of exonerating newspapers from either the basic ethics of their trade or the laws of defamation. As the Grand Chamber of the Court stated in *Fressoz and Roire v. France* ([GC], no. 29183/95, ECHR 1999-I) – the first judgment of the new Court – Article 10 "protects journalists' rights to divulge information on issues of general interest provided that they are acting in good faith and on an accurate factual basis and provide 'reliable and precise' information in accordance with the ethics of journalism" (§ 54).

. . .

Moreover, under Norwegian law the defamation must also be unlawful. This development in Norwegian case-law – described in the judgment of the District Court as "the linchpin of Article 100 of the Norwegian Constitution and . . . essential in a democratic society" – gives the court the possibility to weigh in the balance the respective interests and to find that the public interests involved in publication outweigh the private one in a given case. Norwegian law has thus developed in a manner which has taken into account the principles of Strasbourg case-law. Indeed the District Court followed this approach in the present case but found against the applicants essentially on the grounds that the newspaper focused its attention on sensational headlines and that "sufficient attention was not paid to the protection of other persons in this disclosure" and that the newspaper was well aware that the report had been exempted from public disclosure precisely because of the accusations of wrongdoing. Neither of these factual points can be seriously contested. The *Aftenposten* judgment shows that the test of "unlawfulness" is an important guarantee of press freedom under Norwegian law since it was exactly on this basis that the court found for the defendant newspaper, contrasting that paper's balanced coverage with that of *Bladet Tromsø* in the present case.

Against this background is it for the European Court to say that the District Court's assessment on this point was wrong? Even if the Strasbourg Court should substitute its judgment in this way for that of the national court, on what grounds could this balancing of the interests be called into question? We observe that the Court has previously stated that it is in the first place for the national authorities to determine the extent to which the individual's interest in full protection of his or her reputation should yield to the interests of the community (as regards the investigation of the affairs of large public companies) – *a fortiori* where the reputation of private persons is at stake (see the *Fayed v. the United Kingdom* judgment of 21 September 1994, Series A no. 294-B, p. 55, § 81). Is this not the essence of the margin of appreciation in a case like the present one?

The crux of the Court's reasoning involves essentially a new test that newspapers can be dispensed from verifying the facts of a story depending on (1) the nature and degree of the defamation and (2) whether it was reasonable in the circumstances to rely on the details of the Lindberg report. On both points we find the Court's reasoning to be flawed.

. . .

We accept that if the case concerned the publication of an official report which had been made public by the competent authorities, a newspaper would in principle be entitled to publish it under Article 10 of the Convention without carrying out any further investigation as to the accuracy or precision of the details of the report even if it was damaging to the reputation of private individuals. All that could be expected of a newspaper in such a situation would be to check that the published text corresponded to the official published text.

But the present case does not concern an official public report. On the contrary the report had not immediately been made public by the Ministry precisely because it contained allegations of wrongdoing against the crew members and it was considered only fair and proper to afford them an opportunity to defend themselves and to verify the information. The subsequent series of defamation proceedings and the Commission of Inquiry report vindicated such a cautious approach. Moreover it is clear that the newspaper was aware of this decision but decided nevertheless to go ahead and publish. It was also aware that Mr. Lindberg had previously worked as a freelance journalist on seal hunting issues, having published several of his articles, and did not have the traditional profile of a Ministry inspector.

In our view, judged against this background, the newspaper knew that it was taking the risk of exposing itself to legal action by publishing the articles without taking any steps whatsoever to check the veracity of the claims being made....

. . .

The present judgment's conclusion, that the newspaper was exonerated from the verification of basic factual information by virtue of the degree of defamation involved and the supposedly "official" nature of the Lindberg report, appears to suggest an exceptionally low threshold for the protection of the right to reputation of others where there is an important public interest involved and no public figures. Such an elevation of the public interest in the freedom of the press at the expense of the private individuals caught up in the seal hunting story in this case pays insufficient attention to the national laws on defamation and the balanced freedom of the press-conscious judgments of the domestic courts. It is abundantly clear from the decision of the District Court that the factual basis of the story was inaccurate and that the ethics of journalism were not respected as they ought to have been. Our Court should not, against such a background, reach a different conclusion on these points.

. . .

Questions and Discussion

1. Who is correct? Was this part of the right to environmental information or was it a defamatory accusation of criminal activity that destroyed the reputations of the ship's crew? Could it be both?

2. The Court does not discuss, and the domestic law does not seem to have, the notion of privilege. Has the Court nonetheless established a limited privilege for journalists reporting on issues of public interest?

3. In the subsequent judgment *Thoma v. Luxembourg*, Application No. 38432/97, Eur. Ct. H.R. 2001-III (Mar. 29, 2001), the Court again considered the question of a conviction of defamation for reporting on environmental matters. In this case, a radio journalist presented a weekly program dealing with nature and the environment. During one of his programs, he discussed a written article suggesting that the reforesting of woodlands involved bribery. He was convicted of defamation in civil actions brought by fifty-four forest wardens and nine forestry engineers. He appealed and then challenged his conviction at the European Court

as a violation of freedom of expression. The Court noted the fact that the criticisms were of public officials, not of private individuals, and that journalistic freedom allows recourse to a degree of exaggerations or even provocation. Thus, although the state can limit speech by law to protect the rights and reputation of others, this particular interference was not "necessary in a democratic society" (i.e., meeting a pressing social need, proportionate to the legitimate aim pursued and with relevant and sufficient reasons given). The Court noted in particular that restrictions on freedom of expression are to be strictly construed when they are directed at debate over a problem of general interest.

4. Compare the approach of the Inter-American Court of Human Rights to the issue of environmental information in the following case.

Claude Reyes et al. v. Chile,
Inter-Am. Ct. Hum. Rts. (ser. C) No. 151, Sept. 19, 2006
(some footnotes and internal cross-references omitted)

I

INTRODUCTION OF THE CASE

1. On July 8, 2005, in accordance with the provisions of Articles 50 and 61 of the American Convention, the Inter-American Commission on Human Rights lodged before the Court an application against the State of Chile. This application originated from petition No. 12,108, received by the Secretariat of the Commission on December 17, 1998.

2. The Commission submitted the application for the Court to declare that the State was responsible for the violation of the rights embodied in Articles 13 (Freedom of Thought and Expression) and 25 (Right to Judicial Protection) of the American Convention, in relation to the obligations established in Articles 1(1) (Obligation to Respect Rights) and 2 (Domestic Legal Effects) thereof, to the detriment of Marcel Claude Reyes, Sebastián Cox Urrejola and Arturo Longton Guerrero.

3. The facts described by the Commission in the application supposedly occurred between May and August 1998 and refer to the State's alleged refusal to provide Marcel Claude Reyes, Sebastián Cox Urrejola and Arturo Longton Guerrero with all the information they requested from the Foreign Investment Committee on the forestry company Trillium and the Río Condor Project, a deforestation project to be executed in Chile's Region XII that "c[ould] be prejudicial to the environment and to the sustainable development of Chile." The Commission stated that this refusal occurred without the State "providing any valid justification under Chilean law" and, supposedly, they "were not granted an effective judicial remedy to contest a violation of the right of access to information"; in addition, they "were not ensured the rights of access to information and to judicial protection, and there were no mechanisms guaranteeing the right of access to public information."

4. The Commission requested that, pursuant to Article 63(1) of the Convention, the Court order the State to adopt specific measures of reparation indicated in the application. Lastly, it requested the Court to order the State to pay the costs and expenses arising from processing the case in the domestic jurisdiction and before the body of the inter-American system.

. . .

VI

PROVEN FACTS

. . .

Concerning Marcel Claude Reyes and Arturo Longton Guerrero's request for information from the Foreign Investment Committee and the latter's response

57(12) Marcel Claude Reyes is an economist. In 1983, he worked in the Central Bank as an adviser to the Foreign Investment Committee and in the Environmental Accounts Unit; also, he was Executive Director of the Terram Foundation from 1997 to 2003. One of the purposes of this non-governmental organization was to promote the capacity of civil society to respond to public decisions on investments related to the use of natural resources, and also "to play an active role in public debate and in the production of solid, scientific information . . . on the sustainable development of [Chile]."

57(13) On May 7, 1998, Marcel Claude Reyes, as Executive Director of the Terram Foundation, sent a letter to the Executive Vice President of the Foreign Investment Committee, indicating that the foundation proposed "to evaluate the commercial, economic and social aspects of the [Rio Condor] project, assess its impact on the environment . . . and exercise social control regarding the actions of the State entities that are or were involved in the development of the Río Cóndor exploitation project." In this letter, the Executive Director of the Terram Foundation requested the Foreign Investment Committee to provide the following information "of public interest":

1. "Contracts signed by the State of Chile and the foreign investor concerning the Río Cóndor project, with the date and name of the notary's office where they were signed and with a copy of such contracts.

2. Identity of the foreign and/or national investors in this project.

3. Background information from Chile and abroad that the Foreign Investment Committee had before it, which ensured the soundness and suitability of the investor(s), and the agreements of the Committee recording that this information was sufficient.

4. Total amount of the investment authorized for the Río Cóndor project, method and timetable for the entry of the capital, and existence of credits associated with the latter.

5. Capital effectively imported into the country to date, as the investors' own capital, capital contributions and associated credits.

6. Information held by the Committee and/or that it has requested from other public or private entities regarding control of the obligations undertaken by the foreign investors or the companies in which they are involved and whether the Committee is aware of any infraction or offense.

7. Information on whether the Executive Vice President of the Committee has exercised the power conferred on him by Article 15 bis of D[ecree Law No.] 600, by requesting from all private and public sector entities and companies, the reports and information he required to comply with the Committee's purposes and, if so, make this information available to the Foundation."

. . .

57(19) The State provided Mr. Claude Reyes and Mr. Longton Guerrero with the information corresponding to sections 1, 2, 4 and 5 of the original request for information orally and in writing.

57(20) On April 3, 2006, the Executive Vice President of the Foreign Investment Committee at the time when Mr. Claude Reyes submitted his request for information, stated during the public hearing held before the Inter-American Court, *inter alia*, that he had not provided the requested information:

(a) On section 3, because "the Foreign Investment Committee . . . did not disclose the company's financial data, since providing this information was contrary to the public interest," which was "the country's development." "It was not reasonable that foreign companies applying to the Foreign Investment Committee should have to disclose their financial information in this way; information that could be very important to them in relation to their competitors; hence, this could have been an obstacle to the foreign investment process." It was the Foreign Investment Committee's practice not to provide a company's financial data that could affect its competitiveness to third parties. The Committee and the Vice President defined what was in the public interest;

(b) On section 6, because information on the background material that the Committee could request from other institutions "did not exist" and the Committee "does not having policing functions"; and

(c) On section 7, because "the Foreign Investment Committee had neither the responsibility nor the capacity to evaluate each project on its merits; it had a staff of just over 20 persons. Furthermore, this was not necessary, since the role of the Foreign Investment Committee is to authorize the entry of capitals and the corresponding terms and conditions, and the country had an institutional framework for each sector."

. . .

Concerning the judicial proceedings

[The applicants filed lawsuits seeking redress in domestic courts. The cases were declared inadmissible. – *Eds.*]

. . .

VII

VIOLATION OF ARTICLE 13 OF THE AMERICAN CONVENTION REGARDING TO ARTICLES 1(1) AND 2 THEREOF (FREEDOM OF THOUGHT AND EXPRESSION)

. . .

The Court's findings

61. Article 13 (Freedom of Thought and Expression) of the American Convention establishes, *inter alia*, that:

1. Everyone has the right to freedom of thought and expression. This right includes freedom to seek, receive, and impart information and ideas of all kinds, regardless of frontiers, either orally, in writing, in print, in the form of art, or through any other medium of one's choice.

2. The exercise of the right provided for in the foregoing paragraph shall not be subject to prior censorship but shall be subject to subsequent imposition of liability, which shall be expressly established by law to the extent necessary to ensure:

a. respect for the rights or reputations of others; or
b. the protection of national security, public order, or public health or morals.

3. The right of expression may not be restricted by indirect methods or means, such as the abuse of government or private controls over newsprint, radio broadcasting frequencies, or equipment used in the dissemination of information, or by any other means tending to impede the communication and circulation of ideas and opinions.

. . .

62. Regarding the obligation to respect rights, Article 1(1) of the Convention stipulates that:

The States Parties to this Convention undertake to respect the rights and freedoms recognized herein and to ensure to all persons subject to their jurisdiction the free and full exercise of those rights and freedoms, without any discrimination for reasons of race, color, sex, language, religion, political or other opinion, national or social origin, economic status, birth, or any other social condition.

63. Regarding domestic legal effects, Article 2 of the Convention establishes that:

> Where the exercise of any of the rights or freedoms referred to in Article 1 is not already ensured by legislative or other provisions, the States Parties undertake to adopt, in accordance with their constitutional processes and the provisions of this Convention, such legislative or other measures as may be necessary to give effect to those rights or freedoms.

64. The Court has established that the general obligation contained in Article 2 of the Convention entails the elimination of any type of norm or practice that results in a violation of the guarantees established in the Convention, as well as the issue of norms and the implementation of practices leading to the effective observance of these guarantees.

65. In light of the proven facts in this case, the Court must determine whether the failure to hand over part of the information requested from the Foreign Investment Committee in 1998 constituted a violation of the right to freedom of thought and expression of Marcel Claude Reyes, Sebastián Cox Urrejola and Arturo Longton Guerrero and, consequently, a violation of Article 13 of the American Convention.

66. With regard to the specific issues in this case, it has been proved that a request was made for information held by the Foreign Investment Committee, and that this Committee is a public-law juridical person. Also, that the requested information related to a foreign investment contract signed originally between the State and two foreign companies and a Chilean company (which would receive the investment), in order to develop a forestry exploitation project that caused considerable public debate owing to its potential environmental impact.

. . .

A) *Right to Freedom of Thought and Expression*

75. The Court's case law has dealt extensively with the right to freedom of thought and expression embodied in Article 13 of the Convention, by describing its individual and social dimensions, from which it has deduced a series of rights that are protected by this Article.[2]

76. In this regard, the Court has established that, according to the protection granted by the American Convention, the right to freedom of thought and expression includes "not only the right and freedom to express one's own thoughts, but also the right and freedom to *seek, receive and impart* information and ideas of all kinds."[3] In the same way as the American Convention, other international human rights instruments, such as the Universal Declaration of Human Rights and the International Covenant on Civil and Political Rights, establish a positive right to seek and receive information.

77. In relation to the facts of the instant case, the Court finds that, by expressly stipulating the right to "seek" and "receive" "information," Article 13 of the Convention protects the right of all individuals to request access to State-held information, with the exceptions permitted by the restrictions established in the Convention. Consequently, this article protects the right of the individual to receive such information and the positive obligation of the State to provide it, so that the individual may have access to such information or receive an answer that includes a justification when, for any reason permitted by the Convention, the State is allowed to restrict

---

[2] *Cf. Case of López Álvarez*, Judgment of Feb. 1, 2006 (ser. C) No. 141, para. 163; *Case of Palamara Iribarne*, Judgment of Nov. 22, 2005 (ser. C) No. 135, para. 69; *Case of Ricardo Canese*, Judgment of Aug. 31, 2004 (ser. C) No. 111, paras. 77–80; *Case of Herrera Ulloa*, Judgment of July 2, 2004 (ser. C) No. 107, paras. 108–11; *Case of Ivcher Bronstein*, Judgment of Feb. 6, 2001 (ser. C) No. 74, paras. 146–149; *Case of "The Last Temptation of Christ" (Olmedo Bustos et al.)*, Judgment of Feb. 5, 2001 (ser. C) No. 73, paras. 64–67; *Compulsory Membership in an Association Prescribed by Law for the Practice of Journalism* (arts. 13 and 29 American Convention on Human Rights), Advisory Opinion OC-5/85 of Nov. 13, 1985, (ser. A) No. 5, paras. 30–33 and 43.

[3] *Cf. Case of López Álvarez, supra,* para. 163; *Case of Ricardo Canese, supra,* para. 77; *Case of Herrera Ulloa, supra,* para. 108.

access to the information in a specific case. The information should be provided without the need to prove direct interest or personal involvement in order to obtain it, except in cases in which a legitimate restriction is applied. The delivery of information to an individual can, in turn, permit it to circulate in society, so that the latter can become acquainted with it, have access to it, and assess it. In this way, the right to freedom of thought and expression includes the protection of the right of access to State-held information, which also clearly includes the two dimensions, individual and social, of the right to freedom of thought and expression that must be guaranteed simultaneously by the State.

78. In this regard, it is important to emphasize that there is a regional consensus among the States that are members of the Organization of American States (hereinafter "the OAS") about the importance of access to public information and the need to protect it. This right has been the subject of specific resolutions issued by the OAS General Assembly.[4] In the latest Resolution of June 3, 2006, the OAS General Assembly, "urge[d] the States to respect and promote respect for everyone's access to public information and to promote the adoption of any necessary legislative or other types of provisions to ensure its recognition and effective application."[5]

79. Article 4 of the Inter-American Democratic Charter[6] emphasizes the importance of "[t]ransparency in government activities, probity, responsible public administration on the part of Governments, respect for social rights, and freedom of expression and of the press" as essential components of the exercise of democracy. Moreover, Article 6 of the Charter states that "[i]t is the right and responsibility of all citizens to participate in decisions relating to their own development. This is also a necessary condition for the full and effective exercise of democracy"; therefore, it invites the States Parties to "[p]romot[e] and foster . . . diverse forms of [citizen] participation."

80. In the Nueva León Declaration, adopted in 2004, the Heads of State of the Americas undertook, among other matters, "to provid[e] the legal and regulatory framework and the structures and conditions required to guarantee the right of access to information to our citizens," recognizing that "[a]ccess to information held by the State, subject to constitutional and legal norms, including those on privacy and confidentiality, is an indispensable condition for citizen participation. . . ."[7]

81. The provisions on access to information established in the United Nations Convention against Corruption and in the Rio Declaration on Environment and Development should also be noted. In addition, within the Council of Europe, as far back as 1970, the Parliamentary Assembly made recommendations to the Committee of Ministers of the Council of Europe on the "right of freedom of information,"[8] and also issued a Declaration establishing that, together with respect for the right of freedom of expression, there should be "a corresponding duty for the public authorities to make

---

4 *Cf.* Resolution AG/RES. 1932 (XXXIII-O/03) of June 10, 2003, "Access to Public Information: Strengthening Democracy"; Resolution AG/RES. (XXXIV-O/04) of June 8, 2004, "Access to Public Information: Strengthening Democracy"; Resolution AG/RES. 2121 (XXXV-O/05) of June 7, 2005, "Access to Public Information: Strengthening Democracy"; and AG/RES. 2252 (XXXVI-O/06) of June 6, 2006, "Access to Public Information: Strengthening Democracy."

5 *Cf.* Resolution AG/RES. 2252 (XXXVI-O/06) of June 6, 2006, "Access to Public Information: Strengthening Democracy," second operative paragraph.

6 *Cf.* Inter-American Democratic Charter adopted by the General Assembly of the OAS on Sept. 11, 2001, during the 28th special sess. held in Lima, Peru.

7 *Cf.* Declaration of Nuevo León, adopted on Jan. 13, 2004, by the Heads of State and Government of the Americas, during the Special Summit of the Americas, held in Monterrey, Nuevo León, Mexico.

8 *Cf.* Recommendation No. 582 adopted by the Council of Europe Parliamentary Assembly on Jan. 23, 1970. It recommended instructing the Committee of Experts on Human Rights Experts to consider and make recommendations on:

(i) the extension of the right of freedom of information provided for in Article 10 of the European Convention on Human Rights, by the conclusion of a protocol or otherwise, so as to include freedom to *seek* information (which is included in Article 19(2) of the United Nations Covenant on Civil and Political Rights); there should be a corresponding duty on public authorities to make information available on matters of public interest, subject to appropriate limitations.

available information on matters of public interest within reasonable limits. . . . "⁹ In addition, recommendations and directives have been adopted¹⁰ and, in 1982, the Committee of Ministers adopted a "Declaration on freedom of expression and information," in which it expressed the goal of the pursuit of an open information policy in the public sector.¹¹ In 1998, the "Convention on Access to Information, Public Participation in Decision-Making and Access to Justice in Environmental Matters" was adopted during the Fourth Ministerial Conference "Environment for Europe," held in Aarhus, Denmark. In addition, the Committee of Ministers of the Council of Europe issued a recommendation on the right of access to official documents held by the public authorities,¹² and its principle IV establishes the possible exceptions, stating that "[these] restrictions should be set down precisely in law, be necessary in a democratic society and be proportionate to the aim of protecti[on]."

82. The Court also finds it particularly relevant that, at the global level, many countries have adopted laws designed to protect and regulate the right to accede to State-held information.

83. Finally, the Court finds it pertinent to note that, subsequent to the facts of this case, Chile has made significant progress with regard to establishing by law the right of access to State-held information, including a constitutional reform and a draft law on this right which is currently being processed.

. . .

84. The Court has stated that "[r]epresentative democracy is the determining factor throughout the system of which the Convention is a part," and "a 'principle' reaffirmed by the American States in the OAS Charter, the basic instrument of the inter-American system."¹³ In several resolutions, the OAS General Assembly has considered that access to public information is an essential requisite for the exercise of democracy, greater transparency and responsible public administration and that, in a representative and participative democratic system, the citizenry exercises its constitutional rights through a broad freedom of expression and free access to information.

85. The Inter-American Court referred to the close relationship between democracy and freedom of expression, when it established that:

> Freedom of expression is a cornerstone upon which the very existence of a democratic society rests. It is indispensable for the formation of public opinion. It is also a condition *sine qua non* for the development of political parties, trade unions, scientific and cultural societies and, in general, those who wish to influence the public. It represents, in short, the means that enable the community, when exercising its options, to be sufficiently informed. Consequently, it can be said that a society that is not well informed is not a society that is truly free.¹⁴

86. In this regard, the State's actions should be governed by the principles of disclosure and transparency in public administration that enable all persons subject to its jurisdiction to exercise the democratic control of those actions, and so that they can question, investigate and consider whether public functions are being performed adequately. Access to State-held information of public interest can permit participation in public administration through the social control that can be exercised through such access.

---

⁹ *Cf.* Resolution No. 428 adopted by the Council of Europe Parliamentary Assembly on Jan. 23, 1970.

¹⁰ *Cf.* Resolution No. 854 adopted by the Council of Europe Parliamentary Assembly on Feb. 1, 1979, which recommended the Committee of Ministers "to invite member states which have not yet done so to introduce a system of freedom of information," which included the right to seek and receive information from government agencies and departments; and Directive 2003/4/EC of the European Parliament and Council of Jan. 28, 2003, on public access to environmental information.

¹¹ Declaration on the Freedom of Expression and Information adopted by the Committee of Ministers of Apr. 29, 1982.

¹² *Cf.* Recommendation No. R (2002)2, adopted on Feb. 21, 2002.

¹³ *Cf. Case of YATAMA,* Judgment of June 23, 2005 (ser. C) No. 127, para. 192; *The Word "Laws" in Article 30 of the American Convention on Human Rights,* Advisory Opinion OC-6/86 of May 9, 1986 (ser. A) No. 6, para. 34.

¹⁴ *Cf. Case of Ricardo Canese, supra,* para. 82; *Case of Herrera Ulloa, supra,* para. 112; Advisory Opinion OC-5/85, *supra,* para. 70.

87. Democratic control by society, through public opinion, fosters transparency in State activities and promotes the accountability of State officials in relation to their public activities.[15] Hence, for the individual to be able to exercise democratic control, the State must guarantee access to the information of public interest that it holds. By permitting the exercise of this democratic control, the State encourages greater participation by the individual in the interests of society.

B) *The Restrictions to the Exercise of the Right of Access to State-Held Information Imposed in This Case*

88. The right of access to State-held information admits restrictions. This Court has already ruled in other cases on the restrictions that may be imposed on the exercise of freedom of thought and expression.

89. In relation to the requirements with which a restriction in this regard should comply, first, they must have been established by law to ensure that they are not at the discretion of public authorities. Such laws should be enacted "for reasons of general interest and in accordance with the purpose for which such restrictions have been established." In this respect, the Court has emphasized that:

> From that perspective, one cannot interpret the word "laws," used in Article 30, as a synonym for just any legal norm, since that would be tantamount to admitting that fundamental rights can be restricted at the sole discretion of governmental authorities with no other formal limitation than that such restrictions be set out in provisions of a general nature. . . .
>
> The requirement that the laws be enacted for reasons of general interest means they must have been adopted for the "general welfare" (Art. 32(2)), a concept that must be interpreted as an integral element of public order (*ordre public*) in democratic States. . . .[16]

90. Second, the restriction established by law should respond to a purpose allowed by the American Convention. In this respect, Article 13(2) of the Convention permits imposing the restrictions necessary to ensure "respect for the rights or reputations of others" or "the protection of national security, public order, or public health or morals."

91. Lastly, the restrictions imposed must be necessary in a democratic society; consequently, they must be intended to satisfy a compelling public interest. If there are various options to achieve this objective, that which least restricts the right protected must be selected. In other words, the restriction must be proportionate to the interest that justifies it and must be appropriate for accomplishing this legitimate purpose, interfering as little as possible with the effective exercise of the right.

92. The Court observes that in a democratic society, it is essential that the State authorities are governed by the principle of maximum disclosure, which establishes the presumption that all information is accessible, subject to a limited system of exceptions.

93. It corresponds to the State to show that it has complied with the above requirements when establishing restrictions to the access to the information it holds.

94. In the instant case, it has been proved that the restriction applied to the access to information was not based on a law. At the time, there was no legislation in Chile that regulated the issue of restrictions to access to State-held information.

95. Furthermore, the State did not prove that the restriction responded to a purpose allowed by the American Convention, or that it was necessary in a democratic society, because the authority responsible for responding to the request for information did not adopt a justified decision in writing, communicating the reasons for restricting access to this information in the specific case.

---

[15] *Cf. Case of Palamara Iribarne, supra*, para. 83; *Case of Ricardo Canese, supra*, para. 97; *Case of Herrera Ulloa, supra*, para. 127. Likewise, *cf.* Feldek v. Slovakia, No. 29032/95, § 83, ECHR 2001-VIII; and Surek and Özdemir v. Turkey, Nos. 23927/94 and 24277/94, § 60, ECHR Judgment of July 8, 1999.

[16] *Cf.* Advisory Opinion OC-6/86, *supra*, paras. 26–29.

96. Even though, when restricting the right, the public authority from which information was requested did not adopt a decision justifying the refusal, the Court notes that, subsequently, during the international proceedings, the State offered several arguments to justify the failure to provide the information requested in sections 3, 6 and 7 of the request of May 7, 1998.

97. Moreover, it was only during the public hearing held on April 3, 2006, that the Vice President of the Foreign Investment Committee at the time of the facts, who appeared as a witness before the Court, explained the reasons why he did not provide the requested information on the three sections. Essentially he stated that "the Foreign Investment Committee ... did not provide the company's financial information because disclosing this information was against the collective interest," which was "the country's development," and that it was the Investment Committee's practice not to provide financial information on the company that could affect its competitiveness to third parties. He also stated that the Committee did not have some of the information, and that it was not obliged to have it or to acquire it.

98. As has been proved, the restriction applied in this case did not comply with the parameters of the Convention. In this regard, the Court understands that the establishment of restrictions to the right of access to State-held information by the practice of its authorities, without respecting the provisions of the Convention, creates fertile ground for discretionary and arbitrary conduct by the State in classifying information as secret, reserved or confidential, and gives rise to legal uncertainty concerning the exercise of this right and the State's powers to limit it.

99. It should also be stressed that when requesting information from the Foreign Investment Committee, Marcel Claude Reyes "proposed to assess the commercial, economic and social elements of the [Río Cóndor] project, measure its impact on the environment ... and set in motion social control of the conduct of the State bodies that intervene or intervened" in the development of the "Río Cóndor exploitation" project. Also, Arturo Longton Guerrero stated that he went to request information "concerned about the possible indiscriminate felling of indigenous forests in the extreme south of Chile" and that "[t]he refusal of public information hindered [his] monitoring task." The possibility of Messrs. Claude Reyes and Longton Guerrero carrying out social control of public administration was harmed by not receiving the requested information, or an answer justifying the restrictions to their right of access to State-held information.

. . .

100. Based on the above, the Court finds that the State violated the right to freedom of thought and expression embodied in Article 13 of the American Convention to the detriment of Marcel Claude Reyes and Arturo Longton Guerrero, and failed to comply with the general obligation to respect and ensure the rights and freedoms established in Article 1(1) thereof. In addition, by not having adopted the measures that were necessary and compatible with the Convention to make effective the right of access to State-held information, Chile failed to comply with the general obligation to adopt domestic legal provisions arising from Article 2 of the Convention.

. . .

2) *Application of Article 8(1) of the Convention in relation to the decision of the Santiago Court of Appeal and the right to a simple and prompt recourse, or any other effective recourse, established in Article 25(1) of the Convention*

. . .

137. When State-held information is refused, the State must guarantee that there is a simple, prompt and effective recourse that permits determining whether there has been a violation of the right of the person requesting information and, if applicable, that the corresponding body is ordered to disclose the information. In this context, the recourse must be simple and prompt, bearing in mind that, in this regard, promptness in the disclosure of the information is essential. According to the provisions of Articles 2 and 25(2)(b) of the Convention, if the State Party to the Convention does not have a judicial recourse to protect the right effectively, it must establish one.

138. Regarding the alleged violation of Article 25 of the Convention, Chile merely indicated that "the petitioners filed the application for protection of constitutional guarantees without obtaining results that satisfied their claims," and explained the reforms carried out as of November 1999 which, *inter alia*, established a "specific [judicial] recourse concerning access to information."

139. The Court considers that, in the instant case, Chile failed to guarantee an effective judicial recourse that was decided in accordance with Article 8(1) of the Convention and which resulted in a ruling on the merits of the dispute concerning the request for State-held information; in other words, a ruling on whether the Foreign Investment Committee should have provided access to the requested information.

140. The Court appreciates the efforts made by Chile in 1999 when it established a special judicial recourse to protect access to public information. Nevertheless, it should be pointed out that the violations in this case occurred before the State made this progress in its legislation, so that the State's argument that the alleged victims in this case "could have filed it" is inappropriate since, at the time of the facts of this case, the said recourse had not been established.

141. The Court considers that the three persons who filed the judicial recourse before the Santiago Court of Appeal are victims. They are Marcel Claude Reyes, Arturo Longton Guerrero and Sebastián Cox Urrejola because, although the Court has determined that the right of freedom of thought and expression has been violated only in the case of Marcel Claude Reyes and Arturo Longton Guerrero (*supra*, paras. 69 to 71 and 103), the Chilean judicial body should have issued a ruling if the recourse was inadmissible in the case of one of the appellants owing to active legal standing.

142. Based on the above, the Court concludes that the State violated the right to judicial protection embodied in Article 25(1) of the American Convention, in relation to Article 1(1) thereof, to the detriment of Marcel Claude Reyes, Arturo Longton Guerrero and Sebastián Cox Urrejola, by failing to guarantee them a simple, prompt and effective recourse that would protect them from actions of the State that they alleged violated their right of access to State-held information.

143. The Court also concludes that the said decision of the Santiago Court of Appeal declaring the application for protection inadmissible did not comply with the guarantee that it should be duly justified. Accordingly, the State violated the right to judicial guarantees embodied in Article 8(1) of the Convention, in relation to Article 1(1) thereof, to the detriment of Marcel Claude Reyes, Arturo Longton Guerrero and Sebastián Cox Urrejola.

144. The alleged violation of Articles 8 and 25 of the Convention regarding the regulation of the formal procedure of processing the judicial recourse for the protection of fundamental rights (*supra*, para. 109(b)), was not alleged by the representative at the due procedural opportunity. However, the Court considers it necessary to recall that the regulation of the processing of the recourse referred to in Article 25 of the Convention must be compatible with this treaty.

X

REPARATIONS

APPLICATION OF ARTICLE 63(1) OF THE CONVENTION
OBLIGATION TO REPAIR

. . .

148. In view of the facts described in the preceding chapters, the Court has decided that the State is responsible for the violation of Article 13 of the American Convention in relation to Articles 1(1) and 2 thereof, to the detriment of Marcel Claude Reyes and Arturo Longton Guerrero, and of Articles 8(1) and 25 of the Convention, in relation to Article 1(1) thereof, to the detriment of Marcel Claude Reyes, Arturo Longton Guerrero and Sebastián Cox Urrejola.

In its case law, the Court has established that it is a principle of international law that any violation of an international obligation that has produced damage entails the obligation to repair it adequately. In this regard, the Court has based itself on Article 63(1) of the American Convention, according to which:

> If the Court finds that there has been a violation of a right or freedom protected by this Convention, the Court shall rule that the injured party be ensured the enjoyment of his right or freedom that was violated. It shall also rule, if appropriate, that the consequences of the measure or situation that constituted the breach of such right or freedom be remedied and that fair compensation be paid to the injured party.

Consequently, the Court will now consider the measures necessary to repair the damage caused to Marcel Claude Reyes, Arturo Longton Guerrero and Sebastián Cox Urrejola, owing to these violations of the Convention.

149. Article 63(1) of the American Convention reflects a customary norm that constitutes one of the basic principles of contemporary international law on State responsibility. Thus, when an unlawful act occurs, which can be attributed to a State, this gives rise immediately to its international responsibility, with the consequent obligation to cause the consequences of the violation to cease and to repair the damage caused.

150. Whenever possible, reparation of the damage caused by the violation of an international obligation requires full restitution (*restitutio in integrum*), which consists in the re-establishment of the previous situation. If this is not possible, the international Court must determine measures to guarantee the violated rights, and repair the consequences of the violations. It is necessary to add the measures of a positive nature that the State must adopt to ensure that harmful facts such as those that occurred in the instant case are not repeated. The responsible State may not invoke provisions of domestic law to modify or fail to comply with its obligation to provide reparation, all aspects of which (scope, nature, methods and determination of the beneficiaries) are regulated by international law.

151. Reparations, as the word indicates, consist of measures tending to eliminate the effects of the violations that have been committed. Thus, the reparations established should be proportionate to the violations declared in the preceding chapters of this judgment.

152. In accordance with the probative elements gathered during the proceedings, and in light of the above criteria, the Court will examine the claims submitted by the Commission and the representative regarding reparations, costs and expenses in order to determine the beneficiaries of the reparations and then order the pertinent measures of reparation and costs and expenses.

A) BENEFICIARIES

153. The Court has determined that the facts of the instant case constituted a violation of Article 13 of the American Convention in relation to Articles 1(1) and 2 thereof, to the detriment of Marcel Claude Reyes and Arturo Longton Guerrero, and of Articles 8(1) and 25 of the Convention, in relation to Article 1(1) thereof, to the detriment of Marcel Claude Reyes, Arturo Longton Guerrero and Sebastián Cox Urrejola who, as victims of the said violations, are eligible for the reparations established by the Court.

B) PECUNIARY DAMAGE

155. In the instant case, the victims' representative did not make any statement or request regarding possible pecuniary damage, and the Court has confirmed that the violations declared and the evidence provided did not result in damage of this type that would require reparations to be ordered.

156. The Court considers that this judgment constitutes, *per se*, a significant and important form of reparation and moral satisfaction for the victims. However, in order to repair the non-pecuniary damage in this case, the Court will determine those measures of satisfaction and guarantees of non-repletion that are not of a pecuniary nature, but have public repercussions.

Measures of satisfaction and guarantees of non-repetition

C.1) Request for State-Held Information

157. Regarding the argument that Chile submitted to the Court, according to which there is no longer any interest in providing the information, since the "Río Cóndor" Project was not implemented, it should be indicated that the social control sought through access to State-held information and the nature of the information requested are sufficient motives for responding to the request for information, without requiring the applicant to prove a specific interest or a direct involvement.

158. Therefore, since in this case the State has not provided part of the requested information and has not issued a justified decision regarding the request for information, the Court considers that the State, through the corresponding entity, should provide the information requested by the victims, if appropriate, or adopt a justified decision in this regard.

159. If the State considers that it was not the Foreign Investment Committee's responsibility to obtain part of the information requested by the victims in this case, it should provided a justified explanation of why it did not provide the information.

C.2) Publication of the Pertinent Parts of This Judgment

160. As ordered in other cases as a measure of satisfaction, the State must publish once in the official gazette and in another newspaper with extensive national circulation, the chapter on the Proven Facts of this judgment, . . . which correspond to Chapters VII and VIII on the violations declared by the Court, without the corresponding footnotes, and the operative paragraphs hereof. This publication should be made within six months of notification of this judgment.

C.3) Adoption of the Necessary Measures to Guarantee the Right of Access to State-Held Information

161. The Court also considers it important to remind the State that, in keeping with the provisions of Article 2 of the Convention, if the exercise of the rights and freedoms protected by this treaty is not guaranteed, it has the obligation to adopt the legislative and other measures necessary to make these rights and freedoms effective.

162. The Court appreciates the significant normative progress that Chile has made concerning access to State-held information, that a draft law on access to public information is being processed, and that efforts are being made to create a special judicial recourse to protect access to public information.

163. Nevertheless, the Court finds it necessary to reiterate that the general obligation contained in Article 2 of the Convention involves the elimination of norms and practices of any type that result in violations of the guarantees established in the Convention, as well as the enactment of laws and the development of practices conducive to the effective observance of these guarantees. Hence, Chile must adopt the necessary measures to guarantee the protection of the right of access to State-held information, and these should include a guarantee of the effectiveness of an appropriate administrative procedure for processing and deciding requests for information, which

establishes time limits for taking a decision and providing information, and which is administered by duly trained officials.

C.4) *Training for Public Entities, Authorities and Agents on Access to State-Held Information*

164. In this case, the administrative authority responsible for deciding the request for information of Messrs. Claude Reyes and Longton Guerrero adopted a position that violated the right of access to State-held information. In this regard, the Court observes with concern that several probative elements contributed to the case file reveal that public officials do not respond effectively to requests for information.

165. The Court considers that, within a reasonable time, the State should provide training to public entities, authorities and agents responsible for responding to requests for access to State-held information on the laws and regulations governing this right; this should incorporates the parameters established in the Convention concerning restrictions to access to this information that must be respected.

D) COSTS AND EXPENSES

166. As the Court has indicated previously, costs and expenses are included in the concept of reparations embodied in Article 63(1) of the American Convention, because the activity deployed by the victim in order to obtain justice at both the national and the international levels entails expenditure that must be compensated when the State's international responsibility is declared in a judgment against it. Regarding their reimbursement, the Court must prudently assess their scope, which includes the expenses incurred before the authorities of the domestic jurisdiction, and also those resulting from the proceedings before the inter-American system, taking into account the circumstances of the specific case and the nature of the international jurisdiction for the protection of human rights. This assessment may be based on the principle of equity and taking into account the expenses indicated by the Inter-American Commission and by the representatives, provided the *quantum* is reasonable.

167. The Court takes into consideration that the victims incurred expenses in the course of the measures taken in the domestic judicial sphere, and were represented by a lawyer in this sphere and before the Commission and the Court during the international proceedings. Since there is no documentary evidence to authenticate the expenses incurred in the international proceedings or in the domestic sphere, based on the equity principle, the Court establishes the sum of US$10,000.00 (ten thousand United States dollars) or the equivalent in Chilean currency, which must be delivered in equal parts to Marcel Claude Reyes, Arturo Longton Guerrero and Sebastián Cox Urrejola for costs and expenses, within one year. They will deliver the corresponding amount to their legal representative, in keeping with the assistance he has provided to them.

. . .

Questions and Discussion

1. What is the motivation for this case? Does it actually stop environmental harm from occurring? Could it?
2. What reasons would be sufficient for refusing to provide information? What would not? If the information being sought is protected intellectual property, would that allow it to be withheld? What if it is suspected that the protected secret formula of a product contains hazardous substances? For a list of acceptable reasons drafted by European states, see the Aarhus Convention on Access to Information, Public Participation, and Access to Justice in Environmental Matters, *infra* Section IV.

III. The Right to Public Participation in Decision Making

The major role played by the public in environmental protection is participation in decision making, especially in environmental impact or other permitting procedures. Public participation is based on the right of those who may be affected, including foreign citizens and residents, to have a say in the determination of their environmental future. Participation is also critical to the effectiveness of law. The process by which rules emerge, or how proposed rules become norms and norms become law, is a matter of legitimacy, and legitimacy in turn affects compliance. Legitimacy depends on participation: the governed must have and perceive that they have a voice in governance through representation, deliberation, or some other form of action. Participation may take place through elections, grassroots action, lobbying, public speaking, hearings, and other forms of governance, whereby various interests and communities participate in shaping the laws and decisions that affect them. The major treaty guaranteeing public participation in environmental decision making is the Aarhus Convention, discussed in Section IV *infra*.

A. *Environmental Instruments*

The Rio Declaration refers to public participation not only in Principle 10, mentioned earlier, but also in reference to different groups: women (Principle 20), youths (Principle 21), and indigenous peoples and local communities (Principle 22). Public participation is also emphasized in Agenda 21, the plan of action adopted at the Rio Conference in 1992. The Preamble to Chapter 23 states:

> One of the fundamental prerequisites for the achievement of sustainable development is broad public participation in decision-making. Furthermore, in the more specific context of environment and development, the need for new forms of participation has emerged. This includes the need of individuals, groups, and organizations to participate in environmental impact assessment procedures and to know about and participate in decisions, particularly those that potentially affect the communities in which they live and work. Individuals, groups and organizations should have access to information relevant to environment and development held by national authorities, including information on products and activities that have or are likely to have a significant impact on the environment, and information on environmental protection measures.

Section III of Agenda 21 identifies major groups whose participation is needed: women, youths, indigenous and local populations, nongovernmental organizations, local authorities, workers, business and industry, scientists, and farmers.

Most recent multilateral and many bilateral agreements contain references to or guarantees of public participation.[17] Article 4.1(i) of the Climate Change Convention obliges parties to

---

[17] In addition to the treaties discussed in the text, other agreements referring to public participation are the Protocol to the 1979 Convention on Long-Range Transboundary Air Pollution Concerning the Control of Emissions of Volatile Organic Compounds or Their Transboundary Fluxes (Geneva, Nov. 18, 1991), art. 2(3)(a)(4); Convention on the Protection and Utilization of Transboundary Rivers and Lakes (Helsinki, Mar. 17, 1992), art. 16; Convention on the Transboundary Effects of Industrial Accidents (Helsinki, Mar. 17, 1992), art. 9; Convention for the Protection of the Marine Environment of the Baltic Sea (Helsinki, Apr. 9, 1992), art. 17; Convention for the Prevention of Marine Pollution of the North-East Atlantic (Paris, Sept. 22, 1992), art. 9; Convention on Civil Responsibility for Damage Resulting from Activities Dangerous to the Environment (Lugano, June 21, 1993), arts. 13–16; North American Convention on Cooperation in the Field of the Environment (Washington, D.C., Sept. 14, 1993), arts. 2(1)(a), 14; Convention on Cooperation and Sustainable Development of the Waters of the Danube (Sofia, June 29, 1994), art. 14; Protocol to the 1975 Barcelona Convention on Specially Protected Zones and Biological Diversity in the Mediterranean (Barcelona, June 10, 1995), art. 19; Joint Communique and Declaration on the Establishment of the Arctic Council (Ottawa, Sept. 19, 1996), preamble and arts. 1(a), 2, 3(c); Kyoto Protocol to the U.N. Framework Convention on Climate Change (Dec. 11, 1997), art. 6(3); Convention on Persistent Organic Pollutants (Sept. 22, 2001), art. 10(1)(d), 40 I.L.M. 532 (2001).

promote public awareness and to "encourage the widest participation in this process including that of non-governmental organizations." The Convention on Biological Diversity allows for public participation in environmental impact assessment procedures in its article 14(1)(a). The 1991 Espoo Convention on Environmental Impact Assessment in a Transboundary Context requires states parties to notify the public and to provide an opportunity for public participation in relevant environmental impact assessment procedures regarding proposed activities in any area likely to be affected by transboundary environmental harm. In a final decision on the proposed activities, the state must take due account of the environmental impact assessment, including the opinions of the individuals in the affected area. The U.N. Convention to Combat Desertification goes furthest in calling for public participation, embedding the issue throughout the agreement. Articles 3(a) and (c) begin by recognizing that there is a need to associate civil society with the actions of the state. The treaty calls for an integrated commitment of all actors – national governments, scientific institutions, local communities and authorities, and nongovernmental organizations, as well as international partners, both bilateral and multilateral. Articles 10(2)(e), 13(1)(b), 14(2), 19, and 25.

The 1993 North American Agreement on Environmental Cooperation (NAAEC), also known as the NAFTA side agreement, contains institutional arrangements for public participation. It creates a permanent trilateral body, the Commission for Environmental Cooperation, composed of the Council, the Secretariat, and the Joint Public Advisory Committee (art. 8). The Joint Public Advisory Committee includes fifteen members from the public, five from each member country, and advises the Council as well as provides technical, scientific, and other information to the Secretariat. The Committee also may advise on the annual program and budget, as well as reports that are issued. The NAAEC is also the first environmental agreement to establish a procedure that allows individuals, environmental organizations, and business entities to complain about a state's failure to enforce its environmental law, including those deriving from international obligations.

Recent bilateral agreements also provide for public participation. The Canada–United States Agreement on Air Quality (Ottawa, Mar. 13, 1991), reprinted in 30 I.L.M. 676 (1991), provides that the International Joint Commission established pursuant to an earlier agreement, shall invite comments, including through public hearings as appropriate, on each progress report prepared by the Air Quality Committee established to assist in implementing the agreement. A synthesis of public views and, if requested, a record of such views shall be submitted to the parties. After submission to the parties, the synthesis shall be released to the public. The parties agree to consult on the contents of the progress report, based in part on the views presented to the Commission. Further, according to article 14, the parties shall consult with state or provincial governments, interested organizations, and the public in implementing the agreement.

B. *Human Rights Texts*

As with the right to information, the right to public participation is widely expressed in human rights instruments. Article 21 of the Universal Declaration of Human Rights affirms the right of everyone to take part in governance of his or her country, as does the American Declaration of the Rights and Duties of Man (art. 20) and the African Charter (art. 13). Article 25 of the International Covenant on Civil and Political Rights provides that citizens have the right, without unreasonable restrictions, "to take part in the conduct of public affairs, directly or though freely chosen representatives." The American Convention contains identical language in article 23. These provisions have been invoked far less often than those concerned with information and redress. The European Convention does not contain a broad guarantee of public participation; Protocol I, Article 3, is limited to the right to vote in free and fair elections. *See, e.g., Hirst v. United Kingdom* (No. 2), GC, Reports of Judgments and Decisions 2005-IX (6 Oct. 2005). In Europe, most of the cases concerning the right to participate in environmental decision making arise under national law or the directives of the European Union, for those twenty-seven states that are members of it. *See* GYULA BÁNDI ET AL., THE ENVIRONMENTAL JURISPRUDENCE OF THE EUROPEAN COURT OF JUSTICE 191–203 (2008).

IV. The Rights of Access to Justice and to a Remedy for Environmental Harm

Principle 10 of the Rio Declaration provides that "effective access to judicial and administrative proceedings, including redress and remedy, shall be provided." Agenda 21 calls on governments and legislators to establish judicial and administrative procedures for legal redress to remedy actions affecting the environment that may be unlawful or infringe on rights under the law. They should provide such access to justice to individuals, groups, and organizations with a recognized legal interest. Some instruments make it explicit that the right to a remedy is not limited to nationals of a state. International agreements may contain obligations to grant an injured person or one threatened with harm a right of access to any administrative or judicial procedure equal to that of nationals or residents. Equal access to national remedies has been considered one way of implementing the polluter-pays principle. Article 32 of the 1997 U.N. Convention on the Non-Navigational Uses of International Watercourses formulates the same principle under the name nondiscrimination.

A. *The Right to a Remedy in Human Rights Instruments*

The right to a remedy when a right is violated is itself a right expressly guaranteed by universal and regional human rights instruments. *See Claude Reyes, supra.* It comprises the right of access to justice (i.e., a fair hearing before an impartial and independent tribunal) and the right to redress for harm done. Article 8 of the Universal Declaration of Human Rights affirms that "[e]veryone has the right to an effective remedy by the competent national tribunals for acts violating the fundamental rights granted him by the constitution or laws." The International Covenant on Civil and Political Rights also obliges states to provide remedies. According to its article 2(3):

Each State Party to the . . . Covenant undertakes:

 (a) To ensure that any person whose rights or freedoms as . . . recognized [in the Covenant] are violated shall have an effective remedy notwithstanding that the violation has been committed by persons acting in an official capacity.

 (b) To ensure that any person claiming such a remedy shall have the right thereto determined by competent judicial, administrative or legislative authorities, or by any other competent authority provided for by the legal system of the State, and to develop the possibilities of judicial remedy;

 (c) To ensure that the competent authorities shall enforce such remedies when granted.

The Human Rights Committee has identified the kinds of remedies required, depending on the type of violation and the victim's condition. The Committee has indicated that the state which has engaged in human rights violations, in addition to treating and financially compensating the victim, must undertake to investigate the facts, to take appropriate action, and to bring those found responsible for the violations to justice. The International Labour Organization Convention Concerning Indigenous and Tribal Peoples in Independent Countries, I.L.O. No. 169 (June 27, 1989), specifically refers to "fair compensation for damages" (art. 15(2)), "compensation in money" (art. 16(4)), and full compensation for "any loss or injury" (art. 16(5)).

Declarations, resolutions, and other nontreaty texts also proclaim or discuss the right to a remedy. In some instances, the issue is raised by human rights organs as part of the mechanism of issuing "general comments." The Third General Comment of the Committee on Economic, Social, and Cultural Rights, concerning the nature of state obligations pursuant to article 2(1) of the Covenant, states that appropriate measures to implement the Covenant might include the provision of judicial remedies with respect to rights that may be considered justiciable. It specifically points to the nondiscrimination requirement of the treaty and cross-references the right to a remedy in the Covenant on Civil and Political Rights. A number of other rights are cited as "capable of immediate application by judicial and other organs." United Nations, *Compilation of General Comments and General Recommendations Adopted by Human Rights Treaty Bodies*, U.N. Doc. HRI/GEN/1/Rev.7, at 63, para. 5 (May 12, 2007). *See also* Chapter 4, p. 242.

Regional instruments also contain provisions regarding legal remedies for violations of rights. Article XVII of the American Declaration of the Rights and Duties of Man guarantees every person the right to resort to the courts to ensure respect for legal rights and protection from acts of authority that violate any fundamental constitutional rights. The American Convention on Human Rights entitles everyone to effective recourse for protection against acts that violate the fundamental rights recognized by the constitution "or laws of the state or by the Convention," even where the act was committed by persons acting in the course of their official duties (art. 25). The states parties are to ensure that the competent authorities enforce remedies that are granted.

Article 6 of the European Convention on Human Rights guarantees a fair and public hearing before an international tribunal for the determination of rights and duties. Article 6, paragraph 1, states:

> In the determination of his civil rights and obligations or of any criminal charge against him, everyone is entitled to a fair and public hearing within a reasonable time by an independent and impartial tribunal established by law.

The applicability of article 6 depends on the existence of a dispute concerning a right recognized in the law of the state concerned, including those created by licenses, authorizations, and permits that affect the use of property or commercial activities. *Golder v. United Kingdom*, 18 Eur. Ct. H.R. (ser. A) (1975); *Klass v. Germany*, 28 Eur. Ct. H.R. (ser. A) (1978); *Benthem v. Netherlands*, 97 Eur. Ct. H.R. (ser. A) (1985). In *Oerlemans v. Netherlands*, 219 Eur. Ct. H.R. (ser. A) (1991), article 6 was deemed to apply to a case in which a Dutch citizen could not challenge a ministerial order designating his land as a protected site. For other environmental cases, compare *Zander v. Sweden*, 279B Eur. Ct. H.R. (ser. A) (1993); *Danell et al. v. Sweden* (app. No. 54695/00, judgment of Jan. 17, 2006), and *Brugger v. Austria* (App. No. 76293/01, judgment of Jan. 26, 2006) to the following judgment.

Okyay et al. v. Turkey, 43 Eur. H.R. Rep. 788 (2006), App. No. 36220/97
(judgment of July 12, 2005)

THE FACTS

I. THE CIRCUMSTANCES OF THE CASE

A. Background to the Case

9. The case concerns the national authorities' failure to implement the domestic courts' order to shut down three thermal power plants which pollute the environment in the province of Muğla, in south-west Turkey.

10. The applicants are all lawyers who live and practise in İzmir, a city which is approximately 250 kilometres from the site of the power plants. Relying on Article 56 of the Constitution and section 3(a) of the Environment Act, the applicants argued that it was their constitutional right to live in a healthy and balanced environment, and their duty to ensure the protection of the environment and to prevent environmental pollution.

11. The Yatağan, Yeniköy and Gökova thermal power plants have been operated for many years by the Ministry of Energy and Natural Resources and the public utility company Türkiye Elektrik Kurumu ("TEAŞ") in Muğla, in the Aegean region of Turkey. In the course of their operation, the poor-quality coal used by the plants to produce energy has caused pollution and harmed the region's biological diversity.

[The applicants filed successful administrative actions against the three power plants. The decisions in their favor were upheld by the Supreme Administrative Court by decisions of June 3 and 6, 1998. – *Eds.*]

C. Enforcement of the Administrative Courts' Judgments

35. By virtue of section 28 of the Administrative Procedure Act and of Article 138 § 4 of the Constitution, the administrative authorities are obliged to comply with court decisions and to enforce them within thirty days following service of the decision.

36. By a decision of 3 September 1996, the Council of Ministers, composed of the Prime Minister and other cabinet ministers, decided that the three thermal power plants should continue to operate, despite the administrative courts' judgments. The Council of Ministers reasoned that closure of the plants would give rise to energy shortages and loss of employment and would thus affect the region's income from tourism. Taking the view that the necessary measures were being taken by the authorities with a view to preventing the plants from polluting the environment, the Council of Ministers decided that the plants' operation should not be halted.

37. In letters of 6 and 14 September 1996, the applicants asked the defendant administrative authorities to enforce the judgments of the Aydın Administrative Court.

38. On 11 November 1996 the applicants filed criminal complaints with the offices of the Ankara Chief Public Prosecutor and of the public prosecutors in the jurisdictions in which the plants were situated. They asked the prosecutors to institute criminal proceedings against the members of the Council of Ministers and other relevant administrative authorities for failure to execute the court decisions.

39. In a letter of 20 November 1996, the Ministry of Energy and Natural Resources informed the applicants that the operation of the three thermal power plants would not be halted. It was noted that the power plants were responsible for 7% of the country's total electricity production and that their contribution to the economy was estimated at around five hundred billion Turkish liras. The Ministry further argued that 4,079 people would lose their jobs and the region's tourist sector would be adversely affected if these plants were to cease to operate. It was further claimed

that contracts had already been signed for the installation of new flue gas desulphurisation systems and that the necessary measures were therefore being taken to protect the environment and public health.

40. On 27 November 1996 the Ankara Chief Public Prosecutor issued a decision not to prosecute the Prime Minister and other ministers, having regard to Article 100 of the Constitution[,] which stipulated that the prosecution of these authorities would require a parliamentary investigation.

41. On 25 December 1996 the Yatağan Chief Public Prosecutor issued a decision not to prosecute the director of the Yatağan thermal power plant, given that the Aydın Administrative Court's judgment had not been served on him, and that TEAŞ's directors were not responsible for taking action to comply with the court's judgment.

42. On 12 March 1997 the Milas Chief Public Prosecutor issued a decision not to prosecute the directors of the Yeniköy and Gökova thermal power plants. The Chief Public Prosecutor stated that the directors of the power plants were merely implementing the Council of Ministers' decision of 3 September 1996 and that there were no grounds for considering that they were deliberately refusing to comply with the administrative courts' judgments.

D. Subsequent Developments

43. The applicants submitted a copy of nine judgments given by the Yatağan Magistrates' Court in civil matters (*sulh hukuk mahkemesi*). In these cases, brought against TEAŞ, the plaintiffs, who were farmers living in the vicinity of the Yatağan thermal power plant, alleged that the quality and quantity of their olive and tobacco production had been adversely affected by the poisonous gas and ash emitted by the power plant and that they had therefore suffered pecuniary damage (Files nos. 1998/80, 1998/81, 1999/68, 2000/225, 2000/226, 2000/499, 2001/72, 2001/73, 2001/76; and decisions nos. 1998/108, 1998/113, 1999/339, 2000/164, 2000/183, 2001/59, 2001/75, 2001/78, 2001/79).

44. The Yatağan Magistrates' Court acceded to the plaintiffs' claims and awarded each of them compensation. Relying on expert reports on the plaintiffs' land, the court found that the hazardous gas emitted by the power plant had caused considerable damage to cultivation in the region, in that olive trees and tobacco plants suffered from incomplete leaf growth and were unable to produce a sufficient yield.

45. The Court of Cassation upheld all nine judgments of the Yatağan Magistrates' Court.

II. RELEVANT LAW

A. Domestic Law on Environmental Protection

1. *The Constitution*

46. Article 56 of the Constitution provides:

> Everyone has the right to live in a healthy, balanced environment. It shall be the duty of the State and the citizens to improve and preserve the environment and to prevent environmental pollution. . . . The State shall perform this task by utilising and supervising health and social welfare institutions in both the public and private sectors. . . . "

2. *The Environment Act*

47. Section 3 of the Environment Act (Law no. 2872), published in the Official Gazette on 11 August 1983, reads:

> The general principles governing environmental protection and the prevention of environmental pollution shall be as follows:

(a) Protecting the environment and preventing environmental pollution are the duty of individuals and legal entities as well as of all citizens, and they are required to comply with the measures to be taken and the principles laid down in reference to these matters. . . .

48. Section 10 provides:

"Establishments and concerns which propose to carry out activities which might cause environmental problems shall draw up an environmental impact report. This report shall concern, *inter alia*, the measures proposed to reduce the detrimental effects of waste materials and the necessary precautions to this end.

The types of project for which such a report shall be required, its content and the principles governing its approval by the relevant authorities shall be determined by regulations."

49. Section 28 reads:

Whether or not negligence has occurred, a person who pollutes and harms the environment shall be responsible for the damage resulting from that pollution or the deterioration of the environment.

This liability is without prejudice to any liability which may arise under general provisions.

50. Section 30 provides:

Individuals and legal entities that suffer damage from or have information regarding an activity which pollutes or harms the environment may request that the activity be stopped by applying to the administrative authorities.

B. Relevant International Texts on the Right to a Healthy Environment

51. In June 1992 the United Nations Conference on Environment and Development, meeting in Rio de Janeiro (Brazil), adopted a declaration ("the Rio Declaration on Environment and Development," A/CONF.151/26 (vol. I)) intended to advance the concept of States' rights and responsibilities with regard to the environment. "Principle 10" of this Declaration provides:

Environmental issues are best handled with the participation of all concerned citizens, at the relevant level. At the national level, each individual shall have appropriate access to information concerning the environment that is held by public authorities, including information on hazardous materials and activities in their communities, and the opportunity to participate in decision-making processes. States shall facilitate and encourage public awareness and participation by making information widely available. Effective access to judicial and administrative proceedings, including redress and remedy, shall be provided.

52. On 27 June 2003 the Parliamentary Assembly of the Council of Europe adopted Recommendation 1614 (2003) on environment and human rights. The relevant part of this recommendation states:

9. The Assembly recommends that the Governments of member States:
    i.   ensure appropriate protection of the life, health, family and private life, physical integrity and private property of persons in accordance with Articles 2, 3 and 8 of the European Convention on Human Rights and by Article 1 of its Additional Protocol, by also taking particular account of the need for environmental protection;
   ii.   recognise a human right to a healthy, viable and decent environment which includes the objective obligation for States to protect the environment, in national laws, preferably at constitutional level;

iii.   safeguard the individual procedural rights to access to information, public participation
       in decision making and access to justice in environmental matters set out in the Aarhus
       Convention; . . .

                                           . . .

THE LAW

I. ALLEGED VIOLATION OF ARTICLE 6 § 1 OF THE CONVENTION

60. The applicants alleged that their right to a fair hearing had been breached on account of
the national authorities' failure to implement the administrative courts' judgments. They relied
on Article 6 § 1 of the Convention, the relevant part of which reads:

> In the determination of his civil rights and obligations . . . , everyone is entitled to a fair . . .
> hearing . . . by [a] . . . tribunal. . . .

A. Applicability of Article 6 § 1

61. The Government argued that Article 6 § 1 was not applicable in the present case. Referring to
the Court's considerations in *Balmer-Schafroth and Others v. Switzerland* (judgment of 26 August
1997, *Reports of Judgments and Decisions* 1997–IV, p. 1359, § 40) and *Athanassoglou and Others
v. Switzerland* ([GC], no. 27644/95, § 55, ECHR 2000-IV), as well as *Ünver v. Turkey* ((dec.),
no. 36209/97, 26 September 2000), they submitted that there was no connection between the
impugned power plants' conditions of operation and the alleged infringement of the applicants'
civil rights. In particular, the applicants had failed to show that the power plants' operation
exposed them personally to a danger which was serious, specific and imminent. On the contrary,
the applicants admitted that they had not been personally affected but that they were concerned
about their country's environmental problems and wished to live in a healthy environment. Nor
had they claimed at any stage of the proceedings that they had suffered any economic or other
loss. Accordingly, the result of the proceedings in issue was not directly decisive for any of their
civil rights.

62. The Government further noted that under Turkish law only those whose "rights" had been
violated could claim to be victims, whereas in the instant case the applicants merely alleged a violation of their "interests" before the domestic courts. With reference to the Supreme Administrative
Court's jurisprudence on the subject, the Government pointed out that the concept of "victim"
entailed a violation of a right and not that of an interest. Accordingly, although the applicants
were entitled to bring an action to set aside an administrative act violating their interests, this
did not in itself qualify them as victims. Thus, in the absence of a right at stake, the applicants'
complaints did not concern "civil rights and obligations" within the meaning of Article 6 § 1 of
the Convention.

63. The applicants disputed the Government's submissions and argued that they had been
concerned for the protection of the environment in the Aegean region of Turkey, where they
lived. They also contended that the Government's failure to implement the domestic courts'
decisions had caused them emotional suffering and contravened the principle of the rule of law.

64. The Court reiterates that, for Article 6 § 1 in its "civil" limb to be applicable, there must
be a dispute ("*contestation*" in the French text) over a "civil right" which can be said, at least on
arguable grounds, to be recognised under domestic law. The dispute must be genuine and serious;
it may relate not only to the actual existence of a right but also to its scope and the manner of
its exercise. The outcome of the proceedings must be directly decisive for the right in question;
tenuous connections or remote consequences are not sufficient to bring Article 6 § 1 into play
(see, among other authorities, *Taşkın and Others v. Turkey*, no. 46117/99, § 130, ECHR 2004-X;

Balmer-Schafroth and Others, cited above, p. 1357, § 32; and *Athanassoglou and Others*, cited above, § 43).

65. The Court notes that it is clear from the applications lodged by the applicants with the administrative authorities and the proceedings before the domestic courts that the applicants challenged the operation of the three thermal power plants on account of the damage they had caused to the environment and the risks they posed for the life and health of the Aegean region's population, to which they belonged. While the applicants did not claim to have suffered any economic or other loss, they relied on their constitutional right to live in a healthy and balanced environment. Such a right is recognised in Turkish law, as is clear from the provisions of Article 56 of the Constitution and has been acknowledged by the decisions of the administrative courts. Having regard to the foregoing, the Court is satisfied that the applicants could arguably claim that they were entitled under Turkish law to protection against damage to the environment caused by the power plants' hazardous activities. It follows that there existed a genuine and serious "dispute."

66. It therefore remains to be determined whether the right in issue was a "civil right." In this connection, the Court notes that the environmental pollution caused by the Gökova, Yeniköy and Yatağan thermal power plants through the emission of hazardous gas and ash, and the risk involved for public health, were established by the Aydın Administrative Court on the basis of an expert report. It appears from the findings of the Administrative Court that the hazardous gas emitted by the power plants might extend over an area measuring 2,350 kilometres in diameter. That distance covers the area in which the applicants live and brings into play their right to the protection of their physical integrity, despite the fact that the risk which they run is not as serious, specific and imminent as that run by those living in the immediate vicinity of the plants.

67. Be that as it may, it is to be noted that the applicants, as individuals entitled to live in a healthy and balanced environment and duty bound to protect the environment and prevent environmental pollution, had standing under Turkish law to ask the administrative courts to issue injunctions for the suspension of the power plants' environmentally hazardous activities, and to set aside the administrative authorities' decision to continue to operate them. In addition, the judgments delivered by the administrative courts were favourable to the applicants and any administrative decision to refuse to enforce these judgments or to circumvent them paved the way for compensation (see paragraphs 57 and 58 above and *Taşkın and Others*, cited above, § 133). Accordingly, the outcome of the proceedings before the administrative courts, taken as a whole, may be considered to relate to the applicants' civil rights.

68. That being so, the Court notes that the concept of a "civil right" under Article 6 § 1 cannot be construed as limiting an enforceable right in domestic law within the meaning of Article 53 of the Convention. It is in this respect that the present case differs from the authorities relied on by the Government, notably *Balmer-Schafroth and Others* and *Athanassoglou and Others*, cited above, where the applicants had been unable to secure a ruling by a tribunal on their objections to the extension of the operating permits of nuclear power plants, and *Ünver*, cited above, where the right relied on by the applicant was a procedural right under administrative law and was not related to the defence of any specific right which he may have had under domestic law.

69. In sum, Article 6 of the Convention is applicable in the instant case.

B. Compliance with Article 6 § 1

70. The Government asserted that the administrative authorities had obtained all the necessary licences for the power plants subsequent to the decisions by the administrative courts and, accordingly, had not failed to enforce the decisions in question.

71. The applicants challenged the Government's assertions and contended that the non-enforcement of the administrative courts' decisions was incompatible with the rule of law and contravened the requirements of Article 6 § 1 of the Convention. They also noted that the power

plants still posed a threat to the environment and public health, as demonstrated by the recent judgments given by the administrative courts.

72. The Court reiterates that the execution of a judgment given by a court is to be regarded as an integral part of the "trial" for the purposes of Article 6 of the Convention (see *Hornsby v. Greece*, judgment of 19 March 1997, *Reports* 1997-II, pp. 511–12, § 40). The right of access to a court guaranteed under that Article would be rendered illusory if a Contracting State's legal system allowed a final binding judicial decision or an interlocutory order made pending the outcome of a final decision to remain inoperative to the detriment of one party. This principle is of even greater importance in the context of administrative proceedings concerning a dispute whose outcome is decisive for a litigant's civil rights (ibid.).

73. The Court notes that the administrative authorities failed to comply with the Aydın Administrative Court's interlocutory order of 20 June 1996 suspending the activities of the three thermal power plants (see paragraph 17 above). Furthermore, the decisions of the Supreme Administrative Court upholding the Aydın Administrative Court's judgments of 30 December 1996 were not enforced within the prescribed time-limits. On the contrary, by a decision of 3 September 1996, the Council of Ministers decided that the three thermal power plants should continue to operate despite the administrative courts' judgments. This latter decision had no legal basis and was obviously unlawful under domestic law. It was tantamount to circumventing the judicial decisions. In the Court's opinion, such a situation adversely affects the principle of a law-based State, founded on the rule of law and the principle of legal certainty (see *Taşkın and Others*, cited above, § 136).

74. In the light of the foregoing, the Court considers that the national authorities failed to comply in practice and within a reasonable time with the judgments rendered by the Aydın Administrative Court on 30 December 1996 and subsequently upheld by the Supreme Administrative Court on 3 and 6 June 1998, thus depriving Article 6 § 1 of any useful effect.

75. There has therefore been a violation of Article 6 § 1 of the Convention.

II. APPLICATION OF ARTICLE 41 OF THE CONVENTION

76. Article 41 of the Convention provides:

> If the Court finds that there has been a violation of the Convention or the Protocols thereto, and if the internal law of the High Contracting Party concerned allows only partial reparation to be made, the Court shall, if necessary, afford just satisfaction to the injured party.

77. The applicants did not claim compensation for either pecuniary damage or for costs and expenses. However, they claimed compensation for non-pecuniary damage in respect of the emotional suffering and distress caused by the non-enforcement of the administrative courts' decisions. They left the sum to be awarded to the discretion of the Court.

78. The Government did not comment on the applicants' claims.

79. The Court considers that the applicants must have suffered distress on account of the authorities' failure to comply with the administrative courts' judgments. The applicants, who had already been involved in complex proceedings to obtain favourable decisions from the administrative courts, were compelled to pursue further proceedings in order to ensure that the authorities would comply with those decisions, in violation of the fundamental principles of a State governed by the rule of law (see *Taşkın and Others*, cited above, § 144). While it is difficult to assess damage of this sort, the distress suffered by the applicants cannot be compensated by the mere finding of a violation. Accordingly, making its assessment on an equitable basis, the Court awards each applicant the sum of 1,000 euros.

80. The Court considers it appropriate that the default interest should be based on the marginal lending rate of the European Central Bank, to which should be added three percentage points.

FOR THESE REASONS, THE COURT UNANIMOUSLY

1. *Holds* that there has been a violation of Article 6 § 1 of the Convention;
2. *Holds*
    (a) that the respondent State is to pay each applicant, within three months from the date on which the judgment becomes final according to Article 44 § 2 of the Convention, the sum of EUR 1,000 (one thousand euros) in respect of non-pecuniary damage, to be converted into the national currency of the respondent State on the date of settlement, plus any tax that may be chargeable;
    (b) that from the expiry of the above-mentioned three months until settlement simple interest shall be payable on the above amount at a rate equal to the marginal lending rate of the European Central Bank during the default period plus three percentage points.

Questions and Discussion

1. If the Turkish Constitution did not include the right to a safe and healthy environment, would the applicants have succeeded in their article 6 claim at the European Court of Human Rights? To what extent are procedural rights dependent on substantive ones?

2. Is the remedy adequate in this case? Why doesn't the European Court order the closure of the plants, as the Indian Supreme Court has done in severe pollution cases? Would it have made a difference if the applicants had suffered personal injury or economic loss? In *Case Concerning the Gabčíkovo-Nagymaros Project*, the International Court of Justice refused to enjoin, inter alia, the continued operation of a hydroelectric power plant in Slovakia alleged to pose a continuing source of environmental harm in Hungary. Instead, the Court relied on the concept of sustainable development in the following manner:

    > The Court is mindful that, in the field of environmental protection vigilance and pre-vention are required on account of the often irreversible character of damage to the environment. . . .
    >
    > Throughout the ages, mankind has, for economic and other reasons, constantly inter-fered with nature. In the past, this was often done without consideration of the effects upon the environment. Owing to new scientific insights and to growing awareness of the risks for mankind . . . new norms and standards have been developed. . . . This need to reconcile economic development with protection of the environment is [today] aptly expressed in the concept of sustainable development.
    >
    > For the purposes of the present case, this means that the Parties together should look afresh at the effects on the environment of the operation of the Gabčíkovo power plant. . . .

    Case Concerning the Gabčíkovo-Nagymaros Project (Hungary v. Slovakia), 1997 I.C.J. 7, 78. As a matter of judicial process, ought the principle of sustainable development be available to balance economic interests and environmental harm when the harm results in human rights violations?

3. The right to a remedy extends to compensation for pollution. In *Zimmerman and Steiner v. Switzerland*, 66 Eur. Ct. H.R. (ser. A) (1983), the Court found article 6 applicable to a complaint about the length of proceedings for compensation for injury caused by noise and air pollution from a nearby airport. Article 6 does not, however, encompass a right to judicial review of legislative enactments. In *Braunerheilm v. Sweden*, the commission denied a claim that article 6 was violated when the applicant could not challenge in court

a new law that granted fishing licenses to the general public in waters where the applicant previously had exclusive rights. *Braunerheilm v. Sweden*, App. No. 11764/85 (Mar. 9, 1989). *See* Maguelonne Dejeant-Pons, *Le droit de l'homme a l'environnement, droit fondamental au niveau Européen dans le cadre du Conseil de l'Europe, et la Convention Européenne de sauvegarde des droit de l'homme et des libertés fondamentales*, 4 Revue Juridique De L'environnement (1994).

4. The African Charter contains a broad right to a remedy in article 7, supplemented by "the right to adequate compensation for the spoliation of resources of a dispossessed people." African Charter on Human and Peoples Rights, article 21(2). Article 26 also imposes a duty on states parties to the Charter to guarantee the independence of the courts and to allow the establishment and improvement of appropriate national institutions entrusted with the promotion and protection of rights and freedoms guaranteed by the Charter.

5. Issues of nonenforcement of environmental law and failure to respect rights arise in many contexts. For a comprehensive analysis of the U.S. statutory framework providing a right to a remedy to enforce environmental law, see Edward Lloyd, *Citizen Suits and Defenses Against Them*, American Law Institute – American Bar Association Continuing Legal Education, ALI-ABA Course of Study, June 27–30, 2007 (available on Westlaw). Lloyd's article refers to the numerous federal environmental statutes that allow citizen enforcement actions. *See* Act to Prevent Pollution from Ships, 33 U.S.C. § 1910; Clean Air Act, 42 U.S.C. § 7604; Clean Water Act, 33 U.S.C. § 1365; Comprehensive Environmental Response, Liability, and Cleanup Act, 42 U.S.C. § 9659; Deep Water Port Act, 33 U.S.C. § 1515; Deep Seabed Hard Mineral Resources Act, 30 U.S.C. § 1427; Emergency Planning and Community Right-to-Know Act of 1986, 42 U.S.C. § 11046; Endangered Species Act, 16 U.S.C. § 1540(g); Energy Conservation Program for Consumer Products, 42 U.S.C. § 6305; Marine Protection, Research and Sanctuary Act, 33 U.S.C. § 1415(g); National Forests, Columbia River Gorge National Scenic Area, 16 U.S.C. § 544m(b); Natural Gas Pipeline Safety Act, 49 U.S.C.A. § 1686; Noise Control Act, 42 U.S.C. § 4911; Ocean Thermal Energy Conservation Act, 42 U.S.C. § 9124; Outer Continental Shelf Lands Act, 43 U.S.C. § 1349(a); Powerplant and Industrial Fuel Use Act, 42 U.S.C. § 8435; Resources Conservation and Recovery Act, 42 U.S.C. § 6972; Safe Drinking Water Act, 42 U.S.C. § 300j-8; Surface Mining Control and Reclamation Act, 30 U.S.C. § 1270; Toxic Substances Control Act, 15 U.S.C. § 2619.

6. State citizen-lawsuit statues include Connecticut Environmental Protection Act of 1971, Conn. Gen. Stat. §§ 22a-14 to 20; Florida Environmental Protection Act of 1971, Fla. Stat. Ann. § 403.412; Hawaii, Haw. Const. art. XI, § 9; Illinois, Ill. Const. art. 11, § 2; Indiana, Ind. Code Ann. §§ 13-30-1-1 to -12; Iowa, Iowa Code § 455B. 111; Louisiana, La. Rev. Stat. Ann. § 30:2026; Maryland Environmental Standing Act, Md. Code Ann. Nat. Res. § 1-503; Michigan Environmental Protection Act, Mich. Comp. Laws §§ 324.1701-1706; Minnesota Environmental Rights Act, Minn. Stat. §§ 116B.01-.13; Nevada, Nev. Rev. Stat. §§ 41.540-.570; New Jersey Environmental Rights Act, N.J. Stat. Ann. §§ 2A:35A-1 to 35A-14; North Dakota Environmental Law Enforcement Act of 1975, N.D. Cent. Code §§ 32-40-01 to -11; South Dakota, S.D. Codified Laws Ann. §§ 34A-10-1 to -17; Wyoming Environmental Quality Act, Wyo. Stat. § 35-11-904.

7. For further reading, see Michael D. Axline, Environmental Citizen Suits (1995); Environmental Law Institute, Citizen Suits: An Analysis of Citizen Enforcement Actions Under EPA-Administered Statutes (1984); Susan George, William J. Snape

III, & Rina Rodriguez, *The Public in Action: Using State Citizen Suit Statutes to Protect Biodiversity*, 6 U. BALT. J. ENVTL. L. 1 (1997); Jim Hecker, *The Difficulty of Citizen Enforcement of the Clean Air Act*, 10 WIDENER L. REV. 303 (2004); Edward Lloyd, *Supplemental Environmental Projects or SEPs Have Been Effectively Used in Citizen Suits to Deter Future Violations as Well as to Achieve Significant Supplemental Environmental Benefits*. 10 WIDENER L. REV. 413 (2004); James R. May, *Now More Than Ever: Recent Trends in Environmental Citizen Suits*, 10 WIDENER L. REV. 8 (2004); Jeffery G. Miller, *Private Enforcement of Federal Pollution Control Laws: The Citizen Suit Provisions*, ALI-ABA Course of Study, Environmental Litigation, Boulder, Colo., June 2001; U.S. Environmental Protection Agency, *Policy on the Use of Supplemental Environmental Projects in Enforcement Settlements* (Feb. 12, 1991); Widener University School of Law Symposium, *Environmental Citizen Suits at Thirtysomething: A Celebration & Summit (Apr. 4, 2003)*, 10 WIDENER L. REV. (2003, 2004).

B. *The World Bank Inspection Panel*

As discussed in more detail in Chapter 10, the World Bank Inspection Panel was created in 1994 as a three-member body to increase the accountability of the World Bank for the consequences of the projects it funds. In addition to increasing transparency and accountability, the executive directors specified that one key objective of the Panel would be to ensure that projects were "fully compatible" with World Bank policies and procedures.

The Panel is empowered to receive and investigate requests for inspection from people directly affected by World Bank projects in cases where the Bank has failed to implement and enforce its own policies, procedures, or loan agreements. Two or more affected people in a borrowing country can file to assert that their rights or interests were (or are about to be) directly and adversely affected by an act or omission of the Bank violating a Bank policy or procedure. The applicants must also show that they brought the violations to the attention of Bank management without an adequate response. Claimants can be represented by local nongovernmental organizations in the country where they are located; in exceptional circumstances, they can be represented by international NGOs. In especially serious cases, an executive director of the Bank can also file a claim.

After the claim has been filed, the Panel determines whether the claim is eligible under the Resolution and Panel procedures. If the Panel determines it is eligible, it then registers the claim and starts a preliminary evaluation. Bank management sends its response to the claim to the Board and the Panel, after which the Panel makes a recommendation to the Board about whether there should be a full investigation. The Board must approve an investigation before the Panel can proceed. When the Panel is authorized to investigate, it sends a report with findings to the Board, which will obtain management's response and recommendations. The Board then makes a decision about how to proceed. *See generally* Ibrahim F.I. Shihata, THE WORLD BANK LEGAL PAPERS ch. 23 (2000); Ibrahim F.I. Shihata, *The World Bank Inspection Panel: Its Historical, Legal and Operational Aspects, in* THE INSPECTION PANEL OF THE WORLD BANK: A DIFFERENT COMPLAINTS PROCEDURE 7 (Gudmundur Alfredsson & Rolf Ring eds., 2001).

As of early 2010, sixty-four requests for inspection had been made. The largest number of claims has concerned large dam projects, but other major infrastructure projects have been challenged as well, as the following extract illustrates.

Investigation Report, Ghana: West African Gas Pipeline Project, World Bank Inspection Panel, Report No. 42644-GH, Apr. 25, 2008 (emphasis in original)

Executive Summary

Introduction

On April 27, 2006, the Inspection Panel received a Request for Inspection of the West African Gas Pipeline (WAGP) Project.

The Request was submitted by the Ifesowapo Host Communities Forum of the WAGP Project (the "Association") through their representatives from Olorunda Local Government Area of Lagos State, Nigeria. Additionally, the Panel received a letter from Friends of the Earth Ghana (FoE-Ghana), expressing its support for the Request and asking to be added to the Request. The Association and FoE-Ghana represent local people living in Nigeria and Ghana and are also referred to as the Requesters.

The Project

The Project consists of the construction of a new pipeline system that will transport natural gas from Nigeria to Ghana, Togo and Benin. The Project includes spurs to provide gas-to-power generating units in Ghana, Benin, and Togo, the conversion of existing power generating units to gas, and, as needed, additional compression investments. The new pipeline (678 kilometers long) originates at a connection to the existing Escravos-Lagos Pipeline in Nigeria. Fifty-eight kilometers of pipeline and other ancillary facilities are to be constructed in southwestern Nigeria, and the pipeline then runs off-shore to a terminal point in Takoradi, Ghana.

According to the Project Appraisal Document (PAD), the Project aims to contribute to, *inter alia*, "*improving the competitiveness of the energy sectors in Ghana, Benin, and Togo by promoting the use of cheaper and environmentally cleaner gas from Nigeria in lieu of solid and liquid fuels for power generation and other industrial, commercial uses, and diversifying energy supply sources.*"

The International Development Association (IDA) (hereinafter referred to as "the Bank") has provided a guarantee, in the amount of US$50 million, for certain obligations of Ghana related to the purchase of natural gas from the West African Gas Pipeline Company Limited (WAPCo). The Multilateral Investment Guarantee Agency (MIGA) has provided a US$75 million in political risk guarantee to WAPCo in relation to the construction of the pipeline and associated facilities. The Project is implemented by WAPCo. Current shareholders of WAPCo include Shell, Chevron, Nigerian National Petroleum Corporation (NNPC), Volta River Authority (VRA) of Ghana, BenGaz of Benin, and SotoGaz of Togo (the Sponsors).

The Claims of the Requesters

The Requesters believe that the Bank did not comply with its policies and procedures in relation to the Project, and that the Project will cause irreparable damage to their land and destroy the livelihoods of their communities. Requesters from Nigeria's Delta Region are mainly concerned with the Project's impact on gas flaring reduction and with the safety of an existing pipeline to which WAGP is to be linked. The Requesters and affected communities living near the gas pipeline in Nigeria complain mainly about low compensation rates for the land they had to give up for the pipeline. Those living in southwestern Nigeria, where the pipeline goes under the sea, claim that the construction process hurt their fishing enterprise. The Requesters from Ghana are concerned about inadequate consultation regarding the Project's economic viability, the pipeline's safety, and its impacts on coastal fisheries.

(i) Environmental Assessment and Environmental Issues

The Requesters from Nigeria assert that the Environmental Assessment (EA) for the WAGP should have included the effects of the Project on the existing Escravos-Lagos Pipeline System (ELPS) to which the WAGP will be linked. They believe that the ELPS is unsafe because of its history of poor maintenance and accidents. Moreover, they state that the EA identified the importance of an emergency response system for the construction and operation of the Project. However, they question whether local people will be able to utilize and understand such a system in the case of an accident. They cite several instances of oil and gas related accidents. Similarly, the Requesters from Ghana doubt that Ghana has the capacity to respond to such accidents.

The fishermen among the Requesters in Nigeria believe that the construction of the gas pipeline polluted the water and damaged their nets so that they were no longer able to catch fish in the area. The Requesters in Ghana stress that fishing is essential to their livelihoods and that continued impact assessments should have been conducted to avoid any negative Project impacts on livelihoods and the fisheries ecosystem.

(ii) Economic Evaluation and Gas Flaring

The Requesters from Nigeria question the economic evaluation of the Project and believe that it was based on incorrect assumptions about its impact on the reduction of flaring of "associated gas" (gas recovered when oil is being extracted) in Nigeria. According to them, the assertion that such associated gas would be a significant source for the pipeline is misleading given the actual amount of associated gas to be exported. The Requesters claim that without assurance that the Project will only use associated (otherwise flared) gas rather than less-costly non-associated gas, the Project will not attain its objectives.

The Requesters from Ghana add that Ghana's Energy Commission has also raised concerns about the Project's long term economic benefit to Ghana and the Requesters believe that these concerns have not been taken into account in the consultation process and will not be adequately addressed in the future.

(iii) Disclosure of Information and Consultation

The Requesters claim that the disclosure of relevant information, such as the EA and Resettlement Action Plan (RAP), was inadequate. They also claim that the economic and financial analysis of the Project was never disclosed.

More specifically, they assert that they did not have timely access to the EA. They understand that the EA is now available on the [I]nternet, but assert that the EA is still difficult to access and understand, given the size of the document, the lack of internet access in their area and the low literacy level in their community. As a result, the Requesters claim that many of the stakeholders did not have access to information about the Project and that the members of the communities could not understand the information that was provided.

(iv) Involuntary Resettlement and Poverty Reduction

The Requesters along the Nigerian portion of the pipeline claim that the Bank has failed to comply with its Policy on Involuntary Resettlement. They fear that the Project will negatively impact their livelihoods. They claim that the Project will not restore or improve their standards of living and that the compensation provided is inadequate.

The Requesters assert that compensation does not account for the loss of land, trees and/or other assets, including future income streams, and they express their concern regarding valuation methods to determine compensation rates. Moreover, the Requesters assert that the RAP lacks mechanisms to secure long-term employment for affected members of their communities. As a result, they believe that the people of their communities will become further impoverished.

(v) Supervision

The Requesters claim that many of the above-mentioned problems stem from Management's failure to comply with the Bank's Policy on Supervision.

. . .

The Investigation Report and Applicable Policies and Procedures

This Report concludes the Panel's investigation into the matters alleged in the Request for Inspection. The Chair of the Panel, Werner Kiene, led the investigation. Two expert consultants, on social issues and resettlement, and on environment, assisted the Panel in the investigation.

The Panel reviewed relevant Project documents and other relevant materials provided by the Requesters, Bank Staff, government representatives, local authorities, WAPCo representatives, individuals and communities living in the areas affected by the Project, non-governmental organizations and other sources. The Panel organized three visits to the areas affected by the Project, in June 2006, January 2007 and July 2007, and interviewed Bank staff in Washington and in the offices in Abuja and Accra.

During its visits, the Panel met with Requesters and other individuals and communities, local and national government authorities, WAPCo staff, representatives from nongovernmental organizations, relevant experts and others. The Panel wishes to extend its sincere thanks and appreciation to all of those with whom it met for their time and cooperation.

With respect to this Project, the Panel assessed whether the Bank complied with the following applicable Operational Policies and Procedures:

> OP/BP 4.01 Environmental Assessment
>
> OP/BP 4.12 Involuntary Resettlement
>
> OD 4.15 Poverty Reduction
>
> OP 10.04 Economic Evaluation of Investment Operations
>
> OP/BP 13.05 Project Supervision
>
> World Bank Policy on Disclosure of Information

Context

The Project should be viewed in the broader context of Nigeria's and the region's hydrocarbon economy and its social and environmental dimensions. Nigeria has more than 250 oil and gas fields, including approximately 2,600 producing oil wells that yield about 2 million barrels of oil per day. Worldwide, Nigeria is the ninth largest gas producer and potentially a major gas supplier. However, a large portion of the gas associated with oil production is currently flared. Nigeria is reported to be the world's largest gas flaring country in spite of the government's legislation intended to reduce flaring and completely cease flaring by 2008.

The development of the Nigerian oil industry has affected the country in a number of ways, both positive and negative. Oil has been the foundation for the country's remarkable economic growth, but exploration and production of oil and gas also have had adverse effects on the livelihood and environment of communities living in the production area and near the pipelines.

Social and political conflicts are considered to be rooted in the inequitable social relations that underlie the production and distribution of profits from oil, and its adverse impact on the fragile ecosystem of the Niger Delta. Hydrocarbon extraction in the Niger Delta has caused critical environmental effects such as: contamination of streams and rivers by drill cuttings and drilling fluids; oil spillage from wells, pipelines and tankers; gas flares causing noise, light and air pollution in nearby villages; and effluent discharges from oil and gas installations and refineries.

In 2004, the lost opportunity value of flared gas was estimated at US\$2.5 billion and the adverse environmental costs were similar in scale, including from approximately 70 million metric tons of CO_2 emissions a year. The local-area population reported to the Panel that the impacts of the gas flaring on people and the environment – intense pollution and heat over extended periods of time – are ravaging and extreme.

Social Issues – Analysis of Compliance

In response to the Request, the Panel focused its analysis on displacement issues brought to its attention by Requesters in Nigeria. The development of WAGP involves the displacement of people associated with the land acquisition of 144 hectares for pipeline construction and operation in Nigeria, including the right of way (ROW) and ancillary facilities. The 25 meter-wide ROW traverses 23 western Nigerian communities, including the 12 communities submitting this Request. Other social issues, including impacts relating to gas flaring, are addressed in other Chapters of the Report.

The Panel acknowledges the complexity of land tenure arrangements in West Africa and notes that efforts were made under the Project to address the related social issues. However, in its investigation, the Panel discovered significant flaws and shortcomings in the application of the Bank's Policy on Involuntary Resettlement. *By not ensuring that WAPCo followed important elements of Bank Policy, Management undercut the Bank's development contribution to this Project. More significantly, the necessary measures to avoid impoverishment of the displaced populations were not and still are not in place.*

Baseline Socio-Economic Data

Many of the problems that are raised in the Request can be linked to the lack of adequate socio-economic data on affected communities and households. Without underlying socioeconomic numbers, resettlement planning and mitigation measures risk falling short of what is required by Bank Policies to safeguard affected people, including vulnerable groups, against risks of impoverishment.

The Bank's Policy on Involuntary Resettlement calls for the assessment of these risks, and related mitigation measures, to be based on an accurate census survey with details on current occupants, displaced households, livelihood, expected loss (total and partial) of assets, and vulnerable groups. There should not be a reliance on averages or aggregates as was done in this Project. The Policy requirements cannot be met by general data on the Project affected area or populations, nor by extrapolation from a sample. Additional studies on land tenure, transfer systems, and patterns of social interaction are also required.

The Panel found that Management did not ensure that the requisite socio-economic information was gathered as called for in the Bank Policy. This does not comply with OP 4.12. The Panel finds that the absence of adequate baseline information makes it impossible to ensure that the impacts and potential impoverishment risks facing local people are properly addressed, as required under the Bank's Resettlement Policy.

(i) Number of Displaced Persons

The Panel expert identified methodological problems in the approach to identifying the number of people claiming ownership on the Nigerian ROW, that bring into doubt the size of the affected population. The plots acquired for the Project appear to be portions of extended family holdings. The socio-economic data which led to decisions on resettlement options, however, did not fully reflect the land tenure system along the ROW.

The Panel finds that the complexities of the traditional land tenure system, wherein large extended families control land and the heads of these families distribute user rights among members of the extended family, were not adequately taken into account. This does not comply with OP 4.12. The size and economic holdings of the extended families was – and still is – unknown. Such an analysis would have helped to prevent the lack of transparency in the way compensation payments were made.

The Panel further observes that the number of displaced persons reported in the RAP was determined using a figure for "average" household size which the RAP itself notes is *"surprisingly low."* The Panel expert determined that *the size of the displaced population seems to be underestimated as a result of the methodology used for their identification.*

Similarly, the proportion of the extended family's holdings taken by the WAPCo land acquisition – a direct indication of the degree of disruption to the basic economic unit – is unknown. *It may be the case that the takings had nominal impacts on the overall productive capacity of the extended family. However, it may also be the case that some were disproportionately damaged. Without knowledge of the socio-economic organization, it is impossible to assess the impoverishment risk.*

(ii) Vulnerable Groups

The Bank's Involuntary Resettlement Policy calls for paying particular attention *"to the needs of vulnerable groups among those displaced...."* The RAP prepared for the Project, however, did not contain adequate information on the needs of vulnerable groups that were to be affected by the Project ROW in Nigeria. These included women, the elderly, the poor, and tenants. *The Panel finds that Bank Management failed to ensure that the Sponsor performed an adequate analysis of the socioeconomic risks to vulnerable peoples. This does not comply with Bank Policy on Involuntary Resettlement, and denied these peoples the protections provided under the Policy.*

Since no studies were carried out or mitigation has occurred, population along the ROW remains at risk.

(iii) Land and Productive Assets of Displaced Persons

A critical element in meeting Bank Policy on Involuntary Resettlement is to properly identify the lands and productive assets of the displaced persons. The Panel notes, however, that since such data had not been collected, a questionable "shortcut" was used by dividing the average of land taken by the average household land holdings. On this basis, the Project planners concluded that the Project would take away less than 4 percent of the total land holdings cultivated by the affected households. There were no adequate data available to verify this claim.

On the other hand, in Project documents presented to the Board, it was stated that *"owners lose less than 6 percent of their total land holdings."* This figure was meaningless in terms of identifying the actual risks of any individual household. The same defective methodology was used to report estimated household income losses, resulting from the loss of land, as being less than 2 percent of total household income.

The Panel finds that Management did not ensure that Project planners used reliable and specific data on individuals or households affected by the ROW, rather than assumptions and averages. As a result of these flaws in methodology, the Project documents presented to the Board at the time of Project approval included incorrect and incomplete information on livelihood and impoverishment risks. This was inconsistent with OMS 2.20 and OP 4.12.

Loss of Livelihood, Under-Compensation, and Harm

(i) Land-for-Land Option

The Bank's Involuntary Resettlement Policy gives preference to land-based resettlement strategies for displaced persons whose livelihoods are land-based. *The Panel finds that a land-based resettlement option, described as an alternative within the RAP and encouraged as a preference in OP 4.12, was not effectively offered to the displaced persons as a viable option for livelihood restoration. This is inconsistent with the provisions and objectives of OP 4.12.*

In addition, the critical decision to support the policy option of cash compensation as the method for addressing livelihood risks of a land-based economy was based on an assertion that there existed an active market for land in the affected area – a factor recognized under Bank Policy in determining whether cash compensation is the appropriate method. This assertion, however, was not supported by WAPCo's Environmental and Social Impact Analysis or Estate Surveys. The Panel observed that an active market was apparent in residential plots, but that does not mean that there is an active market in traditional agricultural lands through which the pipeline crosses.

(ii) Livelihood Restoration and Method to Establish Cash Compensation

The RAP states that landowners *"are expected to be able to restore income streams without further assistance once they have received compensation for their land and assets."* Accordingly, *the RAP transferred the burden for the restoration of livelihood onto the displaced persons, once they had obtained cash compensation, without providing additional assistance as called for in Bank Policy. The Panel finds that issues of livelihood restoration, resettlement assistance beyond compensation, and benefit-sharing were not properly negotiated with the displaced persons. This does not comply with Bank Policy on Involuntary Resettlement.*

The RAP further states that compensation negotiations would be based on *"the willing buyer/willing seller arrangement."* The negotiation would take place using an adjusted Nigerian oil-sector (OPTS) rate as a basis for negotiation for land, crops, commercial activities and market squares. WAPCo and the Bank agreed to pay for lost assets and full income restoration through cash compensation. Full compensation, mentioned throughout sections of the RAP, is defined as the OPTS rates for land and crops, adjusted by a 10-fold multiplier and an adjustment for inflation.

The Panel reviewed evidence indicating that those sub-contracted to establish a fair price for the land in question thought that they had to bargain rates down to the lowest level possible. The Panel also heard many concerns about the use of the OPTS rates as a starting point for determining compensation. The OPTS-based approach, combined with multiple references to the national legal framework and evidence of efforts to acquire land at low cost, created a strong likelihood that the affected people would receive less than they were entitled to under the Policy. *The Panel finds that Management failed to comply with the Bank's Policy on Involuntary Resettlement by accepting the use of a formula that is not based on the livelihood restoration objectives of OP 4.12.*

Moreover, the Panel discovered a major flaw in how the stated approach was applied. A Panel review of the compensation payout spreadsheets confirms that the agreed upon 10-fold multiplier in providing compensation was not applied. *As a result, the displaced people were paid one-tenth of what was planned in the RAP. This has resulted in a major failure to comply with Bank Policy on Involuntary Resettlement, and to ensure that the displaced people are at least as well-off as they were before the displacement as required by this Policy.*

Furthermore, the Panel found that *the compensation methodology did not take into account income foregone for the loss of perennial crops.* The loss of perennial crops is different from annual crops, a factor ignored in the estate agent valuations. *In addition, contrary to Bank Policy, the Panel finds that transaction costs were borne by the displaced persons, which further reduced their chances of being as well off after the transaction as before.* In this regard, the Panel also heard reports that a portion of compensation payments made available to the displaced people may have been appropriated, within the community, by local groups of young men, further reducing compensation to the displaced people.

(iii) Remedial Steps

Following the Request for Inspection, the Bank recognized that serious shortcomings existed with respect to the resettlement planning. Among the remedial actions initiated, the Project took steps to hire a legal expert and a valuation expert to assess, across the Nigerian section of the pipeline, the current values of each type of asset lost to the project.

As of the Panel's visit, valuations of income stream losses from agriculture had yet to be calculated. The valuator is collecting sample land plot prices, not individual data from the project-affected persons. The planned updating of the baseline study of the directly affected families, including their progress on income restoration, has yet to be completed. The valuators terms of reference did not include determining whether the compensation rates met OP 4.12 objectives.

The Panel observes that Management and WAPCo recognized that undercompensation occurred, and are preparing for another compensation disbursal. The Panel notes and appreciates these actions.

The Panel is concerned, however, that this is being done without consultation with the displaced peoples, identifying or preparing mitigation for at-risk populations, without setting clear eligibility requirements based on local land tenure, without correction for the transaction cost error discussed above, without benefit-sharing provisions for the displaced population, and without determining whether cash compensation is or is not the appropriate instrument to be used to avoid Project induced impoverishment. In addition, the recommendation for a uniform rate for the entire ROW, adjusted into three zones based on type of land use endangers again the application of the principle of full replacement value.

Development Assistance – Sharing in Project Benefits

To avoid displacement-induced impoverishment, OP 4.12 provides, as one of its objectives, that "resettlement activities should be conceived and executed as sustainable development programs, providing sufficient investment resources to enable the persons displaced by the project to share in project benefits," including through development assistance actions.

The Panel does not question Management's view that community facilities that the Project installed were important for the well-being of the local population. However, the Panel could find no evidence that adequate development assistance, such as land preparation, credit, training or post-construction job opportunities were considered for displaced persons in addition to compensation. *The Panel finds that Management permitted an involuntary resettlement to begin without a development assistance component as required by OP 4.12 that would provide targeted investment resources to enable the persons displaced by the Project to share in Project benefits.*

Disclosure of Information and Consultation

The Bank's Involuntary Resettlement Policy, OP 4.12 states that *"displaced persons should be meaningfully consulted and should have opportunities to participate in planning and implementing resettlement programs."* Bank Policy on Environmental Assessment similarly contains provisions to ensure meaningful consultations with project affected people. The Bank Disclosure Policy requires, *inter alia*, that the Borrower make the draft RAP available before appraisal (i) at the InfoShop and (ii) in-country, at accessible locations and in a form and language that are accessible to potentially affected persons and NGOs.

(i) Findings on Disclosure of Information

The Panel notes that following a review process by Management, the draft RAP was publicly disclosed on July 7, 2004. The Panel found no evidence, however, of attempts to meaningfully present the draft RAP to the displaced persons. On November 2, 2004, Management informed the Board that community members were aware of the existence of an EA and RAP for elements of WAGP, but the Panel found that few had seen them. In Igbesa, the area with the highest concentration of displaced persons, disclosure of many engineering documents in English was evident to the Panel in July 2007, but not of the RAP. *The Panel finds that there was a failure to adequately disclose critical RAP information necessary for the displaced persons to make meaningful, informed choices about livelihood restoration. This does not comply with OP 4.12 on Involuntary Resettlement, or with the Bank's Policy on Disclosure of Information.*

As part of Management's proposed actions in response to the Request for Inspection, a Yoruba translation of the executive summary was prepared about 24 months following the last compensation payment. During its field visit in July 2007, the Panel found no evidence of distribution of this document in the key resettlement area of Igbesa. Regardless of its distribution, *the Panel finds that disseminating such information on livelihood, compensation and other resettlement entitlements years after the displaced persons have made decisions on these matters is neither meaningful nor timely. This does not comply with Bank Policies on Involuntary Resettlement and Disclosure of Information.*

(ii) Findings on Consultation

The Panel notes that the Project sponsors did, in fact, conduct various consultation activities with some of the affected communities during the period in which the RAP was being developed. The records indicated that the focus was on introducing the Project concept, health and safety concerns, and the gathering of public support for the Project. *However, the Panel found only limited evidence that efforts were made to integrate the consultation process into the preparation of the RAP, and in particular to inform the displaced persons of their entitlements under the RAP. This lack of meaningful and timely consultation prevented participation and informed negotiation of resettlement options by the displaced persons as called for in OP 4.12.*

The Panel finds that Management did not provide adequate guidance and instructions to the Project Sponsor to carry out meaningful consultation with the displaced people.

Grievance Mechanism

According to OP 4.12, the Bank requires the Sponsor to make arrangements for affordable and accessible procedures for third-party settlement of disputes arising from resettlement.

In the field the Panel was informed that few grievances have been reported. The Panel notes that without meaningful consultation, including access to the RAP and without an effective disclosure procedure, the displaced persons could not have understood grievance avenues available to them. The Panel notes that external reviews of the RAP section on complaints/grievance resolution identified concerns relating to the lack of procedural clarity with respect to use of the mechanism by affected-people. The Panel notes that recent steps have been taken to provide more information regarding the grievance system, but this has occurred after critical decisions were made in the resettlement process. *The Panel finds that Management failed to ensure that the Sponsor had in place an effective grievance process to identify and redress resettlement issues, as required by OP 4.12.*

Institutional Capacity

In line with OP 4.12, due diligence in relation to the present Project requires that Management and the government determine whether WAPCo had the capacity and financing to carry out a RAP in accord with Bank standards. BP 4.12 further requires the Task Team leader to assess, inter alia, the Borrower's commitment to and capacity for implementing the resettlement instruments.

The Panel notes that Management held a training session on safeguard issues in 2007, only after the Request for Inspection was submitted. This session might have introduced some WAPCo staff to the Policies for the first time. During Panel interviews, WAPCo staff commented, *"had we known what we were supposed to do, we would have done it."* With regard to the Borrower capacity, *the Panel finds that Management did not comply with the requirements of BP 4.12,* including those to assess the Borrower's commitment to and capacity for implementing the resettlement instrument, and mitigating significant risks, including risk of impoverishment, from inadequate implementation of the resettlement instrument. *The Panel further finds that Management did not adequately review and inform the Board of the Sponsor's past experience and limited capacity with implementing operations involving similar involuntary resettlement activities. This is inconsistent with the provisions of OP/BP 4.12 and OMS 2.20.*

Environmental Issues – Analysis of Compliance

Bank Policy OP 4.01 requires environmental assessment (EA) of projects proposed for Bank financing in order to assess the project's potential environmental risks in an integrated way and ensure informed decision-making. According to OP 4.01, the EA should take into account *"the natural environment (air, water, and land); human health and safety; social aspects (involuntary resettlement, indigenous peoples, and physical cultural resources); and transboundary and global environmental aspects."*

Categorization/Screening

Scrutiny of the Regional and Nigerian EA documents shows them to be of good standard and include the elements of Annex B of OP 4.01. *The Panel finds that the Project was correctly assigned "Category A." The Panel further finds that because the Project involves four countries, a consolidated "Regional Assessment" was appropriate.*

Independent Advisory Panel

OP 4.01 provides that for Category A projects that are highly risky or contentious, or involve serious and multidimensional concerns, the Borrower should normally engage an independent advisory panel of internationally recognized specialists.

There is, however, no evidence that the independent advisory panel of internationally recognised environmental specialists was constituted during the planning and design phases of the Project. *The Panel finds that the failure to establish the independent advisory panel during the planning and design stages of the Project, and the delay in its establishment during Project implementation, did not comply with OP 4.01.*

Analysis of Alternatives

The analysis of alternatives is handled comprehensively in the Regional Assessment: chapter 3 of this Assessment deals exclusively with project alternatives while chapter 4 deals with alternatives in project design. Fourteen project alternatives were analysed, eight main alternatives and six variations of these. *The OP 4.01 requirement that alternatives be evaluated has been met. However, the lack of a full economic evaluation of the alternative offshore pipeline route for the Nigerian section is a significant shortcoming and is not consistent with OP 4.01.*

Disclosure of EA Documents and Consultation

The EA documentation is of good quality and is written in sound technical English, but requires a high degree of education to be fully comprehended. For the existing upstream Escravos-Lagos pipeline (ELPS), an Environmental Audit (or risk assessment) in the form of an Integrity Study was undertaken. This document, however, apparently was not placed in the public domain. *The Panel finds that the apparent non-disclosure of this assessment of the ELPS, and the fact that its findings and recommendations are not taken up in the Environmental Assessment Reports, is not in accord with paragraphs 15 and 16 of OP 4.01.* This is of particular significance in the present situation, in light of the many expressions of concern in the Request and by members of local communities about issues relating to the ELPS.

Other EIA reports were made available to the public and to stakeholders as required by the OP 4.01. However, no documentation has been seen that would meet the OP 4.01 requirement that the Borrower provide relevant material in a timely manner *"prior to consultation and in a form and language that are understandable and accessible to the groups being consulted."* Although many meetings were held with communities and stakeholders, the adequacy with which they were prepared to engage meaningfully in the consultation process must be questioned. The Panel observed that affected communities appear not to have been provided with understandable relevant materials on the overall environmental documentation prior to these meetings. *The requirement of OP 4.01 that disclosure be in a form and language that is understandable to the groups being consulted has not been met.*

Assessment of "Upstream" Impacts and the Escravos-Lagos Pipeline System

The Requesters contend that the existing ELPS, to which WAGP connects, is unsafe and that an EIA should be prepared for this existing pipeline. Management states that the project EA covers both the upstream gas source and pipeline safety issues, and that the Project Sponsor prepared an Integrity Study to review the safety of the existing structure. Management further states, however, that the ELPS is not part of the Project's area of influence, and that an EA of the ELPS *"was neither necessary nor appropriate."*

(i) Project Area of Influence

The Panel first considered the scope of the Project's "area of influence" to determine if it includes the upstream Escravos-Lagos pipeline and gas supply system. The determination of area of influence is a basic element of OP 4.01 to ensure that the potential impacts of a project are properly and adequately assessed and addressed.

The Panel notes that although the WAGP is not responsible for the operation of the existing Escravos-to-Lagos pipeline, both the extraction of gas and the operation of the existing ELPS are essential for gas to flow through the WAGP. They are therefore integral to the WAGP initiative. In this regard, the Regional EIA and the Nigeria EIA indicate that WAGP could induce environmental and socioeconomic secondary impacts "upstream" and "downstream" of the Project. For example, upstream of the Project, industry may *"increase oil and gas development in order to supply additional natural gas through WAGP"* by drilling new wells in new fields. It also forecasts that the ELPS has the capacity to deliver gas to WAGP in the next 5–10 years without need for modification, but adds that if gas demand rises above a certain level there might be a need to upgrade the lines feeding into the ELPS, augment surface facilities, and so forth.

The Panel finds that the gas supply system upstream of WAGP is within the Project's area of influence under OP 4.01. The Regional EIA properly flags that the Project might have potential impacts in these upstream areas, but an analysis of their nature and scope has not yet been carried out. The findings of the Integrity Study of the ELPS are noted below.

The Panel also observes that in various Project documents, Bank Management itself makes a linkage between WAGP and the upstream reduction of gas flaring, in this case to highlight a projected benefit of the Project. The Panel considers that this reinforces the view that *the Project and associated facilities and supply areas should be viewed as an inter-connected system for purposes of environmental assessment, considering both potential benefits and adverse impacts. The Panel is concerned that Project documentation was not consistent in defining the Project's area of influence.*

(ii) Integrity Study and Safety of the ELPS

The Management Response states that the ELPS Integrity Study constitutes an environmental audit, which is an appropriate instrument for ELPS given that it is an "existing facility." The Panel notes that OP 4.01 specifies that a range of EA instruments may be used to satisfy the Bank's EA requirement, depending on the project, and that "environmental audits" are an instrument to determine environmental areas of concern at an existing facility. *The Panel finds support for the view that this is an appropriate EA instrument for the ELPS.*

Under OP 4.01, such an EA instrument could be included as part of the overall EA documentation. This would have helped to address a key concern in the Request. *As noted above, however, the Integrity Study of the ELPS was not made part of the EA documentation and apparently has not been publicly disclosed. This has impeded the ability of Requesters and members of the public from being informed of, and providing comments on, this important and controversial subject.*

With respect to the safety issues, the Integrity Study found several shortcomings that led to internal inspection of most sections of the ELPS. This led to a thorough review and inspection as a result of which defects have been detected and corrected, and safety and operational systems modernised. *The Panel's expert concluded that the linkage of the WAGP and ELPS has had the overall effect of improving the safety of the Escravos-Lagos pipeline.*

Emergency Response and Contingency Plans

During the Panel's visit to Nigeria, it was told that before the pipeline carries gas, a series of community meetings would be held to inform persons living near the pipeline of appropriate emergency responses in the case of gas release, fire or explosion. The Panel found that sound and wide ranging emergency response plans have been compiled but, as of July 2007, had not been communicated to communities along the Nigerian portion of WAGP's ROW. *Such emergency response plans will not be effective unless communities are properly informed, both orally and via clear, understandable written text in a form that can be retained and readily accessed, before the pipeline becomes operational.*

Fisheries and Livelihoods of Fishing Communities in Nigeria

The Panel encountered numerous fishermen from the Ajido community who believed that their nets were fouled by a greenish-brown substance during the 2006 fishing season and that this occurred at about the time the pipeline was being drilled under the bed of Badagry Creek. A particle size analysis was undertaken by a researcher the Requesters had hired. This analysis allowed the mass of substance adhering to the nets to be determined but not its biological or chemical composition. Unfortunately no sample of the offending substance was subjected to microscopic or microbiological examination or to chemical analysis to determine its identity and none was preserved to allow for later testing. *Precisely what the offending substance was remains unknown.*

According to the Panel expert, the speculation that Bentonite used as a drilling lubricant for the Horizontal Directional Drilling (HDD) operation caused the net fouling is without scientific foundation. In order for Bentonite to have adhesive qualities a small amount of water must be mixed with a large amount of Bentonite. However, a relatively small amount of Bentonite was used during the drilling operation and according to the operators there was no leakage of it.

There is no record as to whether Management briefed WAPCo as to how the incident was to be investigated and whether or not samples of the offending substance were to be analysed. A lesson to be learned is that project-related incidents need to be comprehensively and rigorously investigated and documented.

Fisheries and Livelihoods of Fishing Communities in Ghana

The Requesters in Ghana claim that an assessment of the Project's impacts on fisheries should be carried out and affected people along the coastline should be consulted. The Panel observed that the first and second season Environmental Baseline Surveys contain considerable detail on fish and fisheries along the route of the pipeline. Both onshore and marine fisheries are considered, and the fisheries components of the two environmental baseline studies are thorough. *The Panel notes that during the Inspection Panel's July 2007 visit to Ghana neither artisanal fishermen nor fisheries regulators expressed concern about potential negative effects of the WAGP on their future livelihoods.*

Project Contribution to Gas Flaring Reduction

In response to the Request, the Panel reviewed Project documents and other data to understand what might be the effect of the Project on the serious problem of gas flaring in Nigeria, and to determine whether this effect had been fairly described in line with Bank Policy – in particular to the public and locally affected communities. *The Panel wishes to note that during its investigation visit, members of communities from the Delta region came to meet with the Panel to describe the serious impacts they endure from the flaring, and ask for all that can be done to reduce and eliminate this problem near their villages.*

This Investigation Report describes apparent inconsistencies in Management documents with respect to the expected contribution of flaring reduction. *The Panel notes the importance of ensuring a transparent monitoring of the impact of the Project on gas flaring. The Panel trusts that Management will specifically address this issue in its Response to this Report.*

The Panel expert also observed that the WAGP may improve air quality due to decreased emissions, but flare reduction due to the Project may largely take place away from villages. The Panel notes that the Project may have given rise to the impression among affected people that the Project would reduce flaring in their areas. *The Panel observes that although a few statements in Management documents were pointing out that the Project impact on overall flaring reduction would not be substantial, the documents included a lot of text on gas flaring that was imprecise and suggestive of much larger benefit.* This raises a systemic issue as discussed in the concluding section of this summary.

Project Implementation and Supervision

OP 13.05 on Supervision states that project supervision covers monitoring, reporting, and other actions to ascertain whether the Borrower is carrying out the project with due diligence, to identify problems and recommend to the Borrower ways to resolve them, to recommend changes, as needed, as the project evolves or circumstances change, and to identify key risks and recommend strategies and actions.

Mission Duration, Frequency and Expertise

The Panel notes that there were long gaps between supervision missions prior to the Request. Furthermore, safeguard staff mainly concerned themselves with Project preparation and were far less involved in the construction phase of the Project. *The Panel finds that Management did not ensure adequate supervision during the construction phase. This did not comply with Bank Policy on Supervision.*

The issues of involuntary resettlement required particular attention in supervision. Though Management identified several problems regarding the compensation process, it was slow to address them. *The Panel finds that Management's lack of diligent supervision created a responsibility vacuum during the RAP implementation. This did not comply with the Bank Policy on Supervision, and led to problems in the resettlement process.*

Systemic Issues

The Panel notes that this investigation revealed some systemic issues that have affected the Bank's overall compliance with its Operational Policies and Procedures in the context of this Project. Some of these issues are noted below.

(i) Supervision of Public-Private Partnership Projects

The Panel notes the Bank's efforts to broaden its portfolio through support of public-private partnerships of the kind funded under this Project. However, as the Report shows, private partners are often chosen for their strong technical competence in a particular field, but may not be well equipped to address the range of Bank Policy requirements absent effective guidance, engagement and project supervision.

In the present case, *the Panel is concerned that Management put too much faith in the Project Sponsor's ability to handle complex social issues* in spite of the troubled history of some of the participating companies' involvement in the Nigerian oil and gas sector.

(ii) Acting on Early Warning Signs – Resources for Supervision

The Panel also observes that a number of warning signs that appeared in the design phases of the Project were not properly interpreted and dealt with. For instance, *Management did not adequately follow up on the warnings relating to the RAP process that were raised and discussed in the monitoring reports.* One important reason is an apparent lack of available supervision resources in terms of funds and safeguards expertise. *Providing sufficient resources and using them for mitigating emerging problems would have been particularly important in a complex Project such as WAGP.*

(iii) Complex Regional Projects

The Panel notes that an on-going regional or in-country presence of Bank Management was initially not considered necessary. However, *the Panel observed serious difficulties in policy oversight "from a distance."* Field presence becomes even more important in large regional projects such as the WAGP. The Panel observes that the regional character of the Project and the absence of a corresponding administrative structure may have contributed to a lack of clarity regarding lines of communication and authority among country staff, regional staff and headquarters. The Panel observes that Management has recently augmented its field presence in Abuja and Accra and that a new approach to regional projects has been developed for the Africa region.

(iv) Raising Expectations About Secondary Benefits

The Panel notes a final systemic issue related to the expected benefits of the Project in reducing gas flaring, as described in various Project documents. Where statements are made to make a project politically attractive, for example by repeated references to secondary benefits, levels of expectation are raised among stakeholders who are mainly interested in these secondary benefits. And, as is brought home by this Request, *when stakeholders do not see their justified expectations fulfilled, they believe that they have been wronged. This also creates a reputational risk for the Bank.*

Questions and Discussion

1. Bank-funded or Bank-assisted projects normally take place in developing countries. Are the policies and procedures with which these countries must comply a form of unwarranted lending conditionality, or are they a useful means to ensure that the Bank itself is not complicit in violating human rights and environmental standards? The Bank can halt or cancel loan disbursements when its policies and conditions are not followed. *See* Int'l Bank for Reconstruction and Development, General Conditions for Loans, sec. 7.02 (July 1, 2005, as amended through Sept. 1, 2007); Int'l Development Association, General Conditions for Credits and Grants, sec. 6.02 (July 1, 2005, as amended through Oct. 1, 2006); *see also* Operational Directive Section 13.40(2), Suspension Unrelated to Payment. In such instances, other lenders may step in that lack either environmental or human rights policies.

2. Who did what wrong in the case of the West Africa pipeline? Note that, in addition to the Bank and the governments involved, private-sector companies participated.

3. Is the Inspection Panel likely to lead to better environmental protection? If you are an officer of the Bank and one of your projects becomes the subject of an Inspection Panel complaint, how might this affect your professional future?

4. Note that the Panel does not propose remedial measures and does not have the power to issue an injunction, to stop a project, or to award financial compensation for harm suffered. The executive directors can take action, however. On August 6, 2008, the Bank's Board of Executive Directors considered the Inspection Panel report on the West Africa pipeline and approved an action plan to respond to the criticisms and violations found. The approved plan includes measures to improve management of resettlement and compensation, to create an effective grievance mechanism, to enhance disclosure of information, and to strengthen field-based supervision.

5. For further reading, see Enrique Carrasco & Alison Guernsey, *The World Bank's Inspection Panel: Promoting True Accountability Through Arbitration*, 41 Cornell Int'l L.J. 577 (2008); World Bank Inspection Panel, Accountability at the World Bank: The Inspection Panel 10 Years On (2003); Dana Clark, *The World Bank and Human Rights: The Need for Greater Accountability*, 15 Harv. Hum. Rts. J. 205 (2002).

V. The Aarhus Convention and Complaints Procedure

The promotion of procedural rights in environmental instruments produced a landmark agreement on June 25, 1998, when thirty-five states and the European Community signed the Convention on Access to Information, Public Participation, and Access to Justice in Environmental Matters. The Convention was sponsored by the U.N. Economic Commission for Europe (UNECE), a regional commission of the United Nations. It has fifty-five members, including all of Europe, as well as the United States, Canada, and states of the former Soviet Union. States having consultative status with the UNECE may also participate and any member of the U.N. may accede with the consent of the parties. The Convention was the first environmental treaty to incorporate and strengthen the language of Stockholm Principle 1, as shown herein.

The Aarhus text mirrors many human rights texts. The Convention's rights-based approach to environmental protection induced the drafters to create compliance procedures and to include public participation at the international level. Primary review of implementation by states parties is conferred on the Meeting of the Parties (MOP), at which nongovernmental organizations "qualified in the fields to which this Convention relates" may participate as observers if they have made a request and not more than one-third of the parties present at the meeting raise objections (art. 10). The Convention (art. 15) also directed the MOP to create a "non-confrontational, non-judicial and consultative" optional arrangement for compliance review, which "shall allow for appropriate public involvement and may include the option of considering communications from members of the public on matters related to this Convention." This tentative language marked the first time a compliance procedure was added to an international environmental agreement, and it led to the innovative complaints procedure of the Aarhus Convention, illustrated by the following case concerning Albania.

**Convention on Access to Information, Public Participation in Decision Making,
and Access to Justice in Environmental Matters, Aarhus, Denmark (June 25, 1998),
U.N. Doc. ECE/CEP/43 (1988), *reprinted in* 38 I.L.M. 515 (1999)**

The Parties to this Convention,

Recalling principle 1 of the Stockholm Declaration on the Human Environment,
Recalling also principle 10 of the Rio Declaration on Environment and Development,

. . .

Affirming the need to protect, preserve and improve the state of the environment and to ensure sustainable and environmentally sound development,

Recognizing that adequate protection of the environment is essential to human well-being and the enjoyment of basic human rights, including the right to life itself,

Recognizing also that every person has the right to live in an environment adequate to his or her health and well-being, and the duty, both individually and in association with others, to protect and improve the environment for the benefit of present and future generations,

Considering that, to be able to assert this right and observe this duty, citizens must have access to information, be entitled to participate in decision-making and have access to justice in environmental matters, and acknowledging in this regard that citizens may need assistance in order to exercise their rights,

Recognizing that, in the field of the environment, improved access to information and public participation in decision-making enhance the quality and the implementation of decisions, contribute to public awareness of environmental issues, give the public the opportunity to express its concerns and enable public authorities to take due account of such concerns,

. . .

Have agreed as follows:

Article 1

OBJECTIVE

In order to contribute to the protection of the right of every person of present and future generations to live in an environment adequate to his or her health and well-being, each Party shall guarantee the rights of access to information, public participation in decision-making, and access to justice in environmental matters in accordance with the provisions of this Convention.

Article 2

DEFINITIONS

For the purposes of this Convention,

. . .

3. "Environmental information" means any information in written, visual, aural, electronic or any other material form on:

(a) The state of elements of the environment, such as air and atmosphere, water, soil, land, landscape and natural sites, biological diversity and its components, including genetically modified organisms, and the interaction among these elements;

(b) Factors, such as substances, energy, noise and radiation, and activities or measures, including administrative measures, environmental agreements, policies, legislation, plans and programmes, affecting or likely to affect the elements of the environment within the scope of subparagraph (a) above, and cost-benefit and other economic analyses and assumptions used in environmental decision-making;

(c) The state of human health and safety, conditions of human life, cultural sites and built structures, inasmuch as they are or may be affected by the state of the elements of the environment or, through these elements, by the factors, activities or measures referred to in subparagraph (b) above;

4. "The public" means one or more natural or legal persons, and, in accordance with national legislation or practice, their associations, organizations or groups;

5. "The public concerned" means the public affected or likely to be affected by, or having an interest in, the environmental decision-making; for the purposes of this definition, non-governmental organizations promoting environmental protection and meeting any requirements under national law shall be deemed to have an interest.

Article 3

GENERAL PROVISIONS

1. Each Party shall take the necessary legislative, regulatory and other measures, including measures to achieve compatibility between the provisions implementing the information, public participation and access-to-justice provisions in this Convention, as well as proper enforcement measures, to establish and maintain a clear, transparent and consistent framework to implement the provisions of this Convention. . . .

5. The provisions of this Convention shall not affect the right of a Party to maintain or introduce measures providing for broader access to information, more extensive public participation in decision-making and wider access to justice in environmental matters than required by this Convention. . . .

7. Each Party shall promote the application of the principles of this Convention in international environmental decision-making processes and within the framework of international organizations in matters relating to the environment.

8. Each Party shall ensure that persons exercising their rights in conformity with the provisions of this Convention shall not be penalized, persecuted or harassed in any way for their involvement. This provision shall not affect the powers of national courts to award reasonable costs in judicial proceedings.

9. Within the scope of the relevant provisions of this Convention, the public shall have access to information, have the possibility to participate in decision-making and have access to justice in environmental matters without discrimination as to citizenship, nationality or domicile and, in the case of a legal person, without discrimination as to where it has its registered seat or an effective centre of its activities.

Article 4

ACCESS TO ENVIRONMENTAL INFORMATION

1. Each Party shall ensure that, subject to the following paragraphs of this article, public authorities, in response to a request for environmental information, make such information available to the public, within the framework of national legislation, including, where requested and subject to subparagraph (b) below, copies of the actual documentation containing or comprising such information:
    (a) Without an interest having to be stated;
    (b) In the form requested unless:
        (i) It is reasonable for the public authority to make it available in another form, in which case reasons shall be given for making it available in that form; or
        (ii) The information is already publicly available in another form.

2. The environmental information referred to in paragraph 1 above shall be made available as soon as possible and at the latest within one month after the request has been submitted, unless the volume and the complexity of the information justify an extension of this period up to two months after the request. The applicant shall be informed of any extension and of the reasons justifying it.

3. A request for environmental information may be refused if:
    (a) The public authority to which the request is addressed does not hold the environmental information requested;
    (b) The request is manifestly unreasonable or formulated in too general a manner; or
    (c) The request concerns material in the course of completion or concerns internal communications of public authorities where such an exemption is provided for in national law or customary practice, taking into account the public interest served by disclosure.

4. A request for environmental information may be refused if the disclosure would adversely affect:
    (a) The confidentiality of the proceedings of public authorities, where such confidentiality is provided for under national law;
    (b) International relations, national defence or public security;
    (c) The course of justice, the ability of a person to receive a fair trial or the ability of a public authority to conduct an enquiry of a criminal or disciplinary nature;
    (d) The confidentiality of commercial and industrial information, where such confidentiality is protected by law in order to protect a legitimate economic interest. Within this framework, information on emissions which is relevant for the protection of the environment shall be disclosed;
    (e) Intellectual property rights;
    (f) The confidentiality of personal data and/or files relating to a natural person where that person has not consented to the disclosure of the information to the public, where such confidentiality is provided for in national law;

(g) The interests of a third party which has supplied the information requested without that party being under or capable of being put under a legal obligation to do so, and where that party does not consent to the release of the material; or

(h) The environment to which the information relates, such as the breeding sites of rare species. The aforementioned grounds for refusal shall be interpreted in a restrictive way, taking into account the public interest served by disclosure and taking into account whether the information requested relates to emissions into the environment.

5. Where a public authority does not hold the environmental information requested, this public authority shall, as promptly as possible, inform the applicant of the public authority to which it believes it is possible to apply for the information requested or transfer the request to that authority and inform the applicant accordingly.

6. Each Party shall ensure that, if information exempted from disclosure under paragraphs 3 (c) and 4 above can be separated out without prejudice to the confidentiality of the information exempted, public authorities make available the remainder of the environmental information that has been requested.

7. A refusal of a request shall be in writing if the request was in writing or the applicant so requests. A refusal shall state the reasons for the refusal and give information on access to the review procedure provided for in accordance with article 9. The refusal shall be made as soon as possible and at the latest within one month, unless the complexity of the information justifies an extension of this period up to two months after the request. The applicant shall be informed of any extension and of the reasons justifying it.

8. Each Party may allow its public authorities to make a charge for supplying information, but such charge shall not exceed a reasonable amount. Public authorities intending to make such a charge for supplying information shall make available to applicants a schedule of charges which may be levied, indicating the circumstances in which they may be levied or waived and when the supply of information is conditional on the advance payment of such a charge.

Article 5

COLLECTION AND DISSEMINATION OF ENVIRONMENTAL INFORMATION

1. Each Party shall ensure that:
   (a) Public authorities possess and update environmental information which is relevant to their functions;
   (b) Mandatory systems are established so that there is an adequate flow of information to public authorities about proposed and existing activities which may significantly affect the environment;
   (c) In the event of any imminent threat to human health or the environment, whether caused by human activities or due to natural causes, all information which could enable the public to take measures to prevent or mitigate harm arising from the threat and is held by a public authority is disseminated immediately and without delay to members of the public who may be affected.

2. Each Party shall ensure that, within the framework of national legislation, the way in which public authorities make environmental information available to the public is transparent and that environmental information is effectively accessible, inter alia, by:
   (a) Providing sufficient information to the public about the type and scope of environmental information held by the relevant public authorities, the basic terms and conditions under which such information is made available and accessible, and the process by which it can be obtained;

(b) Establishing and maintaining practical arrangements, such as:

(i) Publicly accessible lists, registers or files;

(ii) Requiring officials to support the public in seeking access to information under this Convention; and

(iii) The identification of points of contact; and

(c) Providing access to the environmental information contained in lists, registers or files as referred to in subparagraph (b) (i) above free of charge.

3. Each Party shall ensure that environmental information progressively becomes available in electronic databases which are easily accessible to the public through public telecommunications networks. Information accessible in this form should include:

(a) Reports on the state of the environment, as referred to in paragraph 4 below;

(b) Texts of legislation on or relating to the environment;

(c) As appropriate, policies, plans and programmes on or relating to the environment, and environmental agreements; and

(d) Other information, to the extent that the availability of such information in this form would facilitate the application of national law implementing this Convention, provided that such information is already available in electronic form.

4. Each Party shall, at regular intervals not exceeding three or four years, publish and disseminate a national report on the state of the environment, including information on the quality of the environment and information on pressures on the environment.

5. Each Party shall take measures within the framework of its legislation for the purpose of disseminating, inter alia:

(a) Legislation and policy documents such as documents on strategies, policies, programmes and action plans relating to the environment, and progress reports on their implementation, prepared at various levels of government;

(b) International treaties, conventions and agreements on environmental issues; and

(c) Other significant international documents on environmental issues, as appropriate.

6. Each Party shall encourage operators whose activities have a significant impact on the environment to inform the public regularly of the environmental impact of their activities and products, where appropriate within the framework of voluntary eco-labelling or eco-auditing schemes or by other means.

7. Each Party shall:

(a) Publish the facts and analyses of facts which it considers relevant and important in framing major environmental policy proposals;

(b) Publish, or otherwise make accessible, available explanatory material on its dealings with the public in matters falling within the scope of this Convention; and

(c) Provide in an appropriate form information on the performance of public functions or the provision of public services relating to the environment by government at all levels.

8. Each Party shall develop mechanisms with a view to ensuring that sufficient product information is made available to the public in a manner which enables consumers to make informed environmental choices.

9. Each Party shall take steps to establish progressively, taking into account international processes where appropriate, a coherent, nationwide system of pollution inventories or registers on a structured, computerized and publicly accessible database compiled through standardized reporting. Such a system may include inputs, releases and transfers of a specified range of substances and products, including water, energy and resource use, from a specified range of activities to environmental media and to on-site and offsite treatment and disposal sites.

10. Nothing in this article may prejudice the right of Parties to refuse to disclose certain environmental information in accordance with article 4, paragraphs 3 and 4.

Article 6

PUBLIC PARTICIPATION IN DECISIONS ON SPECIFIC ACTIVITIES

1. Each Party:

(a) Shall apply the provisions of this article with respect to decisions on whether to permit proposed activities listed in annex I;

(b) Shall, in accordance with its national law, also apply the provisions of this article to decisions on proposed activities not listed in annex I which may have a significant effect on the environment. To this end, Parties shall determine whether such a proposed activity is subject to these provisions; and

(c) May decide, on a case-by-case basis if so provided under national law, not to apply the provisions of this article to proposed activities serving national defence purposes, if that Party deems that such application would have an adverse effect on these purposes.

2. The public concerned shall be informed, either by public notice or individually as appropriate, early in an environmental decision-making procedure, and in an adequate, timely and effective manner, inter alia, of:

(a) The proposed activity and the application on which a decision will be taken;

(b) The nature of possible decisions or the draft decision;

(c) The public authority responsible for making the decision;

(d) The envisaged procedure, including, as and when this information can be provided:

(i) The commencement of the procedure;

(ii) The opportunities for the public to participate;

(iii) The time and venue of any envisaged public hearing;

(iv) An indication of the public authority from which relevant information can be obtained and where the relevant information has been deposited for examination by the public;

(v) An indication of the relevant public authority or any other official body to which comments or questions can be submitted and of the time schedule for transmittal of comments or questions; and

(vi) An indication of what environmental information relevant to the proposed activity is available; and

(e) The fact that the activity is subject to a national or transboundary environmental impact assessment procedure.

3. The public participation procedures shall include reasonable time-frames for the different phases, allowing sufficient time for informing the public in accordance with paragraph 2 above and for the public to prepare and participate effectively during the environmental decision-making.

4. Each Party shall provide for early public participation, when all options are open and effective public participation can take place.

5. Each Party should, where appropriate, encourage prospective applicants to identify the public concerned, to enter into discussions, and to provide information regarding the objectives of their application before applying for a permit.

6. Each Party shall require the competent public authorities to give the public concerned access for examination, upon request where so required under national law, free of charge and as soon as it becomes available, to all information relevant to the decision-making referred to in this article that is available at the time of the public participation procedure, without prejudice to the right of Parties to refuse to disclose certain information in accordance with article 4, paragraphs 3 and

4. The relevant information shall include at least, and without prejudice to the provisions of article 4:

(a) A description of the site and the physical and technical characteristics of the proposed activity, including an estimate of the expected residues and emissions;

(b) A description of the significant effects of the proposed activity on the environment;

(c) A description of the measures envisaged to prevent and/or reduce the effects, including emissions;

(d) A non-technical summary of the above;

(e) An outline of the main alternatives studied by the applicant; and

(f) In accordance with national legislation, the main reports and advice issued to the public authority at the time when the public concerned shall be informed in accordance with paragraph 2 above.

7. Procedures for public participation shall allow the public to submit, in writing or, as appropriate, at a public hearing or inquiry with the applicant, any comments, information, analyses or opinions that it considers relevant to the proposed activity.

8. Each Party shall ensure that in the decision due account is taken of the outcome of the public participation.

9. Each Party shall ensure that, when the decision has been taken by the public authority, the public is promptly informed of the decision in accordance with the appropriate procedures. Each Party shall make accessible to the public the text of the decision along with the reasons and considerations on which the decision is based.

10. Each Party shall ensure that, when a public authority reconsiders or updates the operating conditions for an activity referred to in paragraph 1, the provisions of paragraphs 2 to 9 of this article are applied mutatis mutandis, and where appropriate.

11. Each Party shall, within the framework of its national law, apply, to the extent feasible and appropriate, provisions of this article to decisions on whether to permit the deliberate release of genetically modified organisms into the environment.

Article 7

PUBLIC PARTICIPATION CONCERNING PLANS, PROGRAMMES AND POLICIES RELATING TO THE ENVIRONMENT

Each Party shall make appropriate practical and/or other provisions for the public to participate during the preparation of plans and programmes relating to the environment, within a transparent and fair framework, having provided the necessary information to the public. Within this framework, article 6, paragraphs 3, 4 and 8, shall be applied. The public which may participate shall be identified by the relevant public authority, taking into account the objectives of this Convention. To the extent appropriate, each Party shall endeavour to provide opportunities for public participation in the preparation of policies relating to the environment.

Article 8

PUBLIC PARTICIPATION DURING THE PREPARATION OF EXECUTIVE REGULATIONS AND/OR GENERALLY APPLICABLE LEGALLY BINDING NORMATIVE INSTRUMENTS

Each Party shall strive to promote effective public participation at an appropriate stage, and while options are still open, during the preparation by public authorities of executive regulations and other generally applicable legally binding rules that may have a significant effect on the environment. To this end, the following steps should be taken:

(a) Time-frames sufficient for effective participation should be fixed;

(b) Draft rules should be published or otherwise made publicly available; and

(c) The public should be given the opportunity to comment, directly or through representative consultative bodies.

The result of the public participation shall be taken into account as far as possible.

Article 9

ACCESS TO JUSTICE

1. Each Party shall, within the framework of its national legislation, ensure that any person who considers that his or her request for information under article 4 has been ignored, wrongfully refused, whether in part or in full, inadequately answered, or otherwise not dealt with in accordance with the provisions of that article, has access to a review procedure before a court of law or another independent and impartial body established by law.

In the circumstances where a Party provides for such a review by a court of law, it shall ensure that such a person also has access to an expeditious procedure established by law that is free of charge or inexpensive for reconsideration by a public authority or review by an independent and impartial body other than a court of law.

Final decisions under this paragraph 1 shall be binding on the public authority holding the information. Reasons shall be stated in writing, at least where access to information is refused under this paragraph.

2. Each Party shall, within the framework of its national legislation, ensure that members of the public concerned

(a) Having a sufficient interest or, alternatively,

(b) Maintaining impairment of a right, where the administrative procedural law of a Party requires this as a precondition, have access to a review procedure before a court of law and/or another independent and impartial body established by law, to challenge the substantive and procedural legality of any decision, act or omission subject to the provisions of article 6 and, where so provided for under national law and without prejudice to paragraph 3 below, of other relevant provisions of this Convention.

What constitutes a sufficient interest and impairment of a right shall be determined in accordance with the requirements of national law and consistently with the objective of giving the public concerned wide access to justice within the scope of this Convention. To this end, the interest of any non-governmental organization meeting the requirements referred to in article 2, paragraph 5, shall be deemed sufficient for the purpose of subparagraph (a) above. Such organizations shall also be deemed to have rights capable of being impaired for the purpose of subparagraph (b) above. The provisions of this paragraph 2 shall not exclude the possibility of a preliminary review procedure before an administrative authority and shall not affect the requirement of exhaustion of administrative review procedures prior to recourse to judicial review procedures, where such a requirement exists under national law.

3. In addition and without prejudice to the review procedures referred to in paragraphs 1 and 2 above, each Party shall ensure that, where they meet the criteria, if any, laid down in its national law, members of the public have access to administrative or judicial procedures to challenge acts

and omissions by private persons and public authorities which contravene provisions of its national law relating to the environment.

4. In addition and without prejudice to paragraph 1 above, the procedures referred to in paragraphs 1, 2 and 3 above shall provide adequate and effective remedies, including injunctive relief as appropriate, and be fair, equitable, timely and not prohibitively expensive. Decisions under this article shall be given or recorded in writing. Decisions of courts, and whenever possible of other bodies, shall be publicly accessible.

5. In order to further the effectiveness of the provisions of this article, each Party shall ensure that information is provided to the public on access to administrative and judicial review procedures and shall consider the establishment of appropriate assistance mechanisms to remove or reduce financial and other barriers to access to justice.

Article 10

MEETING OF THE PARTIES

. . .

2. At their meetings [held at least once every two years], the Parties shall keep under continuous review the implementation of this Convention on the basis of regular reporting by the Parties, and, with this purpose in mind, shall:

(a) Review the policies for and legal and methodological approaches to access to information, public participation in decision-making and access to justice in environmental matters, with a view to further improving them;

. . .

(d) Establish any subsidiary bodies as they deem necessary;

(e) Prepare, where appropriate, protocols to this Convention;

(f) Consider and adopt proposals for amendments to this Convention in accordance with the provisions of article 14;

(g) Consider and undertake any additional action that may be required for the achievement of the purposes of this Convention;

. . .

5. Any non-governmental organization, qualified in the fields to which this Convention relates, which has informed the Executive Secretary of the Economic Commission for Europe of its wish to be represented at a meeting of the Parties shall be entitled to participate as an observer unless at least one third of the Parties present in the meeting raise objections.

6. For the purposes of paragraphs 4 and 5 above, the rules of procedure referred to in paragraph 2 (h) above shall provide for practical arrangements for the admittance procedure and other relevant terms.

. . .

Article 12

SECRETARIAT

The Executive Secretary of the Economic Commission for Europe shall carry out the following secretariat functions:

(a) The convening and preparing of meetings of the Parties;

(b) The transmission to the Parties of reports and other information received in accordance with the provisions of this Convention; and

(c) Such other functions as may be determined by the Parties.

Article 13

ANNEXES

The annexes to this Convention shall constitute an integral part thereof.

. . .

Article 15

REVIEW OF COMPLIANCE

The Meeting of the Parties shall establish, on a consensus basis, optional arrangements of a non-confrontational, non-judicial and consultative nature for reviewing compliance with the provisions of this Convention. These arrangements shall allow for appropriate public involvement and may include the option of considering communications from members of the public on matters related to this Convention.

Article 16

SETTLEMENT OF DISPUTES

1. If a dispute arises between two or more Parties about the interpretation or application of this Convention, they shall seek a solution by negotiation or by any other means of dispute settlement acceptable to the parties to the dispute.

2. When signing, ratifying, accepting, approving or acceding to this Convention, or at any time thereafter, a Party may declare in writing to the Depositary that, for a dispute not resolved in accordance with paragraph 1 above, it accepts one or both of the following means of dispute settlement as compulsory in relation to any Party accepting the same obligation:
    (a) Submission of the dispute to the International Court of Justice;
    (b) Arbitration in accordance with the procedure set out in annex II.

3. If the parties to the dispute have accepted both means of dispute settlement referred to in paragraph 2 above, the dispute may be submitted only to the International Court of Justice, unless the parties agree otherwise.

. . .

ANNEX I

[The Annex contains the list of activities referred to in article 6(1)(a). It includes nearly all industrial processes, including those in the energy sector (mineral oil and gas refineries; thermal and nuclear power stations and other combustion installations; all installations handling radioactive material; production and processing of metals; mineral processing, including any production of asbestos, glass and ceramics); the chemical (organic and inorganic) industry; waste management facilities; paper mills; rail lines and airports; construction of motorways and express roads; construction of a new roads of four or more lanes, or road widening; ports and piers; water canals and groundwater abstraction; oil production; dams and other installations designed for the holding back or permanent storage of water, where a new or additional amount of water held back or stored exceeds 10 million cubic metres; pipelines for the transport of gas, oil or chemicals with a diameter of more than 800 mm and a length of more than 40 km; industrial farming (pigs, poultry); quarries and opencast mining where the surface of the site exceeds 25 hectares, or peat extraction, where the surface of the site exceeds 150 hectares; construction of overhead electrical power lines with a voltage of 220 kV or more and a length of more than 15 km; installations for the storage of petroleum, petrochemical, or chemical products, etc. The final provision opens up the coverage: "20. Any activity not covered by paragraphs 1–19 above where public participation is provided for under an environmental impact assessment procedure in accordance with national legislation."]

REPORT OF THE COMPLIANCE COMMITTEE ON ITS SIXTEENTH MEETING (Addendum),
Meeting of the Parties to the Convention on Access to Information, Public
Participation in Decision-Making and Access to Justice in Environmental Matters,
U.N. Doc. ECE/MP.PP/C.1/2007/4/Add.1 (July 31, 2007) (footnotes omitted)

FINDINGS AND RECOMMENDATIONS WITH REGARD TO COMPLIANCE BY ALBANIA
· · ·

I. BACKGROUND

A. General Issues

3. On 27 April 2005, the Albanian non-governmental organization (NGO) Alliance for the Protection of the Vlora Gulf (also translated as Civil Alliance for the Protection of the Vlora Bay) submitted a communication to the Committee alleging violation by Albania of its obligations under article 3, paragraph 2; article 6, paragraph 2; and article 7 of the Convention.

4. The communication alleged that the Party concerned had failed to notify the public properly and in a timely manner and to consult the public concerned in the decision-making on planning of an industrial park comprising, inter alia, oil and gas pipelines, installations for the storage of petroleum, three thermal power plants and a refinery near the lagoon of Narta, on a site of 560 ha inside the protected National Park. The communicant also alleged that the Party failed to make appropriate provision for public participation in accordance with article 7 of the Convention....

5. The communication was forwarded to the Party concerned on 29 June 2005, following a preliminary determination by the Committee that it was admissible. At the same time, the Committee requested the communicant to present some clarifications and additional information, in particular on any use made of domestic remedies.

6. The Party concerned responded on 25 November 2005, disputing the claim of non-compliance....

7. The Committee discussed the communication at its tenth meeting (5–7 December 2005), with the participation of a representative of the communicant (Mr. Ardian Klosi) who provided additional information. The Party concerned had also been invited to send a representative, but had declined to do so. The communicant was asked to provide additional information and to answer several questions in written form within four weeks. The Committee also asked the secretariat to seek certain additional information from the Government, which was done by letter of 16 December 2005.

8. The communicant answered the questions by letter of 7 January 2006, providing additional information and several documents in Albanian with summaries in English. In its letter, the communicant alleged that there had been no public participation in decisions concerning the proposed industrial energy park. It maintained that there had been only pro forma public participation in the TES project, because most of those who had participated were governmental employees and functionaries from one political party. The communicant also alleged that the State-owned Albanian Electrical Energy Corporation (Korporata Elektroenergjetike Shqiptare, or KESH) had only announced the public discussion on the construction of the TES and the

documents had only been made available in February 2004, after the environmental impact assessment (EIA) process had already been finished. The communicant further alleged that there had been no public information or public participation with respect to the decision-making processes concerning the proposed Albanian-Macedonia-Bulgaria Oil (AMBO) pipeline.

9. The communicant sent a further letter to the Committee on 1 February 2006 containing additional information about alleged plans of the Albanian Government to issue a final license to the Italian-Romanian company La Petrofilera, which would allow it to start operating a large coastal terminal for the storage of oil and oil by-products in the Bay of Vlora without any public participation having taken place.

10. Having received no response from the Party concerned to its request of 16 December 2005 for additional information by the time of its eleventh meeting (29–31 March 2006), the Committee sent a second request on 12 April 2006, asking for additional information and some clarifications.

11. On 12 June 2006, the Party concerned provided the Committee with the text of three decisions of the Council of Territorial Adjustment of the Republic of Albania, all dated 19 February 2003. Decision No. 8 approved the use of the territory for the development of an industrial and energy park; Decision No. 9 approved the construction site for a coastal terminal for the storage of oil and oil by-products and associated port infrastructure in Vlora; and Decision No. 20 approved the construction site of the TES in Vlora. The Party concerned also sent the Committee a chronology of the participation of the public in the decision-making process for the TES, stating that the procedures had been in accordance with national and international law.

12. As the Party concerned had not fully answered the Committee's questions, on 5 September 2006, the secretariat wrote on behalf of the Chairperson requesting it to provide additional information before the thirteenth meeting of the Committee (4–6 October 2006). In its response, sent to the secretariat on 21 October 2006, the Party concerned answered some of the outstanding questions. However, it failed to answer a number of other questions, including on public notification and participation procedures in the decision-making process for the industrial energy park; also, it failed to discuss the time frame for the appeal to the court and to provide a copy of the decision of the Albanian Parliament on funding of the TES.

. . .

15. At its fourteenth meeting (13–15 December 2006), the Committee discussed the case with representatives of both the Party concerned and the communicant, both of whom answered questions, clarified issues, and presented new information. The Party concerned provided information about current status of the TES, namely that no applications for environmental, construction or operating permits had been lodged. Concerning the industrial energy park, the only decision made was about its location. Although some questions remained unanswered, the Committee decided to move to the preparation of draft findings and recommendations.

B. Involvement of International Financial Institutions

16. At its eleventh meeting, the Committee had decided to seek information from the World Bank and the European Bank for Reconstruction and Development (EBRD), as they were two of the main financing institutions for the TES. It noted that the project was subject to their procedures, including procedures related to information and participation issues. The secretariat sent letters to both institutions on 27 July 2006 inviting them to provide any relevant information, including on whether the World Bank's Inspection Panel was or had been addressing the issue.

17. The World Bank office in Tirana responded in a letter dated 2 August 2006 stating that it was not and had never been involved in the development of the industrial park project, but that it had

consistently advised the Government of Albania that the development of any facility planned for such a park should be subject to an appropriate environmental assessment. Regarding the TES in Vlora, the World Bank, EBRD and the European Investment Bank (EIB) had agreed to finance the project and consultants funded by the United States Trade and Development Agency (USTDA) had selected the location based on a detailed siting study, taking into consideration environmental issues. According to the above letter, the siting study had been followed by preparation of a full environmental assessment, during which several scoping sessions and public consultations had been organized, and public input had been taken into account. The World Bank stated that the meetings had been well attended by representatives of governmental agencies, universities, NGOs and the general public, and had been publicized by Albanian television. According to the World Bank, "The entire process was carried out in accordance with Albanian laws and in compliance with applicable European Union and World Bank guidelines."

18. The communicant sent a letter to the Committee on 30 September 2006 commenting on the response by the World Bank. The letter stated that even if the World Bank was not directly involved in the industrial park, it was aware of the other components that were envisaged for the industrial park as well as the intention to expand the TES itself from a capacity of 100 megawatts (MW) up to a capacity of 300 MW. Despite this, public presentations of the project had only addressed the impact and emissions from a 100 MW power station, thus failing to take into account the future cumulative environmental impact of these projects.

. . .

21. In the course of commenting on the draft of these findings and recommendations in May 2007, the World Bank informed the Committee that its Inspection Panel had received a Request for Inspection on the subject of the project.

22. EBRD, in its response of 25 October 2006 to the letter from the secretariat, confirmed that it was providing financing for the construction of the TES and stated that it was not involved in the industrial park. The EBRD Board of Directors had approved the financing for the TES following its review of the project documentation, including reports on compliance with EBRD policies and procedures on public consultation. The project was subject to EIA and public consultations that had been carried out in accordance with Albanian EIA legislation and the World Bank's environmental guidelines, which were comparable to the EBRD EIA requirements.

23. In the course of commenting on the draft of these findings and recommendations in May 2007, the EBRD informed the Committee that on 19 April 2007 a formal complaint by the communicant with regard to this project was registered with the EBRD Independent Inspection mechanism and was being reviewed for eligibility.

C. Admissibility

24. The Committee at its eighth meeting (May 2005) had determined on a preliminary basis that the communication was admissible, subject to review following any comments received from both parties. At its fourteenth meeting (December 2006), the Committee confirmed that the communication was admissible.

. . .

II. SUMMARY OF THE FACTS, EVIDENCE AND ISSUES

30. The communication concerns a proposal to establish an industrial and energy park north of the port of Vlora on the Adriatic coast. The facts relating to the proposed energy park and some of its envisaged components, notably the TES, the oil storage facility and the proposed oil

and gas pipeline, are summarized in the following paragraphs, taking into account that different components relate to different provisions of the Convention.

. . .

III. CONSIDERATION AND EVALUATION BY THE COMMITTEE

56. Albania deposited its instrument of ratification of the Convention on 27 June 2001. The Convention entered into force for Albania on 25 September 2001.

57. The Convention, as a treaty ratified by Albania, is part of the Albanian legal system and is directly applicable, including by the courts. The Party concerned has stated that some aspects of the Convention have been transposed into national law.

A. Admissibility and Use of Domestic Remedies

58. . . . [T]he Committee found the communication to be admissible. Nonetheless, the Committee does have some concerns about the limited extent to which the communicant made use of domestic remedies. The communicant did not try to apply to a court or another independent or impartial body established by law, either about the alleged refusal of the information requests (as entitled under art. 9, para. 1), or about the alleged failure of the public authorities to notify the public concerned about the proposed activities in an adequate, timely and effective manner and to take into account its concerns (under the article 9, para. 2).

59. The communicant attempted to justify this at one point by asserting that Albanian legislation did not provide domestic judicial or similar remedies of the kind envisaged under article 9; at another stage, by reference to its lack of confidence in the ability of the Albanian courts to safeguard its interests in an effective way. Furthermore, it considered its efforts to raise signatures and thereby precipitate a referendum to be a form of domestic remedy, albeit not in a conventional sense.

60. Decision I/7 of the First Meeting of the Parties of the Aarhus Convention says that the Committee should "*take into account* any *available* domestic remedy" (emphasis added). As previously noted by the Committee (MP.PP/C.1/2003/2, para. 37), this is not a strict requirement to exhaust domestic remedies. The Party concerned said in November 2005 that there was no domestic judicial remedy that could be used before the decision was taken, as there was nothing that a court could consider. One year later, the Party concerned presented general information to the effect that according to the Constitution and laws of Albania, there was access to administrative review, the Ombudsman and the courts. The first statement of the Party concerned could be seen to imply that the three decisions the text of which it submitted to the Committee in June 2006 (see para. 9 above) were not subject to appeal, which was also the position of the communicant (see para. 23); by contrast, its second statement indicated that they could have been appealed. In any event, there appears to be a certain lack of clarity with regard to possibilities to appeal certain decisions.

61. The Committee regrets the failure of both the Party concerned and the communicant to provide, in a timely manner, more detailed and comprehensive information on the possibilities for seeking domestic remedies. Furthermore, it does not accept the communicant's assertion that it has tried all possible domestic remedies. Nonetheless, in the face of somewhat incomplete and contradictory information concerning the availability of remedies, also from the side of the Party concerned, the Committee cannot reject the allegations of the communicant that domestic remedies do not provide an effective and sufficient means of redress.

B. Legal Basis

62. As is clear from section I, the case concerns a number of different issues and proposed activities: the energy and industrial park, the TES, the oil storage facility, and the oil and gas pipelines, among others. Each of these issues and proposed activities has its own decision-making processes, and to a certain extent they relate to different provisions of the Convention.

63. During the discussion on the case which took place at the Committee's fourteenth meeting, the communicant indicated that the various decisions of the Albanian authorities referred to in the communication were parts of an overall construction and development plan, about the existence of which the public had not been informed. No evidence or further information to substantiate this allegation has been made available to the Committee. Consequently, the Committee has not addressed this issue in its findings and conclusions. However, it notes that where such overall plans exist, they might be subject to provisions of the Convention and that, in any event, meaningful public participation, generally speaking, implies that the public should be informed that the decisions subject to public participation form parts of an underlying overall plan where this is the case.

64. The Committee decided to concentrate primarily on the issue of public participation with regard to the two decisions made by the Council of Territorial Adjustment of the Republic of Albania on 19 February 2003, namely Decision No. 8 (approving the site of the proposed industrial and energy park) and Decision No. 20 (approving the construction site of the proposed TES). This approach is in line with the Committee's understanding, set out in its first report to the Meeting of the Parties (ECE/MP.PP/2005/13, para. 13), that Decision I/7 does not require the Committee to address all facts and/or allegations raised in a communication. This procedural decision by the Committee to focus on these issues does not prevent it from addressing other aspects of the case.

65. The decisions have in common that they are crucial for the entire decision-making in relation to these sites, constructions and activities. The Committee will first have to consider whether the relevant decisions amount to decisions on specific activities under article 6 of the Convention, or decisions on plans under article 7. In one of its earlier decisions, the Committee, pointed out that "When determining how to categorize a decision under the Convention, its label in the domestic law of a Party is not decisive. Rather, [it] is determined by the legal functions and effects of a decision. . . . " (ECE/MP.PP/C.1/2006/4/Add.2, para. 29). Also, as previously observed by the Committee (ECE/MP.PP/C.1/2006/2/Add.1, para. 28), the Convention does not establish a precise boundary between article 6-type decisions and article 7-type decisions.

66. Decision No 20 concerns activities of types that are explicitly listed in annex I of the Convention. Paragraph 1 of annex I refers to "Thermal power stations and other combustion installations with a heat input of 50 MW or more." As regards Decision No. 8, industrial and energy parks are not listed in annex I as such, even though many of the activities that might typically take place within such parks are listed. If an EIA involving public participation for such a park were required under national legislation, it would be covered by paragraph 20 of annex I.

67. Decision No. 20 simply designates the site where the specific activity will take place and a number of further decisions to issue permits of various kinds (e.g. construction, environmental and operating permits) would be needed before the activities could proceed. Nevertheless, on balance, it is more characteristic of decisions under article 6 than article 7, in that they concern the carrying out of a specific annex I activity in a particular place by or on behalf of a specific applicant.

68. Decision No. 8 on the industrial and energy park, on the other hand, has more the character of a zoning activity, i.e. a decision which determines that within a certain designated territory,

certain broad types of activity may be carried out (and other types may not).[18] This would link it more closely with article 7.

69. The proposed industrial and energy park includes several separate construction projects, each of which would require various kinds of permits. From the information received from the Party concerned and the communicant, it is not clear to what extent the industrial park itself, as distinct from its components, would require further permitting processes, which would in turn allow opportunities for public participation. This too might be a factor distinguishing Decision No. 8 from Decision Nos. 9 and 20, because it is clear that the latter decisions will be followed by further permitting decisions for the respective projects.

70. Taking into account the fact that different interpretations are possible with respect to these issues, the Committee chooses to focus on those aspects of the case where the obligations of the Party concerned are most clear-cut. In this respect, it notes that the public participation requirements for decision-making on an activity covered by article 7 are a subset of the public participation requirements for decision-making on an activity covered by article 6. Regardless of whether the decisions are considered to fall under article 6 or article 7, the requirements of paragraphs 3, 4 and 8 of article 6 apply. Since each of the decisions is required to meet the public participation requirements that are common to article 6 and article 7, the Committee has decided to examine the way in which those requirements have or have not been met.

71. The Committee is aware that at least one of the two decisions that it has chosen to focus on would need to be followed by further decisions on whether to grant environmental, construction and operating permits (and possibly other types of permits) before the activities in question could legitimately commence. However, public participation must take place at an early stage of the environmental decision-making process under the Convention. Therefore, it is important to consider whether public participation has been provided for at a sufficiently early stage of the environmental decision-making processes in these cases.

C. Substantive Issues

1. Industrial and Energy Park

72. The Party concerned has informed the Committee that there was "no complex decision taken on the development of industrial park as a whole." It has emphasized that Decision No. 8 of the Council of Territorial Adjustment of the Republic of Albania "On the Approval of the Industrial and Energy Park – Vlore," which approved the development of "The Industrial and Energy Park – Vlore," was just a location (siting) decision. However, this does not detract from its importance, both in paving the way for more specific decisions on future projects and in preventing other potentially conflicting uses of the land. Several ministries were instructed to carry out this decision. The decision came into force immediately. It is clear to the Committee that this was a decision by a public authority that a particular piece of land should be used for particular purpose, even if further decisions would be needed before any of the planned activities could go ahead.

73. No evidence of any notification of the public concerned, or indeed of any opportunities for public participation being provided during the process leading up to this decision, has been presented to the Committee by the Party concerned, despite repeated requests. The documents

---

[18] In reaching this conclusion, the Committee notes the definition of "plans" in the European Commission Guide for Implementation of Directive 2001/42 on the Assessment of the Effects of Certain Plans and Programmes on the Environment: "Plan is one which sets out how it is proposed to carry out or implement a scheme or a policy. This could include, for example, land use plans setting out how land is to be developed, or laying down rules or guidance as to the kind of development which might be appropriate or permissible in particular areas." Definition of "program" is "the plan covering a set of projects in a given area . . . comprising a number of separate construction projects. . . . "

provided by the Party concerned do not demonstrate that the competent authorities have identified the public that may participate, as requested under article 7 of the Convention, and that they have undertaken the necessary measures to involve the members of the public in the decision-making. To the contrary, the evidence provided suggests that the opponents were not properly notified about the possibilities to participate. The Committee is therefore convinced that the decision was made without effective notification of the public concerned, which ruled out any possibility for the public to prepare and participate effectively during the decision-making process.

74. Given the nature of the decision as outlined in the previous paragraph, even if public participation opportunities were to be provided subsequently with respect to decisions on specific activities within the industrial and energy park, the requirement that the public be given the opportunity to participate at an early stage when all options are open was not met in this case. Because of the lack of adequate opportunities for public participation, there was no real possibility for the outcome of public participation to be taken into account in the decision. Thus the Party concerned failed to implement the requirements set out in paragraphs 3, 4 and 8 of article 6, and consequently was in breach of article 7.

75. The recent modifications in the scope of this decision (see para. 36) may indeed influence its potential impact on the environment, but they do not as such alleviate failures to use proper public consultation provisions on the stage when the site of the park was being determined.

2. Thermal Electric Power Station

76. Contrary to the decision-making process leading up to the designation of the site of the industrial and energy park, the decision-making process relating to the proposed TES involved some elements of public participation, e.g. public notifications, public meetings, availability of EIA documentation and so on. However, as regards Decision No. 20, dated 19 February 2003, which establishes the site of the TES, the only element of public participation in this phase of the process appears to have been the public meeting that took place in Vlora on 28 or 31 October 2002. The issues of who was notified of the meeting and invited to participate in it, the content of the notification, and who actually participated, are therefore important. As mentioned above (para. 37 (a)), the Party concerned asserted that among those who participated in the meeting were "intellectuals and NGOs of Vlora." This assertion has been strongly disputed by the communicant. Unfortunately, despite repeated requests by the Committee, the Party concerned had failed to provide specific information on these points up until May 2007 (see para. 43 (a)). Indeed, even the actual date on which the meeting took place could not be clearly established (see para. 41).

77. Having received the report, minutes and the list of participants of the October 2002 meeting, the Committee, prompted by a correspondence received from the communicant, examined them in comparison with the minutes and the list of participants of the meeting 30 September 2003 (see para. 43 (c)). In this regard the Committee notes that out of 16 questions put forward by the participants of the first meeting and 18 questions raised at the second meeting, 12 are exactly the same. Of these, nine questions received practically verbatim identical replies. Introductions to the meetings and some of the general interventions made by the public officials are also identical. Furthermore, the Committee notes that the lists of participants of the two meetings differ only in the four additional public officials who attended the first meeting. The results of this comparative analysis raise serious concerns regarding the extent to which the report of the meeting can be relied upon as an accurate record of the proceedings as well as regarding the genuine nature of the questions and concerns raised, recorded and subsequently taken into account in the decision-making process.

78. The unclear circumstances surrounding the meeting in October 2002, and the failure of the Party concerned to provide anything to substantiate the claim that the meeting was duly announced and open for public participation, as well as concerns about the quality of the meeting records, lead the Committee to conclude that the Party concerned failed to comply with the requirements for public participation set out in paragraphs 3, 4 and 8 of article 6 of the Convention.

79. A question with regard to the stage of a decision-making process at which public consultations should take place was raised in the commenting on the draft of these findings and recommendations. In this regard, the Committee wishes to make clear that once a decision to permit a proposed activity in a certain location has already been taken without public involvement, providing for such involvement in the other decision-making stages that will follow can under no circumstances be considered as meeting the requirement under article 6, paragraph 4, to provide "early public participation when all options are open." This is the case even if a full environmental impact assessment is going to be carried out. Providing for public participation only at that stage would effectively reduce the public's input to only commenting on how the environmental impact of the installation could be mitigated, but precluding the public from having any input on the decision on whether the installation should be there in the first place, as that decision would have already been taken. The Committee has already expressed this view in some of its earlier findings and recommendations (see ECE/MP.PP/C.1/2005/2/Add.4, para.11 and ECE/MP.PP/C.1/2006/2/Add.1, para.29).

80. The two meetings that took place on 2 April 2003 and 3 September 2003 obviously occurred after the adoption of Decision No. 20, and therefore cannot be considered as events contributing to the involvement of the public in that decision. Thus, they do not mitigate the failure of the Party concerned to comply with the Convention in the process leading to Decision No. 20 of 19 February 2003.

81. Even so, the Committee wishes to make a short comment on these meetings as well, since they also give rise to concern. No information has been provided by the Party concerned to demonstrate that the meetings in April and September 2003 were publicly announced, so as to allow members of the public opposing the project to actively take part in the decision-making. Nor has the Party concerned been able to give any reasonable explanation as to why the rather strong local opposition to the project, indicated by the 14,000 people calling for a referendum, was not heard or represented properly at any of these meetings. This gives raise to concerns that the invitation process also at this stage was selective and insufficient. The only public notification, in the form of newspaper advertisements, that was presented to the Committee related to meetings that took place later in 2004. Thus the Committee notes that, despite some subsequent efforts to improve the means for public participation, there were several shortcomings also in the decision-making process after February 2003.

82. Furthermore, the Committee notes the information provided by the Party concerned in the context of commenting on the draft findings and recommendations that an environmental consent has been issued for the TES in February 2007. Considered together with the fact that as late as 15 December 2006 no application for a permit had been lodged (see para. 48), the issuing of the consent raises a number of serious concerns. These concerns relate to the way in which the provisions of article 6 of the Convention were applied to this decision, in particular in light of the fact that neither the environmental consent issued on 16 February 2007 nor environmental license issued on 3 March 2007 address the issue of public comments or reasons and considerations on which it is based. The Committee notes that the reasons for these concerns appear to resemble those related to decisions Nos. 8 and 20.

3. Oil Storage Terminal and Port Infrastructure

83. With regard to Decision No. 9, approving the construction site for a proposed coastal terminal for storage of oil and by-products and associated port infrastructure, the Committee did not receive information sufficient for it to evaluate the quality of the public participation process in the relevant decision-making. However, the Committee was informed that the capacity of the proposed storage terminal is below the threshold of 200,000 tons stipulated in paragraph 18 of annex I, to the Convention. Thus the requirements for public participation in article 6 do not apply to this decision unless provided for in the national law of the Party concerned, in accordance with either article 6, paragraph 1(b), of the Convention or paragraph 20 of annex I, to the Convention. The Committee is aware that an EIA procedure was in place in Albania at the time of the decision, which could potentially trigger paragraph 20 of annex I, although it has not been able to obtain sufficient information about the situation. However, given this and the fact that the issues raised with regard to Decision No. 9 appear to considerably resemble those in Decisions Nos. 8 and 20, as well as the interest in not further delaying the presentation of its findings with respect to those two decisions, the Committee decides not to further consider this Decision No. 9 at this stage.

4. Oil and Gas Pipelines

84. The Committee notes that pipelines for the transport of gas, oil or chemicals with a diameter of more than 800 mm and a length of more than 40 km are listed in paragraph 14 of annex I of the Convention, and are therefore subject to the full set of public participation requirements under article 6. The AMBO pipeline and other pipeline proposals have not been a particular focus of the Committee's attention, and the Committee has not received sufficient information from the Party concerned or the communicant to be in a position to conclude whether or not there was a failure of compliance with the Convention.

5. Requests for Information, Article 4

85. With regard to the allegations of the communicant that several requests for information were refused or ignored (para. 35), the Committee is concerned that at least some information requests to the Government may not be registered or dealt with properly. In the absence of more concrete evidence, however, including proof that the requests were received by the public authorities in question, the Committee is not in a position to find that there was a failure to comply with article 4 of the Convention.

86. The Committee takes note of the communicant's allegations concerning the failure of the authorities to respond to its requests for information made in 2007 (see para. 51). The Committee, using its discretionary power to focus on what it believes is most important in any given case, does not find it necessary to investigate this matter in any great detail. It does however note that if confirmed, such refusal to provide response to a request for information would be in breach of provisions of article 4, paragraph 1, of the Convention.

6. Clarity of the Framework, Article 3, Paragraph 1

87. The Committee is concerned about the lack of a clear, transparent and consistent framework to implement the provisions of this Convention in Albanian legislation. In particular, there is no clear procedure of early notification of the public (by public announcement or individual invitations, before a decision is made), identification of the public concerned, quality of participation, or

taking the outcome of public meetings into account. Besides the fact that the Committee had difficulties obtaining information from both parties, who did not answer all its questions in a timely and comprehensive manner, and that it still has some questions unanswered, the Committee considers that the Party concerned should take the necessary legislative, regulatory and other measures to achieve compatibility between the provisions implementing the information, public participation and access-to-justice provisions of the Convention.

D. Process of Developing Findings and Recommendations

88. As a general remark on the processing of the communication, the Committee is concerned by the fact that it has taken more than two years to prepare findings and recommendations in this case. This is at least partly attributable to the initial lack of engagement in the process of the Party concerned (as evidenced not least by the fact that it did not accept the invitation to participate the discussion at the eleventh meeting of the Committee), and to the difficulties in obtaining timely, accurate and comprehensive answers from both the Party concerned and the communicant. Indeed, right up to the time of commenting on these findings and recommendations in draft form, i.e. May–June 2007, and despite specific and sometimes repeated requests by the Committee, the Party concerned failed to provide information crucial for correct interpretation of relevant events. The Committee therefore does not exclude a possibility that there is other information relevant to the case that has as yet not been made available to it at this stage.

89. The Committee notes however that the process of compliance review is forward-looking and that its aim is to begin facilitating implementation and compliance at the national level once a need for such is established. It therefore prefers to put forward those conclusions and recommendations which it can make at this stage.

Involvement of international financial institutions

90. Noting that the ultimate responsibility for implementation of and compliance with the provisions of the Convention lies in the hands of individual Parties, the Committee:

(a) Notes with appreciation the constructive contribution of the relevant [international financial institutions, or IFIs], and in particular the World Bank and EBRD, to its process of review of compliance in connection with this communication, which was very useful in establishing many of the facts related to the process under review;

(b) Is mindful of the fact that the involvement of these institutions in the TES project has probably stimulated a gradual increase in the application of the public participation and consultation procedures to the decision-making process by the national authorities;

(c) Also notes with appreciation the interest expressed by both the World Bank and EBRD to support a structured approach to the implementation of the Convention in Albania.

IV. CONCLUSIONS

91. Having considered the above, the Committee adopts the findings and recommendations set out in the following paragraphs.

A. Main Findings with Regard to Non-Compliance

92. With respect to the proposed industrial and energy park (paras. 72–75), the Committee finds that the decision by the Council of Territorial Adjustment of the Republic of Albania to allocate territory for the Industrial and Energy Park of Vlora (Decision No. 8 of 19 February 2003) falls

within the scope of article 7 and is therefore subject to the requirements of article 6, paragraphs 3, 4 and 8. The Party concerned has failed to implement those requirements in the relevant decision-making process and thus was not in compliance with article 7.

93. With respect to the proposed thermal electric power station (paras. 76–82), the Committee finds that the decision by the Council of Territorial Adjustment on the siting of the TES near Vlora (Decision No. 20 of 19 February 2003) is subject to the requirements of article 6, paragraphs 3, 4 and 8. Although some efforts were made to provide for public participation, these largely took place after the crucial decision on siting and were subject to some qualitative deficiencies, leading the Committee to find that the Party concerned failed to comply fully with the requirements in question.

94. By failing to establish a clear, transparent and consistent framework to implement the provisions of the Convention in Albanian legislation, the Party concerned was not in compliance with article 3, paragraph 1, of the Convention (para. 87).

B. Recommendations

95. Noting that the Party concerned has agreed that the Committee take the measure referred to in paragraph 37 (b) of the annex to decision I/7, the Committee, pursuant to paragraph 36 (b) of the annex to decision I/7, has adopted the recommendations set out in the following paragraphs.

95. The Committee recommends that the Party concerned take the necessary legislative, regulatory, administrative and other measures to ensure that:

(a) A clear, transparent and consistent framework to implement the provisions of the Convention in Albanian legislation is established, including a clearer and more effective scheme of responsibility within the governmental administration;

(b) Practical and/or other provisions for the public to participate during the preparation of plans and programmes relating to the environment are in place not only during preparation of individual projects, including through development of detailed procedures and practical measures to implement article 25 of the EIA Law of Albania;

(c) The public which may participate is identified;

(d) Notification of the public is made at an early stage for projects and plans, when options are open, not when decisions are already made;

(e) Notification of the entire public which may participate, including NGOs opposed to the project, is provided, and notifications are announced by appropriate means and in an effective manner so as to ensure that the various categories of the public which may participate are reached, and records kept of such notifications;

(f) The locations where the draft EIA can be inspected by the public before public meetings are publicized at a sufficiently early stage, giving members of the public time and opportunities to present their comments;

(g) Public opinions are heard and taken into account by the public authority making the relevant decisions in order to ensure meaningful public participation;

97. Having regard to paragraph 37 (d), in conjunction with paragraph 36 (b), of the annex to decision I/7, the Committee recommends the Party concerned to take particular care to ensure early and adequate opportunities for public participation in any subsequent phases in the permitting process for the industrial and energy park and the associated projects.

98. The Committee also recommends that the measures proposed in paragraphs 95–97 be taken or elaborated, as appropriate, in consultation with relevant NGOs.

99. The Committee invites the Party concerned to draw up an action plan for implementing the above recommendations and to submit this to the Committee by 15 September 2007.

100. The Committee invites the Party concerned to provide information to the Committee by 15 January 2008 on the measures taken and the results achieved in implementation of the above recommendations.

101. The Committee requests the secretariat, and invites relevant international and regional organizations and financial institutions, to provide advice and assistance to the Party concerned as necessary in the implementation of the measures referred to in paragraphs 95–99.

102. The Committee resolves to review the matter no later than three months before the third meeting of the Parties and to decide what recommendations, if any, to make to the Meeting of the Parties, taking into account all relevant information received in the meantime.

REPORT OF THE COMPLIANCE COMMITTEE ON ITS EIGHTEENTH MEETING, UNECE/MP.PP/C.1/2007/8 (JAN. 25, 2008)

25. The Committee noted with appreciation the action plan for implementing the recommendations contained in its findings and recommendations with regard to compliance by Albania (ECE/MP.PP/C.1/2007/4/Add.1) submitted by the Government of Albania in accordance with paragraph 99 of the findings. The Committee resolved to review any progress made by the Party with respect to implementation of the recommendations, inter alia, on the basis of the report to be submitted by the Party (ECE/MP.PP/C.1/2007/4/Add.1, para.100) at the next meeting, with a view to reflecting this progress in its report to the Meeting of the Parties. In this regard, the Committee noted that it had extended the deadline for the Party to submit the action plan to 3 November 2007. It therefore decided to extend the deadline set out in paragraph 100 of the findings and recommendations to 11 February 2007 so as to allow the Party to make further progress in the implementation of the recommendations. It requested the secretariat to communicate the above to the Government of Albania.

European Environmental Human Rights and Environmental Rights: A Long Time Coming?, 21 GEO. INT'L ENVTL. L. REV. 73, 97–99 (2008) Ole W. Pedersen

In addition to the procedural rights enshrined in the Aarhus Convention, the Compliance Committee established pursuant to Article 15 represents an important and inventive approach to the supervision of international agreements.[19] As in the rest of the Convention, NGOs play an important role in the functioning of the Compliance Committee. The Compliance Committee consists of eight members who serve in a personal capacity rather than as state representatives, and they must be persons of high moral character who are recognized in areas relating to the convention. Candidates for the committee are nominated by parties to the convention as well as NGOs. Complaints may be initiated by a party to the convention, the secretariat, or members of the public, which includes NGOs. Again, the attention given to NGOs is unprecedented for a MEA and falls

---

[19] *See* U.N. Econ. & Soc. Council [ECOSOC], Econ. Comm'n for Europe, *Decision I/7 Review of Compliance*, U.N. Doc. ECE/MP.PP/2/Add.8 (April 2, 2004), *available at* http://www.unece.org/env/pp/documents/mop1/ece.mp.pp.2.add.8.e.pdf [hereinafter ECOSOC, *Review of Compliance*]. . . .

in line with the ethos of the Aarhus Convention. When deciding on a complaint, the Compliance Committee reports to the Meeting of the Parties and can make any number of recommendations: that the Meeting of the Parties provide advice and assistance regarding the implementation of the convention; that the party concerned produce a strategy with a time schedule regarding the compliance with the Aarhus Convention; that the parties issue a declaration of noncompliance; or as a final resort, that the parties suspend the rights and privileges accorded to the offending party under the convention. The Compliance Committee has (as of mid-2008) received twenty-four communications; twenty-three communications from the public and one communication submitted by a party concerning compliance of another party.

Although the Aarhus Convention has been hailed as "the most ambitious venture in the area of environmental democracy so far undertaken under the auspices of the United Nations,"[20] it has received criticism for its obvious weaknesses and shortfalls.[21] Despite the Aarhus Convention's innovative approach in the direction of state obligations towards citizens in an MEA scheme, the major results of the Aarhus Convention would be the use of procedural avenues as a way of achieving substantive outcomes, its strong focus on the empowerment of NGOs, and the possible precedential value of its innovative compliance mechanisms.

The rights in the Aarhus Convention to participation and, in particular, access to justice are not as far-reaching as a first glance might indicate. The reference in Article 9(3) to national law effectively makes the impact of the provision limited. Hopes that it would provide for an "action popularis" appears too optimistic. Nonetheless, the Aarhus Convention, although only regional in scope, represents a landmark in international environmental law for a number of reasons. The Aarhus Convention's focus on procedural rights, as an attempt to facilitate a substantive human right to a healthy environment, is a pioneering approach among MEAs. Furthermore, the geographical scope of the Aarhus Convention and its intentions of furthering environmental protection in former Soviet states have the potential to spread transparency and openness into other policy areas and thus enhance democratic decision-making in those countries. Moreover, the convention has added some weight to the emerging discipline of international administrative law. In addition, the Compliance Committee to the convention is likely to further improve notions of transparency and openness while at the same time being a novel institution in itself.

Questions and Discussion

1. Is the Aarhus Convention a weak or strong agreement? Will it help develop substantive rights and environmental protection or simply offer a limited process to hear complaints?

2. The compliance mechanism has been evaluated by some of its participants. *See, e.g.*, Veit Koester, *Review of Compliance Under the Aarhus Convention: A Rather Unique Compliance Mechanism*, 2 J. EUR. ENVTL. L. & PLANNING L. 31 (2005); Svitlana Kravchenko, *The Aarhus Convention and Innovations in Compliance with Multilateral Environmental Agreements*, 18 COLO. J. INT'L ENVTL. L. & POL'Y 1 (2007).

3. In 2005, the Compliance Committee issued a report finding that Turkmenistan was not compliant with the obligations with the Convention because of the Turkmenistan Act on Public Associations, which requires NGOs to be registered with the state before they can participate in environmental decision making and precludes noncitizens from participating at all. The Compliance Committee recommended that the legislation be amended to eliminate those provisions. The Meeting of Parties under Aarhus endorsed the findings of the Compliance Committee at its second meeting in 2005 and issued a "caution" to the

---

[20] UNECE, Introducing the Aarhus Convention, *available at* http://www.unece.org/env/pp/welcome.html (quoting Kofi A. Annan) (last visited Nov. 2, 2008).

[21] *See* Lord Justice Brooke, David Hall Memorial Lecture, *Environmental Justice: The Cost Barrier*, 18 J. ENVTL. L. 341 (2006).

government of Turkmenistan (which became effective on May 1, 2009) on account of its noncompliance. Another warning was issued by the parties in 2009, but as of May 2010, Turkmenistan has not taken remedial action. What more can be done?

VI. A Combined Process: Prior Informed Consent

Many states and international instruments address issues of environmental justice and the links between human rights and environmental protection through the technique of prior informed consent (PIC). "[Prior informed consent] is generally defined as a consultative process whereby a potentially affected community engages in an open and informed dialogue with individuals or other persons interested in pursuing activities in the area or areas occupied or traditionally used by the affected community." Dan Magraw & Lauren Baker, *Globalization, Communities and Human Rights: Community-Based Property Rights and Prior Informed Consent*, 35 Denv. J. Int'l L. & Pol'y 413, 421 (2007). There are procedural and substantive dimensions to PIC. It depends on respecting the rights of prior information and participation throughout the activity or project cycle, but it also assumes that the community can withhold its consent altogether or condition it on mitigating measures as part of respect for the property, privacy, and other rights of the potentially affected public. Prior informed consent is important in siting hazardous operations, creating protected areas, and controlling access to and benefit sharing of genetic resources. International financial institutions are increasingly requiring "broad" community support for projects that affect indigenous peoples and other local communities. *See* Revised Operational Policy and Bank Procedure on Indigenous Peoples (OP/BP 4.10) (World Bank, 2005); *see also* 1997 Philippine Indigenous Peoples Rights Act, reprinted in Chapter 8, and the U.N. Declaration on the Rights of Indigenous Peoples. In practice, application of PIC may encounter problems, as summarized by Magraw and Baker:

> Despite some initial efforts and successes at applying PIC, in practice there have also been difficulties in the application of this right. States and businesses have sometimes had difficulty determining who to ask for consent, how to do it and what constitutes consent. For example, communities may not have set processes for PIC, or may have procedures that are not clear, transparent or broadly representative. Also, different people within a community may have different or incompatible interests and expectations for a proposed project. Dialogue between communities and outside interests may also be impeded by language, cultural barriers, or distrust. Finally, those seeking access to community land or resources may believe that PIC procedures are unnecessary, or too costly or time-consuming, and thus may resist or engage only minimally in the process.
>
> These difficulties are tractable, but in order to achieve PIC effectively, they must be addressed in specific situations, including drawing from best practices and building capacities of stakeholders involved in the dialogue. It is also extremely valuable to support enabling conditions at the local, State, international and project levels. . . .

Dan Magraw & Lauren Baker, *Globalization, Communities and Human Rights: Community-Based Property Rights and Prior Informed Consent*, 35 Denv. J. Int'l L. & Pol'y 413, 423 (2007). *See also* Anne Perrault et al., *Partnerships for Success in Protected Areas: The Public Interest and Local Community Rights to Prior Informed Consent (PIC)*, 19 Geo. Int'l Envtl. L. Rev. 475–542 (2007); Robert Goodland, *Free, Prior and Informed Consent and the World Bank Group*, 4 Sustainable Development L. & Pol'y 66 (2004); Fergus MacKay, *Indigenous Peoples' Right to Free, Prior and Informed Consent and the World Bank's Extractive Industries Review*, 4 Sust. Dev. L. & Pol'y 43 (2004); L. Mehta & M. Stankovitch, Operationalization

OF FREE, PRIOR INFORMED CONSENT (2000); JUSTICE AND NATURAL RESOURCES: CONCEPTS, STRATEGIES AND APPLICATIONS (Kathryn Mutz et al. eds., 2002).

Rebuked by Internal Investigation, World Bank Plans to Do More in DRC Forest Sector, but Will It Do Better?, Jan. 16, 2008, *available at* http://www.bicusa.org/en/Article.3645.aspx
World Bank Information Center

An Inspection Panel report on the World Bank's safeguard policy violations in its Democratic Republic of Congo (DRC) forest sector operations prompts discussion on new approach and greater role for Pygmies in decision-making about the future of the world's second-largest rainforest.

Last Thursday, January 10, the World Bank's Board of Directors discussed the findings of an Inspection Panel investigation into the Bank's failure to comply with its own safeguard policies in its support for forest sector reforms in the Democratic Republic of Congo (DRC). Although the Board itself issued no formal statement following the meeting, reports indicate that the Executive Directors approved Bank Management's action plan in response to the Panel's conclusions, while noting the need for greater specificity regarding lessons learned and next steps, and expressed their support for three new projects worth $64 million currently under preparation. The Board also requested a progress report on implementation of Management's action plan in one year.

The lesson Bank staff seem to have taken away from the Panel's investigation is "do more," but the question is, will they "do better"? Press releases issued by Bank Management following last Thursday's discussion highlight broad consensus on the need for the Bank to remain engaged in the country's forest sector, but neglect to mention specifics about what the Bank learned from the oversights and failures documented in the Panel report. Such public relations efforts have been a central component in the Bank's proactive communication strategy over the past several years, stepped up in response to mounting public concern about its role in the management of DRC's forests. A closer look at recent press on the case reveals some continued massaging of the facts and suggests a need for a more inclusive dialogue about the Bank's plans going forward.

Background

The investigation by the Bank's internal watchdog garnered considerable attention over its two year span, but the public was kept in the dark about when the Panel's conclusions would be presented to the Bank's Board of Directors. The monthly Board calendar for January, posted on the Bank's external website, did not indicate the date for the discussion of the DRC case, limiting opportunities for interested parties to convey concerns or questions to their representatives on the Board in advance. According to the Inspection Panel's procedures, neither the Panel's report nor Management's response is officially disclosed to the public – or even to the complainants themselves – until after the Board discussion. Although the Panel's findings were summarized in several press accounts in October of last year, after a copy of the report was apparently leaked to journalists, neither the report nor the action plan prepared by Management was made available to the Congolese requestors before being finalized. Neither document is yet available in French.

Twelve Congolese pygmy groups filed the complaint to the Inspection Panel in 2005, concerned about exclusion of indigenous peoples from forest sector reforms supported by the Bank, and about the adverse impacts of increased commercial logging in the vast country, absent a prior participatory land use planning process. The Panel found that the Bank had failed to respect its safeguard policies, including those protecting the rights of indigenous peoples. It also found that the Bank had overestimated the revenues that the Congolese government could earn from timber exports, thereby encouraging logging of the world's second largest rainforest. In addition to supporting the livelihood of 40 million of the country's 60+ million people, DRC's forests hold between 25 and 30 billion tons of carbon dioxide (8% of global carbon stores, according to Greenpeace) – the equivalent of about four years of global emissions.

Shifting Rhetoric and Approach?

Marjory-Anne Bromhead, a manager for environment and natural resources management at the World Bank, quoted in several press articles after last week's Board meeting presented a selective account of the Panel's findings and the actions the Bank plans to take in response. According to those articles and the Bank's own press releases, the Bank is planning to scale up its involvement in the DRC forest sector, with an emphasis on government capacity-building, law enforcement and land use planning. The shift in the Bank's rhetoric and more frequent references to involvement of indigenous peoples and other local communities in forest sector reforms and management seem to suggest that years of civil society advocacy may be beginning to bear fruit. However, questions remain as to just how profound the shift in approach may be and how these planned activities will be sequenced with other logging and infrastructure developments.

The recent press articles failed to mention that, in addition to the three new forestry projects discussed at the Board, the Bank is also supporting a large road rehabilitation project that may pose new risks to forests and forest-dependent peoples. The Pro-Routes project, scheduled for Board approval in March of this year, would help re-open roads in three of the country's most heavily forested provinces. There is no doubt that the DRC needs infrastructure; the question is what kind of infrastructure, and where and when it should be developed? Care must be taken to ensure infrastructure development serves the interests of the local population and protects, rather than endangers, the environment, which is so critical both to local livelihoods and global health.

A Question of Funds or a Matter of Priorities?

Although the Bank has provided nearly $3 billion in support to the DRC since it reengaged in the country in 2001 and approved more than 20 projects since supporting the adoption of the new forest code in 2002, Bromhead insists that the Bank "[hasn't] had the resources yet to help the government implement improved forest management on the ground." One of the chief concerns raised by local and international civil society groups is precisely that over the past six years, the Bank has not directed its funding to enforcement or capacity building to implement reforms, focusing instead on crafting policy language and facilitating a legal review of logging titles designed to streamline the industrial logging sector and allow increased activity in the future.

In its recent communiqués, the Bank has also been quick to highlight the fact that the forest code includes "the principles of community-based forestry and management planning and revenue-sharing with local communities . . . and protects traditional rights of local communities (including Pygmies)." However, the legal measures necessary to put these provisions into practice still have not been adopted. Revenue-sharing does not occur in reality and the legal decrees pertaining to the protection of indigenous rights and community forest management are not finalized, having taken a back-seat to those focused on restarting the timber industry. The Bank itself has acknowledged that, "without the decrees, the Code cannot be truly implemented as it is too general."

Of Words and Action

It is encouraging to read in press accounts of the Board discussion that the Bank and the DRC government both support the maintenance of the moratorium on the allocation of new logging concessions, which is critical to the future of the forests. However, this commitment needs to be concretized in law, and actively enforced – at least until such a time as there is a participatory process for deciding upon zoning of forest lands. As it stands, presidential decrees only require the maintenance of the moratorium until the completion of the forest title review (which many government officials are hoping will conclude shortly, despite significant concerns about the integrity of the process) and the development of a schedule and plan for the allocation of new logging titles. Although the Bank claims it is not encouraging industrial logging in the DRC, its statements do not rule out the possibility that it may do so in the future, once it deems that satisfactory governance conditions and enforcement capacity are in place.

Bank statements place great weight on the role of an independent NGO in improving forest law enforcement. However, the findings of a Bank-supported scoping study on the feasibility of independent forest monitoring in the DRC suggest that such external surveillance is unlikely to be viable today, given the situation of anarchy prevailing in the forest sector, widespread failure to implement or adhere to forest laws and company violations of social responsibility commitments. The report, conducted by Global Witness, recommends "a full moratorium on all industrial-scale logging is necessary as an interim measure whilst forest land use zoning, a comprehensive legal framework, development of meaningful regulatory capacity, and measures to strengthen community rights and participation are completed."

In response to recent criticism, the Bank often repeats the statistic that 25 million hectares of illegal logging concessions were cancelled in 2002. However, it is important to note that many of these concessions have not been "cancelled" as such, but have in fact entered into a process of "legal review" and "conversion" to new-style concessions. Furthermore, some 15 million hectares have been allocated in new concessions since 2002, in breach of the moratorium declared that year. According to a Bank-supported report issued in 2007, "Forests in Post-Conflict Democratic Republic of Congo: Analysis of a Priority Agenda," "the net difference between the total [forest] area under contract in 2002 and 2005 appears to be 2.4 million hectares," and despite the moratorium, "the total number of contracts appears to have increased by 19."

Within a day of the Board discussion, the Bank posted a new "Frequently Asked Questions" document about its forest sector work on its website (see link below). Curiously, among the major threats to the DRC rainforest, the Bank does not list commercial logging. Instead, it names poverty and artisanal logging as the primary causes of rainforest destruction in the DRC, seemingly ignoring the impact of illegal industrial exploitation and the role that logging companies play in purchasing timber from small-scale suppliers. The description of the challenges in the forest sector appears to vilify the very people who live in and depend on the forests of the DRC, while failing to acknowledge the role of multinational companies and international actors in financing or facilitating their activities.

Picking Your Fights . . . and Your Friends?

Finally, the Bank's insistence on "engaging directly with Pygmies," without working through intermediaries, is a not-so-veiled reference to avoiding some of the international organizations that have been heavily involved in advocating for changes in the management of DRC's forests and the inclusion of Pygmy peoples in decision-making about the future of the forests and their own livelihoods. It is critically important that Pygmy peoples and other local communities be directly involved in decisions that affect them. At the same time, the Bank's determination to sideline international groups committed to ongoing work in the DRC should raise questions about the Bank's motivations and the impact of this exclusivity on the diversity of feedback that the Bank will receive from civil society about its forest operations going forward.

If future forest sector operations are to be more successful than past efforts in addressing government capacity to manage the sector and in ensuring participatory land use planning, then the Bank must be willing to engage openly with actors critical of its performance to date, and to be transparent about its plans. As the track record of the Bank's nearly $3 billion portfolio in the DRC would suggest, throwing money at the problems of state capacity-building and law enforcement is not the answer. Given the nature and number of forest sector operations in the DRC to date, some Executive Directors have questioned how strategic the Bank's approach has been. To ensure that the Bank doesn't just do more, but *better* in the future, decision-making about its forest sector operations must not be confined to closed-door Board meetings.

Questions and Discussion

1. What now for the Pygmies? Do they have procedural claims, substantive claims, the right of prior informed consent? What forums would be available to them to further challenge logging in the DRC?
2. Given the recognition that the Pygmies constitute indigenous peoples, are additional rights or remedies available to them? Chapter 8 takes up this issue.

7 Substantive Human Rights and the Environment

I. Introduction

During the nearly four decades since the Stockholm Conference, courts enforcing national and international human rights guarantees have concluded that a safe and healthy environment is a prerequisite to the effective enjoyment of many human rights. Tribunals have come to view environmental protection as essential for the equal enjoyment of, in particular, the rights to life, health, adequate standard of living, home life, and property.

In addition and perhaps in recognition of the linkages, lawmakers in many countries have drafted constitutional and legislative provisions setting forth the right to an environment of a specified quality, such as healthy, safe, secure, clean, or ecologically sound. *See* Barry E. Hill, Steve Wolfson, & Nicholas Targ, *Human Rights and the Environment: A Synopsis and Some Predictions*, 16 Geo. Int'l Envtl. L. Rev. 359, 381–88 (2004) (examining the Constitutions of India, Philippines, Columbia, and Chile); Carl Bruch, Wole Coker, & Chris VanArsdale, *Constitutional Environmental Law: Giving Force to Fundamental Principles in Africa*, 26 Colum. J. Envtl. L. 131 (2001); Edwin Egede, *Human Rights and the Environment: Is There a Legally Enforceable Right of a Clean and Healthy Environment for Peoples of the Niger Delta Under the Framework of the 1999 Constitution of the Federal Republic of Niger?*, 19 Sri Lanka J. Int'l L. 51 (2007); Jan Glazewski, *Environment, Human Rights, and the New South African Constitution*, 7 S. Afr. J. on Hum. Rts. 167 (1991). Two regional human rights treaties also expressly guarantee this right.

Achieving an environment of a quality that is consistent with health and well-being depends on the legal protection and exercise of procedural rights, especially the rights to information, participation in decision making, and access to justice, discussed in Chapter 6. Substantive rights, in addition, place limits on the outcome of the process, ensuring that those in power do not abuse their dominant position to discriminate or cause environmental degradation at a level that infringes on the enjoyment of guaranteed human rights.

II. The Rights to Life and Health

Nearly all major human rights instruments list the right to life first among the international guarantees. It is also among the few rights declared nonderogable in each of the human rights treaties that allow derogations, thus excluding the right to life from those rights that can be suspended in times of national emergency.

The formulation of the right to life is, in general, consistent across global and regional treaties, although the texts differ on the permissibility of capital punishment. The European Convention on Human Rights (art. 2), the American Convention on Human Rights (art. 4), and the African Charter on Human and Peoples' Rights (art. 4) all guarantee that no one shall be arbitrarily deprived of life; they also require states parties to respect the right to life and protect it by law. The International Covenant on Civil and Political Rights (ICCPR, art. 6, para. 1) similarly provides that "[e]very human being has the inherent right to life. This right shall be protected by law. No one shall be arbitrarily deprived of his life."

What constitutes an arbitrary deprivation of life? How far must law and policy go in protecting life? On the one hand, there is agreement that the right to life prohibits governments from practicing summary or extrajudicial executions. On the other hand, it seems clear that the state cannot be an insurer, responsible for all accidental loss of life. How stringent is the state obligation to protect individuals against state or private action that results in loss of life? What is the appropriate standard of care? More specifically, how extensive are the positive obligations for states to take action to prevent loss of life due to environmental degradation?

In General Comment 6 on the right to life, the Human Rights Committee indicated some of the positive measures that States Parties should take:

> 5. . . . [T]he Committee has noted that the right to life has been too often narrowly interpreted. The expression "inherent right to life" cannot properly be understood in a restrictive manner, and the protection of this right requires that States adopt positive measures. In this connection, the Committee considers that it would be desirable for States parties to take all possible measures to reduce infant mortality and to increase life expectancy, especially in adopting measures to eliminate malnutrition and epidemics.

General Comment 6, The Right to Life, adopted Apr. 30, 1982, U.N. Doc. HRI/GEN/1/Rev.7, at 128 (May 12, 2004).

The General Comment's reference to malnutrition and epidemics seems to extend article 6 into matters perhaps more appropriately considered under the right to health, including environmental conditions that might give rise to famine and epidemics. Is this appropriate? Note that the right to health is not in the ICCPR but in the International Covenant on Economic, Social, and Cultural Rights (ICESCR). At the time General Comment 6 was adopted, the ICESCR, unlike the ICCPR, lacked a complaints procedure to adjudicate alleged violations by states parties of the rights and obligations it contains. Could this have influenced the Human Rights Committee?

Human rights treaty provisions on the right to health sometimes mention environmental matters, although most of the provisions were drafted before environmental protection was a prominent issue. The ICESCR, for example, requires states parties to take steps for "the improvement of all aspects of environmental and industrial hygiene" and for "the prevention, treatment and control of epidemic, endemic, occupational, and other diseases" (art. 12). The right to work additionally guarantees the right to safe and healthy working conditions, and the protection of children and young persons includes the right to be free from work harmful to their health (arts. 7(b) and 10(3)). The 1989 Convention on the Rights of the Child, the most widely ratified human rights instrument, goes further.

Convention on the Rights of the Child
(adopted Nov. 20, 1989), G.A. Res. 44/25, U.N. Doc. A/144/149 (1989),
reprinted in 28 I.L.M. 1448 (1989), *corrected at* 29 I.L.M. 1340 (1990)

Article 24
1. States Parties recognize the right of the child to the enjoyment of the highest attainable standard of health and to facilities for the treatment of illness and rehabilitation of health.

States Parties shall strive to ensure that no child is deprived of his or her right of access to such health care services.

2.   States parties shall pursue full implementation of this right and, in particular, shall take appropriate measures:

   (a) To diminish infant and child mortality; . . .

   (b) To combat disease and malnutrition, including . . . through the provision of adequate nutritious foods and clean drinking-water, taking into consideration the dangers and risks of environmental pollution; . . .

   (c) To ensure that all segments of society, in particular parents and children, are informed, have access to education and are supported in the use of basic knowledge of child health and nutrition . . . hygiene and environmental sanitation. . . .

Among environmental agreements, human health is a constant theme, specified as one of the principal aims of environmental protection. In fact, the definition of pollution in many legal texts incorporates concern with human health. Pollution is "the introduction by man, directly or indirectly, of substance or energy into the [environment] resulting in deleterious effects of such a nature as to endanger human health [and] harm living resources."[1] Similarly, the Basel Convention on the Control of Transboundary Movements of Hazardous Wastes and Their Disposal, U.N. Doc. UNEP/WG.190/4 (Mar. 22, 1989) *reprinted in* 28 I.L.M. 657 (1989), expresses the drafters' awareness "of the risk of damage to human health" and "the growing threat to human health" posed by hazardous wastes.

A. U.N. Jurisprudence and Practice

United Nations treaty bodies and Charter organs have taken up environmental degradation when it threatens the rights to life and health. As discussed in Chapter 5, the former U.N. Human Rights Commission appointed a special rapporteur on the adverse effects of the illicit movement and dumping of toxic and dangerous products and wastes on the enjoyment of human rights, whose mandate – continued by the Human Rights Council – includes investigating complaints about illegal waste trade; the issue was framed as one concerning the rights to life and health. *See* Res. 2001/35, *Adverse Effects of the Illicit Movement and Dumping of Toxic and Dangerous Products and Wastes on the Enjoyment of Human Rights*, U.N. Doc. E/CN.4/RES/2001/35 (Apr. 20, 2001). The annual reports of the special rapporteur have documented, inter alia, damage to tissues from arsenic poisoning, risks to health from the dumping of heavy metals, illnesses from pesticide use at banana plantations, deaths from petrochemical dumping, and kidney failure in children due to contaminated pharmaceuticals. *See Report of the Special Rapporteur on the Adverse Effects of the Illicit Movement and Dumping of toxic and Dangerous Products and Wastes on the Enjoyment of Human Rights*, *Addendum*, Human Rights Council, A/HRC/12/26/Add.1 (Aug. 31, 2009). In its resolutions on this matter, the former Commission and the current Council have consistently recognized that such environmental violations "constitute a serious threat to the human rights to life, good health and a sound environment for everyone." Human Rights Council Resolution A/HRC/RES/12/18 (Oct. 12, 2009).

---

[1] Convention on Long-Range Transboundary Air Pollution (Geneva, Nov. 13, 1979), 1302 U.N.T.S. 217, art. 1. *See also* Vienna Convention for the Protection of the Ozone Layer (Vienna, Mar. 22, 1985), UNEP Doc. IG.53/5, art. 1(2); Montreal Protocol on Substances That Deplete the Ozone Layer (Montreal, Sept. 16, 1987), 26 I.L.M. 1550 1987), preamble, para. 3; Convention on the Transboundary Effects of Industrial Accidents (Helsinki, Mar. 17, 1992), 31 I.L.M. 1330, art. 1(c); U.N. Framework Convention on Climate Change (Rio de Janeiro, May 9, 1992), 31 I.L.M. 849, art. 1(1); Convention on the Protection of the Marine Environment of the Baltic Sea Area (Helsinki, Mar. 22, 1974), 13 I.L.M. 546, art. 2(1); Convention for the Prevention of Marine Pollution from Land-Based Sources (Paris, June 4, 1974), 13 I.L.M. 352, art. 1; Convention for the Protection of the Mediterranean Sea against Pollution (Barcelona, Feb. 16, 1976), 15 I.L.M. 290, art. 2(a) and all subsequent regional seas agreements; Convention on the Non-Navigational Uses of International Watercourses (New York, May 31, 1997), 36 I.L.M. 700, art. 21(2).

Treaty bodies monitoring compliance through periodic state reporting have expressed concern over environmental degradation as it affects the enjoyment of human rights. The Committee on the Elimination of All Forms of Discrimination Against Women, in its Concluding Observations on the state report of Romania, expressed its "concern about the situation of the environment, including industrial accidents, and their impact on women's health." U.N. CEDAW, *Concluding Observations on Romania*, U.N. Doc. A/55/38, at p. 89 (Aug. 19, 2000). In 2003–04, the Committee on Economic, Social, and Cultural Rights included references to the environment in its concluding observations on the second periodic report of Ecuador. The Committee voiced concerns "about the negative health and environmental impacts of natural resource extracting companies' activities" on the exercise of land and culture rights by the affected indigenous communities and the equilibrium of the ecosystem. ICESCR, *Concluding Observations on Ecuador* U.N. Doc. E/C.12/1/Add.100, para. 12 (May 14, 2004). See also the Committee's concluding observations on the initial report of Yemen (U.N. Doc. E/C.12/1/Add.92, Dec. 12, 2003). The concluding observations of the Human Rights Committee on, for example, the report of Suriname, U.N. Doc. CCPR/CO/80/SUR, para. 21, March 30, 2004, and of the Committee on the Rights of the Child regarding Jamaica (U.N. Doc. CRC/C/15/Add.210, July 4, 2003), Jordan (U.N. Doc. CRC/C/15/Add.125, at para. 50, June 13, 2000), and South Africa (U.N. Doc. CRC/C/15/Add.122, at para. 30, Feb. 23, 2000) similarly expressed the Committee's concern over environmental degradation. *See also Concluding Observations on Kyrgyzstan*, U.N. Doc. CRC/C/15/Add. 127 (Aug. 9, 2000); *Concluding Observations on Grenada*, U.N. Doc. CRC/15/Add.121 (Feb. 28, 2000); *Solomon Islands*, E/C.12/1/Add.84, at paras. 461, 474 (Nov. 18, 2002).

The individual complaints procedure of the ICCPR Optional Protocol has included claims by applicants alleging that deteriorating environmental conditions threaten their right to life. *See EHP v. Canada*, Communication No. 67/1980, 2 SELECTED DECISIONS OF THE HUMAN RIGHTS COMMITTEE 20 (1990), and *Bordes and Temeharo v. France*, Communication No. 645/1995, CCPR/C/57/D/645/1995 (July 30, 1996). The first mentioned case was declared inadmissible for failure to exhaust local remedies; in the second matter, the petitioners were found to not be victims because of the remoteness of the harm that resulted from atmospheric nuclear testing in the South Pacific. Applicants unsuccessfully attempted to shift the burden of proof to the government, contending that French authorities had been unable to show that the tests would not endanger the health or the environment of the people living in the South Pacific.

Questions and Discussion

1. The Optional Protocol limits standing to "victims" of violations – how imminent and significant does threatened harm have to be to allow standing for an applicant to claim a violation of the right to life? Can this human rights procedure ever be invoked to address the risk of harm? Consider the next case presented here.

2. When is the issue of exhaustion of remedies addressed under the Optional Protocol? If it is only following a determination that a prima facie case is made out, does that suggest that the Human Rights Committee will accept cases like *EHP* case on behalf of the lives of future generations, if local remedies are first exhausted?

3. Is it worth it? Communications submitted pursuant to the ICCPR's Optional Protocol are considered on the basis of written pleadings only, without hearings or on-site investigations. At the conclusion of the process, the Human Rights Committee issues its views, which are published. The Committee lacks the power to award damages or order remedial measures, although it may make recommendations to the state if it finds a violation. There is a

follow-up procedure to monitor compliance with the recommendations made. What is gained by taking a case to the Human Rights Committee? If you were approached by persons made ill by the illicit transfer of hazardous wastes or products, after exhausting local remedies, would you pursue a complaint under the Optional Protocol or would you report the matter to the Special Rapporteur? Can you do both? Like most human rights complaints procedures, the Optional Protocol requires the Committee to determine as a condition of admissibility that "the same matter is not being examined under another procedure of international investigation or settlement." Optional Protocol, art. 5(2)(a). This requirement is generally held not to apply to the mandates of the special rapporteurs.

Brun v. France,
Communication No. 1453/2006 Admissibility, U.N. Doc.
CCPR/C/88/D/1453/2006 (Nov. 23, 2006)

Decision on Admissibility

1.1 The author of the communication, dated 15 November 2005, is André Brun, a French citizen. The author claims to be the victim of violations by France of articles 2, paragraphs 3 (a) and (b), 6, 17 and 25 (a) of the International Covenant on Civil and Political Rights. . . .

. . .

Factual Background

2.1 On 28 April 2000, the Minister of Agriculture issued an order, after consultation with the study group on the dissemination of biomolecularly engineered products, authorizing the company Biogemma to conduct an open–field trial of genetically modified organisms (GMOs). Groups of which the author was a member had demanded that the Minister of Agriculture put a stop to Biogemma's dissemination of GMOs, under threat of destruction of the field trials.

2.2 On 26 August 2001, 200 persons, including the author, met in Cléon d'Andran (France) to demonstrate against the GMO crops. The aim of the demonstration was to destroy a plot of transgenic maize, to dump the uprooted crops in front of the Préfecture and to be received as a delegation by the Préfect. The demonstrators destroyed the plot of transgenic maize.

2.3 Following these events, Biogemma, the company responsible for the destroyed transgenic maize crops, had 10 of the persons who had participated in this action summoned before the Criminal Court of Valence for joint destruction of property belonging to other persons.

2.4 On 8 February 2002, the Criminal Court of Valence imposed fines and prison sentences on the 10 persons. The author received a three months' suspended sentence and a fine of 2,000 euros. On 14 March 2003, the Grenoble Appeal Court upheld the judgement of the court of first instance with regard to the author's conviction, but revised the sentence to a two months' suspended prison sentence and a fine of 300 euros. In a judgement of 28 April 2004, the Court of Cassation rejected the author's appeal. . . .

The Complaint

3.1 The author claims that he is the victim of a violation by France of articles 2, paragraphs 3(a) and (b), 17 and 25(a) of the Covenant. With regard to article 17, the author maintains that, in the context of the uncertainty surrounding GMO open–field trials, the domestic courts should have recognized the legitimacy of the act of destroying the transgenic maize crops and that they had acted out of necessity to protect the environment and health. He argues that the State party has not taken the necessary measures to prevent the violation of article 17 in the broader sense.

The author explains in detail the jurisprudence of the European Court of Human Rights relating to pollution cases. He considers that "the Committee should proceed by analogy, referring to the jurisprudence developed by the European Court of Human Rights, and prepare an extensive interpretation of article 17," under which the concept of private and family life encompasses the right to live in a healthy environment. If the Committee interprets the provision in this way, the author argues that the Committee will find a violation of article 17.

3.2 The author invokes the "precautionary principle" and considers that the medium- and long-term risks of GMOs on health and the environment should be taken into account. He argues that, at present, in the current state of knowledge on the use of GMOs, there has been no precise and coherent response concerning the long–term health and environmental risks. Consequently, the precautionary principle should be applied. In the absence of State intervention, the author considers that, by destroying the field of transgenic maize, the persons convicted at the national level, including the author, acted to prevent risks to public health and the environment associated with experiments which are not subject to any a priori controls.

3.3 The author considers that the planting of transgenic crops in open fields inevitably results in the contamination of conventional crops by genetically modified crops. He argues that the current minimum distances between GMO trial fields and non-GMO fields are ineffective. Thus, the destruction of the transgenic maize crops is necessary to safeguard the assets of conventional and organic farmers.

3.4 The author argues that there is no system of compensation for conventional and organic farmers should their production be found to contain GMOs which they themselves did not introduce. In addition, it is difficult to identify who is responsible, because of the complexity of the legal strategies used by companies to conduct open-field GMO trials.

3.5 The author believes that he acted out of necessity to protect his environment. He recalls that, under French law, the state of necessity arises when a person is in a situation such that, in order to protect an overriding interest, he or she has no other option but to commit an illegal act.

3.6 With regard to article 25, the author considers that in 2001, the year when the act in which he participated was committed, there had been no public debate to allow ordinary citizens to take an active part in the decisions of the public authorities concerning the environment. For this reason, acts of destruction were carried out by groups of farmers and citizens to trigger a debate with the State and the establishment of commissions to consider the question of the use of genetically modified crops and their health and environmental risks. The author claims that a majority of French people (farmers and consumers) is opposed to GMOs, but the State has a very restrictive position in that it continues to allow field trials of GMOs without prior public consultation. He therefore believes that the State party has not respected the provisions of article 25(a) and has exceeded its authority in terms of environmental policy.

3.7 Concerning article 2, paragraphs 3(a) and (b), the author considers that citizens have no legally recognized means of being heard and influencing the decisions of the public authorities concerning GMOs. He argues that the French legislative machinery does not allow him to have effective access to justice prior to the commencement of GMO field trials and that he is therefore unable to challenge the decisions which directly affect him in his private and family life.

3.8 Concerning the exhaustion of domestic remedies, the author argues that he invoked the substance of article 8 of the European Convention on Human Rights, which guarantees respect for private and family life in the same way as article 17 of the Covenant. The author therefore considers domestic remedies to have been exhausted.

. . .

Issues and Proceedings Before the Committee

6.1 Before examining a complaint submitted in a communication, the Human Rights Committee must determine, in accordance with rule 93 of its rules of procedure, whether the communication is admissible under the Optional Protocol to the Covenant.

6.2 In accordance with article 5, paragraph 2(a), of the Optional Protocol, the Committee ascertained that the same matter was not being examined under another procedure of international investigation or settlement.

6.3 Concerning the author's allegations relating to articles 6 and 17 of the Covenant, the Committee observes that no person may, in theoretical terms and by actio popularis, object to a law or practice which he holds to be at variance with the Covenant.[2] Any person claiming to be a victim of a violation of a right protected by the Covenant must demonstrate either that a State party has by an act or omission already impaired the exercise of his right or that such impairment is imminent, basing his argument for example on legislation in force or on a judicial or administrative decision or practice.[3] In the present case, the Committee notes that the author's arguments (see paragraphs 3.2 to 3.5) refer to the dangers allegedly stemming from the use of GMOs and observes that the facts of the case do not show that the position of the State party on the cultivation of transgenic plants in the open field represents, in respect of the author, an actual violation or an imminent threat of violation of his right to life and his right to privacy, family and home. After considering the arguments and material before it the Committee concludes therefore that the author cannot claim to be a "victim" of a violation of articles 6 and 17 of the Covenant within the meaning of article 1 of the Optional Protocol.

6.4 The Committee notes the author's complaint under article 25(a) of the Covenant to the effect that the State party denied him the right and the opportunity to participate in the conduct of public affairs with regard to the cultivation of transgenic plants in the open field. The Committee points out that citizens also take part in the conduct of public affairs by bringing their influence to bear through the public debate and the dialogue with their elected representatives, as well as through their capacity to form associations. In the present case the author participated in the public debate in France on the issue of the cultivation of transgenic plants in the open field; he did this through his elected representatives and through the activities of an association. In these circumstances the Committee considers that the author has failed to substantiate, for purposes of admissibility, the allegation that his right to take part in the conduct of public affairs was violated. This part of the communication is therefore inadmissible under article 2 of the Optional Protocol.[4]

6.5 The Committee points out that article 2 of the Covenant may be invoked by individuals only in relation to other provisions of the Covenant and observes that article 2, paragraph 3(a), provides that each State party shall undertake "to ensure that any person whose rights or freedoms as herein recognized are violated shall have an effective remedy." Article 2, paragraph 3(b), guarantees protection to alleged victims if their complaints are sufficiently well-founded to be arguable under the Covenant. A State party cannot reasonably be required, on the basis of article 2, paragraph 3(b), to make such procedures available in respect of complaints which are less

---

[2] *See* Bordes and Temeharo v. France, Communication No. 645/1995, decision on inadmissibility of July 22, 1996, para. 5.5.

[3] *See* E.W. et al. v. Netherlands, Communication No. 429/1990, decision on inadmissibility of Apr. 8, 1993, para. 6.4; Bordes and Temeharo v. France, Communication No. 645/1995, decision on inadmissibility of July 22, 1996, para. 5.5; Beydon and 19 Other Members of the Association "DIH Mouvement de Protestation Civique" v. France, Communication No. 1400/2005, decision on inadmissibility of Oct. 31, 2005, para. 4.3; and Aalbersberg et al. v. Netherlands, Communication No. 1440/2005, decision on inadmissibility of July 12, 2006, para. 6.3.

[4] See Beydon, *supra*, para. 4.5.

well-founded.[5] Since the author of the present complaint has failed to substantiate his complaint for purposes of admissibility under article 25, his allegation of a violation of article 2 of the Covenant is also inadmissible under article 2 of the Optional Protocol.

7. The Committee therefore decides:

(a) That the communication is inadmissible under articles 1 and 2 of the Optional Protocol; and

(b) That this decision shall be communicated to the State party and to the author.

B. *Regional Jurisprudence*

The *European Convention for the Protection of Human Rights and Fundamental Freedoms* (Nov. 4, 1950) contains a right to life (art. 2) but no right to health; the latter is instead contained in the European Social Charter (revised), E.T.S. No. 163, May 3, 1996, art. 11. Violations of the Social Charter cannot be brought to the European Court of Human Rights; instead, the Charter has a reporting system and an additional protocol providing for a system of collective complaints to the European Committee of Social Rights. E.T.S. No. 158, Nov. 9, 1995. *See* Holly Cullen, *The Collective Complaints System of the European Social Charter: Interpretive Methods of the European Committee of Social Rights*, 9 HUM. RTS. L. REV. 1 (2009).

Complaint No. 30/2005 *Marangopoulos Foundation for Human Rights (MFHR) v. Greece* was the first European Social Charter complaint to concern environmental conditions. It was lodged on April 4, 2005, and claimed violations of article 11 (right to protection of health), article 2(4) (right to reduced working hours or additional holidays for workers in dangerous or unhealthy occupations), article 3(1) (safety and health regulations at work), and article 3(2) (provision for the enforcement of safety and health regulations by measures of supervision) of the European Social Charter. The complaint alleged that in the main areas where lignite is mined, the state had not adequately prevented negative environmental impacts or developed an appropriate strategy to prevent and respond to the health hazards for the population. It also alleged that there was no legal framework guaranteeing security and safety of persons working in lignite mines. The European Committee of Social Rights concluded that there was a violation of articles 2(4), 3(2), and 11 and no violation of article 3(1) of the Charter. It transmitted its decision on the merits to the Committee of Ministers and to the Parties on December 6, 2006. The Committee of Ministers adopted its conclusions on the matter on January 16, 2008. *Resolution CM/ResChS(2008)1, Complaint No. 30/2005 by the Marangopoulos Foundation for Human Rights (MFHR) Against Greece*. On the issue of the right to health (art. 11), the Committee of Ministers stated:

> The Greek National Action Plan for 2005–2007 (NAP1) provides for greenhouse gas emissions for the whole country and all sectors combined to rise by no more than 39.2% until 2010, whereas Greece was committed, in the framework of the Kyoto Protocol, to an increase in these gases of no more than 25% in 2010. When air quality measurements reveal that emission limit values have been exceeded, the penalties imposed are limited and have little dissuasive effect. Moreover, the initiatives taken by DEH (the public power corporation operating the Greek lignite mines) to adapt plant and mining equipment to the "best available techniques" have been slow.

> The Committee finds that Greek regulations satisfy all the requirements concerning information to the public about and their participation in the procedure for approving environmental criteria for projects and activities. However, the circumstances surrounding the granting and extension

---

5 See Kazantzis v. Cyprus, Communication No. 972/2001, decision on inadmissibility of Aug. 7, 2003, para. 6.6; Faure v. Australia, Communication No. 1036/2001, views adopted on Oct. 31, 2005, para. 7.2.

of several authorisations, and the publication on the Internet of such a complex document as the NAP1 for just four days, show that in practice the Greek authorities do not apply the relevant legislation satisfactorily.

The Committee considers that the government does not provide sufficiently precise information to amount to a valid education policy aimed at persons living in lignite mining areas. Finally, very little has so far been done to organise systematic epidemiological monitoring of those concerned and no morbidity studies have been carried out.

A representative of the Greek government responded:[6]

> I have been asked to make clear the important contribution of the Kozani-Ptolemais and Megalopolis power plants in the development of the economy of Greece. The continued use of lignite is well justified by the general public interest since lignite enables the country to maintain its energy independence and offers the entire population access to electricity at a reasonable cost, thus contributing to the economic growth and industrial development of Greece at levels comparable to those of other European Union countries.
>
> Having said that, my government fully acknowledges the importance of ensuring that all adequate measures are taken in order to eliminate any eventual hazardous exposure of citizens to power generation emissions and to secure that the environmental performance of the power plants is constantly being improved.
>
> In this respect, I should like to reassure the Committee of Ministers that the Government of Greece remains fully engaged in further pursuing its efforts to ensure the effective implementation of the rights protected by the European Social Charter.
>
> Moreover, my government acknowledges the significant role that civil society, independent bodies and NGOs play in this field and is convinced of the need to work in close co-operation with them.
>
> I have also been asked to renew the expression of the high esteem in which my authorities hold the valuable work of the European Committee of Social Rights and to assure the latter that its reports and assessments are seriously taken into account. . . .
>
> On the alleged violation of Article 11:
>
>> The state has adopted and implemented a series of measures which do not fall short of European standards and which are constantly being improved. I would only mention the latest progress:
>>
>> - the operation of the highly efficient new Electrostatic Precipitators in Aghios Dimitrios Units I-II, respectively since November and May 2006 (earlier than expected);
>> - the recent issue of new additional IPPC Environmental Permits to power plants in Aghios Dimitrios and Megalopolis;
>> - the significant progress at a fast pace in the construction of the wet-flue-gas desulphurisation system in Megalopolis Unit III.
>
> As regards the global warming issue, there has been a misunderstanding over the National Allocation Plan of Greece for 2005–2007, which defines the national target for the reduction of greenhouse gas emissions. According to the latest press release of the European Commission, Greece is going to reach its Kyoto target, which is the reduction of greenhouse gas emissions by 25% from now to 2010.
>
> As regards local air pollution, all internationally accepted air quality targets and threshold values have been respected and kept under control. There is a constant improvement in ambient air quality, despite the continuous increase of power generation. This is due to the measures imposed

---

[6] [Footnotes omitted. – *Eds.*]

on the Public Power Corporation (DEH) and the adoption of the best available techniques (BAT). The ambient air quality in the Kozani-Ptolemais and Megalopolis areas is satisfactory and comparable to other areas in the country, even non-industrial ones. The air quality in the said regions is being monitored and the relevant data is publicly available, is communicated to the local Prefectures and is submitted regularly – at least annually – to the competent agencies.

As regards the epidemiological studies, despite the methodological difficulties associated with them and the caution with which their findings should be used, Greece acknowledges that their value is important. The Government has financially supported – and continues to do so – the work of independent researchers, specialised laboratories and research institutes renowned for their scientific reliability. The report wrongly states that only two epidemiological studies have been commissioned by the state. The fact is that at least one more has been recently completed in Arcadia and another one is currently [under way] in Florina. The findings of the epidemiological studies carried out have been communicated to the public.

Does this exchange suggest that the complaints procedure can have a positive impact? Why?

The following is the first case brought to the European Court of Human Rights in which environmental conditions led to loss of life; because of the importance of the issues it raised, it was referred to a Grand Chamber of the Court. For further discussion of the jurisprudence of the European Court, see MANUAL ON HUMAN RIGHTS AND THE ENVIRONMENT: PRINCIPLES EMERGING FROM THE CASE-LAW OF THE EUROPEAN COURT OF HUMAN RIGHTS (Council of Europe 2006). *See also* DANIEL GARCÍA SAN JOSÉ, ENVIRONMENTAL PROTECTION AND THE EUROPEAN CONVENTION ON HUMAN RIGHTS (2005).

Öneryildiz v. Turkey,
Application No. 48389/99, 2004-XII Eur. Ct. H.R. 657 [GC] (Nov. 30, 2004) (references omitted).

1. The case originated in an application (no. 48939/99) against the Republic of Turkey lodged with the Court under Article 34 of the Convention for the Protection of Human Rights and Fundamental Freedoms ("the Convention") by two Turkish nationals, Mr. Ahmet Nuri Çınar and Mr. Maşallah Öneryıldız, on 18 January 1999.

. . .

3. Relying on Articles 2, 8 and 13 of the Convention and on Article 1 of Protocol No. 1, the applicants submitted that the national authorities were responsible for the deaths of their close relatives and for the destruction of their property as a result of a methane explosion on 28 April 1993 at the municipal rubbish tip in Ümraniye (Istanbul). They further complained that the administrative proceedings conducted in their case had not complied with the requirements of fairness and promptness set forth in Article 6 § 1 of the Convention.

. . .

THE FACTS

I. THE CIRCUMSTANCES OF THE CASE

9. The applicant was born in 1955 and is now living in the district of Şirvan (province of Siirt), the area where he was born. At the material time he was living with twelve close relatives in the slum quarter (*gecekondu mahallesi*) of Kazım Karabekir in Ümraniye, a district of Istanbul, where he had moved after resigning from his post as a village guard in south-eastern Turkey.

A. The Ümraniye Household-Refuse Tip and the Area in which the Applicant Lived

. . .

10. Since the early 1970s a household-refuse tip had been in operation in Hekimbaşı, a slum area adjoining Kazım Karabekir. On 22 January 1960 Istanbul City Council ("the city council") had been granted use of the land, which belonged to the Forestry Commission (and therefore to the Treasury), for a term of ninety-nine years. Situated on a slope overlooking a valley, the site spread out over a surface area of approximately 35 hectares and from 1972 onwards was used as a rubbish tip by the districts of Beykoz, Üsküdar, Kadıköy and Ümraniye under the authority and responsibility of the city council and, ultimately, the ministerial authorities.

When the rubbish tip started being used, the area was uninhabited and the closest built-up area was approximately 3.5 km away. However, as the years passed, rudimentary dwellings were built without any authorisation in the area surrounding the rubbish tip, which eventually developed into the slums of Ümraniye.

According to an official map covering the areas of Hekimbaşı and Kazım Karabekir, produced by Ümraniye District Council's Technical Services Department, the applicant's house was built on the corner of Dereboyu Street and Gerze Street. That part of the settlement was adjacent to the municipal rubbish tip and since 1978 had been under the authority of a local mayor answerable to the district council.

The Ümraniye tip no longer exists. The local council had it covered with earth and installed air ducts. Furthermore, land-use plans are currently being prepared for the areas of Hekimbaşı and Kazım Karabekir. The city council has planted trees on a large area of the former site of the tip and has had sports grounds laid.

B. Steps Taken by Ümraniye District Council

1. *In 1989*

. . .

11. . . . [O]n 15 December 1989 M.C. and A.C., two inhabitants of the Hekimbaşı area, brought proceedings against the district council in the Fourth Division of the Üsküdar District Court to establish title to land. They complained of damage to their plantations and sought to have the work halted. In support of their application, M.C. and A.C. produced documents showing that they had been liable for council tax and property tax since 1977 under tax no. 168900. In 1983 the authorities had asked them to fill in a standard form for the declaration of illegal buildings so that their title to the properties and land could be regularised (see paragraph 54 below). On 21 August 1989, at their request, the city council's water and mains authority had ordered a water meter to be installed in their house. Furthermore, copies of electricity bills show that M.C. and A.C., as consumers, made regular payments for the power they had used on the basis of readings taken from a meter installed for that purpose.

12. In the District Court, the district council based its defence on the fact that the land claimed by M.C. and A.C. was situated on the waste-collection site; that residence there was contrary to health regulations; and that their application for regularisation of their title conferred no rights on them.

In a judgment delivered on 2 May 1991 (case no. 1989/1088), the District Court found for M.C. and A.C., holding that there had been interference with the exercise of their rights over the land in question.

However, the Court of Cassation set the judgment aside on 2 March 1992. On 22 October 1992 the District Court followed the Court of Cassation's judgment and dismissed M.C.'s and A.C.'s claims.

2. *In 1991*

13. On 9 April 1991 Ümraniye District Council applied to the Third Division of the Üsküdar District Court for experts to be instructed to determine whether the rubbish tip complied with the relevant regulations, in particular Regulation no. 20814 of 14 March 1991 on solid-waste control. A committee was set up for that purpose, composed of a professor of environmental engineering, a land-registry official and a forensic doctor.

According to their report, drawn up on 7 May 1991, the rubbish tip in question did not conform to the technical requirements set forth, *inter alia*, in regulations 24 to 27, 30 and 38 of the Regulations of 14 March 1991 and, accordingly, presented a number of dangers liable to give rise to a major health risk for the inhabitants of the valley, particularly those living in the slum areas: no walls or fencing separated the tip from the dwellings fifty metres away from the mountain of refuse, the tip was not equipped with collection, composting, recycling or combustion systems, and no drainage or drainage-water purification systems had been installed. The experts concluded that the Ümraniye tip "exposed humans, animals and the environment to all kinds of risks." In that connection the report, drawing attention first to the fact that some twenty contagious diseases might spread, underlined the following:

> ... In any waste-collection site gases such as methane, carbon dioxide and hydrogen sulphide form. These substances must be collected and ... burnt under supervision. However, the tip in question is not equipped with such a system. If methane is mixed with air in a particular proportion, it can explode. This installation contains no means of preventing an explosion of the methane produced as a result of the decomposition [of the waste]. May God preserve us, as the damage could be very substantial given the neighbouring dwellings....

On 27 May 1991 the report was brought to the attention of the four councils in question, and on 7 June 1991 the governor was informed of it and asked to brief the Ministry of Health and the Prime Minister's Environment Office ("the Environment Office").

14. Kadıköy and Üsküdar District Councils and the city council applied on 3, 5 and 9 June 1991 respectively to have the expert report set aside. In their notice of application the councils' lawyers simply stated that the report, which had been ordered and drawn up without their knowledge, contravened the Code of Civil Procedure. The three lawyers reserved the right to file supplementary pleadings in support of their objections once they had obtained all the necessary information and documents from their authorities.

As none of the parties filed supplementary pleadings to that end, the proceedings were discontinued.

15. However, the Environment Office, which had been advised of the report on 18 June 1991, made a recommendation (no. 09513) urging the Istanbul Governor's Office, the city council and Ümraniye District Council to remedy the problems identified in the present case:

> ... The report prepared by the committee of experts indicates that the waste-collection site in question breaches the Environment Act and the Regulations on Solid-Waste Control and consequently poses a health hazard to humans and animals. The measures provided for in regulations 24, 25, 26, 27, 30 and 38 of the Regulations on Solid-Waste Control must be implemented at the site of the tip.... I therefore ask for the necessary measures to be implemented ... and for our office to be informed of the outcome.

16. On 27 August 1992 Şinasi Öktem, the mayor of Ümraniye, applied to the First Division of the Üsküdar District Court for the implementation of temporary measures to prevent the city council and the neighbouring district councils from using the waste-collection site. He requested, in particular, that no further waste be dumped, that the tip be closed and that redress be provided in respect of the damage sustained by his district.

On 3 November 1992 Istanbul City Council's representative opposed that request. Emphasising the city council's efforts to maintain the roads leading to the rubbish tip and to combat the spread of diseases, stray dogs and the emission of odours, the representative submitted, in particular, that a plan to redevelop the site of the tip had been put out to tender. As regards the request for the temporary closure of the tip, the representative asserted that Ümraniye District Council was acting in bad faith in that, since it had been set up in 1987, it had done nothing to decontaminate the site.

Istanbul City Council had indeed issued a call for tenders for the development of new sites conforming to modern standards. The first planning contract was awarded to the American firm CVH2M Hill International Ltd, and on 21 December 1992 and 17 February 1993 new sites were designed for the European and Anatolian sides of Istanbul respectively. The project was due for completion in the course of 1993.

17. While those proceedings were still pending, Ümraniye District Council informed the mayor of Istanbul that from 15 May 1993 the dumping of waste would no longer be authorised.

C. The Accident

18. On 28 April 1993 at about 11 a.m. a methane explosion occurred at the site. Following a landslide caused by mounting pressure, the refuse erupted from the mountain of waste and engulfed some ten slum dwellings situated below it, including the one belonging to the applicant. Thirty-nine people died in the accident.

...

III. RELEVANT INSTRUMENTS OF THE COUNCIL OF EUROPE

59. With regard to the various texts adopted by the Council of Europe in the field of the environment and the industrial activities of the public authorities, mention should be made, among the work of the Parliamentary Assembly, of Resolution 587 (1975) on problems connected with the disposal of urban and industrial waste, Resolution 1087 (1996) on the consequences of the Chernobyl disaster, and Recommendation 1225 (1993) on the management, treatment, recycling and marketing of waste, and, among the work of the Committee of Ministers, Recommendation no. R (96) 12 on the distribution of powers and responsibilities between central authorities and local and regional authorities with regard to the environment.

Mention should also be made of the Convention on Civil Liability for Damage resulting from Activities Dangerous to the Environment (ETS no. 150 – Lugano, 21 June 1993) and the Convention on the Protection of the Environment through Criminal Law (ETS no. 172 – Strasbourg, 4 November 1998), which to date have been signed by nine and thirteen States respectively.

60. It can be seen from these documents that primary responsibility for the treatment of household waste rests with local authorities, which the governments are obliged to provide with financial and technical assistance. The operation by the public authorities of a site for the permanent deposit of waste is described as a "dangerous activity," and "loss of life" resulting from the deposit of waste at such a site is considered to be "damage" incurring the liability of the public authorities (see, *inter alia*, the Lugano Convention, Article 2 §§ 1 (c)–(d) and 7 (a)–(b)).

61. In that connection, the Strasbourg Convention calls on the Parties to adopt such measures "as may be necessary to establish as criminal offences" acts involving the "disposal, treatment, storage . . . of hazardous waste which causes or is likely to cause death or serious injury to any person. . . . " and provides that such offences may also be committed "with negligence" (Articles 2 to 4). Although this instrument has not yet come into force, it is very much in keeping with the current trend towards harsher penalties for damage to the environment, an issue inextricably linked with the endangering of human life (see, for example, the Council of the European

Union's Framework Decision no. 2003/80 of 27 January 2003 and the European Commission's proposal of 13 March 2001, amended on 30 September 2002, for a directive on the protection of the environment through criminal law).

Article 6 of the Strasbourg Convention also requires the adoption of such measures as may be necessary to make these offences punishable by criminal sanctions which take into account the serious nature of the offences; these must include imprisonment of the perpetrators.

62. Where such dangerous activities are concerned, public access to clear and full information is viewed as a basic human right; for example, the above-mentioned Resolution 1087 (1996) makes clear that this right must not be taken to be limited to the risks associated with the use of nuclear energy in the civil sector.

THE LAW

I. ALLEGED VIOLATION OF ARTICLE 2 OF THE CONVENTION

63. The applicant complained that the death of nine of his close relatives in the accident of 28 April 1993 and the flaws in the ensuing proceedings had constituted a violation of Article 2 of the Convention, the relevant part of which provides:

> 1. Everyone's right to life shall be protected by law. No one shall be deprived of his life intentionally save in the execution of a sentence of a court following his conviction of a crime for which this penalty is provided by law.

> . . .

64. As they had before the Chamber, the Government disputed that submission.

> . . .

3. *The Court's Assessment*

69. Taking the parties' arguments as a whole, the Court reiterates, firstly, that its approach to the interpretation of Article 2 is guided by the idea that the object and purpose of the Convention as an instrument for the protection of individual human beings requires its provisions to be interpreted and applied in such a way as to make its safeguards practical and effective (see, for example, *Yaşa v. Turkey*, judgment of 2 September 1998, *Reports* 1998-VI, p. 2429, § 64).

70. In the instant case the complaint before the Court is that the national authorities did not do all that could have been expected of them to prevent the deaths of the applicant's close relatives in the accident of 28 April 1993 at the Ümraniye municipal rubbish tip, which was operated under the authorities' control.

71. In this connection, the Court reiterates that Article 2 does not solely concern deaths resulting from the use of force by agents of the State but also, in the first sentence of its first paragraph, lays down a positive obligation on States to take appropriate steps to safeguard the lives of those within their jurisdiction (see, for example, *L.C.B. v. the United Kingdom*, cited above, p. 1403, § 36, and *Paul and Audrey Edwards v. the United Kingdom*, no. 46477/99, § 54, ECHR 2002-II).

The Court considers that this obligation must be construed as applying in the context of any activity, whether public or not, in which the right to life may be at stake, and *a fortiori* in the case of industrial activities, which by their very nature are dangerous, such as the operation of waste-collection sites ("dangerous activities" – for the relevant European standards, see paragraphs 59–60 above).

72. Where the Convention institutions have had to examine allegations of an infringement of the right to the protection of life in such areas, they have never ruled that Article 2 was not applicable. The Court would refer, for example, to cases concerning toxic emissions from a fertiliser factory

(see *Guerra and Others*, cited above, pp. 228–29, §§ 60 and 62) or nuclear tests (see *L.C.B. v. the United Kingdom*, cited above, p. 1403, § 36).

73. In this connection, contrary to what the Government appear to be suggesting, the harmfulness of the phenomena inherent in the activity in question, the contingency of the risk to which the applicant was exposed by reason of any life-endangering circumstances, the status of those involved in bringing about such circumstances, and whether the acts or omissions attributable to them were deliberate are merely factors among others that must be taken into account in the examination of the merits of a particular case, with a view to determining the responsibility the State may bear under Article 2 (ibid., pp. 1403–04, §§ 37–41).

The Court will return to these points later.

74. To sum up, it considers that the applicant's complaint (see paragraph 70 above) undoubtedly falls within the ambit of the first sentence of Article 2, which is therefore applicable in the instant case.

. . .

B. Compliance

. . .

(a) *General Principles Applicable in the Present Case*
(i) Principles relating to the prevention of infringements of the right to life as a result of dangerous activities: the substantive aspect of Article 2 of the Convention

89. The positive obligation to take all appropriate steps to safeguard life for the purposes of Article 2 (see paragraph 71 above) entails above all a primary duty on the State to put in place a legislative and administrative framework designed to provide effective deterrence against threats to the right to life (see, for example, *mutatis mutandis, Osman*, cited above, p. 3159, § 115; *Paul and Audrey Edwards*, cited above, § 54; *İlhan v. Turkey* [GC], no. 22277/93, § 91, ECHR 2000-VII; *Kılıç v. Turkey*, no. 22492/93, § 62, ECHR 2000-III; and *Mahmut Kaya v. Turkey*, no. 22535/93, § 85, ECHR 2000-III).

90. This obligation indisputably applies in the particular context of dangerous activities, where, in addition, special emphasis must be placed on regulations geared to the special features of the activity in question, particularly with regard to the level of the potential risk to human lives. They must govern the licensing, setting up, operation, security and supervision of the activity and must make it compulsory for all those concerned to take practical measures to ensure the effective protection of citizens whose lives might be endangered by the inherent risks.

Among these preventive measures, particular emphasis should be placed on the public's right to information, as established in the case-law of the Convention institutions. The Grand Chamber agrees with the Chamber (see paragraph 84 of the Chamber judgment) that this right, which has already been recognised under Article 8 (see *Guerra and Others*, cited above, p. 228, § 60), may also, in principle, be relied on for the protection of the right to life, particularly as this interpretation is supported by current developments in European standards (see paragraph 62 above).

In any event, the relevant regulations must also provide for appropriate procedures, taking into account the technical aspects of the activity in question, for identifying shortcomings in the processes concerned and any errors committed by those responsible at different levels.

(ii) Principles relating to the judicial response required in the event of alleged infringements of the right to life: the procedural aspect of Article 2 of the Convention

91. The obligations deriving from Article 2 do not end there. Where lives have been lost in circumstances potentially engaging the responsibility of the State, that provision entails a duty for the State to ensure, by all means at its disposal, an adequate response – judicial or otherwise – so that the legislative and administrative framework set up to protect the right to

life is properly implemented and any breaches of that right are repressed and punished (see, *mutatis mutandis, Osman*, cited above, p. 3159, § 115, and *Paul and Audrey Edwards*, cited above, § 54).

92. In this connection, the Court has held that if the infringement of the right to life or to physical integrity is not caused intentionally, the positive obligation to set up an "effective judicial system" does not necessarily require criminal proceedings to be brought in every case and may be satisfied if civil, administrative or even disciplinary remedies were available to the victims (see, for example, *Vo v. France* [GC], no. 53924/00, § 90, ECHR 2004-VIII; *Calvelli and Ciglio*, cited above, § 51; and *Mastromatteo*, cited above, §§ 90 and 94–95).

93. However, in areas such as that in issue in the instant case, the applicable principles are rather to be found in those the Court has already had occasion to develop in relation notably to the use of lethal force, principles which lend themselves to application in other categories of cases.

In this connection, it should be pointed out that in cases of homicide the interpretation of Article 2 as entailing an obligation to conduct an official investigation is justified not only because any allegations of such an offence normally give rise to criminal liability (see *Caraher v. the United Kingdom* (dec.), no. 24520/94, ECHR 2000-I), but also because often, in practice, the true circumstances of the death are, or may be, largely confined within the knowledge of State officials or authorities (see *McCann and Others v. the United Kingdom*, judgment of 27 September 1995, Series A no. 324, pp. 47–49, §§ 157–64, and *İlhan*, cited above, § 91).

In the Court's view, such considerations are indisputably valid in the context of dangerous activities, when lives have been lost as a result of events occurring under the responsibility of the public authorities, which are often the only entities to have sufficient relevant knowledge to identify and establish the complex phenomena that might have caused such incidents.

Where it is established that the negligence attributable to State officials or bodies on that account goes beyond an error of judgment or carelessness, in that the authorities in question, fully realising the likely consequences and disregarding the powers vested in them, failed to take measures that were necessary and sufficient to avert the risks inherent in a dangerous activity (see, *mutatis mutandis, Osman*, cited above, pp. 3159–60, § 116), the fact that those responsible for endangering life have not been charged with a criminal offence or prosecuted may amount to a violation of Article 2, irrespective of any other types of remedy which individuals may exercise on their own initiative (see paragraphs 48–50 above); this is amply evidenced by developments in the relevant European standards (see paragraph 61 above).

94. To sum up, the judicial system required by Article 2 must make provision for an independent and impartial official investigation procedure that satisfies certain minimum standards as to effectiveness and is capable of ensuring that criminal penalties are applied where lives are lost as a result of a dangerous activity if and to the extent that this is justified by the findings of the investigation (see, *mutatis mutandis, Hugh Jordan v. the United Kingdom*, no. 24746/94, §§ 105–09, 4 May 2001, and *Paul and Audrey Edwards*, cited above, §§ 69–73). In such cases, the competent authorities must act with exemplary diligence and promptness and must of their own motion initiate investigations capable of, firstly, ascertaining the circumstances in which the incident took place and any shortcomings in the operation of the regulatory system and, secondly, identifying the State officials or authorities involved in whatever capacity in the chain of events in issue.

95. That said, the requirements of Article 2 go beyond the stage of the official investigation, where this has led to the institution of proceedings in the national courts: the proceedings as a whole, including the trial stage, must satisfy the requirements of the positive obligation to protect lives through the law.

96. It should in no way be inferred from the foregoing that Article 2 may entail the right for an applicant to have third parties prosecuted or sentenced for a criminal offence (see, *mutatis mutandis, Perez v. France* [GC], no. 47287/99, § 70, ECHR 2004-I) or an absolute obligation for

all prosecutions to result in conviction, or indeed in a particular sentence (see, *mutatis mutandis, Tanlı v. Turkey*, no. 26129/95, § 111, ECHR 2001-III).

On the other hand, the national courts should not under any circumstances be prepared to allow life-endangering offences to go unpunished. This is essential for maintaining public confidence and ensuring adherence to the rule of law and for preventing any appearance of tolerance of or collusion in unlawful acts (see, *mutatis mutandis, Hugh Jordan*, cited above, §§ 108 and 136–40). The Court's task therefore consists in reviewing whether and to what extent the courts, in reaching their conclusion, may be deemed to have submitted the case to the careful scrutiny required by Article 2 of the Convention, so that the deterrent effect of the judicial system in place and the significance of the role it is required to play in preventing violations of the right to life are not undermined.

(b) *Assessment of the Facts of the Case in the Light of These Principles*
(i) Responsibility borne by the State for the deaths in the instant case, in the light of the substantive aspect of Article 2 of the Convention

97. In the instant case the Court notes at the outset that in both of the fields of activity central to the present case – the operation of household-refuse tips (see paragraphs 56–57 above) and the rehabilitation and clearance of slum areas (see paragraphs 54–55 above) – there are safety regulations in force in Turkey.

It must therefore determine whether the legal measures applicable to the situation in issue in the instant case call for criticism and whether the national authorities actually complied with the relevant regulations.

98. To that end, the Court considers that it should begin by noting a decisive factor for the assessment of the circumstances of the case, namely that there was practical information available to the effect that the inhabitants of certain slum areas of Ümraniye were faced with a threat to their physical integrity on account of the technical shortcomings of the municipal rubbish tip.

According to an expert report commissioned by the Third Division of the Üsküdar District Court and submitted on 7 May 1991, the rubbish tip began operating in the early 1970s, in breach of the relevant technical standards, and subsequently remained in use despite contravening the health and safety and technical requirements laid down, in particular, in the Regulations on Solid-Waste Control, published in the Official Gazette of 14 March 1991 (see paragraph 56 above). Listing the various risks to which the site exposed the public, the report specifically referred to the danger of an explosion due to methanogenesis, as the tip had "no means of preventing an explosion of methane occurring as a result of the decomposition" of household waste (see paragraph 13 above).

99. On that point, the Court has examined the Government's position regarding the validity of the expert report of 7 May 1991 and the weight to be attached, in their submission, to the applications by Kadıköy and Üsküdar District Councils and Istanbul City Council to have the report set aside (see paragraph 14 above). However, the Court considers that those steps are more indicative of a conflict of powers between different authorities, or indeed delaying tactics. In any event, the proceedings to have the report set aside were in fact abortive, having not been pursued by the councils' lawyers, and the report was never declared invalid. On the contrary, it was decisive for all the authorities responsible for investigating the accident of 28 April 1993 and, moreover, was subsequently confirmed by the report of 18 May 1993 by the committee of experts appointed by the Üsküdar public prosecutor (see paragraph 23 above) and by the two scientific opinions referred to in the report of 9 July 1993 by the chief inspector appointed by the Ministry of the Interior. . . .

100. The Court considers that neither the reality nor the immediacy of the danger in question is in dispute, seeing that the risk of an explosion had clearly come into being long before it was highlighted in the report of 7 May 1991 and that, as the site continued to operate in the same conditions, that risk could only have increased during the period until it materialised on 28 April 1993.

101. The Grand Chamber accordingly agrees with the Chamber (see paragraph 79 of the Chamber judgment) that it was impossible for the administrative and municipal departments responsible for supervising and managing the tip not to have known of the risks inherent in methanogenesis or of the necessary preventive measures, particularly as there were specific regulations on the matter. Furthermore, the Court likewise regards it as established that various authorities were also aware of those risks, at least by 27 May 1991, when they were notified of the report of 7 May 1991. . . .

It follows that the Turkish authorities at several levels knew or ought to have known that there was a real and immediate risk to a number of persons living near the Ümraniye municipal rubbish tip. They consequently had a positive obligation under Article 2 of the Convention to take such preventive operational measures as were necessary and sufficient to protect those individuals (see paragraphs 92–93 above), especially as they themselves had set up the site and authorised its operation, which gave rise to the risk in question.

102. However, it appears from the evidence before the Court that Istanbul City Council in particular not only failed to take the necessary urgent measures, either before or after 14 March 1991, but also – as the Chamber observed – opposed the recommendation to that effect by the Prime Minister's Environment Office (see paragraph 15 above). The Environment Office had called for the tip to be brought into line with the standards laid down in regulations 24 to 27 of the Regulations on Solid-Waste Control, the last-mentioned of which explicitly required the installation of a "vertical and horizontal drainage system" allowing the controlled release into the atmosphere of the accumulated gas (see paragraph 56 above).

103. The city council also opposed the final attempt by the mayor of Ümraniye to apply to the courts, on 27 August 1992, for the temporary closure of the waste-collection site. It based its opposition on the ground that the district council in question was not entitled to seek the closure of the site because it had hitherto made no effort to decontaminate it (see paragraph 16 above).

Besides that ground, the Government also relied on the conclusions in *Chapman*, cited above, and criticised the applicant for having knowingly chosen to break the law and live in the vicinity of the rubbish tip (see paragraphs 23, 43 and 80 above).

However, those arguments do not stand up to scrutiny for the following reasons.

104. In the instant case the Court has examined the provisions of domestic law regarding the transfer to third parties of public property, whether inside or outside the "slum rehabilitation and clearance zones." It has also studied the impact of various legislative initiatives designed to extend in practice the scope *ratione temporis* of Law no. 775 of 20 July 1966 (see paragraphs 54–55 above).

The Court concludes from these legal considerations that, in spite of the statutory prohibitions in the field of town planning, the State's consistent policy on slum areas encouraged the integration of such areas into the urban environment and hence acknowledged their existence and the way of life of the citizens who had gradually caused them to build up since 1960, whether of their own free will or simply as a result of that policy. Seeing that this policy effectively established an amnesty for breaches of town-planning regulations, including the unlawful occupation of public property, it must have created uncertainty as to the extent of the discretion enjoyed by the administrative authorities responsible for applying the measures prescribed by law, which could not therefore have been regarded as foreseeable by the public.

105. This interpretation is, moreover, borne out in the instant case by the administrative authorities' attitude towards the applicant.

The Court observes that between the unauthorised construction of the house in issue in 1988 and the accident of 28 April 1993, the applicant remained in possession of his dwelling, despite the fact that during that time his position remained subject to the rules laid down in Law no. 775, in particular section 18, by which the municipal authorities could have destroyed the dwelling at any time. Indeed, this was what the Government suggested (see paragraphs 77 and 80 above), although they were unable to show that in the instant case the relevant authorities had even envisaged taking any such measure against the applicant.

The authorities let the applicant and his close relatives live entirely undisturbed in their house, in the social and family environment they had created. Furthermore, regard being had to the concrete evidence adduced before the Court and not rebutted by the Government, there is no cause to call into question the applicant's assertion that the authorities also levied council tax on him and on the other inhabitants of the Ümraniye slums and provided them with public services, for which they were charged (see paragraphs 11 and 85 above).

106. In those circumstances, it would be hard for the Government to maintain legitimately that any negligence or lack of foresight should be attributed to the victims of the accident of 28 April 1993, or to rely on the Court's conclusions in *Chapman*, cited above, in which the British authorities were not found to have remained passive in the face of Mrs. Chapman's unlawful actions.

It remains for the Court to address the Government's other arguments relating, in general, to: the scale of the rehabilitation projects carried out by Istanbul City Council at the time in order to alleviate the problems caused by the Ümraniye waste-collection site; the amount invested, which was said to have influenced the way in which the national authorities chose to deal with the situation at the site; and, lastly, the humanitarian considerations which at the time allegedly precluded any measure entailing the immediate and wholesale destruction of the slum areas.

107. The Court acknowledges that it is not its task to substitute for the views of the local authorities its own view of the best policy to adopt in dealing with the social, economic and urban problems in this part of Istanbul. It therefore accepts the Government's argument that in this respect an impossible or disproportionate burden must not be imposed on the authorities without consideration being given, in particular, to the operational choices which they must make in terms of priorities and resources (see *Osman*, cited above, pp. 3159–60, § 116); this results from the wide margin of appreciation States enjoy, as the Court has previously held, in difficult social and technical spheres such as the one in issue in the instant case (see *Hatton and Others v. the United Kingdom* [GC], no. 36022/97, §§ 100–01, ECHR 2003-VIII).

However, even when seen from this perspective, the Court does not find the Government's arguments convincing. The preventive measures required by the positive obligation in question fall precisely within the powers conferred on the authorities and may reasonably be regarded as a suitable means of averting the risk brought to their attention. The Court considers that the timely installation of a gas-extraction system at the Ümraniye tip before the situation became fatal could have been an effective measure without diverting the State's resources to an excessive degree in breach of Article 65 of the Turkish Constitution (see paragraph 52 above) or giving rise to policy problems to the extent alleged by the Government. Such a measure would not only have complied with Turkish regulations and general practice in the area, but would also have been a much better reflection of the humanitarian considerations the Government relied on before the Court.

108. The Court will next assess the weight to be attached to the issue of respect for the public's right to information. . . . It observes in this connection that the Government [has] not shown that any measures were taken in the instant case to provide the inhabitants of the Ümraniye slums with information enabling them to assess the risks they might run as a result of the choices they had made. In any event, the Court considers that in the absence of more practical measures to avoid the risks to the lives of the inhabitants of the Ümraniye slums, even the fact of having respected the right to information would not have been sufficient to absolve the State of its responsibilities.

109. In the light of the foregoing, the Court cannot see any reason to cast doubt on the domestic investigating authorities' findings of fact (see paragraphs 23, 28 and 78 above; see also, for example, *Klaas v. Germany*, judgment of 22 September 1993, Series A no. 269, p. 17, §§ 29–30) and considers that the circumstances examined above show that in the instant case the State's responsibility was engaged under Article 2 in several respects.

Firstly, the regulatory framework proved defective in that the Ümraniye municipal waste-collection site was opened and operated despite not conforming to the relevant technical standards and there was no coherent supervisory system to encourage those responsible to take steps to ensure adequate protection of the public and coordination and cooperation between the various administrative authorities so that the risks brought to their attention did not become so serious as to endanger human lives.

That situation, exacerbated by a general policy which proved powerless in dealing with general town-planning issues and created uncertainty as to the application of statutory measures, undoubtedly played a part in the sequence of events leading to the tragic accident of 28 April 1993, which ultimately claimed the lives of inhabitants of the Ümraniye slums, because the State officials and authorities did not do everything within their power to protect them from the immediate and known risks to which they were exposed.

110. Such circumstances give rise to a violation of Article 2 of the Convention in its substantive aspect; the Government's submission relating to the favourable outcome of the administrative action brought in the instant case (see paragraph 84 above) is of no consequence here, for the reasons set out in paragraphs 151 and 152 below.

(ii) Responsibility borne by the State as regards the judicial response required on account of the deaths, in the light of the procedural aspect of Article 2 of the Convention

111. The Court considers that, contrary to what the Government suggest, it is likewise unnecessary to examine the administrative remedy used to claim compensation (see paragraphs 37, 39–40, 84 and 88 above) in assessing the judicial response required in the present case, as such a remedy, regardless of its outcome, cannot be taken into consideration for the purposes of Article 2 in its procedural aspect (see paragraphs 91–96 above).

112. . . . It remains to be determined whether the measures taken in the framework of the Turkish criminal-law system following the accident at the Ümraniye municipal rubbish tip were satisfactory in practice, regard being had to the requirements of the Convention in this respect. . . .

113. In this connection, the Court notes that immediately after the accident had occurred on 28 April 1993 at about 11 a.m. the police arrived on the scene and interviewed the victims' families. In addition, the Istanbul Governor's Office set up a crisis unit, whose members went to the site on the same day. On the following day, 29 April 1993, the Ministry of the Interior ordered, of its own motion, the opening of an administrative investigation to determine the extent to which the authorities had been responsible for the accident. On 30 April 1993 the Üsküdar public prosecutor began a criminal investigation. Lastly, the official inquiries ended on 15 July 1993, when the two mayors, Mr. Sözen and Mr. Öktem, were committed for trial in the criminal courts.

Accordingly, the investigating authorities may be regarded as having acted with exemplary promptness (see *Yaşa*, cited above, pp. 2439–40, §§ 102–04; *Mahmut Kaya*, cited above, §§ 106–07; and *Tanrıkulu v. Turkey* [GC], no. 23763/94, § 109, ECHR 1999-IV) and as having shown diligence in seeking to establish the circumstances that led both to the accident of 28 April 1993 and to the ensuing deaths.

. . .

116. In the instant case, in a judgment of 4 April 1996, the Istanbul Criminal Court sentenced the two mayors in question to suspended fines of TRL 610,000 (an amount equivalent at the time to approximately 9.70 euros) for negligent omissions in the performance of their duties within the meaning of Article 230 § 1 of the Criminal Code (see paragraph 23 above). Before the Court, the Government attempted to explain why that provision alone had been applied in respect of the two mayors and why they had been sentenced to the minimum penalty applicable (see paragraph 82 above). However, it is not for the Court to address such issues of domestic law concerning individual criminal responsibility, that being a matter for assessment by the national courts, or to deliver guilty or not-guilty verdicts in that regard.

Having regard to its task, the Court would simply observe that in the instant case the sole purpose of the criminal proceedings in issue was to establish whether the authorities could be held liable for "negligence in the performance of their duties" under Article 230 of the Criminal Code, which provision does not in any way relate to life-endangering acts or to the protection of the right to life within the meaning of Article 2.

Indeed, it appears from the judgment of 4 April 1996 that the trial court did not see any reason to depart from the reasoning set out in the committal order issued by the administrative council, and left in abeyance any question of the authorities' possible responsibility for the death of the applicant's nine relatives. The judgment of 4 April 1996 does, admittedly, contain passages referring to the deaths that occurred on 28 April 1993 as a factual element. However, that cannot be taken to mean that there was an acknowledgment of any responsibility for failing to protect the right to life. The operative provisions of the judgment are silent on this point and, furthermore, do not give any precise indication that the trial court had sufficient regard to the extremely serious consequences of the accident; the persons held responsible were ultimately sentenced to derisory fines, which were, moreover, suspended.

117. Accordingly, it cannot be said that the manner in which the Turkish criminal justice system operated in response to the tragedy secured the full accountability of State officials or authorities for their role in it and the effective implementation of provisions of domestic law guaranteeing respect for the right to life, in particular the deterrent function of the criminal law.

118. In short, it must be concluded in the instant case that there has also been a violation of Article 2 of the Convention in its procedural aspect, on account of the lack, in connection with a fatal accident provoked by the operation of a dangerous activity, of adequate protection "by law" safeguarding the right to life and deterring similar life-endangering conduct in future.

[The Court also held by a vote of 15–2 that there had been a violation of the right to property, contained in article 1 of Protocol 1 and of the right to a remedy found in article 13 of the Convention. – Eds.]

Questions and Discussion

1. What standard of care does the Court impose on governments to prevent harm? Does the same standard of care apply to state conduct after loss of life has occurred?

2. Note that the state's obligations extend to activities of state and nonstate actors. Is this too onerous or unreasonable a burden? Contrast the judgments of the U.S. Supreme Court holding that the U.S. Constitution imposes no affirmative obligations on authorities to prevent private violence. *Castle Rock v. Gonzales*, 545 U.S. 748 (2005); *DeShaney v. Winnebago County*, 489 U.S. 189 (1989).

3. When does a state have an obligation to prosecute those responsible for environmental harm? If the state does not fully investigate or take other effective action when the right to life has been violated, is this always a separate violation of the right to a remedy?

4. To what extent does the European Court rely on or incorporate environmental law to establish the content of the state's duties? Is this appropriate?

5. After *Öneryildiz*, can the right to life in article 2 be leveraged to provide environmental protection? What obligations regarding the environment does a state owe individuals in securing the right to life? Does the fact that this is a clearly identifiable, one-time explosion undermine the broader application of the case?

6. No explicit right to receive information about significant environmental health risks is contained in the European Convention on Human Rights. Does the Court in *Öneryildiz* recognize such a right by linking article 2 to a positive duty on the part of states to inform people of potential environmental risks? *See* Daniel García San José, Environmental Protection and the European Convention on Human Rights 64–65 (2005). If so, does this recognition merely explain the nature of the state's duty to secure the right to

life when environmental hazards are present? Would providing information about the risk have been enough or does the state have "to take practical measures, instead of merely informing victims that they risk losing their lives"? *See* Danai Papadopoulou, *Environmental Calamities and the Right to Life: State Omissions and Negligence Under Scrutiny*, 8 ENVTL. L. REV. 59, 63 (2006).

7. On the positive obligations of states, see A.R. MOWBRAY, THE DEVELOPMENT OF POSITIVE OBLIGATIONS UNDER THE EUROPEAN CONVENTION ON HUMAN RIGHTS (2004); D. Shelton, *Private Violence, Public Wrongs, and the Responsibility of States*, 13 FORDHAM INT'L L.J. 1 (1989–90).

C. *National Jurisprudence*

The role of the judiciary in ordering action to protect the environment has been a controversial one, even when life and health are in question. Compare the following two cases.

> *Clean Air Foundation Limited & Gordon David Oldham v. Government of the Hong Kong Special Administrative Region,*
> HCAL 35/2007, Court of First Instance, Constitutional and Administrative Law List, No. 35 of 2007, Judgment of July 26, 2007,
> *available at* http://legalref.judiciary.gov.hk/lrs/common/ju/ju_body.jsp?DIS=57904&AH=&QS=&FN=&currpage=T

[Hartmann, J.:]

Introduction

1. The applicants in this matter have sought leave to apply for judicial review pursuant to O.53, r.3 of the Rules of the High court. Their application, as filed, may be characterized as a broad, frontal attack on what is asserted to be a failure of Government to tackle the problems presented by air pollution.

2. The first applicant is a limited liability company, its principal aim being the protection of the "environmental rights" of Hong Kong people.

3. The second applicant is an environmental advocate. In his supporting affidavit, he has said that he established the Clean Air Foundation in order to galvanize the support of Hong Kong residents in actively promoting the improvement of Hong Kong's air quality.

4. The applicants have contended that Hong Kong's air is so polluted that it is poisoning the people who live near; shortening their lives. It is, in addition, harming Hong Kong as a business and financial centre. They have asserted that Hong Kong's air contains almost three times more particles of soot and other pollutants than the air in New York and Paris and more than double the amount in London.

5. It has been asserted that Government has a legal duty, indeed a duty entrenched in the Basic Law, to guarantee the right to life of all residents. This includes the duty to provide the best possible health care. However, in failing to take more stringent steps to combat air pollution, Government has failed in that duty.

6. It has failed, so it appears to have been asserted, because it has not ensured that there is adequate legislation in place and/or has not pursued effective policies. This failure, it has been said, is not simply an example of poor governance. It goes further and constitutes a breach of this Basic Law, the Bill of Rights and various international covenants which have been extended to Hong Kong.

. . .

11. This judgment goes to the single question of whether leave to apply for judicial review should be given.

. . .

Looking to the Relief Sought

16. The applicants have sought two declarations. The first declaration is intended to be a 'foundation' declaration, setting out the exact nature of the Government's obligations under the Basic law, the Bill of Rights and the international conventions. It is to the following effect:

> Article 28 of the Basic Law and/or Article 2 of the Hong Kong Bill of Rights Ordinance, in proving for protection of a "right to life" and the "right to health," as provided by Article 12 of the International Covenant on Economic, Social and Cultural Rights, imposes upon the Government and affirmative duty to protect the residents and the economy of Hong Kong from the known harmful effects of air pollution. . . .

17. Art. 28 of the Basic Law and art. 2 of the Bill of Rights provide for the right to life in the context of detention, trial and punishment. The question arises, therefore, of whether, on a purposive interpretation, the constitutional protection can be extended to matters of air pollution control. In this respect, Mr. John Scott SC, leading counsel for the applicants, has referred to an emerging international jurisprudence to the effect that the right to life may, depending on the circumstances, impose on public authorities an obligation outside of the context of crime and punishment; for example, to provide vaccines in the case of epidemics or to protect against identified environmental hazards such as nuclear waste. I accept therefore that it is at least *prima facie* arguable that the constitutional right to life may apply in the circumstances advocated by the applicants; that is, by imposing some sort of duty on the Government to combat air pollution.

18. As for art. 12 of the International Covenant on Economic, Social and Cultural Rights, it is more directly in point. It reads:

> 1. The States Parties to the present Covenant recognize the right of everyone to the enjoyment of the highest attainable standard of physical and mental health.
> 2. The steps to be taken by the Stats Parties to the present Covenant to achieve the full realization of this right shall include those necessary for:
>   (a) . . .
>   (b) The improvement of all aspects of environmental and industrial hygiene . . .

19. Art. 12, of course, looks to the progressive achievement of the highest attainable standard of health. Put simply, it recognizes that Rome wasn't built in a day. But that being said, I accept that it must be *prima facie* arguable that it imposes some sort of duty on state authorities to combat air pollution even if it cannot be an absolute duty ensure with immediate effect the end of all pollution.

. . .

22. . . . On a plain reading, the second declaration originally suggested that the entire Air Pollution Control Ordinance and all subsidiary legislation made under it has no force in law. That could not be right. Nor, in fact, did the applicants contend it to be so. There are, for example, regulations which control pollution caused by industrial process, by construction works and the like. It was not suggested that these are legally invalid. Indeed, it must be that they play a very real and effective role in combating air pollution.

23. The amended declaration has sought to be more specific. It has contended that the current legislation fails in respect of two discrete areas. The amendment has been made by adding the following to the original declaration, namely – . . . in that the Government has failed to

take the following steps pursuant to the duty referred to in [the first declaration]; namely, to –

- Adopt up-to-date air quality objectives sufficient for the Secretary for the Environment to discharge his duties pursuant to S.7 of APCO.
- Revise the Air Pollution control (Motor Vehicle Fuel) Regulations, Cap. 311, so as to prohibit the use (as opposed merely the sale) of the pre-Euro and Euro 1diesel in Hong Kong and the importation into Hong Kong of such fuels."

24. In my view, to some degree, the amendment confuses what is, or is not, contained in the legislation with the failure of Government to take steps under that legislation.

25. The amended declaration seeks, first, a declaration that the Air Pollution Control Ordinance and its subsidiary legislation is inconsistent with the Government's obligations under law, not because the legislation is itself lacking but because the government has failed to take action under that legislation; more particularly, s. 7 of the Ordinance, to adopt "up-to-date" air quality objectives.

26. I do not see how it can be *prima facie* argued that s.7 is itself lacking.

27. As I read the section, it makes direct provision for the Secretary for the Environment, in consultation with a statutory body, not only to introduce air quality objectives but to update them whenever necessary. The contention must be, therefore, that the Government has failed to use its powers under the section to introduce what the applicants describe as "up-to-date" air quality objectives.

28. That contention, however, demands an examination of what steps Government has taken to introduce updated air quality objectives and whether, bearing in mind all relevant social, economic and political factors, those steps, whether prudent or not, have been lawful. In short, what is required is an examination of government policy.

29. The amended declaration seeks, second, a declaration that the Air Pollution Control Ordinance and its subsidiary legislation – the Air Pollution Control (Motor Vehicle Fuel) Regulations – is inconsistent with the Government's obligations under law because, while it prohibits the sale of diesel fuel in Hong Kong which does not meet specified levels of purity, it does not prohibit the importation or use of such diesel.

30. What is demanded in respect of this second issue is an examination of why the legislation prohibits the sale of certain diesel fuel but does not prohibit its importation or use. In my view, this also requires an examination of government policy.

Policy

31. Art. 62 of the Basis Law provides that it is for the Government to formulate and implement policies. Art.48 provides that it is for the Chief Executive, once a policy has been formulated, to decide whether, and to what degree, it should be executed.

32. A policy may, of course, be unlawful. But because a policy is considered to be unwise, short-sighted or retrogressive does not make it unlawful. It has long been accepted that policy is a matter for policy-makers and that to interfere with the lawful discretion given to policy-makers would amount to an abuse of the supervisory jurisdiction vested in the courts. . . .

But are matters of policy inherent in this application?

. . .

37. I believe it is inevitable that the two discrete issues contained within the second declaration can only be determined upon an exhaustive analysis of relevant Government policy.

38. Take the first issue, the asserted failure to adopt "up-to-date" air quality objectives. If government has the power under s. 7 of the Air Pollution Control Ordinance to update air quality objectives, either generally or in respect of particular areas, it is inevitable there will

be reasons why – if, in fact, there has been no updating – that it has declined to do so. Those reasons will be based on social and economic factors and, importantly, on an assessment of whether, all matters being taken into account, there is sufficient benefit to be obtained at this time in adopting more stringent objectives.

39. In respect of the second issue, it is obvious that it must turn on an issue of policy. If the sale of certain diesel fuel is prohibited but its importation or use is not, there must be underlying social and economic reasons. And, of course, there are. Fuel may be imported for the purpose only of re-export, presenting no threat of pollution within Hong Kong's borders. As for actual use, ships may come into Hong Kong waters powered by the otherwise prohibited diesel fuel; trucks may deliver produce across the border from the Mainland powered by the same fuel. Are they to be prevented from entering unless that fuel is first jettisoned? Yes, there may be ways of dealing more effectively with the problem. During the course of argument, mention was made of measures adopted in Singapore. But that itself reduces the issue to one of merit rather than one of legality.

40. The applicants, of course, submit that the application does not seek merely to review the wisdom of government's policies in respect of air pollution. This court is not being asked to change its role to some sort of commission of inquiry. This application, it has been said, seeks to determine whether Government has met its obligations in law.

41. I am unable to agree. The real issues here are not issues of legality, they do not go to the Government acing outside of its powers. In my judgment, they go to the merits of the policies adopted by Government; more accurately perhaps, to why Government at this time has not chosen to pursue certain policies.

42. Take for example, the issue of Government prohibiting the sale of certain diesel fuel in Hong Kong but not prohibiting vehicles from the Mainland entering Hong Kong under the power of that diesel. How possibly can this court decide that this decision fails to reach a fair balance between the duty Governments has to protect the right to life and the duty it has to protect the social and economic well-being of the Territory? It cannot do so, not without shouldering aside the discretion vested in Government to decide just how serious a threat those cross-border vehicles present to air pollution and what price must be paid in terms of economic well-being if those vehicles are prevented from entering under the power of the diesel.

Conclusion

43. In all the circumstances, leaving aside the other issues raised in opposition to this application of leave, I am satisfied that it must be refused on the basis that it is fundamentally misconceived. While it purports to seek the determination of issues of law, on an objective assessment it is clear that it seeks in fact to review the merits of policy in an area in which Government must make difficult decisions in respect of competing social and economic priorities and, in law, is permitted a wide discretion to do so. While issues of importance to the community may have been raised, it is not for this court to determine those issues. They are issues for the political process.

Mehta v. Union of India et al., 1988 A.I.R. 1115

VENKATARAMIAH, J.

This is a public interest litigation. The petitioner who is an active social worker has filed this petition *inter alia* for the issue of a writ/order/direction in the nature of mandamus to the respondents other than Respondents 1, and 7 to 9 restraining them from letting out the trade effluents into the river Ganga till such time they put up necessary treatment plants for treating the trade effluents in order to arrest the pollution of water in the said river. Respondent 1 is the Union of India, Respondent 7 is the Chairman of the Central Board for Prevention and Control of Pollution, Respondent 8 is the Chairman, Uttar Pradesh Pollution Control Board and Respondent 9 is the Indian Standards Institute.

Water is the most important of the elements of nature. . . .

. . .

. . . "Environment" includes water, air and land and the inter-relationship which exists among and between water, air and land and human beings, other living creatures, plants, micro-organism and property. (Vide section 2(a) of the Environment (Protection) Act, 1986). Under Section 3(2)(iv) of the said Act the Central Government may lay down standards for emission or discharge of environmental pollutants from various sources whatsoever. Notwithstanding anything contained in any other law but subject to the provisions of the Environment (Protection) Act, 1986, the Central Government may under section S of the 290 Act, in the exercise of its powers and performance of its functions under that Act issue directions in writing to any person, officer or authority and such authority is bound to comply with such directions. The power to issue directions under the said section includes the power to direct the closure, prohibition or regulation of any industry, operation or process or stoppage or regulation of the supply of electricity or water or any other service. Section 9 of the said Act imposes a duty on every person to take steps to prevent or mitigate the environmental pollution. Section 15 of the said Act contains provisions relating to penalties that may be imposed for the contravention of any of the provisions of the said Act or directions issued thereunder. It is to be noticed that not much has been done even under this Act by the Central Government to stop the grave public nuisance caused by the tanneries at Jajmau, Kanpur.

. . .

In the Fiscal Plan for setting up common Effluent Treatment Plants for Indian Tanning Industry (March, 1986) prepared by the committee constituted by the Directorate General of Technical Development (Government of India) it is observed thus: –

> Leather industry is one of the three major industries besides paper and textiles consuming large quantities of water for processing of hides and skins into leather[.] Naturally most of the water used is discharged as wastewater. The wastewater contains putrescible organic and toxic inorganic materials which when discharged as such will deplete dissolved oxygen content of the receiving water courses resulting in the death of all acquatic [*sic*] life and emanating foul odour. Disposal of these untreated effluents on to land will pollute the ground water resources. Discharging of these effluents without treatment into public sewers results in the choking of sewers.
>
> Realising the importance of keeping the environment clean, the Government of India has enacted the Water Pollution Control Act (Central Act 6 of 1974) and almost all the State Government have adopted the Act and implementing the Act by forming the Pollution Control Boards in their respective states. The Pollution Control Boards have been insisting that all industries have to treat their effluents to the prescribed standards and leather industry is no exception to this rule. Tanneries situated all over the country have been faced with the problem of treating their effluents. . . .

. . .

There is a reference to the Jajmau tanneries in "an Action Plan for Prevention of Pollution of the Ganga" prepared by the Department of Environment [which provides]:

4.4.12 Effluent from industries:

> Under the laws of the land the responsibility for treatment of the industrial effluents is that of the industry. While the concept of "Strict Liability" should be adhered to in some cases, circumstances may require that plans for sewerage and treatment systems should consider industrial effluents as well. Clusters of small industries located in a contiguous area near the river bank and causing

direct pollution to the river such as the tanneries in Jajmau in Kanpur is a case in point. In some cases, waste waters from some industrial units may have already been connected to the city sewer and, therefore, merit treatment along with the sewage in the sewage treatment plant. It may also be necessary in some crowded areas to accept wastewaters of industries in a city sewer to be fed to the treatment plant, provided the industrial waste is free from heavy metals, toxic chemicals and is not abnormally acidic or alkaline.

. . .

. . . Just like an industry which cannot pay minimum wages to its workers cannot be allowed to exist a tannery which cannot set up a primary treatment plant cannot be permitted to continue to be in existence for the adverse effect on the public at large which is likely to ensue by the discharging of the trade effluents from the tannery to the river Ganga would be immense and it will outweigh any inconvenience that may be caused to the management and the labour employed by it on account of its closure. Moreover, the tanneries involved in these cases are not taken by surprise. For several years they are being asked to take necessary steps to prevent the flow of untreated wastewater from their factories into the river. Some of them have already complied with the demand. It should be remembered that the effluent discharged from a tannery is ten times noxious when compared with the domestic sewage water which flows into the river from any urban areas on its banks. We feel that the tanneries at Jajmau, Kanpur cannot be allowed to continue to carry on the industrial activity unless they take steps to establish primary treatment plants. In cases of this nature this Court may issue appropriate directions if it finds that the public nuisance or other wrongful act affecting or likely to affect the public is being committed and the statutory authorities who are charged with the duty to prevent it are not taking adequate steps to rectify the grievance. For every breach of a right there should be a remedy. It is unfortunate that a number of tanneries at Jajmau even though they are aware of these proceedings have not cared even to enter appearance in this Court to express their willingness to take appropriate steps to establish the pretreatment plants. So far as they are concerned an order directing them to stop working their tanneries should be passed. . . .

. . .

We issue a direction to the Central Government, the Uttar Pradesh Board, established under the provisions of the Water (Prevention and Control of Pollution) Act, 1974 and the District Magistrate, Kanpur to enforce our order faithfully. Copies of this order shall be cent to them for information. The case is adjourned to 27th October, 1987 to consider the case against the municipal bodies in the State of Uttar Pradesh having jurisdiction over the areas through which the river Ganga is passing.

Questions and Discussion

1. On the basis of the Hong Kong court's analysis, do you think a Hong Kong resident suffering from lung cancer or emphysema would succeed in a damages action against the government for violating the constitutional right to life? How would you address the issue of causation? Would statistical evidence be sufficient to prove the case? *See* Jamie Grodsky, *Genomics and Toxic Torts: Dismantling the Risk-Injury Divide*, 59 STAN. L. REV. 1671 (2007). Could the complaint in that case have been drafted differently to make it more justiciable? As it is, it sought only a declaratory judgment, not specific relief. Was the Court correct in its conclusion? How relevant was the fact that much of the pollution in question was being emitted by Chinese trucks entering Hong Kong?

2. The Supreme Court of India was one of the first courts to insist on protection of the environment as part of the right to life, in the absence of a guaranteed right to a healthy

environment in the constitution. *See Bandhua Mukti Morcha v. Union of India*, 3 S.C.C. 161 (1984) and *Charan Lal Sahu v. Union of India*, AIR 1990 SC 1480). In a subsequent case, the Court observed that the "right to life guaranteed by article 21 includes the right of enjoyment of pollution-free water and air for full enjoyment of life." *Subhash Kumar v. State of Bihar*, AIR 1991 SC 420. A series of judgments between 1996 and 2000 responded to health concerns caused by industrial pollution in Delhi. In some instances, the courts issued orders to cease operations. Compare *Jayal and Others v. India and Others*, (2004) 9 S.C.C. 362, 2003 I.L.D.C. 456 (2003), in which the court found it "necessary to draw a demarcating line between the realm of policy and the permissible areas for judicial interference" and declined to halt development of the Sardar Sarovar Project.

3. Other national courts have similarly implied an obligation for the government to protect the environment as an essential element of the right to life or health. In Costa Rica, a court stated that the rights to health and to the environment are necessary to ensure that the right to life is fully enjoyed. *Presidente de la Sociedad Marlene S.A. v. Municipalidad de Tibas, Sala Constitucional de la Corte Supreme de Justicia* (Constitutional Chamber of the Supreme Court) Decision No. 6918/94 of 25 Nov. 1994. In Bangladesh, the Supreme Court has interpreted the right to life to include the protection and preservation of the environment and ecological balance free from pollution of air and water. *See Dr. Mohiuddin Farooque v. Bangladesh; Dr. Mohiuddin Farooque v. Ministry of Communication, Bangladesh*, 48 D.L.R. 1996.

4. Does it make a difference that the government is a defendant instead of a private company and that the issue is a constitutional right rather than a nuisance? In *Pedro Flores et al. v. Corporación del Cobre*, Supreme Court of Chile, Rol.12.753.FS. 641 (1988), the plaintiff sued a private mining company to enjoin it from dumping tailings into the Pacific Ocean. In affirming the injunction, the Supreme Court held that article 19 of the Chilean Consitution, which provides, inter alia, a right to live in an environment free of pollution, had been violated.

III. A Right to Water

In 2002, the World Summit on Sustainable Development concluded with the participating governments making a commitment to halve by 2015 the number of persons who lack access to safe drinking water and sanitation. *Plan of Implementation of the World Summit on Sustainable Development*, U.N. Doc. A/CONF.199/CRP.7 (Apr. 9, 2002). As you study the material in this section and the nature of a right to water, consider whether this commitment is both sufficient and within what the law requires.

The first text here describes the freshwater problem. The second text reveals the extent to which human rights bodies consider a right to water to be explicitly or implicitly guaranteed as a human right. After reading both texts, consider the following: To what extent will or can a rights-based approach contribute to resolving the water problems outlined in the 2006 Human Development Report? Is a right to water necessary, or would fulfillment of preexisting human rights (e.g., health, housing, adequate standard of living) serve to ensure access to safe drinking water and sanitation? Should water be treated as private property or as a public good? What transboundary obligations, if any, exist? *See also* World Health Organization, *The Global Water Supply and Sanitation Assessment 2000*, Geneva, 2000, at 1; United Nations, Commission on Sustainable Development, *Comprehensive Assessment of the Freshwater Resources of the World*, at 39, U.N. Doc. E/CN.17/1997/9.

A. *Human Rights Law at the Global Level*

Human Development Report 2006. Beyond Scarcity: Power, Poverty, and the Global Water Crisis, U.N. Development Programme, v–vi, 3, 7, 14–17, 19–20 (figures, citations, subheading omitted).

Access to water for life is a basic human need and a fundamental human right. Yet in our increasingly prosperous world, more than 1 billion people are denied the right to clean water and 2.6 billion people lack access to adequate sanitation. These headline numbers capture only one dimension of the problem. Every year some 1.8 million children die as a result of diarrhoea and other diseases caused by unclean water and poor sanitation. At the start of the 21st century unclean water is the world's second biggest killer of children. Every day millions of women and young girls collect water for their families – a ritual that reinforces gender inequalities in employment and education. Meanwhile, the ill health associated with deficits in water and sanitation undermines productivity and economic growth, reinforcing the deep inequalities that characterize current patterns of globalization and trapping vulnerable households in cycles of poverty.

. . . [T]he sources of the problem vary by country, but several themes emerge. First, few countries treat water and sanitation as a political priority, as witnessed by limited budget allocations. Second, some of the world's poorest people are paying some of the world's highest prices for water, reflecting the limited coverage of water utilities in the slums and informal settlements where poor people live. Third, the international community has failed to prioritize water and sanitation in the partnerships for development that have coalesced around the Millennium Development Goals. Underlying each of these problems is the fact that the people suffering the most from the water and sanitation crisis – poor people in general and poor women in particular – often lack the political voice needed to assert their claims to water.

. . .

. . . Water for livelihoods poses a different set of challenges. The world is not running out of water, but many millions of its most vulnerable people live in areas subject to mounting water stress. Some 1.4 billion people live in river basins in which water use exceeds recharge rates. The symptoms of overuse are disturbingly clear: rivers are drying up, groundwater tables are falling and water-based ecosystems are being rapidly degraded. Put bluntly, the world is running down one of its most precious natural resources and running up an unsustainable ecological debt that will be inherited by future generations.

. . .

It is already clear that competition for water will intensify in the decades ahead. Population growth, urbanization, industrial development and the needs of agriculture are driving up demand for a finite resource. Meanwhile, the recognition is growing that the needs of the environment must also be factored in to future water use patterns. Two obvious dangers emerge. First, as national competition for water intensifies, people with the weakest rights – small farmers and women among them – will see their entitlements to water eroded by more powerful constituencies. Second, water is the ultimate fugitive resource, traversing borders through rivers, lakes and aquifers – a fact that points to the potential for cross-border tensions in water-stressed regions. Both dangers can be addressed and averted through public policies and international cooperation – but the warning signs are clearly visible on both fronts.

. . .

Water security is an integral part of [a] broader conception of human security. In broad terms water security is about ensuring that every person has reliable access to enough safe water at an affordable price to lead a healthy, dignified and productive life, while maintaining the ecological systems that provide water and also depend on water. When these conditions are not met, or when access to water is disrupted, people face acute human security risks transmitted through poor health and the disruption of livelihoods.

. . .

The crisis in water and sanitation is – above all – a crisis for the poor. Almost two in three people lacking access to clean water survive on less than $2 a day, with one in three living on less than $1 a day. More than 660 million people without sanitation live on less than $2 a day, and more than 385 million on less than $1 a day.

These facts have important public policy implications. They point clearly towards the limited capacity of unserved populations to finance improved access through private spending. While the private sector may have a role to play in delivery, public financing holds the key to overcoming deficits in water and sanitation.

. . .

Measured on conventional indicators, water stress is increasing. Today, about 700 million people in 43 countries live below the water-stress threshold of 1,700 cubic metres per person – an admittedly arbitrary dividing line. By 2025 that figure will reach 3 billion, as water stress intensifies in China, India and Sub-Saharan Africa. Based on national averages, the projection understates the current problem. The 538 million people in northern China already live in an intensely water-stressed region. Globally, some 1.4 billion people live in river basin areas where water use exceeds sustainable levels.

Water stress is reflected in ecological stress. River systems that no longer reach the sea, shrinking lakes and sinking groundwater tables are among the most noticeable symptoms of water overuse. The decline of river systems – from the Colorado River in the United States to the Yellow River in China – is a highly visible product of overuse. Less visible, but no less detrimental to human development, is rapid depletion of groundwater in South Asia. In parts of India groundwater tables are falling by more than 1 metre a year, jeopardizing future agricultural production.

These are real symptoms of scarcity, but the scarcity has been induced by policy failures. When it comes to water management, the world has been indulging in an activity analogous to a reckless and unsustainable credit-financed spending spree. Put simply, countries have been using far more water than they have, as defined by the rate of replenishment. The result: a large water-based ecological debt that will be transferred to future generations. This debt raises important questions about national accounting systems that fail to measure the depletion of scarce and precious natural capital – and it raises important questions about cross-generational equity. Underpricing (or zero pricing in some cases) has sustained overuse: if markets delivered Porsche cars at give-away prices, they too would be in short supply.

Future water-use scenarios raise cause for serious concern. For almost a century water use has been growing almost twice as fast as population. That trend will continue. Irrigated agriculture will remain the largest user of water – it currently accounts for more than 80% of use in developing countries. But the demands of industry and urban users are growing rapidly. Over the period to 2050 the world's water will have to support the agricultural systems that will feed and create livelihoods for an additional 2.7 billion people. Meanwhile, industry, rather than agriculture, will account for most of the projected increase in water use to 2025.

. . .

Climate change is transforming the nature of global water insecurity. While the threat posed by rising temperatures is now firmly established on the international agenda, insufficient attention has been paid to the implications for vulnerable agricultural producers in developing countries. . . . Few warnings have been more perilously ignored.

Global warming will transform the hydrological patterns that determine the availability of water. Modelling exercises point to complex outcomes that will be shaped by micro-climates. But the overwhelming weight of evidence can be summarized in a simple formulation: many of the world's most water-stressed areas will get less water, and water flows will become less predictable and more subject to extreme events. Among the projected outcomes:

- Marked reductions in water availability in East Africa, the Sahel and Southern Africa as rainfall declines and temperature rises, with large productivity losses in basic food staples. Projections for rain-fed areas in East Africa point to potential productivity losses of up to 33% in maize and more than 20% for sorghum and 18% for millet.
- The disruption of food production systems exposing an additional 75–125 million people to the threat of hunger.
- Accelerated glacial melt, leading to medium term reductions in water availability across a large group of countries in East Asia, Latin America and South Asia.
- Disruptions to monsoon patterns in South Asia, with the potential for more rain but also fewer rainy days and more people affected by drought.
- Rising sea levels resulting in freshwater losses in river delta systems in countries such as Bangladesh, Egypt and Thailand.

· · ·

Looking to the future, one of the greatest challenges is to ensure that strategies for enhancing water productivity extend to the poor. Technology is not neutral in its distributional effects – and the danger is that efforts to get more crop per drop from water resources will bypass poor households.

This does not have to be the case. The revival of small-scale water harvesting programmes in India in response to the groundwater crisis has shown the potential to generate large returns to investment and at the same time to reduce risk and vulnerability. Similarly, micro-irrigation technologies do not have to be geared solely to large capital-intensive producers. Innovative new designs and low-cost technologies for drip irrigation have been taken up extensively. Here, too, the social and economic returns are large. On one estimate the extension of low-cost irrigation technologies to 100 million smallholders could generate net benefits in excess of $100 billion, with strong multiplier effects in income and employment generation.

The way developing country governments address the challenge of balancing equity and efficiency goals in water management will have an important bearing on human development. Putting the interests of the poor at the centre of integrated water resources management policies is an organizing principle. But that principle has to be backed by practical pro-poor policies.

· · ·

. . . [T]he potential for crossboundary tensions and conflict cannot be ignored. While most countries have institutional mechanisms for allocating water and resolving conflict within countries, cross-border institutional mechanisms are far weaker. The interaction of water stress and weak institutions carries with it real risks of conflict.

Hydrological interdependence is not an abstract concept. Two in every five people in the world live in international water basins shared by more than one country. International rivers are a thread that binds countries: 9 countries share the Amazon and 11 the Nile, for example. Rivers also bind the livelihoods of people. The Mekong, one of the world's great river systems, generates power in its upper reaches in China and sustains the rice production and fishery systems that support the livelihoods of more than 60 million people in the lower reaches of its basin.

With hydrological interdependence comes deeper interdependence. As a productive resource, water is unique in that it can never be managed for a single use: it flows between sectors and users. That is true within countries and between them. How an upstream country uses a river inevitably affects the quantity, timing and quality of water available to users downstream. The same interdependence applies to aquifers and lakes.

· · ·

Successful cooperation in the management of shared waters can produce benefits for human development at many levels. Apart from reducing the potential for conflict, cooperation can unlock benefits by improving the quality of shared water, generating prosperity and more secure livelihoods and creating the scope for wider cooperation.

Experience highlights both the potential benefits of cooperation and the costs of noncooperation.

. . .

Report of the U.N. High Commissioner for Human Rights on the Scope and Content of the Relevant Human Rights Obligations Related to Equitable Access to Safe Drinking Water and Sanitation Under International Human Rights Instruments, Human Rights Council, U.N. Doc. A/HRC/6/3 (Aug. 16, 2007) (some citations omitted)

1. In its decision [2/104 of Nov. 27, 2006]), the Human Rights Council requested the Office of the United Nations High Commissioner for Human Rights (OHCHR) " . . . taking into account the views of States and other stakeholders, to conduct, within existing resources, a detailed study on the scope and content of the relevant human rights obligations related to equitable access to safe drinking water and sanitation under international human rights instruments, which includes relevant conclusions and recommendations thereon, to be submitted prior to the sixth session of the Council."

. . .

4. The mandate entrusted to OHCHR by the Human Rights Council limits the sources of international law the study may address to international human rights instruments. These are understood as including international and regional treaties, as well as human rights-related declarations, resolutions, principles and guidelines. While these instruments do not have the same binding force as treaties, they may contain elements that already impose or may come to impose obligations on States under customary international law. They also highlight social expectations and commitments expressed by States and provide useful guidance for interpreting States' obligations under human rights treaties. International plans of action and documents adopted by United Nations treaty bodies will be used as sources of interpretations for these instruments. . . .

5. Access to safe drinking water and sanitation are referred to in a range of instruments which can be grouped as follows:

    (a) Explicit reference in human rights treaties: explicit references to safe drinking water or sanitation are included in the Convention on the Rights of the Child (CRC), the Convention on the Elimination of All Forms of Discrimination against Women (CEDAW), the recently adopted Convention on the Rights of Persons with Disabilities and International Labour Organization (ILO) Convention No. 161 of 1985 on Occupational Health Services. At the regional level, the African Charter on the Rights and Welfare of the Child and the Protocol to the African Charter on Human and Peoples' Rights on the Rights of Women in Africa include specific provisions on access to water. . . .

    (b) Implicit reference in human rights treaties: the close connection between access to safe drinking water and sanitation and a range of other human rights is implicitly addressed in various treaties, notably in relation to the right to life, the prohibition of torture, the right to health, the right to education, the right to adequate housing, the right to food and the right to an adequate standard of living.

    (c) Explicit reference in human rights principles and guidelines: several principles and guidelines adopted by the United Nations and the ILO highlight the obligation to provide safe drinking water or sanitation to particular groups, including prisoners, juveniles deprived of their liberty, internally displaced persons (IDPs), workers living in housing provided by their employers and old persons. The FAO Voluntary Guidelines to support the progressive realization of the right to adequate food in the context of national food security also highlight the fact that access to water in sufficient quantity and quality for all is essential for life and health. . . .

(d) Safe drinking water and sanitation as a human right in declarations and resolutions: access to safe drinking water was first declared a human right by United Nations Member States in the Mar del Plata Action Plan (1977) asserting that irrespective of the level of development, all people "have the right to have access to drinking water in quantities and of a quality equal to their basic needs" [pmbl]. Resolutions adopted by the United Nations General Assembly and the Commission on Human Rights also refer to safe drinking water as a human right.[7] Members of the Non-Aligned Movement, acknowledged the right to water for all in their 14th Summit final document [para. 226]. At the regional level, recommendation 14 of the Committee of Ministers of the Council of Europe to member States on the European Charter on Water Resources provides that everyone has the right to a sufficient quantity of water for his or her basic needs. This being said, the recognition of water as a human right in declarations and resolutions has been uneven.[8]

(e) Expert documents referring to safe drinking water and sanitation as a human right: in 2002, the Committee on Economic, Social and Cultural Rights (CESCR) adopted its general comment No. 15 on the right to water (articles 11 and 12 of the Covenant), defined as the right of everyone to sufficient, safe, acceptable, physically accessible, and affordable water for personal and domestic uses. General comments provide an authoritative interpretation by an expert body on provisions under various international covenants and conventions, including the International Covenant on Economic, Social and Cultural Rights (ICESCR). In 2006, the Sub-Commission for the Promotion and Protection of Human Rights adopted the draft guidelines for the realization of the right to drinking water supply and sanitation (the Sub-Commission's guidelines), which refer to a right to drinking water and sanitation. The Sub-Commission's guidelines are intended to assist Governments, policymakers, international agencies and members of civil society to implement the right to drinking water and sanitation.

(f) Plans of action referring to safe drinking water and sanitation as a human right: a number of plans of action have also referred to water and sanitation as a human right. Agenda 21, adopted at the United Nations Conference on Environment and Development (UNCED) in 1992 states [in ch. 18, para. 47] that "the commonly agreed premise was that 'all peoples, whatever their stage of development and their social and economic conditions, have the right to have access to drinking water in quantities and of a quality equal to their basic needs.'" In the Programme of Action of the International Conference on Population and Development (1994), States affirmed that all people have "the right to an adequate standard of living for themselves and their families, including adequate food, clothing, housing, water and sanitation" [para. 2]. The UN-Habitat Plan of Action (1996) subsequently recognized water and sanitation as a human right [para. 11].

(g) Other recognition of safe drinking water and sanitation as a human right: the former United Nations Secretary-General Kofi Annan emphasized that "access to safe water is

---

[7] General Assembly Res. 54/175, "The right to development," para. 12; Commission on Human Rights Resolutions 2004/17 and 2005/15, "Adverse effects of the illicit movement and dumping of toxic and dangerous products and wastes on the enjoyment of human rights," preamble, paras. 4 and 9.

[8] For instance, water has not been acknowledged as a human right in the U.N. Millennium Declaration or in the ministerial declarations adopted at the World Water Forums.

a fundamental human need and, therefore, a basic human right." In its 2006 Human Development Report, Beyond scarcity: power, poverty and the global water crisis, the United Nations Development Programme (UNDP) stressed the importance of recognizing and implementing the right to water. The United Nations Children's Fund (UNICEF) also stressed that "access to sanitation facilities is a fundamental human right that safeguards health and human dignity." The United Nations Millennium Project Task Force on Water and Sanitation highlighted the importance of the right to water for achieving the Millennium Development Goals (MDGs) related to water and sanitation.[9] National constitutions, legislation and jurisprudence have also recognized water as a human right. National experiences brought to the attention of OHCHR also revealed that many countries have adopted specific legislation regulating access to safe drinking water.

. . .

11. Access to safe drinking water and sanitation can also create equality concerns, notably in relation to women, as limited access tends to disproportionately affect their health, physical and psychological integrity, privacy and access to education. The time burden of collecting and carrying water, which often falls on women and girls, is one explanation for the very large gender gaps in school attendance in many countries, while girls also commonly miss out disproportionately on an education if school sanitation facilities are inadequate. When girls and women have to walk to a place distant from their home for excreta disposal or water collection, they are also vulnerable to harassment and assault. Under the Convention on the Elimination of All Forms of Discrimination against Women (CEDAW), States parties have the obligation to address all forms of discrimination against women, including the elimination of the causes and consequences of their de facto or substantive inequality.

12. A certain number of humanitarian and environmental treaties also entail specific provisions related to access to safe drinking water and sanitation. The Geneva Conventions and their Additional Protocols outline the fundamental importance of access to safe drinking water and sanitation for health and survival in situations of international and non-international armed conflicts. Under the United Nations Economic Commission for Europe (UNECE) Protocol on Water and Health to the 1992 Convention on the Protection and Use of Transboundary Watercourses and International Lakes (UNECE Protocol), States parties have the obligation to take appropriate measures to provide access to drinking water and sanitation and to protect water resources used as sources of drinking water from pollution [Arts 1, 4, paras 2(a)–(b) and 6, para. 1(a)–(b)].

. . .

V. ISSUES REQUIRING FURTHER ELABORATION

43. This section highlights a number of issues that arose throughout the consultation process regarding the nature of human rights obligations in relation to access to safe drinking water and sanitation that might require further elaboration.

A. Access to Safe Drinking Water and Sanitation as a Human Right

44. . . . [H]uman rights treaties entail explicit and implicit obligations in relation to access to safe drinking water and sanitation. Obligations are also found in other human rights instruments, as well as under humanitarian and environmental law treaties. While access to safe drinking water and sanitation is not explicitly recognized as a human right per se in human rights treaties, it has been acknowledged by two expert bodies (CESCR and the

---

[9] *Health, Dignity and Development: What Will It Take?*, U.N. Millennium Project Task Force on Water and Sanitation, 2005, at xiv, available at http://www.unmillenniumproject.org/documents/WaterComplete-lowres.pdf.

Sub-Commission for the Promotion and Protection of Human Rights), as well as by States in several resolutions, declarations and plans of action.

45. However, the debate is still open as to whether access to safe drinking water and sanitation is a human right, notably in relation to the following points: (a) whether access to safe drinking water is a right on its own or whether obligations in relation to access to safe drinking water and sanitation are derived from other human rights, such as the right to life, the right to health, the right to food or the right to an adequate standard of living; (b) the normative content of human rights obligations in relation to access to sanitation.

46. In the High Commissioner's view, international human rights law entails clear obligations in relation to access to safe drinking water. These obligations demand that States ensure everyone's access to a sufficient amount of safe drinking water for personal and domestic uses – defined as water for drinking, personal sanitation, washing of clothes, food preparation and personal and household hygiene – to sustain life and health. It is up to each country to determine what this sufficient amount is, relying on guidance provided by WHO and others. This access should be prioritized over other water uses and should be premised on equality and non-discrimination. States should take steps to ensure that this sufficient amount is of good quality, affordable for all and can be collected within a reasonable distance from a person's home. The primary target should be to ensure everyone's access to a minimum amount of water to prevent disease.

47. While the human rights framework does not dictate a particular form of service delivery or pricing policy, it requires States to adopt adequate measures and to put in place effective regulations to ensure the access of individuals to sufficient, affordable and physically accessible and safe drinking water and sanitation. Effective judicial or other appropriate remedies should be available to individuals who have been denied this access.

48. Given the clarity of these obligations, the open debate as to whether the human right to access safe drinking water is a stand-alone right or is derived from other human rights should not impair the recognition of access to safe drinking water as a human right. As noted in chapter II, the normative content of human rights obligations in relation to access to sanitation would need further elaboration.

C. Private Provision of Water and Sanitation Services

49. A number of submissions to the consultation process for the study have highlighted the potential impact that the private provision of water and sanitation services can have on access to safe drinking water and sanitation. Some submissions suggested that human rights obligations in relation to access to safe drinking water and sanitation should prevent the private provision of these basic services. The approach of United Nations treaty bodies and special procedures has been to stress that the human rights framework does not dictate a particular form of service delivery and leaves it to States to determine the best ways to implement their human rights obligations. While remaining neutral as to the way in which water and sanitation services are provided, and therefore not prohibiting the private provision of water and sanitation services, human rights obligations nonetheless require States to regulate and monitor private water and sanitation providers.

50. An implicit dimension of this duty to regulate is that privatization of water and sanitation services should not take place in the absence of a clear and efficient regulatory framework that can maintain sustainable access to safe, sufficient, physically accessible and affordable water and sanitation. The role of individuals in decision-making on who supplies water and sanitation services, the type of services supplied and how these should be managed raises questions concerning the right to take part in the conduct of public affairs and other rights, and is an important element to take into account when making decisions on private

sector delivery. Further elaboration is needed regarding the human rights response and requirements concerning the private provision of water and sanitation services and the type of regulatory system that States must put in place in that respect.

D. Obligations of Local Authorities

51. Local authorities are often responsible for the supply of safe drinking water and sanitation. Where safe drinking water and sanitation are provided at the local level, the WHO Guidelines outline a certain number of responsibilities of local governments to secure water quality, notably in relation to catchment inspection and consumer education. Local governments represented at the Fourth World Water Forum in Mexico also recognized that all human beings have the right to water in the quantity and quality required to meet their essential needs, as well as to sanitation.

52. Further clarification is needed regarding the role, responsibilities and specific obligations of local authorities responsible for the provision of water and sanitation services. At the same time, as the State remains accountable under international law, its specific responsibilities vis-à-vis local authorities should also be further elaborated upon in the context of human rights obligations in relation to access to safe drinking water and sanitation.

. . .

F. Prioritization Between Various Kinds of Water Use

60. Considering access to safe drinking water from a human rights perspective highlights the need to give precedence in water distribution to water for personal and domestic uses for all. . . .

61. The Plan of Implementation of the World Summit on Sustainable Development (2002) calls for water to be allocated among competing uses in a way that gives priority to the satisfaction of basic human needs. This prioritization of human consumption over other water uses bears certain implications in terms of water management and might require specific systems to manage competing demands and to ensure that access to water for personal and domestic uses is prioritized.

62. Beyond the clear basic principle that safe drinking water for personal and domestic uses should be given precedence over other water uses, questions remain regarding the prioritization between various kinds of water use, particularly in situations of water scarcity. Once a sufficient amount of safe drinking water to prevent disease has been secured for all, allocation of water among various uses – water for personal and domestic uses beyond this sufficient amount, water to produce food, water to sustain livelihoods, or water to ensure environmental hygiene – remains unclear. CESCR General Comment No. 15 notes that priority in the allocation of water should also be given to water resources to prevent starvation and disease and that attention should be given to ensuring that disadvantaged and marginalized farmers have equitable access to water and water management systems. The Human Rights Council may wish to clarify obligations in this regard.

Questions and Discussion

1. Is water an example of the tragedy of the commons? Should it be privatized, included in property rights? Or is it a public good that should be regulated? How?

2. Taking together the recommendations above, can you devise a sustainable water management policy consistent with human rights?

3. In CESCR General Comment 15, the Committee states that "[t]he human right to water entitles everyone to sufficient, safe, acceptable, physically accessible, and affordable water

for personal and domestic uses." U.N. Doc. E/C.12/2002/11, para. 2 (Nov. 26, 2002). Does the right to water exist as a separate right? If so, what are the advantages? Is the Johannesburg Plan of Action mentioned in Chapter 1 in accord with such a right?

4. If the right to water is not a separate right, is it part of the right to life, the right to health, or the right to an adequate standard of living? Or is it straining the meaning of human rights to speak of a right to water?

5. If there is a right to water, is it enforceable? What actions or inactions by a government would constitute a violation of the right?

6. In reviewing periodic state reports, the Committee on Economic, Social, and Cultural Rights has commented on access to water. Do the following comments support the existence of a human right to water? *See also* ICESCR, *Comments of the Committee on Economic, Social, and Cultural Rights*, U.N. Doc. E/C.12/1/Add.84, at paras. 461, 474 (2002) (Solomon Islands).

7. On July 26, 2010, the U.N. General Assembly adopted the Declaration on the Human Right of Water and Sanitation, U.N. Doc. A/64/L.63/Rev.1(2010).

Comments of the Committee on Economic, Social, and Cultural Rights, U.N. Doc. E/2004/22 (March 8, 2004) 42 & 55 at paras. 268, 270, 284–86, 361–62

Israel

268. The Committee is particularly concerned about limited access to and distribution and availability of water for Palestinians in the occupied territories, as a result of inequitable management, extraction and distribution of shared water resources, which are predominantly under Israeli control.

. . .

270. The Committee continues to be concerned about the situation of Bedouins residing in Israel, and in particular those living in villages that are still unrecognized. Despite measures by the State party to close the gap between the living conditions of Jews and Bedouins in the Negev, the quality of living and housing conditions of the Bedouins continues to be significantly lower, with limited or no access to water, electricity and sanitation.

. . .

284. The Committee strongly urges the State party to take immediate steps to ensure equitable access to and distribution of water to all populations living in the occupied territories, and in particular to ensure that all parties concerned participate fully and equally in the process of water management, extraction and distribution. In that connection, the Committee refers the State party to its general comment No. 15 (2002) on the right to water.

285. Reiterating its earlier recommendation, the Committee urges the State party to cease the practices of facilitating the building of Israeli settlements, expropriating land, water and resources, demolishing houses and carrying out arbitrary evictions. . . .

286. The Committee . . . urges the State party to recognize all existing Bedouin villages, their property rights and their right to basic services, in particular water, and to desist from the destruction and damaging of agricultural crops and fields, including in unrecognized villages. The Committee further encourages the State party to adopt an adequate compensation scheme for Bedouins who have agreed to resettle in "townships." . . .

Yemen

361. The Committee is concerned about the living conditions of prisoners and detainees in the State party, especially women, with regard to access to health-care facilities, adequate food and safe drinking water.

362. The Committee is concerned about the persisting water crisis which constitutes an alarming environmental emergency in the State party, and which prevents access to safe and affordable drinking water, particularly for the disadvantaged and marginalized groups of society, and for rural areas.

. . .

B. *The Organization of American States*

Human rights bodies have been monitoring health and environmental conditions related to water quality for a considerable period of time. The mandate of the Inter-American Human Rights Commission includes examining the human rights practices within any member state, even one like Cuba, whose government has been suspended from voting and participation in activities of the Organization of American States (OAS). The normative standards for OAS member states not party to the American Convention on Human Rights are those contained in the American Declaration on the Rights and Duties of Man as explained in Chapter 4. Most countries studies are done through on-site visits, including discussions with government officials and civil society. The following early report on Cuba included consideration of water and sanitation matters.

The Situation of Human Rights in Cuba, Seventh Report, OEA/Ser.L/V/II.61, Doc. 29 rev. 1 (Oct. 4, 1983) (citations omitted)

Chapter XIII. The Right to Health

Environmental Hygiene

41. To preserve and care for a healthy population, an environment conducive to that goal is essential. Certain factors have a significant impact on environmental hygiene: water supply, disposal of industrial or human waste, and the garbage collection system.

a. *Water Supply*

42. In 1953, over three-fourths of rural families in Cuba obtained their water from rivers, wells or springs, many of which were polluted. Only 6.6% of the population had indoor plumbing, although the national average was 55%, whereas in contrast, this figure rose to 79.5% in the cities. A housing census carried out in 1970 revealed that 66.7% of Cubans have access to plumbing (the figure for cities was 88.2%, although for the country it was 26.7%). Therefore, there has been a slight improvement, in particular in rural areas, although growth there has been less marked than in other areas. The absolute number of people without access to plumbing has risen from 508,000 inhabitants in 1953 to 628,000 in 1970.

43. The water has been treated with chlorine. In 1959, only 21% of the water supply to the public was treated, but in the decade of the 1970s, it had risen to 98%. Even so, cases of water pollution are not infrequent. For example, in 1977 typhoid fever struck the oldest section of Havana, when human waste leaked into the water supply system. In the same year, there were 302 cases reported in the capital alone of water pollution, and in the following year 120 cases were reported. Due to the frequency of such cases, the Ministry of Public Health urges the public to boil whatever water it uses.

44. Water shortages have been a persistent and difficult problem. The water supply system has numerous leaks through which a considerable quantity of water is lost, and in addition, they create the risk of pollution. A government report indicates that in 1980 approximately 50% of the water supply was lost due to leaks. In general, water supply pipes are very

old, as are the pumps, which are over 45 years old. The system has not been improved, received maintenance, or been extended because the country's limited financial resources have been allocated to other priorities. As a result, the situation is deteriorating with the passage of time, and at present approximately 300,000 people receive little water in certain neighborhoods of the capital. Furthermore, the hydrostatic level in cities such as Havana and Santiago is becoming progressively lower, while salinity is increasing. Water scarcity has become a persistent complaint throughout the country.

45. Because Cuba has so many rivers, it is logical to think that they would be used as a source of water supply. Unfortunately, most of them have been polluted by industrial waste. Around the city of Havana, the Martín Pérez, Cojimar, Almendares, Luyano, Quibus and Arroyo Tadeo rivers are unusable or nearly unusable due to pollution, as they contain a high number of toxic chemicals as well as hydrocarbons from use for drainage.

46. Pollution of the rivers has in turn led to pollution of bays and coastal waters. The Antonio Nico López oil refinery in Havana, for example, has destroyed nearly all marine life in the port of Havana. Chemical wastes are discharged into the port of Nuevitas, in the beautiful Bay of Cienfuegos, and in the marsh of Zapata, whose ecosystems are at the point of total collapse. There is no longer any marine flora or fauna in the bay of Moa. A Soviet environmental specialist declared "The bays of Havana and Moa are practically dead regions today. It is impossible to obtain any natural resource from them, but they continue to Contaminated the whole Coast. In Santa Maria de Mar it is possible to see a layer of oil floating in the water[:] in Santiago de Cuba[,] over 60% of the water volume is highly polluted[.] In Moa, over 450 cubic meters of processed nickel waste is dumped daily into the water."

47. Despite the enactment of several laws in recent years to solve the problem, little progress has been made.

b. *Sewerage*

48. It is well known that a population's health may be affected by the system used for elimination of human waste. In the 1950s, the existing system was unquestionably inadequate. An author has written that "28% of homes had toilets with running water, and 13.7% were located outside the homes. Over one-third of families had latrines and 23.2% of housing (54.1% in the country) had no sanitary facilities."

49. At present, while a small part of the population enjoys the benefit of proper disposal of human waste, the sewerage system is in such a deplorable condition that it frequently affects the country adversely. The city of Havana is an example of this: its sewerage system was built between 1908 and 1913, and was designed for a maximum population of 600,000 people, who, it was thought, would live within a radius of 25 square miles. At present, the capital has over one million inhabitants and covers over 100 square miles. The sewerage system, to put it mildly, is overloaded; it handles 1.5 times its processing capacity. It is estimated that approximately one million cubic meters of liquid enters the system daily, i.e., approximately six cubic meters per second, but the sewerage system can only efficiently absorb one cubic meter per second. The result is that the pipes burst frequently.

50. It is estimated that the city of Havana requires 300 kilometers of sewerage alone to satisfy demand, but there is little planned to remedy this situation.

· · ·

58. Considerable progress has been made in reducing the rates of stillbirths, infant mortality and the healthy development of children. Prevention, treatment and control of epidemic diseases [have] improved over the years, in particular in terms of mortality, although morbidity rates have risen for some diseases. Nevertheless, the increase in the suicide

rate is a matter of concern and it would be important to explain the above-mentioned increase.

59. Preventive medicine and participation of the community are the cornerstone of the health policy of the country. Prevention, treatment and control of diseases and job accidents leave a great deal to be desired, since sufficient efforts have not been made nor have the necessary resources been allocated to this area.

60. Environmental and industrial health practices require a great deal more attention. Housing, sewerage and water supply require radical improvement. Due to the scarcity of resources, preferential treatment is given to those who are deserving and have the greatest need.

61. Pollution of the soil, air and water is increasing at a dangerous rate, and unless methods are adopted to control it, it could undermine the successes that have been achieved in the health field.

C. *The African Commission on Human and Peoples' Rights*

In *Communications 25/89, 47/90, 56/91 and 100/93 Against Zaire*, the African Commission on Human and Peoples' Rights held that failure by the government to provide basic services such as safe drinking water constituted a violation of article 16. Article 16 of the African Charter states that every individual shall have the right to enjoy the best attainable state of physical and mental health, and that states parties should take the necessary measures to protect the health of their people. The case consolidated four communications asserting torture, killings, arbitrary detention, unfair trials, restrictions on the right to association and peaceful assembly, suppression of freedom of the press, and denial of the rights to education and to health. In regard to the latter, the Commission said:

> The failure of the Government to provide basic services such as safe drinking water and electricity and the shortage of medicine as alleged in communication 100/93 constitutes a violation of Article 16.

AHG/207(XXXII), Annex VIII, at 8

In August 2008, a cholera epidemic began in Zimbabwe. By January 2009, the United Nations Office for the Coordination of Humanitarian Affairs (OCHA) in Geneva reported that the death toll exceeded 1,700, with more than 20,000 made ill. The disease, which spreads through contaminated drinking water, causes severe diarrhoea and dehydration. It is normally easy to treat, provided medical treatment is available. However, supplies and treatment were limited due to inflation; prices were doubling every 24 hours and unemployment reached more than 80 percent. Millions fled to South Africa and neighboring countries is search of work and food. On December 8, UK Prime Minister Gordon Brown called the cholera crisis "an international emergency" and asked the world community to confront Zimbabwe's President Robert Mugabe. Other prominent figures, including Kenyan Prime Minister Raila Odinga and South African Archbishop Desmond Tutu called for Mugabe to go or for peacekeeping troops to be sent to Zimbabwe. Four days later, Mugabe said that doctors had 'arrested' the disease, and said that cholera is not a reason to invade a country. According to *New York Times* reporter Celia Dugger, Zimbabwe's economy, once among the best in Africa, had been virtually destroyed. Water and sanitation services, public schools and hospitals were shut down. See Celia W. Dugger, "Cholera Is Raging, Despite Denial by Mugabe," N.Y. TIMES, Dec. 12, 2008 at A1.

Questions and Discussion

1. What are the human rights issues in Zimbabwe? How should they be addressed? Can claiming a right to safe drinking water assist in any way? See also the discussion of the Responsibility to Protect in Chapter 9.

2. Do the foregoing extracts support the claimed right to water? How might a human rights campaigner employ the observations of the Committee?

D. *National Water Rights*

Water as a Human Right?,
9–10 IUCN Environmental Policy and Law Paper No. 51 (2004)
(some footnotes omitted and renumbered)
John Scanlon, Angela Cassar, & Noemi Nemes

The development of environmental law as a recognised body of law has created an additional source of law for analysis of the existence of a right to water. This is because uniform State practice may provide evidence of *opinio juris*. It is appropriate to consider national constitutions as a source of an emerging right to water and court interpretations of fundamental rights contained in those constitutions. Whilst over 60 constitutions refer to environmental obligations, less than one-half expressly refer to the right of its citizens to a healthy environment.[10] Only the South African Bill of Rights enshrines an explicit right of access to sufficient water. In view of the foregoing, a position that a uniform constitutional practice has emerged is rather doubtful, especially considering the fact that despite the increasing prevalence of constitutional environmental norms, most countries have yet to interpret or apply such norms.[11]

In many countries, particularly those with a civil law tradition, traditionally constitutional rights were not regarded as being self-executing; legislation was required to implement a constitutional provision and to empower a person to invoke protections. However, with the rise of constitutionalism globally, courts increasingly view the constitution as an independent source of rights, enforceable even in the absence of implementing legislation.[12] Thus, courts could and do rely on the environmental provisions of their constitutions when protecting water from pollution or ensuring access to water to meet basic human needs. Where constitutions lack environmental provisions, reliance has been placed on the right to life, a provision contained in most constitutions worldwide. Constitutions many times incorporate "penumbral rights," rights that are not explicitly mentioned in the constitution, but are consistent with its principles and existing rights.[13] These rights could easily adopt emerging fundamental human rights.

Both civil and common-law countries have incorporated the "Public Trust Doctrine" in their constitutions.[14] The doctrine dates back to the Institutes of Justinian ([A.D. 530]) and requires governments to protect certain resources, like water, that the government holds in trust for the public.[15] Many of the US state constitutions have incorporated this doctrine, and courts in at

---

[10] Paula M. Pevato, *A Right to Environment in International Law: Current Status and Future Outlook*, in 8 RECIEL 315 (1999).

[11] Environmental Law Institute Research Report, *Constitutional Environmental Law: Giving Force to Fundamental Principles in Africa* (May 2000), at 6.

[12] Id. at 7.

[13] Id. at 8. E.g., Art. 29 of Eritrea's Constitution: "The right in this Chapter shall not preclude other rights which ensue from the spirit of the Constitution and the principles of a society based on social justice, democracy and the rule of law"; art. 32 of Algeria's Constitution: "The fundamental liberties and the Rights of Man and of citizen are guaranteed."

[14] The public trust doctrine also exists by operation of the common law.

[15] Id. at 23.

least five states have used them to review state action.[16] Similarly, Indian and Sri Lankan courts have relied on the doctrine to protect the environment. In the *M.C. Mehta v. Kamal Nath* Case[17] (1977), which concerned the diversion of a river's flow, the Supreme Court held that the government violated the public trust by leasing the environmentally sensitive riparian forest land to a company. In a landmark decision concerning the Eppawela Phosphate Mining Project, the Sri Lankan Supreme Court said that the "Public Trust Doctrine" on which the petitioners depended was "comparatively restrictive in scope." The court instead put forward a broader doctrine revolving around "Public Guardianship" to protect the site of an ancient kingdom and agricultural lands, and prevent the forced relocation of residents in Sri Lanka's North Central Province. The Court said that "[t]he organs of the State are guardians to whom the people have committed the care and preservation of the resources of the people."[18]

In many cases, courts have applied the provisions of the right to life, environment, etc. where an environmentally destructive activity directly threatened people's health and life. The cases . . . show that while there might not be a constitutional right to water, courts have been prepared to liberally interpret existing constitutional provisions.

Modern Water Rights: Theory and Practice,
FAO Legislative Study No. 92 (2006), at 9–17, 37–39, 45–48, 88–90, 98–102
(section numbers omitted; footnotes omitted or renumbered)
Stephen Hodgson

Throughout history all societies in which water is used have had their own approaches to regulate access to water, their own conceptions of water rights. Such influences are still found in so-called "customary" or "local" law practices as well as influences from religious law such as the Hadiths of Islam. Customary or local law continues to play an important role in water allocation decisions in many developing countries, particularly in rural areas. Nevertheless, as already mentioned, the focus of this review is on formal water rights and the approach of formal legal systems.

. . .

Rights to Surface Water

Under both the common law and civil law traditions, the right to use water depended primarily on the use or ownership of land or structures built on such land. The logic of this approach lies in the fact that historically most water rights, apart from those relating to "instream" uses, related to the use of water on land.

This approach, of conferring a privileged position on the owners of land adjacent to water courses, was one of the elements of Roman water law[,] which had a major influence on the development of water law under the two European legal traditions, prior to the introduction of modern water rights regimes. Indeed some of these influences can still be observed.

Roman law, for example, denied the possibility of private ownership of running water. The Institutes of Justinian published in 533–34 held that running water was a part of the "negative community" of things that could not be owned along with air, the seas and wildlife.[19] It was nevertheless recognized that things in the negative community could be used and that the "usufruct"

---

[16] Id. at 24.

[17] *M.C. Mehta v. Kamal Nath*, 1 S.C.C. 388 (Supreme Court of India, 1977).

[18] *Bulankulama v. Secretary, Ministry of Industrial Development* (2000), Vol. 7, No. 2, S. Asian Envtl. L. Rep. 1. The judgment was delivered on June 2, 2000.

[19] Roman law is not the only legal system that rejects the idea of private ownership of running water. Islamic law, which also takes this approach, plays an important role in shaping legal rules about the use of water.

or right to use the benefit of the resource needed to be regulated to provide order and prevent over-exploitation....

Roman law distinguished the more important, perennial streams and rivers from the less important. The former were considered to be common or public while the latter were private. The right to use a public stream or river was open to all those who had access to them.[20] Roman law, however, recognized the right of the government to prohibit the use of any public water and required an authorization for taking water from navigable streams....

The Common Law Tradition

The countries of the common law tradition did not follow the distinction between public waters and private waters.[21] The common law did, however, maintain the principle of Roman law that flowing waters are *publici juris*. From this basic principle, two divergent approaches to water law and water rights developed: the doctrine of "riparianism" and the doctrine of "prior appropriation."

(a) The Doctrine of Riparianism

The doctrine of riparianism was developed gradually over the years through a series of court decisions and reached its zenith, in terms of its development, in England and the New England states of North America in the course of the nineteenth century.[22] Riparian rights were not considered to be subsidiary land rights, such as easements or servitudes, but were instead an integral part of the right of ownership of the land in question.

Regarding its substantive content, the riparian doctrine held that a riparian right holder had the right to make "ordinary" use of the water flowing in the watercourse. This encompassed the "reasonable use" of that water for domestic purposes and for the watering of livestock and, where those uses of water were made, abstraction could be undertaken without regard to the effect which they might have had on downstream proprietors.... In addition a riparian land owner also had the right to use the water for any other purpose provided that it did not interfere with the rights of other proprietors, upstream or downstream. Such purposes were categorised as being "extraordinary" uses of water. The limits of "extraordinary" water use have never been precisely defined, and are indeed probably incapable of full definition. But it is clear that they are subject to significant restrictions. Specifically, the use of the water must be reasonable, the purpose for which it is taken must be connected with the abstracter's land and the water must be restored to the watercourse substantially undiminished in volume and un-altered in character.

The question whether a particular extraordinary use is reasonable is a question of fact which must be determined by reference to all the circumstances. In addition to such natural riparian rights, a riparian owner could acquire additional rights in the nature of "easements," which are types of land tenure right, in accordance with relevant rules of land tenure.

Notwithstanding its complexity, the doctrine of riparianism spread throughout the English speaking world. As already mentioned, important developments took place in the damp climate of New England, where it still applies in some states. However when the doctrine reached the dry and arid climates of the American West and South West its practical limitations were clearly recognized leading to the development of a new doctrine, that of prior appropriation.

---

[20] Because Roman law did not provide for involuntary servitude of access, it could to that extent be considered a riparian system.

[21] Except to the extent that a distinction is made between the ownership of the banks and bed of tidal and nontidal waters. The banks and bed of former are generally in the private ownership of the riparian landowner, whereas the banks and bed of the latter are owned by the Crown (i.e., the state).

[22] It should, however, be noted that riparian doctrine which was developed by the courts, replaced an earlier conception of water rights based on priority of use which was not as closely tied to land ownership....

(b) The Prior Appropriation Doctrine

The prior appropriation doctrine was developed in the nineteenth century to serve the practical demands of water users in the western United States. It originated in the customs of miners on federal public lands who accorded the best rights to those who first used water just as they had accorded mining rights to those who first located ore deposits. In any event given that their gold washing activities were taking place on federal public lands and not on private land they simply could not seek to apply the doctrine of riparianism.

Nevertheless the prior appropriation doctrine was later extended to farmers and other users, even on private lands. The flexibility of the common law tradition is such that this new, more suitable water rights doctrine, was accepted as the law in a number of states and indeed it continues to apply in the states of Alaska, Arizona, Colorado, Idaho, Montana, Nevada, New Mexico, Utah and Wyoming.... In addition a number of states, including California, have hybrid systems under which both the prior appropriation and riparian doctrines apply simultaneously.

The key significance of the prior appropriation doctrine is that it comprehensively severed the linkage between land and water rights. Water rights are acquired on the basis of beneficial use, rather than land ownership. More specifically, water rights are granted according to where a person applies a particular quantity of water to a particular beneficial use. Those rights continue as long as the beneficial use is maintained.

Most appropriation jurisdictions consider water to be a public resource owned by no one. The right of individuals to use water under the prior appropriation system is based on application of a quantity of water to a beneficial use.

The traditional elements of a valid appropriation are:

- the intention to apply the water to a beneficial use;
- an actual diversion of water from a natural source;
- the application of the water to a beneficial use within a reasonable time period.

The date of the appropriation determines the user's priority to use water, with the earliest user having a superior right. If water is insufficient to meet all needs, those who hold the earliest appropriations (senior appropriators) will obtain all of their allocated water; those who appropriated later (junior appropriators) may receive only some, or none, of the water over which they have rights.

All of the states in which the prior appropriation doctrine applies have statutory administrative procedures to provide an orderly method for appropriating water and regulating established water rights.... In some states appropriators have the option of: (a) applying for a permit; or (b) perfecting a common law appropriation by posting a notice and diverting water. Nowadays it is, however, more typical for state law to require a permit as the exclusive means of making a valid appropriation.

A number of criticisms are made against the prior appropriation doctrine. One criticism is that it tends to discourage water saving by senior appropriators who know that their entitlements are relatively more secure. Furthermore, users have been able to continue seizing water as long as a single drop remained in the stream or aquifer.... While these and other issues have led to calls for water law reform, little progress has been made to date. Indeed what is perhaps most interesting is the fact that being divorced from land tenure rights, trades in water rights have long been accepted, or even encouraged. In fact most of the world's experience of transferable water rights derives from the western states.

. . .

The Civil Law Tradition

The Roman law distinction between public and private waters retained an influence in the countries of the civil law tradition even until quite recently. Generally speaking, while an administrative permission was necessary for the use of public waters this was not necessary in the case of private waters.

For example, the influential French Civil Code, the Code Napoleon, which was promulgated in 1804 after the French Revolution, maintained this distinction. Public waters were those which were considered to be "navigable" or "floatable"[23] and belonged to the public or national domain. Their use required a government permit or authorization.

Private waters, which were those located below, along or upon privately owned land, could be freely utilized subject to certain limitations of a statutory nature such as servitudes and rights of way. The right to use such private waters, both surface and underground, derived from land ownership which recognized the owner's right to use at pleasure the water existing upon his land without any limitation.

Similarly the Spanish Water Act of 1886 considered as private all surface waters, that is waters springing in a private property and rainfall waters, but only for its use on that land and not beyond the limits of that estate.[24] This approach was largely repeated throughout the "civil law" world in Asia, Latin American and parts of Africa. In the Democratic Republic of Congo, for example, the beds of every lake and of all navigable water courses, whether floatable or not, are part of the public land domain and the water of such lakes and water courses as well as groundwater also belongs to the state.[25] Subject, however, to any legal and administrative measures which regulate use or the granting of concessions, the right to use such water is open to everyone.

Finally, the difficulties of accommodating different and competing uses of private waters led the courts to limit the absolute right of use by making it subject to numerous restrictions, particularly as regards the prohibition to pollute water, etc. Gradually the concept of private waters began to lose its force. . . .

It should, however, be noted that in connection with "public waters" a concession has always been required in most jurisdictions of the civil law tradition. Such concessions can be seen as the precursor of modern water rights in the countries of that legal tradition. Of course significant variations existed from jurisdiction to jurisdiction with regard to the constraints placed on the users of private waters but this in outline is the basic position.

Rights to Groundwater

Historically most of the focus of water law and water rights has been on surface water resources. It is only relatively recently, over the last hundred or so years, that specific legal responses have been formulated in water legislation to the issue of groundwater management. As regards the use of ground water both the common law and civil law traditionally also conferred specific benefits on adjacent or, to be more precise, super-adjacent land owners.

The Civil Law Tradition

Traditionally, within the civil law tradition, in accordance with the basic principles of Roman law, groundwater was seen as the property of the owner of the land above it. This basic approach is reflected in article 552 of the French Civil Code[,] which states that:

> Ownership of the ground involves ownership of what is above and below it. An owner may make above all the plantings and constructions which he deems proper, unless otherwise provided for

---

[23] A river is "floatable" if logs can be floated down it.

[24] However there was a possibility of some administrative control reflected in articles 413, 415, and 420–422, which defined private waters as "special property" subject to some restrictive covenants. . . .

[25] In the civil law tradition a distinction is typically made between state owned property in the public domain and state property in the private domain. Property in the latter may, in accordance with specific legislation, be privatized. Property in the former may not unless and until it is transferred to the private domain.

in the Title Of Servitudes or Land Services. He may make below all constructions and excavations which he deems proper and draw from these excavations all the products which they can give, subject to the limitations resulting from statutes and regulations relating to mines and from police statutes and regulations.

The Common Law Tradition

Although the conceptual approach taken by the common law tradition was slightly different, the effect was largely the same. Under the common law there is no property in water percolating through the sub-soil until it has been the object of an appropriation. The effect is that a land owner is entitled to sink a borehole or well on his land to intercept water percolating underneath his property, though the effect is to interfere with the supply of underground water to nearby springs.[26] Yet at the same time, the owner of land through which ground water flows has no right or interest in it which enables him to maintain an action against another landowner whose actions interfere with the supply of water....

In practice, however, as a result of the development and use of modern well drilling techniques and pumps, the approaches of the main legal traditions no longer offer a viable means of effectively regulating the use of groundwater, even though they continue to apply in a number of jurisdictions....

The "Nationalization" of Water Resources

In many jurisdictions the first step in establishing a system of formal rights is to bring water resources within the ownership or control of the state. Because, as described above, the common law has not generally recognized the concept of ownership over flowing water resources even by the state, water legislation in common law jurisdictions has tended to declare a superior state control right over water....

Usually, such state ownership or control applies to all of the water resources within a state's territory thus including both surface water and groundwater.

Having placed water resources under state ownership or control the next step is to address the validity of existing water rights. Apart from provisions that either continue such rights on a deemed basis or provide for their conversion into the new form, an issue returned to below, this is usually achieved by a simple statutory declaration.

Two examples from different Australian jurisdictions are instructive.

Section 8(7) of the Victorian Water Act provides:

> The rights to water conferred by or under this Act on a person who has an interest in land replace any rights:
>> (a) to take or use water;
>> (b) to obstruct or deflect the flow of water; or
>> (c) to affect the quality of any water; or
>> (d) to receive any particular flow of water; or to receive a flow of water of a particular quality that the person might otherwise have been able to enforce against the Crown or any other person because of, or as in incident to, such interests.

This is in those cases where the existing rights would be replaced through the transitory provisions in the new law.

A simpler means of achieving a similar but less comprehensive result appears in section 7(9) of the South Australian Water Resources Act 1997. It provides:

> Rights at common law in relation to the taking of naturally occurring water are abolished....

---

[26] An exception is made, under the common law, for underground water flowing in a defined channel in which case the riparian doctrine applies....

"Free" Uses of Water

Water legislation typically provides a range of exemptions for activities that would otherwise require a water right. Indeed such entitlements are sometimes described in legislation in terms of "rights."[27] Typically, this is done by reference to the type of activity, the volume of water used or a combination of both.[28] . . .

There is no great theoretical justification for exempting such uses from formal water rights regimes. Instead, a value judgement is made by the legislature that takes account of the increased administrative and financial burden of including such uses within the formal framework, their relative value to individual users and their overall impact on the water resources balance.

Similarly as regards groundwater rights, legislation typically provides that a formal right to abstract and use groundwater is not necessary in connection with certain specified purposes provided relatively small volumes of water are used. In Australia, for example, a formal water right is not necessary for the abstraction and use of groundwater for stock and domestic purposes (including household garden irrigation). Such exemptions are usually justified on the basis that their use will have little impact on the total available water supply as well as the administrative burden of seeking to regulate them. However, the sheer number of individual wells can ultimately have a significant negative impact on the quantity (and quality) of groundwater and related surface water resources. . . .

The Introduction of Water Rights

The next step is to introduce modern water rights. As to their legal form, water rights are mostly now created on the basis of a legal instrument issued by the water administration. Such instruments are variously described in legislation as "licences," "permissions," "authorizations," "consents" and "concessions." From a general legal perspective such terms are synonymous. Having said that, in those cases where the word "concession" is used in water legislation this generally relates to cases where a particularly long term of use is envisaged coupled with major investments in infrastructure.

As to their substance, modern water rights are administrative use or usufructory rights. The question arises as to whether or not they are property rights.

Some modern water legislation seeks to make this explicit. . . .

In other jurisdictions the question as to whether or not modern water rights are a form of property is not specified. The fact that they gain their existence from an administrative or regulatory procedure does not by itself preclude them from being property rights. After all, intellectual property rights in the form of trademarks and patents are usually acquired through an administrative procedure.

In conceptualising property both of the main legal traditions differentiate between personal (movable) property such as chattels and real (immovable) property such as land tenure rights. It is also important to note that property rights do not necessarily equate with ownership rights.

Therefore, the fact that water rights may be subject to restrictions, even restrictions on their sale or transfer in some jurisdictions, does not necessarily mean that they are less than property rights. No one would seriously argue, for example, that a right over, say, premises conferred on a lessee pursuant to a lease is anything other than a (real) property right even though it is of limited duration, may specify what the leased premises may be used for and may prevent or restrict assignment of the term.

---

[27] Article 13 of the Albanian Water Law, for example, provides that "[e]veryone has the right to use surface water resources freely for drinking and other domestic necessities and for livestock watering without exceeding its use beyond individual and household needs . . ."

[28] Nevertheless, water legislation usually provides that such "free uses" of water may also be subject to restriction in times of drought.

Consequently it can be said with some confidence that provided they are sufficiently secure and for a sufficiently long duration such water rights are indeed a form of property right.... Finally, it should be emphasized that such rights exist entirely independently to land tenure rights. ...

ENVIRONMENTAL ALLOCATIONS

The basic advantage of modern water rights as far as the environment is concerned is the simple fact that they explicitly specify the volumes of water that may be abstracted or used. This means that it is possible to measure the total amounts of water taken from a given water course or aquifer and thus to calculate the volume of water that is, or should be, left to meet ecological requirements. Such requirements may include ensuring the sustainability of aquatic ecosystems and the use of dilution flows for the enhancement of water quality. Additional benefits may arise from improved riverine ecologies including the possibility of recreational uses as well as aesthetic values.

As already noted, two basic legal techniques are used to ensure that sufficient water is left in a water body.

One is to impose a statutory definition of minimum flows of which the water administration must take account in the issue of new water rights. In Mexico, for example, a minimum streamflow must be established for rivers pursuant to the National Water Law of 1992.

The other technique is to designate a reserve for environmental purposes. Thus the South African National Water Act creates a buffer to protect two of its fundamental tenets – that of ensuring that water is allocated equitably and used beneficially in the public interest, while promoting environmental values. As far as environmental protection is concerned the Reserve is defined to mean "the quantity and quality of water required to protect aquatic ecosystems in order to secure ecologically sustainable development and use of the relevant water resource."...

Of course these kinds of techniques can only be effective as long as the initial assessment of the environmental requirements of a given water body are correct in the first place and do not change significantly over time. Clearly in the context of climate change the requirements of surface water bodies may indeed need to be modified in the future. If water rights are time limited then such revisions can take place when they fall to be renewed or varied. This kind of consideration may militate against the grant of perpetual water rights.

On the other hand, on many water courses around the world, even those on which formal water rights have been granted, it is too late to consider leaving a reserve of minimum stream flow: all of the water is subject to existing water rights.

What solutions are available? In the case of time limited water rights, depending on the urgency of the situation, one solution is simply to wait for the rights to expire. A more costly alternative would be for the water administration to cancel a number of existing rights, partially or wholly, in the public interest so that the water can be re-allocated for environmental ends. However, given that in many jurisdictions compensation would be payable such an approach would likely be expensive. It would also no doubt be controversial not simply because the right holders may be unwilling to give up the water rights in question but also due to the difficulty of agreeing the level of compensation payable. As the experience of compulsory acquisition of land shows, this kind of valuation exercise is invariably difficult and contentious although it is by no means impossible to conclude.

The situation becomes more problematic in those jurisdictions where water rights are of indefinite duration. Thus in Chile given the existence of vested property rights in the use of water it is virtually impossible to reassign water or to develop effective river basin institutions to take account of environment and ecosystem protection....

Thus in a number of the western United States environmental nonconsumptive uses have been found to have economic values that compete with traditional consumptive uses of water. These non-consumptive uses include water for recreation, such as rafting and fishing, fish and wildlife, and water quality maintenance. Both private and public entities have begun to acquire environmental water rights. For example, an NGO called the Nature Conservancy has begun to acquire environmental water rights in Arizona, Colorado and Nevada. The Washington State Legislature has established a "water trust" for the Yakima River and several other rivers to help restore instream flows.... What is particularly interesting is that these uses are starting to compete in the marketplace for traditional water rights demonstrating that there is a genuine willingness on the part of North American society to pay for environmental water uses.

In other words, these examples tend to show that transferable water rights can be used creatively to conserve water resources for environmental and other ends. Similarly in the Edwards Aquifer in Texas the Aquifer Authority has begun a programme of buying back groundwater rights to retire them from use....

CONCLUSION

The key points that emerge from the analysis contained in this paper can be summarized as follows.

First of all traditional land based approaches to water rights, including rights to groundwater, no longer provide a sound basis for the sustainable management and use of water resources. Consequently the need to better manage water resources is usually the underlying reason why modern water rights regimes are introduced.

Effective and widespread consultation can greatly facilitate the introduction of reforms that involve the introduction of modern water rights while at the same time ensuring that those reforms better serve the needs of society and stakeholders.

The fact that water rights are property rights, or quasi property rights, means that primary legislation is usually necessary for sector reform and the introduction of modern water rights. The first formal step in the process of introducing modern water rights is to place water under state ownership or control through such legislation. New institutional arrangements are necessary for the administration of modern water rights. Such arrangements, in the form of a water administration, should include mechanisms for stakeholder participation. A water administration may have competence throughout the relevant jurisdiction. It may alternatively be established specifically to manage a given aquifer or water body. Clearly it is necessary to confer the appropriate powers and legal duties on such an entity if it is to be able to operate effectively....

With the introduction of a modern water rights regime, rights are typically issued to existing water users on the basis of their declared historical use. If following this exercise any remaining water resources remain for allocation, new water rights are issued by the water administration on the basis of a range of statutory steps and measures, including the use of management plans, which are designed to promote rational water use and to prevent arbitrary decision-making. Following the enactment of the necessary legislation, the process of registering water rights is a major administrative and logistical task that may take many years to complete. It is necessary to bear this process in mind during the design of legislation and to take such measures as may be necessary to actively encourage existing water users to claim and register their water rights.

In order to be effective, modern water rights must confer a sufficient degree of security upon right holders both as regards other water users and the state, acting through the water administration. Thus typically water rights may not be modified or cancelled in the absence of fault on the part of the right holder unless compensation is paid. Nevertheless no water right can provide an absolute guarantee that a specific volume of water will always be available in a given resource irrespective of climatic and other natural conditions.

As to their substance, modern water rights typically specify the volume of water that may be abstracted. This may be expressed as a fixed amount or as a proportion of the available water. There is a trend towards limiting the duration of water rights as this makes future re-allocation possible even at the expense of security for rights holders. Furthermore, modern water rights are typically subject to a range of general and specific conditions, including a condition requiring the payment of water fees or charges. Breach of such conditions can lead to the right being lost.

In an increasing number of jurisdictions water rights may be traded. Water rights trades are, however, generally rather carefully regulated by the water administration to minimise negative impacts on third parties and the environment. Most trades in water rights have involved rights relating to surface water. Nevertheless trades in rights to groundwater have taken place in a number of jurisdictions. The evidence suggests that transferable water rights can lead to the economically more efficient use of water resources. Leaving aside arguments over the efficiency of markets for water rights, the fact remains that provided that trades are freely entered into and perceived as beneficial by both parties they do ultimately offer a relatively uncontentious means of re-assigning water from low value to high value uses.

Given that they specify the volume of water that may be abstracted from a given water resource, modern water rights should make it possible to set overall limits on total abstractions so as to permit sustainable resource use. . . .

Notwithstanding these positive conclusions, the fact remains that many countries have yet to introduce modern water rights regimes. Why is that? Of course the precise reasons for this will vary from country to country but such reasons are worth considering in that they may suggest actual, or perceived, disbenefits of moving towards the introduction of modern water rights.

The key issues are probably cost and administrative capacity. It will not have gone un-noticed that many of the examples cited in this paper are from richer countries. The costs in question are not so much those relating to the preparation and adoption of legislation but those of registering and recording water rights as well as the costs of monitoring water resources and enforcing the legislation relating to a water rights regime. Furthermore, implementing a modern water rights regime is a relatively complex process that requires efficient administrators as well as other technical skills.

At first sight, the large number of water users that may be involved (particularly farmers dependant on small land plots) may make the idea of introducing modern water rights in developing countries appear even more daunting. As regards surface water rights, however, if farmers are supplied with water through irrigation schemes, as is often the case, then whatever rights to water they should have are not modern water rights, of the type being discussed here, but rather contractual water rights as discussed in section 2.1 above. There may still be a strong case for the grant of water rights to the operators of such schemes if only to safeguard abstractions for irrigation.

As regards rights to groundwater, the sheer number of actual or potential abstraction points, the issue of cost together with consequential difficulties of monitoring and enforcing abstractions takes on a greater significance. Indeed it seems reasonable to conclude that as concerns groundwater, water rights reforms need to pay particular attention to governance and enforcement mechanisms that involve right holders and other stakeholders in decisionmaking.

Ultimately, though, the costs of introducing a modern water rights regime, and the relative complexity (and thus cost) of whatever regime is chosen, have to be set against the potential costs of inaction. The limitations of traditional water rights are not restricted to richer countries: examples exist in developing countries that do not have modern water rights regimes of new irrigation schemes being built in the upper catchments depriving existing downstream schemes of "their" water as well as of water being diverted from reservoirs built for irrigation to quench the needs of thirsty cities. Needless to say ordinary farmers tend to be the ones who suffer in such cases. As competition for water increases such kinds of conflict are likely only to increase.

In such circumstances policy makers in developing countries may well determine that the costs and resource implications of introducing a modern water rights regime are justified even if for no other reason than to protect the interests of existing water users. Nevertheless even in countries where there is overall water scarcity it will often make sense to focus initially on those basins or aquifers where there are particular problems such as overabstraction/overuse. From a legal perspective this can be done through specific (primary) legislation that applies only to the basins/aquifers in question. Alternatively it may be preferable to enshrine a water rights regime in national (or state) legislation but to provide for its staged implementation (basin by basin, for example) so as to ensure the best use of limited financial and administrative resources.

Even, however, if the hydraulic and economic arguments in favour of the introduction of a modern water rights regime are accepted by policy makers the potential political challenges should not be overlooked, notwithstanding consultation and education exercises undertaken. The first challenge concerns the notion of water privatization. As outlined in this paper, although modern water rights are a form of property right, reforms leading to their adoption do not legally constitute the privatization of water. Indeed in most cases they simply reflect and reinforce existing water rights or uses of water. Nor does the introduction of a system of modern water rights have anything to do with private investment in the urban water sector.

Nevertheless the point is sensitive particularly in developing countries where land and water are the primary livelihood resources. How to allocate water rights on a fair basis that takes account of existing uses of water is a key issue that needs to be addressed from the very beginning (although again most farmers whose land is supplied with water through irrigation schemes need secure contractual water rights rather than modern water rights of the type being discussed here) while safeguarding the interests of the disadvantaged. Another key issue is to distinguish between the notional right to water for personal, household use and the concept of modern water rights. . . .

The issue of tradability or transferability may pose a greater challenge particularly in countries where a large proportion of the population relies on agriculture. Tradability (or the prospect of tradability), which for resource economists may be one of the principal attractions of modern water rights, can be one of the main practical political obstacles to the introduction of such a regime. Indeed, unless the circumstances in which trades can take place, if at all, are carefully regulated from the outset so as to safeguard the interests of the agriculture sector in general and the poor in particular then the introduction of a modern water rights regime may be difficult to achieve. This is not to contradict the findings concerning tradability made earlier in this study but simply to question the extent to which these can be easily translated into the situation of many developing countries.

Questions and Discussion

1. In states whose water law is based on prior appropriation, how would recognition of a right to water change preexisting claims?

2. On October 3, 2008, President Bush signed an agreement, approved by Congress, among the states bordering the Great Lakes, together with the neighboring Canadian provinces, to prevent more distant states from diverting the waters of the lakes. The Great Lakes contain 90 percent of the fresh water of North America. Communities close by the riparian states might obtain access under stringent conditions, but the more arid and distant states of the West will have to live within their water resources. As the populations have grown in Sunbelt desert states like Nevada, Arizona, Utah, and Southern California, there are increasing water pressures. Would a right to water give the populations of these states any claim to Great Lakes water?

3. Some national courts have implied a right to water from constitutional rights guarantees. The Indian Supreme Court has declared that "the right to access to drinking water is fundamental to life and there is a duty on the state under art. 21 to provide clean drinking water to its citizens." *Andhra Pradesh Pollution Control Board-II v. Prof. M.V. Nayudu et al.* [2001] 4 L.R.I. 657. In *Narmada Bachao Andolan v. Union of India*, 2000(7) Scale 34, at

p. 124, the court similarly observed: "Water is the basic need for the survival of human beings and is part of the right to life and human rights as enshrined in art. 21 of the Constitution of India."

4. *See also* ELLI LOUKA, WATER LAW AND POLICY: GOVERNANCE WITHOUT FRONTIERS (2008).

5. Will recognizing a right to water guarantee improved water quality and the ecological balance of hydrographic systems?

IV. Right to Respect for Privacy, Family Life, and Home

As early as 1948, the Universal Declaration of Human Rights recognized:

> No one shall be subjected to arbitrary interference with his privacy, family, home or correspondence. . . .

UDHR, Art. 12. Subsequent human rights treaties have repeated this guarantee, including article 8 of the European Convention on Human Rights.

In the 1980s, applicants in the United Kingdom began invoking article 8 of the European Convention to address issues of noise pollution, in particular from nearby major airports. In *Arrondelle v. United Kingdom*, (1980) 19 D.R. 186; (1982) 26 D.R. 5, the applicant complained of noise from Gatwick Airport and a nearby motorway. The application was declared admissible and eventually settled. *Baggs v. United Kingdom*, (1985) 44 D.R. 13; (1987) 52 D.R. 29, a similar case, was also resolved by friendly settlement. *Powell & Raynor v. United Kingdom*, 1990 Eur.Ct H.R. (ser. A) No. 172, reached the merits. The Court found that aircraft noise from Heathrow Airport constituted a violation of article 8 but was justified under article 8(2) as "necessary in a democratic society" for the economic well-being of the country. Noise was acceptable under the principle of proportionality, if it did not "create an unreasonable burden for the person concerned," a test that could be met by the state if the individual had "the possibility of moving elsewhere without substantial difficulties and losses."

In 2003, a Grand Chamber of the Court considered another challenge to expanding Heathrow's operations, in this case at nighttime, delivering its most extensive examination of the substance and procedure used to balance economic benefits and hardship to individuals. In *Hatton and Others v. United Kingdom*, 2003–VIII Eur. Ct. Hum. Rts. 189 (July 8), the court noted that Heathrow Airport is the busiest airport in Europe and the busiest international airport in the world. Even so, the Court reiterated that "regard must be had to the fair balance that has to be struck between the competing interests of the individual and of the community as a whole. In both contexts the State enjoys a certain margin of appreciation in determining the steps to be taken to ensure compliance with the Convention . . . " (para. 86). The Court added:

99. The Court considers that in a case such as the present one, involving State decisions affecting environmental issues, there are two aspects to the inquiry which may be carried out by the Court. First, the Court may assess the substantive merits of the government's decision, to ensure that it is compatible with Article 8. Secondly, it may scrutinise the decision-making process to ensure that due weight has been accorded to the interests of the individual.

100. In relation to the substantive aspect, the Court has held that the State must be allowed a wide margin of appreciation. In *Powell and Rayner*, for example, it asserted that it was "certainly not for the Commission or the Court to substitute for the assessment of the national authorities any other assessment of what might be the best policy in this difficult

social and technical sphere," namely the regulation of excessive aircraft noise and the means of redress to be provided to the individual within the domestic legal system. The Court continued that "this is an area where the Contracting States are to be recognised as enjoying a wide margin of appreciation" (p. 19, § 44).

101. In other cases involving environmental issues, for example planning cases, the Court has also held that the State must be allowed a wide margin of appreciation. . . .

The Court had no doubt that the implementation of the night flights plan was susceptible of adversely affecting the quality of the applicants' private life and the scope for their enjoying the amenities of their respective homes. The claim thus fell within the rights protected by article 8 of the Convention. However, this case was different from other article 8 claims, because the alleged violation was not predicated on a failure by the national authorities to comply with some aspect of domestic law. The Court explained:

120. . . . This element of domestic irregularity is wholly absent in the present case. The policy on night flights which was set up in 1993 was challenged by the local authorities, and was found, after a certain amount of amendment, to be compatible with domestic law. The applicants do not suggest that the policy (as amended) was in any way unlawful at a domestic level, and indeed they have not exhausted domestic remedies in respect of any such claim. Further, they do not claim that any of the night flights which disturbed their sleep violated the relevant regulations, and again any such claim could have been pursued in the domestic courts under section 76(1) of the Civil Aviation Act 1982.

121. In order to justify the night flight scheme in the form in which it has operated since 1993, the Government refer not only to the economic interests of the operators of airlines and other enterprises as well as their clients, but also, and above all, to the economic interests of the country as a whole. In their submission these considerations make it necessary to impinge, at least to a certain extent, on the Article 8 rights of the persons affected by the scheme. The Court observes that according to the second paragraph of Article 8 restrictions are permitted, *inter alia*, in the interests of the economic well-being of the country and for the protection of the rights and freedoms of others. It is therefore legitimate for the State to have taken the above economic interests into consideration in the shaping of its policy.

122. The Court must consider whether the State can be said to have struck a fair balance between those interests and the conflicting interests of the persons affected by noise disturbances, including the applicants. Environmental protection should be taken into consideration by States in acting within their margin of appreciation and by the Court in its review of that margin, but it would not be appropriate for the Court to adopt a special approach in this respect by reference to a special status of environmental human rights. In this context the Court must revert to the question of the scope of the margin of appreciation available to the State when taking policy decisions of the kind at issue.

. . .

125. Whether in the implementation of that regime the right balance has been struck in substance between the Article 8 rights affected by the regime and other conflicting community interests depends on the relative weight given to each of them. The Court accepts that in this context the authorities were entitled, having regard to the general nature of the measures taken, to rely on statistical data based on average perception of noise disturbance. It notes the conclusion of the 1993 Consultation Paper that due to their small number sleep disturbances caused by aircraft noise could be treated as negligible in comparison to overall normal disturbance rates. However, this does not mean that the concerns of the

people affected were totally disregarded. The very purpose of maintaining a scheme of night flight restrictions was to keep noise disturbance at an acceptable level for the local population living in the area near the airport. Moreover, there was a realisation that in view of changing conditions (increase of air transport, technological advances in noise prevention, development of social attitudes, etc.) the relevant measures had to be kept under constant review.

126. As to the economic interests which conflict with the desirability of limiting or halting night flights in pursuance of the above aims, the Court considers it reasonable to assume that those flights contribute at least to a certain extent to the general economy. The Government have produced to the Court reports on the results of a series of inquiries on the economic value of night flights, carried out both before and after the 1993 Scheme. Even though there are no specific indications about the economic cost of eliminating specific night flights, it is possible to infer from those studies that there is a link between flight connections in general and night flights. . . .

127. A further relevant factor in assessing whether the right balance has been struck is the availability of measures to mitigate the effects of aircraft noise generally, including night noise. A number of measures are referred to above. The Court also notes that the applicants do not contest the substance of the Government's claim that house prices in the areas in which they live have not been adversely affected by the night noise. The Court considers it reasonable, in determining the impact of a general policy on individuals in a particular area, to take into account the individuals' ability to leave the area. Where a limited number of people in an area (2 to 3% of the affected population, according to the 1992 sleep study) are particularly affected by a general measure, the fact that they can, if they choose, move elsewhere without financial loss must be significant to the overall reasonableness of the general measure.

. . .

129. In these circumstances the Court does not find that, in substance, the authorities overstepped their margin of appreciation by failing to strike a fair balance between the right of the individuals affected by those regulations to respect for their private life and home and the conflicting interests of others and of the community as a whole, nor does it find that there have been fundamental procedural flaws in the preparation of the 1993 regulations on limitations for night flights.

130. There has accordingly been no violation of Article 8 of the Convention. . . .

The vote in the Grand Chamber was 12–5. On the issue of article 13 (right to a remedy), the Court agreed with the Chamber that the scope of review by the domestic courts was limited to the classic English public law concepts, such as irrationality, unlawfulness, and patent unreasonableness, and did not at the time allow for consideration of whether the claimed increase in night flights under the 1993 scheme represented a justifiable limitation on the right to respect for the private and family lives or the homes of those who live in the vicinity of Heathrow Airport. In those circumstances, the Court considered that the scope of review by the domestic courts in the case was not sufficient to comply with article 13 on the right of access to justice.

Hatton did not end complaints based on noise pollution. Compare *Ashworth and Others v. U.K.* with *Moreno Gomez v. Spain*, 2004-X Eur. Ct. H.R. 327, 343 (2005). In the Ashworth case, declared inadmissible on January 20, 2004, the applicants complained that the noise caused by low-flying aircraft including aerobatic activity and helicopter training, amounted to an interference with their right to respect for their private and family lives and their homes.

They attempted to distinguish their circumstances from those in *Hatton* in two respects. First, they argued that the economic value of the private airport near Denham was far less than that of Heathrow. Second, they specifically argued diminished property values as a result of the noise. Neither argument was successful. The Court agreed that the noise levels generated by flights at the airport were sufficient to render article 8 applicable. As in *Hatton*, however, the Court noted that there was no failure of compliance with the requirements of domestic law. The Court also reiterated its decision in *Hatton* that it was reasonable to take into consideration the individual's ability to leave the area. Although one applicant asserted that property values had fallen by one-third, the Court pointed to the absence of evidence on this point. Taking these factors into consideration, the Court held the application inadmissible.

In *Moreno Gómez v. Spain*, Application No. 4143/02, Eur. Ct. H.R., 41 EHRR 40 (2005), the applicant succeeded in his claim of noise pollution from 127 bars, pubs, and discotheques near his home. The Court unanimously held that the noise levels were such as to amount to a breach of the rights protected by article 8. The fact that the city council did not enforce its noise abatement measures was seen as contributing to the repeated flouting of the rules that it had established. The fact that the activities in question violated local law was once again a significant factor in the Court's evaluation and holding that no fair balance had been struck. The applicant was awarded her full claim of damages as well as costs and expenses.

Questions and Discussion

1. Does the court reach a fair balance in the *Hatton* case? Should it make a difference whether the applicants moved into their home before night flights were permitted? Do you agree that they can move away without financial loss?

2. Should the government and the European Court have relied on the 1993 study referred to in paragraph 74? Is it relevant that it was commissioned by the British Air Transport industry?

3. Other claims under article 8 have challenged pollution from odors. The following judgment was the first major decision of the European Court of Human Rights on environmental harm as a breach of the right to private life and the home.

López Ostra v. Spain,
Application No. 16798/90 303-C Eur. Ct. H.R. (ser. A). (Dec. 9, 1994)

. . .

7. The town of Lorca has a heavy concentration of leather industries. Several tanneries there, all belonging to a limited company called SACURSA, had a plant for the treatment of liquid and solid waste built with a State subsidy on municipal land twelve metres away from the applicant's home.

8. The plant began to operate in July 1988 without the licence (*licencia*) from the municipal authorities required by Regulation 6 of the 1961 regulations on activities classified as causing nuisance and being unhealthy, noxious and dangerous ("the 1961 regulations"), and without having followed the procedure for obtaining such a licence.

    Owing to a malfunction, its start-up released gas fumes, pestilential smells and contamination, which immediately caused health problems and nuisance to many Lorca people, particularly those living in the applicant's district. The town council evacuated the local residents and rehoused them free of charge in the town centre for the months of July, August and September 1988. In October the applicant and her family returned to their flat and lived there until February 1992.

9. On 9 September 1988, following numerous complaints and in the light of reports from the health authorities and the Environment and Nature Agency (Agencia para el Medio Ambiente y la Naturaleza) for the Murcia region, the town council ordered cessation of one of the plant's activities – the settling of chemical and organic residues in water tanks (*lagunaje*) – while permitting the treatment of waste water contaminated with chromium to continue.

There is disagreement as to what the effects were of this partial shutdown, but it can be seen from the expert opinions and written evidence of 1991, 1992 and 1993, produced before the Commission by the Government and the applicant, that certain nuisances continue and may endanger the health of those living nearby.

B. The Application for Protection of Fundamental Rights

1. *Proceedings in the Murcia Audiencia Territorial*

10. Having attempted in vain to get the municipal authority to find a solution, Mrs. López Ostra lodged an application on 13 October 1988 with the Administrative Division of the Murcia Audiencia Territorial, seeking protection of her fundamental rights (section 1 of Law 62/1978 of 26 December 1978 on the protection of fundamental rights . . .). She complained, inter alia, of an unlawful interference with her home and her peaceful enjoyment of it, a violation of her right to choose freely her place of residence, attacks on her physical and psychological integrity, and infringements of her liberty and her safety (Articles 15, 17 para. 1, 18 para. 2 and 19 of the Constitution) on account of the municipal authorities' passive attitude to the nuisance and risks caused by the waste-treatment plant. She requested the court to order temporary or permanent cessation of its activities.

11. . . . [T]he Audiencia Territorial found against her on 31 January 1989. It held that although the plant's operation could unquestionably cause nuisance because of the smells, fumes and noise, it did not constitute a serious risk to the health of the families living in its vicinity but, rather, impaired their quality of life, though not enough to infringe the fundamental rights claimed. In any case, the municipal authorities, who had taken measures in respect of the plant, could not be held liable. The non-possession of a licence was not an issue to be examined in the special proceedings instituted in this instance, because it concerned a breach of the ordinary law.

[The applicant appealed unsuccessfully to the Supreme Court and the Constitutional Court. – *Eds.*]

. . .

AS TO THE LAW

. . .

II. ALLEGED VIOLATION OF ARTICLE 8 OF THE CONVENTION

44. Mrs. López Ostra first contended that there had been a violation of Article 8 of the Convention, which provides:

> 1. Everyone has the right to respect for his private and family life, his home and his correspondence.

2. There shall be no interference by a public authority with the exercise of this right except such as is in accordance with the law and is necessary in a democratic society in the interests of national security, public safety or the economic well-being of the country, for the prevention of disorder or crime, for the protection of health or morals, or for the protection of the rights and freedoms of others.

The Commission subscribed to this view, while the Government contested it.

. . .

47. Mrs. López Ostra maintained that, despite its partial shutdown on 9 September 1988, the plant continued to emit fumes, repetitive noise and strong smells, which made her family's living conditions unbearable and caused both her and them serious health problems. She alleged in this connection that her right to respect for her home had been infringed.

. . .

51. Naturally, severe environmental pollution may affect individuals' well-being and prevent them from enjoying their homes in such a way as to affect their private and family life adversely, without, however, seriously endangering their health.
Whether the question is analysed in terms of a positive duty on the State – to take reasonable and appropriate measures to secure the applicant's rights under paragraph 1 of Article 8 -, as the applicant wishes in her case, or in terms of an "interference by a public authority" to be justified in accordance with paragraph 2, the applicable principles are broadly similar. In both contexts regard must be had to the fair balance that has to be struck between the competing interests of the individual and of the community as a whole, and in any case the State enjoys a certain margin of appreciation. Furthermore, even in relation to the positive obligations flowing from the first paragraph of Article 8, in striking the required balance the aims mentioned in the second paragraph may be of a certain relevance (see, in particular, the *Rees v. the United Kingdom* judgment of 17 October 1986, Series A no. 106, p. 15, para. 37, and the *Powell and Rayner v. the United Kingdom* judgment of 21 February 1990, Series A no. 172, p. 18, para. 41).

52. It appears from the evidence that the waste-treatment plant in issue was built by SACURSA in July 1988 to solve a serious pollution problem in Lorca due to the concentration of tanneries. Yet as soon as it started up, the plant caused nuisance and health problems to many local people. Admittedly, the Spanish authorities, and in particular the Lorca municipality, were theoretically not directly responsible for the emissions in question. However, as the Commission pointed out, the town allowed the plant to be built on its land and the State subsidised the plant's construction.

53. The town council reacted promptly by rehousing the residents affected, free of charge, in the town centre for the months of July, August and September 1988 and then by stopping one of the plant's activities from 9 September. However, the council's members could not be unaware that the environmental problems continued after this partial shutdown. This was, moreover, confirmed as early as 19 January 1989 by the regional Environment and Nature Agency's report and then by expert opinions in 1991, 1992 and 1993.

54. Mrs. López Ostra submitted that by virtue of the general supervisory powers conferred on the municipality by the 1961 regulations the municipality had a duty to act. In addition, the plant did not satisfy the legal requirements, in particular as regards its location and the failure to obtain a municipal licence.

55. On this issue the Court points out that the question of the lawfulness of the building and operation of the plant has been pending in the Supreme Court since 1991. The Court has consistently held that it is primarily for the national authorities, notably the courts, to interpret and apply domestic law (see, inter alia, the *Casado Coca v. Spain* judgment of 24 February 1994, Series A, no. 285-A, p. 18, para. 43).

At all events, the Court considers that in the present case, even supposing that the municipality did fulfil the functions assigned to it by domestic law, it need only establish whether the national authorities took the measures necessary for protecting the applicant's right to respect for her home and for her private and family life under Article 8 (see, among other authorities and mutatis mutandis, the X *and* Y *v. the Netherlands* judgment of 26 March 1985, Series A no. 91, p. 11, para. 23).

56. It has to be noted that the municipality not only failed to take steps to that end after 9 September 1988 but also resisted judicial decisions to that effect. In the ordinary administrative proceedings instituted by Mrs. López Ostra's sisters-in-law it appealed against the Murcia High Court's decision of 18 September 1991 ordering temporary closure of the plant, and that measure was suspended as a result.

   Other State authorities also contributed to prolonging the situation. On 19 November 1991 Crown Counsel appealed against the Lorca investigating judge's decision of 15 November temporarily to close the plant in the prosecution for an environmental health offence, with the result that the order was not enforced until 27 October 1993.

57. The Government drew attention to the fact that the town had borne the expense of renting a flat in the centre of Lorca, in which the applicant and her family lived from 1 February 1992 to February 1993.

   The Court notes, however, that the family had to bear the nuisance caused by the plant for over three years before moving house with all the attendant inconveniences. They moved only when it became apparent that the situation could continue indefinitely and when Mrs. López Ostra's daughter's paediatrician recommended that they do so. Under these circumstances, the municipality's offer could not afford complete redress for the nuisance and inconveniences to which they had been subjected.

58. Having regard to the foregoing, and despite the margin of appreciation left to the respondent State, the Court considers that the State did not succeed in striking a fair balance between the interest of the town's economic well-being – that of having a waste-treatment plant – and the applicant's effective enjoyment of her right to respect for her home and her private and family life.

There has accordingly been a violation of Article 8.

. . .

IV. APPLICATION OF ARTICLE 50 OF THE CONVENTION

59. Under Article 50,

> If the Court finds that a decision or a measure taken by a legal authority or any other authority of a High Contracting Party is completely or partially in conflict with the obligations arising from the . . . Convention, and if the internal law of the said Party allows only partial reparation to be made for the consequences of this decision or measure, the decision of the Court shall, if necessary, afford just satisfaction to the injured party.

Mrs. López Ostra claimed compensation for damage and reimbursement of costs and expenses.

A. Damage

60. The applicant asserted that the building and operation of a waste-treatment plant next to her home forced her to make radical changes to her way of life. She consequently sought the following sums in reparation of the damage sustained:

(a) 12,180,000 pesetas (ESP) for the distress she suffered from 1 October 1988 to 31 January 1992 while living in her former home;

(b) ESP 3,000,000 for the anxiety caused by her daughter's serious illness;

(c) ESP 2,535,000 for the inconvenience caused from 1 February 1992 by her undesired move;

(d) ESP 7,000,000 for the cost of the new house she was obliged to buy in February 1993 because of the uncertainty of the accommodation provided by the Lorca municipal authorities;

(e) ESP 295,000 for expenses incurred in settling into the new house.

61. The Government considered that these claims were exaggerated. They pointed out that the Lorca municipal authorities had paid the rent for the flat occupied by Mrs. López Ostra and her family in the town centre from 1 February 1992 until she moved into her new house.

62. The Delegate of the Commission found the total sum sought excessive. As regards the pecuniary damage, he considered that while the applicant had theoretically been entitled to claim a new home, she was bound to give her former one in exchange, due allowance being made for any differences in size and characteristics.

63. The Court accepts that Mrs. López Ostra sustained some damage on account of the violation of Article 8. Her old flat must have depreciated and the obligation to move must have entailed expense and inconvenience. On the other hand, there is no reason to award her the cost of her new house since she has kept her former home. Account must be taken of the fact that for a year the municipal authorities paid the rent of the flat occupied by the applicant and her family in the centre of Lorca and that the waste-treatment plant was temporarily closed by the investigating judge on 27 October 1993.

The applicant, moreover, undeniably sustained non-pecuniary damage. In addition to the nuisance caused by the gas fumes, noise and smells from the plant, she felt distress and anxiety as she saw the situation persisting and her daughter's health deteriorating.

The heads of damage accepted do not lend themselves to precise quantification. Making an assessment on an equitable basis in accordance with Article 50, the Court awards Mrs. López Ostra ESP 4,000,000.

B. Costs and Expenses

69. In the light of the criteria laid down in its case-law, the Court considers it equitable to award the applicant ESP 1,500,000 under this head, less the 9,700 French francs paid by the Council of Europe.

Questions and Discussion

1. All international human rights procedures require the applicant to exhaust local remedies. Mrs. López Ostra filed a case in Spanish courts based on the breach of her rights; she did not pursue an administrative remedy under environmental law. Should she have been required to pursue both avenues of possible redress? Does the court indicate what remedies must be exhausted?

2. What might have been the result if the tannery had been operating lawfully under a state license? Would the court still have found a violation? See the *Hatton* case above.

3. Are the remedies in this case adequate? Can the Court issue injunctions? *See* European Convention, art. 41 ("If the Court finds that there has been a violation of the Convention or the protocols thereto, and if the internal law of the High Contracting Party concerned allows only partial reparations to be made, the Court shall, if necessary, afford just satisfaction to the injured party.") If not, is the state simply paying to pollute? *See further* D. SHELTON, REMEDIES IN INTERNATIONAL HUMAN RIGHTS LAW (2d ed. 2004).

4. Note that the Council of Europe's Committee of Ministers oversees compliance with the Court's judgments and insists on general measures to avoid nonrepetition of the violation, as well as payment of any compensation required. The government of Spain reported to the Committee of Ministers that on February 22, 1995, within the time limit set, it had paid the applicant the sum provided for in the judgment and that it had published the judgment and a translation of it. The government added: "In view of the status of the Convention and of the case-law of the Strasbourg organs in Spanish law . . . the Government of Spain is of the opinion that the competent administrative tribunals and municipal authorities will not fail to adapt their practice to the jurisprudence of the Court in the present case." Does this alleviate some of the concern that might arise about the Court's narrow interpretation of its power to issue remedial orders?

5. Could the facts in this case give rise to a claim under article 3, which provides that "no one shall be subjected to torture or to inhuman or degrading treatment or punishment"? Was the pollution serious enough that article 2 could be invoked? What difference does it make? *See Guerra and Others v. Italy*, 1998-I Eur. Ct. Hum. Rts. 210 (1998); Margaret DeMerieux, *Deriving Environmental Rights from the European Convention for the Protection of Human Rights and Fundamental Freedoms*, 21 O.J.L.S. 521, 538–39 (2001); Richard Desgagné, *Integrating Environmental Values into the European Convention on Human Rights*, 89 Am. J. Int'l L. 263, 272–73 (1995).

6. At what point can the European Court take action to halt continuing harm? Note that the European Court, like other international tribunals, has the authority to issue interim or precautionary measures. *See* Rule 39 of the Rules of Court; *cf.* Rule 86 of the Rules of Procedure of the UN Human Rights Committee; Rule 25 of the Rules of Procedure of the Inter-American Commission on Human Rights; article 63(2) of the American Convention on Human Rights. The purpose of the provisions is to avoid possible irreparable damage to the person or persons who present claims. International courts increasingly view such measures as legally binding. *See Mamatkulov & Askarov v. Turkey*, App. Nos. 46827/99 and 46951/99 Eur. Ct. Hum. Rts. (judgment of Feb. 4, 2005), *reprinted in* 44 I.L.M. 759 (2005). Would the facts in López Ostra justify the issuance of interim measures?

7. How much can article 8 contribute to environmental protection? What are the limits on the guarantees afforded to home and family life? The following case explores these questions.

Kyrtatos v. Greece,
2003-VI Eur. Ct. H.R. (May 22)

1. The applicants, who had been granted legal aid, complained, under Article 6 § 1 and Article 8 of the Convention, about the failure of the authorities to comply with two decisions of the Supreme Administrative Court annulling two permits for the construction of buildings near their property. . . .

. . .

2. The applicants were born in 1921 and 1953 respectively and live in Munich. The first applicant is the second applicant's mother.

3. The applicants own real property in the south-eastern part of the Greek island of Tinos, where they spend part of their time. The first applicant is the co-owner of a house and a plot of land on the Ayia Kiriaki-Apokofto peninsula, which is adjacent to a swamp by the coast of Ayios Yiannis.

. . .

4. On 4 December 1985 the prefect of Cyclades redrew the boundaries of the settlement of Ayios Yiannis in the municipality of Dio Horia and of the settlements of Ayia Varvara, Ayios Sostis and Lautaris in the municipality of Triandaru (decision no. 9468/1985). On 6 May 1988 the prefect again redrew the boundaries of the settlements of Ayios Yiannis and Ayios Sostis (decision no. 2400/1988).

5. On 18 March 1993 the town-planning authority of Syros issued building permit no. 620 on the basis of the prefect's decision no. 9468/1985. Another permit (no. 298) had been issued on the same basis by the same authority in 1992.

6. On 21 July 1993 the applicants and the Greek Society for the Protection of the Environment and Cultural Heritage lodged an application for judicial review of the prefect's decisions nos. 9468/1985 and 2400/1988 and of building permit no. 620/1993 with the Supreme Administrative Court. On the same date a second application was lodged by the same persons for judicial review of the prefect's two decisions and of building permit no. 298/1992. The basic argument of the applicants before the Supreme Administrative Court was that the prefect's decisions, and consequently the building permits, were illegal because in the area concerned there was a swamp and Article 24 of the Greek Constitution, which protects the environment, provided that no settlement should be built in such a place.

7. On 10 July 1995 the Supreme Administrative Court considered that the applicants had *locus standi* because they owned property in the area concerned. The court held that it could not review the prefect's decision no. 9468/1985 directly because the application had not been lodged within the time-limit prescribed by law. However, it could review the two building permits issued on the basis of that decision and, in the context of this review, the court was obliged to examine the constitutionality of the prefect's decision. The decision was found to have violated Article 24 of the Constitution, which protects the environment, because the redrawing of the boundaries of the settlements put in jeopardy the swamp in Ayios Yiannis, an important natural habitat for various protected species (such as birds, fishes and sea-turtles). It followed that the building permits were also unlawful and had to be quashed. Moreover, the court quashed the prefect's decision no. 2400/1988 because it had not been published in the Official Gazette in the manner prescribed by law (decisions nos. 3955/1995 and 3956/1995).

8. In 1996 the prefect issued two decisions (nos. DP2315/1996 and DP2316/1996) which excluded the contested buildings from demolition.

9. On 21 April 1997 a special committee of the Supreme Administrative Court found that the authorities had failed to comply with the above decisions. They had not demolished the two buildings constructed on the basis of permits nos. 620/1993 and 298/1992 and had continued issuing building permits in respect of the area that had been included in the settlements further to the unlawful redrawing of the boundaries (minutes no. 6/1997).

. . .

THE LAW

I. ALLEGED VIOLATION OF ARTICLE 6 § 1 OF THE CONVENTION DUE TO THE NON-COMPLIANCE WITH THE JUDGMENTS PRONOUNCED

10. The applicants complained about the failure of the authorities to comply with decisions nos. 3955/1995 and 3956/1995 of the Supreme Administrative Court. They relied on Article 6 § 1 of the Convention[,] which, insofar as relevant, provides:

> In the determination of his civil rights and obligations, . . . everyone is entitled to a fair . . . hearing within a reasonable time by [a] . . . tribunal. . . . "

11. The Government argued that the town-planning authority had taken all the necessary measures to comply with the decisions of the Supreme Administrative Court. In particular, it no longer applied the prefect's decision no. 2400/1988 and had carried out a land-planning study for the area. It was true that the prefect had issued two decisions (nos. DP2315/1996 and DP2316/1996) which excluded the contested buildings from demolition; in this connection the Government submitted that the demolition of the buildings in question was not the only possible way to comply with the decisions of the Supreme Administrative Court. On the contrary, it was admitted both by the relevant legislation and by the general principles of law that the demolition of a building was an extreme measure and had to be avoided, especially when the owner of the building had acted in good faith and had no reason to believe that the building permit on the basis of which construction had taken place would subsequently be annulled. Therefore, the Government concluded that the authorities had complied in substance with decisions nos. 3955/1995 and 3956/1995 of the Supreme Administrative Court.

12. The applicants contested the Government's allegation that the national authorities had complied in substance with the above-mentioned decisions. They were surprised that the Greek Government regarded the exclusion of the contested buildings from demolition as compliance with the annulment of the building permits. They claimed that the only legal consequence of the annulment of the building permits was the demolition of the buildings constructed on the basis of these permits and noted that the Greek authorities had failed to demolish them.

13. The Court reiterates that, according to its established case-law, Article 6 § 1 secures to everyone the right to have any claim relating to his civil rights and obligations brought before a court; in this way it embodies the "right to a court," of which the right of access, namely the right to institute proceedings before courts in civil matters, constitutes one aspect. However, that right would be illusory if a Contracting State's domestic legal system allowed a final, binding judicial decision to remain inoperative to the detriment of one party. Execution of a judgment given by any court must therefore be regarded as an integral part of the "trial" for the purposes of Article 6. Where administrative authorities refuse or fail to comply, or even delay doing so, the guarantees under Article 6 enjoyed by a litigant during the judicial phase of the proceedings are rendered devoid of purpose (see *Hornsby v. Greece*, judgment of 19 March 1997, *Reports of Judgments and Decisions* 1997–II, pp. 510–11, §§ 40–41).

14. In the present case the Court notes that a special committee of the Supreme Administrative Court found that the authorities had failed to comply with its decisions nos. 3955/1995 and 3956/1995. They had not demolished the two buildings constructed on the basis of permits nos. 620/1993 and 298/1992 and had continued issuing building permits in respect of the area that had been included in the settlements further to the unlawful redrawing of the boundaries.

15. Thus, by refraining for more than seven years from taking the necessary measures to comply with two final, enforceable judicial decisions in the present case the Greek authorities deprived the provisions of Article 6 § 1 of the Convention of all useful effect.

There has accordingly been a breach of that Article.

. . .

III. ALLEGED VIOLATION OF ARTICLE 8 OF THE CONVENTION

16. The applicants contended that urban development in the south–eastern part of Tinos had led to the destruction of their physical environment and had affected their life. They relied on Article 8 of the Convention, which provides:

1. Everyone has the right to respect for his private and family life, his home and his correspondence.

2. There shall be no interference by a public authority with the exercise of this right except such as is in accordance with the law and is necessary in a democratic society in the interests of national security, public safety or the economic well-being of the country, for the prevention of disorder or crime, for the protection of health or morals, or for the protection of the rights and

B. The Court's Assessment

17. The Court notes that the applicants' complaint under Article 8 of the Convention may be regarded as comprising two distinct limbs. First, they complained that urban development had destroyed the swamp which was adjacent to their property and that the area where their home was had lost all of its scenic beauty. Second, they complained about the environmental pollution caused by the noises and night-lights emanating from the activities of the firms operating in the area.

18. With regard to the first limb of the applicants' complaint, the Court notes that according to its established case-law, severe environmental pollution may affect individuals' well-being and prevent them from enjoying their homes in such a way as to affect their private and family life adversely, without, however, seriously endangering their health (see *López Ostra v. Spain*, judgment of 9 December 1994, Series A no. 303-C, p. 54, § 51). Yet the crucial element which must be present in determining whether, in the circumstances of a case, environmental pollution has adversely affected one of the rights safeguarded by paragraph 1 of Article 8 is the existence of a harmful effect on a person's private or family sphere and not simply the general deterioration of the environment. Neither Article 8 nor any of the other Articles of the Convention are specifically designed to provide general protection of the environment as such; to that effect, other international instruments and domestic legislation are more pertinent in dealing with this particular aspect.

19. In the present case, even assuming that the environment has been severely damaged by the urban development of the area, the applicants have not brought forward any convincing arguments showing that the alleged damage to the birds and other protected species living in the swamp was of such a nature as to directly affect their own rights under Article 8 § 1 of the Convention. It might have been otherwise if, for instance, the environmental deterioration complained of had consisted in the destruction of a forest area in the vicinity of the applicants' house, a situation which could have affected more directly the applicants' own well-being. To conclude, the Court cannot accept that the interference with the conditions of animal life in the swamp constitutes an attack on the private or family life of the applicants.

20. As regards the second limb of the complaint, the Court is of the opinion that the disturbances coming from the applicants' neighbourhood as a result of the urban development of the area (noises, night-lights, etc.) have not reached a sufficient degree of seriousness to be taken into account for the purposes of Article 8.

21. Having regard to the foregoing, the Court considers that there is no lack of respect for the applicants' private and family life.

There has accordingly been no violation of Article 8.

[In respect to reparations, the Court considered that the applicants "must have suffered feelings of frustration, uncertainty and anxiety as a result of the violations of their rights under the Convention." On an equitable basis, it awarded the first applicant EUR 20,000 and the second applicant EUR 10,000 for the nonpecuniary damage sustained, plus an amount to cover their costs and expenses. – *Eds.*]

PARTLY DISSENTING OPINION OF JUDGE ZAGREBELSKY

I voted against the majority's conclusion that there has been no violation of Article 8 of the Convention. With regret I could not follow the reasoning that convinced the majority of judges to exclude finding any violation of the applicants' private life.

There is no doubt that the environment is not protected as such by the Convention. But at the same time there is no doubt that a degradation of the environment could amount to a violation of a specific right recognised by the Convention (*Powell and Rayner v. the United Kingdom*, judgment of 21 February 1990, Series A no. 172, § 40; *López Ostra v. Spain* (judgment of 9 December 1994, Series A no. 303-C, § 51; *Guerra v. Italy*, judgment of 19 February 1998, *Reports of Judgments and Decisions* 1998-I, § 57).

In the present case it is clear that there was a deterioration in the quality of the environment in which the applicants' house was situated. In particular, it is indisputable that the new urban development has caused damage to the habitat of the fauna which made the swamp area next to the applicants' property near the coast of Ayios Yiannis, exceptionally interesting and agreeable.

In my view, it could hardly be said that the deterioration of the environment did not lead to a corresponding deterioration in the quality of the applicants' life, even without taking into account their special interest in the study of the swamp fauna.

It is obviously difficult to quantify the damage caused to the quality of the applicants' private and family life. But the issue here is whether or not there has been an interference, not how serious the interference was. Certainly we should exclude finding any interference with the applicants' rights if the deterioration concerned is so negligible as to be virtually non-existent. In my view, however, this was not the case. In paragraph 53 the majority accept by way of example that the destruction of a forest bordering the applicants' house could constitute direct interference with private and family life for the purposes of Article 8 of the Convention. I agree, but I see no major difference between the destruction of a forest and the destruction of the extraordinary swampy environment the applicants were able to enjoy near their house.

I am willing to admit that the interference in question was not major, but in my view it is impossible to say that there has been no interference at all. It is true that the importance of the quality of the environment and the growing awareness of that issue cannot lead the Court to go beyond the scope of the Convention. But these factors should induce it to recognise the growing importance of environmental deterioration on people's lives. Such an approach would be perfectly in line with the dynamic interpretation and evolutionary updating of the Convention that the Court currently adopts in many fields.

Article 8 allows even serious and major interferences by the State with the right to private and family life. However, an interference will contravene Article 8 unless it is "in accordance with the law," pursues one or more of the legitimate aims referred to in paragraph 2 and is "necessary in a democratic society" in order to achieve them. In the present case, it is not necessary to examine whether the interference with the applicants' right was necessary and proportionate to the competing economic interests. Here the Court has only to ascertain that, as the Greek courts ruled, the interference was unlawful. Thus, the first and basic condition for the legitimacy of even a minor interference with private or family life has not been fulfilled.

Therefore, I think that the Court should have found a violation of Article 8 of the Convention.

Questions and Discussion

1. Could the foregoing cases have been brought alleging violation of the right to property under article 1 of Protocol No. 1 to the European Convention? That article reads: "Every natural or legal person is entitled to the peaceful enjoyment of his possessions. No one shall be deprived of his possessions except in the public interest and subject to the conditions

provided for by law and by the general principles of international law." *See Buckley v. United Kingdom*, 1996-IV Eur. Ct. H.R. 1271 (1996).

2. The *Kyrtatos* applicants received compensation from the Court for the failure of the authorities to enforce the domestic judgment in their favor. Is that an adequate remedy? What happens to the swamp?

3. Industrial pollution has also been the source of article 8 claims, as the following two cases illustrate. Does the European Court modify its test for a violation in these cases? Note that the *Taşkın* case was decided after a major environmental disaster involving gold mining in Europe. On January 30, 2000, an earth dam impounding gold-mine wastes failed, releasing an estimated one hundred thousand cubic meters of cyanide-contaminated slurry to the Szamos River and then through the Tisza River to the Danube and the Black Sea, leaving a trail of ecological destruction. The Australian and Romanian government-owned venture used an extraction process in which cyanide separated gold from tailings.

Taşkın et al. v. Turkey,
App. No. 46117/99 Eur. Ct. H.R., 2004-X Reports of Judgments and Decisions
(Nov. 10)

. . .

11. The case concerns the granting of permits to operate a gold mine in Ovacýk, in the district of Bergama (İzmir). The applicants live in Bergama and the surrounding villages. . . .

12. The applicants alleged that, as a result of the Ovacýk gold mine's development and operations, they had suffered and continued to suffer the effects of environmental damage; specifically, these include the movement of people and noise pollution caused by the use of machinery and explosives.

. . .

THE LAW

II. ON THE ALLEGED VIOLATION OF ARTICLE 8 OF THE CONVENTION

103. The applicants alleged that both the national authorities' decision to issue a permit to use a cyanidation operating process in a gold mine and the related decision-making process had given rise to a violation of their rights guaranteed by Article 8 of the Convention. . . .

Applicability of Article 8

111. The Court notes, firstly, that the applicants live in Dikili and in the villages of Çamköy and Süleymaniye, localities situated near the Ovacýk gold mine, where gold is extracted by sodium cyanide leaching.

112. Several reports have highlighted the risks posed by the gold mine. On the basis of those reports, the Supreme Administrative Court concluded on 13 May 1997 that the decision to issue a permit had not been compatible with the public interest.

    It found that, given the gold mine's geographical location and the geological features of the region, the use of sodium cyanide in the mine represented a threat to the environment and the right to life of the neighbouring population, and that the safety measures which the company had undertaken to implement did not suffice to eliminate the risks involved in such an activity.

. . .

114. In view of the Supreme Administrative Court's finding in its judgment of 13 May 1997, the Court concludes that Article 8 is applicable.

Compliance with Article 8

. . .

a) The Substantive Aspect

116. The Court has repeatedly stated that in cases raising environmental issues the State must be allowed a wide margin of appreciation (see *Hatton and Others*, cited above, § 100, and *Buckley v. the United Kingdom*, judgment of 25 September 1996, *Reports of Judgments and Decisions* 1996-IV, §§ 74–77).

117. In the instant case, the Court notes that the authorities' decision to issue a permit to the Ovacýk gold mine was annulled by the Supreme Administrative Court. After weighing the competing interests in the present case against each other, the latter based its decision on the applicants' effective enjoyment of the right to life and the right to a healthy environment and concluded that the permit did not serve the public interest (*ibid*). In view of that conclusion, no other examination of the material aspect of the case with regard to the margin of appreciation generally allowed to the national authorities in this area is necessary. Consequently, it remains for the Court to verify whether, taken as a whole, the decision-making process was conducted in a manner which complied with the procedural guarantees in Article 8.

b) The Procedural Aspect

118. The Court reiterates that, according to its settled case-law, whilst Article 8 contains no explicit procedural requirements, the decision-making process leading to measures of inter-ference must be fair and such as to afford due respect to the interests of the individual as safeguarded by Article 8 (see, *mutatis mutandis*, *McMichael v. the United Kingdom*, judgment of 24 February 1995, Series A No. 307-B, p. 55, § 87). It is therefore necessary to consider all the procedural aspects, including the type of policy or decision involved, the extent to which the views of individuals were taken into account throughout the decision-making process, and the procedural safeguards available (see *Hatton and Others*, cited above, § 104). However, this does not mean that decisions can only be taken if comprehensive and measurable data are available in relation to each and every aspect of the matter to be decided.

119. Where a State must determine complex issues of environmental and economic policy, the decision-making process must firstly involve appropriate investigations and studies in order to allow them to predict and evaluate in advance the effects of those activities which might damage the environment and infringe individuals' rights and to enable them to strike a fair balance between the various conflicting interests at stake (see *Hatton and Others*, cited above, § 128). The importance of public access to the conclusions of such studies and to information which would enable members of the public to assess the danger to which they are exposed is beyond question (see, *mutatis mutandis*, *Guerra and Others v. Italy*, judgment of 19 February 1998, *Reports* 1998-I, p. 223, § 60, and *McGinley and Egan v. the United Kingdom*, judgment of 9 June 1998, *Reports* 1998-III, p. 1362, § 97). Lastly, the individuals concerned must also be able to appeal to the courts against any decision, act or omission where they consider that their interests or their comments have not been given sufficient weight in the decision-making process (see, *mutatis mutandis*, *Hatton and Others*, cited above, § 127).

120. In the instant case, the decision to issue a permit to the Ovacýk gold mine, taken on 19 October 1994 by the Ministry of the Environment, was preceded by a series of investigations and studies carried out over a long period. An impact report was drawn up in accordance with section 10 of the Environment Act. On 26 October 1992 a public information meeting was held for the region's inhabitants. During that meeting, the impact study was brought

to the public's attention and participants had an opportunity to present their comments. The applicants and the inhabitants of the region had access to all the relevant documents, including the report in question.

121. When, on 13 May 1997, the Supreme Administrative Court, acting on an application for judicial review, annulled the decision of 19 October 1994, it cited the State's positive obligation concerning the right to life and the right to a healthy environment. Referring to the conclusions of the impact study and the other reports, it held that, due to the gold mine's geographical location and the geological features of the region, the operating permit did not serve the general interest; those studies had outlined the danger of the use of sodium cyanide for the local ecosystem, and human health and safety.

122. The judgment of 13 May 1997 became enforceable at the latest after being served on 20 October 1997; however, the Ovacýk gold mine was not ordered to close until 27 February 1998, i.e. ten months after the delivery of that judgment and four months after it had been served on the authorities.

123. As to the Government's argument that the authorities had complied fully with judicial decisions after 1 April 1998, it does not stand up to scrutiny. Firstly, the long dispute concerning the lawfulness of the permits issued by various ministries following the Prime Minister's intervention on 1 April 2000 was caused solely by the authorities' refusal to comply with the courts' decisions and with the domestic legislation. In fact, in the light of Paragraph 6 of the regulations on impact reports, those permits could have no legal basis in the absence of a decision, based on an impact report, to issue authorisation. Furthermore, no mention is made of any new decision that would replace the decision set aside by the courts.

   Moreover, this argument by the Government has never been accepted by those domestic courts which have been called upon to rule on the lawfulness of subsequent decisions.

124. The Court would emphasise that the administrative authorities form one element of a State subject to the rule of law, and that their interests coincide with the need for the proper administration of justice. Where administrative authorities refuse or fail to comply, or even delay doing so, the guarantees enjoyed by a litigant during the judicial phase of the proceedings are rendered devoid of purpose (see, *mutatis mutandis*, *Hornsby v. Greece*, judgment of 19 March 1997, *Reports* 1997-II, pp. 510–511, § 41).

125. This finding appears all the more necessary in that the circumstances of the case clearly demonstrate that, notwithstanding the procedural guarantees afforded by Turkish legislation and the implementation of those guarantees by judicial decisions, the Council of Ministers, by a decision of 29 March 2002 which was not made public, authorised the continuation of production at the gold mine, which had already begun to operate in April 2001. In so doing, the authorities deprived the procedural guarantees available to the applicants of any useful effect.

c) Conclusion

126. The Court finds, therefore, that the respondent State did not fulfil its obligation to secure the applicants' right to respect for their private and family life, in breach of Article 8 of the Convention. There has consequently been a violation of that provision.

Questions and Discussion

1. The Court also found a violation of article 6(1) resulting from the Turkish authorities' refusal to comply with the judgments of the administrative courts but found it unnecessary to address the complaints based on articles 2 and 13. The Court awarded the applicants EUR

3,000 each in moral damages. The procedural aspects of environmental rights, discussed in this case, are the topic of Chapter 6.

2. What is *Taskin* about? Is it a human rights case, an environmental case, or a rule-of-law case? If it is a human rights case, is it about privacy and home life?

Fadeyeva v. Russia, 2005-IV Eur. Ct. Hum. Rts., App No. 55723/00, Rep. Judgments & Decisions (June 9)

. . .

10. The applicant was born in 1949 and lives in the town of Cherepovets, an important steel-producing centre approximately 300 kilometres north-east of Moscow. In 1982 her family moved to a flat situated at 1 Zhukov Street, approximately 450 metres from the site of the Severstal steel plant ("the plant"). This flat was provided by the plant to the applicant's husband, Mr. Nikolay Fadeyev, under a tenancy agreement.

11. The plant was built during the Soviet era and was owned by the Ministry of Black Metallurgy of the Russian Soviet Federative Socialist Republic (RSFSR). The plant was, and remains, the largest iron smelter in Russia and the main employer for approximately 60,000 people. In order to delimit the areas in which the pollution caused by steel production might be excessive, the authorities established a buffer zone around the Severstal premises – "the sanitary security zone." This zone was first delimited in 1965. It covered a 5,000-metre-wide area around the site of the plant. Although this zone was, in theory, supposed to separate the plant from the town's residential areas, in practice thousands of people (including the applicant's family) lived there. The blocks of flats in the zone belonged to the plant and were designated mainly for its workers, who occupied the flats as life-long tenants. A decree of the Council of Ministers of the RSFSR, dated 10 September 1974, imposed on the Ministry of Black Metallurgy the obligation to resettle the inhabitants of the sanitary security zone who lived in districts nos. 213 and 214 by 1977. However, this has not been done.

12. In 1990 the government of the RSFSR adopted a programme "On improving the environmental situation in Cherepovets." The programme stated that "the concentration of toxic substances in the town's air exceed[ed] the acceptable norms many times" and that the morbidity rate of Cherepovets residents was higher than the average. It was noted that many people still lived within the steel plant's sanitary security zone. Under the programme, the steel plant was required to reduce its toxic emissions to safe levels by 1998. The programme listed a number of specific technological measures to attain this goal. The steel plant was also ordered to finance the construction of 20,000 square metres of residential property every year for the resettlement of people living within its sanitary security zone.

14. In 1993 the steel plant was privatised and acquired by Severstal PLC. In the course of the privatisation the blocks of flats owned by the steel plant that were situated within the zone were transferred to the municipality.

15. On 3 October 1996 the government of the Russian Federation adopted Decree no. 1161 on the special federal programme "Improvement of the environmental situation and public health in Cherepovets" for the period from 1997 to 2010" (in 2002 this programme was replaced by the special federal programme "Russia's ecology and natural resources"). Implementation of the 1996 programme was funded by the World Bank.

The decree . . . stated that "the environmental situation in the city ha[d] resulted in a continuing deterioration in public health." In particular, it stated that over the period from 1991 to 1995 the number of children with respiratory diseases increased from 345 to 945 cases per thousand, those with blood and haematogenic diseases from 3.4 to 11 cases per thousand, and those with skin diseases from 33.3 to 101.1 cases per thousand. The decree also noted that the high level of atmospheric pollution accounted for the increase in respiratory and blood diseases among the city's adult population and the increased number of deaths from cancer.

16. Most of the measures proposed in the programme concerned the functioning of the Severstal steel plant. The decree also enumerated a number of measures concerning the city as a whole: these included the resettlement of 18,900 people from Severstal's sanitary security zone. . . .

17. . . .

18. In 2001 implementation of the 1996 government programme was discontinued and the measures proposed in it were included in the corresponding section of the sub-programme "Regulation of environmental quality" in the special federal programme "Russia's ecology and natural resources (2002–2010)."

19. According to a letter from the mayor of Cherepovets dated 3 June 2004, in 1999 the plant was responsible for more than 95% of industrial emissions into the town's air. According to the State Report on the Environment for 1999, the Severstal plant in Cherepovets was the largest contributor to air pollution of all metallurgical plants in Russia.

[The applicant filed two sets of domestic legal proceedings seeking to be relocated away from the Severstal steel plant. Both proceedings were dismissed. – *Eds.*]

      . . .

THE LAW

I. ALLEGED VIOLATION OF ARTICLE 8 OF THE CONVENTION

64. The applicant alleged that there had been a violation of Article 8 of the Convention on account of the State's failure to protect her private life and home from severe environmental nuisance arising from the industrial activities of the Severstal steel plant. . . .

      . . .

79. The Court reiterates at the outset that, in assessing evidence, the general principle has been to apply the standard of proof "beyond reasonable doubt." Such proof may follow from the coexistence of sufficiently strong, clear and concordant inferences or of similar unrebutted presumptions of fact. It should also be noted that it has been the Court's practice to allow flexibility in this respect, taking into consideration the nature of the substantive right at stake and any evidentiary difficulties involved. In certain instances, only the respondent Government [has] access to information capable of corroborating or refuting the applicant's allegations; consequently, a rigorous application of the principle *affirmanti, non neganti, incumbit probatio* is impossible (see *Aktaş v. Turkey*, no. 24351/94, § 272, ECHR 2003-V).

80. Turning to the particular circumstances of the case, the Court observes that, in the applicant's submission, her health has deteriorated as a result of living near the steel plant. The only medical document produced by the applicant in support of this claim is a report drawn up by a clinic in St Petersburg. The Court finds that this report did not establish any causal link between environmental pollution and the applicant's illnesses. The applicant presented no other medical evidence which would clearly connect her state of health to high pollution levels at her place of residence.

81. The applicant also submitted a number of official documents confirming that, since 1995 (the date of her first recourse to the courts), environmental pollution at her place of residence has constantly exceeded safe levels. According to the applicant, these documents proved that any person exposed to such pollution levels inevitably suffered serious damage to his or her health and well-being.

82. With regard to this allegation, the Court bears in mind, firstly, that the Convention came into force with respect to Russia on 5 May 1998. Therefore, only the period after this date can be taken into consideration in assessing the nature and extent of the alleged interference with the applicant's private sphere.

83. According to the materials submitted to the Court, since 1998 the pollution levels with respect to a number of rated parameters have exceeded the domestic norms. Thus, the data produced by the Government confirm that during the period from 1999 to 2003 the concentration of dust, carbon disulphide and formaldehyde in the air near the applicant's home constantly exceeded the MPLs [maximum permissible limits]. In 1999 the concentration of dust was 1.76 times higher than the MPL, and in 2003 it was 1.13 times higher. In 1999 the concentration of carbon disulphide was 3.74 times higher than the MPL; in 2003 the concentration of this substance had fallen but was still 1.12 times higher than the MPL. The concentration of formaldehyde was 4.53 times higher than the MPL. In 2003 it was 6.3 times higher than the MPL. Moreover, an over-concentration of various other substances, such as manganese, benzopyrene and sulphur dioxide, was recorded during this period.

84. The Court observes further that the figures produced by the Government reflect only annual averages and do not disclose daily or maximum pollution levels. According to the Government's own submissions, the maximum concentrations of pollutants registered near the applicant's home were often ten times higher than the average annual concentrations (which were already above safe levels). The Court also notes that the Government [has] not explained why they failed to produce the documents and reports sought by the Court, although these documents were certainly available to the national authorities. Therefore, the Court concludes that the environmental situation could, at certain times, have been even worse than it appears from the available data.

85. The Court notes further that on many occasions the State recognised that the environmental situation in Cherepovets caused an increase in the morbidity rate for the city's residents. The reports and official documents produced by the applicant, and, in particular, the report by Dr. Mark Chernaik, described the adverse effects of pollution on all residents of Cherepovets, especially those who lived near the plant. Thus, according to the data provided by both parties, during the entire period under consideration the concentration of formaldehyde in the air near the applicant's home was three to six times higher than the safe levels. . . .

86. Finally, the Court pays special attention to the fact that the domestic courts in the present case recognised the applicant's right to be resettled. Admittedly, the effects of pollution on the applicant's private life were not at the heart of the domestic proceedings. However, as follows from the Vologda Regional Court's decision in *Ledyayeva*, it was not contested that the pollution caused by the Severstal facilities called for resettlement in a safer area. Moreover, domestic legislation itself defined the zone in which the applicant's home was situated as unfit for habitation. Therefore, it can be said that the existence of interference with the applicant's private sphere was taken for granted at the domestic level.

87. In summary, the Court observes that over a significant period of time the concentration of various toxic elements in the air near the applicant's home seriously exceeded the MPLs. The Russian legislation defines MPLs as safe concentrations of toxic elements. Consequently, where the MPLs are exceeded, the pollution becomes potentially harmful to the health and well-being of those exposed to it. This is a presumption, which may not be true in a particular case. The same may be noted about the reports produced by the applicant: it is conceivable that, despite the excessive pollution and its proved negative effects on the population as a whole, the applicant did not suffer any special and extraordinary damage.

88. In the instant case, however, the very strong combination of indirect evidence and pre-sumptions makes it possible to conclude that the applicant's health deteriorated as a result of her prolonged exposure to the industrial emissions from the Severstal steel plant. Even assuming that the pollution did not cause any quantifiable harm to her health, it inevitably made the applicant more vulnerable to various illnesses. Moreover, there can be no doubt that it adversely affected her quality of life at home. Therefore, the Court accepts that the actual detriment to the applicant's health and well-being reached a level sufficient to bring it within the scope of Article 8 of the Convention.

. . .

Justification Under Article 8 § 2

1. General Principles

94. The Court reiterates that whatever analytical approach is adopted – the breach of a positive duty or direct interference by the State – the applicable principles regarding justification under Article 8 § 2 as to the balance between the rights of an individual and the interests of the community as a whole are broadly similar (see *Keegan v. Ireland*, judgment of 26 May 1994, Series A no. 290, p. 19, § 49).

95. Direct interference by the State with the exercise of Article 8 rights will not be compatible with paragraph 2 unless it is "in accordance with the law." The breach of domestic law in these cases would necessarily lead to a finding of a violation of the Convention.

96. However, where the State is required to take positive measures, the choice of means is in principle a matter that falls within the Contracting State's margin of appreciation. There are different avenues to ensure "respect for private life," and even if the State has failed to apply one particular measure provided by domestic law, it may still fulfil its positive duty by other means. Therefore, in those cases the criterion "in accordance with the law" of the justification test cannot be applied in the same way as in cases of direct interference by the State.

97. The Court notes, at the same time, that in all previous cases in which environmental questions gave rise to violations of the Convention, the violation was predicated on a failure by the national authorities to comply with some aspect of the domestic legal regime. Thus, in *López Ostra* the waste-treatment plant in issue was illegal in that it operated without the necessary licence, and it was eventually closed down (*López Ostra*, cited above, pp. 46–47, §§ 16–22). In *Guerra and Others* too, the violation was founded on an irregular position at the domestic level, as the applicants had been unable to obtain information that the State was under a statutory obligation to provide (*Guerra and Others*, cited above, p. 219, §§ 25–27). In *S. v. France* (no. 13728/88, Commission decision of 17 May 1990, Decisions and Reports 65, p. 263), the internal legality was also taken into consideration.

98. Thus, in cases where an applicant complains about the State's failure to protect his or her Convention rights, domestic legality should be approached not as a separate and conclusive test, but rather as one of many aspects which should be taken into account in assessing whether the State has struck a "fair balance" in accordance with Article 8 § 2.

2. Legitimate Aim

99. Where the State is required to take positive measures in order to strike a fair balance between the interests of an individual and the community as a whole, the aims mentioned in the second paragraph of Article 8 may be of a certain relevance, although this provision refers only to "interferences" with the right protected by the first paragraph – in other words, it is concerned with the negative obligations flowing therefrom (see *Rees v. the United Kingdom*, judgment of 17 October 1986, Series A no. 106, p. 15, § 37).

100. The Court observes that the essential justification offered by the Government for the refusal to resettle the applicant was the protection of the interests of other residents of Cherepovets who were entitled to free housing under the domestic legislation. In the Government's submissions, since the municipality had only limited resources to build new housing for social purposes, the applicant's immediate resettlement would inevitably breach the rights of others on the waiting list.

101. Further, the Government referred, at least in substance, to the economic well-being of the country. Like the Government, the Court considers that the continuing operation of the steel plant in question contributed to the economic system of the Vologda region and, to that extent, served a legitimate aim within the meaning of paragraph 2 of Article 8 of the Convention. It remains to be determined whether, in pursuing this aim, the authorities have struck a fair balance between the interests of the applicant and those of the community as a whole.

"Necessary in a democratic society"

(a) General Principles

102. The Court reiterates that, in deciding what is necessary for achieving one of the aims mentioned in Article 8 § 2 of the Convention, a margin of appreciation must be left to the national authorities, who are in principle better placed than an international court to evaluate local needs and conditions. While it is for the national authorities to make the initial assessment of necessity, the final evaluation as to whether the justification given by the State is relevant and sufficient remains subject to review by the Court (see, among other authorities, *Lustig-Prean and Beckett v. the United Kingdom*, nos. 31417/96 and 32377/96, §§ 80–81, 27 September 1999).

103. In recent decades environmental pollution has become a matter of growing public concern. As a consequence, States have adopted various measures in order to reduce the adverse effects of industrial activities. When assessing these measures from the standpoint of Article 1 of Protocol No. 1, the Court has, as a rule, accepted that the States have a wide margin of appreciation in the sphere of environmental protection. Thus, in 1991 in *Fredin v. Sweden (no. 1)* (judgment of 18 February 1991, Series A no. 192, p. 16, § 48) the Court recognised that "in today's society the protection of the environment is an increasingly important consideration," and held that the interference with a private property right (revoking the applicant's licence to extract gravel from his property on the ground of nature conservation) was not inappropriate or disproportionate in the context of Article 1 of Protocol No. 1. Later that year, in *Pine Valley Developments Ltd and Others v. Ireland* (judgment of 29 November 1991, Series A no. 222), the Court confirmed this approach.

104. In another group of cases where the State's failure to act was in issue, the Court has also preferred to refrain from revising domestic environmental policies. In a recent Grand Chamber judgment, the Court held that "it would not be appropriate for the Court to adopt a special approach in this respect by reference to a special status of environmental human rights" (see *Hatton and Others*, cited above, § 122). In an earlier case the Court held that "it is certainly not for . . . the Court to substitute for the national authorities any other assessment of what might be best policy in this difficult technical and social sphere. This is an area where the Contracting Parties are to be recognised as enjoying a wide margin of appreciation" (see *Powell and Rayner*, cited above, p. 19, § 44).

105. It remains open to the Court to conclude that there has been a manifest error of appreciation by the national authorities in striking a fair balance between the competing interests of different private actors in this sphere. However, the complexity of the issues involved with

regard to environmental protection renders the Court's role primarily a subsidiary one. The Court must first examine whether the decision-making process was fair and such as to afford due respect to the interests safeguarded to the individual by Article 8 (see *Buckley v. the United Kingdom*, judgment of 25 September 1996, *Reports* 1996-IV, pp. 1292–93, §§ 76–77), and only in exceptional circumstances may it go beyond this line and revise the material conclusions of the domestic authorities (see *Taşkın and Others v. Turkey*, no. 46117/99, § 117, ECHR 2004-X).

. . .

The Court's assessment

(i) The Alleged Failure to Resettle the Applicant

116. The Court notes at the outset that the environmental consequences of the Severstal steel plant's operation are not compatible with the environmental and health standards established in the relevant Russian legislation. In order to ensure that a large undertaking of this type remains in operation, Russian legislation, as a compromise solution, has provided for the creation of a buffer zone around the undertaking's premises in which pollution may officially exceed safe levels. Therefore, the existence of such a zone is a condition *sine qua non* for the operation of an environmentally hazardous undertaking – otherwise it must be closed down or significantly restructured.

117. The main purpose of the sanitary security zone is to separate residential areas from the sources of pollution and thus to minimise the negative effects thereof on the neighbouring population. The Government [has] shown that, in the course of the past twenty years, overall emissions from the Severstal steel plant have been significantly reduced, and this trend can only be welcomed. However, within the entire period under consideration (since 1998), pollution levels with respect to a number of dangerous substances have continued to exceed the safe levels. Consequently, it would only be possible for the Severstal plant to operate in conformity with the domestic environmental standards if this zone, separating the undertaking from the residential areas of the town, continued to exist and served its purpose.

118. The parties argue as to the actual size of the zone. In their later post-admissibility observations and oral submissions to the Court, the Government denied that the applicant lived within its boundaries. However, in their initial observations the Government openly stated that the applicant's home was located within the zone. The fact that the Severstal steel plant's sanitary security zone included residential areas of the town was confirmed in the federal programme of 1996. As regards the applicant's home in particular, the fact that it was located within the steel plant's sanitary security zone was not disputed in the domestic proceedings and was confirmed by the domestic authorities on many occasions. The status of the zone was challenged only after the application had been communicated to the respondent Government. Therefore, the Court assumes that during the period under consideration the applicant lived within Severstal's sanitary security zone.

119. The Government further submitted that the pollution levels attributable to the metallurgic industry were the same if not higher in other districts of Cherepovets than those registered near the applicant's home. However, this proves only that the Severstal steel plant has failed to comply with domestic environmental norms and suggests that a wider sanitary security zone should perhaps have been required. In any event, this argument does not affect the Court's conclusion that the applicant lived in a special zone where the industrial pollution exceeded safe levels and where any housing was in principle prohibited by the domestic legislation.

120. It is material that the applicant moved to this location in 1982 knowing that the environmental situation in the area was very unfavourable. However, given the shortage of housing at that time and the fact that almost all residential buildings in industrial towns belonged to the State, it is very probable that the applicant had no choice other than to accept the flat offered to her family. Moreover, due to the relative scarcity of environmental information at that time, the applicant may have underestimated the seriousness of the pollution problem in her neighbourhood. It is also important that the applicant obtained the flat lawfully from the State, which could not have been unaware that the flat was situated within the steel plant's sanitary security zone and that the ecological situation was very poor. Therefore, it cannot be claimed that the applicant herself created the situation complained of or was somehow responsible for it.

121. It is also relevant that it became possible in the 1990s to rent or buy residential property without restrictions, and the applicant has not been prevented from moving away from the dangerous area. In this respect the Court observes that the applicant was renting the flat at 1 Zhukov Street from the local council as a life-long tenant. The conditions of her rent were much more favourable than those she would find on the free market. Relocation to another home would imply considerable financial outlay[,] which, in her situation, would be almost unfeasible, her only income being a State pension plus payments related to her occupational disease. The same may be noted regarding the possibility of buying another flat, mentioned by the respondent Government. Although it is theoretically possible for the applicant to change her personal situation, in practice this would appear to be very difficult. Accordingly, this point does not deprive the applicant of the status required in order to claim to be a victim of a violation of the Convention within the meaning of Article 34, although it may, to a certain extent, affect the scope of the Government's positive obligations in the present case.

122. The Court observes that Russian legislation directly prohibits the building of any residential property within a sanitary security zone. However, the law does not clearly indicate what should be done with those persons who already live within such a zone. The applicant insisted that the Russian legislation required immediate resettlement of the residents of such zones and that resettlement should be carried out at the expense of the polluting undertaking. However, the national courts interpreted the law differently. The Cherepovets City Court's decisions of 1996 and 1999 established that the polluting undertaking is not responsible for resettlement; the legislation provides only for placing the residents of the zone on the general waiting list. The same court dismissed the applicant's claim for reimbursement of the cost of resettlement. In the absence of any direct requirement of immediate resettlement, the Court does not find this reading of the law absolutely unreasonable. Against the above background, the Court is ready to accept that the only solution proposed by the national law in this situation was to place the applicant on a waiting list. Thus, the Russian legislation as applied by the domestic courts and national authorities makes no difference between those persons who are entitled to new housing, free of charge, on a welfare basis (war veterans, large families, etc.) and those whose everyday life is seriously disrupted by toxic fumes from a neighbouring plant.

123. The Court further notes that, since 1999, when the applicant was placed on the waiting list, her situation has not changed. Moreover, as the applicant rightly pointed out, there is no hope that this measure will result in her resettlement from the zone in the foreseeable future. The resettlement of certain families from the zone by Severstal PLC is a matter of the plant's good faith, and cannot be relied upon. Therefore, the measure applied by the domestic courts makes no difference to the applicant: it does not give her any realistic hope of being removed from the source of pollution.

(ii) The Alleged Failure to Regulate Private Industry

124. Recourse to the measures sought by the applicant before the domestic courts (urgent reset-tlement or reimbursement of the resettlement costs) is not necessarily the only remedy to the situation complained of. The Court points out that "the choice of the means calculated to secure compliance with Article 8 in the sphere of the relations of individuals between themselves is in principle a matter that falls within the Contracting States' margin of appre-ciation. In this connection, there are different ways of ensuring 'respect for private life,' and the nature of the States obligation will depend on the particular aspect of private life that is at issue" (see X *and* Y *v. the Netherlands*, judgment of 26 March 1985, Series A no. 91, p. 12, § 24). In the present case the State had at its disposal a number of other tools capable of preventing or minimising pollution, and the Court may examine whether, in adopting measures of a general character, the State complied with its positive duties under the Convention.

125. In this respect the Court notes that, according to the Government's submissions, the environmental pollution caused by the steel plant has been significantly reduced over the past twenty years. Since the 1970s, air quality in the town has changed for the better. Thus, when the applicant's family moved into the flat in issue in 1982, the overall atmospheric pollution in Cherepovets was more than twice as high as in 2003. Since 1980 toxic emissions from the Severstal steel plant into the town's air have been reduced from 787.7 to 333.2 thousand tonnes. Following the enactment of the 1996 federal programme, the annual overall emissions of air polluting substances attributable to the Severstal facilities have been reduced by 5.7%. The report submitted by the Government indicated that by 2003 the average concentration of certain toxic elements in the air of the town had been significantly reduced; the proportion of "unsatisfactory tests" of the air around the Severstal plant had fallen in the past five years.

126. At the same time, the Court observes that the implementation of the 1990 and 1996 federal programmes did not achieve the expected results: in 2003 the concentration of a number of toxic substances in the air near the plant still exceeded safe levels. Whereas, according to the 1990 programme, the steel plant was obliged to reduce its toxic emissions to a safe level by 1998, in 2004 the chief sanitary inspector admitted that this had not been done and that the new deadline for bringing the plant's emissions below dangerous levels was henceforth 2015.

127. Undoubtedly, significant progress has been made in reducing emissions over the past ten to twenty years. However, if only the period within the Court's competence *ratione temporis* is taken into account, the overall improvement of the environmental situation would appear to be very slow. Moreover, as the Government's report shows, the dynamics with respect to a number of toxic substances are not constant and in certain years pollution levels increased rather than decreased.

128. It might be argued that, given the complexity and scale of the environmental problem around the Severstal steel plant, it cannot be resolved in a short period of time. Indeed, it is not the Court's task to determine what exactly should have been done in the present situation to reduce pollution in a more efficient way. However, it is certainly within the Court's jurisdiction to assess whether the Government approached the problem with due diligence and gave consideration to all the competing interests. In this respect the Court reiterates that the onus is on the State to justify, using detailed and rigorous data, a situation in which certain individuals bear a heavy burden on behalf of the rest of the commu-nity. Looking at the present case from this perspective, the Court notes the following points.

129. The Government referred to a number of studies carried out in order to assess the envi-ronmental situation around the Cherepovets steel plant. However, the Government [has]

failed to produce these documents or to explain how they influenced policy in respect of the plant, particularly the conditions attached to the plant's operating permit. The Court also notes that the Government did not provide a copy of the plant's operating permit and did not specify how the interests of the population residing around the steel plant were taken into account when the conditions attached to the permit were established.

130. The Government submitted that, during the period under consideration, Severstal PLC was subjected to various checks and administrative penalties for different breaches of environmental law. However, the Government did not specify which sanctions had been applied and the type of breaches concerned. Consequently, it is impossible to assess to what extent these sanctions could really induce Severstal to take the necessary measures for environmental protection.

131. The Court considers that it is not possible to make a sensible analysis of the Government's policy *vis-à-vis* Severstal because they have failed to show clearly what this policy consisted of. In these circumstances, the Court has to draw an adverse inference. In view of the materials before it, the Court cannot conclude that, in regulating the steel plant's industrial activities, the authorities gave due weight to the interests of the community living in close proximity to its premises.

132. In sum, the Court finds the following. The State authorised the operation of a polluting plant in the middle of a densely populated town. Since the toxic emissions from this plant exceeded the safe limits established by the domestic legislation and might endanger the health of those living nearby, the State established through legislation that a certain area around the plant should be free of any dwelling. However, these legislative measures were not implemented in practice.

133. It would be going too far to assert that the State or the polluting undertaking were under an obligation to provide the applicant with free housing and, in any event, it is not the Court's role to dictate precise measures which should be adopted by the States in order to comply with their positive duties under Article 8 of the Convention. In the present case, however, although the situation around the plant called for a special treatment of those living within the zone, the State did not offer the applicant any effective solution to help her move away from the dangerous area. Furthermore, although the polluting plant in issue operated in breach of domestic environmental standards, there is no indication that the State designed or applied effective measures which would take into account the interests of the local population, affected by the pollution, and which would be capable of reducing the industrial pollution to acceptable levels.

134. The Court concludes that, despite the wide margin of appreciation left to the respondent State, it has failed to strike a fair balance between the interests of the community and the applicant's effective enjoyment of her right to respect for her home and her private life. There has accordingly been a violation of Article 8 of the Convention.

Questions and Discussion

1. The Court awarded the applicant EUR 6,000 for nonpecuniary damages. For pecuniary losses, the Court noted:

> [T]he violation complained of by the applicant is of a continuing nature. Within the period under consideration the applicant lived in her flat as a tenant and has never been deprived of this title. Although during this time her private life was adversely affected by industrial emissions, nothing indicates that she has incurred any expenses in this connection. Therefore, in respect of the period prior to the adoption of the present judgment the applicant failed to substantiate any material loss. As regards future measures to be adopted by the

Government in order to comply with the Court's finding of a violation of Article 8 of the Convention in the present case, the resettlement of the applicant in an ecologically safe area would be only one of many possible solutions. In any event, according to Article 41 of the Convention, by finding a violation of Article 8 in the present case, the Court has established the Government's obligation to take appropriate measures to remedy the applicant's individual situation. (paras. 141–42).

2. Has the Court's test for a violation of Article 8 changed since *López Ostra*? How would you summarize the test the Court applies? How important is it that the state has complied with the environmental standards it has enacted? How difficult is it for an applicant to win if the state has followed its own law?

3. What evidence was introduced in the case? Is proof beyond a reasonable doubt appropriate in human rights cases? How did the applicant meet this required level of proof?

4. See also the *Case of Giacomelli v. Italy*, Eur. Ct. H.R., Application No. 59909/00 (Nov. 2, 2006). The applicant lived for more than fifty years in a house on the outskirts of Brescia, thirty meters away from a waste treatment plant, Ecoservizi, which began operating in 1982. Following numerous complaints by the applicant and other inhabitants in the area surrounding the plant, the Brescia local heath authority and the Regional Environmental Protection Agency produced a number of reports on Ecoservizi's activities. The reports showed, and judicial authorities were informed, that statutory limits had been exceeded for hazardous substances, such as nickel, lead, nitrogen, and sulphates. Inspections also revealed toxic waste was being improperly handled; the authorities notified the company it was in breach of its license to operate. No EIA was done until seven years after the plant began operating. The applicant invoked Article 8. The European Court found the case admissible and on the merits found that the state authorities had failed to comply with domestic legislation on environmental matters and subsequently had refused to enforce judicial decisions in which the activities in issue had been found to be unlawful, thereby rendering inoperative the procedural safeguards available to the applicant and breaching the principle of the rule of law (citing *Immobiliare Saffi v. Italy* [GC], No. 22774/93, § 63, ECHR 1999-V). In the Court's opinion, even supposing that the domestic law measures and requirements had ultimately been implemented by the relevant authorities and that the necessary steps had been taken to protect the applicant's rights, the fact remained that, for several years, her right to respect for her home was seriously impaired by the dangerous activities carried out at the plant. It concluded that, notwithstanding the margin of appreciation left to the respondent state, "the State did not succeed in striking a fair balance between the interest of the community in having a plant for the treatment of toxic industrial waste and the applicant's effective enjoyment of her right to respect for her home and her private and family life." The Court declined to award pecuniary damages, however, because "the applicant failed to substantiate her claim and did not indicate any causal link between the violation found and the pecuniary damage she had allegedly sustained." It awarded EUR 12,000 in equity for moral damages as well as reimbursement of costs and fees.

V. Right to Property

The Universal Declaration of Human Rights includes the right of every one to own property alone as well as in association with others, and in article 17, it adds that "no one shall be arbitrarily deprived of his property." With the advent of the Cold War, the right to property became a contentious East-West issue, further complicated by the desire of newly independent states to counter what many of their leaders viewed as neocolonial efforts of Western states to retain economic dominance. As a result of the controversies, the right to property was not included in the ICCPR. It is guaranteed, however, by regional human rights instruments. The European Convention's Protocol I, article 1, is set forth earlier here. Article 21 of the American Convention similarly guarantees everyone the right to the use and enjoyment of his property, which may be subordinated to the "interest of society." Any deprivation of property must be established by law, for a public purpose, and justly compensated. The following case represents an unsuccessful effort to use the right to property for nature conservation.

Metropolitan Nature Reserve v. Panama,
Inter-American Human Rights Commission, Rep. No. 88/03, Case No. 11.533
(Inadmissibility) (Oct. 22, 2003) (footnotes omitted)

1. On August 11, 1995, Rodrigo Noriega referred a petition to the Inter-American Commission on Human Rights on behalf of the citizens of the Republic of Panama. The petition charges the Government of Panama with violations of the Panamanian people's right to property as vested in the Metropolitan Nature Reserve following adoption of Public Law 29 on June 23, 1995 which authorized construction of a public roadway through it. Specific violations of Articles 8; 19; 21(1) and (2); 23(1)(a) and (c); 24; and 25(1), (2)(a), (b), and (c) of the American Convention are alleged. These arise given the Nature Reserve's previous designation as a protected area of environmental, scientific, and cultural value for all the citizens of Panama, so established by Public Law 8 in 1985. The petitioner thus considers the Nature Reserve to be their property rather than that of the State. On that basis, he alleges, the State's failure to consult entities responsible for the Nature Reserve about the planned road project in effect constitutes a violation of the citizens' right to maintain that designated area for use by environmental, civic and scientific groups whose interests the construction harms.

2. The State, for its part, declares that it acted under color of constitutional law to relieve Panama City's heavy traffic congestion, and that it properly consulted public and private institutions within the environmental impact study it commissioned to that end. The State adds that in building the North Corridor project aimed at cutting pollution in the city, it has in fact met its duty to promote environmentally sound development.

3. Having analyzed the parties' respective positions, the IACHR concludes that under Article 47 of the American Convention, the petition is inadmissible since it fails to identify individual victims and it is overly broad. The Commission likewise resolves to notify the parties of this decision and to proceed with its publication and inclusion in the Annual Report it will submit to the General Assembly of the OAS.

. . .

II. ANALYSIS OF ADMISSIBILITY

a. Competence of the Commission

26. Article 44 of the American Convention sets forth the Competence of the Commission. It establishes that "[a]ny person or group of persons, or any nongovernmental entity legally recognized in one or more member states of the Organization, may lodge petitions with the Commission containing denunciations or complaints of violation of this Convention by a State Party."

27. It is worth recalling that, unlike other systems designed to protect human rights, the Inter-American System allows various categories of petitioners to submit petitions on behalf of victims. The wording of Article 44 is indeed broad. Referral to the Commission of petitions containing denunciations or complaints of violation of the Convention by a State Party does not require (unlike established practice under the European System or under the United Nations Human Rights Committee) that petitioners be victims *per se*. There is no requirement that petitioners themselves have a direct or indirect personal interest in the adjudication of a petition. Neither is there a requirement that they be legally empowered by the alleged victims to represent those victims.

28. The jurisprudence of this Commission nonetheless establishes that for a petition to be considered admissible, interpretation of Article 44 of the Convention must be construed to mean that there do exist specific, individual and identifiable victims. Petitions filed in the abstract and divorced from the human rights of specific human beings shall not be admissible.

29. An analysis of the Commission's jurisprudence on how Article 44 of the Convention has been applied shows that competence *ratio personae* over individual petitions has been interpreted to encompass the rights of a specific person or of specific persons. . . .

30. In its Report No. 48/96 considering a previously cited Peruvian case, the Commission held that:

> The liberal standing requirement of the inter-American system should not be interpreted, however, to mean that a case can be presented before the Commission *in abstracto*. An individual cannot institute an *actio popularis* and present a complaint against a law without establishing some active legitimation justifying his standing before the Commission. The applicant must claim to be a victim of a violation of the Convention, or must appear before the Commission as a representative of a putative victim of a violation of the Convention by a state party. (Translator's note: Free Translation)

31. The Commission took a like position in its report on the Maria Eugenia Morales de Sierra case of Guatemala, where it specified that:

> . . . in order to initiate the procedures established in Articles 48 and 50 of the American Convention, the Commission requires a petition denouncing a concrete violation with respect to a specific individual. (Translator's Note: Free Translation)

32. That petitions filed as actions for the common good are deemed inadmissible does not imply that the petitioner must always be able to identify with particularity each and every victim on whose behalf the petition is brought. Indeed, it should be noted that the Commission has considered admissible certain petitions submitted on behalf of groups of victims when the group itself was specifically defined, and when the respective rights of identifiable individual members were directly impaired by the situation giving rise to a stated complaint. Such is the case of members of a specific community.

33. Finally, with respect to *the victim*, it must be understood that the concept refers to individuals, the Commission having no standing to consider petitions regarding legal entities.

34. It is clear from an analysis of the case reported here that Rodrigo Noriega filed a petition on behalf of the citizens of Panama alleging that the right to property of all Panamanians has been violated. He points out that those principally affected include environmental, civic and scientific groups such as the Residents of Panama, Friends of the Metropolitan Nature Reserve, the Audubon Society of Panama, United Civic Associations, and the Association for the Research and Protection of Panamanian Species. The Commission, on that basis, holds the present complaint to be inadmissible since it concerns abstract victims represented in an *actio popularis* rather than specifically identified and defined individuals. The Commission

does recognize that given the nature of the complaint, the petition could hardly pinpoint a group of victims with particularity since all the citizens of Panama are described as property owners of the Metropolitan Nature Reserve. The petition is inadmissible, further, because the environmental, civic, and scientific groups considered most harmed by the alleged violations are legal entities and not natural persons, as the Convention stipulates. The Commission therefore rules that it has not the requisite competence *ratione personae* to adjudicate the present matter in accordance with jurisprudence establishing the standard of interpretation for Article 44 of the Convention as applied in the aforementioned cases.

35. Having determined that it lacks standing *ratione personae* to consider the present case, the Commission need not reach the petition's remaining elements of admissibility.

Questions and Discussion

1. Are there any other rights in the American Convention or American Declaration that could be invoked to prevent destruction of a nature preserve or protected area?

2. Would inclusion of the right to a safe and healthy environment change the result in this case? Should it?

3. Consider the new Ecuadoran Constitution, which declares nature to be a legal person and provides that anyone may sue on nature's behalf if the state authorities fail to properly protect it. Although this opens up standing, how would Ecuador's courts decide a case like *Metropolitan Nature Reserve* on the merits?

4. A group of common law countries lack constitutional provisions like those found in other countries that guarantee a right to a healthy environment. Common law constitutions also generally omit any reference to environmental protection as a state policy. Most of them, however, have provisions similar or identical to that found in Kenya's Constitution, chapter V, article 75(6)(a), which provides that the prohibition on taking of property does not apply "in circumstances where it is reasonably necessary so to do because the property is in a dangerous state or injurious to the health of human beings, animals or plants," or "in the case of land, for the purposes of the carrying out thereon of work of soil conservation or the conservation of other natural resources." Do these provisions indirectly guarantee constitutional environmental rights?

Lars and Astrid Fägerskjöld v. Sweden,
Eur. Ct. H.R., Application No. 37664/04 (Admissibility) (Feb. 26, 2008)

The applicants, Mr. Lars Fägerskjöld and Mrs. Astrid Fägerskjöld, are Swedish nationals who were born in 1942 and live in Jönköping. . . .

. . .

COMPLAINTS

The applicants complained under Article 8 of the Convention and Article 1 of Protocol No. 1 to the Convention that the continuous, pulsating noise from the wind turbine and the light reflections from its rotor blades interfered with their peaceful enjoyment of their property and made it impossible for them to enjoy their private and family life. They had bought the property for recreational purposes but the nuisance from the wind turbine had made it difficult to sit outside for long periods of time. Moreover, no independent noise investigation had been carried out despite their repeated requests for one. They further claimed that, as a result of the nuisance, the value of their property had decreased. Lastly, they complained under Article 13 of the Convention that, as the Environment Committee's decision of 4 November 1997 had been taken without their involvement, they had been deprived of an effective domestic remedy for their Convention complaints.

THE LAW

. . .

[On Article 8, the Court found that the noise levels and light reflections in the case were not so serious as to reach the "high threshold established in cases dealing with environmental issues" and it followed that the complaint was manifestly ill founded within the meaning of article 35 § 3 of the Convention. – Eds.]

2. The applicants further complained under Article 1 of Protocol No. 1 to the Convention that the noise and reflections of light from the wind turbine interfered with their peaceful enjoyment of their property and that the nuisance had decreased the value of their property.

The Government submitted that this complaint also should be declared inadmissible for non-exhaustion of domestic remedies since the applicants, if they considered that their property had decreased in value due to the noise and the light reflections from the wind turbine, could have instituted proceedings in an environmental court claiming financial compensation from, *inter alia*, the owners of the land where the wind turbine was located or from the owners of the wind turbine.

In any event, the Government argued that the complaint should be declared inadmissible *ratione materiae* because there had been no deprivation, control of use or interference with the applicants' peaceful enjoyment of their possessions. However, if the Court were to consider that this provision was applicable to the present case, the Government contended that the complaint was manifestly ill-founded. Referring *in extenso* to their submissions under Article 8, the Government insisted that, having regard to the wide margin of appreciation accorded to the Contracting States in matters raising environmental issues, the alleged interference with the applicants' property rights was in accordance with the law, was proportionate and had a legitimate aim. Thus, they were of the opinion that the national authorities and courts had struck a fair balance between the public interest and that of the applicants in the instant case.

The applicants maintained that their rights under Article 1 of Protocol No. 1 had been infringed by the nuisance caused by the wind turbine and that it had decreased the value of their property. They relied on the same grounds as they had for their complaint under Article 8 of the Convention.

Even assuming that the nuisance from the wind turbine can be considered to amount to an inference with the applicants' peaceful enjoyment of their property, and that the complaint thus falls within the ambit of Article 1 of Protocol No. 1, the Court considers that it is manifestly ill-founded, for the reasons below.

Firstly, the Court observes that the original building permit for the third wind turbine, which was granted on 4 November 1997 by the Environment Committee, was repealed and replaced by a new building permit issued on 23 June 1998 by the Committee. This new building permit had been granted only after the applicants and other neighbours within a radius of 500 metres from the wind turbine had been invited to submit their opinions and also had done so. Moreover, the Swedish Civil Aviation Administration, the Swedish Armed Forces and the Board had been heard on the matter and the noise tests of 20 May 1998 had been submitted to the Environment Committee. The Court further notes that this decision was appealed against by the applicants first to the Board and then to the administrative courts. Both the Board and the County Administrative Court heard the appeal on its merits and they also visited the applicants' property and held an oral hearing in the case before rejecting the appeals. The Court also recalls that Swedish legislation allows for building permits to be granted retrospectively and that, if a permit is not granted for a structure which had already been erected, the owners of that structure are obliged to dismantle it. Thus, it is clear to the Court that the building permit was granted in accordance with national law and hence the wind turbine was lawful.

Secondly, to the Court, there is no doubt that the operating of the wind turbine is in the general interest as it is an environmentally friendly source of energy which contributes to the sustainable development of natural resources. It observes that the wind turbine at issue in the present case is capable of producing enough energy to heat between 40 and 50 private households over a one-year period, which is beneficial both for the environment and for society.

Lastly, the Court must decide whether, when granting the retrospective building permit, a fair balance was struck between the competing interests of the individuals affected by the noise from the wind turbine and the community as a whole. In *Hatton and Others* (cited above, § 122) the Court stated that environmental protection should be taken into consideration by Governments in acting within their margin of appreciation and by the Court in its review of that margin. In the present case, this means that the Court must have regard to the positive environmental consequences of wind power for the community as a whole while also considering its negative impact on the applicants. In this respect, it reiterates that in cases raising environmental issues the State must be allowed a wide margin of appreciation (see, among others, *Hatton and Others*, cited above, § 100, and *Taşkın and Others*, cited above, § 116). However, due weight must be given to the individual's interests (*Hatton and Others*, cited above, § 99).

As the Court has already found when examining the complaint under Article 8 of the Convention, the nuisance caused to the applicants by the wind turbine cannot be considered so severe as to affect them seriously or impinge on their enjoyment of their property. In relation to the interests of the community as a whole, the Court reiterates that wind power is a renewable source of energy which is beneficial for both the environment and society. Moreover, the Court attaches weight to the fact that, in order to reduce the noise from the wind turbine, the Environment Committee imposed certain temporary restrictions on its functioning, which were subsequently extended. The Court is aware that the applicants considered these measures to be insufficient but observes that they could have requested, and still can, the imposition of further measures and that they were reminded of this possibility by the Board in its decision of 14 April 1999. Thus, a constant review of the measures already taken and the opportunity to request further measures are available to the applicants through the Environmental Code.

In these circumstances, the Court finds that the alleged interference was proportionate to the aims pursued and, consequently, this part of the complaint must be rejected as being manifestly ill-founded, pursuant to Article 35 §§ 3 and 4 of the Convention.

In so far as concerns the applicants' claim that their property has decreased in value as a result of the noise and light reflections emitted from the wind turbine, the Court finds that they have failed to substantiate this allegation as they have not submitted any evidence that house prices in general or the value of their property in particular have been adversely affected by the wind turbine. In any event, the Court finds that the applicants did not exhaust domestic remedies available to them in this respect as they failed to institute any proceedings at the national level for financial compensation for the alleged loss of value of the property.

Thus, this part of the complaint is inadmissible for non-exhaustion of domestic remedies within the meaning of Article 35 § 1 of the Convention, and must be rejected pursuant to Article 35 § 4.

. . .

In view of the above, it is appropriate to discontinue the application of Article 29 § 3 of the Convention and to reject the application.

Questions and Discussion

1. Are the standards and nature of required proof different for cases brought under article 1 of Protocol I and under article 8?

2. The Court's jurisprudence has been consistent that the right to peaceful enjoyment of possessions guaranteed in article 1 of Protocol 1 does not guarantee the right to enjoy one's property in a pleasant environment. *Fredin v. Sweden*, 13 Eur. H.R. Rep. 784 (1991), App. No. 12033/86.

3. The court repeatedly expresses a positive view of the ecological benefits of wind turbines as an energy source. Some environmental groups are less convinced. Should the Court be willing to accept submissions from amici curiae on this point? How much deference should be given to expert or amicus views, and would it make a difference to the outcome of the case if wind turbines were not ecologically sound?

4. Public authorities are entitled to control the use of property in accordance with the general interest, which means that public authorities can enact environmental measures that restrict the right to peaceful enjoyment of possessions and other property rights. Such restrictions must be lawful and proportionate to the legitimate aim pursued. In *Pine Valley Developments Ltd et al. v. Ireland*, Application No. 12742/87, 222 Eur. Ct. H.R. (ser. A) (Nov. 29, 1991), [1991] 14 Eur. H.R. Rep. 319, government authorities withdrew planning permission for development projects and the developers challenged the actions. The Court found both decisions were proportionate, lawful in domestic law, and pursued the legitimate objective of environmental protection. Similarly, in *Alatulkkila v. Finland*, Application No. 33538/96, 43 Eur. H.R. Rep. 737 (2006), the Court found restrictions on fishing rights in private waters justified and proportionate as a result of the general interest in the conservation of fish stocks. Contrast *Papastavrou et al. v. Greece*, Application No 46372/99, Eur. Ct. H.R. 2003-IV (Apr. 10, 2003) 257, para. 22–39 (holding that public authorities did not strike a fair balance in restricting use of land).

5. The case of *Housing Association of War Disabled and Victims of War of Attica et al. v. Greece* (App. No. 35859/02, Eur. Ct. H.R. (July 13, 2006), [2007] Eur. Ct.H.R. 753 (Sept. 27, 2007) (just satisfaction) involved alleged interference with the property rights of a group of 157 applicants relating to the classification of land as "to be reforested," thereby prohibiting its use. Applicants claimed their title to the property first dated to 1957 when the first applicant bought fifty thousand square meters in the area. In 1960, the Greek government unlawfully requisitioned the land and in 1964 compensated applicants with one hundred thousand square meters of nearby land, with the understanding that the association would be allowed to develop it after the state had issued the appropriate changes to the local planning regulations. Following a series of reclassifications of the land and petitions by the association for development rights to the forest area between 1980 and 1999, the association's case was brought before the Supreme Administrative Court, which dismissed the association's claims.

    The European Court considered that when a decision "could weigh heavily on the property rights of a large number of people," the state's legitimate concern to protect the forests, could not absolve the state of its responsibility to provide adequate protection to the property owners. As "no reasonable balance [was] struck between the public interest and the requirements of the protection of the applicants' rights," the Court found that a violation of article 1 of Protocol No. 1 occurred. On September 27, 2007 the Court issued its judgment on reparations, awarding applicants EUR 5,000,000 for pecuniary damage and EUR 40,000 for costs and expenses.

6. Where environmental measures result in a substantial reduction in the value of property and the owner is not compensated the matter is treated as an issue of expropriation. In the *Case of Pialopoulos et al. v. Greece*, Application No. 37095/97, Eur. Ct. H.R. (Feb. 15, 2001), planning restrictions prevented applicants from building a shopping center on their land. The Court accepted that the impugned measures aimed toward environmental

protection but held that the applicants were entitled to compensation and, because they had not received it, their property rights had been violated.

7. Other rights have been invoked in the European Court. The protection of article 11, on freedom of association, was sought in *Case of Zeleni Balkani v. Bulgaria*, App. No. 63778/00, Eur.Ct.H.R. (Apr. 12, 2007), in which the government was found to have unduly restricted the work of environmental associations by refusing to allow peaceful protests. In *Case of Koretskyy et al. v. Ukraine*, App. No. 40269/02, Eur.Ct.H.R. (Apr. 3, 2008), the Court found a violation of article 11 as a result of the government's refusal to register an environmental association and a nongovernmental organization. In *Marie Chassagnou et al. v. France*, 1999-III Eur.Ct.H.R 65 (Apr. 29, 1999), the Court found a violation of the right to freedom of association as a result of a French law that required certain owners of small areas of land to belong to a hunting association and permit hunting on their property.

VI. The Right to a Healthy or Safe Environment

Given the protections afforded by the substantive rights discussed herein, to which should be added guarantees of equality and nondiscrimination, what is gained by adding a right to a safe or healthy environment to the list of human rights? On nondiscrimination, see the admissibility decision of the Inter-American Commission of Human, Report No. 43/10, Petition 242-05, Mossville Environmental Action Now (United States), *available at* http://www.iachr.org.

A. *International Guarantees*

Article 24 of the African Charter on Human and Peoples' Rights (June 26, 1981) provides that "[a]ll peoples shall have the right to a general satisfactory environment favorable to their development." Article 11 of the Additional Protocol to the American Convention on Human Rights in the Area of Economic, Social, and Cultural Rights (Nov. 17, 1988) proclaims:

1. Everyone shall have the right to live in a healthy environment and to have access to basic public services.
2. The States Parties shall promote the protection, preservation and improvement of the environment.

However, the Protocol permits complaints to be filed only alleging violations of the right to education and the right to trade union freedoms. This creates difficulties for invoking article 11 directly before the inter-American institutions.

The African system has few limits on justiciability and provides very broad standing to file complaints. The first decision of the African Commission on Human and Peoples' Rights concerning environmental quality arose from Communications 25/89, 47/90, 56/91 and 100/93 Against Zaire, summarized herein. Later, the Commission received the much larger case centering on oil exploration and exploitation in the Niger River Delta that is reprinted in Chapter 4. What does the latter decision suggest about the content of the right to environment and the corresponding state duties? For commentaries on the case and the Ogoni conflict generally, see Fons Coomans, *The Ogoni Case Before the African Commission on Human and Peoples' Rights*, 52 INT'L & COMP. L.Q. 749 (2003); Joshua P. Eaton, *The Nigerian Tragedy, Environmental Regulation of Transnational Corporations, and the Human Right to a Healthy Environment*, 15 B.U. INT'L L.J. 261, 293 (1997).

B. *National Guarantees of the Right to a Safe and Healthy Environment*

Some 130 constitutions in the world, including the overwhelming proportion of those amended or written since 1970, include a state obligation to protect the environment or a right to a safe, healthy, ecologically balanced (or other adjective) environment. About half the constitutions take the rights-based approach, and the other half proclaim state duties. This section looks at environmental rights in Europe, the United States, and South Africa.

European Environmental Human Rights and Environmental Rights: A Long Time Coming?, 21 GEO. INT'L ENVTL. L. REV. 73, 108–11 (2008)
(footnotes renumbered)
Ole W. Pedersen

Although the approach to a substantive right to the environment is perhaps one of caution on a regional level in Europe, a number of national constitutions recognize rights to a healthy environment. These constitutional provisions, while effective only on a national level, indicate that the issue is one of increasing importance throughout Europe.[29]

For instance, the French Constitution was amended in 2005 and now includes a Charter of the Environment ("Charter").[30] The Charter affords all citizens of France the right to live in a "balanced environment, favorable to human health."[31] The Charter has been relied upon by the French *Conseil Constitutionnel* in reviewing the constitutionality of ordinary bills. For instance, in a case from 2005 dealing with the establishment of a maritime register the *Conseil Constitutionnel* relied on the Charter although it did not find that the proposed bill violated the Charter's provisions.[32] The Charter was also relied upon by a local administrative court in 2005 when it suspended the granting of an administrative permission to host a rave party in a former airfield, which had subsequently been listed under domestic nature conservation law.[33] Here, the court found that the Charter constituted a "fundamental freedom" of constitutional value allowing for the suspension of the administrative permission under French procedural law.[34]

The French amendment serves to increase the number of European constitutions facilitating a human right to the environment. For example: the Constitution of Belgium, where the right to "lead a worthy life of human dignity" includes "the right to protection of a sound environment";[35] Portugal where the Constitution asserts that "all have the right to a healthy ecologically balanced human environment and the duty to defend it";[36] and Spain where the Constitution states that "everyone has the right to enjoy an environment suitable for the development of the person as well

---

[29] Apart from providing for a specific right, some constitutions contain general provisions on the environment in the shape of broad policy statements. *See, e.g.,* STATUUT NED [Constitution] ch. I, art. 21 (Neth.), *translated in* CONSTITUTIONS OF THE COUNTRIES OF THE WORLD (Rüdiger Wolfrum & Rainer Grote eds., 2005) (stating "it shall be the concern of the authorities to keep the country habitable and to protect and improve the environment").

[30] Legifrance, Charter for the Environment, art. 1, *available at* http://www.legifrance.gouv.fr/html/constitution/const03.htm; *see, e.g.,* David Marrani, *The Second Anniversary of the Constitutionalisation of the French Charter for the Environment: Constitutional and Environmental Implications,* 10 ENVTL. L. REV. 9 (2008); James R. May, *Constituting Fundamental Environmental Rights Worldwide,* 23 PACE ENVTL. L. REV. 113, 113–14 (2005–06).

[31] [Legifrance, Id.]

[32] *See* CC Decision No. 2005–514DC (Apr. 28, 2005), R. 305 (*Loi relative à la création du registre international français*); Marrani, *supra.*

[33] *See* Marrani, *supra,* at 21–22.

[34] Id.

[35] LA CONSTITUTION BELGE art. 23(3)(4) (Belg.), *translated in* CONSTITUTIONS OF THE COUNTRIES OF THE WORLD, *supra; see also* Marc Martens, *Constitutional Right to a Healthy Environment in Belgium,* 16 REV. EUR. CMTY & INT'L ENVTL. L. 287 (2007) (noting that the right in article 23 amounts to a so-called standstill obligation on the state).

[36] CONSTITUIÇÃO DA REPÚBLICA PORTUGUESA [Constitution] art. 66 (Port.), *translated in* CONSTITUTIONS OF THE COUNTRIES OF THE WORLD, *supra.*

as the duty to preserve it."[37] Further north, the Finnish Constitution, adopted in 2000, states that the "public authorities shall endeavor to guarantee for everyone the right to a healthy environment."[38] Likewise, the Norwegian Constitution, altered in 1992, contains a right to "an environment that is conducive to health."[39] In addition, a great number of Eastern European countries have, following the breakdown of the Soviet Union, altered or changed their constitutions to include a substantive right to the environment.[40]

. . .

Thus, the vast number of national constitutions holding provisions on substantive as well as procedural environmental rights adds further impetus to the use of rights to provide for environmental protections. As for the substantive norms, the rights in the national constitutions have the potential to influence debates on the status of a substantive environmental norm under international law. Here it is worth recalling *Taşkin v. Turkey*, where the plaintiff relied on the right to a healthy environment in the Turkish Constitution before the court, which found this to constitute a civil right within the meaning of the ECHR. National constitutional environmental rights are strong indicators of national *opinio juris* and represent the highest level of national law operating as a *lex suprema*. In addition, many of the constitutions changed throughout the last twenty years have been amended to specifically accommodate these rights.

. . .

1. The United States

The U.S. federal constitution is not one of those that mention the environment – unsurprising, given that the constitution was drafted in 1787 – and rights are not often implied as a result of litigation. Nonetheless, in 1968, the same year the government of Sweden proposed to the United Nations that it convene its first international conference on the human environment, U.S. Senator Gaylord Nelson introduced a draft constitutional amendment that would have recognized in the Bill of Rights that "[e]very person has the inalienable right to a decent environment." H.R. J. Res. 1321, 90th Cong., 2d Sess. (1968). The proposal failed, as did later attempts to recognize such a right. H.R. J. Res. 1205, 91st Cong., 2d Sess. (1970). Most recently, Representative Jesse Jackson Jr. proposed a constitutional amendment "respecting the right to a clean, safe, and sustainable environment." H.R.J. Res. 33, 108th Cong. (2003). Each of these proposals sought not only to elevate environmental protection to a constitutional right but also to give the federal government a clear mandate to regulate environmental matters. Without such a mandate, the government has had to rely on the commerce clause and other enumerated powers to assert jurisdiction over natural resources. Thus, the federal government may protect migratory birds that cross state lines, but it lacks jurisdiction to protect all the habitats of such birds, because those habitats include state and

---

[37] C.E. [Constitution] art. 45 (Spain), *translated in* Constitutions of the Countries of the World, *supra*. However, the right enshrined in the Spanish Constitution has been called into question as it has been argued that it serves more as a policy principle. *See* Ernst Brandl & Hartwin Bungert, *Constitutional Entrenchment of Environmental Protection: A Comparative Analysis of Experiences Abroad*, 16 Harv. Envtl. L. Rev.1, 61–63 (1992); Douglas-Scott, *supra*, at 110–11.

[38] Suomen Perustuslaki [Constitution] art. 20 (Fin.), *translated in* Constitutions of the Countries of the World, *supra*. Article 20 stems from a constitutional reform taking place in the mid 1990s in Finland aiming at providing a more "coherent set of fundamental rights" in Finland. *See* Stephen Davies, *In Name or Nature? Implementing International Environmental Procedural Rights in the Post-Aarhus Environment: A Finnish Example*, 9 Envtl. L. Rev. 190 (2007).

[39] Grunnlov [Constitution] art. 110B (Nor.), *translated in* Constitutions of the Countries of the World, *supra*.

[40] These include, among others, Albania, Belarus, Croatia, Czech Republic, Estonia, Hungary, Macedonia, Russia, Slovenia, and Ukraine; *see* May, *supra*, at 129–31. For example, the Hungarian Constitution states, "Hungary recognizes and implements everyone's right to a healthy environment." A Magyar Küztársaság Alkotmánya [Constitution] art. 18 (Hung.), *translated in* Constitutions of the Countries of the World, *supra*; *see also* Gyula Badni, *The Right to Environment in Theory and Practice: The Hungarian Experience*, 8 Conn. J. Int'l L. 439 (1993).

private lands and nonnavigable waters. State opposition to granting this power to the federal government may explain the failure of the proposed amendments.

States in the U.S. have the power to provide their citizens with rights additional to those contained in the federal Constitution, and state constitutions revised or amended from 1970 to the present have added environmental protection among their provisions. *See* ALA. CONST. art. VIII; CAL. CONST. art. X, § 2; FLA. CONST. art. II, § 7; HAW. CONST. art. XI; ILL. CONST. art. XI; LA. CONST. art. IX; MASS. CONST. § 179; MICH. CONST. art. IV, § 52; MONT. CONST. art. IX, § 1; N.M. CONST. art. XX, § 21; N.Y. CONST. art. XIV; N.C. CONST. art. XIV, § 5; OHIO CONST. art. II, § 36; PA. CONST. art. I, § 27; R.I. CONST. art. 1, § 17; TEX. CONST. art. XVI, § 59; UTAH CONST. art. XVIII; VA. CONST. art. XI, § 1. For discussions of these provisions, see A.E. Dick Howard, *State Constitutions and the Environment*, 58 VA. L. REV. 193, 229 (1972); Roland M. Frye Jr., *Environmental Provisions in State Constitutions*, 5 ENVTL. L. REP. 50028–29 (1975); Stewart G. Pollock, *State Constitutions, Land Use, and Public Resources: The Gift Outright*, 1984 ANN. SURV. AM. L. 13, 28–29; Robert A. McLaren, Comment, *Environmental Protection Based on State Constitutional Law: A Call for Reinterpretation*, 12 U. HAW. L. REV. 123, 126–27 (1990); Carole L. Gallagher, *The Movement to Create an Environmental Bill of Rights: From Earth Day 1970 to the Present*, 9 FORDHAM ENVTL. L.J. 107 (1997). For a listing of all environmental provisions in state constitutions, see Bret Adams et al., *Environmental and Natural Resources Provisions in State Constitutions*, 22 J. LAND RESOURCES & ENVTL. L. 73 (2002). The authors take a broad reading of the topic, including all provisions that touch on natural resources. They come to a total of 207 state constitutional provisions in forty-six state constitutions.

The first constitutional recognition of environmental rights appeared in Pennsylvania. Two years after the initial federal constitution effort failed, April 14, 1970 was designated the first Earth Day. *See* Matthew Thor Kirsch, *Upholding the Public Trust in State Constitutions*, 46 DUKE L.J. 1169–1210 (1997). To mark the occasion, the Pennsylvania legislature approved a proposed amendment to the state constitution. The author of the proposal said he intended to "give our natural environment the same kind of constitutional protection that [is] given our political rights." Franklin L. Kury, *The Pennsylvania Environmental Protection Amendment*, PA. B. ASS'N Q., Apr. 1987, at 85, 87, quoted in Kirsch, *supra* n. 30 at 1170. The proposed amendment was approved overwhelmingly by voters in the state, on May 18, 1971. The vote was more than 3–1 in favor of the amendment, with close to 2 million voters. *See* Franklin L. Kury, *The Environmental Amendment to the Pennsylvania Constitution: Twenty Years Later and Largely Untested*, 1 VILL. ENVTL. L.J. 123, 123–24 (1990). The provision, now article I, section 27 of the state constitution, sets forth the following:

> Section 27. Natural resources and the public estate
>
> The people have a right to clean air, pure water, and to the preservation of the natural, scenic, historic and aesthetic values of the environment. Pennsylvania's public natural resources are the common property of all the people, including generations yet to come. As trustee of these resources, the Commonwealth shall conserve and maintain them for the benefit of all the people.

There are several evident features about this text. First, it declares the "people's" right to environmental amenities with a directive to the state to act as a trustee for the "public natural resources" of the state (excluding private property). The resources mentioned are declared to be common property and held for future and present generations.

Following this example, more than thirty of the fifty states in the United States (60 percent) have added constitutional provisions that refer to environmental or natural resource protection as a state constitutional right or governmental duty. The intent of the provisions must be considered in the context of the federal system: unlike the federal government, which must act within the scope of conferred powers, state authorities can act unless prohibited from doing so. Thus, they may regulate the activities harming the environment without mention of the topic in the state constitution. Including provisions in the constitution must serve some other purpose than simply conferring legislative authority over environmental matters. The most compelling explanation is that the amendments were intended to elevate environmental protection as a fundamental value to a constitutional status above the states' legislative and regulatory norms. Another purpose appears in some state debates and constitutional texts: to expand standing to sue to allow public interest litigation on behalf of the environment.

A half dozen other states, like Hawaii, Illinois, Montana, and Texas, followed Pennsylvania in adding a constitutional right to environment. Hawaii's Constitution, article XI, section 9, reads:

> Each person has the right to a clean and healthful environment, as defined by law relating to environmental quality, including control of pollution and resources. Any person may enforce this right against any party, public or private, through appropriate legal proceedings.

Illinois, Massachusetts, and Montana all amended their constitutions in 1972 to similarly provide for a right to a clean and healthful environment. Massachusetts expressly guarantees the right to clean air and water; freedom from excessive and unnecessary noise; and the natural scenic, historic, and aesthetic qualities of their environment. Article XLIX of the Massachusetts state constitution provides:

> The people shall have the right to clean air and water, freedom from excessive and unnecessary noise, and the natural, scenic, historic, and esthetic qualities of their environment; and the protection of the people in their right to the conservation development and utilization of the agricultural, mineral, forest, water, air and other natural resources is hereby declared to be a public purpose.

The Montana Constitution has been enforced by the courts, as the following case illustrates.

Montana Environmental Information Center et al. v. Department of Environmental Quality, 296 Mont. 207, 988 P.2d 1236 (1999)

Justice TERRY N. TRIEWEILER delivered the Opinion of the Court.

¶ 1 The Plaintiffs, Montana Environmental Information Center (MEIC), Clark Fork-Pend Oreille Coalition, and Women's Voices for the Earth, filed an amended complaint in the District Court for the First Judicial District in Lewis and Clark County in which the Department of Environmental Quality (DEQ) for the State of Montana was named as the Defendant and in which Seven-Up Pete Joint Venture (SPJV) subsequently intervened. Plaintiffs alleged, among other claims, that to the extent § 75-5-317(2)(j), MCA (1995) allows discharges of water from watering well or monitoring well tests, which degrade high quality waters without review pursuant to Montana's nondegradation policy found at § 75-5-303(3), MCA (1995), that statute is void for a violation of Article IX, Section 1(1) and (3) of the Montana Constitution. Plaintiffs sought an injunction suspending the exploration license that had been issued by DEQ to SPJV for pump tests to be performed at the site of its proposed gold mine. Both parties moved for summary judgment and following the submission of affidavits and oral testimony, the District Court held that absent a finding of actual injury, § 75-5-317(2)(j), MCA (1995) was not unconstitutional as applied and entered judgment for the DEQ. The Plaintiffs appeal from the judgment of the District Court. We reverse and remand for further review consistent with this opinion.

¶ 2 The issue on appeal is whether the Plaintiffs have demonstrated standing to challenge the constitutionality of § 75-5-317(2)(j), MCA (1995), and, if so, whether the statute implicates either Article II, Section 3 or Article IX, Section 1 of the Montana Constitution.

. . .

Standing

¶ 41 In *Gryczan v. State* (1997), 283 Mont. 433, 442–43, 942 P.2d 112, 118, we held that the following criteria must be satisfied to establish standing:(1) the complaining party must clearly allege past, present, or threatened injury to a property or civil right; and (2) the alleged injury must be distinguishable from the injury to the public generally, but the injury need not be exclusive to the complaining party.

¶ 42 In *Missoula City-County Air Pollution Control Board v. Board of Environmental Review* (1997), 282 Mont. 255, 937 P.2d 463, this Court considered the first prong of the two-part test and concluded that a threatened injury to the Local Board had been established by demonstrating "potential economic injury." *Missoula City-County Air Pollution Control Bd.*, 282 Mont. at 262–63, 937 P.2d at 468. The court accepted the Local Board's argument that "it face[d] potential economic harm from the additional expenses necessary to monitor, collect and analyze data, and to develop a regulatory response which will ensure that Missoula air quality meets minimum federal standards in the face of increased air pollution from Stone Container." *Missoula City-County Air Pollution Control Bd.*, 282 Mont. at 262, 937 P.2d at 468.

¶ 43 The second prong of the test for standing requires that the litigant distinguish his or her injury from injury to the general public. Gryczan, 283 Mont. at 442, 942 P.2d at 118. However, the injury need not be exclusive to the litigant. Gryczan, 283 Mont. at 443, 942 P.2d at 118. In Gryczan we held that the plaintiffs had satisfied the second prong because they "presented evidence of specific psychological effects caused by the statute." We further found it significant that "to deny Respondents standing would effectively immunize the statute from constitutional review." *Gryczan*, 283 Mont. at 446, 942 P.2d at 120.

¶ 44 In Missoula City-County Air Pollution Control Board we held that the Local Board's "interest in the effective discharge of the obligations imposed upon it by law is the equivalent of the personal stake which would support standing of a private citizen of the Missoula airshed." *Missoula City-County Air Pollution Control Bd.*, 282 Mont. at 262, 937 P.2d at 467. We further stated that:

> It is clear to this Court that a citizen of Missoula, as one who breathes the air into which Stone Container is expelling pollutants, would have standing to bring this action. . . . In the same way as a citizen of the Missoula airshed is more particularly affected by the State Board's acts than is a citizen of another area, the interest of the Local Board is distinguishable from and greater than the interest of the public generally.

Missoula City-County Air Pollution Control Bd., 282 Mont. at 262, 937 P.2d at 467–68.

¶ 45 Based on these criteria, we conclude that the allegations in the Plaintiffs' complaint which are uncontroverted, established their standing to challenge conduct which has an arguably adverse impact on the area in the headwaters of the Blackfoot River in which they fish and otherwise recreate, and which is a source for the water which many of them consume. Whether Plaintiffs have demonstrated sufficient harm from the statute and activity complained of to implicate their constitutional rights and require strict scrutiny of the statute they have challenged, is a separate issue.

Constitutional and Statutory Framework

¶ 46 Appellants contend that § 75-5-317(2)(j), MCA (1995), violates their rights guaranteed by Article II, Section 3 and Article IX, Section 1 of the Montana Constitution.

¶ 47 Article II, Section 3 provides in relevant part that:

All persons are born free and have certain inalienable rights. They include the right to a clean and healthful environment. . . .

Mont. Const. art. II, § 3.

¶ 48 Article IX, Section 1 provides in relevant part as follows:

(1) The State and each person shall *maintain and improve* a clean and healthful environment in Montana for present and future generations.

. . .

(3) The legislature shall provide adequate remedies for the protection of the environmental life support system from degradation and provide adequate remedies to prevent unreasonable depletion and degradation of natural resources.

Mont. Const. art. IX, § 1 (emphasis added).

¶ 49. . . .

¶ 50 Plaintiffs contend that the Constitution's environmental protections were violated by the legislature in 1995, when it amended § 75-5-317(2)(j), MCA to provide a blanket exception to the requirements of nondegradation review for discharges from water well or monitoring well tests without regard to the harm caused by those tests or the degrading effect that the discharges have on the surrounding or recipient environment. . . .

. . .

¶ 52 Because discharges containing carcinogenic parameters, (i.e., discharged water containing concentrations of arsenic equal to .009 mg/l) greater than those in the receiving water (i.e., .003 mg/l) were allowed in this case, Plaintiffs contend that the discharges should not have been exempt from nondegradation review by DEQ's own standards and that they have, therefore, demonstrated the necessary harm for strict scrutiny of the blanket exemption provided for in § 75-5-317(2)(j), MCA.

. . .

Constitutional Analysis

¶ 54 In order to address the issue raised on appeal, it is necessary that we determine the threshold showing which implicates the rights provided for by Article II, Section 3 and Article IX, Section 1 of the Montana Constitution and the level of scrutiny to be applied to each provision. DEQ and SPJV contend, and the District Court agreed that actual danger to human health or the health of the environment must first be demonstrated. The Plaintiffs contend that Montana's constitutional provisions are intended to prevent harm to the environment; that degradation to the environment is all that need be shown; and that degradation was established in this case based on the DEQ's own adopted standard.

¶ 55 We have not had prior occasion to discuss the level of scrutiny which applies when the right to a clean and healthful environment guaranteed by Article II, Section 3 or those rights referred to in Article IX, Section 1 are implicated. Nor have we previously discussed the showing which must necessarily be made to establish that rights guaranteed by those two constitutional provisions are implicated. However, our prior cases which discuss other provisions of the Montana Constitution and the debate of those delegates who attended the 1972 Constitutional Convention, guide us in both respects.

¶ 56 In *Butte Community Union v. Lewis* (1986), 219 Mont. 426, 712 P.2d 1309, we held that:

If a fundamental right is infringed or a suspect classification established, the government has to show a "compelling state interest" for its action.

. . .

... in order to be fundamental, a right must be found within Montana's Declaration of Rights or be a right "without which other constitutionally guaranteed rights would have little meaning." *In the Matter of C.H.* (Mont.1984), [210 Mont. 184, 201], 683 P.2d 931, 940, 41 St. Rep. 997, 1007.

Butte Community Union, 219 Mont. at 430, 712 P.2d at 1311.

¶ 57 We held, however, that a middle-tier level of scrutiny will be applied when a right is implicated which, though not contained in our declaration of rights, is referred to in our constitution even though the constitutional provision in question is merely directive to the legislature. We held that:

A benefit lodged in our State Constitution is an interest whose abridgement requires something more than a rational relationship to a governmental objective.

· · ·

... Where constitutionally significant interests are implicated by governmental classification, arbitrary lines should be condemned. Further, there should be balancing of the rights infringed and the governmental interest to be served by such infringement.

Butte Community Union, 219 Mont. at 434, 712 P.2d at 1313–14.

· · ·

¶ 59 We elaborated on the level of scrutiny for statutes or rules which implicate rights guaranteed in our declaration of rights in *Wadsworth v. State* (1996), 275 Mont. 287, 911 P.2d 1165. There we held that, "the inalienable right to pursue life's basic necessities is stated in the Declaration of Rights and is therefore a fundamental right." *Wadsworth*, 275 Mont. at 299, 911 P.2d at 1172.

¶ 60 We also held in Wadsworth that the nature of interest affected by state action dictates the standard of review that we apply and that: "[t]he most stringent standard, strict scrutiny, is imposed when the action complained of interferes with the exercise of a fundamental right or discriminates against a suspect class." *Wadsworth*, 275 Mont. at 302, 911 P.2d at 1174 (citations omitted).

¶ 61 In *Wadsworth*, we gave the following explanation of what is required by strict scrutiny:

Strict scrutiny of a legislative act requires the government to show a compelling state interest for its action. *Shapiro* [*v. Thompson* (1969)], 394 U.S. [618] at 634, 89 S. Ct. [1322] 1331 [22 L. Ed.2d 600]. When the government intrudes upon a fundamental right, any compelling state interest for doing so must be closely tailored to effectuate only that compelling state interest. [*State v.*] *Pastos*, [(1994), 269 Mont. 43, 47] 887 P.2d [199] at 202 (citing *Zablocki v. Redhail* (1978), 434 U.S. 374, 98 S. Ct. 673, 54 L. Ed.2d 618). In addition to the necessity that the State show a compelling state interest for invasion of a fundamental right, the State, to sustain the validity of such invasion, must also show that the choice of legislative action is the least onerous path that can be taken to achieve the state objective. *Pfost v. State* (1985), 219 Mont. 206, 216, 713 P.2d 495, 505.

Wadsworth, 275 Mont. at 302, 911 P.2d at 1174.

¶ 62 Finally, in language relevant to this case, we held in Wadsworth that, "while DOR's conflict of interest policy or rule is at issue rather than a statute, we, nevertheless, apply strict scrutiny analysis since the operation of that rule implicates Wadsworth's fundamental right to the opportunity to pursue employment." *Wadsworth*, 275 Mont. at 303, 911 P.2d at 1174 (emphasis added).

¶ 63 Applying the preceding rules to the facts in this case, we conclude that the right to a clean and healthful environment is a fundamental right because it is guaranteed by the Declaration of Rights found at Article II, Section 3 of Montana's Constitution, and that any statute or rule which implicates that right must be strictly scrutinized and can only survive scrutiny if the State establishes a compelling state interest and that its action is closely tailored to effectuate that interest and is the least onerous path that can be taken to achieve the State's objective.

¶ 64 State action which implicates those rights provided for in Article IX, Section 1 would normally not be subject to strict scrutiny because those rights are not found in Montana's Declaration of Rights. Those rights would normally be subject to a middle-tier of scrutiny because lodged elsewhere in our state constitution. However, we conclude that the right to a clean and healthful environment guaranteed by Article II, Section 3, and those rights provided for in Article IX, Section 1 were intended by the constitution's framers to be interrelated and interdependent and that state or private action which implicates either, must be scrutinized consistently. Therefore, we will apply strict scrutiny to state or private action which implicates either constitutional provision.

¶ 65 A thorough review of the discussion and debate among the delegates to our 1972 Constitutional Convention leads us to the further conclusion that the nature of the environmental rights provided by Articles II and IX cannot be interpreted separately, but that it was the delegates' intention that the two provisions compliment each other and be applied in tandem. Therefore, we look to the records of the convention discussion and debate to determine the showing that must be made before the rights are implicated and strict scrutiny applied.

¶ 66 Article IX, Section 1 was reported to the floor of the constitutional convention by the Natural Resources and Agricultural Committee on March 1, 1972. *Montana Constitutional Convention*, Vol. IV at 1198–99. As originally proposed, however, Article IX, Section 1(1) required that "the state and each person . . . maintain and enhance the Montana environment for present and future generations." *Montana Constitutional Convention*, Vol. IV at 1200, March 1, 1972. It did not provide, as does the current provision, the obligation to "maintain and improve a clean and healthful environment." *See Montana Constitutional Convention*, Vol. IV at 1200, March 1, 1972; Mont. Const. art. IX, § 1(1). The provision, as introduced, was thought by members of the committee to be the strongest environmental protection provision found in any state constitution. Montana Constitutional Convention, Vol. IV at 1200, March 1, 1972. Delegate McNeil explained that descriptive adjectives were not included preceding the word environment such as healthful or unsoiled, because the majority felt that the current Montana environment encompassed all of those descriptive adjectives. *Montana Constitutional Convention*, Vol. IV at 1200, March 1, 1972. He further explained that descriptive adjectives were not originally included because:

> The majority felt that the use of the word "healthful" would permit those who would pollute our environment to parade in some doctors who could say that if a person can walk around with four pounds of arsenic in his lungs or SO2 gas in his lungs and wasn't dead, that that would be a healthful environment. We strongly believe the majority does that our provision or proposal is stronger than using the word "healthful."

Montana Constitutional Convention, Vol. IV at 1201, March 1, 1972.

¶ 67 In discussing the interrelationship of subsections (1) and (3), Delegate McNeil stated:

> Subsection (3) mandates the Legislature to provide adequate remedies to protect the environmental life-support system from degradation. The committee intentionally avoided definitions, to preclude being restrictive. And the term "environmental life support system" is all-encompassing, including but not limited to air, water, and land; and whatever interpretation is afforded this phrase by the Legislature and courts, there is no question that it cannot be degraded.

Montana Constitutional Convention, Vol. IV at 1201, March 1, 1972 (emphasis added).

¶ 68 There were delegates including Delegate Campbell who felt that without descriptive adjectives, such as "clean and healthful" prior to the term "environment," Article IX, Section 1 lacked the force that the majority had intended. *Montana Constitutional Convention*, Vol. IV at 1204, March 1, 1972. However, the proponents of Section 1 as introduced, insisted that the subsection require that the environment not only be maintained but improved. *See* Delegate John Anderson cmts. (*Montana Constitutional Convention*, Vol. IV at 1204, March 1, 1972).

. . .

¶ 73 In concluding remarks in opposition to amending the committee majority's proposed Article IX, Section 1, Delegate McNeil gave the following explanation for the language being recommended:

> We did not want the Supreme Court of this state or the Legislature to be able to say that the environment in Montana, as we know right now, can be degraded to a healthful environment. So our purpose in leaving that word out was to strengthen it. I would like also to remind the delegates that the Illinois provision does not contain subparagraph 3 of the majority proposal, [Article IX, Section 1(3)] which speaks precisely to the point that concerned Jerry Cate so much, and that is there is no provision by which the Legislature can prevent and this is anticipatory can prevent unreasonable depletion of the natural resources. I submit if you will read that majority proposal again and again, you will find that it is the strongest of any constitution. . . .

Montana Constitutional Convention, Vol. V at 1243, March 1, 1972.

¶ 74 Delegate Foster also gave the following defense of the language as originally proposed:

> I feel that if we, as a Constitutional Convention of Montana, use our line of defense on the environment on the basis of healthful, then we, in fact, might as well forget it, because what I'm concerned about in Montana is not a healthful environment. This country is going to have to address itself to the question of a healthful environment. What I'm concerned about is an environment that is better than healthful. If all we have is a survivable environment, then we've lost the battle. We have nothing left of importance. The federal government will see to it one way or another, if it's in its power, that we have an environment in which we can manage to crawl around or to survive or to in some way stay "alive." But the environment that I'm concerned about is that stage of quality of the environment which is above healthful; and if we put in the Constitution that the only line of defense is a healthful environment and that I have to show, in fact, that my health is being damaged in order to find some relief, then we've lost the battle; so I oppose this amendment.

Montana Constitutional Convention, Vol. V at 1243–44, March 1, 1972.

¶ 75 In the end advocates for adding the descriptive language "clean and healthful" prevailed. However, it was not on the basis that they wanted less protection than articulated by Delegates McNeil and Foster, it was because they felt the additional language was necessary in order to assure the objectives articulated by Delegates McNeil and Foster. *See* Delegate Campbell cmts. (*Montana Constitutional Convention*, Vol. V at 1246, March 1, 1972). It was agreed by both sides of the debate that it was the convention's intention to adopt whatever the convention could agree was the stronger language. See Delegate McNeil cmts. (*Montana Constitutional Convention*, Vol. IV at 1209, March 1, 1972).

¶ 76 Although Article IX, Section 1(1), (2), and (3) were all approved by the convention on March 1, 1972 (*Montana Constitutional Convention*, Vol. V at 1251, 1254–55, March 1, 1972) the right to a clean and healthful environment was not included in the Bill of Rights until six days later on March 7, 1972. On that date, Delegate Burkhart moved to add "the right to a clean and healthful environment" to the other inalienable rights listed in Article II, Section 3 of the proposed constitution. *Montana Constitutional Convention*, Vol. V at 1637, March 7, 1972. He explained his intention that it interrelate with those rights provided for and previously adopted in Article IX, Section 1. *Montana Constitutional Convention*, Vol. V at 1637, March 7, 1972. He also stated that it was his intention through the addition of this right to the Bill of Rights to give force to the language of the preamble to the constitution. *Montana Constitutional Convention*, Vol. V at 1637, March 7, 1972. Burkhart stated: "I think it's a beautiful statement, and it seems to me that what I am proposing here is in concert with what's proposed in that Preamble. . . . " *Montana Constitutional Convention*, Vol. V at 1638, March 7, 1972. Delegate Eck concurred that including the additional language in Article II, Section 3, was consistent with the intention of the Natural Resources Committee when it reported Article IX, Section 1. *Montana Constitutional Convention*, Vol. V at 1638, March 7, 1972. The right to a clean and healthy environment was, therefore, included as a fundamental right by a vote of 79 to 7. *Montana Constitutional Convention*, Vol. V at 1640, March 7, 1972. We have previously cited with approval the following language from 16 C.J.S. *Constitutional Laws* § 16 (1984):

> The prime effort or fundamental purpose, in construing a constitutional provision, is to ascertain and to give effect to the intent of the framers and of the people who adopted it. The court, therefore, should constantly keep in mind the object sought to be accomplished . . . and proper regard should be given to the evils, if any, sought to be prevented or remedied. . . .

General Agric. Corp. v. Moore (1975), 166 Mont. 510, 518, 534 P.2d 859, 864.

¶ 77 We conclude, based on the eloquent record of the Montana Constitutional Convention that to give effect to the rights guaranteed by Article II, Section 3 and Article IX, Section 1 of the Montana Constitution they must be read together and consideration given to all of the provisions of Article IX, Section 1 as well as the preamble to the Montana Constitution. In doing so, we conclude that the delegates' intention was to provide language and protections which are both anticipatory and preventative. The delegates did not intend to merely prohibit that degree of environmental degradation which can be conclusively linked to ill health or physical endangerment. Our constitution does not require that dead fish float on the surface of our state's rivers and streams before its farsighted environmental protections can be invoked. The delegates repeatedly emphasized that the rights provided for in subparagraph (1) of Article IX, Section 1 was linked to the legislature's obligation in subparagraph (3) to provide adequate remedies for degradation of the environmental life support system and to prevent unreasonable degradation of natural resources.

¶ 78 We conclude, therefore, that the District Court erred when it held that Montana's constitutional right to a clean and healthy environment was not implicated, absent a demonstration that public health is threatened or that current water quality standards are affected o such an extent that a significant impact has been had on either the Landers Fork or Blackfoot River.

¶ 79 We conclude that the constitutional right to a clean and healthy environment and to be free from unreasonable degradation of that environment is implicated based on the Plaintiffs' demonstration that the pumping tests proposed by SPJV would have added a known carcinogen such as arsenic to the environment in concentrations greater than the concentrations present in the receiving water and that the DEQ or its predecessor after studying the issue and conducting hearings has concluded that discharges containing carcinogenic parameters greater than the concentrations of those parameters in the receiving water has a significant impact which requires review pursuant to Montana's policy of nondegradation set forth at § 75-5-303, MCA. The fact that DEQ has a rule consistent with § 75-5-317(2)(j), MCA (1995), is of no consequence. As we have previously held in Wadsworth, the constitution applies to agency rules as well as to statutes.

¶ 80 We conclude that for purposes of the facts presented in this case, § 75-5-303, MCA is a reasonable legislative implementation of the mandate provided for in Article IX, Section 1 and that to the extent § 75-5-317(2)(j), MCA (1995) arbitrarily excludes certain "activities" from nondegradation review without regard to the nature or volume of the substances being discharged, it violates those environmental rights guaranteed by Article II, Section 3 and Article IX, Section 1 of the Montana Constitution. Our holding is limited to § 75-5-317(2)(j), MCA (1995), as applied to the facts in this case. We have not been asked to and do not hold that this section facially implicates constitutional rights.

¶ 81 Based on these holdings, we reverse the judgment of the District Court and remand to the District Court for strict scrutiny of the statutory provision in question, and in particular for a determination of whether there is a compelling state interest for the enactment of that statute based on the criteria we articulated in Wadsworth v. State.

¶ 82 The judgment of the District Court is reversed and this case is remanded for further proceedings consistent with this opinion.

Questions and Discussion

1. Do you agree with those at the Constitutional Convention who argued that including the word *healthful* weakened the constitutional guarantee? Does it depend on whether the word refers to humans or to the environment being full of health? Does *healthy environment* mean healthy for humans or an environment that is intrinsically healthy? What difference does it make?
2. How would you evaluate the benefits and drawbacks of the Montana constitutional provision in comparison with traditional nuisance law?
3. The Montana Supreme Court further applied its constitutional provision in the case *Cape-France Enterprises v. Estate of Peed*, 29 P.3d 1011 (Mont. 2001), in which it held that "the protections and mandates of this provision to private action – and thus to private parties – as well" as to state action. Thus, "it would be unlawful for Cape-France, a private business entity, to drill a well on its property in the face of substantial evidence that doing so may cause significant degradation of uncontaminated aquifers and pose serious public health risks." The court held that it would be a violation of the state's obligation under the constitution for it to grant specific performance of a contract for the sale of the land in question. *See* Chase Naber, *Murky Waters: Private Action and the Right to a Clean and Healthful Environment – An Examination of Cape-France Enterprises v. Estate of Peed*, 64 MONT. L. REV. 357 (2003); B. Thompson, *Constitutionalizing the Environment: The History and Future of Montana's Environmental Provisions*, 64 MONT. L. REV. 157 (2003).

Comment: Litigating State Constitutional Protections

More than a dozen state constitutions in the United States have enacted provisions that guarantee environmental rights. Not all of them are enforced to the extent of Montana's provision, however. Two major procedural hurdles have been encountered: self-execution and standing.

Self-Execution

Some courts have held that constitutional provisions on the right to environment are non-self-executing and require legislative action before they can be enforced. When a state constitutional environmental provision is ambiguous as to its self-executing status, judges tend to declare that the provisions amount to statements of policy or affirmations of existing legislative authority rather than new, enforceable rights or obligations. When the constitutional provision refers in general to conservation of resources, courts may find the terms too vague to be enforced without the courts being forced to engage in lawmaking in violation of the separation of powers. In such instances, individuals will be barred from invoking constitutional provisions unless and until the legislature enacts measures to establish precise regulations and standards governing the topic.

Courts in Pennsylvania, Louisiana, and Michigan have declared their provisions to be self-executing or have found their provisions executed by legislative action. See *Save Ourselves, Inc. v Louisiana Environmental Control Commission*, 452 So. 2d 1151 (La. 1984); MICH. CONST. art. 4, § 52. In the Pennsylvania case *Commonwealth v. National Gettysburg Battlefield Tower, Inc.*, 302 A.2d 886 (Pa. Commw. Ct.), *aff'd* 311 A.2d 588 (Pa. 1973), the government sued a private company to enjoin its construction of an observation tower overlooking Gettysburg National Military Park. The lower court held that the provision imposed a self-executing duty on the government to protect the environment against private conduct and state action, because "the despoliation of the environment is an act to be expected, in our private ownership society, from public persons." *Id.* at 892. The Court found that the constitutional provision was no vaguer than the guarantees of due process and equal protection and thus could be enforced. On the merits, the trial and appellate courts held that construction of the tower did not violate the constitutional guarantee. The Pennsylvania Supreme Court affirmed but split four ways on the rationale. One justice declined to join any opinion but simply concurred in the result that upheld the decision. Two justices affirmed without discussing the issue of self-execution, and two others concluded that the constitutional provision was not self-executing. The opinion for the Court identified a need for property owners to be able to plan for the use of their property, reasoning that without a more specific standard, "a property owner would not know and would have no way, short of expensive litigation, of finding out what he could do with his property." 311 A.2d at 593. The Court considered that if the vaguely worded provision were "self-executing, action taken under it would pose serious problems of constitutionality, under both the equal protection clause and the due process clause." *Id.* at 595. Two judges dissented, finding the provision self-executing and the proposed tower in violation of it because the provision "installed the common law public trust doctrine as a constitutional right to environmental protection susceptible to enforcement in an action in equity." *Id.* at 596.

A subsequent Pennsylvania case, *Payne v. Kassab*, 21 A.2d 86 (Pa. Commw. Ct. 1973), *aff'd* 361 A.2d 263 (Pa. 1976), affirmed the self-executing nature of section 27 of the Pennsylvania Constitution. Citizens invoked the provision to challenge a street-widening project that would have encroached on a commons area in the town of Wilkes-Barre. As in the earlier case, however, the court decided on the merits that the action did not violate the constitutional guarantee. The Pennsylvania Supreme Court affirmed, 361 A.2d 263 (Pa. 1976), and developed a three-part test for determining violations that "is so weak that litigants using it to challenge environmentally damaging projects are almost always unsuccessful." John Dernbach, *Taking the Pennsylvania Constitution Seriously When It Protects the Environment: Part I – An Interpretive Framework for Article I, Section 27*, 103 DICK. L. REV. 693, 696 (1999).

Standing

Many of the state constitutional provisions appear intended to liberalize standing rules. In Illinois, the constitutional right to a clean and healthful environment creates no new cause of action, *City of Elgin v. County of Cook*, 660 N.E.2d 875 (Ill. 1995), but it does give "standing to an individual to bring an environmental action for a grievance common to members of the public," even in cases where a resident may not be able to demonstrate the "particularized" harm that is normally required. *Glisson v. City of Marion*, 720 N.E.2d 1034, 1041 (Ill. 1999) In *Glisson*, however, the Illinois Court found that the constitutional guarantee was not broad enough to grant standing to an individual who sought to protect biodiversity by obtaining a review of the construction of a dam that would affect two endangered species.

Although not all courts have given effect to this intent, some of them have broadly interpreted the standards in favor of plaintiffs. Pennsylvania courts fall in the latter category. The
state's requirements for standing demand that the plaintiffs have a substantial, direct, and
immediate interest in the subject matter of the litigation. The Pennsylvania Supreme Court
has indicated that environmental litigants may meet this test because "[a]esthetic and environmental well-being are important aspects of the quality of life in our society." *Franklin
Township v. Commonwealth, Department of Environmental Resources*, 452 A.2d 718, 720 (Pa.
1982). Because section 27 establishes a local government's duty to protect its citizen's quality
of life, localities can challenge the state's issuance of a permit for establishment of a toxic
waste disposal site. *Id.* Other decisions have affirmed that section 27 should "normally" be
broadly construed, "especially where a potentially affected locality or private citizen, or specifically empowered watchdog agency, seeks review of an environmental sensitive . . . decision."
*Commonwealth, Pennsylvania Game Commission v. Commonwealth, Department of Envi-
ronmental Resources*, 509 A.2d 877, 883–84 (Pa. Commw. Ct. 1986), *aff'd* 555 A.2d 812 (Pa.
1989).

The Supreme Court of Hawaii has also given broad standing to private individuals to
enforce environmental laws, relying on article XI, section 9, of its constitution. In *Life
of the Land v. Land Use Commission of the State of Hawai'i*, 623 P.2d 431 (Haw. 1981)
the court granted standing to an environmental organization that sought to challenge a
reclassification of certain lands that were not owned by any of the organization's members.
The Supreme Court held that the plaintiffs had standing because of their "aesthetic and
environmental interests," which the court deemed "personal" and "special" interests or rights
guaranteed by article XI, section 9, of the Constitution. Subsequent cases have affirmed that
the constitutional provision gives individuals standing to sue for environmental damage or to
enforce environmental laws. *See Richard v. Metcalf*, 921 P.2d 122 (Haw. 1997); *Kahuna Sunset
Owners Association v. Mahui County Council*, 948 P.2d 122 (Haw. 1997).

Where the procedural hurdles have been overcome or are absent, as in about one-third
of the states with constitutional references to the environment, state courts have enforced
environmental rights. This is also the case in other countries that have enacted constitutional
guarantees of environmental rights, including many developing countries, where the concept
of sustainable development has been critically important. South Africa is one of them.

2. South Africa

Fuel Retailers Association of Southern Africa v. Director-General
Environmental Management, Department of Agriculture, Conservation and
Environment, Mpumalanga Province, et al., Case No. CCT 67/06; ILDC 783
(ZA 2007) (footnotes omitted or renumbered)

Ngcobo J:

Introduction

[1] This application for leave to appeal against the decision of the Supreme Court of Appeal
concerns the nature and scope of the obligations of environmental authorities when they make
decisions that may have a substantial detrimental impact on the environment. In particular, it
concerns the interaction between social and economic development and the protection of the

environment. It arises out of a decision by the Department of Agriculture, Conservation and Environment, Mpumalanga province (the Department), the third respondent, to grant the Inama Family Trust (the Trust) authority in terms of section 22(1) of the Environment Conservation Act, 1989 (ECA) [Act 73 of 1989], to construct a filling station on a property in White River, Mpumalanga (the property).

. . .

Issues Presented

. . .

[34] . . . The questions which fall to be considered in this application are therefore, firstly, the nature and scope of the obligation to consider the social, economic and environmental impact of a proposed development; second, whether the environmental authorities complied with that obligation; and, if the environmental authorities did not comply with that obligation, the appropriate relief.

[35] Before addressing these issues, it is necessary to consider two preliminary matters. The first is the proper cause of action in this application. The other is whether the application raises a constitutional matter, and if so, whether it is in the interests of justice to grant leave to appeal.

The Proper Cause of Action

. . .

[39] . . . In the course of oral argument it became clear that the main ground of attack was that the environmental authorities failed to consider the impact of the proposed filling station on socio-economic conditions, a matter which they were required to consider. The central question in this application therefore is whether the environmental authorities failed to take into consideration matters that they were required to consider prior to granting the authorisation under section 22(1) of ECA.

Does the Application Raise a Constitutional Issue?

[40] Section 24 of the Constitution guarantees to everyone the right to a healthy environment and contemplates that legislation will be enacted for the protection of the environment. ECA and NEMA [the National Environmental Management Act] are legislation which give effect to this provision of the Constitution. The question to be considered in this application is the proper interpretation of the relevant provisions of ECA and NEMA and, in particular, the nature of the obligations imposed by these provisions on the environmental authorities. The proper interpretation of these provisions raises a constitutional issue. So, too, does the application of PAJA [the Promotion of Administrative Justice Act]. It follows therefore that the present application raises a constitutional issue.

Is It in the Interests of Justice to Grant Leave to Appeal?

[41] This case raises an important question concerning the obligation of state organs when making decisions that may have a substantial impact on the environment. In particular, it concerns the nature and scope of the obligation to consider socio-economic conditions. The need to protect the environment cannot be gainsaid. So, too, is the need for social and economic development. How these two compelling needs interact, their impact on decisions affecting the environment and the obligations of environmental authorities in this regard, are important constitutional questions. In

these circumstances, it is therefore in the interests of justice that leave to appeal be granted to consider these issues.

[42] In order to put the issues involved in this case in context and to evaluate the cogency of the constitutional challenge, it is necessary to understand both the constitutional and the legislative frameworks for the protection and management of the environment.

The Relevant Constitutional Provision

[43] The Constitution deals with the environment in section 24 and proclaims the right of everyone –
  (a) to an environment that is not harmful to their health or well-being; and
  (b) to have the environment protected, for the benefit of present and future generations, through reasonable legislative and other measures that –
      (i) prevent pollution and ecological degradation;
      (ii) promote conservation; and
      (iii) secure ecologically sustainable development and use of natural resources while promoting justifiable economic and social development.

Sustainable Development

[44] What is immediately apparent from section 24 is the explicit recognition of the obligation to promote justifiable "economic and social development." Economic and social development is essential to the well-being of human beings.[41] This Court has recognised that socio-economic rights that are set out in the Constitution are indeed vital to the enjoyment of other human rights guaranteed in the Constitution.[42] But development cannot subsist upon a deteriorating environmental base. Unlimited development is detrimental to the environment and the destruction of the environment is detrimental to development. Promotion of development requires the protection of the environment. Yet the environment cannot be protected if development does not pay attention to the costs of environmental destruction. The environment and development are thus inexorably linked. And as has been observed –

> [E]nvironmental stresses and patterns of economic development are linked one to another. Thus agricultural policies may lie at the root of land, water, and forest degradation. Energy policies are associated with the global greenhouse effect, with acidification, and with deforestation for fuelwood in many developing nations. These stresses all threaten economic development. Thus economics and ecology must be completely integrated in decision making and lawmaking processes not just to protect the environment, but also to protect and promote development. Economy is not just about the production of wealth, and ecology is not just about the protection of nature; they are both equally relevant for improving the lot of humankind.[43]

[45] The Constitution recognises the interrelationship between the environment and development; indeed it recognises the need for the protection of the environment while at the same time it recognises the need for social and economic development. It contemplates the integration of environmental protection and socio-economic development. It envisages that environmental

---

[41] Declaration on the Right to Development adopted by General Assembly Resolution 41/128 of Dec. 4, 1986, *available at* http://www.un.org/documents/ga/res/41/a41r128.htm. Article 1 asserts that "[t]he right to development is an inalienable human right." The preamble describes development as "a comprehensive economic, social, cultural and political process, which aims at the constant improvement of the well-being of the entire population."

[42] Government of the Republic of South Africa et al. v. Grootboom et al. 2001 (1) SA 46 (CC); 2000 (11) BCLR 1169 (CC).

[43] *Report of the World Commission on Environment and Development: Our Common Future* (Brundtland Report), *available at* http://www.un.org/esa/sustdev/documents/docs_key_conferences.htm, link: General Assembly 42nd Session: Report of the World Commission on Environment and Development, ch. 1 at para 42.

considerations will be balanced with socio-economic considerations through the ideal of sustainable development. This is apparent from section 24(b)(iii) which provides that the environment will be protected by securing "ecologically sustainable development and use of natural resources while promoting justifiable economic and social development." Sustainable development and sustainable use and exploitation of natural resources are at the core of the protection of the environment.

The Concept of Sustainable Development in International Law

[46] Sustainable development is an evolving concept of international law. Broadly speaking its evolution can be traced to the 1972 Stockholm Conference. That Conference stressed the relationship between development and the protection of the environment, in particular, the need "to ensure that development is compatible with the need to protect and improve [the] environment for the benefit of their population."[44] The principles which were proclaimed at this conference provide a setting for the development of the concept of sustainable development.[45] Since then the concept of sustainable development has received considerable endorsement by the international community.[46] Indeed in 2002 people from over 180 countries gathered in our country for the Johannesburg World Summit on Sustainable Development (WSSD) to reaffirm that sustainable development is a world priority.[47]

[47] But it was the report of the World Commission on Environment and Development (the Brundtland Report) which "coined" the term "sustainable development."[48] The Brundtland Report defined sustainable development as "development that meets the needs of the present without compromising the ability of future generations to meet their own needs." It described sustainable development as –

> [i]n essence . . . a process of change in which the exploitation of resources, the direction of investments, the orientation of technological development; and institutional change are all in harmony and enhance both current and future potential to meet human needs and aspirations.

[48] This report argued for a merger of environmental and economic considerations in decision-making and urged the proposition that "the goals of economic and social development must be defined in terms of sustainability." It called for a new approach to development – "a type of development that integrates production with resource conservation and enhancement, and that links both to the provision for all of an adequate livelihood base and equitable access to resources." The concept of sustainable development, according to the report, "provides a framework for the integration of environment[al] policies and development strategies."

[49] The 1992 Rio Conference made the concept of sustainable development a central feature of its Declaration.[49] The Rio Declaration is especially important because it reflects a real consensus in the international community on some core principles of environmental protection and sustainable development.[50] It developed general principles on sustainable development and provided a framework for the development of the law of sustainable development.

---

44 Principle 13 of the Declaration of the U.N. Conference on the Human Environment, held in Stockholm in 1972, *available at* http://www.unep.org/Documents/Default.asp?DocumentID=97&ArticleID=1503.

45 Separate Opinion of Vice-President Weeramantry in Gabčíkovo-Nagymaros Project (Hungary/Slovakia) 37 I.L.M. 162 (1998).

46 Id.

47 SUSTAINABLE JUSTICE: RECONCILING ECONOMIC, SOCIAL AND ENVIRONMENTAL LAW 561 (Segger & Weeramantry eds., 2005).

48 SANDS PRINCIPLES OF INTERNATIONAL ENVIRONMENTAL LAW 252 (2d ed., 2003).

49 The U.N. Conference on Environment and Development was held in Rio de Janeiro, Brazil on June 3–14, 1992, *available at* http://www.un.org/documents/ga/conf151/aconf15126-1annex1.htm. This Conference adopted, among other instruments, the Rio Declaration on Environment and Development (the Rio Declaration).

50 INTERNATIONAL LAW AND SUSTAINABLE DEVELOPMENT: PAST ACHIEVEMENTS AND FUTURE CHALLENGES 4 (Boyle & Freestone eds., 1999).

[50] At the heart of the Rio Declaration are Principles 3 and 4. Principle 3 provides that "[t]he right to development must be fulfilled so as to equitably meet developmental and environmental needs of present and future generations." Principle 4 provides that "[i]n order to achieve sustainable development, environmental protection shall constitute an integral part of the development process and cannot be considered in isolation from it." The idea that development and environmental protection must be reconciled is central to the concept of sustainable development. At the core of this Principle is the principle of integration of environmental protection and socio-economic development.

[51] Commentators on international law have understandably refrained from attempting to define the concept of sustainable development. Instead they have identified the evolving elements of the concept of sustainable development.[51] These include the integration of environmental protection and economic development (the principle of integration); sustainable utilisation of natural resources (the principle of sustainable use and exploitation of natural resources); the right to development; the pursuit of equity in the use and allocation of natural resources (the principle of intra-generational equity); the need to preserve natural resources for the benefit of present and future generations (the principle of inter-generational and intra-generational equity); and the need to interpret and apply rules of international law in an integrated systematic manner.

[52] The principle of integration of environmental protection and development reflects a –

> . . . commitment to integrate environmental considerations into economic and other development, and to take into account the needs of economic and other social development in crafting, applying and interpreting environmental obligations.

This is an important aspect of sustainable development because "its formal application requires the collection and dissemination of environmental information, and the conduct of environmental impact assessments." The practical significance of the integration of the environmental and developmental considerations is that environmental considerations will now increasingly be a feature of economic and development policy.

[53] The principle of integration of environmental protection and socio-economic development is therefore fundamental to the concept of sustainable development. Indeed economic development, social development and the protection of the environment are now considered pillars of sustainable development. As recognised in the WSSD, States have assumed –

> . . . a collective responsibility to advance and strengthen the interdependent and mutually reinforcing pillars of sustainable development – economic development, social development and environmental protection – at the local, national, regional and global levels.[52]

---

[51] . . . Sands identifies five recurring elements which appear to comprise the legal concept of sustainable development as reflected in international agreements. These are:

- "the need to take into consideration the needs of present and future generations;
- the acceptance, on environmental protection grounds, of limits placed upon the use and exploitation of natural resources;
- the role of equitable principles in the allocation of rights and obligations;
- the need to integrate all aspects of environment and development; and
- the need to interpret and apply rules of international law in an integrated and systemic manner."

[52] U.N. Department of Economic and Social Affairs – Division for Sustainable Development Johannesburg Declaration on Sustainable Development 2002, para. 5, *available at* http://www.un.org/esa/sustdev/documents/WSSD_POI_PD/English/POI_PD.htm.

[54] The concept of sustainable development has received approval in a judgment of the International Court of Justice. This much appears from the judgment of the International Court of Justice in *Gabčíkovo-Nagymaros Project (Hungary/Slovakia)*. . . . [53]

[55] The integration of economic development, social development and environmental protection implies the need to reconcile and accommodate these three pillars of sustainable development. Sustainable development provides a framework for reconciling socio-economic development and environmental protection. This role of the concept of sustainable development as a mediating principle in reconciling environmental and developmental considerations was recognised by Vice-President Weeramantry in a separate opinion in *Gabčíkovo-Nagymaros*, when he said –

> The Court must hold the balance even between the environmental considerations and the development considerations raised by the respective Parties. The principle that enables the Court to do so is the principle of sustainable development.[54]

[56] It is in the light of these developments in the international law of environment and sustainable development that the concept of sustainable development must be construed and understood in our law.

The Concept of Sustainable Development in Our Law

[57] As in international law, the concept of sustainable development has a significant role to play in the resolution of environmentally related disputes in our law. It offers an important principle for the resolution of tensions between the need to protect the environment on the one hand, and the need for socio-economic development on the other hand. In this sense, the concept of sustainable development provides a framework for reconciling socio-economic development and environmental protection.

[58] Sustainable development does not require the cessation of socio-economic development but seeks to regulate the manner in which it takes place. It recognises that socio-economic development invariably brings risk of environmental damage as it puts pressure on environmental resources. It envisages that decision-makers guided by the concept of sustainable development will ensure that socio-economic developments remain firmly attached to their ecological roots and that these roots are protected and nurtured so that they may support future socio-economic developments.

[59] NEMA, which was enacted to give effect to section 24 of the Constitution, embraces the concept of sustainable development. Sustainable development is defined to mean "the integration of social, economic and environmental factors into planning, implementation and decision-making for the benefit of present and future generations." This broad definition of sustainable development incorporates two of the internationally recognised elements of the concept of sustainable development, namely, the principle of integration of environmental protection and socio-economic development, and the principle of inter-generational and intra-generational equity. In addition, NEMA sets out some of the factors that are relevant to decisions on sustainable development. These factors largely reflect international experience. But as NEMA makes it clear, these factors are not exhaustive.[55]

---

53 Gabčíkovo-Nagymaros Project (Hungary/Slovakia) 37 I.L.M. 162, 700 (1998), at para. 140. In a separate opinion, Vice-President Weeramantry held that the concept of sustainable development is part of international customary law. *See* Separate Opinion, at 207.

54 Separate Opinion, at 204.

55 Section 2(4)(a) of NEMA provides:

   "Sustainable development requires the consideration of all relevant factors including the following:

   (i) That the disturbance of ecosystems and loss of biological diversity are avoided, or, where they cannot be altogether avoided, are minimised and remedied;

[60] One of the key principles of NEMA requires people and their needs to be placed at the forefront of environmental management – *batho pele*. It requires all developments to be socially, economically and environmentally sustainable. Significantly for the present case, it requires that the social, economic and environmental impact of a proposed development be "considered, assessed and evaluated" and that any decision made "must be appropriate in the light of such consideration and assessment." This is underscored by the requirement that decisions must take into account the interests, needs and values of all interested and affected persons.

[61] Construed in the light of section 24 of the Constitution, NEMA therefore requires the integration of environmental protection and economic and social development. It requires that the interests of the environment be balanced with socio-economic interests. Thus, whenever a development which may have a significant impact on the environment is planned, it envisages that there will always be a need to weigh considerations of development, as underpinned by the right to socio-economic development, against environmental considerations, as underpinned by the right to environmental protection. In this sense, it contemplates that environmental decisions will achieve a balance between environmental and socio-economic developmental considerations through the concept of sustainable development.

[62] To sum up therefore NEMA makes it abundantly clear that the obligation of the environmental authorities includes the consideration of socio-economic factors as an integral part of its environmental responsibility.[56] It follows therefore that the parties correctly accepted that the Department was obliged to consider the impact of the proposed filling station on socio-economic conditions. It is within this context that the nature and scope of the obligation to consider socio-economic factors, in particular, whether it includes the obligation to assess the cumulative impact of the proposed filling station and existing ones, and the impact of the proposed filling station on existing ones. . . .

The Nature and the Scope of the Obligation to Consider Socio-Economic Conditions

[71] The nature and the scope of the obligation to consider the impact of the proposed development on socio-economic conditions must be determined in the light of the concept of sustainable development and the principle of integration of socio-economic development and the protection of the environment. Once it is accepted, as it must be, that socio-economic development and the protection of the environment are interlinked, it follows that socio-economic conditions have an impact on the environment. A proposed filling station may affect the sustainability of existing filling stations with consequences for the job security of the employees of those filling stations.

(ii) that pollution and degradation of the environment are avoided, or, where they cannot be altogether avoided, are minimised and remedied;

(iii) that the disturbance of landscapes and sites that constitute the nation's cultural heritage is avoided, or where it cannot be altogether avoided, is minimised and remedied;

(iv) that waste is avoided, or where it cannot be altogether avoided, minimised and re-used or recycled where possible and otherwise disposed of in a responsible manner;

(v) that the use and exploitation of non-renewable natural resources is responsible and equitable, and takes into account the consequences of the depletion of the resource;

(vi) that the development, use and exploitation of renewable resources and the ecosystems of which they are part do not exceed the level beyond which their integrity is jeopardised;

(vii) that a risk-averse and cautious approach is applied, which takes into account the limits of current knowledge about the consequences of decisions and actions; and

(viii) that negative impacts on the environment and on people's environmental rights be anticipated and prevented, and where they cannot be altogether prevented, are minimised and remedied."

[56] This principle was considered in the following cases: BP Southern Africa (Pty) Ltd v. MEC for Agriculture, Conservation, Environment and Land Affairs 2004 (5) SA 124 (W), at 140E–151H; Turnstone Trading CC v. Director General Environmental Management, Department of Agriculture, Conservation & Development, Case No. 3104/04 (T), Mar. 11, 2005, unreported, at paras. 17–19; MEC for Agriculture, Conservation, Environment and Land Affairs v. Sasol Oil (Pty) Ltd and Another 2006 (5) SA 483 (SCA), at para. 15.

But that is not all; if the proposed filling station leads to the closure of some or all of the existing filling stations, this has consequences for the environment. Filling stations have a limited end use. The underground fuel tanks and other infrastructure may have to be removed and land may have to be rehabilitated.

[72] Apart from this, the proliferation of filling stations in close proximity to one another may increase the pre-existing risk of adverse impact on the environment. The risk that comes to mind is the contamination of underground water, soil, visual intrusion and light. An additional filling station may significantly increase this risk and increase environmental stress. Mindful of this possibility, NEMA requires that the cumulative impact of a proposed development, together with the existing developments on the environment, socio-economic conditions and cultural heritage must be assessed. The cumulative effect of the proposed development must naturally be assessed in the light of existing developments. A consideration of socio-economic conditions therefore includes the consideration of the impact of the proposed development not only in combination with the existing developments, but also its impact on existing ones.

[73] This approach to the scope of the obligation to consider socio-economic conditions is consistent with the concept of sustainable development under our legislation.

. . .

[78] What must be stressed here is that the objective of considering the impact of a proposed development on existing ones is not to stamp out competition; it is to ensure the economic, social and environmental sustainability of all developments, both proposed and existing ones. Environmental concerns do not commence and end once the proposed development is approved. It is a continuing concern. The environmental legislation imposes a continuing, and thus necessarily evolving, obligation to ensure the sustainability of the development and to protect the environment. As the International Court of Justice observed –

> in the field of environmental protection, vigilance and prevention are required on account of the often irreversible character of damage to the environment and of the limitations inherent in the very mechanism of reparation of this type of damage.

[79] There are two points that must be stressed here. First, the Constitution, ECA and NEMA do not protect the existing developments at the expense of future developments. What section 24 requires, and what NEMA gives effect to, is that socio-economic development must be justifiable in the light of the need to protect the environment. The Constitution and environmental legislation introduce a new criterion for considering future developments. Pure economic factors are no longer decisive. The need for development must now be determined by its impact on the environment, sustainable development and social and economic interests. The duty of environmental authorities is to integrate these factors into decision-making and make decisions that are informed by these considerations. This process requires a decision-maker to consider the impact of the proposed development on the environment and socio-economic conditions.

[80] Second, the objective of this exercise, as NEMA makes it plain, is both to identify and predict the actual or potential impact on socio-economic conditions and consider ways of minimising negative impact while maximising benefit. Were it to be otherwise, the earth would become a graveyard for commercially failed developments. And this in itself poses a potential threat to the environment. One of the environmental risks associated with filling stations is the impact of a proposed filling station on the feasibility of filling stations in close proximity. The assessment of such impact is necessary in order to minimise the harmful effect of the proliferation of filling stations on the environment. The requirement to consider the impact of a proposed development on socio-economic conditions, including the impact on existing developments addresses this concern.

[81] Finally NEMA requires "a risk averse and cautious approach" to be applied by decision-makers. This approach entails taking into account the limitation on present knowledge about the consequences of an environmental decision. This precautionary approach is especially important in the light of section 24(7)(b) of NEMA which requires the cumulative impact of a development on the environmental and socio-economic conditions to be investigated and addressed. An increase in the risk of contamination of underground water and soil, and visual intrusion and light, for example, are some of the significant cumulative impacts that could result from the proliferation of filling stations. Subsection 24(7)(b) specifically requires the investigation of the potential impact, including cumulative effects, of the proposed development on the environment and socio-economic conditions, and the assessment of the significance of that potential impact.[57]

[82] What was required of the environmental authorities therefore was to consider the impact on the environment of the proliferation of filling stations as well as the impact of the proposed filling station on existing ones. This conclusion makes it plain that the obligation to consider the socio-economic impact of a proposed development is wider than the requirement to assess need and desirability under the Ordinance. It also comprehends the obligation to assess the cumulative impact on the environment of the proposed development.

[83] What remains to be considered now is whether the environmental authorities complied with this obligation.

Did the Environmental Authorities Comply with Their Obligations Under NEMA?

[84] It is common cause that the environmental authorities themselves did not consider need and desirability. They took the view that these were matters that must be "proven, argued and considered by the Local Council" when an application for rezoning is made in terms of section 56 of the Ordinance.

. . .

[88] By their own admission therefore the environmental authorities did not consider need and desirability. Instead they relied upon the fact that (a) the property was rezoned for the construction of a filling station; (b) a motivation for need and desirability would have been submitted for the purposes of rezoning; and (c) the town-planning authorities must have considered the motivation prior to approving the rezoning scheme. Neither of environmental authorities claims to have seen the motivation, let alone read its contents. They left the consideration of this vital aspect of their environmental obligation entirely to the local authority. This in my view is manifestly not a proper discharge of their statutory duty. This approach to their obligations, in effect, amounts to unlawful delegation of their duties to the local authority. This they cannot do.

. . .

[91] What must be stressed here is that the question on review is not whether there is evidence that an additional filling station posed undue threat to the environment. The question is whether the environmental authorities considered and evaluated the social and economic impact of the proposed filling station on existing ones and how an additional filling station would affect the environment. Indeed it is difficult to fathom how the environmental authorities could have assessed the threat of overtrading to the environment if they did not apply their minds to this

---

[57] Section 24(7)(b) of NEMA provides:

Procedures for the investigation, assessment and communication of the potential impact of activities must, as a minimum, ensure . . . investigation of the potential impact, including cumulative effects, of the activity and its alternatives on the environment, socio-economic conditions and cultural heritage, and assessment of the significance of that potential impact.

question at all. They could have established such threats if they had applied their mind to this question. They did not do so. Their decision cannot therefore stand.

[92] It is no answer by the environmental authorities to say that had they themselves considered the need and desirability aspect, this could have led to conflicting decisions between the environmental officials and the town-planning officials. If that is the natural consequence of the discharge of their obligations under the environmental legislation, it is a consequence mandated by the statute. It is impermissible for them to seek to avoid this consequence by delegating their obligations to the town-planning authorities. What is of grave concern here is that the environmental authorities did not even have sight of the motivation placed before the local authority relating to need and desirability, let alone read it. Section 24(1) of NEMA makes it clear that the potential impact on socio-economic conditions must be considered by "the organ of state charged by law with authorising, permitting or otherwise allowing the implementation of [a proposed] activity."

. . .

[97] In any event, there is no suggestion that either the town-planning authorities, or the environmental authorities applied their minds to the impact of the proposed filling station on socio-economic conditions. The scoping report was concerned primarily with the financial feasibility of the proposed filling station. In fact, it said nothing about the impact of the proposed filling station on the existing ones. In all the circumstances of this case, the environmental authorities took a narrow view of their obligations and misconstrued their obligations. As a consequence of this, the environmental authorities failed to apply their minds to the impact of the proposed filling station on socio-economic conditions.

[98] Before concluding this judgment, there are two matters that should be mentioned in relation to the duty of environmental authorities which are a source of concern. The first relates to the attitude of Water Affairs and Forestry and the environmental authorities. The environmental authorities and Water Affairs and Forestry did not seem to take seriously the threat of contamination of underground water supply. The precautionary principle required these authorities to insist on adequate precautionary measures to safeguard against the contamination of underground water. This principle is applicable where, due to unavailable scientific knowledge, there is uncertainty as to the future impact of the proposed development. Water is a precious commodity; it is a natural resource that must be protected for the benefit of present and future generations.

[99] In these circumstances one would have expected that the environmental authorities and Water Affairs and Forestry would conduct a thorough investigation into the possible impact of the installation of petrol tanks in the vicinity of the borehole, in particular, in the light of the existence of other filling stations in the vicinity. The environmental authorities did not consider the cumulative effect of the proliferation of filling stations on the aquifer. The Geohydrology division of Water Affairs and Forestry was content with simply stating that the developer must ensure that there is no pollution of water and that there must be monitoring as proposed in the report and in accordance with the regulations. Neither the Water Quality Management nor the Water Utilization divisions of the Water Affairs and Forestry commented on the reports as they did not receive them. They became aware of the development after both the record of decision and the appeal from it had been issued.

[100] The other matter relates to the attitude of the environmental authorities to the objection of the applicant to the construction of the proposed filling station. In the Supreme Court of Appeal they argued that the applicant's opposition to the application for authorisation was motivated by the desire to stifle competition[,] which was "thinly disguised as a desire to protect the environment." In this regard, they pointed to the fact that the main deponent on behalf of the applicant, Mr. Le Roux, owns other filling stations in the area. The Supreme Court of Appeal found that "there appears to be some merit in the contention." Whatever, the merits of the criticism may be, a

matter on which it is not necessary to express an opinion, an environmental authority whose duty it is to protect the environment should welcome every opportunity to consider and assess issues that may adversely affect the environment.

[101] Similarly, the duty of a court of law when the decision of an environmental authority is brought on review is to evaluate the soundness or otherwise of the objections raised. In doing so, the court must apply the applicable legal principles. If upon a proper application of the legal principles, the objections are valid, the court has no option but to uphold the objections. That is the duty that is imposed on a court by the Constitution, which is to uphold the Constitution and the law which they "... must apply impartially and without fear, favour or prejudice." Neither the identity of the litigant who raises the objection nor the motive is relevant.

[102] The role of the courts is especially important in the context of the protection of the environment and giving effect to the principle of sustainable development. The importance of the protection of the environment cannot be gainsaid. Its protection is vital to the enjoyment of the other rights contained in the Bill of Rights; indeed, it is vital to life itself. It must therefore be protected for the benefit of the present and future generations. The present generation holds the earth in trust for the next generation. This trusteeship position carries with it the responsibility to look after the environment. It is the duty of the court to ensure that this responsibility is carried out. Indeed, the Johannesburg Principles adopted at the Global Judges Symposium underscore the role of the judiciary in the protection of the environment.[58]

[103] On that occasion members of the judiciary across the globe made the following statement –

> We affirm our commitment to the pledge made by world leaders in the Millennium Declaration adopted by the United Nations General Assembly in September 2000 "to spare no effort to free all of humanity, and above all our children and grandchildren, from the threat of living on a planet irredeemably spoilt by human activities, and whose resources would no longer be sufficient for their needs."

In addition, they affirmed –

> ... that an independent Judiciary and judicial process is vital for the same implementation, development and enforcement of environmental law, and that members of the Judiciary, as well as those contributing to the judicial process at the national, regional and global levels, are crucial partners for promoting compliance with, and the implementation and the enforcement of, international and national environmental law.

[104] One of these principles expresses –

> A full commitment to contributing towards the realization of the goals of sustainable development through the judicial mandate to implement, develop and enforce the law, and to uphold the Rule of Law and the democratic process ...

Courts therefore have a crucial role to play in the protection of the environment. When the need arises to intervene in order to protect the environment, they should not hesitate to do so.

---

[58] U.N. Environment Programme – Division of Policy Development and Law, Global Judges Symposium on Sustainable Development and the Role of Law – The Johannesburg Principles on the Role of Law and Sustainable Development adopted at the Global Judges Symposium held in Johannesburg, South Africa, Aug. 18–20, 2002, *available at* http://www.unep.org/dpdl/symposium/Principles.htm.

Conclusion

[105] The considerations set out above make it clear that the decision of the environmental authorities is flawed and falls to be set aside as they misconstrued the obligations imposed on them by NEMA. In all the circumstances, the decision by the environmental authorities to grant authorisation for the construction of the filling station under section 22(1) of ECA cannot stand and falls to be reviewed and set aside. It follows that both the High Court and the Supreme Court of Appeal erred, the High Court in dismissing the application for review and the Supreme Court of Appeal in upholding the decision of the High Court.

The Relief

[106] The appropriate relief in this case is to send the matter back to the environmental authorities for them to consider the matter afresh in a manner that is consistent with this judgment.

Costs

[107] Then there is the question of costs. This is a case, in my view, in which the costs should follow the result. However, I do not think that the Trust and its trustees must be saddled with costs. It is true that they opposed the matter – but this was to safeguard their interests. The contest, at the end of the day, was between the applicant and the first, second and third respondents. It is these respondents who should pay the cost of the applicant while the remaining respondents who opposed the matter will have to look after their own costs. The costs payable by the first, second and third respondents must include those that are consequent upon the employment of two counsel.

Questions and Discussion

1. In Argentina, the right is deemed a subjective right entitling any person to initiate an action for environmental protection. *Kattan, Alberto et al. v. National Government*, Juzgado Nacional de la Instancia en lo Contencioso administrativo Federal. No. 2, Ruling of May 10, 1983, La Ley, 1983-D, 576; *Irazu Margarita v. Copetro S.A.*, Cámara Civil y Comercial de la Plata, Ruling of May 10, 1993, *available at* http://www.eldial.com ("The right to live in a healthy and balanced environment is a fundamental attribute of people. Any aggression to the environment ends up becoming a threat to life itself and to the psychological and physical integrity of the person."). *See also Asociación para la Protección de Medio Ambiente y Educación Ecológica "18 de Octubre" v. Aguas Argentinas S.A. et al.*, Federal Appellate Tribunal of La Plata (2003). Colombia also recognizes the enforceability of the right to environment. *Fundepúblico v. Mayor of Bugalagrande et al.*, Juzgado Primero Superior, Interlocutorio No. 032, Tulua (Dec. 19, 1991) ("It should be recognized that a healthy environment is a sina qua non condition for life itself and that no right could be exercised in a deeply altered environment."). For Chilean cases, see *Pablo Orrego Silva et al. v. Empresa Eléctrica Pange, S.A.*, Supreme Court (Aug. 5, 1993); *Antonio Horvath Kiss et al. v. National Commission for the Environment*, Supreme Court (Mar. 19, 1997).

2. Is it necessary or useful to include the right to a safe and healthy environment among human rights guarantees? Or is this simply devaluing the currency, so to speak, by unnecessarily adding desires and claims to the catalog of accepted guarantees? The U.N. General Assembly set forth criteria for adding to the network of international human rights standards in Resolution 41/120 (Dec. 4, 1986). The resolution recognized the value of continuing

efforts to identify specific areas where further international action is required to develop the existing international legal framework, adding that standard setting should be effective and efficient and in accord with the following guidelines:

a. Be consistent with the existing body of international human rights law;
b. Be of fundamental character and derive from the inherent dignity and worth of the human person;
c. Be sufficiently precise to give rise to identifiable and practicable rights and obligations;
d. Provide, where appropriate, realistic, and effective implementation machinery, including reporting systems;
e. Attract broad international support.

Do these guidelines support the further development of the right to a safe and healthy environment?

3. From the readings so far in this chapter, does it seem that the right to environment is widely accepted as a justiciable right? What does it contribute to human rights or to environmental protection?

4. For further reading, see Gudmundur Alfredson and Alexandre Ovsiouk, *Human Rights and the Environment*, 60 NORDIC J. INT'L L. 19 (1991); L. Collins, *Are We There Yet? The Right to Environment in International and European Law*, 2007 McGILL INT'L J. OF SUSTAINABLE DEV. L. & POL'Y 119; Philippe Cullet, *Definition of an Environmental Right in a Human Rights Context*, 13 NETH. Q. HUM. RTS. 25 (1995); Maguelonne Dejeant-Pons, *The Right to Environment in Regional Human Rights Systems*, in HUMAN RIGHTS IN THE TWENTY-FIRST CENTURY 595 (Paul Mahoney & Kathleen Mahoney eds., 1993); Maguelonne Dejeant-Pons & Marc Pallemaerts, DROITS DE L'HOMME ET ENVIRONNEMENT (2002); Richard Desgagné, *Integrating Environmental Values into the European Convention on Human Rights*, 89 AM. J. INT'L L. 263 (1995); Malgosia Fitzmaurice, *The Right of the Child to a Clean Environment*, 23 S. ILL. U. L.J. 611 (1999); Gunther Handl, *Human Rights and Protection of the Environment: A Mildly "Revisionist" View*, in HUMAN RIGHTS AND ENVIRONMENTAL PROTECTION (Antonio A. Cancado Trindade ed., 1992); HUMAN RIGHTS APPROACHES TO ENVIRONMENTAL PROTECTION (Alan Boyle & Michael Anderson eds., 1996); Michael J. Kane, *Promoting Political Rights to Protect the Environment*, 18 YALE J. INT'L L. 389; Alexandre Kiss, *Le droit la conservation de l'environnement*, 1 REVUE UNIVERSELLE DES DROITS DE L'HOMME 445 (1990); John Lee, *The Underlying Legal Theory to Support a Well-Defined Human Right to a Healthy Environment as a Principle of Customary International Law*, 25 COLUM. J. ENVTL. L. 283, 308–09 (2000); James T. McClymonds, *The Human Right to a Healthy Environment: An International Legal Perspective*, 37 N.Y.L.S. L. REV. 583 (1992); Karen E. MacDonald, *Sustaining the Environmental Rights of Children: An Exploratory Critique*, 18 FORDHAM ENVTL. L. REV. 1, 39 (2006); Ole W. Pedersen, *European Environmental Human Rights and Environmental Rights: A Long Time Coming?*, 21 GEO. INT'L ENVTL. L. REV. 73 (2008); Neil Popovic, *In Pursuit of Environmental Human Rights: Commentary on the Draft Declaration of Principles on Human Rights and the Environment*, 27 COLO. HUM. RTS. REV. 487 (1996); Dinah Shelton, *What Happened in Rio to Human Rights?*, 4 Y.B. INT'L ENVTL. L. 75 (1994); Dinah Shelton, *Environmental Rights*, in PEOPLES' RIGHTS (Philip Alston ed., 2001); Melissa Thorme, *Establishing Environment as a Human Right*, 19 DENV. J. INT'L L. & POL'Y 302 (1991); Jon van Dyke, *A Proposal to Introduce the Right to a Healthy Environment into the European Convention Regime*, 13 VA. ENVTL. L.J. 323 (1993).

8 Indigenous Peoples, Rights, and the Environment

I. Introduction

Indigenous peoples are uniquely vulnerable to environmental harm because of the increasing pressures on their lands and resources, as well as the cultural and religious links they maintain with their ancestral territories. There are more than 200 million indigenous people in the world. Most of them live in highly vulnerable ecosystems: the Arctic and tundra, tropical and boreal forests, riverine and coastal zones, and mountains and semiarid rangelands. In the past few decades, traditional indigenous lands have come under increased pressure as outsiders have sought and extracted or converted natural resources to supply a growing global demand. Once hardly accessible, the territories used and occupied by indigenous peoples have become a major source of hydroelectric power, minerals, hardwoods, and pasture lands. Other indigenous regions are being threatened or lost as a result of climate change, as discussed in Chapter 9. For those indigenous and tribal peoples who have remained in their traditional territories, the invasion of the outside world has brought with it disease; exploitation; loss of language and culture; and in too many instances, complete annihilation of the group as a distinct entity. For reports of the U.N. special rapporteur on indigenous peoples, see U.N. Docs. A/HRC/15/37 (2010); A/HCC/12/34 (2009); A/HRC/9/9 (2008); A/HRC/4/32 (2007).

This chapter begins by examining the theoretical approaches to the rights of indigenous peoples. It then looks at the relevant international legal texts before turning to international and domestic jurisprudence. It concludes with an examination of the issue of access to indigenous traditional knowledge and resources in the context of the Convention on Biological Diversity.

II. Theoretical Approaches

Reconciling Five Competing Conceptual Structures of Indigenous Peoples' Claims in International and Comparative Law,
in PEOPLES' RIGHTS 69, 70–71, 73–80, 83–89, 91–92, 96–110
(Philip Alston ed., 2001) (footnotes renumbered)
Benedict Kingsbury

On what conceptual foundations do legal claims made by indigenous peoples rest? Uncertainty on this issue has had the benefit of encouraging the flowering of multiple approaches, but it has also done much to heighten national dissensus on questions involving indigenous peoples, and it has been a serious obstacle to negotiation in the United Nations (U.N.) and the Organization of American States (OAS) of proposed Declarations on the Rights of Indigenous Peoples. This [author] seeks to clarify the debate by distinguishing and exploring five fundamentally different conceptual structures employed in claims brought by indigenous people or members of such groups:

- human rights and non-discrimination claims
- minority claims
- self-determinations claims
- historic sovereignty claims
- claims as indigenous peoples, including claims based on treaties or other agreements between indigenous peoples and states.

... Debates as to the essence of each conceptual structure, and especially as to the boundaries between them, are often proxies for clashes of political interests.... Political interests are scarcely veiled in polar positions taken in arguments as to whether human rights can be held by groups or only by individuals, whether it is correct under the International Covenant on Civil and Political Rights that minorities have no right of self-determination but all peoples do, whether the operative concept is indigenous peoples or indigenous people....

... The forensic point... is that different claims made by indigenous peoples may fall into any of these five categories, or into several at once, and that the totality of these claims as a genre cannot and should not be understood as belonging exclusively to any one or other category. While genuine analytical distinctions underpin this division into categories, these distinctions do not in themselves resolve many of the more difficult problems that arise in practice. Three sets of practical problems arise for consideration.... First, how far and how successfully may the first four, well established categories – which have in large measure been structured by norms and patterns of legal practice not related specifically to indigenous peoples – be adapted to the distinctive features of indigenous peoples' issues? Secondly, how well do these different apparently competing concepts fit together in an integrated legal structure? Thirdly, do the problems and limits of these processes or adaptation and integration of the first four categories suggest, against the background of the increasing salience of indigenous peoples' issues and the rapid evolution of law and policy in this area, that a new legal category of claims of indigenous peoples' has been established, and if so, what is its justification, structure and significance? These questions will be addressed in discussion of each of the five categories. The significance and implications of this five-fold division, including strategies it encourages and the contextual variation and legitimation this fragmentation makes possible, will be considered in the conclusion.

. . .

1. Human Rights and Non-Discrimination

Whether issues raised by indigenous peoples can be addressed exclusively within the existing framework of international human rights law, or whether by contrast a new legal category of indigenous peoples' rights requires recognition, is a fundamental political debate that exemplifies the political tendency to polarize around questions of which legal category applies. Some state representatives in U.N. and OAS negotiations have suggested that the conscientious application of human rights standards is all that is necessary satisfactorily to address problems suffered by members of indigenous groups.

. . .

A fundamental question in human rights claims made by members of indigenous groups against the state is how far the distinctive situation of the indigenous group is relevant. Issues relating to the fair treatment of groups, and the inevitable questions about individual identity and membership which any operational reference to groups entails, are entangled with standard human rights claims based on the suffering of individuals in several existing normative structures. "Genocide" imports issues of harm to groups into the very definition of the crime committed against any individual. The concept of "ethnocide," although not well-developed juridically, is understood by human rights advocates to extend the ambit of genocide to destruction of culture and other conditions essential for the continued distinctive existence of a group. In practice the interaction between individual rights claims and group membership is most systematically established by prohibitions of wrongful discrimination. The strong international policy against racial discrimination has been an important source of leverage in indigenous claims. . . .

A survey of decisions by state courts in countries formally and substantively committed to judicial enforcement of some human rights shows divergent patterns and much uncertainty in addressing the issue whether, and how, the distinctive situation of indigenous groups affects human rights arguments. One line of approach is to deny any distinctive character to indigenous claims on the ground that human rights are universal, not special. An illustration is *Lyng v. Northwest Indian Cemetery Protective Association*,[1] where Indian plaintiffs challenged a proposal by the U.S. Forest Service to build a road on public land in the Chimney Rock area of Northern California, on the ground that the road would effectively destroy the tranquility essential to the continuation of Indian meditative religious practices on this land that had been pursued for many generations. Writing for a majority in the U.S. Supreme Court, Justice O'Connor rejected the argument that the Indians' right to religious freedom under the First Amendment was infringed by road construction. Although federally recognized Indian tribes occupy a special place in the U.S. legal system, and U.S. law recognizes aspects of what is often called "sovereignty" of Indian tribes, Justice O'Connor did not see this as relevant to a First Amendment claim. Her position was that Indians have exactly the same First Amendment rights as anyone else, and that these do not extend to controlling the use of public lands. The historic experience of Indians, including the loss of control of lands they had long used, was not material, nor was the ancient character and spatial location of this particular religious practice. Her argument was that the courts must be neutral as amongst religions, and cannot begin inquiries into the veracity or merits or historical weight of religious claims that would privilege some religious claims over others. But it might well be argued, to the contrary, that the First Amendment jurisprudence does exactly this in privileging understandings of religion that depend not on expanses that since colonization have become "public" lands, but on private buildings protected by a property rights regime that is itself buttressed by First Amendment limits on state action. The process by which land historically used by Indians for religious observance became "public lands," and the weakness of the property rights they enjoy, is integral to evaluating protection of their religious freedom. Supposed neutrality in human rights protection can be, as here, a distortion where the human rights question is separated from the property rights regime and from governance regimes, such as federal trust responsibilities or frameworks for self-government.

A second approach is to start with a requirement of universality but modify it to favour indigenous peoples where disadvantage or past injustices warrant. In *Gerhardy v. Brown*,[2] a defendant who was not a member of the Pitjantjatjara and thus had no right to enter lands restored to Pitjantjatjara communities under the *Pitjantjatjara Land Rights Act* (a South Australian statute), challenged his prosecution for illegal entry onto the lands by arguing that the statutory provision limiting his access infringed the *Racial Discrimination Act* ([an Australian Federal] statute intended to give effect to provisions in the International Convention on the Elimination of All

---

[1] 485 U.S. 439 (1988).
[2] (1985) 159 CLR 70.

Forms of Racial Discrimination). A majority in the High Court of Australia took the view that the South Australian legislation was on its face racially discriminatory in that only Aboriginal people could be Pitjantjatjara and so entitled to free access to the land, whereas non-Pitjantjatjara (including non-Pitjantjatjara Aboriginal people like the defendant) were entitled to access only if other conditions were satisfied (e.g. if they had permission, or were a candidate for election to public office).... The court held, however, that the statutory provision was saved by the provision in the International Convention excluding from the category of racial discrimination: "Special measures taken for the sole purpose of securing adequate advancement of certain racial or ethnic groups or individuals ... in order to ensure such groups or individuals equal enjoyment of human rights and fundamental freedoms ... " The policy of this Convention provision is widely understood to apply even where there is no specific evidence of the effects on particular groups or persons of past discrimination.... Nevertheless, some members of the High Court in *Gerhardy* were strongly influenced in their finding on prima facie discrimination by concern that allowing the government to evade prohibitions of racial discrimination by reference to such criteria as traditional ownership might open a loophole for what Gibbs called "the most obnoxious discrimination." By this he seems to have meant apartheid. His suspicions of "traditional ownership" as a sufficient criterion for excluding non-owners overcame the argument that most owners of property can exclude non-owners; he focused on "the vast area of the lands ... more than one-tenth of the state" to distinguish the situation of the Pitjantjatjara from that of ordinary property holders, although Australian property law protects the exclusionary rights of non-aboriginal holders of very large tracts. This logic—that claims settlements with indigenous peoples for restoration of land to traditional owners may involve racial discrimination against non-members of these groups—is a basis for much political opposition to, and some judicial concerns about, land claims settlements or other historically-grounded arrangements....

A third approach is to uphold special measures by states that benefit indigenous groups precisely because of the distinctive histories and experiences of these groups.

... [The three approaches] have much in common. In each case the questions are framed in terms of state law: the meaning of the First Amendment, the Racial Discrimination Act, the Due Process clause. There is no real indigenous voice in any of the cases; the cases are about Indians and Aborigines, but they themselves do not figure greatly in the judicial opinions. The courts do not demonstrate a close grasp of indigenous experience in relation to religion, land, self-government, or state institutions such as the Bureau of Indian Affairs. This judicial pattern is changing, however, as negotiations and decisions on matters such as land, fisheries, resource management, language, education, and broadcasting evolve into general state acceptance of some degree of indigenous participation, self-government, and voice.... *Delgamuuk v. British Columbia*[3] establishes that indigenous understandings of relations to land and territory, embodied often in oral history, are admissible and relevant in the construction of a concept of aboriginal title that is not simply a creation and sufferance of the state legal system, but embodies both indigenous history and indigenous aspirations.... [T]he situation of indigenous peoples' property in Australia became a substantial *sui generis* issue, with the Commonwealth government seeking at least some aboriginal input through the Australian and Torres Strait Islander Commission before adoption of the *Native Title Act* 1993.[4] The weakness of the public law element became manifest in the retreat from parts of the High Court's jurisprudence in the *Native Title Amendment Act* 1998, government recalcitrance in dealing with and funding the Commission, and the unilateral terms of government policy on matters ranging from "national reconciliation" to the restructuring of aboriginal land councils.[5]

[3] [1997] 3 S.C.R. 1010.
[4] For criticism, see, e.g., Coe, "ATSIC: Self-Determination or Otherwise," 35 RACE AND CLASS (1994).
[5] An overview of public law issues in Australian courts is Clarke, "'Indigenous' People and Constitutional Law," in AUSTRALIAN CONSTITUTIONAL LAW: MATERIALS AND COMMENTARY 50 (P. Hanks & D. Cass eds. 6th ed., 1999).

This review indicates that the adaptation of the category of "human rights" is of fundamental importance in addressing indigenous issues, and that courts and state institutions often prefer to address such issues within this frame, but practice and experience suggest that additional concepts are needed and are often deployed. Issues connected with distinct histories, cultures, and identities animate the search for alternative concepts of international law and national law related to, but going beyond, individual human rights and nondiscrimination. These concepts, increasingly influential in judicial practice and political negotiations relating to indigenous peoples' claims, will be considered in subsequent sections.

2. Minorities

"Minorities" – or more often, a variant such as "national minorities" – has been utilized as a juridical category in international treaty law for several centuries, and was actively promulgated and operationalized by post–World War I legal instruments and League of Nations institutions. After 1945, however, states looked to the lessons of Nazi Germany's irredentist use of disaffected German minorities in neighboring countries, and to the imminent problems of nation-building in post-colonial states, and became reluctant to establish international law standards focused specifically on minorities, preferring instead to build the general human rights programme applicable to all individuals. . . . The body of international legal instruments focused specifically on "minorities" is thus an impoverished one. Recognition of a need to face this deficiency resulted in the early 1990s in the U.N. Declaration on Minorities (1992) and the Council of Europe Framework Convention for the Protection of National Minorities (1995), but neither is very expansive, as many state governments have continued to be unwilling to support general normative provisions that may encourage group demands or inhibit national integration. . . . Article 27 of the International Covenant on Civil and Political Rights (ICCPR), an instrument drafted in the early 1950s and adopted in 1966, thus remains the principal general minority rights treaty text of global application, and it is worded as an individual rights provision, phrased with an aspiration to avoid encouraging new minorities to appear, and seeking to impose only modest duties on states.[6]

If many state governments have been hesitant to see "minorities" operate as a flourishing general legal category, wishing to subsume it into human rights, many indigenous leaders and advocates have insisted on distinguishing themselves from "minorities," arguing that classifying indigenous peoples as minorities is belittling, missing what is distinctive about being indigenous and being a people.[7] . . . In dealing with indigenous issues, [however,] the Human Rights Committee has increasingly interpreted Article 27 in a creative and expansive manner so as to elude some of the strictures states may have hoped to set upon it.[8] This has been reinforced by national courts, and by various national commissions and advisory bodies.

Perhaps the most important juridical application of Article 27 for some indigenous peoples has been a series of holdings that failure of the state to protect indigenous land and resource bases, including the continuing effects of past wrongs, may in certain circumstances amount to a violation of the right to culture protected in Article 27. The leading case is the views of the Human Rights Committee in *Ominayak v. Canada*, where the Committee concluded that the historical inequity of the failure to assure to the Lubicon Lake Band a reservation to which they had a strong claim, and the effect on the band of certain recent developments including oil and timber concessions, "threaten the way of life and culture of the Lubicon Lake Band, and constitute a violation of

---

[6] Article 27 provides: "In those States in which ethnic, religious or linguistic minorities exist, persons belonging to such minorities shall not be denied the right, in community with the other members of their group, to enjoy their own culture, to profess and practise their own religion, or to use their own language."

[7] Such a distinction is partially acknowledged in article 30 of the Convention on the Rights of the Child (1989), which broadly tracks the language of article 27 but refers to minorities "or persons of indigenous origin."

[8] For an overview, see Human Rights Committee General Comment No. 23 (50) on Article 27, U.N. Doc. A/49/40, at 107.

Article 27 so long as they continue."[9] The Committee has incorporated this understanding of Article 27 in numerous discussions of state reports, and has pressed states to adopt this expansive understanding of their Article 27 obligations in national policy. For example, the Committee weighed in to the controversy concerning dam projects on the Biobio [R]iver in Chile, expressing concern that these "might affect the way of life and the rights of persons belonging to the Mapuche and other indigenous communities," and casting doubt on the Chilean government policy of land acquisition and resettlement: "Relocation and compensation may not be appropriate in order to comply with article 27 of the Covenant."[10] This view that Article 27 obligations impose constraints on government economic development policy was applied as the rule of decision by the Supreme Administrative Court of Finland in nullifying deeds for mining claims in Sami areas in a series of cases beginning in 1996.[11] The District Court of Sapporo made similar use of Article 27 in finding in 1997 that the government had improperly failed to consider Ainu culture before proceeding to build the Nibutani Dam.[12]

. . .

Comparing . . . [national cases] indicates that formulation of a noncontextual normative theory governing the striking of such balances is a challenging and probably hazardous undertaking if the theory is intended to be operational in international law. A stimulating attempt is Will Kymlicka's normative distinction, intended to be operational, between external protection that the state should help provide for minority groups to prevent domination by the wider society or other social groups, and internal restrictions that a group imposes on the freedoms of its members, which, he argues, liberalism does not permit. . . . [13] The argument for upholding external protections while considering intervention against a category of "internal restrictions" is deceptively simple. It is stimulating as a parsimonious normative theory in one group of liberal states, but operationalizing it in these simple terms without close attention to history, context, consequences, and prevailing background norms may have unappealing or dangerous results.

Operationalizing such a normative theory involves the questions of who judges, how they judge, and what are the various impacts of different rights protecting institutions.[14] Adjudicative approaches to minority questions have made appreciable contributions, but face inevitable limits, confronted even within the relatively circumscribed scope of Article 27.[15] The case of *Kitok v. Sweden* before the Human Rights Committee typifies the problems encountered by tribunals in using Article 27 as a means to redress wrongs involving land and natural resources. The diminution of areas available for reindeer pasturage due to encroachment by other users, combined with rising living standards, was interpreted by the Sami authorities, whose decisional competence was embodied in Swedish state law, as necessitating restricting some aspiring reindeer herders in order to maintain the viability of the reindeer-herding lifestyle. The decision-making system on reindeer herding among members of the Sami Village *(Sameby)* was reportedly weighted toward those who already had large herds. If it had been clear to the Committee on the complex facts that Ivan Kitok's formal exclusion from entitlement to herd reindeer was an arbitrary exercise of local power, Article 27 might well have provided a basis for intervention, the infringing conduct of the Swedish state being its failure to intervene. But in so far as the *Sameby* policy depriving those who spent more

---

[9] U.N. Doc. A/49/40, annex IX, 1, 27 (1990). Other cases taking this approach include *Länsman v. Finland (No. 1)*, Communication 511/1992, U.N. Doc. CCPR/C/57/1, at 74; *Länsman v. Finland (No.2)*, Communication 671/1995, U.N. Doc. CCPR/C158/D/671/1995; and *Kitok v. Sweden*, Communication 197/1985, 2 HRC OFFICIAL RECORDS 1987–88, at 442.

[10] U.N. Doc. CCPR/C/79/Add.l04, at para. 22 (Mar. 30, 1999).

[11] See especially *Kasivarsi Reindeer Herders' Cooperative v. Ministry of Trade and Industry*, File No. 1447, Helsinki (May 15, 1996). See also the decisions of Mar. 31, 1999, in Cases 692 and 693.

[12] *Kayano and Kaizawa v. Hokkaido Expropriation Committee* (1997), translated by M. Levin, 38 I.L.M. 397 (1999).

[13] MULTICULTURAL CITIZENSHIP: A LIBERAL THEORY OF MINORITY RIGHTS ch. 3 (1995).

[14] Some of these issues are noted in MULTICULTURAL CITIZENSHIP ch. 8.

[15] Johnston, *Native Rights as Collective Rights: A Question of Group Self-Preservation*, 2 CANADIAN JOURNAL OF LAW AND JURISPRUDENCE 19 (1989).

than three years away was a response to the crisis in the long-term viability of reindeer-herding lifestyle and culture, the Swedish state was much more fundamentally implicated in not securing sufficient land, pasturage, and support for the culture to Sami, yet the Committee became more hesitant to intervene. This paradox structures the result in the case, a very uneasy compromise in which no violation of the ICCPR is found because Kitok was in fact being permitted, although not as of right, to herd reindeer, and nothing is said about the systemic assimilationist effects of the diminishing resource base or other aspects of historic Swedish state policy.

Many of the most difficult systemic issues involving minorities are more effectively addressed through negotiations and policy processes, especially in deeply divided societies. In highly charged cases international oversight and conciliation may play an important role, as some of the work of the High Commissioner for National Minorities of the Organization for Security and Cooperation in Europe (OSCE) attests. In cases involving indigenous peoples, international and national regimes of minority rights may set useful minimum standards. Adjudicative or quasi-adjudicative proceedings are significant in upholding fundamental rights, and in some cases may overcome a political impasse or provide impetus to needed policy reforms.

Indigenous claims often have much in common with minority claims. Before the surge of contemporary legal activity concerning indigenous peoples, tribunals frequently conflated the categories. Dealing with (and finding inadmissible) a Sami challenge to a Norwegian government hydro-electric dam project flooding reindeer herding areas in 1983, for example, the legal basis on which the then European Commission on Human Rights proceeded was simply that "a minority group is, in principle, entitled to claim the right to respect for the particular life style it may lead"[16] as private life, family life, or home under Article 8 of the European Convention....

In practice, however, tribunals facing indigenous issues have increasingly found themselves identifying or constructing distinct analytical approaches that go beyond standard minority provisions. This is especially prevalent where claims arise from the distinct historical circumstances of indigenous groups, as such claims are often *sui generis* in the national society.... Where claims are based on maintenance and development of a distinct culture, religion, or language, there may be substantial analogy between indigenous claims and claims of minority groups generally, and the legal techniques used will often overlap. Very often the distinct indigenous element will be integral to such claims too. But there is no universal bright line. Where the substantive differences are contestable, distinctions between indigenous claims and similar claims by other minorities may or may not be legitimate, depending in part on compliance with fundamental human rights standards, and in part on the complex dynamics of different societies.

. . .

3. Self-Determination

Negotiations on international normative instruments relating to indigenous peoples have repeatedly become ensnarled in the question: does the international law of self-determination apply to indigenous peoples? As in other areas, political debate has revolved around the binary issue of the complete applicability or inapplicability of an existing conceptual structure. Representatives of indigenous peoples in international negotiations have insisted as a large group of them put it in a 1993 *demarche* to the U.N. Working Group on Indigenous Populations that "the right of self-determination is the heart and soul of the declaration. We will not consent to any language which limits or curtails the right of self-determination."[17] ... A number of states met this with categorical opposition, asserting that these groups are not peoples, and have no international law right of self-determination....

[16] *G and E v. Norway*, Applications 9278/81 and 9415/81, DR 35 (1984), 30.
[17] Quoted in INDIGENOUS PEOPLE, THE UNITED NATIONS, AND HUMAN RIGHTS 46 (S. Pritchard ed., 1998).

Self-determination has long been a conceptual morass in international law, partly because its application and meaning have not been fully formulated in agreed texts, partly because it reinforces and conflicts with other important principles and specific rules, and partly because the specific international law practice of self-determination does not measure up very well to some of the established textual formulations.[18] The standard international law of self-determination accords to the people of certain territorially-defined units the right to determine the political future of the territory. . . .

A somewhat distinct body of practice confers upon such units, and especially on peoples of independent states as represented by their governments, certain economic rights relating especially to natural resources, and certain protections in relation to title to territory and the use of force.[19] While claims by indigenous peoples may in some cases fall within these categories, for the most part their acceptance would involve some rethinking of existing practice as represented in this summary. Elements of existing interpretations of self-determination, together with increasingly coherent bodies of emerging national and international practice, and the growing support among state governments for initiatives in relation to internal self-determination generally and to indigenous peoples specifically, suggest that the case of indigenous peoples may be one in which innovative normative formulations can be agreed. These will almost certainly not be exhaustive of the issues, probably will not be highly precise, will not be universally respected, and may well be somewhat incoherent. At a minimum, they must not be disastrously dangerous, and within the limits of existing imprecision and incoherence should be consistent with existing formulations relating to self-determination, human rights, and other fundamental principles. If this is to happen, it is suggested that a fundamental reorientation is called for that leaves aside the binary conceptual debate and moves closer to emerging practice. This reorientation involves shifting – not for the purpose of exhaustive statement but merely for the purpose of reaching agreement on partial formulations – from an end-state approach to self-determination.

. . .

The international indigenous movement has been reluctant in international negotiations to move away from the end-state model including possible independence, in order to maintain solidarity with groups unwilling to accept any relationship with an existing state.

. . .

After long hesitation about the application of the provisions on self-determination in Article 1 of the ICCPR to indigenous groups within independent states, the U.N. Human Rights Committee has begun, in dialogues with states parties under the reporting procedure, to express views under the self-determination rubric on the substantive terms of relationships between states and indigenous peoples. It has emphasized in particular the provisions of Article 1(2), which stipulates that all peoples may freely dispose of their natural wealth and resources, and must not be deprived of their own means of subsistence. It has criticized the Canadian government practice of insisting on the inclusion in contemporary claims settlement agreements of a provision extinguishing inherent aboriginal rights, confining aboriginal rights instead to those specified in the agreement.[20] The Committee recommended that this practice "be abandoned as incompatible with Article 1 of the Covenant," an important indication that the Committee believes the Article 1 provisions on self-determination are applicable to indigenous peoples in Canada.[21] The Committee further

---

[18] Some of the problems are surveyed in THE MODERN LAW OF SELF-DETERMINATION (C. Tomuschat ed., 1993).

[19] *See generally* I. BROWNLIE, PRINCIPLES OF PUBLIC INTERNATIONAL LAW 167, 599–602 (5th ed. 1998).

[20] This policy was criticized by the Royal Commission on Aboriginal Peoples in its final report (5 vols., 1996), drawing in turn on an earlier study by Mary Ellen Turpel and Paul Joffe. See ROYAL COMMISSION ON ABORIGINAL PEOPLES, TREATY MAKING IN THE SPIRIT OF CO-EXISTENCE: AN ALTERNATIVE TO EXTINGUISHMENT (1995).

[21] For argument that harsher elements of the policy of extinguishment pursued by the Australian government infringe international law, see Pritchard, *Native Title from the Perspective of International Standards*, 18 AUSTRALIAN Y.B. INT'L L. 127 (1997). The Native Title Amendment Act has been critically considered also by the U.N. Committee on Elimination of Racial Discrimination.

recommended on the basis of Article 1 that the Canadian government implement the Royal Commission report on the need for greater allocation of land and resources to ensure institutions of aboriginal self-government do not fail.[22] Earlier the Committee on Economic, Social and Cultural Rights had made similar substantive recommendations to the government of Canada, without basing itself explicitly on self-determination and the terms of Article 1 of the International Covenant on Social and Cultural Rights (ICESCR).[23] As Article 1 is common to both Covenants, the logic of gradual convergence in interpretation is compelling, and is likely to prevail over differences in institutional dynamics. The intervention of such bodies in the dynamics of state-indigenous relations under Article 1 may be well judged in relation to Canada, where the government accepts the general principle of indigenous self-determination and where the political and policy system has already developed and calibrated possible initiatives. The international bodies, which have scant ability to formulate such detailed policies themselves, are able in such a case to boost one part of a national process. The challenge for these bodies is whether to try to apply such interpretations of self-determination for indigenous peoples to states where the government and the political system are not prepared to accept any such notion, or in situations where there is no carefully crafted and politically legitimate policy document upon which the international body may seize.

The number of state governments accepting principles for relationships with indigenous peoples that incorporate elements of self-determination has gradually increased. Reasonably representative of current positions of Canada, New Zealand, Denmark and other governments is a 1995 statement by the then Australian (Labour) government, that self-determination is "an evolving right which includes equal rights, the continuing right of peoples to decide how they should be governed, the right of people as individuals to participate in the political process (particularly by way of periodic free and fair elections) and the right of distinct peoples within a state to make decisions on and administer their own affairs."[24] The government of Guatemala, formally committed to implementing provisions on land rights, local self-government and national participation in the 1995 Mexico City peace agreement on Identity and Rights of Indigenous Peoples, has taken the position internationally that self-determination of indigenous peoples is possible without threatening national unity.[25] A basis for comparable international positions is provided by the 1991 Colombian Constitution, which in tandem with a series of Constitutional Court decisions envisages significant indigenous autonomy as well as rights in relation to land, resources, consultation, representation, language, and education,[26] and by the Philippines Indigenous Peoples Rights Act of 1997 which expressly endorses indigenous self-governance and self-determination within the state. These legal policies often conflict with other government policies, and may fall far short in implementation and in their real effects, but their normative stance has some genuine support, and reflects a broader if uneven trend. This trend may be necessary to the future success of the state[27] as well as the vitality of indigenous peoples.

. . . Some . . . justify self-determination on human rights grounds, as a necessary precondition and means to the realization of other human rights.[28] In this view, self-determination in finely

---

The New Zealand government's policy of seeking to make contemporary settlements of Maori claims "full and final" has been criticized by Maori leaders and several scholars, including Annie Mikaere and Russell Karu.

[22] Concluding Observations on the Fourth Periodic Report of Canada, U.N. Doc. CCPR/C/79/Add. 105, at para. 8 (Apr. 7, 1999).

[23] Concluding Observations on the Third Periodic Report of Canada, U.N. Doc. E/C.12/1/Add.31, at para. 18 (Dec. 4, 1998).

[24] U.N. Doc. E/CN.4/1995/WG.15/2/Add.2, at para. 8 (Nov. 30, 1995).

[25] Statement at Commission on Human Rights Inter-Sessional Working Group on the Draft Declaration, 1998.

[26] For a short summary, see Wiessner, *Rights and Status of Indigenous Peoples: A Global Comparative and International Legal Analysis*, 12 Harv. Hum. Rts. J. 57, 80, 81 (1999).

[27] *Cf.* A. Milward, The European Rescue of the Nation-State (1992); A. Moravcsik, The Choice for Europe: Social Purpose and State Power from Messina to Maastricht (1998).

[28] Hector Gross Espiell, *The Right to Self-Determination: Implementation of United Nations Resolutions*, U.N. Doc. E/CN.4/Sub.2/405/Rev.1, at para. 59 (1980). McCorquodale, *Self-Determination: A Human Rights Approach*, 43 ICLQ 857 (1994).

nuanced forms is an embodiment of the underlying objectives of human rights – general rights to political participation, for example, or specific rights for the members of religious and linguistic communities collectively to make decisions concerning religious and language matters. This view, while plausible, is far removed from the most common ways in which the idea of "self-determination" is presently used in international practice, although the tide may be moving in this direction. Others look behind the formal rules of self-determination and human rights to find a justification that unites both programmes, such as the realization of freedom and equality through rights accorded to human individuals or collectivities.[29] In this analysis the law of self-determination is the law of remedies for serious deficiencies of freedom and equality, just as the law of human rights is. Comparable arguments can also be made for unifying these categories with minority claims.[30]

. . .

As to the relationship of self-determination to the minorities and indigenous peoples programmes, it has already been noted that the overlap between these latter categories is considerable, and a relational approach is relevant to both. For example, in advocating a view of self-determination as encompassing "the right of distinct peoples within a state to make decisions on and administer their own affairs," the Australian government added that this is "relevant both to indigenous peoples and to national minorities."[31] But the terms of the relationships that evolve will often differ, for reasons that are practical, normative, and in some cases strategic. In some societies, indigenous claims to relational self-determination are legitimate and actionable in a way that comparably extensive claims of minorities might not be, whereas in other societies introducing such a distinction between certain specified groups may be irrelevant or even pernicious. . . .

4. Historic Sovereignty

Accounts and memories of an earlier era of political independence are widespread among indigenous peoples. In many cases this independence was initially recognized by the aspiring colonial power. Treaties between indigenous peoples and colonizing or trading states, made over several centuries, were commonly premised on the capacity of both parties to act. In some cases, this implied recognition of the capacity of the leaders of the indigenous people to act directly in international law. The Treaty of Waitangi, for instance, was one of many such agreements included in standard nineteenth-century European treaty series.[32] The legal basis under which this independence was lost was often not accepted by the indigenous group involved, and even under the legal principles of contemporaneous international law espoused by the colonizers it may have been tainted by illegality. The international law concerning colonialism contained inconsistencies observed by many international lawyers in the nineteenth century and earlier. It is not surprising that leaders of some indigenous groups aspire to rectify wrongs by reviving the previous independence.

. . . Because this programme is not well developed in practice, little attention has been given to fundamental questions. More generally, whereas self-determination is mainly a forward-looking programme, the historic sovereignty programme is organized to be concerned with restoration of the *status quo ante*. This may suggest legal responsibility for wrongful interference with sovereign

---

[29] S.J. Anaya, Indigenous Peoples in International Law (1995); and Anaya, *Self-Determination as a Collective Right Under Contemporary International Law, in* Operationalizing the Right of Indigenous Peoples to Self-Determination 93 (P. Aikio & M. Scheinin eds., 2000).

[30] Some such arguments are evaluated, and carefully sidestepped, in A. Spiliopoulou Akermark, Justifications of Minority Protection in International Law (1997).

[31] U.N. Doc. E/CN.4/1995/WG.15/2/Add.2 (Nov. 30, 1995).

[32] Many such treaties are collected and printed in a separate section in Clive Parry's *Consolidated Treaty Series* (published in the latter part of the twentieth century), but often the original sources intimated no qualitative distinction of this sort.

rights, a class of claim raised in exceptional legal proceedings such as those brought by Nauru and by the U.N. Council for Namibia, and in war reparations arrangements, but otherwise generally sidestepped by former colonial powers and by other military intervenors. Serious problems may also arise in relation to title to territory – little analysis has been undertaken, for example, of the relationship between historic sovereignty claims and the ordering principle of *uti possidetis juris*. Internal administrative boundaries utilized by the larger contemporary state may differ greatly from the boundaries ascribed to the historic entity, yet such internal boundaries have generally governed in the legal practice relating to decolonization and to disintegrating federations. The traditional or ethnic group associated with the historic entity may now be only a minority in the aspiring entity. . . .

. . . Reviving historic sovereignty carries the hope of reversing the consequences of wrongs. In focusing on past dispossession it incorporates a type of moral claim that resonates with liberal principles. But a general argument for independence for indigenous groups based on historic sovereignty goes much further than most groups wish. It takes little account of how things have changed, and its radical implications provoke damaging resistance from states. In practice most indigenous peoples seeking to revive autonomous power utilize more nuanced structures that incorporate some of the same justifications: self-determination, or the emerging conceptual structure of indigenous peoples claims.

5. Indigenous Peoples

The construction and affirmation of a distinct programme of "rights of indigenous peoples," going beyond universal human rights and existing regimes of minority rights, has been one of the objectives of the international indigenous peoples movement. It has received support from some states prepared to recognize the validity of many claims made by indigenous peoples but anxious not simply to endorse the extension of the existing self-determination and historic sovereignty programmes to indigenous peoples without modification. . . .

Crafting substantive legal rules on the basis of their applicability in cases involving a distinct category of indigenous peoples can be a subtle and perilous task if high priority is given to reconciling them with the four existing frameworks already discussed. International Labour Organization (ILO) Conventions 107 (1957) and 169 (1989) are attempts to establish such a concept systematically, although with virtually no involvement of indigenous peoples in the drafting process of Convention 107 in the 1950s, and appreciable but nonetheless limited involvement in the Convention 169 process in the 1980s. Although the assimilationism of Convention 107 and the circumspection of Convention 169 have caused the international indigenous movement to focus energies [elsewhere], these instruments provide significant minimum benchmarks on some issues for states and, in certain circumstances, international organizations. For example, Convention 107 has been invoked by national courts and international bodies to call attention to violations relating to indigenous land rights, displacement, and resettlement,[33] and Convention 169 has been invoked by the Colombian Constitutional Court in determining that consultation with and participation of indigenous people in an oil exploration licensing decision had been inadequate.[34] International development institutions have also begun to use "indigenous peoples" as an operational concept, one that triggers procedural requirements and substantive standards. The logic of the indigenous peoples programme has gradually led these institutions to regard consultation with indigenous peoples as essential in formulating these standards and in certain institutional practices.[35] . . .

---

[33] *Lal Chand* (Supreme Court of India. 1985); B. Morse & T. Berger, Sardar Sarovar: Report of the Independent Review (1992). See also IACHR Ecuador Report (1997).

[34] Petition of Jaime Cordoba Trivino, Defensor del Pueblo, en representación de varias personas integrantes del Grupo Étnico Indígena U'Wa, Sentencia No. SU-039/97 (Feb. 3, 1997).

[35] Kingsbury, *Operational Policies of International Institutions as Part of the Law-Making Process: The World Bank and Indigenous Peoples*, in The Reality of International Law 323 (G. Goodwin-Gill & S. Talmon eds., 1999).

The views of the U.N. Human Rights Committee in *Hopu and Bessert* v. *France* suggest, especially when read in conjunction with *Ominayak* and other cases, that a majority of the Committee are willing to adopt very broad interpretations of established rights in cases where some particular types of groups are involved.[36] . . .

. . . Amongst the ambient population, and many persons who may count themselves as members of indigenous groups, the most powerful argument for a distinctive legal category based on special features of indigenous peoples is wrongful deprivation, above all of land, territory, self-government, means of livelihood, language, and identity. The appeal is thus to history and culture.[37] This justification works well in specific contexts, where it is reasonably clear in broad terms who is indigenous, who is not, what wrongs were done in the past, and why it now seems morally obligatory to respond. But formulating this justification as a rule for hard cases, or as a global abstraction capable of working across different types of societies with intricate identity politics and rapid cultural and economic change, is immensely difficult. Efforts to express culture and history as legal tests have tended to produce feeble and ultimately unconvincing searches to find or not find essentialized culture, and searches to find or not find modern majorities and minorities and peoples and owners as artifacts on the surface of history. Other justifications appeal to special historic and cultural relations with land, or to enduring disadvantage, or to systematic discrimination. These provide strong arguments, but are not exclusively justifications for an indigenous peoples' category.

The construction and justification of a conceptual structure of indigenous peoples' claims is political as well as legal, and threatens to exclude or make difficult other political and legal projects. The indigenous peoples' movement is part of a wider identity politics that may clash with other politics, such as women's movements. As tribal identity becomes more important and a tribe seems more beleaguered, women may feel forced to choose tribal identity and step back from pan-tribal women's movements that were more effective at reforming unequal traditions.[38] Designation of some set of people as "indigenous" may be a simplistic social construction that creates an antonymic identity of "non-indigenous," setting up a structure in which some are privileged and others disadvantaged for unappealing reasons. The justification of history and culture may trigger a search for authenticity that helps some who seem to meet, and may in effect set, such criteria, while taking from others who do not. Resources may go to parts of groups able to maintain a strong political leadership appealing to tribal tradition, rather than to people whose grandparents or parents drifted to urban areas. Or resources may go to new kinds of elites who are able to claim to represent regeneration and revitalization, as opposed to more traditional but less glamorous members of the same descent group. More generally, the indigenous peoples programme implies the insufficiency of other programmes for certain purposes, but its justifications imply more than simply supplementing the other programmes in special cases. The boundaries between this and other programmes are highly permeable in law as in present politics, but hard cases where the programmes clash will continue to arise, perhaps with increasing frequency.

. . .

6. Conclusion

The increasingly rich body of practice in the presentation and negotiation of claims raised by indigenous peoples or members of such groups, and the burgeoning jurisprudence of some national and international courts and tribunals, has not established agreed conceptual foundations for legal analysis and political understanding of indigenous peoples' issues. It has been argued that at least five distinct conceptual structures operate. They make a difference to legal outcomes. . . .

---

[36] U.N. Doc. CCPR/C/60/D/549/1993, views adopted July 29, 1997.
[37] Rosen, *The Right to Be Different*, 107 YALE L.J. 227 (1997).
[38] Sunila Abeysekera has made this point in relation to the North-East Network of North-East Women, an intertribal women's network in Northeast India.

Globally, the range of concepts, and the host of ways in which they can be connected and reconciled, renders unconvincing any insistence on a single homogenizing structure that is alien to the political discourse and social patterns in some societies, or simply unpopular with the regime. If in China the concept of indigenous peoples is not accepted, and human rights discourse has clear limits, the concept of national minorities is well established in the constitutional structure and provides a structure for possible innovation and reform. If in Finland official law and policy does not recognize extensive Sami land rights, state land-use actions incompatible with Sami culture may be controlled under the minority rights programme. If in the U.S. strong minority rights and multiculturalism are viewed with suspicion, attenuated forms of historic sovereignty and self-determination have legal endorsement and political legitimacy, albeit fragile. If New Zealand has also hesitated to move far toward official multiculturalism, biculturalism has been established on the basis of the indigenous peoples programme and the Treaty of Waitangi. This flexibility is far from the absolutism of rights, and allows for evasion and abuse. The risks of delegitimation of indigenous claims jurisprudence through incoherence, and polarization between political forces rallying around competing and utterly unreconciled concepts, are real. But the global system of international law probably does not have the capacity to precisely resolve by agreement difficult questions about the connections between and limits of these conceptual structures.

. . . The international indigenous peoples movement has played an important role in many institutions in raising issues and formulating proposals, and has influenced texts ranging from Agenda 21 to the World Conservation Strategy. But the number of institutions involved far exceeds the present capacities of this movement, and each institution has its own dynamic and its own pressures toward other priorities. General normative instruments . . . have thus played, and if momentum is sustained may continue to play, a fundamental role in articulating norms and justifications that provide a shared reference and source of validation, even while leaving unresolved the more recondite problems of concepts and categories that have been [discussed herein].

Questions and Discussion

1. What difference does it make in practice to the protection of indigenous land, resources, and environment which theoretical approach presented here is adopted?

2. For further reading, see JAMES ANAYA, INDIGENOUS PEOPLES IN INTERNATIONAL LAW (2d ed. 2004); James Anaya & Robert A Williams Jr., *The Protection of Indigenous Peoples' Rights Over Lands and Natural Resources Under the Inter-American Human Rights System*, 14 HARV. HUM. RTS. J. 33 (2001); PATRICK THORNBERRY, INDIGENOUS PEOPLES AND HUMAN RIGHTS (2002); Robert K. Hitchcock, *International Human Rights, the Environment, and Indigenous Peoples*, 1 COLO. J. INT'L ENVTL. L. & POL'Y 1 (1994); William Andrew Shutkin, *International Human Rights Law and the Earth: The Protection of Indigenous Peoples and the Environment*, 31 VA. J. INT'L L. 479 (1991); Lee Swepston, *A New Step in the International Law on Indigenous and Tribal Peoples: ILO Convention 169 of 1989*, 15 OKLA. CITY U. L. REV. 677 (1990); Mario Ibarra, *Traditional Practices in Respect of the Sustainable and Environmentally Sound Self-Development of Indigenous People*, U.N. Doc. E/CN.4/Sub.2/1992/31/Add.1 (May 1, 1992); Siegfried Wiessner, *Rights and Status of Indigenous Peoples: A Global Comparative and International Legal Analysis*, 12 HARV. HUM. RTS. L.J. 57 (1999).

III. International Instruments

No core international human rights treaty mentions indigenous peoples. The Covenant on Civil and Political Rights has two relevant provisions, reprinted herein, and the definition of racial discrimination in the Convention on the Elimination of All Forms of Racial Discrimination is broad enough to include indigenous peoples. Asserting a unique status, indigenous groups for many years have sought legal protection in instruments devoted exclusively to their rights. The International Labour Organization (ILO) first adopted a convention in 1957, which was criticized by many for its assimilationist tenor. This convention was replaced in 1989 by ILO Convention No. 169 Concerning Indigenous and Tribal Peoples in Independent Countries. By mid-2010, the Convention had been ratified by only twenty-two countries. On September 13, 2007, the United Nations completed a two-decade-long negotiating process by adopting the U.N. Declaration on the Rights of Indigenous Peoples, reprinted in this section. Four countries containing large indigenous populations (Australia, Canada, New Zealand, and the United States) declined to support the declaration; as will be seen, each of them has been the subject of human rights complaints about their laws and practices regarding their indigenous populations. On April 3, 2009, the government of Australia announced that it had reversed its opposition to the Declaration, a reversal New Zealand also adopted. Canada and the United States later changed their positions as well.

The Organization of American States (OAS) has been engaged in negotiating its own declaration on the rights of indigenous peoples for many years. For its part, the European system adopted the Framework Convention on National Minorities on November 10, 1994. It is a programmatic treaty that envisages national laws and policies to give effect to its principles. It does not define the term national minorities.

INTERNATIONAL COVENANT ON CIVIL AND POLITICAL RIGHTS,
adopted by G.A. Res. 2200a (xxi)
Dec. 16, 1966, entered into force Mar. 23, 1976

Article 1

1. All peoples have the right of self-determination. By virtue of that right they freely determine their political status and freely pursue their economic, social and cultural development.
2. All peoples may, for their own ends, freely dispose of their natural wealth and resources without prejudice to any obligations arising out of international economic co-operation, based upon the principle of mutual benefit, and international law. In no case may a people be deprived of its own means of subsistence.
3. The States Parties to the present Covenant, including those having responsibility for the administration of Non-Self-Governing and Trust Territories, shall promote the realization of the right of self-determination, and shall respect that right, in conformity with the provisions of the Charter of the United Nations.

Article 27

In those States in which ethnic, religious or linguistic minorities exist, persons belonging to such minorities shall not be denied the right, in community with the other members of their group, to enjoy their own culture, to profess and practise their own religion, or to use their own language.

U.N. Declaration on the Rights of Indigenous Peoples,
adopted by G.A. Res. 61/295 (Sept. 13, 2007)

The General Assembly,

. . .

Affirming that indigenous peoples are equal to all other peoples, while recognizing the right of all peoples to be different, to consider themselves different, and to be respected as such,

Affirming also that all peoples contribute to the diversity and richness of civilizations and cultures, which constitute the common heritage of humankind,

Affirming further that all doctrines, policies and practices based on or advocating superiority of peoples or individuals on the basis of national origin or racial, religious, ethnic or cultural differences are racist, scientifically false, legally invalid, morally condemnable and socially unjust,

Reaffirming that indigenous peoples, in the exercise of their rights, should be free from discrimination of any kind,

Concerned that indigenous peoples have suffered from historic injustices as a result of, inter alia, their colonization and dispossession of their lands, territories and resources, thus preventing them from exercising, in particular, their right to development in accordance with their own needs and interests,

Recognizing the urgent need to respect and promote the inherent rights of indigenous peoples which derive from their political, economic and social structures and from their cultures, spiritual traditions, histories and philosophies, especially their rights to their lands, territories and resources,

. . .

Convinced that control by indigenous peoples over developments affecting them and their lands, territories and resources will enable them to maintain and strengthen their institutions, cultures and traditions, and to promote their development in accordance with their aspirations and needs,

Recognizing that respect for indigenous knowledge, cultures and traditional practices contributes to sustainable and equitable development and proper management of the environment,

. . .

Considering that the rights affirmed in treaties, agreements and other constructive arrangements between States and indigenous peoples are, in some situations, matters of international concern, interest, responsibility and character,

. . .

Bearing in mind that nothing in this Declaration may be used to deny any peoples their right to self-determination, exercised in conformity with international law,

. . .

Recognizing and reaffirming that indigenous individuals are entitled without discrimination to all human rights recognized in international law, and that indigenous peoples possess collective rights which are indispensable for their existence, well-being and integral development as peoples,

Recognizing that the situation of indigenous peoples varies from region to region and from country to country and that the significance of national and regional particularities and various historical and cultural backgrounds should be taken into consideration,

Solemnly proclaims the following United Nations Declaration on the Rights of Indigenous Peoples as a standard of achievement to be pursued in a spirit of partnership and mutual respect:

Article 1

Indigenous peoples have the right to the full enjoyment, as a collective or as individuals, of all human rights and fundamental freedoms as recognized in the Charter of the United Nations, the Universal Declaration of Human Rights and international human rights law.

Article 2

Indigenous peoples and individuals are free and equal to all other peoples and individuals and have the right to be free from any kind of discrimination, in the exercise of their rights, in particular that based on their indigenous origin or identity.

Article 3

Indigenous peoples have the right to self-determination. By virtue of that right they freely determine their political status and freely pursue their economic, social and cultural development.

Article 4

Indigenous peoples, in exercising their right to self-determination, have the right to autonomy or self-government in matters relating to their internal and local affairs, as well as ways and means for financing their autonomous functions.

Article 5

Indigenous peoples have the right to maintain and strengthen their distinct political, legal, economic, social and cultural institutions, while retaining their right to participate fully, if they so choose, in the political, economic, social and cultural life of the State.

. . .

Article 10

Indigenous peoples shall not be forcibly removed from their lands or territories. No relocation shall take place without the free, prior and informed consent of the indigenous peoples concerned and after agreement on just and fair compensation and, where possible, with the option of return.

Article 11

1. Indigenous peoples have the right to practise and revitalize their cultural traditions and customs. This includes the right to maintain, protect and develop the past, present and future manifestations of their cultures, such as archaeological and historical sites, artefacts, designs, ceremonies, technologies and visual and performing arts and literature.
2. States shall provide redress through effective mechanisms, which may include restitution, developed in conjunction with indigenous peoples, with respect to their cultural, intellectual, religious and spiritual property taken without their free, prior and informed consent or in violation of their laws, traditions and customs.

Article 12

1. Indigenous peoples have the right to manifest, practise, develop and teach their spiritual and religious traditions, customs and ceremonies; the right to maintain, protect, and have access in privacy to their religious and cultural sites; the right to the use and control of their ceremonial objects; and the right to the repatriation of their human remains.
2. States shall seek to enable the access and/or repatriation of ceremonial objects and human remains in their possession through fair, transparent and effective mechanisms developed in conjunction with indigenous peoples concerned.

. . .

Article 18

Indigenous peoples have the right to participate in decision-making in matters which would affect their rights, through representatives chosen by themselves in accordance with their own procedures, as well as to maintain and develop their own indigenous decision-making institutions.

Article 19

States shall consult and cooperate in good faith with the indigenous peoples concerned through their own representative institutions in order to obtain their free, prior and informed consent before adopting and implementing legislative or administrative measures that may affect them.

Article 20

1. Indigenous peoples have the right to maintain and develop their political, economic and social systems or institutions, to be secure in the enjoyment of their own means of subsistence and development, and to engage freely in all their traditional and other economic activities.
2. Indigenous peoples deprived of their means of subsistence and development are entitled to just and fair redress.

. . .

Article 23

Indigenous peoples have the right to determine and develop priorities and strategies for exercising their right to development. In particular, indigenous peoples have the right to be actively involved in developing and determining health, housing and other economic and social programmes affecting them and, as far as possible, to administer such programmes through their own institutions.

Article 24

1. Indigenous peoples have the right to their traditional medicines and to maintain their health practices, including the conservation of their vital medicinal plants, animals and minerals. Indigenous individuals also have the right to access, without any discrimination, to all social and health services.
2. Indigenous individuals have an equal right to the enjoyment of the highest attainable standard of physical and mental health. States shall take the necessary steps with a view to achieving progressively the full realization of this right.

Article 25

Indigenous peoples have the right to maintain and strengthen their distinctive spiritual relationship with their traditionally owned or otherwise occupied and used lands, territories, waters and coastal seas and other resources and to uphold their responsibilities to future generations in this regard.

Article 26

1. Indigenous peoples have the right to the lands, territories and resources which they have traditionally owned, occupied or otherwise used or acquired.
2. Indigenous peoples have the right to own, use, develop and control the lands, territories and resources that they possess by reason of traditional ownership or other traditional occupation or use, as well as those which they have otherwise acquired.
3. States shall give legal recognition and protection to these lands, territories and resources. Such recognition shall be conducted with due respect to the customs, traditions and land tenure systems of the indigenous peoples concerned.

Article 27

States shall establish and implement, in conjunction with indigenous peoples concerned, a fair, independent, impartial, open and transparent process, giving due recognition to indigenous peoples' laws, traditions, customs and land tenure systems, to recognize and adjudicate the rights of indigenous peoples pertaining to their lands, territories and resources, including those which were traditionally owned or otherwise occupied or used. Indigenous peoples shall have the right to participate in this process.

Article 28

1. Indigenous peoples have the right to redress, by means that can include restitution or, when this is not possible, just, fair and equitable compensation, for the lands, territories and resources which they have traditionally owned or otherwise occupied or used, and which have been confiscated, taken, occupied, used or damaged without their free, prior and informed consent.

2. Unless otherwise freely agreed upon by the peoples concerned, compensation shall take the form of lands, territories and resources equal in quality, size and legal status or of monetary compensation or other appropriate redress.

Article 29

1. Indigenous peoples have the right to the conservation and protection of the environment and the productive capacity of their lands or territories and resources. States shall establish and implement assistance programmes for indigenous peoples for such conservation and protection, without discrimination.

2. States shall take effective measures to ensure that no storage or disposal of hazardous materials shall take place in the lands or territories of indigenous peoples without their free, prior and informed consent.

3. States shall also take effective measures to ensure, as needed, that programmes for monitoring, maintaining and restoring the health of indigenous peoples, as developed and implemented by the peoples affected by such materials, are duly implemented.

Article 30

1. Military activities shall not take place in the lands or territories of indigenous peoples, unless justified by a relevant public interest or otherwise freely agreed with or requested by the indigenous peoples concerned.

2. States shall undertake effective consultations with the indigenous peoples concerned, through appropriate procedures and in particular through their representative institutions, prior to using their lands or territories for military activities.

Article 31

1. Indigenous peoples have the right to maintain, control, protect and develop their cultural heritage, traditional knowledge and traditional cultural expressions, as well as the manifestations of their sciences, technologies and cultures, including human and genetic resources, seeds, medicines, knowledge of the properties of fauna and flora, oral traditions, literatures, designs, sports and traditional games and visual and performing arts. They also have the right to maintain, control, protect and develop their intellectual property over such cultural heritage, traditional knowledge, and traditional cultural expressions.

2. In conjunction with indigenous peoples, States shall take effective measures to recognize and protect the exercise of these rights.

Article 32

1. Indigenous peoples have the right to determine and develop priorities and strategies for the development or use of their lands or territories and other resources.

2. States shall consult and cooperate in good faith with the indigenous peoples concerned through their own representative institutions in order to obtain their free and informed consent prior to the approval of any project affecting their lands or territories and other

resources, particularly in connection with the development, utilization or exploitation of mineral, water or other resources.

3. States shall provide effective mechanisms for just and fair redress for any such activities, and appropriate measures shall be taken to mitigate adverse environmental, economic, social, cultural or spiritual impact.

Article 33

1. Indigenous peoples have the right to determine their own identity or membership in accordance with their customs and traditions. This does not impair the right of indigenous individuals to obtain citizenship of the States in which they live.

2. Indigenous peoples have the right to determine the structures and to select the membership of their institutions in accordance with their own procedures.

Article 34

Indigenous peoples have the right to promote, develop and maintain their institutional structures and their distinctive customs, spirituality, traditions, procedures, practices and, in the cases where they exist, juridical systems or customs, in accordance with international human rights standards.

. . .

Article 40

Indigenous peoples have the right to access to and prompt decision through just and fair procedures for the resolution of conflicts and disputes with States or other parties, as well as to effective remedies for all infringements of their individual and collective rights. Such a decision shall give due consideration to the customs, traditions, rules and legal systems of the indigenous peoples concerned and international human rights.

. . .

Article 45

Nothing in this Declaration may be construed as diminishing or extinguishing the rights indigenous peoples have now or may acquire in the future.

Article 46

1. Nothing in this Declaration may be interpreted as implying for any State, people, group or person any right to engage in any activity or to perform any act contrary to the Charter of the United Nations or construed as authorizing or encouraging any action which would dismember or impair, totally or in part, the territorial integrity or political unity of sovereign and independent States.

2. In the exercise of the rights enunciated in the present Declaration, human rights and fundamental freedoms of all shall be respected. The exercise of the rights set forth in this Declaration shall be subject only to such limitations as are determined by law and in accordance with international human rights obligations. Any such limitations shall be non-discriminatory and strictly necessary solely for the purpose of securing due recognition and respect for the rights and freedoms of others and for meeting the just and most compelling requirements of a democratic society.

3. The provisions set forth in this Declaration shall be interpreted in accordance with the principles of justice, democracy, respect for human rights, equality, non-discrimination, good governance and good faith.

CONVENTION (NO. 169) CONCERNING INDIGENOUS AND TRIBAL PEOPLES IN INDEPENDENT COUNTRIES, adopted June 27, 1989, by the General Conference of the International Labour Organization at its 67th session, entry into force Sept. 5, 1991

. . .

PART I. GENERAL POLICY

Article 1

1. This Convention applies to:

   (a) Tribal peoples in independent countries whose social, cultural and economic conditions distinguish them from other sections of the national community, and whose status is regulated wholly or partially by their own customs or traditions or by special laws or regulations;

   (b) Peoples in independent countries who are regarded as indigenous on account of their descent from the populations which inhabited the country, or a geographical region to which the country belongs, at the time of conquest or colonisation or the establishment of present State boundaries and who, irrespective of their legal status, retain some or all of their own social, economic, cultural and political institutions.

2. Self-identification as indigenous or tribal shall be regarded as a fundamental criterion for determining the groups to which the provisions of this Convention apply.

3. The use of the term "peoples" in this Convention shall not be construed as having any implications as regards the rights which may attach to the term under international law.

. . .

Article 3

1. Indigenous and tribal peoples shall enjoy the full measure of human rights and fundamental freedoms without hindrance or discrimination. The provisions of the Convention shall be applied without discrimination to male and female members of these peoples.

2. No form of force or coercion shall be used in violation of the human rights and fundamental freedoms of the peoples concerned, including the rights contained in this Convention.

. . .

Article 6

1. In applying the provisions of this Convention, Governments shall:

   (a) Consult the peoples concerned, through appropriate procedures and in particular through their representative institutions, whenever consideration is being given to legislative or administrative measures which may affect them directly;

   (b) Establish means by which these peoples can freely participate, to at least the same extent as other sectors of the population, at all levels of decision-making in elective institutions and administrative and other bodies responsible for policies and programmes which concern them;

   (c) Establish means for the full development of these peoples' own institutions and initiatives, and in appropriate cases provide the resources necessary for this purpose.

2. The consultations carried out in application of this Convention shall be undertaken, in good faith and in a form appropriate to the circumstances, with the objective of achieving agreement or consent to the proposed measures.

Article 7

1. The peoples concerned shall have the right to decide their own priorities for the process of development as it affects their lives, beliefs, institutions and spiritual well-being and the

lands they occupy or otherwise use, and to exercise control, to the extent possible, over their own economic, social and cultural development. In addition, they shall participate in the formulation, implementation and evaluation of plans and programmes for national and regional development which may affect them directly.

. . .

2. Governments shall ensure that, whenever appropriate, studies are carried out, in co-operation with the peoples concerned, to assess the social, spiritual, cultural and environmental impact on them of planned development activities. The results of these studies shall be considered as fundamental criteria for the implementation of these activities.

3. Governments shall take measures, in co-operation with the peoples concerned, to protect and preserve the environment of the territories they inhabit.

. . .

PART II. LAND

Article 13

1. In applying the provisions of this Part of the Convention governments shall respect the special importance for the cultures and spiritual values of the peoples concerned of their relationship with the lands or territories, or both as applicable, which they occupy or otherwise use, and in particular the collective aspects of this relationship.

2. The use of the term "lands" in Articles 15 and 16 shall include the concept of territories, which covers the total environment of the areas which the peoples concerned occupy or otherwise use.

Article 14

1. The rights of ownership and possession of the peoples concerned over the lands which they traditionally occupy shall be recognised. In addition, measures shall be taken in appropriate cases to safeguard the right of the peoples concerned to use lands not exclusively occupied by them, but to which they have traditionally had access for their subsistence and traditional activities. Particular attention shall be paid to the situation of nomadic peoples and shifting cultivators in this respect.

2. Governments shall take steps as necessary to identify the lands which the peoples concerned traditionally occupy, and to guarantee effective protection of their rights of ownership and possession.

3. Adequate procedures shall be established within the national legal system to resolve land claims by the peoples concerned.

Article 15

1. The rights of the peoples concerned to the natural resources pertaining to their lands shall be specially safeguarded. These rights include the right of these peoples to participate in the use, management and conservation of these resources.

2. In cases in which the State retains the ownership of mineral or sub-surface resources or rights to other resources pertaining to lands, governments shall establish or maintain procedures through which they shall consult these peoples, with a view to ascertaining whether and to what degree their interests would be prejudiced, before undertaking or permitting any programmes for the exploration or exploitation of such resources pertaining to their lands. The peoples concerned shall wherever possible participate in the benefits of such activities, and shall receive fair compensation for any damages which they may sustain as a result of such activities.

Article 16

1. Subject to the following paragraphs of this Article, the peoples concerned shall not be removed from the lands which they occupy.
2. Where the relocation of these peoples is considered necessary as an exceptional measure, such relocation shall take place only with their free and informed consent. Where their consent cannot be obtained, such relocation shall take place only following appropriate procedures established by national laws and regulations, including public inquiries where appropriate, which provide the opportunity for effective representation of the peoples concerned.
3. Whenever possible, these peoples shall have the right to return to their traditional lands, as soon as the grounds for relocation cease to exist.
4. When such return is not possible, as determined by agreement or, in the absence of such agreement, through appropriate procedures, these peoples shall be provided in all possible cases with lands of quality and legal status at least equal to that of the lands previously occupied by them, suitable to provide for their present needs and future development. Where the peoples concerned express a preference for compensation in money or in kind, they shall be so compensated under appropriate guarantees.
5. Persons thus relocated shall be fully compensated for any resulting loss or injury.

Article 17

1. Procedures established by the peoples concerned for the transmission of land rights among members of these peoples shall be respected.
2. The peoples concerned shall be consulted whenever consideration is being given to their capacity to alienate their lands or otherwise transmit their rights outside their own community.
3. Persons not belonging to these peoples shall be prevented from taking advantage of their customs or of lack of understanding of the laws on the part of their members to secure the ownership, possession or use of land belonging to them.

Article 18

Adequate penalties shall be established by law for unauthorised intrusion upon, or use of, the lands of the peoples concerned, and governments shall take measures to prevent such offences.

Article 19

National agrarian programmes shall secure to the peoples concerned treatment equivalent to that accorded to other sectors of the population with regard to:
(a) The provision of more land for these peoples when they have not the area necessary for providing the essentials of a normal existence, or for any possible increase in their numbers;
(b) The provision of the means required to promote the development of the lands which these peoples already possess.

. . .

PART IV. VOCATIONAL TRAINING, HANDICRAFTS AND RURAL INDUSTRIES

. . .

Article 23

1. Handicrafts, rural and community-based industries, and subsistence economy and traditional activities of the peoples concerned, such as hunting, fishing, trapping and gathering, shall be recognised as important factors in the maintenance of their cultures and in their economic self-reliance and development. Governments shall, with the participation of

these peoples and whenever appropriate, ensure that these activities are strengthened and promoted.

2. Upon the request of the peoples concerned, appropriate technical and financial assistance shall be provided wherever possible, taking into account the traditional technologies and cultural characteristics of these peoples, as well as the importance of sustainable and equitable development.

Questions and Discussion

1. Do either of the texts above define or explain who is indigenous? Note that adoption of the U.N. Declaration was delayed for a year because of concerns of some African countries about the application of the Declaration to African peoples. Their concerns were not unwarranted. *See* African Commission on Human and Peoples Rights, Case No. 276 / 2003 – *Centre for Minority Rights Development (Kenya) and Minority Rights Group International on behalf of Endorois Welfare Council v. Kenya, infra. See also* the *Sesana* case from Botswana, *infra*.

2. How strong is the protection afforded to the environment and natural resources of indigenous traditional lands? Is there any basis for complaining of transboundary sources of pollution?

IV. The ICCPR and Minority Rights

The Human Rights Committee that oversees compliance with the Covenant on Civil and Political Rights has issued General Comments addressing the meaning and scope of ICCPR's articles 1 and 27. It has also had to interpret and apply the two texts in response to communications filed under its Optional Protocol. Indigenous groups initially tried to invoke article 1 on self-determination; the Committee recharacterized the communication as one under article 27. The rationale for this and the treatment of indigenous environmental claims under article 27 are illustrated by the cases that follow the General Comments. *See also* Committee on the Elimination of All Forms of Racial Discrimination, *General Recommendation No. 23, Rights of Indigenous Peoples*, 51st sess. U.N. Doc. A/52/18, annex V, at para. 4 (Aug. 18, 1997) (calling on states to take certain measures to recognize and ensure the rights of indigenous peoples).

General Comment No. 12: The Right to Self-Determination of Peoples (Mar. 13, 1984)
Human Rights Committee, U.N. Doc. HRI/GEN/1/Rev.9 (Vol. I) (May 27, 2008) at p. 183.

Article 1

1. In accordance with the purposes and principles of the Charter of the United Nations, article 1 of the International Covenant on Civil and Political Rights recognizes that all peoples have the right of self-determination. The right of self-determination is of particular importance because its realization is an essential condition for the effective guarantee and observance of individual human rights and for the promotion and strengthening of those rights. It is for that reason that States set forth the right of self-determination in a provision of positive law in both Covenants and placed this provision as article 1 apart from and before all of the other rights in the two Covenants.

2. Article 1 enshrines an inalienable right of all peoples as described in its paragraphs 1 and 2. By virtue of that right they freely "determine their political status and freely pursue their economic, social and cultural development." The article imposes on all States parties corresponding obligations. This right and the corresponding obligations concerning

its implementation are interrelated with other provisions of the Covenant and rules of international law.

. . .

7. In connection with article 1 of the Covenant, the Committee refers to other international instruments concerning the right of all peoples to self-determination, in particular the Declaration on Principles of International Law concerning Friendly Relations and Co-operation among States in accordance with the Charter of the United Nations, adopted by the General Assembly on 24 October 1970 (General Assembly resolution 2625 (XXV)).

8. The Committee considers that history has proved that the realization of and respect for the right of self-determination of peoples contributes to the establishment of friendly relations and cooperation between States and to strengthening international peace and understanding.

General Comment No. 23: The Rights of Minorities, U.N. Doc. CCPR/C/21/Rev.1/Add.5 (Aug. 4, 1994), reprinted in U.N. Doc. HRI/GEN/1/Rev.9 (Vol. I) (May 27, 2008) at p. 207.

Article 27

1. Article 27 of the Covenant provides that, in those States in which ethnic, religious or linguistic minorities exist, persons belonging to these minorities shall not be denied the right, in community with the other members of their group, to enjoy their own culture, to profess and practise their own religion, or to use their own language. The Committee observes that this article establishes and recognizes a right which is conferred on individuals belonging to minority groups and which is distinct from, and additional to, all the other rights which, as individuals in common with everyone else, they are already entitled to enjoy under the Covenant.

2. In some communications submitted to the Committee under the Optional Protocol, the right protected under article 27 has been confused with the right of peoples to self-determination proclaimed in article 1 of the Covenant. Further, in reports submitted by States parties under article 40 of the Covenant, the obligations placed upon States parties under article 27 have sometimes been confused with their duty under article 2.1 to ensure the enjoyment of the rights guaranteed under the Covenant without discrimination and also with equality before the law and equal protection of the law under article 26.

3.1. The Covenant draws a distinction between the right to self-determination and the rights protected under article 27. The former is expressed to be a right belonging to peoples and is dealt with in a separate part (Part I) of the Covenant. Self-determination is not a right cognizable under the Optional Protocol. Article 27, on the other hand, relates to rights conferred on individuals as such and is included, like the articles relating to other personal rights conferred on individuals, in Part III of the Covenant and is cognizable under the Optional Protocol.

3.2. The enjoyment of the rights to which article 27 relates does not prejudice the sovereignty and territorial integrity of a State party. At the same time, one or other aspect of the rights of individuals protected under that article – for example, to enjoy a particular culture – may consist in a way of life which is closely associated with territory and use of its resources. This may particularly be true of members of indigenous communities constituting a minority.

. . .

6.1. Although article 27 is expressed in negative terms, that article, nevertheless, does recognize the existence of a "right" and requires that it shall not be denied. Consequently, a State party is under an obligation to ensure that the existence and the exercise of this right are protected against their denial or violation. Positive measures of protection are, therefore, required not only against the acts of the State party itself, whether through its legislative, judicial or administrative authorities, but also against the acts of other persons within the State party.

6.2.   Although the rights protected under article 27 are individual rights, they depend in turn on the ability of the minority group to maintain its culture, language or religion. Accordingly, positive measures by States may also be necessary to protect the identity of a minority and the rights of its members to enjoy and develop their culture and language and to practise their religion, in community with the other members of the group. In this connection, it has to be observed that such positive measures must respect the provisions of articles 2.1 and 26 of the Covenant both as regards the treatment between different minorities and the treatment between the persons belonging to them and the remaining part of the population. However, as long as those measures are aimed at correcting conditions which prevent or impair the enjoyment of the rights guaranteed under article 27, they may constitute a legitimate differentiation under the Covenant, provided that they are based on reasonable and objective criteria.

7.   With regard to the exercise of the cultural rights protected under article 27, the Committee observes that culture manifests itself in many forms, including a particular way of life associated with the use of land resources, especially in the case of indigenous peoples. That right may include such traditional activities as fishing or hunting and the right to live in reserves protected by law. The enjoyment of those rights may require positive legal measures of protection and measures to ensure the effective participation of members of minority communities in decisions which affect them.

8.   The Committee observes that none of the rights protected under article 27 of the Covenant may be legitimately exercised in a manner or to an extent inconsistent with the other provisions of the Covenant.

9.   The Committee concludes that article 27 relates to rights whose protection imposes specific obligations on States parties. The protection of these rights is directed towards ensuring the survival and continued development of the cultural, religious and social identity of the minorities concerned, thus enriching the fabric of society as a whole. Accordingly, the Committee observes that these rights must be protected as such and should not be confused with other personal rights conferred on one and all under the Covenant. States parties, therefore, have an obligation to ensure that the exercise of these rights is fully protected and they should indicate in their reports the measures they have adopted to this end.

Ominayak and the Lubicon Lake Band v. Canada,
Communication No. 167/1984, U.N. Doc. CCPR/C/38/D/167/1984 (May 10, 1990)

. . .

2.2   Chief Ominayak is the leader and representative of the Lubicon Lake Band, a Cree Indian band living within the borders of Canada in the Province of Alberta. They are subject to the jurisdiction of the Federal Government of Canada, allegedly in accordance with a fiduciary relationship assumed by the Canadian Government with respect to Indian peoples and their lands located within Canada's national borders. The Lubicon Lake Band is a self-identified, relatively autonomous, socio-cultural and economic group. Its members have continuously inhabited, hunted, trapped and fished in a large area encompassing approximately 10,000 square kilometres in northern Alberta since time immemorial. Since their territory is relatively inaccessible, they have, until recently, had little contact with non-Indian society. Band members speak Cree as their primary language. Many do not speak, read or write English. The Band continues to maintain its traditional culture, religion, political structure and subsistence economy.

2.3   It is claimed that the Canadian Government, through the Indian Act of 1970 and Treaty 8 of 21 June 1899 (concerning aboriginal land rights in northern Alberta), recognized the right of the original inhabitants of that area to continue their traditional way of life. Despite these laws and agreements, the Canadian Government has allowed the provincial government of Alberta to expropriate the territory of the Lubicon Lake Band for the benefit of private corporate interests (e.g., leases for oil and gas exploration). In so doing, Canada is accused of violating the Band's right to determine freely its political status and to pursue its economic, social and cultural development, as guaranteed by article 1, paragraph 1, of the Covenant. Furthermore, energy exploration in the Band's territory allegedly entails a violation of article 1, paragraph 2, which grants all peoples the right to dispose of their natural wealth and resources. In destroying the environment and undermining the Band's economic base, the Band is allegedly being deprived of its means to subsist and of the enjoyment of the right of self-determination guaranteed in article 1.

. . .

Right of Self-Determination

6.1   The Government of Canada submits that the communication, as it pertains to the right of self-determination, is inadmissible for two reasons. First, the right of self-determination applies to a "people" and it is the position of the Government of Canada that the Lubicon Lake Band is not a people within the meaning of article 1 of the Covenant. It therefore submits that the communication is incompatible with the provisions of the Covenant and, as such, should be found inadmissible under article 3 of the Protocol. Secondly, communications under the Optional Protocol can only be made by individuals and must relate to the breach of a right conferred on individuals. The present communication, the State party argues, relates to a collective right and the author therefore lacks standing to bring a communication pursuant to articles I and 2 of the Optional Protocol.

6.2   As to the argument that the Lubicon Lake Band does not constitute a people for the purposes of article I of the Covenant and it therefore is not entitled to assert under the Protocol the right of self-determination, the Government of Canada points out that the Lubicon Lake Band comprises only one of 582 Indian bands in Canada and a small portion of a larger group of Cree Indians residing in northern Alberta. It is therefore the position of the Government of Canada that the Lubicon Lake Indians are not a "people" within the meaning of article 1 of the Covenant.

6.3   The Government of Canada submits that while self-determination as contained in article 1 of the Covenant is not an individual right, it provides the necessary contextual background for the exercise of individual human rights. This view, it contends, is supported by the following phrase from the Committee's general comment on article 1 (CCPR/C/21/Add.3, 5 October 1984), which provides that the realization of self-determination is "an essential condition for the effective guarantee and observance of individual human rights and for the promotion and strengthening of those rights." This general comment, the State party adds, recognizes that the rights embodied in article I are set apart from, and before, all the other rights in the Covenant on Civil and Political Rights and the Covenant on Economic, Social and Cultural Rights. The rights in article 1, which are contained in part I of the Covenant on Civil and Political Rights are, in the submission of Canada, different in nature and kind from the rights in part III, the former being collective, the latter individual. Thus, the structure of the Covenant, when viewed as a whole, further supports the argument that the right of self-determination is a collective one available to peoples. As such, the State party argues, it cannot be invoked by individuals under the Optional Protocol.

6.4   The Government of Canada contends that the Committee's jurisdiction, as defined by the Optional Protocol, cannot be invoked by an individual when the alleged violation concerns a collective right. It therefore contends that the present communication pertaining to self-determination for the Lubicon Lake Band should be dismissed.

. . .

13.1 Before considering a communication on the merits, the Committee must ascertain whether it fulfils all conditions relating to its admissibility under the Optional Protocol.

. . .

13.3 With regard to the State party's contention that the author's communication pertaining to self-determination should be declared inadmissible because "the Committee's jurisdiction, as defined by the Optional Protocol, cannot be invoked by an individual when the alleged violation concerns a collective right," the Committee reaffirmed that the Covenant recognizes and protects in most resolute terms a people's right of self-determination and its right to dispose of its natural resources, as an essential condition for the effective guarantee and observance of individual human rights and for the promotion and strengthening of those rights. However, the Committee observed that the author, as an individual, could not claim under the Optional Protocol to be a victim of a violation of the right of self-determination enshrined in article I of the Covenant, which deals with rights conferred upon peoples, as such.

13.4 The Committee noted, however, that the facts as submitted might raise issues under other articles of the Covenant, including article 27. Thus, in so far as the author and other members of the Lubicon Lake Band were affected by the events which the author has described, these issues should be examined on the merits, in order to determine whether they reveal violations of article 27 or other articles of the Covenant.

14. On 22 July 1987, therefore, the Human Rights Committee decided that the communication was admissible in so far as it might raise issues under article 27 or other articles of the Covenant. The State party was requested, under rule 86 of the rules of procedure, to take interim measures of protection to avoid irreparable damage to Chief Ominayak and other members of the Lubicon Lake Band.

. . .

29.7 Accepting its obligation to provide the Lubicon Lake Band with reserve land under Treaty 8, and after further unsuccessful discussions, the Federal Government, in May 1988, initiated legal proceedings against the Province of Alberta and the Lubicon Lake Band, in an effort to provide a common jurisdiction and thus to enable it to meet its lawful obligations to the Band under Treaty 8. In the author's opinion, however, this initiative was designated for the sole purpose of delaying indefinitely the resolution of the Lubicon land issues and, on 6 October 1988 (30 September, according to the State party), the Lubicon Lake Band asserted jurisdiction over its territory and declared that it had ceased to recognize the jurisdiction of the Canadian courts. The author further accused the State party of "practicing deceit in the media and dismissing advisors who recommend any resolution favourable to the Lubicon people."

29.8 Following an agreement between the provincial government of Alberta and the Lubicon Lake Band in November 1988 to set aside 95 square miles of land for a reserve, negotiations started between the federal Government and the Band on the modalities of the land transfer and related issues. According to the State party, consensus had been reached on the majority of issues, including Band membership, size of the reserve, community construction and delivery of programmes and services, but not on cash compensation, when the [Band] withdrew from the negotiations on 24 January 1989. The formal offer presented at that time by the federal Government amounted to approximately C$45 million in benefits and programmes, in addition to the 95 square mile reserve.

29.9   The author, on the other hand, states that the above information from the State party
         is not only misleading but virtually entirely untrue and that there had been no serious
         attempt by the Government to reach a settlement. He describes the Government's offer
         as an exercise in public relations, "which committed the Federal Government to virtually
         nothing," and states that no agreement or consensus had been reached on any issue. The
         author further accused the State party of sending agents into communities surrounnding
         [*sic*] the traditional Lubicon territory to induce other natives to make competing claims for
         traditional Lubicon land.

29.10   The State party rejects the allegation that it negotiated in bad faith or engaged in improper
         behaviour to the detriment of the interests of the Lubicon Lake Band. It concedes that the
         Lubicon Lake Band has suffered a historical inequity, but maintains that its formal offer
         would, if accepted, enable the Band to maintain its culture, control its way of life and
         achieve economic self-sufficiency and, thus, constitute an effective remedy. On the basis
         of a total of 500 Band members, the package worth C$45 million would amount to almost
         C$500,000 for each family of five. It states that a number of the Band's demands, including
         an indoor ice arena or a swimming pool, had been refused. The major remaining point
         of contention, the State party submits, is a request for C$167 million in compensation for
         economic and other losses allegedly suffered. That claim, it submits, could be pursued in
         the courts, irrespective of the acceptance of the formal offer. It reiterates that its offer to the
         Band stands.

29.11   Further submissions from both parties have, inter alia, dealt with the impact of the Daishowa
         pulp mill on the traditional way of life of the Lubicon Lake Band. While the author states
         that the impact would be devastating, the State party maintains that it would have no serious
         adverse consequences, pointing out that the pulp mill, located about 80 kilometres away
         from the land set aside for the reserve, is not within the Band's claimed traditional territory
         and that the area to be cut annually, outside the proposed reserve, involves less than 1 per
         cent of the area specified in the forest management agreement.

Articles of the Covenant Alleged to Have Been Violated

32.1   The question has arisen of whether any claim under article 1 of the Covenant remains,
         the Committee's decision on admissibility notwithstanding. While all peoples have the
         right of self-determination and the right freely to determine their political status, pursue
         their economic, social and cultural development and dispose of their natural wealth and
         resources, as stipulated in article 1 of the Covenant, the question whether the Lubicon
         Lake Band constitutes a "people" is not an issue for the Committee to address under the
         Optional Protocol to the Covenant. The Optional Protocol provides a procedure under
         which individuals can claim that their individual rights have been violated. These rights
         are set out in part III of the Covenant, articles 6 to 27, inclusive. There is, however, no
         objection to a group of individuals, who claim to be similarly affected, collectively to submit
         a communication about alleged breaches of their rights.

32.2   Although initially couched in terms of alleged breaches of the provisions of article 1 of
         the Covenant, there is no doubt that many of the claims presented raise issues under
         article 27. The Committee recognizes that the rights protected by article 27, include the
         right of persons, in community with others, to engage in economic and social activities
         which are part of the culture of the community to which they belong. Sweeping allegations
         concerning extremely serious breaches of other articles of the Covenant (6, 7, 14, para. 1, and
         26), made after the communication was declared admissible, have not been substantiated
         to the extent that they would deserve serious consideration. The allegations concerning
         breaches of articles 17 and 23, paragraph 1, are similarly of a sweeping nature and will not
         be taken into account except in so far as they may be considered subsumed under the
         allegations which, generally, raise issues under article 27.

32.3   The most recent allegations that the State party has conspired to create an artificial band, the Woodland Cree Band, said to have competing claims to traditional Lubicon land, are dismissed as an abuse of the right of submission within the meaning of article 3 of the Optional Protocol.

Violations and the Remedy Offered

33.   Historical inequities, to which the State party refers, and certain more recent developments threaten the way of life and culture of the Lubicon Lake Band, and constitute a violation of article 27 so long as they continue. The State party proposes to rectify the situation by a remedy that the Committee deems appropriate within the meaning of article 2 of the Covenant.

Questions and Discussion

1.   Do you agree with the Committee's decision that the right of self-determination is nonjusticiable? Did it make a difference in this case?

2.   Was the Canadian government's proposed solution an equitable one that would ensure the rights of the Lubicon Lake Band?

3.   Does the Committee give any indication of how it proposes to resolve disputes over the exploitation of natural resources between the majority in a state and indigenous peoples?

4.   Most of the communications from indigenous groups have come from the Sami, traditional reindeer herders in Scandinavia. *See, e.g., Kitok v. Sweden*, Communication No. 197/1985, II Official Records of the Human Rights Committee 1987/88, U.N. Doc. CCPR/7/Add.1, at 442; *Ilmari Lansman et al. v. Finland*, Communication No. 511/1992, Human Rights Committee, Final Decisions 74, U.N. Doc. CCPR/C/57/1 (1996); *O.S. et al. v. Finland*, Communication No. 431/1990, decision of Mar. 23, 1994; and *Jouni E. Lansmann et al. v. Finland*, Communication No. 671/1995, decision of Oct. 30, 1996.

Apirana Mahuika et al. v. New Zealand, Communication No. 547/1993 decided Nov. 15, 2000, U.N. Doc. CCPR/C/70/D/547/1993 (some notes omitted, others renumbered)

5.1   The Maori people of New Zealand number approximately 500,000, 70% of whom are affiliated to one or more of 81 iwi.[39] The authors belong to seven distinct iwi (including two of the largest and in total comprising more than 140,000 Maori) and claim to represent these. In 1840, Maori and the predecessor of the New Zealand Government, the British Crown, signed the Treaty of Waitangi, which affirmed the rights of Maori, including their right to self-determination and the right to control tribal fisheries. In the second article of the Treaty, the Crown guarantees to Maori:

> The full exclusive and undisturbed possession of their lands, forests, fisheries and other properties which they may collectively or individually possess so long as it is their wish and desire to retain the same in their possession . . .

> The Treaty of Waitangi is not enforceable in New Zealand law except insofar as it is given force of law in whole or in part by Parliament in legislation. However, it imposes obligations on the Crown and claims under the Treaty can be investigated by the Waitangi Tribunal.[40]

. . .

---

[39] *Iwi*: tribe, incorporating a number of constituent *hapu* (subtribes).

[40] The Waitangi Tribunal is a specialized statutory body established by the Treaty of Waitangi Act of 1975 having the status of a commission of enquiry and empowered *inter alia* to inquire into certain claims in relation to the principles of the Treaty of Waitangi.

5.12   On 3 December 1992, the Treaty of Waitangi (Fisheries Claims) Settlement Bill 1992 was introduced. Because of the time constraints involved in securing the Sealords bid,[41] the Bill was not referred to the competent Select Committee for hearing, but immediately presented and discussed in Parliament. The Bill became law on 14 December 1992. . . . According to the Act, the Maori Fisheries Commission was renamed the Treaty of Waitangi Fisheries Commission, and its membership expanded from seven to thirteen members. Its functions were also expanded. In particular, the Commission now has the primary role in safeguarding Maori interests in commercial fisheries.

5.13   The joint venture bid for Sealords was successful. After consultation with Maori, new Commissioners were appointed to the Treaty of Waitangi Fisheries Commission. Since then, the value of the Maori stake in commercial fishing has grown rapidly. In 1996, its net assets had increased to a book value of 374 million dollars. In addition to its 50% stake in Sealords, the Commission now controls also Moana Pacific Fisheries Limited (the biggest in-shore fishing company in New Zealand), Te Waka Huia Limited, Pacific Marine Farms Limited and Chatham Processing Limited. The Commission has disbursed substantial assistance in the form of discounted annual leases of quota, educational scholarships and assistance to Maori input into the development of a customary fishing regime. Customary fishing regulations have been elaborated by the Crown in consultation with Maori.

The complaint:

6.1   The authors claim that the Treaty of Waitangi (Fisheries Claims) Settlement Act confiscates their fishing resources, denies them their right to freely determine their political status and interferes with their right to freely pursue their economic, social and cultural development. It is submitted that the Treaty of Waitangi (Fisheries Claims) Settlement Act 1992 is in breach of the State party's obligations under the Treaty of Waitangi. In this context, the authors claim that the right to self-determination under article 1 of the Covenant is only effective when people have access to and control over their resources.

6.2   The authors claim that the Government's actions are threatening their way of life and the culture of their tribes, in violation of article 27 of the Covenant. They submit that fishing is one of the main elements of their traditional culture, that they have present-day fishing interests and the strong desire to manifest their culture through fishing to the fullest extent of their traditional territories. They further submit that their traditional culture comprises commercial elements and does not distinguish clearly between commercial and other fishing. They claim that the new legislation removes their right to pursue traditional fishing other than in the limited sense preserved by the law and that the commercial aspect of fishing is being denied to them in exchange for a share in fishing quota. . . .

Issues and Proceedings Before the Committee

. . .

9.3   The first issue before the Committee therefore is whether the authors' rights under article 27 of the Covenant have been violated by the Fisheries Settlement, as reflected in the Deed of Settlement and the Treaty of Waitangi (Fisheries Claims) Settlement Act 1992. It is undisputed that the authors are members of a minority within the meaning of article 27 of the Covenant; it is further undisputed that the use and control of fisheries is an essential element of their culture. In this context, the Committee recalls that economic activities may come within the ambit of article 27, if they are an essential element of the culture

[41] [In February 1992, Maori became aware that Sealords, the largest fishing company in Australia and New Zealand was likely to be publicly floated at some time during that year. The Maori Fisheries Negotiators and the Maori Fisheries Commission approached the government with a proposition that the government provide funding for the purchase of Sealords as part of a settlement of Treaty claims to fisheries. – *Eds.*]

of a community. The recognition of Maori rights in respect of fisheries by the Treaty of Waitangi confirms that the exercise of these rights is a significant part of Maori culture. However, the compatibility of the 1992 Act with the treaty of Waitangi is not a matter for the Committee to determine.

9.4   The right to enjoy one's culture cannot be determined *in abstracto* but has to be placed in context. In particular, article 27 does not only protect traditional means of livelihood of minorities, but allows also for adaptation of those means to the modern way of life and ensuing technology. In this case the legislation introduced by the State affects, in various ways, the possibilities for Maori to engage in commercial and non-commercial fishing. The question is whether this constitutes a denial of rights. On an earlier occasion, the Committee has considered that:

> A State may understandably wish to encourage development or allow economic activity by enterprises. The scope of its freedom to do so is not to be assessed by reference to a margin of appreciation, but by reference to the obligations it has undertaken in article 27. Article 27 requires that a member of a minority shall not be denied his right to enjoy his own culture. Thus, measures whose impact amount to a denial of the right will not be compatible with the obligations under article 27. However, measures that have a certain limited impact on the way of life of persons belonging to a minority will not necessarily amount to a denial of the right under article 27.[42]

9.5   The Committee recalls its general comment on article 27, according to which, especially in the case of indigenous peoples, the enjoyment of the right to one's own culture may require positive legal measures of protection by a State party and measures to ensure the effective participation of members of minority communities in decisions which affect them. In its case law under the Optional Protocol, the Committee has emphasised that the acceptability of measures that affect or interfere with the culturally significant economic activities of a minority depends on whether the members of the minority in question have had the opportunity to participate in the decision-making process in relation to these measures and whether they will continue to benefit from their traditional economy. The Committee acknowledges that the Treaty of Waitangi (Fisheries Settlement) Act 1992 and its mechanisms limit the rights of the authors to enjoy their own culture.

9.6   The Committee notes that the State party undertook a complicated process of consultation in order to secure broad Maori support to a nation-wide settlement and regulation of fishing activities. Maori communities and national Maori organizations were consulted and their proposals did affect the design of the arrangement. The Settlement was enacted only following the Maori representatives' report that substantial Maori support for the Settlement existed. For many Maori, the Act was an acceptable settlement of their claims. The Committee has noted the authors' claims that they and the majority of members of their tribes did not agree with the Settlement and that they claim that their rights as members of the Maori minority have been overridden. In such circumstances, where the right of individuals to enjoy their own culture is in conflict with the exercise of parallel rights by other members of the minority group, or of the minority as a whole, the Committee may consider whether the limitation in issue is in the interests of all members of the minority and whether there is reasonable and objective justification for its application to the individuals who claim to be adversely affected.

9.7   As to the effects of the agreement, the Committee notes that before the negotiations which led to the Settlement the Courts had ruled earlier that the Quota Management System was in possible infringement of Maori rights because in practice Maori had no part in it and

---

[42] Committee's Views Case No. 511/1992, Lansmann et al. v. Finland, CCPR/C/52/D/511/1992, para. 9.4

were thus deprived of their fisheries. With the Settlement, Maori were given access to a great percentage of quota, and thus effective possession of fisheries was returned to them. In regard to commercial fisheries, the effect of the Settlement was that Maori authority and traditional methods of control as recognised in the Treaty were replaced by a new control structure, in an entity in which Maori share not only the role of safeguarding their interests in fisheries but also the effective control. In regard to non-commercial fisheries, the Crown obligations under the Treaty of Waitangi continue, and regulations are made recognising and providing for customary food gathering.

9.8   In the consultation process, special attention was paid to the cultural and religious significance of fishing for the Maori, *inter alia*[,] to securing the possibility of Maori individuals and communities to engage themselves in non-commercial fishing activities. While it is a matter of concern that the settlement and its process have contributed to divisions amongst Maori, nevertheless, the Committee concludes that the State party has, by engaging itself in the process of broad consultation before proceeding to legislate, and by paying specific attention to the sustainability of Maori fishing activities, taken the necessary steps to ensure that the Fisheries Settlement and its enactment through legislation, including the Quota Management System, are compatible with article 27.

9.9   The Committee emphasises that the State party continues to be bound by article 27 which requires that the cultural and religious significance of fishing for Maori must deserve due attention in the implementation of the Treaty of Waitangi (Fisheries Claims) Settlement Act. With reference to its earlier case law, the Committee emphasises that in order to comply with article 27, measures affecting the economic activities of Maori must be carried out in a way that the authors continue to enjoy their culture, and profess and practice their religion in community with other members of their group. The State party is under a duty to bear this in mind in the further implementation of the Treaty of Waitangi (Fisheries Claims) Settlement Act.

9.10 The authors' complaints about the discontinuance of the proceedings in the courts concerning their claim to fisheries must be seen in the light of the above. While in the abstract it would be objectionable and in violation of the right to access to court if a State party would by law discontinue cases that are pending before the courts, in the specific circumstances of the instant case, the discontinuance occurred within the framework of a nation wide settlement of exactly those claims that were pending before the courts and that had been adjourned awaiting the outcome of negotiations. In the circumstances, the Committee finds that the discontinuance of the authors' court cases does not amount to a violation of article 14(1) of the Covenant.

9.11 With regard to the authors' claim that the Act prevents them from bringing claims concerning the extent of their fisheries before the courts, the Committee notes that article 14(1) encompasses the right to access to court for the determination of rights and obligations in a suit at law. In certain circumstances the failure of a State party to establish a competent court to determine rights and obligations may amount to a violation of article 14(1). In the present case, the Act excludes the courts' jurisdiction to inquire into the validity of claims by Maori in respect to commercial fishing, because the Act is intended to settle these claims. In any event, Maori recourse to the Courts to enforce claims regarding fisheries was limited even before the 1992 Act; Maori rights in commercial fisheries were enforceable in the Courts only to the extent that s. 88(2) of the Fisheries Act expressly provided that nothing in the Act was to affect Maori fishing rights. The Committee considers that whether or not claims in respect of fishery interests could be considered to fall within the definition of a suit at law, the 1992 Act has displaced the determination of Treaty claims in respect of fisheries by its specific provisions. Other aspects of the right to fisheries, though, still give the right to access to court, for instance in respect of the allocation of quota and of the regulations governing customary fishing rights. The authors have not substantiated the claim that the enactment of the new legislative framework has barred their access to court in any matter falling within the scope of article 14, paragraph 1. Consequently, the Committee finds that the facts before it do not disclose a violation of article 14, paragraph 1.

10. The Human Rights Committee, acting under article 5, paragraph 4, of the Optional Protocol to the International Covenant on Civil and Political Rights, is of the view that the facts before it do not reveal a breach of any of the articles of the Covenant.

V. The OAS and the Development of *Sui Generis* Rights

The inter-American human rights system created by the Organization of American States extends to all independent states in the Western Hemisphere, from the Arctic to Patagonia. The population of each state in the region includes descendants of "precontact" indigenous populations and tribal peoples, who continue to suffer exclusion, poverty, and loss of their lands and resources. Over time, the Inter-American Commission on Human Rights and the Inter-American Court of Human Rights have evolved a doctrine of unique rights for indigenous and tribal peoples and articulated the special obligations of states toward them.

One of the earliest cases bringing the Commission's attention to the plight of the indigenous was *Yanomami v. Brazil*, Case 7615 (Brazil), 1984–1985 *Annual Report of the Inter-American Commission on Human Rights* 24, OEA/Ser.L/V/II.66, doc. 10, rev. 1 (1985). The petition alleged that the government violated the American Declaration of the Rights and Duties of Man by constructing a highway through Yanomami territory and authorizing exploitation of the territory's resources. These actions led to the influx of nonindigenous, who brought contagious diseases that remained untreated because of a lack of medical care. The Commission found that the government had violated the Yanomani's rights to life, liberty, and personal security guaranteed by article 1 of the Declaration, as well as the right of residence and movement (article 8) and the right to the preservation of health and well-being (article 11). Subsequently, the Commission issued a country report on human rights in Ecuador that expanded on the duties of the state toward indigenous peoples, especially in the context of development projects. They Commission placed its emphasis on the procedural rights of information, participation, and redress. Later cases have added substantive protections.

Report on the Situation of Human Rights in Ecuador,
OEA/Ser.L/V/II.96, Doc. 10 rev. 1, Apr. 24, 1997 (footnotes omitted, some renumbered).

. . .

Ecuadorean law provides that all subsurface minerals are the property of the State. Consequently, the State exploits oil and mineral deposits, either directly through the state-owned oil company PetroEcuador, or indirectly, through concessions and service contracts with foreign oil companies.

The exploitation of oil resources in the Oriente since the 1960's, when commercially viable deposits were first discovered, has had a profound impact on the region and its people. . . . Current Oriente operations involve, inter alia, over 300 producing wells, regional oil refineries, secondary pipelines, transfer lines and gas lines, and the network of roads that serves the industry.

. . .

The Commission was advised by representatives of communities near oil development sites that, as a result of exposure to contaminated water, soil and air, some of their members suffered from skin diseases, rashes, chronic infections and fevers, gastrointestinal problems, and that the children particularly suffered frequent bouts of diarrhea. . . .

In addition, a number of people told the delegation that contamination of the physical environment was hindering their ability to feed their families. The Commission has received reports that the pollution of local rivers, streams and lakes has contaminated the fish residents depend on as a dietary staple, and that development activities and contamination have driven away the wildlife they hunt as an important source of protein. In a number of instances, separation stations, exploratory or production wells, and waste pits are located immediately adjacent to or even within local communities. Many facilities, including those the Commission observed, are not fenced in or otherwise secured. Settlers reported that animals they raise to eat and to sell had become sick from drinking contaminated water, or had died after drinking from or becoming trapped in local waste pits. In several cases, the Commission received reports from settlers who had lost animals, fields or crops due to oil spills which had spread onto their land.

The inhabitants allege that the Government has failed to regulate and supervise the activities of both the state-owned oil company and of its licensee companies. They further allege that the companies take few if any measures to protect the affected population, and refuse to implement environmental controls or to utilize existing technologies employed in other countries. Those who spoke before the delegation indicated that the Government had failed to ensure that oil exploitation activities were conducted in compliance with existing legal and policy requirements. Throughout its travels in the Oriente, the delegation received claims that the Government of Ecuador has violated and continues to violate the constitutionally protected rights of the inhabitants of the region to life and to live in an environment free from contamination.

. . .

The Applicable Legal Framework

. . .

Ecuador is Party to or has supported a number of instruments which recognize the critical connection between the sustenance of human life and the environment, including: the Additional Protocol to the American Convention in the Area of Economic, Social and Cultural Rights, the ICCPR and the ICESCR, the Stockholm Declaration, the Treaty for Amazonian Cooperation, the Amazon Declaration, the World Charter for Nature, the Convention on Nature Protection and Wildlife Preservation in the Western Hemisphere, the Rio Declaration on Environment and Development) and the Convention on Biological Diversity.

2. Relevant Inter-American Law

The realization of the right to life, and to physical security and integrity is necessarily related to and in some ways dependent upon one's physical environment. Accordingly, where environmental contamination and degradation pose a persistent threat to human life and health, the foregoing rights are implicated.

The American Declaration of the Rights and Duties of Man, which continues to serve as a source of international obligation for all member states, recognizes the right to life, liberty and personal security in Article I, and reflects the interrelationship between the rights to life and health in Article XI, which provides for the preservation of the health and well being of the individual. This priority concern for the life and physical preservation of the individual is reflected in the American Convention in Article 4, which guarantees the right to life, and Article 5, which guarantees the right to physical, mental and moral integrity.

The right to life recognized in Article 4 of the American Convention is . . . fundamental in the sense that it is nonderogable and constitutes the basis for the realization of all other rights. Article 4 protects an individual's right to have his or her life respected: "This right shall be protected by law . . . [n]o one shall be arbitrarily deprived of his life." The right to have one's life respected is not, however, limited to protection against arbitrary killing. States Parties are required to take certain positive measures to safeguard life and physical integrity. Severe environmental pollution may pose a threat to human life and health, and in the appropriate case give rise to an obligation on the part of a state to take reasonable measures to prevent such risk, or the necessary measures to respond when persons have suffered injury.

Analysis

The Commission recognizes that the right to development implies that each state has the freedom to exploit its natural resources, including through the granting of concessions and acceptance of international investment. However, the Commission considers that the absence of regulation, inappropriate regulation, or a lack of supervision in the application of extant norms may create serious problems with respect to the environment which translate into violations of human rights protected by the American Convention.

. . .

According to the Government's own figures, billions of gallons of untreated toxic wastes and oil have been discharged directly into the forests, fields and waterways of the Oriente. The resulting consequences for the inhabitants of the affected areas have been and remain grave. The right to life and the protection of the physical integrity of the individual are norms of an imperative nature. Article 2 of the American Convention requires that where these rights are not adequately ensured through legislative and other means, the State must take the necessary corrective measures. Where the right to life, to health and to live in a healthy environment is already protected by law, the Convention requires that the law be effectively applied and enforced.

The information analyzed above on the impact of oil exploitation activities on the health and lives of the affected residents raises serious concern, and prompts the Commission to encourage the State of Ecuador to take the measures necessary to ensure that the acts of its agents, through the State-owned oil company, conform to its domestic and inter-American legal obligations. Moreover, the Commission encourages the State to take steps to prevent harm to affected individuals through the conduct of its licensees and private actors. The State of Ecuador must ensure that measures are in place to prevent and protect against the occurrence of environmental contamination which threatens the lives of the inhabitants of development sectors. Where the right to life of Oriente residents has been infringed upon by environmental contamination, the Government is obliged to respond with appropriate measures of investigation and redress.[43]

CONCLUSIONS

The American Convention on Human Rights is premised on the principle that rights inhere in the individual simply by virtue of being human. Respect for the inherent dignity of the person is the principle which underlies the fundamental protections of the right to life and to preservation of physical well-being. Conditions of severe environmental pollution, which may cause serious physical illness, impairment and suffering on the part of the local populace, are inconsistent with the right to be respected as a human being.

In the context of the situation under study, protection of the right to life and physical integrity may best be advanced through measures to support and enhance the ability of individuals to safeguard and vindicate those rights. The quest to guard against environmental conditions which threaten human health requires that individuals have access to: information, participation in relevant decision-making processes, and judicial recourse.

Access to information is a prerequisite for public participation in decision-making and for individuals to be able to monitor and respond to public and private sector action. Individuals have a right to seek, receive and impart information and ideas of all kinds pursuant to Article 13 of

---

[43] While the Commission has analyzed the human rights situation in the Oriente through the example of oil exploitation activities, it must be noted that other types of development activities raise similar factual and legal concerns. One pertinent example concerns the effects of gold mining in the interior. The processes employed involve various types of chemicals, including cyanide and mercury, which may be emitted into streams and rivers.

the American Convention. Domestic law requires that parties seeking authorization for projects which may affect the environment provide environmental impact assessments and other specific information as a precondition. However, individuals in affected sectors have indicated that they lack even basic information about exploitation activities taking place locally, and about potential risks to their health. The Government should ensure that such information as the law in fact requires be submitted is readily accessible to potentially affected individuals.

Public participation in decision-making allows those whose interests are at stake to have a say in the processes which affect them. Public participation is linked to Article 23 of the American Convention, which provides that every citizen shall enjoy the right "to take part in the conduct of public affairs, directly or through freely chosen representatives," as well as to the right to receive and impart information. As acknowledged in Decree 1802, while environmental action requires the participation of all social sectors, some, such as women, young people, minorities and indigenous peoples, have not been able to directly participate in such processes for diverse historical reasons. Affected individuals should be able to be informed about and have input into the decisions which affect them.

The right to access judicial remedies is the fundamental guarantor of rights at the national level. Article 25 of the American Convention provides that "[e]veryone has the right to simple and prompt recourse, or any other effective recourse, to a competent court or tribunal for protection against acts that violate his fundamental rights recognized by the constitution or laws of the state concerned or by this Convention. . . . " This means that individuals must have access to judicial recourse to vindicate the rights to life, physical integrity and to live in a safe environment, all of which are expressly protected in the Constitution. Individuals and [NGOs] have indicated to the Commission that, for various reasons, judicial remedies have not proven an available or effective means for individuals threatened by environmental pollution to obtain redress.

The norms of the inter-American human rights system neither prevent nor discourage development; rather, they require that development take place under conditions that respect and ensure the human rights of the individuals affected. As set forth in the Declaration of Principles of the Summit of the Americas: "Social progress and economic prosperity can be sustained only if our people live in a healthy environment and our ecosystems and natural resources are managed carefully and responsibly."

As the Commission observed at the conclusion of its observation in loco: "Decontamination is needed to correct mistakes that ought never to have happened." Both the State and the companies conducting oil exploitation activities are responsible for such anomalies, and both should be responsible for correcting them. It is the duty of the State to ensure that they are corrected.

Mayagna (Sumo) Awas Tingni Community v. Nicaragua,
Inter-Am. Court Hum. Rts (ser. C) No. 79 (Aug. 31, 2001)
(footnotes omitted or renumbered).

. . .

[The Awas Tingni Community is an indigenous group of more than six hundred persons located in the Northern Atlantic Autonomous Region (Región Autónoma Atlántico Norte RAAN) of Nicaragua. The community subsists on the basis of family farming and communal agriculture, as well as gathering fruit and medicinal plants, hunting, and fishing, carried out within traditional lands and with a traditional collective form of organization. The community had no real property title deed to the lands, although the right to indigenous lands was recognized in the Nicaraguan constitution. On March 26, 1992, the Awas Tingni Community and Maderas y Derivados de Nicaragua, S.A. (MADENSA) signed a contract for the comprehensive management of the forest. The contract was revised in May 1994 to facilitate the definition of communal lands and to avoid undermining the community's territorial claims. On March 13, 1996, the state, through MARENA, granted a thirty-year concession to SOLCARSA to manage and use the forest in an area of roughly sixty-two thousand hectares located in the RAAN. The company was later sanctioned for having illegally felled trees "on the site of the Kukulaya community" and for having carried out works without an environmental permit. On February 27, 1997, the Constitutional Panel of the Supreme Court of Justice declared the concession granted to SOLCARSA to be unconstitutional because it had not been approved by the plenary of the Regional Council of the RAAN. On July 11, 1995, María Luisa Acosta Castellón, representing the community, submitted a letter to the minister of MARENA, with a request that no further steps be taken to grant the concession to SOLCARSA without an agreement with the community. The community then sought legal recognition of its territorial claims without success, and the state granted another forestry concession to SOLCARSA without the community's consent. – Eds.]

. . .

IX VIOLATION OF ARTICLE 21

142. Article 21 of the Convention declares that:

1. Everyone has the right to the use and enjoyment of his property. The law may subordinate such use and enjoyment to the interest of society.
2. No one shall be deprived of his property except upon payment of just compensation, for reasons of public utility or social interest, and in the cases and according to the forms established by law.
3. Usury and any other form of exploitation of man by man shall by prohibited by law.

143. Article 21 of the American Convention recognizes the right to private property. In this regard, it establishes: a) that "[e]veryone has the right to the use and enjoyment of his property"; b) that such use and enjoyment can be subordinate, according to a legal mandate, to "social interest"; c) that a person may be deprived of his or her property for reasons of "public utility or social interest, and in the cases and according to the forms established by law"; and d) that when so deprived, a just compensation must be paid.

144. "Property" can be defined as those material things which can be possessed, as well as any right which may be part of a person's patrimony; that concept includes all movables and immovables, corporeal and incorporeal elements and any other intangible object capable of having value.

145. During the study and consideration of the preparatory work for the American Convention on Human Rights, the phrase "[e]veryone has the right to the use and enjoyment of *private property*, but the law may subordinate its use and enjoyment to public interest" was replaced by "[e]veryone has the right to the *use and enjoyment* of his property. The law may subordinate such use and enjoyment to the social interest." In other words, it was decided to refer to the "use and enjoyment of his *property*" instead of "private property."

146. The terms of an international human rights treaty have an autonomous meaning, for which reason they cannot be made equivalent to the meaning given to them in domestic law. Furthermore, such human rights treaties are live instruments whose interpretation must adapt to the evolution of the times and, specifically, to current living conditions.[44]

147. Article 29(b) of the Convention, in turn, establishes that no provision may be interpreted as "restricting the enjoyment or exercise of any right or freedom recognized by virtue of the laws of any State Party or by virtue of another convention to which one of the said states is a party."

148. Through an evolutionary interpretation of international instruments for the protection of human rights, taking into account applicable norms of interpretation and pursuant to

---

44 Cf. *The Right to Information on Consular Assisstance* [sic] *in the Framework of Guarantees for Due Legal Process* Advisory Opinion OC-16/99 of Oct. 1, 1999. A Series No. 16, para. 114.

article 29(b) of the Convention – which precludes a restrictive interpretation of rights –, it is the opinion of this Court that article 21 of the Convention protects the right to property in a sense which includes, among others, the rights of members of the indigenous communities within the framework of communal property, which is also recognized by the Constitution of Nicaragua.

149. Given the characteristics of the instant case, some specifications are required on the concept of property in indigenous communities. Among indigenous peoples there is a communitarian tradition regarding a communal form of collective property of the land, in the sense that ownership of the land is not centered on an individual but rather on the group and its community. Indigenous groups, by the fact of their very existence, have the right to live freely in their own territory; the close ties of indigenous people with the land must be recognized and understood as the fundamental basis of their cultures, their spiritual life, their integrity, and their economic survival. For indigenous communities, relations to the land are not merely a matter of possession and production but a material and spiritual element which they must fully enjoy, even to preserve their cultural legacy and transmit it to future generations.

150. In this regard, Law No. 28, published on October 30, 1987 in La Gaceta No. 238, the Official Gazette of the Republic of Nicaragua, which regulates the Autonomy Statute of the Regions of the Atlantic Coast of Nicaragua, states in article 36 that:

> Communal property are the lands, waters, and forests that have traditionally belonged to the Communities of the Atlantic Coast, and they are subject to the following provisions:
>
> 1. Communal lands are inalienable; they cannot be donated, sold, encumbered nor taxed, and they are inextinguishable.
> 2. The inhabitants of the Communities have the right to cultivate plots on communal property and to the usufruct of goods obtained from the work carried out.

151. Indigenous peoples' customary law must be especially taken into account for the purpose of this analysis. As a result of customary practices, possession of the land should suffice for indigenous communities lacking real title to property of the land to obtain official recognition of that property, and for consequent registration.

152. As has been pointed out, Nicaragua recognizes communal property of indigenous peoples, but has not regulated the specific procedure to materialize that recognition, and therefore no such title deeds have been granted since 1990. Furthermore, in the instant case the State has not objected to the claim of the Awas Tingni Community to be declared owner, even though the extent of the area claimed is disputed.

153. It is the opinion of the Court that, pursuant to article 5 of the Constitution of Nicaragua, the members of the Awas Tingni Community have a communal property right to the lands they currently inhabit, without detriment to the rights of other indigenous communities. Nevertheless, the Court notes that the limits of the territory on which that property right exists have not been effectively delimited and demarcated by the State. This situation has created a climate of constant uncertainty among the members of the Awas Tingni Community, insofar as they do not know for certain how far their communal property extends geographically and, therefore, they do not know until where they can freely use and enjoy their respective property. Based on this understanding, the Court considers that the members of the Awas Tingni Community have the right that the State carry out the delimitation, demarcation, and titling of the territory belonging to the Community; and abstain from carrying out, until that delimitation, demarcation, and titling have been done, actions that might lead the agents of the State itself, or third parties acting with its

acquiescence or its tolerance, to affect the existence, value, use or enjoyment of the property located in the geographical area where the members of the Community live and carry out their activities.

143. Based on the above, and taking into account the criterion of the Court with respect to applying article 29(b) of the Convention, the Court believes that, in light of article 21 of the Convention, the State has violated the right of the members of the Mayagna Awas Tingni Community to the use and enjoyment of their property, and that it has granted concessions to third parties to utilize the property and resources located in an area which could correspond, fully or in part, to the lands which must be delimited, demarcated, and titled.

154. Together with the above, we must recall what has already been established by this court, based on article 1(1) of the American Convention, regarding the obligation of the State to respect the rights and freedoms recognized by the Convention and to organize public power so as to ensure the full enjoyment of human rights by the persons under its jurisdiction. According to the rules of law pertaining to the international responsibility of the State and applicable under International Human Rights Law, actions or omissions by any public authority, whatever its hierarchic position, are chargeable to the State which is responsible under the terms set forth in the American Convention.

155. For all the above, the Court concludes that the State violated article 21 of the American Convention, to the detriment of the members of the Mayagna (Sumo) Awas Tingni Community, in connection with articles 1(1) and 2 of the Convention.

. . .

XI Application of Article 63(1)

. . .

162. Article 63(1) of the American Convention establishes that

> [i]f the Court finds that there has been a violation of a right or freedom protected by this Convention, the Court shall rule that the injured party be ensured the enjoyment of his right or freedom that was violated. It shall also rule, if appropriate, that the consequences of the measure or situation that constituted the breach of such right or freedom be remedied and that fair compensation be paid to the injured party.

156. In the instant case the Court established that Nicaragua breached articles 25 and 21 of the Convention in relation to articles 1(1) and 2 of the Convention. In this regard, the Court has reiterated in its constant jurisprudence that it is a principle of international law that any violation of an international obligation which has caused damage carries with it the obligation to provide adequate reparation for it.

164. For the aforementioned reason, pursuant to article 2 of the American Convention on Human Rights, this Court considers that the State must adopt the legislative, administrative, and any other measures required to create an effective mechanism for delimitation, demarcation, and titling of the property of indigenous communities, in accordance with their customary law, values, customs and mores. Furthermore, as a consequence of the aforementioned violations of rights protected by the Convention in the instant case, the Court rules that the State must carry out the delimitation, demarcation, and titling of the corresponding lands of the members of the Awas Tingni Community, within a maximum term of 15 months, with full participation by the Community and taking into account its customary law, values, customs and mores. Until the delimitation, demarcation, and titling of the lands of the members of the Community have been carried out, Nicaragua must abstain from acts which might lead the agents of the State itself, or third parties acting

with its acquiescence or its tolerance, to affect the existence, value, use or enjoyment of the property located in the geographic area where the members of the Awas Tingni Community live and carry out their activities.

165. In the instant case, the Court notes that the Commission did not prove that there were material damages caused to the members of the Mayagna Community.

166. The Court considers that this Judgment is, in and of itself, a form of reparation to the members of the Awas Tingni Community.

167. The Court considers that due to the situation in which the members of the Awas Tingni Community find themselves due to lack of delimitation, demarcation, and titling of their communal property, the immaterial damage caused must also be repaired, by way of substitution, through a monetary compensation. Under the circumstances of the case it is necessary to resort to this type of compensation, setting it in accordance with equity and based on a prudent estimate of the immaterial damage, which is not susceptible of precise valuation. Due to the above and taking into account the circumstances of the cases and what has been decided in similar cases, the Court considers that the State must invest, as reparation for the immaterial damages, in the course of 12 months, the total sum of US$50,000 (fifty thousand United States dollars) in works or services of collective interest for the benefit of the Awas Tingni Community, by common agreement with the Community and under the supervision of the Inter-American Commission.

Questions and Discussion

1. Is it appropriate for an international human rights court to order a country to award land to an indigenous group? What evidence should be required to demonstrate sufficient links with territory to obtain communal property rights? How should land claims that cross international boundaries be resolved?

2. It took a while, but the government of Nicaragua complied with the Court's judgment. The Commission issued the following press release, No. 62/08, on December 18, 2008:

    The Inter-American Commission on Human Rights (IACHR) praises the demarcation and titling of ancestral lands belonging to Nicaragua's Mayagna Awas Tingni Indigenous Community.

    On Sunday, December 14, the government of Nicaragua gave the Awas Tingni Community the property title to 73,000 hectares of its territory, located on the country's Atlantic Coast. This marked a critical step forward in the resolution of a case the IACHR took to the Inter-American Court in 1998, the first case on indigenous peoples' collective property rights that the Commission had asked the Court to hear. The judgment handed down on August 31, 2001, by the Inter-American Court became a historic milestone in the recognition and protection of the rights of indigenous peoples around the world, and an important legal precedent in international human rights law.

3. If indigenous land and resource claims are recognized, are all indigenous groups entitled to recover lost lands? What about the rights of intervening purchasers?

4. New indigenous land and resource claims were brought to the Inter-American Commission and Court following the *Awas Tingni* decision. First, the Court decided the case of the *Indigenous Community Yakye Axa v. Paraguay*, Merits, Reparations and Costs, Inter-Am. Ct. Hum. Rts (ser. C) No. 125 (June 17, 2005). Nine months later, the *Case of the Sawhoya-maxa Indigenous Community v. Paraguay*, Inter-Am. Court Hum. Rts. (ser. C) No. 146 (Mar. 29, 2006), addressed the difficult issue of returning indigenous lands after they had been sold to and occupied by others. The Court summed up its earlier jurisprudence: (1) traditional possession of their lands by indigenous people has equivalent effects to those

of a state-granted full property title; (2) traditional possession entitles indigenous people to demand official recognition and registration of property title; (3) the members of indigenous peoples who have unwillingly left their traditional lands, or lost possession thereof, maintain property rights thereto, even though they lack legal title, unless the lands have been lawfully transferred to third parties in good faith; and (4) the members of indigenous peoples who have unwillingly lost possession of their lands, when those lands have been lawfully transferred to innocent third parties, are entitled to restitution thereof or to obtain other lands of equal extension and quality. Consequently, possession is not a requisite conditioning the existence of indigenous land restitution rights. The court addressed the temporal element as follows:

131. The second issue under analysis refers to whether the right to the restitution of traditional lands lasts indefinitely in time. In order to solve this matter, the Court takes into consideration that the spiritual and material basis for indigenous identity is mainly supported by their unique relationship with their traditional lands. As long as said relationship exists, the right to claim lands is enforceable, otherwise, it will lapse. Said relationship may be expressed in different ways, depending on the particular indigenous people involved and the specific circumstances surrounding it, and it may include the traditional use or presence, be it through spiritual or ceremonial ties; settlements or sporadic cultivation; seasonal or nomadic gathering, hunting and fishing; the use of natural resources associated with their customs and any other element characterizing their culture.

132. It is to be further considered that the relationship with the land must be possible. For instance, in situations like in the instant case, where the relationship with the land is expressed, *inter alia*, in traditional hunting, fishing and gathering activities, if the members of the indigenous people carry out few or none of such traditional activities within the lands they have lost, because they have been prevented from doing so for reasons beyond their control, which actually hinder them from keeping up such relationship, such as acts of violence or threats against them, restitution rights shall be deemed to survive until said hindrances disappear.

133. As it stems from the Proven Facts Chapter in the instant judgment, the members of the Sawhoyamaxa Community, in spite of having been dispossessed and of being denied access to the claimed lands, still carry out traditional activities in them and still consider them their own. . . .

134. Based on the foregoing, the Court considers that the land restitution right of the members of the Sawhoyamaxa Community has not lapsed.

138. . . . [T]he Court considers that the fact that the claimed lands are privately held by third parties is not in itself an "objective and reasoned" ground for dismissing *prima facie* the claims by the indigenous people. Otherwise, restitution rights become meaningless and would not entail an actual possibility of recovering traditional lands, as it would be exclusively limited to an expectation on the will of the current holders, forcing indigenous communities to accept alternative lands or economic compensations. In this respect, the Court has pointed out that, when there be conflicting interests in indigenous claims, it must assess in each case the legality, necessity, proportionality and fulfillment of a lawful purpose in a democratic society (public purposes and public benefit), to impose restrictions on the right to property, on the one hand, or the right to traditional lands, on the other.

. . .

186. Considering the aforesaid, the Court finds that the State violated Article 4(1) of the American Convention, as regards to Article 1(1) thereof, since it has not adopted the necessary positive measures within its powers, which could reasonably be expected to prevent or avoid risking the right to life of the members of the Sawhoyamaxa Community.

As for restitution of the Community's lands owned by third parties, the Court concluded that:

212. ... [T]he State must consider the possibility of purchasing these lands or the lawfulness, need and proportionality of condemning these lands in order to achieve a lawful purpose in a democratic society, as reaffirmed in paragraphs 135 to 141 of the instant Judgment and paragraphs 143 to 151 of the judgment entered by the Court in the *Case of the Indigenous Community Yakye Axa*. If restitution of ancestral lands to the members of the Sawhoyamaxa Community is not possible on objective and sufficient grounds, the State shall make over alternative lands, selected upon agreement with the aforementioned Indigenous Community, in accordance with the community's own decision-making and consultation procedures, values, practices and customs. In either case, the extension and quality of the lands must be sufficient to guarantee the preservation and development of the Community's own way of life.

5. The next case was the first to focus extensively on the rights of indigenous and tribal peoples to control major development projects within indigenous and tribal lands.

Case of the Saramaka People v. Suriname,
Inter-Am. Ct. Hum. Rts. (ser. C) No. 172 (Nov. 28, 2007)
(footnotes omitted or renumbered)

· · ·

2. The application submits to the Court's jurisdiction alleged violations committed by the State against the members of the Saramaka people, an allegedly tribal community living in the Upper Suriname River region. The Commission alleged that the State has not adopted effective measures to recognize their right to the use and enjoyment of the territory they have traditionally occupied and used, that the State has allegedly violated the right to judicial protection to the detriment of such people by not providing them effective access to justice for the protection of their fundamental rights, particularly the right to own property in accordance with their communal traditions, and that the State has allegedly failed to adopt domestic legal provisions in order to ensure and guarantee such rights to the Saramakas.

· · ·

78. The Commission and the representatives alleged that the Saramaka people make up a tribal community and that international human rights law imposes an obligation on the State to adopt special measures to guarantee the recognition of tribal peoples' rights, including the right to collectively own property. The State disputed whether the Saramaka people could be defined as a tribal community subject to the protection of international human rights law regarding their alleged right to collectively own property. The Court must therefore analyze whether the members of the Saramaka people make up a tribal community, and if so, whether it is subject to special measures that guarantee the full exercise of their rights.

79. First of all, the Court observes that the Saramaka people are not indigenous to the region they inhabit; they were instead brought to what is now known as Suriname during the colonization

period. Therefore, they are asserting their rights as alleged tribal peoples, that is, not indigenous to the region, but that share similar characteristics with indigenous peoples, such as having social, cultural and economic traditions different from other sections of the national community, identifying themselves with their ancestral territories, and regulating themselves, at least partially, by their own norms, customs, and traditions.

The Members of the Saramaka People as a Distinct Social, Cultural and Economic Group with a Special Relationship with Its Ancestral Territory

80. According to the evidence submitted by the parties, the Saramaka people are one of the six distinct Maroon groups in Suriname whose ancestors were African slaves forcibly taken to Suriname during the European colonization in the 17th century. Their ancestors escaped to the interior regions of the country where they established autonomous communities. The Saramaka people are organized in twelve matrilineal clans (*lös*), and it is estimated that the contemporary size of the Saramaka population ranges from 25,000 to 34,000, which is spread over 63 communities on the Upper Suriname River and in a number of displaced communities located to the north and west of said area.

81. Their social structure is different from other sectors of society inasmuch as the Saramaka people are organized in matrilineal clans (*lös*), and they regulate themselves, at least partially, by their own customs and traditions. Each clan (*lö*) recognizes the political authority of various local leaders, including what they call Captains and Head Captains, as well as a *Gaa'man*, who is the community's highest official.

82. Their culture is also similar to that of tribal peoples insofar as the members of the Saramaka people maintain a strong spiritual relationship with the ancestral territory[45] they have traditionally used and occupied. Land is more than merely a source of subsistence for them; it is also a necessary source for the continuation of the life and cultural identity of the Saramaka people. The lands and resources of the Saramaka people are part of their social, ancestral, and spiritual essence. In this territory, the Saramaka people hunt, fish, and farm, and they gather water, plants for medicinal purposes, oils, minerals, and wood. Their sacred sites are scattered throughout the territory, while at the same time the territory itself has a sacred value to them. In particular, the identity of the members of the Saramaka people with the land is inextricably linked to their historical fight for freedom from slavery, called the sacred "first time." . . .

83. Furthermore, their economy can also be characterized as tribal. According to the expert testimony of Dr. Richard Price, for example, "the very great bulk of food that Saramaka eat comes from . . . farms [and] gardens" traditionally cultivated by Saramaka women. The men, according to Dr. Price, fish and "hunt wild pig, deer, tapir, all sorts of monkeys, different kinds of birds, everything that Saramakas eat." Furthermore, the women gather various fruits, plants and minerals, which they use in a variety of ways, including making baskets, cooking oil, and roofs for their dwellings.

84. Thus, in accordance with all of the above, the Court considers that the members of the Saramaka people make up a tribal community whose social, cultural and economic characteristics are different from other sections of the national community, particularly because of their special relationship with their ancestral territories, and because they regulate themselves, at least partially, by their own norms, customs, and/or traditions. Accordingly, the Court will now address whether

---

45 By using the term *territory* the Court is referring to the sum of traditionally used lands and resources. In this sense, the Saramaka territory belongs collectively to the members of the Saramaka people, whereas the lands within that territory are divided among and vested in the twelve Saramaka clans. *Cf.* Affidavit of Head Captain and Fiscali Eddie Fonkie, Apr. 5, 2007 (case file of affidavits and observations thereto, appendix 4, folio 1911); Expert opinion of Professor Richard Price (transcription of public hearing, pp. 60–61), and Professor Richard Price, "Report in support of Provisional Measures."

and to what extent the members of the tribal peoples require special measures that guarantee the full exercise of their rights.

SPECIAL MEASURES OF PROTECTION OWED TO MEMBERS OF THE TRIBAL COMMUNITY THAT GUARANTEE THE FULL EXERCISE OF THEIR RIGHTS

85. This Court has previously held, based on Article 1(1) of the Convention, that members of indigenous and tribal communities require special measures that guarantee the full exercise of their rights, particularly with regards to their enjoyment of property rights, in order to safeguard their physical and cultural survival. Other sources of international law have similarly declared that such special measures are necessary.[46] . . .

86. The Court sees no reason to depart from this jurisprudence in the present case. Hence, this Tribunal declares that the members of the Saramaka people are to be considered a tribal community, and that the Court's jurisprudence regarding indigenous peoples' right to property is also applicable to tribal peoples because both share distinct social, cultural, and economic characteristics, including a special relationship with their ancestral territories, that require special measures under international human rights law in order to guarantee their physical and cultural survival.

. . .

102. Two additional related arguments submitted by the State as to why it has failed to legally recognize and protect the land-tenure systems of indigenous and tribal communities are the alleged "complexities and sensitivities" of the issues involved, and the concern that legislation in favor of indigenous and tribal peoples may be perceived as being discriminatory towards the rest of the population. Regarding the first issue, the Court observes that the State may not abstain from complying with its international obligations under the American Convention merely because of the alleged difficulty to do so. The Court shares the State's concern over the complexity of the issues involved; nevertheless, the State still has a duty to recognize the right to property of members of the Saramaka people, within the framework of a communal property system, and establish the mechanisms necessary to give domestic legal effect to such right recognized in the Convention, as interpreted by this Tribunal in its jurisprudence.

103. Furthermore, the State's argument that it would be discriminatory to pass legislation that recognizes communal forms of land ownership is also without merit. It is a well-established principle of international law that unequal treatment towards persons in unequal situations does not necessarily amount to impermissible discrimination.[47] Legislation that recognizes said differences

---

[46] As early as 1972, in the resolution the Commission adopted on "Special Protection for Indigenous Populations – Action to Combat Racism and Racial Discrimination," the Commission proclaimed that "for historical reasons and because of moral and humanitarian principles, special protection for indigenous populations constitutes a sacred commitment of states." *Cf.* Resolution on Special Protection for Indigenous Populations. Action to Combat Racism and Racial Discrimination, OEA/Ser.L/V/II.29 Doc. 41 rev. 2 (Mar. 13, 1973), cited in Inter-American Commission on Human Rights, *Report 12/85, Case No. 7615, Yanomami. Brazil* (Mar. 5, 1985), para. 8. *Cf.* Inter-American Commission on Human Rights, Report on the Situation of Human Rights in Ecuador, OAS/Ser.L/V/II.96 Doc.10 rev. 1, at ch. 9 (Apr. 24, 1997) (stating that "within international law generally, and inter-American law specifically, special protections for indigenous peoples may be required for them to exercise their rights fully and equally with the rest of the population. Additionally, special protections for indigenous peoples may be required to ensure their physical and cultural survival – a right protected in a range of international instruments and conventions"); UNCERD, *General Recommendation No. 23, Rights of Indigenous Peoples (Fifty-first session, 1997)*, U.N. Doc. A/52/18, annex V, at para. 4 (Aug. 18, 1997) (calling upon States to take certain measures in order to recognize and ensure the rights of indigenous peoples); and ECHR, *Case of Connors v. The United Kingdom*, Judgment of May 27, 2004, Application No. 66746/01, para. 84 (declaring that States have an obligation to take positive steps to provide for and protect the different lifestyles of minorities as a way to provide equality under the law).

[47] *Cf., e.g.,* ECHR, *Connors v. United Kingdom*, . . . para. 84 (declaring that States have an obligation to take positive steps to provide for and protect the different lifestyles of minorities as a way to provide equality under the law). *Cf. also* Inter-American Commission on Human Rights, Report on the Situation of Human Rights in Ecuador, . . . (stating that "within international law

is therefore not necessarily discriminatory. In the context of members of indigenous and tribal peoples, this Court has already stated that special measures are necessary in order to ensure their survival in accordance with their traditions and customs. Thus, the State's arguments regarding its inability to create legislation in this area due to the alleged complexity of the issue or the possible discriminatory nature of such legislation are without merit.

. . .

D. *The Right of the Members of the Saramaka People to Use and Enjoy the Natural Resources That Lie on and Within Their Traditionally Owned Territory*

118. An issue that necessarily flows from the assertion that the members of the Saramaka people have a right to use and enjoy their territory in accordance with their traditions and customs is the issue of the right to the use and enjoyment of the natural resources that lie on and within the land, including subsoil natural resources. In the present case, both the State and the members of the Saramaka people claim a right to these natural resources. The Saramakas claim that their right to use and enjoy all such natural resources is a necessary condition for the enjoyment of their right to property under Article 21 of the Convention. The State argued that all rights to land, particularly its subsoil natural resources, are vested in the State, which can freely dispose of these resources through concessions to third parties. The Court will address this complex issue in the following order: first, the right of the members of the Saramaka people to use and enjoy the natural resources that lie on and within their traditionally owned territory; second, the State's grant of concessions for the exploration and extraction of natural resources, including subsoil resources found within Saramaka territory; and finally, the fulfillment of international law guarantees regarding the exploration and extraction concessions already issued by the State.

119. First, the Court must analyze whether and to what extent the members of the Saramaka people have a right to use and enjoy the natural resources that lie on and within their traditionally owned territory. The State does not contest that the Saramakas have traditionally used and occupied certain lands for centuries, or that the Saramakas have an "interest" in the territory they have traditionally used in accordance with their customs. The controversy lies regarding the nature and scope of said interest. In accordance with Suriname's legal and constitutional framework, the Saramakas do not have property rights *per se*, but rather merely a privilege or permission to use and occupy the lands in question. According to Article 41 of the Constitution of Suriname and Article 2 of its 1986 Mining Decree, ownership rights of all natural resources vest in the State. For this reason, the State claims to have an inalienable right to the exploration and exploitation of those resources. On the other hand, the customary laws of the Saramaka people allegedly vest in its community a right over all natural resources within and subjacent to or otherwise pertaining to its traditional territory. In support of this assertion, the Court heard testimony from a Saramaka Captain to the effect that the Saramaka people have a general right to "own everything, from the very top of the trees to the very deepest place that you could go under the ground."

generally, and Inter-American law specifically, special protections for indigenous peoples may be required for them to exercise their rights fully and equally with the rest of the population. Additionally, special protections for indigenous peoples may be required to ensure their physical and cultural survival – a right protected in a range of international instruments and conventions"). *Cf. also* U.N. International Convention on the Elimination of All Forms of Racial Discrimination, art. 1.4 (stating that "[s]pecial measures taken for the sole purpose of securing adequate advancement of certain racial or ethnic groups or individuals requiring such protection as may be necessary in order to ensure such groups or individuals equal enjoyment or exercise of human rights and fundamental freedoms shall not be deemed racial discrimination"), and UNCERD, *General Recommendation No. 23, Rights of Indigenous Peoples*, . . . para. 4 (calling upon States to take certain measures in order to recognize and ensure the rights of indigenous peoples).

120. In this regard, this Court has previously held that the cultural and economic survival of indigenous and tribal peoples, and their members, depend on their access and use of the natural resources in their territory "that are related to their culture and are found therein," and that Article 21 protects their right to such natural resources.[48] Nevertheless, the scope of this right needs further elaboration, particularly regarding the inextricable relationship between both land and the natural resources that lie therein, as well as between the territory (understood as encompassing both land and natural resources) and the economic, social, and cultural survival of indigenous and tribal peoples, and thus, of their members.

121. In accordance with this Court's jurisprudence as stated in the *Yakye Axa* and *Sawhoyamaxa* cases, members of tribal and indigenous communities have the right to own the natural resources they have traditionally used within their territory for the same reasons that they have a right to own the land they have traditionally used and occupied for centuries. Without them, the very physical and cultural survival of such peoples is at stake. Hence the need to protect the lands and resources they have traditionally used to prevent their extinction as a people. That is, the aim and purpose of the special measures required on behalf of the members of indigenous and tribal communities is to guarantee that they may continue living their traditional way of life, and that their distinct cultural identity, social structure, economic system, customs, beliefs and traditions are respected, guaranteed and protected by States.

122. As mentioned above, due to the inextricable connection members of indigenous and tribal peoples have with their territory, the protection of their right to property over such territory, in accordance with Article 21 of the Convention, is necessary to guarantee their very survival. Accordingly, the right to use and enjoy their territory would be meaningless in the context of indigenous and tribal communities if said right were not connected to the natural resources that lie on and within the land. That is, the demand for collective land ownership by members of indigenous and tribal peoples derives from the need to ensure the security and permanence of their control and use of the natural resources, which in turn maintains their very way of life. This connectedness between the territory and the natural resources necessary for their physical and cultural survival is precisely what needs to be protected under Article 21 of the Convention in order to guarantee the members of indigenous and tribal communities' right to the use and enjoyment of their property. From this analysis, it follows that the natural resources found on and within indigenous and tribal people's territories that are protected under Article 21 are those natural resources traditionally used and necessary for the very survival, development and continuation of such people's way of life.

123. Thus, in the present case, the Court must determine which natural resources found on and within the Saramaka people's territory are essential for the survival of their way of life, and are thus protected under Article 21 of the Convention. Consequently, the Court must also address whether and to what extent the State may grant concessions for the exploration and extraction of those and other natural resources found within Saramaka territory.

---

[48] The Court also takes notice that the African Commission, as well as the Canadian Supreme Court and the South African Constitutional Court, have ruled that indigenous communities' land rights are to be understood as including the natural resources therein. Nevertheless, according to the African Commission and the Canadian Supreme Court, these rights are not absolute, and may be restricted under certain conditions. *Cf.* African Commission on Human and Peoples' Rights, *The Social and Economic Rights Action Center and the Center for Economic and Social Rights v. Nigeria*, Communication 155/96 (2001), paras. 42, 54 and 55, and *Delgamuukw v. British Columbia*, [1997] 3 S.C.R. 1010 (December 11, 1997), paras. 194, 199 and 201. The South African Constitutional Court, citing a domestic law that required the return of land to owners who had been dispossessed by racially discriminatory policies, affirmed the right of an indigenous peoples to the mineral resources in its lands. *Cf. Alexkor Ltd. and the Government of South Africa v. Richtersveld Community et al.*, CCT/1903 (October 14, 2003), para. 102.

E. The State's Grant of Concessions for the Exploration and Extraction of Natural Resources Found on and Within Saramaka Territory

124. The Commission and the representatives alleged that land concessions for forestry and mining awarded by the State to third parties on territory possessed by the Saramaka people, without their full and effective consultation, violates their right to the natural resources that lie on and within the land. The State asserted that all land ownership, including all natural resources, vests in the State, and that, as such, the State may grant logging and mining concessions within alleged Saramaka territory, while respecting as much as possible Saramaka customs and traditions.

E.1) RESTRICTIONS ON THE RIGHT TO PROPERTY

125. This brings the Court to the issue of whether and to what extent the State may grant concessions for the exploration and extraction of natural resources found within Saramaka territory. In this regard, the State argued that, should the Court recognize a right of the members of the Saramaka people to the natural resources found within traditionally owned lands, this right must be limited to those resources traditionally used for their subsistence, cultural and religious activities. According to the State, the alleged land rights of the Saramakas "would not include any interests on forests or minerals beyond what the Tribe traditionally possesses and uses for subsistence (agriculture, hunting, fishing etc.), and the religious and cultural needs of its people."

126. The State seems to recognize that resources related to the subsistence of the Saramaka people include those related to agricultural, hunting and fishing activities. This is consistent with the Court's previous analysis on how Article 21 of the Convention protects the members of the Saramaka people's right over those natural resources necessary for their physical survival. Nevertheless, while it is true that all exploration and extraction activity in the Saramaka territory could affect, to a greater or lesser degree, the use and enjoyment of some natural resource traditionally used for the subsistence of the Saramakas, it is also true that Article 21 of the Convention should not be interpreted in a way that prevents the State from granting any type of concession for the exploration and extraction of natural resources within Saramaka territory. Clean natural water, for example, is a natural resource essential for the Saramakas to be able to carry out some of their subsistence economic activities, like fishing. The Court observes that this natural resource is likely to be affected by extraction activities related to other natural resources that are not traditionally used by or essential for the survival of the Saramaka people and, consequently, its members. Similarly, the forests within Saramaka territory provide a home for the various animals they hunt for subsistence, and it is where they gather fruits and other resources essential for their survival. In this sense, wood-logging activities in the forest would also likely affect such subsistence resources. That is, the extraction of one natural resource is most likely to affect the use and enjoyment of other natural resources that are necessary for the survival of the Saramakas.

127. Nevertheless, the protection of the right to property under Article 21 of the Convention is not absolute and therefore does not allow for such a strict interpretation. Although the Court recognizes the interconnectedness between the right of members of indigenous and tribal peoples to the use and enjoyment of their lands and their right to those resources necessary for their survival, said property rights, like many other rights recognized in the Convention, are subject to certain limitations and restrictions. In this sense, Article 21 of the Convention states that the "law may subordinate [the] use and enjoyment [of property] to the interest of society." Thus, the Court has previously held that, in accordance with Article 21 of the Convention, a State may restrict the use and enjoyment of the right to property where the restrictions are: a) previously established by law; b) necessary; c) proportional, and d) with the aim of achieving a legitimate objective in a democratic society. In accordance with this Article, and the Court's jurisprudence, the State will

be able to restrict, under certain circumstances, the Saramakas' property rights, including their rights to natural resources found on and within the territory.

128. Furthermore, in analyzing whether restrictions on the property right of members of indigenous and tribal peoples are permissible, especially regarding the use and enjoyment of their traditionally owned lands and natural resources, another crucial factor to be considered is whether the restriction amounts to a denial of their traditions and customs in a way that endangers the very survival of the group and of its members. That is, under Article 21 of the Convention, the State may restrict the Saramakas' right to use and enjoy their traditionally owned lands and natural resources only when such restriction complies with the aforementioned requirements and, additionally, when it does not deny their survival as a tribal people.[49]

E.2) SAFEGUARDS AGAINST RESTRICTIONS ON THE RIGHT TO PROPERTY THAT DENY THE SURVIVAL OF THE SARAMAKA PEOPLE

129. In this particular case, the restrictions in question pertain to the issuance of logging and mining concessions for the exploration and extraction of certain natural resources found within Saramaka territory. Thus, in accordance with Article 1(1) of the Convention, in order to guarantee that restrictions to the property rights of the members of the Saramaka people by the issuance of concessions within their territory does not amount to a denial of their survival as a tribal people, the State must abide by the following three safeguards: First, the State must ensure the effective participation of the members of the Saramaka people, in conformity with their customs and traditions, regarding any development, investment, exploration or extraction plan (hereinafter "development or investment plan")[50] within Saramaka territory. Second, the State must guarantee that the Saramakas will receive a reasonable benefit from any such plan within their territory. Thirdly, the State must ensure that no concession will be issued within Saramaka territory unless and until independent and technically capable entities, with the State's supervision, perform a prior environmental and social impact assessment. These safeguards are intended to preserve, protect and guarantee the special relationship that the members of the Saramaka community have with their territory, which in turn ensures their survival as a tribal people.

130. These safeguards, particularly those of effective participation and sharing of benefits regarding development or investment projects within traditional indigenous and tribal territories, are consistent with the observations of the Human Rights Committee, the text of several international instruments, and the practice in several States Parties to the Convention.[51] In *Apirana Mahuika*

---

[49] *Cf., e.g.,* UNHRC, *Länsman et al. v. Finland (Fifty-second session, 1994),* Communication No. 511/1992, U.N. Doc. CCPR/C/52/D/511/1994, at para. 9.4 (Nov. 8, 1994) (allowing States to pursue development activities that limit the rights of a minority culture as long as the activity does not fully extinguish the indigenous people's way of life).

[50] By "development or investment plan" the Court means any proposed activity that may affect the integrity of the lands and natural resources within the territory of the Saramaka people, particularly any proposal to grant logging or mining concessions.

[51] *Cf., e.g.,* I.L.O. Convention No. 169, article 15(2) (stating that "[i]n cases in which the State retains the ownership of mineral or sub-surface resources or rights to other resources pertaining to lands, governments shall establish or maintain procedures through which they shall consult these peoples, with a view to ascertaining whether and to what degree their interests would be prejudiced, before undertaking or permitting any programmes for the exploration or exploitation of such resources pertaining to their lands."). Similar requirements have been put in place by the World Bank, *Revised Operational Policy and Bank Procedure on Indigenous Peoples (OP/BP 4.10).* Other documents more broadly speak of a minority's right to participate in decisions that directly or indirectly affect them. *Cf., e.g.,* UNHRC, *General Comment No. 23: The Rights of Minorities (Art. 27), supra,* para. 7 (stating that the enjoyment of cultural rights under Article 27 of the ICCPR "may require positive legal measures of protection and measures to ensure the effective participation of members of minority communities in decisions which affect them"); UNCERD, *General Recommendation No. 23, Rights of indigenous peoples, supra* note [49], para. 4(d) (calling upon States parties to "[e]nsure that members of indigenous peoples have equal rights in respect of effective participation in public life and that no decisions directly relating to their rights and interests are taken without their informed consent").

et al. v. New Zealand, for example, the Human Rights Committee decided that the right to culture of an indigenous population under Article 27 of the ICCPR could be restricted where the community itself participated in the decision to restrict such right. The Committee found that "the acceptability of measures that affect or interfere with the culturally significant economic activities of a minority depends on whether the members of the minority in question have had the opportunity to participate in the decision-making process in relation to these measures and whether they will continue to benefit from their traditional economy."[52]

131. Similarly, Article 32 of the United Nations Declaration on the Rights of Indigenous Peoples, which was recently approved by the U.N. General Assembly with the support of the State of Suriname, states the following:[53]

1. Indigenous peoples have the right to determine and develop priorities and strategies for the development or use of their lands or territories and other resources.
2. States shall consult and cooperate in good faith with the indigenous peoples concerned through their own representative institutions in order to obtain their free and informed consent prior to the approval of any project affecting their lands or territories and other resources, particularly in connection with the development, utilization or exploitation of mineral, water or other resources.
3. States shall provide effective mechanisms for just and fair redress for any such activities, and appropriate measures shall be taken to mitigate adverse environmental, economic, social, cultural or spiritual impact.

132. More importantly, the District Commissioner of Sipaliwini in Suriname, who testified before the Court on behalf of the State, recognized the importance of consulting with the traditional authorities of the Saramaka people prior to authorizing concessions that may affect "communities in the direct vicinities." Nonetheless, the Court considers that the actual scope of the guarantees concerning consultation and sharing of the benefits of development or investment projects requires further clarification.

E.2.a) *Right to Consultation, and Where Applicable, a Duty to Obtain Consent*

133. First, the Court has stated that in ensuring the effective participation of members of the Saramaka people in development or investment plans within their territory, the State has a duty to actively consult with said community according to their customs and traditions. This duty requires the State to both accept and disseminate information, and entails constant communication between the parties. These consultations must be in good faith, through culturally appropriate procedures and with the objective of reaching an agreement. Furthermore, the Saramakas must be consulted, in accordance with their own traditions, at the early stages of a development or investment plan, not only when the need arises to obtain approval from the community, if such is the case. Early notice provides time for internal discussion within communities and for proper feedback to the State. The State must also ensure that members of the Saramaka people are aware of possible risks, including environmental and health risks, in order that the proposed development or investment plan is accepted knowingly and voluntarily.

---

[52] UNHRC, *Apirana Mahuika et al. v. New Zealand (Seventieth session, 2000)*, U.N. Doc. CCPR/C/70/D/547/1993, at para. 9.5 (Nov. 15, 2000).

[53] The Court observes that, in explaining the position of the State in favor of this text, the representative of Suriname is reported to have specifically alluded to the aforementioned text of Article 32 of such instrument. The U.N. Press Release states the following: "[The representative of Suriname] said his Government accepted the fact that the States should seek prior consultation to prevent a disregard for human rights. The level of such consultations depended on the specific circumstances. Consultation should not be viewed as an end in itself, but should serve the purpose of respecting the interest of those who used the land," http://www.un.org/News/Press/docs/2007/ga10612.doc.htm.

Finally, consultation should take account of the Saramaka people's traditional methods of decision-making.[54]

134. Additionally, the Court considers that, regarding large-scale development or investment projects that would have a major impact within Saramaka territory, the State has a duty, not only to consult with the Saramakas, but also to obtain their free, prior, and informed consent, according to their customs and traditions. The Court considers that the difference between "consultation" and "consent" in this context requires further analysis.

135. In this sense, the U.N. Special Rapporteur on the situation of human rights and fundamental freedoms of indigenous people has similarly observed that:

> [w]herever [large-scale projects] occur in areas occupied by indigenous peoples it is likely that their communities will undergo profound social and economic changes that are frequently not well understood, much less foreseen, by the authorities in charge of promoting them.... The principal human rights effects of these projects for indigenous peoples relate to loss of traditional territories and land, eviction, migration and eventual resettlement, depletion of resources necessary for physical and cultural survival, destruction and pollution of the traditional environment, social and community disorganization, long-term negative health and nutritional impacts as well as, in some cases, harassment and violence.[55]

Consequently, the U.N. Special Rapporteur determined that "[f]ree, prior and informed consent is essential for the [protection of] human rights of indigenous peoples in relation to major development projects."[56]

136. Other international bodies and organizations have similarly considered that, in certain circumstances, and in addition to other consultation mechanisms, States must obtain the consent of indigenous and tribal peoples to carry out large-scale development or investment projects that have a significant impact on the right of use and enjoyment of their ancestral territories.[57]

137. Most importantly, the State has also recognized that the "level of consultation that is required is obviously a function of the nature and content of the rights of the Tribe in question." The Court agrees with the State and, furthermore, considers that, in addition to the consultation that is always required when planning development or investment projects within traditional Saramaka territory, the safeguard of effective participation that is necessary when dealing with major development or investment plans that may have a profound impact on the property rights of the members of the Saramaka people to a large part of their territory must be understood to additionally require the free, prior, and informed consent of the Saramakas, in accordance with their traditions and customs.

---

[54] Similarly, in *Maya Indigenous Communities of the Toledo District v. Belize*, the Inter-American Commission observed that States must undertake effective and fully informed consultations with indigenous communities with regard to acts or decisions that may affect their traditional territories. In said case, the Commission determined that a process of "fully informed consent" requires "at a minimum, that all of the members of the community are fully and accurately informed of the nature and consequences of the process and provided with an effective opportunity to participate individually or as collectives." *Cf.* Inter-American Commission on Human Rights, *Report* 40/04, *Merits. Case* 12.052. *Maya Indigenous Communities of the Toledo District, supra*, para. 142. *Cf. also* Equator Principles, Principle 5.

[55] U.N., *Report of the Special Rapporteur on the Situation of Human Rights and Fundamental Freedoms of Indigenous People, supra*, p. 2.

[56] U.N., *Report of the Special Rapporteur on the Situation of Human Rights and Fundamental Freedoms of Indigenous People, supra*, para. 66.

[57] The UNCERD has observed that "[a]s to the exploitation of the subsoil resources of the traditional lands of indigenous communities, the Committee observes that merely consulting these communities prior to exploiting the resources falls short of meeting the requirements set out in the Committee's general recommendation XXIII on the rights of indigenous peoples. The Committee therefore recommends that the prior informed consent of these communities be sought." *Cf.* UNCERD, *Consideration of Reports submitted by States Parties Under Article 9 of the Convention, Concluding Observations on Ecuador (Sixty-second session, 2003)*, U.N. Doc. CERD/C/62/CO/2, at para. 16 (June 2, 2003).

E.2.b) *Benefit-Sharing*

138. The second safeguard the State must ensure when considering development or investment plans within Saramaka territory is that of reasonably sharing the benefits of the project with the Saramaka people. The concept of benefit-sharing, which can be found in various international instruments regarding indigenous and tribal peoples' rights,[58] can be said to be inherent to the right of compensation recognized under Article 21(2) of the Convention, which states that

> [n]o one shall be deprived of his property except upon payment of just compensation, for reasons of pubic utility or social interest, and in the cases and according to the forms established by law.

139. The Court considers that the right to obtain compensation under Article 21(2) of the Convention extends not only to the total deprivation of property title by way of expropriation by the State, for example, but also to the deprivation of the regular use and enjoyment of such property. In the present context, the right to obtain "just compensation" pursuant to Article 21(2) of the Convention translates into a right of the members of the Saramaka people to reasonably share in the benefits made as a result of a restriction or deprivation of their right to the use and enjoyment of their traditional lands and of those natural resources necessary for their survival.

140. In this sense, the Committee on the Elimination of Racial Discrimination has recommended not only that the prior informed consent of communities must be sought when major exploitation activities are planned in indigenous territories, but also "that the equitable sharing of benefits to be derived from such exploitation be ensured."[59] Similarly, the Special Rapporteur on the situation of human rights and fundamental freedoms of indigenous peoples has suggested that, in order to guarantee "the human rights of indigenous peoples in relation to major development projects, [States should ensure] mutually acceptable benefit sharing.... "[60] In this context, pursuant to Article 21(2) of the Convention, benefit sharing may be understood as a form of reasonable equitable compensation resulting from the exploitation of traditionally owned lands and of those natural resources necessary for the survival of the Saramaka people.

F. *The Fulfillment of the Guarantees Established Under International Law in Relation to the Concessions Already Granted by the State*

141. Having declared that the Saramakas' right to use and enjoy their traditionally owned lands necessarily implies a similar right with regards to the natural resources that are necessary for their survival, and having set safeguards and limitations regarding the State's right to issue concessions that restrict the use and enjoyment of such natural resources, the Court will now proceed to analyze whether the concessions already issued by the State within Saramaka territory complied with the safeguards mentioned above.

142. In the present case, the evidence before the Court demonstrates that between 1997 and 2004, the State issued at least four logging concessions and a number of mining concessions to both Saramaka and non-Saramaka members and foreign companies within territory traditionally

---

[58] U.N. Declaration on the Rights of Indigenous Peoples, *supra*, article 32 (stating that "States shall consult and cooperate in good faith with the indigenous peoples concerned through their own representative institutions in order to obtain their free and informed consent prior to the approval of any project affecting their lands or territories and other resources, particularly in connection with the development, utilization or exploitation of mineral, water or other resources"), and I.L.O. Convention No. 169, ... article 15(2) (stating that "[t]he peoples concerned shall wherever possible participate in the benefits of such activities, and shall receive fair compensation for any damages which they may sustain as a result of such activities").

[59] UNCERD, *Consideration of Reports Submitted by States Parties Under Article 9 of the Convention, Concluding Observations on Ecuador, supra*, para. 16.

[60] U.N., *Report of the Special Rapporteur on the Situation of Human Rights and Fundamental Freedoms of Indigenous People, supra*, para. 66.

owned by members of the Saramaka community. Witness Rene Somopawiro, the acting director of the State's Foundation for Forest Management and Production Control, recognized in his testimony before the Court that the State had issued concessions within Saramaka territory. District Commissioner Strijk also declared that, during his tenure, at least one logging concession was issued by the State within Saramaka territory and that this concession was held by a non-Saramaka person or corporation.

143. As mentioned above, Article 21 of the Convention does not *per se* preclude the issuance of concessions for the exploration and exploitation of natural resources in indigenous or tribal territories. Nonetheless, if the State wants to restrict, legitimately, the Saramakas' right to communal property, it must consult with the communities affected by the development or investment project planned within territories which they have traditionally occupied, reasonably share the benefits with them, and complete prior assessments of the environmental and social impact of the project.

F.1) LOGGING CONCESSIONS

144. Thus, with regard to timber logging, a question arises as to whether this natural resource is one that has been traditionally used by the members of the Saramaka people in a manner inextricably related to their survival. In this regard, Dr. Richard Price, an anthropologist who gave his expert opinion during the public hearing in the present case, submitted a map in which the Saramaka people made hundreds of marks illustrating the location and variety of trees they use for different purposes. For example, the Saramakas use a special type of tree from which they build boats and canoes to move and transport people and goods from one village to another. The members of the Saramaka community also use many different species of palm trees to make different things, including roofing for their houses, and from which they obtain fruits that they process into cooking oil. When referring to the forest, one of the witnesses stated during the public hearing that it "is where we cut trees in order to make our houses, to get our subsistence, to make our boats . . . ; everything that we live with." Another witness addressed the importance of wood-cutting for the Saramaka people and how they care about their environment:

> When we cut trees, we think about our children, and our grandchildren, and future generations. . . . When we go into the forest for any purpose, we think about what we're doing, we think about saving the environment. We are very careful not to destroy anything that is in the forest. We take the wood that we need for our purposes, and we are very careful not to destroy the environment.

145. Additionally, the evidence before the Tribunal suggests that the members of the Saramaka people also rely on timber logging as part of their economic structure. In this regard, the State emphasized that some individual Saramaka members have requested logging concessions from the State on their own individual behalf. When asked during the public hearing why he, for example, had requested an individual logging concession from the State, Captain Cesar Adjako, of the Matjau clan (*lö*), responded that he did so "because the government made a new law saying that if you wanted to sell the wood you cut, you had to have your name on a concession. Otherwise you were not allowed to sell the wood. . . . Once I have a concession, all my children are able to cut the wood." That is, the request for a personal concession was intended to allow the members of the Saramaka people to legally continue selling wood, as they have traditionally done for subsistence purposes.

146. This evidence shows that the members of the Saramaka people have traditionally harvested, used, traded and sold timber and non-timber forest products, and continue to do so until the present day. Thus, in accordance with the above analysis regarding the extraction of natural resources that are necessary for the survival of the Saramaka people, and consequently, its members, the State

should not have granted logging concessions within Saramaka territory unless and until the three safeguards of effective participation, benefit-sharing, and prior environmental and social impact assessments were complied with.

F.1.a) *Effective Participation*

147. In this case, regarding the logging concessions granted within Saramaka territory, the State did not guarantee the effective participation of the Saramakas in advance, through their traditional decision-making processes, nor did it share the benefits with the members of said people. According to District Commissioner Strijk, who testified before this Tribunal, it was "not necessary" to consult with or obtain the consent of the Saramakas in relation to the logging concessions in question because there were no reported traditional Saramaka sites in the area. In the words of District Commissioner Strijk, "if there are sacred sites, cemeteries, and agricultural plots, then we have consultation, if there are no sacred sites, [cemeteries,] and agricultural plots, then consultation doesn't take place." This procedure evidently fails to guarantee the effective participation of the Saramaka people, through their own customs and traditions, in the process of evaluating the issuance of logging concessions within their territory. As mentioned above, the question for the State is not whether to consult with the Saramaka people, but whether the State must also obtain their consent.

F.1.b) *Prior Environmental and Social Impact Assessments*

148. The State further argued that the "concessions which were provided to third parties did not affect [Saramaka] traditional interests." The evidence before the Tribunal suggests not only that the level of consultation referred to by the State was not enough to guarantee the Saramakas' effective participation in the decision-making process, but also that the State did not complete environmental and social impact assessments prior to issuing said concessions, and that at least some of the concessions granted did affect natural resources necessary for the economic and cultural survival of the Saramaka people. The Court once again observes that when a logging concession is granted, a variety of non-timber forest products, which are used by the members of the Saramaka people for subsistence and commercial purposes, are also affected.

149. In this regard, a map produced by expert witness Dr. Peter Poole and submitted to the Court depicts Saramaka occupation and use of lands and resources in the concessions granted within Saramaka territory to non-Saramaka members. This evidence shows that members of the Saramaka people were extensively using the areas granted to the logging companies as hunting and fishing grounds, as well as a source of a variety of forest products.

150. Head Captain Wazen Eduards, Captain Cesar Adjako, Ms. Silvi Adjako, and Mr. Hugo Jabini, for example, all testified that the activities of the logging companies within traditional Saramaka territory were highly destructive and caused massive damage to a substantial area of the Saramaka people's forest and the ecological and cultural functions and services it provided. Ms. Silvi Adjako, for instance, declared that the logging companies "caused much destruction in our forest and made parts of our land useless because they blocked the creeks and made the water sit on the earth. Before then we were able to use the forest freely and quietly, and it was a great comfort to us and supported us." This statement is also supported by the declaration of Mr. Hugo Jabini, who added that these companies "left a totally ruined forest where they worked. Big parts of the forest cannot be used anymore for farming, and animals will stay away from these areas as well. The creeks are all blocked and the area is flooded and turning into a swamp. It is useless and the spirits are greatly offended."

151. The observations of the Saramaka witnesses are corroborated by the research of expert witnesses Dr. Robert Goodland and Dr. Peter Poole, both of whom visited the concessions and surrounding

areas between 2002 and 2007. In general, Dr. Goodland stated that "the social, environmental and other impacts of the logging concessions are severe and traumatic," and that the "[l]ogging was carried out below minimum acceptable standards for logging operations." Dr. Goodland characterized it as "among the worst planned, most damaging and wasteful logging possible." Dr. Poole added that it was "immediately apparent to [him] that the logging operations in these concessions were not done to any acceptable or even minimum specifications, and sustainable management was not a factor in decision-making."

152. Dr. Goodland and Dr. Poole both testified that the logging companies built substandard bridges in their concessions and that these bridges unnecessarily blocked numerous creeks. Because these creeks are the primary source of potable water used by members of the Saramaka people, "water necessary for drinking, cooking, washing, irrigation, watering gardens, and catching fish is not available. [Furthermore,] subsistence farms become less productive or so unproductive that they have to be abandoned." According to Dr. Goodland, these large areas of standing water render the forest incapable of producing traditional Saramaka agricultural crops. Dr. Poole reached the same conclusions.

F.1.c) *Benefit-Sharing*

153. Not only have the members of the Saramaka people been left with a legacy of environmental destruction, despoiled subsistence resources, and spiritual and social problems, but they received no benefit from the logging in their territory. Government statistics submitted into evidence before the Court prove that a considerable quantity of valuable timber was extracted from the territory of the Saramaka people without any compensation.

. . .

154. In conclusion, the Court considers that the logging concessions issued by the State in the Upper Suriname River lands have damaged the environment and the deterioration has had a negative impact on lands and natural resources traditionally used by members of the Saramaka people that are, in whole or in part, within the limits of the territory to which they have a communal property right. The State failed to carry out or supervise environmental and social impact assessments and failed to put in place adequate safeguards and mechanisms in order to ensure that these logging concessions would not cause major damage to Saramaka territory and communities. Furthermore, the State did not allow for the effective participation of the Saramakas in the decision-making process regarding these logging concessions, in conformity with their traditions and customs, nor did the members of the Saramaka people receive any benefit from the logging in their territory. All of the above constitutes a violation of the property rights of the members of the Saramaka people recognized under Article 21 of the Convention, in connection with Article 1.1 of said instrument.

F.2) GOLD-MINING CONCESSIONS

155. The Court must also analyze whether gold-mining concessions within traditional Saramaka territory have affected natural resources that have been traditionally used and are necessary for the survival of the members of the Saramaka people. According to the evidence submitted before the Court, the members of the Saramaka people have not traditionally used gold as part of their cultural identity or economic system. Despite possible individual exceptions, members of the Saramaka people do not identify themselves with gold nor have demonstrated a particular relationship with this natural resource, other than claiming a general right to "own everything, from the very top of the trees to the very deepest place that you could go under the ground." Nevertheless, as stated above, because any gold mining activity within Saramaka territory will necessarily affect other natural resources necessary for the survival of the Saramakas, such as waterways, the State has a

duty to consult with them, in conformity with their traditions and customs, regarding any proposed mining concession within Saramaka territory, as well as allow the members of the community to reasonably participate in the benefits derived from any such possible concession, and perform or supervise an assessment on the environmental and social impact prior to the commencement of the project. The same analysis applies regarding other concessions within Saramaka territory involving natural resources which have not been traditionally used by members of the Saramaka community, but that their extraction will necessarily affect other resources that are vital to their way of life.

156. The Court recognizes that, to date, no large-scale mining operations have taken place within traditional Saramaka territory. Nevertheless, the State failed to comply with the three safeguards when it issued small-scale gold mining concessions within traditional Saramaka territory. That is, such concessions were issued without performing prior environmental and social impact assessments, and without consulting with the Saramaka people in accordance with their traditions, or guaranteeing their members a reasonable share in the benefits of the project. As such, the State violated the members of the Saramaka peoples' right to property under Article 21 of the Convention, in conjunction with Article 1(1) of such instrument.

157. With regard to the concessions within Saramaka territory that have already been granted to private parties, including Saramaka members, the Court has already declared that "when indigenous communal property and individual private property are in real or apparent contradiction, the American Convention itself and the jurisprudence of the Court provide guidelines to establish admissible restrictions to the enjoyment and exercise of those rights."[61] Thus, the State has a duty to evaluate, in light of the present Judgment and the Court's jurisprudence, whether a restriction of these private property rights is necessary to preserve the survival of the Saramaka people.

   . . .

158. From all of the above considerations, the Court concludes the following: first, that the members of the Saramaka people have a right to use and enjoy the natural resources that lie on and within their traditionally owned territory that are necessary for their survival; second, that the State may restrict said right by granting concessions for the exploration and extraction of natural resources found on and within Saramaka territory only if the State ensures the effective participation and benefit of the Saramaka people, performs or supervises prior environmental and social impact assessments, and implements adequate safeguards and mechanisms in order to ensure that these activities do not significantly affect the traditional Saramaka lands and natural resources; and finally, that the concessions already issued by the State did not comply with these safeguards. Thus, the Court considers that the State has violated Article 21 of the Convention, in conjunction with Article 1 of such instrument, to the detriment of the members of the Saramaka people.

REPARATIONS

   . . .

C. Measures of Redress

194. In order to guarantee the non-repetition of the violation of the rights of the members of the Saramaka people to the recognition of their juridical personality, property, and judicial protection, the State must carry out the following measures:

---

[61] *Case of the Indigenous Community Yakye Axa, supra*, para. 144. *Cf. also* UNHRC, *Ivan Kitok v. Sweden*, Communication No. 197/1985, U.N. Doc. CCPR/C/33/D/197/1985, at para. 9.8 (Aug. 10, 1988).

a) delimit, demarcate, and grant collective title over the territory of the members of the Sara-
    maka people, in accordance with their customary laws, and through previous, effective
    and fully informed consultations with the Saramaka people, without prejudice to other
    tribal and indigenous communities. Until said delimitation, demarcation, and titling of
    the Saramaka territory has been carried out, Suriname must abstain from acts which
    might lead the agents of the State itself, or third parties acting with its acquiescence or
    its tolerance, to affect the existence, value, use or enjoyment of the territory to which
    the members of the Saramaka people are entitled, unless the State obtains the free,
    informed and prior consent of the Saramaka people. With regards to the concessions
    already granted within traditional Saramaka territory, the State must review them, in light
    of the present Judgment and the Court's jurisprudence, in order to evaluate whether a mod-
    ification of the rights of the concessionaires is necessary in order to preserve the survival
    of the Saramaka people. The State must begin the process of delimitation, demarcation
    and titling of traditional Saramaka territory within three months from the notification
    of the present Judgment, and must complete this process within three years from such
    date;

b) grant the members of the Saramaka people legal recognition of their collective juridical
    capacity, pertaining to the community to which they belong, with the purpose of ensuring
    the full exercise and enjoyment of their right to communal property, as well as collective
    access to justice, in accordance with their communal system, customary laws, and traditions.
    The State must comply with this reparation measure within a reasonable time;

c) remove or amend the legal provisions that impede protection of the right to property of
    the members of the Saramaka people and adopt, in its domestic legislation, and through
    prior, effective and fully informed consultations with the Saramaka people, legislative,
    administrative, and other measures as may be required to recognize, protect, guarantee
    and give legal effect to the right of the members of the Saramaka people to hold collective
    title of the territory they have traditionally used and occupied, which includes the lands
    and natural resources necessary for their social, cultural and economic survival, as well as
    manage, distribute, and effectively control such territory, in accordance with their customary
    laws and traditional collective land tenure system, and without prejudice to other tribal and
    indigenous communities. The State must comply with this reparation measure within a
    reasonable time;

d) adopt legislative, administrative and other measures necessary to recognize and ensure
    the right of the Saramaka people to be effectively consulted, in accordance with their
    traditions and customs, or when necessary, the right to give or withhold their free,
    informed and prior consent, with regards to development or investment projects that
    may affect their territory, and to reasonably share the benefits of such projects with the
    members of the Saramaka people, should these be ultimately carried out. The Sara-
    maka people must be consulted during the process established to comply with this form
    of reparation. The State must comply with this reparation measure within a reasonable
    time;

e) ensure that environmental and social impact assessments are conducted by independent
    and technically competent entities, prior to awarding a concession for any development
    or investment project within traditional Saramaka territory, and implement adequate safe-
    guards and mechanisms in order to minimize the damaging effects such projects may have
    upon the social, economic and cultural survival of the Saramaka people, and

f) adopt legislative, administrative and other measures necessary to provide the members
    of the Saramaka people with adequate and effective recourses against acts that violate
    their right to the use and enjoyment of property in accordance with their communal land

tenure system. The State must comply with this reparation measure within a reasonable time.

195. Additionally, the Court considers that the present Judgment *per se* is a form of reparation that should be understood as a form of satisfaction that recognizes that the rights of the members of the Saramaka people addressed in the present Judgment have been violated by the State.

196. [Publish and broadcast the judgment].

. . .

C.2.a) *Material Damages*

199. According to the evidence submitted before the Tribunal, a considerable quantity of valuable timber was extracted from Saramaka territory without any consultation or compensation. Additionally, the evidence shows that the logging concessions awarded by the State caused significant property damage to the territory traditionally occupied and used by the Saramakas. For these reasons, and based on equitable grounds, the Court considers that the members of the Saramaka people must be compensated for the material damage directly caused by these activities in the amount of US$75,000.00 (seventy-five thousand United States dollars). This amount shall be added to the development fund described *infra*.

C.2.b) *Immaterial Damages*

200. In the previous chapter the Court described the environmental damage and destruction of lands and resources traditionally used by the Saramaka people, as well as the impact it had on their property, not just as it pertains to its subsistence resources, but also with regards to the spiritual connection the Saramaka people have with their territory. Furthermore, there is evidence that demonstrates the suffering and distress that the members of the Saramaka people have endured as a result of the long and ongoing struggle for the legal recognition of their right to the territory they have traditionally used and occupied for centuries, as well as their frustration with a domestic legal system that does not protect them against violations of said right, all of which constitutes a denigration of their basic cultural and spiritual values. The Court considers that the immaterial damage caused to the Saramaka people by these alterations to the very fabric of their society entitles them to a just compensation.

201. For these reasons, and on equitable grounds, the Court hereby orders the State to allocate US$600,000.00 for a community development fund created and established for the benefit of the members of the Saramaka people in their traditional territory. Such fund will serve to finance educational, housing, agricultural, and health projects, as well as provide electricity and drinking water, if necessary, for the benefit of the Saramaka people. The State must allocate said amount for this development fund in accordance with paragraph 208 of the present Judgment.

202. An implementation committee composed of three members will be responsible for designating how the projects will be implemented. The implementation committee shall be composed of a representative appointed by the victims, a representative appointed by the State, and another representative jointly appointed by the victims and the State. The Committee shall consult with the Saramaka people before decisions are taken and implemented. Furthermore, the members of the fund's implementation committee must be selected within six months from the notification of the present Judgment. Should the State and the representatives fail to reach an agreement as to the members of the implementation committee within six months after notice of the present Judgment, the Court may convene a meeting to resolve the matter.

. . .

Questions and Discussion

1. Where does the Inter-American Court's jurisprudence fit in the theoretical approaches outlined by Benedict Kingsbury at the beginning of this chapter? Do you agree with the Court's approach? Is the concept of unique or special rights merely a way to avoid discussing the right of self-determination? To what extent does this case give indigenous and tribal peoples a right to say no to resource use on their lands?

2. For further on the rights of indigenous peoples, see the 2007 Annual Report of the IACHR, OEA/Ser.L/V/II.130, doc. 22, rev. 1 (Dec. 29, 2007), paras. 55 et seq. The Commission notes that, as early as 1972, it had maintained that, for historical reasons and for moral and humanitarian principles, states had a duty to provide "special protection" for indigenous peoples. In 1990, the Commission established the special rapporteurship on the rights of indigenous peoples, with the purpose of focusing special attention on indigenous peoples in the Americas. In November 2009, the Commission adopted a report prepared by the special rapporteur, focusing on indigenous land, territory, and resource rights. In 2010, the Inter-American Court returned to the situation of indigenous in Paraguay with its judgment in the *Case of the Xákmok Kásek Indigenous Community. v. Paraguay* Inter-Am. Ct Hum Rts. (ser. C) No. 214 (Aug. 24, 2010).

3. An Australian nongovernmental organization (NGO) has documented human rights violations and environmental destruction stemming from corruption in the foreign-dominated logging industry in Papua New Guinea, similar to the issues raised by the cases in the OAS. Does it suggest that such problems are common to poor, rural communities and not limited to indigenous peoples? *See* Australian Conservation Foundation, Bulldozing Progress: Human Rights Abuses and Corruption in Papua New Guinea's Large Scale Logging Industry (2007). How important is NGO monitoring and reporting on human rights abuses? Is a report like that done by the Australian NGO likely to have an impact on its target audiences? Who is most likely to respond?

VI. African Regional Law

Like the United Nations Covenants, but unlike other regional human rights treaties, the African Charter on Human and Peoples' Rights contains a right of self-determination, adopted in large part to promote decolonization and majority rule in apartheid-era South Africa. The extent to which there are indigenous peoples in independent African states has been a matter of controversy. In 2009, the African Commission on Human and Peoples Rights faced a conflict between purported environmental protection measures and the rights of indigenous peoples in Kenya. *Centre for Minority Rights Development (Kenya) and Minority Rights Group International on behalf of Endorois Welfare Council v Kenya.* Afr. Comm'n HPR, Case 276/2003 (Feb. 4, 2010). The complaint on behalf of the Endorois Community alleged that the government of Kenya forcibly removed the Endorois from their ancestral lands without proper prior consultations or adequate and effective compensation when the government created the Lake Hannington Game Reserve in 1973, and re-gazetted the Lake Bogoria Game Reserve in 1978. After domestic litigation failed to provide redress in 2000, parts of the Endorois' ancestral land was allegedly demarcated and sold by the state to third parties. In 2002, concessions for ruby mining on Endorois traditional land were granted to a private company. The petitioners further alleged that the process of evicting them from their traditional land severed their spiritual, cultural, and economic ties to the land. In sum, the complaint asserted that in the creation of the Game Reserve, the government disregarded national law, Kenyan Constitutional provisions, and rights guaranteed in the African Charter, including the right to property, the right to free disposition of natural resources, the right to religion, the right to cultural life, and the right to development. The Endorois sought restitution of their land, with legal title and clear demarcation and compensation to the community for all their losses.

The government disputed the characterization of the Endorois as a community/sub-tribe or clan on their own. In response, the African Commission noted that while the terms "peoples" and "indigenous community" arouse emotive debates, the Commission, through its Working Group of Experts on Indigenous Populations/Communities, had set out four criteria for identifying indigenous peoples.[62] These are: the occupation and use of a specific territory; the voluntary perpetuation of cultural distinctiveness; self-identification as a distinct collectivity, as well as recognition by other groups; an experience of subjugation, marginalization, dispossession, exclusion or discrimination. After studying all the submissions of the complainants and the respondent state, the African Commission concluded that the Endorois culture, religion, and traditional way of life are intimately intertwined with their ancestral lands, that Lake Bogoria and the Monchongoi Forest are central to the Endorois' way of life, and without access to their ancestral land, the Endorois are unable to fully exercise their cultural and religious rights, and feel disconnected from their land and ancestors.

On the merits of the complaint, the government maintained that the action of the government to gazette the Game Reserve was for purposes of conserving the environment and wildlife, including the cultural grounds of the Endorois. The government did not deny that the Endorois' had been removed from their ancestral land in this context. The African Commission agreed that in some situations it may be necessary to place some form of limited restrictions on a right protected by the African Charter, but the raison d'être for a particularly harsh limitation on the right to practice religion, such as that experienced by the Endorois, must be based on exceptionally good reasons, and it is for the respondent state to prove that such interference is not only proportionate to the specific need on which it is predicated, but is also reasonable. The African Commission was "not convinced that removing the Endorois from their ancestral land was a lawful action in pursuit of economic development or ecological protection. The African Commission [wa]s of the view that allowing the Endorois to use the land to practice their religion would not detract from the goal of conservation or developing the area for economic reasons." Id., para. 173.

The government also claimed an objective of ensuring that wildlife is managed and conserved, to yield to the nation in general and to individual areas in particular, optimum returns in terms of cultural, aesthetic, and scientific gains, as well as economic gains as are incidental to proper wildlife management and conservation. It argued that National Reserves are subject to agreements as to restrictions or conditions relating to the provisions of the area covered by the reserve. In this case, communities living around the National Reserves had in some instances been allowed to drive their cattle to the Reserve for the purposes of grazing, provided they did not cause harm to the environment and the natural habitats of the wild animals. Thus, the community's right of access was not extinguished.

According to the government, the "Forests (Tugen-Kamasia) Rules" enabled the inhabitants of the Baringo District, including the Endorois, to enjoy some privileges of access for some purposes. The Rules "allowed the community to collect dead wood for firewood, pick wild berries and fruits, take or collect the bark of dead trees for thatching beehives, cut and

---

[62] Report of the African Commission's Working Group of Experts on Indigenous Populations/Communities (adopted at the Twenty-eighth Session, 2003).

remove creepers and lianes for building purposes, take stock, including goats, to watering places as may be approved by the District Commissioner in consultation with the Forest Officer, enter the Forest for the purpose of holding customary ceremonies and rites, but no damage shall be done to any tree, graze sheep within the Forest, graze cattle for specified periods during the dry season with the written permission of the District Commissioner or the Forest Officer and to retain or construct huts within the Forest by approved forest cultivators among others." Id., para. 180. The government also said that the complainants were at liberty to practice their religion and culture. Further, it stated that the due process of law regarding compensation was followed at the time of the said gazettement.

On the right to property, the African Commission decided that the first step in the protection of traditional African communities is the acknowledgment that the rights, interests and benefits of such communities in their traditional lands constitute "property" under the Charter and that special measures may have to be taken to secure such "property rights." Thus, although the Endorois did not have registered property, they either had their own houses constructed on the land of their ascendants or lived in the houses owned by their fathers and cultivate the land belonging to the latter. The Court further noted that the applicants had unchallenged rights over the common land in the village, such as the pasture, grazing, and the forest land, and that they earned their living from stockbreeding and tree-felling. The African Commission concluded that the Endorois property rights were encroached upon, in particular by the expropriation and the effective denial of ownership of their land. "It agrees with the complainants that the Endorois were never given the full title to the land they had in practice before the British colonial administration. Their land was instead made subject to a trust, which gave them beneficial title, but denied them actual title. The African Commission further agreed that though for a decade they were able to exercise their traditional rights without restriction, the trust land system had proved inadequate to protect their rights." Id. para. 199. The African Commission's conclusions on the rights of indigenous peoples in the context of environmental protection are reprinted in the following extract.

Centre for Minority Rights Development (Kenya) and Minority Rights Group International on behalf of Endorois Welfare Council v Kenya. **Afr. Comm'n HPR, Case 276/2003 (Feb. 4, 2010)**

209. In the view of the African Commission, the following conclusions could be drawn: (1) traditional possession of land by indigenous people has the equivalent effect as that of a state-granted full property title; (2) traditional possession entitles indigenous people to demand official recognition and registration of property title; (3) the members of indigenous peoples who have unwillingly left their traditional lands, or lost possession thereof, maintain property rights thereto, even though they lack legal title, unless the lands have been lawfully transferred to third parties in good faith; and (4) the members of indigenous peoples who have unwillingly lost possession of their lands, when those lands have been lawfully transferred to innocent third parties, are entitled to restitution thereof or to obtain other lands of equal extension and quality. Consequently, possession is not a requisite condition for the existence of indigenous land restitution rights. The instant case of the Endorois is categorised under this last conclusion. The African Commission thus agrees that the land of the Endorois has been encroached upon.

210. That such encroachment has taken place could be seen by the Endorois' inability, after being evicted from their ancestral land, to have free access to religious sites and their traditional land to graze their cattle. The African Commission is aware that access roads, gates, game lodges and a hotel have all been built on the ancestral land of the Endorois community around Lake Bogoria and imminent mining operations also threatens to cause irreparable damage to the land.

The African Commission has also been notified that the Respondent State is engaged in the demarcation and sale of parts of Endorois historic lands to third parties.

211. The African Commission is aware that encroachment in itself is not a violation of Article 14 of the Charter, as long as it is done in accordance with the law. Article 14 of the African Charter indicates a two-pronged test, where that encroachment can only be conducted – 'in the interest of public need or in the general interest of the community' and 'in accordance with appropriate laws'. The African Commission will now assess whether an encroachment 'in the interest of public need' is indeed proportionate to the point of overriding the rights of indigenous peoples to their ancestral lands. The African Commission agrees with the Complainants that the test laid out in Article 14 of the Charter is *conjunctive*, that is, in order for an encroachment not to be in violation of Article 14, it must be proven that the encroachment was in the interest of the public need/general interest of the community *and* was carried out in accordance with appropriate laws.

212. The 'public interest' test is met with a much higher threshold in the case of encroachment of indigenous land rather than individual private property. In this sense, the test is much more stringent when applied to ancestral land rights of indigenous peoples. In 2005, this point was stressed by the Special Rapporteur of the United Nations Sub-Commission for the Promotion and Protection of Human Rights who published the following statement:

> Limitations, if any, on the right to indigenous peoples to their natural resources must flow only from the most urgent and compelling interest of the state. Few, if any, limitations on indigenous resource rights are appropriate, because the indigenous ownership of the resources is associated with the most important and fundamental human rights, including the right to life, food, the right to self-determination, to shelter, and the right to exist as a people.[63]

213. Limitations on rights, such as the limitation allowed in Article 14, must be reviewed under the principle of proportionality. The Commission notes its own conclusions that " . . . the justification of limitations must be strictly proportionate with and absolutely necessary for the advantages which follow.[64]

214. The African Commission is of the view that any limitations on rights must be proportionate to a legitimate need, and should be the least restrictive measures possible. In the present Communication, the African Commission holds the view that in the pursuit of creating a Game Reserve, the Respondent State has unlawfully evicted the Endorois from their ancestral land and destroyed their possessions. It is of the view that the upheaval and displacement of the Endorois from the land they call home and the denial of their property rights over their ancestral land is disproportionate to any public need served by the Game Reserve.

215. It is also of the view that even if the Game Reserve was a legitimate aim and served a public need, it could have been accomplished by alternative means proportionate to the need. From the evidence submitted both orally and in writing, it is clear that the community was willing to work with the Government in a way that respected their property rights, even if a Game Reserve was being created. The African Commission agrees that the Respondent State has not only denied the Endorois community all legal rights in their ancestral land, rendering their property rights essentially illusory, but in the name of creating a Game Reserve and the subsequent eviction of the Endorois community from their own land, the Respondent State has violated the very essence

---

[63] Erica-Irene Daes, "Indigenous Peoples' Right to Land and Natural Resources" in Minorities, Peoples, and Self-Determination (Nazila Ghanea and Alexandra Xanthaki eds., 2005). Martinrs Nijhoff Publishers.
[64] *Constitutional Rights Project, Civil Liberties Organisation and Media Rights Agenda v. Nigeria*, African Commission on Human and Peoples' Rights, Comm Nos. 140/94, 141/94, 145/95 (1999), para. 42 (hereinafter *The Constitutional Rights Project Case 1999*).

of the right itself, and cannot justify such an interference with reference to "the general interest of the community" or a "public need."

. . .

218. The African Commission also notes that the 'disproportionate' nature of an encroachment on indigenous lands – therefore falling short of the test set out by the provisions of Article 14 of the African Charter – is to be considered an even greater violation of Article 14, when the displacement at hand was undertaken by force. Forced evictions, by their very definition, cannot be deemed to satisfy Article 14 of the Charter's test of being done 'in accordance with the law'. This provision must mean, at the minimum, that both Kenyan law and the relevant provisions of international law were respected. Where such removal was forced, this would in itself suggest that the 'proportionality' test has not been satisfied.

. . .

225. Two further elements of the 'in accordance with the law' test relate to the requirements of consultation and compensation.

226. In terms of consultation, the threshold is especially stringent in favour of indigenous peoples, as it also requires that *consent* be accorded. Failure to observe the obligations to consult and to seek consent – or to compensate - ultimately results in a violation of the right to property.

. . .

228. In the instant case, the African Commission is of the view that no effective participation was allowed for the Endorois, nor has there been any reasonable benefit enjoyed by the community. Moreover, a *prior* environment and social impact assessment was not carried out. The absence of these three elements of the 'test' is tantamount to a violation of Article 14, the right to property, under the Charter. The failure to guarantee effective participation and to guarantee a reasonable share in the profits of the Game Reserve (or other adequate forms of compensation) also extends to a violation of the right to development.

. . .

231. The African Commission is of the view that the Respondent State did not pay the prompt, full compensation as required by the Constitution. It is of the view that Kenyan law has not been complied with and that though some members of the Endorois community accepted limited monetary compensation that did not mean that they accepted it as full compensation, or indeed that they accepted the loss of their land.

232. The African Commission notes the observations of the United Nations Declaration on the Rights of Indigenous Peoples, which, amongst other provisions for restitutions and compensations, states:

> Indigenous peoples have the right to restitution of the lands, territories and resources which they have traditionally owned or otherwise occupied or used; and which have been confiscated, occupied, used or damaged without their free and informed consent. Where this is not possible, they have the right to just and fair compensation. Unless otherwise freely agreed upon by the peoples concerned, compensation shall take the form of lands, territories and resources equal in quality, size and legal status.[65]

233. In the case of *Yakye Axa v Paraguay* the [Inter-America] Court established that any violation of an international obligation that has caused damage entails the duty to provide appropriate reparations. . . .

---

[65] Declaration on the Rights of Indigenous Peoples, preambular para. 5, E/CN.4/Sub.2/1994/2/Add.1 (1994).

234. The Court said that once it has been proved that land restitution rights are still current, the State must take the necessary actions to return them to the members of the indigenous people claiming them. However, as the Court has pointed out, when a State is unable, on objective and reasonable grounds, to adopt measures aimed at returning traditional lands and communal resources to indigenous populations, it must surrender alternative lands of equal extension and quality, which will be chosen by agreement with the members of the indigenous peoples, according to their own consultation and decision procedures.[66] This was not the case in respect of the Endorois. The land given them is not of equal quality.

235. The reasons of the Government in the instant Communication are questionable for several reasons including: (a) the contested land is the site of a conservation area, and the Endorois – as the ancestral guardians of that land - are best equipped to maintain its delicate ecosystems; (b) the Endorois are prepared to continue the conservation work begun by the Government; (c) no other community have settled on the land in question, and even if that is the case, the Respondent State is obliged to rectify that situation,[67] (d) the land has not been spoliated and is thus inhabitable; (e) continued dispossession and alienation from their ancestral land continues to threaten the cultural survival of the Endorois' way of life, a consequence which clearly tips the proportionality argument on the side of indigenous peoples under international law.

. . .

248. The African Commission is of the opinion that the Respondent State has a higher duty in terms of taking positive steps to protect groups and communities like the Endorois,[68] but also to promote cultural rights including the creation of opportunities, policies, institutions, or other mechanisms that allow for different cultures and ways of life to exist, develop in view of the challenges facing indigenous communities. These challenges include exclusion, exploitation, discrimination and extreme poverty; displacement from their traditional territories and deprivation of their means of subsistence; lack of participation in decisions affecting the lives of the communities; forced assimilation and negative social statistics among other issues and, at times, indigenous communities suffer from direct violence and persecution, while some even face the danger of extinction.[69]

249. In its analysis of Article 17 of the African Charter, the African Commission is aware that unlike Articles 8 and 14, Article 17 has no claw-back clause. The absence of a claw-back clause is an indication that the drafters of the Charter envisaged few, if any, circumstances in which it would be appropriate to limit a people's right to culture. It further notes that even if the Respondent State were to put some limitation on the exercise of such a right, the restriction must be proportionate to a legitimate aim that does not interfere adversely on the exercise of a community's cultural rights. Thus, even if the creation of the Game Reserve constitutes a legitimate aim, the Respondent

---

[66] See case of the Indigenous Community Yakye *Axa*, para. 149.

[67] Indeed, at para 140 of the *Sawhoyamaxa Indigenous Community v. Paraguay* case, the Inter-American Court stresses that: "Lastly, with regard to the third argument put forth by the State, the Court has not been furnished with the aforementioned treaty between Germany and Paraguay, but, according to the State, said convention allows for capital investments made by a contracting party to be condemned or nationalized for a "public purpose or interest", which could justify land restitution to indigenous people. Moreover, the Court considers that the enforcement of bilateral commercial treaties negates vindication of non-compliance with state obligations under the American Convention; on the contrary, their enforcement should always be compatible with the American Convention, which is a multilateral treaty on human rights that stands in a class of its own and that generates rights for individual human beings and does not depend entirely on reciprocity among States.

[68] See UN Declaration on the Rights of Persons Belonging to National or Ethnic, Religious and Linguistic Minorities, Article 4(2): States shall take measures to create favourable conditions to enable persons belonging to minorities to express their characteristics and to develop their culture, language, religion, traditions and customs; CERD General Recommendation XXIII, Article 4(e): Ensure that indigenous communities can exercise their rights to practise and revitalize their cultural traditions and customs and to preserve and to practise their languages; International Covenant on Economic, Social and Cultural Rights, Article 15(3).

[69] See statement by Mr. Sha Zukang Under-Secretary General for Economic and Social Affairs and Coordinator of the Second International Decade of the World's Indigenous People to the Third Committee of the General Assembly on the Item "Indigenous Issues" New York, 20 October 2008.

State's failure to secure access, as of right, for the celebration of the cultural festival and rituals cannot be deemed proportionate to that aim. The Commission is of the view that the cultural activities of the Endorois community pose no harm to the ecosystem of the Game Reserve and the restriction of cultural rights could not be justified, especially as no suitable alternative was given to the community.

. . .

252. The Complainants allege that in violation of art. 21, the Endorois community has been unable to access the vital resources in the Lake Bogoria region since their eviction from the Game Reserve.

253. The Respondent State denies the allegation. It argues that it is of the view that the Complainants have immensely benefited from the tourism and mineral prospecting activities. . . .

254. The Respondent State also argue that the community has been holding consultations with Corby Ltd., as evidence by the agreement between them is a clear manifestation of the extent to which the former participants in the decisions touch on the exploitation of the natural resources and the sharing of the benefits emanating therefrom.

256. The African Commission notes that proceeds from the Game Reserve have been used to finance a lot of useful projects, 'a fact' that the Complainants do not contest. The African Commission, however, refers to cases in the Inter-American Human Rights system to understand this area of the law. The American Convention does not have an equivalent of the African Charter's Article 21 on the Right to Natural Resources. It therefore reads the right to natural resources into the right to property (Article 21 of the American Convention), and in turn applies similar limitation rights on the issue of natural resources as it does on limitations of the right to property. The "test" in both cases makes for a much higher threshold when potential spoliation or development of the land is affecting indigenous land.

. . .

267 In the instant case of the Endorois, the Respondent State has a duty to evaluate whether a restriction of these private property rights is necessary to preserve the survival of the Endorois community. The African Commission is aware that the Endorois do not have an attachment to ruby. Nevertheless, it is instructive to note that the African Commission decided in *The Ogoni case* that the right to natural resources contained within their traditional lands vested in the indigenous people. This decision made clear that a people inhabiting a specific region within a state can claim the protection of Article 21.[70] Article 14 of the African Charter indicates that the two-pronged test of 'in the interest of public need or in the general interest of the community' and 'in accordance with appropriate laws' should be satisfied.

275. Responding to the allegation that the Game Reserve made it particularly difficult for the Endorois to access basic herbal medicine necessary for maintaining a healthy life, the Respondent State argues that the prime purpose of gazetting the National Reserve is conservation. Also responding to the claim that the Respondent State has granted several mining and logging concessions to third parties, and from which the Endorois have not benefited, the Respondent State asserts that the community has been well informed of those prospecting for minerals in the area. It further states that the community's mining committee had entered into an agreement with the Kenyan company prospecting for minerals, implying that the Endorois are fully involved in all community decisions.

276. The Respondent State also argues that the community is represented in the Country Council by its elected councillors, therefore presenting the community the opportunity to always be

---

[70] The Ogoni Case (2001), paras 56–58.

represented in the forum where decisions are made pertaining to development. The Respondent State argues that all the decisions complained about have had to be decided upon by a full council meeting.

281. The African Commission notes that its own standards state that a Government must consult with respect to indigenous peoples especially when dealing with sensitive issues as land.[71] The African Commission agrees with the Complainants that the consultations that the Respondent State did undertake with the community were inadequate and cannot be considered effective participation. The conditions of the consultation failed to fulfil the African Commission's standard of consultations in a form appropriate to the circumstances. It is convinced that community members were informed of the impending project as a *fait accompli*, and not given an opportunity to shape the policies or their role in the Game Reserve.

290. In the instant Communication, even though the Respondent State says that it has consulted with the Endorois community, the African Commission is of the view that this consultation was not sufficient. It is convinced that the Respondent State did not obtain the prior, informed consent of all the Endorois before designating their land as a Game Reserve and commencing their eviction. The Respondent State did not impress upon the Endorois any understanding that they would be denied all rights of return to their land, including unfettered access to grazing land and the medicinal salt licks for their cattle. The African Commission agrees that the Complainants had a legitimate expectation that even after their initial eviction, they would be allowed access to their land for religious ceremonies and medicinal purposes – the reason, in fact why they are in front of the African Commission.

291. Additionally, the African Commission is of the view that any development or investment projects that would have a major impact within the Endorois territory, the State has a duty not only to consult with the community, but also to obtain their free, prior, and informed consent, according to their customs and traditions.

. . .

294. In relation to benefit sharing, the IACtHR in the Saramaka case said that benefit sharing is vital both in relation to the right to development and by extension the right to own property. The right to development will be violated when the development in question decreases the well-being of the community. The African Commission similarly notes that the concept of benefit-sharing also serves as an important indicator of compliance for property rights; failure to duly compensate (even if the other criteria of legitimate aim and proportionality are satisfied) result in a violation of the right to property.

297. The African Commission is convinced that the inadequacy of the consultations left the Endorois feeling disenfranchised from a process of utmost importance to their life as a people. Resentment of the unfairness with which they had been treated inspired some members of the community to try to reclaim the Mochongoi Forest in 1974 and 1984, meet with the President to discuss the matter in 1994 and 1995, and protest the actions in peaceful demonstrations. The African Commission agrees that if consultations had been conducted in a manner that effectively involved the Endorois, there would have been no ensuing confusion as to their rights or resentment that their consent had been wrongfully gained. It is also convinced that they have faced substantive losses - the actual loss in well-being and the denial of benefits accruing from the Game Reserve. Furthermore, the Endorois have faced a significant loss in choice since their eviction from the

---

[71] Report of the African Commission's Working Group of Experts on Indigenous Populations/Communities (Twenty-eighth session, 2003). See also ILO Convention 169 which states: "Consultations carried out in application of this Convention shall be undertaken, in good faith and in a form appropriate to the circumstances, with the objective of achieving agreement or consent to the proposed measures."

land. It agrees that the Endorois, as beneficiaries of the development process, were entitled to an equitable distribution of the benefits derived from the Game Reserve.

298. The African Commission is of the view that the Respondent State bears the burden for creating conditions favourable to a people's development.[72] It is certainly not the responsibility of the Endorois themselves to find alternate places to graze their cattle or partake in religious ceremonies. The Respondent State, instead, is obligated to ensure that the Endorois are not left out of the development process or benefits. The African Commission agrees that the failure to provide adequate compensation and benefits, or provide suitable land for grazing indicates that the Respondent State did not adequately provide for the Endorois in the development process. It finds against the Respondent State that the Endorois community has suffered a violation of Article 22 of the Charter.

Recommendations

1. In view of the above, the African Commission finds that the Respondent State is in violation of Articles 1, 8, 14, 17, 21 and 22 of the African Charter. The African Commission recommends that the Respondent State:(a) Recognise rights of ownership to the Endorois and restitute Endorois ancestral land. (b) Ensure that the Endorois community has unrestricted access to Lake Bogoria and surrounding sites for religious and cultural rites and for grazing their cattle.(c) Pay adequate compensation to the community for all the loss suffered; (d) Pay royalties to the Endorois from existing economic activities and ensure that they benefit from employment possibilities within the Reserve. (e) Grant registration to the Endorois Welfare Committee. (f) Engage in dialogue with the Complainants for the effective implementation of these recommendations. (g) Report on the implementation of these recommendations within three months from the date of notification. 2. The African Commission avails its good offices to assist the parties in the implementation of these recommendations.

VII. National Laws and Jurisprudence

Various national laws also protect indigenous land and resource rights. Some of the approaches taken, like those in international law, emphasize procedural rights; others incorporate international human rights standards and recognize communal land rights for indigenous groups. A few examples follow.

A. Australia

Mabo et al. v. Queensland (No. 2), High Court of Australia, (1992) 175 CLR 1, 14–77, 99–119, 217; (1992) 107 ALR 1; (1992) 66 ARLJ 408 (footnotes omitted and citations added)

BRENNAN J.

. . .

The Murray Islands lie in the Torres Strait, at about 10 degrees S. Latitude and 144 degrees E. Longitude. They are the easternmost of the Eastern Islands of the Strait. Their total land area is of the order of 9 square kilometres. The biggest is Mer (known also as Murray Island), oval in shape about 2.79 kms long and about 1.65 kms across. A channel about 900 m. wide separates Mer from the other two islands, Dauar and Waier, which lie closely adjacent to each other to the south of Mer. The Islands are surrounded for the most part by fringing reefs. The people

---

[72] Declaration on the Right to Development, Article 3.

who were in occupation of these Islands before first European contact and who have continued to occupy those Islands to the present day are known as the Meriam people. Although outsiders, relatively few in number, have lived on the Murray Islands from time to time and worked as missionaries, government officials, or fishermen, there has not been a permanent immigrant population. Anthropological records and research show that the present inhabitants of the Islands are descended from the people described in early European reports. The component of foreign ancestry among the present population is small compared with most communities living in the Torres Strait. The Meriam people of today retain a strong sense of affiliation with their forbears and with the society and culture of earlier times. They have a strong sense of identity with their Islands. The plaintiffs are members of the Meriam people. In this case, the legal rights of the members of the Meriam people to the land of the Murray Islands are in question.

. . .

On analysis, the defendant's argument is that, when the territory of a settled colony became part of the Crown's dominions, the law of England so far as applicable to colonial conditions became the law of the colony and, by that law, the Crown acquired the absolute beneficial ownership of all land in the territory so that the colony became the Crown's demesne and no right or interest in any land in the territory could thereafter be possessed by any other person unless granted by the Crown. Perhaps the clearest statement of these propositions is to be found in *Attorney-General v. Brown* (1847) 1 Legge 312, at p. 316, when the Supreme Court of New South Wales rejected a challenge to the Crown's title to and possession of the land in the Colony....

The proposition that, when the Crown assumed sovereignty over an Australian colony, it became the universal and absolute beneficial owner of all the land therein, invites critical examination. If the conclusion at which Stephen C.J. arrived in *Attorney-General v. Brown* be right, the interests of indigenous inhabitants in colonial land were extinguished so soon as British subjects settled in a colony, though the indigenous inhabitants had neither ceded their lands to the Crown nor suffered them to be taken as the spoils of conquest.... Judged by any civilized standard, such a law is unjust and its claim to be part of the common law to be applied in contemporary Australia must be questioned. This Court must now determine whether, by the common law of this country, the rights and interests of the Meriam people of today are to be determined on the footing that their ancestors lost their traditional rights and interests in the land of the Murray Islands on 1 August 1879.

. . .

The Acquisition of Sovereignty

> The acquisition of territory by a sovereign state for the first time is an act of state which cannot be challenged, controlled or interfered with by the courts of that state.

This principle, stated by Gibbs J. in the Seas and Submerged Lands Case, *New South Wales v. The Commonwealth* (1975) 135 CLR, at p. 388, precludes any contest between the executive and the judicial branches of government as to whether a territory is or is not within the Crown's Dominions. The Murray Islands were annexed by an exercise of the prerogative evidenced by the Letters Patent; a mode of acquisition recognized by the common law as a valid means of acquiring sovereignty over foreign territory. The recognition is accorded simply on the footing that such a prerogative act is an act of State the validity of which is not justiciable in the municipal courts....

Although the question whether a territory has been acquired by the Crown is not justiciable before municipal courts, those courts have jurisdiction to determine the consequences of an acquisition under municipal law. Accordingly, the municipal courts must determine the body of law which is in force in the new territory. By the common law, the law in force in a newly-acquired territory depends on the manner of its acquisition by the Crown. Although the manner in which a sovereign state might acquire new territory is a matter for international law, the common law has had to march in step with international law in order to provide the body of law to apply in a territory newly acquired by the Crown.

International law recognized conquest, cession, and occupation of territory that was *terra nullius* as three of the effective ways of acquiring sovereignty. No other way is presently relevant. See E. Evatt, "The Acquisition of Territory in Australia and New Zealand" in (1968) *Grotian Society Papers*, p. 16, who mentions only cession and occupation as relevant to the Australasian colonies. The great voyages of European discovery opened to European nations the prospect of occupying new and valuable territories that were already inhabited. As among themselves, the European nations parcelled out the territories newly discovered to the sovereigns of the respective discoverers, provided the discovery was confirmed by occupation and provided the indigenous inhabitants were not organized in a society that was united permanently for political action. *Worcester v. Georgia* (1832) 6 Pet 515, at pp. 543–544 (31 U.S. 350, at p. 369); Lindley, *The Acquisition and Government of Backward Territory in International Law*, (1926), Chs. III and IV. To these territories the European colonial nations applied the doctrines relating to acquisition of territory that was *terra nullius*. They recognized the sovereignty of the respective European nations over the territory of "backward peoples" and, by State practice, permitted the acquisition of sovereignty of such territory by occupation rather than by conquest. See Lindley, ibid., p. 47. Various justifications for the acquisition of sovereignty over the territory of "backward peoples" were advanced. The benefits of Christianity and European civilization had been seen as a sufficient justification from mediaeval times. See Williams, *The American Indian in Western Legal Thought*, (1990), pp. 78ff; and *Johnson v. McIntosh* (1823) 8 Wheat 543, at p. 573 (21 U.S. 240, at p. 253). Another justification for the application of the theory of *terra nullius* to inhabited territory – a justification first advanced by Vattel at the end of the 18th century – was that new territories could be claimed by occupation if the land were uncultivated, for Europeans had a right to bring lands into production if they were left uncultivated by the indigenous inhabitants. Vattel, *The Law of Nations* (1797), bk. I, pp. 100–101. See Castles, *An Australian Legal History* (1982), pp. 16–17. It may be doubted whether, even if these justifications were accepted, the facts would have sufficed to permit acquisition of the Murray Islands as though the Islands were *terra nullius*. The Meriam people were, as Moynihan J. found, devoted gardeners. In 1879, having accepted the influence of the London Missionary Society, they were living peacefully in a land-based society under some sort of governance by the Mamoose and the London Missionary Society. However that may be, it is not for this Court to canvass the validity of the Crown's acquisition of sovereignty over the Islands which, in any event, was consolidated by uninterrupted control of the Islands by Queensland authorities. 10 *Encyclopaedia of Public International Law* (1987), p. 500; cf. J. Crawford, "The Criteria for Statehood in International Law," (1977) 48 *The British Year Book of International Law* 93, at p. 116.

The enlarging of the concept of *terra nullius* by international law to justify the acquisition of inhabited territory by occupation on behalf of the acquiring sovereign raised some difficulties in the expounding of the common law doctrines as to the law to be applied when inhabited territories were acquired by occupation (or "settlement," to use the term of the common law). Although Blackstone commended the practice of "sending colonies (of settlers) to find out new habitations," he wrote

> so long as it was confined to the stocking and cultivation of desert uninhabited countries, it kept strictly within the limits of the law of nature. But how far the seising on countries already peopled, and driving out or massacring the innocent and defenceless natives, merely because they differed from their invaders in language, in religion, in customs, in government, or in colour; how far such a conduct was consonant to nature, to reason, or to Christianity, deserved well to be considered by those, who have rendered their names immortal by thus civilizing mankind.

Commentaries on the Laws of England, 17th ed. (1830), bk. II, ch. 1, p. 7.

As we shall see, Blackstone's misgivings found a resonance in international law after two centuries. *Advisory Opinion on Western Sahara* (1975) 1 ICJR 12. But he was unable to declare any rule by which the laws of England became the laws of a territory which was not a "desert uninhabited" country when the Crown acquired sovereignty over that territory by discovery and occupation as terra nullius. As the British acquisition of sovereignty over the Colony of New South Wales was regarded as dependent upon the settlement of territory that was terra nullius consequent on discovery, . . . and as the law of New South Wales is the source of the law applicable to the Murray Islands, we must next examine the basis on which the common law was received as the law of the Colony of New South Wales.

. . .

The Basis of the Theory of Universal and Absolute Crown Ownership

It is one thing for our contemporary law to accept that the laws of England, so far as applicable, became the laws of New South Wales and of the other Australian colonies. It is another thing for our contemporary law to accept that, when the common law of England became the common law of the several colonies, the theory which was advanced to support the introduction of the common law of England accords with our present knowledge and appreciation of the facts. . . .

The facts as we know them today do not fit the "absence of law" or "barbarian" theory underpinning the colonial reception of the common law of England. That being so, there is no warrant for applying in these times rules of the English common law which were the product of that theory. It would be a curious doctrine to propound today that, when the benefit of the common law was first extended to Her Majesty's indigenous subjects in the Antipodes, its first fruits were to strip them of their right to occupy their ancestral lands. . . .

As the indigenous inhabitants of a settled colony were regarded as "low in the scale of social organization," they and their occupancy of colonial land were ignored in considering the title to land in a settled colony. . . . The theory that the indigenous inhabitants of a "settled" colony had no proprietary interest in the land thus depended on a discriminatory denigration of indigenous inhabitants, their social organization and customs. As the basis of the theory is false in fact and unacceptable in our society, there is a choice of legal principle to be made in the present case. This Court can either apply the existing authorities and proceed to inquire whether the Meriam people are higher "in the scale of social organization" than the Australian Aborigines whose claims were "utterly disregarded" by the existing authorities or the Court can overrule the existing authorities, discarding the distinction between inhabited colonies that were terra nullius and those which were not.

The theory of *terra nullius* has been critically examined in recent times by the International Court of Justice in its Advisory Opinion on Western Sahara (1975) ICJR, at p. 39. . . .

. . .

If the international law notion that inhabited land may be classified as terra nullius no longer commands general support, the doctrines of the common law which depend on the notion that native peoples may be "so low in the scale of social organization" that it is "idle to impute to such people some shadow of the rights known to our law" can hardly be retained. If it were permissible in past centuries to keep the common law in step with international law, it is imperative in today's world that the common law should neither be nor be seen to be frozen in an age of racial discrimination.

The fiction by which the rights and interests of indigenous inhabitants in land were treated as non-existent was justified by a policy which has no place in the contemporary law of this country. . . . Whatever the justification advanced in earlier days for refusing to recognize the rights and interests in land of the indigenous inhabitants of settled colonies, an unjust and discriminatory doctrine of that kind can no longer be accepted. The expectations of the international community accord in this respect with the contemporary values of the Australian people. The opening up of international remedies to individuals pursuant to Australia's accession to the Optional Protocol to the International Covenant on Civil and Political Rights brings to bear on the common law the powerful influence of the Covenant and the international standards it imports. The common law does not necessarily conform with international law, but international law is a legitimate and important influence on the development of the common law, especially when international law declares the existence of universal human rights. A common law doctrine founded on unjust discrimination in the enjoyment of civil and political rights demands reconsideration. It is contrary both to international standards and to the fundamental values of our common law to entrench a discriminatory rule which, because of the supposed position on the scale of social organization of the indigenous inhabitants of a settled colony, denies them a right to occupy their traditional lands. . . .

. . .

The acquisition of territory is chiefly the province of international law; the acquisition of property is chiefly the province of the common law. The distinction between the Crown's title to territory and the Crown's ownership of land within a territory is made as well by the common law as by international law. . . . The general rule of the common law was that ownership could not be acquired by occupying land that was already occupied by another.

It was only by fastening on the notion that a settled colony was terra nullius that it was possible to predicate of the Crown the acquisition of ownership of land in a colony already occupied by indigenous inhabitants. It was only on the hypothesis that there was nobody in occupation that it could be said that the Crown was the owner because there was no other. If that hypothesis be rejected, the notion that sovereignty carried ownership in its wake must be rejected too. Though the rejection of the notion of terra nullius clears away the fictional impediment to the recognition of indigenous rights and interests in colonial land, it would be impossible for the common law to recognize such rights and interests if the basic doctrines of the common law are inconsistent with their recognition.

A basic doctrine of the land law is the doctrine of tenure, to which Stephen C.J. referred in *Attorney-General v. Brown*, and it is a doctrine which could not be overturned without fracturing the skeleton which gives our land law its shape and consistency. It is derived from feudal origins.

The Feudal Basis of the Proposition of Absolute Crown Ownership

. . .

Accepting the doctrine of tenure, it was an essential postulate that the Crown have such a title to land as would invest the Sovereign with the character of Paramount Lord in respect of a tenure created by grant and would attract the incidents appropriate to the tenure, especially the Crown's right to escheat. The Crown was invested with the character of Paramount Lord in the colonies by attributing to the Crown a title, adapted from feudal theory, that was called a radical, ultimate or final title. The Crown was treated as having the radical title to all the land in the territory over which the Crown acquired sovereignty. The radical title is a postulate of the doctrine of tenure and a concomitant of sovereignty. As a sovereign enjoys supreme legal authority in and over a territory, the sovereign has power to prescribe what parcels of land and what interests in those parcels should be enjoyed by others and what parcels of land should be kept as the sovereign's beneficial demesne.

. . .

Recognition of the radical title of the Crown is quite consistent with recognition of native title to land, for the radical title, without more, is merely a logical postulate required to support the doctrine of tenure (when the Crown has exercised its sovereign power to grant an interest in land) and to support the plenary title of the Crown (when the Crown has exercised its sovereign power to appropriate to itself ownership of parcels of land within the Crown's territory). Unless the sovereign power is exercised in one or other of those ways, there is no reason why land within the Crown's territory should not continue to be subject to native title. It is only the fallacy of equating sovereignty and beneficial ownership of land that gives rise to the notion that native title is extinguished by the acquisition of sovereignty.

. . .

Once it is accepted that indigenous inhabitants in occupation of a territory when sovereignty is acquired by the Crown are capable of enjoying – whether in community, as a group or as individuals – proprietary interests in land, the rights and interests in the land which they had theretofore enjoyed under the customs of their community are seen to be a burden on the radical title which the Crown acquires. The notion that feudal principle dictates that the land in a settled colony be taken to be a royal demesne upon the Crown's acquisition of sovereignty is mistaken. . . .

. . .

The Need for Recognition by the Crown of Native Title

The defendant contests the view that the common law recognizes the possession of rights and interests in land by indigenous inhabitants of British colonies and submits that, by the common law governing colonization, pre-existing customary rights and interests in land are abolished upon colonization of inhabited territory, unless expressly recognized by the new sovereign. There is a formidable body of authority, mostly cases relating to Indian colonies created by cession, to support this submission. *Secretary of State for India v. Bai Rajbai* (1915) LR 42 Ind App 229, at pp. 237, 238–239; *Vajesingji Joravarsingji v. Secretary of State for India* (1924) LR 51 Ind App 357, at pp. 360, 361; *Secretary of State for India v. Sardar Rustam Khan* (1941) AC 356, at pp. 370–372. . . .

The proposition that pre-existing rights and interests in land must be established, if at all, under the new legal system introduced on an acquisition of sovereignty is axiomatic, and the proposition that treaties do not create rights enforceable in municipal courts is well established. . . . However, the relevant question is whether the rights and interests in land derived from the old regime survive the acquisition of sovereignty or do they achieve recognition only upon an express act of recognition by the new sovereign? Lord Dunedin's view in *Vajesingji Joravarsingji*, (1924) LR 51 Ind App, at p. 361 was that recognition by the sovereign of rights and interests possessed under the old regime was a condition of their recognition by the common law. . . . Lord Dunedin's view does not accord with the rule stated by Viscount Haldane in *Amodu Tijani* (1921) 2 AC, at p. 407:

> A mere change in sovereignty is not to be presumed as meant to disturb rights of private owners; and the general terms of a cession are prima facie to be construed accordingly.

His Lordship does not limit the generality of the first sentence to acquisitions by cession; rather, he appears to be construing the terms of a cession in the light of the general principle by which private proprietary rights survive a change in sovereignty by whatever means. Despite his judgment in *Vajesingji Joravarsingji*, Viscount Dunedin subsequently accepted [in Sakariyawo Oshodi v. Moriamo Dakolo (1930) AC 667, at p. 668] that the decision in *Amodu Tijani* laid down that the cession of Lagos in 1861 "did not affect the character of the private native rights." . . . We are not concerned here with compensation for expropriation but we are concerned with the survival of private rights and interests in land and their liability to be extinguished by action of the Crown. The rule in *Amodu Tijani* was followed by the Privy Council in *Sobhuza II. v. Miller* (1926) AC, at p. 525 where the title of an indigenous community, which their Lordships thought to be generally usufructuary in character, was held to survive as "a mere qualification of a burden on the radical or final title of whoever is sovereign," capable of being extinguished "by the action of a paramount power which assumes possession or the entire control of land."

. . .

The preferable rule, supported by the authorities cited, is that a mere change in sovereignty does not extinguish native title to land. (The term "native title" conveniently describes the interests and rights of indigenous inhabitants in land, whether communal, group or individual, possessed under the traditional laws acknowledged by and the traditional customs observed by the indigenous inhabitants.) The preferable rule equates the indigenous inhabitants of a settled colony with the inhabitants of a conquered colony in respect of their rights and interests in land and recognizes in the indigenous inhabitants of a settled colony the rights and interests recognized by the Privy Council in *In re Southern Rhodesia* as surviving to the benefit of the residents of a conquered colony.

. . .

The Nature and Incidents of Native Title

Native title has its origin in and is given its content by the traditional laws acknowledged by and the traditional customs observed by the indigenous inhabitants of a territory. The nature and incidents of native title must be ascertained as a matter of fact by reference to those laws and customs. The ascertainment may present a problem of considerable difficulty, as Moynihan J. perceived in the present case. It is a problem that did not arise in the case of a settled colony so long as the fictions were maintained that customary rights could not be reconciled "with the institutions or the legal ideas of civilized society" *In re Southern Rhodesia* (1919) AC, at p. 233, that there was no law before the arrival of the British colonists in a settled colony and that there was no sovereign law-maker in the territory of a settled colony before sovereignty was acquired by the Crown. These fictions denied the possibility of a native title recognized by our laws. But once it is acknowledged that an inhabited territory which became a settled colony was no more a legal desert than it was "desert uninhabited" in fact, it is necessary to ascertain by evidence the nature and incidents of native title. Though these are matters of fact, some general propositions about native title can be stated without reference to evidence.

First, unless there are pre-existing laws of a territory over which the Crown acquires sovereignty which provide for the alienation of interests in land to strangers, the rights and interests which constitute a native title can be possessed only by the indigenous inhabitants and their descendants. Native title, though recognized by the common law, is not an institution of the common law and is not alienable by the common law. Its alienability is dependent on the laws from which it is derived. If alienation of a right or interest in land is a mere matter of the custom observed by the indigenous inhabitants, not provided for by law enforced by a sovereign power, there is no machinery which can enforce the rights of the alienee. The common law cannot enforce as a proprietary interest the rights of a putative alienee whose title is not created either under a law which was enforceable against the putative alienor at the time of the alienation and thereafter until the change of sovereignty or under the common law. And, subject to an important qualification, the only title dependent on custom which the common law will recognize is one which is consistent with the common law. Thus, in *The Case of Tanistry*, (1608) Davis (80 ER); 4th ed. Dublin (1762) English translation, at pp. 94–99, the Irish custom of tanistry was held to be void because it was founded in violence and because the vesting of title under the custom was uncertain. The inconsistency that the court perceived between the custom of tanistry known to the Brehon law of Ireland and the common law precluded the recognition of the custom by the common law. At that stage in its development, the common law was too rigid to admit recognition of a native title based on other laws or customs, but that rigidity has been relaxed, at least since the decision of the Privy Council in *Amodu Tijani*. The general principle that the common law will recognize a customary title only if it be consistent with the common law is subject to an exception in favour of traditional native title.

Of course, since European settlement of Australia, many clans or groups of indigenous people have been physically separated from their traditional land and have lost their connexion with it. But that is not the universal position. It is clearly not the position of the Meriam people. Where a clan or group has continued to acknowledge the laws and (so far as practicable) to observe the customs based on the traditions of that clan or group, whereby their traditional connexion with the land has been substantially maintained, the traditional community title of that clan or group can be said to remain in existence. The common law can, by reference to the traditional laws and customs of an indigenous people, identify and protect the native rights and interests to which they give rise. However, when the tide of history has washed away any real acknowledgment of traditional law and any real observance of traditional customs, the foundation of native title has disappeared. A native title which has ceased with the abandoning of laws and customs based on tradition cannot be revived for contemporary recognition. Australian law can protect the interests of members of an indigenous clan or group, whether communally or individually, only in conformity with the traditional laws and customs of the people to whom the clan or group belongs and only where members of the clan or group acknowledge those laws and observe those customs (so far as it is practicable to do so). Once traditional native title expires, the Crown's radical title expands to a full beneficial title, for then there is no other proprietor than the Crown.

It follows that a right or interest possessed as a native title cannot be acquired from an indigenous people by one who, not being a member of the indigenous people, does not acknowledge their laws and observe their customs; nor can such a right or interest be acquired by a clan, group or member of the indigenous people unless the acquisition is consistent with the laws and customs of that people. Such a right or interest can be acquired outside those laws and customs only by the Crown [citations omitted]. Once the Crown acquires sovereignty and the common law becomes the law of the territory, the Crown's sovereignty over all land in the territory carries the capacity to accept a surrender of native title. The native title may be surrendered on purchase or surrendered voluntarily, whereupon the Crown's radical title is expanded to absolute ownership, a plenum dominium, for there is then no other owner.... If native title were surrendered to the Crown in expectation of a grant of a tenure to the indigenous title holders, there may be a fiduciary duty on the Crown to exercise its discretionary power to grant a tenure in land so as to satisfy the expectation, but it is unnecessary to consider the existence or extent of such a fiduciary duty in this case. Here, the fact is that strangers were not allowed to settle on the Murray Islands and, even after annexation in 1879, strangers who were living on the Islands were deported. The Meriam people asserted an exclusive right to occupy the Murray Islands and, as a community, held a proprietary interest in the Islands. They have maintained their identity as a people and they observe customs which are traditionally based. There was a possible alienation of some kind of interest in 2 acres to the London Missionary Society prior to annexation but it is unnecessary to consider whether that land was alienated by Meriam law or whether the alienation was sanctioned by custom alone. As we shall see, native title to that land was lost to the Meriam people in any event on the grant of a lease by the Crown in 1882 or by its subsequent renewal.

Secondly, native title, being recognized by the common law (though not as a common law tenure), may be protected by such legal or equitable remedies as are appropriate to the particular rights and interests established by the evidence, whether proprietary or personal and usufructuary in nature and whether possessed by a community, a group or an individual. The incidents of a particular native title relating to inheritance, the transmission or acquisition of rights and interests on death or marriage, the transfer of rights and interests in land and the grouping of persons to possess rights and interests in land are matters to be determined by the laws and customs of the indigenous inhabitants, provided those laws and customs are not so repugnant to natural justice, equity and good conscience that judicial sanctions under the new regime must be withheld: *Idewu Inasa v. Oshodi* (1934) AC 99, at p. 105. Of course in time the laws and customs of any people will change and the rights and interests of the members of the people among themselves will change too. But so long as the people remain as an identifiable community, the members of whom are identified by one another as members of that community living under its laws and customs, the communal native title survives to be enjoyed by the members according to the rights and interests to which they are respectively entitled under the traditionally based laws and customs, as currently acknowledged and observed. Here, the Meriam people have maintained their own identity and their own customs. The Murray Islands clearly remain their home country. Their land disputes have been dealt with over the years by the Island Court in accordance with the customs of the Meriam people.

Thirdly, where an indigenous people (including a clan or group), as a community, are in possession or are entitled to possession of land under a proprietary native title, their possession may be protected or their entitlement to possession may be enforced by a representative action brought on behalf of the people or by a sub-group or individual who sues to protect or enforce rights or interests which are dependent on the communal native title. Those rights and interests are, so to speak, carved out of the communal native title. A sub-group or individual asserting a native title dependent on a communal native title has a sufficient interest to sue to enforce or protect the communal title. *Australian Conservation Foundation v. The Commonwealth* [1979] HCA 1; (1980) 146 CLR 493, at pp. 530–531, 537–539, 547–548; *Onus v. Alcoa of Australia Ltd.* [1981] HCA 50; (1981) 149 CLR 27, at pp. 35–36, 41–42, 46, 51, 62, 74–75. A communal native title enures for the benefit of the community as a whole and for the sub-groups and individuals within it who have particular rights and interests in the community's lands.

The recognition of the rights and interests of a sub-group or individual dependent on a communal native title is not precluded by an absence of a communal law to determine a point in contest between rival claimants. By custom, such a point may have to be settled by community consensus or in some other manner prescribed by custom. A court may have to act on evidence which lacks specificity in determining a question of that kind. That is statutorily recognized in the case of the Murray Islands. The jurisdiction conferred on the Island Court by s.41(2)(b) of the *Community Services (Torres Strait) Act* 1984–1990 (Q.) includes a jurisdiction which must be exercised in accordance with the customs of the Meriam people. . . .

Whatever be the precision of Meriam laws and customs with respect to land, there is abundant evidence that land was traditionally occupied by individuals or family groups and that contemporary rights and interests are capable of being established with sufficient precision to attract declaratory or other relief. Although the findings made by Moynihan J. do not permit a confident conclusion that, in 1879, there were parcels of land in the Murray Islands owned allodially by individuals or groups, the absence of such a finding is not critical to the final resolution of this case. If the doctrine of Attorney-General v. Brown were applied to the Murray Islands, allodial ownership would have been no bar to the Crown's acquisition of universal and absolute ownership of the land and the extinguishing of all native titles. But, by applying the rule that the communal proprietary interests of the indigenous inhabitants survive the Crown's acquisition of sovereignty, it is possible to determine, according to the laws and customs of the Meriam people, contests among members of the Meriam people relating to rights and interests in particular parcels of land.

. . .

These propositions leave for resolution by the general law the question of the validity of any purported exercise by the Crown of the power to alienate or to appropriate to itself waste lands of the Crown. In Queensland, these powers are and at all material times have been exercisable by the Executive Government subject, in the case of the power of alienation, to the statutes of the State in force from time to time. The power of alienation and the power of appropriation vested in the Crown in right of a State are also subject to the valid laws of the Commonwealth, including the Racial Discrimination Act. Where a power has purportedly been exercised as a prerogative power, the validity of the exercise depends on the scope of the prerogative and the authority of the purported repository in the particular case.

. . .

Dean and Gaudron JJ.

. . .

The numbers of the Aboriginal inhabitants of the Australian continent in 1788, the relationship between them and the lands on which they lived, and the content of the traditional laws and customs which governed them are still but incompletely known or imperfectly comprehended. The following broad generalizations must, however, now be accepted as beyond real doubt or intelligent dispute at least as regards significant areas of the territory which became New South Wales. As has been said, it is clear that the numbers of Aboriginal inhabitants far exceeded the expectations of the settlers. The range of current estimates for the whole continent is between three hundred thousand and a million or even more. Under the laws or customs of the relevant locality, particular tribes or clans were, either on their own or with others, custodians of the areas of land from which they derived their sustenance and from which they often took their tribal names. Their laws or customs were elaborate and obligatory. The boundaries of their traditional lands were likely to be long-standing and defined. The special relationship between a particular tribe or clan and its land was recognized by other tribes or groups within the relevant local native system and was reflected in differences in dialect over relatively short distances. In different ways and to varying degrees of intensity, they used their homelands for all the purposes of their lives: social, ritual, economic. They identified with them in a way which transcended common law notions of property or possession. As was the case in other British Colonies[, s]ee, e.g., *Amodu Tijani* (1921) 2 AC, at p. 404; *Sobhuza II. V. Miller* (1926) AC, at p. 525, the claim to the land was ordinarily that of the tribe or other group, not that of an individual in his or her own right.

In the context of the above generalizations, the conclusion is inevitable that, at the time of the establishment of the Colony of New South Wales in 1788, there existed, under the traditional laws or customs of the Aboriginal peoples in the kaleidoscope of relevant local areas, widespread special entitlements to the use and occupation of defined lands of a kind which founded a presumptive common law native title under the law of a settled Colony after its establishment. Indeed, as a generalization, it is true to say that, where they existed, those established entitlements of the Australian Aboriginal tribes or clans in relation to traditional lands were no less clear, substantial and strong than were the interests of the Indian tribes and bands of North America, at least in relation to those parts of their traditional hunting grounds which remained uncultivated.

It follows from what has been said in earlier parts of this judgment that the application of settled principle to well-known facts leads to the conclusion that the common law applicable to the Colony in 1788, and thereafter until altered by valid legislation, preserved and protected the pre-existing claims of Aboriginal tribes or communities to particular areas of land with which they were specially identified, either solely or with others, by occupation or use for economic, social or ritual purposes. Under the law of the Colony, they were entitled to continue in the occupation or use of those lands as the holders of a common law native title which was a burden upon and reduced the title of the Crown. The Crown and those acting on behalf of the Crown were bound by that native title notwithstanding that the Crown's immunity from action and the fiction that the King could do no wrong precluded proceedings against the Crown to prevent, or to recover compensation for, its wrongful infringement or extinguishment. In accordance with the basic principles of English constitutional law applicable to a settled Colony, the sovereignty of the British Crown did not, after the act of State establishing the Colony was complete, include a prerogative right to extinguish by legislation or to disregard by executive act the traditional Aboriginal rights in relation to the land which were recognized and protected by the common law as true legal rights. The combined effect of (i) the personal nature of those rights, (ii) the absence of any presumption of a prior grant to the Aboriginal title-holders, and (iii) the applicable principles of English land law was that native title would be extinguished by a subsequent inconsistent grant of the relevant land by the Crown which was not invalid on its face. That extinguishment would, however, involve a wrongful infringement by the Crown of the rights of the Aboriginal title-holders.

It is unnecessary for the purposes of this judgment, and probably now impracticable, to seek to ascertain what proportion of the lands of the continent were affected by such common law native titles. Obviously, the proportion was a significant one. Conceivably, it was the whole.

(x) *The "Dispossession of the Original Inhabitants"*

. . .

In the very early days, the explanation of the disregard of Aboriginal claims and the resulting dispossession and conflict may have been that the new arrivals were ignorant of the fact that, under pre-existing local law or custom, particular tribes or clans had established entitlements to the occupation and use of particular areas of land. That explanation is not, however, a plausible one in respect of later events. Increasingly, the fact that particular tribes or clans enjoyed traditional entitlements to the occupation and use of particular lands for ritual, economic and social purposes was understood. Increasingly, that fact was even acknowledged by government authorities and in formal despatches. . . . Thus, on 14 March 1841, James Stephen, probably the most knowledgeable of all the nineteenth century permanent heads of the Imperial Colonial Office, noted on a despatch received from South Australia, Colonial Office Records, Australian Joint Copying Project, File No.13/16, Folio 57:

> It is an important and unexpected fact that these Tribes had proprietary rights in the Soil – that is, in particular sections of it which were clearly defined or well understood before the occupation of their country.

Two years later, Stephen wrote of the "dispossession of the original Inhabitants."

Nor can it be said that it did not occur to the Imperial and local authorities that the dispossession of the Aboriginal inhabitants might involve the infringement of rights recognized by the common law. The story of the development of South Australia, including the ineffective reservation in the Letters Patent of 1836 protecting "the rights of any Aboriginal Natives (of South Australia) to the actual occupation or enjoyment in their own persons or in the persons of their descendants of any land therein now actually occupied or enjoyed by such Natives," demonstrates that the contrary was the case. . . .

Inevitably, one is compelled to acknowledge the role played, in the dispossession and oppression of the Aborigines, by the two propositions that the territory of New South Wales was, in 1788, terra nullius in the sense of unoccupied or uninhabited for legal purposes and that full legal and beneficial ownership of all the lands of the Colony vested in the Crown, unaffected by any claims of the Aboriginal inhabitants. Those propositions provided a legal basis for and justification of the dispossession. They constituted the legal context of the acts done to enforce it and, while accepted, rendered unlawful acts done by the Aboriginal inhabitants to protect traditional occupation or use. The official endorsement, by administrative practice and in judgments of the courts, of those two propositions provided the environment in which the Aboriginal people of the continent came to be treated as a different and lower form of life whose very existence could be ignored for the purpose of determining the legal right to occupy and use their traditional homelands.

. . .

(xii) *The Nature, Incidents and Limitations of the Common Law Native Title of Australian Aborigines*

To a large extent, the nature, incidents and limitations of the rights involved in the common law native title of Australian Aborigines appear from what has been written above. It would, however, seem desirable to identify them in summary form at this stage of this judgment.

Ordinarily, common law native title is a communal native title and the rights under it are communal rights enjoyed by a tribe or other group. It is so with Aboriginal title in the Australian States and internal Territories. Since the title preserves entitlement to use or enjoyment under the traditional law or custom of the relevant territory or locality, the contents of the rights and the identity of those entitled to enjoy them must be ascertained by reference to that traditional law or custom. The traditional law or custom is not, however, frozen as at the moment of establishment of a Colony. Provided any changes do not diminish or extinguish the relationship between a particular tribe or other group and particular land, subsequent developments or variations do not extinguish the title in relation to that land.

The rights of an Aboriginal tribe or clan entitled to the benefit of a common law native title are personal only. The enjoyment of the rights can be varied and dealt with under the traditional law or custom. The rights are not, however, assignable outside the overall native system. They can be voluntarily extinguished by surrender to the Crown. They can also be lost by the abandonment of the connection with the land or by the extinction of the relevant tribe or group. It is unnecessary, for the purposes of this case, to consider the question whether they will be lost by the abandonment of traditional customs and ways. Our present view is that, at least where the relevant tribe or group continues to occupy or use the land, they will not.

The personal rights conferred by common law native title do not constitute an estate or interest in the land itself. They are extinguished by an unqualified grant of an inconsistent estate in the land by the Crown, such as a grant in fee or a lease conferring the right to exclusive possession. They can also be terminated by other inconsistent dealings with the land by the Crown, such as appropriation, dedication or reservation for an inconsistent public purpose or use, in circumstances giving rise to third party rights or assumed acquiescence. The personal rights of use and occupation conferred by common law native title are not, however, illusory. They are legal rights which are infringed if they are extinguished, against the wishes of the native title-holders, by inconsistent grant, dedication or reservation and which, subject only to their susceptibility to being wrongfully so extinguished, are binding on the Crown and a burden on its title.

(xiii) *Legislative Powers with Respect to Common Law Native Title*

Like other legal rights, including rights of property, the rights conferred by common law native title and the title itself can be dealt with, expropriated or extinguished by valid Commonwealth, State or Territorial legislation operating within the State or Territory in which the land in question is situated. To put the matter differently, the rights are not entrenched in the sense that they are, by reason of their nature, beyond the reach of legislative power. The ordinary rules of statutory interpretation require, however, that clear and unambiguous words be used before there will be imputed to the legislature an intent to expropriate or extinguish valuable rights relating to property without fair compensation. . . .

There are, however, some important constraints on the legislative power of Commonwealth, State or Territory Parliaments to extinguish or diminish the common law native titles which survive in this country. In so far as the Commonwealth is concerned, there is the requirement of s.51(xxxi) of the Constitution that a law with respect to the acquisition of property provide "just terms." Our conclusion that rights under common law native title are true legal rights which are recognized and protected by the law would, we think, have the consequence that any legislative extinguishment of those rights would constitute an expropriation of property, to the benefit of the underlying estate, for the purposes of s.51(xxxi). An even more important restriction upon legislative powers to extinguish or diminish common law native title flows from the paramountcy of valid legislation of the Commonwealth Parliament over what would otherwise be valid State or Territory legislation. In particular, as *Mabo v. Queensland* [1988] HCA 69; (1988) 166 CLR 186 has demonstrated, the provisions of the *Racial Discrimination Act* 1975 (Cth) represent an important restraint upon State or Territory legislative power to extinguish or diminish common law native title.

It is unnecessary and would be impracticable to seek to identify the extent to which particular legislative provisions have clearly and unambiguously extinguished or adversely affected common law native title in different areas of this country. That being so, the general comments about enforcement and protection in the next section of this judgment must necessarily be read as subject to the provisions of any valid applicable legislation.

(xiv) *The Enforcement and Protection of Common Law Native Title*

As has been seen, common law native title-holders in an eighteenth century British Colony were in an essentially helpless position if their rights under their native title were disregarded or wrongly extinguished by the Crown. Quite apart from the inherent unlikelihood of such title-holders being in a position to institute proceedings against the British Crown in a British court, the vulnerability of the rights under native title resulted in part from the fact that they were personal rights susceptible to extinguishment by inconsistent grant by the Crown and in part from the immunity of the Crown from court proceedings. The vulnerability persists to the extent that it flows from the nature of the rights as personal. On the other hand, as legislative reforms increasingly subjected the Crown or a nominal defendant on its behalf to the jurisdiction of the courts and to liability for compensatory damages for a wrong done to a subject, the ability of native title-holders to protect and vindicate the personal rights under common law native title significantly increased. If common law native title is wrongfully extinguished by the Crown, the effect of those legislative reforms is that compensatory damages can be recovered provided the proceedings for recovery are instituted within the period allowed by applicable limitations provisions. If the common law native title has not been extinguished, the fact that the rights under it are true legal rights means that they can be vindicated, protected and enforced by proceedings in the ordinary courts.

In a case where the Crown or a trustee appointed by the Crown wrongly denies the existence or the extent of an existing common law native title or threatens to infringe the rights thereunder (e.g. by an inconsistent grant), the appropriate relief in proceedings brought by (or by a representative party or parties on behalf of) the native title-holders will ordinarily be declaratory only since it will be apparent that the Crown or the trustee, being bound by any declaration, will faithfully observe its terms. Further relief is, however, available where it is necessary to protect the rights of the title-holders. One example of such further relief is relief by way of injunction. See, e.g., *Nireaha Tamaki v. Baker* (1901) AC, at p. 578. Notwithstanding their personal nature and their special vulnerability to wrongful extinguishment by the Crown, the rights of occupation or use under common law native title can themselves constitute valuable property. Actual or threatened interference with their enjoyment can, in appropriate circumstances, attract the protection of equitable remedies. Indeed, the circumstances of a case may be such that, in a modern context, the appropriate form of relief is the imposition of a remedial constructive trust framed to reflect the incidents and limitations of the rights under the common law native title. The principle of the common law that pre-existing native rights are respected and protected will, in a case where the imposition of such a constructive trust is warranted, prevail over other equitable principles or rules to the extent that they would preclude the appropriate protection of the native title in the same way as that principle prevailed over legal rules which would otherwise have prevented the preservation of the title under the common law. In particular, rules relating to requirements of certainty and present entitlement or precluding remoteness of vesting may need to be adapted or excluded to the extent necessary to enable the protection of the rights under the native title.

. . .

[ORDER]

In lieu of answering the questions reserved for the consideration of the Full Court,

   (1)   *declare that the land in the Murray Islands is not Crown land within the meaning of that term in s. 5 of the Land Act 1962 (Q.);*

(2) *putting to one side the Islands of Dauer and Waier and the parcel of land leased to the Trustees of the Australian Board of Missions and those parcels of land (if any) which have validly been appropriated for use for administrative purposes the use of which is inconsistent with the continued enjoyment of the rights and privileges of the Meriam people under native title, declare that the Meriam people are entitled as against the whole world to possession, occupation, use and enjoyment of the lands of the Murray Islands;*

(3) *declare that the title of the Meriam people is subject to the power of the Parliament of Queensland and the power of the Governor in Council of Queensland to extinguish that title by valid exercise of their respective powers, provided any exercise of those powers is not inconsistent with the laws of the Commonwealth.*

Questions and Discussion

1. In response to the *Mabo* II judgment, the Australian Federal Parliament enacted the Native Title Act of 1993 (Cth). The Act codified a statutory definition of native title, based on the opinion of Justice Brennan. It also established the Native Title Tribunal and a procedure for obtaining compensation and determining native title.

2. In Australia, as well as other countries, courts have had to balance indigenous rights with environmental protection, especially in the enforcement of endangered species laws. In *Yanner v. Eaton*, (1999) 201 CLR 351; (1999) 166 ALR 258; (1999) 73 ALRJ 1518, the Court considered the collision between Aboriginal cultural and religious practices, which involved their taking and eating of protected juvenile estuarine crocodiles in violation of the Fauna Conservation Act of 1994 (Qld). The Court found that the law did not entirely deprive the Aboriginal community of the ability to exercise traditional rights but merely regulated particular aspects and thus could be enforced against them.

B. *The United States*

During the two and a quarter centuries since the United States became independent, its laws and policies concerning Native Americans have often changed. During many periods they were overtly racist, with legal measures sometimes aggressively assimilationist, at other times protectionist. As the laws have evolved, the legal status of Native Americans has differentiated among three major groups: continental American Indians, Alaskan native groups (primarily Inuit), and native Hawaiians. The latter two groups live in territories that were acquired rather late in U.S. history, and their legal status thus evolved separately from that of continental American Indians.

The status of American Indians has always been unique in the U.S. federal structure. They have a special relationship with the federal government, which has a duty to protect tribes and their properties. See WILLIAM C. CANBY JR., AMERICAN INDIAN LAW (3d ed. 1998). Before independence and at the beginning of the United States' history, Indian tribes were considered as foreign sovereign nations, and relations were largely governed by treaty. The Constitution granted Congress the power to "regulate Commerce with the Indian Tribes," and the president was given the power, with the advice and consent of the Senate, to make treaties. U.S. CONST., art I, s. 8, cl. 3; art. II, s. 2, cl. 2. Trade and Intercourse Acts, from 1 Stat. 137 (1790) to 4 Stat. 729 (1834).

As the non-Indian population grew, the policy of separation became a pretext for the expulsion of Indians from their lands east of the Mississippi River. The U.S. Supreme Court began formulating a doctrine of the dependence of Indian tribes that justified the taking of Indian land. In 1823, the Court announced that European discovery gave European sovereigns the right to acquire native territory either by purchase or by conquest.[73] Indians retained only the right of occupancy and only so long as it was not extinguished by the federal government. A subsequent U.S. Supreme Court case, in which the Cherokee Nation sought to challenge its removal from traditional lands, resulted in a judgment that the Cherokee Nation could not bring suit as a "foreign state," although it had concluded treaties with the United States, because "it may well be doubted whether those tribes which reside within the acknowledged boundaries of the United States can, with strict accuracy, be denominated foreign nations. They may, more correctly, perhaps, be denominated domestic dependent nations."[74] A year later, the same court announced that within the territories occupied by the Cherokees "is a distinct community, occupying its own territory, with boundaries accurately described, in which the laws of [a state] can have no force."[75] In effect, Indian tribes became subject to the guardianship of the U.S. government but outside the regulation of the various states and local non-Indian communities.

The forced removal of Indian tribes west of the Mississippi led to further restrictions on land rights, as the federal government began to designate specific reservations, usually after concluding a treaty in which the tribe ceded the major part of its lands to the federal government. Once most of these lands were acquired, Congress denied Indian tribes further recognition as independent nations with whom treaties could be concluded.[76] Thereafter, reservations were created by statute or executive order.

Reservations soon came to be seen as the key for ensuring Indian adaptation to non-Indian culture. A supervising Indian "agent" appointed by the government but heavily influenced by religious groups created Indian schools beginning in 1865 with the goal of instructing pupils in Christianity. In 1878, boarding schools were established to educate Indian children away from their tribal cultures and environments. Although Indian communities retained civil and criminal jurisdiction over offenses committed on the reservations and by members of the tribe,[77] Congress eventually passed the Major Crimes Act to declare murder and other serious crimes federal offenses to be prosecuted in federal court.

The reservations policy was opposed by many for sound and unsound reasons, the latter mostly based on a desire for even more Indian land. In 1887, the federal government fundamentally altered its policy and began to press for total assimilation of all Indians into mainstream U.S. culture. The result was the catastrophic General Allotment Act of 1887, also know as the Dawes Act.[78] The Act carved up the reservations to create small landholdings for individuals Indians, held in trust for the first twenty-five years by the government and afterward owned freely by the individuals. The Act provided that those who received the land allotments would become U.S. citizens, as would other Indians residing apart from their tribes and adopting "the habits of civilized life."[79] All "excess" land not allotted was to be disposed of by the government in negotiations with the tribe.

No consent was required of the Indian tribes or individual Indians before the Act was applied. Its primary effect was to reduce the holdings of Indian lands by almost two-thirds, from 138 million acres in 1887 to 48 million acres in 1934, of which almost half was desert or

---

[73] *Johnson v. McIntosh*, 21 U.S. (8 Wheat.) 543 (1823).

[74] *Cherokee Nation v. Georgia*, 30 U.S. (5 Pet.) 1 (1831).

[75] *Worcester v. Georgia*, 31 U.S. (6 Pet.) 515, 557 (1832).

[76] 25 U.S.C. § 71 (1871). The constitutionality of this law is questionable and has never been tested in court.

[77] *See* Ex parte Crow Dog, 109 U.S. 556 (1883).

[78] Indian General Allotment Act (Dawes Act), ch. 119, 24 Stat. 388 (1887) (codified as amended in scattered sections of 25 U.S.C. (1994)).

[79] Not until 1924 was U.S. citizenship conferred on all Indians born in the United States. 8 U.S.C. § 1401(b).

semidesert. By 1928, the failure of the policy was clear, and a federal report[80] led to another major change in policy, through adoption of the Indian Reorganization Act of 1934.[81] This Act was the first in U.S. history that sought to preserve Indian tribes and cultures by protecting the land base and permitting tribes to set up self-government. The policy of allotments ended and the Act authorized the secretary of the interior to restore the "excess" lands taken under the Dawes Act.

Although the 1934 Act was largely successful in stimulating the revival of Indian tribes, the post–World War II period brought another wave of assimilationist policies. In 1953, Congress formally adopted a preference for "termination" of Indian tribes, to "make the Indians within the territorial limits of the United States subject to the same laws and entitled to the same privileges and responsibilities as are applicable to other citizens of the United States," and to end their status as protected peoples.[82] Statutes terminated the legal recognition of several tribes, who suffered economic ruin as a result. Although termination was in place as official policy, the federal Bureau of Indian Affairs sought to "relocate" individual Indians off the reservations.

By the late 1960s, the policy of termination, like the earlier Dawes Act, was viewed as a serious failure. Assimilation was rejected in favor of cultural diversity, and Congress passed the Indian Civil Rights Act of 1968.[83] The Act extended the Constitution's Bill of Rights to Indian tribes. Two years later, the U.S. president declared termination a failed policy and urged a program of self-government for Indians. A series of congressional measures followed that strengthened the status of tribes as permanent, self-governing institutions.[84] In 1988, Congress declared a commitment to "the development of strong and stable tribal governments."[85] Finally, in 1994, President Clinton instructed the federal agencies to conduct relations with tribal governments as though in a "government-to-government" relationship.[86] Thus, the United States has come almost full circle, once again to accept that Indian tribes are nations entitled to self-governance in a pluralist society and possessing cultures that are entitled to respect and protection by the federal government.

In summary, over time, as a result of forced relocation, killings, assimilation, and sterilization, the estimated population of 10 million Native Americans at European arrival has declined to approximately 2.4 million. Lindsay Glauner, *The Need for Accountability and Reparation: 1830–1976 – The United States Government's Role in the Promotion, Implementation and Execution of the Crime of Genocide Against Native Americans*, 51 DePaul L. Rev. 911 (2002).

Legally today, recognized Indian tribes are considered independent entities with inherent powers of self-government subject to regulation by Congress. Thus, Indian tribes are not subject to regulation, including taxation, by the component states of the United States, unless the federal Congress delegates particular legislative power to the states. Despite this constitutionally mandated structure, states have periodically sought to assert their power over Indian tribes, whereas the scope afforded tribes for self-government has frequently shifted according to congressional dictates.

---

[80] Institute for Government Research, The Problem of Indian Administration (1928).

[81] Also known as the Wheeler-Howard Act, 25 U.S.C. § 461.

[82] H.Con.Res. 108, 83rd Cong., 1st Sess., 67 Stat. B132 (1953).

[83] 82 Stat. 77, 25 U.S.C.A. § 1301 et seq.

[84] *See, e.g.*, The Indian Financing Act of 1974, 25 U.S.C. §§ 1451 et seq.; the Indian Self-Determination and Education Assistance Act, 25 U.S.C., §§ 450 et seq.; and the Indian Tribal Government Tax Status Act of 1982, 96 Stat. 2607.

[85] 25 U.S.C. § 450a(b).

[86] 59 Fed.Reg. 22951 (1994).

It has been estimated that the status and rights of Native Americans in the United States are governed by nearly four hundred treaties, as well as domestic statutory and case law. Walter R. Echohawk, *Justice and the American Indian*, 3 CONTACT 33 (1973). Treaty-based claims often concern land rights. Native Hawaiians continue to demand redress for the loss of their independence, lands, and culture. They have filed state law claims based on the overthrow of the government in 1893, seeking back payment of trust revenues and to enjoin negotiation, settlement, and execution of a release by trustees. *Office of Hawaiian Affairs v. State of Hawaii*, Civ. No. 94–0205-01; *Ka-ai-ai v. Drake*, Civ. No. 92–3742-10 (1st Cir. 1992); *Kealoha v. Hee*, Civ. No. 94–0118-1 (1st Cir.).

Other claims commonly asserted concern cultural property, grave goods, and traditional knowledge. The names of Native American tribes and historical personages, for example, are carried by sports teams, T-shirts, and alcoholic beverages, which has led to considerable litigation. See Rosemary T. Coombe, *The Properties of Culture and the Politics of Possessing Identity: Native Claims in the Cultural Appropriation Controversy*, 6 CAN. J.L. & JURIS. 249 (1993). Where, as in the Hopi culture, the ritual or information is considered sacred, or restricted only to initiates, its uncontrolled public dissemination is directly contrary to the tribe's cultural precepts. *See* David Howes, *Introduction: Commodities and Cultural Borders*, in CROSS-CULTURAL CONSUMPTION: GLOBAL MARKETS, LOCAL REALITIES at 143–44 (David Howes ed., 1996).

In the United States, as early as 1946, the Indian Claims Commission was given jurisdiction to hear and resolve claims arising from the seizure of Indian property and treaty breaches by the United States. Act of Aug. 13, 1946, ch. 959, s. 1, 60 Stat. 1049 (West 1999). The 1971 Alaska Native Claims Settlement Act granted indigenous Alaskans monetary relief as well as land. 43 U.S.C. §1601 (1998). The Alaskan Native Claims Settlement Act awarded US$1 billion and 44 million acres of land that had been wrongfully seized. In March 2003, the U.S. Supreme Court upheld a 1999 federal court decision awarding damages to Native Americans for trust fund mismanagement by the U.S. Department of the Interior and Treasury. *United States v. White Mountain Apache Tribe*, 537 U.S. 465, 123 S. Ct. 1126 (2003). *See also Cobell v. Norton*, 240 F.3d 1081 (CADC, 2001). The fund had been established in the 1830s to compensate Native Americans for earlier injustices, including deprivation of land. For an analysis of indigenous claims in the United States, see Nell Jessup Newton, *Indian Claims in the Courts of the Conqueror*, 41 AM. U.L. REV. 753 (1992); Robert T. Coulter, *The Failure of Indian Rights Advocacy*, in RETHINKING INDIAN LAW 103 (National Lawyer's Guild Committee on Native American Struggles ed., 1982).

Disputes over land and resource claims have continued and have led to a case against the United States at the Inter-American Commission on Human Rights. The decision explains the difficulties facing unrecognized tribes and the difficult process of determining rights over lands and resources.

Mary and Carrie Dann v. United States,
Inter-Am. Comm'n Hum. Rts,
Case 11.140, Rep. 75–02 (Dec. 27, 2002) (some footnotes omitted)

[The petitioners, members of the Western Shoshone tribe in Nevada, claimed that the United States interfered with their use and occupation of their ancestral lands by appropriating the lands as federal property and by physically removing their livestock from the lands, as well as by permitting or acquiescing in gold-prospecting activities in Western Shoshone traditional territory. The applicants claimed violations of the American Declaration (the United States is not a party to the American Convention on Human Rights or ILO Convention No. 169 but is a member of the Organization of American States) – *Eds.*].

1. The Western Shoshone People and Mary and Carrie Dann

100. According to the observations of both the Petitioners and the State in this matter, the Western Shoshone "people" or "nation" constitutes a collective of individuals of native descent who have traditionally occupied the vast and arid territory of approximately 24,000,000 acres that is now primarily the state of Nevada in the United States. There appears to be no dispute between the parties as to the indigenous status of the Western Shoshone or of their historical occupation and use of this territory and its resources. Moreover, the parties agree that at some point the Western Shoshone had title to this territory as their ancestral lands. Rather, in the Commission's estimation, the point of contention in this case involves the question of whether any or all of those property rights subsist and the proper method of determining and respecting any such rights.

101. Also according to the record in this matter, the Western Shoshone nation is comprised of numerous relatively decentralized bands or tribes, including the Temoak Shoshone Band, the Ely Shoshone Band, and the Yomba Shoshone Band. Each band is comprised primarily of groups and individuals who have an extended family relationship and who have traditionally occupied the same area within the Western Shoshone ancestral territory.

102. The Western Shoshone and the U.S. government are parties to an existing treaty, the Treaty of Ruby Valley of 1863, 1863 (Treaty Between the United States of America and Western Bands of Shoshone Indians, ratified by the U.S. in 1866, and proclaimed on October 21, 1869, 18 Stat. 689). The Petitioners claim that under this treaty, the United States recognized certain Western territories as "Western Shoshone country" but granted the United States certain privileges such as building a railway to California, engaging in mining, and establishing mining towns and settlements. Moreover, the Petitioners contend that an encroachment by the U.S. on Western Shoshone territory transpired in the late 19th and early 20th centuries and that this occurred in violation of the terms of the Treaty of Ruby Valley.

103. In terms of the relation of the Western Shoshone to their ancestral lands, the Petitioners have contended the existence of a system of aboriginal land title that has historically been communal in nature and based upon land and resource use patterns. These patterns have been influenced by the fact that the Western Shoshone bands live in sparsely populated communities located far from each other in the vast territory and that in order to sustain themselves, bands have hunted, fished, and raised cattle and horses, and engaged in commerce with their neighbors. The State has not specifically contested this characterization of the Western Shoshone's traditional occupation and use of their ancestral lands.

104. With respect to the Dann family in particular, the parties have indicated that the Danns live on a ranch on Dann band land close to the small rural community of Crescent Valley, Nevada, where they raise livestock. Their ranch is the Danns' sole means of support, as they raise their own food and all of their needs are met by the sale of livestock, goods and produce to neighboring Western Shoshone and to non-Indians. The parties have also indicated that the Dann band is not among the federally-chartered Western Shoshone tribes with which the United States government maintains official relations. There appears to be no dispute, however, that the Dann band, and the Dann sisters themselves, are considered a part of the Western Shoshone people who have traditionally occupied a particular region of the Western Shoshone ancestral territory, and as such share in the history and status of the Western Shoshone as an aboriginal people. Similarly, the Petitioners have claimed, and the State has not contested, that the Dann family has traditionally occupied and used a

region broader than their individual ranch and that this constitutes part of the Dann Band land.

. . .

115. According to the information before the Commission, in 1951 the Temoak Band on behalf of the "Western Shoshone Identifiable Group" filed a claim with the [Indian Claims Commission (ICC)] against the United States based upon the United States having taken a vast expanse of Western Shoshone ancestral territory in Nevada and California. *Shoshone Tribe v. United States*, 11 I.C.C. 387 (1962). *See also United States v. Dann*, 706 F.2d 919 (1983). The claim alleged that from time to time the federal government had extinguished the Western Shoshone's title by confiscation.

116. In 1962, the ICC found that the Western Shoshone Tribe had held aboriginal title to a total of 24,396,403 acres in Nevada, and that their title to most of this land was extinguished over an unspecified period of time by gradual encroachment of both the federal government and third parties. In 1966, the Temoak claimants and the government agreed to stipulate an average extinguishment date of July 1, 1872 in order to determine the amount of compensation due, and the ICC agreed upon the date. Subsequently in 1977 the ICC completed the compensation phase of the proceeding and awarded the Western Shoshone with $26 million in compensation. This finding was based on the value of the property at the time of the alleged extinguishment, $.10 to $.15 per acre, without interest. In 1979 the Court of Claims affirmed this award on appeal.

117. In 1974, however, a group of Western Shoshone including the Danns attempted to intervene in the ICC process in order to remove a portion of the 24,000,000 acres of Western Shoshone property from the pending process. This included the lands that were the subject of the separate trespass action by the United States against the Danns in the federal courts. The interveners argued that any lands to which they claimed aboriginal title, including lands which they continued to occupy and use, should be excluded from the determination of the final award. The ICC rejected the intervention and that ruling was affirmed by the Court of Claims, which viewed the attempted intervention as an intra-tribal disagreement over the proper litigation strategy. *Western Shoshone Legal Defense & Education Ass'n v. United States*, 531 F.2d 495 (Ct. Cl. 1976), cert. denied, 429 U.S. 885 (1976). *See also United States v. Dann*, 706 F.2d 919 (1983) at 922–923.

118. In 1975 and 1976, the Temoak Band dismissed their attorney and adopted a position similar to that of the Danns, namely that aboriginal title to the lands in question had never been extinguished and that the Band's previous attorney had not presented them with the choice of whether to include all of the ancestral lands in the claim or to assert that title to a portion of the lands was not extinguished. Accordingly, they attempted to stay the proceedings in the ICC and before the Court of Claims to further address this issue. However, the ICC denied the stay and entered a final judgment, and on appeal the Court of Claims affirmed the ICC's ruling on the basis that it was too late for the Temoak Band to change their litigation strategy. *Temoak Band v. United States*, 593 F.2d at 996–999 (Ct. Cl.).

119. In December 1979 the Clerk of the Court of Claims certified the Commission's award to the U.S. General Accounting Office, which automatically appropriated the amount of the award and deposited it for the tribe in an interest-bearing trust account in the Treasury of the United States. According to the most recent information before the Commission this award has not yet been paid out, although a bill was introduced before Congress in mid-2000 to authorize the Secretary of the Interior to make a per capita distribution of the funds.

120. Outside of the process before the ICC, in 1974 the United States brought an action in trespass in the federal courts against the Danns, in relation to grazing that the Danns had

undertaken without a permit in the Northeast corner of Nevada. In response to the action, the Danns argued that the land had been in their possession and the possession of their ancestors since time immemorial and that their aboriginal title in the property precluded the State from requiring grazing permits.

121. The U.S. District Court rejected the Danns' argument, on the basis that the Danns' aboriginal title in the property had been extinguished by the collateral claims process before the ICC and that the United States had acquired all twenty-two million acres of Western Shoshone land through the estoppel effect of the ICC's 1962 judgment. On appeal, the Ninth Circuit Court of Appeals reversed the District Court decision and remanded the matter back, on the basis that the extinguishment issue had not been litigated or decided in the ICC proceedings. *United States v. Dann*, 572 F.2d 222 at 226 (9th Cir. 1978). On remand, the District Court held in 1980 that aboriginal title in the land in issue was extinguished when the final ICC award was certified for payment, and on further appeal the Ninth Circuit in a 1983 judgment once again reversed the District Court, reiterating its previous holding that the Dann band was not estopped from raising aboriginal title as a defense because the issue of extinguishment of title had not actually been litigated before the ICC. *United States v. Dann*, 706 F.2d 919 (9th Cir. 1983). Moreover, the Court held that the title of the Western Shoshone had never been extinguished by prior application of public land laws or by the creation of a Western Shoshone reservation because in the Court's view these actions did not evince a clear indication of congressional intent to extinguish aboriginal title.

122. On further review by the U.S. Supreme Court, the Ninth Circuit decision was reversed, on the basis that "payment" of the award could be taken to have occurred when the monies were appropriated to the U.S. Treasury and thus to have discharged all claims and demands involving the Western Shoshone land claim. On this basis, the U.S. Supreme Court determined that the Danns were estopped from raising aboriginal title as a defense to the U.S. trespass action. *United States v. Dann*, 470 U.S. 36.

123. The matter was once again remanded to the District Court and on further appeal to the Ninth Circuit, it was finally decided by that Court that the U.S. Supreme Court's finding of preclusion was decisive on precluding the issue of aboriginal title collectively and accordingly accepted the ICC's determination of July 1, 1872 as the appropriate date for the extinguishment of Western Shoshone land rights. In reaching this conclusion, the Court stated:

> *It is true that the taking was not actually litigated* ... but the payment of the claim award establishes conclusively that a taking occurred. From the claims litigation, we can only conclude that the taking occurred in the later part of the nineteenth century. [emphasis added]

C. Indigenous Peoples' Human Rights Principles and the American Declaration on the Rights and Duties of Man

130. Of particular relevance to the present case, the Commission considers that general international legal principles applicable in the context of indigenous human rights to include:
   - the right of indigenous peoples to legal recognition of their varied and specific forms and modalities of their control, ownership, use and enjoyment of territories and property;[87]

---

[87] The U.N. Committee on the Elimination of All Forms of Racism has similarly recognized that the "land rights of indigenous peoples are unique and encompass a tradition and cultural identification of the indigenous peoples with their lands that has been generally recognized," CERD decision 2(54) on Australia, para. 4. In this decision, the Committee criticized amendments to Australia's Native Title Act as incompatible with Australia's obligations under the Race Convention, particularly Articles 2 and

- the recognition of their property and ownership rights with respect to lands, territories and resources they have historically occupied;[88] and
- where property and user rights of indigenous peoples arise from rights existing prior to the creation of a state, recognition by that state of the permanent and inalienable title of indigenous peoples relative thereto and to have such title changed only by mutual consent between the state and respective indigenous peoples when they have full knowledge and appreciation of the nature or attributes of such property. This also implies the right to fair compensation in the event that such property and user rights are irrevocably lost.

131.   Based upon the foregoing analysis, the Commission is of the view that the provisions of the American Declaration should be interpreted and applied in the context of indigenous petitioners with due regard to the particular principles of international human rights law governing the individual and collective interests of indigenous peoples. Particularly pertinent provisions of the Declaration in this respect include Article II (the right to equality under the law), Article XVIII (the right to a fair trial), and Article XXIII (the right to property). As outlined above, this approach includes the taking of special measures to ensure recognition of the particular and collective interest that indigenous people have in the occupation and use of their traditional lands and resources and their right not to be deprived of this interest except with fully informed consent, under conditions of equality, and with fair compensation. The Commission wishes to emphasize that by interpreting the American Declaration so as to safeguard the integrity, livelihood and culture of indigenous peoples through the effective protection of their individual and collective human rights, the Commission is respecting the very purposes underlying the Declaration which, as expressed in its Preamble, include recognition that "[s]ince culture is the highest social and historical expression of that spiritual development, it is the duty of man to preserve, practice and foster culture by every means within his power.

132.   The Commission will therefore interpret and apply the provisions of the American Declaration to the Petitioners' claims of violations of the American Declaration in light of above principles.

. . .

D. Application of International Human Rights Norms and Principles in the Circumstances of Mary and Carrie Dann

135.   In the context of the procedural history in the Dann case outlined above, two factual issues of particular significance to the issues raised in this case appear to be the subject of conflicting submissions by the parties and require determination by the Commission based upon the record before it.

5, due in part to the inclusion of provisions that extinguish or impair the exercise of indigenous title rights and interests in order to create legal certainty for governments and third parties at the expense of indigenous title. Article 5(c) of the Race Convention in particular calls upon State Parties to "recognize and protect the rights of indigenous peoples to own, develop, control and use their common lands, territories and resources."

[88]   See Draft Inter-American Indigenous Declaration, *supra*, Art. XVIII(2). See similarly CERD General Recommendation XXIII (51) concerning Indigenous Peoples (Aug. 18, 1997) (calling upon states parties to the Race Convention to "recognize and protect the rights of indigenous peoples to own, develop, control and use their communal lands, territories and resources."); ILO Convention (No. 169), *supra*, Art. 14(1) (providing that "[t]he rights of ownership and possession of the peoples concerned over the lands which they traditionally occupy shall be recognized. In addition, measures shall be taken in appropriate cases to safeguard the right of the peoples concerned to use lands not exclusively occupied by them, but to which they have traditionally had access for their subsistence and traditional activities. Particular attention shall be paid to the situation of nomadic peoples and shifting cultivators in this respect."); Art. 15(1) (stating that "[t]he rights of the peoples concerned to the natural resources pertaining to their lands shall be specially safeguarded. These rights include the right of these peoples to participate in the use, management and conservation of these resources.").

136. First, the Petitioners contend that the Danns did not authorize or participate in the ICC claim submitted by the Temoak Band before the ICC, and that when they and several other bands subsequently sought to intervene in the proceedings, they were unsuccessful. The State submits conversely that throughout the proceedings before the ICC the Western Shoshone were kept fully apprised through regular meetings held with members of the tribe. The only such meetings specifically referred to by the State, however, were meetings convened by the attorney for the Temoak Band in 1965, 14 years after the ICC proceedings commenced and 3 years after the ICC issued its extinguishment finding. In the absence of evidence to the contrary the Commission accepts that the Danns did not play a full or effective role in retaining, authorizing or instructing the Western Shoshone claimants in the ICC process.

137. In addition, there appears to be some conflict between the parties' positions as to whether the subsistence of Western Shoshone title to all or part of its ancestral territory was the subject of litigation and determination by the ICC. Based upon the record before it, the Commission finds that the determination as to whether and to what extent Western Shoshone title may have been extinguished was not based upon a judicial evaluation of pertinent evidence, but rather was based upon apparently arbitrary stipulations as between the U.S. government and the Temoak Band regarding the extent and timing of the loss of indigenous title to the entirety of the Western Shoshone ancestral lands. In reaching this conclusion, the Commission has considered in particular the 1983 judgment of the U.S. Court of Appeals for the Ninth Circuit in which that Court concluded on the evidence available that Western Shoshone title had not been extinguished. In this respect, the Ninth Circuit was the only judicial body to review the substance of the ICC's finding of "extinguishment" of Western Shoshone title, but its findings were reversed by the U.S. Supreme Court without consideration of the merits of the Ninth Circuit's findings on this point. This effectively left the issue of title to Western Shoshone lands without definitive substantive adjudication by the U.S. courts.

138. In evaluating the Petitioners' claims in light of these evidentiary findings, the Commission first wishes to expressly recognize and acknowledge that the State, through the development and implementation of the Indian Claims Commission process, has taken significant measures to recognize and account for the historic deprivations suffered by indigenous communities living within the United States and commends the State for this initiative. As both the Petitioners and the State have recognized, this process provided a more efficient solution to the sovereign immunity bar to Indian land claims under U.S. law and extended to indigenous communities certain benefits relating to claims to their ancestral lands that were not available to other citizens, such as extended limitation periods for claims.

139. Upon evaluating these processes in the facts as disclosed by the record in this case, however, the Commission concludes that these processes were not sufficient to comply with contemporary international human rights norms, principles and standards that govern the determination of indigenous property interests.

140. The Commission first considers that Articles XVIII and XXIII of the American Declaration specially oblige a member state to ensure that any determination of the extent to which indigenous claimants maintain interests in the lands to which they have traditionally held title and have occupied and used is based upon a process of fully informed and mutual consent on the part of the indigenous community as a whole. This requires at a minimum that all of the members of the community are fully and accurately informed of the nature and consequences of the process and provided with an effective opportunity to participate individually or as collectives. In the case of the Danns, however, the record indicates that the land claim issue was pursued by one band of the Western Shoshone people [with] no apparent mandate from the other Western Shoshone bands or members. There is also

no evidence on the record that appropriate consultations were held within the Western Shoshone at the time that certain significant determinations were made. This includes in particular the ICC's finding that the entirety of the Western Shoshone interest in their ancestral lands, which interests affect the Danns, was extinguished at some point in the past.

141. To the contrary, despite the fact that it became clear at the time of the Danns' request to intervene that the collective interest in the Western Shoshone territory may not have been properly served through the proceedings pursued by the Temoak Band, the courts ultimately did not take measures to address the substance of these objections but rather dismissed them based upon the expediency of the ICC processes. In the Commission's opinion and in the context of the present case, this was not sufficient in order for the State to fulfill its particular obligation to ensure that the status of the Western Shoshone traditional lands was determined through a process of informed and mutual consent on the part of the Western Shoshone people as a whole.

142. The insufficiency of this process was augmented by the fact that, on the evidence, the issue of extinguishment was not litigated before or determined by the ICC, in that the ICC did not conduct an independent review of historical and other evidence to determine as a matter of fact whether the Western Shoshone properly claimed title to all or some of their traditional lands. Rather, the ICC determination was based upon an agreement between the State and the purported Western Shoshone representatives as to the extent and timing of the extinguishment. In light of the contentions by the Danns that they have continued to occupy and use at least portions of the Western Shoshone ancestral lands, and in light of the findings by the Ninth Circuit Court of Appeals as to the merits of the ICC's extinguishment finding, it cannot be said that the Danns' claims to property rights in the Western Shoshone ancestral lands were determined through an effective and fair process in compliance with the norms and principles under Articles XVIII and XXIII of the American Declaration.

143. Further, the Commission concludes that to the extent the State has asserted as against the Danns title in the property in issue based upon the ICC proceedings, the Danns have not been afforded their right to equal protection of the law under Article II of the American Declaration. The notion of equality before the law set forth in the Declaration relates to the application of substantive rights and to the protection to be given to them in the case of acts by the State or others. Further, Article II, while not prohibiting all distinctions in treatment in the enjoyment of protected rights and freedoms, requires at base that any permissible distinctions be based upon objective and reasonable justification, that they further a legitimate objective, regard being had to the principles which normally prevail in democratic societies, and that the means are reasonable and proportionate to the end sought.

144. The record before the Commission indicates that under prevailing common law in the United States, including the Fifth Amendment to the U.S. Constitution, the taking of property by the government ordinarily requires a valid public purpose and the entitlement of owners to notice, just compensation, and judicial review. In the present case, however, the Commission cannot find that the same prerequisites have been extended to the Danns in regard to the determination of their property claims to the Western Shoshone ancestral lands, and no proper justification for the distinction in their treatment has been established by the State. In particular, as concluded above, any property rights that the Danns may have asserted to the Western Shoshone ancestral lands were held by the ICC to have been "extinguished" through proceedings in which the Danns were not effectively represented and where the circumstances of this alleged extinguishment were never actually litigated nor the merits of the finding finally reviewed by the courts. And while compensation for this extinguishment was awarded by the ICC, the value of compensation was calculated

based upon an average extinguishment date that does not on the record appear to bear any relevant connection to the issue of whether and to what extent all or part of Western Shoshone title in their traditional lands, including that of the Danns, may no longer subsist. Further, the Commission understands that the amount of compensation awarded for the alleged encroachment upon Western Shoshone ancestral lands did not include an award of interest from the date of the alleged extinguishment to the date of the ICC decision, thus leaving the Western Shoshone uncompensated for the cost of the alleged taking of their property during this period.

145. All of these circumstances suggest that the Danns have not been afforded equal treatment under the law respecting the determination of their property interests in the Western Shoshone ancestral lands, contrary to Article II of the Declaration. While the State has suggested that the extinguishment of Western Shoshone title was justified by the need to encourage settlement and agricultural developments in the western United States, the Commission does not consider that this can justify the broad manner in which the State has purported to extinguish indigenous claims, including those of the Danns, in the entirety of the Western Shoshone territory. In the Commission's view, this is particularly apparent in light of evidence that the Danns and other Western Shoshone have at least until recently continued to occupy and use regions of the territory that the State now claims as its own.

V. PROCEEDINGS SUBSEQUENT TO REPORT 113/01

. . .

148. By communication dated December 17, 2001 and received by the Commission on December 19, 2001 the State delivered a response to the Commission's request for information, in which it rejected the Commission's report in its entirety and asserted that Mary and Carrie Dann had been accorded the right to equality before the law, the right to a fair trial, and the right to own property.

. . .

150. . . . The United States made four principal arguments in rejecting the conclusions and recommendations in the Commission's report. It first contended that the Danns' complaints regarding the alleged lack of due process in the Indian Claims Commission proceedings were fully and fairly litigated in the United States courts and should not be reconsidered by the Commission. Second, the State argued that the Commission lacked jurisdiction to evaluate processes established under the 1946 Indian Claims Act since the Act predated the U.S. ratification of the OAS Charter. Third, the State claimed that the Commission erred in interpreting the principles of the American Declaration in light of Article XVIII of the OAS draft Declaration on the Rights of Indigenous Peoples, which had not yet been adopted by the political organs of the OAS. Finally, the State rejected the Commission's findings on the basis that the American Declaration is not a legally binding instrument and therefore cannot be the object of violations by the United States.

151. In elaborating upon the arguments in its response, the United State[s] provided an overview of the history of litigation in U.S. domestic courts pertaining to the Western Shoshone lands.

152. The State also refers to the trespass action commenced by the United States government against the Danns in 1974 alleging that they were grazing livestock on certain public lands in Nevada without a permit as required by regulations promulgated by the Secretary of the Interior under the Taylor Grazing Act. The United States notes in particular that according to the U.S. Supreme Court, the finality under section 22(a) of the 1946 Indian Claims Commission Act of the ICC's judgment and award in the Western Shoshone litigation precluded the Danns from continuing to assert aboriginal title, since the award had been

placed in a trust fund account for the benefit of members of the Western Shoshone. The Supreme Court also observed that only tribal, but not individual, aboriginal rights were precluded by the Indian Claims Commission proceedings, although the Court declined to address the issue of individual aboriginal title further since it had not been addressed by the lower courts. On remand, the U.S. Court of Appeals for the Ninth Circuit ruled that the Danns would be able to assert individual aboriginal title as a defense in the trespass action to the extent that such rights were acquired prior to the withdrawal of the lands from the public grazing legislation in 1934 and continuously exercised since that time. However, the Danns subsequently withdrew their claims of individual aboriginal title as a defense in the trespass action, and as a result the U.S. federal courts have ordered the Danns to comply with the United States' grazing regulations.

153. In disputing the findings in the Commission's report, the State first contends that the Commission has violated the "fourth instance" procedural rule by advancing the same arguments that have been adjudicated, reviewed and rejected by federal courts in the above litigation in accordance with U.S. federal law and, in the State's view, the provisions of international law, contemporary or otherwise.

154. In this connection, the State identifies as a "fundamental error" throughout the Commission's decision its factual assumption that the land at issue in the Indian Claims Commission litigation represented an aggregation of individual claims and not a collective tribal claim of the Western Shoshone. The State asserts that the claim before the Indian Claims Commission was in fact a collective tribal claim regarding all of the communal tribal lands and not an aggregation of related individual claims, a characteristic recognized by the U.S. Court of Claims and by the "firmly established principle" under U.S. law that tribes, not individuals, have authority over communal tribunal land. As a consequence, the Danns were not entitled to be individually represented in the Indian Land Claims proceeding.

155. The State also contends that the Commission committed a fundamental factual error by concluding that at the time of the Danns' request to intervene, the collective interest in the Western Shoshone territory may not have been properly served through the proceedings pursued by the Temoak Band. Rather, the State argues that U.S. Court of Claims properly concluded that the Temoak Band was the appropriate representative of the entire Western Shoshone and that the allegations of fraud and collusion levied by the Danns and other petitioners against the Temoak Band were unfounded. The State notes in particular that the U.S. Court of Claims viewed the dispute by the Danns and other petitioners raised in their application to intervene as a dispute "over the proper strategy to follow in this litigation." The State observes in this regard that the U.S. Court of Claims also held that during the title phase of the proceeding before the Indian Claims Commission there had been a judicial evaluation of the pertinent evidence pertaining to the issue of extinguishment of Western Shoshone title, whereby the Indian Claims Commission made its own determination that the Western Shoshone lands were held by separate Shoshone entities and that Indian title to the area was extinguished by encroachment. The U.S. Court of Claims considered in particular that it was proper for the parties to agree to stipulate that the Nevada lands be valued as of July 1, 1872 rather than having a further "burdensome" trial of the dates of disposals of each separate tract.

156. Based upon these findings by the U.S. Court of Claims, the State argues that the Commission erred in finding that the Temoak band did not properly serve the interests of the Western Shoshone, but rather that the U.S. courts fully examined this question and properly concluded that the Temoak Band was the proper representative of the Western Shoshone and that they had fully litigated their claim.

157. Another factual error that the United States alleges on the part of the Commission is the finding that the Danns were not fully apprised of the litigation strategy that had been

employed by the organized entity of the Western Shoshone group. The State points in this regard to a finding by the U.S. Court of Claims that the Danns were for a very long time quite aware of the position with respect to the Nevada land taken before the Indian Claims Commission by the Temoak Band and its counsel. The State also points to findings in the same U.S. Court of Claims decision that the attorney for the Temoak Band reported that Western Shoshone General Council meetings occurred in 1947, three years before the ICC action was filed, in 1959, three years before the ICC issued its extinguishment finding, and in 1965, five years before the ICC issued its decision awarding $26,154,600 to the Western Shoshone, and therefore that the Commission erred in finding that there was no evidence on the record that appropriate consultations were held within the Western Shoshone at the time that certain significant determinations were made.

158. Further, the State disputes the Commission's finding that the U.S. courts did not take the measures necessary to address the substance of the Danns' request for intervention but dismissed them based upon the expediency of the ICC proceedings. The State relies in this regard upon the U.S. Court of Claims' denial of the intervention based upon the "unjustified tardiness of the request for intervention," which occurred 23 years after the litigation was initiated. The State therefore contends that in light of the Court of Claims' determination that no adequate excuse was offered for the long delay, and the fact that any other litigant in U.S. federal courts would be subject to equivalent procedural requirements concerning timeliness, neither the United States Courts procedural ruling nor the preclusive effect of that Congress has assigned to the judgment of the Indian Claims Commission offends due process. The State therefore maintains that the processes employed in the Western Shoshone Indian Claims Commission litigation did provide due process guarantees required by the U.S. Constitution and reflected in the American Declaration, and indeed afforded them an even greater opportunity to press their claims than would be available to a non-Indian seeking compensation for the taking of their land, as the Commission in part recognized.

159. In its response to the Commissions' report, the United States also contended that the processes established under the Indian Claims Act of 1946 did not violate contemporary norms of international law. The State first argues that the Commission lacked jurisdiction over events that resulted solely from the passage of the Indian Claims Commission Act, since that statute only extended jurisdiction to the Indian Claims Commission for claims arising from the taking of aboriginal lands prior to August 13, 1946, while the United States did not ratify the OAS Charter until after the Indian Claims Commission Act was signed into law on August 13, 1946.

160. The State further complains that the evaluation of the processes established under the 1946 Indian Claims Commission Act in light of contemporary international norms is an impermissible inter-temporal application of law, according to which the State claims that "it is not permissible to import into the legal evaluation of a previously existing situation, or of an old treaty, doctrines of modern law that did not exist and were not accepted at the time, and only resulted from the subsequent development or evolution of international law." In the State's view, the Commission has violated the principle of inter-temporal law because the Indian Claims Proceedings concerning the Western Shoshone were completed in 1977 and the Indian Claims Commission itself was dissolved on September 30, 1978.

161. The State's second objection to the Commission's legal approach challenges the Commission's conclusion that aspects of Article XVIII of the OAS draft Declaration on the Rights of Indigenous Peoples reflect general international legal principles developing out of and applicable inside and outside of the inter-American system and could therefore be relied upon in interpreting and applying the provisions of the American Declaration in the context of indigenous peoples. In support of its position that Article XVIII of the

draft declaration does not reflect general international legal principles, the State cites the 1999 advice of the Inter-American Juridical Committee that "[i]nternational law does not recognize the indigenous person's right of ownership and use of lands as defined in this article," and objects that the Commission makes no effort to reconcile its position with that of the Inter-American Juridical Committee.

162.   The State also relies upon its own previously-expressed view, and that of other OAS member states, that draft Article XVIII does not reflect general international legal principles. The State therefore rejects what it characterizes as the application of substantive norms that may or may not emerge in a non-binding document that has not yet been agreed to by member states of the OAS to processes established by the United States in 1946. The State adds that it is not relevant to analyze whether the United States violated general norms of international law since the Commission is not an international tribunal, and further objects that treaties cited by the Commission, including the International Covenant on Civil and Political Rights and the Convention on the Elimination of Racial Discrimination, are not binding upon the United States to the disputed situation since they were ratified long after the litigation in question was completed.

163.   The Commission has the following brief observations in respect of the State's objections to the conclusions and recommendations in the Commission's preliminary merits report in this matter. Beginning with the State's final objection relating to the legal status of the American Declaration, the State claims that the Commission erred in finding that the United States has violated provisions of the American Declaration because the Commission's competence, as defined through the 1967 amendment of the OAS Charter and the 1979 Statute of the Inter-American Commission approved by OAS Resolution No. 447, October 1979, "does not turn a non-binding document such as the American Declaration into a treaty that can be considered to be legally binding upon the United States." The State's observations fail to consider, however, the well-established and long-standing jurisprudence and practice of the inter-American system according to which the American Declaration is recognized as constituting a source of legal obligation for OAS members states, including in particular those states that are not parties to the American Convention on Human Rights. These obligations are considered to flow from the human rights obligations of member states under the OAS Charter, which member states have agreed are contained in and defined by the American Declaration, as well as from the customary legal status of the rights protected under many of the Declaration's core provisions. As a source of legal obligation, therefore, it is appropriate for the Commission to consider and, where substantiated, find violations of that instrument attributable to a member state of the OAS, including the United States.

164.   The Commission also observes that many of the State's objections relate to the extent to which and manner in which the Commission evaluated issues, facts and evidence that, according to the State, had already been the subject of consideration and determination by the domestic courts. What the State must recognize in this connection, however, is that the Commission has an independent obligation to evaluate the facts and circumstances of a complaint as elucidated by the parties in light of the principles and standards under the American Declaration. This includes such matters as the adequacy of the procedures through which the petitioners' property interests in the Western Shoshone ancestral land were purported to be determined. While proceedings or determinations at the domestic level on similar issues can be considered by the Commission as part of the circumstances of a complaint, they are not determinative of the Commission's own evaluation of the facts and issues in a petition before it. This is particularly significant in cases such as the present, where neither the courts [nor] the state itself regarded the matters raised in the case as human rights issues, but rather as questions regarding land title and land use. The Commission hastens to add in this connection that, contrary to what the State appears

to contend in its response, the domestic courts did not reach consistent or clear decisions on certain central aspects of the petitioners' complaints relating to the Western Shoshone ancestral land, including particularly the question of whether the alleged extinguishment of indigenous title in the land had ever been litigated before domestic authorities as well as whether the Danns' due process rights were properly respected in the domestic process. It was therefore not only appropriate, but crucial, for the Commission to reach conclusions on these matters, in light of the significant implications of this aspect of the circumstances of the complaint upon the State's obligations under Articles II, XVIII and XXIII of the American Declaration in connection with indigenous property interests.

165. Specifically with regard to the adequacy of the Danns' participation in the process by which title to the Western Shoshone ancestral lands was purported to be determined, the Commission considers it important to emphasize, as it noted in its decision on the merits, that the collective interests of indigenous peoples in their ancestral lands is not to be asserted to the exclusion of the participation of individual members in the process. To the contrary, the Commission has found that any determination of the extent to which indigenous peoples may maintain interests in the lands to which they have traditionally held title and have occupied and used must be based upon a process of fully informed and mutual consent on the part of the indigenous community as a whole. And as the Commission concluded on the circumstances of this case, the process by which the property interests of the Western Shoshone were determined proved defective in this respect. That only proof of fraud or collusion could impugn the Temoak Band's presumed representation of the entire Western Shoshone people, and that Western Shoshone General Council meetings occurred on only three occasions during the 18 year period between 1947 and 1965, fails to discharge the State's obligation to demonstrate that the outcome of the ICC process resulted from the fully informed and mutual consent of the Western Shoshone people as a whole.

166. The State's objections to the Commission's competence, relating both to the fourth instance formula and its jurisdiction *ratione temporis* concerning the 1946 Indian Claims Commission Act, were not raised by the State before or in response to the Commission's admissibility report, in which the Commission concluded that it had competence to consider the Petitioners' complaints, and the Petitioners have had no notice of or opportunity to respond to these new allegations. Consequently, it is not open to the State to raise these objections at this stage of the process. In any event, the Commission considers that the fourth instance formula has no application in this case. According to the fourth instance formula, the Commission in principle will not review the judgments issued by the domestic courts acting within their competence and with due judicial guarantees. The fourth instance formula does not, however, preclude the Commission from considering a case where the Petitioner's allegations entail a possible violation of any of the rights set forth in instruments of the inter-American human rights system. In the present case, the Petitioners have alleged, and the Commission in fact found, discrete violations of the principles and standards under the American Declaration of the Rights and Duties of Man based upon its evaluation of the facts and evidence as presented by the parties in the proceeding before it, and therefore the fourth instance formula does not apply. Moreover, the notion that the Commission is precluded from addressing an issue merely because the domestic courts of a member state may have addressed the same matter is plainly inconsistent with the exhaustion of domestic remedies requirement and must be rejected on this ground as well. Concerning the fact that the Indian Claims Commission Act was promulgated in 1946, it is well established that a state remains responsible for any violations of a human rights instrument that pre-dated its ratification or accession to the instrument, to the extent that those violations continue to have effects or are not manifested until after the date of ratification. In the present case,

the facts as determined by the Commission clearly indicate that the Indian Claims Commission Act applied to and had effects upon the Petitioners well after the United States' ratification of the OAS Charter in 1951, and indeed continue to do so, and consequently the State properly remains responsible for the effects of the application of that legislation upon the petitioners to the extent they are inconsistent with the petitioners' rights under the American Declaration.

167. As for the alleged impermissible inter-temporal application of law, the State's submissions in this regard rely upon the mistaken premise that the Commission is addressing a "previously existing situation" in evaluating the Danns' complaint. While it may be the case that the ICC process itself took place more than 30 years ago, the Petitioners' complaints concerning indigenous title to the property, including alleged improprieties in the ICC process, remained the subject of controversy and continued to effect the Petitioners' interests at the time their petition was lodged and continue to do so. Moreover, the American Declaration, as an embodiment of existing and evolving human rights obligations of member states under the OAS Charter, is not to be interpreted and applied as the law that existed at the time of the Declaration's adoption but rather in light of ongoing developments in the rights protected under those instruments. Consequently, it is appropriate to evaluate the Petitioners' complaints in light of developments in the corpus of international human rights law more broadly since the American Declaration was first composed. To the extent that the Danns remain the victims of an on-going violation of their rights under Articles II and XXIII of the Declaration, then, the State is obliged to resolve the situation in light of its contemporary obligations under international human rights law and not those applicable at the time when the ICC process took place, to the extent that the law may have evolved.

168. The State's criticisms of the Commission's reference to the draft Inter-American Declaration on the Rights of Indigenous Peoples and of contemporary international human rights standards to the Danns' situation, like its objections to the Commission's jurisdiction, are untimely and not properly the subject of argument at this stage of the process, particularly since the basis of these objections were clearly in issue during the processing of the complaint before the Commission. As the Commission observed in its preliminary merits report, however, the provisions of the draft Indigenous Declaration are properly considered in interpreting and applying the provisions of the American Declaration in the context of indigenous peoples to the extent that the basic principles reflected in provisions of the draft Declaration, including aspects of Article XVIII, reflect general international legal principles developing out of and applicable inside and outside of the inter-American system.

169. Based upon the State's response, the Commission must conclude that no measures have been taken to comply with the Commission's recommendations. On this basis, and having considered the State's observations, the Commission has decided to ratify its conclusions and reiterate its recommendations, as set forth below.

VII. RECOMMENDATIONS

. . .

1. Provide Mary and Carrie Dann with an effective remedy, which includes adopting the legislative or other measures necessary to ensure respect for the Danns' right to property in accordance with Articles II, XVIII and XXIII of the American Declaration in connection with their claims to property rights in the Western Shoshone ancestral lands.

2. Review its laws, procedures and practices to ensure that the property rights of indigenous persons are determined in accordance with the rights established in the American Declaration, including Articles II, XVIII and XXIII of the Declaration.

Questions and Discussion

1. The Commission does not discuss the issue of overgrazing on marginal Western lands and the impact this has on the environment. Should the United States have raised the issue? Should that have an impact on the outcome of the case? How do you balance indigenous cultural and resource rights with environmental protection if they come into conflict?

2. Indigenous religious rites and/or rights have also given rise to litigation when they involve the use of endangered species, such as eagle feathers. After the courts proved unreceptive to claimed exceptions to the application of the Endangered Species Act, Congress enacted the American Indian Religious Freedom Act, 42 U.S.C. § 1996, "to protect and preserve for American Indians their inherent right of freedom to believe, express, and exercise the traditional religions of the American Indian, Eskimo, Aleut, and Native Hawaiians, including but not limited to access to sites, use and possession of sacred objects, and the freedom to worship through ceremonials and traditional rites." Section 2 provided that the president direct the various federal departments, agencies, and other instrumentalities responsible for administering relevant laws to evaluate their policies and procedures in consultation with native traditional religious leaders to determine changes necessary to preserve Native American religious cultural rights and practices. In 1997, the secretaries of the interior and commerce issued Secretarial Order No. 3206 pursuant to the Endangered Species Act of 1973, 16 U.S.C. 1531. It said the following about accommodating Native American religious practices:

    > Principle 4. THE DEPARTMENTS SHALL BE SENSITIVE TO INDIAN CULTURE, RELIGION AND SPIRITUALITY.
    >
    > The Departments shall take into consideration the impacts of their actions and policies under the Act on Indian use of listed species for cultural and religious purposes. The Departments shall avoid or minimize, to the extent practicable, adverse effects upon the noncommercial use of listed sacred plants and animals in medicinal treatments and in the expression of cultural and religious beliefs by Indian tribes. When appropriate, the Departments may issue guidelines to accommodate Indian access to, and traditional uses of, listed species, and to address unique circumstances that may exist when administering the Act.
    >
    > Principle 5. THE DEPARTMENTS SHALL MAKE AVAILABLE TO INDIAN TRIBES INFORMA-
    > TION RELATED TO TRIBAL TRUST RESOURCES AND INDIAN LANDS, AND, TO FACILITATE
    > THE MUTUAL EXCHANGE OF INFORMATION, SHALL STRIVE TO PROTECT SENSITIVE TRIBAL
    > INFORMATION FROM DISCLOSURE.
    >
    > . . .
    >
    > Sec. 8. Special Study on Cultural and Religious Use of Natural Products. The Departments recognize that there remain tribal concerns regarding the access to, and uses of, eagle feathers, animal parts, and other natural products for Indian cultural and religious purposes. Therefore, the Departments shall work together with Indian tribes to develop recommendations to the Secretaries within one year to revise or establish uniform administrative procedures to govern the possession, distribution, and transportation of such natural products that are under federal jurisdiction or control.

3. The Supreme Court decisions on point established a five-prong test that needed to be satisfied before conservation measures could be applied to restrict Native American treaty hunting and fishing rights. The test was adopted as federal policy for applying incidental take

restrictions under the Endangered Species Act. The Secretarial Order restated this federal enforcement policy as applied to incidental take of listed species. Presumptively favoring Native American use while asserting that the Endangered Species Act applies to everyone, the policy requires an analysis and determination that all the following standards have been met: (1) the restriction is reasonable and necessary for conservation of the species at issue; (2) the conservation purpose of the restriction cannot be achieved by reasonable regulation of non-Indian activities; (3) the measure is the least restrictive alternative available to achieve the required conservation purpose; (4) the restriction does not discriminate against Indian activities, either as stated or applied; and (5) voluntary tribal measures are not adequate to achieve the necessary conservation purpose. Therefore, conservation restrictions may be imposed on Indian tribes only when all five standards have been met. Is this a reasonable accommodation?

4.   Native Alaskans were not included in Secretarial Order No. 3206 because of concerns about their subsistence hunting of whales. Note that, under the International Convention for the Regulation of Whaling (1946), to which the United States is a party, the International Whaling Commission has granted an exemption from the general prohibition on whale hunting for the purpose of enabling harvests in perpetuity appropriate to the cultural and nutritional requirements of aboriginal subsistence. The exemption applies to indigenous groups in Denmark, Russia, St. Vincent and the Grenadines, and the United States.

C. *Botswana*

As noted earlier, several African countries asked for last minute changes in the draft U.N. Declaration on the Rights of Indigenous Peoples, in part reflecting concern about litigation from some of their own peoples. A few states, such as Namibia and Botswana, are inhabited by the San, or Bushmen, as they were formerly known. This group is among the oldest cultures on the earth and has lived in the area around the Kalahari Desert far longer than tribal groups that arrived at a later time, though still before European colonial regimes came to power. Legal conflicts over land and resources in sub-Saharan Africa today often center on access of local groups to the resources of nature preserves and parks that are valuable governmental assets for tourism, as well as necessary to protect endangered species and their habitats. The following case was decided shortly before the adoption of the U.N. Declaration on the Rights of Indigenous Peoples and exemplifies what some consider a potential conflict between environmental protection and human rights.

Sesana and Others v. Attorney General, High Court,
Misc. No 52 of 2002; ILDC 665
(BW 2006), Judgment of Dec. 13, 2006

[The San in this case contested efforts to remove and exclude them from the Central Kgalagadi Game Reserve (CKGR), a protected area created in 1961 during the British colonial administration. The CKGR is a unique wilderness exceeding 52,000 square kilometers. At the time of its creation, the CKGR was the largest game reserve in Africa. It is now the third largest in Africa and the largest game reserve in Botswana. The CKGR originally had a double purpose, to conserve nature and to carve out a large portion of the inner part of the Kgalagadi desert, where Basarwa and some Bakgalagadi were resident, so that the communities could continue to follow their traditional hunting and gathering way of life. At the time of the creation of the reserve, however, because of apartheid South Africa, it was considered politically unacceptable to create a human reserve, so a deliberate decision was made to create a game reserve without reference to the San. It has a harsh climate, with limited and unreliable rainfall, but still home to a significant population of wildlife, as well as some of the few remaining descendants of hunting and gathering peoples in the world. The judges issued three separate opinions, but agreed on the conclusions respecting most of the issues raised, as indicated in the Order that begins the case-*Eds.*]

M. Dibotelo, J.:

. . .

55. [I]n view of the decisions reached by each of us, the court makes the following Order:

1. The termination in 2002 by the Government of the provision of basic and essential services to the Applicants in the Central Kgalagadi Game Reserve (CKGR) was neither unlawful nor unconstitutional. (Dow J dissenting).

2. The Government is not obliged to restore the provision of such services to the Applicants in the CKGR. (Dow J dissenting)

3. Prior to 31 Jan 2002, the Applicants were in possession of the land, which they lawfully occupied in their settlements in the CKGR. (unanimous decision)

4. The Applicants were deprived of such possession by the Government forcibly or wrongly and without their consent. (Dibotelo J dissenting)

5. The Government refusal to issue special game licenses to the Appellants is unlawful (unanimous decision)

6. The Government refusal to issue special game licenses to the Applicants is unconstitutional (Dibotelo dissenting)

7. The Government refusal to allow the Applicants to enter the CKGR unless they are issued with permits is unlawful and unconstitutional. (Dibotelo dissenting)

8. Each party shall pay their own costs. (Dow dissenting).

Dow J.:

. . .

H. Conclusions on the Issues

H. 1. Introduction:

5. First, I take the position that the fact the Applicants belong to a class of peoples that have now come to be recognized as "indigenous peoples" is of relevance and more particularly, I find relevant that:

a. Botswana has been a party to The Convention of the Elimination of All Forms of Racial Discrimination since 1974. The Race Committee[89] adopted Recommendation XXIII, which requires of state parties to: "ensure that members of indigenous peoples have equal rights in respect of effective participation in public life and that no decisions directly relating to their rights and interests are taken without their informed consent."

b. The current wisdom, which should inform all policy and direction in dealing with indigenous peoples is the recognition of their special relationship to their land. Jose R. Martinez Cobo,[90] states:

---

[89] Committee on the Elimination of All Forms of Racial Discrimination, General Comment XXIII, U.N. Doc A/52/18, Annex V, at para. 4(d).

[90] The Study of the Problem of Discrimination Against Indigenous Populations, Vol. V, No. E.86.XIV.3 (U.N. publication).

> It is essential to know and understand the deeply spiritual relationship between indigenous peoples and their land as basic to their existence as such and to all their beliefs, customs, traditions and culture.

> For such peoples the land is not merely a possession and a means of production. The entire relationship between the spiritual life of indigenous peoples and Mother Earth, and their land, has a great many deep-seated implications. Their land is not a commodity which can be acquired, but a material element to be enjoyed freely.

Paras. 196 and 197.

. . .

H.5. The Issue:

Whether the Applicants were in lawful possession of the land they occupied in the CKGR.

H.6. Reasoning:

. . .

10. It is reasonable to conclude that one could only claim hunting rights in the CKGR if one could claim right of residence. Such right can only flow from one either having been born in the Reserve or having been born to persons who themselves could claim residence there.

11. The right of the residents of the CKGR to reside therein without the requirement of a permit and the right of the Government to exclude others, if such exclusion is necessary for their protection, was at the time of the creation of the Reserve, contained in the legislation or the interpretation of the legislation that created the Reserve.

12. At independence, this special right of residence in the Reserve and the right to exclude others if need be, found its way into the Constitution after much debate by the Colonial Government about the matter.

13. The Constitution provides as follows at Section 14(1) and 14(3)(c):

> No person shall be deprived of his freedom of movement, and for the purpose of this section the said freedom means the right to move freely throughout Botswana, the right to reside in any part of Botswana, the right to enter Botswana and immunity from expulsion from Botswana. . . .

> Nothing contained in or done under the authority of any law shall be held to be [in]consistent with or in contravention of this section to the extent that the law in question makes provision –

> for the imposition of restrictions on the entry into or residence within defined areas of Botswana of persons who are not Bushmen to the extent that such restrictions are reasonably required for the protection or well being of Bushmen.

14. Section 14(3)(c) is a derogation clause, in that it curtails or sets limits to the right to freedom of movement granted under Section 14(1).

. . .

17. Section 14(c) allows for unequal protection of the law or discrimination, in that it allows the Respondent to exclude non-Bushmen from defined areas, if such exclusion can be justified on the grounds of the protection of the well being of Bushmen.

18. Under the operation of Sections 14(3)(c) and Section 15(7) therefore, the Respondent had full authority to regulate the entry into the Reserve of persons who were not Bushmen, if such regulation, could be justified on the basis that it was for the latter's protection.

19. The CKGR is a "defined area" within the meaning of Section 14(3)(c) and I so hold for the reason that there cannot be any doubt that that portion of the Constitution was informed by the concerns about the future of the Bushman then resident in the CKGR at the time leading up to independence.

20. The Constitution could hardly protect that which was unlawful to begin with, thus residence by the Bushmen in the Reserve was lawful as at the time of the adoption of the independence Constitution and nothing since has been done, either by way of policy or legislation, to change that.

21. In fact, quite to the contrary, the Respondent has over the years adopted policies, regulations and practices and promulgated laws, that have supported human residence in the Reserve.

22. The residents whose residence in the Reserve the Respondent has supported and facilitated through policies, laws and practices are the "Bushmen" who in 1961 were to be protected by the creation of the Reserve and their descendants and such residents and their descendants, as were, either by marriage or other social ties, ordinarily resident in the Reserve at the time of the 2002 relocations. The Applicants fall within this category.

23. The provision of services to residents in the Reserve, without questioning their right to reside there is an act that supports the proposition that the Respondent accepts the lawfulness of the Applicants' residence in the CKGR.

24. The policy of not seeking to regulate the entry and exit of the residents of the Reserve through the issuance of permits is yet another indicator that Respondent did not, at least until 2002, question the lawfulness of the residence of the Applicants in the Reserve

25. Section 45(1) of the Wildlife Conservation and National Parks (Regulations) recognizes that there were residents with the CKGR at the time of its establishment and gives those residents and as well as persons who "can rightly lay claim to hunting rights" in the Reserve, an opportunity to hunt therein. Parliament would hardly facilitate that which is unlawful.

26. Section 18(1) of the Wildlife Conservation and National Parks Act (Regulations) provide for the creation of Community Use Zones within national parks and game reserves of for the benefit of communities living in or immediately adjacent to such parks or game reserves.

. . .

28. The intent and purpose of the provisions above was to recognize rights of residence and hunting that existed prior to the establishment of the CKGR and to facilitate continued enjoyment of those rights.

29. It has been said that the CKGR is State land and so it is. So are Gaborone Township, Lobatse Township and other areas not falling within tribal territories. That fact alone does not make residence therein unlawful. Residence within Gaborone Township is guided by land use policies, regulations and laws, just as residence in the CKGR is. But there is one difference, residence in the CKGR of Bushmen, is specially protected, in that others may be excluded.

30. The CKGR is a piece of State land with two primary uses that pre-dates 1966, the year of Botswana's independence. The uses are game conservation and residence by a specified community of people.

31. The Respondent has long recognized this dual use of the land, and that explains the policies, laws and practices if has adopted over the years.

32. At no point during the discussions about relocations has the Respondent suggested that residence within the Reserve was in any way unlawful.

33. It has been said that human residence within the Reserve is inconsistent with the Respondent's policy of total preservation of wildlife. That may be so, and in that case, the Respondent has adopted a policy that cannot be realized. Alternatively, the Respondent policy must be read as an ideal with certain acknowledged limitations, one of them being the reality of human residence within the Reserve. After all, the policy came after the people.

H.7. Decision:

The Applicants were in lawful possession of the land they occupied in their settlements.

H.8. The Issue:

Whether the Applicants were deprived of such possession by the Government forcibly or wrongly and without their consent

. . .

H.9.3. The Relevance of the Relative Powerlessness of the Applicants to the issue of Consent:

1. In view of the position of the Applicant, in terms of their ethnicity, their literacy levels and political and economic clout, to obtain true consent to relocate, that is, to be sure that it had "persuaded but not forced" anyone to relocate, common sense dictated that the Respondent acknowledged and addressed the relative powerlessness of the Applicants.

2. The Basarwa and to some extent the Bakgalagadi, belong to an ethnic group that is not socially and politically organised in the same manner as the majority of other Tswana speaking ethnic groups and the importance of this is that programmes and projects that have worked with other groups in the country will not necessarily work when simply cut and pasted to the Applicants' situation. A model of consultations that assumed that the calling of a "kgotla" meeting as one would in a Tswana village was sufficient consultation may not necessarily have been the best. This is not to hold as a matter of fact that the "kgotla" meeting model was not proper consultation in all instances, but it is certainly a questioning of that process. What, for example, constitutes a "kgotla" meeting in a settlement like Gope, where there was no chief, or in Kikao, where the entire settlement is basically one family or in Gugamma where the headman was away sick in Salajwe?

3. The Applicants belong to an ethnic group that has been historically looked down-upon, often considered to be no more than cheap, disposable labour, by almost all other numerically superior ethnic groups in Botswana. Until recently, perhaps it is still the case, "Mosarwa," "Lesarwa," "Lekgalagadi," and "Mokgalagadi" were common terms of insult, in the same way as "Nigger" and "Kaffir" were/are. Any adult Motswana who pretends otherwise is being dishonest in the extreme. The relevance of this fact is that those Applicants who had been politicised through their involvement with FPK, Ditshwanelo and the Negotiating Team were bound to see any action that smelled of a top-down approach as yet another act of disrespect by the initiators of the action. On the other hand, the average non-politicised Applicant, illiterate, dependant upon Government services, without political representation at the high political level, was hardly in a position to give genuine consent. It was the Respondent's obligation to put in place mechanisms that promoted

and facilitated true and genuine consent by individuals, families and communities. Groups like Ditshwanelo or the Negotiating Team could have been invited to ensure some levelling out of the negotiation playing field.

4. The Respondent has charged that Roy Sesana and "his international friends"... who will not leave "us" alone, are really the cause of the problems. The Applicants wanted to move, the Respondent says, but FPK, The Negotiating Team and Survival International have intimidated them into not relocating. Here is an African Government – is the essence of the complaint – that has the best interests of its citizens at heart, that has built clinics and schools, has sunk boreholes to ensure clean portable water, has granted title to land and granted choices of cattle or goats. It has plans to facilitate and promote private enterprise within the re-settlement villages, and a bunch of latter-day-colonialists are scuttling all that, with their talk of indigenousness, culture and land rights. What is a Government to do?

5. How can one not sympathise with the Respondent on this point, it might be asked? After all;

6. Slavery carted black people across the seas and the ripples are still felt today.

7. Colonialism carved up Africa, including the CKGR, for European benefit. In the case of Botswana, when it officially ended, the country was one of the poorest five in the world and boasted the legendary 12 miles of tar road, in a country the size of France.

8. Apartheid's wounds are still oozing, not quite healed. And Apartheid was thriving and well and the colonial government was managing Botswana from its bosom, when it was deciding whether or not to carve out a piece of land for residence of Basarwa and what to call it once it had been carved out.

9. When the Respondent's own advisers (The Mission Report) suggested the partitioning of the CKGR into two, keeping one part for the residents another part for wildlife, the views of the European Union were relevant to the rejection of that proposition. The European Union had money to offer and the African government had designs on that money, so that plan, not to say it was a good plan, never saw the light of day. And donor money often comes with consultants to offer advice and counsel, and the case of Phillip Marshall, the author of the early versions of the CKGR Management Plans, is a case in point.

10. Since the relocations started in 1996, the Respondent has had to assure diplomats of one Western country or another that it will do that and it will not do that as regards the future of the CKGR and its residents.

11. Then, an act that has irked the Respondent enough to find mention in various of its affidavits and witness summaries; Survival International threw its weight behind, the Respondent will say, in front of, the Applicants. Yet another Western player, insinuating itself between a people and their Government, the Respondent says.

12. Then, a British lawyer, a thing that has irritated Mr. Pilane, flew from England to represent the Applicants. Will it ever stop; you can almost hear the cry, this continued and continuous interference from the West? What is a Government to do?

13. The case being judged, though is not whether slavery was brutish, which it was, or whether colonialism was a system fuelled by a racist and arrogant ideology, which [it] was or whether apartheid was diabolical, which it was. It is not even about how high the Botswana Government should jump when a Western diplomat challenges or questions its decision. I think it is only fair to observe that African governments will continue to do quite a bit of jumping as long the global economic and political arrangements remain the way they are. But that is not the case before us.

. . .

16. What is a Government to do? The Government can be as irritated and/or annoyed as it wants to be at what it considers outside interference in its affairs, but it cannot, it should not, in response to such irritations disadvantage its own people. More than anything else, a Government that hears sounds of discontent is obligated to pause and listen and ask itself why it is that a course of action it thought reasonable and rational is attracting dissent and disquiet.

17. Even assuming that it had believed that the Applicants were keen to relocate, once there appeared to be some resistance, once the FPK, The Negotiating Team and Ditshwanelo started to seek a revision of the relocation decision, once the lawyers were instructed and litigation was threatened, the Respondent was obligated to pause and listen.

18. After all, the Respondent's interest must ultimately be the welfare of its people, and its people include the Applicants. The decision to terminate the services, to relocate the Applicants, to terminate the issuance of special game licences, to refuse the Applicants re-entry into the reserve, are ultimately resource management and allocation and welfare promotion decisions.

19. Such decisions require a balancing of rights, a consideration of who benefits and who is adversely affected when one path or other is followed. Such a balancing exercise would have necessarily involved a comparative analysis of the expected losses and the benefits to the Applicants, as well as the expected losses and the benefits to the nation, of relocations.

. . .

26. It is not difficult to see how, at a personal level, an individual might well have decided that it was better to be poor at home, than to be poor in a new and unfamiliar place.

27. It is not hard to see how a person from Kikao, might have been less enthusiastic about moving to New Xade, than a person from Old Xade. After all in 1985, the dry season population of Kikao was 4 people and that of Old Xade was 860. In 2001, the population of Kikao was 31 and that of New Xade, all of Old Xade having been relocated, was 1094.

28. This is not to say that the Respondent did not have the interests of the Applicants at heart, but it is to say that they ought to have listened more carefully at what motivated or was likely to motivate the Applicants' decisions and choices.

. . .

31. Operating under the [belief] that relocation to centres offering "secure" land tenure, the opportunity to rear cattle, better healthcare, educational and other facilities has to be something everyone wants, the Respondent was unable to appreciate the reasons behind the persistent resistance to relocate and finally explained it away as the result of bad advice by busybodies meddling in matters that did not affect them.

. . .

33. Respondent might want to pause and consider whether the disappearance of a people and their culture isn't too high a price to pay for the gain of offering those people services at a centralised location. It might want to consider, whether with Botswana's relatively small population of 1.6 [million] people, regard being had to its land size and its relative wealth, cannot, faced with a unique culture on the verge of extinction as it is, afford to be innovative in its development programmes. The failure of economic projects at Kaudwane and New Xade may well have something to do with the culture and pattern of life of those who relocated there. Perhaps they do not even like tomatoes and in that case, no matter how much money is poured into the horticulture projects, the projects will not thrive. Perhaps never having reared cattle in the Reserve, being given five cattle to take care of is more of a challenge than a benefit. Perhaps the community that made

up Kikao would have been persuaded to move to a game ranch of its own, than to growing tomatoes in Kaudwane. And this is not a fanciful idea; the Respondent current policies actually have programmes and projects that allow for individuals to own large tracts of land for game and/or cattle farming. This is not to make definitive findings on these point, but it is to say that I am not convinced, on the evidence, that the decision to terminate services and relocate the Applicants and what to offer them once they has been relocated, took into consideration such relevant considerations as the potential disruptions to their culture and the threat to their very survival as a people. I note the Respondent's position that it does not discriminate on ethic lines, but equal treatment of un-equals can amount to discrimination.

34. The Respondent allowed its annoyance with the involvement of groups who were themselves not residents of the CKGR, especially the involvement of Survival International, to influence its dealings with the Applicants and ultimately the Respondent changed course too swiftly and without allowing the Applicants an opportunity to be heard on the matter.

. . .

H.9.7. The Relevance of the Termination of the Issuance of Special Game Licenses (SGLs) to Consent:

1. On the 17th January 2002, the Respondent, through the office of the [Department of Wildlife and National Parks (DWNP)], issued a blanket instruction to the effect that no more SGLs would be issued and further that existing ones would be withdrawn. The instruction was based on the reasoning that "In view of the recent Government decision to terminate services to the residents of the . . . Reserve . . . the Department is obliged to conform. The Department has considered the services it offers in the . . . Reserve and it has decided to cease issuance of Special Game Licences to people residing inside the Reserve."

2. The motivation could not have been cost, since the Director of DWNP has not remotely suggested that cost was a motivator.

3. The motivation could not have been conservation of wildlife, since the Director did not avert his mind to that issue before terminating the issuance of the licences and withdrawing already issued licences.

4. The motivation could not have been disease control, since that issue does not seem to have exercised the Director's mind until he came to give evidence in this case. Dr. Alexander's views of disease transmission from domestic animals to wild animals and vice-versa were not sought during the many months that the DWNP was developing a plan to manage the Reserve.

5. The motivation could not have been anything that the Applicants had done; for the Director would then have dealt with individual offenders.

. . .

7. The plan, therefore, was that by the end of 31st January 2002, there would be no water, no food, and no hunting, within the Reserve. Life would simply be very hard, if not outright impossible.

. . .

H.10. Decision:

Those Applicants who relocated in 2002, whether they had registered to relocate or relocated with their families were deprived of possession of the settlements they lawfully occupied by the Government forcibly, wrongly and without their consent.

. . .

H.17. The Issue:

Whether the Government refusal to issue special game licenses to the Applicants is unlawful and unconstitutional:

H.18. Reasoning:

1. The powers of the Director of DWNP to issue SGLs was in terms of Sections 26 and 30 of the Wildlife Conservation and National Parks (The Act) and Section 45 (1) of the National Parks and Game Reserves Regulations of 2000 (The Regulations) and Section 9 of the Wildlife Conservation (Hunting and Licensing) Regulations (The Hunting Regulations) and the Director was obligated to exercise the powers granted to him reasonably, rationally and fairly.

2. In terms of the Act, and The Hunting Regulations, persons who were entitled to be issued with SGLs were persons who were "principally dependent on hunting and gathering veld produce for their food." (Section 30 (1)).

3. In terms of Regulations, persons who were resident within the CKGR at the time of its establishment or those who could lay claim to hunting rights in the CKGR could be permitted to hunt therein.

4. Prior to the 2002 relocations, the Respondent had determined that the Applicants fell within one or more of the above categories and had issued them with SGLs. The licence purports to have been issued in terms of Section 30, thus bringing Segootsane, for example, within the category of persons "principally dependent on hunting and gathering" for food.

5. The Director's decisions not to issue special game licences, as well as to render invalid those already issued, was not based on the need to conserve or to protect wildlife, but rather on the view by the then Director of DWNP that a special game licence[] was a service subject to withdrawal in terms of the Respondent's decision to withdraw services to the residents of the CKGR.

6. The Director should have been guided by the provisions of the Act and the Regulations, as opposed to what he heard over the radio, on how to exercise powers granted to him under the said Act and Regulations.

7. The Act and the Regulations contemplate a situation where the Director would evaluate, on a case-by-case basis, whether an individual or a household, fell within the category of persons described by the said Act and/or the Regulations and the Director failed to do that.

8. The Director thus acted outside the powers granted to him by law or at the very least failed to act as the law directed him to act.

9. In any event, the DWNP had no power to withdraw already issued licenses; such an act would constitute a wrongful deprivation of a right to property without an opportunity to be heard.

10. An existing SLG conferred a right and the taking away of that right without an opportunity to be heard was unlawful.

H.19. Conclusion:

The Respondent refusal to issue special game licenses to the Applicants unlawful and unconstitutional.

H.20. The Issue:

Whether the Government refusal to allow the Appellants to enter the CKGR unless they are issued with a permit is unlawful and unconstitutional.

H.21. The Reasoning:

1. The Respondent position seems to be that only those who did not relocate and it says there are 17 of them, may remain in, and if they leave, re-enter the Reserve without permits and that all others, are caught by Section 49 of the National Parks and Game Reserves Regulations, 2000 (The Regulations). This group would include every one who vacated the Reserve during the 2002 relocations, whether they "registered" to relocate or not. For those who "relocated" it appears that their right to return to the Reserve without a permit depends on whether they have been "compensated." This policy is contained in the 30th October 2002 Presidential Directive which states on this point, "All those people who have relocated and were compensated should not be allowed to resettle in the CKGR." . . .

. . .

5. The Respondent's policy though is far from clear. On the very same matter, the Respondent has advanced the position that; "There are however, a few who have returned to the game reserve with their new livestock. . . . Their decision to resettle in the game reserve has placed them in breach of the agreement that they voluntarily entered into with the Government to relocate outside the game reserve. However, in line with its declared policy of persuasion, the Government of Botswana has not done anything to force these people to leave the reserve."

6. The question becomes; is the Respondent policy to persuade or to prosecute? It can hardly be both.

7. Since it is Respondent's position that those who never relocated, and by this it is meant those who were not transported by the Respondent out of the Reserve during the 2002 relocations, can remain, exit and re-enter without permits, it must be the Respondent's position that it was their act of relocating, and perhaps coupled with the acceptance of compensation, that extinguished their rights to re-enter without permits. It must then, also be the Respondent's case that, prior to the relocations, the Applicants had a right to live in the Reserve.

8. Whatever the Respondent says is the basis of the continuing right of those Applicants who did not relocate and the right, prior to relocation, of those who did, to reside in the Reserve, there are various problems with the proposition that relocations or relocations coupled with acceptance of compensations, extinguished the right of those who relocated to re-enter the Reserve without permits.

9. The first problem is that for the people who "registered" to relocate, the extinction of their right to relocate must be said to have occurred when they accepted the terms of the relocation. What were those terms? When did the Respondent communicate those terms to the Applicants? [Were] these new terms, applicable only to the 2002 relocations and not to earlier relocations? After all, some people who had relocated before had returned to the Reserve and no demands for permits were made . . . then.

. . .

17. In any event, flowing from the holdings that the Applicants were in lawful occupation of their settlements and that the entire relocation exercise was wrongful, unlawful and without the necessary consent, any rights that were lost as a result thereof were lost wrongfully and unlawfully.

Any attempt to regulate the enjoyment of those rights by permits, when such permits were not, prior to the 2002 relocations, a feature of the enjoyment of such right is an unlawful curtailment of the right of movement of the Applicants. It is unlawful and constitutional.

18. There can not be any doubt that the Respondent, through the DWNP, was always entitled, as part of its management of the Reserve, to monitor and regulate traffic, especially vehicular traffic, into the Reserve. In the case of the Applicants, such monitoring and regulation might well include keeping records of identities and numbers of the residents, the incidence of entry and exit from the Reserve, the nature and impact on the Reserve of the transportation they used for such entry and exit. But such management cannot be used as a means of denying the Applicants to right to reside in the Reserve.

. . .

H.22. Conclusion:

The Respondent's refusal to allow the Appellants to enter the CKGR unless they are issued with a permit is unlawful and unconstitutional.

I. Directions on the Way-Forward

1. In conclusion, it seems to me that this case invites the concluding comments. This Court has been invited to resolve a dispute, which at first blush is about the termination of water and other named services to a few hundred people, who are demanding access to a specified piece of land and the right to hunt in that piece of land. While that is indeed correct, this dispute cannot be resolved, will not be resolved, unless the Respondent acknowledges and addresses its deeper context, its nub, and its heart.

2. This is a case that questions the meaning of "development" and demands of the Respondent to take a closer look at its definition of that notion. One of colonialism's greatest failings was to assume that development was, in the case of Britain, Anglicising, the colonised. All the current talk about African renaissance is really a twisting and turning at the yokes of that ideology. Botswana has a unique opportunity to do things differently.

3. The case is thus, ultimately about a people demanding dignity and respect. It is a people saying in essence, "our way of life may be different but it worthy of respect. We may be changing and getting closer to your way of life, but give us a chance to decide what we want to carry with us into the future." Did any one even think to record settlements on video and/or film, before they disappeared into the grassland? Did any one consider that perhaps a five-year old being relocated may one day wish to know where she/he came from? Or perhaps the Respondent lifestyle was seen as a symbol of poverty that was worth preserving.

4. The Respondent's failure has been in assuming that a cut and paste process, where what has worked in someplace else, and even then taking short cuts at times, would work with the Applicants. When the case started, Mr. Pilane was full of talk about how the services belonged to the Respondent and how the Respondent had a right to do what it wished with them. This prompted some Applicants to say that in that case, the Government could take the services and leave them in their land. That, in my view, is a very unfortunate view of the role of governments. Governments exist for one reason only; to manage the people's resources for the people's benefit, period. They do this guided by policies and laws and they put in place structures and agencies that make this possible. In doing so, they very often have to make very difficult decisions about resource allocations. But the resources do not belong to governments to do what they wish with them. They belong to the people.

5. The world over, non-governmental organisations are increasingly being recognised as legitimate and important actors in civil society. The Applicants have identified Ditshwanelo, FPK and the Negotiating Team as their representatives. The Respondent should see this as offering an opportunity for the promotion of true consultation between the parties, as opposed to a meddling by third parties.

PHUMAPHI J:

72. . . . [I]n this jurisdiction, the Constitution which embodies the fundamental human rights, is the supreme law of the land and all laws and all acts of the State are tested against it. In considering the Mabo case, this Court has to bear in mind the limitations that constrained the High Court of Australia.

73. The Mabo case discusses the notion that, once a country is colonised, all land in the colony belongs to the Crown and prior rights held by indigenous inhabitants are extinguished upon colonisation.

. . .

79. The reasoning of the Australia Court is quite persuasive, but this Court would not readily endorse any action taken by the State to extinguish the "native rights" of citizens, unless it is done in accordance with the Constitution of the Republic of Botswana. I have earlier said the evidence indicates that the Bushmen were in the area now known as the CKGR prior to 1910, when the Ghanzi Crown land which included the CKGR was proclaimed. It therefore follows that they must have claimed "native rights" to land, which has since become the CKGR, as they keep referring to it in their evidence as "their land," like many other inhabitants of the then Bechuanaland, who claimed rights to the land they occupied. The question to be answered is whether such rights were ever extinguished by,

(a) the proclamation of the land they occupied a Crown land or

(b) the declaration of the land they occupied a game reserve.

80. Dealing with the first question, the 1910 Proclamation was silent on rights of the people who occupied the land that was proclaimed Crown land. It does not even allude to their presence on the land. This is hardly surprising in light of what has been discussed above, that the colonial power's modus operandi, was to pretend that the land it grabbed did not belong to anyone, yet, in reality it was inhabited by people who had rights.

81. The rights of the Bushmen in the CKGR were not affected by the proclamation of the land they occupied to be Crown land, as they continued to live on it, and exploit it without interference from the British Government. They continued to hunt and wander about the land, without let or hindrance except, if they moved to Ghanzi farms, where they were considered a nuisance to the white farmers.

82. Not only is the British Government presumed . . . to have respected the "native rights" of the Bushmen in the CKGR upon proclamation of the Crown land, but the fact that it considered providing them with water, so that they could remain in the CKGR, is a clear indication that it did not extinguish their "native rights" with respect to the CKGR. The "native rights" of the Bushmen in the CKGR were therefore not extinguished in 1910 when the Crown land was declared.

83. Did the declaration of the land occupied by the Bushmen to be a game reserve (CKGR) extinguish their rights in respect thereof?

84. There is copious documentary evidence indicating that, the British Government intended the CKGR to be a free hunting area for the resident Bushmen. However, it got itself entangled in a

diplomatic web and ended up declaring a game reserve in which the Bushmen had no hunting rights, quite contrary to the ostensible reason for creating the reserve. . . .

87. The plain language of the Game Reserve Proclamation in terms of which CKGR was declared a game reserve, made it quite clear that hunting in the CKGR was forbidden for everyone including the Bushmen indigenous to the CKGR. This was so, despite the fact that there is abundant evidence above, to the effect that, when the idea of declaring the game reserve was conceived, the intention was that it would serve a dual purpose: viz. (i) to protect game from poachers, and (ii) to provide land for the Bushmen where they could hunt freely to satisfy their nutritional needs without interference from outsiders.

. . .

91. The independence Constitution of the Republic of Botswana recognised the presence of Bushmen in the CKGR by making a special provision in respect of them (section 14(3)(c)). There was never a time when the CKGR Bushmen were considered trespassers in the CKGR, either by the British Government or the Botswana Government. That explains why when the Botswana Government decided a policy to relocate them, the policy was "persuade but do not force." If their presence in the CKGR offended against any law, the Government would have been within its right to hand the matter to the Botswana Police to deal with them. The 1963 Regulations make it plain that they are exempt from producing permits to enter the CKGR.

92. I therefore find that creation of the CKGR did not extinguish the "native title" of the Bushmen to the CKGR. It follows that since I have come to the conclusion that, neither the declaration of the Ghanzi Crown land nor of CKGR extinguished the native rights of the Bushmen to CKGR, the Applicants who are part of the natives of the CKGR, were in possession of the land which they lawfully occupied in their settlements in the CKGR subsequent to the 31st January 2002.

VIII. Indigenous Rights in Environmental Agreements

There are few environmental agreements that focus on the rights of indigenous peoples. One that does, and in an innovative manner, is the Declaration on the Establishment of the Arctic Council (Sept. 19, 1996), *reprinted in* 35 I.L.M. 1382 (1996). A political undertaking of the eight circumpolar states, the Council was the first international body to include indigenous peoples as permanent participants on the basis of "recognition of the special relationship and unique contributions to the Arctic of indigenous peoples and their communities" (preamble). Three indigenous organizations are specifically mentioned in the Declaration: the Inuit Circumpolar Conference; the Sami Council; and the Association of Indigenous Minorities of the North, Siberia, and the Far East of the Russian Federation. The intent is to ensure full participation and consultation with Arctic indigenous representatives in the fulfillment of the Arctic Environmental Protection Strategy, adopted in 1991, and other environmental objectives of the Council.

A. *The Convention on Biological Diversity*

The Convention on Biological Diversity (CBD) is one of the few global environmental agreements to address some of the concerns of indigenous peoples, albeit without mentioning indigenous rights. In fact, the Convention asserts the sovereign rights of states over biological resources and places governments in charge of determining access to the resources (art. 15, para. 1). The Convention calls for prior informed consent as a basis for access but appears to refer to the consent of the state, not local communities dependent on the resources. Article 8j of the CBD calls for protecting traditional knowledge and practices consistent with sustainable development, but it contains no protection respecting indigenous lands and resources. Decision VI/1 of the Sixth Conference of the Parties emphasized the need to consult indigenous and local communities in order to conserve the sustainable use biological resources. The Decision specifically recommended that environmental, social, and cultural impact assessments be done for developments proposed to take place on or likely to impact lands and waters traditionally occupied or used by indigenous and local communities. Annex II of the Decision set forth recommendations for conducting the assessments. The other major decision of the Sixth Meeting of the Parties is reprinted here.

Bonn Guidelines on Access to Genetic Resources and Fair and Equitable Sharing of the Benefits Arising out of their Utilization, Convention on Biological Diversity, COP Decision VI/24 (adopted at the Sixth Conference of the Parties, The Hague, April 2002).

I. GENERAL PROVISIONS

. . .

C. Scope

. . .

9. All genetic resources and associated traditional knowledge, innovations and practices covered by the Convention on Biological Diversity and benefits arising from the commercial and other utilization of such resources should be covered by the guidelines, with the exclusion of human genetic resources.

. . .

E. Objectives

10. The objectives of the Guidelines are the following:
     a. To contribute to the conservation and sustainable use of biological diversity;
     b. To provide Parties and stakeholders with a transparent framework to facilitate access to genetic resources and ensure fair and equitable sharing of benefits;
     c. To provide guidance to Parties in the development of access and benefit-sharing regimes;
     d. To inform the practices and approaches of stakeholders (users and providers) in access and benefit-sharing arrangements;
     e. To provide capacity-building to guarantee the effective negotiation and implementation of access and benefit-sharing arrangements, especially to developing countries, in particular least developed countries and small island developing States among them;
     f. To promote awareness on implementation of relevant provisions of the Convention on Biological Diversity;
     g. To promote the adequate and effective transfer of appropriate technology to providing Parties, especially developing countries, in particular least developed countries and small island developing States among them, stakeholders and indigenous and local communities;
     h. To promote the provision of necessary financial resources to providing countries that are developing countries, in particular least developed countries and small island

developing States among them, or countries with economies in transition with a view to contributing to the achievement of the objectives mentioned above;

i. To strengthen the clearing-house mechanism as a mechanism for cooperation among Parties in access and benefit-sharing;

j. To contribute to the development by Parties of mechanisms and access and benefit-sharing regimes that recognize the protection of traditional knowledge, innovations and practices of indigenous and local communities, in accordance with domestic laws and relevant international instruments;

k. To contribute to poverty alleviation and be supportive to the realization of human food security, health and cultural integrity, especially in developing countries, in particular least developed countries and small island developing States among them;

l. Taxonomic research, as specified in the Global Taxonomy Initiative, should not be prevented, and providers should facilitate acquisition of material for systematic use and users should make available all information associated with the specimens thus obtained.

11. The Guidelines are intended to assist Parties in developing an overall access and benefit-sharing strategy, which may be part of their national biodiversity strategy and action plan, and in identifying the steps involved in the process of obtaining access to genetic resources and sharing benefits.

II. ROLES AND RESPONSIBILITIES IN ACCESS AND BENEFIT-SHARING PURSUANT TO ARTICLE 15 OF THE CONVENTION ON BIOLOGICAL DIVERSITY

A. National Focal Point

12. Each Party should designate one national focal point for access and benefit-sharing and make such information available through the clearing-house mechanism. The national focal point should inform applicants for access to genetic resources on procedures for acquiring prior informed consent and mutually agreed terms, including benefit-sharing, and on competent national authorities, relevant indigenous and local communities and relevant stakeholders, through the clearing-house mechanism.

B. Competent National Authority(ies)

13. Competent national authorities, where they are established, may, in accordance with applicable national legislative, administrative or policy measures, be responsible for granting access and be responsible for advising on:

a. The negotiating process;

b. Requirements for obtaining prior informed consent and entering into mutually agreed terms;

c. Monitoring and evaluation of access and benefit-sharing agreements;

d. Implementation/enforcement of access and benefit-sharing agreements;

e. Processing of applications and approval of agreements;

f. The conservation and sustainable use of the genetic resources accessed;

g. Mechanisms for the effective participation of different stakeholders, as appropriate for the different steps in the process of access and benefit-sharing, in particular, indigenous and local communities;

h. Mechanisms for the effective participation of indigenous and local communities while promoting the objective of having decisions and processes available in a language understandable to relevant indigenous and local communities.

14. The competent national authority(ies) that have the legal power to grant prior informed consent may delegate this power to other entities, as appropriate.

C. Responsibilities

15. Recognizing that Parties and stakeholders may be both users and providers, the following balanced list of roles and responsibilities provides key elements to be acted upon:

    a. Contracting Parties which are countries of origin of genetic resources, or other Parties which have acquired the genetic resources in accordance with the Convention, should:

        i. Be encouraged to review their policy, administrative and legislative measures to ensure they are fully complying with Article 15 of the Convention;

        ii. Be encouraged to report on access applications through the clearing-house mechanism and other reporting channels of the Convention;

        iii. Seek to ensure that the commercialization and any other use of genetic resources should not prevent traditional use of genetic resources;

        iv. Ensure that they fulfil their roles and responsibilities in a clear, objective and transparent manner;

        v. Ensure that all stakeholders take into consideration the environmental consequences of the access activities;

        vi. Establish mechanisms to ensure that their decisions are made available to relevant indigenous and local communities and relevant stakeholders, particularly indigenous and local communities;

        vii. Support measures, as appropriate, to enhance indigenous and local communities' capacity to represent their interests fully at negotiations;

    b. In the implementation of mutually agreed terms, users should:

        i. Seek informed consent prior to access to genetic resources, in conformity with Article 15, paragraph 5, of the Convention;

        ii. Respect customs, traditions, values and customary practices of indigenous and local communities,

        iii. Respond to requests for information from indigenous and local communities;

        iv. Only use genetic resources for purposes consistent with the terms and conditions under which they were acquired;

        v. Ensure that uses of genetic resources for purposes other than those for which they were acquired, only take place after new prior informed consent and mutually agreed terms are given;

        vi. Maintain all relevant data regarding the genetic resources, especially documentary evidence of the prior informed consent and information concerning the origin and the use of genetic resources and the benefits arising from such use;

        vii. As much as possible endeavour to carry out their use of the genetic resources in, and with the participation of, the providing country;

        viii. When supplying genetic resources to third parties, honour any terms and conditions regarding the acquired material. They should provide this third party with relevant data on their acquisition, including prior informed consent and conditions of use and record and maintain data on their supply to third parties. Special terms and conditions should be established under mutually agreed terms to facilitate taxonomic research for non-commercial purposes;

        ix. Ensure the fair and equitable sharing of benefits, including technology transfer to providing countries, pursuant to Article 16 of the Convention arising from the commercialization or other use of genetic resources, in conformity with the mutually agreed terms they established with the indigenous and local communities or stakeholders involved;

c. Providers should:

   i. Only supply genetic resources and/or traditional knowledge when they are entitled to do so;
   ii. Strive to avoid imposition of arbitrary restrictions on access to genetic resources.

d. Contracting Parties with users of genetic resources under their jurisdiction should take appropriate legal, administrative, or policy measures, as appropriate, to support compliance with prior informed consent of the Contracting Party providing such resources and mutually agreed terms on which access was granted. These countries could consider, *inter alia*, the following measures:

   i.   Mechanisms to provide information to potential users on their obligations regarding access to genetic resources;
   ii. Measures to encourage the disclosure of the country of origin of the genetic resources and of the origin of traditional knowledge, innovations and practices of indigenous and local communities in applications for intellectual property rights;
   iii. Measures aimed at preventing the use of genetic resources obtained without the prior informed consent of the Contracting Party providing such resources;
   iv. Cooperation between Contracting Parties to address alleged infringements of access and benefit-sharing agreements;
   v.   Voluntary certification schemes for institutions abiding by rules on access and benefit-sharing;
   vi. Measures discouraging unfair trade practices;
   vii. Other measures that encourage users to comply with provisions under subparagraph 16 (b) above.

III. PARTICIPATION OF STAKEHOLDERS

16. Involvement of relevant stakeholders is essential to ensure the adequate development and implementation of access and benefit-sharing arrangements. However, due to the diversity of stakeholders and their diverging interests, their appropriate involvement can only be determined on a case-by-case basis.

17. Relevant stakeholders should be consulted and their views taken into consideration in each step of the process, including:

a. When determining access, negotiating and implementing mutually agreed terms, and in the sharing of benefits;
b. In the development of a national strategy, policies or regimes on access and benefit-sharing.

18. To facilitate the involvement of relevant stakeholders, including indigenous and local communities, appropriate consultative arrangements, such as national consultative committees, comprising relevant stakeholder representatives, should be made.

19. The involvement of relevant stakeholders should be promoted by:

a. Providing information, especially regarding scientific and legal advice, in order for them to be able to participate effectively;
b. Providing support for capacity-building, in order for them to be actively engaged in various stages of access and benefit-sharing arrangements, such as in the development and implementation of mutually agreed terms and contractual arrangements.

20. The stakeholders involved in access to genetic resources and benefit-sharing may wish to seek the support of a mediator or facilitator when negotiating mutually agreed terms.

IV. STEPS IN THE ACCESS AND BENEFIT-SHARING PROCESS

. . .

C. Prior Informed Consent

21. As provided for in Article 15 of the Convention on Biological Diversity, which recognizes the sovereign rights of States over their natural resources, each Contracting Party to the Convention shall endeavour to create conditions to facilitate access to genetic resources for environmentally sound uses by other Contracting Parties and fair and equitable sharing of benefits arising from such uses. In accordance with Article 15, paragraph 5, of the Convention on Biological Diversity, access to genetic resources shall be subject to prior informed consent of the contracting Party providing such resources, unless otherwise determined by that Party.

. . .

C. Role of Intellectual Property Rights in the Implementation of Access and Benefit-Sharing Arrangements

The Conference of the Parties

1. Invites Parties and Governments to encourage the disclosure of the country of origin of genetic resources in applications for intellectual property rights, where the subject matter of the application concerns or makes use of genetic resources in its development, as a possible contribution to tracking compliance with prior informed consent and the mutually agreed terms on which access to those resources was granted;

2. Also invites Parties and Governments to encourage the disclosure of the origin of relevant traditional knowledge, innovations and practices of indigenous and local communities relevant for the conservation and sustainable use of biological diversity in applications for intellectual property rights, where the subject matter of the application concerns or makes use of such knowledge in its development;

3. Requests the Executive Secretary, with the help of other international and intergovernmental organizations such as the World Intellectual Property Organization and through the Ad Hoc Open-ended Inter-Sessional Working Group on Article 8(j) and Related Provisions of the Convention, where appropriate, to undertake further information gathering and analysis with regard to:

    a. Impact of intellectual property regimes on access to and use of genetic resources and scientific research;

    b. Role of customary laws and practices in relation to the protection of genetic resources and traditional knowledge, innovations and practices, and their relationship with intellectual property rights;

    c. Consistency and applicability of requirements for disclosure of country of origin and prior informed consent in the context of international legal obligations;

    d. Efficacy of country of origin and prior informed consent disclosures in assisting the examination of intellectual property rights applications and the re-examination of intellectual property rights granted;

    e. Efficacy of country of origin and prior informed consent disclosures in monitoring compliance with access provisions;

f.   Feasibility of an internationally recognized certificate of origin system as evidence of prior informed consent and mutually agreed terms; and

g.   Role of oral evidence of prior art. in the examination, granting and maintenance of intellectual property rights;

4.   Invites the World Intellectual Property Organization to prepare a technical study, and to report its findings to the Conference of the Parties at its seventh meeting, on methods consistent with obligations in treaties administered by the World Intellectual Property Organization for requiring the disclosure within patent applications of, *inter alia*:

a.   Genetic resources utilized in the development of the claimed inventions;

b.   The country of origin of genetic resources utilized in the claimed inventions;

c.   Associated traditional knowledge, innovations and practices utilized in the development of the claimed inventions;

d.   The source of associated traditional knowledge, innovations and practices; and

e.   Evidence of prior informed consent;

5.   Requests the Executive Secretary to collect, compile and disseminate information on the matters specified in paragraphs 3 and 4 above, including through the clearing-house mechanism of the Convention and other appropriate means;

6.   Invites Parties and Governments to submit case-studies that they consider relevant to the issues specified in paragraphs 3 and 4; and

7.   Requests the Executive Secretary to gather information and prepare a report on national and regional experiences;

8.   Invites other relevant international organizations (such as the Food and Agriculture Organization of the United Nations, the United Nations Conference on Trade and Development, the World Intellectual Property Organization, the World Trade Organization, and the United Nations Commission on Human Rights), as well as regional organizations, Parties and Governments to contribute to the further study and analysis of the issues specified in paragraphs 3 and 4;

9.   Encourages the World Intellectual Property Organization to make rapid progress in the development of model intellectual property clauses which may be considered for inclusion in contractual agreements when mutually agreed terms are under negotiation;

10. Recognizes the importance of the work being undertaken by the World Intellectual Property Organization on international models and encourage the World Intellectual Property Organization to also consider means by which Parties could collaborate to protect traditional knowledge for further consideration by the Conference of the Parties;

11. Urges the World Intellectual Property Organization to provide to the Conference of the Parties with the results of its deliberations of relevance to access to genetic resources and benefit-sharing related to traditional knowledge;

12. Encourages Parties to facilitate the participation of indigenous and local communities and other relevant stakeholders in the various forums, in particular the World Intellectual Property Organization, the Convention on Biological Diversity, the World Trade Organization, the United Nations Conference on Trade and Development and regional forums, as well as in the preparation of national strategies, policies, regulatory frameworks and legislation related to access to genetic resources and benefit-sharing, from a very early stage;

13. Requests the Executive Secretary to compile information, and to make it available through the clearing-house mechanism of the Convention and other means, on the principles, legal mechanisms and procedures for obtaining prior informed consent of indigenous and local communities under national access regimes for genetic resources, and also on assessments of the effectiveness of such mechanisms and procedures, and requests Parties to provide such information to assist the Executive Secretary.

Questions and Discussion

1. Plants are the source of most of the pharmaceuticals on the market today, many of them developed from indigenous knowledge acquired by trial and error and transmitted for generations. How should the various rights and interests of indigenous communities and their states, pharmaceutical companies and their states, environmental activists, and those seeking access to inexpensive and effective medicines be balanced? What if the indigenous knowledge is confidential, restricted to religious leaders?

2. Does it make sense to grant intellectual property rights to indigenous and local communities to ensure equitable benefit sharing when their knowledge and plant resources are used? Or should we return to a system where intellectual property laws cannot protect pharmaceuticals because of the public interest?

3. What policies are most likely to further environmental protection and secure the rights of indigenous peoples? Are the two aims in conflict?

4. On December 30, 2010, the Nagoya Protocol on Access to Genetic Resources and the Fair and Equitable Shoring of Benefits Arising from Their Utilization to the CBD Convention was opened for Signature, when it comes into force it will supercede the Bonn Guidelines.

5. For further reading on this issue, see Frederico Lenzerini, *Indigenous Peoples' Cultural Rights and the Controversy over Commercial Use of Their Traditional Knowledge*, in CULTURAL HUMAN RIGHTS 119–49 (Francisco Francioni & Martin Scheinin eds., 2008); Charles R. McManis, *Intellectual Property, Genetic Resources, and Traditional Knowledge Protection: Thinking Globally, Acting Locally*, 11 CARDOZO J. INT'L & COMP. L. 547 (2003); Dinah Shelton, *Fair Play, Fair Pay: Preserving Traditional Knowledge and Biological Resources*, 5 Y.B. INT'L ENVTL. L. 77 (1995).

B. *Climate Change, Reducing Emissions from Deforestation in Developing Countries, and Forest Peoples*

Reducing Emissions from Deforestation in Developing Countries (REDD) was agreed to at UNFCCC's COP-11 in Montreal in 2005, after "Compensated Reduction" was formally proposed by Papua New Guinea and Costa Rica "on behalf of many supportive Nations." This group, now negotiating as the Coalition for Rainforest Nations (CFRN), has pushed for "voluntary carbon emission reductions by conserving forests in exchange for access to international markets for emissions trading." COP-13, held in Bali in December 2007, was the scene of significant developments in relation to REDD. Governments agreed that REDD should be included in the negotiations toward a second commitment period for the Kyoto Protocol (UNFCCC, 2008). From the start, indigenous and forest peoples have been skeptical of REDD, viewing it as another potential device to remove control of their lands and resources from them. Some of the controversy is reflected in the material that follows a description of REDD.

United Nations Collaborative Programme on Reducing Emissions from Deforestation and Forest Degradation in Developing Countries,
available at http://www.un-redd.org UN-REDD Program

Deforestation and forest degradation, through agricultural expansion, conversion to pastureland, infrastructure development, destructive logging, fires[,] etc., account for nearly 20% of global greenhouse gas emissions, more than the entire global transportation sector and second only to the energy sector. It is now clear that in order to constrain the impacts of climate change within limits that society will reasonably be able to tolerate, the global average temperatures must be stabilized within two degrees Celsius. This will be practically impossible to achieve without reducing emissions from the forest sector, in addition to other mitigation actions.

REDD – Reducing Emissions from Deforestation and Forest Degradation in Developing Countries – is an effort to create a financial value for the carbon stored in forests, offering incentives for developing countries to reduce emissions from forested lands and invest in low-carbon paths to sustainable development.

It is predicted that financial flows for greenhouse gas emission reductions from REDD could reach up to US$30 billion a year. This significant North-South flow of funds could reward a meaningful reduction of carbon emissions and could also support new, pro-poor development, help conserve biodiversity and secure vital ecosystem services.

Further, maintaining forest ecosystems can contribute to increased resilience to climate change. To achieve these multiple benefits, REDD will require the full engagement and respect for the rights of Indigenous Peoples and other forest-dependent communities.

To "seal the deal" on climate change, REDD activities in developing countries must complement, not be a substitute for, deep cuts in developed countries' emissions. The decision to include REDD in a post-Kyoto regime must not jeopardize the commitment of Annex I countries to reduce their own emissions. Both will be critical to successfully address climate change.

Supporting Countries to Get Ready for REDD

Reducing Emissions from Deforestation and Forest Degradation (REDD) is increasingly likely to be included in a post-2012 climate agreement, yet many questions remain unanswered. How will the REDD mechanism link to existing national development strategies? How can forest communities and indigenous peoples participate in the design, monitoring and evaluation of national REDD programmes? How will REDD be funded, and how will countries ensure that benefits are distributed equitably among all those who manage the forests? Finally, how will the amount of carbon stored and sequestrated as a result of REDD be monitored?

The UN-REDD Programme was created to assist developing countries to answer just these kinds of questions and help them get ready to participate in a future REDD mechanism. Through its nine initial country programme activities in Africa, Asia and Latin America, the UN-REDD Programme supports the capacity of national governments to prepare and implement national REDD strategies with the active involvement of all stakeholders, including indigenous peoples and other forest-dependent communities.

In-Country and Global Support for REDD Readiness

The UN-REDD Programme works both at the national and at the international level.

Within countries, the UN-REDD Programme supports processes for REDD readiness and contributes to the development of national REDD strategies. Guided by principles of country ownership and leadership, the Programme provides technical advice on ways to address deforestation and forest degradation, methods and tools for measuring and monitoring greenhouse gas emissions and forest carbon flows. It promotes REDD financing as an opportunity to develop low-carbon growth and helps countries access financial and technical support. The Programme promotes and facilitates broad-ranging consultations among stakeholders, including indigenous peoples and other forest-dependent communities, and helps establish linkages with existing national programmes in the areas of governance, development, poverty reduction, food security and natural resource management.

So far, the formulation process of UN-REDD national programmes has proved quick and efficient, allowing for the approval of most of the initial nine national programmes.

At the international level, the UN-REDD Programme seeks to build consensus and knowledge about REDD and raise awareness about the importance of including a REDD mechanism in a post-2012 climate change agreement. It also provides opportunities for dialogue between governments, civil society organizations and technical experts, to ensure that REDD efforts are based on science and take into account the views and needs of all stakeholders.

The UN-REDD Programme brings together technical teams from around the world to develop common approaches, analyses and guidelines on issues such as measurement, reporting and verification (MRV) of carbon emissions and flows, remote sensing, and greenhouse gas inventories. It provides guidance on how best to design and implement REDD, to ensure that forests continue to provide multiple benefits for livelihoods and biodiversity to societies while storing carbon at the same time. Other areas of work include national forest assessments and monitoring of in-country policy and institutional change.

The UN-REDD Programme also documents, analyzes and disseminates successes and key challenges emerging from its activities, and provides numerous face-to-face opportunities for learning and sharing of experience.

Working Together

The UN-REDD Programme builds on the convening power and expertise of the Food and Agriculture Organization of the United Nations (FAO), the United Nations Development Programme (UNDP) and the United Nations Environment Programme (UNEP).

The UN-REDD Programme works in close coordination with the Forest Carbon Partnership Facility (FCPF) and the Forest Investment Program (FIP) both at the international level – harmonizing normative frameworks and organizing joint events – and at the national level, where joint missions and sharing of information result in coordinated support interventions. The Programme also works with the Secretariat of the United Nations Framework Convention on Climate Change (UNFCCC) and the Global Environment Facility (GEF), as well as the United Nations Forum on Forests (UNFF), members of the Collaborative Partnership on Forests (CPF), donors, civil society, non-governmental organizations, and academia.

The UN-REDD Programme is governed by a Policy Board composed of representatives from partner countries, donors to the multi-donor trust fund, civil society, indigenous peoples and FAO, UNDP and UNEP. All members have an equal voice in decisions on overall leadership, strategic directions and financial allocations. Current funding amounts to US$75 million contributed by the governments of Norway, Spain and Denmark.

REDD Myths: A Critical Review of Proposed Mechanisms to Reduce Emissions from Deforestation and Degradation in Developing Countries,
114 CLIMATE AND DEFORESTATION 5–8 (2008)
Friends of the Earth

United Nations negotiations on Reducing Emissions from Deforestation in Developing countries (REDD) are in fast forward mode, both in the negotiating halls and on the ground. This is partly because of the considerable sums of money being discussed – figures of tens of billions of dollars per year are the norm. Yet many critical questions remain unanswered. Will REDD help to mitigate climate change or actually negate efforts that have been made so far? Who will really benefit from REDD funds? How might trading in forest carbon credits impact on REDD-related policies and projects?

From a climate change point of view, the overall goal is to stabilize the atmospheric concentration of CO_2 at as low a level as possible. This can partly be achieved by stopping deforestation, which is responsible for some 18% of carbon emissions to the atmosphere. But REDD is not intended to stop deforestation. A detailed analysis shows that "reducing emissions from deforestation" is actually a dramatically different approach that could have significant negative impacts on people, on biodiversity and even on our climate.

Firstly, in current REDD scenarios it is perfectly plausible that deforestation could be allowed to continue at or return to unacceptable rates, with prolonged damage to biodiversity and the risk that forests will be tipped into a process of dieback.

This is because the atmospheric concentration of CO_2 can also be reduced by *deferring* deforestation: even if deforestation rates return to their original level after a certain period, there will still have been a beneficial effect on CO_2 concentrations. This rather undermines one of the key arguments used to promote REDD: that it will be good for biodiversity. In addition, REDD could also be used to reward those engaged in logging and industrial agriculture, whilst ignoring those countries and communities that have low deforestation rates.

This is because REDD is primarily intended to create financial incentives that will prompt those engaged in deforestation to switch to managing standing forests. Most calculations of how much REDD will cost focus on the profits that would be forfeited by those engaged in deforestation. This "opportunity cost" approach also implies that REDD will be used to channel public funds, through facilities such as the World Bank's Forest Carbon Partnership Facility, to pay the polluter. REDD is also likely to provide lucrative opportunities for those with money to invest, including forest carbon finance companies.

These opportunity cost calculations, and others that look at the potential income that could be generated from simply conserving carbon stocks (in countries with low rates of deforestation, for example) have another major drawback. They give the impression that completely stopping deforestation would be prohibitively expensive. But this is *only* the case if those engaged in deforestation are compensated. It would be more useful to focus on the opportunity costs to government revenue streams, jobs and value-added industries. This approach would still provide the necessary positive incentives to governments considering changing their policies with respect to deforestation.

Critically, REDD will also hamper much-needed efforts to mitigate climate change so long as it is based on a definition of forests than includes plantations. Plantations are not forests. Large-scale monoculture tree plantations cause serious environmental, social and economic problems. Furthermore, plantations store only 20% of the carbon that intact natural forests do. It thus seems inconceivable that the U.N. Framework Convention on Climate Change (UNFCCC) would sanction any process that allows natural forests to be replaced with plantations. Yet this is exactly what is being proposed in REDD.

Some countries even support a "net deforestation" approach: this would allow them to continue logging and cutting forest to make way for agricultural commodities (including agrofuels) in some areas, whilst conserving forests and/or extending plantations in others.

A further major concern is that REDD could actually negate existing efforts to mitigate climate change if it is funded by the sale of forest carbon credits on the international compliance markets.

If REDD is funded through carbon offsetting it will undermine current and future emissions reductions agreed to by industrialized countries. Allowing countries with carbon intensive lifestyles to continue consuming inequitably and unsustainably, by permitting them to fund cheaper forest carbon "offsets" in developing countries, diverts critical resources and attention away from measures to address fossil fuel consumption and the real underlying causes of deforestation.

REDD also refocuses attention on a key moral and legal dilemma – to whom, if anyone, do forests belong to? And who has the rights to sell forest carbon credits? It is certainly clear that in the absence of secure land rights, Indigenous Peoples and other forest-dependent communities have no guarantees that they will receive any form of REDD "incentive" or reward for their extensive forest conservation efforts.

Whether national or project-based, REDD policies will trigger a rapid expansion in lands set aside for REDD projects. In many countries, governments and others are likely to ignore the customary and territorial rights of Indigenous Peoples, as they seek to protect an increasingly valuable resource from "outside" interference, violently or otherwise. The simple fact that forests are becoming an increasingly valuable commodity means that they are more likely to be wrested away from local people. Previous experiences, with the Clean Development Mechanism, voluntary carbon offset projects and payments for environmental services schemes, indicate that there is little reason for optimism, especially for already marginalized communities living in the forests.

Commodifying forest carbon is also inherently inequitable, since it discriminates against people, and especially women, who previously had free access to the forest resources they needed to raise and care for their families, but cannot afford to buy forest products or alternatives. Any REDD projects that deny local communities and Indigenous Peoples access to forests risk having grave impacts on poverty and the achievement of the Millennium Development Goals.

Indigenous Peoples and forest-dependent communities may also find it hard to benefit from REDD even if they actively wish to participate in REDD projects.

Firstly, if they are not engaged in unsustainable deforestation they may not qualify for REDD incentives.

Secondly, they may be disadvantaged by uncertainties or conflicts over land tenure (and these conflicts are even less likely to be resolved in their favour if forests increase in value).

Thirdly, because of the uncertainties associated with deforestation projects (because of storms or forest fires, for example) project managers are likely to find themselves saddled with the projects' risks and liabilities. They may also find themselves responsible for finding upfront funding and operational costs to tide them over until they are paid at the end of the project period. Either way, larger and richer organizations operating to economies of scale can deal with these difficulties much more easily, than Indigenous Peoples and local communities, who may therefore find themselves in a poor negotiating position right from the start. They may also have to address language barriers and hire or find assistance to deal with the technical complexities involved in establishing, monitoring and verifying REDD projects.

An additional suite of risks arise if REDD is to be funded through compliance carbon markets. Many observers assume that REDD is synonymous with carbon trading and offsetting, but this is not the case (so far, at least). Although using the markets to fund REDD has been favoured by a majority of governments (or was, before the global financial crisis erupted onto the global scene) it has still been a contentious issue.

Nevertheless, the full range of risks associated with using carbon offsetting to fund REDD has not been properly considered. In addition to the fundamental problem of equating forest and fossil carbon it could:

- Hold REDD hostage to the vagaries of markets and the activities of speculators, and generally lead to funding that is unstable and unpredictable.
- Reduce developing countries' sovereignty over their natural resources, by prioritising investment decisions that focus on maximising profits and allowing foreign investors to buy up forest "services."
- Allow richer, industrialized countries to continue polluting and divert resources and attention away from measures that could address the real underlying causes of deforestation.
- Foster an "armed protection" mentality that could lead to the displacement of millions of forest-dependent people, including by force.
- Facilitate corruption and poor governance in countries with tropical forests, because of the large sums of money proposed and the complex nature of the financial mechanisms likely to be involved.
- Prioritize "least cost" measures, which increase the likelihood of environmentally and socially damaging activities and push liability for failed projects onto local communities.
- Flood carbon markets, reducing the price of carbon and thereby stalling other climate change mitigation programmes.
- See most funding channelled to countries such as Brazil and Indonesia, which have high deforestation rates or large areas of forest cover.

- Be so complex and have such high transaction costs that only the largest companies operating to economies of scale are able to participate.

In addition to concerns about financing, it has long been known that there are numerous methodological problems associated with deforestation projects. Although there have now been some technological improvements (especially in satellite imaging technology), most of these problems and associated risks remain, meaning that REDD might fail even if the large sums of money being discussed are raised and distributed.

An enduring problem is whether REDD can address "leakage" concerns. A project-level approach, for example, could mean that deforestation activities simply shift to another area in the same country (depending on the specific causes of deforestation in that country). One obvious solution to this predicament is to focus efforts at the national level and to involve as many countries as possible. Even so, a question still remains about possible leakage from tropical forests to boreal and temperate forests. Ultimately, the only real solution is to remove the underlying causes of deforestation.

Measuring degradation is also problematic, but important. If degradation is not included in REDD, great quantities of carbon could be lost without the system recognising it. In some countries, such as those in the Congo Basin, losses from degradation tend to be much higher than those from deforestation. However, the fact that degradation data may be less reliable – and is more expensive to acquire – is likely to discourage carbon finance investors, which may mean negotiators choose to exclude degradation in order to accommodate carbon trading. This dilemma seems to be yet another cogent practical argument for using publicly rather than privately sourced finance.

In conclusion, efforts to reduce emissions from deforestation and degradation, being discussed in the post-2012 negotiations, must be replaced with a mechanism to stop deforestation. Governments are already committed to this under the Climate Change Convention and in other agreements such as the Convention on Biological Diversity.

Renewed efforts to achieve this goal should be founded on the ecosystems approach, climate justice and the rights and role of Indigenous Peoples and local communities. They should also address biodiversity and poverty effectively and challenge the underlying causes of deforestation directly, nailing down demand-side drivers in importing countries and resolving governance, poverty and land tenure issues in forested countries. It is particularly important that stopping deforestation is seen as more than just a carbon counting exercise; and that plantations are removed from the equation. In so far as funding is required to stop deforestation, financing should be invested in national programmes and infrastructure that directly support alternative rights-based forms of forest conservation, sustainable management, natural regeneration and ecosystem restoration, such as community-based forestry.

Funding – from whatever source – should address the needs of developing countries, but should not directly increase the financial value of forests. Benefits to governments could be tied to national commitments to cease commercial deforestation and to restructure logging, pulp and paper and other industries, possibly over a number of years.

It is important to bear in mind that financing is not everything. There are other important and relatively cheap options that could help to prevent deforestation, including deforestation bans and moratoria and a global forest fire fighting fund and expertise bank, to assist countries unable to prevent or stop forest fires.

It could also be useful to focus on developing transition funds that would help developing countries match lost tax revenue streams, jobs and value-added industries. This approach could provide the necessary positive incentives to governments considering changing their policies with respect to deforestation, but would be additional to the costs associated with tackling the underlying causes of deforestation.

Carbon markets cannot be used to fund efforts to stop deforestation: they will simply negate existing efforts to reduce reliance on fossil fuels. There are alternative sources of funds that do not rely on voluntary assistance or on carbon trading, such as taxing fossil fuel use and diverting fossil fuel energy subsidies in industrialized countries. These would be true win[-]win options, since they would also, in themselves, work to reduce greenhouse gas emissions. They would also provide a predictable source of transition funding.

Furthermore, all funding should be grant-based only: any concessional loans could mean that developing countries are pushed into increasing their debt burden because of climate change, a problem for which they are not responsible. Neither the World Bank nor the Global Environment Facility (so long as it is unduly influenced by the World Bank) should be permitted to drive this process forward. Instead, a transparent, accountable and participative fund-based mechanism should be established within the U.N.

Some of the official documentation on REDD can be found in the following materials:

- FAO, UNDP & UNEP, *U.N. Collaborative Program on Reducing Emissions from Deforestation and Forest Degradation in Developing Countries: Framework Document* (2008), *available at* http://www.undp.org/mdtf/UN-REDD/docs/Annex-A-Framework-Document.pdf;
- *Statement from the International Indigenous Peoples Forum on Climate Change*, Accra Climate Change Talks, Ghana, Aug. 21–27 2008. *available at* http://www.tebtebba.org/index.php?option=com_content&view=article&id=30:statement-from-the-iipfcc-accra-climate-talks&catid=51:ip-declarations;
- UNFCC, *Views on Outstanding Methodological Issues Related to Policy Approaches and Positive Incentives to Reduce Emissions from Deforestation and Forest Degradation in Developing Countries: Submissions from Parties* (2008), *available at* http://unfccc.int/resource/docs/2008/sbsta/eng/misc04.pdf; and
- Global Forest Coalition, *Effective Policies to Reduce Emissions from Deforestation in Developing Countries Must Address Leakage and Incorporate Social Impact Criteria* (2008), *available at* http://unfccc.int/resource/docs/2008/smsn/ngo/016.pdf.
- A related and similarly controversial approach to conservation is payment for ecosystem services (PES).

For further reading on REDD and PES, see Mirjam Macchi, *Indigenous and Traditional Peoples and Climate Change*, IUCN, (2008), *available at* http://cmsdata.iucn.org/downloads/indigenous_peoples_climate_change.pdf; Katharina Kunzmann, *The Non-Legally Binding Instrument on Sustainable Management of All Types of Forests – Towards a Full Legal Regime for Sustainable Forest Management?*, 9 German L.J. 981 (2008); Ezequiel Logo, *Ecosystem Services, The Millennium Ecosystem Assessment, and the Conceptual Difference Between Benefits Provided by Ecosystems and Benefits Provided by People*, 23 J. Land Use & Envtl. L. 243, 255–61(2008); Brian C. Steed, *Government Payments for Ecosystem Services – Lessons from Costa Rica*, 23 J. Land Use & Envtl. L. 177 (2007); James Salzman, *A Field of Green? The Past and Future of Ecosystem Services*, 21 J. Land Use & Envtl. L. 133, 146–49 (2006); Justin K. Holcombe, *Protecting Ecosystems and Natural Resources by Revising Conceptions of Ownership, Rights, and Valuation*, J. Land Resources & Envtl. L. 83, 89–92 (2005); Kristen Hite, *Back to the Basics: Improved Property Rights Can Help Save Ecuador's Rainforests*, 16 Geo. Int'l Envtl. L. Rev. 763 (2004); Stefano Pagiola, *Payments for Environmental Services: An Introduction*, Environment Department, World Bank (2006), *available at* http://siteresources.worldbank.org/INTEEI/Resources/IntroToPES.pdf.

9 Humanitarian Crises: Armed Conflicts and Other Disasters

I. Introduction

Neither human rights nor environmental protection fare well during crises, whether the event is a tsunami or a civil war. Laws cannot prevent the former and have not succeeded in eliminating the latter. Law and policy can attempt, however, to minimize the harmful consequences of such catastrophes. The efforts to ameliorate the violent impact of armed conflict constitute the field of humanitarian law. And increasingly, the legal treatment of disasters outside of armed conflict has started to emerge, although it is probably too early to proclaim a field of international disaster law.

This chapter examines the problem of protecting the environment and the enjoyment of human rights in periods of crisis. It first considers the range of laws that aim to protect non-combatants and the environment during armed conflict, including issues of war crimes and accountability. It then turns to "natural" disasters, including industrial accidents of human origin. The final section concerns the rights of displaced persons, including environmental refugees. Before examining any of these issues, however, it is well to consider the similarities and differences between disasters and conflicts.

> *Natural Disaster and Conflict-Induced Displacement: Similarities, Differences, and Inter-Connections*, BROOKINGS INSTITUTION (Mar. 27, 2008), available at http://www.brookings.edu/speeches/2008/0327_displacement_ferris.aspx
>
> Elizabeth Ferris
>
> . . .

A Conceptual Problem

A natural disaster is defined by the U.N. as: "the consequences of events triggered by natural hazards that overwhelm local response capacity and seriously affect the social and economic development of a region." There is a burning debate in the humanitarian field about just how "natural" are natural disasters – which raises interesting opportunities to relate to those working on human-induced climate change. For example, landslides are reportedly becoming more common in Nepal. This may be the result of environmental factors (climate change) – as warmer temperatures are leading to melting of glaciers – but it may also be the result of deforestation which is an activity carried out by humans.

The terms "slow-onset" and "rapid-onset" disasters are often used by those working on natural disasters to distinguish between, for example, desertification on the one hand and typhoons on the other. Anki Strauss argues that the scale of migration resulting from gradual changes is likely to be far greater than the displacement resulting from individual catastrophic events. She also argues that long-term environmental change is more likely to cause permanent migration than sudden catastrophes. This makes intuitive sense. But the term "slow-onset" cries out for further clarification: how slow is slow? Does it occur over years? Decades? Longer? How does this term relate to concepts such as increasing poverty or environmental degradation or social marginalization and exclusion?

Since the beginning of recorded history, people have migrated because of environmental factors – floods, drought, famine – usually because they could no longer survive in their places of origin. Are all environmental changes to be considered as slow-onset natural disasters? If so, the distinctions between displacement caused by natural disasters and economic migration become more difficult.

Yet another conceptual problem is that the differences between natural disasters and conflicts are usually not clear-cut. Government policies, for example, can both contribute to and mitigate the effects of natural disasters. For example, the Cuban government has developed an impressive response to mitigating the effects of hurricanes, including grassroots-based early warning and evacuation systems. Other countries in the region which are also prone to frequent hurricanes, such as Haiti, experience far greater casualty figures. Government policies can also both contribute to and mitigate the effects of conflict. In some countries, governments are active participants in civil conflicts, e.g.[,] Sudan and Sri Lanka. In others, such as Colombia, the government has adopted exemplary legislation to protect the human rights of those affected by conflict, but there are major shortcomings in implementing them. In still others, governments simply do not have the capacity to protect people displaced by war, e.g.[,] Somalia and Iraq.

Similarities

Let me begin by noting three over-arching similarities between those displaced by natural disasters and by conflicts.

1. The human experiences of those displaced by natural disasters and conflicts are very similar. People displaced, for example, by both flooding and by fighting often lose family members, endure family separation, lose their possessions, and experience trauma and depression. They have similar protection and assistance needs. They lose important documents[,] which limits their access to public services. They lose property and it may take years (if ever) before they receive compensation for their loss. In both cases, vulnerable groups suffer more. For example, globally, for every one adult male who drowns in a flood, there are 3–4 women who die. Sexual abuse and rape of women is often a tool of war while gender-based violence is unfortunately common among women displaced by both natural disasters and conflict. Children displaced by both natural disasters and conflicts are often more susceptible to recruitment by armed forces. Vulnerable groups also frequently experience discrimination in the provision of assistance. In many camps where persons displaced by conflict live, food is – at least initially – more likely to go to healthy and strong men than to children or the disabled. And in New Orleans, the elderly, the immigrants and African-American communities suffered the effects of Hurricane Katrina disproportionately.

A report by the Urban Institute on hospitals during Hurricane Katrina found that 1,749 patients occupied the eleven New Orleans-area hospitals that were surrounded by floodwaters, yet there were no city or state plans for moving patients in the event of a catastrophe.

The problems that are often encountered by persons affected by the consequences of natural disasters include: unequal access to assistance; discrimination in aid provision; enforced relocation; sexual and gender-based violence; loss of documentation; recruitment of children into fighting forces; unsafe or involuntary return or resettlement; and issues of property restitution. These are similar to the problems experienced by those displaced by conflicts.

2. Most people displaced by either conflicts or natural disasters remain within the borders of their country. They are internally displaced persons (IDPs), defined in the Guiding Principles on Internal Displacement as:

> Persons or groups of persons who have been forced or obliged to flee or to leave their homes or places of habitual residence, in particular as a result of or in order to avoid the effects of armed conflict, situations of generalized violence, violations of human rights or natural or human-made disasters, and who have not crossed an internationally recognized State border.

While there are some 10 million refugees in the world – people fleeing persecution or conflict who have crossed an international border – the number of conflict-induced IDPs is estimated at 25 million. This trend is likely to grow as governments of both developing and industrialized countries are making it more difficult for people fleeing violence to seek safety in their territories.

Those who are displaced by either natural disasters or conflicts are entitled to basic human rights as citizens of their countries and as guaranteed by various international human rights conventions. The Guiding Principles on Internal Displacement set out these human rights as applicable to the displaced. As internally displaced persons, it is their national governments [that] are responsible for protecting and assisting them during displacement and for facilitating durable solutions for their displacement. Another similarity is that governments often do not meet these obligations – whether the precipitating cause of displacement is a hurricane or a civil war.

3. Poverty makes things worse for both victims of natural disasters and conflict. Of the 10 lowest ranking countries on the Human Development Index, five are currently experiencing displacement because of conflict (Democratic Republic of Congo, Ethiopia, Chad, Central African Republic, and Sierra Leone.) Several of the others are particularly susceptible to natural disasters: Mozambique, Mali, Niger, Guinea-Bissau, Burkina Faso. Or to take another comparison: on 10 December 1988, an earthquake registering 6.9 on the Richter scale hit Armenia, killing some 55,000 people and leaving 500,000 homeless. Less than a year later, in October 1989, an even stronger earthquake, 7.1 on the Richter scale, hit San Francisco, California, killing 62 and leaving 12,000 homeless. Chances of surviving a natural disaster are much higher in developed countries.

. . .

Similarly, there is a relationship between poverty and conflict. An analysis of state weakness in the developing world found a strong relationship between poverty and failed states which are more likely to have conflict-induced displacement. "Thus a substantial majority of the world's failed and critically weak states are also the world's poorest, with GNI per capita in the bottom quintile of developing nations." The 10 weakest states, according to economic, political security, and social welfare indicators are (in order of weakest to less weak): Somalia, Afghanistan, DRC, Iraq, Burundi, Sudan, Central African Republic, Zimbabwe, Liberia and Côte d'Ivoire – all countries which have experienced major civil conflict – which has generated many displaced persons – in recent years.

Other Less Obvious Similarities

1. Natural disasters, almost by definition, have environmental effects. But so do conflicts – and displacement itself. Refugee camps, for example, can quickly deplete forests and developing countries which host the majority of the world's refugees and IDPs often pay a high environmental cost. A degraded environment is also more likely to suffer the consequences of natural disasters. For example, Martine and Guzman found that Central America's vulnerability to hurricanes and other natural disasters is a product of social, economic, and environmental causes. Another example is the fact that the disappearance of the wetlands in southern Louisiana intensified the effects of Hurricane Katrina.

2. The international response system to both natural disasters and conflict is fairly well-developed. In both cases, there seems to be a greater initial response to high-profile crises[,] which diminishes as situations become protracted. While comparative analyses are lacking, there seems to be support for the fact that donor response to both natural disaster – and conflict-induced displacement – is largely influenced by strategic concerns rather than the absolute need of the IDPs. For example, Drury et al used a sample of 2,337 cases of disaster assistance between 1964 and 1995 to test the role of political influence in U.S. disaster assistance overseas. They conclude that "foreign policy and domestic factors not only influence disaster assistance and allocations but that they are the overriding determinant." It would be useful to test this with the other major donors in the disaster relief system.

The weakest point in the international system for both natural disasters and conflicts is in prevention or mitigation. In the case of natural disasters, early warning systems have been developed – although of course, more could be done. But early warning systems alone are not enough. In the case of natural disasters, the international humanitarian community has come up with the Hyogo Plan of Action and the International Strategy for Disaster Risk Reduction. These offer concrete suggestions for reducing the human impact of natural disasters, but are unfortunately not yet priorities for most national governments or for international donors. In the field of conflict-prevention, there are many initiatives underway – by civil society, governments, international organizations – but the lack of political will and the pesky issue of sovereignty at times create insurmountable obstacles. Human rights activists, for example, long warned that the political situation in Rwanda was explosive just as humanitarian workers warned of an upcoming famine in Ethiopia as early as 1983. Early warning without early action does not prevent displacement.

Differences – or Differences in Degree?

Although research is scarce, there appear to be some differences between conflict-induced and natural disaster-induced displacement – although in most cases, the differences are not absolute, but rather are differences in degree.

1. Solutions may be different for those displaced by natural disasters and by conflicts. For all IDPs, the Guiding Principles on Internal Displacement spell out three solutions – return to the place of origin, integration into the place of displacement, and settlement in another part of the country – and stress that IDPs should have the right to choose the solution. In some natural disasters, IDPs do not have the option of return, e.g.[,] Montserrat and those displaced by riverbank erosion. If predictions are correct that sea levels will rise as a result of climate change, the option of return for those displaced is likely to be difficult or non-existent. For IDPs displaced by conflict, return to the community of origin remains an option – even though it may be politically difficult and may take a long time to realize.

2. Another possible difference is that generally those displaced by natural disasters are more likely to return home more rapidly than those displaced by conflicts. One of the few studies to systematically compare duration of displacement by its cause found in four South Asian countries that 80% of those displaced by natural disasters had been displaced for one year or less, while 57% of those displaced by armed conflict and 66% of those displaced by development projects had been displaced for more than 5 years. There is a growing literature on protracted refugee and conflict-induced IDP situations, indicating that in about two-thirds of these cases, displacement lasts more than 5 years. In the case of refugees, the average length of displacement is 17 years. . . .

3. Those displaced by conflict may – or may not – have more notice than those displaced by natural disasters, at least sudden-onset disasters.

4. Although systematic data are lacking, the number of people who cross national borders because of natural disasters seems to be much lower than those displaced internally. In many cases, conflicts force people to leave not only their communities, but also their countries. Thus, it

is common to have both refugees and IDPs from the same conflict, e.g.[,] Sudanese displaced in Darfur and Sudanese refugees in neighboring Chad, Iraqi refugees in neighboring countries and Iraqi IDPs.

Those who are forced to flee their countries solely because of natural disasters are not considered to be refugees under international law. In the case of the eruption of the volcano on Montserrat in 1995, which (unusually) permanently displaced about half of the country's inhabitants, the response to the displaced was developed by Caribbean and the U.K. governments. In other cases where people have crossed national borders because of natural disasters, such as those fleeing the Ethiopian famine in 1984–85, the humanitarian community has responded as if they were indeed refugees. However, in most cases the cause of famine is due as much to governmental policies as to natural disasters.

5. Governments may be more likely to accept international assistance for people displaced by natural disasters than for those displaced by conflicts. However, this is not absolute as indicated by the example of Hurricane Katrina where the U.S. government was unwilling – or unable – to accept immediate offers of assistance. And access to conflict areas, even in times of natural disasters, may be limited by authorities.

The role of the military – either national or international forces in providing assistance to the displaced – is more generally accepted in natural disasters than in conflict. However, as Kälin pointed out with respect to tsunami-affected countries:

> While it is often the case that the military is the national institution most equipped with the logistics, personnel and supplies to undertake initial rescue and humanitarian response to large disasters, ongoing military control of aid and of camps can also endanger beneficiaries, because it can heighten the IDPs' vulnerability to sexual exploitation and abuse as well as children's military recruitment, and dampen displaced persons' ability to control decisions affecting their lives. This risk is especially high in situations of internal armed conflict, where the proximity of the military can render the camps a military target for no-state armed groups.

In conflict situations, multinational forces have been used in a number of situations, such as Bosnia, Afghanistan and Iraq to protect the delivery of humanitarian relief. But their presence is often controversial as many humanitarian actors feel that the involvement of military forces contradicts humanitarian principles of neutrality and independence.

Inter-Connections

Natural disasters can cause conflicts and can help resolve them. Conflicts often develop over scarce natural resources, which are exacerbated by natural disasters such as flooding and desertification. U.N. Secretary-General, Ban Ki Moon for example, highlighted the impact of slow-onset natural disasters, intensified by climate change, as a causal factor in the conflict in Darfur. Many researchers have commented on the fact that conflicts over water in the Middle East could intensify in the region.

II. Human Rights, the Environment, and Armed Conflict

Environmental damage is common during war and can harm both present and future generations. Persons who live in or near a combat zone can ingest persistent toxins or be exposed to radiation or other carcinogenic or mutagenic substances. Military action can contaminate air, water, and soil or disrupt ecological processes, thereby generating streams of refugees who flee the damage only to find new forms of environmental degradation associated with large refugee camps. Ecological damage also can hamper or prevent the rebuilding of communities after cessation of the conflict.

Throughout history, militaries have deliberately harmed the environment as a wartime strategy. From the Roman salting of lands around Carthage during the Third Punic War to Iraqi-set oil fires during the 1991 Gulf War, nature and its resources have been targets of attack or turned into weapons. Throughout the twentieth century, the scope for destruction increased with the development of weapons of mass destruction. The potential for harm was evidenced during the Vietnam War when widespread use of chemical defoliants destroyed entire ecosystems and led to public health concerns in the United States and Vietnam. To many observers, the severity of the environmental impacts in Vietnam revealed a need for new international law to mitigate the ecological consequences of armed conflict.

Principle 24 of the Rio Declaration affirms that warfare is inherently destructive of sustainable development. The Declaration calls on states to respect international law concerning the environment in times of armed conflict and cooperate in its further development, as necessary. Humanitarian law consists of customary international law and treaties, codified in the Hague Conventions of 1899 and October 18, 1907, and the Geneva Conventions of August 12, 1949. In 1976, states adopted the first treaty specifically aimed to protect the environment against military assault: the Environmental Modification Convention (ENMOD, Dec. 10, 1976). A year later, Additional Protocol I to the 1949 Geneva Conventions added to the body of law on environmental protection during wartime.

The following materials look at the role of natural resources and the environment in the emergence and resolution of conflicts. The subsequent sections address the law of armed conflict, claims for environmental damage, and the decisions of the International Court of Justice on this issue. Before examining these issues, however, preliminary questions must be addressed: What is the relationship between humanitarian law and human rights law? Do they overlap, or is there a clear demarcation between the applicability of one set of norms and the other?

A. *The Relationship of Humanitarian Law to Human Rights Law*

Scholars and activists have debated the relationship between human rights and humanitarian law for several decades. Does human rights law apply only in peacetime? Does humanitarian law apply to all conflicts from riots to world wars? How does the notion that states may derogate from certain guaranteed rights in time of national emergency fit within the two bodies of law? In 2004, the International Court of Justice discussed the scope of humanitarian law and human rights law in response to a request from the U.N. General Assembly for an advisory opinion on Israel's international legal obligations in the occupied Palestinian territories; an extract is printed herein. The legal adviser to the International Committee of the Red Cross also addressed the issue the following year.

Statement by Emanuela-Chiara Gillard, ICRC Legal Adviser,
International Association of Refugee Law Judges World Conference
(Stockholm, Apr. 21–23, 2005)

While international humanitarian law only applies in times of armed conflict, human rights law applies at *all* times; in times of peace and in times of armed conflict. The concurrent application of these two bodies of law has been expressly recognised by various international tribunals, including the International Court of Justice, the U.N. Human Rights Committee, the European Court of

Human Rights, the Inter-American Commission on Human Rights and, of course, numerous national courts.

This being said, some human rights treaties permit states to derogate from certain rights in times of public emergency. Certain key rights may never be suspended, including the right to life and the prohibition of torture or cruel, inhuman or degrading treatment or punishment. Moreover, unless and until they have issued derogations in accordance with the relevant procedures states are bound by the entirety of their conventional obligations even in times of armed conflict.

The scope of application of the two bodies of law is slightly different. International humanitarian law binds all actors in armed conflicts: states, organised armed groups and individuals. Human rights law, on the other hand, lays down rules that regulate states in their relations with *individuals*. While there is a growing body of opinion according to which organised armed groups – particularly if they exercise government-like functions – must also respect human rights the issue remains unsettled. Although individuals do not have specific obligations under human rights law, the most serious violations of human rights, such as genocide, crimes against humanity and torture, are criminalised by international law and are often crimes under national criminal law.

The essence of some of the rules of international humanitarian law and human rights law is similar. For example, both bodies of law aim to protect human life. prohibit torture or cruel treatment, prescribe basic rights for persons facing criminal proceedings and prohibit discrimination. However, care must be taken to ensure the proper articulation of the relationship between the two sets of rules.

As stated by the International Court of Justice in its advisory opinion on *Nuclear Weapons*, in situations of armed conflict, international humanitarian law is *lex specialis*. What does this mean? The precise interplay depends on the rules in question.

There may be certain matters for which international humanitarian law lays down a "self-contained" set of rules. In these cases the provisions of international humanitarian law apply to the exclusion of human rights. A case in point are the rules relating to prisoners of war found in the Third Geneva Convention[,] which, with regard to most matters, is a self-contained system. For example, this means that prisoners of war can be deprived of their liberty until the end of hostilities and a right to challenge the deprivation of liberty cannot be inferred from human rights law. [Article 5 of Third Geneva Convention does give captured combatants a right to have their entitlement to prisoner of war status determined by a competent tribunal. – *Eds.*]

On the other hand, international humanitarian law can be vague or silent on particular questions, in which case it is proper to turn to human rights law for guidance to interpret the rules in question. This is most notable in relation to fair trial provisions, where international humanitarian law only contains general provisions, like a reference to entitlement to "judicial guarantees recognised as indispensable by civilised peoples." The precise contents of such guarantees can be inferred from human rights law. Human rights law is also an important source of rules and protection in non-international armed conflicts, where the international humanitarian law treaty rules are few.

Finally, there may be issues addressed by *both* bodies of law. As international humanitarian law is *lex specialis*, the human rights norm must be interpreted through the prism of international humanitarian law. What do I mean by this? The right to life can serve as an example. What constitutes an "unlawful killing" in situations of armed conflict must be assessed on the basis of the relevant rules of international humanitarian law, including the fact that combatants or other persons taking a direct part in hostilities may be attacked – even with lethal force; and that killing of civilians in certain circumstances may not be prohibited. They may be permissible "collateral damage." The lawfulness of such deaths must be assessed pursuant to international humanitarian law's principle of proportionality[,] which requires a balancing of the incidental loss of civilian life or injury to civilians with the concrete and direct military advantage expected from a particular attack.

In recent years we have been seeing the emergence of extremely interesting and important case law from human rights and national courts as they grapple with this complex relationship. The analysis is not rendered any easier by the question of the extent of extra-territorial application of human rights.

Legal Consequences of the Construction of a Wall in the Occupied Palestinian Territory, Advisory Opinion, 2004 I.C.J. 136 (July 9)

[On December 10, 2003, the secretary-general of the United Nations notified the ICJ of the decision taken by the General Assembly to submit the question set forth in its resolution ES-10/14, adopted on 8 December 2003, for an advisory opinion on the following question:

> What are the legal consequences arising from the construction of the wall being built by Israel, the occupying Power, in the Occupied Palestinian Territory, including in and around East Jerusalem, as described in the report of the Secretary-General, considering the rules and principles of international law, including the Fourth Geneva Convention of 1949, and relevant Security Council and General Assembly resolutions?

The excerpt here contains the Court's treatment of humanitarian law and the issue of the applicability of human rights law in the Occupied Palestinian territory. – Eds.]

. . .

89. As regards international humanitarian law, the Court would first note that Israel is not a party to the Fourth Hague Convention of 1907, to which the Hague Regulations are annexed. The Court observes that, in the words of the Convention, those Regulations were prepared "to revise the general laws and customs of war" existing at that time. Since then, however, the International Military Tribunal of Nuremberg has found that the "rules laid down in the Convention were recognized by all civilized nations, and were regarded as being declaratory of the laws and customs of war" (Judgment of the International Military Tribunal of Nuremberg, 30 September and 1 October 1946, p. 65). The Court itself reached the same conclusion when examining the rights and duties of belligerents in their conduct of military operations (Legality of the Threat or Use of Nuclear Weapons, Advisory Opinion, I. C. J. Reports 1996 (1), p. 256, para. 75). The Court considers that the provisions of the Hague Regulations have become part of customary law, as is in fact recognized by all the participants in the proceedings before the Court.

90. Secondly, with regard to the Fourth Geneva Convention, differing views have been expressed by the participants in these proceedings. Israel, contrary to the great majority of the other participants, disputes the applicability de jure of the Convention to the Occupied Palestinian Territory. In particular, in paragraph 3 of Annex 1 to the report of the Secretary-General, entitled "Summary Legal Position of the Government of Israel," it is stated that Israel does not agree that the Fourth Geneva Convention "is applicable to the occupied Palestinian Territory," citing "the lack of recognition of the territory as sovereign prior to its annexation by Jordan and Egypt" and inferring that it is "not a territory of a High Contracting Party as required by the Convention."

. . .

93. . . . Subsequently, the Israeli authorities have indicated on a number of occasions that in fact they generally apply the humanitarian provisions of the Fourth Geneva Convention within the occupied territories. However, according to Israel's position as briefly recalled in paragraph 90 above, that Convention is not applicable de jure within those territories because, under Article 2, paragraph 2, it applies only in the case of occupation of territories

falling under the sovereignty of a High Contracting Party involved in an armed conflict. Israel explains that Jordan was admittedly a party to the Fourth Geneva Convention in 1967, and that an armed conflict broke out at that time between Israel and Jordan, but it goes on to observe that the territories occupied by Israel subsequent to that conflict had not previously fallen under Jordanian sovereignty. It infers from this that that Convention is not applicable *de jure* in those territories.

. . .

95. The Court notes that, according to the first paragraph of Article 2 of the Fourth Geneva Convention, that Convention is applicable when two conditions are fulfilled: that there exists an armed conflict (whether or not a state of war has been recognized); and that the conflict has arisen between two contracting parties. If those two conditions are satisfied, the Convention applies, in particular, in any territory occupied in the course of the conflict by one of the contracting parties.

The object of the second paragraph of Article 2 is not to restrict the scope of application of the Convention, as defined by the first paragraph, by excluding therefrom territories not falling under the sovereignty of one of the contracting parties. It is directed simply to making it clear that, even if occupation effected during the conflict met no armed resistance, the Convention is still applicable.

This interpretation reflects the intention of the drafters of the Fourth Geneva Convention to protect civilians who find themselves, in whatever way, in the hands of the occupying Power. Whilst the drafters of the Hague Regulations of 1907 were as much concerned with protecting the rights of a State whose territory is occupied, as with protecting the inhabitants of that territory, the drafters of the Fourth Geneva Convention sought to guarantee the protection of civilians in time of war, regardless of the status of the occupied territories, as is shown by Article 47 of the Convention.

. . .

96. The Court would moreover note that the States parties to the Fourth Geneva Convention approved that interpretation at their Conference (on 15 July 1995). They issued a statement in which they "reaffirmed the applicability of the Fourth Geneva Convention to the Occupied Palestinian Territory, including East Jerusalem." Subsequently, on 5 December 2001, the High Contracting Parties, referring in particular to Article 1 of the Fourth Geneva Convention of 1949, once again reaffirmed the "applicability of the Fourth Geneva Convention to the Occupied Palestinian Territory, including East Jerusalem." They further reminded the Contracting Parties participating in the Conference, the parties to the conflict, and the State of Israel as occupying Power, of their respective obligations.

97. Moreover, the Court would observe that the ICRC, whose special position with respect to execution of the Fourth Geneva Convention must be "recognized and respected at all times" by the parties pursuant to Article 142 of the Convention, has also expressed its opinion on the interpretation to be given to the Convention. In a declaration of 5 December 2001, it recalled that "the ICRC has always affirmed the *de jure* applicability of the Fourth Geneva Convention to the territories occupied since 1967 by the State of Israel, including East Jerusalem."

. . .

101. In view of the foregoing, the Court considers that the Fourth Geneva Convention is applicable in any occupied territory in the event of an armed conflict arising between two or more High Contracting Parties. Israel and Jordan were parties to that Convention when the 1967 armed conflict broke out. The Court accordingly finds that that Convention is applicable in the Palestinian territories which before the conflict lay to the east of the Green Line and which, during that conflict, were occupied by Israel, there being no need for any enquiry into the precise prior status of those territories.

102.   The participants in the proceedings before the Court also disagree whether the international human rights conventions to which Israel is party apply within the Occupied Palestinian Territory. Annex 1 to the report of the Secretary-General states:

> 4. Israel denies that the International Covenant on Civil and Political Rights and the International Covenant on Economic, Social and Cultural Rights, both of which it has signed, are applicable to the occupied Palestinian territory. It asserts that humanitarian law is the protection granted in a conflict situation such as the one in the West Bank and Gaza Strip, whereas human rights treaties were intended for the protection of citizens from their own Government in times of peace.

Of the other participants in the proceedings, those who addressed this issue contend that, on the contrary, both Covenants are applicable within the Occupied Palestinian Territory.

103.   On 3 October 1991 Israel ratified both the International Covenant on Economic, Social and Cultural Rights of 19 December 1966 and the International Covenant on Civil and Political Rights of the same date, as well as the United Nations Convention on the Rights of the Child of 20 November 1989. It is a party to these three instruments.

104.   In order to determine whether these texts are applicable in the Occupied Palestinian Territory, the Court will first address the issue of the relationship between international humanitarian law and human rights law and then that of the applicability of human rights instruments outside national territory.

105.   In its Advisory Opinion of 8 July 1996 on the *Legality of the Threat or Use of Nuclear Weapons*, the Court had occasion to address the first of these issues in relation to the International Covenant on Civil and Political Rights. In those proceedings certain States had argued that "the Covenant was directed to the protection of human rights in peacetime, but that questions relating to unlawful loss of life in hostilities were governed by the law applicable in armed conflict" (*I. C.J. Reports 1996* (I), p. 239, para. 24).

The Court rejected this argument, stating that:

> the protection of the International Covenant of Civil and Political Rights does not cease in times of war, except by operation of Article 4 of the Covenant whereby certain provisions may be derogated from in a time of national emergency. Respect for the right to life is not, however, such a provision. In principle, the right not arbitrarily to be deprived of one's life applies also in hostilities. The test of what is an arbitrary deprivation of life, however, then falls to be determined by the applicable *lex specialis*, namely, the law applicable in armed conflict which is designed to regulate the conduct of hostilities. (Ibid, p. 240, para. 25.)

106.   More generally, the Court considers that the protection offered by human rights conventions does not cease in case of armed conflict, save through the effect of provisions for derogation of the kind to be found in Article 4 of the International Covenant on Civil and Political Rights. As regards the relationship between international humanitarian law and human rights law, there are thus three possible situations: some rights may be exclusively matters of international humanitarian law; others may be exclusively matters of human rights law; yet others may be matters of both these branches of international law. In order to answer the question put to it, the Court will have to take into consideration both these branches of international law, namely human rights law and, as *lex specialis*, international humanitarian law.

107.   It remains to be determined whether the two international Covenants and the Convention on the Rights of the Child are applicable only on the territories of the States parties thereto or whether they are also applicable outside those territories and, if so, in what circumstances.

108.   The scope of application of the International Covenant on Civil and Political Rights is defined by Article 2, paragraph 1, thereof, which provides:

> Each State Party to the present Covenant undertakes to respect and to ensure to all individuals within its territory and subject to its jurisdiction the rights recognized in the present Covenant, without distinction of any kind, such as race, colour, sex, language, religion, political or other opinion, national or social origin, property, birth or other status.

This provision can be interpreted as covering only individuals who are present within a State's territory and subject to that State's jurisdiction. It can also be construed as covering both individuals present within a State's territory and those outside that territory but subject to that State's jurisdiction. The Court will thus seek to determine the meaning to be given to this text.

109.   The Court would observe that, while the jurisdiction of States is primarily territorial, it may sometimes be exercised outside the national territory. Considering the object and purpose of the International Covenant on Civil and Political Rights, it would seem natural that, even when such is the case, States parties to the Covenant should be bound to comply with its provisions.

The constant practice of the Human Rights Committee is consistent with this. Thus, the Committee has found the Covenant applicable where the State exercises its jurisdiction on foreign territory. It has ruled on the legality of acts by Uruguay in cases of arrests carried out by Uruguayan agents in Brazil or Argentina (case No. 52/79, *Lopez Burgos v. Uruguay*; case No. 56/79, *Lilian Celiherti de Cusariego v. Uruguay*). It decided to the same effect in the case of the confiscation of a passport by a Uruguayan consulate in Germany (case No. 106181, *Montero v. Uruguay*).

The *travaux préparatoires* of the Covenant confirm the Committee's interpretation of Article 2 of that instrument. These show that, in adopting the wording chosen, the drafters of the Covenant did not intend to allow States to escape from their obligations when they exercise jurisdiction outside their national territory. They only intended to prevent persons residing abroad from asserting, vis-à-vis their State of origin, rights that do not fall within the competence of that State, but of that of the State of residence (see the discussion of the preliminary draft in the Commission on Human Rights, EICN.4lSR.194, para. 46; and United Nations, *Official Records of the General Assembly, Tenth Session, Annexes*, A12929, Part II, Chap. V, para. 4 (1955)).

         . . .

111.   In conclusion, the Court considers that the International Covenant on Civil and Political Rights is applicable in respect of acts done by a State in the exercise of its jurisdiction outside its own territory.

112.   The International Covenant on Economic, Social and Cultural Rights contains no provision on its scope of application. This may be explicable by the fact that this Covenant guarantees rights which are essentially territorial. However, it is not to be excluded that it applies both to territories over which a State party has sovereignty and to those over which that State exercises territorial jurisdiction. Thus Article 14 makes provision for transitional measures in the case of any State which "at the time of becoming a Party, has not been able to secure in its metropolitan territory or other territories under its jurisdiction compulsory primary education, free of charge."

It is not without relevance to recall in this regard the position taken by Israel in its reports to the Committee on Economic, Social and Cultural Rights. In its initial report to the Committee of 4 December 1998, Israel provided "statistics indicating the enjoyment of the rights enshrined in the Covenant by Israeli settlers in the occupied Territories." The Committee noted that, according to Israel, "the Palestinian population within the same jurisdictional areas were excluded from both the report and the protection of the Covenant"

(E/C.12/1/Add.27, para. 8). The Committee expressed its concern in this regard, to which Israel replied in a further report of 19 October 2001 that it has "consistently maintained that the Covenant does not apply to areas that are not subject to its sovereign territory and jurisdiction" (a formula inspired by the language of the International Covenant on Civil and Political Rights). This position, continued Israel, is "based on the well-established distinction between human rights and humanitarian law under international law." It added: "the Committee's mandate cannot relate to events in the West Bank and the Gaza Strip, inasmuch as they are part and parcel of the context of armed conflict as distinct from a relationship of human rights" (E/1990/6/Add.32, para. 5). In view of these observations, the Committee reiterated its concern about Israel's position and reaffirmed "its view that the State party's obligations under the Covenant apply to all territories and populations under its effective control" (E/C.12/1Add.90, paras. 15 and 31).

For the reasons explained in paragraph 106 above, the Court cannot accept Israel's view. It would also observe that the territories occupied by Israel have for over 37 years been subject to its territorial jurisdiction as the occupying Power. In the exercise of the powers available to it on this basis, Israel is bound by the provisions of the International Covenant on Economic, Social and Cultural Rights. Furthermore, it is under an obligation not to raise any obstacle to the exercise of such rights in those fields where competence has been transferred to Palestinian authorities.

113. As regards the Convention on the Rights of the Child of 20 November 1989, that instrument contains an Article 2 according to which "States Parties shall respect and ensure the rights set forth in the . . . Convention to each child within their jurisdiction. . . . " That Convention is therefore applicable within the Occupied Palestinian Territory.

Questions and Discussion

1. Can you explain how *lex specialis* would apply in the event of conflict between a human right and norm of humanitarian law? Does it always mean that in a conflict situation that humanitarian law will prevail? Would the *lex generalis* retain any relevance? For instance, could it be looked to for guidance in interpreting the *lex specialis* rule? The Human Rights Committee has observed that

   the Covenant [ICCPR] applies also in situations of armed conflict to which the rules of international humanitarian law are applicable. While, in respect of certain Covenant rights, more specific rules of international humanitarian law may be specially relevant for the purposes of the interpretation of Covenant rights, both spheres of law are complementary, not mutually exclusive.

   U.N. Human Rights Committee, General Comment No. 31[80] *Nature of the General Legal Obligation Imposed on States Parties to the Covenant*, CCPR/C/21/Rev.1/Add.13, at para. 11 (May 26, 2004). If these areas of law are "complementary, not mutually exclusive," is *lex specialis* ever relevant?

2. Tribunals other than the International Court of Justice have also applied human rights contained in treaties over which they have jurisdiction to situations of armed conflict. In *Bamaca Velásquez v. Guatemala*, Petition No 11.129/1993 (Judgment, Nov. 25, 2000), the Inter-American Court on Human Rights also applied international human rights law in a situation of armed conflict:

   The Court considers that it has been proved that, at the time of the facts of this case, an internal conflict was taking place in Guatemala. . . . As has previously been stated . . . instead of exonerating the State from its obligations to respect and guarantee human rights, this fact obliged it to act in accordance with such obligations.

Id. at para. 207. The European Court of Human Rights notably applied the European Convention on Human Rights to the conflict in the Russian Federation in *Isayeva, Yusupova and Bazayeva v. Russia*, Application Nos. 57947/00, 57948/00 and 57949/00, 41 Eur. H.R. Rep. 39 (Feb. 24, 2005) and to Turkish occupation of Northern Cyprus, in *Cyprus v. Turkey*, Application No. 25781/94 (May 10, 2001). For further discussion, see Christine Byron, *A Blurring of Boundaries: The Application of International Humanitarian Law by Human Rights Bodies*, 48 Va. J. Int'l L. 839 (2007).

B. *The Role of Natural Resources and the Environment in Armed Conflicts*

To what extent is control of natural resources a source of conflict? Can rules respecting shared natural resources help avoid conflict? How serious are the predictions of future water wars? There is considerable debate over these issues, and efforts are being made to garner the empirical evidence necessary to understand the relationships among natural resources, the environment, and armed conflict. The U.N. Environment Programme has taken a first look at these questions in the following extract.

From Conflict to Peacebuilding: The Role of Natural Resources and the Environment, Consultation Draft, at 5, 6, 8, 15, 19 (Sept. 2008) U.N. Environment Programme

Since 1990 at least eighteen violent conflicts have been fuelled by the exploitation of natural resources. In fact, recent research suggests that over the last sixty years at least forty percent of all intrastate conflicts have a link to natural resources. Civil wars such as those in Liberia, Angola and the Democratic Republic of Congo have centered on "high-value" resources like timber, diamonds, gold, minerals and oil. Other conflicts, including those in Darfur and the Middle East, have involved control of scarce resources such as fertile land and water.

As the global population continues to rise, and demand for resources continues to grow, there is significant potential for conflicts over natural resources to intensify in the coming decades. In addition, the potential consequences of climate change for water availability, food security, prevalence of disease, coastal boundaries, and population distribution may aggravate existing tensions and generate new conflicts.

Environmental factors are rarely, if ever, the sole cause of violent conflict. Ethnicity, adverse economic conditions, low levels of international trade and conflict in neighboring countries are all significant drivers of violence. However, the exploitation of natural and related environmental stresses can be implicated in all phases of the conflict cycle, from contributing to the outbreak and perpetuation of violence to undermining prospects for peace. In addition, the environment itself can fall victim to conflict, as direct and indirect environmental damage, coupled with the collapse of institutions, can lead to environmental risks that threaten people's health, livelihoods and security.

Because the way that natural resources and the environment are governed has a determining influence on peace and security, these issues can also contribute to a relapse into conflict if they are not properly managed in post-conflict situations. Indeed, preliminary findings from a retrospective analysis of intrastate conflicts over the past sixty years indicate that conflicts associated with natural resources are twice as likely to relapse into conflict in the first five years. Nevertheless, fewer than a quarter of peace negotiations aiming to resolve conflicts linked to natural resources have addressed resource management mechanisms.

. . .

Integrating environment and natural resources into peacebuilding is no longer an option – it is a security imperative. . . .

. . .

The 2004 report of the United Nations High-Level Panel on Threats, Challenges and Change highlighted the fundamental relationship between the environment, security, and social and economic development in the pursuit of global peace in the 21st century, while a historical debate at the U.N. Security Council in June 2007 concluded that poor management of "high-value" resources constituted a threat to peace. . . . The potential for conflicts to be ignited by the environmental impacts of climate change is also attracting international interest in this topic. . . . As a result, no serious discussion of current or emerging threats to security can take place without considering the role of natural resources and the environment.

. . .

The relationship between natural resources, the environment and conflict is thus multi-dimensional and complex, but three principal pathways can be drawn:

a) Contributing to the outbreak of conflict: Attempts to control natural resources or grievances caused by inequitable wealth sharing or environmental degradation can contribute to the outbreak of violence. Countries that depend on the export of a narrow set of primary commodities may also be more vulnerable to conflict.

b) Financing and sustaining conflict: Once conflict has broken out, extractive "high-value" resources may be exploited to finance armed forces, or become strategic considerations in gaining territory. In such cases, the duration of conflict is extended in the availability of new sources of financing, or complicated by efforts to gain control over resource-rich areas.

c) Undermining peacemaking: The prospect of a peace agreement may be undermined by individuals or splinter groups that could lose access to the revenues generated by resource exploitation if peace were to prevail. Once a peace agreement is in place, the exploitation of natural resources can also threaten political reintegration and reconciliation by providing economic incentives that reinforce political and social divisions.

. . .

The environment has always been a silent casualty of conflict. To secure a strategic advantage, demoralize local populations or subdue resistance, water wells have been polluted, crops torched, forests cut down, soils poisoned, and animals killed. In some cases, such as the draining of the marshlands of the Euphrates-Tigris Delta by Saddam Hussein during the 1980s and 1990s, ecosystems have also been deliberately targeted to achieve political and military goals. During the Vietnam war, nearly 72 million litres of the dioxin-containing defoliant Agent Orange were sprayed over the country's forests, resulting in entire areas being stripped of all vegetation. Some of these areas remain unsuitable for any form of agricultural use today. . . .

While numerous other examples of natural resources being used as a weapon of war exist, the majority of the environmental damage that occurs in times of conflict is collateral, or related to the preparations and execution phases of wars and to the coping strategies of local populations. In this regard, impacts of conflict on the environment can be divided into three main pathways:

a) Direct impacts: are caused by the physical destruction of ecosystems and wildlife or the release of polluting and hazardous substances into the natural environment during conflict.

b) Indirect impacts: result from the coping strategies used by local and displaced populations to survive the socio-economic disruption and loss of basic services caused by conflict. This often entails the liquidation of natural assets for immediate survival income, or the overuse of marginal areas, which can lead to long-term environmental damage.

c) Institutional impacts: Conflict causes a disruption of state institutions, initiatives, and mech-anisms of policy coordination, which in turn creates space for poor management, lack of investment, illegality, and the collapse of positive environmental practice. At the same time, financial resources are diverted away from investments in public infrastructure and essential services towards military objectives.

. . .

Whether a war-torn society can maintain peace after a conflict ceases depends on a broad range of factors, including the conditions that led to the onset of war, the characteristics of the conflict itself, the nature of the peace settlement, and the influence of external forces (i.e., global economic or political pressures).

The previous sections have shown that natural resources can be an important contributing factor in the outbreak of conflict, in financing and sustaining conflict, and in spoiling peacemaking prospects. Increasing demand for resources, population growth and environmental stresses including climate change, will likely compound these problems. At the same time, conflicts cause serious environmental impacts, which need to be addressed to protect health and livelihoods.

In peacebuilding, it is therefore critical that the environmental drivers and impacts of conflict are managed, that tensions are defused, and that natural assets are used sustainably to support stability and development in the longer term. Indeed, there can be no durable peace if the natural resources that sustain livelihoods and ecosystem services are damaged, degraded or destroyed. As mentioned above, conflicts associated with natural resources are twice as likely to relapse into conflict in the first five years. Despite this, fewer than a quarter of peace negotiations aiming to resolve conflicts linked to natural resources have addressed resource management mechanisms.

Furthermore, the U.N. has not effectively integrated environment and natural resource considerations into its peacebuilding interventions. Priorities typically lie in meeting humanitarian needs, demobilization, disarmament, and reintegration, supporting elections, restoring order and the rule of law, and opening the economy to foreign investment. The environment and natural resources are often framed as issues to be addressed at a later stage.

This is a mistaken approach, which fails to take into account the changing nature of the threats to national and international security. Rather, integrating these issues into peacebuilding should be considered a security imperative, as deferred action or poor choices made early on often establish unsustainable trajectories of recovery that may undermine long-term peace and stability.

To ensure that environmental and natural resource issues are successfully integrated across the range of peacebuilding activities, it is critical that they are not treated in isolation, but instead form an integral part of the analyses and assessments that guide peacebuilding interventions. Indeed, it is only through a cross-cutting approach that these issues can be tackled effectively as part of peacebuilding measures to address the factors that may trigger a relapse of violence or impede the peace consolidation process. . . .

a) Supporting economic recovery: With the crucial provision that they are properly governed and carefully managed – "high-value" resources (such as hydrocarbons, minerals, metals, stones and export timber) hold out the prospect of positive economic development, employment and budget revenue. The risk, however, is that the pressure to kick-start development and earn foreign exchange can lead to rapid uncontrolled exploitation of such resources at sub-optimal prices, without due attention to environmental sustainability and the equitable distribution of revenues. When the benefits are not shared, or when environmental degradation occurs as a consequence of exploitation, there is serious potential for conflict to resume.

b) Developing sustainable livelihoods: Durable peace fundamentally hinges on the development of sustainable livelihoods, the provision of basic services, and on the recovery and sound management of the natural resource base. Environmental damage caused by conflicts, coping strategies, and chronic environmental problems that undermine livelihoods must therefore be addressed from the outset. Minimizing vulnerability to natural hazards and climate change through the management of key natural resources and the introduction of appropriate technologies should also be addressed.

c) Contributing to dialogue, cooperation and confidence-building: The environment can be an effective platform or catalyst for enhancing dialogue, building confidence, exploiting shared interests and broadening cooperation between divided groups as well as within and between states.

Questions and Discussion

1. Given the UNEP's conclusions, what measures would you include in a peace program for Iraq? Consider the question again after reading the UNEP's 2003 "Desk Study" of the environmental problems in Iraq stemming from recent conflicts, reprinted at section D of this Chapter *infra*.

2. Should environmental protection be considered a part of national security? What difference would it make in law and policy?

3. For further reading, see K. BALLENTINE & H. NITZSCHKE, PROFITING FROM PEACE: MANAGING THE RESOURCE DIMENSIONS OF CIVIL WAR (2005); J. BARNETT, THE MEANING OF ENVIRONMENTAL SECURITY: ECOLOGICAL POLITICS AND POLICY IN THE NEW SECURITY ERA (2001); O. Brown et al., *Climate Change: The New Security Threat*, 83 INT'L AFF. 1141 (2007); NATURAL RESOURCES AND VIOLENT CONFLICT: OPTIONS AND ACTIONS (P. COLLIER & I. BANNON EDS., 2003); P. DIEHL & N.P. GLEDITSCH, ENVIRONMENTAL CONFLICTS (2001); GLOBAL WITNESS, SINEWS OF WAR – ELIMINATING THE TRADE IN CONFLICT RESOURCES (2006); T. HOMER-DIXON, ENVIRONMENT, SCARCITY, AND VIOLENCE (1999); UNDERSTANDING ENVIRONMENT, CONFLICT AND COOPERATION (S. LONERGAN ED., 2004); A. SALEEM, PEACE PARKS: CONSERVATION AND CONFLICT RESOLUTION (2007).

C. *The Law of Armed Conflict*

State practice and religious traditions have long prohibited deliberate attacks on certain objects, such as the destruction of trees during war. Grotius, in his classic *On the Law of War and Peace*, contended that the law of nations forbids the poisoning of water; in a chapter on moderation in laying waste, he also supported the principle later known as military necessity, a principle that prohibits wanton destruction. Until the U.S. Civil War (1861–1864), however, states had not approved any agreement setting forth the laws of war. During that conflict, the U.S. Army adopted the Lieber Code of 1863, which imposed rules on the treatment of civilians and prisoners of war and set limits on the means and methods of warfare. Four principles emerged from the Lieber Code to become generally accepted in state practice and international agreements:

- military necessity;
- proportionality;
- prevention of unnecessary suffering; and
- discrimination between civilian and military targets.

These principles are given detailed elaboration in the law of armed conflict, including in agreements on treatment of wounded and prisoners of war, bans on certain weapons, the duties of occupying powers, and specific rules for different theaters of conflict (land, air, sea). Among the legal instruments governing armed conflict are several that contain provisions relevant to environmental protection:

- St. Petersburg Declaration Renouncing the Use, in Time of War, of Explosive Projectiles under 400 Grammes in Weight, St. Petersburg, Nov. 29, 1868, AM. J. INT'L L. 1 (Supp.) 95;

- Hague Convention (No. IV) Respecting the Laws and Customs of War on Land (1907), The Hague, Oct. 18, 1907, 36 Stat. 2277, T.S. No. 539;
- Geneva Protocol for the Prohibition of the Use in War of Asphyxiating, Poisonous or Other Gases and of Bacteriological Methods of Warfare (1925), Geneva, June 17, 1925, 26 U.S.T. 571, T.I.A.S. No. 8061, 14 I.L.M. 49 (1975);
- Convention Relative to the Protection of Civilian Persons in Time of War (Geneva, Aug. 12, 1949), 6 U.S.T. 3516, T.I.A.S. No. 3365, 75 U.N.T.S. 287 (Geneva Convention (IV)) and Additional Protocol I Relating to the Protection of Victims of International Armed Conflicts, June 8, 1977, 1125 U.N.T.S. 3, *reprinted in* 16 I.L.M. 1391 (1977);
- Treaty Banning Nuclear Weapon Tests in the Atmosphere, in Outer Space and Under Water, Moscow, Aug. 5, 1963, 480 U.N.T.S. 43 (1963) and Comprehensive Test Ban Treaty, Sept. 24, 1996;
- Convention on Military or Any Other Hostile Use of Environmental Modification Techniques (ENMOD), May 18, 1977, 1108 U.N.T.S. 151 (1977);
- Protocols II and III to the 1980 U.N. Convention on Certain Conventional Weapons, restricting mines and incendiary weapons;
- Convention on the Prohibition of the Development, Production, Stockpiling and Use of Chemical Weapons and on their Destruction, Paris, Jan. 13, 1993, 32 I.L.M. 800 (1993).

Most of these texts do not explicitly mention the environment, but they contain general principles and provisions that may be applied to promote environmental protection. Any action lacking a military purpose is unlawful.

The 1907 Hague Convention, with its annexed regulations, prohibits the use of poison or poisoned weapons and requires occupying states to refrain from overexploiting resources such as forests. Convention (No. IV) Respecting the Laws and Customs of War on Land, with Annex of Regulations (The Hague, Oct. 18, 1907), arts. 23(a), 55, 36 Stat. 2277 (1911). These rules emerged from a general agreement of the parties that "the right of belligerents to adopt means of injuring the enemy is not unlimited." Hague Convention (IV) Respecting the Laws and Customs of War on Land, art. 22, annex, § 2, ch. I. Several customary international norms enshrined in the Hague Convention could provide potentially far-reaching environmental protection, including the fundamental principles of necessity, proportionality, and discrimination between military and civilian targets.

Perhaps most important, the preamble to the Convention recites the well-known Martens clause, which reads:

> Until a more complete code of the laws of war has been issued, the High Contracting Parties deem it expedient to declare that, in cases not included in the Regulations adopted by them, the inhabitants and the belligerents remain under the protection and the rule of the principles of the law of nations, as they result from the usages established among civilized peoples, from the laws of humanity, and the dictates of the public conscience.

The clause has been repeated in subsequent treaties, including the 1949 Geneva Conventions, the 1977 Additional Protocols I and II, and the 1980 Convention on Certain Conventional Weapons. In the aftermath of the 1991 Gulf War, the International Committee of the Red Cross (ICRC) and the U.N. General Assembly asserted the relevance of the Martens clause to environmental protection.

The Geneva Conventions of 1949 supplemented the provisions of the 1907 Hague Regulations and, like them, protect property, including property owned collectively or by the state or other public authorities. Article 147 of Geneva Convention (IV), on the protection of civilians, includes among "grave breaches" of the Convention any extensive destruction and appropriation of property not justified by military necessity and carried out unlawfully and wantonly. It is unclear whether the term *property* includes public goods, such as water resources, public lands, and air. The Geneva Conventions apply to international armed conflict and not to civil wars. Only one article extends the protections to internal armed conflicts, as described by Frits Kalshoven and Liesbeth Zegveld, in *Constraints on the Waging of War: An Introduction to International Humanitarian Law* (ICRC, 2001):

Common Article 3

Article 3 common to the Conventions of 1949, as the only article especially written for non-international armed conflict, has been described either as a "mini-convention" or as a "convention within the conventions." It provides rules which parties to an internal armed conflict are "bound to apply, as a minimum." Given that in present times the majority of armed conflicts fall within this category, the article has assumed an importance the drafters could hardly have foreseen.

The article presents a peculiar problem in that armed opposition groups are not (and indeed, formally cannot become) parties to the Conventions. They may use this as an argument to deny any obligation to apply the article. A strong argument to encourage armed opposition groups to adopt a more positive attitude is that application of Article 3 is likely to entail an improvement of their "image," in the country and in the eyes of the outside world as well, and thus may work to their advantage.

Another aspect of the same problem is that governments often do not wish to recognise insurgents as an official "party to the conflict," or even as a separate entity. They may therefore wish to avoid any statement officially acknowledging that Article 3 is applicable, for fear that this would be read as a recognition of the insurgents as an adverse party. In an attempt to meet this objection, Article 3(4) stipulates that application of its provisions "shall not affect the legal status of the Parties to the conflict." Evidently, this form of words cannot prevent the potential effect the application of the article may have, or be perceived to have, on the political status of the insurgents.

A government faced with this dilemma might realise that even though a refusal on its part to recognise the application of Article 3 may be one possible device for withholding political status from the insurgents, such a refusal in the face of obvious facts may at the same time do serious damage to its own "image," again, both in the eyes of its own population and in those of the outside world. For, as we shall see, the rules contained in Article 3 are minimum standards in the most literal sense of the term; standards, in other words, no respectable government could disregard for any length of time without losing its aura of respectability. It should be noted that Article 3 is applicable in all conflicts not of an international character. These include not only conflicts which see the government opposed to an armed opposition group but also conflicts between two armed opposition groups to which the government is not a party.

The article prescribes the humane treatment, without discrimination, of all those who take no active part in the hostilities, including members of armed forces (regular or otherwise) who "have laid down their arms" or are hors de combat as a consequence of "sickness, wounds, detention, or any other cause." With respect to all these persons: the following acts are and shall remain prohibited at any time and in any place whatsoever:

(a) violence to life and person, in particular murder of all kinds, mutilation, cruel treatment and torture;
(b) taking of hostages;
(c) outrages upon personal dignity, in particular humiliating and degrading treatment;
(d) the passing of sentences and the carrying out of executions without previous judgment pronounced by a regularly constituted court, affording all the judicial guarantees which are recognised as indispensable by civilised peoples.

Note that the terms "respect" and "protection" do not figure in this text: the provision of humane treatment is the only requirement. Furthermore, there is no reference to prisoner-of-war status, no matter for whom; nor is punishment merely for participation in hostilities excluded, the only conditions being those of a fair trial (which, of course, may be the difference between life and death).

As regards humanitarian assistance, Article 3 requires no more than that "the wounded and sick shall be collected and cared for." Matters such as registration, information, or the status of medical personnel, hospitals and ambulances, are not mentioned at all.

In the penultimate paragraph, the parties to the conflict are encouraged "to bring into force, by means of special agreements, all or part of the other provisions" of the Conventions. The parties may actually be prepared to do this when they have a shared interest, for instance, in organising an exchange of prisoners who are a burden on their hands. The conclusion of such agreements will often come about through the intermediary of the ICRC.

Other treaties include specific measures relating to the environment, *inter alia*, article I of the Convention on Military or Any Other Hostile Use of Environmental Modification Techniques (ENMOD), articles 35(3) and 55(1) of the 1977 Additional Protocol I to the Geneva Convention, and article 2 of Protocol III to the U.N. Conventional Weapons Convention. The ENMOD Convention is primarily concerned with the use of nature as a weapon of war. Environmental modification, defined in article II, means "any technique for changing – through the deliberate manipulation of natural processes – the dynamics, composition or structure of the Earth, including its biota, lithosphere, hydrosphere and atmosphere, or of outer space." Article 1 prohibits all "hostile use of environmental modification techniques having widespread, long-lasting or severe effects as the means of destruction, damage or injury" to the opposing side. A contemporaneous understanding of the Conference of the U.N. Committee on Disarmament defined *widespread* to mean an area on the scale of several hundred square kilometers. *Longlasting* means a period of months, approximately a season, and *severe* is defined as "involving serious or significant disruption or harm to human life, natural and economic resources or other assets."

Additional Protocol I to the 1949 Geneva Convention significantly advanced the law concerning environmental protection during warfare. It contains several provisions directly related to protection of the environment and noncombatants.

Protocol Additional to the Geneva Conventions of 12 August 1949, and Relating to the Protection of Victims of International Armed Conflicts (Protocol 1),

Adopted June 8, 1977, by the Diplomatic Conference on the Reaffirmation and Development of International Humanitarian Law applicable in Armed Conflicts, entry into force December, 7 1979

PART III SECTION I. – METHODS AND MEANS OF WARFARE

Article 35. – Basic Rules

1. In any armed conflict, the right of the Parties to the conflict to choose methods or means of warfare is not unlimited.
2. It is prohibited to employ weapons, projectiles and material and methods of warfare of a nature to cause superfluous injury or unnecessary suffering.

3. It is prohibited to employ methods or means of warfare which are intended, or may be expected, to cause widespread, long-term and severe damage to the natural environment.

Article 53. – Protection of Cultural Objects and of Places of Worship

Without prejudice to the provisions of the Hague Convention for the Protection of Cultural Property in the Event of Armed Conflict of 14 May 1954, and of other relevant international instruments, it is prohibited:
  (a) To commit any acts of hostility directed against the historic monuments, works of art or places of worship which constitute the cultural or spiritual heritage of peoples;
  (b) To use such objects in support of the military effort;
  (c) To make such objects the object of reprisals.

Article 54. – Protection of Objects Indispensable to the Survival of the Civilian Population

1. Starvation of civilians as a method of warfare is prohibited.
2. It is prohibited to attack, destroy, remove or render useless objects indispensable to the survival of the civilian population, such as foodstuffs, agricultural areas for the production of foodstuffs, crops, livestock, drinking water installations and supplies and irrigation works, for the specific purpose of denying them for their sustenance value to the civilian population or to the adverse Party, whatever the motive, whether in order to starve out civilians, to cause them to move away, or for any other motive.
3. The prohibitions in paragraph 2 shall not apply to such of the objects covered by it as are used by an adverse Party:
    (a) As sustenance solely for the members of its armed forces; or
    (b) If not as sustenance, then in direct support of military action, provided, however, that in no event shall actions against these objects be taken which may be expected to leave the civilian population with such inadequate food or water as to cause its starvation or force its movement.
4. These objects shall not be made the object of reprisals.
5. In recognition of the vital requirements of any Party to the conflict in the defence of its national territory against invasion, derogation from the prohibitions contained in paragraph 2 may be made by a Party to the conflict within such territory under its own control where required by imperative military necessity.

Article 55. – Protection of the Natural Environment

1. Care shall be taken in warfare to protect the natural environment against widespread, long-term and severe damage. This protection includes a prohibition of the use of methods or means of warfare which are intended or may be expected to cause such damage to the natural environment and thereby to prejudice the health or survival of the population.
2. Attacks against the natural environment by way of reprisals are prohibited.

Article 56. – Protection of Works and Installations Containing Dangerous Forces

1. Works or installations containing dangerous forces, namely dams, dykes and nuclear electrical generating stations, shall not be made the object of attack, even where these objects are military objectives, if such attack may cause the release of dangerous forces and consequent severe losses among the civilian population. Other military objectives located at or in the

vicinity of these works or installations shall not be made the object of attack if such attack may cause the release of dangerous forces from the works or installations and consequent severe losses among the civilian population.

2. The special protection against attack provided by paragraph 1 shall cease:

    (a) For a dam or a dyke only if it is used for other than its normal function and in regular, significant and direct support of military operations and if such attack is the only feasible way to terminate such support;

    (b) For a nuclear electrical generating station only if it provides electric power in regular, significant and direct support of military operations and if such attack is the only feasible way to terminate such support;

    (c) For other military objectives located at or in the vicinity of these works or installations only if they are used in regular, significant and direct support of military operations and if such attack is the only feasible way to terminate such support.

3. In all cases, the civilian population and individual civilians shall remain entitled to all the protection accorded them by international law, including the protection of the precautionary measures provided for in Article 57. If the protection ceases and any of the works, installations or military objectives mentioned in paragraph I is attacked, all practical precautions shall be taken to avoid the release of the dangerous forces.

4. It is prohibited to make any of the works, installations or military objectives mentioned in paragraph 1 the object of reprisals.

5. The Parties to the conflict shall endeavour to avoid locating any military objectives in the vicinity of the works or installations mentioned in paragraph 1. Nevertheless, installations erected for the sole purpose of defending the protected works or installations from attack are permissible and shall not themselves be made the object of attack, provided that they are not used in hostilities except for defensive actions necessary to respond to attacks against the protected works or installations and that their armament is limited to weapons capable only of repelling hostile action against the protected works or installations.

6. The High Contracting Parties and the Parties to the conflict are urged to conclude further agreements among themselves to provide additional protection for objects containing dangerous forces.

7. In order to facilitate the identification of the objects protected by this article, the Parties to the conflict may mark them with a special sign consisting of a group of three bright orange circles placed on the same axis, as specified in Article 16 of Annex I to this Protocol. The absence of such marking in no way relieves any Party to the conflict of its obligations under this Article.

· · ·

Additional Protocol I to the Geneva Convention applies only to land warfare and to sea or air warfare that affects the land. The Protocol does not protect the atmosphere generally or the air above the land if the land below is not affected. Moreover, articles 35(3) and 55 set a high threshold for prohibited acts, banning only those that cause "widespread, longterm and severe damage." Protocol I defines *long term* to be a period of decades. The Conference Committee clearly stated that the terms of Protocol I must be interpreted in accordance with the meaning specified in the Protocol and not in light of similar terms contained in other instruments, such as ENMOD.

The majority of states have accepted Protocol I, but several key states have withheld ratification. The rules embodied in the Protocol can only be binding on nonsignatories if the rules constitute or become customary international law. A further limiting factor arises from the fact that Protocol I applies only to international armed conflicts. Additional Protocol

II to the Geneva Conventions specifically applies to noninternational armed conflicts and contains no provision concerning the environment.

Some treaties address specific weapons systems. The Convention on the Prohibition of the Development, Production, Stockpiling and Use of Chemical Weapons and on Their Destruction (Paris, Jan. 13, 1993) contains far-reaching provisions on control of national chemical production facilities and international verification of state obligations. Contracting states must destroy all chemical weapons and all production facilities within ten years of the Agreement's entry into force. Each state party must provide access to any chemical weapons destruction facility for the purpose of on-site systematic verification and monitoring. The treaty covers all toxic chemicals and their precursors, listed in three schedules or annexes. Several bilateral agreements have been concluded that also may contribute to the environmentally sound destruction of chemical weapons. The U.S.-Russian Agreement Concerning the Safe, Secure and Ecologically Sound Destruction of Chemical Weapons (July 30, 1992) included a pledge by the United States to provide up to $55 million to assist Russia to destroy chemical weapons. An agreement of December 1992 between Russia and Germany enabled the construction of a plant to destroy specific materials.

Other specific weapons systems have been restricted because of their indiscriminate effects or the excessive injuries they cause. In particular, nuclear weapons and antipersonnel land mines have been targeted by the international community. In 1996, the conference of state parties to the Convention on Prohibitions or Restrictions on the Use of Certain Conventional Weapons adopted a protocol on the use of mines, booby traps, and other devices. Protocol II to the Convention on Prohibitions on the Use of Certain Conventional Weapons Which May Be Deemed to Be Excessively Injurious or to Have Indiscriminate Effects (Geneva, May 3, 1996), 35 I.L.M. 1206 (1996). The Protocol applies to international and to internal armed conflicts. It limits the types of weapons that can be used and calls on each contracting party to clear, remove, or destroy all mines, booby traps, and similar devices.

Another weapons treaty, the Convention on the Prohibition of the Use, Stockpiling, Production and Transfer of Anti-Personnel Mines and on Their Destruction (Oslo, Sept. 18, 1997), mentions the environment, but its purpose is to end the casualties caused by land mines. According to article 5 of the Convention, each state party must clear all mines in areas under its jurisdiction or control at the latest within ten years following the entry into force of the Convention. The Convention does not require an environmental impact assessment before mine clearance activities, although this may be necessary pursuant to other international agreements or national law. Each state party is required to report to the U.N. secretary-general within 180 days of the entry into force of the Convention for that party on numerous matters related to mines and mined areas. Included in the reporting obligation is information regarding the status of programs for the destruction of antipersonnel mines, including details of the methods to be used in destruction, the location of all destruction sites, and the applicable safety and environmental standards to be observed. Art. 7(1)(f).

Throughout the 1990s, various international organizations attempted to consider the impacts of armed conflict on the environment and to propose new rules. The International Atomic Energy Agency (IAEA) General Conference adopted a resolution on September 21, 1990, recognizing that attacks or threats of attack on nuclear facilities devoted to peaceful purposes could jeopardize the development of nuclear energy, affirmed the importance and reliability of its nuclear safeguard procedures. IAEA GC (XXXIV) RES/533 (Sept. 21, 1990). The U.N. General Assembly supported the IAEA with its own Resolution 45/581 (Dec. 4, 1990), in which it expressed its conviction of the need to prohibit armed attacks on nuclear installations.

On November 25, 1992, the General Assembly affirmed that environmental considerations are one of the elements to be taken into account in implementing the principles of law applicable in armed conflict. In referring to the Iraqi occupation of Kuwait, it condemned the destruction of hundreds of oil-well heads and the release and waste of crude oil into the sea and noted that existing provisions of international law prohibit such acts. G.A. Res. 47/37 (Nov. 25, 1992). It stressed that destruction of the environment, not justified by military necessity and carried out wantonly, is clearly contrary to existing international law. The Resolution invited the ICRC to report on activities undertaken by the Committee and other relevant bodies with regard to the protection of the environment in times of armed conflict. The ICRC produced two reports, the second of which included model guidelines for military manuals. "Protection of the Environment in Time of Armed Conflict," submitted by the U.N. Secretary-General to the 48th session of the General Assembly. U.N. Doc. A/48/269 (July 29, 1993); Guidelines for Military Manuals and Instructions on the Protection of the Environment in Times of Armed Conflict, U.N. Doc. A/49/323 Annex (Aug. 19, 1994). The General Assembly did not formally approve the guidelines, but invited states to disseminate them widely. G.A. Res. 49/50, at para. 11 (Dec. 9, 1994).

In 1994, the UNEP established the Working Group on Liability and Compensation for Environmental Damage Arising from Military Activities, as part of its Montevideo Program for the Development and Periodic Review of Environmental Law (II-1993). According to the Report, a state that has committed an act of aggression cannot rely on the rules of international law allowing for exclusions or exemptions of responsibility and liability but will be fully liable for damage to the environment. The Working Group also proposed a comprehensive definition of *environmental damage* and methods of valuation. UNEP/ENV.LAW/3/info.1 (Oct. 15, 1996), 27 E.P.L. 134 (1997).

Another expert has summarized the state of the law on environmental protection during armed conflict.

Protection of the Natural Environment in Time of Armed Conflict,
285 Int'l Rev. Red Cross 567–78 (1991) (footnotes omitted)

Antoine Bouvier

I. Introduction

. . .

The rules of IHL for the protection of the environment . . . aim not to prevent damage altogether, but rather to limit it to a level deemed tolerable. Unfortunately, there is reason to fear that the use of particularly devastating means of warfare (whose effects are often still unknown) could wreak such large-scale destruction as to render illusory the protection afforded civilians under IHL. Indeed, severe environmental damage could seriously hamper or even prevent the implementation of provisions to protect the victims of armed conflict (the *wounded,* the *sick, prisoners of war or civilians*). For these reasons alone, respect for and compliance with the rules of IHL for the protection of the environment are crucial.

All these issues suddenly assumed new urgency during the conflict that set the Middle East ablaze in 1990–91.

In the wake of that crisis, many questions were raised about the content and scope of and possible shortcomings in the rules of IHL for the protection of the environment in time of armed conflict. These questions were discussed at several meetings of experts in humanitarian law and environmental protection. In spite of the high level of the discussions, it proved impossible to reach any final conclusions because of the difficulty in establishing various basic data, such as a scientific assessment of the environmental damage caused by modern warfare and a thorough analysis of the content and limitations of the rules in force.

However, the following provisional conclusions were drawn:

(a) the 1990–1991 Middle East conflict is too narrow a frame of reference for setting standards since environmental damage in wartime can take many forms;

(b) certain issues should nevertheless be examined with a view to solving problems of interpretation of the rules in force and possibly filling loopholes in the law;

(c) the rules of IHL currently in force could substantially limit environmental damage, providing they are correctly complied with and fully respected.

II. Rules of Law for the Protection of the Environment in Time of Armed Conflict

Most of the customary rules, treaty provisions and general principles for the protection of the environment in time of armed conflict are mentioned below, and the most important are discussed in some detail.

It should be pointed out here that, although the concept of the environment as it is understood today did not emerge until the 1970s, many of the general rules and principles of IHL (often dating much further back) contribute to protecting the environment in wartime.

A. General Principles

The most important general principle of humanitarian law in the present context is the one according to which the right of the Parties to the conflict to choose methods or means of warfare is not unlimited. This basic principle, which was first set forth in the Declaration of St. Petersburg in 1868, has been frequently reiterated in IHL treaties, most recently in Protocol I of 1977 additional to the Geneva Conventions (Art. 35, para. 1).

The rule of proportionality is another basic principle of IHL which underlies many of its provisions. Like the first principle mentioned, it clearly applies as well to protection of the environment in time of armed conflict.

B. Treaties Affording the Environment Indirect Protection

First of all the term "indirect protection" of the environment should be defined. Until the early 1970s IHL was "traditionally . . . anthropocentric in scope and focus." Indeed, IHL texts adopted before then made no reference to the environment as such (the concept did not even exist at the time). Nevertheless various provisions relating, for example, to private property or the protection of the civilian population, afforded the environment some protection.

. . .

C. Treaties Affording the Environment Specific Protection

Two treaties are of major importance:

• the Convention on the Prohibition of Military or Any Other Hostile Use of Environmental Modification Techniques ("ENMOD" Convention adopted by the United Nations on 10 December 1976);

• Protocol I of 1977 additional to the Geneva Conventions of 1949.

. . .

3. Link Between the Provisions of Protocol I and the Rules of the Convention on the Prohibition of the Use of Environmental Modification Techniques ("ENMOD")

These two treaties prohibit different types of environmental damage. While Protocol I prohibits recourse to environmental warfare, i.e. the use of methods of warfare likely to upset vital balances of nature, the "ENMOD" Convention prohibits what is known as geophysical warfare, which implies the deliberate manipulation of natural processes and may trigger "hurricanes, tidal waves, earthquakes, and rain or snow."

Far from overlapping, these two international treaties are complementary. However, they give rise to tricky problems of interpretation stemming in particular from the fact that they attribute different meanings to identical terms, such as "widespread, long-term and severe." To give but one example of such semantic difficulties, the definition of "long-term" ranges from several months or a season for the United Nations Convention to several decades for the Protocol.

Moreover, the conditions of being widespread, long-term and severe are cumulative in Protocol I, whereas each condition is sufficient in and of itself for the "ENMOD" Convention to apply.

There is a danger that such discrepancies might hamper the implementation of these rules. It is therefore to be hoped that the work currently being carried out in the field of environmental protection in wartime will lead to harmonization of the two treaties.

D. Protection of the Environment in Situations of Non-International Armed Conflict

Despite the obvious threat posed by situations of non-international armed conflict, none of the rules of IHL applicable to such situations provide specifically for protection of the environment. A proposal was made at the CDDH to introduce into Protocol II a provision analogous to Article 35, para. 3, and Article 55 of Protocol I, but the idea was ultimately rejected.

However, the concept of environmental protection is not totally absent from Protocol II. Article 14 ("Protection of objects indispensable to the survival of the civilian population"), which prohibits attacks against "foodstuffs, agricultural areas for the production of foodstuffs, crops, livestock, drinking water installations and supplies and irrigation works," and Article 15, which prohibits any attack against "installations containing dangerous forces . . . if such attack may cause the release of [such] forces," unquestionably contribute to protecting the environment in time of non-international armed conflict.

III. Conclusion

The destructive potential of the methods and means of warfare already in use or available in the world's arsenals today represents a threat to the environment of a magnitude unprecedented in the history of humanity. Special emphasis must therefore be placed on compliance with and constant development of the rules of IHL for the protection of the environment in time of armed conflict.

Unlike certain other authors, we are not convinced of the need at present to revise all the provisions of IHL for the protection of the environment, although this would become indispensable should new means of warfare be introduced.

Certain issues nevertheless merit detailed study. In particular, attention should be paid . . . to protection of the environment in time of non-international armed conflict and to the formulation of rules applicable between a State party to a conflict and a State not party thereto whose natural environment may be affected by the conflict. Further thought should also be given to the suggestion put forward by some experts that nature reserves should be declared demilitarized zones in the event of conflict.

It is generally agreed that the rules of IHL currently in force . . . could considerably limit environmental damage in warfare, providing they are correctly applied and fully respected. Therefore, rather than initiating a new and possibly unproductive codification process, a special effort should be made to ensure that these rules are adopted by as many States as possible. It is of paramount importance to ensure implementations of and respect for the existing rules, so that future generations will not be faced with insurmountable problems resulting from damage caused to the environment in time of conflict.

Questions and Discussion

1. Do you agree that the current rules are adequate? If not, what should be added?
2. For further reading, see Frits Kalshoven & Liesbeth Zegveld, CONSTRAINTS ON THE WAGING OF WAR: AN INTRODUCTION TO INTERNATIONAL HUMANITARIAN LAW (2001); Jozef Goldblat, *The Mitigation of Environmental Disruption by War: Legal Approaches*, in ENVIRONMENT HAZARDS OF WAR 53–55 (A. Westing ed., 1990); Alexander Kiss, *Les Protocoles additionnels aux Conventions de Genéve de 1977 et la protection des biens de l'environnement*, in ÉTUDES ET ESSAIS SUR LE DROIT INTERNATIONAL HUMANITAIRE 182 (1985); THE HANDBOOK OF HUMANITARIAN LAW IN ARMED CONFLICTS (Dieter Fleck ed., 2008); John Carey & William Dunlap, INTERNATIONAL HUMANITARIAN LAW: ORIGINS (2003); W.M. Arkin et al., MODERN WARFARE AND THE ENVIRONMENT: A CASE STUDY OF THE GULF WAR (1991); THE ENVIRONMENTAL CONSEQUENCES OF WAR: LEGAL, ECONOMIC, AND SCIENTIFIC PERSPECTIVES (J.E. Austin & Carl Bruch eds., 2000); G. Plant, ENVIRONMENTAL PROTECTION AND THE LAWS OF WAR (1993).

D. *Claims for Environmental Damage*

In January 1991, the Iraqi military occupying Kuwait detonated more than seven hundred Kuwaiti oil wells, igniting more than six hundred of them. Smoke from the fires affected not only Kuwait but also Iran, Turkey, Jordan, and Saudi Arabia, and oil that spilled into the desert seeped into the underground aquifer. Iraq also opened valves at several oil terminals and pumped perhaps as much as 11 million barrels of crude oil into the Persian Gulf. Subsequent bombing of the terminals by the U.S. and its allies halted the flow of oil. Other oil slicks appeared, apparently caused by damage to tankers and oil-storage facilities. Oil refineries, oil-gathering stations, and power and water desalination plants were all damaged or destroyed. Letter of July 12, 1991, from the Chargé d'Affaires of the Permanent Mission of Kuwait to the United Nations to the Secretary-General, July 15, 1991; U.N. Doc. A/45/1035, S/22787, at 2. The U.N. Security Council reacted to the Iraqi destruction in paragraph 16 of Resolution 687, which affirmed that Iraq

> is liable under international law for any direct loss, damage, including environmental damage and the depletion of natural resources, or injury to foreign Governments, nationals and corporations, as a result of Iraq's unlawful invasion and occupation of Kuwait.

Questions have been raised about the appropriateness of the Security Council adopting an adjudicative or quasi-adjudicative role in making a finding of liability on its own. *See* JOHN COLLIER & VAUGHAN LOWE, THE SETTLEMENT OF INTERNATIONAL DISPUTES IN INTERNATIONAL LAW: INSTITUTIONS AND PROCEDURES 41–44 (1999). Do you see any problem? In any event, paragraph 18 of the Resolution created a fund from the export sale of Iraqi oil for the payment of claims and established a commission to administer the fund. This was the first time that an international body has been charged with compensating for wartime environmental damage.

The U.N. Compensation Commission (UNCC) established its procedures regarding claims in a series of decisions taken by its Governing Council. Council Decision 7 provides that payments are to be made available with respect to direct environmental damage and the depletion of natural resources, including losses or expenses resulting from

(a) Abatement and prevention of environmental damage, including expenses directly relating to fighting oil fires and stemming the flow of oil in coastal and international waters;
(b) Reasonable measures already taken to clean and restore the environment or future measures which can be documented as reasonably necessary for that purpose;
(c) Reasonable monitoring and assessment of environmental damage for the purpose of evaluating and abating harm and restoring the environment;
(d) Reasonable monitoring of public health and performing medical screening for the purposes of investigation and combating increased health risks as a result of the environmental damage; and
(e) Depletion of or damage to natural resources.

UNCC, Governing Council Decision 7, para. 35, revised Mar. 16, 1992, S/AC.26/1991/7/Rev.1. The list is not exhaustive.

Following completion of earlier categories of cases, such as those concerned with individual personal injuries, the UNCC turned to the environmental claims. In 1996, the UNCC approved a payout of US$610,048,547 to the Kuwait Oil Company on behalf of the public oil sector as a whole for the well blowout. *See Decision Concerning the Well Blowout Control Claim*, Governing Council of the UNCC, 66th mtg., Dec. 17, 1996, S/AC.26/Dec. 40 (Dec. 18, 1996).

In December 1998, the Governing Council of the UNCC appointed a three-member panel to review other claims for losses resulting from environmental damage and the depletion of natural resources submitted by governments and by public-sector enterprises. On June 22, 2001, the UNCC delivered its first set of awards on 107 claims for monitoring and assessment of environmental damage, depletion of natural resources, monitoring of public health, and performing medical screenings for the purposes of investigation and combating increased health risks (the "monitoring and assessment claims"). The total amount of the claims exceeded US$1 billion ($1,007,412,574), with Kuwait and Saudi Arabia each claiming close to $500 million. See UNCC, *Report and Recommendations Made by the Panel of Commissioners Concerning the First Installment of "F4" Claims*, U.N. Doc. S/AC.26/2001/16 (June 22, 2001). The environmental claims reported in the first installment concerned monitoring and assessment related to damage from air pollution; depletion of water resources and damage to groundwater; damage to "cultural heritage resources"; oil pollution to the Persian Gulf; damage to coastlines; damage to fisheries; damage to wetlands and rangelands; damage to forestry, agriculture, and livestock; and damage or risk of damage to public health. In addition to the claims that were expected to be filed related to oil fires and released oil from destroyed wells, claims were filed over disruption of desert and coastal ecosystems as a result of the movement of military vehicles, personnel, and ordnance, as well as adverse impacts on the environment resulting from the transit and settlement of persons who departed Iraq and Kuwait as a result of the invasion.

The claims for monitoring and assessment presented special problems because they were heard before any substantive claims were considered. The Panel accepted that the claims for monitoring and assessment should be determined first, however, because the results of the monitoring and assessment could be critical in enabling claimants to establish the existence of damage and evaluate the quantum of compensation to be claimed. The claims for monitoring and assessment were thus permitted to generate evidence of substantive harm. At the same time, the panel sought a "nexus between the activity and environmental damage or risk of damage that may be attributed directly to Iraq's invasion and occupation of Kuwait." Para. 31.

In assessing the nexus and reasonableness of the monitoring and assessment activity, the Panel considered

- causality (i.e., the plausibility that pollutants released during the invasion and occupation could have impacted the territories of the claimants);
- whether the areas or resources in question could have been affected by pollutants resulting from the conflict;
- whether there is evidence of environmental damage or risk of damage; and
- whether the monitoring and assessment might produce results that could assist the panel in determining substantive claims.

According to the Panel, the mere fact that monitoring and assessment activity did not establish conclusively that environmental damage had been caused did not necessarily supply a valid reason for rejecting a claim for expenses of the monitoring activity, because it could be of benefit even if no evidence of war-caused damage was found. This was also held to be the case if the results show that damage has occurred, but no restoration or remediation was possible or feasible.

To be within the UNCC mandate, any proven damage had to be attributable to Iraq's invasion and occupation. As in other liability proceedings, separating out the causation was a difficult matter, particularly in the absence of baseline information. In assessing each claim, the panel considered the circumstances of the claim, including the nature of the damage to be assessed and the location and purpose of the monitoring and assessment activity and the appropriateness of the activity by reference to generally accepted scientific criteria and methodologies. Where supporting evidence and documentation was lacking, the Panel rejected claims. The successful claimant states had to submit periodic progress reports on environmental monitoring and assessment.

The Panel reported a second installment of environmental claims in late 2002, including nineteen claims from states outside the region (Australia, Canada, Germany, the Netherlands, United Kingdom, and United States). *Concerning the Second Installment of "F4" Claims*, U.N. Doc. S/AC.26/2002/26 (Oct. 3, 2002). The thirty claims totaled some US$872,760,534 for expenses incurred for measures to abate and prevent environmental damage, to clean and restore the environment, to monitor and assess environmental damage, and to monitor public health risks alleged to have resulted from Iraq's invasion and occupation of Kuwait.

The second-installment claims involved some novel issues, and by Procedural Order Nos. 7 and 8, both dated February 1, 2002, the Panel informed Iraq and the regional claimants that oral proceedings would be held to focus on, inter alia, whether the phrase "environmental damage and the depletion of natural resources" under Security Council Resolution 687 (1991) and Governing Council Decision 7 included loss or damage to elements such as cultural property, human health, aesthetic values of landscapes, and so on. After oral and written proceedings, the Panel gave an expansive reading to Governing Council Decision 7 on the meaning of *environmental damage*. In the view of the Panel, the term *environmental damage*, in paragraph 16 of Security Council Resolution 687 (1991), could cover, for example, expenses incurred as a result of measures undertaken to prevent or abate harmful impacts of airborne contaminants on property or human health, provided that the losses or expenses were a direct result of Iraq's invasion and occupation of Kuwait.

Regarding the prevention and abatement claims of states from outside the region, the Panel found that neither Security Council Resolution No. 687 nor Governing Council Decision 7 restricted eligibility for compensation to losses or expenses incurred by the countries in which the environmental damage occurred or by countries located in the Persian Gulf region. In the view of the panel, expenses resulting from assistance rendered to countries in the Persian Gulf region to respond to environmental damage, or threat of damage to the environment or public health, qualified for compensation. The Panel then turned to evaluating the claims.

Governing Council Report and Recommendations Made by the Panel of Commissioners Concerning the Third Installment of "F4" Claims, U.N. Compensation Commission, 43 I.L.M. 704 (2004) (Dec. 18, 2003)

1. The Governing Council of the United Nations Compensation Commission (the "Commission"), at its thirtieth session held from 14 to 16 December 1998, appointed the "F4" Panel . . . to review claims for direct environmental damage and depletion of natural resources resulting from Iraq's invasion and occupation of Kuwait. This is the third report of the Panel. It contains the recommendations of the Panel to the Governing Council on the third installment of "F4" claims submitted pursuant to article 38(e) of the Provisional Rules for Claims Procedure (S/AC.26/1992/10).

2. The third "F4" installment consists of three claims by the Government of the State of Kuwait and two claims by the Government of the Kingdom of Saudi Arabia. . . . The claims were submitted to the Panel in accordance with article 32 of the Rules on 20 March 2002.

3. . . . The total compensation sought in the claims reviewed in this report is 10,004,219,582 United States dollars (USD).

. . .

I. Overview of the Third "F4" Installment

5. The claims in the third "F4" installment are for expenses resulting from measures already taken or to be undertaken in the future to clean and restore environment alleged to have been damaged as a direct result of Iraq's invasion and occupation of Kuwait.

6. The Claimants seek compensation for expenses resulting from cleaning and restoration measures undertaken or to be undertaken by them to remediate damage from:

(a) Oil released from damaged oil wells in Kuwait;
(b) Pollutants released from oil well fires and firefighting activities in Kuwait;
(c) Oil spills into the Persian Gulf from pipelines, offshore terminals and tankers;
(d) Laying and clearance of mines;
(e) Movements of military vehicles and personnel; and
(f) Construction of military fortifications.

. . .

III. Legal Framework

A. Mandate of the Panel

18. The mandate of the Panel is to review the "F4" claims and, where appropriate, recommend compensation.

19.   In discharging its mandate, the Panel has borne in mind the observations of the Secretary-General of the United Nations, in his report to the Security Council of 2 May 1991, that:

> "The Commission is not a court or an arbitral tribunal before which the parties appear; it is a political organ that performs an essentially fact-finding function of examining claims, verifying their validity, evaluating losses, assessing payments and resolving disputed claims. It is only in this last respect that a quasi-judicial function may be involved. Given the nature of the Commission, it is all the more important that some element of due process be built into the procedure. It will be the function of the commissioners to provide this element."

> "Report of Secretary-General pursuant to paragraph 19 of Security Council resolution 687 (1991)," S/22559, paragraph 20.

B. Applicable Law

20.   Article 31 of the Rules sets out the applicable law for the review of claims, as follows:

> In considering the claims, Commissioners will apply Security Council resolution 687 (1991) and other relevant Security Council resolutions, the criteria established by the Governing Council for particular categories of claims, and any pertinent decisions of the Governing Council. In addition, where necessary, Commissioners shall apply other relevant rules of international law.

21.   Paragraph 16 of Security Council resolution 687 (1991) reaffirms that Iraq is "liable under international law for any direct loss, damage, including environmental damage and the depletion of natural resources, or injury to foreign Governments, nationals and corporations, as a result of Iraq's unlawful invasion and occupation of Kuwait."

C. Compensable Losses or Expenses

22.   Governing Council decision 7 (S/AC.26/1991/7/Rev. 1) provides guidance regarding the losses or expenses that may be considered as "direct loss, damage, or injury" resulting from Iraq's invasion and occupation of Kuwait, in accordance with paragraph 16 of Security Council resolution 687 (1991).

23.   Paragraph 34 of Governing Council decision 7 provides that "direct loss, damage, or injury" includes any loss suffered as a result of:

(a) Military operations or threat of military action by either side during the period 2 August 1990 to 2 March 1991;
(b) Departure of persons from or their inability to leave Iraq or Kuwait (or a decision not to return) during that period;
(c) Actions by officials, employees or agents of the Government of Iraq or its controlled entities during that period in connection with the invasion or occupation;
(d) The breakdown of civil order in Kuwait or Iraq during that period; or
(e) Hostage-taking or other illegal detention.

24.   Paragraph 35 of Governing Council decision 7 provides that "direct environmental damage and the depletion of natural resources" includes losses or expenses resulting from:

(a) Abatement and prevention of environmental damage, including expenses directly relating to fighting oil fires and stemming the flow of oil in coastal and international waters;

    (b) Reasonable measures already taken to clean and restore the environment or future measures which can be documented as reasonably necessary to clean and restore the environment;

    (c) Reasonable monitoring and assessment of the environmental damage for the purposes of evaluating and abating the harm and restoring the environment;

    (d) Reasonable monitoring of public health and performing medical screenings for the purposes of investigation and combating increased health risks as a result of the environmental damage; and

    (e) Depletion of or damage to natural resources.

25. As the Panel observed in its report on the second installment of "F4" claims (the "second 'F4' report"), paragraph 35 of Governing Council decision 7 does not purport to give an exhaustive list of the activities and events that can give rise to compensable losses or expenses; rather it should be considered as providing guidance regarding the types of activities and events that can result in compensable losses or expenses.. "Report and recommendations made by the Panel of Commissioners concerning the second installment of 'F4' claims," S/AC.26/2002/26 ("second 'F4' report"), paragraph 22.

D. Evidentiary Requirements

26. Article 35(1) of the Rules provides that "[e]ach claimant is responsible for submitting documents and other evidence which demonstrate satisfactorily that a particular claim or group of claims is eligible for compensation pursuant to Security Council resolution 687 (1991)." Article 35(1) also provides that it is for each panel to determine "the admissibility, relevance, materiality and weight of any documents and other evidence submitted."

27. Article 35(3) of the Rules provides that category "F" claims "must be supported by documentary and other appropriate evidence sufficient to demonstrate the circumstances and amount of the claimed loss." In addition, Governing Council decision 46 (S/AC.26/Dec.46 (1998)) states that, for category "F" claims, "no loss shall be compensated by the Commission solely on the basis of an explanatory statement provided by the claimant."

28. When recommending compensation for environmental damage or loss that has been found to be a direct result of Iraq's invasion and occupation of Kuwait, the Panel has in every case assured itself that the applicable evidentiary requirements regarding the circumstances and amount of the damage or loss claimed have been satisfied.

E. Legal Issues

29. In reviewing the claims in the third "F4" installment, the Panel considered a number of legal issues relating to the claims. Some of these issues were raised by Iraq in its written responses or in submissions during the oral proceedings and were commented upon by the Claimants during the oral proceedings.

1. Amendment of Claims Based on Results of Monitoring and Assessment Activities

30. The Claimants have submitted amendments to some of the claims based on results of monitoring and assessment activities. In some cases, these amendments increase the amount of compensation claimed, while others decrease the claimed amounts.

31. Iraq has questioned these amendments. It contends that the amendments and the data on which they are based should not be accepted by the Panel because they were submitted after the expiry of the applicable time limits.

32. In its report on the first installment of "F4" claims (the "first 'F4' report"), the Panel anticipated that the results of some monitoring and assessment activities would assist its review of related substantive claims. [para. 39] The Panel recalled that "the Governing Council's decision to authorize expedited review of monitoring and assessment claims was, in large part, intended to make funds available to claimants to finance activities that might produce information to support their substantive 'F4' claims." [Ibid.] The view of the Panel, the possibility that the amounts claimed might increase or decrease in the light of data and information obtained from monitoring and assessment activities is implicit in the decision of the Governing Council to authorize separate funding for monitoring and assessment activities prior to the review of related substantive claims. The Panel, therefore, finds that it is appropriate to receive and consider amendments to the amounts claimed, provided that such amendments are based on information and data obtained from monitoring and assessment activities.

2. Threshold for Compensable Damage

33. Security Council resolution 687 (1991) provides that Iraq is "liable under international law for any direct loss, damage, including environmental damage and the depletion of natural resources . . . as a result of Iraq's unlawful invasion and occupation of Kuwait." According to Iraq, this means that the Panel must have regard to the applicable rules of international law in determining whether any environmental damage or loss alleged to have resulted from "Iraq's invasion and occupation of Kuwait" qualifies for compensation in accordance with Security Council resolution 687 (1991). Specifically, Iraq argues that damage resulting from the invasion and occupation of Kuwait is not compensable unless it reaches the "threshold" that is generally accepted in international law for compensation in cases of state responsibility for transboundary environmental damage. According to Iraq, the applicable threshold is that the damage must be at least "significant," and no compensation should be awarded for damage that is below this threshold.

34. As noted in paragraph 20, the primary sources of the law to be applied by the Panel in the review of claims for compensation are listed in article 31 of the Rules. These are "Security Council resolution 687 (1991) and other relevant Security Council resolutions, the criteria established by the Governing Council for particular categories of claims, and any pertinent decisions of the Governing Council." "[O]ther relevant rules of international law" are to be applied "where necessary." In the view of the Panel, this means that recourse to "other relevant rules of international law" is necessary where the Security Council resolutions and the decisions of the Governing Council do not provide sufficient guidance for the review of a particular claim.

35. For the claims in the third "F4" installment, the Panel finds that Security Council resolution 687 (1991) and the relevant decisions of the Governing Council provide sufficient guidance. Resolution 687 states clearly that compensation is payable for "any direct loss, damage . . . or injury" that resulted from Iraq's invasion and occupation of Kuwait. In addition, paragraph 35 of Governing Council decision 7 states that "direct environmental damage and the depletion of natural resources" include losses or expenses resulting from "reasonable measures already taken to clean and restore the environment or future measures which can be documented as reasonably necessary to clean and restore the environment." In the view of the Panel, the key issues for decision in connection with the claims in the third "F4" installment are: (a) whether the environmental damage for which compensation is sought resulted directly from Iraq's invasion and occupation of Kuwait; (b) whether measures already taken by a claimant to remediate environmental damage were "reasonable"; and

(c) whether measures proposed to be undertaken by a claimant qualify as "future measures which can be documented as reasonably necessary to clean and restore the environment."

36. In considering the reasonableness of remediation measures, it is appropriate to have regard to the extent of the damage involved. However, in the view of the Panel, this is not the only factor to be considered. Other factors, such as the location and nature of the damage and its actual or potential effects on the environment may also be relevant. Thus, for example, where damage that might otherwise be characterized as "insignificant" is caused to an area of special ecological sensitivity, or where the damage, in conjunction with other factors, poses a risk of further or more serious environmental harm, it may not be unreasonable to take remediation measures in order to prevent or minimize potential additional damage.

3. Parallel or Concurrent Causes of Environmental Damage

37. Iraq contends that some of the damage for which compensation is sought by the Claimants cannot be attributed solely to "Iraq's invasion and occupation of Kuwait." It alleges that some of the damage resulted from other factors that existed before and after the invasion and occupation of Kuwait. According to Iraq, the environment in the claimant countries was not in "pristine condition" prior to the invasion and occupation. In particular, Iraq refers to exploration for oil, the operation of refineries and petrochemical industries and the large number of oil tankers operating in the Persian Gulf as sources of environmental damage both before and after the invasion and occupation. With respect to Kuwait's claim for damage to its terrestrial resources from military activities, Iraq asserts that any damage still remaining is the result of mismanagement and destructive land use, especially the failure to control livestock grazing and the use of off-road vehicles in sensitive areas of the desert. Iraq maintains, therefore, that "it is impossible to limit the causes of environmental pollution in a particular region to one cause and hold one state liable for that and oblige it to compensate the damages, especially when many factors and states contributed to the pollution."

38. With regard to Iraq's liability for environmental damage where there are parallel or concurrent causes, the Panel recalls that in its second "F4" report it notes that "Iraq is, of course, not liable for damage that was unrelated to its invasion and occupation of Kuwait, nor for losses or expenses that are not a direct result of the invasion and occupation. However, Iraq is not exonerated from liability for loss or damage that resulted directly from the invasion and occupation simply because other factors might have contributed to the loss or damage. Whether or not any environmental damage or loss for which compensation is claimed was a direct result of Iraq's invasion and occupation of Kuwait will depend on the evidence presented in relation to each particular loss or damage." [Second "F4" report, paragraph 25].

In reviewing each of the claims in the third "F4" installment, the Panel has considered whether, and if so to what extent, the evidence available indicates that the damage for which compensation is sought was wholly or partly the result of factors unrelated to Iraq's invasion and occupation of Kuwait. It has also considered whether the claimant has aggravated or otherwise contributed to the damage, either by failing to take appropriate steps to mitigate damage or by negligent or other improper action. Where, on the basis of the evidence, the Panel finds that damage resulted from causes wholly unconnected with Iraq's invasion and occupation of Kuwait, no compensation is recommended for such damage or loss. Where the evidence shows that damage resulted directly from Iraq's invasion and occupation of Kuwait but that other factors have contributed to the damage for which compensation is claimed, due account is taken of the contribution from such other factors in order to determine the level of compensation that is appropriate for the portion of the damage which is directly attributable to Iraq's invasion and occupation of Kuwait. [First "F4" report, paragraphs 33–34; second "F4" report, paragraph 40.]

4. Duty of the Claimant to Prevent and Mitigate Environmental Damage

40. Iraq also argues that some of the damage for which the Claimants seek compensation has been caused or contributed to by the Claimants themselves, either because they failed to take steps to mitigate damage resulting from the invasion and occupation of Kuwait or because the damage had been aggravated by the acts or omissions of the Claimants after the invasion and occupation. For example, Iraq claims that Saudi Arabia's failure to remove oil from its coastal areas over 12 years after the end of the invasion and occupation constitutes a breach of Saudi Arabia's obligation under international law to mitigate the damage. Iraq claims that Saudi Arabia's failure to act has allowed a sediment layer to form over the oil contamination, thus doubling the quantity of material to be remediated. Iraq also alleges that any damage to Kuwait's groundwater resources must be attributed to the negligence of Kuwait. It claims, first, that Kuwait was negligent in constructing oil recovery pits in areas above its aquifers and, secondly, that Kuwait should have taken action to remove oil recovery pits and oil lakes from above the aquifers as soon as it became aware that they had the potential to contaminate groundwater.

41. According to Iraq, failure by a claimant to take reasonable and timely measures to mitigate damage from the invasion and occupation of Kuwait amounts to contributory negligence and justifies rejection of the claim for compensation or a corresponding reduction in the compensation to be awarded to the claimant. Iraq also contends that action by a claimant that causes additional damage or aggravates damage from the invasion and occupation constitutes an intervening factor that breaks the chain of causation so that the damage involved can no longer be attributed to "Iraq's invasion and occupation of Kuwait."

42. The Panel stresses that each claimant has a duty to mitigate environmental damage to the extent possible and reasonable in the circumstances. Indeed, in the view of the Panel, that duty is a necessary consequence of the common concern for the protection and conservation of the environment, and entails obligations towards the international community and future generations. The duty to mitigate damage encompasses both a positive obligation to take appropriate measures to respond to a situation that poses a clear threat of environmental damage as well as the duty to ensure that any measures taken do not aggravate the damage already caused or increase the risk of future damage. Thus, if a claimant fails to take reasonable action to respond to a situation that poses a clear threat of environmental damage, the failure to act may constitute a breach of the duty to mitigate and could provide justification for denying compensation in whole or in part. By the same token, where a claimant takes measures that are unreasonable, inappropriate or negligent in the circumstances and thereby aggravates the damage or increases the risk of damage, the claimant may be required to bear some responsibility for the portion of the loss or damage that is attributable to its own acts or omissions.

43. In the view of the Panel, whether an act or omission of a claimant constitutes failure to mitigate damage depends on the circumstances of each claim and the evidence available. The test is whether the claimant acted reasonably, having regard to all the circumstances with which it was confronted. Where a claimant fails to respond to a crisis that presents a clear threat of environmental damage, such inaction should rightly be considered as a breach of the claimant's duty to mitigate damage. On the other hand, a claimant confronted with a situation that poses multiple threats of serious environmental damage may not be able to deal with all the threats at the same time or in the same way. In such a situation, a decision by the claimant to take or not to take measures, based on its judgment of the

urgency of the various threats, would not necessarily constitute a violation of the duty to mitigate damage. As previously noted by the Panel, the reasonableness or appropriateness of the measures taken or not taken by a claimant in such a situation must be evaluated by reference to the circumstances in which the decision was taken. For example, in its second "F4" report, the Panel found that the decision taken by the contractors engaged by Kuwait for mine clearance to detonate some unexploded ordnance where it was found, instead of recovering and storing the ordnance in an appropriate facility, was reasonable in the circumstances, given the dangerous conditions present at the time.[Paras. 100–101.] The Panel also found that the decision of Kuwait "to select contractors from a limited number of specially designated countries was . . . not unreasonable, particularly in view of the special circumstance in which the decision was taken." [Second "F4" report, para. 94.] The same considerations apply to the decisions of claimants regarding measures to prevent or mitigate environmental damage resulting from Iraq's invasion and occupation of Kuwait.

5. Remediation Objectives

44. The Claimants state that the objective of the remediation measures taken or proposed by them is to restore the environment to the condition in which it would have been if Iraq's invasion and occupation of Kuwait had not occurred.

45. While accepting this objective in principle, Iraq argues that, in determining the appropriate objectives of remediation, due account should be taken of the fact that the environment in the claimant countries was not in "pristine condition" prior to the invasion and occupation of Kuwait. According to Iraq, it should not be held responsible for expenses to remediate damage that predated the invasion and occupation of Kuwait. Consequently, Iraq maintains that any compensation awarded for remediation should be limited to the damage that resulted directly from the invasion and occupation. According to Iraq, compensation should not be awarded for measures to restore the environment to a "pristine condition," because that could result in "unjust enrichment" for the Claimants.

46. Iraq further argues that, in any case, remediation is justified only where environmental assessment, risk assessment and analysis of alternatives show that the risks posed by the environmental damage exceed the potential risks posed by the proposed remediation measures. In particular, due consideration should be given to the possibility of natural recovery. Furthermore, Iraq maintains that remediation measures that involve "grossly disproportionate costs" are unreasonable and should be rejected in favour of less expensive measures.

47. With respect to the claims in the third "F4" installment, the Panel considers that the appropriate objective of remediation is to restore the damaged environment or resource to the condition in which it would have been if Iraq's invasion and occupation of Kuwait had not occurred. In applying this objective to a particular claim, regard must be had to a number of considerations. These include, *inter alia*, the location of the damaged environment or resource and its actual or potential uses; the nature and extent of the damage; the possibility of future harm; the feasibility of the proposed remediation measures; and the need to avoid collateral damage during and after the implementation of the proposed measures. In the view of the Panel, such an approach is appropriate even where there is evidence that the environment was not in pristine condition prior to Iraq's invasion and occupation of Kuwait. The contribution of any pre-existing or subsequent causes of damage (where such causes can be identified) should be considered, not in determining the restoration objective to be achieved by remediation, but in determining the proportion of the costs of remediation that can reasonably be attributed to Iraq's invasion and occupation of Kuwait.

48. The Panel considers that, in assessing what measures are "reasonably necessary to clean or restore" damaged environment, primary emphasis must be placed on restoring the environment to pre-invasion conditions, in terms of its overall ecological functioning rather than on the removal of specific contaminants or restoration of the environment to a particular physical condition. For, even if sufficient baseline information were available to determine the exact historical state of the environment prior to Iraq's invasion and occupation of Kuwait, it might not be feasible or reasonable to fully recreate pre-existing physical conditions.

6. Duty to Consider Transboundary Impacts of Remediation Measures

49. Iraq asserts that, in considering remediation measures proposed by the Claimants, account should be taken of the potential impacts of such measures in third States. According to Iraq, remediation measures with potential transboundary impacts are subject to the requirements of international law relating to notification to the States concerned, and the Claimants have the obligation to consult with such third States, with a view to preventing or minimizing any adverse transboundary impacts.

50. The Panel recognizes the need for claimants to consider the potential adverse impacts of remediation measures that they undertake to respond to environmental damage in their respective territories. In particular, the Panel emphasizes that claimants have the obligation under international law to ensure that the remediation measures that they take do not cause damage to the environment in other States or in areas beyond the limits of national jurisdiction. In the view of the Panel, it is the responsibility and right of each claimant to decide on the measures and procedures that are necessary and appropriate to ensure compliance with its international obligations.

IV. Review of the Third "F4" Installment Claims

51. Article 36 of the Rules provides that a panel of Commissioners may "(a) in unusually large or complex cases, request further written submissions and invite individuals, corporations or other entities, Governments or international organizations to present their views in oral proceedings" and "(b) request additional information from any other source, including expert advice, as necessary." Article 38(b) of the Rules provides that a panel of Commissioners "may adopt special procedures appropriate to the character, amount and subject-matter of the particular types of claims under consideration."

52. In view of the complexity of the issues raised by the claims and the need to consider scientific, engineering and cost issues in evaluating the claims, the Panel sought the assistance of a multi-disciplinary team of independent experts retained by the Commission ("expert consultants"). Expert consultants were retained, *inter alia*, in the fields of desert ecology, desert botany, terrestrial and marine remediation techniques, marine biology, coastal ecology, coastal geomorphology, geology, hydrogeology, water quality, indoor air quality, health risk assessment, chemistry, water treatment engineering, coastal engineering, civil engineering and ordnance disposal.

53. At the direction of the Panel, the Panel's expert consultants undertook on-site inspections in Kuwait and in Saudi Arabia. The purpose of the inspections was to enable the expert consultants to obtain information that would assist the Panel to:

   (a) Assess the nature and extent of environmental damage resulting from Iraq's invasion and occupation of Kuwait;
   (b) Evaluate the technical feasibility, reasonableness and cost-effectiveness of the remediation measures proposed by the Claimants; and
   (c) Identify possible remediation alternatives.

54. Where necessary, the Panel requested additional information from the Claimants to clarify their claims.

55. In reaching its findings and formulating its recommendations on the claims, the Panel has taken due account of all the information and evidence made available to it, including the evidence and information provided by the Claimants in the claim documents and in response to requests for additional information; the information and views submitted by Governments in response to article 16 reports; the written responses submitted by Iraq; the views presented by Iraq and the Claimants during the oral proceedings; and the reports of the Panel's expert consultants.

56. In order to avoid multiple recovery of compensation, the Panel instructed the secretariat to carry out cross-claim and cross-category checks of the claims. On the basis of these checks, the Panel is satisfied that there is no risk of duplication of awards of compensation.

57. In considering future measures proposed by a claimant to clean and restore the damaged environment, the Panel has evaluated the reasonableness of the measures by reference to, *inter alia*, the potential of the measures to achieve the remediation objectives set out in paragraphs 47 and 48; potential adverse environmental impacts of the proposed measures; and the cost of the measures as compared with other remediation alternatives. In some cases, the Panel has found that certain modifications to the measures proposed are necessary or desirable to take account of these considerations. Details of such modifications are set out in the relevant technical annexes to this report. The amounts recommended for the claims are based on the proposed measures as modified. This is consistent with the approach adopted by the Panel in its previous reports.

. . .

V. Claims of the State of Kuwait

A. Overview

60. In the third "F4" installment, Kuwait submitted three claims for expenses for measures to remediate environmental damage that it alleges resulted from Iraq's invasion and occupation of Kuwait. Claim No. 5000256 is for future measures to remediate damage to groundwater resources. Claim No. 5000450 is for future measures to remediate damage to terrestrial resources. Claim No. 5000452 is for expenses incurred for the cleaning and restoration of the exterior of the Central Bank of Kuwait's building.

61. Kuwait alleges that the detonation of oil wells by Iraqi forces during the final days of their occupation of Kuwait resulted in the release of over 1 billion barrels of crude oil into the environment, much of which was ignited and burned for many months. According to Kuwait, fallout from the burning oil, in the form of soot and oil droplets, contaminated the soil as well as buildings and other structures in Kuwait. In addition, sea water used to fight the oil well fires, together with oil and dissolved hydrocarbons, seeped into the soil and infiltrated the aquifers in Umm-Al Aish and Raudhatain in the north-east of the country.

62. According to Kuwait, the desert soil and vegetation were severely disrupted by the construction of military fortifications, including ditches, berms, bunkers, trenches, and pits; the laying and clearance of mines; and the extensive movement of military vehicles and personnel. These activities are alleged to have resulted in, *inter alia*, accelerated soil erosion, increased sand movement and increased incidence of dust and sand storms. Kuwait asserts that the construction of military fortifications and movement of military vehicles and personnel also caused significant damage to natural vegetation and wildlife.

B. Claim No. 5000256 – Damage to Groundwater Resources

63. Kuwait seeks compensation in the amount of USD 185,167,546 for the expense of future measures to remediate two freshwater aquifers that it alleges have been contaminated as a result of Iraq's invasion and occupation of Kuwait. This amount represents an increase in the original amount claimed, reflecting an amendment requested by Kuwait on the basis of new information obtained from its monitoring and assessment projects.

64. Kuwait states that during efforts to extinguish burning oil wells, pits were dug to hold firefighting water from the Persian Gulf. After the fires were extinguished, oil that had spilled from damaged wells was diverted into some of these pits and stored until the oil was recovered by Kuwait Oil Company. Additional pits dedicated to the recovery of spilled oil were constructed. Kuwait refers to all the pits for the recovery of spilled oil as "oil recovery pits."

65. Kuwait alleges that the Umm Al-Aish aquifer, near the Sabriyah oil field, and the Raudhatain aquifer, located near the Raudhatain oil field, have been contaminated by oil from damaged oil wells and by sea water used to fight the oil fires. According to Kuwait, large quantities of hydrocarbons and sea water from the surface reached the aquifers through infiltration. Kuwait adds that, since 1991, the oil recovery pits, contaminated wadis and oil lakes have continued to act as conduits of pollution of these aquifers.

66. According to Kuwait, Raudhatain and Umm Al-Aish are the only two aquifers in the country that contain freshwater. In both aquifers, freshwater lenses sit on top of brackish water. Kuwait states that water from the freshwater lenses of the two aquifers was potable prior to Iraq's invasion and occupation of Kuwait, but some of it is no longer suitable for drinking due to contamination.

67. Kuwait has submitted results of monitoring and assessment studies which show contamination by total petroleum hydrocarbons ("TPH") and total dissolved solids ("TDS") in the northern part of the Umm Al-Aish aquifer and the southern part of the Raudhatain aquifer.

68. Iraq argues that Kuwait has not provided evidence to support the claim of damage to the freshwater lens of the Raudhatain aquifer. Iraq also contends that the presence of TPH in the aquifers is not sufficient proof of environmental damage or health risks because, according to it, there are no established TPH standards for drinking water.

69. In any case, Iraq contends that TPH and TDS contamination in the aquifers is not the result of Iraq's invasion and occupation of Kuwait. According to Iraq, any groundwater contamination in Kuwait is the result of mismanagement and improper land use. In particular, Iraq asserts that the increased salinity of the water in the aquifers has been caused by over-pumping of water from the aquifers prior to 1990. Iraq also contends that Kuwait was negligent in locating oil recovery pits above the aquifers.

70. In the view of the Panel, some of the data presented by Kuwait to support this claim are difficult to interpret. In particular, the methods used to identify and measure the levels of TPH and TDS raise issues regarding quality assurance, data comparability and data interpretation. Furthermore, the absence of pre-invasion data on TPH levels makes it difficult to assess the full significance of post-invasion data.

71. In spite of these shortcomings, the Panel finds, on the totality of the evidence presented to it, that there is TPH and TDS contamination in the freshwater lenses of the northern Umm Al-Aish and southern Raudhatain aquifers, and that this contamination resulted from the infiltration of large quantities of sea water used to fight the oil well fires and contaminants from the oil recovery pits and the oil lakes. Analysis of TDS in the aquifers suggests that the contamination resulted from infiltration of sea water used to fight the oil well fires rather than from over-pumping of water from the aquifers.

72. In the view of the Panel, the TPH and TDS contamination makes this water unsuitable for human consumption and it is, therefore, reasonable for Kuwait to take measures to improve the quality of the water. Moreover, considering the urgent need for quick action to extinguish the oil well fires and to control the release of oil from the damaged oil wells, Kuwait was neither unreasonable nor negligent in constructing the oil recovery pits close to where the firefighting and oil recovery activities were being undertaken.

73. With regard to Iraq's assertion that Kuwait had failed to take timely and appropriate steps to remove the oil lakes and oil recovery pits, the Panel notes that removal was initially prevented by mine clearance and further delayed by oil field reconstruction operations. Until recently, there was also a lack of monitoring data identifying the location, nature and extent of surface and groundwater contamination. Although earlier removal of oil lakes and pits might have reduced the degree and volume of contaminated groundwater, the failure to do so was not unreasonable in light of the factors noted above.

74. Accordingly, the Panel finds that contamination of the Raudhatain and Umm Al-Aish aquifers by oil from damaged oil wells and by sea water used to fight the oil well fires constitutes environmental damage directly resulting from Iraq's invasion and occupation of Kuwait, and a programme to remediate the damage would constitute reasonable measures to clean and restore the environment.

75. Kuwait proposes to remediate the two aquifers by pumping contaminated groundwater from the aquifers, treating it in a dedicated facility and re-injecting the treated water into the aquifers. Treatment would include carbon adsorption to remove high molecular weight hydrocarbons; treatment to remove natural organic matter; and a membrane process, utilizing ultrafiltration followed by reverse osmosis, to reduce salinity levels to drinking water standards. Kuwait also proposes to flush residual contamination from the soil and vadose zone above the aquifers.

76. Iraq questions the appropriateness of the model used by Kuwait to determine the location and extent of the contaminated plumes because the model has not been calibrated with site-specific parameters and data. It states that the values used in the model to calculate the rate of natural recharge of freshwater in the aquifers are too low.

77. Iraq also maintains that more complete monitoring and assessment results are needed before any remediation programmes are undertaken. It states that, in any case, other and more appropriate remediation alternatives should be considered.

78. In the view of the Panel, restoration of water quality in the aquifers is an appropriate objective, and the remediation measures proposed by Kuwait are reasonable, subject to some modifications based on alternative approaches. The Panel considers that extraction of contaminated groundwater and its replacement with injected potable water is a reasonable remediation measure. However, treatment of the contaminated groundwater in a dedicated facility might not be necessary. As an alternative, contaminated groundwater could be pumped into holding ponds and allowed to evaporate. Potable water would be obtained from other sources to recharge the freshwater lenses. Following the development of more specific information on the identity of the contaminants in the groundwater, Kuwait may decide to treat the extracted groundwater for reuse. Furthermore, the available evidence indicates that flushing of the vadose zone is not necessary because there is little risk to the aquifers from any residual contaminants in that zone. Details of these modifications are set out in annex I.

79. The Panel finds that, with the modifications outlined in annex I, the remediation measures proposed by Kuwait constitute measures that are reasonably necessary to clean and restore the environment, within the meaning of paragraph 35(b) of Governing Council decision 7.

80. The expenses of the remediation measures have been adjusted to take account of the modifications in annex I including:

   (a) The reduced volume of water that needs to be extracted from the aquifers;
   (b) The elimination of a dedicated treatment facility;
   (c) The elimination of the flushing of the vadose zone; and
   (d) The extra cost of continuous monitoring of the remediation measures.

81. Accordingly, the Panel recommends compensation in the amount of USD 41,531,463 for this claim.

82. For the reasons indicated in paragraph 196, no date of loss for the purposes of interest is indicated for the recommended award.

83. The Panel has not considered the issue of compensation for loss of use of groundwater resources. This issue will be considered in the fifth installment of "F4" claims as part of claim No. 5000460.

C. Claim No. 5000450 – Damage to Terrestrial Resources

1. Introduction

84. Kuwait seeks compensation in the amount of USD 5,050,105,158 for expenses of future measures to remediate damage to its terrestrial environment resulting from Iraq's invasion and occupation of Kuwait. This amount represents a decrease in the original amount claimed, reflecting amendments made by Kuwait on the basis of new information obtained from its monitoring and assessment projects.[1]

85. Claim No. 5000450 comprises five claim units for future measures to be undertaken by Kuwait to remediate environmental damage alleged to have resulted from Iraq's invasion and occupation of Kuwait. Kuwait requested the Panel to consider these claim units as separate claims. However, the Panel decided to treat claim No. 5000450 as a single claim but to review the claim units separately. Accordingly, the Panel's recommendations on the claim units are presented separately in this report.

· · ·

2. Remediation of Areas Damaged by Military Fortifications

92. Kuwait seeks compensation in the amount of USD 14,170,924 for future measures to remediate areas damaged by the construction and backfilling of military fortifications.

93. According to Kuwait, over 240,000 military fortifications, comprising antitank ditches, berms, bunker trenches and pits, were constructed in Kuwait by the military forces of Iraq during their invasion and occupation of Kuwait. Kuwait submitted data, collected during operations to clear mines and other remnants of war, to support these numbers.

94. Kuwait alleges that the fortifications have caused damage to its desert environment. It states that the construction and subsequent backfilling of these fortifications, representing a total area of approximately 6.25 square kilometers scattered over a large area of its desert, exposed soil and other materials to wind erosion which adversely affected the desert ecosystem, including its biodiversity, soil-water relationships and the long-term productivity of the soil. Kuwait also submitted information to support its contention that the construction and

---

[1] The decrease in claimed costs is primarily due to Kuwait's decision to use less costly remediation techniques for tarcrete-affected areas and areas that need to be revegetated. This decision was based on information produced by monitoring and assessment projects that were funded by awards in the first installment of "F4" claims for Claim Nos. 5000433 and 5000434 (*see* table 7 of first "F4" report).

backfilling of military fortifications have contributed to increased sand mobilization in the affected areas.

95. Iraq contends that the location of the military fortifications is unclear and that the estimate of the average size of fortifications lacks "tangible evidence." Iraq also claims that uncontrolled livestock grazing is the "principal issue that affects sand movement, vegetation cover and the ability of the desert to repair itself." Indeed, Iraq asserts that areas that have been fenced since 1991 "show remarkable levels of vegetation."

96. Iraq also argues that Kuwait "does not provide clear evidence that persistent environmental damage linked to the Conflict and post-Conflict activities is still present." Iraq states that, given the general climatic conditions and dust and sand storm activities in the region, military fortifications in such small areas could have only a negligible impact on sand movements in Kuwait. Iraq also asserts that natural revegetation has occurred in desert areas in Iraq which were similarly damaged.

97. As noted by the Panel in its second "F4" report, there is evidence that Iraqi forces fortified the country against military action by the Allied Coalition Forces. There is also evidence that the construction and backfilling of military fortifications adversely affected plant growth and soil functioning, and increased wind erosion and sand mobilization. The evidence also shows that there has been very little natural recovery at military fortification sites that have been protected from livestock grazing. The Panel, therefore, concludes that construction and backfilling of military fortifications was the major cause of environmental damage at these sites. However, the Panel observes that uncontrolled livestock grazing, both before and after Iraq's invasion and occupation of Kuwait, also caused damage in unfenced areas where military fortifications were located. Accordingly, the Panel finds that the ecological impacts are not attributable solely to Iraq's invasion and occupation of Kuwait.

98. Based on the evidence available, the Panel considers that Kuwait's estimate of the total area affected by military fortifications is reasonable. Moreover, although the small area affected by military fortifications is unlikely to be a major contributor to sand mobilization, the Panel is satisfied that the construction and backfilling of military fortifications have caused environmental damage through destabilization or compaction of different soil types.

99. The Panel, therefore, finds that damage to Kuwait's desert areas from the construction and backfilling of military fortification sites constitutes environmental damage directly resulting from Iraq's invasion and occupation of Kuwait, and a programme to remediate the damage would constitute reasonable measures to clean and restore the environment.

100. Kuwait proposes to stabilize the areas damaged by the construction and backfilling of military fortifications by applying a 2.5-centimetre layer of gravel to control erosion and encourage the re-establishment of indigenous species.

101. Iraq argues that the proposed gravel stabilization "is not technically documented" and "will have significant adverse environmental effects." Iraq suggests that Kuwait should instead address damage to the desert through "a national plan to organize and efficiently manage grazing."

102. The Panel considers that gravel stabilization is an established remediation technique; and it is appropriate for those soil types in Kuwait where there is clear evidence of the presence of a physical soil crust and low concentrations of loose sand upwind of the areas to be remediated. Gravel application can be accomplished with little negative environmental impact by using lightweight, low-impact equipment.

103. The Panel finds that, with the modifications outlined in annex II, the remediation measures proposed by Kuwait constitute measures that are reasonably necessary to clean and restore the environment, within the meaning of paragraph 35(b) of Governing Council decision 7. The Panel emphasizes that in order to ensure the success of the remediation measures, it

will be necessary for Kuwait to adopt appropriate measures to protect vulnerable areas, such as fencing to control grazing and the use of off-road vehicles.

104. The expenses of the proposed remediation measures have been adjusted to take account of the Panel's finding, in paragraph 97, that uncontrolled livestock grazing contributed to the damage. An adjustment has also been made to take account of the decreased area and reduced cost of the remediation measures, as indicated in annex II.

105. Accordingly, the Panel recommends compensation in the amount of USD 9,019,717 for this claim unit.

3. Remediation of Areas in and Around Wellhead Pits

106. Kuwait seeks compensation in the amount of USD 34,276,192 for expenses of future measures to remediate areas in and around wellhead pits constructed for the storage of sea water used for fighting the oil well fires. Some of the wellhead pits were subsequently backfilled with material from adjacent areas.

107. Kuwait alleges that releases from the damaged oil wells contaminated the areas in and around the wellhead pits. Kuwait also states that the material used to backfill the wellhead pits was contaminated with petroleum hydrocarbons from these releases.

108. According to data from satellite imagery and field research submitted by Kuwait, a total of 163 wellhead pits are located in oil-contaminated areas. Ninety-eight pits are in the Burgan oil field and 65 pits are in the Raudhatain and Sabriyah oil fields.

109. Iraq argues that Kuwait has not provided sufficient evidence to demonstrate the number, location and size of the wellhead pits. Iraq contends that Kuwait has provided only indirect evidence of oil contamination in the wellhead pits and that no evidence has been provided of damage to the soil surrounding the wellhead pits.

110. In the view of the Panel, data from Kuwait's remote sensing and field verification have provided sufficient evidence to demonstrate the number of wellhead pits and the areas that have been affected by contamination from these pits. The Panel finds that, given the location of the pits and the material used to backfill them, there is a real risk of contamination to the areas in and around the pits from petroleum hydrocarbons in the pits and the backfill material. The pits and backfill material also pose a risk of contamination to groundwater where the pits are located above the aquifers. Consequently, it is reasonable for Kuwait to take measures to remediate the areas in and around the wellhead pits.

111. The Panel, therefore, finds that damage to areas in and around wellhead pits from oil contamination constitutes environmental damage directly resulting from Iraq's invasion and occupation of Kuwait, and a programme to remediate the damage would constitute reasonable measures to clean and restore the environment.

112. Kuwait proposes to excavate contaminated soil and treat it, using high temperature thermal desorption to remove the petroleum contamination. The treated soil would be used to backfill the wellhead pits, and the top of the pits would be stabilized with gravel. Kuwait also proposes to revegetate the remediated areas. The claim unit relating to the revegetation programme of these areas is reviewed in paragraphs 149 to 150 of this report.

113. Iraq contends that using high temperature thermal desorption to treat excavated soil could have serious adverse environmental impacts. Iraq also questions the use of gravel to stabilize the remediated areas.

114. In the view of the Panel, treatment of excavated soil by high temperature thermal desorption is not warranted in the circumstances of this claim. Other remediation alternatives, such as landfilling, have proven to be equally effective, and they involve significantly less expense.

115. As stated in paragraph 102, the Panel considers that the use of gravel stabilization is an appropriate remediation technique.

116.   The Panel has indicated modifications to the remediation programme that dispense with high temperature thermal desorption treatment of contaminated soil. Moreover, as stated in paragraph 149, the Panel considers that revegetation is not warranted in these areas. The areas involved are relatively small and can be expected to revegetate naturally, if protected from grazing and off-road vehicles. Details of the modifications are set out in annex III.

117.   The Panel finds that, with the modifications outlined in annex III, the remediation measures proposed by Kuwait constitute measures that are reasonably necessary to clean and restore the environment, within the meaning of paragraph 35(b) of Governing Council decision 7.

118.   The expenses of the proposed remediation programme have been adjusted to take account of the modifications in annex III, including:

(a) Reduction in the volume of soil to be excavated;

(b) Elimination of high temperature thermal desorption treatment of excavated material; and

(c) Landfilling of excavated material.

119.   Accordingly, the Panel recommends compensation in the amount of USD 8,252,657 for this claim unit.

4. Remediation of Areas Damaged by Tarcrete

120.   Kuwait seeks compensation in the amount of USD 928,820,719 for expenses of future measures to remediate areas damaged by tarcrete.

121.   According to Kuwait, contamination from the oil well fires was deposited over approximately 271 square kilometers of its desert areas, where it formed tarcrete. Kuwait alleges that the tarcrete degraded the desert ecosystem and resulted in plant death and loss of vegetative cover. Kuwait also states that tarcrete interferes with the growth and reproduction of some species, and alters the composition of desert vegetation.

122.   Kuwait provided evidence to show that the presence of tarcrete has resulted in chemical contamination of the affected desert areas. Kuwait also provided data from soil sampling to define the chemical composition of tarcrete and tarcrete-affected soils.

123.   Iraq argues that the area alleged to be affected by tarcrete is "ill-defined and unclear." Iraq also argues that there is no evidence that tarcrete poses a risk of long-term environmental damage. Indeed, Iraq claims that tarcrete could have a positive effect in promoting soil stabilization, and it alleges that tarcrete has in fact contributed to an increase in the vegetative cover in some parts of Kuwait. Iraq further asserts that, in any case, Kuwait has not undertaken an appropriate risk assessment to demonstrate that there is need for remediation.

124.   The Panel finds that monitoring and assessment information submitted by Kuwait has provided a reasonably accurate approximation of the areas damaged by tarcrete. There is clear evidence that tarcrete can impair ecological recovery. While there has been natural recovery in some areas, large areas of tarcrete remain and this has impaired ecological functions such as water infiltration, nutrient cycling and the growth of vegetation.

125.   The Panel, therefore, finds that damage to Kuwait's desert areas from tarcrete constitutes environmental damage directly resulting from Iraq's invasion and occupation of Kuwait, and a programme to remediate the damage would constitute reasonable measures to clean and restore the environment.

126.   Kuwait proposes to remove tarcrete by hand and treat it by high temperature thermal desorption. It proposes to dispose of the treated material in existing quarries and pits near the oil fields. The areas from which tarcrete is removed would be stabilized with gravel and revegetated. The revegetation component of the remediation programme is discussed in paragraphs 151 to 152.

127. Iraq claims that the proposed remediation will cause "additional damage." It states that "tarcrete is stable and does not present a risk whereas the excavation of tarcrete for treatment will be destructive to vegetation and soils." Instead, it suggests that consideration should be given to alternative remediation approaches that would accelerate the recovery process.

128. In the view of the Panel, the physical removal of tarcrete could damage the affected soil, impair natural recovery and reduce the chances of successful revegetation. Furthermore, treatment of excavated soil by high temperature thermal desorption is not warranted in the circumstances.

129. The Panel has outlined a modified remediation programme that involves fragmentation of the tarcrete, instead of removal and treatment by high temperature thermal desorption. Furthermore, as indicated in paragraph 151, the Panel does not consider that any revegetation measures are warranted in the areas damaged by tarcrete. After fragmentation of the tarcrete, natural recovery can be accelerated by the application of organic amendments to provide additional nutrients. Details of the modified remediation programme are set out in annex IV.

130. The Panel finds that, with the modifications outlined in annex IV, the remediation measures proposed by Kuwait constitute measures that are reasonably necessary to clean and restore the environment, within the meaning of paragraph 35(b) of Governing Council decision 7.

131. The expenses of the proposed remediation programme have been adjusted to take account of the modifications in annex IV, including:

    (a) On-site manual fragmentation of tarcrete for part of the affected areas;
    (b) Elimination of high temperature thermal desorption treatment; and
    (c) Addition of organic soil amendments to all affected areas.

132. Accordingly, the Panel recommends compensation in the amount of USD 166,513,110 for this claim unit.

5. Revegetation of Damaged Terrestrial Ecosystems

133. Kuwait seeks a total compensation in the amount of USD 4,039,217,642 for expenses of future measures to revegetate areas of its desert that it alleges have been damaged as a result of Iraq's invasion and occupation of Kuwait.

134. This compensation is sought for a comprehensive and integrated programme to revegetate the areas alleged to have been affected by military activities; the areas in and around the wellhead pits; and the areas alleged to have been damaged by tarcrete. Kuwait states that such a programme is necessary because vegetative cover provides an essential mechanism for desert surface stabilization. It also helps to regulate the distribution of rainfall and provides sustenance for wildlife.

(a) Areas Affected by Military Activities

135. Kuwait alleges that the construction and backfilling of military fortifications, mine laying and mine clearance, movement of vehicles and personnel and construction of berms and sand walls (collectively referred to as "military activities"), caused soil compaction which "disrupts the soil's natural permeability and infiltration properties, resulting in reduced water storage capacity." Kuwait further alleges that military activities increased wind erosion of the soil, which "inhibits the regeneration of stabilizing vegetation." Kuwait also states that these activities led to a "sudden and dramatic increase in sand mobilization."

136. Iraq argues that "the degree to which military activity during the Conflict has contributed to an increase in dust storms is not documented." Iraq also contends that there are other

sources of sand mobilization, such as overgrazing, which Kuwait has failed to take into account.

137. Although overgrazing is a well-documented problem in Kuwait, the Panel considers that the military activities were the primary cause of the increase in sand mobilization during the years immediately following the end of Iraq's occupation of Kuwait.

138. The Panel, therefore, finds that damage to Kuwait's desert areas from these military activities constitutes environmental damage directly resulting from Iraq's invasion and occupation of Kuwait, and a programme to remediate the damage would constitute reasonable measures to clean and restore the environment.

139. Kuwait proposes to revegetate areas affected by military activities. Kuwait states that vegetation in these areas has not recovered from the effects of Iraq's invasion and occupation of Kuwait and a revegetation programme is necessary to restore biological productivity and to "address the large-scale mobilization of sand."

140. The revegetation programme proposed by Kuwait involves the establishment of 70 revegetation islands, covering 420 square kilometers. Each revegetation island would cover an area of 6 square kilometers. Half of each island would be designated for active revegetation by the "planting of shrubs, grasses, and forbs tailored to the specific revegetation island location and ecosystem type." The remaining half of each revegetation island would be left to revegetate naturally. To minimize damage by livestock grazing, Kuwait proposes to fence each of the revegetation islands.

141. In order to stabilize and control sand movement and encroachment, Kuwait also proposes to construct 70 shelter belts, covering an area of 385 square kilometers. Each shelter belt would be 5 kilometers long. The shelter belts would be located upwind of the revegetation islands to control sand movement in the disturbed areas where increased sand movement has been observed.

142. Iraq states that the revegetation methods proposed for areas affected by military activities "are over-elaborate [and] may well have negative effects on the biodiversity of Kuwait." Iraq argues that no active revegetation is necessary and that fencing and security maintenance would be sufficient.

143. The Panel finds that revegetation of the areas damaged by military activities is appropriate. In the view of the Panel, fencing alone would not ensure timely restoration of areas experiencing serious sand mobilization.

144. The Panel considers that Kuwait's proposal for establishing shelter belts and revegetation islands is a reasonable approach for restoration of the affected areas. However, this programme should rely more on natural revegetation processes and avoid the introduction of non-native species which could have negative environmental impacts. A modified revegetation programme based on these considerations is outlined in annex V.

145. The Panel finds that, with the modifications outlined in annex V, the remediation measures proposed by Kuwait constitute measures that are reasonably necessary to clean and restore the environment, within the meaning of paragraph 35(b) of Governing Council decision 7.

146. The expenses of the proposed revegetation programme for areas affected by military activities have been adjusted to take account of the modifications indicated in annex V.

147. The Panel has made a further adjustment to the costs of the revegetation programme to take account of the contribution of other factors unrelated to Iraq's invasion and occupation of Kuwait including, in particular, uncontrolled livestock grazing and the use of off-road vehicles in sensitive desert areas. In the view of the Panel, the need for revegetation is due, in part, to these other factors.

148. Accordingly, the Panel recommends compensation in the amount of USD 460,028,550 for this unit of the claim.

(b) Areas Damaged in and Around Wellhead Pits

149. Kuwait proposes a revegetation programme for the areas in and around wellhead pits. In its review of the remediation programme for these areas, the Panel has recommended an award that includes remediation measures that rely on natural revegetation (*see* paragraph 116). Accordingly, the Panel does not consider that a revegetation programme is necessary for these areas.

150. Consequently, the Panel recommends no compensation for this segment of the claim.

(c) Areas Damaged by Tarcrete

151. Kuwait proposes a revegetation programme for the areas affected by tarcrete. In its review of the remediation programme for the areas affected by tarcrete, the Panel has recommended an award that includes remediation measures that rely on natural vegetation (*see* paragraph 129). Accordingly, the Panel finds no need for a revegetation programme for these areas.

152. Consequently, the Panel recommends no compensation for this segment of the claim.

6. Cleaning of Government Buildings

153. Kuwait seeks compensation in the amount of USD 33,619,681 for expenses to clean and repair 2,066 government buildings alleged to have been damaged as a result of Iraq's invasion and occupation of Kuwait.

154. Kuwait alleges that the buildings require repairs "as a result of damages associated with oil fires and smoke." According to Kuwait, the facades of the buildings were contaminated by air pollution. Kuwait also alleges that some of the contaminants entered the air conditioning systems and that this could have long-term adverse health consequences for the occupants of the buildings.

155. The Panel finds that damage to government building facades and air conditioning systems by releases from the oil well fires would constitute environmental damage directly resulting from Iraq's invasion and occupation of Kuwait. However, Kuwait has not presented evidence sufficient to demonstrate the circumstances and amount of the claimed loss. Consequently, the Panel finds that Kuwait has failed to meet the evidentiary requirements for compensation specified in article 35(3) of the Rules.

156. Accordingly, the Panel recommends no compensation for this claim unit.

7. Recommended Award for Claim No. 5000450

157. The Panel's recommendation for compensation for claim No. 5000450 is summarized in Table 2.

Table 2. *Recommended Award for Claim No. 5000450*

Claim No.	Claim Unit	Amount Claimed (USD)	Amount Recommended (USD)
	Remediation of areas damaged by military fortifications	14,170,924	9,019,717
	Remediation of areas in and around wellhead pits	34,276,192	8,252,657
5000450	Remediation of areas damaged by tarcrete	928,820,719	166,513,110
	Revegetation of damaged terrestrial ecosystems	4,039,217,642	460,028,550
	Cleaning of government buildings	33,619,681	nil
Total		5,050,105,158	643,814,034

158.   The Panel has not considered the issue of compensation for loss of use of terrestrial resources. This issue will be considered in the fifth installment of "F4" claims as part of claim No. 5000460.

159.   For the reasons indicated in paragraph 196, no date of loss for the purposes of interest is indicated for this recommended award.

                                                    . . .

VI. Claims of the Kingdom of Saudi Arabia

A. Claim No. 5000451 – Damage to Coastal Resources

169.   Saudi Arabia seeks compensation in the amount of USD 4,748,292,230 for expenses of future measures to remediate damage to its coastal environment resulting from Iraq's invasion and occupation of Kuwait. This amount represents a decrease of the original amount claimed, reflecting amendments made by Saudi Arabia on the basis of new information obtained from its monitoring and assessment projects. The decrease in claimed costs is primarily due to a reduction in Saudi Arabia's estimated volume of contaminated sediment to be excavated and treated by the high temperature thermal desorption process. The reduction in estimated sediment volume was primarily based on data collected as part of the monitoring and assessment programme which was funded by the award for claim No. 5000409 . . . , as well as modifications to the proposed remediation programme. Relevant information was produced by monitoring and assessment projects that were funded by awards in the first installment of "F4" claims for claim Nos. 5000359, 5000363, 5000409 and 5000411. . . .

170.   Saudi Arabia states that its coastal environment was damaged by (a) more than 10 million barrels of oil deliberately released into the Persian Gulf by Iraqi forces; (b) contaminants released from oil wells in Kuwait that were set on fire by Iraqi forces; and (c) other releases of oil into the Persian Gulf as a result of Iraq's invasion and occupation of Kuwait.

171.   Saudi Arabia asserts that the oil released as a result of Iraq's invasion and occupation of Kuwait dwarfed all previous inputs of oil into the Persian Gulf from spills, refinery operations, natural seeps, exploration and production activities, operational discharges from vessels, urban run-offs and similar sources.

172.   According to Saudi Arabia, the 1991 oil spills caused extensive oil contamination to a total of more than 600 kilometers of shoreline, from the border with Kuwait to Abu Ali. Saudi Arabia states that chemical analysis ("biomarker fingerprinting") of over 3,000 sediment samples, collected in the areas it proposes to remediate, indicates that the oil currently found in that area is predominantly of Kuwaiti origin. The chemical analysis and collection of underlying data were carried out as part of a survey of the entire affected shoreline that was funded by an award in the first installment of "F4" claims.

173.   Saudi Arabia explains that the damage to its shoreline results from the toxicological effects of chemical constituents of oil as well as the physical effects resulting from smothering of sediment layers by oil. According to Saudi Arabia, the continued presence of layers of oil-contaminated sediments and tar mat at many sites on the shoreline is preventing natural recolonization and ecological recovery in sections of the supra-littoral and intertidal regions. As a result, many areas of the shoreline are almost devoid of plant and animal life or show significant reduction in biological diversity.

174.   Iraq states that "there is no dispute that the oil spill occurred or that it had immediately caused environmental damage to wildlife and the beaches and habitats of the coast of Saudi Arabia." However, Iraq contends that the damage to Saudi Arabia's shoreline cannot be

attributed solely to the events in 1991. It points out that the region "is constantly exposed both to accidental spills and routine ongoing pollution." It refers in particular to the large spill "associated with a well at Nowruz, Iran that resulted in 1.9 million barrels of oil being dumped in the northern section of the Gulf" in 1983. Iraq also contends that it is not liable for damage caused by oil releases that resulted from bombing of Iraqi tankers by the Allied Coalition Forces or for damage from oil that was released from oil wells in Kuwait "long after [Iraqi forces] had withdrawn from Kuwait."

175.   Iraq refers to a study funded by the European Union, which it contends found "significant recovery of all habitat types in the Jubail area after five years (end of 1995). The only exceptions were some areas of salt marshes." Iraq claims that this is "the only long-term research ever undertaken on the impacted coastline." It also states that a "survey team in 1991 made much more modest assessments of the extent of the damage than currently claimed" by Saudi Arabia. Iraq further asserts that biological assessment studies submitted by Saudi Arabia are incomplete, rely on a "coarse" methodology, and have been misinterpreted by Saudi Arabia.

176.   As noted in paragraph 23, Governing Council decision 7 states that "direct loss, damage, or injury" includes any loss suffered as a result of military operations by either side during the period 2 August 1990 to 2 March 1991.Accordingly, damage caused by oil releases are compensable whether they resulted from military operations by Iraq or the Allied Coalition Forces. In the view of the Panel, evidence available from a variety of sources supports the conclusion that the overwhelming majority of the oil currently present in the areas which Saudi Arabia proposes to remediate resulted from Iraq's invasion and occupation of Kuwait.

177.   The Panel observes that, while there has been some attenuation of oil contamination since Iraq's invasion and occupation of Kuwait, recent studies indicate that there are still areas with high levels of oil contamination. Saudi Arabia submitted shoreline survey data on the presence of oil and on the biological conditions along its shoreline. The data, which were collected at more than 19,500 sampling sites in the area proposed for remediation, indicate that there are large areas where oil contamination continues to impair coastal resources and where there has been little or no biological recovery.

178.   The Panel, therefore, finds that damage from oil contamination to the shoreline between the Kuwait border and Abu Ali constitutes environmental damage directly resulting from Iraq's invasion and occupation of Kuwait, and a programme to remediate the damage would constitute reasonable measures to clean and restore the environment.

179.   Saudi Arabia proposes to remediate 20 areas, totalling approximately 73 square kilometers, along the coastline between the Kuwait border and Abu Ali. In these areas it proposes to excavate and remove visibly contaminated material. During the excavation, salt marsh and tidal flat areas would be isolated from the sea by the construction of sea walls and dikes; these would be progressively removed as work is completed in each area. Following sediment excavation, residual contamination in remaining sediments would be treated with bio-remediation techniques. The excavated material would be treated using high temperature thermal desorption at a number of facilities to be constructed for that purpose. Treated sediments would be blended with dredged subtidal sediments and replaced in excavated areas. The salt marshes would be revegetated after bio-remediation treatment. Saudi Arabia states that it will review and modify the remediation programme as additional information from its monitoring and assessment studies becomes available.

180.   Iraq states that the proposed remediation would have "large scale and deleterious environmental impacts," and argues that Saudi Arabia has failed to assess these impacts. It also asserts that high temperature thermal desorption is not a suitable method for remediation of the oil-contaminated coastal sediments.

181.   The Panel has some concerns with the remediation programme proposed by Saudi Arabia. The extensive excavation proposed by Saudi Arabia poses a risk of causing substantial environmental harm to areas that are already experiencing natural recovery, as well as to other sensitive areas where excavation may cause more harm than good. Furthermore, the extensive infrastructural work related to this excavation, such as construction and deconstruction of numerous seawalls, dikes and access roads for the transport of excavated material could have considerable adverse impacts on the coastal and marine environment. The Panel also considers that the problems relating to the disposal of excavated material and the backfilling of excavated sites have not been adequately addressed.

182.   The Panel does not consider that treatment of oil-contaminated material by high temperature thermal desorption is warranted in the circumstances of this claim. The evidence presented does not justify the use of high temperature thermal desorption rather than other disposal options, such as landfilling, which is an accepted waste management practice throughout the world and is routinely utilized for the disposal of oil-contaminated material.

183.   The Panel has evaluated a modified remediation programme that will target the impediments to ecological recovery and accelerate natural recovery without posing unacceptable risks of adverse environmental impacts. Details of the modified programme are set out in annex VI.

184.   The Panel finds that, with the modifications outlined in annex VI, the remediation measures proposed by Saudi Arabia constitute measures that are reasonably necessary to clean and restore the environment, within the meaning of paragraph 35(b) of Governing Council decision 7.

185.   The expenses of the proposed remediation programme have been adjusted to take account of the modifications in annex VI, including:

    (a) Reduction in the total area and volume of materials to be remediated;
    (b) Emphasis on *in situ* treatment methods;
    (c) Elimination of high temperature thermal desorption treatment of excavated material; and
    (d) Landfilling of excavated material.

186.   The recommended award includes provision for long-term monitoring of the remediation activities. The Panel considers it appropriate to integrate continuous monitoring into the design and implementation of the remediation programme. This will make the programme flexible and more able to respond to new information.

187.   The Panel, therefore, recommends compensation in the amount of USD 463,319,284 for this claim.

188.   For the reasons indicated in paragraph 196, no date of loss for the purposes of interest is indicated for this recommended award.

189.   The Panel has not considered the issue of compensation for loss of use of coastal resources. This issue will be considered, as necessary, in the fifth installment of "F4" claims as part of claim No. 5000463.

B. Claim No. 5000360 – Monitoring of Coastal Remediation Activities

190.   Saudi Arabia seeks compensation in the amount of USD 20,602,177 for a project to assess the effectiveness of clean-up and remediation measures in coastal areas affected by oil pollution resulting from Iraq's invasion and occupation of Kuwait, and to determine whether additional remediation is required. This amount represents an increase in the original amount claimed, reflecting an amendment requested by Saudi Arabia on the basis of new information obtained from its monitoring and assessment projects.

191. As indicated in paragraph 186, the Panel has included appropriate provision for the costs of long-term monitoring of the remediation activities in the award recommended for claim No. 5000451.

192. Accordingly, the Panel recommends no compensation for this claim.

––––––––––

The precedent of the Gulf War stimulated international organizations and civil society to monitor and document environmental damage in subsequent conflicts. *See, e.g.*, REGIONAL ENVIRONMENTAL CENTER FOR CENTRAL AND EASTERN EUROPE, ASSESSMENT OF THE ENVIRONMENTAL IMPACT OF MILITARY ACTIVITIES DURING THE YUGOSLAVIA CONFLICT: PRELIMINARY FINDINGS (June 1999). The 1999 Kosovo conflict allegedly included poisoning of wells, scorched-earth tactics, and indiscriminate bombing, thus leading the UNEP to establish an expert task force that included NGO representatives to assess the environmental damage. The UNEP also examined the environmental consequences of the conflicts in Iraq. The full reports of the UNEP's assessments can be downloaded from the UNEP Post-Conflict Assessment Unit's Web site at http://postconflict.unep.ch.

Desk Study on the Environment in Iraq, UNEP 2003, at 8–9, 13–14, 28–29, 37–39, 52–84; http://postconflict.unep.ch/publications/Iraq_DS.pdf

Lessons learned from UNEP's post-conflict assessments demonstrate that environmental contamination and degradation have critical humanitarian consequences requiring consideration at an early stage in relief and recovery operations. Failure to do so can lead to additional degradation of air, soil and water resources, causing long-term threats to both human health and sustainable livelihoods. Furthermore, the assessments have revealed the critical need to build institutional capacities for environmental management immediately after the conflict in order to screen the potential environmental impacts of reconstruction and development projects, and to ensure their sustainability.

Prior to the 1991 Gulf War, Iraq enjoyed a high standard of living, with a majority of the population making up a relatively wealthy middle class. In fact, in 1990, the United Nations Development Programme (UNDP) listed Iraq as 67th on its Human Development Index based on the country's (then) high levels of education, access to potable water and sanitation, as well as low infant mortality figures. However, when revenues from the oil industry fell dramatically due to the application of U.N. sanctions the humanitarian situation deteriorated, with dwindling food and water supplies and greatly reduced access to healthcare and education.

The country's medical infrastructure is in a very poor state. Many facilities are only partially operational because of inadequate maintenance of buildings and equipment, and a lack of vital spare parts. Prior to the outbreak of renewed military conflict in March 2003, essential medicines and equipment had been made available under the oil-for-food program, contributing to an improvement in the overall situation, but there were still shortages of antibiotics, anaesthetics and intravenous fluids, as well as detergents and disinfectants.

Health problems faced by the Iraqi population include malnutrition, nutritional anaemia, deficiencies of vitamin A and iodine, malaria, acute respiratory infections, leishmaniasis, and measles. Morbidity rates among children under five are very high, with acute respiratory tract infections and diarrhoeal disease representing over 70% of deaths.

. . .

Over the last decade, the water distribution system has steadily deteriorated, due mainly to a lack of spare parts and maintenance. As a consequence, the amount of water available for distribution has fallen by more than half, and much of the remaining resource never reaches the final consumer because of leakages. Furthermore, the rivers that most Iraqis rely on for their water are increasingly contaminated with raw sewage, as waste treatment plants fall into disrepair.

. . .

There were more than 128,100 refugees and about 700,000 internally displaced persons in Iraq in 2001. Displacement and redistribution was a policy pursued by the regime, which has resulted in crowded and ethnically unbalanced cities both in the north as well as in western and southern parts of the country. The refugees included about 23,700 from Iran and 13,100 from Turkey (in both cases mostly Kurds), about 90,000 Palestinians, and about 1,300 refugees of other nationalities. An estimated 600,000 internally displaced persons in the Kurdish controlled northern governorates included more than 100,000 people expelled by the Iraqi regime from Kirkuk and surrounding districts. At least another 100,000 persons were internally displaced elsewhere in Iraq, mostly in the southeastern marshlands. In 2001, an estimated one to two million Iraqis living outside Iraq were believed to be at risk of persecution if they returned, although only about 300,000 had any formal recognition as refugees or asylum seekers.

3.1 Overview

Iraq is confronted with a range of environmental problems that are both immediate and severe. Some can be directly linked with the effects of recent military conflicts. . . .

3.2 Water Resources

Main problems:

- the adverse downstream impact of large dams in the upper Tigris and Euphrates basin
- deliberate drainage of Iraqi wetlands
- severe contamination of surface water by sewage and other waste
- inadequately maintained and war-damaged water distribution network
- land salinization and waterlogging due to unsustainable irrigation practices and poor maintenance
- potential contamination of groundwater by oil spills.

The Significance of the Tigris and Euphrates Rivers to Iraq

Iraq is traversed by two major rivers, the Tigris and the Euphrates, both of which rise in the eastern mountains of Turkey and enter Iraq along its northwestern borders. Before their confluence just north of Basra, the Euphrates flows for about 1,000 km and the Tigris for some 1,300 km within Iraqi territory. Downstream from this point, the combined rivers form the tidal Shatt al-Arab waterway, which flows 190 km into the Gulf. The southern Shatt al-Arab forms the border between Iraq and Iran and represents the symbolic boundary of Arab culture and language.

The Euphrates basin (579,314 km2) embraces parts of Iraq (roughly 49% of the basin), Turkey (21%), Syria (17%) and Saudi Arabia (13%). The Euphrates River does not receive water from permanent tributaries within Iraqi territory and is fed only by seasonal runoff from wadis. The Tigris basin (371,562 km2) covers parts of the territories of Iran (47.2% of the basin), Iraq (38%), Turkey (14%) and Syria (0.3%). Within Iraq, the Tigris River receives water from four main tributaries, the Khabour, Great Zab, Little Zab and Diyala, which rise in the mountains of eastern Turkey and northwestern Iran and flow in a southwesterly direction until they meet the Tigris. A seasonal river, Al Authaim, rising in the highlands of northern Iraq, also flows into the Tigris, and is the only significant tributary entirely within Iraq.

The great alluvial plains of the Tigris and Euphrates Rivers comprise more than a quarter of Iraq's surface area. Topographically, the region is extremely flat, with a fall of only 4 cm/km over the lower 300 km of the Euphrates and 8 cm/km along the Tigris. Under natural conditions, the region was rich in wetlands and subject to annual flooding of up to 3 m. In recent years, this seasonal flooding has occurred on a much smaller scale because of dams constructed upstream, particularly on the Euphrates in Turkey and Syria, and due to largescale drainage works in Iraq itself.

Until the mid-20th century, most efforts to regulate the Tigris and Euphrates were primarily concerned with irrigation, but development plans in the 1960s and 1970s were increasingly devoted to reduction of flooding, though expansion of irrigation in upstream parts of the river basins was also an important goal.

In 1980, a Joint Technical Committee on Regional Waters was created by Turkey and Iraq, on the basis of a 1946 protocol concerning the control and management of the Euphrates and the Tigris. Syria joined the committee in 1982.

Transboundary issues concerning the Euphrates are critical to Iraq's water strategy as more than 90% of the river's water comes from outside the country (as opposed to 50% for the Tigris).

Under the terms of a 1990 agreement between Syria and Iraq, Iraq shares the Euphrates' waters with Syria on a 58% (Iraq) and 42% (Syria) basis, based on the flow received by Syria at its border with Turkey. Since Turkey has unilaterally promised to provide a minimum flow of 15.8 km3/year at its border, this agreement would *de facto* represent approximately 9.2 km3/year for Iraq. However, there is not yet any trilateral binding agreement between the three countries.

. . .

Sanitation

Due to the collapse of sewage treatment systems, huge quantities of raw sewage, mixed with industrial waste (as there is no separate system for industrial discharges) are being discharged into water bodies every day, with a large part of this being released into the Tigris in Baghdad, the city's only source of water. The pumping of wastewater to sewage treatment plants relies on a network of pumping stations in the city, and few of these stations have backup generators for operation in the event of disruption to the main electricity supply. In the north of the country, most sewage disposal takes place through a system of cesspools and septic tanks that are not dependent on power supplies.

Water Supply

Prior to the 1991 Gulf War, potable water was supplied to all urban centres, but only 54% of rural areas. The situation has deteriorated subsequently, due *inter alia* to poor maintenance and the banning of chlorine imports – required for water treatment – under U.N. sanctions for potential "dual use" substances. This has led to the spread of a wide range of water-borne illnesses such as typhoid, dysentery, cholera and polio, the latter re-emerging after nearly being eradicated prior to the sanctions. Significant quantities of water are lost through leakages.

Irrigation and Salinity

Irrigation in what is now Iraq dates back some 7,500 years to the time when the Sumerians built a canal to irrigate wheat and barley on land between the Tigris and the Euphrates. It was estimated in 1990 that over 5.5 million ha of Iraqi territory are potentially suitable for irrigation, with 63% of this land occurring in the Tigris basin, 35% in the Euphrates basin, and 2% along the Shatt al-Arab. However, irrigation development depends to a large extent on the volume of water released by the upstream countries.

The risk of elevated soil salinity and waterlogging as a consequence of poor irrigation practices has long been a priority concern in the country, and was already recorded as a cause of crop yield reductions some 3,800 years ago. It is estimated that in 1970 half the irrigated areas in central and southern Iraq were degraded in this way. In 1978, a land rehabilitation programme was initiated, comprising concrete lining for irrigation canals and the installation of field drains and collector drains. By 1989, a total of 700,000 ha had been rehabilitated at a cost of around U.S.$2,000/ha.

Military Waste, Including Waste from Chemical, Biological and Nuclear Weapons Programmes

The multiple military conflicts during the past quarter of a century have resulted in large and widespread quantities of military debris (including unexploded ordnance, spent cartridges/shells/penetrators, military vehicles etc), toxic and radioactive material (depleted uranium), contaminated soils and demolition waste (e.g., containing chemicals or asbestos), human and animal remains (leading to elevated disease risks, especially in urban areas), and packaging from military and humanitarian supplies.

3.5 Ecosystem Degradation

Main problems:

- destruction of the Mesopotamian Marshes and degradation of the Shatt al-Arab
- mismanagement of wetlands in general;
- high risk of desertification exacerbated by unsustainable agricultural practices, and overgrazing, as well as by land degradation from military movements and use of munitions;
- lack of information on the current status of Iraq's natural forest cover.

Destruction of the Mesopotamian Marshes

The destruction of the Mesopotamian marshlands has been documented in a UNEP report *The Mesopotamian Marshlands: Demise of an Ecosystem*. This study reveals that the wetlands in the middle and lower basin of the Tigris and Euphrates Rivers in Iraq were, until recently, the most extensive wetland ecosystems in the Middle East. In their lower courses, the rivers created a vast network of wetlands – the Mesopotamian Marshes – covering up to 20,000 km2. These comprised a complex of tall reeds, seasonal marshes, dominated by desert shrub and grasses, shallow and deep-water lakes, slightly brackish seasonal lagoons, and regularly inundated mudflats. The wetlands extended from Basra in the south to within 150 km of Baghdad, but the core of the system was located around the confluence of the Tigris and Euphrates rivers.

Massive drainage works in southern Iraq in the late 1980s and early 1990s, together with the effects of major upstream damming devastated the wetlands (overall loss of 90%), such that only minor and fragmented parcels remain today. Satellite images taken in 1973–1976 reveal that the wetlands were then more or less intact. However, the UNEP study shows that massive loss and degradation had taken place by 2000, with the greatest change occurring between 1991 and 1995. The central and Al Hammar marshlands had been almost completely destroyed, with 97% and 94% of their respective cover transformed into bare land and salt crusts. The water-filtering role of the marshland had ceased and the remaining drainage canals carried polluted irrigation wastewater directly toward the Gulf, with potentially harmful impacts on local fish resources.

The entire Marsh Arab community has suffered huge social and economic upheaval as a result of the marshlands' destruction, with about 40,000 people forced to flee to southwest Iran and hundreds of thousands internally displaced within Iraq.

The impact on biodiversity has also been catastrophic. Prominent losses include possible extinction of the endemic smooth-coated otter *Lutra perspicillata maxwellii*, bandicoot rat *Nesokia bunnii*, long-fingered bat *Myotis capaccinii* and an endemic species of barbel fish *Barbus sharpeyi*.

Several waterbirds are critically threatened, including African darter *Anhinga rufa* and sacred ibis *Threskiornis aethiopica*, which may now be extinct in the Middle East. A further 66 bird species are considered to be at risk. A wide range of migratory aquatic species have been affected – including penaied shrimp, and Hilsa shad *Tenualosa ilisha* (a fish), which migrate between the Gulf and nursery grounds in the marshlands – with serious economic consequences for coastal fisheries. Increasing salinity in the Shatt al-Arab estuary (due to upstream hydrotechnical works) has also damaged the breeding grounds of another important fish species, silver pomfret *Pampus argenteus*.

A new study conducted by UNEP indicates that, of the remnant wetlands surviving in 2000, one-third had disappeared by 2002. UNEP experts predict that unless urgent action is taken to reverse the trend and rehabilitate the marshlands, the entire wetland system is likely to be lost within three to five years. This will only be feasible through regional cooperation.

Environmental Impacts of Military Conflicts

· · ·

4.2 Iran-Iraq War, 1980–1988

The Iraq-Iran War began in September 1980. Iraq commenced a ground assault on Iran, and launched air strikes on strategic targets. However, Iranian resistance proved strong, and all Iraqi troops had withdrawn from the occupied portions of Iran by early 1982. Iran then initiated a series of offensives that Iraq responded to with the deployment of chemical weapons in 1983.

Chemical and Biological Weapons

The Organisation for the Prohibition of Chemical Weapons (OPCW) states that "During the Iran-Iraq war . . . there were various unconfirmed reports that Iraq had used chemical weapons, but the international community was slow to react at first. Eventually, however, U.N. factfinding teams confirmed that Iraq was indeed using chemical weapons on a massive scale and that Iran had suffered thousands of casualties as a result of these attacks."

Iraq's use of chemical weapons during the war can be divided into three distinct phases:

- 1983 to 1986 – use against advancing Iranian forces. In 1984, Iraq became the first country known to have used a nerve agent on the battlefield when it deployed aerial bombs filled with the nerve agent tabun. Some 5,500 Iranians were killed by this means between March 1984 and March 1985. Some 16,000 Iranians were reported killed by the toxic blister agent mustard gas between August 1983 and February 1986.
- 1986 to early 1988 – use adapted to target the preparation of Iranian offensives.
- Early 1988 to conclusion of the war – integration of large nerve agent strikes into Iraq's overall offensive operations.

. . . The chemical weapons deployed by Iraq reportedly included mustard gas and the nerve gases sarin, tabun and GF, which have environmental persistence times ranging from thirty minutes, in the case of tabun, to as much as two years in the case of mustard gas. At the time of the attacks, both countries were parties to the 1925 Geneva Protocol, a treaty banning the use of chemical weapons against another contracting party (Protocol for the Prohibition of the Use in War of Asphyxiating, Poisonous, or other Gases, and of Bacteriological Methods of Warfare, signed at Geneva on 19 June 1925). A U.N. expert team, which conducted investigations between 1984 and 1988, confirmed that chemical weapons had been used by Iraq.

The degree of environmental contamination and the extent of deaths and injuries, both during and after a chemical weapons attack, depend on the following factors:

- Method of weapon deployment
- Toxicity and persistence of the agent used

- Toxicity and persistence of possible breakdown products
- Intensity of solar radiation
- Wind velocity and air turbulence
- Temperature, precipitation and humidity
- Topography and soil conditions.

Towards the end of the war, Iraq's use of chemical weapons was not confined to military targets. During 1987 and 1988, it was alleged that numerous chemical attacks had been launched against Kurdish villages in the north of the country. Clinical evidence and soil samples confirmed the use of mustard gas and the nerve agent tabun against the Kurdish population in 1987. The most infamous attack occurred on 16 March 1988 in the town of Halabja, where up to 5,000 Kurdish civilians and Iranian soldiers died from the effects of sarin nerve gas and mustard gas. Later that year, chemical weapon agents were again used against the Kurds, forcing many thousands to flee to Iran and Turkey.

The U.N. Secretary-General requested Iraq's permission for a U.N. investigation but this was denied. suggesting that Iraq may also have used biological weapons. Furthermore, according to some toxicological tests, mycotoxins were found in samples of body fluids taken from Iranian gas victims. However, neither of these reports was verified, and the use of biological weapons by Iraq against Iran remains unconfirmed.

The most likely biological agents to be used as weapons agents are:

● Anthrax ● Smallpox ● Botulin toxin ● Tularaemia ● Plague

Beyond the immediate concerns for the health of affected individuals, livestock and crops, the potentially longer-term ecological implications associated with the use of biological weapons represent an important risk element.

. . .

4.4 Environmental Impacts and Risks from the Conflict of March/April 2003

. . . When reviewing this preliminary summary it is essential to keep in mind that Iraq's environment was already subject to a range of both chronic and acute environmental problems arising from:

- impacts of the Iran-Iraq War and 1991 Gulf War . . . ;
- low priority attached to the environment by the Iraqi government;
- unintended effects of U.N. sanctions (imports of many spare parts and chemicals required for maintaining essential environmental services such as sanitation and water supply were restricted because of their "dual use" nature; only in May 2002 were new procedures set in place by Security Council resolution 1409 for the processing of contracts for humanitarian supplies).

In addition to the key issues outlined below, it can be expected that additional risks will arise from unexploded ordnance and land mines. At the time of writing, there have been no reports of any major marine pollution incidents in the Gulf, nor have there been mass movements of displaced persons across international borders. However, all these, and additional potential environmental stresses, will need to be kept under continual review.

The U.S. air force stated that, as of 15 April 2003, coalition air forces had used 18,275 precision – guided munitions (67% of all munitions deployed) and around 8,975 unguided munitions. Over 800 Tomahawk cruise missiles had been fired as of 12 April. This compares with 288 fired during the 1991 Gulf War.

Disruption of Power Supplies, Water and Sanitation

... [T]he Iraqi population has become highly urbanized in recent years, meaning that most citizens are dependent on municipal power, water and sanitation services. Baghdad, Basra and other cities have experienced extended power cuts, with serious impacts on already inadequate water distribution and sanitation systems that have been subject to further degradation during the conflict. Millions of civilians have been deprived of basic services and there is likely to be an elevated risk of disease epidemics, as well as an increased pollution burden on the Tigris River.

Electricity supplies to central Baghdad were cut at approximately 17.00 GMT on 3 April and, at the time of finalizing this report (22 April), have not been re-established. The cause of the blackout is unknown, with coalition forces saying that they had not deliberately targeted the city's power supply. On 9 April, the ICRC estimated that only 20% of Baghdad's five million citizens had access to electricity, while the following day the organization was planning to visit the Medical City hospital complex (650 beds), which was "still experiencing water shortages." The ICRC was also attempting to fill public water tanks in areas of the capital currently not connected to the water-supply network.98 On 16 April, ICRC reported that Al-Rashad hospital in the east of Baghdad "lacks sufficient drinking water, has no water for washing or cleaning ... and only limited food is available for patients." ICRC provided 30,000 litres of water for drinking and cleaning.

In Basra, the ICRC and coalition forces had partially reconnected the city's water supply by the end of March. However, on 10 April the ICRC stated that "the water supply to parts of Basra and reportedly also to most towns in southern Iraq remains disrupted." A week earlier, the BBC reported the water and humanitarian situation in the southern town of Umm Qasr to be "a shambles."100 The ICRC, working with local technicians, restored supplies to the Al-Sadr region of Baghdad on 17 April, coinciding with a call from the U.N. Secretary General for coalition forces to do everything possible to ease the humanitarian situation.

Waste Management and Disease

The conflict will have exacerbated an already critical waste management situation. The longterm consequences of inadequate waste systems will be supplemented by acute health and safety risks associated with the accumulation of waste in populated areas, especially major town and cities. These risks include disease vectors (vermin, insects, dogs, pathogens) sourced to human remains, clinical waste, and food waste, and exposure to dust and debris potentially containing asbestos and other hazardous materials.

Oil-Well Fires in Southern Iraq and Oil-Filled Trenches Around Baghdad

Reports of oil wells having been deliberately set on fire in the Rumeila oilfield of southern Iraq began to emerge on 20 March, while a thick haze of dark smoke could be seen from Kuwait City the following day. Pentagon officials indicated that the fires were at wellheads, rather than from oil-filled trenches. Initial reports of up to 30 fires were later scaled back to nine. On 25 March Reuters stated that three of the fires had been extinguished, while on 27 March the Associated Press reported "as many as five fires were still burning," although a spokesperson for the Kuwaiti oil industry said that only three fires remained. Specialist contractors from Canada and the U.S. were preparing to tackle these sites. British forces cast doubt on initial claims that many of the wellheads had been sabotaged, reporting only very limited evidence of tampering. Only two fires were still burning on 3 April, while the last fire was reportedly extinguished on 15 April.

Oil-filled trenches in and around Baghdad were set alight in an attempt to impede coalition weapons and prevent aerial and satellite surveillance. These fires, together with fires at targeted sites, generated large quantities of dense black smoke, containing a range of toxic substances, with potential health risks for local people. The trenches also cause soil pollution and potentially threaten contamination of groundwater bodies and drinking water supplies. The number, extent and intensity of oil fires (whether from wells or trenches) were far smaller than during the 1991 Gulf War, and it can be expected that damage to the environment and/or human health has been at a lower level. However, further studies are needed to confirm this tentative conclusion.

As of 22 April, there have been no reports of any major oil (or petroleum product) spills, either on land or into water bodies (including offshore waters). This again contrasts with the severe environmental damage that occurred during the 1991 Gulf War.

Environmental Impacts of Oil Fires

Crude oil is a mixture of about one thousand different hydrocarbons, with exact composition (notably the ratio of heavy and light components) varying from one reserve to another. The products of uncontrolled oil fires, whether at a wellhead, a storage area or in trenches, will depend on the type of crude oil, local climate conditions, the content of hydrogen sulphide (H_2S), water and/or natural gas, and the presence of naturally occurring radioactivity, especially dissolved radon isotopes as products of the natural uranium decay series.

The broad categories of contaminants from oil fires are:

- extreme heat
- carbon monoxide
- unburned hydrocarbons
- poly aromatic hydrocarbons (PAHs)
- polychlorinated-dibenzo-dioxins and furans
- carbon soot
- oxides of sulphur
- oxides of nitrogen
- carbon dioxide
- radon

Of these, the first two are lethal, capable of causing immediate death upon exposure, even for a short duration. However, this would happen only within the immediate vicinity of the fire. The other pollutants have more chronic effects and some (PAHs, carbon soot) are carcinogenic. Other than potential impacts on human and animal health, the contaminants from oil fires may also damage vegetation (including crops), landscapes, and human artefacts (including buildings and archaeological sites). A normal oil-well fire will generally have only a limited footprint, though damage within this area may be very severe. However, many Iraqi oil fields are high producers (>5,000 bpd) by industry standards, and liable to generate very substantial quantities of pollutants. Plumes can potentially extend hundreds of kilometres and possibly enter neighbouring countries, depending on wind direction. Multiple large well fires, as occurred in Kuwait in 1991, may result in large-scale regional impacts, reduced penetration of sunlight, accumulated tar on ground surface, exposure of the general populace to pollutants, and widespread damage to vegetation.

Assuming that a typical well produces 5,000 bpd, and that there may be up to ten fires burning simultaneously, the level of fuel load could have been around 50,000 bpd. This equates to the pollution from 8 million diesel cars burning fuel at 99% efficiency.

Environmental Impacts of Unburned Oil from Wells and Trenches

The impacts of unburnt crude oil spilled onto the ground will depend on the type of crude (light/heavy), the presence of hydrogen sulphide, microclimatic conditions (temperature and wind direction) and the permeability of the ground. In the case of light crude oil (or its products), an explosive mixture of volatile hydrocarbons is soon formed in the area, putting people and the environment at risk. Hydrogen sulphide has the potential to cause instant death at concentrations above 500 ppm and high concentrations are known to occur at many oil and gas wells in the region.

The broad categories of contaminants from unburnt oil leaks/pools are as follows:

- volatile hydrocarbons, including aromatics (BTEX)
- hydrogen sulphide
- highly saline water
- naturally occurring radioactivity.

Since the aromatic hydrocarbons (benzene etc.), which are known carcinogens, are the most volatile of hydrocarbons, exposure even at low levels can be very harmful. Exposure can occur some kilometres from the point of the leak/pool depending on the prevailing wind conditions. Hydrocarbons may be very mobile in the ground especially in fractured/permeable soil (though percolation of crude is typically slower than that of oil products such as petrol and diesel), with a risk of widespread aquifer contamination, which is very expensive and time-consuming to remediate. There was significant aquifer contamination in Kuwait as a result of oil released during the Gulf War.

Oil mist can be carried for a few hundred metres before dropping back to ground, causing smothering of plant leaves, damage to buildings and artefacts, and depriving oxygen from ground microfauna.

Tackling deliberate and accidental oil spillages is extremely difficult, the more so in a conflict situation. If hydrogen sulphide is present, it will not be advisable to approach the area without special breathing apparatus. Secondly, due to the potentially explosive mixture of volatile hydro-carbons, it may not be safe for people to work in the area, either with our without breathing apparatus. Overall, therefore, oil trenches that have not been burnt, though less spectacular in terms of media imagery, are probably more damaging from a health and environment control and clean-up perspective.

Damage to Industrial Sites

UNEP's experience in the Balkans showed that direct or indirect damage to industrial sites can threaten human health and the environment. However, as of 22 April, no detailed information was available concerning the impacts of the recent conflict on industrial sites and potential releases of hazardous substances into the environment.

On 29 March, a coalition airstrike on a factory close to Al Rasheed water treatment plant caused damage to buildings within the treatment plant compound.

Targeting of Military Sites, Including Sites Related to the Production of Chemical, Biological and Nuclear Weapons

The coalition targeted numerous Iraqi military facilities, including ammunition storage sites and the logistical supply chains for Iraqi forces. Any of the sites targeted could present hazards to the environment and/or human health from a range of risk factors, including possible presence of unexploded ordnance, toxic or radioactive substances, and pollutants such as oil and petroleum products.

Several military targets were identified during coalition media briefings. For example, on 31 March it was reported that the Al-Kindi rocket and missile development site, located at Mosul near the Tigris River some 400 km north of Baghdad, was targeted by a coalition airstrike. This site had been visited by IAEA and UNVOMIC inspectors on four occasions between December 2002 and February 2003.

On 1 April, the Pentagon stated that a "former terrorist training camp" believed to have been "developing poisons for use against civilians in Europe and the United States" at Khurmal in Northeastern Iraq had been targeted with Tomahawk cruise missiles during the last week of March.

Several media reports raised concerns about the security of nuclear material at a storage facility near the Tuwaitha Nuclear Research Centre entered by U.S. forces during the conflict, although it was unclear how, when and by whom the site had first been entered. The U.S. subsequently provided assurances to IAEA that the nuclear material located there would be properly protected and access to the site restricted.

IAEA inspectors had been monitoring and inspecting the facility since 1991. It contained nuclear material that, under the terms set out by the U.N. Security Council, IAEA was not required to remove from Iraq after the Gulf War because the material could not be used directly for nuclear weapons purposes. Nevertheless, IAEA applied seals on the drums containing the nuclear materials and on the building itself.

During weapons inspections in Iraq from November 2002 until March 2003, IAEA inspectors visited the Tuwaitha Centre many times. In some buildings, the inspectors had documented higher than normal radiation levels, attributable to Iraq's past nuclear weapons programme and the presence of radioisotopes.

Speaking on 11 April 2003, IAEA's Director General said that, "as soon as circumstances permit, IAEA should return to verify that there has been no diversion of this material." IAEA has also underlined that radiation levels remain high and that great care must be taken when entering the facility. As of 22 April, the potential environmental consequences at any of the above-mentioned sites of possible releases of toxic/hazardous substances, including chemicals and heavy metals, are unknown.

Physical Degradation of Ecosystems

Intensive military activities will have caused widespread degradation of fragile desert ecosystems that may take many decades to recover. This will increase erosion, loss of top soil, and vulnerability to sand storms.

Depleted Uranium

Depleted uranium, a by-product from the process that enriches natural uranium ore for use as fuel in nuclear reactors and nuclear weapons, has both defensive and offensive military applications. Its high density makes it suitable as a component of armour plating (e.g., for part of the turrets of U.S. Abrams M1 main battle tanks), as well as for piercing armour plating. DU munitions are currently manufactured for use by aircraft (including helicopters) and tanks.

Many Iraqi tanks and armoured personnel carriers (APCs) were targeted during the conflict by U.S. A10 Thunderbolt ("warthog" or "tankbuster") aircraft, used throughout the military campaign. Use of DU by coalition forces was confirmed by U.S. Central Command on 26 March. A10s are equipped with conventional missiles, but also with guns that fire rounds of depleted uranium (DU). Television pictures broadcast by media on 8 April showed A10 aircraft attacking both the Planning and Information Ministries in Baghdad. Expert observers considered that DU munitions were used in these attacks. In other incidents, U.S. Abrams tanks are known to have burned, with likely releases of DU to the environment.

Overall, it is likely that significant amounts of DU rounds have been fired (around 290 metric tons were reportedly fired during the 1991 Gulf War[111]), with additional DU released into the environment from the burning of armour plating. This may involve any or all of the following potential risks to the environment and human health, based on UNEP's findings in the Balkans:

- Inhalation of DU dust at the time of munition impact, leading to a potentially serious additional health risk to anyone in the immediate vicinity who survived the initial blast and subsequent fire;
- Widespread, low-level contamination of the ground surface by DU;
- Presence of intact DU penetrators buried in soft ground (which might be dug up and handled by unprotected individuals, leading to a low-level but unnecessary beta radiation dose to the skin);
- Presence of DU penetrator fragments on the ground surface (which might be picked up and handled by unprotected individuals, including "souvenir" hunters, leading to a low-level but unnecessary radiation dose);
- Possible migration of DU into ground water (and from there into drinking water supplies), through corrosion and dissolution of penetrators and penetrator fragments.

However, it must be stressed that UNEP's work in the Balkans was undertaken some years after conflict had occurred, during which time dispersion of DU dust had occurred. Currently, in Iraq, there will be fresh surface contamination around sites targeted with DU in March and April 2003. UNEP experts expect there to be a high risk of inhaling DU dust when entering within a radius of about 150 m of such sites, unless high quality dust masks are worn. Inhalation of DU dust within this radius could result in health risks due to both the potential chemical toxicity of uranium, and to its radioactive nature.

It is also important to underline that the environmental conditions in Iraq (especially climate, soil, geology and vegetation) are very different to those prevailing in the Balkans and there may be important differences in the rates of corrosion and in the environmental pathways for DU. Consequently, it is important that independent scientific investigations are made if local people, military personnel, and those otherwise present in affected areas in the weeks, months and years ahead are to be given appropriate and accurate advice concerning risks to human health and the environment.

DU was reportedly used extensively in the vicinity of Basra during the 1991 Gulf War, so it is likely that future field investigations may detect sites where DU contamination is present from two conflicts 12 years apart. DU was also used in Kuwait in 1991 and IAEA conducted a study of affected sites in 2002.

Chemical and/or Biological Weapons

As of 22 April 2003, there is no evidence that chemical or biological weapons have been used at any time during the conflict, though the discovery of protective clothing at Iraqi military positions, and – in a Nasiriya hospital – of drugs used to counteract the effects of chemical weapons, led to coalition speculation that the Iraqi regime was prepared to deploy such weapons.

Several reported finds by coalition forces of chemical weapons facilities were later discounted.

On 22 April, the U.S. stated that no weaponized chemicals, biological agents or any nuclear devices had so far been found. Some potential "dual use" materials had been located, but the quantities and substances did not indicate weaponization.

Speaking on 10 April, the U.N. Secretary General stated his view that the mandate of U.N. weapons inspectors was still valid, having only been suspended because of the war. He expected that inspectors would be able to return as soon as possible to resume their work.

The Chairman of UNMOVIC has also indicated his belief that U.N. weapons inspectors can play a key role. Effective weapon inspections will be an important element in safeguarding Iraq's future environment.

Unexploded Ordnance (UXO)

As in the 1991 conflict, it can be expected that significant quantities of UXO are present, especially in and around heavily targeted areas such as Baghdad and Basra. One recent media report detailed the removal of an unexploded smart bomb from the grounds of Basra's main hotel. Unless strictly controlled and monitored, the open burning and detonation of UXO could pose risks to the environment and human health.

5.1 Overview

The post-conflict situation in Iraq, following the events of March and April 2003, presents immediate challenges in the fields of humanitarian assistance, reconstruction and administration. The humanitarian consequences of the conflict, including the disruption of water, sanitation and power supplies, mean that environmental issues must be accorded high priority. This report has highlighted many of the environmental risks and vulnerabilities now confronting Iraq. However, as a consequence of the ongoing conflict, it was not possible to gather information at the field level – an essential precondition for preparing effective postconflict environmental assistance. This is why UNEP advocates that early steps should be taken towards assembling more detailed knowledge of the current situation on the ground, through a series of specialized field missions. However, restoring security and the rule of law will be needed before these activities can be undertaken. The environmental situation in Iraq was already of serious concern prior to the most recent outbreak of conflict. This had resulted from a combination of successive wars, the low priority attached to environmental concerns by the former Iraqi government, and the unintended impact of U.N. sanctions, such as restrictions on the import of chemicals used for treating drinking water.

The conflict of March and April 2003 has been markedly different from the 1991 Gulf War, having been focused on major urban areas in Iraq, especially Baghdad and Basra. As result, the environmental consequences have also been very different, with the most obvious problems being air pollution from oil-trench fires and the damage to essential services such as water and electricity supplies.

This does not mean, however, that the consequences have been negligible. Among the known categories of impacts are physical damage to environmental infrastructure, (e.g., water and sanitation systems), targeting of military and industrial infrastructure, and consequent releases of potentially hazardous substances, air pollution from oil-well and oil-trench fires, damage to ecosystems and landscapes from military activities and use of depleted uranium (DU) ordnance, which is likely to have resulted in widespread environmental contamination of as yet unknown levels or consequences.

Questions and Discussion

1. From what is stated in the foregoing, does it appear that the coalition complied with international humanitarian law respecting the environment?
2. Does the United States have any obligation to clean up the depleted uranium before it leaves Iraq? For purposes of preventing future conflicts, how much attention should be devoted to cleanup and environmental protection?
3. If a state's use of force is illegal, is it strictly liable for all resulting environmental harm? Was that what the Security Council said in 1991?

4. Where a military alliance uses force, are the states individually liable for environmental and human rights consequences? Who has jurisdiction? Do individuals have human rights claims?

Behrami & Behrami v. France; Saramati v. France, Germany & Norway, Eur. Ct. Hum. Rts. (GC), Apps. 71412/01, 78166/01 (May 2, 2007) (Admissibility decision)

THE FACTS

. . .

I. RELEVANT BACKGROUND TO THE CASES

2. The conflict between Serbian and Kosovar Albanian forces during 1998 and 1999 is well documented. On 30 January 1999, and following a decision of the North Atlantic Council ("NAC") of the North Atlantic Treaty Organisation ("NATO"), NATO announced air strikes on the territory of the then Federal Republic of Yugoslavia ("FRY") should the FRY not comply with the demands of the international community. Negotiations took place between the parties to the conflict in February and March 1999. The resulting proposed peace agreement was signed by the Kosovar Albanian delegation but not by the Serbian delegation. The NAC decided on, and on 23 March 1999 the Secretary General of NATO announced, the beginning of air strikes against the FRY. The air strikes began on 24 March 1999 and ended on 8 June 1999 when the FRY troops agreed to withdraw from Kosovo. On 9 June 1999 "KFOR," the FRY and the Republic of Serbia signed a "Military Technical Agreement" ("MTA") by which they agreed on FRY withdrawal and the presence of an international security force following an appropriate U.N. Security Council Resolution ("UNSC Resolution").

3.UNSC Resolution 1244 of 10 June 1999 provided for the establishment of a security presence (KFOR) by "Member States and relevant international institutions," "under U.N. auspices," with "substantial NATO participation" but under "unified command and control." NATO pre-deployment to The Former Yugoslav Republic of Macedonia allowed deployment of significant forces to Kosovo by 12 June 1999 (in accordance with OPLAN 10413, NATO's operational plan for the UNSC Resolution 1244 mission called "Operation Joint Guardian"). By 20 June FRY withdrawal was complete. KFOR contingents were grouped into four multinational brigades ("MNBs") each of which was responsible for a specific sector of operations with a lead country. They included MNB Northeast (Mitrovica) and MNB Southeast (Prizren), led by France and Germany, respectively. Given the deployment of Russian forces after the arrival of KFOR, a further agreement on 18 June 1999 (between Russia and the United States) allocated various areas and roles to the Russian forces.

4. UNSC Resolution 1244 also decided on the deployment, under U.N. auspices, of an interim administration for Kosovo (UNMIK) and requested the Secretary General ("SG"), with the assistance of relevant international organisations, to establish it and to appoint a Special Representative to the SG ("SRSG") to control its implementation. UNMIK was to coordinate closely with KFOR. UNMIK comprised four pillars corresponding to the tasks assigned to it. Each pillar was placed under the authority of the SRSG and was headed by a Deputy SRSG. Pillar I (as it was at the relevant time) concerned humanitarian assistance and was led by UNHCR before it was phased out in June 2000. A new Pillar I (police and justice administration) was established in May 2001 and was led directly by the U.N., as was Pillar II (civil administration). Pillar III, concerning democratisation and institution building, was led by the Organisation for Security and Co-operation in Europe ("OSCE") and Pillar IV (reconstruction and economic development) was led by the European Union.

II. THE CIRCUMSTANCES OF THE BEHRAMI CASE

5. On 11 March 2000 eight boys were playing in the hills in the municipality of Mitrovica. The group included two of Agim Behrami's sons, Gadaf and Bekim Behrami. At around midday, the group came upon a number of undetonated cluster bomb units ("CBUs") which had been dropped during the bombardment by NATO in 1999 and the children began playing with the CBUs. Believing it was safe, one of the children threw a CBU in the air: it detonated and killed Gadaf Behrami. Bekim Behrami was also seriously injured and taken to hospital in Pristina (where he later had eye surgery and was released on 4 April 2000). Medical reports submitted indicate that he underwent two further eye operations (on 7 April and 22 May 2000) in a hospital in Bern, Switzerland. It is not disputed that Bekim Behrami was disfigured and is now blind.

6. UNMIK police investigated. They took witness statements from, *inter alia*, the boys involved in the incident and completed an initial report. Further investigation reports dated 11, 12 and 13 March 2000 indicated, *inter alia*, that UNMIK police could not access the site without KFOR agreement; reported that a French KFOR officer had accepted that KFOR had been aware of the unexploded CBUs for months but that they were not a high priority; and pointed out that the detonation site had been marked out by KFOR the day after the detonation. The autopsy report confirmed Gadaf Behrami's death from multiple injuries resulting from the CBU explosion. The UNMIK Police report of 18 March 2000 concluded that the incident amounted to "unintentional homicide committed by imprudence."

7. By letter dated 22 May 2000 the District Public Prosecutor wrote to Agim Behrami to the effect that the evidence was that the CBU detonation was an accident, that criminal charges would not be pursued but that Mr. Behrami had the right to pursue a criminal prosecution within eight days of the date of that letter. On 25 October 2001 Agim Behrami complained to the Kosovo Claims Office ("KCO") that France had not respected UNSC Resolution 1244. The KCO forwarded the complaint to the French Troop Contributing Nation Claims Office (TCNCO"). By letter of 5 February 2003 that TCNCO rejected the complaint stating, *inter alia*, that the UNSC Resolution 1244 had required KFOR to supervise mine clearing operations until UNMIK could take over and that such operations had been the responsibility of the U.N. since 5 July 1999.

III. THE CIRCUMSTANCES OF THE SARAMATI CASE

8. On 24 April 2001 Mr. Saramati was arrested by UNMIK police and brought before an investigating judge on suspicion of attempted murder and illegal possession of a weapon. On 25 April 2001 that judge ordered his pre-trial detention and an investigation into those and additional charges. On 23 May 2001 a prosecutor filed an indictment and on 24 May 2001 the District Court ordered his detention to be extended. On 4 June 2001 the Supreme Court allowed Mr. Saramati's appeal and he was released.

9. In early July 2001 UNMIK police informed him by telephone that he had to report to the police station to collect his money and belongings. The station was located in Prizren in the sector assigned to MNB Southeast, of which the lead nation was Germany. On 13 July 2001 he so reported and was arrested by UNMIK police officers by order of the Commander of KFOR ("COMKFOR"), who was a Norwegian officer at the time.

10. On 14 July 2001 detention was extended by COMKFOR for 30 days.

11. On 26 July 2001, and in response to a letter from Mr. Saramati's representatives taking issue with the legality of his detention, KFOR Legal Adviser advised that KFOR had the authority to detain under the UNSC Resolution 1244 as it was necessary "to maintain a safe and secure environment" and to protect KFOR troops. KFOR had information concerning Mr. Saramati's alleged involvement with armed groups operating in the border region between Kosovo and the Former Yugoslav Republic of Macedonia and was satisfied that Mr. Saramati represented a threat to the security of KFOR and to those residing in Kosovo.

12. On 26 July 2001 the Russian representative in the UNSC referred to "the arrest of Major Saramati, the Commander of a Kosovo Protection Corps Brigade, accused of undertaking activities threatening the international presence in Kosovo."

13. On 11 August 2001 Mr. Saramati's detention was again extended by order of COMKFOR. On 6 September 2001 his case was transferred to the District Court for trial, the indictment retaining charges of, *inter alia*, attempted murder and the illegal possession of weapons and explosives. By letter dated 20 September 2001, the decision of COMKFOR to prolong his detention was communicated to his representatives.

14. During each trial hearing from 17 September 2001 to 23 January 2002 Mr. Saramati's representatives requested his release and the trial court responded that, although the Supreme Court had so ruled in June 2001, his detention was entirely the responsibility of KFOR.

15. On 3 October 2001 a French General was appointed to the position of COMKFOR.

16. On 23 January 2002 Mr. Saramati was convicted of attempted murder under Article 30 § 2(6) of the Criminal Code of Kosovo in conjunction with Article 19 of the Criminal Code of the FRY. He was acquitted on certain charges and certain charges were either rejected or dropped. Mr. Saramati was transferred by KFOR to the UNMIK detention facilities in Pristina.

17. On 9 October 2002 the Supreme Court of Kosovo quashed Mr. Saramati's conviction and his case was sent for re-trial. His release from detention was ordered. A re-trial has yet to be fixed.

. . .

THE LAW

63. Messrs Behrami invoked Article 2 of the Convention as regards the impugned inaction of KFOR troops. Mr. Saramati relied on Articles 5, 6 and 13 as regards his detention by, and on the orders of, KFOR. The President of the Court agreed that the parties' submissions to the Grand Chamber could be limited to the admissibility of the cases. . . .

A. The Issue to Be Examined by the Court

66. The applicants maintained that there was a sufficient jurisdictional link, within the meaning of Article 1 of the Convention, between them and the respondent States and that their complaints were compatible *ratione loci*, *personae* and *materiae* with its provisions.

67. The respondent and third party States disagreed.

. . .

E. The Court's Assessment

121. The Court has adopted the following structure in its decision set out below. It has, in the first instance, established which entity, KFOR or UNMIK, had a mandate to detain and de-mine, the parties having disputed the latter point. Secondly, it has ascertained whether the impugned action of KFOR (detention in *Saramati*) and inaction of UNMIK (failure to de-mine in *Behrami*) could be attributed to the U.N.: in so doing, it has examined whether there was a Chapter VII framework for KFOR and UNMIK and, if so, whether their impugned action and omission could be attributed, in principle, to the U.N.. The Court has used the term "attribution" in the same way as the ILC in Article 3 of its draft Articles on the Responsibility of International Organisations. Thirdly, the Court has then examined whether it is competent *ratione personae* to review any such action or omission found to be attributable to the U.N..

122. In so doing, the Court has borne in mind that it is not its role to seek to define authoritatively the meaning of provisions of the U.N. Charter and other international instruments: it must nevertheless examine whether there was a plausible basis in such instruments for the matters impugned before it (*mutatis mutandis*, *Brannigan and McBride v. the United Kingdom*, judgment of 26 May 1993, Series A no. 258-B, § 72).

It also recalls that the principles underlying the Convention cannot be interpreted and applied in a vacuum. It must also take into account relevant rules of international law when examining questions concerning its jurisdiction and, consequently, determine State responsibility in conformity and harmony with the governing principles of international law of which it forms part, although it must remain mindful of the Convention's special character as a human rights treaty (Article 31 § 3 (c) of the Vienna Convention on the Law of Treaties of 23 May 1969; *Al-Adsani v. the United Kingdom* [GC], no. 35763/97, § 55, ECHR 2001-XI; and the above-cited decision of *Banković and Others*, at § 57).

1. The Entity with the Mandate to Detain and to De-Mine

123. The respondent and third party States argued that it made no difference whether it was KFOR or UNMIK which had the mandate to detain (the *Saramati* case) and to de-mine (the *Behrami* case) since both were international structures established by, and answerable to, the UNSC. The applicants maintained that KFOR had the mandate to both detain and de-mine and that the nature and structure of KFOR was sufficiently different to UNMIK as to engage the respondent States individually.

124. Having regard to the MTA (notably paragraph 2 of Article 1), UNSC Resolution 1244 (paragraph 9 as well as paragraph 4 of Annex 2 to the Resolution) as confirmed by FRAGO997 and later COMKFOR Detention Directive 42 (see paragraph 51 above), the Court considers it evident that KFOR's security mandate included issuing detention orders.

125. As regards de-mining, the Court notes that Article 9(e) of UNSC Resolution 1244 provided that KFOR retained responsibility for supervising de-mining until UNMIK could take over, a provision supplemented by, as pointed out by the U.N. to the Court, Article 11(k) of the Resolution. The report of the SG to the UNSC of 12 June 1999 confirmed that this activity was a humanitarian one (former Pillar I of UNMIK) so UNMIK was to establish UNMACC pending which KFOR continued to act as the *de facto* coordination centre. When UNMACC began operations, it was therefore placed under the direction of the Deputy SRSG of Pillar I. The U.N. submissions to this Court, the above-cited Evaluation Report, the Concept Plan, FRAGO 300 and the letters of the Deputy SRSG of August and October 1999 to KFOR confirm, in the first place, that the mandate for supervising de-mining was *de facto* and *de jure* taken over by UNMACC, created by UNMIK, at the very latest, by October 1999 and therefore prior to the detonation date in the *Behrami* case and, secondly, that KFOR remained involved in de-mining as a service provider whose personnel therefore acted on UNMIK's behalf.

126. The Court does not find persuasive the parties' arguments to the contrary. Whether, as noted by the applicants and the U.N. respectively, NATO had dropped the CBUs or KFOR had failed to secure the site and provide information thereon to UNMIK, this would not alter the mandate of UNMIK. The reports of the SG to the UNSC cited by the applicants may have referred to UNMACC as having been set up jointly by KFOR and the U.N., but this described the provision of assistance to UNMIK by the previous *de facto* co-ordination centre (KFOR): it was therefore transitional assistance which accorded with KFOR's general obligation to support UNMIK (paragraphs 6 and 9(f) of UNSC Resolution 1244) and such assistance in the field did not change UNMIK's mandate. The report of the International Committee of the Red Cross relied upon by the applicants, indicated (at p. 23) that mine clearance in Kosovo was coordinated by UNMACC which in turn fell under the aegis of UNMIK. Finally, even if KFOR support was, as a matter of fact, essential to the continued presence of UNMIK (the applicants' submission), this did not alter the fact that the Resolution created separate and distinct presences, with different mandates and responsibilities and, importantly, without any hierarchical relationship or accountability between them (U.N. submissions).

127. Accordingly, the Court considers that issuing detention orders fell within the security mandate of KFOR and that the supervision of de-mining fell within UNMIK's mandate.

2. Can the Impugned Action and Inaction Be Attributed to the U.N.?

(a) The Chapter VII Foundation for KFOR and UNMIK

128. As the first step in the application of Chapter VII, the UNSC Resolution 1244 referred expressly to Chapter VII and made the necessary identification of a "threat to international peace and security" within the meaning of Article 39 of the Charter. The UNSC Resolution 1244, *inter alia*, recalled the UNSC's "primary responsibility" for the "maintenance of international peace and security." Being "determined to resolve the grave humanitarian situation in Kosovo" and to "provide for the safe and free return of all refugees and displaced persons to their homes," it determined that the "situation in the region continues to constitute a threat to international peace and security" and, having expressly noted that it was acting under Chapter VII, it went on to set out the solutions found to the identified threat to peace and security.

129. The solution adopted by UNSC Resolution 1244 to this identified threat was, as noted above, the deployment of an international security force (KFOR) and the establishment of a civil administration (UNMIK).

In particular, that Resolution authorised "Member States and relevant international organisations" to establish the international security presence in Kosovo as set out in point 4 of Annex 2 to the Resolution with all necessary means to fulfil its responsibilities listed in Article 9. Point 4 of Annex 2 added that the security presence would have "substantial [NATO] participation" and had to be deployed under "unified command and control." The UNSC was thereby delegating to willing organisations and members states . . . the power to establish an international security presence as well as its operational command. Troops in that force would operate therefore on the basis of U.N. delegated, and not direct, command. In addition, the SG was authorised (Article 10) to establish UNMIK with the assistance of "relevant international organisations" and to appoint, in consultation with the UNSC, a SRSG to control its implementation (Articles 6 and 10 of the UNSC Resolution). The UNSC was thereby delegating civil administration powers to a U.N. subsidiary organ (UNMIK) established by the SG. Its broad mandate (an interim administration while establishing and overseeing the development of provisional self-government) was outlined in Article 11 of the Resolution.

130. While the Resolution referred to Chapter VII of the Charter, it did not identify the precise Articles of that Chapter under which the UNSC was acting and the Court notes that there are a number of possible bases in Chapter VII for this delegation by the UNSC: the non-exhaustive Article 42 (read in conjunction with the widely formulated Article 48), the non-exhaustive nature of Article 41 under which territorial administrations could be authorised as a necessary instrument for sustainable peace; or implied powers under the Charter for the UNSC to so act in both respects based on an effective interpretation of the Charter. In any event, the Court considers that Chapter VII provided a framework for the above-described delegation of the UNSC's security powers to KFOR and of its civil administration powers to UNMIK (see generally and *inter alia*, White and Ulgen, *"The Security Council and the Decentralised Military Option: Constitutionality and Function,"* Netherlands Law Review 44, 1997, 386; Sarooshi, *"The United Nations and the Development of Collective Security: The Delegation by the U.N. Security Council of its Chapter VII powers,"* Oxford University (1999); Chesterman, *"Just War or Just Peace: Humanitarian Intervention and International Law,"* (2002) Oxford University Press, pp. 167–169 and 172); *Zimmermann and Stahn,* cited above; De Wet, *"The Chapter VII Powers of the United Nations Security Council,"* 2004, pp. 260–265; Wolfrum *"International Administration in Post-Conflict Situations by the United Nations and other International Actors,"* Max Planck UNYB Vol. 9 (2005), pp. 667–672; Friedrich, *"UNMIK in Kosovo: struggling with Uncertainty,"* Max Planck UNYB 9 (2005) and the references

cited therein; and *Prosecutor v. Duško Tadić*, Decision of 2.10.95, Appeals Chamber of ICTY, §§ 35–36).

131. Whether or not the FRY was a U.N. member state at the relevant time (following the dissolution of the former Socialist Federal Republic of Yugoslavia), the FRY had agreed in the MTA to these presences. It is true that the MTA was signed by "KFOR" the day before the UNSC Resolution creating that force was adopted. However, the MTA was completed on the express basis of a security presence "under U.N. auspices" and with U.N. approval and the Resolution had already been introduced before the UNSC. The Resolution was adopted the following day, annexing the MTA and no international forces were deployed until the Resolution was adopted.

(b) Can the Impugned Action Be Attributed to KFOR?

132. While Chapter VII constituted the foundation for the above-described delegation of UNSC security powers, that delegation must be sufficiently limited so as to remain compatible with the degree of centralisation of UNSC collective security constitutionally necessary under the Charter and, more specifically, for the acts of the delegate entity to be attributable to the U.N. (as well as Chesterman, de Wet, Friedrich, Kolb and Sarooshi all cited above, see Gowlland-Debbas *"The Limits of Unilateral Enforcement of Community Objectives in the Framework of U.N. Peace Maintenance"* EIL (2000) Vol. 11, No. 2 369–370; Niels Blokker, *"Is the authorisation Authorised? Powers and Practice of the U.N. Security Council to Authorise the Use of Force by "Coalition of the Able and Willing,"* EJIL (2000), Vol. 11 No. 3; pp. 95–104 and *Meroni v. High Authority* Case 9/56, [1958] ECR 133).

Those limits strike a balance between the central security role of the UNSC and two realities of its implementation. In the first place, the absence of Article 43 agreements which means that the UNSC relies on States (notably its permanent members) and groups of States to provide the necessary military means to fulfil its collective security role. Secondly, the multilateral and complex nature of such security missions renders necessary some delegation of command.

133. The Court considers that the key question is whether the UNSC retained ultimate authority and control so that operational command only was delegated. This delegation model is now an established substitute for the Article 43 agreements never concluded.

134. That the UNSC retained such ultimate authority and control, in delegating its security powers by UNSC Resolution 1244, is borne out by the following factors.

In the first place, and as noted above, Chapter VII allowed the UNSC to delegate to "Member States and relevant international organisations." Secondly, the relevant power was a delegable power. Thirdly, that delegation was neither presumed nor implicit, but rather prior and explicit in the Resolution itself. Fourthly, the Resolution put sufficiently defined limits on the delegation by fixing the mandate with adequate precision as it set out the objectives to be attained, the roles and responsibilities accorded as well as the means to be employed. The broad nature of certain provisions could not be eliminated altogether given the constituent nature of such an instrument whose role was to fix broad objectives and goals and not to describe or interfere with the detail of operational implementation and choices. Fifthly, the leadership of the military presence was required by the Resolution to report to the UNSC so as to allow the UNSC to exercise its overall authority and control (consistently, the UNSC was to remain actively seized of the matter, Article 21 of the Resolution). The requirement that the SG present the KFOR report to the UNSC was an added safeguard since the SG is considered to represent the general interests of the U.N..

While the text of Article 19 of UNSC Resolution 1244 meant that a veto by one permanent member of the UNSC could prevent termination of the relevant delegation, the Court does not consider this factor alone sufficient to conclude that the UNSC did not retain ultimate authority and control.

135. Accordingly, UNSC Resolution 1244 gave rise to the following chain of command in the present cases. The UNSC was to retain ultimate authority and control over the security mission

and it delegated to NATO (in consultation with non-NATO member states) the power to establish, as well as the operational command of, the international presence, KFOR. NATO fulfilled its command mission *via* a chain of command (from the NAC, to SHAPE, to SACEUR, to CIC South) to COMKFOR, the commander of KFOR. While the MNBs were commanded by an officer from a lead TCN, the latter was under the direct command of COMKFOR. MNB action was to be taken according to an operational plan devised by NATO and operated by COMKFOR in the name of KFOR.

136. This delegation model demonstrates that . . . direct operational command from the UNSC is not a requirement of Chapter VII collective security missions.

137. However, the applicants made detailed submissions to the effect that the level of TCN control in the present cases was such that it detached troops from the international mandate and undermined the unity of operational command. They relied on various aspects of TCN involvement including that highlighted by the Venice Commission and noted KFOR's legal personality separate to that of the TCNs.

138. The Court considers it essential to recall at this point that the necessary donation of troops by willing TCNs means that, in practice, those TCNs retain some authority over those troops (for reasons, *inter alia*, of safety, discipline and accountability) and certain obligations in their regard (material provision including uniforms and equipment). NATO's command of operational matters was not therefore intended to be exclusive, but the essential question was whether, despite such TCN involvement, it was "effective."

139. The Court is not persuaded that TCN involvement, either actual or structural, was incompatible with the effectiveness (including the unity) of NATO's operational command. The Court does not find any suggestion or evidence of any actual TCN orders concerning, or interference in, the present operational (detention) matter. Equally there is no reason to consider that the TCN structural involvement highlighted by the applicants undermined the effectiveness of NATO's operational control. Since TCN troop contributions are in law voluntary, the continued level of national deployment is equally so. That TCNs provided materially for their troops would have no relevant impact on NATO's operational control. It was not argued that any NATO rules of engagement imposed would not be respected. National command (over own troops or a sector in Kosovo) was under the direct operational authority of COMKFOR. While individual claims might potentially be treated differently depending on which TCN was the source of the alleged problem (national commanders decided on whether immunity was to be waived, TCNs had exclusive jurisdiction in (at least) disciplinary and criminal matters, certain TCNs had put in place their own TCNCOs and at least one TCN accepted civil jurisdiction (the above-cited *Bici* case)), it has not been explained how this, of itself, could undermine the effectiveness or unity of NATO command in *operational* matters. The Court does not see how the failure to conclude a SOFA between the U.N. and the host FRY could affect, as the applicants suggested, NATO's operational command. That COMKFOR was charged exclusively with issuing detention orders amounts to a division of labour and not a break in a unified command structure since COMKFOR acted at all times as a KFOR officer answerable to NATO through the above-described chain of command.

140. Accordingly, even if the U.N. itself would accept that there is room for progress in co-operation and command structures between the UNSC, TCNs and contributing international organisations (see, for example, Supplement to an Agenda for Peace: Position paper of the SG on the Occasion of the 50th Anniversary of the U.N., A/50/60 – S/1995/1; the *Brahami* report, cited above; UNSC Resolutions 1327 (2000) and 1353 (2001); and Reports of the SG of 1 June and 21 December 2001 on the Implementation of the Recommendations of the Special Committee on Peacekeeping Operations and the Panel on U.N. Peace Operations (A/55/977, A/56/732)), the Court finds that the UNSC retained ultimate authority and control and that effective command of the relevant operational matters was retained by NATO.

141. In such circumstances, the Court observes that KFOR was exercising lawfully delegated Chapter VII powers of the UNSC so that the impugned action was, in principle, "attributable" to the U.N. within the meaning of the word outlined at paragraphs 29 and 121 above.

(c) Can the Impugned Inaction Be Attributed to UNMIK?

142. In contrast to KFOR, UNMIK was a subsidiary organ of the U.N. Whether it was a subsidiary organ of the SG or of the UNSC, whether it had a legal personality separate to the U.N., whether the delegation of power by the UNSC to the SG and/or UNMIK also respected the role of the UNSC for which Article 24 of the Charter provided, UNMIK was a subsidiary organ of the U.N. institutionally directly and fully answerable to the UNSC (see ILC report at paragraph 33 above). While UNMIK comprised four pillars (three of which were at the time led by UNHCR, the OSCE and the EU), each pillar was under the authority of a Deputy SRSG, who reported to the SRSG who in turn reported to the UNSC (Article 20 of UNSC Resolution 1244).

143. Accordingly, the Court notes that UNMIK was a subsidiary organ of the U.N. created under Chapter VII of the Charter so that the impugned inaction was, in principle, "attributable" to the U.N. in the same sense.

3. Is the Court Competent Ratione Personae?

144. It is therefore the case that the impugned action and inaction are, in principle, attributable to the U.N.. It is, moreover, clear that the U.N. has a legal personality separate from that of its member states (*The Reparations case*, ICJ Reports 1949) and that that organisation is not a Contracting Party to the Convention.

145. In its *Bosphorus* judgment (cited above, §§152–153), the Court held that, while a State was not prohibited by the Convention from transferring sovereign power to an international organisation in order to pursue cooperation in certain fields of activity, the State remained responsible under Article 1 of the Convention for all acts and omissions of its organs, regardless of whether they were a consequence of the necessity to comply with international legal obligations, Article 1 making no distinction as to the rule or measure concerned and not excluding any part of a State's "jurisdiction" from scrutiny under the Convention. The Court went on, however, to hold that where such State action was taken in compliance with international legal obligations flowing from its membership of an international organisation and where the relevant organisation protected fundamental rights in a manner which could be considered at least equivalent to that which the Convention provides, a presumption arose that the State had not departed from the requirements of the Convention. Such presumption could be rebutted, if in the circumstances of a particular case, it was considered that the protection of Convention rights was manifestly deficient: in such a case, the interest of international cooperation would be outweighed by the Convention's role as a "constitutional instrument of European public order" in the field of human rights (*ibid.*, §§ 155–156).

146. The question arises in the present case whether the Court is competent *ratione personae* to review the acts of the respondent States carried out on behalf of the U.N. and, more generally, as to the relationship between the Convention and the U.N. acting under Chapter VII of its Charter.

147. The Court first observes that nine of the twelve original signatory parties to the Convention in 1950 had been members of the U.N. since 1945 (including the two Respondent States), that the great majority of the current Contracting Parties joined the U.N. before they signed the Convention and that currently all Contracting Parties are members of the U.N. Indeed, one of the aims of this Convention (see its preamble) is the collective enforcement of rights in the Universal Declaration of Human Rights of the General Assembly of the U.N. More generally, it is further recalled, as noted at paragraph 122 above, that the Convention has to be interpreted in the light of any relevant rules and principles of international law applicable in relations between

its Contracting Parties. The Court has therefore had regard to two complementary provisions of the Charter, Articles 25 and 103, as interpreted by the International Court of Justice.

148. Of even greater significance is the imperative nature of the principle aim of the U.N. and, consequently, of the powers accorded to the UNSC under Chapter VII to fulfil that aim. In particular, it is evident from the Preamble, Articles 1, 2 and 24 as well as Chapter VII of the Charter that the primary objective of the U.N. is the maintenance of international peace and security. While it is equally clear that ensuring respect for human rights represents an important contribution to achieving international peace (see the Preamble to the Convention), the fact remains that the UNSC has primary responsibility, as well as extensive means under Chapter VII, to fulfil this objective, notably through the use of coercive measures. The responsibility of the UNSC in this respect is unique and has evolved as a counterpart to the prohibition, now customary international law, on the unilateral use of force.

149. In the present case, Chapter VII allowed the UNSC to adopt coercive measures in reaction to an identified conflict considered to threaten peace, namely UNSC Resolution 1244 establishing UNMIK and KFOR.

Since operations established by UNSC Resolutions under Chapter VII of the U.N. Charter are fundamental to the mission of the U.N. to secure international peace and security and since they rely for their effectiveness on support from member states, the Convention cannot be interpreted in a manner which would subject the acts and omissions of Contracting Parties which are covered by UNSC Resolutions and occur prior to or in the course of such missions, to the scrutiny of the Court. To do so would be to interfere with the fulfilment of the U.N.'s key mission in this field including, as argued by certain parties, with the effective conduct of its operations. It would also be tantamount to imposing conditions on the implementation of a UNSC Resolution which were not provided for in the text of the Resolution itself. This reasoning equally applies to voluntary acts of the respondent States such as the vote of a permanent member of the UNSC in favour of the relevant Chapter VII Resolution and the contribution of troops to the security mission: such acts may not have amounted to obligations flowing from membership of the U.N. but they remained crucial to the effective fulfilment by the UNSC of its Chapter VII mandate and, consequently, by the U.N. of its imperative peace and security aim.

. . .

There exists, in any event, a fundamental distinction between the nature of the international organisation and of the international cooperation with which the Court was there concerned and those in the present cases. As the Court has found above, UNMIK was a subsidiary organ of the U.N. created under Chapter VII and KFOR was exercising powers lawfully delegated under Chapter VII of the Charter by the UNSC. As such, their actions were directly attributable to the U.N., an organisation of universal jurisdiction fulfilling its imperative collective security objective.

152. In these circumstances, the Court concludes that the applicants' complaints must be declared incompatible *ratione personae* with the provisions of the Convention.

Questions and Discussion

1. Do you agree? Note that the United Nations has immunity from suit in the national courts of member states and that neither individuals nor international organizations have standing at the International Court of Justice. Does this mean that international peacekeeping troops can act with impunity?
2. On the substance, are international organizations bound by human rights and environmental norms? The laws of war? They may or may not have treaty-making power, but international organizations in practice do not adhere to multilateral agreements on any of these topics. Are they bound by customary international law?

E. *ICJ Opinions and Judgments*

In 1995, the U.N. General Assembly requested an advisory opinion on the question of whether the threat or use of nuclear weapons is a violation of international law, in light of their impacts on health and the environment. *Request for an Advisory Opinion from the International Court of Justice on the Legality of the Threat or Use of Nuclear Weapons*, G.A. Res. 49/75K, U.N. GAOR, 49th sess., Supp. No. 49, at 71, U.N. Doc. A/49/49 (1995). In fact, transnational civil society, in the form of a coalition of nongovernmental organizations and individuals calling themselves the World Court Project, was behind the request, having successfully exerted pressure on the General Assembly to make the request to the Court. The Court decided it had jurisdiction to answer the General Assembly's questions and did so on July 8, 1996. Also before the Court, in a separate proceeding, was an effort to reopen a contentious case filed by Australia and New Zealand against France, challenging the legality of nuclear testing in the South Pacific. The Court held that the proceedings were definitively terminated but noted that its conclusion was "without prejudice to the obligations of states to respect and protect the natural environment." See Request for an Examination of the Situation in Accordance with Paragraph 63 of the Court's Judgment of Dec. 20, 1974 in the *Nuclear Tests (New Zealand v. France)* Case, Order of Sept. 22, 1995, 1995 ICJ para. 64.

In the advisory opinion on the legality of nuclear weapons, the Court was intensely divided on some issues and unanimous in regard to others. Given the complexity of the matter, it is perhaps not surprising that, for the first time in its history, each judge issued a separate declaration or opinion. Several holdings were closely linked to international environmental law. First, the Court found by a vote of 11–3 that neither customary nor conventional international law – including international environmental law – prohibits the existence of nuclear weapons *as such. Legality of the Threat of Use of Nuclear Weapons*, at 36, para. 105(2)(B). The three dissenting judges found that nuclear weapons, in all their probable uses, are so devastating that they would be likely to breach human rights and environmental standards and thus are prohibited as such. The Court unanimously agreed that "[a] threat or use of nuclear weapons should . . . be compatible with . . . the principles and rules of international humanitarian law, as well as with specific obligations under treaties and other undertakings which expressly deal with nuclear weapons." *Id.* at 36, para. 105(2)(D).

The Court's final determination was the most divided. The Court's vote was 7–7, necessitating a deciding vote of the President holding that "the threat or use of nuclear weapons would generally be contrary to the rules of international law applicable in armed conflict and, in particular, the principles and rules of humanitarian law." *Id.* at para. 105(2)(E). The Court went on, however, to say that it could not conclude definitively whether or not extreme self-defense, in which the life of the state would be at stake, would allow the threat or use of nuclear weapons. The Court recognized that "the use of nuclear weapons could constitute a catastrophe for the environment," the latter representing "not an abstraction but . . . the living space, the quality of life and the very health of human beings, including generations unborn." Given this, the Court held that states must take environmental considerations into account in assessing what is necessary and proportionate in the pursuit of military objectives. The Court noted that the provisions of Additional Protocol I to the 1949 Geneva Conventions embody a general obligation to protect the natural environment against widespread, long-term, and severe environmental damage; the prohibition of methods and means of warfare that are intended or may be expected to cause such damage; and the prohibition of attacks against the natural environment by way of reprisals. Thus, although no specific provision prohibits the use of nuclear weapons, humanitarian law indicates that important environmental factors should be taken into account in the use of such weaponry in armed conflicts.

F. *Accountability*

The air campaign conducted by members of the North Atlantic Treaty Organization (NATO) against Yugoslavia during the Kosovo conflict produced allegations that the environmental and other impacts of the bombing made the attacks illegal under international humanitarian law. The prosecutor for the International Criminal Tribunal for the Former Yugoslavia appointed a committee to advise as to whether to conduct a formal investigation. The June 14, 2000, report of the committee recommended against an investigation, having assessed both the law and the available evidence that were relevant to its mandate. *See* Final Report of the Committee Established to Review the NATO Bombing Campaign Against the Federal Republic of Yugoslavia, *available at* http://www.un.org/icty/pressreal/nato/061300.htm. On the first matter, the Committee considered articles 35(3) and 55 of Additional Protocol I to state the "basic" legal provisions applicable to environmental protection during armed conflict. Significantly, the Committee asserted that article 55 "may . . . reflect current customary law" (para. 16), despite a suggestion from the International Court of Justice four years earlier that it does not. *See Advisory Opinion on the Threat or Use of Nuclear Weapons,* 1996 I.C.J. 242, para. 31. Turning to the facts, the Committee found that the bombing campaign caused some environmental damage through attacks on industrial facilities, such as chemical plants and oil installations that released pollutants. Final Report, para. 14. But given the duty to find cumulative conditions fulfilled (long-term, widespread, and severe damage) and acknowledging the high threshold set by those conditions, the Committee concluded that it would be difficult to assess whether such a threshold was reached in this case, "even if reliable environmental assessments were to give rise to legitimate concern concerning the impact of the NATO bombing campaign." *Id.* at para. 15. The Committee concluded by expressing its opinion that, according to the information in its possession, "the environmental damage caused during the NATO bombing campaign does not reach the Additional Protocol I threshold." *Id.* at para. 17.

The conclusion did not end the matter, because the Committee estimated that the legality of the attacks also had to be tested in light of the principles of military necessity and proportionality. It would appear that there was little debate over the issue of military necessity, because most of the discussion in the Report concerns proportionality. The Committee states that, in applying this principle, "it is necessary to assess the importance of the target in relation to the incidental damage expected: if the target is sufficiently important, a greater degree of risk to the environment may be justified." *Id.* Regretting the lack of concrete guidelines on what constitutes excessive damage, the Committee said that, "at a minimum, actions resulting in massive environmental destruction, especially when they do not serve a clear and important military purpose, would be questionable." *Id.* at para. 22. Though recommending that no investigation proceed, the Committee considered that, independent of the principle of proportionality, there is a duty to take precautionary measures to minimize collateral damage to the environment. "If there is a choice of weapons or methods of attack available, a commander should select those which are most likely to avoid, or at least minimize incidental damage. In doing so, however, he is entitled to take account of factors such as stocks of different weapons and likely future demands, the timeliness of attack and risks to his own forces." *Id.* at para. 21. Thus, the general principles of international humanitarian law play as great a role as do the more recent provisions that specifically mention environmental protection. *See* Ida Bostian, *The Environmental Consequences of the Kosovo Conflict and the NATO Bombing of Serbia*, 1999 COLO. J. INT'L ENVTL. L. & POL'Y 230 (2000).

Note that the Rome Statute of the International Criminal Court (July 17, 1998), 37 I.L.M. 999 (1998), gives the ICC jurisdiction over war crimes, defined as grave breaches of the 1949 Geneva Conventions on the Law of Armed Conflict or "other serious violations of the laws and customs applicable in international armed conflict, within the established framework of international law." Among the enumerated offenses in article 8(2)(b)(iv) is the following:

> intentionally launching an attack in the knowledge that such attack will cause incidental loss of life or injury to civilians or damage to civilian objects or widespread, long-term and severe damage to the natural environment which would be clearly excessive in relation to the concrete and direct overall military advantage anticipated.

Do the conflicts described in the previous section suggest any commission of war crimes within this definition?

III. Environmental Disasters and Their Aftermath

States are not insurers against environmental harm from accidents or unavoidable degradation, either with respect to those in their territory and jurisdiction or across borders. Although it is accepted that international environmental law imposes "the general obligation of states to ensure that activities within their jurisdiction and control respect the environment of other states or of areas beyond national control," this duty is one of due diligence to prevent transboundary harm caused by human activities. *See Legality of the Threat or Use of Nuclear Weapons*, Advisory Opinion, I.C.J. Reports 1996, at 241–42, para 29. Emergency preparedness can mitigate harm from natural disasters and provide assistance to those who are affected. Industrial accidents should be preventable, but incidents occur nonetheless. Both types of catastrophes can result in severe environmental degradation, as well as loss of life, health, and property. Internal and transboundary movements of displaced persons may cause further humanitarian and environmental crises. This section looks at the international obligations of states and emerging concepts addressing environmental disasters and their impacts on human rights. We look first at hazardous activities and then at natural disasters.

A. *Industrial Accidents*

Following the April 26, 1986, explosion in Reactor Number 4 of the Chernobyl nuclear power plant in the Ukraine (then part of the Soviet Union), the resulting fire melted a portion of the uranium fuel. Although there was no nuclear explosion and the core of the reactor did not melt, the serious fire that engulfed the reactor released a large quantity of radioactive material into the air. Fallout occurred near the plant and spread beyond. Between April 27 and May 8, nearly fifty thousand persons were evacuated from towns located within a thirty-kilometer radius of the plant. Two persons were immediately killed by the explosion, twenty-nine died shortly after, and hundreds were afflicted with radiation poisoning. The foreign consequences were also severe, even though no deaths were immediately attributed to the accident. Following rapid changes in the wind direction, the radioactive cloud that had formed over Chernobyl crossed the airspace of a series of countries, beginning with those of Scandinavia. Four days after the incident, radiation measurements along the Swedish coast were ten times higher than normal. The radioactive cloud moved south, crossing Germany,

Austria, Switzerland, Yugoslavia, and Italy. See Linda Malone, *The Chernobyl Accident: A Case Study in International Law Regulating State Responsibility for Transboundary Nuclear Pollution*, 12 COLO. J. ENVT'L L. 203, 222 (1987).

No international treaty regulated the plant or actions to be taken in the event of an accident. The interpretation then given to the Convention on Long-Range Transboundary Air Pollution (Geneva, Nov. 13, 1979) excluded pollution by radioactivity. The Soviet Union was not a contracting party to the Vienna Convention on Civil Liability for Nuclear Damage (May 21, 1963). Indeed, among the states that suffered effects from the radioactive cloud, only Yugoslavia had signed and ratified the Convention. There remained, therefore, only the recourse to customary international law.

After consideration, none of the affected states presented a claim for damages to the Soviet Union. They instead requested that the Governing Council of the International Atomic Energy Agency (IAEA) convene an extraordinary session to elaborate measures to reinforce international cooperation in the field of nuclear security and radioactive protection. This meeting, which took place in Vienna from July 21 to August 15, 1986, drafted two conventions that were adopted one month later by the IAEA General Conference. The Convention on Early Notification of a Nuclear Accident (Sept. 26, 1986) entered into force on October 27; the Convention on Assistance in the Case of a Nuclear Accident or Radiological Emergency was signed the same day and rapidly ratified by the signatories.

The instrument on assistance traces a general framework for cooperation between states on the one hand and between the states and the IAEA on the other hand, in the case of nuclear accident or other radiological emergency (i.e., any danger caused by radiation, whatever the cause). Had the Convention on Assistance existed at the time of the Chernobyl incident, any state exposed to radiation could have claimed assistance, whether or not the accident or emergency originated in its territory, under its jurisdiction, or under its control. Art. 2, para. 1. It is clear, however, that states parties did not accept any obligation other than cooperating among themselves and with the Agency to facilitate early response. Art. 1, para. 1.

Apparently no government pushed to conclude rules on state liability for accidental environmental harm. Negotiations would no doubt have been lengthy and perhaps unsuccessful over such matters as proximate harm and mitigation of damages. The difficulty of evaluating the consequential costs of the Chernobyl accident, especially with respect to the precautionary measures taken by the affected countries, also may have led states to avoid the issue of state responsibility. It also reflects the general reticence of states toward rules imposing strict liability for harm caused by a state or its citizens. The emphatic preference remains for measures of prevention.

More than a decade later, the U.N. International Law Commission (ILC) completed its Draft Articles on the Responsibility of States for Internationally Wrongful Acts, which the U.N. General Assembly "took note of" in Res. 56/83 (Dec. 2001). According to article 2 of the ILC Draft Articles, there is an internationally wrongful act when a state's conduct (an action or omission) constitutes a breach of an international obligation of the state. Article 3 adds that the characterization of an act as internationally wrongful is governed by international law. In other words, the primary rules of conduct for states (i.e., their rights and duties established by treaties and custom, for example) establish whether an act or omission constitutes a wrongful act. At present, only a handful of treaties make states strictly liable for any harm that occurs, and those treaties primarily address state-operated hazardous activities, such as space launches.

Since 1978, the International Law Commission has considered the topic of "international liability for injurious consequences arising out of acts not prohibited by international law," or strict liability. In 1997, the ILC decided to deal only with the question of prevention of transboundary damage from hazardous activities. Within four years it presented to the U.N. General Assembly a completed set of nineteen articles on the topic. *See* Draft Articles on Prevention of Transboundary Harm from Hazardous Activities, *in Report of the International Law Commission on the Work of Its Fifty-Third Session*, U.N. GAOR, 56th sess. Supp. No. 10, U.N. Doc. A/56/10 370 (2001). The General Assembly reviewed the articles and, pressed by certain member states, asked the ILC to continue working on the topic of international liability, "bearing in mind the interrelationship between prevention and liability." Res. 56/82 of Jan. 18, 2002. By July 2004, a draft set of Principles on Allocation of Loss in the Case of Transboundary Harm Arising out of Hazardous Activities was provisionally adopted by the Commission on first reading, and after comments by states, adopted on second reading in May 2006. See *Draft Report of the International Law Commission on the Work of its Fifty-Eighth Session*, "Chapter V: International Liability for Injurious Consequences Arising out of Acts Not Prohibited by International Law (International Liability in Case of Loss from Transboundary Harm Arising out of Hazardous Activities)," U.N. Doc. A/CN.4/L.693/Add.1 (June 9, 2006). To a large extent, these efforts can be seen as supplementing and completing the ILC Articles on State Responsibility, although the content of the adopted rules appears largely to repudiate strict liability when the state has complied with the Draft Articles on Prevention.

The Draft Principles approach the issue as one of allocating the risk of loss due to harm resulting from lawful economic or other activities, when the relevant state has complied with its due diligence obligations to prevent transboundary harm. The articles provide a general framework for states to adopt domestic law or conclude international agreements to ensure prompt and adequate compensation for the victims of transboundary damage caused by lawful hazardous activities.

**Draft Principles on the Allocation of Loss in the Case
of Transboundary Harm Arising out of Hazardous Activities,**
2 Yearbook of the International Law Commission, 2006 pt. 2

. . .

Principle 1 Scope of Application

The present draft principles apply to transboundary damage caused by hazardous activities not prohibited by international law.

Principle 2 Use of Terms

For the purposes of the present draft principles:

(a)   "damage" means significant damage caused to persons, property or the environment; and includes:

    (i) loss of life or personal injury;

    (ii) loss of, or damage to, property, including property which forms part of the cultural heritage;

    (iii) loss or damage by impairment of the environment;

    (iv) the costs of reasonable measures of reinstatement of the property, or environment, including natural resources;

    (v) the costs of reasonable response measures;

(b) "environment" includes natural resources, both abiotic and biotic, such as air, water, soil, fauna and flora and the interaction between the same factors, and the characteristic aspects of the landscape;

(c) "hazardous activity" means an activity which involves a risk of causing significant harm;

(d) "State of origin" means the State in the territory or otherwise under the jurisdiction or control of which the hazardous activity is carried out;

(e) "transboundary damage" means damage caused to persons, property or the environment in the territory or in other places under the jurisdiction or control of a State other than the State of origin;

(f) "victim" means any natural or legal person or State that suffers damage;

(g) "operator" means any person in command or control of the activity at the time the incident causing transboundary damage occurs.

Principle 3 Purposes

The purposes of the present draft principles are:

(a) to ensure prompt and adequate compensation to victims of transboundary damage; and

(b) to preserve and protect the environment in the event of transboundary damage, especially with respect to mitigation of damage to the environment and its restoration or reinstatement.

Principle 4 Prompt and Adequate Compensation

1. Each State should take all necessary measures to ensure that prompt and adequate compensation is available for victims of transboundary damage caused by hazardous activities located within its territory or otherwise under its jurisdiction or control.

2. These measures should include the imposition of liability on the operator or, where appropriate, other person or entity. Such liability should not require proof of fault. Any conditions, limitations or exceptions to such liability shall be consistent with draft principle 3.

3. These measures should also include the requirement on the operator or, where appropriate, other person or entity, to establish and maintain financial security such as insurance, bonds or other financial guarantees to cover claims of compensation.

4. In appropriate cases, these measures should include the requirement for the establishment of industry-wide funds at the national level.

5. In the event that the measures under the preceding paragraphs are insufficient to provide adequate compensation, the State of origin should also ensure that additional financial resources are made available.

Principle 5 Response Measures

Upon the occurrence of an incident involving a hazardous activity which results or is likely to result in transboundary damage:

(a) the State of origin shall promptly notify all States affected or likely to be affected of the incident and the possible effects of the transboundary damage;

(b) the State of origin, with the appropriate involvement of the operator, shall ensure that appropriate response measures are taken and should, for this purpose, rely upon the best available scientific data and technology;

(c) the State of origin, as appropriate, should also consult with and seek the cooperation of all States affected or likely to be affected to mitigate the effects of transboundary damage and if possible eliminate them;

(d) the States affected or likely to be affected by the transboundary damage shall take all feasible measures to mitigate and if possible to eliminate the effects of such damage;

(e) the States concerned should, where appropriate, seek the assistance of competent interna-
     tional organizations and other States on mutually acceptable terms and conditions.

Principle 6 International and Domestic Remedies

1. States shall provide their domestic judicial and administrative bodies with the necessary
    jurisdiction and competence and ensure that these bodies have prompt, adequate and
    effective remedies available in the event of transboundary damage caused by hazardous
    activities located within their territory or otherwise under their jurisdiction or control.
2. Victims of transboundary damage should have access to remedies in the State of origin
    that are no less prompt, adequate and effective than those available to victims that suffer
    damage, from the same incident, within the territory of that State.
3. Paragraphs 1 and 2 are without prejudice to the right of the victims to seek remedies other
    than those available in the State of origin.
4. States may provide for recourse to international claims settlement procedures that are
    expeditious and involve minimal expenses.
5. States should guarantee appropriate access to information relevant for the pursuance of
    remedies, including claims for compensation.

Principle 7 Development of Specific International Regimes

1. Where, in respect of particular categories of hazardous activities, specific global, regional
    or bilateral agreements would provide effective arrangements concerning compensation,
    response measures and international and domestic remedies, all efforts should be made to
    conclude such specific agreements.
2. Such agreements should, as appropriate, include arrangements for industry and/or State
    funds to provide supplementary compensation in the event that the financial resources of
    the operator, including financial security measures, are insufficient to cover the damage
    suffered as a result of an incident. Any such funds may be designed to supplement or replace
    national industry-based funds.

Principle 8 Implementation

1. Each State should adopt the necessary legislative, regulatory and administrative measures
    to implement the present draft principles.
2. The present draft principles and the measures adopted to implement them shall be applied
    without any discrimination such as that based on nationality, domicile or residence.
3. States should cooperate with each other to implement the present draft principles.

Questions and Discussion

1. As can be seen, the draft principles support existing state practice, which largely channels
    liability to the owner or operator and demands financial guarantees against harm. The
    articles do not support strict liability for states, unless the state itself is the operator of the
    hazardous activity. The lack of any serious consideration of state liability may be under-
    stood in the context of the articles on prevention: failure to fulfill the due diligence duty to
    prevent is considered to breach an international obligation and shifts the applicable legal
    regime to one of state responsibility. *See* P.S. Rao, *First Report on the Legal Regime for
    Allocation of Loss in Case of Transboundary Harm Arising out of Hazardous Activities*, U.N.
    Doc. A/CN.4/531, at 7 (August 2003, 55th ILC Sess.). The ILC appears to have decided that

strict liability of states does not have support even as a measure of progressive development in the law. See P.S. Rao, *Third Report on the Legal Regime for Allocation of Loss in Case of Transboundary Harm Arising out of Hazardous Activities,*" U.N. Doc. A/CN.4/566, at para. 31 (March 2006, 58th ILC Sess.). *See also* Pemmaraju Sreenivasa Rao, *International Liability for Transnational Harm,* 34 ENVTL. POL'Y & L. 224 (2004); Robin R. Churchill, *Facilitating (Transnational) Civil Liability Litigation for Environmental Damage by Means of Treaties: Problems and Progress,* 12 Y.B. INT'L ENVTL. L. 1, 35–36 (2001); A. Kiss & D. Shelton, *Strict Liability in International Environmental Law,* in LAW OF THE SEA, ENVIRON-MENTAL LAW AND SETTLEMENT OF DISPUTES 1131, 1140 (T.M. Ndiaye & R. Wolfrum eds., 2007).

2. If the draft principles had been concluded in a legally binding form before Chernobyl, what would have been the obligations of the Soviet Union? Would the principles have helped avoid any of the harm that occurred? Would compensation have been due?

3. If international environmental law and state responsibility impose only limited obligations on states to prevent and redress industrial accidents, can human rights law fill any gaps and provide greater protection? Consider the next case: does it contribute to preventing or redressing harm from natural/industrial disasters?

Case of Budayeva et al. v. Russia,
Application Nos. 15339/02, 21166/02, 20058/02, 11673/02 and 15343/02,
Eur. Ct. H.R. (Mar. 20, 2008)

The case originated in five applications against the Russian Federation lodged with the Court under Article 34 of the Convention for the Protection of Human Rights and Fundamental Freedoms by six Russian nationals, Ms. Khalimat Khuseyevna Budayeva and Ms. Fatima Khuseynovna Atmurzayeva on 15 March 2002, by Ms. Raya Meliyevna Shogenova on 10 April 2002, by Ms. Nina Nikolayevna Khakhlova on 18 February 2002 and by Mr. Andrey Aleksandrovich Shishkin and Ms. Irina Ilyinichna Shishkina on 9 March 2002.

. . .

3. Relying on Articles 2, 8 and 13 of the Convention and on Article 1 of Protocol No. 1 to the Convention, the applicants alleged that the national authorities were responsible for the death of Mr. Budayev, for putting their lives at risk and for the destruction of their property, as a result of the authorities' failure to mitigate the consequences of a mudslide which occurred in Tyrnauz on 18–25 July 2000, and that no effective domestic remedy was provided to them in this respect.

THE FACTS

I. THE CIRCUMSTANCES OF THE CASE

A. The Circumstances Concerning the Mudslide
1. Background Facts

13. The town of Tyrnauz is situated in the mountain district adjacent to Mount Elbrus, in the central Caucasus. Its population is about 25,000 inhabitants. The general urban plan of the town was developed in the 1950s as part of a large-scale industrial construction project. Two tributaries of the Baksan River passing through Tyrnauz, the Gerhozhansu and the Kamyksu, are known to be prone to causing mudslides.

14. The first documentary evidence of a mudslide in the Gerhozhansu River dates back to 1937. Subsequently mudslides were registered almost every year; occasionally they hit the town, causing damage. The heaviest mudslides registered prior to 2000 occurred on 1 August 1960, on 11 August 1977 and on 20 August 1999. According to the Government, the series of mudslides of 18–25 July 2000 were the strongest and most destructive of all.

15. The inhabitants and authorities of Tyrnauz are generally aware of the hazard, and are accustomed to the mudslides which usually occur in the summer and early autumn.

16. The first technical research into a scheme to protect Tyrnauz from the mudslides was carried out in the 1950s, and by 1959 a number of proposals had been made. The scheme chosen by the authorities following a comparative feasibility study provided for the construction of a feed-through mud retention collector. Construction work began, but in 1960 this was disrupted by an exceptionally strong mudslide, and the project had to be corrected and extended accordingly. The construction of the collector was finished in 1965 and operated successfully for 35 years, apparently providing sufficient defence against the mudslides. In 1977 a technical review was carried out following a particularly strong mudslide which seriously damaged some sections of the collector, and it was considered necessary to carry out repair work. The collector was fully repaired by 1982.

17. In addition, in early 1999 the local authorities put into operation a mud retention dam in the river gorge of Gerhozhan, upstream from the mud retention collector. The dam was intended to enhance the protection of Tyrnauz from mud and debris flows. It measured 160 m × 38 m × 40 m and was built with 6,000 cubic metres of reinforced concrete and 2,000 tons of metal structures.

2. The Condition of the Dam in the Summer of 2000

18. On 20 August 1999 a mud and debris flow hit the dam, seriously damaging it.

19. On 30 August 1999 the director of the Mountain Institute, a state agency whose mandate included monitoring weather hazards in high-altitude areas, called for an independent survey of the damage caused to the dam by the mudslide. He made recommendations to the Minister responsible for Disaster Relief of the KBR [Republic of Kabardino-Balkariya] concerning the composition of a State Commission for the survey.

20. On the same day he also sent a letter to the President of the KBR, calling for emergency clean-up and restoration work to the dam and for an early warning system to be set up to raise the alarm in the event of a mudslide. . . .

21. On 17 January 2000 the acting director of the Mountain Institute sent a letter to the Prime Minister of the KBR, warning about the increased risk of mudslides in the coming season. He stated that the dam was seriously damaged, that its reconstruction appeared unfeasible at that stage and that, consequently, the only way to avoid casualties and mitigate the damage was to establish observation posts to warn civilians in the event of a mudslide, for which he requested a mandate and financial support. . . .

22. On 7 March 2000 the Head of the Elbrus District Administration sent a letter to the Prime Minister of the KBR in which he referred to the imminent large-scale mudslide and requested financial aid to carry out certain emergency work on the dam. In his request he invoked possible "record losses" and casualties. . . .

23. On 7 July 2000 the assistant director and the head of research of the Mountain Institute attended a session at the Ministry for Disaster Relief of the KBR. At the meeting they reiterated the warning about the risk of mudslides in that period and requested that observation points be set up in the upper sections of the Gerhozhansu River, in order to monitor the river at all times and to issue an emergency warning in the event of a mudslide.

24. On 10 July 2000 the assistant director of the Mountain Institute reported to the agency director that he had warned the Ministry for Disaster Relief of the KBR of the forthcoming mudslide and requested the setting up of twenty-four hour observation posts.

25. It would appear that none of the above measures were ever implemented.

3. The Mudslide of 18–25 July 2000

26. At about 11 p.m. on 18 July 2000 a flow of mud and debris hit the town of Tyrnauz and flooded some of the residential quarters.

27. According to the Government, this first wave caused no casualties. However, the applicants alleged that at least one person was killed. In particular, the second applicant claimed to have witnessed the death of her neighbour Ms. B, born in 1934, who was trapped in the debris and drowned in the mud before anybody could help her. She also alleged that she had witnessed a Zhiguli vehicle with four men in it being carried away by the mudslide.

28. According to the Government, following the mudslide of 18 July 2000 the authorities ordered the emergency evacuation of the residents of Tyrnauz. The police and local officials went round people's homes to notify them of the mudslide and to help evacuate the elderly and disabled. In addition, police vehicles equipped with loudspeakers drove round the town, calling on residents to evacuate because of the mud hazard.

29. The Government did not specify when exactly these measures were taken. The applicants agreed that the alarm was indeed raised through loudspeakers once the mudslide had struck, but no advance warning was given. They claimed that they had been unaware of the order to evacuate and doubted that any had been issued. They also alleged that there had been no rescue forces or other organised on-the-spot assistance at the scene of the disaster, which became a cauldron of chaos and mass panic.

30. In the morning of 19 July 2000 the mud level lowered and the residents returned to their homes. The Government alleged that they did so in breach of the evacuation order, while the applicants claimed that they were not aware that the mudslide alert was still active, pointing out that there were no barriers or warnings to prevent people from returning to their homes. They did not spot any police or emergency officers near their homes, but could see that their neighbours were all at home and children were playing outside. Water, gas and electricity supplies had been reconnected after being cut off during the night.

31. At 1 p.m. on the same day a second, more powerful, mudslide hit the dam and destroyed it. Mud and debris instantly descended on the town, sweeping the wreckage of the dam before them. At 17 Otarova Street the mudslide destroyed part of a nine-storey block of flats, with four officially reported casualties. Several other buildings were damaged. It also caused the river to overflow, flooding the residential quarters on the right bank.

32. The town was hit by a succession of mudslides until 25 July 2000.

33. Eight people were officially reported dead. According to the applicants, a further 19 persons allegedly went missing.

34. According to the Government, on 3 August 2000 the Prosecutor's Office of the Elbrus District decided not to launch a criminal investigation into the accident. The applicants claimed that they were unaware of this. No copy of this decision was made available to the Court.

35. On 12 August 2000 the Government of the KBR adopted a directive on the payment of compensation for loss of housing to the victims of the mudslide. It established the general principles for the provision of new accommodation and the guidelines for calculating compensation for those who wished to settle outside Tyrnauz. The loss of a 1-room flat gave rise to payment of up to 15,000 roubles (RUB), of a 2-room flat – to up to RUB 20,000 and of a 3-room flat – to up to RUB 45,000. Alternately, victims could opt for housing vouchers

that would entitle families of more than one person to free housing of at least 18 sq. m per family member, and single-person families – to 33 sq. m.

36.   On 20 December 2000 the Department of Disaster Relief of the Elbrus District issued a written statement, apparently in connection with individual lawsuits, that it had received no advance warning concerning the Tyrnauz mudslide in 2000, either from the Ministry for Disaster Relief of the KBR or from any other authority.

37.   On the same day the Elbrus District Administration also issued a written statement that it had received no warning of a mudslide at any time during the past two years.

38.   On 14 February 2001, apparently following an enquiry from the district administration, the Finance Department of the Elbrus District reported that no funds had been allocated in the district budget for the restoration work required after the 1999 mudslide.

B. The Circumstances of the Individual Applicants

[The applications suffered property losses and physical and emotional injuries, and one suffered the loss of life of her husband. All sued unsuccessfully for damages in local courts-Eds.]

. . .

THE LAW

. . .

II. ALLEGED VIOLATION OF ARTICLE 2 OF THE CONVENTION

116.   The applicants complained that the authorities had failed to comply with their positive obligations to take appropriate measures to mitigate the risks to their lives against the natural hazards. The first applicant complained that the domestic authorities were responsible for the death of her husband in the mudslide of July 2000. She and the other applicants also complained that the domestic authorities were responsible for putting their lives at risk, as they had failed to discharge the State's positive obligations and had been negligent in the maintenance of the dam, in monitoring the hazardous area and in providing an emergency warning or taking other reasonable measures to mitigate the risk and the effects of the natural disaster. They also complained that they had had no redress, in particular they had not received adequate compensation in respect of their pecuniary and non-pecuniary damage. They relied on Article 2 of the Convention which, in so far as relevant, provides:

> "1. Everyone's right to life shall be protected by law. No one shall be deprived of his life intentionally save in the execution of a sentence of a court following his conviction of a crime for which this penalty is provided by law. . . . "

. . .

B. The Court's assessment
1. General Principles Applicable in the Present Case

(a) Applicability of Article 2 of the Convention and General Principles Relating to the Substantive Aspect of That Article

128.   The Court reiterates that Article 2 does not solely concern deaths resulting from the use of force by agents of the State but also, in the first sentence of its first paragraph, lays down a positive obligation on States to take appropriate steps to safeguard the lives of those within their jurisdiction (see, for example, *L.C.B. v. the United Kingdom*, cited above, p. 1403, § 36, and *Paul and Audrey Edwards v. the United Kingdom*, no. 46477/99, § 54, ECHR 2002-II).

129. This positive obligation entails above all a primary duty on the State to put in place a legislative and administrative framework designed to provide effective deterrence against threats to the right to life (see, for example, *mutatis mutandis*, *Osman v. the United Kingdom*, judgment of 28 October 1998, *Reports* 1998-VIII, p. 3159, § 115; *Paul and Audrey Edwards*, cited above, § 54; *İlhan v. Turkey* [GC], no. 22277/93, § 91, ECHR 2000-VII; *Kılıç v. Turkey*, no. 22492/93, § 62, ECHR 2000-III; and *Mahmut Kaya v. Turkey*, no. 22535/93, § 85, ECHR 2000-III).

. . .

134. As to the choice of particular practical measures, the Court has consistently held that where the State is required to take positive measures, the choice of means is in principle a matter that falls within the Contracting State's margin of appreciation. There are different avenues to ensure Convention rights, and even if the State has failed to apply one particular measure provided by domestic law, it may still fulfil its positive duty by other means (see, among other cases, *Fadeyeva v. Russia*, no. 55723/00, § 96, ECHR 2005-IV).

135. In this respect an impossible or disproportionate burden must not be imposed on the authorities without consideration being given, in particular, to the operational choices which they must make in terms of priorities and resources (see *Osman*, cited above, pp. 3159–60, § 116); this results from the wide margin of appreciation States enjoy, as the Court has previously held, in difficult social and technical spheres (see *Hatton and Others v. the United Kingdom* [GC], no. 36022/97, §§ 100–01, ECHR 2003-VIII, and *Öneryıldız*, cited above, § 107). This consideration must be afforded even greater weight in the sphere of emergency relief in relation to a meteorological event, which is as such beyond human control, than in the sphere of dangerous activities of a man-made nature.

136. In assessing whether the respondent State had complied with the positive obligation, the Court must consider the particular circumstances of the case, regard being had, among other elements, to the domestic legality of the authorities' acts or omissions (see *López Ostra v. Spain*, judgment of 9 December 1994, Series A no. 303-C, pp. 46–47, §§ 16–22, and *Guerra and Others v. Italy*, judgment of 19 February 1998, *Reports* 1998-I, p. 219, §§ 25–27), the domestic decision-making process, including the appropriate investigations and studies, and the complexity of the issue, especially where conflicting Convention interests are involved (see *Hatton and others*, cited above, § 128, and *Fadeyeva*, cited above, §§ 96–98).

137. In the sphere of emergency relief, where the State is directly involved in the protection of human lives through the mitigation of natural hazards, these considerations should apply in so far as the circumstances of a particular case point to the imminence of a natural hazard that had been clearly identifiable, and especially where it concerned a recurring calamity affecting a distinct area developed for human habitation or use (see, *mutatis mutandis*, *Murillo Saldias and others*, cited above). The scope of the positive obligations imputable to the State in the particular circumstances would depend on the origin of the threat and the extent to which one or the other risk is susceptible to mitigation.

(b) Principles Relating to the Judicial Response Required in the Event of Alleged Infringements of the Right to Life: The Procedural Aspect of Article 2 of the Convention

138. The obligations deriving from Article 2 do not end there. Where lives have been lost in circumstances potentially engaging the responsibility of the State, that provision entails a duty for the State to ensure, by all means at its disposal, an adequate response – judicial or otherwise – so that the legislative and administrative framework set up to protect the right to life is properly implemented and any breaches of that right are repressed and punished

(see, *mutatis mutandis*, *Osman*, cited above, p. 3159, § 115, and *Paul and Audrey Edwards*, cited above, § 54).

139.　In this connection, the Court has held that if the infringement of the right to life or to physical integrity is not caused intentionally, the positive obligation to set up an "effective judicial system" does not necessarily require criminal proceedings to be brought in every case and may be satisfied if civil, administrative or even disciplinary remedies were available to the victims (see, for example, *Vo v. France* [GC], no. 53924/00, § 90, ECHR 2004-VIII; *Calvelli and Ciglio v. Italy* [GC], no. 32967/96, § 51, ECHR 2002-I; and *Mastromatteo v. Italy* [GC], no. 37703/97, §§ 90 and 94–95, ECHR 2002-VIII).

140.　However, in the particular context of dangerous activities, the Court considered that an official criminal investigation is indispensible given that public authorities are often the only entities to have sufficient relevant knowledge to identify and establish the complex phenomena that might have caused an incident. It held that where the authorities in question, fully realising the likely consequences and disregarding the powers vested in them, failed to take measures that were necessary and sufficient to avert the risks inherent in a dangerous activity, the fact that those responsible for endangering life have not been charged with a criminal offence or prosecuted may amount to a violation of Article 2, irrespective of any other types of remedy which individuals may exercise on their own initiative (see *Öneryıldız*, cited above, § 93).

141.　The approach taken by the Court in a case brought by victims of a natural disaster, namely campers caught in a flood at an official camping site, was consistent with that in the area of dangerous activities. The Court found that successful proceedings for damages before an administrative tribunal, preceded by comprehensive criminal proceedings, were an effective remedy for the purposes of Article 35 § 1 of the Convention (see *Murillo Saldias and others*, cited above).

142.　Accordingly, the principles developed in relation to judicial response following incidents resulting from dangerous activities lend themselves to application also in the area of disaster relief. Where lives are lost as a result of events engaging the State's responsibility for positive preventive action, the judicial system required by Article 2 must make provision for an independent and impartial official investigation procedure that satisfies certain minimum standards as to effectiveness and is capable of ensuring that criminal penalties are applied to the extent that this is justified by the findings of the investigation (see, *mutatis mutandis*, *Hugh Jordan v. the United Kingdom*, no. 24746/94, §§ 105–09, 4 May 2001, and *Paul and Audrey Edwards*, cited above, §§ 69–73). In such cases, the competent authorities must act with exemplary diligence and promptness and must of their own motion initiate investigations capable of, firstly, ascertaining the circumstances in which the incident took place and any shortcomings in the operation of the regulatory system and, secondly, identifying the State officials or authorities involved in whatever capacity in the chain of events in issue (see *Öneryıldız*, cited above, § 94).

143.　Moreover, the requirements of Article 2 go beyond the stage of the official investigation, where this has led to the institution of proceedings in the national courts: the proceedings as a whole, including the trial stage, must satisfy the requirements of the positive obligation to protect lives through the law (see *Öneryıldız*, cited above, § 95).

144.　It should in no way be inferred from the foregoing that Article 2 may entail the right for an applicant to have third parties prosecuted or sentenced for a criminal offence (see, *mutatis mutandis*, *Perez v. France* [GC], no. 47287/99, § 70, ECHR 2004-I) or an absolute obligation for all prosecutions to result in conviction, or indeed in a particular sentence (see, *mutatis mutandis*, *Tanlı v. Turkey*, no. 26129/95, § 111, ECHR 2001-III). In the particular context of disaster relief the Court found that the adequacy of the domestic judicial response was not undermined by the fact that no official was found criminally liable (see *Murillo Saldias and others*, cited above).

145. The Court's task therefore consists in reviewing whether and to what extent the courts, in reaching their conclusion, may be deemed to have submitted the case to the careful scrutiny required by Article 2 of the Convention, so that the deterrent effect of the judicial system in place and the significance of the role it is required to play in preventing violations of the right to life are not undermined (see *Öneryıldız*, cited above, § 93).

2. Application of the General Principles in the Present Case

146. The Court will begin by noting that although only one of the present applications, brought by Ms. Budayeva, concerns the death of a family member, the circumstances of the case in respect of the other applicants leave no doubt as to the existence of a threat to their physical integrity (see, *mutatis mutandis*, *Makaratzis v. Greece* [GC], no. 50385/99, §§ 52–55, ECHR 2004-XI). This brings their complaints within the ambit of Article 2 of the Convention. Moreover, the applicability of Article 2 has not been contested by the Government. Turning to the applicants' specific complaints, the Court observes that they accused the authorities of having allowed three major shortcomings in the functioning of the system for protection against natural hazards in Tyrnauz, which led to casualties and losses in July 2000. Firstly, they alleged a negligent failure to maintain mud-protection engineering facilities, notably to restore the mud-retention dam damaged in 1999 and to clear the mud-retention collector blocked by the leftover debris. Secondly, they complained about the lack of a public warning about the approaching disaster that would help to avoid casualties, injuries and mass panic. Finally, they complained that these events, despite their scale and devastating consequences, did not give rise to an enquiry that would assess the effectiveness of the authorities' conduct before and during the mudslide, in particular whether everything possible had been done to mitigate the damage. The Court will consider each of these aspects in the light of the general principles set out above.

(a) Alleged Failure to Maintain Defence and Warning Infrastructure: Substantive Aspect of Article 2

147. The Court, first, observes that the town of Tyrnauz is situated in an area prone to mudslides. The regular occurrence of this calamity in the summer season and the prior existence of defence schemes designed to protect the area indicate that the authorities and the population reasonably assumed that a mudslide was likely in the summer of 2000. This is in fact not in dispute between the parties. What they disagree on is the authorities' prior knowledge that the mudslide in 2000 was likely to cause devastation on a larger scale than usual.

148. The Court notes that in the year immediately preceding the mudslide of August 2000 the authorities of the KBR received a number of warnings that should have made them aware of the increasing risks. The first warning, issued in 30 August 1999 by the competent surveillance agency, the Mountain Institute, informed the Minister for Disaster Relief of the KBR about the need to repair the mud-protection dam, damaged by a strong mudslide, and calling for the setting-up of an early warning system that would allow the timely evacuation of civilians in the event of a mudslide. The second warning from the same agency was sent on 17 January 2000 to the Prime Minister of the KBR. It stated that even if restoration of the dam was not feasible, it was indispensable to set up observation posts to ensure the functioning of the warning system in the summer of 2000. The next warning was sent by the Head of the Elbrus District Administration to the Prime Minister of the KBR on 7 March 2000. This warning restated the previous ones and, moreover, referred to possible record

losses and casualties in the event of a failure to take the indicated measures. Finally, on 7 July 2000 the Mountain Institute sent another warning to the Minister for Disaster Relief of the KBR calling for urgent installation of the observation posts.

149.   It follows that the authorities of the KBR at various levels were aware that any mudslide, regardless of its scale, was capable of causing devastating consequences in Tyrnauz because of the state of disrepair in which the defence infrastructure had been left after the previous mudslide. It is also clear that there was no ambiguity about the scope or the timing of the work that needed to be performed. However, the Government gave no reasons why no such steps were taken. On the basis of the documents submitted by the applicant, it appears that after the 1999 mudslide there was no allocation of funds for these purposes (see paragraph 38 above). It follows from the Government's observations that such funds were only made available after the 2000 disaster. In the absence of any explanation on the part of the Government the Court cannot but conclude that the demands for the restoration of the defence infrastructure after the 1999 mudslide were not given proper consideration by the decision-making and budgetary bodies prior to the hazardous season of 2000.

150.   Moreover, it does not appear that at the material time the authorities were implementing any alternative land-planning policies in the area that would dispense with the concept of the mud-defence facilities or suspend their maintenance.

151.   Consequently, the Court sees no justification for the authorities' failure to prepare the defence infrastructure for the forthcoming hazardous season in 2000.

152.   In such circumstances the authorities could reasonably be expected to acknowledge the increased risk of accidents in the event of a mudslide that year and to show all possible diligence in informing the civilians and making advance arrangements for the emergency evacuation. In any event, informing the public about inherent risks was one of the essential practical measures needed to ensure effective protection of the citizens concerned.

153.   The applicants consistently maintained that they had not received any warning until the mudslide actually arrived in the town. It also follows from the Government's submissions that the alarm was raised during the first wave of the mudslide on 18 July 2000, but not before. According to the Government, the evacuation order continued on the following day, 19 July 2000, when the most severe destruction occurred. This is contested by the applicants, who claimed that there had been no sign of any evacuation order when they were returning to their flats. They submitted witness statements confirming that people who returned to their homes on 19 July 2000 saw no warning against doing so. Given that the Government did not specify how the order, if it was issued, was publicised or otherwise enforced, the Court may only assume that the population was not made sufficiently aware of it, as the applicants allege.

154.   The Court further notes that, in order to be able to inform the neighbourhood of the mudslide hazard, the authorities would need to set up temporary observation posts in the mountains. However, the persistent requests of the specialised surveillance agency indicating that such posts were indispensible for ensuring the residents' safety were simply ignored. By the beginning of the mudslide season the authorities thus found themselves short of means to estimate the time, force or probable duration of the mudslide. Accordingly, they were unable to give advance warning to the residents or to efficiently implement the evacuation order.

155.   Since the Government have not put forward any explanation for the failure to set up temporary observation posts, the Court concludes that the authorities' omission in ensuring the functioning of the early warning system was not justified in the circumstances.

156.   Finally, having regard to the authorities' wide margin of appreciation in matters where the State is required to take positive action, the Court must look beyond the measures specifically referred to by the applicants and consider whether the Government envisaged

other solutions to ensure the safety of the local population. On order to do so the Court has requested the Government to provide information on the regulatory framework, land-planning policies and specific safety measures implemented at the material time in Tyrnauz for deterring natural hazards. The information submitted in response related exclusively to the creation of the mud-retention dam and the mud-retention collector, facilities that, as the Court has established above, were not adequately maintained. Accordingly, in exercising their discretion as to the choice of measures required to comply with their positive obligations, the authorities ended up by taking no measures at all up to the day of the disaster.

157. It is noteworthy that, as the Government pointed out in their observations, in 2001 budgetary allocations were made for the reconstruction of the defence infrastructure. This yields further support to the applicants' argument that implementing safety measures could have, and should have, taken place earlier, but only the catastrophic consequences of the 2000 mudslide put pressure on the authorities to do so.

158. In the light of the above findings the Court concludes that there was no justification for the authorities' omissions in implementation of the land-planning and emergency relief policies in the hazardous area of Tyrnauz regarding the foreseeable exposure of residents, including all applicants, to mortal risk. Moreover, it finds that there was a causal link between the serious administrative flaws that impeded their implementation and the death of Vladimir Budayev and the injuries sustained by the first and the second applicants and the members of their family.

159. The authorities have thus failed to discharge the positive obligation to establish a legislative and administrative framework designed to provide effective deterrence against threats to the right to life as required by Article 2 of the Convention.

160. Accordingly, there has been a violation of Article 2 of the Convention in its substantive aspect.

(b) Judicial Response Required in the Event of Alleged Infringements of Right to Life: Procedural Aspect of Article 2

161. The mudslide of 19–25 July 2000 killed eight people, including the first applicant's husband, Vladimir Budayev, and threatened the lives of an uncertain number of other residents of Tyrnauz.

162. Within a week of the incident the prosecutor's office decided to dispense with a criminal investigation into the circumstances of Vladimir Budayev's death. However, in conducting the inquest the prosecutor's office confined itself to establishing the immediate cause of his death, which was found to be the collapse of the building, and did not enter into the questions of safety compliance or the possible engagement of the authorities' responsibility. Moreover, it does not appear that those questions were the subject of any enquiry, whether criminal, administrative or technical. In particular, no action has been taken to verify the numerous allegations made in the media and in the victims' complaints concerning the inadequate maintenance of the mud-defence infrastructure or the authorities' failure to set up the warning system.

163. In so far as the question of State liability has been raised in certain individual civil actions, the Court notes that in order to be successful in these proceedings the plaintiffs would have to demonstrate to what extent the damage attributable to the State's alleged negligence exceeded what was inevitable in the circumstances of a natural disaster. Indeed, the applicants' claims for damages were dismissed precisely for the failure to do so (see paragraphs 49–50, 60, 67, 76 and 85 above). However, this question could only be answered, if at all, by a complex expert investigation involving the assessment of technical and administrative

aspects, as well as by obtaining factual information available to the authorities alone. The claimants were thus required to discharge a burden of proof in respect of facts that were beyond the reach of private individuals. Accordingly, without the benefit of an independent criminal enquiry or expert assessment the victims would inevitably fall short of means to establish civil liability on the part of the State.

164. Moreover, the domestic courts deciding on the applicants' claims did not make full use of the powers they possessed in order to establish the circumstances of the accident. In particular, they dispensed with calling any witnesses, whether officials or ordinary citizens, or seeking an expert opinion which would have enabled them to establish or to disprove the authorities' responsibility, despite the plaintiffs' requests. The courts' reluctance to exercise their powers to establish the facts does not appear justified in view of the evidence already produced by the applicants, including the official reports suggesting that their concerns were also shared by certain officials. Accordingly, these proceedings were not capable of providing the judicial response required by the deaths caused by the mudslide in Tyrnauz.

165. Having found that the question of State responsibility for the accident in Tyrnauz has never as such been investigated or examined by any judicial or administrative authority, the Court concludes that there has also been a violation of Article 2 of the Convention in its procedural aspect.

III. ALLEGED VIOLATION OF ARTICLE 1 OF PROTOCOL NO. 1 TO THE CONVENTION

166. The applicants complained that the authorities' failure to maintain the mud-defence infrastructure, to monitor the hazardous area, to provide an emergency warning or to take other reasonable measures to mitigate the risk and the effects of the natural disaster also constituted a violation of their right to protection of property. They complained, in particular, that they had not received adequate compensation in respect of their losses. They relied on Article 1 of Protocol No. 1 to the Convention, which provides:

> Every natural or legal person is entitled to the peaceful enjoyment of his possessions. No one shall be deprived of his possessions except in the public interest and subject to the conditions provided for by law and by the general principles of international law.
>
> The preceding provisions shall not, however, in any way impair the right of a State to enforce such laws as it deems necessary to control the use of property in accordance with the general interest or to secure the payment of taxes or other contributions or penalties.

. . .

172. The Court notes, first, that the applicants were the lawful owners and occupants of the flats destroyed by the mudslide, and of all of the destroyed belongings comprising their households. In fact, the existence of "possessions" within the meaning of Article 1 of Protocol No. 1 to the Convention, or the list of objects that have been destroyed, are not in dispute between the parties. The Court will therefore proceed to examine to what extent the authorities were under an obligation to take measures for the protection of these possessions and whether this obligation has been complied with in the present case.

173. The Court reiterates that allegations of a failure on the part of the State to take positive action in order to protect private property should be examined in the light of the general rule in the first sentence of the first paragraph of Article 1 of Protocol No. 1 to the Convention, which lays down the right to the peaceful enjoyment of possessions (see *Beyeler v. Italy* [GC], no. 33202/96, § 98, ECHR 2000-I, and *Öneryıldız*, cited above, § 133). It also reiterates that genuine, effective exercise of the right protected by Article 1 of Protocol No. 1 to the Convention does not depend merely on the State's duty not to interfere, but may require positive measures of protection, particularly where there is a direct link between

the measures an applicant may legitimately expect from the authorities and his effective enjoyment of his possessions (see *Bielectric S.r.l. v. Italy* (dec.), no. 36811/97, 4 May 2000, and *Öneryıldız*, cited above, § 134).

. . .

174. In the present case, however, the Court considers that natural disasters, which are as such beyond human control, do not call for the same extent of State involvement. Accordingly, its positive obligations as regards the protection of property from weather hazards do not necessarily extend as far as in the sphere of dangerous activities of a man-made nature.

175. For this reason the Court considers that for the purposes of the present case a distinction must be drawn between the positive obligations under Article 2 of the Convention and those under Article 1 of Protocol No. 1 to the Convention. While the fundamental importance of the right to life requires that the scope of the positive obligations under Article 2 includes a duty to do everything within the authorities' power in the sphere of disaster relief for the protection of that right, the obligation to protect the right to the peaceful enjoyment of possessions, which is not absolute, cannot extend further than what is reasonable in the circumstances. Accordingly, the authorities enjoy a wider margin of appreciation in deciding what measures to take in order to protect individuals' possessions from weather hazards than in deciding on the measures needed to protect lives.

176. In the present case the Court found that the measures invoked by the applicants, that is, the maintenance of the mud-defence infrastructure and the setting up of the early warning system, were vital for the protection of the lives and well-being of the civilians. However, it cannot be said that the causal link between the State's failure to take these measures and the extent of the material damage is similarly well-established.

177. The Court notes, and it is not in dispute between the parties, that the mudslide of 2000 was exceptionally strong, and the extent to which the proper maintenance of the defence infrastructure could have mitigated its destructive effects remains unclear. There is also no evidence that a functioning warning system could have prevented damage to the apartment blocks or the applicants' other possessions.

178. As regards the alleged lack of an independent enquiry and judicial response, the Court considers that this procedural duty does not have the same significance with regard to destroyed property as in the event of loss of life. Moreover, the extent of the material damage attributable to State negligence might not be susceptible to accurate evaluation in circumstances of outstanding complexity, as in the present case. In fact, providing redress by means of tort action may not always be the most appropriate response to a large-scale calamity. Considerations of urgency and efficiency may lead the authorities to give priority to other general and individual measures, such as providing emergency assistance and allotting benefits to all victims irrespective of the actual losses.

179. In the present case, the domestic courts found that the applicants were all granted free substitute housing and a lump-sum emergency allowance and that the authorities carried out emergency repairs of public facilities to restore the living conditions in residential quarters.

180. In so far as the applicants argued that these benefits did not fully cover their pecuniary losses, the Court observes that the terms of compensation have previously been found an essential element in cases concerning the taking of property under the second sentence of the first paragraph of Article 1 of Protocol No. 1. The Court found that while the absence of compensation would usually be incompatible with this provision, it does not guarantee a right to full compensation in all circumstances, since legitimate objectives of "public interest" may call for less than reimbursement of the full market value (see *Papachelas v. Greece* [GC], no. 31423/96, § 48, ECHR 1999-II).

181. Moreover, payment of full compensation cannot be regarded as a prerequisite for compliance with the first rule set out in the first sentence of the first paragraph. In order to be compatible with the general rule an interference with the right to the peaceful enjoyment of possessions must strike a "fair balance" between the demands of the general interest of the community and the requirements of the protection of the individual's fundamental rights (see *Beyeler*, cited above, § 107). Compensation terms under the relevant legislation are material to the assessment of whether the contested measure respects the requisite fair balance, and notably, whether it does not impose a disproportionate burden on the applicant (see *Former King of Greece and Others v. Greece*, [GC], no. 25701/94, § 89, ECHR 2000-XII).

182. The Court considers that the positive obligation on the State to protect private property from natural disasters cannot be construed as binding the State to compensate the full market value of destroyed property. In the present case, the damage in its entirety could not be unequivocally attributed to State negligence, and the alleged negligence was no more than an aggravating factor contributing to the damage caused by natural forces. In such circumstances the terms of compensation must be assessed in the light of all the other measures implemented by the authorities, account being taken of the complexity of the situation, the number of affected owners, and the economic, social and humanitarian issues inherent in the provision of disaster relief.

183. The Court observes that the disaster relief payable to the mudslide victims under the directive of 12 August 2000 entitled the applicants to free housing and an allowance of RUB 13,200 (then an equivalent of about 530 euros). The victims had equal, direct and automatic access to these benefits, which did not involve a contentious procedure or a need to prove the actual losses. As regards the first, the fourth, the fifth and the sixth applicants, the size of the free housing they received was equivalent to their perished flats. As regards the second applicant, she opted to receive free housing vouchers issued on the basis of the number of family members. She applied as a single-person family and received a voucher for 33 sq. m, as opposed to the 54 sq. m that she could have received had she applied as a family of three. She did not elaborate on the reasons for doing so. As regards the third applicant, she initially received monetary compensation that took account of the size of the perished flats. However, she later exchanged this for a housing voucher, with which she bought housing in the Moscow region which she resold shortly afterwards. Since she did not disclose the details of this transaction, the Court cannot assess her resulting losses or benefits.

184. On the basis of the foregoing, the Court concludes that the housing compensation provided to the applicants was not manifestly out of proportion to their lost accommodation. Given the importance of this asset, the large number of affected persons and the scale of emergency relief to be handled by the authorities in such circumstances, the cap of RUB 13,200 on compensation for household belongings appears justified. In sum, the Court considers that the conditions under which victims were granted compensation for possessions lost in the mudslide did not impose a disproportionate burden on the applicants.

185. It follows that there has been no violation of Article 1 of Protocol No. 1 to the Convention.

[The Court unanimously held that there was a violation of article 2 and no violation of article 1 of Protocol 1. It awarded compensation to each of the applicants. – *Eds.*]

Questions and Discussion

1. In the *Budayeva* case, the Russian government took action to relieve the losses of the villagers who suffered from the mudslides, although the European Court found both the

preventive and responsive actions inadequate. The Court says that the obligations on the state should not be too onerous in the face of a natural disaster. Has it struck a proper balance?

2. Note that, in 1993, European states concluded the Lugano Convention on Civil Liability for Damages Resulting from the Exercise of Activities Dangerous for the Environment (June 21). The Convention broadly imposes responsibility on all persons and companies and the state and all agencies exercising control over dangerous activities, irrespective of the place of the harm. Anyone who is in control of a dangerous activity is responsible for damages caused by that activity. Liability is not imposed if damage occurs as a result of armed conflict, a natural disaster, an intentional act of a third party, or "pollution of a level acceptable having regard to the relevant local circumstances," or if the activity was taken for the benefit of the person damaged.

3. What if the government of a state took minimal or no action following a catastrophe? Would other states have the right to intervene to protect individuals from loss of life, health, and property? Is there a duty to do so? The next section examines this issue.

B. *Natural Disasters and the Responsibility to Protect*

In 2001, the International Commission on Intervention and State Sovereignty, formed by the Canadian Government, issued the report *Responsibility to Protect: Report of the International Commission on Intervention and State Sovereignty*. The Report emphasized the duties of governments to protect all persons from massive human rights abuses and other humanitarian crises. This responsibility rests primarily on each individual state with respect to its territory, but the Report concludes that when states "manifestly fail" to protect their populations, the international community shares a collective responsibility to respond through the United Nations, especially through the Security Council. The U.N. Summit Outcome Document, issued by governments at the conclusion of the 2005 High-level Plenary Meeting of the General Assembly, endorsed the "responsibility to protect" and made commitments to strengthen international institutions. In December 2007, the U.N. Security Council approved the creation of a position of special adviser on the responsibility to protect.

On April 28, 2006, the Security Council made its first explicit reference to the responsibility to protect in Resolution 1674 on the Protection of Civilians in Armed Conflict, reaffirming provisions of the World Summit Outcome Document regarding the responsibility to protect populations but limited the responsibility to cases of genocide, war crimes, ethnic cleansing, and crimes against humanity.

The content and criteria for applying the responsibility to protect remain controversial with some governments, which are hesitant to accept this new version of humanitarian intervention. It remains an evolving concept. *See* SUSAN C. BREAU, HUMANITARIAN INTERVENTION: THE UNITED NATIONS AND COLLECTIVE RESPONSIBILITY (2005). Some NGOs and observers claimed that the responsibility to protect should have been invoked after the government of Myanmar refused entry to aid organizations following a massive cyclone devastated areas of the country. The following extracts discuss the legality of humanitarian intervention as part of the responsibility to protect: in one case, the aid of the international community was actively sought (Haiti); in the other, it was resisted (Myanmar). Should states be able to intervene if the government deliberately refuses aid? Whose view is more convincing?

The Responsibility to Protect Haiti, ASIL INSIGHT, Mar. 10, 2010, *available at*
http://www.asil.org/files/insight100310pdf.pdf (footnotes omitted)
Linda A. Malone

On January 12, 2010, a massive earthquake struck Haiti, essentially destroying the Haitian government infrastructure. According to remarks by Rene Magloire, former Minister of Justice and
Special Advisor to the President and Ministry of Justice, the presidential palace, the ministry of justice building, and the legislative palace were destroyed. Police stations and prisons were damaged,
allowing thousands of detainees and prisoners to escape. More than 200 thousand died, more than
300 thousand were injured, more than 450 thousand became refugees, more than 400 thousand
homes were destroyed, more than 120 thousand homes damaged, and more than a million people
were left without shelter. . . .

Consensual Relief Efforts

As early as 1991, the United Nations Environmental Program ("UNEP"), in response to mounting disquietude over environmental security, established the United Nations Center for Urgent
Environmental Assistance ("UNCUEA") to assess and respond to man-made environmental
emergencies in cooperation with other United Nations agencies. To address acute environmental emergencies specifically, UNEP has now coordinated with the United Nations Office for
the Coordination of Humanitarian Affairs (OCHA) to create the Joint UNEP/OCHA Environment Unit (JEU). A month after the earthquake in Haiti, John Holmes, the head of OCHA,
wrote a confidential email to his top U.N. relief agency coordinators highly critical of the
U.N. relief efforts and weak implementation of its humanitarian "cluster strategy" for delivering relief in twelve sectors of need, including water, health care, and shelter. He emphasized
that "with the rainy season looming, these unmet needs are taking on additional urgency, not
least from the health and protections points of view, and given the potential consequences
in terms of both politics and security of large demonstrations in some sensitive places." He
stated that there was an urgent need for better coordination "(1) to ensure close coordination
with the efforts of national authorities; (2) to channel the contributions of the private sector;
and (3) to make maximum use of the logistical support and other assistance provided by the
military."

   In a natural disaster like that in Haiti, there are significant logistical problems in coordination of U.N. and multilateral relief efforts, even with a totally cooperative and consenting
state. Legal problems are less significant with a consenting state, as there is no need to justify relief efforts as lawful "intervention." Providing relief assistance in an uncooperative or
failed state, however, may present legal problems. Even the Security Council is subject to the
Article 2(7) prohibition on intervention in states' domestic jurisdiction when it recommends
relief assistance under Chapter VI. If the state in which the environmental problem originates
is uncooperative, the Security Council, instead of resorting to Chapter VII, might choose to
issue precautionary and ameliorative recommendations for emergency response action applicable only in the territory of consenting states, but which could nevertheless be interpreted by
the state of origin as "intervention" in its domestic jurisdiction. For example, routine monitoring or exchange of information on the transboundary effects of an environmental disaster, taken
pursuant to a Security Council recommendation that there be such collection and exchange of
information, might be objectionable to the state of origin. In this regard, it is relevant to note
that Russian counter-intelligence agents in 1995 accused a "[w]estern ecological organization
of divulging military secrets and . . . suggested that foreign environmental groups are fronts for
espionage."

Environmental disasters with transboundary effects, loss of a vital global resource, or actions in violation of international environmental law may no longer be regarded as matters of "domestic" jurisdiction. An interpretation of "domestic" jurisdiction that excludes environmental disasters with international ramifications is also consistent with the current widespread recognition that "domestic" jurisdiction does not encompass large scale deprivation of basic human rights. Otherwise even the most well intended relief efforts by states or the U.N. might be characterized as unlawful intervention in uncooperative or failed states.

Humanitarian Intervention

Even when working with a fully cooperative government in Haiti, the head of U.N. relief operations has acknowledged a disturbing inadequacy of the U.N. to provide and coordinate voluntary relief assistance. In the first critical hours during the Haiti earthquake, or in the next environmental disaster, what government is available to consent to such efforts? Do the international community and the U.N. have to await consent from a state unable to respond? The Security Council may authorize action without consent if there is a "threat to peace," and recent precedents of humanitarian intervention and acknowledgment of refugee problems as a threat to peace may lend themselves to invocation of Chapter VII, but not decisively so.

The legality of unilateral and multilateral humanitarian intervention by states continues to be highly disputed, given the Charter limitation on states' use of force as "self-defense." It would be difficult for a state to justify military intervention in a natural disaster in another state as self-defense. Similarly, "breach of peace, threat to peace, or an act of aggression" under Chapter VII for purposes of Security Council authorization of enforcement measures does not effortlessly lend itself to authorizing humanitarian intervention, much less in natural disasters.

In the absence of real or threatened military conflict, can environmental destruction be sufficient to trigger the Council's Chapter VII powers? Is a threat to ecological security a threat to international peace and security? The Security Council has declared that non-military sources of instability in the economic, humanitarian, and ecological fields may become a threat to peace and security. Should environmental degradation threaten to lead to conflict between states or take place in an ongoing military conflict, there would be no need to resort to a separate notion of ecological security or humanitarian intervention in order to trigger authority in the Security Council under Chapter VII. Absent real or potential military conflict, however, there are many conceivable scenarios in which the state of origin of an environmental disaster might be unable or unwilling to cooperate with the Security Council or other states (e.g., the Soviet Union during Chernobyl and Myanmar after the tsunami), thereby exacerbating the transboundary effects of an environmental disaster and jeopardizing the lives of its own populace by refusing to cooperate with the international community in remedial action.

Security Council enforcement action with respect to preservation of human rights is analogous to Security Council enforcement action to protect individuals from environmental catastrophes. For example, the humanitarian mission to Somalia, the economic sanctions and authorization of a multinational force for Haiti in 1993, the placement of relief operations in Iraqi territory for the Kurdish population, and the establishment of the international criminal tribunals for Rwanda and the former Yugoslavia are examples of humanitarian intervention by the Security Council in order to remedy gross and systematic deprivation of human rights. Although each of these precedents (with the notable exception of Haiti) can be legitimized by pointing to the background conflicts present, such a position would ignore the humanitarian justifications given in the relevant resolutions for the Security Council's actions. Notably, the political tension created by mass migration of refugees has also been a factor in the Council's invocation of Chapter VII. These examples indicate that the Security Council members and the global community are at least somewhat receptive to a policy-oriented, constitutive approach to interpreting the Charter even when such interpretation expands the obligations and duties of member states beyond the original intent of the Charter.

Any analogy to the Security Council's exercise of humanitarian intervention under Chapter VII is complicated by the fact that, under international law, there has yet to be clear and unequivocal recognition of a right to a safe and healthful environment. This lack of recognition is particularly troublesome in that whatever authority the Security Council might have under Chapter VII, the scope of its activities is confined by the stated purposes of the United Nations in Article 1. Article 1 explicitly mentions human rights as one of the fundamental purposes of the United Nations. Absent a threat to military peace and security, or recognition of the concept of ecological security, legitimacy of any Security Council enforcement measures in responding to natural disasters on humanitarian grounds will be attenuated so long as there is no explicit and clear recognition of a fundamental right to a safe and healthful environment.

The Responsibility to Protect

The gap between this periodic need for the international community to intervene in a state's management of environmental disasters and the prohibition on intervention could be filled by an extension of a relatively new norm to this situation. On September 16, 2005, the United Nations General Assembly adopted by consensus a resolution recognizing the "responsibility to protect." The core of the responsibility to protect is that "[e]ach individual State has the responsibility to protect its populations from genocide, war crimes, ethnic cleansing and crimes against humanity." The international community has the responsibility to use diplomatic, humanitarian and other peaceful means, and if those fail, may take "collective action, in a timely and decisive manner, through the Security Council, in accordance with the Charter, including Chapter VII, on a case-by-case basis" when "national authorities are manifestly failing to protect their populations" from the four crimes.

. . .

However, U.N. officials, including the Secretary-General, have been quick to deny that the responsibility to protect applies to environmental crises.

From State Security to Human Security

Would the responsibility to protect, if accepted as a norm of international law, alter the calculation by requiring the Security Council or states to act? Ultimately, the difference between Chapter VII precedents, the U.N. formulation of the responsibility to protect, and ICISS Report may be one of affirmative obligation versus permissive authority, and timing. A natural disaster, which results in massive loss of life and population displacement, can be characterized as a "threat to peace" such that the Security Council may authorize enforcement action. The Security Council would not have an affirmative responsibility to protect, unless the situation deteriorates into the commission of war crimes, genocide, ethnic cleansing, or crimes against humanity. Under the ICISS formulation, states and the U.N. would have an affirmative obligation to respond whenever a population is suffering serious harm, and the U.N. would have an affirmative obligation to do so with military force when there is a large scale loss of life, "actual or apprehended which is the product of deliberate state action, neglect or inability to act, or a failed state situation. . . . " Haiti, seeking to "rise from the ashes," in the words of King Henri Christophe, the leader of the 1804 Haitian revolution, may provide a litmus test for which approach, prevention or remediation, is to be the international practice.

Myanmar Faces Pressure to Allow Major Aid Effort, New York Times, May 8, 2008, at
http://www.nytimes.com/2008/05/08/world/asia/08iht-08myanmar.12682654.html
Seth Mydans

BANGKOK: As hungry, shivering survivors waited among the dead for help after a huge cyclone in Myanmar, aid agencies and diplomats said Wednesday that the delivery of relief supplies was being slowed by the reluctance of the country's secretive military leaders to allow an influx of outsiders.

With conditions growing worse in the vast, flooded Irrawaddy Delta region, the top United States diplomat in Myanmar estimated that the death toll could rise as high as 100,000, from the official tally of 22,500. An accurate assessment might take days or weeks to emerge.

Relief workers and survivors described scenes of horror as people huddled on spits of dry ground surrounded by bodies and animal carcasses floating in the murky water or lodged in mangrove trees.

With Myanmar mostly closed to foreign journalists, information was coming from aid agencies, residents and diplomats based there. Witnesses spoke of fights over dwindling supplies of food and clean water, of hordes of people overwhelming the few shops still open.

Four days after the cyclone passed, entire villages on Wednesday lay under water after being submerged by a 12-foot storm surge that obliterated houses and buried unsuspecting residents in a wall of water.

The scenes and the scale of the devastation recalled Asia's last great natural disaster, the 2004 tsunami, which claimed 181,000 lives in several countries.

The storm and its aftermath posed a severe challenge to the military government, which in September violently suppressed a pro-democracy movement led by monks, killing at least 31 people and probably many more.

It was not clear what effect the disaster would have on the junta's grip on power, with angry residents complaining about a lack of warning and a slow response by the government, and with the possibility of an influx of foreigners into the closed and tightly controlled country.

· · ·

Despite the emerging scale of the disaster, the Myanmar government has let in little aid and has restricted movement in the delta, aid agencies say. It has not granted visas to aid workers, even though supplies are being marshalled in nearby countries like Thailand.

In response, the French foreign minister, Bernard Kouchner, suggested that the United Nations should invoke its "responsibility to protect" civilians as the basis for a resolution to allow the delivery of international aid even without the junta's permission.

"We are seeing at the United Nations if we can't implement the responsibility to protect, given that food, boats and relief teams are there, and obtain a United Nations resolution which authorizes the delivery and imposes this on the Burmese government," Kouchner told reporters in Paris.

But the United Nations' under secretary general for humanitarian affairs, John Holmes, resisted the idea of taking action to force Myanmar to open its doors, though he said 50 to 100 United Nations aid workers were awaiting word on visa applications.

· · ·

Myanmar told United Nations officials that it dedicated 7 helicopters and 80 ships to relief work. "Seven is a very small number considering the enormous logistical needs," said Paul Risley, spokesman for the World Food Program's Asia operations.

The political party of the opposition leader Daw Aung San Suu Kyi, who is under house arrest, has called for international aid. But the generals who run Myanmar are obviously reluctant to allow large numbers of foreigners in, especially with a referendum looming on a proposed Constitution backed by the military.

· · ·

Myanmar – Responsibility to Protect? Doctors Without Borders (May 21, 2008), *available at* http://www.doctorswithoutborders.org/publications/article.cfm?id=2740&cat=ideas-opinions
Françoise Bouchet-Saulnier

Is There a Legal Framework for International Humanitarian Assistance in the Case of Natural Disasters?

As established by resolutions of the U.N. General Assembly, the rules applicable during natural disasters are based on two key notions: the responsibility of the affected State to coordinate and provide aid to the populations on its territory and to facilitate the operations of aid organizations; and, international solidarity to support affected countries and strengthen their ability to act when it is inadequate.

However, neither a right nor obligation of international control exists for distributing aid. Thus, there is no provision for a case in which a State refuses this cooperation and no authorization to override such a refusal. NGOs and States may not ignore the government in question, even when it is an authoritarian regime, and must negotiate with it regarding the possibility and forms of intervention.

The only entity that may legally impose a decision on a State is the Security Council of the United Nations, which may decide to use force under Chapter VII of the U.N. Charter; that is, under its powers in the case of threats to peace.

Thus, there is no legal rule that would make it possible to force the Myanmar government to allow international aid workers into the country to set up aid operations following Cyclone Nargis.

. . .

Reconciling R2P with IDP Protection,
1 Global Responsibility to Protect 15–37
(2010) (some footnotes omitted)
Roberta Cohen

The concept of the responsibility to protect (R2P) developed in large measure from efforts to design an international system to protect internally displaced persons (IDPs).

. . .

When first counted in 1982, 1.2 million IDPs could be found in 11 countries; by 1995, the number had surged to 20 to 25 million.[2]

The international system, however, set up after the Second World War, focused almost exclusively on refugees – persons who fled across borders to escape persecution. The 1951 Refugee Convention and the U.N. High Commissioner for Refugees (UNHCR) provided international protection to people who were outside their countries of origin and deprived of the protection of their own governments. As UNICEF's Executive Director observed, "The world has established a minimum safety net for refugees," but "This is not yet the case with respect to internally displaced populations."[3]

. . .

---

[2] Roberta Cohen & Francis M. Deng, Masses in Flight: The Global Crisis of Internal Displacement 3 (1998).

[3] James P. Grant, *Refugees, Internally Displaced and the Poor: An Evolving Ethos of Responsibility*, address at the Round Table on the Papal Document, UNICEF, Mar. 9, 1993.

It was not until the 1990s that this gap in treatment was challenged and the international community began in a concerted way to try to assist and protect people uprooted inside their countries.

. . .

International Protection for IDPs

A complex mix of motivations produced the broader international approach that seeks to protect and assist people uprooted within their own countries. The growing number of IDPs was a key consideration as was the risk that conflict and displacement in one country could spill over borders and disrupt regional and international stability. International preoccupation with preventing refugee flows also lent support to protecting people inside their countries. So too did the Cold War's end, which facilitated access and was accompanied by an erosion in traditional notions of sovereignty. From 1991 on, Security Council resolutions began to demand access to IDPs and other affected populations, and sometimes authorised the establishment of relief corridors and cross-border operations or the use of force to reach IDPs and others in need.

The international response to IDP emergencies, however, initially focused on providing food, medicine and shelter to the displaced. In 1989, U.N. Resident Coordinators were assigned the task of coordinating "assistance" to IDPs in the field. But with the displacement of Kurds, Bosnians and Somalis, it became clear that security was as overriding a priority as food. . . .

IDPs began to look to the international community for protection when their states collapsed or when their governments proved unable or unwilling to provide them with elemental security.

The Refugee Policy Group (RPG), a small think tank in Washington DC, took the lead in pointing out that United Nations mechanisms to coordinate assistance to IDPs would prove ineffective unless there were comparable "measures to protect the human rights of those displaced."[4] The assumption that because IDPs were within the borders of their countries their governments would protect them was proving erroneous. Before a special meeting of delegates of the U.N. Commission on Human Rights in 1990, RPG argued that when governments do not have the willingness or ability to protect their displaced populations, international involvement becomes essential. . . .

. . .

Sovereignty as Responsibility and the Guiding Principles on Internal Displacement

It fell to Francis M. Deng, who became Representative of the Secretary-General on IDPs in 1992, to undertake the work of developing the conceptual and legal framework for the international protection of IDPs. Deng put forward the concept of sovereignty as responsibility as the most appropriate protection framework for people displaced inside their countries. . . .

The concept posits primary responsibility for the welfare and safety of IDPs with their governments. However, when governments are unable to fulfill their responsibilities, they should request and accept offers of aid from the international community. If they refuse or deliberately obstruct access and put large numbers at risk, the international community has a right and even a responsibility to take a series of calibrated actions. These range from "diplomatic demarches

---

4 *See* Roberta Cohen, Refugee Policy Group, *U.N. Human Rights Bodies Should Deal with the Internally Displaced*, Statement before delegates to the U.N. Commission on Human Rights, organized by the Quaker U.N. Office and the World Council of Churches, Geneva, Feb. 7, 1990. *See also* ROBERTA COHEN & JACQUES CUENOD, IMPROVING INSTITUTIONAL ARRANGE-MENTS FOR THE INTERNALLY DISPLACED 6–7 (Brookings Institution, Refugee Policy Group Project on Internal Displacement 1995); and THOMAS WEISS & DAVID A. KORN, INTERNAL DISPLACEMENT: CONCEPTUALIZATION AND ITS CONSEQUENCES 11–29 (2006).

to political pressures, sanctions, or, as a last resort, military intervention." State failure to provide protection and life-supporting assistance "legitimized the involvement of the international
community."[5]

The Guiding Principles on Internal Displacement, introduced by Deng into the U.N. in 1998,[6]
are based on the concept of sovereignty as responsibility. They set forth the rights of IDPS and the
responsibilities of governments and international organisations toward these populations. They
affirm that primary responsibility for displaced populations rests with their governments (Principles
3, 25); but if governments are unable to provide life-supporting protection and assistance, they
are expected to request assistance from the international community. In such cases, offers of
aid shall not be regarded "as an unfriendly act or an interference in a State's internal affairs"
(Principle 25); nor shall offers of aid be "arbitrarily withheld" when the authorities concerned are
"unable or unwilling" to provide the required assistance. The Principles do not explicitly state that
international aid can be provided without the consent of the affected country but according to
Deng and the author, the . . . obligation imposed on states by humanitarian and human rights law
to refrain from refusing reasonable offers of international assistance makes it difficult to dispute
the existence of a duty to accept such offers.[7]

The Principles further emphasise that in providing assistance, international humanitarian organisations should pay attention to the "protection needs and human rights" of IDPs and take "measures" in this regard (Principle 27). IDPs therefore must have access not only to material assistance
from the international community but also to protection from violence and abuse when governments fail to provide these to its citizens.

Challenges of R2P's Application to IDPs

When R2P was adopted by the U.N. General Assembly in 2005, it was generally expected that the
concept would enhance security for IDPs since the concept of sovereignty as responsibility was
recognised as its antecedent,21 and IDPs were so often the victims of R2P related crimes.

Like its antecedent, R2P places primary responsibility on the state to protect its population
and calls on the international community to support states in discharging that responsibility. But
if states fail in that obligation, responsibility shifts to the international community. There is an
international responsibility to take "collective action" when people are threatened by genocide,
crimes against humanity, war crimes, and ethnic cleansing. Such action can include "diplomatic,
humanitarian, and other peaceful means," to be followed if necessary by the use of force on a case
by case basis under Chapter VII of the U.N. Charter.

. . .

Exclusion of Disaster IDPs. In a speech in Berlin in 2008, the U.N. Secretary-General warned
that "Extending the principle [of R2P] to cover other calamities, such as HIV/AIDS, climate
change, or response to natural disasters, would undermine the 2005 consensus and stretch the
concept beyond recognition or operational utility."[8] By the stroke of a pen the Secretary-General
thus ruled out of R2P's potential protection the millions of persons expected to be uprooted by
disasters and climate change. The exclusion is said to accord with the World Summit Outcome
document which omits natural disasters from the R2P formulation even though the ICISS report
upon which R2P was based recommended as a criteria for R2P's application, . . . overwhelming

---

[5] COHEN & DENG, MASSES IN FLIGHT, at 7.
[6] U.N. Commission on Human Rights, The Guiding Principles on Internal Displacement, U.N. Doc. E/CN.4/1998/53/Add.2
(Feb. 11, 1998).
[7] COHEN AND DENG, MASSES IN FLIGHT, at 277.
[8] Ban Ki-moon, Address of the U.N. Secretary General at event on Responsible Sovereignty: International Cooperation for a
Changed World, Berlin, July 15, 2008.

natural or environmental catastrophes, where the state concerned is either unwilling or unable to cope, or call for assistance, and significant loss of life is occurring or threatened.[9]

The Secretary-General's Special Adviser Edward Luck reinforced this exclusion with the argument that R2P could only be triggered if "murder or extermination committed as part of 'a widespread or systematic attack' against the civilian population" were to take place.[10] However, if, in the context of a natural disaster, a government were to deliberately cause serious injury to the physical and mental health of massive numbers of the civilian population through blatant neglect, its action (or inaction) could well be said to constitute an attack on that population as postulated by Luck. Indeed, the Burmese government's "reckless indifference" toward the victims of Cyclone Nargis in 2008 made it possible to argue that it was intentionally causing suffering on a massive scale and possibly crimes against humanity.[11] Former Canadian Foreign Minister Lloyd Axworthy argued that Burma's "actively impeding the timely arrival of assistance and medications to more than one million people" should have invoked R2P: "What is the moral distinction between closing the door of rescuing people from death by machete and closing the door of life-saving aid?"[12]

When the definition of IDPs was first debated in the 1990s, similar controversies arose. Those opposed to the inclusion of disaster victims argued that this would broaden the concept and make it less meaningful. Disaster IDPs were said not to have the same protection needs as those uprooted by conflict. However, the majority pointed out that governments sometimes responded to disasters by persecuting or neglecting certain groups on political or ethnic grounds. In Ethiopia, in the mid 1980s, the Derg, under the pretext of responding to a natural disaster, forcibly and brutally relocated hundreds of thousands of highland Tigreans whom it considered political opponents into lowland malaria-infested areas; large numbers died as a result. In Sudan, the government refused to declare a state of emergency or request international aid during drought-related famines until it was forced to by the international community because of the widespread sickness and death.

A number of scholars, moreover, have pointed out that the mere invoking of R2P can prove valuable to protecting those at risk. Its mention at the time of Cyclone Nargis reportedly made the Burmese government more responsive to the victims and the international community more actively engaged.[13]

Tensions between human rights and humanitarian protection of IDPs. R2P's emphasis on human rights protection has at times created tensions with humanitarian programs for IDPs. When French Foreign Minister Bernard Kouchner called for R2P's application during Cyclone Nargis, and French, British and U.S. warships neared Burma's coast, U.N. Emergency Relief Coordinator Holmes strongly protested against any form of coercion to protect the IDPs as this could undermine international and regional efforts to bring in humanitarian aid. Military force, he did not believe "would be helpful to the people we are actually trying to help."[14] R2P was even opposed as an umbrella for the non-military actions taken by the Secretary-General, the U.N. and the Association of Southeast Asian Nations (ASEAN). It was argued that negotiation and cooperation with the authorities without reference to R2P was the most effective means of gaining access to affected areas. . . .

---

[9] ICISS, THE RESPONSIBILITY TO PROTECT, at 33.

[10] Edward C. Luck, Testimony before Subcommittee on International Development, Foreign Assistance, Economic Affairs and International Environmental Protection, Committee on Foreign Relations, U.S. Senate, June 17, 2008.

[11] Under the Rome Statute of the International Criminal Court, adopted in Rome, Italy on July 27, 1998 (entered into force July 2, 2002), inhumane acts "intentionally causing great suffering, or serious injury to body or to mental or physical health" are included under crimes against humanity when committed as part of "a widespread or systematic attack directed against any civilian population." Gareth Evans, *Facing Up to Our Responsibilities*, GUARDIAN, May 12, 2008. *See also* Roberta Cohen, *The Burma Cyclone and the Responsibility to Protect*, 1 GLOBAL RESPONSIBILITY TO PROTECT 253–57 (2009).

[12] Lloyd Axworthy & Allen Rock, *Responsibility to Protect? Yes*, GLOBE & MAIL, May 9, 2008.

[13] Haacke, *Myanmar, the Responsibility to Protect, and the Need for Practical Assistance*, at 169.

[14] World Federalist Movement Institute for Global Policy, *The Responsibility to Protect and Its Application*, May 9, 2009.

For the Executive Director of Médecins Sans Frontières USA, Nicholas de Torrente, the integration of humanitarian aid into broader political and security frameworks risks politicising and jeopardising relief operations. It also identifies aid workers with one side of a conflict and can expose them to attacks. Many humanitarian aid workers have expressed difficulty as well with the very concept of "protection," arguing that going beyond delivering food, medicine and shelter could lead to denial of access, the expulsion of staff and interfere with relationships with governments on humanitarian and development issues. Other aid workers, however, consider protection essential to their work, and argue that when genocide and atrocity crimes are being committed, neutrality is not an option.

The extent to which R2P will encourage humanitarian organisations to engage more actively in protecting the physical safety and human rights of IDPs caught up in humanitarian emergencies remains to be seen. Nor is it clear whether U.N. human rights bodies will move beyond monitoring to play more of an actual protection role in the field.

Questions and Discussion

1. Is there a "best" approach to disaster relief? Should the U.N. create green helmets who could quickly respond?
2. Is the responsibility to protect a reformulation of the doctrine of humanitarian intervention, or are there significant differences? Should either apply in the case of environmental disasters?

IV. Refugees

In 2003, the U.N. reported that for the first time in history, the number of environmental refugees had surpassed the number of political and war refugees. According to some scholars, 50 million people worldwide will be displaced by 2010 because of rising sea levels, desertification, dried-up aquifers, weather-induced flooding, and other serious environmental changes. *See* MOLLY CONISBEE & ANDREW SIMMS, ENVIRONMENTAL REFUGEES: THE CASE FOR RECOGNITION (2003). The U.N. University agrees and notes that Red Cross research shows that more people are now displaced by environmental disasters than war.

Those displaced have been referred to as environmental refugees, defined as "people who can no longer gain a secure livelihood in their homelands because of drought, soil erosion, desertification, deforestation and other environmental problems, together with associated problems of population pressures and profound poverty." N. Myers, *Environmental Refugees: An Emergent Security Issue*, OSCE, 13th Economic Forum, Prague (2005). Yet international refugee conventions do not recognize the category of environmental refugee. In 1951, the U.N. General Assembly adopted the Convention relating to the Status of Refugees (Res. 429), which defined refugees as those having

> well-founded fear of being persecuted for reasons of race, religion, nationality, membership of a particular social group or political opinion, is outside the country of his nationality and is unable, or owing to such fear, is unwilling to avail himself of the protection of that country; or who, not having a nationality and being outside the country of his former habitual residence as a result of such events, is unable or, owing to such fear, is unwilling to return to it.

The definition of *refugee* was extended later to people who "are forced to move for a complex range of reasons including persecution, widespread human rights abuses, armed conflict and generalized violence." U.N. HIGH COMMISSIONER FOR REFUGEES, PARTNERSHIP: AN OPERATIONS MANAGEMENT HANDBOOK FOR UNHCR'S PARTNERS (2003).

The main goal of refugee law and policy is repatriation, or return of refugees to their original homes. If this is impossible or undesirable, resettlement is the only alternative. Until a permanent home can be established, the United Nations, helped by numerous nongovernmental organizations and states, provides food, shelter, medical care, and other basic services to the refugees.

Critics claim that the concept of environmental refugee is unsound and unworkable. Richard Black argues that, "although environmental degradation and catastrophe may be important factors in the decision to migrate, and issues of concern in their own right, their conceptualization as a primary cause of forced displacement is unhelpful and unsound intellectually, and unnecessary in practical terms." R. Black, *Environmental Refugees: Myth or Reality?* New Issues in Refugee Research Working Paper No. 34, at 2 (2001). States are also unwilling to extend protection to an ill-defined category, yet the problems continue to expand. This section examines the plight of displaced persons, the rights of refugees, and the concept of environmental refugees.

Environmental Refugees: How Many, How Bad?,
CSA Discovery Guide, June 2006, at 6–7, 8–9, 12–13
Ethan Goffman

Environmental, economic, and political degradation are undoubtedly connected. Categories remain permeable, for instance in ongoing migrations to the United States; "Though nominally economic migrants, many of the estimated 1 million people who flood illegally into the United States annually from Mexico are in part driven by declining ecological conditions in a country where 60 percent of the land is classified as severely degraded."[15]

One classification may cause the other or, more likely, each drives the other in a vicious circle of reinforcing degradations. "Environmental refugee as a term is, today, basically perceived as a way of simplifying the understanding of a situation that is usually much more complex than what can be illustrated by environmental explanations," argues one social scientist.[16]

All of this would leave the term "environmental refugee" looking problematic, yet the term is useful for describing numerous real-world situations. It would, for instance, be pointless to define refugees from the recent Asian Tsunami, or from the devastation of New Orleans by Hurricane Katrina, solely via the 1951 United Nations definition, although political factors certainly influence the make-up, duration, and long-term fate of the refugees. In such cases, the term "environmental refugee" seems the best one.

. . .

Classifying Environmental Refugees

From the various schemes categorizing environmental refugees, it is possible to derive a few clear types derived from human history and organization, at least speaking theoretically. Natural disasters are the most obvious, and have the longest history. Since the start of *Homo sapiens*, forest fires, hurricanes, floods, volcanic eruptions, and earthquakes have caused human dislocation, both temporary and permanent. While these would seem to be out of human control, decisions to live in disaster-prone areas intensify the danger. For instance, for economic and aesthetic reasons, a

---

[15] UNEP, *Migration and Tourism*, Our Planet Mag., 2000.
[16] R. Haug, *Forced Migration, Processes of Return and Livelihood Construction Among Pastoralists in Northern Sudan*, 26 Disasters 70–84, at 74 (2002).

large proportion of people choose to live in coastal areas, and therefore make themselves more vulnerable to floods and hurricanes.

In a hunter-gatherer society, in which nomadism is often a way of life, it might be difficult to say when migration is part of a "normal" pattern and when it achieves environmental refugee status. Drought has always been with human beings, with the response generally being to move on to the next watering hole, fresh spring, lake, or other water source. Of course in contemporary times drought takes on a whole new context, and must be looked at in regional, national, and international contexts. Lester Brown, for instance, worries that on a global level we are drawing down our overall water supply.[17]

Ever since humans adopted agriculture, and largely abandoned a nomadic way of life, over the last 10,000 years or so, we have made ourselves vulnerable to another kind of environmental dislocation, that caused by land degradation, of which the dust bowl is but one example. Drought, erosion, and soil depletion threaten the stability of agricultural societies. Some environmentalists believe that modern agricultural methods, depending largely on a very few crop types, have permanently altered ecosystems and left us vulnerable to massive crop failure, although continual technological changes might very well offset this.

The industrial age brought forth pollution, yet another kind of environmental stress, at times leading to refugees. Pollution, depending upon how one defines the word, had always existed, both from natural sources and from human garbage, yet not of the kind or concentration generated by industry. Evolving technology has led to new chemical wastes, with varied and often unpredictable effects. Brown describes New York state's Love Canal, site of "21,000 tons of toxic waste" that led to "birth defects and other illnesses," as the site of "the first toxic-waste refugees." Although this may be exaggerated, such toxic events as the Chernobyl nuclear disaster periodically mar our world. Most pollution, however, leads to a kind of slow degradation, a decrease in health, rather than a mass exodus.

Finally, global climate change caused by humans is an extremely recent phenomena that seems to have created only a few refugees, but almost certainly will increase future numbers, perhaps exponentially. The most obvious way is through raising sea levels, as may already be happening in the Pacific. And global climate change has the potential to interact with other environmental problems. Recent scientific papers, for instance, suggest that hurricanes may become (or may already be) larger and fiercer than those in the past. Changes in climate also make agricultural output unpredictable; techniques that grow bounteous crops in one climate may not work as well in another, making planning for best practices in a given area increasingly difficult.

In sum, then, while natural disasters have been always with us, human innovation leads to increases in the quality of life, but also to unexpected consequences and periodic waves of refugees.

. . .

The Fate of Small Islands: Perchance to Drown?

Flooding is only one of several ways in which climate change may spur environmental refugees; drought, forest fires, disease, and massive hurricanes are other possible side effects of global warming. For small island chains such as Tuvalu, Vanuatu, and the Maldives, however, flooding is the current danger; these island nations may be early victims of rising sea levels. In 2005 a small Vanuatu community was moved inland to escape flooding.

Tuvalu has made plans to abandon their nine island nation, although haven for the entire population of 11,000 has yet to be secured. New Zealand has already become a refuge for many Tuvaluans, and both New Zealand and Australia are debating how to handle future refugees.

---

[17] L. Brown, Outgrowing the Earth 99ff. (2004).

Erosion and disruption of fresh water are likely to affect those portions of small islands that remain above sea level. The Maldives are particularly threatened. According to a United Nations report, "with about three-quarters of the land area of Maldives less than a meter above mean sea level, the slightest rise in sea level will prove extremely threatening." With tide variation, environmental impacts are increased: "Many islands already suffer inundation and shoreline erosion" that lead "to freshwater shortages and disease outbreaks."[18]

Still, the timing, nature, and causes of environmental impacts are difficult to pinpoint. According to one report, "changes in sea level are related to a multitude of variables and no realistic trend can be detected from the data for many years to come."[19] Indeed, skeptics about global climate change argue that small island nations use the possibility of rising sea levels as a tool to garner aid, and cite studies that "sea level around Tuvalu has been falling precipitously for the last half-century" before it began to rise.[20] And the causes of any geographic – or time-specific rise in sea level may always be contested.

More important than short-term trends, however, is the longer-term consensus among the vast majority of climate scientists that global climate change is, indeed, happening. If this is so, an environmental justice issue here is whether wealthy countries that generate large amounts of greenhouse gases should take in large numbers of refugees from climate change induced events. Explains a climate change guidebook, "while small islands are not responsible for the causes of climate change, they are likely to be the first to experience the worst effects of climate change, particularly through sea-level rise on low lying islands or through water shortages on porous and low lying islands."[21] The Alliance of Small Island States "claims that metropolitan countries will need to pay damages to their countries and must begin meaningful reductions of greenhouse gases without further delay." Of course sorting out the long-term causes of such events, who is responsible, and how they should compensate, is far easier said than done. Most developed nations have thus far foregone responsibility for island nation refugees.

Statement by Emanuela-Chiara Gillard, ICC Legal Adviser,
International Association of Refugee Law Judges,
World Conference Stockholm, Apr. 21–23, 2005

B. Interface Between International Humanitarian Law and Refugee Law

Armed conflict and international humanitarian law are of relevance to refugee law and refugee protection in a number of ways.

First, to determine who is a refugee. Many asylum seekers are persons fleeing armed conflict and often violations of international humanitarian law. Does this make them refugees? Not every person fleeing an armed conflict automatically falls within the definition of the 1951 Refugee Convention, which lays down a limited list of grounds for persecution. While there may be situations, notably in conflicts with an ethnic dimension, where persons are fleeing because of a fear of persecution based on their "race, religion, nationality or membership of a particular social group," this is not always the case.

---

[18] UNEP. *Maldives: State of the Environment. Part III, Key Environmental Issues.* UNEP Regional Resource Centre for Asia and the Pacific (2002).

[19] Ministerial Conference on Environment and Development in Asia and the Pacific (2000). Climate Change and the Pacific Islands. U.N. Economic and Social Commission for Asia and the Pacific.

[20] P. MICHAELS, DON'T BOO-HOO FOR TUVALU (2001).

[21] E. TOMPKINS ET AL., SURVIVING CLIMATE CHANGE IN SMALL ISLANDS – A GUIDEBOOK (2005).

Recognising that the majority of persons forced to leave their state of nationality today are fleeing the indiscriminate effect of hostilities and the accompanying disorder, including the destruction of homes, foodstocks and means of subsistence – all violations of international humanitarian law – but with no specific element of persecution, subsequent regional refugee instruments, such as the 1969 OAU Refugee Convention and the 1984 Cartagena Declaration on Refugees have expanded their definitions to include persons fleeing armed conflict.

Moreover, states that are not party to these regional instruments have developed a variety of legislative and administrative measures, such as the notion of "temporary protection" for example, to extend protection to persons fleeing armed conflict.

A second point of interface between international humanitarian law and refugee law is in relation to issues of exclusion. Violations of certain provisions of international humanitarian law are war crimes and their commission may exclude a particular individual from entitlement to protection as a refugee.

Protection of Refugees Under International Humanitarian Law

International humanitarian law offers refugees who find themselves in a state experiencing armed conflict a two-tiered protection. First, provided that they are not taking a direct part in hostilities, as civilians refugees are entitled to protection from the effects of hostilities. Secondly, in addition to this general protection, international humanitarian law grants refugees additional rights and protections in view of their situation as aliens in the territory of a party to a conflict and their consequent specific vulnerabilities.

a. General Protection

If respected, international humanitarian law operates so as to *prevent* displacement of civilians and to ensure their protection during displacement, should they nevertheless have moved.

i. The Express Prohibition of Displacement

Parties to a conflict are expressly prohibited from displacing civilians. This is a manifestation of the principle that the civilian population must be spared as much as possible from the effects of hostilities.

During occupation, the Fourth Geneva Convention prohibits individual or mass forcible transfers, both within the occupied territory and beyond its borders, either into the territory of the occupying power or, as is more often the case in practice, into third states.

There is a limited exception to this rule, which permits an occupying power to "evacuate" the inhabitants of a particular area if this is necessary for the security of the civilian population or for imperative military reasons. Even in such cases the evacuations should not involve the displacement of civilians *outside* the occupied territory unless this is impossible for material reasons. Moreover, displaced persons must be transferred back to their homes as soon as the hostilities in the area in question have ceased.

The prohibition on displacing the civilian population for reasons related to the conflict unless the security of the civilians or imperative military reasons so demand also applies in non-international armed conflicts.

ii. Protection from the Effects of Hostilities in Order to *Prevent* Displacement

In addition to these express prohibitions, the rules of international humanitarian law which shield civilians from the effects of hostilities also play on important role in the *prevention* of displacement, as it is often violations of these rules which are at the root of displacements in situations of armed conflict.

Of particular relevance are:

- the prohibition to attack civilians and civilian property and of indiscriminate attacks;
- the duty to take precautions in attack to spare the civilian population;
- the prohibition of starvation of the civilian population as a method of warfare and of the destruction of objects indispensable to its survival; and
- and the prohibition on reprisals against the civilian population and its property.

Also of relevance are the prohibition on collective punishments which, in practice have often taken form of destruction of homes, leading to displacement; and the rules requiring parties to a conflict, as well as all other states, to allow the unhindered passage of relief supplies and assistance necessary for the survival of the civilian population.

iii. Protection During Displacement

Although prohibited by international humanitarian law, displacement of civilians frequently occurs in practice. Once displaced or evacuated civilians are entitled to various protections and rights. Thus we find rules regulating the manner in which evacuations must be effected: transfers must be carried out are in satisfactory conditions of hygiene, health, safety and nutrition; during displacement persons must be provided with appropriate accommodation and members of the same family must not be separated.

Although these provisions relate to conditions to be ensured on situations of evacuation – i.e. "lawful" displacements for the safety of the persons involved security or for imperative military necessity – these conditions should be applicable *a fortiori* in situations of unlawful displacement.

In addition to these special provisions relating specifically to persons who have been displaced, such persons are civilians and, as such, entitled, even during displacement, to the whole range of protection appertaining to civilians.

b. Specific Protection of Refugees

In addition to this general protection, international humanitarian law affords refugees further specific protection. In international armed conflicts refugees are covered by the rules applicable to aliens in the territory of a party to a conflict generally as well as by the safeguards relating specifically to refugees.

i. Protection as Aliens in the Territory of a Party to a Conflict

Refugees benefit from the protections afforded by the Fourth Geneva Convention to aliens in the territory of a party to a conflict, including:

- the entitlement to leave the territory in which they find themselves unless their departure would be contrary to the national interests of the state of asylum;
- the continued entitlement to basic protections and rights to which aliens had been entitled before the outbreak of hostilities;
- guarantees with regards to mean of existence, if the measures of control applied to the aliens by the party to the conflict means that they are unable to support themselves.

While recognising that the party to the conflict in whose control the aliens find themselves may, if its security makes this absolutely necessary, intern the aliens or place them in assigned residence, the Convention provides that these are the strictest measures of control to which aliens may be subjected.

Finally, the Fourth Convention also lays down limitations on the power of a belligerent to transfer aliens. Of particular relevance is the rule providing that a protected person may in no circumstances be transferred to a country where he or she may have reason to fear persecution for his or her political opinions or religious beliefs; a very early expression of the principle of *non refoulement*.

ii. Additional Protections for Refugees

In addition to the aforementioned rules for the benefit of all aliens in the territory of a party to a conflict, the Fourth Geneva Convention contains two further provisions expressly for the benefit of refugees. The first provides that refugees should not be treated as enemy aliens – and thus susceptible to the measures of control – solely on the basis of their nationality. This recognises the fact refugees no longer have a link of allegiance with that state and are thus not automatically a potential threat to their host state.

The second specific provision deals with the precarious position in which refugees may find themselves if the state which they have fled occupies their state of asylum. In such circumstances, the refugees may only be arrested, prosecuted, convicted or deported from the occupied territory by the occupying power for offences committed *after* the outbreak of hostilities, or for offences unrelated to the conflict committed before the outbreak of hostilities which, according to the law of the now occupied state of asylum, would have justified extradition in time of peace. The objective of this provision is to ensure that refugees are not punished for acts – such as political offences – which may have been the cause of their departure from their state of nationality, or for the mere fact of having sought asylum.

All of this being said, who is a refugee for the purposes of international humanitarian law? Although the Fourth Geneva Convention expressly refers to refugees, it does not define this term. Instead, it focuses on their *de facto* lack of protection from any government.

The matter was developed in Additional Protocol I. This provides that persons who, before the beginning of hostilities, were considered refugees under the relevant international instruments accepted by the parties concerned or under the national legislation of the state of refuge or of residence are to be considered "protected persons" within the meaning of the Fourth Convention in all circumstances and without any adverse distinction.

Questions and Discussion

1. What additional legal guarantees would refugee status add for those displaced by environmental conditions? Does it make sense for those whose states may disappear? Does it guarantee a right of entry into another state?

2. Can the term *environmental refugee* be defined with sufficient precision to make it a workable concept acceptable to states?

3. In addition to the problems of displacement due to environmental catastrophe or degradation, temporary refugee camps themselves are a source of environmental and human rights abuse. Wendy Vanasselt described the problems:

    > Refugees searching for safe haven can burden the ecosystems in their country of asylum and complicate environmental decision-making. In 2001, there were about 20 million uprooted people worldwide. Some 12 million were refugees and 5 million were "internally displaced persons" – people forced to flee their homes, but still living in their original country (UNHCR 2002:12, 19, 22).

    > Often, refugees are forced to settle in resource-scarce areas, putting further pressure on trees, land, water, and wildlife. The unstable in – and outflow of displaced people affects established patterns of rural cropping and food production, and upsets long-term agricultural investments (Messer et al. 2000). When rural communities are forced to flee, they may

take with them knowledge of the harvest cycles of locally adapted seeds and the informal networks of seed swapping that help preserve the genetic diversity of agriculture (PRTADG 1999:12–14). Streams of refugees can overburden infrastructure for living quarters, clean water supplies, and waste systems.

When it is time to make decisions about natural resource use and conservation, refugees are unable to have a voice in those decisions because they are not citizens. Even if they return to their original homes, they may lose their say in land use and management decisions due to land ownership disputes or postwar changes in national land policy. For example, in postwar Mozambique, the government awarded commercial land concessions in many areas when local communities were still absent or were struggling to re-establish their livelihoods, and were thus unable to effectively join in the decision (Hatton et al. 2001:64). In addition, documentation regarding legal land rights and property ownership is often misplaced or confiscated during conflicts, as occurred in the southern Balkans when Kosovo Albanians fled to Albania and the former Yugoslav Republic of Macedonia in 1999 (UNEP and UNCHS 1999:5).

World Resources 2002–2004, Chapter 2, Box 2.1. at 25-27 (United Nations Development Programme, United Nations Environment Programme, World Bank, World Resources Institute, 2003) [citing: J. HATTON, M. COUTO, & J. OGLETHORPE, BIODIVERSITY AND WAR: A CASE STUDY FROM MOZAMBIQUE (Biodiversity Support Program 2001); E. Messer, M. Cohen, & J. D'Costa, *Armed Conflict and Hunger*, HUNGER NOTES ONLINE, Fall 2000; Paul Richards Technology & Agricultural Development Group (PRTADG), *The Silent Casualties of War*, UNESCO COURIER, July–Aug. 1999,at 12–14; U.N. ENVIRONMENT PROGRAMME & U.N. CENTRE FOR HUMAN SETTLEMENTS, THE KOSOVO CONFLICT: CONSEQUENCES FOR THE ENVIRONMENT AND HUMAN SETTLEMENTS (1999); U.N. HIGH COMMISSION ON REFUGEES, STATISTICAL YEARBOOK 2001 (2002)].

4. A UNEP Study on the environmental impacts of Kosovar refugee camps in Albania points out a few of the problems.

MANAGING THE KOSOVO REFUGEE CRISIS: ENVIRONMENTAL CONSEQUENCES (2000) UNEP BALKANS 2000

Background to the Crisis

In March 1998, a stream of refugees began entering Albania to escape conflicts within the province of Kosovo in the Federal Republic of Yugoslavia (FRY). This number increased in May and June 1998, and by the end of that year, UNHCR estimated that approximately 21,800 refugees from Kosovo had entered Albania. During the first three months of 1999, a slow but steady influx continued.

On March 24, 1999, the Rambouillet peace talks having broken down, NATO commenced air strikes against FRY. Virtually overnight, hundreds of thousands of refugees fled Kosovo to Albania, the Former Yugoslav Republic of Macedonia, Montenegro and Bosnia-Herzegovina. The sudden refugee influx posed a formidable relief challenge to Albania and the rest of the international community.

Albania responded by accommodating as many refugees as resources would permit, welcoming hundreds of thousands of refugees into their homes and communities for as long as was required. Many partners, including U.N. agencies, international organizations, donors and nongovernmental organizations, supported the Albanian relief operations.

On June 3rd 1999, after more than two months of intensive air bombardment by NATO, FRY agreed to an international peace plan and the withdrawal of its military forces from Kosovo.

The population of refugees in Albania peaked on June 9, 1999, when humanitarian aid was extended to some 460,000. According to UNHCR, an estimated 61% of these refugees stayed with 30,000 host families; 18% lived in 50 tented camps, and 21% resided in 300 collective centers.

On June 10, 1999, following continued negotiations, NATO suspended its military operations and the U.N. Security Council adopted Resolution 1244, the Kosovo Peace Plan. With the Kosovo conflict ended, the refugees began to return to their homes.

Refugee Crisis Management

Despite national and international contingency planning, no one was prepared for the speed and magnitude of the refugee crisis in Albania. The Government and the international community made extraordinary efforts to respond. Still, in analyzing the consequences of the crisis, it is important to recognize the lack of time that was available for adequate environmental planning.

When the crisis began, the government of Albania established the Emergency Management Group (EMG). The EMG's role was to serve as an information clearinghouse and to coordinate the delivery of services and humanitarian aid to refugees. The group was based out of the Office of the Prime Minister, and included representatives from various government agencies, municipalities, and inter-governmental organizations. Regional Environmental Agency representatives provided input on environmental matters through prefectures and local governments.

The EMG was an innovative attempt to centralize management of the refugee crisis. In practice, however, the EMG did not play a strong role in strategic decisions. Municipalities, prefectures and aid agencies for example, took the lead in camp site selection, often without the direct involvement of the Government or UNHCR. Unfortunately, environmental criteria were frequently not taken into consideration during this process due to information gaps, a lack of local expertise and inadequate time.

Other refugee coordination and management activities were spread over multiple agencies. Some camps were managed by UNHCR, others by local authorities, non-governmental organizations and military entities. Although Regional Environmental Agency officials and UNHCR staff members advised camp managers on environmental protection, standards varied considerably among the camps.

Post-emergency coordination activities were addressed by a combination of the EMG, UNHCR, UNDP and ECAT. UNHCR, however, did not issue formal guidelines on the closure, cleanup and rehabilitation of the camps until July 8, 1999. By then, the majority of the refugees had already left most camps and the attention of donors and the international community was shifting to other situations. Although all UNHCR-managed camps were cleaned, officials interviewed by UNEP reported that numerous other sites were not adequately cleaned or rehabilitated.

The Environmental Dimension of the Refugee Influx

In the context of a conflict, the provision of refugee relief is the first and foremost priority. Food, housing, health care – these basic needs and others must be provided without delay. In the wake of refugee influxes, however, it is worthwhile to examine their impacts, if any, on the environment and to understand whether lessons for the future can be derived.

In Albania, the Government and the international community met the basic needs of some 460,000 people, an overwhelming success in the provision of emergency relief. In spite of the time and pressure posed by the influx, UNHCR and the EMG took measures to ensure protection of Albania's environment. Undoubtedly, the success of these measures is to some degree reflected in the fact that impacts to Albania's environment were minimal.

Nevertheless, after the Kosovo conflict ended, concerns were raised that the refugees may have placed a heavy and lasting burden on the country's environmental management infrastructure. As a result, one of the key aims of the assessment was to determine the overall environmental impacts of the refugee influx and to consider what steps can be taken to further integrate environmental protection into future refugee operations. UNEP's observations and conclusions follow. General and site-specific recommendations are contained in Chapter 7.

SOLID WASTE

Vast quantities of solid wastes are inevitably produced as the basic living needs of refugees are met. Excessive packaging of food aid and other basic goods is the principle cause. The successful management and disposal of such wastes largely depends on the waste management infrastructure of the host country.

During the crisis in Albania, municipalities, with the support of UNHCR and donors, collected and transported solid waste from refugee camps to local landfills. Wastes produced by refugees staying with host families were also managed by municipal services. Despite this increased load, baseline municipal services were maintained throughout the crisis, and significant impacts on the existing waste management infrastructure were not evident. Nevertheless, UNEP observed waste scattered in the Tirana City Park near the Olympic Camp and also lining the banks of Lake Shkodër in downtown Shkodër. According to local experts, these sites were not degraded before the refugee crisis.

In some rural areas and townships, illegal dumpsites used by the local population were also used for refugee wastes. In some cases, whole new sites were established. These illegal dumpsites, located primarily in parks and along water bodies, continue to be used by the local population at the expense of human health and the environment. Beaches and coastal forests in the districts of Durrës, Golem, Diyjake and Lezhe were among the areas polluted by illegal dumping.

Comprehensive statistics are not available on the amounts of solid wastes produced by each camp and host family. However, based on data obtained from three camps (Austrian, Caritas, and Islamic Relief), each refugee in those camps produced an average of 1.7 kilograms of solid wastes per day. By contrast, the residents of Tirana reportedly produced a daily average of 0.7 kilograms of solid waste per person that same year. This difference suggests that adequate measures may not have been taken to minimize the generation of refugee solid wastes.

WASTEWATER

Albania's lack of wastewater treatment facilities was reflected in the refugee camps and collective centers. Facilities that could not be connected to municipal sewage lines used soak-away pit latrines to collect wastewater. It is unclear what proportion of these latrines were properly lined. After the refugees were repatriated, the majority of these pits were buried and their contents left on-site. The potential of these pits to contaminate groundwater and soil remains unknown.

The Municipality of Tirana maintains a 540-kilometer wastewater collection system. Pipes collecting wastewater from the Olympic Camp in Tirana were connected with the municipal system. Due to hookups by nearby houses that were illegally constructed, however, the camp's sewage pipes were blocked and disconnected from the municipal system. Instead, the wastewater generated was spread over a nearby, poorly drained field.

In Shkodër, wastewater generated by the Islamic Relief Camp was discharged into a small stormwater drainage canal that connected with Lake Shkodër. Lake Shkodër and its adjoining wetlands boast high biological production and diversity. Part of the area is being considered for designation as a national protected area. In such a sensitive aquatic environment, the disposal of the camp's wastewater should have been more carefully considered. A hookup to the municipal wastewater collection system would have been a preferable option.

During the peak crisis period, the refugees accommodated by host families put an additional burden on urban wastewater collection systems. These additional wastewaters increased the amount of untreated chemical and biological pollution entering local receiving waters.

WATER SUPPLY

Water appears to have been provided to refugees without long-term impact to the majority of supply systems. Rural camps were supplied either by tanker trucks or artesian wells. Urban and suburban refugee camps were generally supplied by nearby city and municipal systems.

The refugee influx exacerbated the country's water supply problems. Increased demand strained pipelines and created supply shortages. Although water rationing was imposed, some urban water supply systems may have experienced increased losses due to the crisis.

FORESTS AND BIODIVERSITY

In Albania, illegal timber harvesting and animal poaching by refugees was minimized by the provision of meals and wood from local suppliers. Minor incidences of animal poaching and timber harvesting were reported at some of the campsites. Long-term impacts, however, are not evident.

The National Environment Agency and its regional representatives actively attempted to minimize the number of camps located in or near protected areas. Due to their efforts, only six camps were eventually built in the vicinity of protected areas, and two camps were prevented from being established. While some illegal harvesting of timber occurred in these areas, there is no evidence of long-term ecological impacts or loss of biodiversity. The disposal of solid wastes in these areas, however, may have contaminated soil and groundwater and adversely impacted local wildlife.

Forest and biodiversity impacts have not been associated with refugees that stayed with host families or in collective centers.

AGRICULTURAL AREAS

During the process of campsite selection, flat and well-drained locations are generally preferred for construction. Unfortunately, agricultural lands often allow camps to be established quickly and at the lowest cost. The Albanian Ministry of Agriculture and Food reports that a total of 500 hectares of agricultural lands were used for refugee campsites. This included 379 hectares of productive state land, 87 hectares of productive private land, and 34 hectares of non-productive state land. Campsites ranged in capacity between 120 and 20,000 people, with a typical capacity of 2,000 to 6,000 people.

Some of these areas have been cleaned by UNHCR. On the majority of sites, however, gravel remains, inhibiting future agricultural production. As of the time of the UNEP mission, 80% of the agricultural land used required rehabilitation. The lost productivity from these lands is expected to have significant economic impacts on families that had farmed them. A report published by the Food and Agriculture Organization of the United Nations, entitled *The Impact of the Kosovo Crisis on Albanian Agriculture and the Environment*, provides a comprehensive assessment of the agricultural impacts of the crisis.

URBAN GREEN SPACES AND RECREATION AREAS

The majority of refugees stayed with host families, in camps, or in collective centers. Some makeshift shelters, however, were established in urban green spaces and recreation areas. Much of the vegetation in these areas was trampled or removed, reducing their aesthetic benefit to the community. Garbage disposal and timber removal were also significant problems. The community park in Fier and the City Park in Tirana were among those subjected to minor degradation.

Recommendations

. . .

10. The shortcomings of the EMG underscore the need to establish a single coordination body at the outset of a refugee crisis. Government-based coordinating bodies must have precise legal mandates covering all activities-from the delivery of humanitarian aid, to camp site selection, management and rehabilitation-as well as the full support of U.N. agencies, inter-governmental organizations, and NGOs. The experience and expertise of UNHCR should be used as much as possible during refugee operations.

11. "Life cycle assessment" should be used as a planning tool during refugee crises. This approach requires consideration of a site's future use during the site selection process and in subsequent management decisions. The goal is to ensure that the technologies used on site will facilitate redevelopment and minimize rehabilitation costs. Redeveloping sites with significant benefit to local communities should be a priority.

12. UNHCR has developed environmental guidelines and policies to minimize the environmental impacts of refugees. These documents, however, were not distributed in a timely or comprehensive manner to some relevant agencies and camp managers. Improved efforts should therefore be taken by UNHCR to distribute these materials at the outset of refugee operations.

13. Rehabilitation efforts were supported by the UNHCR Quick Impact Projects (QIPs) program for refugee-affected areas, as well as numerous other agencies and donors. Despite these efforts, the majority of refugee-affected agricultural lands were not rehabilitated. Funding of future reha-bilitation projects should be justified against the overall environmental management needs and priorities of the country. Any future rehabilitation work should involve the National Environment Agency and relevant municipal authorities.

14. At the outset of any humanitarian emergency, environmental technology, including GIS inventory and other "state of the art" data, should be used to identify environmentally sensitive areas in the country. This would make possible the selection of sites with low environmental impacts and high redevelopment potential. It would also enable the use of technologies to minimize environmental impacts on sensitive areas selected. UNEP's Environmental Information Services, UNHCR and other international agencies could assist in this process. The camp site selection process should also consider guidance from competent national environmental agencies, as well as from non-governmental and intergovernmental organizations, and municipalities.

15. In order to minimize the production of solid wastes, aid and donor agencies should adopt poli-cies requiring that the food products and durable goods they procure use minimal or biodegradable packaging. Buying in bulk and distributing food via reusable containers is recommended. Prefer-ence should be given to goods that are produced` in a sustainable way and that can be used locally following the repatriation of the refugees.

16. In order to minimize the potential for contamination by wastewaters, metal tanks should be used as the default method for wastewater management. Soak-away pits may be considered if, according to specialized assessment, unique environmental conditions and topography would prevent seepage into groundwater channels.

17. In order to assess the site-specific environmental impacts of refugee camps, standardized photographs should be taken from permanently marked camera locations both before, during

and after refugee occupation. This technique, known as Photopoint Monitoring, would help to document site conditions throughout refugee operations and minimize the potential for false claims of damage.

18. *Site-Specific Recommendations*

a) Spitalle Camp Site, Durrës: Situated on a former wetland, the area has been cleaned, but natural regeneration has been hampered by the soil's high salt content and, possibly, by heavy metal contamination from the nearby former chemical factory (see Chapter 3). Rehabilitation of the site needs to be considered in the context of the wider environmental strategy for the area. (See recommendations above re Chemical plant, Durrës.) A pilot project to establish a forest on the site would provide information about vegetative stabilization of the area and help remediation if soil contamination and salinity levels are found to be excessively high.

b) Harmmalaj 3 (Spanish Camp Site), Durrës: Although this site has been cleaned, latrine pits and water supply channels are unfilled, and extensive gravel areas remain. Rehabilitation was hampered by land ownership disputes. Any rehabilitation funds that are made available to this site should be redirected towards addressing local environmental priorities.

c) Rrushkull 1 Camp Site, Durrës: The site has been cleaned and vegetation is regenerating, but two concrete buildings and multiple concrete tent pads remain. The NEA recommends that the site be restored to a nature reserve for migratory birds. This proposal requires funds for a feasibility assessment and implementation. An alternative proposal is to develop the site into Department of Forestry facilities for scientific research. At a minimum, the concrete structures on site should be removed.

d) Austrian Camp/Airfield Camp, Shkodër: Gravel roads, concrete septic pits, unfilled drainage channels, and garbage from refugee occupation remain on site. Funds should be directed toward clearing an unofficial riverside dumpsite that developed near downtown Shkodër during the crisis. The municipality of Shkodër and private investors should investigate the potential of re-opening the airport at the former camp site.

e) Islamic Relief Camp Site, Shkodër: Wastewaters from this camp flowed into an open drainage channel that discharged into Shkodër Lake. The Lake has high levels of biological diversity and provides critical habitat for a variety of waterfowl. No additional rehabilitation is required; private construction work has been initiated.

f) Hope Camp, Fier: Located on lands prone to flooding. Infrastructure was removed and basic cleanup performed, but gravel-filled drainage channels, gravel roads, concrete-encased latrines and slabs remain. Topsoil removed from drainage ditches and latrine pits was piled into two large mounds. Any rehabilitation funds that are made available to this site should be redirected towards addressing local environmental priorities.

g) Olympic Collective Center: The camp houses up to 150 refugees in prefabricated accommodations and relies on a soak-away septic field to manage wastewaters. The field is unlined, and the potential for groundwater contamination is unknown. The local health authority should conduct a preliminary assessment to detect possible contamination from the septic field. When refugee operations have finished, the area could be developed into recreation and sport facilities.

h) Tirana City Park and Lake: The park and lake represent a valuable recreation area for local citizens. The lack of solid waste infrastructure has led to the creation of numerous illegal dump-sites in the park and along the lakeshore. Refugees exacerbated the problem and also harvested wood illegally. An environmental management plan should be developed for the park and lake area. Citizens should be educated in pollution prevention practices. Deforested areas should be replanted. Park management strategies should be adapted from successful models elsewhere.

———————

In the past two decades, the U.N. General Assembly has noted and expressed concern at the deleterious effect of the presence of refugees on the environment of host countries. Numerous provisions recognize the need to incorporate in the plans of assistance to refugees, returnees, and displaced persons measures to remedy the environmental deterioration in host countries and to welcome the efforts of UNHCR to resolve such problems. Other provisions call on UNHCR to enhance coordination with relevant parties to address refugee-related environmental problems and request that all countries and U.N. agencies assist in restoring the ecological balance of host countries. Several provisions request that the secretary-general study the environmental impact of the prolonged presence of refugees, with a view to rehabilitating those areas.

General Assembly Resolutions 42/127 (Dec. 7, 1987), 43/147 (Dec. 8, 1988), 44/152 (Dec. 15, 1989), and 45/154, PP8 (Dec. 18, 1990) all had preambular paragraphs:

> *Noting with concern* the deleterious effect of the refugee presence on the environment, which has resulted in widespread deforestation, soil erosion and the threat of destruction to an already fragile economic balance,

The G.A. Resolution 44/139 (Dec. 15, 1989) added an operative paragraph on the issue:

> *Recognizing* the need to incorporate in the plans of assistance to refugees, returnees and displaced persons measures to restore the ecological balance and the rational utilization of the natural resources in the areas of the countries affected,
>
> . . .
>
> 7. *Calls upon* the co-operating countries and the relevant agencies of the United Nations system to assist in restoring the ecological balance of the areas in the countries of asylum affected by the massive presence of refugees, in order to provide the populations of those areas with the conditions conducive to development; . . .

Resolution 45/141 (Dec. 14, 1990):

> 5. *Agrees* on the need for projects in favour of refugees, returnees and displaced persons to promote, inter alia:
>
> . . .
>
> (d) The protection of the environment;

Resolution 46/108 (Dec. 16, 1991) put forth:

> *Realizing* the importance of assisting the host countries, in particular those countries that have been hosting refugees for a longer time, to remedy environmental deterioration and the negative impact on public services and the development process,
>
> . . .
>
> 10. *Requests* the Secretary-General to study and assess the environmental and socio-economic impact of the prolonged presence of refugees in the host countries with a view to rehabilitating those areas; . . .

Resolution 47/105 (Dec. 16, 1992):

> 10. Requests the Secretary-General to study and assess the environmental and socio-economic impact of the prolonged presence of refugees in the host countries with a view to rehabilitating those areas;

> GA Res. 48/116 of 20 Dec 1993, GA Res. 49/119 of 23 Dec. 1994 and GA Res. 50/152 of 21 Dec. 1995:

> 13. *Reaffirms* the importance of incorporating environmental considerations into the programmes of the Office of the High Commissioner, especially in the least developed countries, in view of the impact on the environment of the large numbers of refugees and displaced persons of concern to the High Commissioner;

Resolution 52/101 (Dec. 12, 1997) and 53/126 (Dec. 9, 1998):

> 15. *Welcomes* the ongoing efforts undertaken by the Office of the United Nations High Commissioner for Refugees with host Governments, the United Nations and non-governmental organizations and the international community, in concentrating on the environment and eco-systems of countries of asylum;

Resolution 56/135 (Dec. 19, 2001) and 57/183 (Dec. 18, 2002):

> 2. *Notes with concern* that the deteriorating socio-economic situation, compounded by political instability, internal strife, human rights violations and natural disasters, has led to increased numbers of refugees and displaced persons in some countries of Africa, and remains particularly concerned about the impact of large-scale refugee populations on the security, socio-economic situation and environment of countries of asylum;

> . . .

> 22. *Welcomes* the programmes carried out by the Office of the High Commissioner with host Governments, the United Nations, nongovernmental organizations and the international community to address the environmental and socio-economic impact of refugee populations;

> 23. *Calls upon* the international donor community to provide material and financial assistance for the implementation of programmes intended for the rehabilitation of the environment

---

For further reading, there are numerous articles on the environment and refugees. *See, e.g.*, CHRISTOPHER J. BARROW, LAND DEGRADATION: DEVELOPMENT AND BREAKDOWN OF TERRESTRIAL ENVIRONMENTS (1991); Michael M. Cernea, *Disaster-Related Refugee Flows and Development-Caused Population Displacement*, in ANTHROPOLOGICAL APPROACHES TO INVOLUNTARY RESETTLEMENT POLICY, PRACTICE AND THEORY 375–99 (Michael M. Cernea and Scott Guggenheim eds. 1993); Robert Chambers, *Hidden Losers: The Impact of Rural Refugees and Refugee Programs on Poorer Hosts*, 20 INT'L MIGRATION REV. 245–63 (1986); ESSAM EL-HINNAWI, ENVIRONMENTAL REFUGEES (1985); U.N. HIGH COMMISSIONER FOR REFUGEES, INTERIM GUIDELINES ON THE ENVIRONMENT GENEVA (1994); Arthur H. Westing, *Environmental Refugees – A Growing Category of Displaced Persons*, 19 ENVTL. CONSERVATION 201–07 (1988).

10 Environmental Rights and International Finance: The World Bank Example

I. Intergovernmental Financial Institutions and Their Origins

This chapter examines the performance of intergovernmental financial institutions in relation to how well the projects they finance respect human rights and limit harmful environmental impacts. These financial institutions are commonly known as multilateral development banks (MDBs). There are five such banks in existence today. One, the World Bank, is global in scope. The four others are regional: the African Development Bank, the Asian Development Bank, the European Bank for Reconstruction and Development, and the Inter-American Development Bank. In addition, there are six subregional banks (for East Africa, West Africa, the Caribbean, Central America, and the Black Sea), whose membership is typically limited to borrowing nations. This tells us the number of MDBs, but what exactly are multilateral development banks? The following excerpt provides some guidance.

The World Bank Group traces its origins to the historic U.N. Monetary and Financial Conference of July 1944, where representatives of forty-five governments met to produce the modern system of international trade and economic cooperation that was the basis for the global postwar expansion. This conference is commonly known as the Bretton Woods conference, after the New Hampshire town where the conference was held.

The understanding that economic rivalries between the major industrial powers in the 1930s had led to the eruption of war predominated at the Bretton Woods conference. With victory imminent for the Allied powers, the conference attendees sought to establish an international framework in which restrictions on international trade favoring individual states were removed. The conference attendees also agreed on the establishment of international financial institutions to which distressed nations could turn as an alternative to military violence. The British delegation to the Bretton Woods conference was headed by the influential economic theorist John Maynard Keynes.

The Bretton Woods conference produced the International Monetary Fund (IMF), the General Agreement on Tariffs and Trade (GATT), and the International Bank for Reconstruction and Development (IBRD), each with a different role in the newly established economic order. The IMF was charged with monitoring the balance of payments accounts of member states, or the flow of money between each state and other states, as well as with providing loans as a last resort to countries with payment imbalances. The IMF has since developed a large infrastructure for analyzing and reporting economic data and providing advice to member nations. The GATT was a major treaty that aimed to reduce tariffs and other restrictions on international trade, and it was succeeded by the modern World Trade Organization (WTO) in 1995.

The IBRD, the first of five institutions that now constitute the World Bank Group, was created at Bretton Woods and charged with providing loans and technical advice to the governments of developing states for the purposes of development and reconstruction.

IBRD Articles of Agreement: Article I, as amended effective Feb. 16, 1989, http://siteresources.worldbank.org/EXTABOUTUS/Resources/ibrd-articlesofagreement.pdf

The purposes of the Bank are:

(i) To assist in the reconstruction and development of territories of members by facilitating the investment of capital for productive purposes, including the restoration of economies destroyed or disrupted by war, the reconversion of productive facilities to peacetime needs and the encouragement of the development of productive facilities and resources in less developed countries.

(ii) To promote private foreign investment by means of guarantees or participations in loans and other investments made by private investors; and when private capital is not available on reasonable terms, to supplement private investment by providing, on suitable conditions, finance for productive purposes out of its own capital, funds raised by it and its other resources.

(iii) To promote the long-range balanced growth of international trade and the maintenance of equilibrium in balances of payments by encouraging international investment for the development of the productive resources of members, thereby assisting in raising productivity, the standard of living and conditions of labor in their territories . . .

The Bank shall be guided in all its decisions by the purposes set forth above.

Questions and Discussion

1. In addition to the IBRD, which makes loans directly to developing states in return for guarantees by the state that the loan will be repaid, four other banks now constitute the WBG.

   The International Development Association (IDA), created in 1960, provides various forms of interest-free loans or grants (i.e., concessional financing) to the poorest states in the world. The IDA obtains most of its resources to make these loans by contributions from the governments of member countries, whereas the IBRD raises resources on the global financial markets. The IBRD and the IDA are together known as the World Bank. As of 2008, the IBRD has 185 member states and the IDA has 168.

   The International Finance Corporation (IFC), created in 1956, provides loans without requiring a guarantee by a state that the loan will be repaid. The IFC loans primarily in the private sector but may also loan in the public sector to government agencies at a subnational level. The IFC's capital is provided by member states, of which there are 181.

   The International Centre for Settlement of Investment Disputes (ICSID), created in 1966, provides arbitration, on a voluntary basis, of disputes between member countries and investors who are nationals of different member countries. Many bilateral investment treaties (BITs) contain provisions mandating arbitration in the ICSID. As of 2008, 143 countries were parties to the convention establishing the ICSID.

   The Multilateral Investment Guarantee Agency (MIGA) was created in 1988 for the purpose of encouraging foreign direct investment into developing countries. In addition to providing analysis and advice to investors and governments, MIGA provides insurance to international investors against political risk. Among the political risks for which the MIGA provides insurance are restrictions placed on the investor's assets in the host country, expropriation of the investor's assets by the host country, war and civil disturbance in the host country, and breach of contract by the host country. There are 173 member states of the MIGA.

The IBRD, IDA, IFC, MIGA, and ICSID are together known as the World Bank Group (WBG).

2. In the immediate aftermath of World War II, the IBRD made a number of large loans to states devastated by the war for the purpose of reconstruction. Today, the World Bank makes loans to states for a diverse array of objectives, including developing agriculture, education, energy infrastructure, gender equality, public health, telecommunications, mining, poverty reduction programs, transportation, urban infrastructure, and water resources. In 2007, the World Bank made loans totaling $23.6 billion for 279 projects.

3. Although the WBG is part of the U.N. organization, it is not subject to control by U.N. bodies. Instead, the bank is controlled by a Board of Governors, consisting of one governor from each member state, which meets annually. To be a member state, the prospective member must also become a member of the IMF. A controversial internal voting system provides that each member state's vote be weighed according to that member state's financial contributions. Each state receives 250 votes and an additional vote for each share it obtains in the bank's capital stock. Accordingly, the lion's share of the voting power falls to a short list of the wealthiest countries Table 10.1.

The Board of Governors meets only once per year, so the day-to-day operations of the WBG are delegated to twenty-four executive directors. France, Germany, Japan, the United Kingdom, and the United States each can appoint an executive director; other member countries nominate the remaining nineteen executive directors. By tradition, the United

Table 10.1 *IBRD Subscriptions and Voting Power: November 1, 2008[a]*

Member	Amount[b] (Percentage)	Votes (Percentage)
Afghanistan	30.0 (0.02%)	550 (0.03%)
Australia	2,446.4 (1.55%)	24,714 (1.53%)
China	4,479.9 (2.85%)	45,059 (2.78%)
El Salvador	14.1 (0.01%)	391 (0.02%)
France	6,939.7 (4.41%)	69,647 (4.30%)
Germany	7,239.9 (4.60%)	72,649 (4.49%)
Iran	2,368.6 (1.51%)	23,936 (1.48%)
Japan	12,700.0 (8.07%)	127,250 (7.86%)
Mexico	1,880.4 (1.20%)	19,054 (1.18%)
Russian Federation	4,479.5 (2.85%)	45,045 (2.78%)
United Kingdom	6,939.7 (4.41%)	69,647 (4.30%)
United States	26,496.9 (16.84%)	265,219 (16.38%)

[a] Millions of 1944 U.S. dollars.
[b] *See* http://siteresources.worldbank.org/BODINT/Resources/278027–1215524804501/
IBRDCountryVotingTable.pdf.

States nominates the World Bank president, who serves as chair of the Board of Governors, subject to the approval of the Board of Governors.

Amendments to the bank's Articles of Agreement, which provide for this organizational structure, require three-fifths of the governors and 85 percent of the voting power. Note that the United States, with 16.38 percent of the voting power, is the only country that can unilaterally block an amendment to the Articles of Agreement.

The World Bank President Paul Wolfowitz (2005–07), former secretary of state in the administration of U.S. President George W. Bush, resigned after a World Bank ethics committee found that a relationship between Wolfowitz and Shaha Ali Riza, World Bank senior communications officer (and acting manager of external affairs) for the Middle East and North Africa Regional Office, placed him in a conflict of interest in violation of the World Bank's Code of Conduct. Wolfowitz was replaced as president of the World Bank by Robert B. Zoellick on July 1, 2007; until the time of his nomination, Zoellick was serving as deputy secretary of the U.S. State Department.

4. From 1944 until the early 1990s, there was no official channel through which to pursue redress inside the World Bank Group if a bank was in violation of internal policies. Intense international scrutiny of projects in which the World Bank Group was involved, including by environmental NGOs, led to the creation of the World Bank Inspection Panel in 1993 and the office of the Compliance Advisor Ombudsman in 1999.

Multilateral Development Banks and Burma, Bank Information Center 1–7 (Oct. 2004) (tables and boxes omitted), http://www.bicusa.org/en/Article.1629.aspx

[Multilateral development banks] say that their operations and projects are intended to reduce poverty and to encourage economic development. Critics argue, however, that MDBs tend to impose economic principles that favor liberalization and privatization regardless of whether such principles are best suited for the situation in the country receiving assistance. Further, MDB projects are conducted often without genuine consultation with the affected people and civil society in the recipient country. MDB funding often fall[s] prey to corruption. MDB-funded projects also have caused severe damage on the local environment and population. Because of MDB projects, citizens in many countries are facing problems such as reduction in jobs, rising cost of water, environmental degradation, and involuntary resettlement without adequate compensation.

. . .

[MDBs] provide financial support and advice for economic and social development activities in developing countries. MDBs are called "banks" but they are different from commercial banks in that they give grants in addition to loans. The grants and loans generally are for countries, not individual people. Here, "multilateral" means multiple countries, and MDBs are owned by different countries that pay money to be members (shareholders) of the MDBs. Assistance from MDBs is similar to economic aid from developed countries, but because the MDBs are owned by different countries, the decision-making process of MDBs is more complex.

MDBs give financial support to activities and projects in the context of national development of the recipient country. For example, MDBs may extend loans for an infrastructure[-]building program (e.g. highway or a dam), or for reforming sectors in the recipient country's so that the sectors will be administered more efficiently (e.g. water sector or agricultural sector). For developing countries, MDBs generally are a significant source of financial support for their development plans.

The founding document of each MDB set forth the MDB's purpose, organization, and operations. To become a member, a country must: (1) sign the founding document; (2) meet the requirements set forth in the founding document; and (3) buy shares of the MDB. Countries must buy shares regardless of whether it is a donor country or a borrowing country.

MDBs extend grants and loans, conduct research, and provide policy advice to developing country members. The financial assistance may be for specific activities aimed at poverty reduction and sustainable development, or for structural reforms in a sector or the economy of the country as a whole.

The world's low-income countries that cannot borrow money in international markets may receive grants, interest-free loans, and technical assistance from MDBs. MDBs have a certain process through which qualified countries may receive assistance on concessionary terms (low-interest loans with a long time to repay, and a long grace period). The International Development Association (IDA) at the World Bank and the Asian Development Fund at the ADB provide such concessional loans.

MDBs also conduct research on a country's sectors and economy. The result of the research is reflected in the assistance strategies for that country. The assistance strategies become a basis for the level and content of the MDBs' financial assistance to be provided to that country.

MDB projects are conceived, designed, and implemented according to a "project cycle." After a proposal for a project is fully developed, it is usually submitted to the Board for formal approval.

Different documents are developed at each stage of the project cycle. Documents concerning the protection of the environment or the livelihoods of local peoples (such as resettlement plans or environmental impact assessments) are generated during project preparation. The formal decision to finance the project (approval) is usually made by the Board of Executive Directors.

"Policies" guide the work of the MDBs. The MDBs are required to comply with the policies when they operate. Some of the policies are relevant to preventing or mitigating negative environmental and social impacts in the project area or local peoples.

II. The World Bank and Environmental Rights

A. *The Debate over Bank Policies*

For many years, the projects and activities funded by the major banks have been heavily criticized. *See* BRUCE RICH, MORTGAGING THE EARTH: THE WORLD BANK, ENVIRONMENTAL IMPOVERISHMENT, AND THE CRISIS OF DEVELOPMENT (1994). In recent years, even critics have recognized at least some progress. See John W. Head, *For Richer or For Poorer: Assessing the Criticism Direct at the Multilateral Development Banks*, 52 U. KAN. L. REV. 241 (2004) Yet criticisms remain. In this chapter, we focus on the World Bank as an exemplar both of problems and progress.

Sustainable Development: Rhetoric and Reform at the World Bank 4
TRANSNAT'L L. & CONTEMP. PROBS. 253, 255–70 (1994)
(selected footnotes omitted and replaced)

Kevin Huyser

. . .

WORLD BANK STRUCTURE AND OPERATIONS

Under the Bank's Articles of Agreement, all powers of the Bank are vested in a Board of Governors, consisting of one governor appointed by each member country. Unlike other international organizations, the Bank employs a weighted voting system in which a country's voting power is determined by the number of Bank shares owned. The Board of Governors then selects a Board of Executive Directors, which is delegated authority to carry out general operations of the Bank. The Executive Directors approve all loans and policy decisions of the Bank, though formal votes are rare; decisions are normally reached by consensus. The Executive Directors also select a President to serve as chief of the Bank's operating staff. Unlike the requirements in some other U.N. agencies, the Bank president is not limited by geographical quotas in selecting officers and staff, which contributed to the Bank's favorable reputation as an efficient international institution.

. . .

Under the Articles of Agreement, the Executive Directors are to "function in continuous session at the principal office of the Bank and shall meet as often as the business of the Bank may require." Though this provision suggests the Executive Directors exercise a fair amount of control over the Bank's operations, the staff is largely independent of the Executive Directors' intervention and influence because the staff works so closely with individual projects. This fact, coupled with the increasing numbers and complexity of proposed projects, gives the staff "considerable discretion to accept or resist new approaches, even if these approaches are 'sponsored' by the executive leadership."

The staff's discretion exists despite the existence of a formalized process of cost-benefit analysis for proposed projects–the Project Cycle. The first stage in this process is the Identification Phase. The concern here is the identification of projects suitable for Bank financing. Although borrowing countries are to bear the responsibility of identifying appropriate projects, in practice, the Bank staff often plays a large and influential role.

The second stage of the Project Cycle is the Preparation Phase. Here, the Bank and borrower "consider technical, institutional, financial, and economic conditions necessary to achieve a particular project's objectives." The Appraisal Phase follows and is the sole responsibility of the Bank. Bank staff members review all aspects of the project, and a resulting report serves as the basis for loan negotiations between the Bank and borrowing country. By this time, the Bank staff has worked closely with the project and its many technicalities, and, as a result, the Executive Directors usually place great confidence in the staff's appraisal of a particular project.

The Negotiations Phase is the fourth stage, with the Bank and borrower agreeing on the measures and legal obligations necessary to ensure success of the project. The Bank has complete discretion in setting terms on loans and guarantees. However, the Bank's apolitical nature is intended to limit this latitude. The Articles of Agreement state that the Bank and its officers shall not be "influenced in their decisions by the political character of the member or members concerned. . . . Only economic considerations shall be considered." In the past, the Bank has avoided attaching political conditions to loans, stressing instead economic criteria. Arguably, this apolitical nature allows the Bank to avoid many of the negative effects of politicization that have plagued international efforts of the United Nations and its specialized agencies in the past.

In the Implementation Phase, the borrower makes the majority of the decisions, though still subject to the terms of the loan agreement. The Bank's role is one of supervision and technical assistance. In the final stage, the Evaluation Phase, the Bank's project staff prepares a completion report, and the Bank's Operations Evaluation Department, an office separate from the operating staff and reporting directly to the Executive Directors, conducts an independent audit of the project.

Over the years, the Bank has slowly evolved from an international organization with an uncertain purpose to one with the primary role of reconstruction, only to later shift its focus to developmental aid. There can be little doubt today that the Bank is an enormously powerful and influential international organization. With its weighted voting system and arguably apolitical nature, the Bank has managed to avoid many of the shortcomings of other international agencies and organizations and has earned a degree of respect among many in the international financial community.

. . .

Negative Environmental Impact and the Bank's Response

Though the Bank experienced success in the rebuilding of a war-ravaged Europe, enabling it to shift its focus to aiding the development of DCs and LDCs, Bank funding of such projects resulted in numerous, costly environmental catastrophes.[1] Indeed, critics charge that the Bank's "development" projects have produced nothing but human misery and environmental wrongs.[2] Whether it be the predicted forced displacement of nearly 70,000 people and the flooding of some 875,000 acres of forest due to the Bank's support of the Narmada Valley Dam project in India or the acceleration of deforestation by capital-intensive agriculture and jungle colonization in the Bank's funding of the Polonoreste project in Brazil, the impact of the Bank's loans has been devastating.[3]

Yet despite its participation in such large-scale ecological disasters and its apparent disregard for the environment, the Bank was the first international organization to confront environmental concerns, recognizing and voicing the need to incorporate environmental safeguards into its development programs.[4] Indeed, by 1970 the Bank established the post of Environmental Advisor to evaluate the potential environmental effects of every investment project.[5] Though the Bank's move was no doubt largely a rhetorical response to environmental problems (especially in light of the numerous environmental disasters the Bank funded throughout the 1970s and 1980s), it was not until 1972 that the 114 nations participating in the United Nations Conference on the Human Environment in Stockholm placed the protection of the environment on the official agenda of international law and policy.[6]

In 1971, the Bank expanded its environmental staff by establishing the Office of Environmental Affairs.[7] At the time, identified projects under consideration were sent to the Office of Environmental Affairs early in the Project Cycle, and, if the project warranted it, the Bank conducted a detailed investigation into a project's potential environmental problems.[8] If more serious issues were discovered, the Bank conducted further evaluations in order to determine what solutions to include in the project's specifications.[9] The Bank consolidated and outlined its general guidelines and environment-related principles in an Operational Manual Statement (OMS) in 1984.[10] Again,

---

[1] See generally Bruce M. Rich, Multilateral Development Banks, Environmental Policy, and the United States, 12 Ecology L.Q. 681, 688 (1985) (discussing the adverse impact of projects planned and financed by the Bank resulting in the aggravation of massive deforestation, erosion, and desertification problems in DCs and LDCs).

[2] Dianne Dumanoski, A New Run on the World Bank's Policies, Boston Globe, Oct. 5, 1986, at A25.

[3] Id. See also Environmental Impact of World Bank Lending (Vol. I), Hearing Before the Subcomm. on Human Rights and International Organizations, and on International Economic Policy and Trade of the House Comm. on Foreign Affairs, 101st Cong., 1st sess. 99, 87 (1989) [hereinafter Hearing].

[4] See Note, Providing for Environmental Safeguards in the Development Loans Given by the World Bank Group to the Developing Countries, 5 Ga. J. Int'l & Comp. L. 540, 544 (1974).

[5] Robert McNamara, Speech to the U.N. Conference on Human Development (June 8, 1972), in The McNamara Years at the World Bank 197 (1981) [hereinafter McNamara Speech].

[6] Stockholm Declaration of the U.N. Conference on the Human Environment, June 16, 1972, U.N. Doc. A/CONF. 48/14 (1972), 11 I.L.M. 1416 (1972) [hereinafter Stockholm Declaration; see also Lynton K. Caldwell, International Environmental Policy 55 (1990).

[7] McNamara Speech, supra note 6, at 199.

[8] Ibrahim F.I. Shihata, The World Bank and the Environment: A Legal Perspective, 16 Md. J. Int'l L. & Tr. 1, 4 (1992).

[9] McNamara Speech, supra note 6, at 199; see also Shihata, supra note 10, at 5 (claiming that, according to reports maintained by the Office of Environmental Affairs, between July 1, 1971, and June 30, 1978, "63% of Bank-financed projects (1,342) revealed no apparent or potential environmental issues . . . [and projects that did] were dealt with through special studies carried out by Bank staff or consultants or by other agencies. . . . ").

[10] Shihata, supra note 9, at 5–6. The guiding principles of OMS No. 2.36 stated that the Bank:

    a. endeavors to ensure that each project affecting renewable natural resources does not exceed the regenerative capacities of the environment;

    b. will not finance projects that cause severe or irreversible environmental deterioration, including species extinctions without mitigatory measures acceptable to the Bank;

    c. will not finance projects that unduly compromise the public's health and safety;

    d. will not finance projects that displace people or seriously disadvantage certain vulnerable groups without undertaking mitigatory measures acceptable to the Bank;

the rhetoric of the policies and guidelines the Bank claimed to follow far exceeded the Bank's actual commitment to environmental protection.[11]

Between 1986 and 1990, when Mr. Barber Conable served as Bank president, a series of major environmental initiatives took place. In 1987 the Bank underwent a major reorganization, establishing an environmental department in each of the four regional divisions, as well as a central environmental department in the policy complex of the Bank.[12] In addition, the central environmental department instituted a broad-based environmental training program for Bank staff members.[13] The main reason for the reorganization and training "was to ensure that environmental considerations were fully integrated into all aspects of the Bank's operations."[14]

In 1990, the Bank, in conjunction with other international organizations, established the Global Environmental Facility (GEF).[15] This is an aid-funneling program administered by the United Nations Environment Program, the United Nations Development Program, and the Bank.[16] The GEF, a three-year pilot program, supports projects in developing countries by addressing four environmental concerns—ozone depletion, climate change, biodiversity, and the protection of international waters.[17]

Recognizing the need for greater incorporation of environmental concerns into development operations, the Bank issued its Operational Directive on Environmental Assessment (ODEA) 4.00 in 1989, and a subsequent revision in 1991.[18] The main purpose of the ODEA "is to standardize and formalize a process in which all projects to be financed by the Bank undergo a specific assessment."[19] With the issuance of the ODEAs, the Bank purported the environmental impact assessment to be as much a standard part of project preparation as economic, financial, institutional, and engineering analysis.[20]

Environmental review begins in the Identification Phase. The Bank screens all new projects and assigns each to one of four categories based upon the nature, magnitude, and sensitivity of environmental issues:[21]

---

e. will not finance projects that contravene any international environmental agreement to which the member country concerned is a party;

f. will not finance projects that could significantly harm the environment of a neighboring country without the consent of that country. The Bank is willing to assist neighboring members to find an appropriate solution in cases where such harm could result;

g. will not finance projects which would modify natural areas designated by international conventions as World heritage sites or Biosphere Reserves, by national legislation as national parks, wildlife refuges, or other protected areas; and

h. endeavors to ensure that projects with unavoidable adverse consequences for the environment are located in areas where the environmental damage is minimized, even at somewhat greater initial costs.

Id.

[11] For example, in early 1985, the Bank approved the Narmada Valley Dam project in India, yet neither the Staff Appraisal Reports nor the President's Reports to the Executive Directors addressed the project's environmental effects in great detail. GRAHAM SEARLE, MAJOR WORLD BANK PROJECTS 5, 23 (1987). According to the Bank, the project would flood nearly 825,000 acres of land and require the evacuation of approximately seventy thousand people. Id. at 27.

[12] Shihata, *supra* note 9, at 7.

[13] WORLD BANK, STRIKING A BALANCE: THE ENVIRONMENTAL CHALLENGE OF DEVELOPMENT 7 (1989) [hereinafter STRIKING A BALANCE].

[14] Shihata, *supra* note 9, at 7.

[15] WORLD BANK, THE WORLD BANK ANNUAL REPORT 1992, at 59 (1992).

[16] Id.

[17] Id.

[18] Id. at 58–59; see also Dennis J. Scott, *Making a Banking Turn*, 9 ENVTL. F. 21 (1992).

[19] Shihata, *supra* note 9, at 9.

[20] WORLD BANK, THE WORLD BANK ANNUAL REPORT 1990, at 65 (1990) [hereinafter 1990 ANNUAL REPORT].

[21] *Operational Directive 4.0-Annex A*, in THE WORLD BANK, TECH. PAPER NO. 139, ENVIRONMENTAL ASSESSMENT SOURCEBOOK 27, 30 (1991); R.J.A. GOODLAND, *The World Bank's Environmental Assessment Policy*, 14 HASTINGS INT'L & COMP. L. REV. 811, 816 (1991).

Category A – projects that may have a diverse and significant impact on the environment and thus require a full and complete environmental assessment.[22]

Category B – projects that may have only limited, specific environmental effects that should be investigated but do not warrant a complete, in-depth environmental analysis.[23]

Category C – projects for which an environmental analysis is not normally necessary.[24]

Category D – environmental projects that do not require an assessment, because environmental development is the planned focus.[25]

If required by the Bank's categorization of the project, the borrowing country conducts an environmental assessment, with any necessary assistance from the Bank, in the Preparation Phase.

During the Appraisal Phase, the Bank reviews the assessment with the borrower and determines whether the recommendations have been properly incorporated into the project design and economic analysis. The assessments also provide the basis for supervising the environmental considerations of project implementation. Borrowing countries must report compliance with environmental conditions, the status of mitigating measures, and the findings of monitoring program.

In the Evaluation Phase, project-completion reports are required to evaluate environmental effects. The reports are to take particular note of whether the original assessment anticipated the environmental effects, as well as determine the effectiveness of mitigating measures employed.

One of the most important elements of the revised ODEA, in contrast to its predecessor, is the Bank mandate that borrowing governments "take the views of affected groups and local nongovernmental organizations (NGOs) fully into account in project design and implementation, and in particular in the preparation of environmental assessments." In addition, the Bank claims it is unlikely that it will proceed with a project if a potential borrower "demurs or indicates that it is not in a position to release the report."

. . .

Questions and Discussion

1. The World Bank Group (WBG) is formally a specialized agency of the United Nations, but it is not subject to oversight in its activities by any U.N. organ. As we see in the following, the IBRD and the IDA are subject to a form of regulation by the World Bank Inspection Panel and the IFC and MIGA or are subject to the Office of the Compliance Advisor Ombudsman (CAO). Where the Inspection Panel or the CAO finds that a member bank of the WBG is involved in activity that is inconsistent with the bank's lending policies, the Inspection Panel or the CAO can make a recommendation to the bank's executive leadership to take action with regard to the project. Affected persons or their proper representatives concerned that a member bank of the WBG is violating an environmental right in contravention of the bank's lending policies may have recourse in either of these semi-independent channels. See Eisuke Suzuki & Suresh Nanwani, *Responsibility of International Organizations: The*

---

[22] *Operational Directive 4.0-Annex A, supra* note 23, at 30; GOODLAND, *supra* note 23, at 816. Projects typical of this group include dams and reservoirs, large-scale irrigation and drainage, land clearing and leveling, transportation projects, and projects that run the risk of causing a serious environmental accident. 1990 ANNUAL REPORT, *supra* note 23, at 64–65.

[23] *Operational Directive 4.0-Annex A, supra* note 23, at 30; GOODLAND, *supra* note 23, at 816. Projects typical of this group include development projects similar to those in category A but on a smaller scale. 1990 ANNUAL REPORT, *supra* note 23, at 64–65.

[24] *Operational Directive 4.0-Annex A, supra* note 23, at 30; GOODLAND, *supra* note 23, at 816. Such projects include those directed towards education, family planning, health, nutrition, institutional development, and technical assistance. 1990 ANNUAL REPORT, *supra* note 22, at 64–65.

[25] *Operational Directive 4.0-Annex A, supra* note 23, at 30. Under the 1991 revision of the ODEA, category D is eliminated.

Accountability Mechanisms of Multilateral Development Banks, 27 MICH. J. INT'L L. 177, 203–18 (2005).

2. Should the World Bank's Articles of Agreement be amended to include the assistance of sustainable development and the prevention of environmental harm in its stated purposes, objectives, and powers?

3. The most severe critic of the World Bank is perhaps Bruce Rich, an attorney for the Environmental Defense Fund, whose book MORTGAGING THE EARTH: THE WORLD BANK, ENVIRONMENTAL IMPOVERISHMENT, AND THE CRISIS OF DEVELOPMENT (1994) takes the World Bank to task for its environmental insensitivity. Rich's criticism is summarized as follows:

> The book starts with a richly painted scenario: the 1991 meeting of the World Bank and International Monetary Fund (IMF) nations in Bangkok, Thailand. Rich chronicles the Thai government's expensive charade, which was intended to make the delegates believe that Bangkok is an economic growth wonderland by forcibly relocating slum neighborhoods and by redirecting services from the disadvantaged local people to the meeting delegates. Rich contrasts the luxurious facade of the World Bank/IMF meeting to a "People's Forum" organized by more than 200 Thai NGOs held simultaneously with the World Bank/IMF extravaganza.
>
> Rich uses speakers at the People's Forum to introduce the kinds of World Bank development activities largely responsible for environmentally problematic development. First, he notes hydroelectric development in Thailand and elsewhere. Through these scenarios he posits ill-conceived population resettlement programs as a significant problem caused by the Bank's "high-handed technocratic negligence," Rich explains how the World Bank seduced the Thai government in the 1950s into creating an independent power agency, the Electric Generating Authority of Thailand (EGAT), and describes how EGAT in turn perpetuated forced resettlements of thousands of Thais with the end result that they were plunged further into poverty in the name of "development."
>
> In *Mortgaging the Earth* Rich repeatedly cites resettlement programs as a prime example of how World Bank projects accentuate the poverty of those who either are already impoverished or exist at the margin. The author, however, does give somewhat grudging approval to a 1980 World Bank policy requiring borrowers to develop resettlement and rehabilitation plans – in consultation with and the approval of the affected population – intended to place them in no worse an economic situation than before resettlement. Notwithstanding this policy, Rich consistently criticizes these Bank resettlement programs as implemented.
>
> Rich calls misguided resettlement programs a problem of "superfluous people . . . a new class of poor, uprooted from every traditional link to the land and the local community" increasing with "almost demonic intensity" in the name of large-scale development activities. He places heavy blame for this problem on borrowing governments and their agencies for playing down the costs of resettlement to make projects seem more financially attractive and at times for their "sheer incompetence and corruption."
>
> After introducing the resettlement issue, Rich returns to the Bangkok People's Forum to describe the mistrust of the assembled villagers for EGAT's then-newest project, the Pak Mun dam. Rich begins with a discussion of some conclusions that recur throughout *Mortgaging the Earth:* World Bank projects usually do not perform as well as advertised as to their basic purpose – here irrigation and power production – or economic development in general; they often have serious adverse environmental consequences, and World Bank development is cloaked in secrecy – particularly from populations indigenous to the geographic area of the project.
>
> In the case of the Pak Mun dam, Rich describes a twelve-thousand signature petition to the World Bank to stop the project, EGAT's unwillingness to make environmental documentation generally available, and EGAT's threat of reprisals against villagers who

continued to protest the project. By citing what apparently is a Thai NGO study, Rich then comments on the failure of Thai dam projects – many funded by the World Bank – to meet their objectives. This study notes that the nine major irrigation dams provided water to less than half of their planned areas and that only one of the "numerous" hydroelectric dams achieved or exceeded its power production goals in the past decade. The discussion then launches into one of the subthemes of the book, that pure supply-sided power projects are misguided and that more emphasis should be placed on energy efficiency or conservation measures, or "demand-side" projects. Rich cites to a U.S. AID researcher's estimate that demand-side projects could have the same effect as the Pak Mun dam project at less than a quarter of the cost.

Rich returns again to the People's Forum to introduce the next category of what he believes is misguided development: "destructive World Bank-fostered agricultural policies." This includes development of export crops – for example, sugar cane, palm oil, rubber, and timber – as well as programs such as industrial shrimp farming. In one paragraph Rich criticizes programs leading to widescale erosion. Several paragraphs later he criticizes a reforestation program despite its beneficial effects on erosion because it also included a large resettlement effort and because the new forests would be used to create industrial pulp for export trade. While Rich describes his views as to potential problems with World Bank programs broadly, he defines acceptable solutions narrowly. With regard to deforestation, however, he suggests that he would support reforestation efforts through community forestry programs run by local farmers using local tree species.

Rich's recitation of development horrors continues throughout the book: deforestation and hydroelectric projects in Brazil; transmigration (large-scale forced population resettlement) in Indonesia; coal-fired power projects and irrigation projects in India; agriculture and livestock projects in Rwanda; and forest clearing in Malaysia.

Laurent R. Hourcle, Book Review, 28 GEO. WASH. J. INT'L L. & ECON. 721, 725–27 (1995) (footnotes omitted).

4.   Two World Bank officials, present the Bank's point of view:

Financial flows to developing countries alone do not by any means ensure sustainable development, but adequate financial resources are essential for a sustainable future in these countries. There are two reasons for this, one general and one specific. First, economic development and environmental health are mutually dependent. While the links between population growth, poverty, and environmental damage are still not fully understood, the vicious cycle of poverty and environmental degradation is well-illustrated throughout the developing world. The world's poor directly suffer from environmental degradation, in the forms of soil erosion, polluted air and water, and declining fish stocks, for example. While at the same time, people living on less than one dollar per day tend to cause much of the environmental damage, such as depleting agricultural resources, their only source of sustenance, by overworking marginal lands.

. . .

Second, additional targeted investments, estimated by the World Bank to represent roughly two percent of Gross Domestic Product, are required to address priority environmental concerns. These include programs to remedy past environmental damage, such as cleaning up waste sites and replanting trees, as well as programs to avoid future damage, such as creating protected areas or building wastewater treatment plants.

[Multilateral Financial Institutions (MFIs)] are currently reshaping their lending patterns to help meet this need. World Bank financing for targeted environmental programs has risen by $5.6 billion since the Rio Earth Summit, to a total of over $10 billion. Because the World Bank only funds a portion of each project, this portfolio represents some $25 billion in investments supported by the World Bank. Moreover, because the World Bank, like all MFIs, finances its lending program by borrowing through the international bond markets, where its bonds are listed with the highest possible rating, it can provide loans at rates otherwise unavailable to developing countries. Thus, MFIs are the principal and most efficient mechanism for directing savings, mostly from industrialized countries, toward investments with high environmental and social, if not always short-term financial, pay-offs in developing countries.

                                         . . .

While financial flows are important, in the long run they are less important than the policy and institutional changes encouraged and enabled by such flows. Investments in air pollution control technology in the former Soviet Union, for example, are less important in terms of their long-term effects than reducing subsidies for energy or setting up a regulatory agency. Similarly, however plentiful the goodwill and financial resources directed at reducing deforestation in Africa, the creation of parks will fail if other incentives in the economy encourage people to cut down trees. Issues such as property rights, price regimes for farm products, and social equity all need to be addressed more broadly. Finally, ensuring that a specific project strictly adheres to Western environmental standards, such as environmental assessment requirements, is less important than developing standards appropriate to the country in question and building the capacity within that country to strengthen, monitor, and enforce those standards. MFIs play a unique role in supporting the policy reforms and institution-building required to achieve these wider objectives. First, MFIs' constituencies are the very economic, planning, and line ministries most able to effect the changes needed. Second, through initiating discussions with decisionmakers during project design, MFIs have a natural vehicle, or point-of-entry, for supporting such reforms. For example, the World Bank, through its energy loans in Eastern Europe, is aiming to promote the price regimes and regulatory frameworks that will increase energy efficiency and conservation. Similarly, loans to the Baltic States for the improvement of municipal water supplies and wastewater management have been used by the respective country's governments and supported by the World Bank as a first step in reconsidering comprehensive, regional strategies for river basin, wetland, and coastal-zone management. Third, their development experience and rapidly growing environmental portfolios and skills base give MFIs an important advantage, learning from experience what works and what does not. The World Bank is able to benefit from its experience in implementing environmental projects in sixty-two countries throughout the world. MFIs employ the largest group of environmental specialists in the world.

Surprisingly, MFIs are able to effect the most positive and durable changes through their technical and analytical work and not through their financial might. Environmental assessments (EAs) are a particularly good example. Since 1984 the World Bank has screened all of its projects for their environmental consequences, and since 1989, those projects deemed to have a potentially serious impact on the environment are subject to a full assessment to identify and evaluate likely impacts, analyze alternatives from an environmental perspective, and provide mitigation and management measures to eliminate or minimize any negative environmental effects. Also since 1989, and particularly since the Rio Earth Summit, governments, other development institutions, non-governmental organizations (NGOs), and increasingly the private sector, have established EA policies and procedures and are implementing them in a wide range of development projects.

Indeed, it is now unlikely that any major investment decision will be made without taking potential environmental consequences into account.

Andrew Steer & Jocelyn Mason, *A View from the World Bank*, 3 Ind. J. Global Legal Stud. 35, 37–41 (1995) (footnotes omitted).

B. *The World Bank Inspection Panel*

1. Beginnings

In June 1992, the World Bank published an independent review of its role in the Sardar Sarovar dam project on the Narmada River in India. The review was commissioned following broad international scrutiny of the negative environmental and social consequences of the Narmada River project, which involved 30 large, 135 medium, and 3,000 small dams, as well as $450 million in loans from the World Bank. For further details about the project, see Case Study II in the online Case Studies that accompany this text. The published review, known as the Morse Commission Report after its chair Bradford Morse, was an important step toward the establishment of channels of redress inside the World Bank.

Sardar Sarovar: The Report of the Independent Review

Letter from Bradford Morse (Chairman) and Thomas R. Berger (Deputy Chairman) to Lewis T. Preston (President, The World Bank) of June 18, 1992.

Dear Mr. President:

On 1 September 1991 we began our Independent Review of the Sardar Sarovar dam and irrigation projects in India. Since then we have spent much time in India; we conferred with ministers and officials of the Government of India and of the Governments of Gujarat, Maharashtra and Madhya Pradesh; we met with nongovernment organisations and concerned citizens; we received hundreds of submissions, We travelled throughout the Narmada valley, to villages and relocation sites, to the dam site, the upstream area, the command area, and downstream. We also visited Kachchh and other drought-prone areas of Gujarat.

We have talked to whomever we thought could help us in the task assigned to us, that is, to conduct an assessment of the measures being taken to resettle and rehabilitate the population displaced or otherwise affected by the Sardar Sarovar Projects, and of the measures being taken to ameliorate the environmental impact of the Projects.

The World Bank has made an important contribution to the advancement of human and environmental concerns by developing policies for the resettlement and rehabilitation of people displaced or otherwise affected by Bank supported projects and for the mitigation of the environmental effects of such projects. Similarly the government of India has developed a comprehensive environmental regime to reduce the environmental impact of public works projects. In spite of these positive factors, however, we believe that the situation is very serious. We have discovered fundamental failures in the implementation of the Sardar Sarovar Projects.

We think the Sardar Sarovar Projects as they stand are flawed, that resettlement and rehabilitation of all those displaced by the Projects is not possible under prevailing circumstances, and that the environmental impacts of the Projects have not been properly considered or adequately addressed. Moreover, we believe that the Bank shares responsibility with the borrower for the situation that has developed.

. . .

In 1985 the Bank entered into credit and loan agreements with the Government of India and the Governments of Gujarat, Madhya Pradesh and Maharashtra relating to the construction of the dam and the canal. Under these agreements the Bank has treated only the people whose villages will be affected by the submergence as "project-affected" persons entitled to be resettled and rehabilitated. Our first task has been to consider the measures being taken for the resettlement and rehabilitation of these people. But our Terms of Reference [the writ of the commission] refer to persons "displaced/affected by the reservoir and infrastructure." We were also asked by [World Bank] President Conable to consider, under our Terms of Reference, the status of resettlement and compensation for "canal-affected persons."

On the environmental side, our Terms of Reference require us to consider measures being taken to ameliorate the impact of "all aspects of the Projects." To do this we have reviewed the extent to which there has been compliance with the Bank's and India's requirements for the Projects. We have also considered hydrology and water management issues and their relationship to environmental impact upstream, downstream, and in the command area. Without an understanding of these matters it is impossible to appreciate what the environmental impact of the Projects may be, and thus to determine what ameliorative measures are appropriate.

. . .

Our Terms of Reference require us, in making our assessment, to consider all of the Bank's existing operational directives and guidelines, bearing in mind that the credit and loan agreements were approved in 1985. Under Bank policy at that time resettlement and rehabilitation and environmental impact had to be appraised at the threshold of a project. Yet there was no proper appraisal made of the Sardar Sarovar Projects; no adequate appraisals of resettlement and rehabilitation or of environmental impact, were made prior to approval. The Projects proceeded on the basis of an extremely limited understanding of both human and environmental impact, with inadequate plans in place and inadequate mitigative measures under way.

It is noteworthy that the Bank has seen fit to establish our review. The Bank has provided us with all necessary documents, has engaged in the frankest discussions with us, and has given us the latitude we needed to do our job. We think it unlikely that any other international aid organisation has ever established a review with a mandate as sweeping as ours in connection with a project, no matter how controversial. The Bank's willingness to do so is a tribute to its determination to understand what has gone wrong with the Projects. Similarly, we have had the cooperation of the Government of India, of the Governments of Gujarat Maharashtra and Madhya Pradesh, of NGOs, and of people affected by the Projects.

. . .

In 1990 the Bank announced a comprehensive resettlement policy applying to oustees generally, and in 1991 a specific resettlement policy relating to tribals. These policy statements reiterated and elaborated the principles laid down a decade earlier.

These Bank policies reflect the global adoption of new concepts of human rights. They constitute a recognition that large-scale projects, especially in rural, forested and frontier areas, may displace people just as do war and natural calamities. They focus on people who are being displaced by the advance of development, and require that in any project the human rights of the oustees must be respected. According to ILO 107, these are rights not to be impaired on grounds of national sovereignty or national interest. These considerations may justify undertaking a project but, according to ILO 107, they do not justify the nullification of these human rights if a project goes ahead. The governments of the three States claim that they are prepared to implement the Award of the Tribunal and to live by the Bank credit and loan agreements. There is disagreement, however, over interpretation. Gujarat, which has 4,700 oustee families, adopted a policy in 1988 which offers two hectares of land to all landed oustees. It also offers two hectares of land to those designated as landless; tribals and others who may be cultivating encroached land therefore receive two hectares of land. Under Gujarat's policy, in keeping with the Tribunal's Award, major sons also receive two hectares.

The Government of Gujarat and the Governments of Madhya Pradesh and Maharashtra contend that Gujarat's policy goes beyond the requirements set out in the Tribunal Award and the Bank agreements. Maharashtra, which may have as many as 3,000 families to be resettled, and Madhya Pradesh, with as many as 23,000 families to be resettled, are prepared to offer two hectares of land to landed oustees. But they are not willing to provide two hectares for major sons. Neither Madhya Pradesh nor Maharashtra acknowledges any rights of encroachers to adequate land on resettlement.

This disparity in State policies has resulted in a dispute over the meaning of the Tribunal Award and the requirements of the Bank credit and loan agreements. The dispute may seem technical but upon its outcome depends the chances of thousands of oustees to land on resettlement.

The first aspect of the dispute relates to major sons. It is said that Madhya Pradesh and Maharashtra are obliged under the Tribunal Award to provide two hectares for major sons of families displaced from revenue lands. Yet the direction by the Tribunal that every major son be treated as a separate family stands without qualification, express or implied. What other purpose would this provision serve except to enable each major son to claim the same entitlement as the family to which he belongs? In our view the failure of Madhya Pradesh and Maharashtra to provide a minimum of two hectares of land to each major son in any landed family constitutes non-compliance with the Tribunal Award.

Of course, even if the Tribunal's Award were to be adopted, as regards major sons, by Madhya Pradesh and Maharashtra, it would still benefit only the major sons of landed families, for the Tribunal did not acknowledge any right in encroachers to be treated as landed.

This brings us to the second aspect of the disagreement, relating to encroachers. As noted above, Madhya Pradesh and Maharashtra say that encroachers must be treated as landless oustees with no entitlement to adequate land for cultivation on resettlement. The dispute here is whether tribal people, holding their land by customary usage, are entitled to be treated as landed oustees. Madhya Pradesh and Maharashtra say they are not, that they are illegal occupiers.

The result is that, in Madhya Pradesh and Maharashtra, thousands of tribal families, who are classified as landless but who are in fact cultivating land, may not receive any or adequate land on resettlement. Both States have provided that encroachers who can prove that they were cultivating encroached land prior to a certain date (in Maharashtra, 1978; in Madhya Pradesh, 1987) will be entitled to have their interests recorded. But these arrangements depend on documented proof which does not often exist. We estimate that, under the States' view, at least 60 per cent of tribal oustees engaged in cultivating land in Madhya Pradesh and Maharashtra will not receive adequate land on resettlement.

There are more than 60 million tribal people in India, many of them dependent on land they and their forebears have cultivated for generations. In 1987 the United Nations World Commission on Environment and Development (the Brundtland Commission) addressed the need for respect for indigenous and tribal land and resource rights. It said:

> The starting point for a just and humane policy for such groups is the recognition and protection of their traditional rights to land and the other resources that sustain their way of life – rights they may define in terms that do not fit into standard legal systems.

Central to the Bank's credit and loan agreements with India and the three States is the objective requiring that *all* oustees, including those described as landless, be enabled as a result of resettlement and rehabilitation measures taken on their behalf, to *'improve or at least regain* the standard of living they were enjoying prior to their displacement' (emphasis added). How can this be guaranteed in the case of oustees for whom cultivation is their one skill and at the heart of their social, economic, and cultural lives, except by providing them, on resettlement, with land to cultivate? In 1984 the Narmada Control Authority, established to oversee the Projects, declared: 'For tribals, there is no rehabilitation more effective than providing land as the source of livelihood'. We have concluded that it is in fact the only way to ensure that they improve or at least regain their standard of living. The result of classifying encroachers as landless oustees means that people who are in fact cultivating land they regard as their own will become landless labourers. This is not rehabilitation. It does not leave them at least as well off as before.

The tribal people in Madhya Pradesh and Maharashtra are aware of the issue, and what it will mean for them if they are resettled as landless labourers. When we visited Bamni, a tribal village in Maharashtra, the people told us, 'We are farmers, not labourers'. In our view Maharashtra and Madhya Pradesh, in failing to provide adequate land on resettlement for rehabilitation of encroachers, have not complied with the Bank credit and loan agreements.

The States point out that under the Award and World Bank agreements all oustees have the right to resettle in Gujarat, where landed and landless oustees alike are to receive two hectares of irrigable land. Madhya Pradesh and Maharashtra contemplate that a very large number of oustees will therefore resettle in Gujarat. In fact, under Madhya Pradesh's plan for resettlement, its resettlement sites are to provide only 10 per cent of the land needed for its oustees.

But many oustees do not wish to go to Gujarat, for reasons which have to do with language, culture and other ties to their region. . . .

. . .

This raises questions about the right of choice provided for in the Tribunal Award and by the Bank agreements. That right ensures that displaced families, though obliged to leave their homes, ought not to be compelled to leave their home State. It is true that the bare right of choice remains. But the disparity in benefits means that they must choose between migrating to Gujarat or giving up their standard of living.

The only resettlement policy applicable to all three States is the Bank's. But Bank policy has not been respected. The Projects were not appraised in accordance with Bank requirements, basic information had not been gathered and adequate plans for resettlement and rehabilitation were not in place.

Notwithstanding Gujarat's success in providing land for submergence oustees, it has not provided land on resettlement for those oustees displaced in 1960–61, when the lands of six villages of Kevadia were expropriated to establish the construction site for the dam. To be sure, some of these villagers have received a measure of cash compensation. But since 1985 these people have been covered by the Bank agreements. Their entitlement to land should have been acknowledged seven years ago, yet the Bank has failed to secure an acknowledgment by Gujarat of their entitlement under the Bank agreements, let alone conveyance of appropriate lands.

Indeed, it is only recently that the Bank has urged – though it has never insisted – that India and the States comply with the 1979 Tribunal Award regarding major sons, and develop policies to match the overarching objective of the Bank agreements in order to ensure land for encroachers.

Nor is it only that the Bank has failed to enforce the Award and agreements. It has, in the case of the canal, failed to obtain a covenant in its agreement with Gujarat to require compliance with Bank policy. What about those villagers living in the path of the canal? Construction of the canal and irrigation system will affect as many as 140,000 families, of whom perhaps 13,000 – no one knows how many – will lose much or all of their land. People losing land to the canal and irrigation system are offered compensation under the Land Acquisition Act of 1984. The number of such persons is a matter of competing estimates. But this much is clear: acquisition of land under the Land Acquisition Act has often meant that farmers losing land have been compensated at rates substantially lower than replacement costs.

The responsibility in this regard appears to us to rest with the Bank. It did not include resettlement benefits for canal oustees in the 1985 credit and loan agreements, even though such had been a part of Bank policy for five years. Evolving respect for human rights has established new norms for resettlement and rehabilitation. The Bank's policies have been influential in establishing these norms, and India has adopted many of them. It ratified ILO 107 in 1958. India and the three riparian States signed the 1985 credit and loan agreements with the Bank.

At the end of the day, however, the failure of India and the States to enforce the relevant provisions of the Tribunal Award and the Bank agreements, and the Bank's failure to enshrine its policies in the agreements, mean that involuntary resettlement resulting from the Sardar Sarovar Projects offends recognised norms of human rights – human rights that India and the Bank have been in the forefront to secure.

In 1972, after the Stockholm Conference, a new consciousness of environmental issues emerged. In India, as elsewhere, in the 1970s and 1980s this was reflected in new environmental laws, guidelines and practices. We have already noted the absence in India of a national policy in the field of resettlement and rehabilitation (the matter is regarded as a State responsibility). In the environmental field, however, the Government of India has developed a comprehensive structure of policies for environmental protection and assessment of environmental impact.

In 1983 environmental clearance for the Sardar Sarovar Projects was not forthcoming from India's Ministry of Environment and Forests because of a lack of information on environmental impact. In 1985 the Bank approved the credit and loan for the Projects. An appropriate environmental assessment was not made. In the Bank's 1985 Staff Appraisal Report no mention is made of the controversy that was holding up environmental clearance in India. The Bank required an environmental work plan by December 1985. It was not done. The date was extended to 1989. The work plan is still not available.

It was not until 1987 that a conditional environmental clearance for the Projects was given by India's Ministry of Environment and Forests. It was provided in the clearance that, instead of environmental impact studies being done before approval of the Projects, they were to be done pari passu, that is, concurrently with construction – an approach that we believe undermines the very basis for environmental planning. There was, however, an explicit schedule providing for the completion of the environmental impact studies by 1989. Most of the studies were not completed by 1989. Many have still not been completed. Without proper data and studies, proper assessments of environmental impact cannot be made and effective ameliorative measures cannot be developed.

The history of the environmental aspects of Sardar Sarovar is a history of noncompliance. There is no comprehensive impact statement. The nature and magnitude of environmental problems and solutions remain elusive. This feeds the controversy surrounding the Projects. As with the resettlement and rehabilitation issues, this has placed our review in a difficult position. To complete our work, we have had to assemble basic ecological information to establish the likely effects of the Projects upstream, downstream and in the command area. This work should have been done by others before the Projects were approved.

The design and operation of a multi-purpose project like the Sardar Sarovar Projects depends on the hydrology of the river. Understanding impacts, therefore, begins with an understanding of the hydrology and the nature of the changes that will be caused by the engineering works.

During the proceedings before the Narmada Water Disputes Tribunal, the States agreed on a figure of 28 MAF as the average annual stream flow to be expected three years out of four. The Tribunal accepted this figure as a basis for the apportionment of the benefits of the Projects. It also provided a benchmark for design of the dam and canal.

We found discrepancies in basic hydrological information related to these works. We therefore examined the streamflow data and did our own analysis. We found that there is good reason to believe that the Projects will not perform as planned. The problems relate to the sequence and timing of streamflows and the capacity of the dam and canal to store and divert water. The effects of Sardar Sarovar upstream, downstream and in the command area, therefore, will be different from what has been assumed to date whether or not the upstream NSP is built as planned. A realistic operational analysis upon which to base an environmental assessment is lacking. This alarmed us and it should alarm others, especially for a megaproject with such far-reaching implications as Sardar Sarovar.

For the area upstream of the dam there are piecemeal studies that suggest that the impact on biodiversity will be minimal. But there has been no attempt properly to assess the cumulative impacts arising from the NSP. Although the NSP is not within our terms of reference, the resulting cumulative impacts will almost certainly be serious. The Bank has placed itself in a difficult position by agreeing to proceed with the SSP before the environmental implications of directly related projects upstream are understood.

Programmes in the upstream region for compensatory afforestation and catchment area treatment are under way. We believe that these programmes, however successful in the short term, are likely to fail because of the lack of participation by local people. It is our view that achieving the necessary cooperation is not likely to be possible within the construction schedule imposed by Sardar Sarovar.

The backwater effect of sedimentation upstream of the dam is also an issue which has been ignored. Our analysis indicates this effect could mean a rapid, continuing, and cumulative rise in water level in the river above the reservoir. This can cause flooding to extensive areas of densely populated farmland. The human and environmental impacts could well be severe.

The construction of a dam on a free-flowing river has obvious implications for the downstream ecosystem, all the more so when proposed developments upstream will divert most of the river flows. But we found that no assessment of downstream impact has been done. Some of the basic information is only now being gathered. The implications of the Sardar Sarovar Projects for the geomorphology of the lower reaches of the river and its estuary and for the fishery and the people living in the region are unknown. We were able to assemble enough information to indicate that the impacts will be serious. It is likely, for example, that the hilsa fishery, the largest on the west coast, on which thousands of people depend, will suffer severe losses or be eliminated completely. The mitigative measures currently proposed are inadequate.

The shortcomings we have found in environmental assessment also extend into the command area. Although properly integrated studies are lacking, we have found that there are likely to be serious problems with waterlogging and salinity. Assumptions used in design of the canal and irrigation network, and on the development of mitigative measures, are questionable. We can only conclude that, when taken together, the problems that will arise in the command area will be quite similar to those identified by the Bank in many other irrigation projects in its 1991 India Irrigation Sector Review.

The priority water use is domestic consumption. We were surprised therefore to find that the plans for the delivery of water to the people in the villages and other centres in the drought-prone regions of Gujarat were only in the earliest stages of development. Apart from guidelines and intentions, we had little to review. We could not make any proper assessment as required by our Terms of Reference.

We have been conscious throughout our review of the close connection between the Projects' engineering design and the human and environmental impacts. This can be most clearly observed in the field of public health.

Large-scale irrigation projects such as the Sardar Sarovar Projects are known to carry health risks. From the first phases of construction, through creation of canals and ponds, to establishment of the reservoir itself, there are inevitable dangers, of a large-scale increase in water-borne diseases. These have been documented since the 1930s, and World Bank-assisted projects have witnessed some of the problems that can occur.

Yet, as recently as January 1992, we find that the Bank's consultant says that the Sardar Sarovar Projects appear to have been 'planned, designed and executed without incorporation of Health Safeguards'. He describes various parts of the Projects as 'death traps' and as 'taking Malaria to the doorsteps of the villagers' and as creating' ideal breeding sites' for malarial mosquitoes. He reported a total collapse of vector control measures. The incidence of malaria has risen sharply in villages near the dam; local clinics have recorded deaths from malaria. The failure to anticipate and prevent malarial hazards is a part of the failure to implement measures to mitigate the impacts of the Projects.

The Bank is now proposing a Narmada Basin Development Project, and is considering providing a US $90 million credit for this purpose. The connections between this project and Sardar Sarovar are many. Although the Basin Development Project appears to address many of the problems raised during our review, and we recognise that some parts have merit, we have concluded that it will not succeed in meeting the stated objective as 'a comprehensive programme to tackle the growth and sustainability needs of the basin'. Furthermore, the staff appraisal report for the proposed Basin project fails to acknowledge the linkages that also exist with the NSP. The Bank may be moving incrementally towards involvement in another major development project without prior consideration of the possible social and environmental consequences.

In spite of non-compliance with Bank resettlement and environmental requirements, the Sardar Sarovar Projects are proceeding – in the words of Chief Minister Patel of Gujarat – as 'an article of faith'. It seems clear that engineering and economic imperatives have driven the Projects to the exclusion of human and environmental concerns. Social and environmental tradeoffs have been made that seem insupportable today.

The Bank has followed what it describes as an incremental strategy, in an attempt to secure compliance with its resettlement policies. India has done much the same in its adoption of the pari passu principle with regard to environmental issues. These approaches, however, have failed to achieve their objectives. Moreover, they signify that these crucial matters – resettlement and environment – are of only secondary importance.

We are well aware of the scale of the development task facing India, of the importance India places on irrigation in increasing production in the agricultural sector, and of the longstanding partnership between India and the Bank in this endeavour. But our Terms of Reference are specific. They require us to consider the Bank's policies, India's environmental regime, and the credit and loan agreements. These emerge from the context of Bank-India relations just as surely as does the longstanding partnership in the enhancement of agricultural production between the Bank and India. If there was no intention of following Bank policy or India's regulatory regime, it would have been appropriate to acknowledge this. In any event, the incremental strategy has been counter-productive.

The Bank, in crafting our Terms of Reference, invited specific recommendations which "should include, as appropriate, any recommendations for improvement of project implementation.".... If essential data were available, if impacts were known, if basic steps had been taken, it would be possible to know what recommendations to make. But we cannot put together a list of recommendations to improve resettlement and rehabilitation or to ameliorate environmental impact, when in so many areas no adequate measures are being taken on the ground or are even under consideration.

Important assumptions upon which the Projects are based are now questionable or are known to be unfounded. Environmental and social trade-offs have been made and continue to be made, without a full understanding of the consequences. As a result, benefits tend to be overstated, while social and environmental costs are frequently understated. Assertions have been substituted for analysis.

Every decision as to the Sardar Sarovar Projects has always been, and will continue to be, a decision for India and the States involved. Together, they have spent a great deal of money. The foundations of the dam are in, the dam wall is going up, the turbines have been ordered and the canal is completed to the Mahi River. No one wants to see this money wasted. But we caution that it may be more wasteful to proceed without full knowledge of the human and environmental costs. We have decided that it would be irresponsible for us to try to patch together a series of recommendations on implementation when the flaws in the Projects are as obvious as they appear to us. As a result, we think that the wisest course would be for the Bank to step back from the Projects and consider them afresh. The failure of the Bank's incremental strategy should be acknowledged.

Whatever decisions the Bank makes about its role in the Projects, it must bear in mind the critical importance of consultation with the people of the valley and along the route of the canal. Such consultation would be in accord with the Brundtland Report, which said that in the case of tribal people, "they must be given a decisive voice in the formulation of resource policy in their areas." The same must be achieved for non-tribals as well. As Prime Minister Rajiv Gandhi said to the United Nations on the adoption by the General Assembly of the Brundtland Report, "The search for the right answers must go on relentlessly. It is a worldwide endeavour to which [I]ndia pledges its unstinting support."

Chapter 17: Findings and Recommendations

We have completed an assessment of resettlement and environmental aspects of the Sardar Sarovar Projects. In this chapter we draw together the findings of our review, already explained in the preceding chapters, and set forth the recommendations which, in our judgment, are appropriate to these findings.

Resettlement and Rehabilitation

- The Bank and India both failed to carry out adequate assessments of human impacts of the Sardar Sarovar Projects. Many of the difficulties that have beset implementation of the Projects have their origin in this failure.
- There was virtually no basis, in 1985, on which to determine what the impacts were that would have to be ameliorated. This led to an inadequate understanding of the nature and scale of resettlement.
- This inadequate understanding was compounded by a failure to consult the people potentially to be affected.
- Failure to consult the people has resulted in opposition to the Projects, on the part of potentially affected people, supported by activists. This opposition has created great obstacles to successful implementation.
- In drafting the terms and conditions of the 1985 credit and loan agreements, the Bank failed to take adequate account of the fact that a large proportion of those at risk from the development of the Sardar Sarovar Projects are tribal people. This meant that insufficient account was taken of the principles enshrined in the Bank's 1982 Operational Manual Statement outlining its policies regarding tribal people.
- In these and other ways, the Bank failed to follow the principles and policies it set out in 1980 and 1982. In addition, the Bank's overarching principle embodied in the 1985 credit and loan agreements by which resettlement and rehabilitation were to be judged, namely that oustees improve or at least regain their standard of living as quickly as possible, was not consistently advanced or insisted upon with sufficient force or commitment.
- The Bank failed to consider the effects of the Projects on people living downstream of the dam. We recommend that the Bank develop a policy to deal with the plight of persons affected downstream. They may not come within the rubric of resettlement, but their situation should be addressed.
- As a result of both the inadequate database and the failure to incorporate provisions of the Bank's policies in the 1985 credit and loan agreements, the provisions for resettlement and rehabilitation do not adequately address the real needs of those to be affected.
- In particular, the agreements allowed a distinction between 'landed' and 'landless' oustees which failed to recognise the realities of life in the submergence villages.
- Similarly, the rights of encroachers were not acknowledged. The only way of implementing resettlement policy, at least in the case of the Sardar Sarovar Projects, in a way that restores

oustees' previous standard of living is by provision of adequate land. This is of special relevance to the oustees of Maharashtra and Madhya Pradesh.

- The people of the six villages affected by construction and development of Kevadia Colony were not appropriately and adequately compensated. The Bank failed to ensure that this be done as required by the 1985 agreements. We recommend that the Bank require India to provide land for the families of the six villages, with an adjustment for cash compensation received in the interim, as appropriate.
- Relocation and resettlement of the people of the rock-filled dyke villages was implemented in a way that meant that the Bank's overarching principle of resettlement and rehabilitation, i.e. that no one should suffer a fall in standard of living, was not likely to be achieved.
- The Bank failed to ensure that those affected by construction of the canal and irrigation system would be entitled to resettlement benefits.
- We recommend that the Bank should use its good offices to ensure that Gujarat provides resettlement benefits to canal-affected persons, especially those farmers who are rendered marginal or landless.
- The policies of the riparian States failed to anticipate the needs of major sons, and adopted what we regard as an unduly restrictive interpretation of the Tribunal Award's provision for major sons. Maharashtra and Madhya Pradesh continue to maintain this interpretation and provide inadequate benefits to major sons of landed families.
- In 1987–88 the Government of Gujarat expanded its resettlement and rehabilitation policies to provide two hectares of irrigable land to all oustees including the landless, encroachers and major sons. This represented a policy package that came nearer than any thus far set out anywhere in India to establishing a basis for successful resettlement.
- Despite Gujarat's improved policy, Maharashtra and Madha Pradesh continued to limit the provision of two hectares of land to 'landed' oustees. This means encroachers and major sons (including the major sons of landed oustees) are not entitled to benefits in their own States that meet the Bank's overarching principle of resettlement and rehabilitation. The proportion of oustees thus vulnerable to a reduced standard of living is at least 60 per cent.
- The disparity between Gujarat's policy and the policies of Maharashtra and Madhya Pradesh has meant that oustees' right to choose between relocation in Gujarat and their own State has been rendered meaningless.
- Implementation of resettlement in Maharashtra has been limited by both policy deficiencies and availability of irrigable land.
- Implementation of resettlement in Madhya Pradesh has been limited by policy deficiencies, inadequate institutional commitment, continuing failure of consultation and limited availability of suitable resettlement land.
- This state of affairs in Madhya Pradesh has produced a situation in which, even if Madhya Pradesh were to adopt a policy with benefits equal to Gujarat's, such a policy could not now be implemented, given the time necessary to meet the requirements of the Sardar Sarovar Projects.
- Resettlement of oustees in Gujarat has entailed a scattering of families and villages among many different sites. This is in part a result of choices made by oustees. It is also a result of inadequate land at resettlement sites to accommodate all oustees who wish to have land there. This has contributed to some separation of families, especially in the case of oustees from the rock filled dyke villages.
- Gujarat is unlikely to be able to resettle a large proportion of oustees from Maharashtra and Madhya Pradesh. Even if land were available for relocation sites, resettlement and rehabilitation at these sites presents major problems.

- The record of resettlement and rehabilitation in India, which has been unsatisfactory in virtually every project with a large resettlement component, should reasonably have prompted the Bank to adopt a less flexible standard for resettlement and rehabilitation of project-affected people. In this context, the Bank's incremental strategy to obtain compliance, made explicit in 1989, greatly undermines prospects for achieving successful resettlement and rehabilitation.

Environment

- Measures to anticipate and mitigate environmental impact were not properly considered in the design of the Projects because of a lack of basic data and consultation with the affected people.
- The Bank's appraisal took no account of the fact that environmental clearance in India was not forthcoming in 1983 from the Ministry of Environment and Forests because of insufficient information.
- Under the 1985 credit and loan agreements, the Bank required an environmental work plan to be developed by the end of 1985, later extended to 1989. It is still not available, resulting in a disjointed, piecemeal approach to environmental planning that is both inefficient and ineffective.
- In 1987 India's environmental clearance for the Projects was given, despite the fact that the information required prior to the Projects' clearance was unavailable. In order to overcome this deficiency, studies were to be conducted pari passu with construction. The clearance was conditional on completion of these basic studies by 1989. Most remain to be completed. We believe that the pari passu policy greatly undermines the prospects for achieving environmental protection.
- Significant discrepancies in the hydrological data and analyses indicate that the Sardar Sarovar Projects will not perform as planned either with or without the upstream NSP. A realistic operational analysis of the Projects upon which to base an impact assessment has not been done.
- The cumulative impacts of the SSP together with the related upstream developments, especially the NSP, are very likely to be far reaching, yet they have not been studied.
- The afforestation and catchment area treatment programmes proposed upstream are unlikely to succeed within the timetable of the Projects because of the lack of consultation with, and participation of, villagers in the affected areas.
- The compensatory afforestation approach being taken by Gujarat in Kachchh, if continued, will lead to a steady decline in the quality of forests. The practice of replanting marginal forest lands in substitution for better lands that will be submerged, means that the forests will be diminished in value.
- The impact associated with the backwater effect of sedimentation in the upper reaches of the reservoir has not been considered. Our assessment has concluded that it will be significant.
- The downstream ecological implications of dam construction have not been considered. Important but limited data have only recently begun to be collected. The downstream impacts are likely to be significant, including severe losses to, if not the elimination of, the last important hilsa fishery in western India.
- There has been no comprehensive environmental assessment of the canal and water delivery system in the command area. Information we have gathered leads us to believe that there will be serious problems with waterlogging and salinity. We also found that many of the assumptions used in project design and for the development of mitigative measures are suspect.
- Despite the stated priority of delivery of drinking water, there were no plans available for review.
- The existing threat from malaria within the command area is serious. The Projects have been designed and executed without appropriate safeguards. The failure to adopt measures to reduce

the likelihood of the spread of malaria illustrates the breakdown between assurances offered by the Bank and India and the reality on the ground. We recommend that the Bank use its good offices to ensure that preventive measures are taken as a matter of urgency to address the public health problems posed by water-borne diseases in the Projects area.

- The newly proposed Narmada Basin Development Project, although it appears to address some of the problems highlighted in our review, fails to address key issues, many of which are the same as have caused problems with the Sardar Sarovar Projects. Although some specific elements have merit, the Basin Development Project adopts a piecemeal approach, falling far short of the work that the Bank's own missions have said is needed for proper basin development. The implications of Narmada Sagar for basin development are overlooked.

- Bank requirements that the Basin Development Project not entail forced relocation and proceed on the basis of a participatory approach to forest management and catchment area treatment, as proposed, are laudable but unrealistic, given the hostility towards the Projects in the region and the time frames envisaged by the Projects.

The Bank

We have made findings that reveal a failure to incorporate Bank policies into the 1985 credit and loan agreements and subsequent failure to require adherence to enforceable provisions of these agreements. Much of what has gone wrong with Sardar Sarovar Projects is the result of such failures over a range of resettlement and rehabilitation and environmental matters.

How did this happen?

It is apparent that there has been, and continues to be, deep concern among Bank officers and staff that India should have the means to enhance agricultural production. The Sardar Sarovar Projects were seen as offering enormous benefits, especially in terms of delivery of drinking water and irrigation.

There developed an eagerness on the part of the Bank and India to get on with the job. Both, it seems, were prepared to ease, or even disregard, Bank policy and India's regulations and procedures dealing with resettlement and environmental protection in the hope of achieving much-needed benefits.

Experience worldwide, in developed as well as developing countries, has shown that by factoring m and allowing for human and environmental considerations at the outset, projects can be substantially improved. To be effective, resettlement and environmental planning must be integrated into the design of projects; otherwise they become costly and burdensome addons.

These considerations lead to an examination of issues that focus on the Bank itself. Our work in conducting the independent review has encouraged us to make a number of observations which may be of value. Embedded in the World Bank's operational directives is a resolve to establish ex ante project assessment. This requires an investment by the Bank of time and money and personnel with appropriate expertise, with on-the-ground studies and consultation as part of the planning of a project.

There should be a review of Bank procedures to ensure that the full reach of the Bank's policies is being implemented. The Bank should establish whether the problems we have found in the case of Sardar Sarovar are at issue in other projects m India and elsewhere. Our findings on this project may well indicate a need on the part of the Bank to strengthen quality control.

The Projects

The Terms of Reference provided that our assessment should include as appropriate, recommendations for improvement of implementation. The absence of proper impact assessments and the paucity of undisputed data have limited our ability confidently to make project-specific recommendations of the kind that were contemplated. We have limited ourselves to recommendations with respect to the Kevadia villagers, the canal oustees, downstream policy, and the protection of public health, that should be carried through regardless of the fate of the Projects.

Our findings indicate that the Sardar Sarovar Projects are beset by profound difficultly. These difficulties have their genesis in the earliest phase of the Bank's involvement in the Projects, for they turn on the absence of an adequate database and failure to consult with the people whose lives and environment were and continue to be affected.

Lack of data meant that the Bank was not able, in the early 1980s, to appraise the Projects properly. No one is sure about the impacts of the reservoir and the canal on either people or the land. Without knowing what impacts were likely to be, we find it difficult to the point of impossibility to assess measures by which they might be alleviated; much of our work has therefore been devoted to gathering our own limited information base.

People who live in the villages and depend on the resources of the valley should have played a central part in determining the Project's impact. Both their knowledge and their vulnerabilities are integral to any understanding of what is at issue. At the same time, failure to consult has fuelled intense opposition to the projects which, as we have pointed out, has itself become a serious obstacle to design and implementation of mitigative measures.

These factors – absence of adequate data, failure of consultation, and hostility towards the Projects in the Narmada Valley – bear on every aspect of implementation. Our Terms of Reference invite us to recommend measures to improve implementation. It seems to us that the essential condition, the very starting point of any such recommendation, requires that these underlying difficulties be addressed.

But the underlying difficulties – the failures that reach back to the origin of the Projects – cannot be overcome by a patchwork of studies. The limited information base which we constructed is inadequate for the purpose. Nor is it a question of applying more intense pressure to Maharashtra and Madhya Pradesh in order to secure improved resettlement policies. As we say, the difficulties are profound. The Bank's incremental strategy and India's pari passu policy, adopted to deal with resettlement and environmental problems, have for the most part failed. A further application of the same strategy, albeit in a more determined or aggressive form, would also fail. As long as implementation continues in these ways, problems will be compounded rather than mitigated.

Absence of human and environmental assessment ab initio creates the impression that the demands of engineering carry far more weight in the Bank than the needs of the people to be affected or of the environment. The Bank's incremental strategy (and the Bank's concurrence in India's pari passu policy) strengthen[s] this impression. Readiness to bear with non-compliance thereafter confirms it.

Decisions as to the future of the Sardar Sarovar Projects and the Bank's participation in them are within the exclusive domains of India and the Bank. But implementation of the Projects requires measures that go to the heart of the problems in which the resettlement and environmental components of the Sardar Sarovar Projects have become mired. We have been at pains in the section of this chapter summarising our findings to demonstrate how those problems of human and environmental impact encompass all aspects of the Projects, including the uncertainties of hydrology, the upstream questions, the impact downstream, the command area issues, the health risks, the deficiencies in resettlement policy and implementation in each of the three States as well as the canal. None of these issues can he ignored.

It seems to us that the matters we have raised are fundamental. It would be prudent if the necessary studies were done and the data made available for informed decision-making before further construction takes place. Implementation requires that the Bank take a step back. Otherwise, the possibility of making sound decisions will be further compromised.

Little can be achieved while construction continues. What would a step back achieve? First, it would afford an opportunity to design the kinds of human and environmental impact studies that are still needed. Second, it would permit the assessment of the results of such studies, to see whether modifications of the Projects might be in order. Third, it would provide a chance to consider what resettlement and rehabilitation policies might meet the needs of the oustees, and how these could be implemented in a way that is consistent with the Bank's policies and principles as set out in its Operational Manuals and Directives.

Even though proponents describe Sardar Sarovar as the most studied and least implemented project in India, we do not agree. The Projects may well be the most talked about in India, but the fact is that their human and environmental consequences have not been studied, and their engineering, design and operation would profit from further analysis.

There is a need to consider Sardar Sarovar in the social and environmental context of the Narmada valley as a whole, to consult, inform and involve the people affected by the Projects throughout the Narmada valley, those affected in the command area, and those living downstream. The opposition, especially in the submergence area, has ripened into hostility. So long as this hostility endures, progress will be impossible except as a result of unacceptable means.

A way must be found to rebuild confidence, to demonstrate goodwill, and to send out an unambiguous message that the Bank continues to be committed to its principles and its policies.

Reflections

In the case of the Sardar Sarovar Projects, India has bound itself to meet standards for resettlement and rehabilitation more exacting than any it had agreed to in the past.

We do not expect perfect justice; in an imperfect world it cannot be obtained. There is no doubt that in the national interest, people can be required to resettle. However, India, in conformity with the development of international standards of human rights, has subscribed to certain minimum conditions that must be observed even when the national interest is involved. They reflect the inalienable human rights of the oustees. We believe that these norms must be adhered to.

Nor do we insist upon an unattainable standard in environmental impact assessment and mitigation. However, to construct the Sardar Sarovar Projects, India has availed itself of world-class engineering technology. Should it settle for less than adequate standards in the application of social and environmental science?

We are aware of the statement in the eleventh principle of the Rio Declaration presented to the 1992 United Nations Conference on Environment and Development:

> Standards applied by some countries may be inappropriate and of unwarranted economic and social cost to other countries, in particular developing countries.

But the environmental standards for the Sardar Sarovar Projects were established by India itself. On the resettlement side, standards were determined by the Narmada Water Disputes Tribunal and agreed to by India and the States m the credit and loan agreements.

We have felt obliged to illuminate what we think are flaws in the Sardar Sarovar Projects. It should not be thought that these would only be found in India or confined to the Sardar Sarovar Projects. The fragile assumptions which have supported this project can be found elsewhere. Failure to consider the human rights of 'the displaced and failure to consider environmental impacts occur in the development of megaprojects in both developed and developing countries.

If the human rights obligations identified by ILO Convention 107 and in Bank policy are acknowledged and respected, if the commitment to the environment is real, and if these are properly integrated into project design at the outset, more effective and equitable development will ensue. Some believe that these requirements make it more difficult, often more costly, to build megaprojects like Sardar Sarovar. This implies that human and environmental costs are to be heavily discounted in project planning and execution. But hard lessons from the past have taught us that this is unacceptable. In some cases it may be that alternatives to projects that cause compulsory relocation on a large scale or severe environmental impact may have to be sought.

We have found it difficult to separate our assessment of resettlement and rehabilitation and environmental protection from a consideration of the Sardar Sarovar Projects as a whole. The issues of human and environmental impact bear on virtually every aspect of large-scale development projects. Ecological realities must be acknowledged, and unless a project can be carried out in accordance with existing norms of human rights – norms espoused and endorsed by the Bank and many borrower countries – the project ought not to proceed.

The Bank must ensure that in projects it decides to support the principles giving priority to resettlement and environmental protection are faithfully observed. This is the only basis for truly sustainable development.

Questions and Discussion

1. For more detailed study, you should review Case Study II in the online Case Studies that accompany this text and the questions that follow.
2. The revelations in the Morse Commission Report, and in particular the discovery that the Bank had widely failed to implement its own policies and agreements with respect to the environment and resettlement in the Sardar Sarovar project, precipitated a flood of demands from member countries and NGOs to implement measures to prevent a recurrence of the Sardar Sarovar mistakes. The Bank's critics pointed out that the Morse Commission had uncovered problems that were deeper than the Sardar Sarovar project alone; the Morse Commission Report noted that "problems besetting the Sardar Sarovar projects are more the rule than the exception to resettlement operations supported by the Bank." In response to international pressure following the Morse Commission Report, the World Bank executive directors created the Inspection Panel in September 1993, which in many ways was modeled after the Morse Commission.

2. Establishment of the Inspection Panel

IBRD Resolution 93–10 and IDA Resolution 93–6, adopted by the Bank's Board of Executive Directors on Sept. 22, 1993, *reprinted in* 34 I.L.M. 503, 520 (1995)

The Executive Directors:
Hereby resolve:

1. There is established an independent Inspection Panel (hereinafter called the Panel), which shall have the powers and shall function as stated in this resolution.

Composition of the Panel

2. The Panel shall consist of three members of different nationalities from Bank member countries. The President, after consultation with the Executive Directors, shall nominate the members of the Panel to be appointed by the Executive Directors.
3. The first members of the Panel shall be appointed as follows: one for three years, one for four years and one for five years. Each vacancy thereafter shall be filled for a period of five years,

provided that no member may serve for more than one term. The term of appointment of each member of the Panel shall be subject to the continuity of the inspection function established by this Resolution.

4. Members of the Panel shall be selected on the basis of their ability to deal thoroughly and fairly with the requests brought to them, their integrity and their independence from the Bank's Management, and their exposure to developmental issues and to living conditions in developing countries. Knowledge and experience of the Bank's operations will also be desirable.

5. Executive Directors, Alternates, Advisors and staff members of the Bank Group may not serve on the Panel until two years have elapsed since the end of their service in the Bank Group. For purposes of this Resolution, the term "staff" shall mean all persons holding Bank Group appointments as defined in Staff Rule 4.01 including persons holding consultant and local consultant appointments.

6. A Panel member shall be disqualified from participation in the hearing and investigation of any request related to a matter in which he/she has a personal interest or had significant involvement in any capacity.

7. The Panel member initially appointed for five years shall be the first Chairperson of the Panel, and shall hold such office for one year. Thereafter, the members of the Panel shall elect a Chairperson for a period of one year.

8. Members of the Panel may be removed from office only by decision of the Executive Directors, for cause.

9. With the exception of the Chairperson who shall work on a full-time basis at Bank head-quarters, members of the Panel shall be expected to work on a full-time basis only when their workload justifies such an arrangement, as will be decided by the Executive Directors on the recommendation of the Panel.

10. In the performance of their functions, members of the Panel shall be officials of the Bank enjoying the privileges and immunities accorded to Bank officials, and shall be subject to the requirements of the Bank's Articles of Agreement concerning their exclusive loyalty to the Bank and to the obligations of subparagraphs (a) and (d) of paragraph 3.1 and paragraph 3.2 of the Principles of Staff Employment concerning their conduct as officials of the Bank. Once they begin to work on a full-time basis, they shall receive remuneration at a level to be determined by the Executive Directors upon a recommendation of the President, plus normal benefits available to Bank fixed-term staff. Prior to that time, they shall be remunerated on a *per diem* basis and shall be reimbursed for their expenses on the same basis as the members of the Bank's Administrative Tribunal. Members of the Panel may not be employed by the Bank Group, following the end of their service on the Panel.

11. The President, after consultation with the Executive Directors, shall assign a staff member to the Panel as Executive Secretary, who need not act on a full-time basis until the workload so justifies. The Panel shall be given such budgetary resources as shall be sufficient to carry out its activities.

Powers of the Panel

12. The Panel shall receive requests for inspection presented to it by an affected party in the territory of the borrower which is not a single individual (i.e., a community of persons such as an organization, association, society or other grouping of individuals), or by the local representative of such party or by another representative in the exceptional cases where the party submitting the request contends that appropriate representation is not locally available and the Executive Directors so agree at the time they consider the request for

inspection. Any such representative shall present to the Panel written evidence that he is acting as agent of the party on behalf of which the request is made. The affected party must demonstrate that its rights or interests have been or are likely to be directly affected by an action or omission of the Bank as a result of a failure of the Bank to follow its operational policies and procedures with respect to the design, appraisal and/or implementation of a project financed by the Bank (including situations where the Bank is alleged to have failed in its follow-up on the borrower's obligations under loan agreements with respect to such policies and procedures) provided in all cases that such failure has had, or threatens to have, a material adverse effect. In view of the institutional responsibilities of Executive Directors in the observance by the Bank of its operational policies and procedures, an Executive Director may in special cases of serious alleged violations of such policies and procedures ask the Panel for an investigation, subject to the requirements of paragraphs 13 and 14 below. The Executive Directors, acting as a Board, may at any time instruct the Panel to conduct an investigation. For purposes of this Resolution, "operational policies and procedures" consist of the Bank's Operational Policies, Bank Procedures and Operational Directives, and similar documents issued before these series were started, and does not include Guidelines and Best Practices and similar documents or statements.

13. The Panel shall satisfy itself before a request for inspection is heard that the subject matter of the request has been dealt with by the Management of the Bank and Management has failed to demonstrate that it has followed, or is taking adequate steps to follow the Bank's policies and procedures. The Panel shall also satisfy itself that the alleged violation of the Bank's policies and procedures is of a serious character.

14. In considering requests under paragraph 12 above, the following requests shall not be heard by the Panel:

    (a) Complaints with respect to actions which are the responsibility of other parties, such as a borrower, or potential borrower, and which do not involve any action or omission on the part of the Bank.

    (b) Complaints against procurement decisions by Bank borrowers from suppliers of goods and services financed or expected to be financed by the Bank under a loan agreement, or from losing tenderers for the supply of any such goods and services, which will continue to be addressed by staff under existing procedures.

    (c) Requests filed after the Closing Date of the loan financing the project with respect to which the request is filed or after the loan financing the project has been substantially disbursed. [This will be deemed to be the case when at least ninety five percent of the loan has been disbursed.]

    (d) Requests related to a particular matter or matters over which the Panel has already made its recommendation upon having received a prior request, unless justified by new evidence or circumstances not known at the time of the prior request.

15. The Panel shall seek the advice of the Bank's Legal Department on matters related to the Bank's rights and obligations with respect to the request under consideration.

Procedures

16. Requests for inspection shall be in writing and shall state all relevant facts, including, in the case of a request by an affected party, the harm suffered by or threatened to such party or parties by the alleged action or omission of the Bank. All requests shall explain the steps already taken to deal with the issue, as well as the nature of the alleged actions or omissions and shall specify the actions taken to bring the issue to the attention of Management, and Management's response to such action.

17. The Chairperson of the Panel shall inform the Executive Directors and the President of the Bank promptly upon receiving a request for inspection.

18. Within 21 days of being notified of a request for inspection, the Management of the Bank shall provide the Panel with evidence that it has complied, or intends to comply with the Bank's relevant policies and procedures.

19. Within 21 days of receiving the response of the Management as provided in the preceding paragraph, the Panel shall determine whether the request meets the eligibility criteria set out in paragraphs 12 to 14 above and shall make a recommendation to the Executive Directors as to whether the matter should be investigated. The recommendation of the Panel shall be circulated to the Executive Directors for decision within the normal distribution period. In case the request was initiated by an affected party, such party shall be informed of the decision of the Executive Directors within two weeks of the date of such decision.

20. If a decision is made by the Executive Directors to investigate the request, the Chairperson of the Panel shall designate one or more of the Panel's members (Inspectors) who shall have primary responsibility for conducting the inspection. The Inspector(s) shall report his/her (their) findings to the Panel within a period to be determined by the Panel taking into account the nature of each request.

21. In the discharge of their functions, the members of the Panel shall have access to all staff who may contribute information and to all pertinent Bank records and shall consult as needed with the Director General, Operations Evaluation Department and the Internal Auditor. The borrower and the Executive Director representing the borrowing (or guaranteeing) country shall be consulted on the subject matter both before the Panel's recommendation on whether to proceed with the investigation and during the investigation Inspection in the territory of such country shall be carried out with its prior consent.

22. The Panel shall submit its report to the Executive Directors and the President The report of the Panel shall consider all relevant facts, and shall conclude with the Panel's findings on whether the Bank has complied with all relevant Bank policies and procedures.

23. Within six weeks from receiving the Panel's findings, Management will submit to the Executive Directors for their consideration a report indicating its recommendations in response to such findings. The findings of the Panel and the actions completed during project preparation also will be discussed in the Staff Appraisal Report when the project is submitted to the Executive Directors for financing. In all cases of a request made by an affected party, the Bank shall, within two weeks of the Executive Directors' consideration of the matter, inform such party of the results of the investigation and the action taken in its respect, if any.

Decisions of the Panel

24. All decisions of the Panel on procedural matters, its recommendations to the Executive Directors on whether to proceed with the investigation of a request, and its reports pursuant to paragraph 22, shall be reached by consensus and, in the absence of a consensus, the majority and minority views shall be stated.

Reports

25. After the Executive Directors have considered a request for an inspection as set out in paragraph 19, the Bank shall make such request publicly available together with the recommendation of the Panel on whether to proceed with the inspection and the decision of the Executive Directors in this respect. The Bank shall make publicly available the report submitted by the Panel pursuant to paragraph 22 and the Bank's response thereon within two weeks after consideration by the Executive Directors of the report.

26. In addition to the material referred to in paragraph 25, the Panel shall furnish an annual report to the President and the Executive Directors concerning its activities. The annual report shall be published by the Bank.

Review

27. The Executive Directors shall review the experience of the inspection function established by this Resolution after two years from the date of the appointment of the first members of the Panel. . . .

Questions and Discussion

1. In most courts, the complaining party must show something like a sufficient level of interest in the matter being litigated, or a close enough relation to the harm alleged, to be entitled to any relief. Paragraphs 12–14 set out a number of eligibility criteria that parties bringing requests for inspection before the Inspection Panel must meet. The requesting party must either be an "an affected party in the territory of the borrower" or a representative of that party. If the requesting party is a representative, that representative must be local unless "the party submitting the request contends that appropriate representation is not locally available" and the executive directors agree. In other words, an environmental NGO located in the United States desirous of representing a party affected by a World Bank project in Nepal before the Inspection Panel could do so only in the rare case that the executive directors agreed that local representation was not available in Nepal.

   Paragraph 12 requires that the complaining party be prepared to demonstrate that "its rights or interests have been or are likely to be directly affected by an action or omission of the Bank as a result of a failure of the Bank to follow its operational policies and procedures with respect to the design, appraisal, and/or implementation of a project financed by the Bank" where that failure "has had, or threatens to have, a material adverse effect." Paragraph 13 further requires that the issue being complained of "has been dealt with by the Management of the Bank and Management has failed to demonstrate that it has followed, or is taking adequate steps to follow the Bank's policies and procedures." The Inspection Panel is instructed also to "satisfy itself that the alleged violation of the Bank's policies and procedures is of a serious character."

   Procedural requirements for complaining parties can be found in paragraph 16, which requires that the request for inspection be "in writing," include "all relevant facts" regarding the substantive matters discussed here, "explain the steps already taken to deal with the issue," and "specify the actions taken to bring the issue to the attention of Management" as well as management's response. For further discussion of the standing and eligibility requirements, see the 1996 and 1999 reviews of the Inspection Panel, note 3.

2. Notice that unlike a court applying a national constitution or statute that explicitly recognizes a right as creating a cause of action, the Inspection Panel and the Compliance Advisor and Ombudsman (CAO) may apply only the bank's written policy documents. See Sec. C below. In other words, environmental rights are recognized by the Inspection Panel and the CAO only where they are recognized, implicitly or explicitly, in the bank policy documents. Instead of hearing disputes between states or other parties, the Inspection Panel and the CAO hear complaints only when a member bank is alleged to have been engaged in misconduct and where the complaining party meets eligibility and standing requirements. The remedies available through the Inspection Panel and the CAO are also limited; the Inspection Panel and the CAO can only make recommendations to a bank's executive leadership, which may or may not adopt them. However, the World Bank Group structure,

including the Inspection Panel and the CAO, was created pursuant to international legal treaties, and the operation of those treaties with respect to environmental rights is included in the corpus of international law.

3. The Inspection Panel is composed of three inspectors who sit for staggered terms of three years. Individuals may not serve as inspectors if they have worked inside the WBG over the prior two years. Each new inspector is nominated by the World Bank president and appointed by the Executive Board. In practice, this involves the preparation of a slate of candidates by a selection committee for the president to choose from. This process has drawn some criticism, because it is the directors of the very banks the Inspection Panel is charged with monitoring that select the inspectors.

The first Inspection Panel consisted of a chair, Ernst Gunther Bröder of Germany, former president of the European Investment Bank; Richard E. Bissell of the United States, former senior official with the U.S. Agency for International Development; and Álvaro Umaña-Quesada of Costa Rica, former minister of natural resources for that country. Despite his banking background, Bröder provided strong, independent leadership for the Panel, which has had continuing salutary institutional impacts.

4. Paragraph 27 of the resolution establishing the Inspection Panel required the executive directors to review the "experience of the inspection function" of the Inspection Panel after two years. The executive directors actually completed two reviews. The first review was completed in October 1996 and included several important clarifications regarding the original resolution.

Review of the Resolution Establishing the Inspection Panel: Clarification of Certain Aspects of the Resolution (Oct. 17, 1996), *The World Bank Operational Manual, Bank Procedures*, BP 17–55, ann. B

. . .

The Resolution establishing the Inspection Panel calls for a review after two years from the date of appointment of the first panel members. On October 17, 1996, the Executive Directors of the Bank and IDA completed the review process. . . . The Inspection Panel and Management are requested by the Executive Directors to observe the clarifications in their application of the Resolution. The clarifications are set out below.

The Panel's Function

Since the Resolution limits the first phase of the inspection process to ascertaining the eligibility of the request, this phase should normally be completed within the 21 days stated in the Resolution. However, in cases where the Inspection Panel believes that it would be appropriate to undertake a "preliminary assessment" of the damages alleged by the requester (in particular when such preliminary assessment could lead to a resolution of the matter without the need for a full investigation), the Panel may undertake the preliminary assessment and indicate to the Board the date on which it would present its findings and recommendations as to the need, if any, for a full investigation. If such a date is expected by the Panel to exceed eight weeks from the date of receipt of Management's comments, the Panel should seek Board approval for the extension, possibly on a "no-objection" basis. What is needed at this preliminary stage is not to establish that a serious violation of the Bank's policy has actually resulted in damages suffered by the affected party, but rather to establish whether the complaint is *prima facie* justified and warrants a full investigation because it is eligible under the Resolution.

Panel investigations will continue to result in "findings" and the Board will continue to act on investigations on the basis of recommendations of Management with respect to such remedial action as may be needed.

Eligibility and Access

It is understood that the "affected party" which the Resolution describes as "a community of persons such as an organization, association, society or other grouping of individuals" includes any two or more persons who share some common interests or concerns. . . .

The Panel's mandate does not extend to reviewing the consistency of the Bank's practice with *any* of its policies and procedures, but, as stated in the Resolution, is limited to cases of alleged failure by the Bank to follow its operational policies and procedures *with respect to the design, appraisal and/or implementation of projects*, including cases of alleged failure by the bank to follow-up on the borrowers' obligations under loan agreements, with respect to such policies and procedures. . . .

Outreach

Management will make its response to requests for inspection available to the public within three days after the Board has decided on whether to authorize the inspection. Management will also make available to the public opinions of the General Counsel related to Inspection Panel matters promptly after the Executive Directors have dealt with the issues involved, unless the Board decides otherwise in a specific case. . . .

Role of the Board

The Board will continue to have authority to (i) interpret the Resolution; and (ii) authorize inspections. In applying the Resolution to specific cases, the Panel will apply it as it understands it, subject to the Board's review. As stated in the Resolution, "[t]he Panel shall seek the advice of the Bank's Legal Department on matters related to the Bank's rights and obligations with respect to the request under consideration."

————

In 1999, the Executive Board released the Second Review of the experience and function of the Inspection Panel, which included some significant changes to the Inspection Panel's function and procedure. This Second Review, together with the First Review and the Resolution establishing the Inspection Panel, constitute the complete writ of the Inspection Panel as it operates today.

Conclusions of the Board's Second Review of the Inspection Panel
(Apr. 20, 1999), *reprinted in* 39 I.L.M. 249 (2000)

The Executive Directors approved today, April 20, 1999, with immediate effect, the report of the Working Group on the Second Review of the Inspection Panel, as revised in light of the extensive consultations that took place after the report was first circulated. The report confirms the soundness of the Resolution establishing the Inspection Panel . . . and provides clarifications for its application.

These clarifications supplement the clarifications issued by the Board on October 17, 1996 and prevail over them in case of conflict. The report's recommendations approved by the Board are as follows:

1. The Board reaffirms the Resolution, the importance of the Panel's function, its independence and integrity.

2. Management will follow the Resolution. It will not communicate with the Board on matters associated with the request for inspection, except as provided for in the Resolution. It will thus direct its response to the request, including any steps it intends to take to address its failures, if any, to the Panel. Management will report to the Board any recommendations it may have, after the Panel completes its inspection and submits its findings, as envisaged in paragraph 23 of the Resolution.

3. In its initial response to the request for inspection, Management will provide evidence that

   (a) it has complied with the relevant Bank operational policies and procedures; or that
   (b) there are serious failures attributable exclusively to its own actions or omissions in complying, but that it intends to comply with the relevant policies and procedures; or that
   (c) the serious failures that may exist are exclusively attributable to the borrower or to other factors external to the Bank; or that
   (d) the serious failures that may exist are attributable both to the Bank's non-compliance with the relevant operational policies and procedures and to the borrower or other external factors. The Inspection Panel may independently agree or disagree, totally or partially, with Management's position and will proceed accordingly.

4. When Management responds, admitting serious failures that are attributable exclusively or partly to the Bank, it will provide evidence that it has complied or intends to comply with the relevant operating policies and procedures. This response will contain only those actions that the Bank has implemented or can implement by itself.

5. The Inspection Panel will satisfy itself as to whether the Bank's compliance or evidence of intention to comply is adequate, and reflect this assessment in its reporting to the Board.

6. The Panel will determine the eligibility of a request for inspection independently of any views that may be expressed by Management. With respect to matters relating to the Bank's rights and obligations with respect to the request under consideration, the Panel will seek the advice of the Bank's Legal Department as required by the Resolution.

7. For its recommendation on whether an investigation should be carried out, the Panel will satisfy itself that all the eligibility criteria provided for in the Resolution have been met. It will base its recommendation on the information presented in the request, in the Management response, and on other documentary evidence. The Panel may decide to visit the project country if it believes that this is necessary to establish the eligibility of the request. In respect of such field visits, the Panel will not report on the Bank's failure to comply with its policies and procedures or its resulting material adverse effect; any definitive assessment of a serious failure of the Bank that has caused material adverse effect will be done after the Panel has completed its investigation.

8. The original time limit, set forth in the Resolution for both Management's response to the request and the Panel's recommendation, will be strictly observed except for reasons of force majeure, i.e., reasons that are clearly beyond Management's or the Panel's control, respectively, as may be approved by the Board on a no objection basis.

9.   If the Panel so recommends, the Board will authorize an investigation without making a judgement on the merits of the claimants' request, and without discussion except with respect to the following technical eligibility criteria:

   (a) The affected party consists of any two or more persons with common interests or concerns and who are in the borrower's territory (Resolution para. 12).

   (b) The request does assert in substance that a serious violation by the Bank of its operational policies and procedures has or is likely to have a material adverse effect on the requester (Resolution paras. 12 and 14a).

   (c) The request does assert that its subject matter has been brought to Management's attention and that, in the requester's view, Management has failed to respond adequately demonstrating that it has followed or is taking steps to follow the Bank's policies and procedures (Resolution para. 13).

   (d) The matter is not related to procurement (Resolution para. 14b).

   (e) The related loan has not been closed or substantially disbursed (Resolution para. 14c).

   (f) The Panel has not previously made a recommendation on the subject matter or, if it has, that the request does assert that there is new evidence or circumstances not known at the time of the prior request (Resolution para. 14d).

10. Issues of interpretation of the Resolution will be cleared with the Board.

11. The "preliminary assessment" concept, as described in the October 1996 Clarification, is no longer needed. The paragraph entitled "The Panel's Function" in the October 1996 "Clarifications" is thus deleted.

12. The profile of Panel activities, in-country, during the course of an investigation, should be kept as low as possible in keeping with its role as a fact-finding body on behalf of the Board. . . .

13. As required by the Resolution, the Panel's report to the Board will focus on whether there is a serious Bank failure to observe its operational policies and procedures with respect to project design, appraisal and/or implementation. The report will include all relevant facts that are needed to understand fully the context and basis for the panel's findings and conclusions. The Panel will discuss in its written report only those material adverse effects, alleged in the request, that have totally or partially resulted from serious Bank failure of compliance with its policies and procedures. If the request alleges a material adverse effect and the Panel finds that it is not totally or partially caused by Bank failure, the Panel's report will so state without entering into analysis of the material adverse effect itself or its causes.

14. For assessing material adverse effect, the without-project situation should be used as the base case for comparison, taking into account what baseline information may be available. Non-accomplishments and unfulfilled expectations that do not generate a material deterioration compared to the without-project situation will not be considered as a material adverse effect for this purpose. As the assessment of material adverse effect in the context of the complex reality of a specific project can be difficult, the Panel will have to exercise carefully its judgement on these matters, and be guided by Bank policies and procedures where relevant. . . .

Questions and Discussion

1.   After a claim, or request for inspection, is filed, the Inspection Panel first determines whether the party bringing the request meets the eligibility requirements set out in paragraphs 12 to 14. If the Inspection Panel is satisfied that the requirements have been met, then it

"registers" the request. Within 21 days, the Bank management makes a response to the request. Before the 1999 review, the Inspection Panel made a preliminary investigation into the substance of the request, but now preliminary inspection is restricted to a determination of eligibility. If the Inspection Panel concludes that the matter should be investigated, then on the basis of the request and the management response the Inspection Panel makes a recommendation to the Bank's Executive Board. If the Board approves the investigation, then one of the inspectors (members of the Inspection Panel) is assigned to the case. The inspector to whom the matter was assigned conducts an investigation and submits a report, the bank management has an opportunity to reply to the report, and the Board (not the Inspection Panel) makes a final decision. The length of time that the board has to prepare the report can be adjusted based on the nature of the request. Within two weeks of the Board's final decision, the Inspection Panel's report and management's reply are published. Note that before this time, none of the documents generated by the Inspection Panel and management are published. For further discussion of this process, see *Yacyretá Hydroelectric Project Argentina/Paraguay, infra,* and discussion.

2. According to paragraph 12 of the resolution creating the Inspection Panel, the party requesting an inspection must show the Bank deviated from "its operational policies and procedures" in the course of the project. To do this, the requesting party should refer to the *World Bank Operational Manual,* which includes operational policies (OPs), bank procedures (BPs), and interim instructions to staff (OpMemos). Operational policies are numerous and cover a broad range of topics, many of which are directly concerned with the environmental impact of the project. The Inspection Panel and Management may disagree about whether a particular policy or procedure applies in a particular case. Consider the following table, reproduced from World Bank Operational Policy 4.00, for a sample of what these policies may look like.

3. Table 10.2 page 814 is excerpted from a much larger table summarizing the Bank's policies and objectives. Recall that according to paragraph 12 of the resolution creating the Inspection Panel, a party is eligible to request an inspection when that party can show that it suffered a material adverse effect because the Bank deviated from "its operational policies and procedures" in the course of a project. Do you think the "operational policies and procedures" therefore constitute rights? Does the policy, for example, to "[p]revent and, where not possible to prevent, at least minimize, or compensate for adverse project impacts" create a right to compensation? Does the policy to "[d]isclose draft EA in a timely manner, before appraisal formally begins" create a right to information? If the operational policies and procedures do create rights, how would you establish a violation of each, and what relief is available? How would you show that the denial of this right resulted in material adverse effect? Remember that the Inspection Panel cannot itself order compensation but can investigate and make recommendations where policies have been violated. Remember also paragraph 14 of the Second Review (when "assessing material adverse effect, the without-project situation should be used as the base case for comparison").

4. On the basis of the resolution establishing the Inspection Panel and the policy objectives reproduced above, do you think the directors of the World Bank Group have addressed the problem presented by the Sardar Sarovar controversy? If not, how would you have advised the directors to proceed following the publication of the Morse Commission Report? What measures, if any, would you have recommended instead? How do you think all the parties involved in the Sardar Sarovar controversy (e.g., Bank staff, construction firms, local government, environmental NGOs, displaced individuals) reacted to the establishment of the Inspection Panel? In other words, how were they affected?

Table 10.2. *Environmental and Social Safeguard Policies – Policy Objectives and Operational Principles*

Objectives	Operational Principles

A. Environmental Assessment

To help ensure the environmental and social soundness and sustainability of investment projects.	1. Use a screening process for each proposed project, as early as possible, to determine the appropriate extent and type of environmental assessment (EA) so that appropriate studies are undertaken proportional to potential risks and to direct, and, as relevant, indirect, cumulative, and associated impacts. Use sectoral or regional environmental assessment when appropriate.
To support integration of environmental and social aspects of projects into the decision making process.	2. Assess potential impacts of the proposed project on physical, biological, socio-economic and physical cultural resources, including transboundary and global concerns, and potential impacts on human health and safety.
	3. Assess the adequacy of the applicable legal and institutional framework, including applicable international environmental agreements, and confirm that they provide that the cooperating government does not finance project activities that would contravene such international obligations.
	4. Provide for assessment of feasible investment, technical, and siting alternatives, including the "no action" alternative, potential impacts, feasibility of mitigating these impacts, their capital and recurrent costs, their suitability under local conditions, and their institutional, training and monitoring requirements associated with them.
	5. Where applicable to the type of project being supported, normally apply the Pollution Prevention and Abatement Handbook (PPAH). Justify deviations when alternatives to measures set forth in the PPAH are selected.
	6. Prevent and, where not possible to prevent, at least minimize, or compensate for adverse project impacts and enhance positive impacts through environmental management and planning that includes the proposed mitigation measures, monitoring, institutional capacity development and training measures, an implementation schedule, and cost estimates.
	7. Involve stakeholders, including project-affected groups and local nongovernmental organizations, as early as possible, in the preparation process and ensure that their views and concerns are made known to decision makers and taken into account. Continue consultations throughout project implementation as necessary to address EA-related issues that affect them.
	8. Use independent expertise in the preparation of EA where appropriate. Use independent advisory panels during preparation and implementation of projects that are highly risky or contentious or that involve serious and multi-dimensional environmental and/or social concerns.
	9. Provide measures to link the environmental assessment process and findings with studies of economic, financial, institutional, social, and technical analyses of a proposed project.
	10. Provide for application of the principles in this Table to subprojects under investment and financial intermediary activities.
	11. Disclose draft EA in a timely manner, before appraisal formally begins, in an accessible place and in a form and language understandable to key stakeholders.

Objectives	Operational Principles

. . .

F. Forests

To realize the potential of forests to reduce poverty in a sustainable manner, integrate forests effectively into sustainable economic development, and protect the vital local and global environmental services and values of forests.

1. Screen as early as possible for potential impacts on forest health and quality and on the rights and welfare of the people who depend on them. As appropriate, evaluate the prospects for new markets and marketing arrangements.
2. Do not finance projects that would involve significant conversion or degradation of critical forest areas or related critical natural habitats, or that would contravene applicable international environmental agreements.
3. Do not finance natural forest harvesting or plantation development that would involve any conversion or degradation of critical forest areas or related critical natural habitats.
4. Support projects that adversely impact noncritical natural forests or related natural habitats only if viable alternatives to the project are not available and only if appropriate conservation and mitigation measures are in place.
5. Support commercial, industrial-scale forest harvesting only when the operation is certified, under an independent forest certification system, as meeting, or having a time-bound action plan to meet, internationally recognized standards of responsible forest management and use.
6. Ensure that forest restoration projects maintain or enhance biodiversity and ecosystem functionality and that all plantation projects are environmentally appropriate, socially beneficial, and economically viable.
7. Give preference to small-scale community-level management approaches where they best reduce poverty in a sustainable manner.
8. Support commercial harvesting by small-scale landholders, local communities or entities under joint forest management where monitoring with the meaningful participation of local communities demonstrates that these operations achieve a standard of forest management consistent with internationally recognized standards of responsible forest use or that they are adhering to an approved time-bound plan to meet these standards.
9. Use forest certification systems that require: (a) compliance with relevant laws; (b) recognition of, and respect for, legal or customary land tenure and use rights as well as the rights of Indigenous Peoples and workers; (c) measures to enhance sound community relations; (d) conservation of biological diversity and ecological functions; (e) measures to maintain or enhance environmentally sound multiple benefits from the forest; (f) prevention or minimization of environmental impacts; (g) effective forest management planning; (h) active monitoring and assessment of relevant forest management areas; and (i) independent, cost effective, third-party assessment of forest management performance against measurable performance standards defined at the national level and compatible with

(*continued*)

Table 10.2 (continued)

Objectives	Operational Principles
	internationally accepted principles and criteria of sustainable forest management through decision-making procedures that are fair, transparent, independent, designed to avoid conflict of interest and involve the meaningful participation of key stakeholders, including the private sector, Indigenous Peoples, and local communities.
	10. Disclose any time-bound action plans in a timely manner, before appraisal formally begins, in an accessible place and in a form and language that are understandable to key stakeholders.
	. . .
H. Safety of Dams	
To assure quality and safety in the design and construction of new dams and the rehabilitation of existing dams, and in carrying out activities that may be affected by an existing dam.	1. Identify existing dams and dams under construction that can influence the performance of the project and implement necessary safety measures/remedial works.
	2. Use experienced and competent professionals to design and supervise the construction, operation, and maintenance of dams and associated works.
	3. Develop detailed plans, including for construction supervision, instrumentation, operation and maintenance and emergency preparedness.
	4. Use independent advice on the verification of design, construction, and operational procedures and appoint independent panels of experts for large or high hazard dams.
	5. Use contractors that are qualified and experienced to undertake planned construction activities.
	6. Carry out periodic safety inspections of new/rehabilitated dams after completion of construction/rehabilitation, review/monitor implementation of detailed plans and take appropriate action as needed.

The reaction among environmental NGOs to the establishment of the Inspection Panel was generally positive, although many think the Bank still has a long way to go to fully address the problem:

> The World Bank's Executive Directors and management should be credited with creating the inspection panel. In adopting the complaint mechanism, the Executive Directors have made the Bank the only international institution explicitly accountable to citizens. As such, the panel is a remarkable advancement in international law. But for the inspection panel to have a truly independent and credible voice and thus aid the Bank in meeting the challenges of the future, the Bank must empower the panel and respect its decisions. Oversight by environmental and other groups will help to ensure that the panel does not perpetuate business as usual at the Bank.

Lori Udall & David Hunter, *The World Bank's New Inspection Panel: Will It Increase Accountability?*, Center for International Environmental Law Issue Brief No. 1 (Apr. 1994).

3. As of March 2010, there have been sixty-four requests for inspection submitted to the Inspection Panel. As of June 30, 2007 (surprisingly, the last record produced by the Bank), forty-one

of those requests have been "registered." In other words, the Inspection Panel found that the party requesting an inspection satisfied the standing and eligibility requirements in a majority of cases, even in 2007. To that time, the Inspection Panel recommended inspection in roughly twenty cases. As you have seen, however, it remains with the Executive Board to accept or reject the Panel's recommendation. The Panel issues annual reports that are available online. The reports contain detailed information on all requests for inspection. It also released an internal analysis of the Panel in 2009. WORLD BANK, ACCOUNTABILITY AT THE WORLD BANK: THE INSPECTION PANEL AT 15 YEARS (2009).

3. The Inspection Panel in Action

The following Inspection Panel recommendation, involving land that was seized to build a dam access road in Nepal, followed from the first request the Inspection Panel received.

Nepal: Proposed Arun III Hydroelectric Project and Restructuring of the Arun III Access Road Project (Credit 2029-NEP) Request No. RQ94/1, Inspection Panel (Dec. 16, 1994) (Washington, D.C.)

Proposed Project

1. Management of IDA is planning to seek approval for an SDR [World Bank "Standard Drawing Rights," about two-thirds per U.S. dollar – *Eds.*] 99.5 million development credit to the Kingdom of Nepal ("HMG/N" – the borrower) and the restructuring of an existing credit for SDR 24.4 million (Arun III Access Road Project – Cr. 2029-NEP) to help finance the proposed Arun III Hydroelectric Project. The revised project components include a 122 kilometer access road through the Arun Valley, construction of a 201 MW [megawatt] run-of-river (including a 68 meter dam) hydroelectric power scheme (the first phase of the Arun III 402 MW scheme) in the Sankhuwa-Sava District and 122 kilometers of transmission lines from there to Duhabi. The Arun basin is about 170 kilometers east of Kathmandu.

2. The proposed credit would be on standard IDA terms with a 40 year maturity....

3. Total project costs are estimated at about US$800 million. The project would be cofinanced by the Asian Development Bank, Kreditanstalt für Weideraufbau, the Government of France, the Swedish Agency for International Technical and Economic Cooperation, the Finnish International Development Agency and other donors.

The Request

4. *Summary:* The Panel received a Request, dated October 24, 1994, from citizens of Nepal (the "Requesters") who claim that their rights and interests have been or likely are to be materially and adversely affected by the acts or omissions of IDA during the design and appraisal of Arun III. Two of the Requesters claim that they have been directly and adversely affected by the design and implementation of the resettlement program related to Arun III. The Requesters claim to be, or likely to be affected by alleged violations of provisions of, inter-alia, the following policies and procedures.

- Operational Policy/Bank Procedure 10.04: *Economic Evaluation of Investment Operations*
- *The World Bank Policy on Disclosure of Information*, September 1994; Bank Procedures 17.50 and 10.00 . . .
- Operational Directive 4.01: *Environmental Assessment*

- Operational Directive 4.30: *Involuntary Resettlement*
- Operational Directive 4.20: *Indigenous Peoples*

5. The two Requesters from the now abandoned Hill Route asked for anonymity and, in accordance with Nepalese law, appointed Messrs. Siwatoki and Ghimire of Kathmandu, Nepal (the other two Requesters) to represent them. . . .

6. *Eligibility Issues*: para. 17 of the Procedures requires the Chairman to register the Request [if] "the Request appears to contain sufficient required information. . . . " While recognizing that there were deficiencies in the formalities, in accordance with this para, the Chairman, on November 3, 1994, registered the Request in the Panel Register; notified the Requester, the Executive Directors and the President of IDA of the registration; and transmitted to the President a copy of the original Request together with fixed copies of the attachments and evidence of registration. Upon receipt, on November 8, of the originals of the accompanying documentation, copies were forwarded to the President of IDA.

7. The Panel judged that the serious nature of the substance of the Request as a whole and its timing in relation to the project process outweighed outright rejection of the Request on the grounds of doubts on the standing of the Requesters and incomplete compliance with formal procedures. Management apparently came to the same conclusion since, as noted before, it addressed the substance of the Request without questioning its eligibility under the applicable terms of the Resolution.

Operational Policies and Procedures

8. Given that a period of about seven years has elapsed since the inception of Arun III, the evolving nature of IDA policies and procedures and the timing of their application in relation to various stages of this proposed project is a source of disagreement between the Request and Response. . . .

B. The Request and the Response

9. The request lists a number of statements of policies and procedures which the Requesters believe IDA has failed to follow in the course of the design, appraisal and initial implementation of Arun III. The Response provides information indicating that Management believes it has not failed to follow the relevant policies and procedures. The Request and the Response are reviewed briefly and are followed by the Panel's initial comments.

I. Economic Analysis of Investment Operations

Alternatives

10. *The Request* states that IDA "has violated its operational policies regarding the Economic Evaluation of Investment Operations, as a basic criterion for acceptability. For the project to be acceptable on economic grounds, 'the expected present value of the project's net benefits must be higher than or equal to the expected net present value of mutually exclusive project alternatives.' By not undertaking the relevant studies of the alternatives . . . , the World Bank has not fulfilled this very basic criteria for acceptability of the project."

11. The Request also complains that IDA violated this Directive throughout the project cycle by not considering alternative sequencing until 1993/94 and that the study is incomplete as the comparison was made with only very preliminary costs for the alternative schemes; that the earlier

Least Cost Generation Expansion Plans ("LCGEP") of 1987 and 1990 failed to take into account that the same amount of power generated from Arun III could also be generated from a series of smaller alternatives in the 1 MW to 100 MW range; and that by not completing feasibility studies of the 30 or more smaller alternatives identified by HMG/N, IDA has not fulfilled the policy requirement to compute the LCGEP for additional power generation for Nepal. The Request also states that "there is every reason to believe that once the detailed studies are completed, the smaller alternatives can be built at prices lower than or competitive with Arun III."

12. *The Response*, while answering the Request in line with OP/BP 10.04 suggests, in its Annex A, that this policy was not in effect at the time of identification and appraisal: that only those instructions in this OP/BP which are identical to those in force at the time are applicable. It indicates that the basis for the LCGEP was the initial consideration of "some 3000" alternative generation and expansion plans of which 11 individual hydro investment project candidates of varying sizes were examined to the pre-feasibility level or "beyond." However, "in response to questions, additional alternative strategies were investigated in order to check the robustness of the standard least-cost analysis. This involved the consideration of project candidates that preliminary analysis has previously screened out." The Response concludes that the cost of an alternative was higher than the cost of HMG/N's proposed program.

13. *The Response* also states that there are no hard and fast rules on how many alternative proposals should be investigated to the "pre-feasibility" stage, it is a question of professional judgment. The number of hydro candidates explored to the pre-feasibility level is considered to represent "a very respectable effort for a country such as Nepal" – given that the determining factors are the extra cost and associated delays. Noting that the project contains funding for further pre-feasibility and feasibility work for smaller hydro projects – which, if attractive, will be accommodated periodically into the LCGEP – it is pointed out that there is no evidence that such further study would displace Arun III from the LCGEP.

Risk Analysis

14. *The Request* complains that the risk analysis is faulty, in particular that:

- one large natural catastrophe would virtually ruin the Nepalese economy;
- no account has been taken of the risk of undertaking such a large project in relation to the size of the Nepalese economy;
- while over 80% of the catchment area of the Arun River lies under the control of China and a proposed Changsun Basin Irrigation Project is pending, no account of upstream developments (riparian rights) has been included; and
- there is no bilateral agreement with India even though Phase II of Arun III and future development in the valley depend on surplus power sales to India.

15. *The Response* explains that

- under OP 10.04 treatment of risks associated with large projects is not mentioned and there is no explicit policy with respect to the valuation of risks – as distinguished from the analysis and/or management of risks – associated with large projects. But "recognition of Arun's magnitude and importance to the Nepalese economy was what led the Bank to undertake such comprehensive analysis of the project";
- the analysis does not consider the risks to project viability of the possible construction of the Changsuo Basin Irrigation Project because the appraisal team judged these risks to be minimal;

recently the Chinese authorities have reconfirmed their non-objection to the project and that the small size of the project is likely to have no effect on downstream water users; and

• with respect to sales to India: in the past bilateral agreements have not been necessary and suggests that even if no surplus sales occur, there would only be a 1% drop in the projects economic rate of return which remains above the project's opportunity cost of capital.

Poverty Reduction

16. *The Request* suggests that there will be immediate and threatened long-term irreversible impacts on the already absolute [*sic*] poor inhabitants of the Arun Valley, as a result, in particular, of NEA's [Nepal Electricity Authority] lack of capacity to implement environmental and social safeguards.

17. At the national level, the Request suggests that the large size of the project in relation to Nepal's annual national budget will not directly benefit the poor as its high cost will crowd out investments in social services and targeted poverty interventions.

18. *The Response* acknowledges that 450,000 inhabitants of the Arun Valley lead a "harsh subsistence life;" it states that the primary objective of the project is to meet Nepal's growing power requirements in the medium term at least cost so that this constraint on growth and poverty reduction can be overcome. Referring to the Environmental Action Plan the Response suggests that it aims to limit negative direct impacts and to maximize the Valley's prospects for sustainable growth and poverty reduction.

Alternatives

19. [The Panel notes that with] respect to examination of alternatives . . . previous policies and procedures would appear to be applicable. A preliminary review . . . of those policies and procedures suggests that the fundamental requirements are substantially the same as those in OP/BP 10.04. In particular it is noted that OMS 2.21, para. 8, states that: "Consideration of alternatives is the single most important feature of proper project analysis throughout the project cycle, from the development plan for the particular sector through identification to appraisal." It is also noted that the Response deals with the issues of alternatives and analysis of project risks in the context of the requirements of OP 10.04.

20. It is clear that Nepal's hydropower potential is considerable (estimated at 25,000 MW). However less than 1 % of the resource has been developed and there is no complete inventory that could be used reliably for long term planning.

21. Out of about 107 potential hydroelectric sites that have been identified, technical and economic screening criteria yielded only 18 projects for which pre-feasibility or further engineering studies have been carried out. The latest LCGEP considered only 11 projects. It is a matter of judgment whether this is an adequate number of options that should have been considered in the 30–80 MW range.

22. The Panel notes that the MOP [a Memorandum and Recommendation on the project circulated by the President to the Board, dated August 29, 1994] recognizes that: "The only realistic alternative to the hydropower investment program proposed by the Government is a series of hydro investments in the range of 10 MW to 100 MW. While these are certainly small projects by international standards, most are similar in magnitude to the two previous major hydro investments made in Nepal; namely, Kulekhani (60 and 32 MW) and Marsyangdi (69 MW). Past preinvestment studies in Nepal's major river systems have identified a large number of such potential investments. Pre-feasibility and feasibility work has been done on some 18 of the 93 sites identified. About half of

the 18 are under 100 MW; these have already been taken into account in the least cost generation analysis. Hence, the effort to develop an alternative hydropower investment program has had to draw from among those projects, mostly in the 30 to 80 MW range, which had previously been screened out (on the basis of rather crude technical and economic criteria) as less attractive than those for which pre-feasibility work has been commissioned. The alternative investment program thus identified has been labelled Plan B.... The costs of Plan B are estimated to be about 5% higher than the Government's proposed investment program under assumptions about the future considered most likely, and 5% less in the scenario where demand growth follows the low load forecast."

23. There is reason to believe that if a less restrictive assessment, including a wider range of hydro resources, could be undertaken it would result in expanding the number of economically and environmentally acceptable options.

Risk Analysis

24. IDA policies provide for evaluation of investment projects to ensure that they promote the borrower's development goals and that the economic analysis be conducted to determine whether the project creates more net benefits to the economy than other mutually exclusive options for the use of the resources in question; and state that assessing sustainability includes evaluating the project's financial impact on the implementing/sponsoring institution and estimating the direct effect on public finances of the project's capital outlays and recurrent costs. This process also includes an analysis of the sources, magnitude and effects of the risks associated with the proposed project.

25. The Panel notes that, with the information available, the comparison of the risks associated with the project and its alternatives is very difficult due to the large number of factors involved including:

- natural catastrophic events such as Glacial Lake Outburst Floods (GLOF) and high monsoon rains leading to high river floods which constitute a permanent risks in the project area. These risks were considered a major factor in the original decision to choose a Hill Route for the access road;
- the steep tariff rate increases that NEA must implement, likely cost overruns, lower economic growth;
- major risks associated with the economic performance of the project are associated with the rate of growth of demand, which in turn is related to the unforeseeable response to price increases and export sales The lack of a long term power sales agreement with India poses a potential long term risk to the project. This risk has been highlighted by IDA, particularly in the case of Nepal, in the 1986 Project Performance Audit Report for the Kulekhani Hydroelectric Project... which concludes that: "Agreements on export would be required prior to the start of any large scale development, and because most countries are reluctant to be dependent on others for electrical energy, negotiations on such matters may last over extended periods of time." The MOP contains a rather detailed discussion of risks and concludes that: "Comparison of the overall risks of the alternative strategies shows that both have problems requiring careful management. There is simply no low risk way to meet Nepal's power requirements over the next decade or so."

26. All power development options require careful risk management unprecedented in Nepal and therefore institutional capacity building is critical to the success of any strategy. Major risks

associated with institutional capacity in the NEA and HMG/N emerge as significant in a variety of ways: to oversee construction, long-term O&M [operations and management]; reorganization of the power sector management, and ability to sustain appropriate tariff increases. Each could endanger the viability of Arun III at any time. While funding agencies can supplement institutional capacity in the short-term, the strengthening of institutions will still have to develop rapidly and extensively.

27. The Request cites, as a potential risk, the fact that 80 percent of the river lies in China. The Response refers to the small size of the proposed Changsuo Basin Irrigation Project. At the request of the Panel, Management has provided satisfactory evidence showing that the Government of China does not oppose Arun III.

28. Risk assessment must include all factors that might have a bearing on the project, and compare them with those of the alternatives. IDA has attempted to deal with those issues, but, the environmental and social impacts of the alternative have not been systematically analyzed; therefore a realistic comparison of risks associated with the proposed project and its alternatives could not have been carried out.

Poverty Alleviation

29. OP 10.04 states that the economic analysis examines the project's consistency with IDA'S poverty reduction strategy.

30. The Panel recognizes two levels of potential impacts on poverty. The first relates to the localized effect of Arun III on the Arun basin's poor, particularly the people whose land, like that of the Requesters on the abandoned Hill Route, was expropriated; and those on the proposed Valley Route whose land might be expropriated. The second relates to the likely macroeconomic impacts on the country as a whole due to the large size of the investment to be undertaken in relation to the size of the economy. These impacts on a national level might result in: (a) an initial increase in poverty because the opportunity cost of capital to address poverty directly and the resources needed for other targeted interventions may be consumed by Arun III; (b) a reduced consumption due to the effect of rising electricity tariffs on consumers as they devote a larger share of their disposable income to electricity; and (c) a constraint on public expenditure and investment – as noted in a recent Bank document: "The power sector as a whole is expected to absorb 15 percent of local resources and 40 percent of foreign resources, and AHP [Arun III] alone will absorb close to 20 percent of total development resources during the peak implementation phase in FY [Fiscal Year] 97-FY99."

31. The high priority of poverty alleviation in Nepal has been reiterated by the Bank. However, steps already taken by IDA and HMG/N suggest it will be more difficult to implement the policies on poverty. Future steps, such as further cancellation of "low priority projects" in social sectors and the large fiscal demands of Arun III may contribute to the risk that policies on poverty cannot be implemented.

II. Environmental Assessment

Alternatives

32. *The Request* states that the environmental and social issues and available alternatives to Arun III were not integrated into decisions on whether to proceed with the project. Citing the 1991 Basinwide Environmental Impacts Study ("RAP"), it states that: "the road alignment [hill route] and dam site were already decided and the study team did not have the mandate to change these

decisions;" and the 1992 study" of the valley route was conducted to determine whether it "might provide time and cost savings in providing access to the Arun III hydropower site. Serving the needs of the population . . . is a secondary consideration . . . and that the need for and the siting of the power project and therefore the justification for the road, is taken as a given." It is noted that, in response to pressure to investigate alternatives adequately, and after the EIA process was completed, the Bank commissioned a study known as Plan B which was conducted from the standpoint of whether Arun III is the "least cost" option for Nepal – without consideration of the environmental and social costs of either Arun III or its alternatives.

33. The Request also points out that: "[t]he so-called EIA of the Valley route of the access road fails to take into consideration and compare from environmental standpoint any alternative approach to build this road. For example, applying environmentally friendly approach in building the roads in the Himalayan foothills by employing simple and conservation-oriented techniques and labor intensive methods have been proved successful. The pace of the proposed construction of the road and the approach adopted, thus, is a serious environmental concern that the EIA ignores.

34. *The Response* questions the applicability of the policy on Environmental Assessment for timing reasons but then states that Management nevertheless proceeded as if it were applicable. As evidence of compliance, the Response cites the consideration of three dam sites in the Arun valley and two different access roads. The Response notes that the 1993 Environmental Assessment Executive Summary' ("EA Summary") clearly states that identification of Arun III was based on least cost studies undertaken up to 1990 and that "these studies addressed environmental/social issues at the reconnaissance level for all feasible sites."

35. [The Panel] notes that while the current policy was not in effect when the Credit 2029 for the Hill Access Road Project was approved, it was in effect at the time when it was decided to change the access road to the Valley Route. The 1993 EA Summary states that: "The Arun III . . . was identified as the best major hydropower scheme for early addition to the Nepal Interconnected System under the LCGEP completed by the NEA in 1987. . . . [This] choice was confirmed by an LCGEP Update Study completed in 1990. . . . This study included estimates of resettlement costs in its comparative analysis of the various projects, but not the costs of other environmental impacts or economic benefits."

36. The Panel notes that the major environmental and social impacts of the Arun project are due to the construction of the access road, and not due to the hydroelectric generating facility itself. Given the timing of the change of the choice of road alignment the social impact has been magnified and the environmental impact assessment studies dealt primarily with the original route (Hill Route).

37. The Panel finds it necessary to look at this decision in more detail, particularly in view of the fact that almost all of the land of the families on the Hill Route had already been acquired.

Access Road Alignment

38. In 1987, a detailed feasibility study was carried out by the Department of Roads for the so-called "Hill Route." Detailed designs and tender documents were completed in 1988, in anticipation of an early start of construction, and further refined in the following years. The final alignment chosen, designs and construction methods were referred to in the SAR [Staff Appraisal Report of August 19, 1994] as environmentally the "state of the art" for a major road project in Nepal.

39. The SAR for the Arun III Access Road Project of May 12, 1989 refers to the selection of alignment for the access road in para. 3.08: "The route selected as being most economical in

terms of construction and maintenance, consistent with sound environmental planning, is in mountainous terrain and follows the ridges wherever possible, descending only for crossings of the Piluwa Khola near Chainpur, the Sabhaya Khola at Tumlingtar and at the sites of the powerhouse, adit [horizontal subterranean entrance] and dam. The streams and rivers of this area are unpredictable and can be very violent and destructive. They cause excessive steepening of the valley sides and consequent instability of the slopes. The route has therefore been chosen to avoid rivers as far as possible, and to follow the contours closely in order to minimize the quantities of cut and fill, and to reduce negative environmental impact. The contract documents for road construction also incorporate environmental conservation measures."

40. The Panel notes that within three years of this decision, the project design for the road took the opposite approach, selecting a route where more than 50 percent runs close to the previously described unstable, steep, unpredictable and hazardous slopes of the Arun River.

41. In 1992, according to the EA Summary, following a decision to revise Arun III's design and reduce initial expenditure and given the sole criterion of providing access to the power sites as quickly as possible, the feasibility of a "Valley" route was investigated again. Engineering and construction planning studies had shown that although the construction costs would be similar to those of the Hill Route, there would be a time saving of one year and a total length construction of only 122 km. The EA Summary points out however, that: "The speed of construction of a project can have a considerable effect on its environmental impact. Slower construction of the access road would allow a less capital intensive approach with a higher local labor demand (and therefore local benefits), and modified construction techniques with lower physical impact. Slower construction of the hydropower components of Arun III would reduce the size of the labour force required, reduce the volumes of spoil to be excavated and disposed of annually, and permit more gradual institutional development.."..

42. The proposed change in routes was presented to the Panel of Experts (POE) and approved in principle by them. However, the POE pointed to the apparent disadvantages of the Valley Route:

- "increase of forested land in the RoW [right of way] and possibly less disturbed and higher quality forest and protected wildlife habitat in the RoW: approximately 209 ha [hectares] vs. 145 ha
- closer proximity to the Makalu-Barun Conservation Area
- losses and uncertainties resulting from the circumstance that land compensation for the hill route is already 94 percent completed
- additional impacts associated with future construction of spur roads or other connections to hill villages that would have been connected by the hill route."

The POE also concluded, inter alia, that: "The recommendation from the environmental perspective therefore is to proceed with the design and tendering of the project using the valley route, to drop the hill route from further consideration at this time, to establish a clear and equitable policy concerning the families within the hill route who have already received compensation, and to update and amend project environmental documents, in parallel with the detailed engineering and along the following lines, to reflect the change in route.

1. It would be useful if the September 1992 Joint Venture EIA of the valley route would make a more detailed comparison of the impacts of the hill route and the valley route, including implications for associated changes in transmission line impacts, if any, and options and implications for families within the RoW of the hill route who have already received compensation.

2. Regardless of which route is adopted, the recommendations and cost estimates (about US$14 million) of the King Mahendra Trust report on "Environmental Management and Sustainable Development in the Arun Basin" should be released to the public, reviewed, screened and prioritized to facilitate the development of an action plan for implementation. Without such a plan there will be no mechanism in place for controlling off-site impacts (especially encroachment on forests and wildlife) in the vicinity of the access road and power station, south and east of the Makalu-Banin Conservation Area."

43. The decision to pursue the Valley Route led NEA to commission a study to "revise and update the existing environmental impact assessment study of the access road in accordance with World Bank guidelines" (Terms of Reference for JV Consultants). This update was supposed to be carried out in a period of four months although the road alignment had not been completed. The following clause was included in the Terms of Reference: "In order to complete the update of the EIA within the four months of Period A, it is mandatory to have a preliminary alignment or alignment options available at the latest six weeks after the commencement of the services with respect to the access road, and in the first week of August [1992] regarding the transmission line." Also included in the terms of reference is the following disclaimer: "The time available will not allow it to perform a detailed socio-economic and ecological survey along the entire alignment. Rather, surveys will be of a qualitative nature and will concentrate on selected areas from which conclusions will have to be drawn to the total length of alignment."

44. The Environmental Impact Assessment for Arun Access Road-Valley Route published in September, 1992, concludes that the impact on biological resources is significant since the Valley Route transverses forested areas for the major part of its length (71 Km out of 124 Km), and that most of the areas show high species diversity and presence of rare, endemic and endangered species of trees and other plants. In addition, the loss of habitat will result in significant impact on vertebrae. The EIA for the access road concludes that: "The road runs close to the Arun River for 67 km and therefore construction of the road will have direct impact on mammalian and reptilian wildlife due to direct habitat, severance of territory, disturbance and increased access to hunting. Quantitative data on population sizes are not available."

45. The Panel finds the process of choosing the access road has created uncertainties of a serious nature with regard to IDAS ability to follow OD 4.01 on environmental assessment. The Response cites three major components to the Environmental Action Plan: an Environmental Mitigation Plan, A Land Acquisition Resettlement and Compensation Plan and a Regional Action Plan ("RAP"). During consultations with the proposed borrower and executing entity, the Panel learned that the updated RAP will not be completed until January 1995. On the basis of the evidence reviewed, the Panel concludes that the environmental assessment and processing of the proposed loan do not appear to be consistent with the provisions of OD 4.01 and its annexes. The potential of direct, serious long-term damage is significant.

Cumulative Effects and Inadequacies

46. *The Request* states that cumulative impacts of all three Arun Valley hydropower schemes (i.e. Arun III, Upper Arun and Lower Arun) have not been evaluated and that there should be a comprehensive study of the long term effects including those of additional road construction; that other inadequacies of the EIA include no thorough assessment of the impact of the transmission lines, mitigation plans for natural disasters, effects on fish and disposal of construction spoils.

47. *The Response* refers to the 1991 basin-wide environmental sustainability study as meeting the Bank's requirement. "The effects of Upper Arun which are likely to be environmentally more sensitive than Arun III were studied separately in a 1991 feasibility study." It notes that Lower Arun

"is generally recognized to have less significant impacts"; it is acknowledged that further work will be undertaken in the first year of the project to verify that effects on fisheries are minimal and identify mitigation measures as necessary.

48. Mention is also made of the approval of environmental mitigation measures by the project's POE....

49. [The Panel] *observes* that, according to the SAR, the POE included a single "expert in environmental management and resettlement" and that in June 1994 a decision was made to "reconstitute the POE by the end [of] December 1994 for review of assistance and guidance on the critical technical and safety aspects and dam safety monitoring during construction and supervision." It is also noted that the reconstituted Panel will be "expanded to include environmental expertise to advise effectively on detailed RAP and resettlement issues. In addition the MOP states that a POE, "both international and Nepali, will advise, on, inter alia, the RAP and resettlement implementation, and propose modifications where appropriate." It is pointed out that the reconstituted Panel will "include a core of specialists in area development, resettlement, biodiversity and agriculture management;" and that other experts will be consulted as needed.

50. Applicable IDA policies provide for Regional Environmental Assessments and special provisions relating to Dam and Reservoir projects. In particular Environmental Advisory Panels are recommended: "For major, highly risky, or contentious projects with serious and multi-dimensional environmental concerns, the borrower should normally engage an advisory panel of independent, internationally recognized, environmental specialists to advise on (a) the terms of reference (TORS) for the EA, (b) key issues and methods for preparing the EA, (c) recommendations and findings of the EA, (d) implementation of the EAs recommendations, and (e) development of environmental management capacity in the implementing agency."

51. Given that OD 4.01 was applicable when the Valley Route was chosen and the Arun III Hydroelectric Project appraised, the environmental assessment should have included a comprehensive approach to the Arun basin, including a long term perspective that also considered the Upper and Lower Arun Projects, access roads (including the Valley Route and additional spurs), as well as transmission lines. Environmental assessments should be integrated into project design from its inception and, must go beyond descriptive studies, focusing on the interaction of all project components and decisions that affect the natural and social environment, including mitigation plans and the institutional capacity to develop, implement and monitor them. It is not clear that the composition of the POE properly reflected the requirements set out by IDA policies.

52. Given the nature and complexity of the environmental and social risks of the project, IDA policy would appear to require the existence of a POE solely devoted to environmental and social issues. Instead, IDA and the borrower agreed in 1994 to consolidate planning for such an environmental panel into the existing POE.

III. Disclosure of Information

53. *The World Bank Policy on Disclosure of Information*, September 1993, states in part that the Bank "recognizes and endorses the fundamental importance of accountability and transparency.... Dissemination of information to local groups affected by the projects supported by the Bank, including non-governmental organizations, particularly as it will facilitate the participation of those groups in Bank-financed projects, is essential for the effective implementation and sustainability of the projects.... It follows that there is a presumption in favor of disclosure."

Project Identification Document ("PID")

54. *The Request* complains that the PID was not prepared before January 24, 1994 and has subsequently not been updated to include all the information required by BP 10.00 Annex A.

55. *The Response* states that the "content and dissemination of the Arun PID were substantially in line with Bank policy and procedures."

56. [*The Panel* notes that] IDA's Procedures for operations in which major changes are made after appraisal, require preparation of a final revision of the PID following appraisal.

57. The Panel notes that the PID is an effective means of providing timely and concise information on proposed projects. It is highly desirable, for projects that command this degree of interest at the national and international level, that this document be updated in accordance with emerging Bank policies. The September 1993 BP 17.50 Annex D required a completed PID for all projects beyond the IEPS stage but not yet presented to the Board by January 1, 1994. The document was not available at the Public Information Center ("PIC") until March. . . .

Environmental Assessment ("EA")

58. *The Request* asserts that this provision was not followed by IDA and notes that the environmental impact assessment was one of the documents for which release was requested in the law suit filed with the Supreme Court [of Nepal] on December 31, 1993. [On May 8, 1994, the Supreme Court ordered the government to release the requested information. There is a right to information in the Constitution of Nepal. *Eds.*]

59. *The Response* claims that the "dissemination of the results of the Environmental Assessment was substantially in line with Bank policies and procedure."

60. [*The Panel* notes that] the 1993 procedures on information disclosure require that "before the Bank proceeds to appraisal, the EA [Environmental Assessment] must be made available in the borrowing country at some public place accessible to affected groups and local NGOs."

61. The Panel notes that the EA for the Hill Route (the RAP in this case) was completed in 1991; that the EA Summary was published in Kathmandu in May 1993, and the "Due Process Manual" prepared in Nepali by NEA in November 1993 is restricted to information on land acquisition and compensation procedures. While the Response provides detailed information on the timing and applicability of specific IDA policies on disclosure of information, it does not refer to the relevant policies relating to Environment Assessment.

62. Considerable efforts have been made to gather and release environmental data about the project and the IDA appears to have made substantial efforts to make it available in Washington. However, much of the relevant information was not available in Nepal.

Factual Technical Information

63. *The Request* claims that factual technical information was requested during project preparation to enable the Requesters to have an input into the design and promote alternatives but such information was received too late (after appraisal) to allow input. In particular it is noted that the study of alternatives was not released until after appraisal and the completion of loan negotiation.

64. *The Response* mentions initial delays in implementing the new disclosure policy in this respect but notes that sections of the SAR [Staff Appraisal Report] have been available at the PIC [Public Information Center] since September 1994.

65. [The Panel notes that] IDA policy allows for the release, by the Country Director concerned, of additional factual technical information for projects under preparation through the PIC.

66. The Panel notes Management's prompt disclosure of relevant parts of the SAR but the Request suggests this is not available in Nepal. In light of the high degree of interest in the project in Nepal it appears unfortunate that delays in implementing the new policy occurred and that no mention is made in the Response of supplying such factual technical information to NEA's Arun Information Center.

67. The Panel is concerned about the serious problem of enforcing release of information in borrowing countries; and notes a gap in the availability of information in Washington, on the one hand, and in the country where the project is located on the other – in particular in the actual project area.

68. With regard to overall disclosure of information, the Panel recognizes the progress made by the Management in last two years in relation to projects such as Arun III. In the borrowing countries progress varies, as evidenced by the need to take cases to the Nepalese Supreme Court twice this year to obtain release of project information.

69. Disclosure is not an end in itself according to Bank policy, but rather a means of enhancing the ability of affected people to participate in the design and consideration of project alternatives.

70. Meeting the requirements of Bank policy on release of information in Nepal appears to have been difficult. The Panel urges continued attention to this evolving issue.

IV. Involuntary Resettlement

71. *The Request* claims that (a) specific violations of IDA's policies or involuntary resettlement have occurred (Hill Route) and that (b) violations of the policies are likely to occur (Valley Route).

Hill Route

72. With reference to the cash compensation raised by two of the Requesters it is claimed that the central objective of improving or at least restoring affected people to former living standards has already been violated. It points out that the effect of ACRP [Acquisition, Compensation, and Rehabilitation Plan] has been to inflate prices far beyond compensated value; and that in violation of para. 14 of the policy, land has been undervalued. The Request also criticizes the fact that land for land compensation was not appropriately offered.

Valley Route

73. *The Request* notes that the proposed project benefits will be electricity but affected people will not benefit that employment benefits will be temporary but the adverse effects of displacement are permanent – SPAFs [Seriously Project Affected Family] are to be given only first priority for employment on road construction. The request also notes that the EIA shows that cash compensation was already failing in case of the Hill Route and that the Valley Route people will have even less ability to deal with cash because they are poorer: this raises whole question of land for land compensation and actual implementation. According to the Request the law is basically limited to cash compensation and PAFs are not being informed of a land option. The

Requesters are not aware that any socio-economic survey has been done to determine value of land. In addition the Request notes a violation of the policy as no resettlement plan has been established before appraisal for those to be displaced by the transmission lines.

74. *The Response* explains IDA's compliance with the Operational Directive ("OD") on Involuntary Resettlement in relation to the Valley Route, noting that implementation arrangements have been agreed at negotiations; SPAFs are to be offered and are to chose replacement land to be purchased by NEA; PAFs [Project Affected Family]will receive cash Compensation; a cadastral [real property] survey of all areas expected to be affected by the project was completed prior to land acquisition.

75. Furthermore, *the Response* suggests that the OD contains no requirements as to how project benefits should be shared; nor does it require that permanent employment be provided to displaced persons but in this case the ACRP provides that at least one person from every SPAF is to be offered temporary employment by NEA; full socioeconomic surveys covering all PAFs were carried out for the Hill Route in 1990 and the Valley Route in 199356; resettlement planning was timely and that only 8 families will be affected by transmission lines. The Response refers to preparation of a Due Process Manual in Nepali which describes the ACRP policies and procedures and designed to inform affected people of their rights.

76. [The Panel notes that the] Staff Appraisal Report for the original Access Road (Credit 2029-NEP) describes the resettlement plan: "*Resettlement.* To provide necessary compensation and rehabilitation measures for the population whose land, buildings and means of livelihood would be either temporarily or permanently affected by the road/dam construction, the project includes implementation of an ACRP. The ACRP contains an overall plan for the resettlement to be carried out under the project as well as details on the nature and magnitude of the operation, compensation packages offered to the affected families, development plans for relocation sites, transfer/transport arrangements, implementation timetable and costs. The legislative basis for implementing the ACRP is contained in the Land Acquisition Guidelines 2045 approved by HMG on January 5, 1989."

77. When the Hill road was designed IDA approved a resettlement plan regarded as a model at that time. The resettlement plan for the proposed Valley route is based on it.

Hill Route

78. A very large number of families (estimated at about 1600) were deprived of their land for purposes of this project. After the change in access route alignment it appears that this land is not needed for project purposes. Nevertheless, the "Hill Route RoW will be retained in government ownership for future road construction purposes."

79. The POE Report No. 7 pointed out that among the apparent disadvantages of the Valley Route were "losses and uncertainties resulting from the circumstance that land compensation for the hill route is already 94 percent completed," and concluded that "[if the valley route is selected, NEA's 'Environmental Assessment and Management Executive Summary' should be updated and amended to reflect the selection of the valley route, [and] address the issue of impacts on families within the RoW of the hill route who have already received compensation."

80. A decision was made, in 1992, to change the Arun access road to the Valley Route. The Panel notes that apart from the reference to completion of a socio-economic survey, the Response does not address the issue of impacts on families within the ROW of the now abandoned Hill Route who have already received compensation. Those affected appear to have been forgotten which gives rise to a number of issues:

- land has been purchased from those who will not longer share in any benefits the construction of an access road might confer
- there is no systematic information on what adverse impacts the acquisition has caused except for the claims of the two Requesters
- there does not yet appear to be any mitigation plan for the Hill Route people
- under Nepalese law it appears that HMG/N is supposed to return land no longer needed for the project for which it was acquired.

Valley Route

81. Although no foreign exchange resources have been utilized under the Arun III Access Road Project of 1989. this project triggered actions by HMG/N that could have negative impacts on local populations since the land of a large number of families was expropriated for the RoW of the original route.

82. By the time the change of route was introduced in 1992, most of the land purchases had been completed for the original route, According to the Panel of Experts' Report No.7, by September 1992, 94 percent of the land purchases of the RoW had been completed, supposedly according to specific Land Acquisition Guidelines approved by HMG/N. The total number of affected families by the Hill Route is estimated at 1661.

83. Therefore, the comparison between the number of families affected by the Hill and Valley Routes must clarify the fact that over 1600 families have already been affected in the Hill Route, while an additional 1146 families will also be affected by the RoW of the Valley route.

84. The Panel has received a specific request from two people who claim to be directly and adversely affected by acquisition of their land for the now abandoned Hill Route. This claim requires further study. Prima facie these material adverse effects appear to be a direct result of omissions by IDA during preparation and appraisal of the project and appear to be a serious violation of IDA s resettlement policies.

85. Because this gives rise to uncertain future implications regarding implementation of the resettlement process for the proposed Valley Route, steps need to be taken to ensure the apparent adverse effects of the Hill Route will not be repeated.

V. Indigenous Peoples

86. *The Request* claims that there are no benefits provided for the Indigenous peoples, who will suffer only adverse impacts and lists those impacts; there is no mitigation or indigenous peoples plan – it is unclear whether documents contain actual work plans or just recommendations – many recommendations in EIA are not taken into consideration; there are many issues to be resolved in bidding documents – which are secret; mitigation of negative effects on indigenous peoples does not constitute a development plan; land appropriation on the Hill Route started before completion of the cadastral survey; the policy on participation in the decision making process was violated as stated in 1991 EIA – "the road alignment and dam site were already decided and the study team did not have mandate to change these decisions."

87. *The Response* explains that all aspects of the policy have been met, mostly by reference to documents. It notes that the cadastral survey is nearing completion in Sankhuwasabha and acknowledges that, despite all precautions "a close watch will be necessary throughout project implementation to ensure that the objectives of the OD are met. To this end, the project supervision plan involves careful monitoring and evaluation of the impact of project related activities on vulnerable groups in the valley."

88. IDAS policy on Indigenous Peoples requires a specific "Indigenous Peoples Development Plan" that is comprehensive, that avoids or mitigates potentially adverse effects and ensures that the indigenous people receive culturally, socially and economically compatible benefits.

89. [The Panel notes that there] are a variety of different ethnic groups along the Arun basin. The original regional action plan (RAP) which focuses on the Hill Route reviews an extensive range of social and environmental issues including vulnerable groups, indigenous peoples and women. Some of these groups are unfamiliar with a cash economy which poses additional risks to their welfare requiring special attention.

90. IDA s policy is that an Indigenous Peoples development plan should be prepared. The NEA has informed the Panel that a revised RAP [Regional Action Plan for the Arun III Project] will be ready in January 1995: it may be that this will contain an appropriate Indigenous Peoples development plan and provisions for implementation. Provision for technical assistance to support the RAP Secretariat at base cost of US$2 million aimed at facilitating implementation of the RAP was introduced and agreed during June 1994 negotiations.

Questions and Discussion

1. The Arun River flows from Nepal through Tibet and China, where it joins the Ganges. Lori Udall, of International Rivers Network, summed up the problem facing the Arun dam project this way:

> It is a five-day walk from the nearest road to get to the proposed site of the Arun III Dam in the Arun River valley. A planned 74.4-mile-long access road to be constructed through the valley and the influx of up to 10,000 construction workers and their families will jeopardize the lives and cultures of 450,000 indigenous people and threaten over one hundred species of endangered and rare flora and fauna. The Arun III project is the first in a series of three dams to be built in the valley, and yet there has been no cumulative environmental impact assessment for the entire scheme.

> Lori Udall, *The Arun III Dam: A Test Case in World Bank Accountability*, 26 BULL. CONCERNED ASIAN SCHOLARS 82 (No. 4, 1994).

    More than 1,600 families along the original access road route were deprived of their land before it was decided to build the road along a different route, and although some 1,100 families lost their land along the new route, the land was not returned to the families on the original route. The Inspection Panel found environmental assessments were not properly conducted; alternatives were not fully considered, and if a "less restrictive assessment, including a wider range of hydro resources, could be undertaken, it would result in expanding the number of economically and environmentally acceptable options." The Inspection Panel also noted that information regarding the project was available in Washington but not in Nepal.

2. In its first opportunity to address the question of eligibility, the Inspection Panel appears to adopt a lenient standard (see paragraphs 6 and 7). The Panel simply comments that "the serious nature of the substance of the Request as a whole and its timing in relation to the project process outweighed outright rejection of the Request on the grounds of doubts on the standing of the Requesters and incomplete compliance with formal procedures." This balancing doctrine was addressed by the Executive Board in the subsequent 1999 Second Review, *supra*: "For its recommendation on whether an investigation should be carried out, the Panel will satisfy itself that all the eligibility criteria provided for in the Resolution have been met."

3. In Arun, the resolution creating the Inspection Panel and defining its functions was put
    into practice for the first time. The request for an inspection in this case was filed by the
    Arun Concerned Group, a coalition of Nepalese NGOs, in October 1994. The Inspection
    Panel registered the request and recommended an inspection. The Board approved the
    recommendation, and the Panel produced a report. In August 1995, the Bank withdrew its
    support for the project. *See* Richard Bissel, *Recent Practice of the Inspection Panel of the
    World Bank*, 91 AM. J. INT'L L. 741, 741 (1997).
       Arun's reception was generally positive:

    > Professor Daniel Bradlow of the Washington College of Law (WCL), whose proposal for
    > appointing an ombudsman at the Bank served as a model for the Panel, [described] the
    > Panel's report as "diligent and thoughtful," and one that "makes a superb effort to respond
    > to all the issues in the complaint in a very serious and determined way." He [encouraged]
    > affected people and groups representing them to take advantage of the opportunities pro-
    > vided by the Panel, and thereby to enhance the Panel's ability to hold the Bank accountable
    > for its development strategies."

    > Samir Desai, *Inspection Panel Responds to Nepal Dam Complaint: First Against World
    > Bank*, 2 HUM. RTS. BRIEF 2 (No. 2, 1995).

4. What happens if the Executive Board does not approve an Inspection Panel Recommen-
    dation? To answer this question, consider the following case.

Yacyretá Hydroelectric Project Argentina/Paraguay Panel Report and Recommendation to the Executive Directors of the IBRD Inspection Panel (Dec. 26, 1996) (Washington, D.C.)

Below is (A) Background information, (B) Discussion, and (C) Recommendation of the Inspection
Panel ("Panel") on whether or not there should be an investigation ("Recommendation") into
allegations made in the above-referenced Request for Inspection ("Request")....

A. Background

1. On September 30, 1996[,] the Panel received a Request which alleged violations by Management
of policies and procedures of the International Bank for Reconstruction and Development ("Bank")
in relation to the Yacyretá Hydroelectric Project ("Yacyretá" or "Project"). The Bank has been
involved in the design and implementation of Yacyretá since the mid[-]1970s. A number of
agreements and amendments between the Bank and the Republics of Argentina and Paraguay,
a bi-national entity established by both governments, and other entities, relate fully or in part
to Yacyretá.... [The] total amount of Bank financing for Yacyretá [to date is] $895.1 million.
In addition, in February 1995 the Board approved a loan for $46.5 million to the Republic of
Paraguay ... of which $1.2 million is to finance civil works related to the resettlement activities
under the Yacyretá Project.

The Request for Inspection

2. The Request was filed by an organization called SOBREVIVENCIA – located in Asunción,
Paraguay – representing persons who live in Encarnación, Paraguay (the "Requesters"). The
Request claims that the environment as well as the standards of living, health and economic
well-being of people in the Yacyretá area have been, and may potentially be, directly and adversely
affected as a result of the filling of the Yacyretá reservoir to 76 meters above sea level ("masl") and
the failure of the Bank to ensue – through supervision and enforcement of legal covenants – the

adequate execution of the environmental mitigation and resettlement activities included in the Project.

3. The Requesters allege that filling the reservoir inter alia has:

- caused the water to become stagnant and polluted which has contaminated the groundwater supplies used for drinking water;
- affected sanitation systems through discharge of untreated sewage into now stagnant waters that creates health hazards;
- destroyed crops;
- inundated and destroyed island communities and ecosystems;
- flooded farmlands and wildlands;
- displaced local people and wildlife; and
- disrupted fish migration through damming the river, with dramatic impact on subsistence diets and biodiversity.

4. Alleged adverse socioeconomic impacts include:

- loss of jobs, livelihood, and forced resettlement to low quality homes;
- those involved in fishing, ceramics, bakery and laundry services have lost their jobs or their earning capacity has been greatly diminished through loss of fish, top quality clay and loss of customers due to concerns over the poor water quality; and
- distances of resettlement areas from former job sites or sources of income has resulted in additional economic losses due to remoteness and the relatively high cost of transportation.

5. The Requesters claim that the direct and material adverse effects described above result from the Bank's omissions and failures in the preparation and implementation of the Project which violate its policies and procedures including inter alia, the following;

- Environmental Aspects of Bank Work (OMS 2.36)
- Environmental Policy for Dam and Reservoir Projects (OD 4.00 Annex B)
- Environmental Assessment (OD 4.01)
- Indigenous Peoples (OD 4.20)
- Involuntary Resettlement (OD 4.30)
- Project Monitoring and Evaluation (OD 10.70)
- Wildlands Policy (OPN 11.02)
- Cultural Property (OPN 11.03)
- Project Supervision (OD 13.05)
- Suspension of Disbursements (OD 13.40)

6. The Requesters also claim that procedural aspects incorporated in many of such polices, such as basic rights of participation and access to information, have been denied or ignored in the preparation and execution of Yacyretá.

7. In addition the Requesters claim that:

- the Environmental Trust Fund referred to in para. 2.16 of the Staff Appraisal Report ("SAR") for Loan 3520-AR3h as neither been established nor properly funded;
- the Bank has been lax in supervising the Project; and

- the Bank has failed to enforce its rights under the several agreements that it has entered into with the Governments of Argentina ("GOA"), Paraguay ("GOP") and the Yacyretá Binational Authority (Entidad Binacional Yacyretá "EBY").

8. On October 1, 1996 the Panel notified the Executive Directors and Bank President of receipt of the Request (meaning "Registration" under the Panel's *Operating Procedures*). On November 1,1996 the Panel received the Management response ("Response") to the Request.

Management Response

9. The substance of the Response . . . reads as follows: "We do not agree that the problems which have occurred and their possible consequences for the local population are the result of any alleged Management violation of the Bank's policies and procedures. The salient features of the Management Response are:

- Yacyretá made economic sense when conceived and, even though the economic realities have since changed, it still makes more sense to complete Yacyretá than to stop it.
- all resettlement and environmental mitigation activities required prior to reaching the current reservoir of 76 masl have been met (except some pending matters which are being addressed through appropriate financing and supervision).
- the impacts of increasing the operating level of the reservoir above 76 masl have not yet occurred and are covered by sufficient legal covenants in full compliance with Bank policies.
- although counterpart funding shortfalls have delayed Project implementation, they have not caused harmed impacts, precisely because the reservoir has not been raised beyond its initial operating level.
- the delay in increasing the operating level of the reservoir is, in part, attributable to the Bank's supervision efforts to ensure compliance with resettlement and environmental management activities, supporting the essential principle of Bank operations that the exercise of available legal remedies is not a requirement but a discretionary tool, to be applied only after other reasonable means of persuasion have failed."

Panel: Initial Study

10. After receipt of the Response the Panel decided that an initial field study was needed both to verify the eligibility of the Request and assess the adequacy of the Response. [The latter purpose was foreclosed by the 1999 Second Review. – *Eds.*]

11. The Panel considered information obtained during Mr. Alvaro Umaña Quesada's ("Inspector") review conducted in the Project area from December 2–6, 1996. The Inspector consulted with the Governments of Argentina and of Paraguay, EBY, people in the Project area and their representatives from SOBREVIVENCIA. The Panel consulted with the Bank Executive Director representing Argentina and Paraguay.

12. As provided in the recent review of the Resolution [the 1996 First Review], the Panel indicated to the Board that it would evaluate the Inspector's findings and would then submit its recommendation as to the need, if any, for an Investigation. Subsequently, the Panel again interviewed Regional Management, staff and others.

B. Discussion

13. The discussion below is based on the Panel's preliminary review of the Request and Response and takes into account the information provided through subsequent interviews in the field and in Washington, D.C.

14. Pursuant to para. 19 of the Resolution it is the responsibility of the Panel to "determine whether the request meets the eligibility criteria set out in paragraphs 12 to 14" after it has received the Response and the Executive Directors have expressed the hope that the Panel process will not focus on "narrow technical grounds" with regard to eligibility. . . .

15. The Panel is satisfied that the Request meets the eligibility criteria set out in paragraph 12 of the Resolution and that those signing the Request (i) represent communities that feel negatively affected by the design and implementation of the Yacyretá Project; and (ii) properly authorized SOBREVIVENCIA as their legitimate representative. The Inspector verified the identity of the "anonymous" Requesters and obtained first hand knowledge of some of the alleged material harm on the spot during his field visit.

Preliminary Evidence of Material Harm

16. The Response maintains that the Requesters have not suffered the material harm they allege but the Panel notes that the following [Management] statements, for example, appear to indicate otherwise: "there is *little* evidence of harm having been done to the affected parties" (para. 2 of Cover Memorandum from Mr. Wolfensohn to Mr. Bissell); and that "Socio-economic outcomes of the relocation of the population affected by operation of the reservoir at level 76 masl are *mostly* satisfactory" (2.8) [Emphases added by the Panel].

17. During his field visit the Inspector interviewed groups of people in the Project area. These discussions and his initial observations prima facie confirm some of the allegations of harm made in the Request. For example:

- Quality clay resources seem to be now under water which has an impact on the brick and tile industry. In addition, the 1200 ceramic workers-unlike other affected people-have not been regarded as eligible for compensation.
- Discharges of raw sewage and slaughterhouse waste into streams that used to flow freely have exposed nearby populations to health risks associated with deteriorating sanitary conditions caused by the rise in reservoir level to 76 masl.
- Rise in groundwater levels has contaminated drinking water wells and caused latrines to backup rendering them useless and potentially a health risk.
- People interviewed in one housing resettlement area claim that they have not been fully compensated and that commercial structures to replace their shops or businesses have not been built.
- In the Barrio San Pedro resettlement the Inspector observed leaky roofs and inferior construction materials.

18. A review of these and many other allegations of harm-including damage to wildlife and fisheries-in the Request would require investigation.

Alleged Acts or Omissions

19. The Request claims in substance that the act of filling the reservoir to 76 masl but at the same time failing to implement adequately the required resettlement, environmental and social mitigation measures has harmed them and their environment. In addition they express their deep concern about future damage that may occur if the water level is raised to the 78 masl and 83 masl as envisaged in the Project.

20. Management Response admits to delays in resettlement and environmental actions required prior to filling the reservoir to the 76 mas1 level and provides various explanations for the Project's difficulties and delays.

21. The Panel notes that:

- the SAR for Yacyretá II explains that [the Bank's loan] is supporting the resettlement program required for raising the level to 76 masl because "It was expected that the resettlement program would have been completed under the Electric Power Sector Project."..
- The SAR emphasizes the proper sequencing of project components: "It is particularly important that the resettlement and environment mitigation measures needed to protect the affected population be executed *prior* to the reservoir rise, and in compliance with defined standards. It would be appropriate to determine whether these have been accomplished in the first semester of 1994 when the Bank would conduct with EBY a mid-term review of the Project. Consequently, the Bank plans to monitor carefully EBY's performance in this area *before* the level is raised to 76m, and again to 78m. [Emphases added by Panel].

22. The Panel observes that the Resettlement and Environmental Management Plans ("REMP') included a specific sequence of actions for a variety of critical areas such as relocation, compensation, wildlife, compensatory reserves, environmental health and fisheries. At the time the reservoir was filled to 76 masl in 1994 a number of key environmental and resettlement actions had not been completed and many of them now at the end of 1996 still await completion.

23. Quoting the SAR the Response notes that among the three major risks associated with Yacyretá were "failure to implement the resettlement and environmental mitigation activities satisfactorily." Despite the occurrence of such failures Management does not seem to have regarded it as a "major risk" since it agreed to let the reservoir be filled to 76 masl. Much later an internal memorandum from staff working on environmental aspects warned Regional Management of the deteriorating situation:

> The situation is serious, in that the Bank "no objection" to filling the reservoir to elevation 76 meters was conditioned upon the agreement that all pending environmental and resettlement actions, which were not complete at the time of the reservoir filling, would be completed in the course of 1995. The necessary resources to complete the resettlement and environmental pending actions for elevation 76 m have not been provided, despite repeated Bank reiteration of the same request and repeated borrower representations of an intention to do so.

This memorandum was prepared in June 1996 – nearly two years after filling the reservoir to 76 masl. Without a more detailed study – that is only possible in the context of an investigation – it is difficult to understand how the imbalance developed between progress in civil works and the REM was allowed to grow without an effective response from Management. This is one of the very actions and omission which the Requesters claim has adversely affected them.

Alleged Policy Violations

24. The Request claims that the Bank's act of authorizing the filling of the reservoir to 76 masl and omission in not insisting on completion of the resettlement, environmental and social mitigation measures are violations of various Bank policies and procedures: as a result of this failure groups of local people have suffered material harm.

25. Management Response appears to suggest that even if there has been harm, it is not the result of any policy violations. It refers to "problems which have occurred and their possible consequences for the local population" but does not agree that they are "the result of any alleged Management violation of the Bank's policies and procedures."

26. The Panel observes that both the Resettlement and Environmental policies require an appropriate sequence of actions to prevent harm to both potentially affected populations and the environment. The sequence of actions in this Project – designed for masl levels 76, 78 and 83 – was allowed to slip badly when counterpart funding became unavailable and when an eventual privatization became an option to fund Yacyretá.

27. The Panel notes all the other policy violations alleged by the Requesters. However, given this large and complex Request, the Panel has focused only on what appear to be two serious and initially verifiable policy allegations. Even though Management has addressed the complaints, the Panel is not convinced that there has been substantial compliance with the relevant policies and procedures.

Supervision

28. The Request also alleges that Management has failed to supervise adequately the Project and to enforce several covenants related to environmental mitigation and resettlement activities.

29. The Response argues that the exercise of available legal remedies is not a requirement, but a discretionary tool, to be applied only after other reasonable means of persuasion have failed....

30. The Panel, knowing that Management has flexibility in deciding whether to exercise available legal remedies, must note that the Resolution itself defines as an instance of failure in the compliance of Bank policies and procedures situations where the Bank has "failed in its follow-up on the borrower's obligations under loan agreements with respect to such policies or procedures" (para. 12). In other words, according to Bank policy, compliance is not achieved by merely including covenants in Loan Agreements but rather by ensuring that their provisions are implemented in a timely fashion by the borrower and executing entities.

31. The attention of the Panel was drawn to the discretionary use of legal remedies by an excellent OED [World Bank Operations Evaluation Department] analysis. The recent OED Performance Audit Report for two of the loans providing financing for Yacyretá states that: "the Bank accepted repeated violations of major covenants;" and adds that: "[c]ovenanted actions are a precarious way to ensure the viability of a financing plan in light of the Bank's willingness to 'accommodate' non-compliance and the added difficulty of stopping a large unitary project once it has reached a certain stage of implementation."

32. The Response denies that the provision of funds for the implementation of pending actions has constituted a problem. The evidence reviewed so far by the Panel suggests otherwise. Damage related to noncompliance with covenants appears to have occurred. A more detailed analysis – which is only possible under an investigation – would be required to ascertain whether there has been a violation of Bank policy through failure to enforce legal covenants, as stated by

the Requesters, or compliance thereof has been achieved through "other reasonable means of persuasion" as claimed by Management.

33. The Management Response includes "Pending Actions.".. : "With respect to compliance with pending actions related to elevating the reservoir to the current operating level of 76 mad, a time-bound Action Plan, supported by a Special Account, has been put in place to complete all pending actions no later than December 1997." The Response states that "These activities will be completed by the end of 1997, thus concluding the resettlement and environmental mitigation measures required for raising the operating level of the reservoir to 76 masl.."..

34. The Request as noted above at para. 7 complains that the Environmental Trust Fund to finance the REMP has neither been established nor properly funded.

35. The Response states that the claim is incorrect: that the Trust Fund (to finance all REMP activities) was established by EBY in November 1994 and that while "amounts deposited in this Fund were not precisely those agreed with the Bank, the Borrower has funded the required REMP activities up to elevation 76 masl through the Fund and otherwise.."..

36. Further clarifications by the staff explain that the Trust Fund referred to in the SAR was never established but rather an account for receiving funds for the execution of the REMP was opened and an initial deposit of about $3 million made on January 13, 1995: this is in reality the "Trust Fund" referred to in the Response. This account was used during 1995 but as the GOA contributions to EBY were reduced and later on ceased, the account "lost its purpose."

37. Two other accounts have since been established for similar purposes:

- a so-called "special account" opened in August 1996 with an initial deposit of $4 million (for which the Panel has been unable to obtain operating documentation); and
- an "Escrow Account" just opened on December 10, 1996[,] with an initial deposit of $5.4 million and with further deposits expected to reach a total of $8.2 million to finance certain specified REMP activities that were supposed to be carried out before the reservoir reached the 76 masl level. (The Panel has received documents relating to this account).

38. The Panel notes the importance attached to funding the Environmental Trust Fund for this component in the SAR . . . : "Given the underlying importance of satisfactorily completing the Resettlement and Environmental Management Programs required for *different reservoir operation levels*, during negotiations EBY agreed to establish by November 1994, and, thereafter maintain an Environmental Trust Fund on terms and conditions satisfactory to the Bank by depositing therein the amounts necessary to finance in a timely manner all activities under these programs and for the Arroyos protection works, *such amounts* to be derived from the sales of electricity or any other resource and *be at least US $18.3 million in 1995, US $60.9 million in 1996, US $101.6 million in 1997, and US $2.7 million in 1998* . . . withdrawals from such account would be made exclusively to finance these activities." [Emphases added by Panel]

39. As evidenced by the above SAR data, neither the $8 million already deposited, nor the $16 million in funding anticipated by the Management Response appear to be adequate to implement pending activities of the REMP that may be necessary to meet the policy requirements and the Requesters' concerns. The December 20, 1996, Back to Office Report confirms the seriousness of the financial gap facing the Project at my operating level.

C. Recommendation

40. The Yacyretá Hydroelectric Project has represented a massive effort spanning over twenty years, exceeding $8 billion in cost and including a large number of highly complex issues and uncertainties. It is now uncertain whether or when the Project will reach its original design level and generating capacity and what would be the sources of the funding to complete the Project including the REMP. The Panel has been informed that, to date, while the main civil work infrastructure components are almost complete, only about a fifth of the housing in the resettlement component has been completed and other activities and social mitigation measures lag far behind. This is an unusual imbalance.

41. Based on the preliminary review the Panel is satisfied that there have been material adverse effects which many have resulted from policy violations of a serious nature.

42. The recommendation below for an investigation represents the Panel's preliminary conclusion that the Request is eligible for investigation. It will be necessary to conduct an investigation in order to determine whether the harm claimed or likely to occur and the allegations of serious violations of policy are well founded.

43. Based on the foregoing the Panel recommends that the Executive Directors authorize an investigation into the violations of Bank policies and procedures alleged in the Request.

Questions and Discussion

1. The huge Yacyretá hydroelectric project was initiated by a 1973 treaty between Paraguay and Argentina. The 808-meter, $11 billion dam is situated on the Paraná River, which forms part of the boundary between the two countries, in the area of Yacyretá Island. The project was plagued by decades of cost overruns, political recriminations between the two countries, and allegations of corruption. The dam itself operated far below capacity for many years, and in early 2010, it operates at 60 percent of its potential.

   Critics of the dam project alleged that tens of thousands of local inhabitants were displaced by the project without adequate compensation for the loss of their homes, jobs, and crops; the drinking water supply was polluted; communities were broken up; and wildlife was decimated and endangered. The Bank took measures, often in the form of contracts with third parties, to alleviate the harm caused by the project. However, as the Panel suggests, the measures were not always carried out.

2. The requesting parties in the Yacyretá case chose to remain anonymous because they feared retaliation from their respective governments and from the Bank's agents and contractors. In this case, the anonymous individuals have designated Sobrevivencia as their agent. The Inspection Panel permits anonymous requests, so long as during the twenty-one-day preliminary review the Panel can verify that the anonymous individuals are eligible. The Management response in the Yacyretá case concedes that anonymity may be appropriate:

   > The identity of those individuals that Sobrevivencia claims to represent is being held confidential by the Panel at the request of the NGO [Sobrevivencia]. Although the Board Resolution itself does not address the issue of claimant anonymity, Management understands that there have been Panel precedents in this regard. Nevertheless, it is important to note that such anonymity imposes serious constraints on Management's ability to respond. . . . [26]

[26] Response para. 1.2(d)

3. Recall that according to the resolution establishing the Inspection Panel, for an investigation to proceed, the Board must accept the Panel's recommendation. Consider the following account of what happened after the Inspection Panel produced the report and recommendation you just read:

> At their first informal meeting to discuss the recommendation in early February 1997, the Board split over whether to approve an inspection, with the [donor] countries in favor and [borrower] countries opposed. While Board deliberations are confidential, the Directors' positions on Yacyretá were no secret. The Argentine Executive Director, Julio Nogues, launched the strongest attack, mobilizing opposition to the Panel, the claim and the claimants from other borrowing countries. Mr. Nogues'[s] statement at the Board meeting objected to an investigation and accused the Panel of operating outside its own resolution, and of placing the country in a precarious financial situation owing to the recent financial crisis. He also took issue with the claimants' eligibility because they are Paraguayan. There was also a strong reaction from the [borrower] countries to the term "investigation," which to some implied wrongdoing. They were concerned especially that the Panel process would focus on the role of the government in causing harm, rather than on the role of the Bank.
>
> However for the first time in a Panel deliberation the donor country Directors unanimously supported the Panel's recommendation. The strongest advocates for an investigation included the U.S., Netherlands and Switzerland. Apparently President Wolfensohn supported an investigation as well, but was searching for a consensus and it was clear that one would not be reached. The Board had split completely between North and South. Given the fact that the [donor] countries own more than 50% of the Bank and thus have more than 50% of the votes, if a vote had been taken to authorize an inspection, the outcome would have been different. But the Board rarely votes. To do so in the case of Yacyretá may have been seen by some Directors, and certainly by President Wolfensohn, to be too costly for the Bank. The decision about the Panel's recommendation was thus postponed.
>
> During this period, NGOs conducted a vigorous international campaign aimed at lobbying the Executive Directors to support the claim. The main intent was to ensure that the Board understood that the international NGO community was paying close attention to their process and that anything short of a decision to accept the Panel's recommendation would damage the Bank's credibility. . . .
>
> The Board met again in late February. In addition to deliberating over the Panel's Recommendation, the Board heard a presentation from Bank management of a new EBY-generated Action Plan. The Plan had two parts: Plan A addressed those environment and resettlement actions that were to have been completed prior to filling the reservoir to level 76 masl and Plan B proposed actions that would be necessary for "continued operation of the reservoir at 76 masl in an environmentally sound manner."
>
> While it is important to note that effective actions, or remedies, are a desired outcome of the claims process, the Board's acceptance of the Action Plan undermined the Panel process in two important ways. First, it gave management direct access to the Board in order to present their point of view of the claim without making a similar allowance for claimants, who had not seen the Action Plan and were unable to respond to it either in person or in writing. The balance of power in the deliberation thus resided with management. Second, directing the Panel to look at the efficacy of the Action Plan deflected the Panel away from focusing on specific Bank policy violations.
>
> The Board was also unable to reach consensus on the term "investigation," and instead authorized the Panel "to undertake a review of the existing problems of the Yacyretá project in the areas of environment and resettlement and provide an assessment of the adequacy of the Action Plan as agreed between the Bank and the two countries concerned."[27]

---

[27] Kay Treakle, *Accountability at the World Bank: What Does It Take?* (BANK INFORMATION CENTER 1998).

The resulting Inspection Panel report was delivered to the Board in September 1997, and concluded, "Despite extensive but inconsistent supervision efforts, the Bank has failed to bring the project into compliance with relevant Bank policies and procedures due to a poorly conceived Project design in the first place, compounded by changing standards and regulations over time, EBY bureaucratic procedures and lack of financial resources."

4. The Inspection Panel's final report was not the final word in the Yacyretá case. Isabel Guerrero, World Bank acting vice president for Latin America and the Caribbean, addressed a letter to Yacyretá claimant Pedro Arzamendia on behalf of World Bank President Wolfensohn. The letter, which appeared in the Paraguayan newspaper *Última Hora* in March 1998, included these words: "the Bank is satisfied with the conclusions of the report which affirm that its policies on resettlements, environment, community participation, and others were fully respected and applied in the case of Yacyretá." It also said, "We have complete confidence in the institutions and people that work with us to implement the Action Plan agreed to." The letter, which misrepresented the findings of the report, was subsequently retracted. President Wolfensohn met personally with representatives of Sobrevivencia to apologize.

5. On May 17, 2002, a separate claim was filed with the Inspection Panel involving the Yacyretá Dam: Paraguay/Argentina: Reform Project for the Water and Telecommunication Sectors, SEGBA V Power Distribution Project (Yacyretá 2002). The Panel registered the Request and recommended inspection. The recommendation was approved by the Board, and a report was delivered to the Board on February 24, 2004. The Board approved an action plan to address the situation, and a management progress report on the action plan was reviewed by the Inspection Panel on February 10, 2005. This review noted, "The Panel again observes that a number of essential but costly social and environmental activities have yet to be completed as the water level of the Yacyretá reservoir is to be raised further."

6. How would you characterize the problem presented by the Yacyretá case? What accounts for the Board's reluctance to act on the panel's recommendations on the first Yacyretá claim? What can prevent the Bank's directors from simply ignoring the findings of the Inspection Panel? How can the situation that developed in Yacyretá be avoided in the future?

C. *Office of Compliance Advisor and Ombudsman*

Democratizing Multilateral Development Banks, in THE NEW "PUBLIC":
THE GLOBALIZATION OF PUBLIC PARTICIPATION 151-164
(Environmental Law Institute 2002)
Nathalie Bernasconi-Osterwalder and David Hunter

When the Inspection Panel was created, neither the IFC [International Finance Corporation] nor MIGA [Multilateral Investment Guarantee Agency] had any environmental or social policies. Accordingly, the Panel's jurisdiction did not extend to their operations. In 1999, after the IFC adopted its safeguard policies, World Bank President James Wolfensohn announced the creation of an office of the Compliance Advisor and Ombudsman (CAO). . . .

The CAO has two goals: "first, to help the IFC and MIGA address – in a manner that is fair, objective, and constructive – complaints made by people who have been or may be affected by projects in which the IFC and MIGA play a role; and second, to enhance the social and environmental outcomes of those projects." To achieve those goals, the CAO has three related roles: (i) Responding to complaints by persons who are affected by projects and attempting to resolve issues raised using a flexible, problem solving approach (the ombudsman role);

(ii) Providing a source of independent advice to the President and the management of IFC and MIGA. CAO provides advice both in relation to particular projects and in relation to broader environmental and social policies, guidelines, procedures, and systems (the advisory role); (iii) Overseeing audits of IFC's and MIGA's social and environmental performance, both overall and in relation to sensitive projects, to ensure compliance with policies, guidelines, procedures, and systems (the compliance role).

Any individual, group, community, entity, or other party affected or likely to be affected by the social or environmental impacts of an IFC or MIGA project may make a complaint to the Ombudsman's office.

The Ombudsman process tries to resolve the concerns raised by the affected communities through a variety of possible conflict resolution methodologies, including, for example, consultation, dialogue, or mediation. The focus is not necessarily on determining whether the IFC or MIGA have been at fault in the design or implementation of the project. Because IFC and MIGA projects involve private sector companies, the Ombudsman can more easily play an intermediary role using IFC/ MIGA leverage with the project sponsor to address legitimate concerns of affected people.

The CAO may bring the complaint process to a close either when a settlement agreement has been reached or when it has determined that further investigation or problem-solving efforts are not going to be productive. At that point, the CAO will inform the complainant and report to the President of the World Bank Group. The report to the President may include specific recommendations the CAO believes could help to solve problems raised by the complaint. The CAO may also decide to conduct a compliance audit to address non-compliance issues identified in the course of responding to the complaint or may refer any policy issues to the advisory role of the CAO's office.

The CAO's compliance role may be triggered through the ombudsman's process, at the request of management or on the CAO's own initiative. The purpose of a compliance audit is to determine whether IFC, MIGA, or in some cases the project sponsor have complied with the environmental and social safeguard policies of the respective institution. The compliance report may also contain specific recommendations for improving compliance both in the specific project and more generally. A report from each compliance audit is provided to the President.

Given the relatively short period of time in which the CAO has been operating, there is insufficient experience to determine its long-term success in resolving the problems of project-affected people or in improving the IFC's and MIGA's policy compliance. In several cases, however, the affected people have been satisfied with the outcomes of the process or at least the preliminary assessments that have validated their concerns.

According to the CAO Operational Guidelines "Any individual, group, community, entity, or other party that believes it is affected – or potentially affected – by the social and/or environmental impacts of an IFC/MIGA project may make a complaint to the CAO Ombudsman." The CAO Guidelines explains the three functions the CAO performs:

- Ombudsman role (CAO Ombudsman): Responding to complaints by individual(s), group(s) of people, or organization(s) that are affected by IFC/MIGA projects.... The focus of the CAO ombudsman role is on helping to resolve complaints, ideally by improving social and environmental outcomes on the ground.
- Compliance role (CAO Compliance): Overseeing audits of the social and environmental performance of IFC and MIGA, particularly in relation to sensitive projects....
- Advisory role (CAO Advisor): Providing a source of independent advice to the President of the World Bank Group and the management of IFC and MIGA....

CAO Operational Guidelines (Apr. 2007), *available at* http://www.cao-ombudsman.org/ html-english/documents/WEBEnglishCAO06.08.07Web.pdf.

A complaint to the CAO because of the human rights and environmental impacts of an IFC-funded project can assist in focusing attention on the particular problems associated with the project. However, the CAO does not have the authority to find fault or withdraw a loan. It uses a "flexible, problem-solving approach," which brings the parties together to negotiate a solution. The CAO would not require any specific action from the multinational corporations; it can only make recommendations.

The following complaint from Tanzania illustrates the "spotlight" function of the CAO, as well as its inherent limitations.

LEAT *Bulyanhulu Complaint to IFC/MIGA Compliance Advisor/Ombudsman* (Jan. 14, 2002), *available at* http://www.leat.or.tz/activities/buly/miga.complaint.php

We[,] Lawyers' Environmental Action Team ("LEAT")[,] lodge a complaint concerning the Bulyanhulu Gold Mine project. This complaint is made on our own behalf and on behalf of our clients, communities of former small-scale miners and landholders of the Bulyanhulu area organized under the Bulyanhulu Small-Scale Gold Miners' Committee ("the Bulyanhulu complainants"). LEAT is a public interest environmental law organization that has been working with and on behalf of the Bulyanhulu complainants.

. . .

Project Description

1. The Bulyanhulu Gold Mine in Bulyanhulu area of Kahama District, Shinyanga Region is a large-scale underground gold mine that also produces silver and copper.
2. The Multilateral Investment Guarantee Agency ("MIGA") is involved with the project through the provision of a political risk guarantee in the sum of United States Dollars 172 million approved in August 2000.
3. The projector sponsor is Kahama Mining Corporation Limited of Dar es Salaam, Tanzania, which is a wholly-owned subsidiary of Barrick Gold Corporation of Toronto, Canada ("the project sponsors").

Background to the Complaint

a. The Bulyanhulu complainants formerly lived and worked for gain as small-scale miners, small traders, peasant farmers and livestock keepers in an area called Bulyanhulu in Kahama District, Shinyanga Region in central western Tanzania. However, in September 1994, the project sponsors laid a claim over the Bulyanhulu area on the basis of a license granted by the Government of Tanzania on August 5, 1994, a copy of which is annexed hereto and marked "B" to form part of this complaint.
b. Relying on this license, the project sponsors caused the Canadian High Commission in Tanzania to put diplomatic pressure on the Tanzanian Government to evict the Bulyanhulu complainants. (The Complainants shall refer to documents obtained from the Canadian Department of Foreign Affairs and International Trade (DFAIT) under the Canadian Access to Information Act and collectively marked "C" in support of this contention.)
c. The project sponsors also commenced judicial proceedings against the Bulyanhulu complainants in the High Court of Tanzania to have the Bulyanhulu complainants evicted by

judicial orders. (Copies of the ruling and order of the High Court of Tanzania in these proceedings is annexed hereto and marked "D" to form part of this complaint.)

d. Following adverse ruling by the High Court of Tanzania, the project sponsors first appealed to the Court of Appeal of Tanzania (Tanzania's highest appellate court) but later withdrew the appeal and reverted to using diplomatic and administrative pressure to evict the Bulyanhulu complainants. (Copies of an application by the project sponsors' lawyers to the court of Appeal of Tanzania and the corresponding order of the Chief Justice are annexed hereto and collectively marked "E" to form part of this complaint.) The Bulyanhulu complainants shall also make reference to contemporaneous press reports copies of which are annexed hereto and collectively marked "F" to form part of this complaint.

e. On July 30, 1996, the Tanzanian Government issued orders that the Bulyanhulu complainants should vacate their lands, settlements and property within 24 hours. Paramilitary police units and demolition equipment belonging to the project sponsors and operated by their employees were then stationed in the Bulyanhulu complainants' villages and settlements. The next day the eviction of the Bulyanhulu complainants and the destruction of their settlements and immovable property began and went on for much of August 1996. (See Annexes "C" and "F," and copies of videotapes taken by the project sponsors and the Tanzanian police annexed hereto and collectively marked "G" to form part of this complaint.)

f. In so doing, the project sponsors and the Government of Tanzania went contrary to the order of the High Court of Tanzania attached hereto and marked "D." The Bulyanhulu complainants shall also refer to official statements of the Tanzanian Government relating to the matters in question annexed hereto and marked "H" to form part of this complaint. The Bulyanhulu complainants shall, in addition refer to project documents prepared by and/or for the project sponsors and submitted to MIGA which are collectively marked "I" in support of this complaint.

g. The Bulyanhulu complainants were, thus, forced to leave the area and currently live in Kakola Village, Kahama Town, Mwabomba and Kezeria mining areas, all in Kahama District. Those who have remained in the Bulyanhulu area of which Kakola village is part have continued to live in fear of forcible and uncompensated eviction as correspondence between the project sponsors and the Government of Tanzania, and court documents all of which are marked "J" to form part of this complaint show.

The Complaint

4. The Bulyanhulu complainants have been, are being and/or are likely to be affected by social and environmental impacts of the project in the following ways:

Forced Evictions and Displacement When Project Sponsor Took Control of the Mine Site

a. We believe that potentially hundreds of thousands of the Bulyanhulu complainants were forcibly evicted and displaced from the Bulyanhulu area when the project sponsors illegally and irregularly entered into the Bulyanhulu complainants' lands, settlements and mining areas with the help of the security forces of the Government of Tanzania.

b. We believe that the project sponsors and the Government of Tanzania failed or neglected to plan, finance and implement any resettlement or relocation plan and to provide alternative lands or settlements or alternative sources of livelihoods for the Bulyanhulu complainants.

c. We believe that the project sponsors and the Government of Tanzania failed and/or refused to pay any or adequate, fair, just and prompt compensation for loss of agricultural and grazing lands; destruction of settlements including residential and commercial property; expropriation of mineral rights and investment in mining equipment, machinery and mining shafts; and loss of income generated through employment in small-scale mining operations.

Ongoing Threats of Eviction and Displacement

d. We believe that the project sponsors and the Government of Tanzania have continued to use force or threats of use of force to evict and displace additional numbers of the Bulyanhulu complainants.

e. We believe that the project sponsor and the Government of Tanzania have continued to violate and/or otherwise interfere with the peaceful enjoyment of the property rights of the remaining Bulyanhulu complainants such as by preventing the Bulyanhulu complaints from productively using their agricultural and grazing lands; and prohibiting them from building residential and commercial houses in their existing lands and settlements.

f. We believe that the project sponsors and the Government of Tanzania have failed and/or neglected to pay any or adequate, fair, just and prompt compensation for the violation of, and/or interference with, the peaceful enjoyment of the property rights by the Bulyanhulu.

Negative Impacts on the Economy of the Bulyanhulu Area

g. We believe that the project sponsors destroyed the local economy of the Bulyanhulu area and even beyond, depopulated the Bulyanhulu area and the impoverished the Bulyanhulu complainants as a result of expropriation of agricultural and grazing lands; destruction of residential and commercial property and settlements; expropriation of investment in mining shafts, machinery and equipment and loss of employment opportunities;

h. We believe that the project sponsors failed to provide comparable or better settlements; comparable or better sources of livelihoods in the form of economic activities and employment opportunities for the remaining Bulyanhulu complainants;

i. We believe that the project sponsors' investment does not help the national poverty alleviation efforts by its failure to contribute significantly and fairly to government revenue in the form of taxes, royalties and other charges.

j. We believe that having destroyed employment opportunities that were available prior to their acquisition of the Bulyanhulu area, the project sponsors have failed to create any significant or comparable employment opportunities thereby undermining the national poverty alleviation goals.

Project Sponsors' Failure to Observe Laws of Tanzania in Their Takeover of the Bulyanhulu Mine Site

k. We believe that the project sponsors failed and/or neglected to secure a license that correctly and properly described the area of their concession;

l. We believe that the project sponsors and the Government of Tanzania failed and/or neglected to follow proper procedures to extinguish and/or interfere with the property rights of the Bulyanhulu complainants;

m. We believe that having decided to take the Bulyanhulu complainants to the Tanzanian courts, the project sponsors then failed and/or neglected to abide by the lawful orders and decisions of the Tanzanian courts;

n. We believe that the project sponsors also committed acts or failed and/or neglected to commit acts complained of in paragraphs a-f as stated.

Environmental and Social Impacts Assessments Inaccurate and Inadequate

o. We believe that the project sponsors failed and/or neglected to carry out any environmental impacts assessment studies and processes prior to their entry into and acquisition of the Bulyanhulu area and prior to the eviction and displacement of the Bulyanhulu complainants;

p. We believe that the project sponsors failed and/or neglected to carry out adequate and meaningful consultations with the Bulyanhulu complainants prior to their entry into and acquisition of the Bulyanhulu area;

q. We believe that the project sponsors commissioned, financed, published and submitted to MIGA, the Government of Tanzania and the general public environmental impacts statements, environmental management plan and social development plan that were materially inaccurate; and contained erroneous, false and misleading information and conclusions concerning their acquisition, possession and operation of the Bulyanhulu Gold Mine.

r. We believe that having later decided to make material changes to the design and the implementation of the project, the project sponsors failed to prepare, publish and/or submit to MIGA, the Government of Tanzania and the general public any additional environmental impacts assessment statements and/or environmental management plans concerning any material changes to the design and/or implementation of the project that might have significant environmental impacts to the Bulyanhulu complainants.

Non-Disclosure of Material Information

s. We believe that the project sponsors failed to prepare for, and/or disclose to, MIGA, the Government of Tanzania and the general public all material information as to the facts and circumstances pertaining to the acquisition, possession and operation of the Bulyanhulu Gold Mine including all acts and omissions enumerated in the foregoing paragraphs.

t. We believe that the project sponsors failed to disclose in environmental impacts statements, environmental management plan and social development plan submitted to MIGA, the Government of Tanzania and the general public the existence of the very serious allegations of human rights atrocities implicating the project sponsors and the Government of Tanzania as regards the manner of the project sponsor's acquisition, possession and operation of the project.

u. We believe that the project sponsors failed and/or neglected to disclose and/or to acknowledge in environmental impacts statements, environmental management plan and social development plan the existence of any reports or information concerning any investigations of the allegations of human rights abuses against the Bulyanhulu complainants that may have established the innocence of the project sponsors and the Government of Tanzania.

v. We believe that the project sponsors failed to and/or neglected to disclose to MIGA, the Government of Tanzania and the general public additional environmental impacts statements and/or environmental management plans, if any, concerning any material changes to the design and/or implementation of the project that might have significant environmental impacts to the Bulyanhulu complainants.

MIGA's Inadequate Due Diligence Investigations

w. We believe that MIGA failed to carry out a thorough and competent due diligence investigation pertaining to the facts and circumstances surrounding the project sponsor's acquisition, possession and operation of the Bulyanhulu Gold Mine in order to establish the veracity of the information submitted and soundness of the conclusions drawn by the project sponsors prior to making the decision to provide political risk guarantee for the project.

MIGA's Violation of Its Information Disclosure Policies

    x.   We believe that MIGA failed to prepare and/or disclose to the complainants and other interested parties all material information pertaining to the facts and circumstances surrounding the project sponsor's acquisition, possession and operation of the project in spite of repeated requests from the complainants and other interested parties to do so.

Actions Taken by Complainants

    5.   The following actions have been taken by us to try to resolve these issues:

    a.   We have twice written to His Excellency Benjamin William Mkapa, President of the United Republic of Tanzania on both occasions requesting him and his government to address themselves to these matters and to right any or all of the wrongs that may have been committed against the Bulyanhulu communities; as well as to see to it that any violations of the laws of Tanzania are thoroughly investigated and where, necessary and appropriate, punished in accordance with the laws of Tanzania. Copies of the letters are annexed hereto and collectively marked "K" to form part of this complaint.

    b.   We have twice written to the Director of Criminal Investigations Department in the Tanzanian Police Force detailing some of the wrongs enumerated herein and requesting him to see to it that these wrongs are thoroughly investigated and, where necessary and appropriate, punished in accordance with the laws of Tanzania. We shall collectively refer to this correspondence as "L" in support of this complaint.

    c.   We have twice written to MIGA and once to Canada's Export Development Corporation ("EDC") requesting the two institutions to address these issues and to see to it that any/or all wrongs enumerated herein are thoroughly and independently investigated and, where necessary and appropriate, any wrongs righted in accordance with MIGA policies and the regulations governing the EDC. These correspondence is annexed hereto and collectively marked "M" to form part of this complaint.

    d.   We have also written to the project sponsor requesting to be supplied with copies of relevant reports and the evidence in the project sponsor's possession. See letter to the project sponsors annexed hereto and marked "N" to form part of this complaint.

    e.   We have met and held discussions pertaining to these issues with officials from MIGA, the World Bank and the EDC; the project sponsors; and with elected and/or appointed officials of the Governments of Tanzania, Canada, the United States, Great Britain and the Netherlands.

Actions Taken by Project Sponsor, MIGA and Government of Tanzania

    6.   The following actions have been taken the Project Sponsor, MIGA and the Government of Tanzania in response to the actions of the complainants:

Project Sponsor

    a.   The Project Sponsor has responded by denying all allegations of wrongdoing on its part.

    b.   The Project Sponsor has taken steps to level all the areas where alleged human rights abuses took place in what appears to be attempts to destroy any evidence of any wrongdoing on its part.

    c.   The Project Sponsor has furnished false and/or misleading information as to independent investigations and conclusions therefrom concerning allegations of human rights abuses. We shall refer to correspondence from the project sponsors concerning these matters which is attached hereto and collectively marked "O" to form part of this complaint.

MIGA

    d. MIGA has also responded by vigorously defending the Project Sponsor's actions and conduct and denied all allegations of any wrongdoing on its and Project Sponsor's part.

    e. MIGA has furnished false and/or misleading information as to independent investigations and the conclusions therefrom concerning allegations of human rights abuses. We shall refer to correspondence and project documents from MIGA which is attached hereto and collectively marked "P" to form part of this complaint.

Government of Tanzania

    f. The Government of Tanzania has responded by denying all allegations concerning its own and Project Sponsor's conduct in the acquisition, possession and operation of the Bulyanhulu Gold Mine.

    g. The Government of Tanzania has responded by furnishing false, misleading and contradictory information concerning its investigation of the allegations of human rights abuses. We shall refer to official statements from the Government of Tanzania which are annexed hereto and marked "Q" to form part of this complaint.

    h. The Government of Tanzania has also taken steps to harass, intimidate and/or threaten the complainants and any other person or persons who have tried to investigate or question the facts and circumstances surrounding the Project Sponsor's acquisition, possession and operation of the Bulyanhulu mine site. The Government actions have included police raids and searches of LEAT offices and the homes of LEAT officers; arrests and detention of LEAT officers and other critics of the Government's handling of the Bulyanhulu evictions and allegations of human rights abuses; and threats to commence criminal prosecutions against the complainants and other persons attempting to investigate and/or question the Government's handling of the evictions and allegations of human rights allegations. We shall refer to contemporaneous press reports which are collectively marked "R" in support of this complaint.

7. The names of the contact persons at MIGA are:

    a. Mr. Gerald T. West
    b. Mr. Marcus Williams
    c. Ms. Moina Varkie

8. The following are details of MIGA policies, guidelines or procedures that we believe have not been complied with:

    a. Involuntary Resettlement: In order for this project to proceed, hundreds of thousands of people had to be relocated. This was done forcibly and without any resettlement plan. Involuntary resettlement is continuing without any resettlement plan.

    b. environmental Assessment Policy: The Environmental impact assessment processes were carried out after the forced relocation and displacement of the Bulyanhulu complainants and thereby failed to take account of their concerns and interests.

    c. Public Consultation: Public consultations were done after the Bulyanhulu complainants had been forcibly evicted and were, therefore, of no meaning to the Bulyanhulu complainants. The consultations were also limited to government functionaries and departments with no or minimal participation by local and national NGOs.

    d. Social Safeguard Policy: No social safeguards were taken to deal with the social and economic impacts of the forced relocation of the Bulyanhulu complainants nor have any safeguards been taken to mitigate the continuing negative social and economic impacts the project is having on neighboring communities.

e. Information Disclosure Policy: MIGA has consistently declined requests to disclose to the public any information or documents it may have collected in its due diligence investigation and that it relied upon in making its decision to approve the political risk guarantee for the project.

f. Article 12(d) of MIGA's Convention that states that "in guaranteeing an investment, the Agency shall satisfy itself as to the economic soundness of the investment and its contribution to the development of the host country.

g. Article 12(d) of the MIGA Convention also states that in guaranteeing an investment, the Agency shall satisfy itself as to the "compliance of the investment with the host country's laws and regulations.

9. We would like to see this complaint resolved in the following way:

a. Full, fair and just compensation should be paid to all Bulyanhulu complainants who were involuntarily resettled without any resettlement plan.

b. Full, fair and just compensation should be paid to all Bulyanhulu complainants whose agricultural and grazing lands were expropriated; residential and commercial property and settlements destroyed; investment in mining shafts, machinery and equipment confiscated; and employment opportunities lost.

c. Full, fair and just compensation should be paid to all remaining Bulyanhulu complainants whose property rights continue to be violated and/or interfered with by the actions of the project sponsors. In the alternative, the project sponsors should desist from any continuing or future acts that violate or otherwise interfere with the enjoyment by the Bulyanhulu complainants of their property rights.

d. The CAO should review MIGA's actual process of due diligence investigation, in order to assess whether MIGA properly investigated the foregoing issues, and whether it took the steps necessary to ensure that this project complied with MIGA policies before it approved the political risk guarantee for the Bulyanhulu Gold Mine.

e. The CAO should review the environmental and social impacts information the project sponsors has submitted to MIGA, and compare it with the information contained in this complaint in order to establish the adequacy and the veracity of the environmental and social impacts information and the soundness of the conclusions drawn in the environmental information submitted to MIGA and the Government of Tanzania.

f. The CAO should investigate the ongoing threats of eviction and displacement, and the negative social and economic impacts the Bulyanhulu mine project is having on neighboring communities.

g. The CAO should assess whether MIGA has complied with its safeguard policies, particularly its policy on involuntary resettlement, and should assess whether or how MIGA's financing of this project advances its poverty alleviation goals.

h. The CAO should review MIGA's compliance with its information disclosure policies in responding to requests for information regarding this project and should direct MIGA to fully disclose all documentation save for that protected by the confidentiality clauses to allow for full public participation in the process of resolving this complaint.

i. The CAO should lend its voice for calls for establishment of an independent commission of inquiry agreeable to the Bulyanhulu complainants as well as to the project sponsors and the Government of Tanzania to independently, transparently and thoroughly inquire into the facts and circumstances pertaining to the acquisition, possession and operation of the project and, where necessary and appropriate, make recommendations for the resolution of this complaint.

j. The CAO should investigate whether MIGA performed proper due diligence prior to its approval of the guarantee with respect to the economic and social benefits accruing to local communities in the Bulyanhulu area and to the Tanzanian national in terms of employment opportunities; and revenue from taxes, royalties and other charges. In addition the CAO should investigate whether MIGA considered in its due diligence investigations any viable alternatives to the project that might have had greater or comparable social and economic benefits but lesser negative impacts.

We are mindful of the fact that Barrick Gold Corporation, the current parent company of the project sponsors, and MIGA did not become directly involved with this project until the spring of 1999 when most of the events complained of had already taken place. We believe, however, that there is a direct relationship between the events of the pre-1999 period and the current mining operations undertaken by the project sponsors at the Bulyanhulu area. There is a direct relationship because those events were a precondition for the development of the project sponsors' current mining operations. The project would not have moved forward without having first to address the issue of the hundreds of thousands of people who were living and working in the disputed area.

We believe that this direct relationship exists regardless of the amount of time that passed between the events complained of on the one hand, and Barrick's and MIGA's involvement in the project on the other hand. This direct relationship also exists regardless of the ownership structure of the project sponsors for the reason that the current owners of the project and MIGA have benefited, are benefiting and will benefit financially from the pre-1999 events complained of. Indeed, we are aware that changes in the ownership structure have not changed the legal personality or identity of the project sponsors.

We, therefore, believe that the circumstances surrounding the pre-1999 events fall within any reasonable definition of the "scope" of the project. Therefore, these events fall within the scope of the due diligence that should have been conducted by both the project sponsors and MIGA. It is our hope that the CAO will share our belief that MIGA's due diligence requirements during project preparation must apply to events that precede its involvement in a given project if those events are directly relevant to the project's development. It is imperative that the World Bank Group not send the message that possible improprieties in project preparation are acceptable provided they occur prior to MIGA's direct involvement or under the ownership of an entity other than the immediate project sponsor.

. . .

CAO Assessment Report Summary, Complaint Regarding
MIGA's Guarantee of the Bulyanhulu Gold Mine, Tanzania (2002),
available at http://www.cao-ombudsman.org/cases/document-links/
documents/bulyfinal.Englishpdf.pdf

The CAO was unable to find any basis for the allegations of present day intimidation, interference or undermining of the community by the mine. Clearly the development dynamics around an investment of this type and character in an area devoid of other economic opportunities and social services are difficult and the challenges severe. The mine is however stepping up its work in partnership with the community and other NGO partners and with the government in the region.

Conclusions

. . . The CAO is also concerned that MIGA did not carry out a more thorough review of the project following IFC's pre-appraisal visit. Simply reviewing documents without a site visit, especially with changes in the project and with a gap in time between IFC's and MIGA's reviews, is inadequate. In this case MIGA has been well served by a mine and a project sponsor that appear to be committed to best practice. It is for this reason and not as the result of the supervision or due diligence by MIGA that the mine is performing to environmental and social standards that are in line with those expected of an investment of the World Bank Group....

To date no environment or social specialist on contract to MIGA has visited Bulyanhulu. Moreover, in conversations with the mine management and staff there was an expression of interest in other examples of best practice in social development, areas where the World Bank Group positions itself as a leader. MIGA should examine its capacity and willingness to support its clients to replicate and develop best practices and to act as a source of information and support where clients are inclined to do so.

The CAO does not believe that the project merits a compliance audit and was impressed with the way in which the mine was developing its social and environmental capacity. The questions of revenue management and distribution and the disparities between an investment of the size of Bulyanhulu in one of the poorest regions of Tanzania, and how maximum benefits can be captured for local people is a perennial one for IFC and MIGA.

Once again, there would seem to be room for more coordinated approaches on this issue between MIGA and the World Bank and other agencies active in Tanzania. Without guidance from MIGA, Barrick Gold has established meaningful partnerships with international aid and development organizations to reinforce its social development activities and these should be supported and their development impact monitored.

The CAO does not believe that it can play any further useful role in this case. The CAO respectfully urges the complainants and their international counterparts to assess carefully the way in which they use information and the emphasis they place on substantiation. Advocacy on behalf of local people who may lack the means to make their voices heard to government and international authorities has been a tried and tested method of forcing change. International advocacy NGOs in the environment, development and human rights fields have a proud record of propelling the World Bank Group towards more rigorous approaches to environment and social assessment among other policy initiatives. Similarly, human rights NGOs play an important role in acting as a global conscience and have brought about changes in attitudes in the private sector, including in resource extraction industries. But the CAO believes there is a responsibility that goes with this role.

ASSESSMENT SUMMARY OF THE COMPLAINT REGARDING MIGA's GUARANTEE OF THE BULYANHULU GOLD MINE, TANZANIA (Dec. 2, 2002), *available at* http://www.leat.or.tz/activities/buly/leat.response.to.cao.pdf

We are in receipt of your 11-page Summary Report dated October 21, 2002. In view of the astonishing findings, conclusions and numerous disparaging assertions contained in this Summary Report we write to request that you retract certain statements which, we believe, were outside the scope of the investigation, and several statements which are inaccurate, misleading and unfair. We wish to start at the earliest moment of our engagement with your office as we think this provides a fitting background to your Summary Report and our response.

1. MISREPRESENTATION OF FACTS IN THE COMPLAINT

As you may remember, LEAT first approached your Office with regard to the guarantee by MIGA of the Bulyanhulu Gold Mine in late August of 2001. That first meeting, held in your office, was also attended by representatives of Washington DC-based NGOs such as Friends of the Earth (FoE-US), the Center for International Environmental Law (CIEL), Oxfam America, Bank Information Center (BIC) and the Natural Resources Defense Council (NRDC). You will no doubt recall that LEAT had wanted your Office to investigate the widespread allegations of human rights abuses including alleged killings of artisanal miners when the security forces of the Government of Tanzania and officials of Sutton Resources/Kahama Mining Corporation Ltd., moved in to evict the artisanals from the Bulyanhulu gold mines in July and August 1996. We wanted you to investigate those and subsequent events at Bulyanhulu with a view to establishing whether MIGA had undertaken proper due diligence investigation prior to its approval of political risk guarantee for the Bulyanhulu Gold Mine now owned by Barrick Gold Corporation.

However, as you may recall, you made it very clear that the issue of the killings was outside your Office's mandate, which, as you informed those present, was limited to investigating complaints related to breaches of MIGA's social and environmental safeguard policies and due diligence procedures. If, therefore, LEAT wished to submit a complaint to the CAO, it should ensure that that complaint was confined to allegations of breaches of those policies and procedures only. Your investigative team comprised of Ms. Rachel Kyte – who also attended that first meeting – and Mr. John Ambrose would reiterate this position in subsequent meeting with LEAT in Dar es Salaam and again in public meetings with the Bulyanhulu villagers and complainants in late March 2002.

As you correctly point out in your Report, an independent investigation of the allegations of killings has been and remains one of LEAT's and the Bulyanhulu complainants' key demands. That being the case, it took months of agonized discussions and wide-ranging consultations with the complainants and our international counterparts to ultimately decide to drop the allegations of killings in order to present a complaint to your Office. The complaint was finally lodged with your Office on January 15, 2002 and followed, on February 11, by a supplement detailing further grounds for the complaint.

LEAT's letter of complaint carefully followed the model letter provided in the CAO's Operational Guidelines that you provided us with. We invited you to investigate several major areas of concern with regard to the Bulyanhulu Gold Mine that we believe are within your mandate, namely;

a. Forced evictions and displacement of potentially hundreds of thousands of Bulyanhulu villagers and complainants and failure to plan, finance and implement any resettlement or to compensate property loss.
b. Ongoing evictions and forced displacements or threats thereof and uncompensated interference with property rights of the complainants.
c. Negative impacts on the local economy including the destruction of the social and economic fabric of the communities, and the undermining of national poverty alleviation goals.
d. Failure to observe the laws of Tanzania when the project sponsors took control of the Bulyanhulu Gold Mine.
e. Submitting inadequate, inaccurate and misleading social and environmental impacts information including failure to account for material changes to the design or implementation of the Bulyanhulu Gold Mine.
f. Non-disclosure by project sponsors of material information pertaining to the acquisition of the project.
g. MIGA's failure to carry out any or adequate due diligence investigation in order to verify the information submitted and soundness of conclusions drawn by project sponsors prior to issuing a guarantee.
h. MIGA's violation of its own information disclosure policies.

In support of these grounds were three volumes of documentary evidence in the form of relevant company records, government papers of both the governments of Tanzania and Canada, police records, court records of both the High Court and the Court of Appeal of Tanzania and extant newspaper reports of the events of July and August 1996 at Bulyanhulu. As well as these were a wide array of correspondence between LEAT and the government of Tanzania, the police force, MIGA and the Export Development Corporation of the government of Canada (EDC).

We are therefore deeply disappointed that you largely ignored the record before you but, instead, introduced matters or issues that you had insisted the complainants leave out as a condition to submitting the complaint. For example, you state, at page 2 of the Summary Report, that your assessment was undertaken "in relation to the complaint." Indeed, your own summary of the grounds of the complaint correctly frames the grounds and the issues that we invited you to investigate (see page 3 of the Summary Report). None of those grounds raised the issue of the alleged killings, which are nowhere even mentioned in the complaint. Yet you assert that the complaint 'repeats allegations regarding events of late July and early August 1996 *that include misconduct and murder made against government authorities and the mine.*" (p. 4) More specifically, "LEAT alleges that the *manner in which the land was cleared on July 30 and following days resulted in 52 unnamed individuals being buried alive in the pits that they worked.* "(p. 5) And at page 7 we find the following: "*The complaint alleges that 52 people were killed in the process of land clearance, trapped alive in their pits by the mine and local administration staff as they plugged and filled the mine shafts,* etc., etc. Since the complaint does not make any of the above assertions, we, therefore, respectfully request that these comments be removed from the report because they are outside the express language and scope of the complaint.

The same applies to your entire discussion of the videotape evidence at page 4 of the Summary Report. You start that discussion by inaccurately stating that although "the allegations made and repeated by LEAT in its complaint to the CAO are not new... *LEAT asserts that it has new evidence, namely a video which, it states, is a contemporaneous record of bodies being exhumed from small scale miners' pits.*" Yet, as the complaint clearly shows, the only reference to the videotapes in the entire complaint was made in connection with the manner in which the eviction order against the Bulyanhulu communities was made and executed by government authorities and Kahama Mining officials and the consequent destruction of villages, settlements and property belonging to the communities (See paragraph "e" of the background to the complaint).

That notwithstanding, you then proceed to examine this aspect of the alleged complaint: "The CAO cannot be sure that the video shows that which LEAT maintains [i]t shows. The location, date, timing and detail cannot be verified. Therefore, it is not clear that the video shows small scale miners suffocated as a result of the clearing of the land in the days following the July 30 announcement. Further, the CAO found witnesses and other contemporaneous documentation that would refute the version of events that LEAT contends the video supports. During the field mission to Bulyanhulu small scale miners introduced to the CAO team who knew of the video were sure of the location where the events were filmed and took the CAO to the spot. However, they could not be sure that the miners shown being dragged from mine shafts had been killed as a result of that land clearance and were unable to support the version of events that LEAT alleged the video revealed."

With regard to allegations of the 52 deaths, you inaccurately allege that "*the CAO has asked for a list of the names of the 52 people who were killed in the first days of August 1996 as stated in the complaint. Neither LEAT, nor the (Small Scale Miners' Committee) have been able to supply the list of names.... The CAO is left to reflect that if a list cannot be produced by local people, the local administration, or the (Small Scale Miners' Committee) that is the complainant in this case, this casts doubt on the veracity of the allegations that these people died as a result of the filling in of mine shafts in early August 1996.*" It was, however, not necessary for you to ask since LEAT had already given the list to the CAO in the supporting documentation for the complaint.

As you know, your Operational Guidelines require complainants to state other steps or actions they may have taken to try to resolve their grievances prior to approaching the CAO. In our case, we stated – at paragraph 5(a) of the complaint – that we had written to President Mkapa of Tanzania on two occasions asking him to intervene to address these matters. One of those letters, which we attached to the complaint as Annexe "K," had a list of the names of 36 persons who up to that time were alleged to have died as a result of the events of July and August 1996. You may also know that the list has been in the public domain since September 27, 2001 when our second letter to President Mkapa was published in the Tanzanian press. That list has also been made available to any and all persons who have asked for it including the Tanzanian police force. We are confirmed in our belief that your Office never asked for the list because we have also thoroughly checked our records but failed to locate any communication from your office requesting this list. Since there is no record of any communication in this connection we respectfully urge you to remove that assertion from your Summary Report because it inaccurately alleges facts whose existence is, at best, in question.

Still on the subject of the killings, you assert that your investigative team met with local people who stated that their relatives were among the 52 killed. Whereas it is true that your investigators did meet with numerous complainants who alleged that their relations were among the missing and feared dead, you inaccurately assert that "... their neighbors took pains to tell the CAO team that these relatives were alive and well or in one case had died in a mine accident prior to August 1996. In other cases, the Tanzanian press has found people alive in other parts of the country, who it is alleged died at this time" (p. 7). As you may know, when your investigative team visited Bulyanhulu, a LEAT representative served as the team's sole interpreter. For three days that the team visited various localities and villages and talked to hundreds of villagers in public meetings, that representative was the team's sole link with the Bulyanhulu communities and the complainants. And in meeting after public meeting in which dozens of villagers narrated the mayhem and chaos that broke out following the order to disperse of July 30, 1996 not a single person came forward who contradicted the testimony that there were killings. Not a single villager came forward to contradict the story that some mothers told of how their sons perished in the Bulyanhulu goldfields that fateful August. And, we believe, our representative was in a much better position to understand the complainants' testimony than Ms. Kyte or Mr. Ambrose who did not speak or understand Swahili, the only medium of communication during those meetings. Our representative also stayed in the same hotel with the team and would have known had villagers with different testimony approached your investigators.

It may be that your investigators may have heard the testimony you allege during the team's final two days it spent inside the Bulyanhulu mine complex. That was where your investigators met with both the company and government officials. In sharp contrast to the various meetings with the complainants and the villagers, the meetings inside the mine complex were not open to the public or to the complainants or their representatives. We believe that the claims of contradictory testimony that you refer to may have emanated from those closed meetings with company and government officials. We, therefore, respectfully request that you remove your statement that inaccurately implies that the complainants' testimony was contradicted by other witnesses during the public meetings your investigators held with hundreds of Bulyanhulu villagers and complainants. Or, at the very least, we urge you to make public your sources of information or substantiation for this particular information.

Regarding your claim that the Tanzanian press has found people alive who are alleged to have died in August 1996, we have the following to say. When in early April 2002 Tanzanian newspapers reported that a person claiming to be a Turo Masanja, one of the dead miners in our list, had come forward to deny that there were any killings, we immediately became suspicious. The said person was introduced at a political rally in Kahama town organized by the ruling CCM party and addressed by a member of its National Executive Committee. Upon investigating the story, we found that this "Turo Masanja" was not only an impostor but also that he was one of about ten people who had apparently been paid or promised to be paid by senior police officers from Dares Salaam to pose as the dead men in our list. We found others who had similarly been promised compensation by "Canadians" for their property losses should they recant their testimonies regarding the alleged deaths of their relatives.

We also found that the political rally where this person was produced had been organized specifically for the media with the sole purpose of discrediting LEAT and thwarting calls for an independent inquiry that were then gaining greater momentum. We further learned that Barrick Gold had in fact actively participated in this subterfuge, flying several journalists from Dar es Salaam in its aircraft specifically to cover this event and then circulated the resulting press reports to various organizations in the US and Canada as evidence that the allegations of killings were fabricated.

We feared that Barrick Gold would also seek to use the press reports it had engineered to influence the outcome of the CAO's investigation of our complaint. And so on July 10, we wrote to Ms. Kyte a lengthy expose of this event and asked her to bear this fact in mind should Barrick Gold ever seek to raise the issue with your Office. Ms. Kyte never acknowledged receipt of our letter then nor have you done so in your Summary Report. On the contrary you seem to have uncritically accepted whatever Barrick Gold operatives may have told you or your investigators regarding this matter. We would, therefore, respectfully request you to remove any reference of this matter not only because it was not germane to your investigation, but also because your version of that event has been challenged. Should you feel inclined to keep it, we respectfully urge you to acknowledge that LEAT did submit a rejoinder to the story and give reasons why you deem LEAT's version unworthy of belief.

2. WHITEWASHING HUMAN RIGHTS ABUSES

Bearing in mind that you had declined to investigate allegations of human rights abuses including allegations of killings, LEAT had nevertheless requested you to lend your voice to calls "for establishment of an independent commission of inquiry agreeable to the Bulyanhulu complainants as well as the project sponsors and the Government of Tanzania to independently, transparently and thoroughly inquire into the facts and circumstances pertaining to the acquisition, possession and operation of the project and, where necessary and appropriate, make recommendations for the resolution of this complaint" (para. 9(i) of the complaint).

You have declined that request, arguing that "without a list of victims, with a video that cannot be verified as showing what it is alleged to show, and with so much contradictory evidence as to what happened on the days concerned, (you do not)... find that the case has been made for the CAO to recommend an independent inquiry" (p. 7) In addition, you contend, "... after reviewing the material that is available (the CAO) has not found that there is a compelling case for an inquiry" (ibid.) These conclusions have to be measured not only in the light of the issues we have raised herein, but also in the light of an unsolicited admission that you *did not undertake a full scale inquiry, nor did (you) engage in the techniques of human rights investigation which would be necessary to try and prove or disprove many of the allegations repeated in the complaint, such as the exhumation of closed mine shafts, for example*" (p. 2).

Implicitly suggesting that you may not have seen or been shown all of the available evidence, your Summary Report "... *urges all sides to make public any information they may have that sheds further light on the events of July-August 1996 (as) this can help resolve the continual tension around the allegations at the core of the complaint, so that the mine and the people of Kakola and the surrounding area are able to live in peace*" (ibid.) This suggests that your conclusion that the case for an independent inquiry has not been made may have been arrived at too hastily to be considered conclusive.

In addition to bringing up matters you had expressly prohibited LEAT from raising, you disputed LEAT's claim and the evidence that "potentially hundreds of thousands of the Bulyanhulu complainants were forcibly evicted and displaced from the Bulyanhulu area (para. 4(a) of the complaint) Speculating, but without offering any proofs, that gold deposits had largely been exhausted by the time of the July and August 1996 events, you expressed your confidence that the number of displaced communities "is somewhere between 200 and 2000 people" (p. 5). The evidence that LEAT submitted in this regard was taken from Barrick Gold's own environmental impact studies of the area undertaken by a Canadian consulting firm Norecol, Dames & Moore and submitted to MIGA by Barrick Gold.

According to these documents, the discovery of the Bulyanhulu gold deposits in 1975 "...attracted some small-scale artisanal mining to the site."(Barrick Gold and Kahama Mining (1999), *Social Development Plan for Bulyanhulu Gold Mine, Tanzania*, p.4). However, following a visit to the area by then President Ali Hassan Mwinyi in February 1993, "artisanal miners requested the right to resume artisanal activities at Bulyanhulu," which "permission was given by the President As a result of this permission, that same year there was *"a massive influx, in which some 30,000 – 400,000 artisanal miners, associated entrepreneurs and 'opportunists' arrived'* (ibid., 21). Elsewhere in that document, Barrick Gold argued that although no records were kept of the number of artisanal miners, *"estimates range between 30,000 and 400,000"* (ibid., 20).

Barrick Gold's high estimates of the Bulyanhulu population during this period are broadly supported by estimates given by Tanzania government sources both before and after the events of August 1996. For example, two years earlier then District Commissioner for Kahama had protested to then Minister for Water, Energy and Minerals that the grant of mineral rights to Sutton Resources would result in the eviction of over three hundred thousand people in the area who were "earning a living as well as contributing to the national economy."

In addition, just four days before the removals were ordered, the then Member of Parliament for the area denounced the planned eviction of his constituents, telling a session of the Tanzanian Parliament that about 200,000 artisanal miners, peasant farmers and their families were threatened with eviction in Bulyanhulu.2 Hardly three weeks after the removals and with the allegations of killings making front-page news in the Tanzanian press, the Inspector General of Police issued a press release denying the allegations of killings but supporting the MP's estimate that about 200,000 people had already been evicted from the Bulyanhulu area.3 Extant press reports that broke the news of the killings also estimated the population that had just been dispersed from the area at between 200,000 and 300,000.

All this evidence was included in the three volumes of supporting documentation made available to your Office. Both Barrick Gold that paid for the EIA studies referred to above and submitted them to MIGA, and MIGA that accepted them did not object to these statistics prior to the launching of LEAT's campaign for an independent inquiry in July 2001. Since then, however, Barrick Gold has attempted to play down the number of people who were affected by the removals and, hence, the historical significance of these removals. Realizing the significance of these numbers, the company now does not want critics to make any reference to its own project documents anymore. It now accuses civil society organizations that have referred to them of "misleading people into thinking that the number of people who... were evicted from (the Bulyanhulu) concession was 200,000" Without first expressly disowning its project documents, the company now claims that unspecified "contemporaneous documents" show "there were fewer than approximately 15,000 people on the site at the time of the events in question."

We are troubled by the fact that you appear to have uncritically and without any substantiation bought headlong into Barrick Gold's case. Taking aim at what you call "the numbers game," you charge that figures from studies of the area "have been embellished and exaggerated over the years" (p. 5). However, you have not disclosed the parties responsible for "embellishing and exaggerating" these figures or their reasons for doing so. We fail to understand, for instance, why would consultants commissioned and paid for by Barrick Gold seek to embellish or exaggerate the area's population figures as this would, obviously, not be in their employer's interest. Nor can we understand what an elected representative of the community, or a District Commissioner and the chief of the national police force – both government officials appointed by the President of Tanzania – would seek to gain by exaggerating these figures and thereby casting the government in a negative light. In any case, as we have argued, these figures were in circulation both before and after the evictions were effected and were never contested by Barrick Gold or the Tanzanian authorities until recently.

We are disappointed by your apparent unwillingness to examine the mass of documentary evidence we submitted to you that showed that the Tanzanian government at the highest levels was well aware of the mass displacement of people that would and did result from the removals. For example, you argue that the *"movements of thousands of people, if not tens of thousands, in caravans in the space of just a few days, would have attracted attention of central government and international agencies in the area. Yet no one can substantiate such a large internal displacement"* (p. 5). Yet had you taken the trouble to look carefully at the *Social Development Plan for the Bulyanhulu Gold Mine,* prepared by Barrick Gold after its takeover of the Bulyanhulu area in March 1999, you would have noticed the company's unsolicited admission that *"the removal of a large number of artisanal miners from the Bulyanhulu site in 1996 by the government has meant that the area has already received regional and national political attention"* (ibid., p.41).

We are also unable to understand your disturbing reluctance to examine or comment on the documentary evidence made available to you that showed widespread concern amongst Tanzanian government officials, Canadian government representatives and senior company officials at the lengthy coverage by the Tanzanian press of the events at Bulyanhulu. We, therefore, respectfully urge you to rectify this record or, at the very least, give reasons why you think the project documents prepared by Barrick Gold and submitted to MIGA, as well as Tanzanian government sources are unworthy of belief.

3. SEEING OR HEARING NO EVIL

The LEAT complaint had alleged widespread illegal behaviour by the Canadian investors prior to, during and subsequent to the events of July and August 1996. In support of these allegations, LEAT submitted extensive documentary evidence including copies of the license that the project sponsors relied upon for their claim of right over the Bulyanhulu gold deposits; court records of proceedings in lawsuits between the companies and the Bulyanhulu communities; and excerpts of the various statutory laws that were violated when the artisanal miners and peasant farmers were driven off from Bulyanhulu. As well as this was evidence of more recent acts of illegal behaviour when, in May of 2000, Barrick Gold operatives and government authorities forcibly removed some families from the site of the Mine's current tailings dam.

Your response to these allegations was to gloss over, evade or – in certain instances – manipulate or distort well-known and uncontested facts. For example, LEAT had alleged that Kahama Mining and Sutton Resources never had a license over the Bulyanhulu concession and introduced copy of the only license that these companies ever had. That license did not even mention the Bulyanhulu area referring, instead, to another area in another district in another region. In the subsequent supplementary information filed with your Office on February 11, we provided an exhaustive legislative history of the Bulyanhulu area. This showed that these companies should never have been in Bulyanhulu in the first place, as the area had since the early 1980s been legally set aside for the exclusive and beneficial use of the artisanal miners.

Even though you were well aware of this aspect of the complaint, you completely failed to investigate or deal with it. Instead, you chose to believe, without proof or further explanation, that *"in 1994 the Government of Tanzania.,. granted a prospecting license to Kahama Mining . . . a subsidiary of Sutton Resources"* (p. 1). And as far the legislative history of the area is concerned, this is completely ignored in the Summary Report, which does not even acknowledge receiving the supplementary information let alone its existence.

Your attitude regarding allegations and evidence of illegality on the part of the Canadian companies or Tanzanian government authorities seems to have been to disavow any power or mandate to investigate these allegations. For example, when presented with the fact that the July 30, 1996 order issued by the Minister of Energy and Minerals most probably violated a High Court injunction issued on September 29, 1995 you dodged the issue by claiming that you had "no mandate to opine on the validity of this decree" (p. 6). Yet you showed no such hesitation in concluding that "*the issue of compensation paid to small scale miners at the time of the order to vacate the land in 1996 is one between the (Government of Tanzania) and the small scale miners and falls within the (Government of Tanzania's) exclusive jurisdiction*" (p. 7).

As with the license and other matters, the issue of compensation was governed by the 1979 Mining Act whose excerpted copies we had presented you with. For the record, paragraph 1(d) of the supplementary complaint we submitted to you on February 11 referred to section 81(1) of the 1979 Act that had obligated "the registered holder of the Mining Right or the holder of the prospecting right or claim . . . to pay to the lawful occupier of any land, fair and reasonable compensation in respect of the disturbance or damage to any crops, trees, buildings, stock or works thereon resulting from the activities of the holder of a mining or prospecting right or claim. On this basis, it was the sole legal responsibility of the companies that claimed mineral rights over the Bulyanhulu area to pay compensation to the complainants. Your conclusion in this regard is, therefore, wrong and we respectfully urge you to rectify the error or at the very least give reasons should you choose not to do so. We also doubt whether your disavowal of a mandate to investigate allegations of violations of Tanzanian laws with regard to the Bulyanhulu Mine can be sustained in view of the provisions of

Article 12(d) of the MIGA Convention that obliges MIGA to satisfy itself as to the "compliance of the investment with the host country's laws and regulations."

You also seem to have missed or ignored simple and uncontested facts. It is, for example, a well-documented fact that it was Kahama Mining and Sutton Resources that took the artisanal miners to the Tanzanian courts on June 20, 1995. It is also a well-established fact that when, in September of 1995, the High Court of Tanzania showed unwillingness to serve as a tool to achieve these companies' ends, the latter chose – in the High Court's memorable phrase – "to short-circuit the law by using the executive wing of government Once the evictions started on July 31, the miners' leaders successfully sought the intervention of the High Court. The Court issued another temporary injunction order against both the company and the Tanzanian government on August 2.

It is a matter of historical record that this injunction was not overturned by the Court of Appeal of Tanzania until February 26, 1997, some six months after the forced removals. Copies of these court documents were made available to you. That the removals had proceeded regardless of, and in violation of, the High Court injunction order is confirmed by internal documents of the Canadian companies that LEAT was able to obtain in the course of its investigation also made available to you. For example, in an August 6, 1996 memo faxed to the Vancouver headquarters of Sutton Resources, Jim Hylands, then the company's Exploration Manager at Bulyanhulu explains that the Inspector General of Police told the Regional Police Commander for Shinyanga Region that the police are to remove the miners by whatever means required; and . . . that there is to be no more discussion of this operation – he had his orders, carry them out – and ignore any noise he hears from Tabora." Tabora is the seat of the High Court of Tanzania for the Western Zone, The LEAT complaint provided an exhaustive documentation of these matters which you ought to have considered. But surprisingly, we read in the Summary Report that "the (Government of Tanzania's) decree (for the artisanal miners to leave the Bulyanhulu area) was challenged in court by (the Small Scale Miners Committee). On July 30, 1996, the (Government of Tanzania) announced a process of clearance, and issued a final decree that the concession area be vacated by 'illegal miners.' That decree was challenged by the (Small Scale Miners' Committee) and *an injunction was issued on July 3151. This was overturned on August 2, 1996* and the process went ahead" (p. 2). No evidence is given for any of these wrong assertions nor are reasons given as to why you found LEAT's documentary evidence unworthy of belief. We would likewise urge you to rectify this record as even Barrick Gold and the Tanzanian government authorities have, to our knowledge, not contested our version of these facts.

With regard to allegations in the complaint of illegal behavior that directly implicated Barrick Gold, we are dissatisfied by the factual basis for your conclusions. LEAT submitted documents showing that on May 13, 2000, 16 families were forcibly evicted from the current site of the mine's tailings dam following a 24-hour notice from the Kahama District Commissioner. We presented a copy of that order as part of the supporting documentation in the complaint. There was also evidence that the forced evictions were carried out regardless of the fact that the 16 families had challenged Barrick Gold's plans and the case was still pending in the Court of Appeal of Tanzania.

The CAO investigative team was taken to the site just outside Kakola town where these families were dumped after their eviction. It was given copies of documents showing that the mostly illiterate villagers had been made to thumb-print documents written in complex legal jargon in English stating that they had agreed to forever relinquish all rights over their ancestral lands to Barrick Gold's subsidiary in return for compensation averaging $100 per family! The families told the team how they were unable to grow food crops for the very real fear that they would be evicted again as they were still living within the bounds of Barrick Gold's concession. They also took the team to where their boreholes were destroyed and fenced off when they were evicted and now they have no reliable water sources for their domestic use and for their livestock. The Summary Report is, however, evasive on these questions. It, instead, seeks to absolve Barrick Gold of wrongdoing by changing the facts regarding the year 2000 evictions, wrongly asserting that they took place in 1998, before Barrick Gold took over at Bulyanhulu.

You accept the fact that the evicted families were found to be living in "poor conditions" and in "insecurity," as the complaint had alleged. You found that "there was insecurity within these families as they expected to be moved again in the near future and therefore were disinclined to plant and cultivate" (p. 8). Playing down Barrick Gold's responsibility for these "poor conditions" and "insecurity" – and ignoring entirely the issue of whether or not the evictions complied with World Bank safeguard policies – you found no evidence "of a coordinated policy or opposition by the mine to people living on the concession growing crops (ibid.) However, the Summary Report tacitly agrees that Barrick Gold may not have adequately and meaningfully consulted with the communities. Thus we read: "There is clearly room for greater communication by the mine with these families still living on the concession and clarity on what they may or may do [*sic*] on this land and on their future status" (ibid.)

In Kakola, your investigators heard testimony of how Barrick Gold was planning to demolish villagers' houses in order to expand the road going into the mine complex. The villagers testified that they were not consulted regarding the road's expansion and the planned demolitions. In fact the team was shown houses that had already been marked with red ink ready for demolition. The team was also informed of the mine's opposition to construction by the villagers of their places of religious worship within the town and that the villagers are now forced to walk for miles to bury their dead outside the concession. Barrick Gold has repeatedly boasted of supplying potable water to thousands of villagers in Bulyanhulu. However, the villagers testified to the team that Kakola, with an estimated population of 12,000, and which is the closest settlement to the mine complex was yet to see a drop of water supplied by the company. This was also the case with Stamico, another community of about 3,000 just across the river to the north of the mine complex and Nyakagwe, another settlement to the west of the Mine.

The CAO investigative team asked very pointed questions regarding these questions and took copious notes of the testimony. However, you state that you are "unable to find any basis for the allegations of present day intimidation, interference or undermining of the community by the mine." Rather, the admittedly "severe challenges" that communities such as Kakola were suffering from were a result of "the development dynamics around an investment of this type and character in an area devoid of other economic opportunities and social services (p. 9) When decoded, this means the poverty evident in Kakola and other communities today resulted from the investors taking control of the communities' main economic resource without providing them with an alternative source of livelihoods.

And this was the basis of our contention in the complaint that the investors had destroyed the local economy, impoverished communities and thereby undermined the national poverty alleviation goals. Indeed, Barrick Gold has itself admitted in project documents submitted to MIGA that *"the closure of small-scale mining had a major negative effect on economic activity, population and social development, which has been felt beyond the immediate mining area"* (see Kahama Mining (1998) *Environmental Impact Statement for the Bulyanhulu Gold Project*, Vol. 1, p. 8–2; and Barrick Gold and Kahama Mining, op. cit., p. 36). In view of these admissions in Barrick Gold's own project documents, we respectfully request you to give reasons for your disagreement with our contention that the MIGA guarantee is inconsistent with the requirements of Article 12(d) of the MIGA Convention that obligates MIGA to "satisfy itself as to the economic soundness of the investment and its contribution to the development of the host country."

4. SLAP ON THE WRIST FOR MIGA

The LEAT complaint had drawn attention to serious flaws in the process and outcome of the social and environmental impacts assessments that had been submitted to MIGA by Barrick Gold. It was our case that these studies should have been carried out before the 1996 removals for consultations with communities to be of any meaningful value. That was not done. Instead, the companies waited until the Bulyanhulu communities were driven off from the area then purported to undertake an EIA. Even then the information based on these studies that Barrick Gold submitted to MIGA was materially inaccurate, erroneous and misleading. And MIGA, without first carrying out a thorough and competent due diligence investigation to establish the veracity of this information and the soundness of its conclusions, approved millions of dollars in political risk guarantees for the Bulyanhulu mine.

Your Summary Report acknowledges that the EIA for the project had been found not to meet the World Bank Group requirements by an earlier IFC mission. Among the areas that this EIA was found wanting related to "issues of resettlement and compensation related to the pipeline, the tailings dam and the mine In addition, that EIA "did not address past issues of land clearance" (p. 8). Without providing any details, the Summary Report states that the IFC team "noted in detail the remedies that would be required to bring the project into compliance with IFC policies and notes the reputational issues in the 1996 alleged incidents. The IFC recommended an addendum to the EIA be prepared detailing what would be required along the themes outlined above" (ibid., pp. 8–9).

The Summary Report also acknowledges that MIGA was made aware of these concerns after Barrick Gold approached it for guarantee. However, and crucially, *"beyond this, the CAO has been unable to find any correspondence from MIGA to Bamck Gold or to ascertain from MIGA or Barrick staff that the issues raised in the IFC back-to-office report had been acted on by MIGA."* In other words you were not able to find evidence that MIGA and Barrick Gold had acted on any of the IFC mission's recommendations that included resettlement, compensation, and past events of land clearance. Although you failed to explicitly say so, it is on record that Barrick Gold submitted to MIGA precisely the same EIA documents that the IFC mission had condemned as inadequate.

It is also clear from the Summary Report that MIGA did not carry out any due diligence investigation whatsoever. Nor, prior to the CAO's visit had MIGA ever carried out a site visit or sent any environmental or social specialist to visit the area! By all accounts, it seems, all MIGA did was to be "comfortable" with Barrick's assurances that all was well at Bulyanhulu. This, according to you, was unsatisfactory: "At issue . . . is whether MIGA sought to or felt it should seek independent verification of critical issues surrounding the viability of a Category A project for guarantee. The purpose and intent of environmental and social due diligence in the World Bank Group is to provide that independent verification, precisely so that the Group is not left to 'trust' the sponsor" (p. 9). You also rejected the notion that the IFC mission amounted to due diligence investigation. According to the Summary Report, a back-to-office report "cannot qualify as 'due diligence' and IFC made clear to MIGA its status" (ibid.)

Having concluded that MIGA did not carry out any due diligence investigation, you seem to have failed or avoided to draw the obvious conclusion: That the guarantee should never have been approved, bearing in mind that the IFC mission had found the project wanting with regard to the World Bank Group policies. Although you found fault with MIGA for "trusting" the project sponsor by taking Barrick Gold's assurances at their face value, you fell into the same trap with your conclusion that you had "no reason" to doubt Barrick Gold's assurances to MIGA. This is especially strange considering that Barrick Gold had submitted to MIGA precisely the same project documents IFC had criticized even after the project design had been changed! It is even stranger given the allegations and evidence of wrongdoing by Barrick Gold that was presented to your investigators. We respectfully invite you to explain what is reassuring about a company that paid an average of $100 in compensation for every family that was evicted in May 2000. We would also like to know what is reassuring about a company that sprays people's houses with red ink to mark them for demolition without even telling the owners about its plans. Or that refuses to supply communities nearest to it with potable water but does so to communities further from the mine. We respectfully wish to know what would amount to evidence of a coordinated policy if not the evidence presented above.

. . .

6. CONCLUSION

We understand from your Summary Report that you no longer desire to play any role in this matter. While we intend to respect your decision in this regard, we cannot pass the opportunity to respectfully request you to rectify the Summary Report in the manner we have suggested above. We would like to believe that it is not in the best interests of all concerned that the CAO's legacy in the Bulyanhulu matter be poisoned by the inaccuracies, factual errors, unsupported claims and unsubstantiated conclusions that have unfortunately characterized your Summary Report.

Questions and Discussion

1. It has been observed that the CAO has a broader mandate than the Inspection Panel. The CAO not only examines the compliance of IFC and MIGA projects with the Banks' policies and procedures, but the CAO is also supposed to play a problem solving (ombudsman) role and an advisory role to IFC/MIGA management. Could anything more have been done by the CAO in connection with the complaints about the Bulyanhulu Gold Mine?

2. It is important to recognize that both the CAO and Inspection Panel may only investigate and suggest corrective actions for acts or omissions by the World Bank Group. Neither has authority over actions of the Bank Group's clients, that is, borrower governments or private companies. This limitation means that the mechanisms may not fully address the needs of some complainants, since the local implementing agency, be it a government or private-sector company, should also be held accountable for harms to people and the environment.

11 Human Rights, the Environment, and Corporate Accountability

> The only social responsibility of a corporation is to make money. Period.
>
> Milton Friedman

The effort to establish enforceable human rights obligations on nonstate actors, including corporations, has persisted since the beginning of attempts to protect human rights through law. *See* Steven R. Ratner, *Corporations and Human Rights: A Theory of Legal Responsibility*, 111 YALE L.J. 443, 452–54 (2001). Originally, though, international human rights obligations were viewed as governing only states, because of entrenched international legal doctrine related to legal personality. Lauterpacht, writing in the mid-twentieth century observed that "[t]he orthodox positivist doctrine has been explicit in the affirmation that only States are subjects of international law." H. Lauterpacht, *The Subjects of the Law of Nations*, 63 L.Q. REV. 438, 439 (1947). *See also* L. OPPENHEIM, 1 INTERNATIONAL LAW 341 (1905) ("[s]ince the Law of Nations is a law between States only and exclusively, States only and exclusively are subjects of the Law of Nations"). Individuals and other nonstate actors were viewed as objects, not subjects, of the international legal system. Recall the discussion in Chapter 4 about the human rights obligations to "respect" and "ensure" and "take steps" contained in article 2 of the International Covenant on Civil and Political Rights and the International Covenant on Economic, Social, and Cultural Rights. Those obligations, of course, rest on states for their fulfillment. However, this does not necessarily mean that nonstate actors cannot be held accountable for human rights violations on other grounds.

In practice, the dividing line between states as exclusive international legal persons (with sole possession of international rights and duties) and all others lacking personality has never been as clear-cut as the traditional rule on personality maintained. Even Lauterpacht, at the time he was writing, rejected the historical view as "antiquated and no longer tenable." Lauterpacht, *Id.* at n. 2. It is true, however, that the expansion of international legal personality is dependent on state consent (as influenced by a host of political, economic, and social interests and externalities). States still retain principal control over international lawmaking, and it is by norms of international law produced by states that legal personality is conferred on nonstate actors – including by establishing enforceable rights for individuals and legal persons or by imposing corporate obligations giving rise to liability for their breach.

In this chapter, we take up consideration of the idea of corporations as protectors and promoters of human rights and the ways in which corporations may be held accountable as violators of human rights. This may seem counterintuitive, because the two areas of law have been distant. Indeed, a recent text on commercial law and human rights begins: "'Commercial law *and* human rights?' The title of this book is apt to produce some incredulity." COMMERCIAL LAW AND HUMAN RIGHTS vii (Stephen Bottomley & David Kinley eds., 2002). The reason for this disconnect can be attributed to what has been called the myth of the two sectors: "[N]o reference is so common, so accepted, as that to the two sectors of the economic and political world. There is the private sector and there is the public sector." JOHN KENNETH GALBRAITH, THE ECONOMICS OF INNOCENT FRAUD: TRUTH FOR OUR TIME 33 (2004). Historically, corporate activity has been perceived as part of the private sector, liable to "discipline" only by market forces. Human rights, the argument runs, falling outside of notions of the market, find no place in the private sector and must instead be located in the public realm, imposing obligations for their protection and promotion exclusively on the state. In fact, to some extent, the division between the sectors has been more illusory than real, and certainly over the past twenty years has become increasingly blurred, as traditional public functions are carried out by corporate actors. *See, e.g.*, Martha Minow, *Public and Private Partnerships: Accounting for the New Religion*, 116 HARV. L. REV. 1229 (2003).

In general, the multinational corporation has been largely immune from international regulation, and human rights have been no exception. Even in municipal legal systems, holding multinational corporations accountable for human rights violations has been difficult. Several explanations have been offered about the nature of the corporate form that helps thwart effective human rights regulation of corporate behavior. First of all, the distinct legal status and personality of a corporation set up by municipal law allows it to broadly allocate risks associated with activities by forming corporate groups of enterprises connected by cross-shareholding and common directorships, or by establishing subsidiary and holding company relationships. This makes "[t]racing a unique nationality of a corporation . . . difficult, if not impossible." Eric W. Orts, *The Legitimacy of Multinational Corporations, in* PROGRESSIVE CORPORATE LAW 247 (Lawrence E. Mitchell ed., 1995). Ordinarily, each distinct enterprise is entitled to a distinct and separate legal status, regardless of its relationship to a parent or other enterprises in the group. Distinct legal status and limited liability also allows for the avoidance of responsibility for actions in a corporate group as well as the deployment of procedural strategies, notably the doctrine of *forum non conveniens*, to obtain judicial postures favorable to their interests. *See* Stephen Bottomley, *Corporations and Human Rights, in* COMMERCIAL LAW AND HUMAN RIGHTS 51–55 (Stephen Bottomley & David Kinley eds., 2002).

What follows in this chapter is an examination of three different approaches that have been developed to engage corporate attention to human rights. The first approach by international lawyers has been to craft international regulation (mostly still *lex ferenda* outside of the International Labour Organization) to attempt to superintend corporate activities and actions that bear, either positively or negatively, on human rights. *See, e.g.*, Danwood Mzikenge Chirwa, *The Long March to Binding Obligations of Transnational Corporations in International Human Rights Law*, 22 S. AFR. J. ON HUM. RTS. 76 (2006). A second approach, perhaps in response to attempts at international regulation, was developed by the corporate community itself. Its focus is on voluntary self-regulation through various codes of conduct, independent certification programs, and ethical investment pressure of shareholders. This approach emphasizes corporate social responsibility. These voluntary codes have emerged on a company-by-company basis, as well as across industries. *See, e.g.*, Sean D. Murphy, *Taking Multinational Corporate Codes to the Next Level*, 43 COLUM. J. TRANSNAT'L L. 389 (2005). A third approach has been a tactical response to the perceived ineffectiveness of the first and second approaches by lawyers with human rights and environmental law backgrounds. These lawyers have promoted legislation and deployed litigation in municipal courts as a means of pressure and redress in response to human rights abuses. *See, e.g.*, Beth Stephens, *Corporate Liability: Enforcing Human Rights Through Domestic Litigation*, 24 HASTING INT'L & COMP. L. REV. 401 (2001). Consumer action through boycotts, labeling campaigns (e.g., Rugmark), and procurement policies like anti-sweatshop initiatives must also be noted. Stockholder challenges to corporate policies were important during the anti-apartheid campaign. Before we turn to these approaches, however, we first consider the nature and operations of multinational corporations in today's world.

I. Multinational Corporations

The Legitimacy of Multinational Corporations, in Progressive Corporate Law 247–66
(Lawrence E. Mitchell ed., 1995) (footnotes omitted)
Eric W. Orts

One of the great historical changes of the last half of the 20th century is the rise of multinational corporations. The multinational corporation has a "diverse nationality joined together by ties of common ownership and responsive to a common management strategy." It takes a variety of legal forms. Most commonly, a parent company headquartered in a "home" country owns, wholly or partially, subsidiaries incorporated in "foreign" countries. Increasingly, however, it is difficult to distinguish intelligibly between home and foreign corporations. Finance, share ownership, management, employees, production facilities, and markets for customers and suppliers are all subject to "internationalization." Tracing a unique nationality of a corporation becomes difficult, if not impossible. Modem joint ventures, for example, go beyond the model of a home corporation owning foreign subsidiaries. Often, they blur national distinctions by bringing together companies with different "home" nationalities in strategic alliances. Cross-border licensing agreements and other international contractual arrangements also contribute to a general tendency toward global business. In light of this trend, Robert Reich refers somewhat apocalyptically to "the coming irrelevance of corporate nationality."

. . .

The Rise of Multinational Corporations

Multinational corporations find their roots in late 19th century antecedents in the United States, Europe, and Japan. Although nobody foretold their rapid rise to power in the 20th century, large multinational corporations expanded like ancient empires. Growth in international investment was nothing short of "spectacular." A highpoint was reached in the decade before World War I. In 1913, about one-third of total world investment was international." The catastrophes of two world wars and a global depression interrupted international economic development, but global political conditions after World War II fostered another especially rapid growth of multinational enterprise. From 1950 to 1968, United States private investment abroad rose from almost $20 billion to over $100 billion, and corresponding foreign investment in the United States rose from $8 billion to over $40 billion. Although again interrupted occasionally by recessions and oil shocks, growth in international investment continued for the balance of the century. Another especially robust expansion occurred in the decade of the 1980s. From 1983 to 1989, foreign direct investment, which measures the amount of capital invested by "home" companies in "foreign" subsidiaries or affiliates, increased by an annual rate of almost twenty-nine percent. In 1985, total sales of the 350 largest multinational corporations accounted for one-third of the combined gross national products of industrialized countries. By 1990, world "international production," which describes the "intricate pattern of goods and services that reach consumers after crossing borders or through local companies whose ownership and financing originates elsewhere," totaled $5.5 trillion. This figure represents $1.5 trillion more than $4.5 trillion of traditional international trade denominated in exports of goods and services. In other words, international production through multinationals has become quantitatively more important than international trade. International production and international trade put together amount to about half the gross global multinational corporations have foreign assets of at least $6 trillion.

Corresponding to the expansion of international investment and production, the number of multinational corporations also increased rapidly in the latter half of the 20th century. From 1969 to 1990, the number of multinationals with "homes" in the top fourteen industrial countries more than tripled, increasing from around 7,000 to almost 24,000. By 1994, a conservative estimate of the number of multinational corporations put the total at around 37,000, which accounted for more than 200,000 foreign subsidiaries or affiliates.

In the period immediately following World War II, most multinationals had parent companies based in the United States or Great Britain. Even as late as 1970, more than half of all multinational corporations were based in these two countries. However, the number of "home" countries for multinational corporations has recently expanded greatly. . . . Significant numbers of multinational parents are now located in the emerging economies of Brazil, China, Hong Kong, and Korea, among others. Still, almost half of all multinationals have their parents in only four countries: the United States, Germany, Japan, and Great Britain. Multinationals based in these four countries account for approximately seventy percent of all foreign direct investment. All of the largest 100 multinational corporations have their parents in developed countries.

At least four general factors have contributed to the historical growth of multinational corporations. They relate to technology, economics, politics, and law.

First, technological improvements made doing business across great distances cheap and convenient. Air travel, telephones, telecopiers, and computers formed a technical web of fast transportation and communication. Like the technology of steamships, railroads, and the telegraph in the late 19th century, the new technologies of the 20th century set the stage for the emergence of a world-wide business web. Businesses grew multinational as new technologies overcame impediments to efficient organization and coordination over distances. The "revolution in transportation and communication," as Eric Hobsbawm writes, "virtually annihilated time and distance." Economies of scale and scope that might otherwise have gone unexploited came more easily within reach.

Second, improved technology enhanced the ability of multinational firms to exploit economic advantages. Several interrelated economic factors are at work. Managing a firm across multinational markets and with techniques of international production provides significant economic flexibility. As Bruce Kogut writes, "[t]he primary advantage of the multinational firm, as differentiated from the national corporation, lies in its flexibility to transfer resources across borders through a globally maximizing network. Multinational flexibility allows firms to perform regulatory arbitrage, that is, to shift operations among countries to take advantage of differing legal requirements, for example, lower labor costs due to absence of minimum wage laws or unions, more flexible antitrust or tax law, or weaker environmental law. It also permits firms to capture cost externalities associated with international management, such as recruiting personnel and scanning for new markets, and to achieve joint production economies in global marketing and manufacturing. In addition, multinational scope allows for hedging of financial risks, such as currency exchange and interest rate changes, within a single firm, rather than through the portfolios of investors who may be more averse to these risks.

Third, the economic advantages of multinational corporations depend on assurance of global political stability. The post-World War II political structure provided for a sufficient "peace" among the leading industrialized nations to allow for the development of close economic ties. Compatible democratic governments in Europe, North America, and Japan allowed trade and investment to develop among them without significant fear of ideological uncertainty. The Cold War between the United States and the Soviet Union played an important role. The East-West conflict downplayed differences among the democratic nations. The long "peace" among leading industrial nations extending from the end of World War II through the Cold War established a global unity that helped to spawn a "Golden Age" of explosive economic growth. The global economic expansion engendered by the Cold Peace of the Cold War enabled relatively "free trade, free capital movements and stable currencies. These conditions engendered "an increasingly transnational economy" characterized by the emergence of an international division of labor and the rise of multinational corporations.

Fourth, the role of law in the creation and maintenance of the global economy is more important than is sometimes recognized. Prevalence of a free-market ideology and an understanding of the political need for global economic integration in the post-World War II period resulted in important international agreements.

Bilateral investment treaties proliferated between home and host countries. Among other things, these treaties pledged signatory nation-states to recognize their respective legal business forms. In combination with stable domestic legal regimes, bilateral investment treaties helped to provide the predictability needed for increasing levels of international investment and the confidence often needed for parent corporations to establish foreign subsidiaries. Bilateral agreements among "the American alliance," namely, the United States, Great Britain, Germany, and Japan (along with less powerful allies such as Canada and Australia), were especially important.

. . .

Without some basic mutual recognition of the rights of foreign firms to conduct business in a country, multinational corporations could not persist. As Detlev Vagts observes, the legal prerequisites for foreign subsidiaries are as follows: "(1) the parent corporation must have power to own shares of the stock of another corporation, and (2) it must be possible for the shares of the subsidiary to be owned by one corporation to an extent sufficient to confer effective control. These legal relationships between parent and subsidiary must be recognized by both the home government of the parent and the foreign government in which the subsidiary is operating. The principle of mutual recognition or, stated more broadly, "free choice of means," applies also to other forms of doing international business. Free choice of means refers to the legal rights of businesses to engage in different methods of accessing particular markets. In addition to rights to establish subsidiaries in foreign countries, this general principle covers cross-border licensing, non-controlling financial investments, joint ventures, franchising, and trade. Free choice of means looks toward assuring a broad range of business choices, independent of particular national legal environments.

. . .

The International Legitimacy of Multinational Corporations

At present, the legitimacy of multinational corporations remains tenuous. . . . I have argued that the legitimacy of corporate forms of business enterprise depends directly on the legitimacy of governments which set up corporate statutes and courts which administer corporate law. As I use the term, legitimacy relates to three different levels of analysis. First, legitimacy refers to legal validity. A corporation is legitimate in this sense if it complies with the applicable laws governing its creation and operation. Empirical legitimacy refers to a second level. The popular acceptance of the legal authority establishing and regulating corporations determines the extent of empirical legitimacy. Third, systemic legitimacy refers to a critical assessment of whether a corporation acquires and exercises its power according to justifiable rules and with evidence of consent. From the perspective of law in the United States, business corporations are legitimate, according to these criteria, given (1) legally valid creation and adherence to the rules of the game established by corporate law, (2) empirical acceptance of the corporate form by the American public, and (3) a relatively open, democratic, and effective legal system, which embraces a number of moral and technical dimensions of corporate law and allows for criticism and reform. In the international context, however, it is more difficult to answer the question, "Why are multinational corporations legitimate?" The problem stems from the fact that the activities of multinational corporations are often subject to a relatively inchoate international legal regime, to potentially conflicting national laws, or to no applicable law at all.

. . .

Corporations cannot break free entirely of nation-states, dependent as they are for their legal existence on corporate laws of home and host countries. But a world of relative freedom of economic movement creates conditions that permit businesses to function in a sense above the law of any particular nation-state. Multinational corporations become stateless to the extent they define their economic interests in terms of a number of nation-states. When multinational corporations become truly global in this sense, with a significant presence in many nation-states, regulatory arbitrage becomes increasingly feasible. At the same time, a single multinational corporation may increasingly find itself subject to conflicting legal obligations imposed by two or more nation-states. In either event, multinationals with not only "global reach" but "global presence" begin to owe allegiance to more than one nation-state or, what is worse, to none.

In the 21st century, I believe the geographical focus of corporate law will begin to broaden to take account of this new reality. An increasingly global economy will demand a more holistic and international treatment of corporate law. Already, multinational corporations rival the power of nation-states in terms of the dynamics of the international political economy, and their relative power is likely to increase in the next century. "As more and more enterprises have been drawn into the competitive game of world markets," writes Susan Strange, "multinationals have come to occupy a larger and larger part of the current picture of international relations. They are no longer playing walk-on parts, auxiliaries to the real actors. They are at center stage, right up there with governments." Therefore, the legal foundations of multinationals will become increasingly important to understand. Not only will greater understanding of multinationals broaden the academic perspective of corporate law, it will begin to address larger concerns of an emerging "global business civilization."

Given the large role that multinational corporations will likely play in global society in the 21st century, what is their legal basis? Where do they come from as a matter of law? . . .

. . .

. . . Corporate groups first appeared in the late 19th century, primarily as a method of linking together railroad, steel, and oil companies, as well as public utilities." Corporate groups with a "holding company" structure of parents holding stock in subsidiaries were invented in the early 20th century as an antidote to restrictive antitrust legislation." Since then, the model of the corporate group has been transported abroad to form the basic structure of the multinational corporation. Robert Reich's dramatic prediction of the "coming irrelevance of corporate nationality" in the 21st century therefore actually traces its legal origins to the 19th century. Corporate groups are now recognized in most, if not all, industrialized countries. . . .

Consonant with Detlev Vagts's observation that a prerequisite for multinational corporations is the initial recognition of a parent, a subsidiary, and a legal right of parental control of the subsidiary, Phillip Blumberg recognizes the historical development of the holding company as the key legal requirement for the evolution of multinational corporate groups." Recognition of corporate groups means that a parent company, as one legal entity, can own a subsidiary, which is recognized as a separate legal entity. This development enables a corporate enterprise to split its legal identity across national borders. For certain purposes, a foreign subsidiary is recognized as a foreign legal entity; for other purposes, it is recognized as a legal entity within the parental home company in this manner, the multinational "string[s] together corporations created by the laws of different states."

As a practical legal matter, the innovation of corporate groups avoids the difficult question of determining the nationality of a multinational corporation as a whole. Choice of law often follows a rule of *lex incorporationis*; that is, internal governance of a corporation is governed by the state of incorporation. Different choice of law rules may apply in different cases and different countries to determine corporate nationality for different purposes. Depending on the circumstances, choice of law may look to the nationality of controlling shareholders, the nationality of managers, the principal place of business, or the principal place of managerial control....

Whatever the choice of law rule, recognition of corporate groups allows for two key claims. First, a multinational parent can control operations of the whole from a home parent, exerting control over its governance and internal affairs. Second, the multinational is able to benefit from legal recognition, and often control, of its subsidiaries abroad. As a result, writes John Kozyris,

> [Although the] increasing number of multinational corporations active world-wide and the question of their relationships to the home and the host nationals have provoked extensive and heated discussions in recent years[,]...[t]he question of what law should govern the internal affairs of these corporations hardly surfaces at all in these debates. There are plausible explanations for this indifference. First, the typical multinational corporation does not consist of one corporate entity but of a complex group of parents, subsidiaries, and affiliates, each of which is incorporated under and identified with the law of one country. Thus, there is no single internal corporate law governing the entire enterprise; the law applicable to each component unit can be determined under separate choice-of-law criteria. Second, it is generally assumed that the internal corporate relationship is of a private nature among the owners and managers of the enterprise and that the public objectives of the nations affected can be best pursued through external regulation and control rather than internal intervention.

...I suggest an approach to thinking about the problem of the legitimacy of multinational corporations that employs the three criteria for legitimacy outlined above. My analysis considers the legal validity, empirical legitimacy, and systemic legitimacy of multinational corporations.

First, multinational corporations are legally valid to the extent they comport with the positive laws of the countries in which they operate and any applicable international law. Foreign subsidiaries are legitimate, in this sense, according to the rules laid down by the laws of the nation-states in which they are located and under international law. Multinational groups themselves are similarly legitimated by the cross-cutting standards of national and international laws. The role of positive law in providing legitimacy even at this basic level, however, is somewhat vague.

International law, despite considerable advances in recent years, is not highly developed on the question of multinational corporations. Although academics and activists have called for an international regulatory framework for multinationals at least since 1970..., the last twenty-five years have witnessed little concrete progress along these lines. However, an intricate quilt of bilateral investment treaties has blanketed the world, providing for a certain level of legal protection for multinational investment. These treaties provide basic rights to foreign businesses, including protection against expropriation by nationalization, international dispute resolution (usually through arbitration), and some level of mutual recognition and free choice of means, such as provided by "most-favored-nation" status or some other standard of "fair and equal treatment." Also, the... World Trade Organization (WTO), has adopted provisions governing Trade-Related Investment Measures (TRIMs). Essentially, TRIMs restrict signatory countries from adopting local content or export level requirements on foreign-owned or foreign-controlled firms or joint ventures. None of these international laws, however, provides unified coverage of governance of multinational corporations. At this level, only "soft law," which is not legally binding, governs. This soft law includes the Guidelines for Multinational Enterprises developed by the Organization for Economic Cooperation and Development (OECD), the United Nations Draft Code on Transnational Corporations, and the World Bank's Guidelines on the Treatment of Foreign Direct Investment. For the most part, this soft law of multinational corporations amounts to "ineffectual hortatory declarations." The OECD Guidelines, for example, specify that they are "voluntary and not legally enforceable." Although sundry activities of multinational corporations are regulated internationally, there is a hole in the international legal fabric of corporate governance.

National laws do not fill the void left by incomplete international regulation. Applicable national laws often conflict or provide incomplete regulatory coverage. National laws cover various subjects that touch on multinational operations and activities, including regulation of foreign direct investment, transfer of technology, privatization, government procurement, taxation, antitrust, labor law, environmental law, and litigation (including jurisdictional issues). Corporations involved in particular countries must take care to comply with applicable laws. However, when extraterritorial reach of national laws is asserted, it runs into objections from other nation-states, either under international law or politically. National law alone cannot encompass – and therefore cannot legitimate – the multinational enterprise as a whole.

Split across international borders, with legitimate business forms recognized in multiple countries, the multinational entity itself appears as something of a moving target above a somewhat confused, conflicting, and incomplete mass of uncoordinated law. Conceived as a whole, which is how they are usually managed, multinational corporations often seem like ghosts escaping the various national and international laws that reach out impotently to claim them. At other times and in other circumstances, multinationals seem instead like unlucky football players who are "double hit" when they get caught between the conflicting laws of two nation-states or between international obligations on one side and conflicting national duties on the other. To the extent multinationals take care to comply with the validly enacted regulations of various states and any applicable international law, they are legitimate at the basic level of legal validity. But to the extent that multinationals fall between the cracks of national and international law, their legitimacy seems sorely wanting.

At the second level of empirical legitimacy, the situation of multinational corporations is also problematic. It is probably fair to say that many people in the world – particularly people living in poor regions of the globe – distrust the activity of multinational corporations. Multinationals may in fact play an important role in improving global standards of living. But billions of people are left out of the emerging global business civilization. For them, the benefits of what has been called "the Global Shopping Mall" and "the Global Work Place" lie out of reach. Here, an empirical gap in the legitimacy of multinational corporations arises. In the long run, this gap of empirical legitimacy threatens to undermine the stability of the global business civilization that appears otherwise to be rapidly developing.

Perhaps somewhat paradoxically, revealing the distance between normative and empirical reality, I believe the systemic legitimacy of multinational corporations is in somewhat better shape than their empirical legitimacy. From a critical perspective, the recognition of multinational corporate entities in various countries forms the basis for the systemic legitimacy of international business. If particular countries do not like the activities of multinational corporations, they remain free to restrict them, unless they endorse an international legal regulation to the contrary. Regulation of multinational corporations is imperfect, combining as it does a host of national legal regimes within a patchwork of international law. A flexible international scheme of mutual recognition and free choice of means can, however, provide a legitimate basis for the multinational corporation – at least to the extent one can say that international law adheres to critical standards of democratic government."

. . .

In the 21st century, multinational corporations will retain their empirical legitimacy only to the extent they contribute generally to a rising of all boats. The time has passed for strictly financial or strictly legal accounts of corporate enterprise. Corporations that adhere to a "business only" view of the world may continue to prosper economically. But the bleaker visions of the 21st century make clear that they should add at least two major policy issues to their radar screens.

First, global ecological crisis can no longer be ignored. Legal systems alone cannot meet the challenges presented. Conflict at the international level among nation-states has too often rendered international environmental law a cruel joke. Multinational corporations should, in their internal management and in their lobbying efforts, help to pick up the slack. The stakes – survival of the natural environment as we have known it and perhaps even survival of the human species – are too great for a "business as usual" attitude.

Second, the increasing division between the world's rich and poor will likely pose a threat to the emerging world business civilization about which many dream. Emerging economies are crucial. Multinational corporations must see themselves as citizens of the world. They should work toward a more equitable distribution of global prosperity than exists at present.

Regarding particular reform proposals for multinational corporate regulation, the time may now be ripe, at the [start] of the 21st century, to adopt a . . . World Investment Organization in conjunction with the new WTO. The international negotiating problems should not prove too difficult, especially given the increasingly strong waves of internationalization that have been sweeping over all aspects of business. At least, the regulation of multinational corporations should cease to concern only the internationalists. Corporate law should with increasing frequency turn its attention outward. It should address the economic well-being not only of the shareholders and managers in rich industrialized countries, but also those many others with whom they share the planet. Corporate law scholars should cultivate a global sensibility and, in their work, contribute to the development of basic legal rules of mutual recognition and free choice of means – along with sensitivity toward inclusion of all groups and nationalities – that will sustain the emergence of a prosperous and egalitarian world civilization in the next century.

II. The Rights of Corporations

Before considering corporate responsibilities, it must be emphasized that corporations, as legal persons, are deemed protected by some international human rights instruments, including the European Convention of Human Rights and Fundamental Freedoms. The enjoyment of the guaranteed rights and petitions to protect those rights can either support environmental protection or challenge measures with that aim. The following cases provide examples.

Case of Verein Gegen Tierfabriken Schweiz (Vgt) v. Switzerland,
2001-VI Eur. Ct Hum. Rts, App. No. 24699/94
Reports of Judgments and Decisions (June 28, 2001)

THE FACTS

I. THE CIRCUMSTANCES OF THE CASE

8. The aim of the applicant association is the protection of animals, with particular emphasis on animal experiments and industrial animal production.

9. As a reaction to various television commercials of the meat industry, the applicant association prepared a television commercial lasting fifty-five seconds and consisting of two scenes.

10. The first scene of the film showed a sow building a shelter for her piglets in the forest. Soft orchestrated music was played in the background, and the accompanying voice referred, *inter alia*, to the sense of family which sows had. The second scene showed a noisy hall with pigs in small pens, gnawing nervously at the iron bars. The accompanying voice stated, *inter alia*, that the rearing of pigs in such circumstances resembled concentration camps, and that the animals were pumped full of medicaments. The film concluded with the exhortation: "Eat less meat, for the sake of your health, the animals and the environment!"

11. On 3 January 1994 the applicant association, wishing this film to be broadcast in the programmes of the Swiss Radio and Television Company (*Schweizerische Radio- und Fernse-hgesellschaft*), sent a videocassette to the then Commercial Television Company (AG für das Werbefernsehen, now called Publisuisse) responsible for television advertising.

12. On 10 January 1994 the Commercial Television Company informed the applicant association that it would not broadcast the commercial in view of its "clear political character." The company pointed out that an alternative solution would be a film showing the merits of a decent rearing of animals and informing viewers that they were free to enquire into the origin of the meat which they were buying.

. . .

THE LAW

. . .

II. ALLEGED VIOLATION OF ARTICLE 10 OF THE CONVENTION

35. The applicant association complained that the refusal to broadcast its commercial had infringed Article 10 of the Convention, which provides:

1. Everyone has the right to freedom of expression. This right shall include freedom to hold opinions and to receive and impart information and ideas without interference by public authority and regardless of frontiers. This Article shall not prevent States from requiring the licensing of broadcasting, television or cinema enterprises.

2. The exercise of these freedoms, since it carries with it duties and responsibilities, may be subject to such formalities, conditions, restrictions or penalties as are prescribed by law and are necessary in a democratic society, in the interests of national security, territorial integrity or public safety, for the prevention of disorder or crime, for the protection of health or morals, for the protection of the reputation or rights of others, for preventing the disclosure of information received in confidence, or for maintaining the authority and impartiality of the judiciary.

36. The Government contested that submission.

A. Responsibility of the Respondent State

37. Before the substance of the matter can be examined, the Court must consider whether responsibility can be attributed to the respondent State. . . .

44. It is not in dispute between the parties that the Commercial Television Company is a company established under Swiss private law. The issue arises, therefore, whether the company's refusal to broadcast the applicant association's commercial fell within the respondent State's jurisdiction. In this respect, the Court notes in particular the Government's submission according to which the Commercial Television Company, when deciding whether or not to acquire advertising, was acting as a private party enjoying contractual freedom.

45. Under Article 1 of the Convention, each Contracting State "shall secure to everyone within [its] jurisdiction the rights and freedoms defined in . . . [the] Convention." As the Court stated in *Marckx v. Belgium* (judgment of 13 June 1979, Series A no. 31, pp. 14–15, § 31; see also *Young, James and Webster v. the United Kingdom*, judgment of 13 August 1981, Series A no. 44, p. 20, § 49), in addition to the primarily negative undertaking of a State to abstain from interference in Convention guarantees, "there may be positive obligations inherent" in such guarantees. The responsibility of a State may then be engaged as a result of not observing its obligation to enact domestic legislation.

46. The Court does not consider it desirable, let alone necessary, to elaborate a general theory concerning the extent to which the Convention guarantees should be extended to relations between private individuals *inter se*.

47. Suffice it to state that in the instant case the Commercial Television Company and later the Federal Court in its decision of 20 August 1997, when examining the applicant association's request to broadcast the commercial at issue, both relied on section 18 of the Swiss Federal Radio and Television Act, which prohibits "political advertising." Domestic law, as interpreted in the last

resort by the Federal Court, therefore made lawful the treatment of which the applicant association complained (see *Marckx* and *Young, James and Webster*, cited above). In effect, political speech by the applicant association was prohibited. In the circumstances of the case, the Court finds that the responsibility of the respondent State within the meaning of Article 1 of the Convention for any resultant breach of Article 10 may be engaged on this basis.

B. Whether There Was an Interference with the Applicant Association's Rights Under Article 10 of the Convention

48. The responsibility of the respondent State having been established, the refusal to broadcast the applicant association's commercial amounted to an "interference by public authority" in the exercise of the rights guaranteed by Article 10.

49. Such an interference will infringe the Convention if it does not meet the requirements of paragraph 2 of Article 10. It is therefore necessary to determine whether it was "prescribed by law," motivated by one or more of the legitimate aims set out in that paragraph, and "necessary in a democratic society" to achieve them.

C. Whether the Interference Was "Prescribed by Law"

50. The applicant association submitted that there was no sufficient legal basis for the interference in its rights by the Commercial Television Company. The commercial which it intended to broadcast could not be considered as "political." It merely contained pictures without any linguistic elements explaining how pigs behaved in natural surroundings and how, in contrast to this, they were kept by human beings, in cramped pens. At most, this qualified as information. The fact that such information could lead to political consequences did not make it political advertising. The primary task of information was to enlighten and to disseminate knowledge that ultimately led to the correct political decisions.

51. The Government contended that any interference with the applicant association's rights was "prescribed by law" within the meaning of Article 10 § 2 of the Convention in that it was based on section 18(5) of the Federal Radio and Television Act, the latter having been duly published and, therefore, accessible to the applicant association. While the term "political" was somewhat vague, absolute precision was unnecessary, and it fell to the national authorities to dissipate any doubts as to the interpretation of the provisions concerned. In the present case, the Federal Court in its decision of 20 August 1997 considered that the commercial at issue, denouncing the meat industry, was not of a commercial character and in fact had to be placed in the more general framework of the applicant association's militancy in favour of the protection of animals.

52. The Court recalls its case-law according to which the expression "prescribed by the law" not only requires that the impugned measure should have some basis in domestic law, but also refers to the quality of the law in question, requiring that it should be accessible to the person concerned and foreseeable as to its effects (see *Amann v. Switzerland* [GC], no. 27798/95, ECHR 2000-II). However, it is primarily for the national authorities, notably the courts, to interpret and apply domestic law (see *Kopp v. Switzerland*, judgment of 25 March 1998, *Reports* 1998-II, p. 541, § 59, and *Kruslin v. France*, judgment of 24 April 1990, Series A no. 176-A, pp. 21–22, § 29).

53. In the present case, the Federal Court in its judgment of 20 August 1997 relied as a legal basis for the refusal to broadcast the applicant association's commercial on section 18(5) of the Federal Radio and Television Act prohibiting "political advertising." Section 15 of the Radio and Television Ordinance reiterates this prohibition.

54. It is not in dispute between the parties that these laws, duly published, were accessible to the applicant association. The issue arises, however, whether the rules were foreseeable as to their effects.

55. The Court reiterates that a norm cannot be regarded as a "law" within the meaning of Article 10 § 2 unless it is formulated with sufficient precision to enable any individual – if need be with appropriate advice – to foresee, to a degree that is reasonable in the circumstances, the consequences which a given action may entail. Those consequences need not be foreseeable with absolute certainty. Again, whilst certainty is desirable, it may bring in its train excessive rigidity and the law must be able to keep pace with changing circumstances. Accordingly, many laws are inevitably couched in terms which, to a greater or lesser extent, are vague and whose interpretation and application are questions of practice. . . .

56. In the present case, it falls to be examined whether the term "political advertising" in section 18(5) of the Federal Radio and Television Act was formulated in a manner such as to enable the applicant association to foresee that it would serve to prohibit the broadcasting of the proposed television commercial. The latter depicted pigs in a forest as well as in pens in a noisy hall. The accompanying voice compared this situation with concentration camps and exhorted television viewers to "eat less meat, for the sake of [their] health, the animals and the environment."

57. In the Court's opinion the commercial indubitably fell outside the regular commercial context inciting the public to purchase a particular product. Rather, with its concern for the protection of animals, expressed partly in dramatic pictures, and its exhortation to reduce meat consumption, the commercial reflected controversial opinions pertaining to modern society in general and also lying at the heart of various political debates. Indeed, as the Federal Court pointed out in its judgment of 20 August 1997 (see paragraph 23 above), the applicant association had filed a disciplinary complaint with the Swiss Federal Parliament in respect of these matters.

58. As such, the commercial could be regarded as "political" within the meaning of section 18(5) of the Federal Radio and Television Act. It was, therefore, "foreseeable" for the applicant association that its commercial would not be broadcast on these grounds. It follows that the interference was thus "prescribed by law" within the meaning of Article 10 § 2 of the Convention.

D. Whether the Interference Pursued a Legitimate Aim

59. The applicant association further maintained that there was no legitimate aim which justified the interference with its rights.

60. The Government submitted that the refusal to broadcast the commercial at issue aimed at enabling the formation of public opinion protected from the pressures of powerful financial groups, while at the same time promoting equal opportunities for the different components of society. The refusal also secured for the press a segment of the advertising market, thus contributing towards its financial autonomy. In the Government's opinion, therefore, the measure was justified "for the protection of the . . . rights of others" within the meaning of Article 10 § 2 of the Convention.

61. The Court notes the Federal Council's message to the Swiss Federal Parliament in which it was explained that the prohibition of political advertising in section 18(5) of the Swiss Radio and Television Act served to prevent financially powerful groups from obtaining a competitive political advantage. The Federal Court in its judgment of 20 August 1997 considered that the prohibition served, in addition, to ensure the independence of broadcasters, spare the political process from undue commercial influence, provide for a degree of equality of opportunity among the different forces of society and to support the press, which remained free to publish political advertisements.

62. The Court is, therefore, satisfied that the measure aimed at the "protection of the . . . rights of others" within the meaning of Article 10 § 2 of the Convention.

E. Whether the Interference Was "Necessary in a Democratic Society"

63. The applicant association submitted that the measure had not been proportionate, as it did not have other valid means at its disposal to broadcast the commercial at issue. The television programmes of the Swiss Radio and Television Company were the only ones to be broadcast and seen throughout Switzerland. The evening news programme and the subsequent national weather

forecasts had the highest ratings, namely between 50% and 70% of all viewers. Even with the use of considerable financial resources it would not be possible to reach so many persons via the private regional channels or the foreign channels which could be received in Switzerland.

64. The Government considered that the measure was proportionate as being "necessary in a democratic society" within the meaning of Article 10 § 2 of the Convention. It was not up to the Court to take the place of the national authorities; indeed, Contracting States remained free to choose the measures which they considered appropriate, and the Court could not be oblivious of the substantive or procedural features of their respective domestic laws . . . In the present case, the Federal Court in its judgment of 20 August 1997 was called upon to examine conflicting interests protected by the same basic right: namely the freedom of the applicant association to broadcast its ideas, and the freedom of the Commercial Television Company and the Swiss Radio and Television Company to communicate information. To admit the applicant association's point of view would be to grant a "right to broadcast," which right would substantially interfere with the right of the Commercial Television Company and the Swiss Radio and Television Company to decide which information they chose to bring to the attention of the public. In fact, Article 10 would then oblige a third party to broadcast information which it did not wish to. Finally, the public had to be protected from untimely interruptions in television programmes by commercials.

65. In this respect the Government pointed out the various other possibilities open to the applicant association to broadcast the information at issue, namely by means of local radio and television stations, the print media and internet. Moreover, the Commercial Television Company had offered the applicant association the possibility of discussing the conditions for broadcasting its commercials, but this had been categorically refused by the latter.

66. The Court recalls that freedom of expression constitutes one of the essential foundations of a democratic society and one of the basic conditions for its progress and for each individual's self-fulfilment. Subject to paragraph 2 of Article 10, it is applicable not only to "information" or "ideas" that are favourably received or regarded as inoffensive or as a matter of indifference, but also to those that offend, shock or disturb. Such are the demands of pluralism, tolerance and broadmindedness without which there is no "democratic society." As set forth in Article 10, this freedom is subject to exceptions. Such exceptions must, however, be construed strictly, and the need for any restrictions must be established convincingly, particularly where the nature of the speech is political rather than commercial. . . .

67. Under the Court's case-law, the adjective "necessary," within the meaning of Article 10 § 2, implies the existence of a "pressing social need." The Contracting States have a certain margin of appreciation in assessing whether such a need exists, but it goes hand in hand with a European supervision, embracing both the legislation and the decisions applying it, even those given by an independent court. The Court is therefore empowered to give the final ruling on whether a "restriction" is reconcilable with freedom of expression as protected by Article 10.

68. The Court's task, in exercising its supervisory jurisdiction, is not to take the place of the competent national authorities but rather to review under Article 10 the decisions they delivered pursuant to their power of appreciation. This does not mean that the supervision is limited to ascertaining whether the respondent State exercised its discretion reasonably, carefully and in good faith; what the Court has to do is to look at the interference complained of in the light of the case as a whole and determine whether it was "proportionate to the legitimate aim pursued" and whether the reasons adduced by the national authorities to justify it are "relevant and sufficient". . . . In doing so, the Court has to satisfy itself that the national authorities applied standards which were in conformity with the principles embodied in Article 10 and, moreover, that they relied on an acceptable assessment of the relevant facts. . . .

69. It follows that the Swiss authorities had a certain margin of appreciation to decide whether there was a "pressing social need" to refuse the broadcasting of the commercial. Such a margin of

appreciation is particularly essential in commercial matters, especially in an area as complex and fluctuating as that of advertising. . . .

70. However, the Court has found above that the applicant association's film fell outside the regular commercial context inciting the public to purchase a particular product. Rather, it reflected controversial opinions pertaining to modern society in general. . . . The Swiss authorities themselves regarded the content of the applicant association's commercial as being "political" within the meaning of section 18(5) of the Federal Radio and Television Act. Indeed, it cannot be denied that in many European societies there was, and is, an ongoing general debate on the protection of animals and the manner in which they are reared.

71. As a result, in the present case the extent of the margin of appreciation is reduced, since what is at stake is not a given individual's purely "commercial" interests, but his participation in a debate affecting the general interest. . . .

72. The Court will consequently examine carefully whether the measure in issue was proportionate to the aim pursued. In that regard, it must balance the applicant association's freedom of expression, on the one hand, with the reasons adduced by the Swiss authorities for the prohibition of political advertising, on the other, namely to protect public opinion from the pressures of powerful financial groups and from undue commercial influence; to provide for a certain equality of opportunity among the different forces of society; to ensure the independence of broadcasters in editorial matters from powerful sponsors; and to support the press.

73. It is true that powerful financial groups can obtain competitive advantages in the area of commercial advertising and may thereby exercise pressure on, and eventually curtail the freedom of, the radio and television stations broadcasting the commercials. Such situations undermine the fundamental role of freedom of expression in a democratic society as enshrined in Article 10 of the Convention, in particular where it serves to impart information and ideas of general interest, which the public is moreover entitled to receive. Such an undertaking cannot be successfully accomplished unless it is grounded in the principle of pluralism of which the State is the ultimate guarantor. This observation is especially valid in relation to audio-visual media, whose programmes are often broadcast very widely. . . .

74. In the present case, the contested measure, namely the prohibition of political advertising as provided in section 18(5) of the Federal Radio and Television Act, was applied only to radio and television broadcasts, and not to other media such as the press. The Federal Court explained in this respect in its judgment of 20 August 1997 that television had a stronger effect on the public on account of its dissemination and immediacy. In the Court's opinion, however, while the domestic authorities may have had valid reasons for this differential treatment, a prohibition of political advertising which applies only to certain media, and not to others, does not appear to be of a particularly pressing nature.

75. Moreover, it has not been argued that the applicant association itself constituted a powerful financial group which, with its proposed commercial, aimed at endangering the independence of the broadcaster; at unduly influencing public opinion or at endangering equality of opportunity among the different forces of society. Indeed, rather than abusing a competitive advantage, all the applicant association intended to do with its commercial was to participate in an ongoing general debate on animal protection and the rearing of animals. The Court cannot exclude that a prohibition of "political advertising" may be compatible with the requirements of Article 10 of the Convention in certain situations. Nevertheless, the reasons must be "relevant" and "sufficient" in respect of the particular interference with the rights under Article 10. In the present case, the Federal Court, in its judgment of 20 August 1997, discussed at length the general reasons which justified a prohibition of "political advertising." In the Court's opinion, however, the domestic authorities have not demonstrated in a "relevant and sufficient" manner why the grounds generally advanced in support of the prohibition of political advertising also served to justify the interference in the particular circumstances of the applicant association's case.

76. The domestic authorities did not adduce the disturbing nature of any particular sequence, or of any particular words, of the commercial as a ground for refusing to broadcast it. It therefore mattered little that the pictures and words employed in the commercial at issue may have appeared provocative or even disagreeable.

77. In so far as the Government pointed out that there were various other possibilities to broadcast the information at issue, the Court observes that the applicant association, aiming at reaching the entire Swiss public, had no other means than the national television programmes of the Swiss Radio and Television Company at its disposal, since these programmes were the only ones broadcast throughout Switzerland. The Commercial Television Company was the sole instance responsible for the broadcasting of commercials within these national programmes. Private regional television channels and foreign television stations cannot be received throughout Switzerland.

78. The Government have also submitted that admitting the applicant association's claim would be to accept a "right to broadcast" which in turn would substantially interfere with the rights of the Commercial Television Company to communicate information. Reference was further made to the danger of untimely interruptions in television programmes by means of commercials. The Court recalls that its judgment is essentially declaratory. Its task is to determine whether the Contracting States have achieved the result called for by the Convention. Various possibilities are conceivable as regards the organisation of broadcasting television commercials; the Swiss authorities have entrusted the responsibility in respect of national programmes to one sole private company. It is not the Court's task to indicate which means a State should utilise in order to perform its obligations under the Convention....

79. In the light of the foregoing, the measure in issue cannot be considered as "necessary in a democratic society." Consequently, there has been a violation of Article 10 of the Convention.

The case returned to the Court in 2009 and resulted in the following Grand Chamber judgment delivered on June 30, 2009:

. . .

78. Unlike the Chamber, the Grand Chamber considers it appropriate to examine the present case from the standpoint of the positive obligation on the respondent State to take the necessary measures to allow the television commercial to be broadcast.

79. Article 1 of the Convention provides that the Contracting States "shall secure to everyone within their jurisdiction the rights and freedoms defined in . . . [the] Convention." As the Court stated in *Marckx* . . . , in addition to the primarily negative undertaking of a State to abstain from interference in Convention guarantees, "there may be positive obligations inherent" in such guarantees.

. . .

81. In determining whether or not a positive obligation exists, regard must be had to the fair balance that has to be struck between the general interest of the community and the interests of the individual, the search for which balance is inherent throughout the Convention. The scope of this obligation will inevitably vary, having regard to the diversity of situations obtaining in Contracting States and the choices which must be made in terms of priorities and resources. However, this obligation must not be interpreted in such a way as to impose an impossible or disproportionate burden on the authorities....

82. Moreover, the boundaries between the State's positive and negative obligations under the Convention do not lend themselves to precise definition. The applicable principles are nonetheless similar. Whether the case is analysed in terms of a positive duty on the State or in terms of interference by a public authority which needs to be justified, the criteria to be applied do not

differ in substance. In both contexts regard must be had to the fair balance to be struck between the competing interests at stake. . . .

. . .

91. The Court must ascertain whether, in view of the importance of the execution of its judgments in the Convention system and the applicable principles, the respondent State had a positive obligation to take the necessary measures to allow the television commercial in issue to be broadcast following the Court's finding of a violation of Article 10. In determining whether such an obligation exists, regard must be had to the fair balance that has to be struck between the general interest of the community and the interests of the individual.

92. The Court reiterates that there is little scope under Article 10 § 2 of the Convention for restrictions on political speech or, as in this case, on debate of questions of public interest. . . . This applies all the more in the instant case, having regard to the Court's judgment of 28 June 2001. Moreover, the television commercial concerned battery pig-farming. Accordingly, as it related to consumer health and to animal and environmental protection, it was undeniably in the public interest.

93. The Court further notes that the television commercial was never broadcast, even after the Court's judgment had found that the refusal to broadcast it infringed freedom of expression. However, prior restraints on publication entail such dangers that they call for the most careful scrutiny. . . .

94. Furthermore, the Court has already found, in its judgment of 28 June 2001, that the interference in issue was not necessary in a democratic society, among other reasons because the authorities had not demonstrated in a relevant and sufficient manner why the grounds generally advanced in support of the prohibition of "political" advertising could serve to justify the interference in the particular circumstances of the case. . . . The Federal Court subsequently dismissed the applicant association's application to reopen the proceedings on the ground that the association had not provided a sufficient indication of its position as to the nature of "the amendment of the judgment and the redress being sought," as it was formally required to do by section 140 of the former Federal Judicature Act. . . . On this point, the Grand Chamber shares the view expressed in paragraph 62 of the Chamber judgment that this approach is overly formalistic in a context in which it is clear from the circumstances as a whole that the association's application necessarily concerned the broadcasting of the commercial in question, which had been prohibited by the Federal Court itself on 20 August 1997.

95. The Federal Court further held that the applicant association had not sufficiently shown that it still had an interest in broadcasting the commercial. As the Chamber observed in paragraph 62 of its judgment, the Federal Court thereby took the place of the applicant association, which alone was competent at that stage to judge whether there was still any purpose in broadcasting the commercial. The Grand Chamber shares that view. It further observes that the public interest in dissemination of a publication does not necessarily decrease with the passing of time. . . . Moreover, the Federal Court did not offer its own explanation of how the public debate on battery farming had changed or become less topical since 1994, when the commercial was initially meant to have been broadcast. Nor did it show that after the Court's judgment of 28 June 2001 the circumstances had changed to such an extent as to cast doubt on the validity of the grounds on which the Court had found a violation of Article 10. Lastly, the Court must also reject the argument that the applicant association had alternative options for broadcasting the commercial in issue, for example via private and regional channels, since that would require third parties, or the association itself, to assume a responsibility that falls to the national authorities alone: that of taking appropriate action on a judgment of the Court.

96. Furthermore, the argument that the broadcasting of the commercial might be seen as unpleasant, in particular by consumers or meat traders and producers, cannot justify its continued prohibition. The Court reiterates in this connection that freedom of expression is applicable not

only to "information" or "ideas" that are favourably received or regarded as inoffensive or as a matter of indifference, but also to those that offend, shock or disturb. Such are the demands of pluralism, tolerance and broadmindedness without which there is no "democratic society"....

97. The Court notes, lastly, that the Contracting States are under a duty to organise their judicial systems in such a way that their courts can meet the requirements of the Convention.... This principle also applies to the execution of the Court's judgments. Accordingly, it is equally immaterial in this context to argue, as the Government did, that the Federal Court could not in any event have ordered that the commercial be broadcast following the Court's judgment. The same is true of the argument that the applicant association should have instituted civil proceedings.

(iv) Conclusion

98. Having regard to the foregoing, the Court considers that the Swiss authorities failed to comply with their positive obligation under Article 10 of the Convention in the instant case. There has therefore been a violation of that Article. [By a vote of 11–6 – Eds.]

Case of Pine Valley Developments Ltd and Others v. Ireland,
Eur. Ct Hum. Rts., App. No. 12742/87 (Nov. 29, 1991)

I. THE PARTICULAR CIRCUMSTANCES OF THE CASE

A. Introduction

8. The first and second applicants, Pine Valley and Healy Holdings, used to have as their principal business the purchase and development of land. The first of these companies, which was a wholly-owned subsidiary of the second, was struck off the register of companies on 26 October 1990 and dissolved on 6 November 1990, for failure to file annual returns for more than eight years. Since 1981 Healy Holdings too has filed no annual returns; on 14 October and 29 November 1985 a receiver to this company was appointed by two secured creditors. The third applicant, Mr. Daniel Healy, is the managing director of Healy Holdings and its sole beneficial shareholder; on 19 July 1990, by order of an English court, he was adjudged bankrupt.

9. On 15 November 1978 Pine Valley had agreed to purchase for IR £550,000 21½ acres of land at Clondalkin, County Dublin. It did so in reliance on an outline planning permission ... for an industrial warehouse and office development on the site. This permission, which was recorded in the official planning register ..., had been granted on 10 March 1977 by the Minister for Local Government to the then owner, Mr. Patrick Thornton, on his appeal against the refusal, on 26 April 1976, by the planning authority (Dublin County Council) of full planning permission. One of the grounds for that refusal was that the site was in an area zoned for the further development of agriculture so as to preserve a green belt.

10. On 15 September 1980 Dublin County Council refused the detailed planning approval ... for which Pine Valley had applied on 16 July 1980 in reliance on the outline permission. Pine Valley thereupon sought a conditional order of mandamus, directing the council to grant such approval; such an order was granted on 8 December 1980 and was made absolute by the High Court by a decision of 27 May 1981.

11. On 17 July 1981 Pine Valley sold the land to Healy Holdings for IR £550,000.

[The applicant unsuccessfully sought relief in domestic courts. – Eds.]

· · ·

II. ALLEGED VIOLATION OF ARTICLE 1 OF PROTOCOL NO. 1 (P1–1)

50. The applicants submitted that, as a result of the Supreme Court's decision holding the outline planning permission to be invalid, coupled with the respondent State's alleged failure to validate that permission retrospectively or its failure to provide compensation for the reduction in

value of their property, they had been victims of a breach of Article 1 of Protocol No. 1 (P1–1) to the Convention, which provides:

> Every natural or legal person is entitled to the peaceful enjoyment of his possessions. No one shall be deprived of his possessions except in the public interest and subject to the conditions provided for by law and by the general principles of international law.
>
> The preceding provisions shall not, however, in any way impair the right of a State to enforce such laws as it deems necessary to control the use of property in accordance with the general interest or to secure the payment of taxes or other contributions or penalties.

This submission, which was contested by the Government, was not accepted by the Commission.

A. Whether There Was an Interference with a Right of the Applicants

51. Bearing in mind that in the first Pine Valley case... the Supreme Court held that the outline planning permission granted to Mr. Thornton was a nullity ab initio, a first question that arises in this case is whether the applicants ever enjoyed a right to develop the land in question which could have been the subject of an interference.

Like the Commission, the Court considers that this question must be answered in the affirmative. When Pine Valley purchased the site, it did so in reliance on the permission which had been duly recorded in a public register kept for the purpose and which it was perfectly entitled to assume was valid.... That permission amounted to a favourable decision as to the principle of the proposed development, which could not be reopened by the planning authority.... In these circumstances it would be unduly formalistic to hold that the Supreme Court's decision did not constitute an interference. Until it was rendered, the applicants had at least a legitimate expectation of being able to carry out their proposed development and this has to be regarded, for the purposes of Article 1 of Protocol No. 1 (P1–1), as a component part of the property in question (see, mutatis mutandis, the Fredin judgment of 18 February 1991, Series A no. 192, p. 14, para. 40).

52. The Government contended that there had been no interference with any right of the applicants under Article 1 of Protocol No. 1 (P1–1) since the outline planning permission had been retrospectively validated by section 6(1) of the 1982 Act....

The Court recalls that it is in the first place for the national authorities, notably the courts, to interpret and apply domestic law (see, amongst various authorities, the Eriksson judgment of 22 June 1989, Series A no. 156, p. 25, para. 62). In the present case, a number of the members of the Supreme Court expressed the opinion, in the second Pine Valley case, that the applicants were excluded from the benefit of section 6(1)...; furthermore, a different view was not taken by the other national authorities involved, namely Dublin County Council and the Planning Board....

The Government maintained, however, that the question of the interpretation of section 6 of the 1982 Act was not before the Supreme Court for decision and that the observations made by its members on this subject were no more than obiter dicta.

The Court must, whatever the weight of those observations in domestic law, be guided by such pronouncements of the national authorities as exist on the subject, especially those emanating from members of the highest court of the land. Bearing also in mind that in the second Pine Valley case the defendants (one of whom was the State) accepted, at least tacitly, that the applicants did not have the benefit of section 6(1) of the 1982 Act..., it cannot now be claimed that their outline planning permission was retrospectively validated by that provision. The Court must therefore proceed on the basis that it was not.

53. The applicants accepted the Commission's view that there had been no interference with the rights of Pine Valley since it had sold the land in question before the Supreme Court's

decision in the first Pine Valley case . . . , with the result that the losses were borne by the other applicants.

Whilst the existence of a violation is conceivable even in the absence of detriment (see, inter alia, the Groppera Radio AG and Others judgment of 28 March 1990, Series A no. 173, p. 20, para. 47), the Court concurs in the result. Pine Valley had parted with ownership of the land, without retaining any right thereover that was protected by Article 1 of Protocol No. 1 (P1–1). That provision, whether taken alone (P1–1) or in conjunction with Article 14 (art. 14+P1–1) of the Convention, therefore did not apply to this applicant.

54. The Court thus concludes that there was an interference with the right of Healy Holdings and Mr. Healy to the peaceful enjoyment of their possessions.

This conclusion is not affected by three other points on which the Government relied[:]

(a) Firstly, the possibility open to the applicants of seeking some other planning permission does not alter the fact that they lost the benefit of the one they already had.

(b) Secondly, the fact that the Minister for Local Government acted bona fide in granting permission to Mr. Thornton has no bearing whatsoever on the effects of the Supreme Court's decision in the first Pine Valley case.

(c) Thirdly, the applicants' failure to seek compensation under section 55 of the 1963 Act . . . cannot be regarded as excluding the existence of an interference, since this remedy might, at most, have provided redress for the consequences after the event. Besides, the Government did not cite any case-law contradicting the applicants' view that this section was not applicable to a refusal of planning approval, neither have they clearly established that the quantum of compensation payable would have covered the entirety of the applicants' losses.

B. The Article 1 (P1–1) Rule Applicable to the Case

55. The applicants contended that the interference in question, by annulling the outline planning permission, constituted a "deprivation" of possessions, within the meaning of the second sentence of the first paragraph of Article 1 of Protocol No. 1 (P1–1). The Commission, on the other hand, saw it as a "control of the use of property," within the meaning of the second paragraph of that provision.

56. There was no formal expropriation of the property in question, neither, in the Court's view, can it be said that there was a de facto deprivation. The impugned measure was basically designed to ensure that the land was used in conformity with the relevant planning laws and title remained vested in Healy Holdings, whose powers to take decisions concerning the property were unaffected. Again, the land was not left without any meaningful alternative use, for it could have been farmed or leased. Finally, although the value of the site was substantially reduced, it was not rendered worthless, as is evidenced by the fact that it was subsequently sold in the open market (see paragraph 13 above).

Accordingly, as for example in the Fredin case (see the above-mentioned judgment, Series A no. 192, pp. 14–15, paras. 42–47), the interference must be considered as a control of the use of property falling within the scope of the second paragraph of Article 1 (P1–1).

C. Compliance with the Conditions Laid Down in the Second Paragraph of Article 1 (P1–1)

1. Lawfulness and Purpose of the Interference

57. The applicants did not dispute that the interference was in conformity with planning legislation and, like that legislation, was designed to protect the environment (see paragraph 9 above). This, in the Court's view, is clearly a legitimate aim "in accordance with the general interest" for the purposes of the second paragraph of Article 1 (P1–1) (see the same judgment, p. 16, para. 48).

2. Proportionality of the Interference

58. The applicants maintained that, in the absence of compensation or retrospective validation of their outline planning permission, the interference complained of could not be described as proportionate to the aim pursued.

59. Although the annulment by the Supreme Court of the planning permission was pronounced in proceedings to which the applicants were party, its consequences were not confined to them, as is evidenced by the fact that legislation – the 1982 Act – was subsequently passed with the intention of validating retrospectively the permissions affected. Indeed, the applicants would have found themselves in the same position if a similar decision had been handed down in a case in which they had not been involved.

The interference was designed and served to ensure that the relevant planning legislation was correctly applied by the Minister for Local Government not simply in the applicants' case but across the board. The decision of the Supreme Court, the result of which was to prevent building in an area zoned for the further development of agriculture so as to preserve a green belt . . . , must be regarded as a proper way – if not the only way – of achieving that aim.

The applicants were engaged on a commercial venture which, by its very nature, involved an element of risk (see, mutatis mutandis, the Håkansson and Sturesson judgment of 21 February 1990, Series A no. 171-A, pp. 17–18, paras. 53 and 55, and the above-mentioned Fredin judgment, Series A no. 192, pp. 17–18, para. 54) and they were aware not only of the zoning plan but also of the opposition of the local authority, Dublin County Council, to any departure from it. . . . This being so, the Court does not consider that the annulment of the permission without any remedial action being taken in their favour can be regarded as a disproportionate measure.

D. Conclusion

60. The Court thus concludes that there has been no violation of Article 1 of Protocol No. 1 (P1–1) as regards any of the applicants.

III. ALLEGED VIOLATION OF ARTICLE 14 OF THE CONVENTION, TAKEN TOGETHER WITH ARTICLE 1 OF PROTOCOL NO. 1 (ART. 14+P1–1)

61. The applicants alleged that since the remedial action taken by the legislature in the shape of section 6 of the 1982 Act benefited all the holders of permissions in the relevant category other than themselves, they had been victims of discrimination contrary to Article 14 of the Convention, taken in conjunction with Article 1 of Protocol No. 1. The former provision reads as follows:

> The enjoyment of the rights and freedoms set forth in [the] Convention shall be secured without discrimination on any ground such as sex, race, colour, language, religion, political or other opinion, national or social origin, association with a national minority, property, birth or other status.

This allegation was contested by the Government, but accepted by the Commission as regards Healy Holdings and Mr. Healy.

62. The Court recalls that, for the reasons set out in paragraph 53 above, Article 14 (art. 14) is not applicable as far as Pine Valley is concerned.

63. The Government contended, in this context also, that the applicants' outline planning permission had been validated by the 1982 Act and that, accordingly, no question of discrimination arose. The Court has already dealt with this contention in paragraph 52 above and rejects it on the grounds there stated.

64. The Government did not rely on the observations made by certain members of the Supreme Court in this connection . . . nor did they advance any other justification for the difference of

treatment between the applicants and the other holders of permissions in the same category as theirs.

The Court therefore finds that there has been a violation of Article 14 of the Convention, taken together with Article 1 of Protocol No. 1 (art. 14+P1–1), as regards Healy Holdings and Mr. Healy.

Matos e Silva, Lda., et al. v. Portugal,
Eur. Ct Hum. Rts., App. No. 15777/89,
Judgment of Sept. 16, 1996

. . .

9. The first applicant, Matos e Silva, Lda. ("Matos e Silva"), is a private limited company entered in the companies' register at Loulé (Portugal). It, alone among the applicants, was a party to the domestic proceedings. . . . The second and third applicants, Mrs. Maria Sofia Machado Perry Vidal and Teodósio dos Santos Gomes, Lda., another company, are the only shareholders in and owners of Matos e Silva. The second applicant manages both companies.

A. The Background to the Case

10. Matos e Silva works land in the municipality of Loulé. It cultivates the land, extracts salt and breeds fish.

11. It owns part of this land, having bought the parcels in question on different occasions. The remainder was worked under a concession granted under a royal decree of 21 July 1884 to Basilio de Castelbranco. Article 2 of the decree provided that the parcels of land over which the concession had been granted could be expropriated without any right to compensation for the grantees. In 1886 Basilio de Castelbranco assigned the concession to the Compagnia Exploradora de Terrenos Salgados do Algarve. When that company was wound up, some of its former shareholders purchased the concession. They formed the Matos e Silva company whose object was in particular to purchase and work part of the salt marshes which were the subject matter of the concession. On 12 August 1899 that company executed a sale and purchase agreement before a notary in respect of those parcels of land.

On 16 September 1899 it had the agreement recorded in the Loulé land register in the following terms: "1899 – 16 September. . . . The transfer of the usable area of the third glebe of the Ludo parcel [*prazo*] . . . together with the parcels of land known as Ludo and Marchil . . . is registered in favour of the Matos e Silva company . . . , which purchased them . . . for a total price of 79,500 $ 000 reis [*sic*]. . . . " Since then Matos e Silva has acted in respect of that land uti dominus, paying the taxes and duties provided for by Portuguese legislation on land ownership.

12. On 2 May 1978, by Decree no. 45/78, the Portuguese Government created a nature reserve for animals (Reserva Natural da Ria Formosa) on the Algarve coast (municipalities of Loulé, Olhão and Faro), including the parcels of Matos e Silva's land known as "Herdade do Muro do Ludo," or "Quinta do Ludo" or again "Herdade do Ludo." The Government took various measures in connection with this scheme, including the five contested by the applicants.

. . .

AS TO THE LAW

. . .

III. ALLEGED VIOLATION OF ARTICLE 1 OF PROTOCOL NO. 1 (P1–1)

71. The applicants also complained of three expropriation measures and of two measures similar to expropriation. They considered that they amounted to a breach of Article 1 of Protocol No. 1 (P1–1), which provides:

Every natural or legal person is entitled to the peaceful enjoyment of his possessions. No one shall be deprived of his possessions except in the public interest and subject to the conditions provided for by law and by the general principles of international law.

The preceding provisions (P1–1) shall not, however, in any way impair the right of a State to enforce such laws as it deems necessary to control the use of property in accordance with the general interest or to secure the payment of taxes or other contributions or penalties.

A. Whether There Was a "Possession"

72. The Government devoted most of their submissions to arguing that the applicants did not have any "possessions" within the meaning of Article 1 of Protocol No. 1 (P1–1). Matos e Silva's legal position as owner of the land in question was debatable under domestic law. Consequently, the applicants could not allege an infringement of a property right that had not been established.

73. The applicants denied that there was an issue in Portuguese law. They pointed out that part of the land had never been included in the royal concession. Ownership of the land previously covered by the 1884 concession derived from the presumption in law created by the fact that their purchase in 1899 had been entered in the land register; the validity of that entry had never been contested.

In any event, the 1884 concession had itself already transferred ownership to the grantee at the time. Besides, the State had always regarded Matos e Silva as owner of the land since it had, for example, acquired for value a very large tract of it as the site for Faro airport in 1969 and had at all times collected property taxes on all the land. In any case, Matos e Silva had become the owner by adverse possession. Lastly, State Counsel himself, in his pleadings of 8 March 1995 in the proceedings concerning Legislative Decree no. 173/84, had recognised the company's ownership of the "Quinta do Ludo."

74. The Commission considered that for the purposes of the instant case Matos e Silva was to be regarded as owner of the land in question.

75. Like the Commission, the Court notes that the ownership of part of the land is not contested.

As to the other part (see paragraph 11 above), the Court agrees with the Government that it is not for the Court to decide whether or not a right of property exists under domestic law. However, it recalls that the notion "possessions" (in French: "biens") in Article 1 of Protocol No. 1 (P1–1) has an autonomous meaning (see the Gasus Dosier- und Fördertechnik GmbH v. the Netherlands judgment of 23 February 1995, Series A no. 306-B, p. 46, para. 53). In the present case the applicants' unchallenged rights over the disputed land for almost a century and the revenue they derive from working it may qualify as "possessions" for the purposes of Article 1 (P1–1).

B. Whether There Was an Interference

76. In the applicants' submission, it was not in doubt that there had been an interference with their right to the peaceful enjoyment of their possessions. The land in question was subject to several restrictions. Apart from a ban on building and easements and restrictions affecting development of the land, the profitability of the land was currently about 40% less than it had been in 1983. Furthermore, it was impossible to sell the land because potential purchasers would be deterred by the legal position. The suspension of the effects of Legislative Decree no. 173/84 would have no influence on the restrictions on ownership brought about by successive Government measures since 1 March 1983. Lastly, the State had never paid or offered any compensation.

77. The Government maintained that there had not been a deprivation of property. The expropriation procedure had never been set in motion and no action had ever been taken with respect to the

land, whose status was the same as before. Under Articles 9 et seq. of the 1976 Expropriations Code, a public-interest declaration was a preliminary to expropriation proceedings. By itself it did not affect the content of ownership and did not make it impossible to dispose of the land concerned, especially as it lapsed after two years. For that reason, during that period, the declarations had not caused any interference or a transfer of or change to the title on the basis of which the applicants worked the land. In addition, Legislative Decree no. 173/84 had rendered the earlier measures nugatory and prevented them from being of any effect in the future. It had merely brought about a withdrawal of the concession, not an expropriation. Its effects had been suspended by a judgment of the Supreme Administrative Court on 18 July 1985 and it had not caused any interference. In conclusion neither the legal title by virtue of which the applicants cultivated the land in question nor the conditions in which the land was worked in practice had really changed.

78. The Commission expressed the view that the measures in issue amounted to an interference with the peaceful enjoyment of possessions. In particular, the applicants' control of the land in issue had, in practical terms, been substantially restricted as farming, fish farming and salt production could not be developed and building on the land was prohibited.

79. Like the Commission, the Court notes that although the disputed measures have, as a matter of law, left intact the applicants' right to deal with and use their possessions, they have nevertheless greatly reduced their ability to do so in practice. They also affect the very substance of ownership in that three of them recognise in advance the lawfulness of an expropriation. The other two measures, the one creating and the other regulating the Ria Formosa Nature Reserve, also incontestably restrict the right to use the possessions. For approximately thirteen years the applicants have thus remained uncertain what would become of their properties. The result of all the disputed decisions has been that since 1983 their right over the possessions has become precarious. Although a remedy in respect of the contested measures was available, the position was in practice the same as if none existed.

In conclusion, the applicants have suffered an interference with their right to the peaceful enjoyment of their possessions. The consequences of that interference were, without any doubt, aggravated by the combined use of the public-interest declarations and the creation of a nature reserve over a long period. . . .

C. Whether the Interference Was Justified

80. It remains to be determined whether or not this interference contravenes Article 1 (P1–1).

1. The applicable rule

81. Article 1 (P1–1) guarantees in substance the right of property. It comprises three distinct rules. The first, which is expressed in the first sentence of the first paragraph (P1–1-1) and is of a general nature, lays down the principle of peaceful enjoyment of property. The second rule, in the second sentence of the same paragraph (P1–1-1), covers deprivation of possessions and makes it subject to certain conditions. The third, contained in the second paragraph (P1–1-2), recognises that the Contracting States are entitled, amongst other things, to control the use of property in accordance with the general interest, by enforcing such laws as they deem necessary for the purpose. However, the rules are not "distinct" in the sense of being unconnected: the second and third rules are concerned with particular instances of interference with the right to peaceful enjoyment of property. They must therefore be construed in the light of the general principle laid down in the first rule. . . .

82. The applicants submitted that the combined effects of the five measures had resulted in a de facto expropriation of their possessions. The first two measures were indeed expropriation measures since, under Portuguese law, a public-interest declaration set in motion the expropriation

procedure and was followed merely by an enforcement measure. The third measure was actually entitled expropriation. Yet no compensation was paid to the applicants. The owner lost all right to sell his property in its previous condition; he could only transfer precarious rights. In any event, it was no longer possible to work normally land that was subject to three public-interest declarations, several prohibitions including one on building, several easements and an authorisation enabling the State to take immediate possession of the land.

. . .

85. In the Court's opinion, there was no formal or de facto expropriation in the present case. The effects of the measures are not such that they can be equated with deprivation of possessions. As the Delegate of the Commission stated, the position was not irreversible. . . . The restrictions on the right to property stemmed from the reduced ability to dispose of the property and from the damage sustained by reason of the fact that expropriation was contemplated. Although the right in question had lost some of its substance, it had not disappeared. The Court notes, for example, that all reasonable manner of exploiting the property had not disappeared seeing that the applicants continued to work the land. The second sentence of them first paragraph (P1–1-1) is therefore not applicable in the instant case.

Although the measures did not all have the same legal effect and had different aims, they must be looked at together in the light of the first sentence of the first paragraph of Article 1 of Protocol No. 1 (P1–1-1).

2. Compliance with the Rule Set Forth in the First Sentence of the First Paragraph (P1–1-1)

86. For the purposes of the first sentence of the first paragraph (P1–1-1), the Court must determine whether a fair balance was struck between the demands of the general interest of the community and the requirements of the protection of the individual's fundamental rights (see the Sporrong and Lönnroth judgment previously cited, p. 26, para. 69).

(a) The General Interest

87. According to the applicants, a scrutiny of the five measures does not indicate any coherent strategy with regard to their possessions.

88. Even though the purpose for which the applicants' possessions were intended was changed several times, the Court, like the Commission, accepts that the measures pursued the public interest relied on by the Government, that is to say town and country planning for the purposes of protecting the environment.

(b) Whether a Fair Balance Was Struck Between the Opposing Interests

89. In the applicants' submission, the measures taken were never necessary in the public interest as they had never been followed up. The Portuguese State did not implement the programmes which the three expropriation measures should have enabled it to launch. It did not at any stage build an aquaculture station or establish a single reserve for migrant birds or a general nature reserve.

90. The Government maintained that the decisions concerned struck an adequate and reasonable balance between the public interest pursued and the various private interests as regards individual use of and profit from the land. In this instance, the State had a duty to prevent improper and speculative uses of the land. The length of the proceedings could not be taken into account.

91. As to proportionality, the Commission considered that the length of the proceedings, coupled with the fact that it had so far been impossible for the applicants to obtain even partial compensation for the damage sustained, upset the balance which should be struck between protection of the right of property and the requirements of the general interest.

92. The Court recognises that the various measures taken with respect to the possessions concerned did not lack a reasonable basis. However, it observes that in the circumstances of the case the measures had serious and harmful effects that have hindered the applicants' ordinary enjoyment of their right for more than thirteen years during which time virtually no progress has been made in the proceedings. The long period of uncertainty both as to what would become of the possessions and as to the question of compensation further aggravated the detrimental effects of the disputed measures.

As a result, the applicants have had to bear an individual and excessive burden which has upset the fair balance which should be struck between the requirements of the general interest and the protection of the right to the peaceful enjoyment of one's possessions.

93. Having regard to all these considerations, the Court dismisses the Government's preliminary objections with respect to this part of the case and holds that there has been a violation of Article 1 of Protocol No. 1 (P1–1).

V. APPLICATION OF ARTICLE 50 OF THE CONVENTION (ART. 50)

97. Article 50 of the Convention (art. 50) provides:

> If the Court finds that a decision or a measure taken by a legal authority or any other authority of a High Contracting Party is completely or partially in conflict with the obligations arising from the . . . Convention, and if the internal law of the said Party allows only partial reparation to be made for the consequences of this decision or measure, the decision of the Court shall, if necessary, afford just satisfaction to the injured party.

A. Damage

98. The applicants submitted that reparation for the alleged pecuniary damage should put them in a situation equivalent to the one which they would have been in had the unlawful measures not been implemented. The sum awarded should correspond to compensation in kind. It should take into account the current value of the compensation due by reason of the disputed measures, the loss of enjoyment suffered and the loss of profit resulting from the fact that they were unable to benefit from the development of tourism on the Algarve and had lost opportunities to expand their activities.

In order to assess the damage thus identified, they continued, it was necessary to determine what would have been their financial position had the State not intervened. To this end, the applicants produced a detailed estimate of the pecuniary loss showing that the amount of the compensation due in 1983, capitalised at the rates set out in the 1976 Expropriations Code, came to 20,458,463,000 escudos (PTE).

An identical sum would be due were the Court to consider that the expropriation in 1983 was lawful. The current value of the property was PTE 12,687,240,000, to which should be added PTE 7,771,223,000 for the loss of real sale opportunities.

The applicants also claimed non-pecuniary damage. The dispute had caused them feelings of frustration, powerlessness, suffering and revolt given the brutal manner in which their rights had been "trampled on" and the discriminatory treatment they had received. They claimed PTE 60,000,000 under this head.

They further submitted that these amounts should be increased by interest at the statutory annual rate of 15% to run from the date on which their memorial was lodged until the date of payment.

99. In the Government's submission, reparation in kind remained an adequate means of redress. Furthermore, the applicants' claim was unfounded. The land in question had never had and never would have the potential on which the applicants' evaluation was based. It was not suitable

for building or development for tourism purposes. Moreover, for thirty years the land had been subject to an obligation not to hinder air traffic. The national public works authority had recently valued the land in question at PTE 300,000,000 to be increased if appropriate by 10% to 15%. Furthermore, so long as the proceedings remained pending, the applicants were unable to claim a loss of profit, such loss being hypothetical. With regard to the possible damage sustained on account of the length of the proceedings, the applicants could bring an action for damages against the State in the domestic courts.

As regards the alleged non-pecuniary damage, the Government considered that only individuals could suffer anxiety and distress because of the uncertainty into which the length of proceedings plunged them. In any event, the amount claimed was unreasonable. The Government left it to the Court to make an assessment ex aequo et bono.

100. The Delegate of the Commission considered the applicants' claims excessive.

101. The Court points out that there has been no expropriation or situation tantamount to a deprivation of property, but a reduced ability to dispose of the possessions in question. The methods of assessment proposed by the applicants are therefore not appropriate. The breaches found of Article 1 of Protocol No. 1 (P1–1) and Article 6 para. 1 of the Convention (art. 6–1) make it incumbent on the Court to assess the damage as a whole having regard to the uncertainty created by the length of the proceedings and to the interferences with the free use of the property. Assessing the various items of damage on an equitable basis, the Court considers that the applicants should be awarded satisfaction of PTE 10,000,000.

. . .

FOR THESE REASONS, THE COURT UNANIMOUSLY

1. Decides to join the Government's preliminary objections to the merits, and dismisses them after examining the merits;

2. Holds that there has not been a violation of Article 13 (art. 13) or of Article 6 para. 1 of the Convention (art. 6-1) on account of the lack of access to a tribunal;

3. Holds that there has been a violation of Article 6 para. 1 of the Convention (art. 6-1) on account of the length of the proceedings;

4. Holds that there has been a violation of Article 1 of Protocol No. 1 (P1–1);

5. Holds that it is not necessary to examine the allegation of a violation of Article 14 of the Convention taken in conjunction with Article 1 of Protocol No. 1 (art. 14+P1–1);

6. Holds that the respondent State is to pay the applicants taken together, within three months, 10,000,000 (ten million) escudos for damage and 6,000,000 (six million) escudos for costs and expenses, on which sums simple interest at an annual rate of 10% shall be payable from the expiry of the above-mentioned three months until settlement;

7. Dismisses the remainder of the claim for just satisfaction.

III. International Attempts to Regulate Corporations

There have been several efforts to develop generally applicable norms to govern the activities of transnational corporations. As the foregoing reading indicates, almost all of these lawmaking efforts have had "soft law" results (aside from treaties negotiated under the auspices of the International Labor Organization). The resulting documents often do not bind either states or nonstate corporate actors.

Report of the U.N. High Commissioner on Human Rights and Responsibilities of Transnational Corporations and Related Business Enterprises with Regard to Human Rights, U.N. Doc. E/CN.4/2005/91 (Feb. 15, 2005)

What Are the Responsibilities of Business with Regard to Human Rights?

27. In considering the responsibilities of business with regard to human rights, it is important to reiterate that States are the primary duty bearers of human rights. While business can affect the enjoyment of human rights significantly, business plays a distinct role in society, holds different objectives, and influences human rights differently to States. The responsibilities of States cannot therefore simply be transferred to business; the responsibilities of the latter must be defined separately, in proportion to its nature and activities.

28. The Global Compact has identified responsibilities of business in connection with two principles:

(a)   Principle One: Businesses should support and respect the protection of internationally proclaimed human rights;

(b)   Principle Two: Businesses should make sure that they are not complicit in human rights abuses.

29. This provides a useful starting point for understanding the responsibilities of business with regard to human rights, suggesting three forms of responsibility. The first two responsibilities – to "respect" and to "support" human rights – relate to the acts and omissions of the business entity itself. The third responsibility on business entities – to "make sure they are not complicit" in human rights abuses – concerns the relationship between business entities and third parties.

30. A responsibility to "respect" human rights is comparatively unproblematic and requires business to refrain from acts that could interfere with the enjoyment of human rights. For example, a private detention centre institution should refrain from inflicting cruel, inhuman and degrading treatment on people detained.

31. More complex issues arise in relation to the responsibility to "support" human rights. For example, the responsibility to "support" human rights suggests that business entities carry positive responsibilities to promote human rights. On the one hand, business entities have a great and sometimes untapped potential to promote human rights through investment, and promotion of economic growth and the underlying conditions required for the enjoyment of human rights. A responsibility to "support" human rights could help channel this. On the other hand, accepting that business has positive responsibilities to use its influence to promote human rights could sit uneasily with the traditional discretion of States to make appropriate choices and exercise balance in designing policies to fulfil human rights. In this context, it is relevant to note that business entities already carry positive responsibilities in other areas of national law, for example in the law of negligence when discharging a duty of care to employees or local communities. This could provide guidance when clarifying the positive responsibilities on business to "support" human rights.

32. Similarly, subdividing the responsibility to "support" human rights into subcategories of responsibilities could be helpful. For example, the Committee on Economic, Social and Cultural Rights has subdivided the obligations of States parties to the International Covenant on Economic, Social and Cultural Rights into obligations to respect, protect and fulfil (promote, provide and facilitate) economic, social and cultural rights. The responsibilities to "support" human rights could therefore be clarified by considering what business could do to protect, promote, provide and facilitate human rights. These sub-responsibilities could then be classified as "essential," "expected," or "desirable" conduct of business entities.

33. The responsibility on business entities to "make sure they are not complicit in human rights abuses" similarly raises complex issues. Corporations often act with other partners in joint ventures or with national and local governments which could lead to allegations of complicity if the partner itself has abused human rights. One definition of "complicity" states that a company is complicit in human rights abuses if it authorizes, tolerates, or knowingly ignores human rights abuses committed by an entity associated with it, or if the company knowingly provides practical assistance or encouragement that has a substantial effect on the perpetration of human rights abuse.

34. Four situations illustrate where an allegation of complicity might arise against a company. First, when the company actively assists, directly or indirectly, in human rights violations committed by others; second, when the company is in a partnership with a Government and could reasonably foresee, or subsequently obtains knowledge, that the Government is likely to commit abuses in carrying out the agreement; third, when the company benefits from human rights violations even if it does not positively assist or cause them; and fourth, when the company is silent or inactive in the face of violations. As with the responsibility to "support" human rights, the duty on business to act or not act in each of these situations might not always be clear. Questions arise as to the extent of knowledge that the business entity had or should have had in relation to the human rights abuse and the extent to which it assisted through its acts or omissions in the abuse.

35. National and international criminal law has elaborated the doctrine of complicity as a basis for criminal liability, including criminal liability for legal persons for their complicity in crimes. The doctrine of complicity under national and international criminal law could therefore provide guidance in the further elaboration of this responsibility.

What Are the Boundaries of the Responsibilities of Business with Regard to Human Rights?

36. In contrast to the limits on States' human rights obligations, the boundaries of the human rights responsibilities of business are not easily defined by reference to territorial limits. While a small business might have relatively limited influence over the enjoyment of human rights within a particular country, a large company might influence the enjoyment of human rights across boundaries. Defining the boundaries of business responsibility for human rights therefore requires the consideration of other factors such as the size of the company, the relationship with its partners, the nature of its operations, and the proximity of people to its operations.

37. A helpful means to understand the scope and boundaries of the responsibilities of business is the non-legal concept of "sphere of influence." The concept has not been defined authoritatively; however the "sphere of influence" of a business entity tends to include the individuals to whom it has a certain political, contractual, economic or geographic proximity. Every business entity, whatever its size, will have a sphere of influence; the larger it is, the larger the sphere of influence is likely to be. It is relevant to note that the Global Compact asks participating business entities "to embrace, support and enact, within their sphere of influence" its ten principles.

38. The notion of "sphere of influence" could be useful in clarifying the extent to which business entities should "support" human rights and "make sure they are not complicit in human rights abuses" by setting limits on responsibilities according to a business entity's power to act. Importantly, "sphere of influence" could help clarify the boundaries of responsibilities of business entities in relation to other entities in the supply chain such as subsidiaries, agents, suppliers and buyers by guiding an assessment of the degree of influence that one company exerts over a partner in its contractual relationship – and therefore the extent to which it is responsible for the acts or omissions or a subsidiary or a partner down the supply chain.'[3] At the same time, "sphere of influence" should help draw the boundaries between the responsibilities of business and the obligations on States so that business entities do not take on the policing role of Government. Finally,

the notion of "sphere of influence" could ensure that smaller business entities are not forced to undertake over-burdensome human rights responsibilities, but only responsibilities towards people within their limited sphere of influence.

39. The Commission might wish to consider and develop further the concept of "sphere of influence."

In Relation to Which Human Rights Does Business Have Responsibility?

40. There are many sources of human rights that could be relevant to defining the rights for which business has responsibilities. At the global level, international human rights law provides the primary source. Importantly, the Universal Declaration of Human Rights has become a point of reference for many initiatives and standards on business and human rights. The International Covenant on Civil and Political Rights, the International Covenant on Economic, Social and Cultural Rights and the other main human rights treaties provide a further source. While human rights coverage is not equal across nations due to varying levels of ratification, it is important to note that all States have ratified at least one human rights treaty. Significantly, the Convention on the Rights of the Child, which recognizes all civil, cultural, economic, political and social rights in relation to children, has achieved almost universal acceptance with 191 ratifying States. Similarly, some human rights have become norms of customary international law and can therefore be considered to have universal application.

41. The international instruments give little guidance as to which human rights are relevant to the activities of business. In principle, the responsibility to "respect" human rights could apply to all recognized rights; business entities should therefore refrain from interfering with the enjoyment of any rights. However, to the extent that business entities have positive responsibilities to "support" human rights, the rights applicable to business are necessarily narrower than those applicable to States, given the very different nature of business and the role it plays in society. Importantly, rights that require sensitive balancing decisions in the public interest or intervention by a public authority would be outside the scope of business responsibilities. For example, some rights such as the rights relating to criminal trials, the right to asylum and political rights are wholly within the public functions of the State and therefore less directly relevant to business.

42. A non-exhaustive list of human rights more relevant to business could include: the prohibition of discrimination, the right to life, liberty and security of the person, freedom from torture, the right to privacy, freedom of opinion and expression, the right to seek, receive and impart information, freedom of association, the right to organize, the prohibition of bonded or forced labour, the prohibition of forms of child labour, the right to health, the right to an adequate standard of living and the right to education. Similarly, the rights of certain groups of people particularly affected by the activities of business are relevant – such as the rights of women, children, employees, indigenous peoples and migrant workers and their families.

How Can the Responsibilities of Business with Regard to Human Rights Be Guaranteed?

43. Ensuring that business respects human rights is first a matter of State action at the domestic level. States have undertaken international obligations to respect the rights of individuals and groups of individuals and to protect those rights against the actions of third parties; those third parties include business entities. Many countries have introduced human rights implementing legislation that regulates business entities in areas such as discrimination and workers' human rights. Courts and quasi-judicial tribunals enforce these laws.

44. Companies also have an important role to play in ensuring that they protect human rights standards in their own operations. Voluntary initiatives on business and human rights can help to promote a culture of respect for human rights from within the company and can give human

rights standards practical meaning while motivating positive change in support of human rights. Companies can also promote human rights in their relationships with business partners through the inclusion of contractual terms stipulating respect for human rights as part of a business deal. Similarly, markets mechanisms have a role to play in ensuring respect for human rights through the use of environmental and social indices and public reporting on social responsibility which rates the performance of business entities, which in turn can affect market confidence and motivate better performance.

45. Nonetheless, company and market initiatives have their limits and are not necessarily comprehensive in their coverage nor a substitute for legislative action. Importantly, while voluntary business action in relation to human rights works for the well-intentioned and could effectively raise the standard of other companies, there remains scepticism amongst sectors of civil society as to their overall effectiveness.

46. There is also a question of how to ensure respect for human rights in situations where effective governance or accountability are absent because the State is unwilling or unable to protect human rights – for example due to a lack of control over its territories, weak judiciary, lack of political will or corruption. A lack of appropriate regulation and enforcement by the State could fail to check human rights abuses adequately while also encourage a climate of impunity. A particularly complex issue involves the regulation of companies headquartered in one country, operating in a second and having assets in a third. There is concern that business entities might evade the jurisdictional power of States in some situations, which could lead to negative consequences for the enjoyment of human rights.

47. Increasing attention is being given to whether and to what extent parent companies should be subject to the law and jurisdiction of their home countries in relation to their operations abroad. The United States Alien Tort Claims Act provides one example of a home country measure which gives courts power to hear civil claims by foreign citizens for injuries caused by actions in violation of the law of nations or a treaty of the United States although other examples also exist. Subjecting parent companies to their home jurisdiction for alleged human rights abuses against claimants of the host country raises questions of respect for the national sovereignty of the host country while also highlighting several complex legal questions which require further examination. Nonetheless, home country regulation could provide an effective means of protecting human rights in situations where accountability gaps exist.

. . .

Annex

II. DESCRIPTION OF A SELECTION OF EXISTING INITIATIVES AND STANDARDS ON BUSINESS AND HUMAN RIGHTS

Of the many existing initiatives and standards on business and human rights, the following list identifies those mentioned most prominently in the consultations.

. . .

Business Leaders' Initiative for Human Rights (BLIHRA). BLIHR brings together ten companies (ABB, Barclays plc, Gap, Hewlett-Packard Company, National Grid Transco plc, Novartis, Novo Nordisk, MTV Networks Europe, Statoil and the Body Shop International plc) for a three-year period beginning in May 2003 to explore the ways that human rights standards and principles can inform issues of corporate responsibility and corporate governance. During the first year of the initiative, BLIHR worked together in collaboration with leading human rights and corporate responsibility experts and organizations to examine a range of relevant standards and initiatives, with a particular focus on the draft Norms described above.

. . .

Voluntary Principles on Security and Human Rights for the Extractive and Energy Sectors. The Governments of the United States and the United Kingdom, companies in the extractive and energy sectors and non-governmental organizations developed a set of voluntary principles to provide practical guidance to strengthen human rights safeguards in company security arrangements in the extractive sector. The Voluntary Principles are the basis of a global standard for the extractive sector and address three areas of mutual concern to both companies and civil society, namely: engagement with private security; engagement with public security; and risk assessment supporting security arrangements consistent with human rights. While the Voluntary Principles are essentially voluntary, they have also been annexed to contracts and can therefore also potentially become legally enforceable.

. . .

Worldwide Responsible Apparel Production (WRAP). WRAP is a certification programme, requiring manufacturers to comply with 12 universally accepted principles including principles, relating to compliance with laws and workplace relations; the prohibition of forced labour; prohibition of harassment and abuse; compensation and benefits; hours of work; prohibition of discrimination; health and safety; freedom of association and collective bargaining; environment; customs' compliance and security. The programme's objective is to monitor independently and certify compliance with these socially responsible global standards for manufacturing and ensure that sewn products are produced under lawful, humane and ethical conditions. . . .

SA8000. Social Accountability International, a non-profit organization based in the United States, established the SA8000 certification scheme in 1999 as a way for retailers, brand companies, suppliers and other organizations to maintain just and decent working conditions throughout the supply chain. SA8000 is based on international workplace norms derived from ILO Conventions, the Universal Declaration of Human Rights and the Convention on the Rights of the Child, and includes standards on child labour, forced labour, workplace health and safety, freedom of association and collective bargaining, non-discrimination, discipline, working hours, compensation, and management systems. . . .

Kimberley Process Certification Scheme. In 2002, 36 States and the European Union, representing countries that mine, trade and cut rough diamonds, formally adopted the Kimberley Process Certification Scheme with the ultimate aim of putting an end to trade in conflict diamonds. A declaration outlines all the steps that Governments should take to ensure certification of diamonds under the scheme. Steps include the creation of systems of internal control – including penalties for violations – to prevent conflict diamonds entering shipments of rough cut diamonds. The signatory Governments have also undertaken to monitor effectively diamond trade in order to detect and prevent trade in conflict diamonds. The Kimberley Process is ongoing and participating Governments rotate the chairpersonship of the process on an annual basis.

The Global Sullivan Principles. The Global Sullivan Principles were developed as a voluntary code of conduct for companies doing business in apartheid – South Africa. The Principles aim to have companies and organizations of all sizes, in widely disparate industries and cultures, working toward the common goals of human rights, social justice and economic opportunity. Each endorser of the Principles makes a commitment to work towards the goals of the Principles, including through the implementation of internal policies, procedures, training and reporting structures. Endorsing companies and organizations are asked to take part in an annual reporting process to document and share their experiences in relation to implementation of the Principles.

Global Reporting Initiative (GRI). GRI started in 1997 as a multi-stakeholder process and independent institution to develop and disseminate a globally applicable framework for reporting an organization's sustainability performance. The framework presents reporting principles and specific content indicators to guide the preparation of organization-level sustainability reports. The framework of principles and guidelines is for voluntary use by organizations for reporting on the economic, environmental, and social dimensions of their activities, products, and services. GRI is an official collaborating centre of UNEP and works in cooperation with the Global Compact.

. . .

The Extractive Industry Transparency Initiative. In 2002, the United Kingdom Government announced the Extractive Industries Transparency Initiative at the World Summit on Sustainable Development in Johannesburg. The initiative aims to increase transparency over payments by companies to governments and Government-linked entities, as well as transparency over revenues by those host country Governments through voluntary reporting submitted to an independent third party. The initiative is multi-stakeholder and seeks the involvement of small, medium and multi-national businesses, industry groups, intergovernmental and non-governmental organizations as well as host and home country Governments.

Caux Round Table Principles for Business. Designed in 1994 by a network of business leaders, the Caux Round Table Principles aim to express a standard to measure business behaviour through the identification of shared values and the reconciliation of differing values. The Principles set out responsibilities of business in relation to a range of issues including respect for the environment, avoidance of illicit operations and respect for customers, employees, investors, suppliers, competitors and communities. The Principles identify the responsibility of business to respect human rights and democratic institutions and promote them wherever possible. The Caux Round Table promotes the Principles through a range of networks that includes employer associations, civil society and the Global Compact Office.

. . .

The Danish Institute for Human Rights (DIHR) Human Rights and Business Project. Since 1999, the Human Rights and Business Project of DIHR, in joint sponsorship with the Confederation of Danish Industries and the Industrial Fund for Developing Countries, has focused on clarifying the responsibility of business in relation to human rights through the development of concrete tools which can be used by companies to evaluate their human rights performance. DIHR has focused in particular on the development of the Human Rights Compliance Assessment tool – a diagnostic test, consisting of individual indicators which companies run to ensure that their practices remain compliant with human rights.

FTSE4Good Index. FTSE Group, an independent company whose sole business is the creation and management of indices and associated data services, has developed the FTSE4Good index series to measure the performance of companies that meet globally recognized corporate responsibility standards and to facilitate investment in those companies. For inclusion in the company assessment process, a company must meet criteria requirements in three areas: working towards environmental sustainability; developing positive relationships with stakeholders; and upholding and supporting universal human rights.

Goldman Sachs Energy Environmental and Social Index. Goldman Sachs, a global investment banking, securities and investment management firm, has developed an environmental and social index for the oil and gas industry to identify specific environmental and social issues likely to be material for company competitiveness and reputation. The index relies on 30 criteria over 8 categories, namely: climate change; pollution; human rights; management diversity and incentives; investment in the future; workforce; safety; and transparency and vision. Goldman Sachs published its first index in 2004.

. . .

Questions and Discussion

1. In 2008, the special representative of the secretary-general extended the ideas contained in his report excerpted here. In particular, he suggested a framework for regulating multinational corporations built around a state duty to protect human rights, a corporate responsibility to respect human rights, and adequate access to remedies for those whose rights have been violated. In focusing on corporate responsibility to respect, the special representative writes:

51. When it comes to the role companies themselves must play, the main focus in the debate has been on identifying a limited set of rights for which they may bear responsibility. For example, the draft norms on the responsibilities of transnational corporations and other business enterprises with regard to human rights generated intense discussions about whether its list of rights was too long or too short, and why some rights were included and others not. At the same time, the norms would have extended to companies essentially the entire range of duties that States have, separated only by the undefined concepts of "primary" versus "secondary" obligations and "corporate sphere of influence." This formula emphasizes precisely the wrong side of the equation: defining a limited list of rights linked to imprecise and expansive responsibilities, rather than defining the specific responsibilities of companies with regard to all rights.

. . .

54. In addition to compliance with national laws, the baseline responsibility of companies is to respect human rights. Failure to meet this responsibility can subject companies to the courts of public opinion – comprising employees, communities, consumers, civil society, as well as investors – and occasionally to charges in actual courts. Whereas governments define the scope of legal compliance, the broader scope of the responsibility to respect is defined by social expectations – as part of what is sometimes called a company's social licence to operate.

55. The corporate responsibility to respect exists independently of States' duties. Therefore, there is no need for the slippery distinction between "primary" State and "secondary" corporate obligations – which in any event would invite endless strategic gaming on the ground about who is responsible for what. Furthermore, because the responsibility to respect is a baseline expectation, a company cannot compensate for human rights harm by performing good deeds elsewhere. Finally, "doing no harm" is not merely a passive responsibility for firms but may entail positive steps – for example, a workplace anti-discrimination policy might require the company to adopt specific recruitment and training programmes.

. . .

56. To discharge the responsibility to respect requires due diligence. This concept describes the steps a company must take to become aware of, prevent and address adverse human rights impacts. Comparable processes are typically already embedded in companies because in many countries they are legally required to have information and control systems in place to assess and manage financial and related risks.

57. If companies are to carry out due diligence, what is its scope? The process inevitably will be inductive and fact-based, but the principles guiding it can be stated succinctly. Companies should consider three sets of factors. The first is the country contexts in which their business activities take place, to highlight any specific human rights challenges they may pose. The second is what human rights impacts their own activities

may have within that context – for example, in their capacity as producers, service providers, employers, and neighbours. The third is whether they might contribute to abuse through the relationships connected to their activities, such as with business partners, suppliers, State agencies, and other non-State actors. How far or how deep this process must go will depend on circumstances.

58. For the substantive content of the due diligence process, companies should look, at a minimum, to the international bill of human rights and the core conventions of the ILO, because the principles they embody comprise the benchmarks against which other social actors judge the human rights impacts of companies.

59. The Special Representative's research and consultations indicate that a basic human rights due diligence process should include the following.

. . .

60. Companies need to adopt a human rights policy. Broad aspirational language may be used to describe respect for human rights, but more detailed guidance in specific functional areas is necessary to give those commitments meaning.

Impact Assessments

61. Many corporate human rights issues arise because companies fail to consider the potential implications of their activities before they begin. Companies must take proactive steps to understand how existing and proposed activities may affect human rights. The scale of human rights impact assessments will depend on the industry and national and local context. While these assessments can be linked with other processes like risk assessments or environmental and social impact assessments, they should include explicit references to internationally recognized human rights. Based on the information uncovered, companies should refine their plans to address and avoid potential negative human rights impacts on an ongoing basis.

Integration

62. The integration of human rights policies throughout a company may be the biggest challenge in fulfilling the corporate responsibility to respect. As is true for States, human rights considerations are often isolated within a company. That can lead to inconsistent or contradictory actions: product developers may not consider human rights implications; sales or procurement teams may not know the risks of entering into relationships with certain parties; and company lobbying may contradict commitments to human rights. Leadership from the top is essential to embed respect for human rights throughout a company, as is training to ensure consistency, as well as capacity to respond appropriately when unforeseen situations arise.

Tracking Performance

63. Monitoring and auditing processes permit a company to track ongoing developments. The procedures may vary across sectors and even among company departments, but regular updates of human rights impact and performance are crucial. Tracking generates information needed to create appropriate incentives and disincentives for employees and ensure continuous improvement. Confidential means to report non-compliance, such as hotlines, can also provide useful feedback.

. . .

72. In short, the scope of due diligence to meet the corporate responsibility to respect human rights is not a fixed sphere, nor is it based on influence. Rather, it depends on

the potential and actual human rights impacts resulting from a company's business activities and the relationships connected to those activities.

. . .

73. The corporate responsibility to respect human rights includes avoiding complicity. The concept has legal and non-legal pedigrees, and the implications of both are important for companies. Complicity refers to indirect involvement by companies in human rights abuses – where the actual harm is committed by another party, including governments and non-State actors. Due diligence can help a company avoid complicity.

Protect, Respect and Remedy: A Framework for Business and Human Rights, Report of the Special Representative of the Secretary-General on the Issue of Human Rights and Transnational Corporations and Other Business Enterprises, U.N. Doc. A/HRC/8/5 (Apr. 7, 2008). See also the Special Representative's subsequent report, *Business and Human Rights: Towards Operationalizing the "Protect, Respect and Remedy" Framework*, U.N. Doc. A/HRC/11/13 (Apr. 22, 2009).

2. As you make your way through this chapter, consider this: if you were corporate counsel to a multinational corporation, how you would advise the board of directors on human rights and environmental limits to corporate activity? Consider also whether you would advocate for the company to develop a corporate code of conduct on human rights and the environment and/or join an industrywide code of conduct.

A. OECD Guidelines

The "Guidelines for Multinational Enterprises" were first adopted by the Organization for Economic Co-operation and Development (OECD) in 1976 (15 I.L.M. 969 (1976)) and were revised in 2000 (40 I.L.M. 237 (2001)). The OECD Guidelines are recommendations addressed by governments to multinational enterprises. They provide voluntary principles and standards for responsible business conduct consistent with applicable laws.

OECD Guidelines for Multinational Enterprises,
DAFFE/IME/WPG (2000) 15/FINAL (Oct. 31, 2001)

. . .

I. Concepts and Principles

1. The Guidelines are recommendations jointly addressed by governments to multinational enterprises. They provide principles and standards of good practice consistent with applicable laws. Observance of the Guidelines by enterprises is voluntary and not legally enforceable.

2. Since the operations of multinational enterprises extend throughout the world, international co-operation in this field should extend to all countries. Governments adhering to the Guidelines encourage the enterprises operating on their territories to observe the Guidelines wherever they operate, while taking into account the particular circumstances of each host country.

3. A precise definition of multinational enterprises is not required for the purposes of the Guidelines. These usually comprise companies or other entities established in more than one country and so linked that they may co-ordinate their operations in various ways. While one or more of these entities may be able to exercise a significant influence over the activities of others, their degree of autonomy within the enterprise may vary widely from one multinational enterprise to another. Ownership may be private, state or mixed. The Guidelines are addressed to all the

entities within the multinational enterprise (parent companies and/or local entities). According to the actual distribution of responsibilities among them, the different entities are expected to co-operate and to assist one another to facilitate observance of the Guidelines.

4. The Guidelines are not aimed at introducing differences of treatment between multinational and domestic enterprises; they reflect good practice for all. Accordingly, multinational and domestic enterprises are subject to the same expectations in respect of their conduct wherever the Guidelines are relevant to both.

5. Governments wish to encourage the widest possible observance of the Guidelines. While it is acknowledged that small- and medium-sized enterprises may not have the same capacities as larger enterprises, governments adhering to the Guidelines nevertheless encourage them to observe the Guidelines recommendations to the fullest extent possible.

6. Governments adhering to the Guidelines should not use them for protectionist purposes nor use them in a way that calls into question the comparative advantage of any country where multinational enterprises invest.

7. Governments have the right to prescribe the conditions under which multinational enterprises operate within their jurisdictions, subject to international law. The entities of a multinational enterprise located in various countries are subject to the laws applicable in these countries. When multinational enterprises are subject to conflicting requirements by adhering countries, the governments concerned will co-operate in good faith with a view to resolving problems that may arise.

8. Governments adhering to the Guidelines set them forth with the understanding that they will fulfil their responsibilities to treat enterprises equitably and in accordance with international law and with their contractual obligations.

9. The use of appropriate international dispute settlement mechanisms, including arbitration, is encouraged as a means of facilitating the resolution of legal problems arising between enterprises and host country governments.

10. Governments adhering to the Guidelines will promote them and encourage their use. They will establish National Contact Points that promote the Guidelines and act as a forum for discussion of all matters relating to the Guidelines. The adhering Governments will also participate in appropriate review and consultation procedures to address issues concerning interpretation of the Guidelines in a changing world.

II. General Policies

Enterprises should take fully into account established policies in the countries in which they operate, and consider the views of other stakeholders. In this regard, enterprises should:

1. Contribute to economic, social and environmental progress with a view to achieving sustainable development.

2. Respect the human rights of those affected by their activities consistent with the host government's international obligations and commitments.

3. Encourage local capacity building through close co-operation with the local community, including business interests, as well as developing the enterprise's activities in domestic and foreign markets, consistent with the need for sound commercial practice.

4. Encourage human capital formation, in particular by creating employment opportunities and facilitating training opportunities for employees.

5. Refrain from seeking or accepting exemptions not contemplated in the statutory or regulatory framework related to environmental, health, safety, labour, taxation, financial incentives, or other issues.

6. Support and uphold good corporate governance principles and develop and apply good corporate governance practices.

7. Develop and apply effective self-regulatory practices and management systems that foster a relationship of confidence and mutual trust between enterprises and the societies in which they operate.

8. Promote employee awareness of, and compliance with, company policies through appropriate dissemination of these policies, including through training programmes.

9. Refrain from discriminatory or disciplinary action against employees who make bona fide reports to management or, as appropriate, to the competent public authorities, on practices that contravene the law, the Guidelines or the enterprise's policies.

10. Encourage, where practicable, business partners, including suppliers and sub-contractors, to apply principles of corporate conduct compatible with the Guidelines.

11. Abstain from any improper involvement in local political activities.

III. Disclosure

1. Enterprises should ensure that timely, regular, reliable and relevant information is disclosed regarding their activities, structure, financial situation and performance. This information should be disclosed for the enterprise as a whole and, where appropriate, along business lines or geographic areas. Disclosure policies of enterprises should be tailored to the nature, size and location of the enterprise, with due regard taken of costs, business confidentiality and other competitive concerns.

2. Enterprises should apply high quality standards for disclosure, accounting, and audit. Enterprises are also encouraged to apply high quality standards for non-financial information including environmental and social reporting where they exist. The standards or policies under which both financial and non-financial information are compiled and published should be reported.

3. Enterprises should disclose basic information showing their name, location, and structure, the name, address and telephone number of the parent enterprise and its main affiliates, its percentage ownership, direct and indirect in these affiliates, including shareholdings between them.

4. Enterprises should also disclose material information on:
   a) The financial and operating results of the company;
   b) Company objectives;
   c) Major share ownership and voting rights;
   d) Members of the board and key executives, and their remuneration;
   e) Material foreseeable risk factors;
   f) Material issues regarding employees and other stakeholders;
   g) Governance structures and policies.

5. Enterprises are encouraged to communicate additional information that could include:

   a) Value statements or statements of business conduct intended for public disclosure including information on the social, ethical and environmental policies of the enterprise and other codes of conduct to which the company subscribes. In addition, the date of adoption, the countries and entities to which such statements apply and its performance in relation to these statements may be communicated;
   b) Information on systems for managing risks and complying with laws, and on statements or codes of business conduct;
   c) Information on relationships with employees and other stakeholders.

. . .

V. Environment

Enterprises should, within the framework of laws, regulations and administrative practices in the countries in which they operate, and in consideration of relevant international agreements, principles, objectives, and standards, take due account of the need to protect the environment, public health and safety, and generally to conduct their activities in a manner contributing to the wider goal of sustainable development. In particular, enterprises should:

1. Establish and maintain a system of environmental management appropriate to the enterprise, including:
   a) Collection and evaluation of adequate and timely information regarding the environmental, health, and safety impacts of their activities;
   b) Establishment of measurable objectives and, where appropriate, targets for improved environmental performance, including periodically reviewing the continuing relevance of these objectives; and
   c) Regular monitoring and verification of progress toward environmental, health, and safety objectives or targets.

2. Taking into account concerns about cost, business confidentiality, and the protection of intellectual property rights:
   a) Provide the public and employees with adequate and timely information on the potential environment, health and safety impacts of the activities of the enterprise, which could include reporting on progress in improving environmental performance; and
   b) Engage in adequate and timely communication and consultation with the communities directly affected by the environmental, health and safety policies of the enterprise and by their implementation.

3. Assess, and address in decision-making, the foreseeable environmental, health, and safety related impacts associated with the processes, goods and services of the enterprise over their full life cycle. Where these proposed activities may have significant environmental, health, or safety impacts, and where they are subject to a decision of a competent authority, prepare an appropriate environmental impact assessment.

4. Consistent with the scientific and technical understanding of the risks, where there are threats of serious damage to the environment, taking also into account human health and safety, not use the lack of full scientific certainty as a reason for postponing cost-effective measures to prevent or minimise such damage.

5. Maintain contingency plans for preventing, mitigating, and controlling serious environmental and health damage from their operations, including accidents and emergencies; and mechanisms for immediate reporting to the competent authorities.

6. Continually seek to improve corporate environmental performance, by encouraging, where appropriate, such activities as:
   a) Adoption of technologies and operating procedures in all parts of the enterprise that reflect standards concerning environmental performance in the best performing part of the enterprise;
   b) Development and provision of products or services that have no undue environmental impacts; are safe in their intended use; are efficient in their consumption of energy and natural resources; can be reused, recycled, or disposed of safely;
   c) Promoting higher levels of awareness among customers of the environmental implications of using the products and services of the enterprise; and
   d) Research on ways of improving the environmental performance of the enterprise over the longer term.

7. Provide adequate education and training to employees in environmental health and safety matters, including the handling of hazardous materials and the prevention of environmental accidents, as well as more general environmental management areas, such as environmental impact assessment procedures, public relations, and environmental technologies.

8. Contribute to the development of environmentally meaningful and economically efficient public policy, for example, by means of partnerships or initiatives that will enhance environmental awareness and protection.

. . .

VII. Consumer Interests

When dealing with consumers, enterprises should act in accordance with fair business, marketing and advertising practices and should take all reasonable steps to ensure the safety and quality of the goods or services they provide. In particular, they should:

1. Ensure that the goods or services they provide meet all agreed or legally required standards for consumer health and safety, including health warnings and product safety and information labels.

2. As appropriate to the goods or services, provide accurate and clear information regarding their content, safe use, maintenance, storage, and disposal sufficient to enable consumers to make informed decisions.

3. Provide transparent and effective procedures that address consumer complaints and contribute to fair and timely resolution of consumer disputes without undue cost or burden.

4. Not make representations or omissions, nor engage in any other practices, that are deceptive, misleading, fraudulent, or unfair.

5. Respect consumer privacy and provide protection for personal data.

6. Co-operate fully and in a transparent manner with public authorities in the prevention or removal of serious threats to public health and safety deriving from the consumption or use of their products.

VIII. Science and Technology

Enterprises should:

1. Endeavour to ensure that their activities are compatible with the science and technology (S&T) policies and plans of the countries in which they operate and as appropriate contribute to the development of local and national innovative capacity.

2. Adopt, where practicable in the course of their business activities, practices that permit the transfer and rapid diffusion of technologies and know-how, with due regard to the protection of intellectual property rights.

3. When appropriate, perform science and technology development work in host countries to address local market needs, as well as employ host country personnel in an S&T capacity and encourage their training, taking into account commercial needs.

4. When granting licenses for the use of intellectual property rights or when otherwise transferring technology, do so on reasonable terms and conditions and in a manner that contributes to the long term development prospects of the host country.

5. Where relevant to commercial objectives, develop ties with local universities, public research institutions, and participate in co-operative research projects with local industry or industry associations.

Questions and Discussion

1. In 2008, the U.N. special representative on business and human rights expressed reservations about the OCED Guidelines. He stated that the current OECD "human rights provisions not only lack specificity, but in key respects have fallen behind the voluntary standards of many companies and business organizations." He concluded that the revision of the Guidelines was required. *Protect, Respect, and Remedy: A Framework for Business and Human Rights*, U.N. Doc. A/HRC/8/5, at 13 (Apr. 7, Apr. 7, 2008). Do you agree? In March 2010, the OECD, responding to these and other concerns announced:

    > Since the last review of the Guidelines in 2000, the landscape for international investment and multinational enterprises has continued to change rapidly. The world economy has witnessed new and more complex patterns of production and consumption. Non-OECD countries are attracting a larger share of world investment and multinational enterprises from non-adhering countries have grown in importance. At the same time, the financial and economic crisis and the loss in confidence in open markets, the need to address climate change, and reaffirmed international commitments to development goals have prompted renewed calls from governments, the private sector and social partners for high standards of responsible business conduct.
    >
    > At their 2009 Annual Meeting, National Contact Points (NCPs) responsible for the implementation of the Guidelines recommended that adhering countries review the experience gained with this instrument with a view to defining terms of reference for its possible update. At the June 2009 OECD Council Meeting at Ministerial level, ministers from OECD and non-member countries welcomed "further consultation on the updating of the OECD Guidelines to increase their relevance and clarify private sector responsibilities."
    >
    > The first step in this process took place on 8 December 2009 with a consultation which sought the views of stakeholders and non-adhering governments on the priority areas for an update. In Spring 2010, adhering governments will decide on terms of reference for an update in light of the outcomes of the consultations.

    OCED Press Release, 2010 Update of the OCED Guidelines on Multinational Enterprises (Mar. 1, 2010), *available at* http://www.oecd.org/document/33/0,3343,en_2649_34889_44086753_1_1_1_1,00.html

2. The U.N. Commission and Centre on Transnational Corporations has worked on the promulgation of a Code of Conduct for Transnational Corporations. The difficulty of coming to agreement on the norms of international law to be established under such a Code is typified by the following excerpt from the 1985 Report of the Centre on Transnational Corporations:

    > There are at least two different schools of thought on this matter. The first maintains that the code should allow for the applicability of customary international legal principles in relevant areas to amplify or qualify the broad standards enunciated in the code: According to this view, the applicability of international law to the relations between States and transnational corporations is not Limited to international obligations expressly founded on conventions, treaties or other international agreements. In addition, customary international law is seen as prescribing principles and rules with respect to such matters as jurisdiction over transnational corporations, permanent sovereignty of States over their

natural wealth and resources, renegotiation of State contracts, nationalization and compensation, non-discriminatory treatment of transnational corporations, diplomatic protection of aliens and alien property, and procedures for the settlement of disputes between Governments and transnational corporations. It follows that the provisions of the code would not derogate from the application of those customary principles of international law, subject of course to the express undertakings of the States concerned under conventions, treaties and other international agreements concluded by such States. The proponents of this view accordingly maintain that the code ought to take into account the relevance of international law by incorporating stipulation's with respect to its applicability to the relations between Governments and transnational corporations.

The second school of thought questions the existence of universally recognized principles of customary international law governing the treatment of transnational corporations or foreign investors. Adherents to that school maintain that this area falls primarily within the purview of national law, subject to international legal norms and specific undertakings and obligations expressly stipulated in international instruments, such as codes of conduct and conventions, treaties and other international agreements, to which the States concerned have freely subscribed.

U.N. Centre on Transnational Corporations, Report on Work on the Formulation of the United Nations Code of Conduct on Transnational Corporations, E/C.1O/1985/s/2, at 12–13 (1985).

3.   Most codes of conduct for transnational enterprises focus on economic and social issues rather than protection of the environment. See Robert Grosse, *Codes of Conduct for Multinational Enterprises*, 16 J. WORLD TRADE L. 414 (1982). Exceptions can be found, such as the Bonn Guidelines on Access to Genetic Resources adopted in the framework of the Convention on Biological Diversity. For discussions of the legal effects of codes of conduct, see A.A. Fatouros, *On the Implementation of International Codes of Conduct*, 30 AM. U. L. REV. 941 (1981); Hans W. Baade, *The Legal Effects of Codes of Conduct for Multinational Enterprises*, 22 GER. Y.B. INT'L L. 11 (1979); Steven K. Chance, *Codes of Conduct for Multinational Corporations*, 33 BUS. LAW. 1799 (1978).

B. ILO *Tripartite Declaration*

Tripartite Declaration of Principles Concerning Multinational Enterprises and Social Responsibility (as amended in 2000), 83 ILO OFFICIAL BULL. http://www.ilo.org/wcmsp5/groups/public/—ed_emp/—emp_ent/— multi/documents/publication/wcms_094386.pdf (2000) (footnotes omitted)

*1. Multinational enterprises play an important part in the economies of most countries and in international economic relations. This is of increasing interest to governments as well as to employers and workers and their respective organizations. Through international direct investment and other means such enterprises can bring substantial benefits to home and host countries by contributing to the more efficient utilization of capital, technology and labour. Within the framework of development policies established by governments, they can also make an important contribution to the promotion of economic and social welfare; to the improvement of living

* Paragraphs 1-7, 8, 10, 25, 26, and 52 (formerly paragraph 51) have been the subject or interpretation under the Procedure for the examination of disputes concerning the application of the Tripartite Declaration of Principles concerning Multinational Enterprises and Social Policy....

standards and the satisfaction of basic needs; to the creation of employment opportunities, both directly and indirectly; and to the enjoyment of basic human rights, including freedom of association, throughout the world. On the other hand, the advances made by multinational enterprises in organizing their operations beyond the national framework may lead to abuse of concentrations of economic power and to conflicts with national policy objectives and with the interest of the workers. In addition, the complexity of multinational enterprises and the difficulty of clearly perceiving their diverse structures, operations and policies sometimes give rise to concern either in the home or in the host countries, or in both.

2. The aim of this Tripartite Declaration of Principles is to encourage the positive contribution which multinational enterprises can make to economic and social progress and to minimize and resolve the difficulties to which their various operations may give rise, taking into account the United Nations resolutions advocating the establishment of a New International Economic Order.

3. This aim will be furthered by appropriate laws and policies, measures and actions adopted by the governments and by cooperation among the governments and the employers' and workers' organizations of all countries.

4. The principles set out in this Declaration are commended to the govern-merits, the employers' and workers' organizations of home and host countries and to the multinational enterprises themselves.

5. These principles are intended to guide the governments, the employers' and workers' organizations and the multinational enterprises in taking such measures and actions and adopting such social policies, including those based on the principles laid down in the Constitution and the relevant Conventions and Recommendations of the ILO, as would further social progress.

6. To serve its purpose this Declaration does not require a precise legal definition of multinational enterprises; this paragraph is designed to facilitate the understanding of the Declaration arid not to provide such a definition. Multinational enterprises include enterprises, whether they are of public, mixed or private ownership, which own or control production, distribution, services or other facilities outside the country in which they are based. The degree of autonomy of entities within multinational enterprises in relation to each other varies widely from one such enterprise to another, depending on the nature of the links between such entities and their fields of activity end having regard to the great diversity in the form of ownership, in the size, in the nature and location of the operations of the enterprises concerned. Unless otherwise specified, the term "multinational enterprise" is used in this Declaration to designate the various entities (parent companies or local entities or both or the organization as a whole) according to the distribution of responsibilities among them. in the expectation that they will cooperate and provide assistance to one another as necessary to facilitate observance of the principles laid down in the Declaration.

7. This Declaration sets out principles in the fields of employment, training, conditions of work and life and industrial relations which governments, employers' and workers' organizations and multinational enterprises are recommended to observe on a voluntary basis: its provisions shall not limit or otherwise affect obligations arising out of ratification of any ILO Convention.

GENERAL POLICIES

8. All the parties concerned by this Declaration should respect the sovereign rights of States, obey the national laws and regulations, give due consideration to local practices and respect relevant international standards. They should respect the Universal Declaration of Human Rights and the corresponding International Covenants adopted by the General Assembly of the United Nations as well as the Constitution of the International Labour Organization and its principles according to which freedom of expression arid association are essential to sustained progress. They should contribute to the realization of the ILO Declaration on Fundamental Principles and Rights at Work and its Follow-up, adopted in 1998. They should also honour commitments which

they have freely entered into, in conformity with the national law and accepted international obligations.

9. Governments which have not yet ratified Conventions Nos. 87, 98, 111, 122, 138 and 182 are urged to do so and in any event to apply, to the greatest extent possible, through their national policies, the principles embodied therein and in Recommendations Nos. ill, 119, 122, 146 and 190....

10. Multinational enterprises should take fully into account established general policy objectives of the countries in which they operate. Their activities should be in harmony with the development priorities and social aims arid structure of the country in which they operate. To this effect, consultations should he held between multinational enterprises, the government and, wherever appropriate, the national employers' and workers' organizations concerned.

11. The principles laid down in this Declaration do not aim at introducing or maintaining inequalities of treatment between multinational and national enterprises. They reflect good practice for all. Multinational and national enterprises, wherever the principles of this Declaration are relevant to both, should be subject to the same expectations in respect of their conduct in general and their social practices in particular.

12. Governments of home countries should promote good social practice in accordance with this Declaration of Principles, having regard to the social and labour law, regulations and practices in host countries as well as to relevant international standards. Both host and home country governments should be prepared to have consultations with each other, whenever the need arises, on the initiative of either.

. . .

CONDITIONS OF WORK AND LIFE

Safety and Health

37. Governments should ensure that both multinational and national enterprises provide adequate safety and health standards for their employees....

38. Multinational enterprises should maintain the highest standards of safety and health, in conformity with national requirements, bearing in mind their relevant experience within the enterprise as a whole, including any knowledge of special hazards. They should also make available to the representatives of the workers in the enterprise, and upon request, to the competent authorities and the workers' and employers' organizations in all countries in which they operate information on the safety and health standards relevant to their local operations, which they observe in other countries, In particular they should make known to those concerned any special hazards and related protective measures associated with new products and processes. They, like comparable domestic enterprises, should be expected to play a leading role in the examination of causes of industrial safety and health hazards and in the application of resulting improvements within the enterprise as a whole.

39. Multinational enterprises should cooperate in the work of international organizations concerned with the preparation arid adoption of international safety and health standards,

40. In accordance with national practice multinational enterprises should cooperate fully with the competent safely and health authorities, the representatives of the workers and their organizations, and established safety and health organizations. Where appropriate, matters relating to safety and health should be incorporated in agreements with the representatives of the workers and their organizations.

Questions and Discussion

1. Why should the International Labour Organization be concerned with the environment? How does the Tripartite Declaration protect human rights? The environment? How might it be implemented?

2. What are the direct obligations of multinational corporations under the Tripartite Declaration?

3. Even if the Tripartite Declaration remains weak, it is important to emphasize that the ILO has been instrumental in linking human rights concerns with labor concerns. In particular, through a series of treaties and recommendations, it has established international minimum standards in free association, collective bargaining, and equality of opportunity and treatment. Specific ILO treaties have focused on particularly vulnerable or marginalized populations, including children, women, and indigenous peoples.

C. *Norms on the Responsibilities of Transnational Corporations*

Norms on the Responsibilities of Transnational Corporations
and Other Business Enterprises with Regard to Human Rights,
97 Am. J. Int'l L. 901, 907–15 (2003)
David Weissbrodt & Muria Kruger

On August 13, 2003, the United Nations Sub-Commission on the Promotion and Protection of Human Rights approved the "Norms on the Responsibilities of Transnational Corporations and Other Business Enterprises with Regard to Human Rights" (Norms) in its Resolution 2003/16....

. . .

II. Issues Raised in Preparing Human Rights Norms for Businesses

. . .

Content of the Norms

[T]he Norms largely reflect, restate, and refer to existing international norms, in addition to specifying some basic methods for implementation.

... [T]he very first principle, entitled "General Obligations," states, as dearly as possible, that the Norms are in no manner intended to reduce the obligations of governments to promote, secure the fulfillment of, respect, ensure respect for, or protect human rights. The Norms would be misused if they were employed by a government to justify failing to protect human rights fully or to provide appropriate remedies for human rights violations. This idea is reinforced by the saving clause in paragraph 19, which states that nothing in the Norms should be construed as diminishing states' obligations to protect and promote human rights or as limiting rules or laws that provide greater protection of human rights.

The Norms contain some basic implementation procedures and anticipate that they may eventually he supplemented by other techniques and processes. First, the Norms expect companies to adopt and implement their own internal rules of operation to ensure the protections set forth in the instrument. Second, the Norms indicate that businesses will be subject to periodic monitoring that is independent and transparent, and includes input from relevant stakeholders. Further, ... the[re is] a norm calling upon businesses to provide adequate reparations to anyone harmed by conduct that was inconsistent with the standards in the Norms. The addition of this principle indicates the ... intent not only to prevent conduct that violates human rights standards, but also to repair past harms. It can be further read to indicate the ... intent not only to make a statement about the appropriate conduct of businesses, but also to require action on their part.

The Nonvoluntary Nature of the Guidelines

The Norms as adopted are not a voluntary initiative of corporate social responsibility. The many implementation provisions show that they amount to more than aspirational statements of desired conduct. Further, the Sub-Commission's Resolution 2003/16 called for the creation of a mechanism for NGOs and others to submit information about businesses that are not meeting the minimum standards of the Norms. The nonvoluntary nature of the Norms therefore goes beyond the voluntary guidelines found in the U.N. Global Compact, the ILO Tripartite Declaration, and the OECD Guidelines for Multinational Enterprises.

Although not voluntary, the Norms are not a treaty, either. . . .

The legal authority of the Norms derives principally from their sources in treaties and customary international law, as a restatement of international legal principles applicable to companies. The United Nations has promulgated dozens of declarations, codes, rules, guidelines, principles, resolutions, and other instruments, in addition to treaties, that interpret the general human rights obligations of member stales under Articles 55 and 56 of the [U.N.] Charter and may reflect customary international law. The Universal Declaration of Human Rights is the most prominent of those instruments; it not only serves as an authoritative, comprehensive, and nearly contemporaneous interpretation of the human rights obligations under the Charter, but also contains provisions chat have been recognized as reflective of customary international law.

. . .

. . . The Norms could be adopted and promulgated (1) by the Commission on Human Rights, like "Protection of Human Rights in the Context of Human Immunodeficiency Virus (HIV) and Acquired Immunodeficiency Syndrome (AIDS)"; (2) by the Economic and Social Council, like the "Principles on the Effective Prevention and Investigation of Extra-Legal, Arbitrary and Summary Executions"; and, of course, (3) by the General Assembly, like the "Declaration on the Elimination of Violence Against Women. Obviously, the higher the U.N. body and the closer to consensus the vote in adopting soft-law principles such as the Norms, the greater the authority they would obtain. But the principles will derive authority from broad acceptance in international practice as well.

Hence, the legal authority of the Norms now derives principally from their sources in international law as a restatement of legal principles applicable to companies, but they have room to become more binding in the future. The level of adoption within the United Nations, further refinement of implementation methods by the working group, and increasingly broad acceptance of the Norms will continue to play an important role in the development of their binding nature.

. . .

Norms on the Responsibilities of Transnational Corporations and Other Business Enterprises with Regard to Human Rights, U.N. Doc. E/CN.4/Sub.2/2003/12/Rev.2 (26 August 2003)

Preamble

Bearing in mind the principles and obligations under the Charter of the United Nations, in particular the preamble and Articles 1,2,55 and 56, inter alia to promote universal respect for, and observance of, human rights and fundamental freedoms,

Recalling that the Universal Declaration of Human Rights proclaims a common standard of achievement for all peoples and all nations, to the end that Governments, other organs of society and individuals shall strive, by teaching and education to promote respect for human rights and freedoms, and, by progressive measures, to secure universal and effective recognition and observance, including of equal rights of women and men and the promotion of social progress and better standards of life in larger freedom,

Recognizing that even though States have the primary responsibility to promote, secure the fulfilment of, respect, ensure respect of and protect human rights, transnational corporations and other business enterprises, as organs of society, are also responsible for promoting and securing the human rights set forth in the Universal Declaration of Human Rights,

. . .

A. General Obligations

1. States have the primary responsibility to promote, secure the fulfilment of, respect, ensure respect of and protect human rights recognized in international as well as national law, including ensuring that transnational corporations and other business enterprises respect human rights. Within their respective spheres of activity and influence, transnational corporations and other business enterprises have the obligation to promote, secure the fulfilment *of*, respect, ensure respect of and protect human rights recognized in international as well as national law, including the rights and interests of indigenous peoples and other vulnerable groups.

B. Right to Equal Opportunity and Non-Discriminatory Treatment

2. Transnational corporations and other business enterprises shall ensure equality of opportunity and treatment, as provided in the relevant international instruments and national legislation as well as international human rights law, for the purpose of eliminating discrimination based on race, colour, sex, language, religion, political opinion, national or social origin, social status, indigenous status, disability, age – except for children, who may be given greater protection – or other status of the individual unrelated to the inherent requirements to perform the job, or of complying with special measures designed to overcome past discrimination against certain groups.

C. Right to Security of Persons

3. Transnational corporations and other business enterprises shall not engage in nor benefit from war crimes, crimes against humanity, genocide, torture, forced disappearance, forced or compulsory labour, hostage-taking, extrajudicial, summary or arbitrary executions, other violations of humanitarian law and other international crimes against the human person as defined by international law, in particular human rights and humanitarian law.

4. Security arrangements for transnational corporations and other business enterprises shall observe international human rights nouns as well as the laws and professional standards of the country or countries in which they operate.

D. Rights of Workers

5. Transnational corporations and other business enterprises shall not use forced or compulsory labour as forbidden by the relevant international instruments and national legislation as well as international human rights and humanitarian law.

6. Transnational corporations and other business enterprises shall respect the rights of children to be protected from economic exploitation as forbidden by the relevant international instruments and national legislation as well as international human rights and humanitarian law.

7. Transnational corporations and other business enterprises shall provide a safe and healthy working environment as set forth in relevant international instruments and national legislation as well as international human rights and humanitarian law.

8. Transnational corporations and other business enterprises shall provide workers with remuneration that ensures an adequate standard of living for them and their families. Such remuneration shall take due account of their needs for adequate living conditions with a view towards progressive improvement.

9. Transnational corporations and other business enterprises shall ensure freedom of association and effective recognition of the right to collective bargaining by protecting the right to establish and, subject only to the rules of the organization concerned, to join organizations of their own choosing without distinction, previous authorization, or interference, for the protection of their employment interests and for other collective bargaining purposes as provided in national legislation and the relevant conventions of the International Labour Organization.

E. Respect for National Sovereignty and Human Rights

10. Transnational corporations and other business enterprises shall recognize and respect applicable nouns of international law, national laws and regulations, as well as administrative practices, the rule of law, the public interest, development objectives, social, economic and cultural policies including transparency, accountability and prohibition of corruption, and authority of the countries in which the enterprises operate.

11. Transnational corporations and other business enterprises shall not offer, promise, give, accept, condone, knowingly benefit from, or demand a bribe or other improper advantage, nor shall they be solicited or expected to give a bribe or other improper advantage to any Government, public official, candidate for elective post, any member of the armed forces or security forces, or any other individual or organization. Transnational corporations and other business enterprises shall refrain from any activity which supports, solicits, or encourages States or any other entities to abuse human rights. They shall further seek to ensure that the goods and services they provide will not be used to abuse human rights.

12. Transnational corporations and other business enterprises shall respect economic, social and cultural rights as well as civil and political rights and contribute to their realization, in particular the rights to development, adequate food and drinking water, the highest attainable standard of physical and mental health, adequate housing, privacy, education, freedom of thought, conscience, and religion and freedom of opinion and expression, and shall refrain from actions which obstruct or impede the realization of those rights.

F. Obligations with Regard to Consumer Protection

13. Transnational corporations and other business enterprises shall act in accordance with fair business, marketing and advertising practices and shall take all necessary steps to ensure the safety and quality of the goods and services they provide, including observance of the precautionary principle. Nor shall they produce, distribute, market, or advertise harmful or potentially harmful products for use by consumers.

G. Obligations with Regard to Environmental Protection

14. Transnational corporations and other business enterprises shall carry out their activities in accordance with national laws, regulations, administrative practices and policies relating to the preservation of the environment of the countries in which they operate, as well as in accordance with relevant international agreements, principles, objectives, responsibilities and standards with regard to the environment as well as human rights, public health and safety, bioethics and the precautionary principle, and shall generally conduct their activities in a manner contributing to the wider goal of sustainable development.

H. General Provisions of Implementation

15. As an initial step towards implementing these Norms, each transnational corporation or other business enterprise shall adopt, disseminate and implement internal rules of operation in compliance with the Norms. Further, they shall periodically report on and take other measures fully to

implement the Norms and to provide at least for the prompt implementation of the protections set forth in the Norms. Each transnational corporation or other business enterprise shall apply and incorporate these Norms in their contracts or other arrangements and dealings with contractors, subcontractors, suppliers, licensees, distributors, or natural or other legal persons that enter into any agreement with the transnational corporation or business enterprise in order to ensure respect for and implementation of the Norms.

16. Transnational corporations and other business enterprises shall be subject to periodic monitoring and verification by United Nations, other international and national mechanisms already in existence or yet to be created, regarding application of the Norms. This monitoring shall be transparent and independent and take into account input from stakeholders (including non-governmental organizations) and as a result of complaints of violations of these Norms. Further, transnational corporations and other business enterprises shall conduct periodic evaluations concerning the impact of their own activities on human rights under these Norms.

17. States should establish and reinforce the necessary legal and administrative framework for ensuring that the Norms and other relevant national and international laws are implemented by transnational corporations and other business enterprises.

18. Transnational corporations and other business enterprises shall provide prompt, effective and adequate reparation to those persons, entities and communities that have been adversely affected by failures to comply with these Norms through, inter alia, reparations, restitution, compensation and rehabilitation for any damage done or property taken. In connection with determining damages, in regard to criminal sanctions, and in all other respects, these Norms shall be applied by national courts and/or international tribunals, pursuant to national and international law.

19. Nothing in these Norms shall be construed as diminishing, restricting, or adversely affecting the human rights obligations of States under national and international law, nor shall they be construed as diminishing, restricting, or adversely affecting more protective human rights nouns, nor shall they be construed as diminishing, restricting, or adversely affecting other obligations or responsibilities of transnational corporations and other business enterprises in fields other than human rights.

Questions and Discussion

1. The Norms were transmitted from the Sub-Commission to the Commission, which was not warmly receptive and never endorsed them. To what extent do you think that the assertion of the "nonvoluntary" nature of the Norms might have contributed to this negative reaction?
2. Note that paragraphs 1 and 3 of the Norms seem to link accountability with a corporation's influence and benefit. Products liability in tort has long been justified on the economic benefit a company derives from the sale of its goods. *See, e.g.,* Francis H. Bolen, *Liability of Manufacturers to Persons Other Than Their Immediate Vendees*, 45 L.Q. Rev. 343 (1929). Ordinarily, however, the liability of a business organization rests on the narrower ground of corporate "control" over an act or omission.
3. As noted, governments have been tepid in their response to the Norms because of the limit-pushing nature of the instrument. Given that implementation is primarily directed at corporations in the hope that the Norms will be internalized, is state involvement really necessary? Is the approach of the norms realistic?
4. The controversy surrounding the Norms prompted the U.N. secretary-general to appoint a special representative on human rights and transnational corporations and other business enterprises. The special representative has continued forward momentum on eventual *lex*

lata international regulation. In his 2006 Report to the 62nd Session of the old Human Rights Commission, the special representative made the following observations about the Norms.

Promotion and Protection of Human Rights,
Interim Report of the Special Representative of the Secretary-General on the Issue of Human Rights and Transnational Corporations and other Business Enterprises, U.N. Doc. E/CN.4/2006/97 (Feb. 22, 2006)

. . .

56. . . . The Sub-Commission approved the Norms in Resolution 2003/16 of August 13, 2003. The Commission, in Resolution 2004/116 of 20 April 2004, expressed the view that, while the Norms contained "useful elements and ideas" for its consideration, as a draft the proposal had no legal standing.

. . .

60. The Norms are said merely to "reflect" and "restate" international legal principles applicable to business with regard to human rights. At the same time, they are also said to be the first such initiative at the international level that is "non-voluntary" in nature, and thus in some sense directly binding on corporations. But taken literally, the two claims cannot both be correct. If the Norms merely restate established international legal principles then they cannot also directly bind business because, with the possible exception of certain war crimes and crimes against humanity, there are no generally accepted international legal principles that do so. And if the Norms were to bind business directly then they could not merely be restating international legal principles; they would need, somehow, to discover or invent new ones. What the Norms have done, in fact, is to take existing state-based human rights instruments and simply assert that many of their provisions now are binding on corporations as well. But that assertion itself has little authoritative basis in international law – hard, soft, or otherwise.

. . .

65. There are legitimate arguments in support of the proposition that it may be desirable in some circumstances for corporations to become direct bearers of international human rights obligations, especially where host governments cannot or will not enforce their obligations and where the classical international human rights regime, therefore, cannot possibly be expected to function as intended. Moreover, there are no inherent conceptual barriers to states deciding to hold corporations directly responsible, either by extraterritorial application of domestic law to the operations of their own firms, or by establishing some form of international jurisdiction. But these are not propositions about established law; they are normative commitments and policy preferences about what the law should become that require state action for them to take effect.

66. A second problematic feature of the Norms concerns their imprecision in allocating human rights responsibilities to states and corporations. While it may be useful to think of corporations as "organs of society," in the preambular language of the Universal Declaration, they are specialized organs, performing specialized functions. They are not a microcosm of the entire social body. By their very nature, therefore, corporations do not have a general role in relation to human rights like states, but a specialized one. The Norms do allow that some civil and political rights may not pertain to companies. But they articulate no actual principle for differentiating human rights responsibilities based on the respective social roles performed by states and corporations. Indeed, in several instances, and with no justification, the Norms end up imposing higher obligations on corporations than states, by including as standards binding on corporations instruments that not all states have ratified or have ratified conditionally, and even some for which states have adopted no international instrument at all.

67. Lacking a principled basis for differentiating responsibilities, the concept of "spheres of influence" is left to carry the burden. But in legal terms, this is a burden it cannot sustain on its own. The concept has productive practical applicability, as we saw in the discussion of company human rights policies, and as the SRSG will elaborate more fully in his final report. But it has no legal pedigree; it derives from geopolitics. Neither the text of the Norms nor the Commentary offers a definition, nor is it clear what one would look like that could pass legal liability tests. Case law searches to date have found no explicit references to it, and nothing that corresponds to it beyond fairly direct agency-like relationships. So the strictly legal meaning of the concept remains elusive, hardly a suitable basis for establishing binding obligations.

68. In addition, without a principled differentiation, in actual practice the allocation of responsibilities under the Norms could come to hinge entirely on the respective capacities of states and corporations in particular situations – so that where states are unable or unwilling to act, the job would be transferred to corporations. While this may be desirable in special circumstances and in relation to certain rights and obligations, as a general proposition it is deeply troubling. The issue is not simply one of fairness to companies, or of inviting endless strategic gaming by states and companies alike. Far more profound is the fact that corporations are not democratic public interest institutions and that making them, in effect, co-equal duty bearers for the broad spectrum of human rights – and for "the obligation to promote, secure the fulfilment of, respect, ensure respect and protect" those rights, as the General Obligations of the Norms put it – may undermine efforts to build indigenous social capacity and to make governments more responsible to their own citizenry.

69. Nothing that has been said here should be taken to imply that innovative solutions to the challenges of business and human rights are not necessary, or that the further evolution of international and domestic legal principles in relation to corporations will not form part of those solutions. Likewise, normative undertakings and advocacy are essential ingredients for the continued development of the human rights regime, in relation to business no less than other domains. But it is to conclude that the flaws of the Norms make that effort a distraction from rather than a basis for moving the SRSG's mandate forward. Indeed, in the SRSG's view the divisive debate over the Norms obscures rather than illuminates promising areas of consensus and cooperation among business, civil society, governments, and international institutions with respect to human rights.

IV. Self-Regulation

With the ascendance of public concern over both human rights and the environment, a growing number of business enterprises have found it in their self-interest (in terms of competition for consumers, attractiveness of investment, and public relations) to make voluntary commitments to the protection of human rights and the environment. In playing to the market, enterprises have branded their products as sensitive to such concerns (e.g. "fair-trade" coffee). Transnational corporations have also developed voluntary codes of conduct for human rights and the environment. A number of instruments mentioned in the Report of the High Commissioner for Human Rights at the beginning of this chapter belong to the category of voluntary codes.

Voluntary codes of practice for transnational corporations first made their appearance in the 1970s, gained acceptance in the 1980s, and continue to be developed. The Sullivan Principles reflect the first major set of voluntary corporate guidelines. The Principles were drafted in 1977 by the Reverend Leon Sullivan, at the time a Baptist minister and member of the Board of Directors of General Motors. The Principles were originally limited in scope to pressuring American companies operating in apartheid South Africa to abide by antidiscrimination and labor standards in their South African activities. Picking up on the idea of lifting international labor standards, the MacBride Principles followed in 1984. Developed in the context of the Northern Ireland problem of employment discrimination based on religion, the MacBride Principles urge American companies operating in Northern Ireland to pursue affirmative action and antidiscrimination goals. These early codes were established in the United States and applicable to U.S. corporations. However, global public concern about ethical behavior by business actors worldwide has resulted in more widely applicable codes and an appreciation by companies of the need to take public concerns seriously. *See further* Christopher McCrudden, *Human Rights Codes for Transnational Corporations: The Sullivan and MacBride Principles*, in COMMITMENT AND COMPLIANCE: THE ROLE OF NON-BINDING NORMS IN THE INTERNATIONAL LEGAL SYSTEM 418 (Dinah Shelton ed., 2000).

Business and Human Rights: Mapping International Standards of Responsibility and Accountability for Corporate Acts, **Report of the Special Representative of the Secretary-General on the Issue of Human Rights and Transnational Corporations and Other Business Enterprises, U.N. Doc. No. A/HRC/4/35 (Feb. 19, 2007)**

. . .

V. SELF-REGULATION

In addition to legal standards, hard or soft, the mandate of the Special Representative includes evolving social expectations regarding responsible corporate citizenship, including human rights. One key indicator consists of the policies and practices that business itself adopts voluntarily, triggered by its assessment of human rights-related risks and opportunities, often under pressure from civil society and local communities. . . .

However, mapping the entire universe of business enterprises is impossible. More than 77,000 transnational corporations currently span the globe, with roughly 770,000 subsidiaries and millions of suppliers. Those numbers are dwarfed by local firms, and an even bigger informal sector in developing countries.

Therefore, the Special Representative conducted studies of a subset of business entities to determine how they perceive corporate responsibility and accountability regarding human rights. One was a questionnaire survey of the *Fortune* Global 500 firms (FG500), which are under social scrutiny as the world's largest companies. The second ("business recognition study") consisted of three parts: actual policies, rather than questionnaire responses, of a broader cross-section of firms from all regions (including developing countries) screened as likely to have policies that include human rights; eight collective initiatives that include human rights standards, like the Fair Labor Association (FLA) or the International Council on Metals and Mining (ICMM); and the human rights criteria employed by five socially responsible investment funds (SRI funds).

Such a mapping could barely have been done five years ago because few corporate human rights policies existed. Uptake has been especially rapid among large global firms, a group still predominantly domiciled in Europe, North America and Japan. Newer entrants from other regions lag behind, although it is unclear whether this lag reflects a fundamental difference or merely timing. Numerous firms in the business recognition study only recently joined initiatives like the Global Compact and are only beginning to develop human rights policies. . . .

All FG500 respondents, irrespective of region or sector, included non-discrimination as a core corporate responsibility, at minimum meaning recruitment and promotion based on merit. Workplace health and safety standards were cited almost as frequently. More than three quarters recognized freedom of association and the right to collective bargaining, the prohibition against child and forced labour, and the right to privacy. European firms were more likely than their United States counterparts to recognize the rights to life, liberty, and security of person; health; and an adequate standard of living. . . .

Companies referenced international instruments in formulating their policies. Among the FG500, ILO declarations and conventions topped the list, followed by the Universal Declaration of Human Rights. United Nations human rights treaties were mentioned infrequently. The Global Compact was cited by just over 50 per cent, the OECD Guidelines by just under 50 per cent. More than 80 per cent also said they worked with external stakeholders on their human rights policies. NGOs topped that list, followed by industry associations. . . .

The broader cross-section of companies paralleled the FG500 in recognizing labour standards. But their recognition of other rights was consistently lower: the highest, at 16 percent, was the right to security of the person, encompassing both the right to life and the freedom from cruel and unusual punishment. For areas covered by social, economic, and cultural rights these companies tended to emphasize their philanthropic contributions.

Firms in both samples participated in one of the eight collective initiatives. The recognition of rights by these initiatives closely reflected industry sectors: for example, those in manufacturing focused more on labour rights, whereas the extractive initiatives emphasized community relations and indigenous rights. Moreover, they drew on international standards: the FLA and Social Accountability 8000 meet or exceed most core ILO rights, while Equator banks track the IFC's performance standards. The SRI indices mirrored the overall high recognition of labour rights, and several exhibited a particular concern for rights related to indigenous peoples, as well as the right to a family life.

How do these companies and other business entities respond to social expectations regarding accountability? Most FG500 firms said they had internal reporting systems to monitor their human rights performance. Three quarters indicated that they also reported externally, but of those fewer than half utilized a third-party medium like the Global Reporting Initiative (GRI). Some form of supply chain monitoring was relatively common. But only one third said they routinely included human rights criteria within their social/environmental impact assessments. . . .

In short, leading business players recognize human rights and adopt means to ensure basic accountability. Yet even among the leaders, certain weaknesses of voluntarism are evident. Companies do not necessarily recognize those rights on which they may have the greatest impact. And while the rights they do recognize typically draw on international instruments, the language is rarely identical. Some interpretations are so elastic that the standards lose meaning, making it difficult for the company itself, let alone the public, to assess performance against commitments. . . .

Where self-regulation remains most challenged, however, is in its accountability provisions. . . .

. . . The number of firms reporting their social, environmental and human rights profiles, called "sustainability reporting," has risen exponentially. But quality has not matched quantity. Far fewer companies report systematically on how their core business strategies and operations impact on these sustainability issues. Instead, anecdotal descriptions of isolated projects and philanthropic activity often prevail. . . . The GRI provides standardized protocols to improve the quality and comparability of company reporting, but fewer than 200 firms report in accordance with GRI guidelines, another 700 partially do so, while others claim to use them informally.

Assurance helps people to know whether companies actually do what they say. A growing proportion of sustainability reports (circa 40 per cent) include some form of audit statement, typically provided by large accounting firms or smaller consultancies. . . .

Supply chain assurance faces the greatest credibility challenges. Global brands and retailers, among others, have developed supplier codes to compensate for weak or unenforced standards in some countries, because global social expectations require them to demonstrate adherence to minimum standards. However, without independent external assurance of some sort these systems lack credibility, especially for companies with questionable performance records. Standards for supply chain auditing are highly variable. Among the most trusted are the brand certification and SA8000 factory certification systems of the Fair Labor Association (FLA), both of which involve multi-stakeholder governance structures. . . .

For several reasons, the initiatives described in this section have not reached all types of companies. First, because many of the tools were developed for large national and transnational firms, they are not directly suitable for small- and medium-sized enterprises. Existing tools need to be adapted or new ones developed. Second, as noted, large developing country firms are just beginning to be drawn into this arena. Third, a more serious omission may be major state-owned enterprises based in some emerging economies: with few exceptions, they have not yet voluntarily associated themselves with such initiatives, nor is it well understood when the rules of State attribution apply to their human rights performance. Finally, as is true of all voluntary – and many statutory initiatives– determined laggards find ways to avoid scrutiny. This problem is not unique to human rights, nor is it unprecedented in history. But once a tipping point is reached, societies somehow manage to mitigate if not eliminate the problem. The trick is getting to the tipping point. . . .

Questions and Discussion

On April 20, 2010, the *Deepwater Horizon* oil well blew out in the Gulf of Mexico off the coast of Louisiana. The well continued to spew massive amounts of oil and gas into the Gulf for nearly five months, until September 18 when it was finally declared "dead." This is an environmental disaster that is still drastically affecting the marine and coastline ecosystems in the Gulf of Mexico, but it also raises civil and criminal liability, penalties and damages on the part of a number of multinational corporations, including BP.

Nineteen years ago, the *Exxon Valdez* ran aground on Bligh Reef in Alaska's Prince William Sound and spilled up to 750,000 barrels of oil in a pristine, remote environment. Widely viewed as on the worst environmental disasters in U.S. history at the time, it prompted the Coalition for Environmentally Responsible Economies (CERES) – a collection of environmental NGOs and pension funds – to develop and campaign for a ten-point corporate code known as the "Valdez Principles." Under the code, corporations voluntarily assume responsibility for environmental protection by implementing adequate policies and procedures. Many companies were reluctant, at least initially to put their name to the Principles. See Stephen C. Jones & Brad A. DeVore, *Companies Adopt Exxon Valdez Principles*, NAT'L L.J., Sept. 2, 1991, at 1. British Petroleum was one of the corporations that resisted. Jennifer Nash & John Erhenfeld, *Codes of Environmental Management Practice: Assessing Their Potential as a Tool for Change*, 22 ANN. REV. ENERGY ENVT. 487, 514 (1997). Can you suggest why? After you review the Valdez Principles, can you suggest ways they might have application, either before or after, the *Deepwater Horizon* incident?

The Valdez Principles, *reprinted in* **Rajib N. Sanyal & Joao S. Neves,**
The Valdez Principles: Implications for Corporate Social Reponsibility,
10 J. BUS. ETHICS 883, 888–89 (1991)

1. Protection of the biosphere.
We will minimize and strive to eliminate the release of any pollutant that may cause environmental damage to the air, water or earth and its inhabitants. We will safeguard habitats in rivers, lakes, wetlands, coastal zones and oceans and will minimize contributing to the greenhouse-effect, depletion of the ozone layer, acid rain, or smog.

2. Sustainable use of natural resources.
We will make sustainable use of renewable natural resources, such as water, soils and forests. We will conserve non-renewable natural resources through efficient use and careful planning. We will protect wildlife habitat, open spaces and wilderness while protecting biodiversity.

3. Reduction and disposal of waste.

We will minimize the creation of waste, especially hazardous waste, and wherever possible recycle materials. We will dispose of all wastes through safe and responsible methods.

4. Wise use of energy

We will make every effort to use environmentally safe and sustainable energy sources to meet our needs. We will invest in improved energy efficiency and conservation in our operations. We will maximize the energy efficiency of products we produce or sell.

5. Risk reduction

We will minimize the environmental, health and safety risks to our employees and the communities in which we operate by employing safe technologies and operating procedures and by being constantly prepared for emergencies.

6. Marketing of safe products and services

We will sell products or services that minimize adverse environmental impacts and that are safe as consumers commonly use them. We will inform consumers of the environmental impacts of our products or services.

7. Damage compensation

We will take responsibility for any harm we cause to the environment by making every effort to fully restore the environment and to compensate those persons who are adversely affected.

8. Disclosure

We will disclose to our employees and to the public incidents relating to our operations that cause environmental harm or pose health or safety hazards. We will disclose potential environmental, health or safety hazards posed by our operations, and we will not take any action against employees who report any condition that creates a danger to the environment or poses health and safety hazards.

9. Environmental directors and managers.

At least one member of the Board of Directors will be a person qualified to present environmental interests. We will commit management resources to implement these Principles, including the funding of an office of vice president for environmental affairs or an equivalent executive position, reporting directly to the CEO, to monitor and report upon our implementation efforts.

10. Assessment and annual audit

We will conduct and make public an annual self-evaluation of our progress in implementing these Principles and in complying with all applicable laws and regulations throughout our worldwide operations. We will work toward the timely creation of independent environmental audit procedures which we will complete annually and make available to the public.

Questions and Discussion

1. In an effort to attract more corporations to sign the principles, the name of the Valdez Principles has been changed to the CERES Principles, after their sponsor, the Coalition for Environmentally Responsible Economics (CERES). In addition, a number of provisions that received criticism by corporations were modified:

     The original Valdez Principles included the requirement that firms institute a process for third-party environmental auditing. The new principles replaced this provision with the requirement that companies publish an annual "CERES Report," a response to approximately 100 questions about environmental performance and practices posed by the coalition. The Valdez Principles required that each member company create a board-level environmental committee and appoint an environmentalist as a director. The revised principles instead call upon companies to consider demonstrated environmental commitment as a factor in choosing a director. While CERES had originally asked companies to sign its principles, it now asked companies to endorse them. The coalition added a disclaimer stating that endorsing in no way constituted a legal commitment. Wording changes were made allowing companies to "attempt" or "strive" for environmental improvements but not necessarily eliminate problems. And the new principles called for environmental restoration rather than damage compensation.

Jennifer Nash & John Erhenfeld, *Codes of Environmental Management Practice: Assessing Their Potential as a Tool for Change*, 22 ANN. REV. ENERGY ENVT. 487, 514 (1997).

2. Another influential code is the International Chamber of Commerce's Business Charter for Sustainable Development, which calls for providing "appropriate information to shareholders" so that investments informed by a company's human rights and environmental practice are possible.

3. The Office of the Secretary-General of the United Nations also launched an initiative in 2000, *The Global Compact*, to promote human rights, workers' rights, and the protection of the environment by multinational companies. *Global Compact* attempts to bring multinational corporations into the fold of responsible international citizens. Secretary-General Kofi Annan endorsed the Compact in his Millennium Report, titled *We the Peoples: The Role of the United Nations in the Twenty-First Century*, Report of the Secretary-General, U.N. Doc. A/54/2000 (Mar. 27, 2000). *Global Compact* is sponsored by the International Labour Organization, the U.N. Environment Programme, and the Office of the U.N. High Commissioner for Human Rights. The Compact originally comprised nine principles (now ten) aimed at the promotion by corporations of equitable labor standards, respect for human rights generally, and protection of the environment. Companies can join the Compact by addressing a letter to the Office of the U.N. Secretary-General and agreeing to implement the ten principles:

Human Rights

Principle 1: Businesses should support and respect the protection of internationally proclaimed human rights; and

Principle 2: make sure that they are not complicit in human rights abuses.

Labour Standards

Principle 3: Businesses should uphold the freedom of association and the effective recognition of the right to collective bargaining;

Principle 4: the elimination of all forms of forced and compulsory labour;

Principle 5: the effective abolition of child labour; and

Principle 6: the elimination of discrimination in respect of employment and occupation.

Environment

Principle 7: Businesses should support a precautionary approach to environmental challenges;

Principle 8: undertake initiatives to promote greater environmental responsibility; and

Principle 9: encourage the development and diffusion of environmentally friendly technologies

Anti-Corruption

Principle 10: Businesses should work against all forms of corruption, including extortion and bribery

4. It is worth noting that compliance with the *Global Compact* is monitored. *See further* United Nations, *The Global Compact: Corporate Citizenship in the World Economy* (Global Compact Office 2003).

5. In addition to voluntary codes of conduct, do you think the insurance industry has a role to play in fostering better business practices? Should liability insurance be priced to reflect social responsibility? For instance, in connection with risks associated with climate change, Munich RE, a large European reinsurer, sponsored the Climate Change and Liability Workshop in October 2008 to explore insurance pricing by addressing a number of underlying questions, including to what extent should, and how can, the insurance industry respond to damages associated with climate change? And, who ultimately must take the blame for losses attributable to climate change?

Anita Margrethe Halvorssen, *Book Review*, CHANGING COURSE: A GLOBAL BUSINESS PERSPECTIVE ON DEVELOPMENT AND THE ENVIRONMENT, BY STEPHEN SCHMIDHEINY WITH THE BUSINESS COUNCIL FOR SUSTAINABLE DEVELOPMENT (MIT Press, 1992), 4 COLO. J. INT'L ENVTL. L. & POL'Y, 241, 243–48 (1993) (footnotes omitted)

The Business Council for Sustainable Development (BCSD)] . . . stresses that the key to sustainable development is a system of open, competitive markets in which prices include the cost of environmental resources. Competition, the BCSD states, is the driving force for new technology, which is needed to enable more efficient use of natural resources and pollution reduction. Giving the right market signals, steering businesses toward sustainable development, is only possible if environmental costs of producing and distributing goods are integrated into economic decision-making. The lack of such a pricing system, the BCSD reasons, is why industrialization has generally operated using resources in an unsustainable manner and creating high levels of pollution. The difficult issue, of course, is how to determine the true environmental costs. The BCSD believes that responsibility for determining those costs lies with government, not the companies, so that those costs may be applied in an internationally harmonized manner. The report emphasizes that many governments do just the opposite by subsidizing polluting activities, such as energy, transportation, and agriculture.

The BCSD endorses the use of the "polluter pays principle," which requires the polluter to pay for all damage caused in the production process, as the starting point for internalizing environmental costs.' However, the report states that the implementation of such a principle is at present unclear and somewhat random. It adds that governments need to clarify the issue of past damage.

Three well-known mechanisms for internalizing environmental costs are analyzed in the report: government regulations (command and control), self-regulation, and economic instruments. The BCSD states that regulations are needed to create a basic regulatory framework in all countries." However, it feels that most countries rely too heavily on the command and control mechanism. Self-regulation could prove less costly than the other mechanisms but could also lead to the creation of cartels and protectionism. The third mechanism, economic instruments, receives the most favorable reviews. The BCSD characterizes economic instruments as those that involve government intervention in the form of taxes and charges, to create incentives or disincentives, for the purpose of changing behavior. In addition to being more cost efficient than government regulations, they provide the incentive for polluters to change to cleaner technologies rather than requiring the use of a specific technology, which, the report states, is often the case of command approaches.

. . .

The BCSD supports the changes economists have been suggesting in the national accounting systems as a way to promote the internalization of environmental costs. Currently, the Gross

National Product (GNP) does not take account of environmental degradation. But the report states that "[i]f countries were run like businesses, there would be an accounting for depletion of valuable assets such as forests, oil, topsoil, and water." Systems for natural resource accounting and budgeting were first established in Norway in 1974 and France in 1978. In Japan, the net national welfare measurement (NNW) adjusts national income for several factors, including the environment.

CHANGING COURSE proposes a new energy policy based upon increased energy efficiency, a more sustainable combination of the different energy sources and consumption patterns, and a long-term energy strategy for developing countries. The BCSD suggests that some "no-regrets" policies – measures that make sense no matter what the risk of global warming – should be adopted immediately. The report argues that actions such as energy efficiency make good business sense. This statement is particularly true as the environmental costs are internalized.

The BCSD provides an in-depth description of how energy efficiency can be increased in areas such as electricity generation, transportation, and industry. In addition, it sets out priorities for a rational energy strategy and argues for developing an energy accounting system to help assess the total "cradle to grave" energy aspects of products.

. . .

The BCSD suggests replacing the term "technology transfer" with a new concept: "technology cooperation." Technology cooperation is described as having a broader range of objectives than technology transfer, emphasizing long-term business development with a focus on developing infrastructure, wealth-generating capacities, and a country's competitiveness. Given the historical criticisms of how multinationals have operated in developing countries, this would seem to be a novel approach indeed. The report explains how a large number of official development aid projects have failed because they focused on capital-intensive hardware; using a contractor; and did not include environmental, maintenance, operating, and other know-how (or "software") by the supplier.

CHANGING COURSE promotes technology cooperation between two companies establishing a long-term partnership in a commercial setting – using joint ventures or direct investments – as the best solution.

Questions and Discussion

1. The European Union has adopted Regulation 1836/93 (EEC) which provides for voluntary eco-audits by participating companies that are willing to report on corporate environmental performance. In Australia, a number of states have enacted legislation that empowers state Environmental Protection Authorities to require mandatory environmental audits for certain pollution license holders in the case of poor environmental performance. *See, e.g., Protection of the Environment (Operations) Act 1997* (New South Wales); *Environment Protection Act 1970* (Victoria).

2. Are these codes of conduct useful? What are their advantages and disadvantages? Should they be compulsory?

V. Domestic Regulation

In this section, we turn our attention to attempts by individual states to unilaterally regulate the activities of multinational corporations at the national level. These regulatory attempts have taken two principal forms. One is targeted legislation involving specific countries (e.g., South Africa during apartheid) or reprehensible activities (e.g., forced child labor). The other employs civil litigation to enjoin or recover damages for acts or omissions that breach human rights and damage the environment.

On the legislative front, over the past several decades, states around the world have leveraged activities of multinational corporations as a tool of foreign policy. Realizing the importance of foreign direct investment to recipient countries and corporations alike, states have passed legislation designed to pressure both governments and corporations in situations in which respect for human rights and/or environmental protection is lacking. No municipal law exists anywhere that establishes comprehensive regulation for multinational corporations, but four major legislative approaches have been employed.

First, a law may prohibit all corporate presence in a country (or trade associated with that country) in which human rights are subject to gross violation. *See, e.g., Comprehensive Anti-Apartheid Act* of 1986, Pub. L. 99–40, 100 Stat. 1086, 22 U.S.C. §§ 5000–116 et seq. (Supp. IV 1986) (now repealed). Second, a statute can restrict access to governmental contracts and market access (or similar benefits) unless a corporation is in compliance with human rights and environmental norms. *See, e.g.,* LOS ANGELES, CAL., ADMIN. CODE div. 10, ch. 1, art. V (1986) (requiring city to refuse contracts to companies doing business with South Africa). Third, a law or executive regulation can operate directly and compel the observance of certain standards such as those related to occupational safety and health. *See, e.g.,* Exec. Order 13,126 Prohibition of Acquisition of Products Produced by Forced or Indentured Child Labor, 64 Fed. Reg. 32383 (1999). Finally, statues, especially as they relate to investment securities, can require that offshore activities that have a potential impact on the bottom line (including human rights and environmental problems) be fully disclosed. *See, e.g., Corporate Code of Conduct Bill* 2000 (Cth) (proposed Australian law requiring Australian companies operating overseas to report to the Australian Securities and Investment Commission (i) social, ethical, and environmental polices; (ii) environmental impact of operations offshore, and (iii) any breach of host state environmental and human rights laws). *See generally* Cynthia Williams, *The SEC and Corporate Social Transparency,* 112 HARV. L. REV. 1197 (1999).

As explained earlier, in addition to these direct legislative regulatory strategies, there exists in some states – including notably in the United States – the ability to reach the international activities of multinationals through civil litigation. In the United States, this civil litigation is mostly premised on the Alien Tort Statute (ATS), 28 U.S.C. §1350, which provides: "the district courts shall have original jurisdiction of any civil action for a tort only, committed in violation of the law of nations or a treaty of the United States." The ATS has become a recognized vehicle for attempting to protect human rights and environmental values. However, it is important to note that the ATS is jurisprudentially limited at present. In 2006, the special representative of the secretary-general on human rights and transnational corporations observed:

> It is worth noting, therefore, that of the thirty-six [ATS] cases to date involving companies, twenty have been dismissed, three settled, and none decided in favor of the plaintiffs; the rest are ongoing. In its only [ATS] decision, the U.S. Supreme Court, while reaffirming the standing of customary international law norms in principle, stipulated demanding tests for proving their existence: they must be "specific," "obligatory," and "universal." Moreover, the majority opinion advised lower courts to exercise restraint in "applying internationally generated norms" and leave the decision to create novel forms of liability "to legislative judgment in the great majority of cases." Thus, [ATS's] influence has been mainly existential: the mere fact of providing the possibility of a remedy has made a difference. But it remains a limited tool, even more so after the Supreme Court ruling; it is difficult and expensive to use, especially for plaintiffs; and it is unique.

Promotion and Protection of Human Rights Interim Report of the Special Representative of the Secretary-General on the Issue of Human Rights and Transnational Corporations and other Business Enterprises, U.N. Doc. E/CN.4/2006/97 at 16, ¶ 62 (Feb. 22, 2006).

Questions and Discussion

1. In studying the following materials in this section, consider the extent to which it is legitimate for a state to unilaterally attempt to legislate its morality beyond its territorial jurisdiction. What, if anything, distinguishes a global leader from an extraterritorial bully?

2. Consider, too, whether the national approaches we are considering apply equally to all multinational corporations or whether liability is limited in some way, thus putting particular corporations at a competitive disadvantage.

A. National Legislative Measures

Recall the discussion about Burma (today Myanmar) and the responsibility to protect doctrine in Chapter 9. The human rights violations outlined there, unfortunately, are symptomatic of a very poor broader record on human rights by the Burmese government. A number of states, including the United States, have enacted national measures to bring pressure on the leaders in Burma to improve conditions. What follows is a historical summary of the situation in Burma and the U.S. legislative response.

First Do No Harm: Myanmar Trade Sanctions and Human Rights,
5 Nw. Univ. J. Int'l Hum. Rts. 153, 154–58 (2007) (footnotes omitted)
Michael Ewing-Chow

II. A Recent History of Myanmar

Myanmar [Burma] was once one of the wealthiest countries in Southeast Asia and was believed to be on a fast track to development because of significant natural resources. However, in 1962 General Ne Win overthrew the elected civilian government and replaced it with a repressive military government. The military government isolated Myanmar from the international community and formed a centrally planned economy under the slogan "the Burmese way to socialism." Socialism led to the nationalization of all major foreign and domestically owned businesses and also of many smaller shops and stalls. Production soon declined under government control and towards the end of the 1960s the country, once Asia's largest rice exporter, was facing food deficits. Despite strong economic growth in the Southeast Asian region, Myanmar applied and was declared a Least Developed Country by the U.N. in l987.

The present ruling military junta, the State Peace and Development Council (SPDC) . . . has been criticized by much of the international community since the SPDC used force to respond to the demonstrations in 1988 and it refused to honor the results of the 1990 elections. In those elections, the National League for Democracy (NLD) led by Aung San Suu Kyi received 62 percent of the votes cast, taking some 80 percent of the 485 seats contested.

More recently, in May 2003 following an attack on Aung San Suu Kyi's motorcade and subsequent crackdown on the NLD, in which a number of people were killed, Aung San Suu Kyi was placed under house arrest.

Then on October 19, 2004, Myanmar again became the focus of international attention with the sudden and unexpected removal of Prime Minister Khin Nyunt. The Prime Minister had played a leading role in negotiations with ethnic nationality groups as well as with Aung San Suu Kyi in the lead up to the National Convention. Khin Nyunt has been placed under house arrest allegedly for corruption and replaced by the more conservative Lt. Gen. (later General) Soe Win.

The regime appears increasingly isolationist, as illustrated by its November 7, 2005 announcement of the sudden and abrupt relocation of its capital to the remote town of Pyinmana.

Finally, in May 2006, despite U.N. Secretary-General Kofi Annan's appeal to General Than Shwe and the military government to release Aung San Suu Kyi, her house arrest was extended once again.

The political problems of Myanmar are reflected in the wider problems faced by its people, with both a poor standard of living and poor economic prospects, Healthy life expectancy at birth is only 49.9 for males and 53.5 for females and, although figures vary widely, per capita income for 2005 is estimated to be U.S.$145 at a realistic exchange rate.

The military government has been accused of grave violations of basic human rights including forced labor, the use of child soldiers, forced relocation, summary executions, torture and the rape of women and girls, particularly of members of ethnic minorities. In addition the junta's policies and decisions have caused or exacerbated a host of ills for the entire Southeast Asian region, from large refugee outflows, to the spread of HIV/AIDS and other infectious diseases and the trafficking of drugs and human beings.

III. The Responses

Soon after the military government responded to demonstrations with force in 1988, President George H.W. Bush revoked Myanmar's benefits under the Generalized System of Preferences (GSP) ostensibly because of Myanmar's violations of internationally recognized workers' rights. In 1990, the Customs and Trade Act of 1990 was passed by the U.S. Senate and Congress, requiring the U.S. President to impose economic sanctions against Myanmar or as the U.S. prefers to call it, Burma, "if specific conditions were not met, including progress on human rights and suppression of the outflow of narcotics." Subsequently, on July 22, 1991, President Bush invoked the Customs and Trade Act and refused to renew the bilateral textile agreement with Myanmar that had expired on December 31, 1990.

On September 30, 1996, President Clinton signed the 1997 Foreign Operations Act, which prohibits the U.S. from giving any new assistance to Myanmar. The Act gave the U.S. President the discretion to prohibit individuals in the United States from initiating "new investments" in Myanmar. This was followed soon after by President Clinton's signing of an executive order implementing the provisions in the Foreign Operations Appropriations Bill on May 20, 1997, which prohibited new investment by U.S. persons in Myanmar and barred any modification or expansion of existing trade commitments.

On March 31, 2003, the U.S. State Department released its report "Burma: Country Reports on Human Rights Practices – 2002" which accused the ruling SPDC of very serious human rights abuses including rape, torture and murder. Two months later, on May 31, the SPDC placed the pro-democracy activist Aung San Suu Kyi in "protective custody."

The U.S. response to the report and the imprisonment of Aung San Suu Kyi was the Burmese Freedom and Democracy Act of 2003 (BFDA). The BFDA was passed by the U.S. House of Representatives on July IS 2003 by a vote of 418–2 and by the U.S. Senate on 16 July 2003 by a vote of 94–1.

President George W. Bush signed the BFDA and issued an Executive Order implementing the legislation on July 29, 2003. The BFDA contains a clause allowing the U.S. President to waive the application of any provision deemed contrary to "national security interests." To date, no waivers have been made.

The BFDA bans the importation of any goods produced, manufactured, grown or assembled in Myanmar, requires the U.S. treasury to direct U.S. financial institutions to freeze assets in the United States of "those individuals who hold senior positions in the SPDC," and expands a ban on visas to the U.S. for officials of the SPDC. The BFDA states that the U.S. will also block any application by Myanmar for soft loans from the IMF and the World Bank.

The BFDA provides that the ban will remain in effect until the U.S. President determines and certifies to Congress that the Myanmar military government has made "substantial and measurable progress to end violations of internationally recognized human rights including rape." To have the ban lifted, the BFDA requires that the U.S. Secretary of State consult with the Secretary General of the International Labor Organization (ILO) and other relevant nongovernmental organizations and report to the appropriate congressional committees that the SPDC "no longer systematically violates workers' rights, including the use of forced and child labor, and conscription of child soldiers.

The U.S. President must also declare that the SPDC has made "measurable and substantial progress toward implementing a democratic government," and before the U.S. President will do so, the SPDC is required to release all political prisoners, and allow freedoms of speech and press freedom, and freedom of association and religion. In addition, the SPDC would have to reach an agreement with the NLD and other democratic forces in that country, including Burma's ethnic nationalities, "on the transfer of power to a civilian government accountable to the Burmese people through democratic elections under the rule of law.

. . .

It should be noted that in the debate on the bill, U.S. senators stressed the need for a multilateral approach to sanctions on Myanmar but were content to approve the immediate unilateral sanctions found in the BFDA.

Burmese Freedom and Democracy Act of 2003, Pub. L. 108–61 (July 28, 2003); 50 U.S.C. §1701 note

. . .

SEC. 2. FINDINGS.

Congress makes the following findings:

(1) The State Peace and Development Council (SPDC) has failed to transfer power to the National League for Democracy (NLD) whose parliamentarians won an overwhelming victory in the 1990 elections in Burma.

(2) The SPDC has failed to enter into meaningful, political dialogue with the NLD and ethnic minorities and has dismissed the efforts of United Nations Special Envoy Razali bin Ismail to further such dialogue.

(3) According to the State Department's `Report to the Congress Regarding Conditions in Burma and U.S. Policy Toward Burma' dated March 28, 2003, the SPDC has become `more confrontational' in its exchanges with the NLD.

(4) On May 30, 2003, the SPDC, threatened by continued support for the NLD throughout Burma, brutally attacked NLD supporters, killed and injured scores of civilians, and arrested democracy advocate Aung San Suu Kyi and other activists.

(5) The SPDC continues egregious human rights violations against Burmese citizens, uses rape as a weapon of intimidation and torture against women, and forcibly conscripts child-soldiers for the use in fighting indigenous ethnic groups.

(6) The SPDC is engaged in ethnic cleansing against minorities within Burma, including the Karen, Karenni, and Shan people, which constitutes a crime against humanity and has directly led to more than 600,000 internally displaced people living within Burma and more than 130,000 people from Burma living in refugee camps along the Thai-Burma border.

(7) The ethnic cleansing campaign of the SPDC is in sharp contrast to the traditional peaceful coexistence in Burma of Buddhists, Muslims, Christians, and people of traditional beliefs.

(8) The SPDC has demonstrably failed to cooperate with the United States in stopping the flood of heroin and methamphetamines being grown, refined, manufactured, and transported in areas under the control of the SPDC serving to flood the region and much of the world with these illicit drugs.

(9) The SPDC provides safety, security, and engages in business dealings with narcotics traffickers under indictment by United States authorities, and other producers and traffickers of narcotics.

(10) The International Labor Organization (ILO), for the first time in its 82-year history, adopted in 2000, a resolution recommending that governments, employers, and workers

organizations take appropriate measures to ensure that their relations with the SPDC do not abet the government-sponsored system of forced, compulsory, or slave labor in Burma, and that other international bodies reconsider any cooperation they may be engaged in with Burma and, if appropriate, cease as soon as possible any activity that could abet the practice of forced, compulsory, or slave labor.

(11) The SPDC has integrated the Burmese military and its surrogates into all facets of the economy effectively destroying any free enterprise system.

(12) Investment in Burmese companies and purchases from them serve to provide the SPDC with currency that is used to finance its instruments of terror and repression against the Burmese people.

(13) On April 15, 2003, the American Apparel and Footwear Association expressed its 'strong support for a full and immediate ban on U.S. textiles, apparel and footwear imports from Burma' and called upon the United States Government to 'impose an outright ban on U.S. imports' of these items until Burma demonstrates respect for basic human and labor rights of its citizens.

(14) The policy of the United States, as articulated by the President on April 24, 2003, is to officially recognize the NLD as the legitimate representative of the Burmese people as determined by the 1990 election.

(15) The United States must work closely with other nations, including Thailand, a close ally of the United States, to highlight attention to the SPDC's systematic abuses of human rights in Burma, to ensure that nongovernmental organizations promoting human rights and political freedom in Burma are allowed to operate freely and without harassment, and to craft a multilateral sanctions regime against Burma in order to pressure the SPDC to meet the conditions identified in section 3(a) (3) of this Act.

SEC. 3. BAN AGAINST TRADE THAT SUPPORTS THE MILITARY REGIME OF BURMA.

(a) General Ban –

(1) IN GENERAL – Notwithstanding any other provision of law, until such time as the President determines and certifies to Congress that Burma has met the conditions described in paragraph (3), beginning 30 days after the date of the enactment of this Act, the President shall ban the importation of any article that is a product of Burma.

(2) BAN ON IMPORTS FROM CERTAIN COMPANIES – The import restrictions contained in paragraph (1) shall apply to, among other entities –

(A) the SPDC, any ministry of the SPDC, a member of the SPDC or an immediate family member of such member;

(B) known narcotics traffickers from Burma or an immediate family member of such narcotics trafficker;

(C) the Union of Myanmar Economics Holdings Incorporated (UMEHI) or any company in which the UMEHI has a fiduciary interest;

(D) the Myanmar Economic Corporation (MEC) or any company in which the MEC has a fiduciary interest;

(E) the Union Solidarity and Development Association (USDA); and

(F) any successor entity for the SPDC, UMEHI, MEC, or USDA.

(3) CONDITIONS DESCRIBED – The conditions described in this paragraph are the following:

(A) The SPDC has made substantial and measurable progress to end violations of internationally recognized human rights including rape, and the Secretary of State, after consultation with the ILO Secretary General and relevant nongovernmental organizations, reports to the appropriate congressional committees that the SPDC no longer systematically violates workers rights, including the use of forced and child labor, and conscription of child-soldiers.

(B) The SPDC has made measurable and substantial progress toward implementing a democratic government including–

(i) releasing all political prisoners;

(ii) allowing freedom of speech and the press;

(iii) allowing freedom of association;

(iv) permitting the peaceful exercise of religion; and

(v) bringing to a conclusion an agreement between the SPDC and the democratic forces led by the NLD and Burma's ethnic nationalities on the transfer of power to a civilian government accountable to the Burmese people through democratic elections under the rule of law.

(C) Pursuant to section 706(2) of the Foreign Relations Authorization Act, Fiscal Year 2003 (Public Law 107–228), Burma has not been designated as a country that has failed demonstrably to make substantial efforts to adhere to its obligations under international counternarcotics agreements and to take other effective counternarcotics measures, including, but not limited to (i) the arrest and extradition of all individuals under indictment in the United States for narcotics trafficking, (ii) concrete and measurable actions to stem the flow of illicit drug money into Burma's banking system and economic enterprises, and (iii) actions to stop the manufacture and export of methamphetamines.

(4) APPROPRIATE CONGRESSIONAL COMMITTEES – In this subsection, the term `appropriate congressional committees' means the Committees on Foreign Relations and Appropriations of the Senate and the Committees on International Relations and Appropriations of the House of Representatives.

(b) WAIVER AUTHORITIES – The President may waive the prohibitions described in this section for any or all articles that are a product of Burma if the President determines and notifies the Committees on Appropriations, Finance, and Foreign Relations of the Senate and the Committees on Appropriations, International Relations, and Ways and Means of the House of Representatives that to do so is in the national interest of the United States.

. . .

SEC. 5. LOANS AT INTERNATIONAL FINANCIAL INSTITUTIONS.

The Secretary of the Treasury shall instruct the United States executive director to each appropriate international financial institution in which the United States participates, to oppose, and vote against the extension by such institution of any loan or financial or technical assistance to Burma until such time as the conditions described in section 3(a)(3) are met.

. . .

Questions and Discussion

1. Why do you suppose that the casebook authors can find no pure example of a national measure that requires or encourages the cessation of environmental degradation permitted by a state in violation of human rights? The so-called Pelosi Amendment, 22 U.S.C. § 262m-7, requires the U.S. executive director for each multilateral development bank to refrain from voting in favor of any proposed action by the bank that would have a significant effect on the human environment unless an environmental impact assessment has been prepared and circulated at least 120 days before the date of the vote. For instance, why have not states unilaterally legislated to require multinational oil companies and others to quit

Nigeria and cease all transactions with its government until it satisfactorily deals with the rights of the Ogoni people, dealt with in Chapter 4? Is there anything in particular that might make states reluctant to take such unilateral measures? Note that multilateral agreements requiring trade bans, like the Convention on International Trade in Endangered Species, are enforced by national laws and regulations.

2. States do sometimes use economic incentives to promote environmental protection. The so-called Lome Agreements between the European Community and some seventy African, Caribbean, and Pacific states have included provisions on protection of the environment and conservation of natural resources. The OECD also adopted measures to link environmental protection to development assistance. In NAFTA, Chapter 11 contains investment rules that operate in parallel with trade rules to regulate investors and foreign investment activities. *See* Alexandre Kiss & Dinah Shelton, INTERNATIONAL ENVIRONMENTAL LAW 763–64, 771 (3d ed., 2004). Unilaterally, the U.S. Export-Import Bank has incorporated environmental considerations in its lending practices (12 USC § 635i-5), whereas legislation requires the U.S. Overseas Investment Corporation (OPIC) to take account of the environmental effects of projects in determining whether to provide insurance, financing, or reinsurance for a development project. 22 U.S.C.A. § 2191(n).

3. The Burmese Freedom and Democracy Act of 2003 has been reauthorized a number of times, including most recently in Block Burmese JADE (Junta's Anti-Democratic Efforts) Act of 2008, Pub. L. 110–286 (2008). The Burmese junta, at the time of writing, remains in power. What, if anything, does this indicate about the effectiveness of unilateral sanctions?

4. What if a state or province within a federal country decided that it, too, wanted to legislate on Burma to preclude multinational corporations doing business with Burma from bidding on contracts with the state? In *Crosby v. National Foreign Trade Council*, 530 U.S. 363, 120 S. Ct. 2288, 147 L. Ed. 2d 352 (2000), the U.S. Supreme Court held that the Massachusetts Act Regulating State Contracts with Companies Doing Business with or in Burma was preempted by an earlier version of the federal Act because it conflicted "with Congress's specific delegation to the President of flexible discretion, with limitation of sanction to a limited scope of actions and actors, and with direction to develop a comprehensive, multinational strategy under the federal Act. . . . "

5. As the following section discusses, private litigation has provided a further avenue to hold corporations accountable. With respect to Burma, the significant case of *Doe v. Unocal*, 110 F. Supp. 2d 1294 (C.D. Cal. 2000) resulted in a settlement following accusations that a joint venture between the defendant oil company and the military junta was engaged in human rights violations and environmental destruction in building an oil pipeline through Burma.

B. *Civil Litigation – The U.S. Alien Tort Statute Example*

The First Congress of the United States passed an Act in 1789 as part of the first Judiciary Act, ch. 20, §9, 1 Stat. 73–93, that remained little noticed and little used until the fourth quarter of the twentieth century. That Act is known as both the Alien Tort Statute (ATS) and the Alien Tort Claims Act. 28 U.S.C. §1350. The ATS allows any alien to sue in federal district court for a tort committed in violation of customary international law or a treaty of the United States. Since it became active, the ATS has been controversial and has engendered debate about its necessity and effectiveness. *Compare* Anne-Marie Burley, *The Alien Tort Statue of and the Judiciary Act of 1789: A Badge of Honor*, 83 AM. J. INT'L L. 461 (1989) *with* Curtis A. Bradley & Jack L. Goldsmith, *Rights Case Gone Wrong: A Ruling Imperils Firms and U.S. Diplomacy*, WASH. POST, Apr. 19, 2009, at A19.

1. The Alien Tort Statute

Transnational Public Law Litigation,
100 YALE L.J. 2347–72 (1991) (footnotes omitted)
Harold Hongju Koh

Several years ago, I called attention to the burgeoning of "transnational public law litigation": suits brought in United States courts by individual and governmental litigants challenging violations of international law. As recent examples of this phenomenon, I included international human rights suits brought by aliens against foreign and United States governments and officials under the Alien Tort Statute, as well as actions by foreign governments against individual, American government, and corporate defendants.

. . .

As in traditional domestic litigation, transnational public lawsuits focus retrospectively upon achieving compensation and redress for individual victims. But as in traditional international law litigation, the transnational public law plaintiff pursues a prospective aim as well: to provoke judicial articulation of a *norm* of transnational law, with an eye toward using that declaration to promote a political settlement in which both governmental and nongovernmental entities will participate. Thus, although transnational public law plaintiffs routinely request retrospective damages or even prospective injunctive relief, their broader strategic goals are often served by a declaratory or default judgment announcing that a transnational norm has been violated. . . .

I. THE EVOLUTION OF TRANSNATIONAL PUBLIC LAW LITIGATION

. . .

As England became the preeminent global power, the law of nations was domesticated first into English common law, then applied to the American colonies, and subsequently incorporated into United States law. With American independence, the law of nations became part of the common law of the United States. The Continental Congress resolved to send a diplomatic letter stating that the United States would cause "the law of nations to be most strictly observed." The Federalist Papers made extensive mention of the law of nations' role in United States courts. In Article I of the Constitution, the Framers expressly gave Congress the power to define and punish "Piracies . . . committed on the high Seas, and Offences against the Law of Nations." Moreover, Article III extended the judicial power of the United States not simply to cases arising under the Constitution and laws of the United States, but also to cases arising under treaties, and a large class of international cases – those affecting Ambassadors, public Ministers and consuls, admiralty and maritime cases, and cases involving foreign parties.

The Framers never expected such cases and controversies to be decided solely under domestic law. As Professor White has recounted, "[t]he Framers' Constitution anticipated that international disputes would regularly come before the United States courts, and that the decisions in those cases could rest on principles of international law, without any necessary reference to the common law or to constitutional doctrines." All three branches quickly recognized the applicability of the law of nations in American courts. Executive officials such as Thomas Jefferson heralded the law of nations as "an integral part . . . of the laws of the land." Congress immediately enacted as part of the First Judiciary Act the Alien Tort Statute, which gave the district courts jurisdiction "of all causes where an alien sues for a tort only in violation of the law of nations or a treaty of the United States." Shortly thereafter, Congress passed statutes criminalizing piracy and assaults upon ambassadors. American courts regularly decided cases under the law of nations, particularly those involving piracies and prize jurisdiction (captures of enemy ships as prizes of war), and applied and clarified international law principles in cases concerning offenses against the law of nations, acquisition and control of territory, boundary disputes, questions of nationality, foreign sovereign immunity, and principles of war and neutrality. . . .

. . . [T]hroughout the early nineteenth century, American courts regularly construed and applied the unwritten law of nations as part of the "general common law," particularly to resolve commercial disputes, without regard to whether it should be characterized as federal or state. . . .

. . .

[I]n 1895, Justice Gray . . . proclaim[ed] in *Hilton v. Guyot* [159 U.S. 113 (1895).] that:

> International law, in its widest and most comprehensive sense – including not only questions of right between nations, governed by what has been appropriately called the law of nations; but also questions arising under what is usually called private international law, or the conflict of laws, and concerning the rights of persons within the territory and dominion of one nation, by reason of acts, private or public, done within the dominions of another nation – is part of our law, and must be ascertained and administered by the courts of justice, as often as such questions are presented in litigation between man and man, duly submitted to their determination.

Although conceding that treaties or statutes provided American courts with "[t]he most certain guide . . . for the decision of such questions," when "there is no written law upon the subject," Justice Gray repeated, "the duty still rests upon the judicial tribunals of ascertaining and declaring what the law is, whenever it becomes necessary to do so, in order to determine the rights of parties to suits regularly brought before them."

. . .

As the twentieth century opened, Justice Gray repeated almost verbatim his words from *Hilton* in a famous prize case, *The Paquete Habana*, [175 U.S. 677, 700 (1900)]. But over the first half of this century, the scope of the law of nations applied in American courts substantially narrowed. . . . As the century proceeded, the courts increasingly invoked three concerns to mitigate their duty to declare the law of nations: *comity*, *separation of powers*, and *judicial incompetence*. . . .

. . .

Modern transnational public law litigation began with the 1946 war crimes trials at Nuremburg and Tokyo, which redefined the permissible party structures, claims, and fora of international litigation.

. . .

. . . Tokyo and Nuremburg pierced the veil of state sovereignty and dispelled the myth that international law is for states only, re-declaring that individuals are subjects, not just objects, of international law. Thereafter, private citizens, government officials, nongovernmental organizations and multinational enterprises could all be rightsholders and responsible actors under international law, and hence, proper plaintiffs and defendants in transnational actions. . . . Tokyo and Nuremberg galvanized the international human rights movement: the drive for global human rights standards that has provided transnational public law litigation with its authoritative texts.

. . .

Chief Justice Marshall first drew that line [between self-executing and nonself-executing treaties] in *Foster & Elam v. Neilson*, [27 U.S. (2 Pet.) 253 (1829).] which declared that a treaty becomes the law of the land unless its terms "import a contract" or "either of the parties engages to perform a particular act," in which case legislative implementation is necessary "before it can become a rule for the Court." *Foster* was reversed on its own facts only four years later and went largely ignored until the late nineteenth century. Moreover, Marshall clearly intended nonself-executing treaties to be the exception, not the rule. Nevertheless, post-Nuremburg courts revitalized and expanded the doctrine to hold a series of human rights treaties nonself-executing. Avoiding the sole relevant question – whether the plaintiff has stated a claim upon which relief can be granted – courts have fragmented the nonself-executing treaty doctrine into a series of preliminary obstacles that litigants must now overcome to enforce treaties through the courts.

The second judicial barrier to transnational public law litigation solidified in 1964, when the Court recast the Act of State doctrine into its modern form in *Banco Nacional de Cuba v. Sabbatino* [376 U.S. 398 (1964).]. An odd coalition of the judicial restraint and anticolonialist elements on the Court formed an eight-Justice majority that voted not simply to defer to a Cuban expropriatory decree, but also to *enforce* it against an expropriated company's American owners. Although *Sabbatino* was technically a commercial case, replete with vertical elements, the Court declined even to apply international law to review the validity of the act of a recognized foreign sovereign fully executed within its own territory. By so saying, the Court went far beyond the comity rationale that had guided its previous Act of State decisions, now emphasizing separation of powers and judicial incompetence as the main reasons why American courts should not adjudicate cases under international law.

By explicitly linking the Act of State Doctrine to separation of powers, *Sabbatino* implied that determinations regarding the legality of foreign state acts are quasi-political questions, whose decision is appropriately confided in the Executive Branch or Congress, not the courts. Moreover, the Court concluded that courts have limited competence to find the law in international cases, a conclusion belied both by Justice White's powerful dissent and extensive judicial precedents. *Sabbatino* especially urged abstention in customary international law cases where no clear consensus exists on the content of the rule in question. Together with the self-executing treaty doctrine, *Sabbatino* thus cast a profound chill upon the willingness of United States domestic courts to interpret or articulate norms of international law – both customary and treaty-based – in both private and public cases....

...The courts soon read *Sabbatino*, together with earlier precedents regarding judicial deference to executive discretion in foreign affairs and political question notions imported from the domestic electoral context, as a general directive to stay out of foreign affairs adjudication. This chill stimulated a period of American judicial withdrawal from the arena of public international norm-enunciation that lasted for more than a decade....

. . .

As the 1970s closed, however, two complementary trends engendered a new generation of transnational public law cases in United States judicial fora. The first was the by now well-chronicled rise of *domestic* public law litigation: a growing acceptance by litigants of United States courts as instruments of social change....

This growing faith in the capacity of the courts to engage in domestic public law litigation coincided with a second trend: the explosion of *transnational commercial* litigation in United States courts. As nations increasingly entered the marketplace, and the United States adopted the doctrine of restrictive sovereign immunity by statute, federal courts became increasingly obliged to adjudicate commercial suits brought by individuals and private entities against foreign governments. This plethora of transnational suits not only returned domestic courts to the business of adjudicating international law, from which they had largely excluded themselves since *Sabbatino*, but also stimulated a reawakening of the bench's and bar's interest in the black-letter doctrine of international and foreign relations law.

. . .

In 1980, these trends came together in the Second Circuit's landmark decision in *Filartiga v. Pena-Irala*630 F.2d 876, 884, n. 15 (2d Cir. 1980). *Filartiga* held that the Alien Tort Statute conferred district court jurisdiction over a suit by Paraguayans versus a Paraguayan official who had tortured their relative to death in Paraguay, while acting under color of governmental authority. On remand, the federal district court awarded judgment of nearly $ 10.4 million, comprising compensatory damages based on Paraguayan law and punitive damages based on United States cases and international law....

. . .

... [T]he core issue in the case was quintessentially legal: whether the victims had a right to be free from torture that was actionable in federal court. Resolution of that question required standard legal determinations – judicial construction of the Alien Tort Statute and human rights treaties – and a conclusion that the customary international law norm against torture was definable, obligatory, and universal....

Since *Filartiga*, transnational public law litigation has followed two tracks: cases brought by individual plaintiffs and those brought by nation-states. The individual suits may themselves be subdivided into "international tort" suits, in which plaintiffs have sought compensation, norm-enunciation, and deterrence through judicial declarations of international law violations, and more ambitious "institutional reform" suits, in which plaintiffs have sought not simply retrospective redress and prospective declarations, but affirmative reform of United States foreign policy programs.

International tort suits have generated the greatest activity in United States courts. *Filartiga* provided the paradigm for a series of Alien Tort Statute suits by alien plaintiffs against foreign officials acting under color of governmental authority, claiming violations of the plaintiffs' internationally recognized human rights. Although no *Filartiga*-type plaintiff has apparently collected full compensation for his injuries, many have expressed satisfaction simply to have won default judgments announcing that the defendant had transgressed universally recognized norms of international law. These small successes encouraged Alien Tort Statute plaintiffs to expand the class of defendants beyond foreign government officials to a second group, foreign governments.

. . .

The most novel development in transnational public law litigation has been its expansion beyond individual to state plaintiffs. The litigation brought by the Government of India against Union Carbide in United States and Indian courts in the wake of the Bhopal tragedy provides the most dramatic example. Following an environmental disaster, the importing state sued a private multinational entity in domestic, rather than international, court, making complex claims based on transnational law. India sued as *parens patriae* for its citizens, claiming to seek judicial reparations for their injuries, but its apparent motive in turning to American courts was not so much to win enforceable relief, as to obtain a judicial declaration of Union Carbide's strict liability for the disaster. Although India hoped to use such a declaration to provoke a political settlement that would potentially bind Union Carbide, India, the United States, as well as the private Indian plaintiffs, that ambition was not realized.

. . .

Transnational public law litigation thus constitutes a novel and expanding effort by both state and individual plaintiffs to fuse international legal rights with domestic judicial remedies. Transnational litigation, which originated in the context of private commercial suits against foreign governments, has now migrated into the realm of public human rights suits against the United States and foreign governments and officials. State-initiated litigation, once restricted to international tribunals, has also migrated into American courts, reflecting failing faith in international adjudication as a process for obtaining meaningful remedies.

Questions and Discussion

1. A major source of controversy has been about how the ATS is invoked against multinational corporations on the basis of a theory of complicity with foreign governments that have

committed human rights abuses. In *Doe v. Unocal Corp.*, 395 F.3d 932 (9th Cir. 2002), it was alleged that Unocal, a Burmese subsidiary of the Union Oil Company of California, directly or in complicity with the Burmese military subjected the population of a village over which an oil pipeline was being constructed to forced labor, murder, rape, and torture. A three-judge panel reversed the District Court's summary judgment but established a high burden of proof. It ruled that an ATS plaintiff needs to show that a corporation alleged to be complicit "provided knowing practical assistance or encouragement" to a government perpetrating violations. *Id.* at 947. The decision was vacated for a rehearing en banc, but the case settled before a new decision. *Doe I v. Unocal*, 395 F.3d 978 (9th Cir. 2003). *See further* Richard L. Herz, *The Liberalizing Effects of Tort: How Corporate Complicity Liability Under the Alien Tort Statute Advances Constructive Engagement*, 21 HARV. HUM. RTS. J. 207 (2008); Paul L. Hoffman & Daniel A. Zaheer, *The Rules of the Road: Federal Common Law and Aiding and Abetting Under the Alien Tort Claims Act*, 26 LOY. L.A. INT'L & COMP. L. REV. 47 (2003).

2. It is important to be aware that the ATS does not supersede the Foreign Sovereign Immunities Act (FSIA), 28 U.S.C. §1330 et seq. The FSIA does contain a tort exception to sovereign immunity, but it applies only to torts committed in the United States. *See, e.g., Argentina v. Amerada Hess Shipping Corp.*, 488 U.S. 428, 109 S. Ct. 683, 102 L. Ed. 2d 818 (1989). Accordingly, most ATS actions have been brought against individuals. This does not mean a government official acting outside of the scope of his or her authority as a government official cannot be sued under the ATS. For example, if a government official commits torture without an explicit order or authority from the government, an ATS action will lie. *See, e.g., In re Estate of Marco Litigation*, 978 F.2d 493, 498 (9th Cir. 1992).

3. In 2004, the U.S. Supreme Court interpreted the ATS for the first time in a case concerning a Mexican national who had allegedly been arbitrarily arrested and detained in violation of international law. The case follows.

Sosa v. Alvarez-Machain, 542 U.S. 692, 124 S. Ct. 2739, 159 L. Ed. 2d 718 (2004) (footnotes omitted)

Justice SOUTER delivered the opinion of the Court.

I

... In 1985, an agent of the Drug Enforcement Administration (DEA), Enrique Camarena-Salazar, was captured on assignment in Mexico and taken to a house in Guadalajara, where he was tortured over the course of a 2-day interrogation, then murdered.... DEA officials in the United States came to believe that respondent Humberto Alvarez-Machain (Alvarez), a Mexican physician, was present at the house and acted to prolong the agent's life in order to extend the interrogation and torture.

In 1990, a federal grand jury indicted Alvarez for the torture and murder of Camarena-Salazar, and the United States District Court for the Central District of California issued a warrant for his arrest.... [T]he DEA approved a plan to hire Mexican nationals to seize Alvarez and bring him to the United States for trial. As so planned, a group of Mexicans, including petitioner Jose Francisco Sosa, abducted Alvarez from his house, held him overnight in a motel, and brought him by private plane to El Paso, Texas, where he was arrested by federal officers....

... [Alvarez's] case was tried in 1992, and ended at the close of the Government's case, when the District Court granted Alvarez's motion for a judgment of acquittal.

In 1993, after returning to Mexico, Alvarez began the civil action before us here. He sued Sosa [and several others]...under the ATS [Alien Tort Statute] for a violation of the law of nations.... The [ATS] provides in its entirety that "[t]he district courts shall have original jurisdiction of any civil action by an alien for a tort only, committed in violation of the law of nations or a treaty of the United States."...

The District Court...awarded summary judgment and $25,000 in damages to Alvarez on the ATS claim. A three-judge panel of the Ninth Circuit then affirmed the ATS judgment....

A divided en banc court came to the same conclusion.... As for the ATS claim, the court called on its own precedent, "that [the ATS] not only provides federal courts with subject matter jurisdiction, but also creates a cause of action for an alleged violation of the law of nations."... The Circuit then relied upon what it called the "clear and universally recognized norm prohibiting arbitrary arrest and detention"...to support the conclusion that Alvarez's arrest amounted to a tort in violation of international law.

. . .

IV

We think it is correct...to assume that the First Congress understood that the district courts would recognize private causes of action for certain torts in violation of the law of nations, though we have found no basis to suspect Congress had any examples in mind beyond those torts corresponding to Blackstone's three primary offenses.... We assume, too, that no development in the two centuries from the enactment of § 1350 to the birth of the modern line of cases beginning with *Filartiga v. Pena-Irala*, 630 F.2d 876 (C.A.2 1980), has categorically precluded federal courts from recognizing a claim under the law of nations as an element of common law.... Still, there are good reasons for a restrained conception of the discretion a federal court should exercise in considering a new cause of action of this kind. Accordingly, we think courts should require any claim based on the present-day law of nations to rest on a norm of international character accepted by the civilized world and defined with a specificity comparable to the features of the 18th-century paradigms we have recognized. This requirement is fatal to Alvarez's claim.

A

A series of reasons argue for judicial caution when considering the kinds of individual claims that might implement the jurisdiction conferred by the early statute. First, the prevailing conception of the common law has changed since 1789 in a way that counsels restraint in judicially applying internationally generated norms. When § 1350 was enacted, the accepted conception was of the common law as "a transcendental body of law outside of any particular State but obligatory within it unless and until changed by statute." *Black and White Taxicab & Transfer Co. v. Brown and Yellow Taxicab & Transfer Co.*, (1928) (Holmes, J., dissenting). Now, however, in most cases where a court is asked to state or formulate a common law principle in a new context, there is a general understanding that the law is not so much found or discovered as it is either made or created....

Second, along with, and in part driven by, that conceptual development in understanding common law has come an equally significant rethinking of the role of the federal courts in making it. *Erie R. Co. v. Tompkins*, 304 U.S. 64, (1938), was the watershed in which we denied the existence of any federal "general" common law.... [T]he general practice has been to look for legislative guidance before exercising innovative authority over substantive law. It would be remarkable to take a more aggressive role in exercising a jurisdiction that remained largely in shadow for much of the prior two centuries.

Third, this Court has recently and repeatedly said that a decision to create a private right of action is one better left to legislative judgment in the great majority of cases.... [T]he possible collateral consequences of making international rules privately actionable argue for judicial caution.

Fourth, the subject of those collateral consequences is itself a reason for a high bar to new private causes of action for violating international law, for the potential implications for the foreign relations of the United States of recognizing such causes should make courts particularly wary of impinging on the discretion of the Legislative and Executive Branches in managing foreign affairs.... Since many attempts by federal courts to craft remedies for the violation of new norms of international law would raise risks of adverse foreign policy consequences, they should be undertaken, if at all, with great caution....

The fifth reason is particularly important in light of the first four. We have no congressional mandate to seek out and define new and debatable violations of the law of nations, and modern indications of congressional understanding of the judicial role in the field have not affirmatively encouraged greater judicial creativity.

. . .

C

We must still, however, derive a standard or set of standards for assessing the particular claim Alvarez raises, and for this action it suffices to look to the historical antecedents. Whatever the ultimate criteria for accepting a cause of action subject to jurisdiction under § 1350, we are persuaded that federal courts should not recognize private claims under federal common law for violations of any international law norm with less definite content and acceptance among civilized nations than the historical paradigms familiar when § 1350 was enacted. See, e.g., *United States v. Smith*, 5 Wheat. 153, 163–180, n. 8 (1820) (illustrating the specificity with which the law of nations defined piracy)....

Thus, Alvarez's detention claim must be gauged against the current state of international law, looking to those sources we have long, albeit cautiously, recognized. "[W]here there is no treaty, and no controlling executive or legislative act or judicial decision, resort must be had to the customs and usages of civilized nations; and, as evidence of these, to the works of jurists and commentators, who by years of labor, research and experience, have made themselves peculiarly well acquainted with the subjects of which they treat. Such works are resorted to by judicial tribunals, not for the speculations of their authors concerning what the law ought to be, but for trustworthy evidence of what the law really is." *The Paquete Habana* [175 U.S. 677, 700 (1900)].

To begin with, Alvarez cites two well-known international agreements that, despite their moral authority, have little utility under the standard set out in this opinion. He says that his abduction by Sosa was an "arbitrary arrest" within the meaning of the Universal Declaration of Human Rights (Declaration).... And he traces the rule against arbitrary arrest not only to the Declaration, but also to article nine of the International Covenant on Civil and Political Rights (Covenant), Dec. 16, 1966, 999 U.N.T.S. 171..., to which the United States is a party, and to various other conventions to which it is not. But the Declaration does not of its own force impose obligations as a matter of international law.... And, although the Covenant does bind the United States as a matter of international law, the United States ratified the Covenant on the express understanding that it was not self-executing and so did not itself create obligations enforceable in the federal courts.... Accordingly, Alvarez cannot say that the Declaration and Covenant themselves establish the relevant and applicable rule of international law. He instead attempts to show that prohibition of arbitrary arrest has attained the status of binding customary international law....

Alvarez . . . invokes a general prohibition of "arbitrary" detention defined as officially sanctioned action exceeding positive authorization to detain under the domestic law of some government, regardless of the circumstances. Whether or not this is an accurate reading of the Covenant,

Alvarez cites little authority that a rule so broad has the status of a binding customary norm today.[1] . . .

Alvarez's failure to marshal support for his proposed rule is underscored by the Restatement (Third) of Foreign Relations Law of the United States (1986), which says in its discussion of customary international human rights law that a "state violates international law if, as a matter of state policy, it practices, encourages, or condones . . . prolonged arbitrary detention." 2 *Id.*, § 702. Although the Restatement does not explain its requirements of a "state policy" and of "prolonged" detention, the implication is clear. Any credible invocation of a principle against arbitrary detention that the civilized world accepts as binding customary international law requires a factual basis beyond relatively brief detention in excess of positive authority. Even the Restatement's limits are only the beginning of the enquiry, because although it is easy to say that some policies of prolonged arbitrary detentions are so bad that those who enforce them become enemies of the human race, it may be harder to say which policies cross that line with the certainty afforded by Blackstone's three common law offenses. . . .

Whatever may be said for the broad principle Alvarez advances, in the present, imperfect world, it expresses an aspiration that exceeds any binding customary rule having the specificity we require.[2] Creating a private cause of action to further that aspiration would go beyond any residual common law discretion we think it appropriate to exercise. . . . It is enough to hold that a single illegal detention of less than a day, followed by the transfer of custody to lawful authorities and a prompt arraignment, violates no norm of customary international law so well defined as to support the creation of a federal remedy.

The judgment of the Court of Appeals is
Reversed.

Questions and Discussion

1. The court rules that "courts should require any claim based on the present-day law of nations to rest on a norm of international character accepted by the civilized world and defined with a specificity comparable to the features of the 18th-century paradigms" the court discusses. Could Sosa have offered any further proof?

2. Are there any environmental rights that have the requisite acceptance and specificity? Which ones?

3. Note 20 in the Sosa judgment left open the question of corporate accountability: "A related consideration is whether international law extends the scope of liability for a violation of a given norm to the perpetrator being sued, if the defendant is a private actor such as a corporation or individual." *Compare Tel-Oren v. Libyan Arab Republic*, 726 F.2d 774, 791–95 (C.A.D.C.1984) (Edwards, J., concurring) (insufficient consensus in 1984 that torture by private actors violates international law), with *Kadic v. Kardzíc*, 70 F.3d 232, 239–41

---

[1] Specifically, he relies on a survey of national constitutions . . . ; a case from the International Court of Justice, *United States v. Iran*, 1980 I.C.J. 3, 42; and some authority drawn from the federal courts. . . . None of these suffice. The [constitutional] survey does show that many nations recognize a norm against arbitrary detention, but that consensus is at a high level of generality. The *Iran* case, in which the United States sought relief for the taking of its diplomatic and consular staff as hostages, involved a different set of international norms and mentioned the problem of arbitrary detention only in passing; the detention in that case was, moreover, far longer and harsher than Alvarez's . . . . And the authority from the federal courts, to the extent it supports Alvarez's position, reflects a more assertive view of federal judicial discretion over claims based on customary international law than the position we take today.

[2] It is not that violations of a rule logically foreclose the existence of that rule as international law. *Cf. Filartiga v. Pena-Irala*, 630 F.2d 876, 884, n. 15 (C.A.2 1980) ("The fact that the prohibition of torture is often honored in the breach does not diminish its binding effect as a norm of international law"). Nevertheless, that a rule as stated is as far from full realization as the one Alvarez urges is evidence against its status as binding law; and an even clearer point against the creation by judges of a private cause of action to enforce the aspiration behind the rule claimed.

(C.A.2 1995) (sufficient consensus in 1995 that genocide by private actors violates international law).

Laying One Bankrupt Critique to Rest: Sosa v. Alvarez Machain *and the Future of Human Rights Litigation in U.S. Courts,* 57 VAND. L. REV. 2241, 2283–87 (2004) Ralph Steinhardt

IV. THE NEXT FRONTIER IN ALIEN TORT LITIGATION

The first significant battle over the interpretation of *Alvarez-Machain II* will come in a variety of cases testing whether corporate actors may be liable under the ATS for their complicity in human rights abuses by the government with which they do business. Many such cases have been dismissed on jurisdictional, political, or factual grounds, and others have been derailed under the *forum non conveniens* doctrine. Especially in the context of cases arising out of World War II against Japanese and German government entities or corporations, the treaties ending the war have been interpreted to render additional compensation or reparations a matter for the executive branch. If anything, the corporate cases that have actually been decided reaffirm that the courts have the necessary tools to distinguish non justiciable or frivolous claims from those that are meritorious.

No part of *Alvarez-Machain II* turned on the circumstances under which a corporation faces liability for a breach of international law, but the government and a coalition of business interests had urged the Court to interpret the ATS so as to bar such actions. The Court implicitly rejected the propositions that corporations are *in principle* immune from liability under international law or that the prospect of abusive lawsuits required a narrow interpretation of the ATS. Instead, the Court reasoned only that "the determination whether a norm is sufficiently definite to support a cause of action" is "related [to] whether international law extends the scope of liability for a violation of a given norm to the perpetrator being sued, if the defendant is a private actor such as a corporation or individual." For these purposes, the Court contrasted torture, which does require state action in order to be a violation of international law,196 with genocide, which does not.'97 The Court also noted a particular set of pending class actions "seeking damages from various corporations alleged to have participated in, or abetted, the regime of apartheid that formerly controlled South Africa," but rather than decide that all such cases were beyond the reach of the ATS, the Court declared instead that "[i]n such cases, there is a strong argument that federal courts should give serious weight to the Executive Branch's view of the case's impact on foreign policy."

For centuries, the imposition of individual liability for certain international wrongs (e.g., piracy) has generated little controversy. Certainly the framers of the First Judiciary Act of 1789 had little doubt that private citizens who infringed the rights of ambassadors or diplomats could be sued under Section 1350. Pirates, the exemplar of intended defendants under the ATS, were not always or necessarily considered state actors, but there was never any question that their actions violated international law; indeed, one of the earliest exercises of jurisdiction under the ATS involved an unlawful seizure of property by a non state actor. The statute subsequently provided jurisdiction over a child custody dispute that involved a breach of the law of nations. In settings other than *Alvarez-Machain II*, the executive branch has concluded that corporations are in principle capable of violating the law of nations or a treaty of the United States for purposes of the ATS, and that conclusion is consistent with well-established international norms to which the United States has given its assent. Specific treaties establish that private actors may be punished for acts of genocide, slavery, and war crimes. These regimes do not distinguish between natural and juridical individuals, and corporations that engage in the slave trade or commit acts of genocide or provide corporate cover for war crimes would not as a matter of law be exempt from liability. "Certain forms of conduct violate the law of nations whether undertaken by those acting under the auspices of a state or only as private individuals."

This suggests that there are at least two distinct circumstances in which a corporation (or any other private actor) might bear international responsibility: (1) a category of *per se* wrongs, in which the corporation – like any individual – commits one of that narrow class of wrongs identified by treaty or custom as not requiring state action to be considered wrongful; and (2) a category of contextual wrongs, in which the corporation's conduct is sufficiently infused with state action as to engage international standards. To date, no corporation has been found liable under the ATS under either theory, but both remain viable in the aftermath of *Alvarez-Machain II*, despite the strong position staked out by business groups as *amici curiae*.

2. Litigating Environmental Claims Under the ATS

Litigating Environmental Abuses Under the Alien Tort Claims Act: A Practical Assessment, 40 Va. J. Int'l L. 545 (2000)
Richard L. Herz

All too often, transnational corporations (TNCs) and governments inflict devastating environmental harms on local people in developing countries. Typically, the damage is obvious and preventable, but ignored by those who cause it. Texaco's oil development in the Ecuadorian Amazon and Freeport-McMoRan's copper and gold mine in the highlands of Irian Jaya, Indonesia are noteworthy examples. Texaco drilled oil in the Ecuadorian Amazon for twenty years, ending in 1992. During that time, the company opened over 300 wells and cut 18,000 miles of trail and 300 miles of road in pristine rainforest. Disregarding the established industry practice of pumping wastes back into wells, Texaco dumped massive quantities of toxic byproducts onto roads and into streams and wetlands local people used for drinking, fishing and bathing. Texaco also filled over 600 pits with toxic waste, which often washed out in heavy rain. A farmer, describing the rupture of just one of these pits, stated, "[i]t has been three years, and my wife is still covered with rashes. I have eight children. All of them have been sick with rashes, flus, their stomachs, swollen throats. We did not have that before the spill. The rupture also ruined his farm and water supply. At least 30,000 people have suffered injuries similar to those experienced by that farmer and his family as a result of Texaco's Amazonian operations.

Freeport's practices are equally outrageous. The company has removed the top 400 feet of a mountain sacred to the local Amungme people. It currently dumps 160,000 tons of untreated, toxic mine tailings into the local waterways each day, a figure that will soon rise to 285,000 tons, the equivalent of a ten ton dump truck-full every three seconds. This massive release of sediment has created an artificial floodplain on a local river, destroying the river and inundating surrounding rainforests. The mine has also devastated lakes and polluted ground and surface water with toxins. This damage has threatened the lives and health of the entire Amungme people, through starvation, exposure to toxic chemicals, pollution of their water, and destruction of their lands.

. . .

... [T]he Alien Tort Claims Act (ATCA)... opens federal courts to civil suits by aliens for torts committed in violation of customary international law, even when the case involves acts perpetrated in another country by a non-U.S. citizen. Recently, courts have recognized that under certain circumstances, ATCA permits suits against TNCs for human rights abuses associated with their projects. Given this development, the time is ripe to determine whether ATCA can provide redress to victims of TNCs' massive environmental degradation....

The stakes in such suits are enormous. For the plaintiffs, an ATCA action might represent the only means even theoretically available to prevent or receive some compensation for the loss of their livelihoods, cultures, health and even lives. Conversely, because corporations like Freeport and Texaco cause such extensive harm, the costs of a judgment involving damages, remediation and/or the future operation of a project in an environmentally responsible manner would be high. More generally, these suits challenge the impunity with which TNCs have heretofore destroyed the environments of unwilling communities. Indeed, the very existence of ATCA suits may cause at least some TNCs to reevaluate the way they do business abroad in order to avoid potential liability.

Benal v. Freeport-McMoran, Inc., 197 F.3d 161 (5th Cir. 1999) (footnotes omitted)

CARL E. STEWART, Circuit Judge:

Tom Beanal ("Beanal") brought suit against the defendants in federal district court for alleged violations of international law. The district court dismissed Beanal's claims pursuant to FED. R. CIV. PROC. 12(b) (6). After a careful review of Beanal's pleading, we affirm the district court.

I. FACTUAL & PROCEDURAL HISTORY

This case involves alleged violations of international law committed by domestic corporations conducting mining activities abroad in the Pacific Rim. Freeport – McMoran, Inc., and Freeport – McMoran Copper & Gold, Inc., ("Freeport"), are Delaware corporations with headquarters in New Orleans, Louisiana. Freeport operates the "Grasberg Mine," an open pit copper, gold, and silver mine situated in the Jayawijaya Mountain in Irian Jaya, Indonesia. The mine encompasses approximately 26,400 square kilometers. Beanal is a resident of Tamika, Irian Jaya within the Republic of Indonesia (the "Republic"). He is also the leader of the Amungme Tribal Council of Lambaga Adat Suki Amungme (the "Amungme")In August 1996, Beanal filed a complaint against Freeport in federal district court in the Eastern District of Louisiana for alleged violations of international law. Beanal invoked jurisdiction under (1) 28 U.S.C. §1332, (2) the Alien Tort Statute, 28 U.S.C. §1350 note. In his First Amended Complaint, he alleged that Freeport engaged in environmental abuses, human rights violations and cultural genocide. Specifically, he alleged that Freeport mining operations had caused harm and injury to the Amungme's environment and habitat. He further alleged that Freeport engaged in cultural genocide by destroying the Amungme's habitat and religious symbols, thus forcing the Amungme to relocate. Finally, he asserted that Freeport's private security force acted in concert with the Republic to violate international human rights. Freeport moved to dismiss Beanal's claims under Fed.R.Civ.Proc12(b) (6). The district court in April 1997 issued a thorough forty-nine page Opinion and Order dismissing Beanal's claims without prejudice and with leave to amend. *See Beanal v. Freeport-McMoran*, 969 F. Supp. 362 (E.D. La. 1997). Pursuant to Rule 12(e), the district court instructed Beanal to amend his complaint to state more specifically his claims of genocide and individual human rights violations. In August 1997, the district court granted Freeport's motion to strike Beanal Second Amended Complaint because Beanal inappropriately attempted to add third parties. At the motion to strike hearing, the court again instructed Beanal to please facts sufficient to support his allegations of genocide and individual human rights violations. In March 1998, the district court granted Freeport's motion to strike Beanal's Third Amended Complaint and dismissed his claims with prejudice. Beanal now appeals the district court's rulings below.

. . .

A. *Alien Tort Statute*

Beanal claims that Freeport engaged in conduct that violated the Alien Tort Statute (the "ATS" or "§1350"). Under §1350:

> The district courts shall have original jurisdiction of any civil action by an alien for a tort only, committed in violation of the law of nations or a treaty of the United States.

Section 1350 confers subject matter jurisdiction when the following conditions are met; (1) an alien sues, (2) for a tort, (3) that was committed in violation of the "law of nations" or a treaty of the United States. *See Kaclic v. Karadzic*, 70 F.3d 232, 238 (2d Cir.1995). Beanal does not claim that Freeport violated a United States treaty. Thus, the issue before us is whether Beanal states claims upon which relief can be granted for violations under the "law of nations," i.e., international law.

We observed in 1985, [t]he question of defining 'the law of nations' is a confusing one which is hotly debated, chiefly among academics." *Carmichael v. United Technologies Corp.*, 835 F.2d 109, 113 (5th Cir.1985). However, in *Cohen v. Hart man.*, 634 F.2d 318, 319 (5th Cir. 1981) (per curiam), we "held that the standards by which nations regulate their dealings with one another *inter se* constitutes the 'law' of nations.'" These standards include the rules of conduct which govern the affairs of this nation, acting in its national capacity, in relationships with any other nation. *See id.* (quoting *Valanga v. Metropolitan Life Ins. Co.*, 259 F.Supp. 324 (E.D. Pa.1966)). The law of nations is defined by customary usage and clearly articulated principles of the international community. One of the means of ascertaining the law of nations is "by consulting the work of jurists writing professedly on public law or by the general usage and practice of nations; or by judicial decisions recognizing and enforcing that law." *See Carmichael* 835 F.2d at 113 (citing *United States v. Smith*, 18 U.S. (5 Wheat) 153, 160–61, 5 L. Ed. 57 (1820)), *see also Kadic* 70 F.3d at 238; *Filartiga v. Pena-Irala*, 630 F.2d 876, 880 (2d Cir. 1980). Courts "must interpret international law not as it was in 1789, but as it has evolved and exists among the, nations of the world to-day." *Kadic* 70 F.3d at 238; *Filartiga*, 630 F.2d at 881. Although Beanal's claims raise complex issues of international law; nonetheless, the task before us does not require that we resolve them. We are only required to determine whether the pleadings on their face state a claim upon which relief can be granted. Although the day may come when we will have to join other jurisdictions who have tackled head-on complex issues involving international law, "[t]his case, however,' does not require that we stand up and be counted." *Carmichael*, 835 F.2d. at 113. Beanal's allegations under the ATS can be divided into three categories: 1) individual human rights violations; (2) environmental torts; and (3) genocide and cultural genocide. We address each in turn.

1. Individual Human Rights Violations

First, Beanal claims that his pleadings sufficiently state claims for individual human rights violations. Essentially, Beanal complains that Freeport engaged in the following conduct; (1) surveillance; (2) mental torture; (3) death threats; and (4) house arrest. *See* Third Amended Complaint ¶ 25. However, Freeport argues that Beanal's allegations fail to give adequate notice under the federal pleading requirements. Also, Freeport claims that Beanal failed to plead the requisite state action to support his claims under the ATS. The district court found that Beanal merely made nominal changes to his Third Amended Complaint in an attempt to comply with its order to provide a more definite statement of what had happened to him individually. As such, the district court ruled that Beanal's complaint failed to provide a more definite statement of his claims.

After reviewing Beanal's pleadings de novo, we agree with the district court's ruling. Beanal's complaint merely makes conclusory allegations. Beanal's claims are devoid of names, dates, locations, times or any facts that would put Freeport on notice as to what conduct supports the nature of his claims) Furthermore, after comparing Beanal's' Third Amended Complaint with his Second Amended Complaint, we agree with the district court's observation in that, "B canal has made a superficial effort to personalize his complaint in order to comply with the court's April and August Order" Although Beanal argues that the district court inappropriately subjected his complaint to a heightened pleading standard, nonetheless, the notice requirements under Rule 8 require more that "bare bone allegations that a wrong has occurred." *See South Cent. Bell Tel. Co.*, 904 F.2d at 277. Because we affirm the district court's dismissal of Beanal's claims of individual human rights violations under the ATS on the ground that his complaint fails to provide adequate factual specificity as to what had happened to him individually, we need not address whether state-action is required to sustain an action for individual human rights violation under the ATS.

2. *Environmental Torts and Abuses*

Next, Beanal argues that Freeport through its mining activities engaged in environmental abuses which violated international law. In his Third Amended Complaint, Beanal alleges the following:

> FREEPORT, in connection with its Grasberg operations, deposits approximately 100,000 tons of tailings per day in the Aghwagaon, Otomona and Ajkwa Rivers. Said tailings have diverted the natural flow of the rivers and have rendered the natural waterways of the plaintiff unusable for traditional uses including bathing and drinking. Furthermore, upon information and belief, the heavy metal content of the tailings have and/or will affect the body tissue of the aquatic life in said rivers. Additionally, tailings have blocked the main flow of the Ajkwa River causing overflow of the tailings into lowland rain forest vegetation destroying the same....

> FREEPORT, in connection with its Grasberg operations has diverted the aforesaid rivers greatly increasing the chance of future flooding in Timika, the home of the plaintiff, Tom Beanal....

> FREEPORT, in connection with its Grasberg mining operations has caused or will cause through the course of its operations 3 Billion tons of "overburden" to be dumped into the upper Wanagon and Carstensz creating the likely risk of massive landslides directly injurious to the plaintiff. Furthermore, said "overburden" creates acid rock damage which has created acid streams and rendering the Lake Wanagon an "acid lake" extremely high in copper concentrations....

However, Freeport argues that Beanal's allegations of environmental torts are not cognizable under the "law of nations" because Beanal fails to show that Freeport's mining activities violate any universally accepted environmental standards and norms. Furthermore, Freeport argues that it would be improper for a United States tribunal to evaluate another country's environmental practices and policies. The district court conducted a thorough survey of various international law principles, treaties, and declarations and concluded that Beanal failed to articulate environmental torts that were cognizable under international law.

Beanal and the *amici* refer the court to several sources of international environmental law to show that the alleged environmental abuses caused by Freeport's mining activities are cognizable under international law. Chiefly among these are the *Principles of International Environmental Law I: Frameworks, Standards and Implementation* 183 – 18 (Phillip Sands ed,. 1995) ("Sands"), and the *Rio Declaration on Environment and Development,* June 13, 1992, U.N. Doc. A/CONF. 15 1/5 rev.1 (1992) (the "Rio Declaration").

Nevertheless, "[i]t is only where the nations of the world have demonstrated that the wrong is of mutual and not merely several, concern, by means of express international accords, that a wrong generally recognized becomes an international law violation in the meaning. of the [ATS]." *Filartiga,* 630 F.2d at 888. Thus, the ATS "applies only to shockingly egregious 'violations of universally recognized principles 'of international law." *See Zapata v. Quinn,* 707 F.2d 691, 692 (2d Cir. 1983) (per curiam). Beanal fails to show that these treaties and agreements enjoy universal acceptance in the international community. The sources of international law cited by Beanal and the *amici* merely refer to a general sense of environmental responsibility and state abstract rights and liberties devoid of articulable or discernable standards and regulations to identify practices that constitute international environmental abuses or torts. Although the United States has articulable standards embodied in federal statutory law to address environmental violations domestically, *see* The National Environmental Policy Act (42 U.S.C. § 4321 *et seq.*) and The Endangered Species Act (16 U.S.C. § 1532), nonetheless, federal courts should exercise extreme caution when adjudicating environmental claims under international law to insure that environmental policies of the United States do not displace environmental policies of other governments. Furthermore, the argument to abstain from interfering in a sovereign's environmental practices carries persuasive force especially when the alleged environmental torts and abuses occur within the sovereign's borders and do not affect neighboring countries. Therefore, the district court did not err when it concluded that Beanal failed to show in his pleadings that Freeport's mining activities constitute environmental torts or abuses under international law.

3. Genocide and Cultural Genocide

Beanal claims that Freeport engaged in acts of genocide and cultural genocide. In his First Amended Complaint, Beanal alleged that Freeport's mining operations caused the Amungme to be displaced and relocate to other areas of the country. He also alleged that Freeport's mining activities destroyed the Amungme's habitat. As such, Beanal asserted that Freeport purposely engaged in activity to destroy the Amungme's cultural and social framework. However, Freeport attacked Beanal's allegations claiming that cultural genocide is not recognized as a discrete violation of international law. The district court relying chiefly on the express language of Article II of the Convention on the Prevention and Punishment of the Crime of Genocide, 78 U.T.S. 277 (the "Convention on Genocide"), concluded that cultural genocide was not recognized in the international community as a violation of international law. The district court then instructed Beanal to amend his complaint to allege genocide. Specifically, the court instructed Beanal to allege facts that would demonstrate that "he [was] the victim of acts committed with the intent to destroy the people of the Amungme tribe...." Consequently, the district court found that Beanal's Third Amended Complaint failed to comply with express instructions.

A review of Beanal's Third Amended Complaint reveals that his claim of genocide suffers from the same pleading defects that plagued his other claims of individual human rights violations.. Beanal's complaint is saturated with conclusory allegations devoid of underlying facts top support his claim of genocide. Although the pleading requirements under Rule 8 are to be liberally construed in favor of the plaintiff, nevertheless, the rule requires more that "bare bones allegations" *See Walker* 904 F.2d at 277.

Notwithstanding Beanal's failure to allege facts to support sufficiently his claims of genocide, Beanal and the *amici* in their respective briefs urge this court to recognize cultural genocide as a discrete violation of international law. Again, they refer the court to several international conventions, agreements. And declarations. Nevertheless, a review of these documents reveals that the documents make pronouncements and proclamations of an amorphous right to "enjoy culture," or a right to "freely pursue" culture, or a right to cultural development. They nonetheless fail to proscribe or identify conduct that would constitute an act of cultural genocide. As such, it would be problematic to apply these vague and declatory international documents to Beanal's claim because they are devoid of discernible means to define or identify conduct that constitutes a violation of international law. Thus, it would be imprudent for a United States tribunal to declare an amorphous cause of action under international law that has failed to garner universal acceptance....

. . .

B. Torture Victim Protection Act

Beanal claims that his allegations of individual human rights violations are also actionable under the TVPA. The TVPA provides an explicit cause of action for torture and extrajudicial killings. *See* 28 U.S.C. § 1350, note; § 2. In pertinent part, the statute declares that any individual who, under actual or apparent authority, or color of law, of any foreign nation subjects an individual torture or extrajudicial killing shall, in a civil action, be liable for damages. *Id.* § 2(a) (1), and (2). Freeport argues that the TVPA does not apply to corporations; In other words, an "individual" is not a corporation under the TVPA. The district court applied a plain language interpretation of the statute and reviewed the legislative history and ruled that the TVPA does not apply to corporations.

Beanal's allegations of individual human rights violations under the TVPA are essentially predicated on the same claims of individual human rights violations under the ATS. Because we find that Beanal fails to state with the requisite specificity and definiteness his claims of individual human rights violations under the ATS, we find that his allegations under the TVPA also suffer from the same pleading defects. Beanal fails to provide sufficient underlying facts to support his claims. Thus, we affirm the district court's dismissal of Beanal's claims under the TVPA on the ground that his allegations fail to provide the requisite factual specificity and definiteness to survive a Rule 12(b) motion to dismiss. Therefore, we need not reach the question of whether a cause of action for individual human rights violations is actionable against a corporation under the TVPA.

. . .

CONCLUSION

We acknowledge that the district court exercised considerable judgment, discretion, and patience below. In light of the gravity and far ranging implications of Beanal's allegations, not only did the court give Beanal several opportunities to amend his complaint to conform with the minimum requisites as set forth in the federal rules, the court also conscientiously provided Beanal with a road-map as to how to amend his complaint to survive a motion to dismiss assuming that Beanal could marshal facts sufficient to comply with the federal rules. Nevertheless, Beanal was unable to put before the court a complaint that met minimum pleading requirements under the federal rules. Accordingly, we AFFIRM the district court.

Esther Kiobel, et al. v. Royal Dutch Petroleum Co.,
621 F.3d 111 (2d. Cir. 2010) (some footnotes omitted)

JOSÉ A. CABRANES, CIRCUIT JUDGE:

. . . .

Plaintiffs, who are, or were, residents of the Ogoni Region of Nigeria, allege that defendants Royal Dutch Petroleum Company ("Royal Dutch") and Shell Transport and Trading Company PLC ("Shell"), through a subsidiary named Shell Petroleum Development Company of Nigeria, Ltd. ("SPDC"), aided and abetted the Nigerian government in committing human rights abuses directed at plaintiffs. Royal Dutch and Shell are holding companies incorporated respectively in the Netherlands and the United Kingdom. SPDC is incorporated in Nigeria. All defendants are corporate entities – that is, "juridical" persons, rather than "natural" persons.

SPDC has been engaged in oil exploration and production in the Ogoni region of Nigeria since 1958. In response to SPDC's activities residents of the Ogoni region organized a group named the "Movement for Survival of Ogoni People" to protest the environmental effects of oil exploration in the region. According to plaintiffs, in 1993 defendants responded by enlisting the aid of the Nigerian government to suppress the Ogoni resistance. Throughout 1993 and 1994, Nigerian military forces are alleged to have shot and killed Ogoni residents and attacked Ogoni villages – beating, raping, and arresting residents and destroying or looting property – all with the assistance of defendants. Specifically, plaintiffs allege that defendants, *inter alia*, (1) provided transportation to Nigerian forces, (2) allowed their property to be utilized as a staging ground for attacks, (3) provided food for soldiers involved in the attacks, and (4) provided compensation to those soldiers.

Plaintiffs brought claims against defendants under the ATS for aiding and abetting the Nigerian government in alleged violations of the law of nations. Specifically plaintiffs brought claims of aiding and abetting (1) extrajudicial killing; (2) crimes against humanity; (3) torture or cruel, inhuman, and degrading treatment; (4) arbitrary arrest and detention; (5) violation of the rights to life, liberty, security, and association; (6) forced exile; and (7) property destruction.

. . .

... [T]his appeal presents a question that has been lurking for some time in our ATS jurisprudence. Since our first case upholding claims brought under the ATS in 1980, *see Filartiga v. Pena-Irala*, 630 F.2d 876 (2d Cir.1980), our Court has never directly addressed whether our jurisdiction under the ATS extends to civil actions against corporations, *see Presbyterian Church of Sudan v. Talisman Energy, Inc.*, 582 F.3d 244, 261 n. 12 (2d Cir.2009) (assuming, without deciding, that corporations may be liable for violations of customary international law); *Khulumani v. Barclay Nat'l Bank Ltd.*, 504 F.3d 254, 282–83 (2d Cir.2007) (Katzmann, J., concurring) (noting that, because defendants did not raise the issue, the Court need not reach the question of whether corporations may be liable for violations of customary international law); *id.* at 321–25 (Korman, J., concurring in part and dissenting in part) (expressing the view that corporations cannot be held liable under the ATS). We have, in the past, decided ATS cases involving corporations without addressing the issue of corporate liability. ... But that fact does not foreclose consideration of the issue here. As the Supreme Court has held, "when questions of *jurisdiction* have been passed on in prior decisions *sub silentio*," the Court "has never considered itself bound when a subsequent case finally brings the jurisdictional issue before [it]." ... The same rule applies here.

In answering the question presented we proceed in two steps. First, we consider which body of law governs the question – international law or domestic law – and conclude that international law governs.[1] Second, we consider what the sources of international law reveal with respect to whether corporations can be subject to liability for violations of customary international law. We conclude that those sources lead inescapably to the conclusion that the customary international law of human rights has not to date recognized liability for corporations that violate its norms.

I. Customary International Law Governs Our Inquiry

The ATS grants federal district courts jurisdiction over claims "by an alien for a tort only, committed in violation of the law of nations or a treaty of the United States." 28 U.S.C. § 1350. In 2004, the Supreme Court held in *Sosa* that the ATS is a jurisdictional statute only; it creates no cause of action, Justice Souter explained, because its drafters understood that "the common law would provide a cause of action for the modest number of international law violations with a potential for personal liability at the time." 542 U.S. at 724. Indeed, at the time of its adoption, the ATS "enabled federal courts to hear claims in a very limited category defined by the law of nations and recognized at common law." *Id.* at 712. These included "three specific offenses against the law of nations addressed by the criminal law of England [and identified by Blackstone]: violation of safe conducts, infringement of the rights of ambassadors, and piracy" – each a rule "binding individuals for the benefit of other individuals[, which] overlapped with the norms of state relationships." *Id.* at 715 (citing 4 W. Blackstone, *Commentaries on the Laws of England* 68 (1769)).

The Supreme Court did not, however, limit the jurisdiction of the federal courts under the ATS to those three offenses recognized by the law of nations in 1789. Instead, the Court in *Sosa* held that federal courts may recognize claims "based on the present-day law of nations" provided that the claims rest on "norm[s] of international character accepted by the civilized world and defined with a specificity comparable to the features of the 18th-century paradigms [the Court had] recognized." *Id.* at 725.

---

[1] The Supreme Court has long recognized that "where there is no treaty and no controlling executive or legislative act or judicial decision," customary "[i]nternational law is part of our law." *The Paquete Habana*, 175 U.S. 677, 700, 20 S.Ct. 290, 44 L.Ed. 320 (1900). In *Sosa*, the Court explained that the ATS was enacted "on the understanding that the *common law* would provide a cause of action for the modest number of international law violations with a potential for personal liability." 542 U.S. at 724 (emphasis added).

The Supreme Court cautioned that "the determination whether a norm is sufficiently definite to support a cause of action should (and, indeed, inevitably must) involve an element of judgment about the practical consequences of making that cause available to litigants in the federal courts." *Id.* at 732–33 (footnote omitted). The Court also observed that "a related consideration is whether *international law* extends the scope of liability for a violation of a given norm to the perpetrator being sued, if the defendant is a private actor such as a corporation or an individual." *Id.* at 732 n. 20 (emphasis added). We conclude – based on international law, *Sosa*, and our own precedents – that international law, and not domestic law, governs the scope of liability for violations of customary international law under the ATS.

. . . .

II. Corporate Liability Is Not a Norm of Customary International Law

To attain the status of a rule of customary international law, a norm must be "specific, universal, and obligatory." *Sosa*, 542 U.S. at 732 (quoting with approval the statement of a lower court) (internal quotation marks omitted); *see also Flores*, 414 F.3d at 248 ("[C]ustomary international law is composed only of those rules that States universally abide by, or accede to, out of a sense of legal obligation and mutual concern."); Restatement (Third) § 102(2) ("Customary international law results from a general and consistent practice of states followed by them from a sense of legal obligation."). Defining such norms "is no simple task," as "[c]ustomary international law is discerned from myriad decisions made in numerous and varied international and domestic arenas." *Flores*, 414 F.3d at 247. The sources consulted are therefore of the utmost importance.

. . . Agreements or declarations that are merely aspirational, and that "do[ ] not of [their] own force impose obligations as a matter of international law," are of "little utility" in discerning norms of customary international law. *Sosa*, 542 U.S. at 734 (discussing the limited utility of the Universal Declaration of Human Rights, G.A. Res. 217A (III), U.N. Doc. A/810 (1948)).[2]

In this Circuit we have long recognized as authoritative the sources of international law identified in Article 38 of the Statute of the International Court of Justice ("ICJ Statute"). *See Filartiga*, 630 F.2d at 880–81 & n. 8 (describing Article 38 as consistent with the Supreme Court's historical approach to sources of international law); *see also* J.L. Brierly, *The Law of Nations* 56 (Sir Humphrey Waldock ed., 6th ed.1963) (referring to Article 38 as "a text of the highest authority"); Restatement (Third) § 103 (describing similar sources as evidence of international law). . . .

A. International Tribunals

Insofar as international tribunals are established for the specific purpose of imposing liability on those who violate the law of nations, the history and conduct of those tribunals is instructive. We find it particularly significant, therefore, that no international tribunal of which we are aware has *ever* held a corporation liable for a violation of the law of nations.

. . .

---

[2] Our holding in *Flores* is consistent with the Supreme Court's rejection of the proposition that the Universal Declaration of Human Rights is an authoritative source of customary international law. 414 F.3d at 259–62 (explaining that the Universal Declaration of Human Rights is "not [a] proper source[ ] of customary international law because [it is] merely aspirational and [was] never intended to be binding on member States of the United Nations"). And it is consistent with the views of several of our sister Circuits. *See, e.g., Igartúa-De La Rosa v. United States*, 417 F.3d 145, 150 (1st Cir.2005) (en banc) ("The Universal Declaration of Human Rights is precatory: that is, it creates aspirational goals but not legal obligations, even as between states."); *Haitian Refugee Ctr. v. Gracey*, 809 F.2d 794, 816 n. 17 (D.C.Cir.1987) (noting that the Universal Declaration of Human Rights "is merely a nonbinding resolution, not a treaty, adopted by the United Nations General Assembly").

Since Nuremberg, international tribunals have continually declined to hold corporations liable for violations of customary international law. For example, the charters establishing both the International Criminal Tribunal for the former Yugoslavia, or "ICTY," and the International Criminal Tribunal for Rwanda, or "ICTR," expressly confined the tribunals' jurisdiction to "natural persons." *See* International Criminal Tribunal for the Former Yugoslavia Statute, S.C. Res. 827, U.N. Doc. S/RES/827 (May 25, 1993), *adopting* The Secretary-General, Report Pursuant to Paragraph 2 of Security Council Resolution 808 ("Report of the Secretary-General"), art. 6, U.N. Doc. S/25704 (May 3, 1993) ("The International Tribunal shall have jurisdiction over *natural persons* . . . ."); Statute of the International Tribunal for Rwanda, art. 5, S.C. Res. 955, U.N. Doc. S/RES/955 (Nov. 8, 1994) (same); *cf. Khulumani*, 504 F.3d at 274 (Katzmann, J., concurring) ("[T]he ICTY Statute is particularly significant because the 'Individual Criminal Responsibility' section of that statute was intended to codify existing norms of customary international law.").

. . . .

More recently, the Rome Statute of the ICC also limits that tribunal's jurisdiction to "natural persons." *See* The Rome Statute of the International Criminal Court ("Rome Statute") art. 25(1), *opened for signature* July 17, 1998, 37 I.L.M. 1002, 1016; *see also* Albin Eser, *Individual Criminal Responsibility, in* 1 *The Rome Statute of the International Criminal Court* 767, 778 (Antonio Cassese et al. eds., 2002) ("[W]hen reading paragraphs (1), (2), and (3) of Article 25 of the ICC Statute together, there can be no doubt that by limiting criminal responsibility to individual natural persons, the Rome Statute implicitly negates – at least for its own jurisdiction – the punishability of corporations and other legal entities."). Significantly, a proposal to grant the ICC jurisdiction over corporations and other "juridical" persons was advanced by the French delegation, but the proposal was rejected. *See* Eser, *ante*, at 779. As commentators have explained, the French proposal was rejected in part because "criminal liability of corporations is still rejected in many national legal orders" and thus would pose challenges for the ICC's principle of "complementarity." *Id*; [other citations omitted] . . . For some delegations the whole notion of corporate criminal responsibility was simply 'alien', raising problems of complementarity." (emphasis added)). The history of the Rome Statute therefore confirms the absence of any generally recognized principle or consensus among States concerning corporate liability for violations of customary international law.

In sum, modern international tribunals make it abundantly clear that, since Nuremberg, the concept of corporate liability for violations of customary international law has not even begun to "ripen[ ]" into a universally accepted norm of international law. *Cf. The Paquete Habana*, 175 U.S. at 686 (explaining that a practice can "gradually ripen[ ] into a rule of international law" through "usage among civilized nations").

B. International Treaties

Treaties "are proper evidence of customary international law because, and insofar as, they create *legal obligations* akin to contractual obligations on the States parties to them." *Flores*, 414 F.3d at 256. Although all treaties ratified by more than one State provide *some* evidence of the custom and practice of nations, "a treaty will only constitute *sufficient proof* of a norm of *customary international law* if an overwhelming majority of States have ratified the treaty, *and* those States uniformly and consistently act in accordance with its principles." *Id.* (second emphasis added). . . . That a provision appears in one treaty (or more), therefore, is not proof of a well-established norm of *customary* international law.

One district court in our Circuit erroneously overvalued the importance of a number of international treaties in finding that corporate liability has attained the status of customary international law. *See Presbyterian Church of Sudan v. Talisman Energy, Inc.*, 244 F.Supp.2d 289, 316–17 (S.D.N.Y.2003) (denying defendants' motion to dismiss). *But see Presbyterian Church of Sudan v. Talisman Energy, Inc.*, 453 F.Supp.2d 633 (S.D.N.Y.2006) (granting summary judgment to defendants on different grounds), *affirmed by* 582 F.3d 244 (2d Cir.2009). None of the treaties relied upon in the district court's 2003 *Presbyterian Church* opinion has been ratified by the United States, and most of them have not been ratified by other States whose interests would be most profoundly affected by the treaties' terms.[3] *Cf. Flores*, 414 F.3d at 256–57.... Those treaties are therefore insufficient – considered either individually or collectively – to demonstrate that corporate liability is universally recognized as a norm of customary international law.

Even if those specialized treaties had been ratified by an "overwhelming majority" of states, *id.* at 256 – as some recent treaties providing for corporate liability have been, *see, e.g.*, Convention Against Transnational Organized Crime, art. 10(1), *adopted* Nov. 15, 2000, S. Treaty Doc. 108–16; Convention on Combating Bribery of Foreign Public Officials in International Business Transactions, art. 2, *done* Dec. 17, 1997, S. Treaty Doc. No. 105–43 – the fact that those treaties impose obligations on corporations in the context of the treaties' particular subject matter tells us nothing about whether corporate liability for, say, violations of *human rights*, which are not a subject of those treaties, is universally recognized as a norm of *customary international law.* Significantly, to find that a treaty embodies or creates a rule of customary international law would mean that the rule applies beyond the limited subject matter of the treaty and *to nations that have not ratified it. See* 1 *Oppenheim's International Law* § 626, at 1261. To construe those treaties as so-called "law-making" treaties – that is, treaties that codify existing norms of customary international law or crystallize an emerging rule of customary international law – would be wholly inappropriate and without precedent. *See id.* § 583, at 1203–04 (discussing "law-making" treaties).

As noted above, there is no historical evidence of an existing or even nascent norm of customary international law imposing liability on corporations for violations of human rights. It cannot be said, therefore, that those treaties on specialized questions codify an existing, general rule of customary international law. Nor can those recent treaties, in light of their limited number and specialized subject matter, be viewed as crystallizing an emerging norm of customary international law. *See id.* § 583, at 1204 (explaining that "relatively extensive participation in a treaty, coupled with a *subject matter of general significance* and stipulations which accord with the general sense of the international community, do establish for some treaties an influence far beyond the limits of formal participation in them" (footnote omitted)). Furthermore, even if, as a general rule, treaties on a specialized subject matter could be viewed as crystallizing a norm of customary international law (which they generally cannot), it would be inappropriate to do so in this case in light of the recent *express rejection* in major multilateral treaties of a norm of corporate liability in the context of human rights violations. *See, e.g.*, Rome Statute, *ante*, art. 25.

· · ·

... Provisions on corporate liability in a handful of specialized treaties cannot be said to have a "fundamentally norm-creating character." Moreover, as the history of the Rome Statute demonstrates, "still unresolved controversies as to the exact meaning and scope of this notion" of corporate liability "raise further doubts as to the potentially norm-creating character of the rule." *Id.* Accordingly, provisions imposing corporate liability in some recent specialized treaties have not established corporate liability as a norm of customary international law.

---

3 The district court relied on the following treaties: (1) Convention Concerning the Application of the Principles of the Right to Organise and to Bargain Collectively, *adopted* July 1, 1949, 96 U.N.T.S. 257 (not ratified by the United States); (2) Convention on Third Party Liability in the Field of Nuclear Energy, *done* July 29, 1960, amended Jan. 28, 1964, 956 U.N.T.S. 263 (not ratified by the United States, China, the Soviet Union, or Germany); (3) International Convention on Civil Liability for Oil Pollution Damage, *done* Nov. 29, 1969, 973 U.N.T.S. 3 (not ratified by the United States, China, or the Soviet Union)); (4) Vienna Convention on Civil Liability for Nuclear Damage, *done* May 21, 1963, 1063 U.N.T.S. 265 (not ratified by the United States, China, France, Germany, or the United Kingdom); (5) Convention Relating to Civil Liability in the Field of Maritime Carriage of Nuclear Material, *done* Dec. 17, 1971, 974 U.N.T.S. 255 (not ratified by the United States, China, the Soviet Union, or the United Kingdom); and (6) Convention on Civil Liability for Oil Pollution Damage Resulting from Exploration for and Exploitation of Seabed Mineral Resources, *done* Dec. 17, 1976, *reprinted at* 16 I.L.M. 1450 (signed by six States but ratified by none). *Presbyterian Church*, 244 F.Supp.2d at 317.

In reaching the contrary conclusion in *Presbyterian Church*, the judge to whom the case was originally assigned in the district court acknowledged that "most treaties *do not* bind corporations" but reasoned that "[i]f corporations can be liable for unintentional torts such as oil spills or nuclear accidents, *logic would suggest* that they can be held liable for intentional torts such as complicity in genocide, slave trading, or torture." *Presbyterian Church*, 244 F.Supp.2d at 317 (emphases added). In addition to the reasons discussed above, the district court's conclusion was flawed by its use of an improper methodology for discerning norms of customary international law: customary international law does not develop through the "logical" expansion of existing norms. *Cf. Yousef*, 327 F.3d at 103–04 ("The strictly limited set of crimes subject to universal jurisdiction cannot be expanded by drawing an analogy between some new crime . . . and universal jurisdiction's traditional subjects."). Rather, as the Supreme Court has explained, it develops, if at all, through the custom and practice "among civilized nations . . . gradually ripening into a rule of international law." *Sosa*, 542 U.S. at 715 (quoting *The Paquete Habana*, 175 U.S. at 686).[4]

. . .

We conclude, therefore, that the relatively few international treaties that impose particular obligations on corporations do not establish corporate liability as a "specific, universal, and obligatory" norm of customary international law. *Id.* at 732 (internal quotation marks omitted). Although those treaties suggest a trend towards imposing corporate liability in *some special* contexts, no trend is detectable outside such narrow applications in specialized treaties, and there is nothing to demonstrate that corporate liability has yet been recognized as a norm of the customary international law of human rights.

C. Works of Publicists

Although the works of publicists (*i.e.*, scholars or "jurists") can be a relevant source of customary international law, "[s]uch works are resorted to by judicial tribunals, not for the speculations of their authors concerning what the law ought to be, but for trustworthy evidence of what the law really is." *Sosa*, 542 U.S. at 734 (quoting *The Paquete Habana*, 175 U.S. at 700); *see also* ICJ Statute, *ante*, art. 38(1)(d), 59 Stat. at 1060 (directing the ICJ to apply "judicial decisions and the teachings of the most highly qualified publicists of the various nations, as *subsidiary means for the determination of rules of law*." (emphasis added)). . . .

In light of the evidence discussed above, it is not surprising that two renowned professors of international law, Professor James Crawford and Professor (now Judge) Christopher Greenwood, forcefully declared in litigation argued before this panel on the same day as this case, that customary

---

[4] Another district court in our Circuit has similarly allowed claims against corporate defendants to proceed under the ATS despite acknowledging the "strength of authority supporting" the argument that corporate liability is *not* recognized as a norm of customary international law. *In re Agent Orange Prod. Liability Litig.*, 373 F.Supp.2d 7, 56 (E.D.N.Y.2005) (Weinstein, J.); *id.* at 57 (noting that "in the Nuremberg trials, this point of lack of corporate liability appeared to have been explicitly stated"). Judge Weinstein rejected the argument that corporations cannot be liable under the ATS because, among other things, "[l]imiting civil liability to individuals while exonerating the corporation . . . *makes little sense* in today's world," and "[d]efendants present[ed] *no policy reason* why corporations should be uniquely exempt from tort liability under the ATS," and "even if it were not true that international law recognizes corporations as defendants" they could still be sued under the ATS because "an ATS claim is a federal common law claim and it is a bedrock tenet of American law that corporations can be held liable for their torts." *Id.* at 58, 59 (emphases added).

Customary international law, however, is developed through the customs and practices of States, not by what "makes . . . sense" to a judge, by the "policy reason[s]" recognized by a judge, or by what a judge regards as "a bedrock tenet of American law." *See Sosa*, 542 U.S. at 738 (refusing to accept plaintiff's argument because "in the present, imperfect world, it expresses an aspiration that exceeds any binding customary rule having the specificity we require"); *accord Nestle*, No. CV 05-5133, slip op. at 135 ("*Sosa* prohibits courts from substituting abstract aspirations – or even pragmatic concerns – in place of specific international rules.").

Nor is customary international law developed through "parity of reasoning," as some scholars have suggested. *See* Harold Hongju Koh, *Separating Myth from Reality About Corporate Responsibility Litigation*, 7 J. Int'l Econ. L. 263, 265 (2004) (suggesting that because corporations may have some "rights" under international law, "by parity of reasoning, they must have duties as well").

international law does not recognize liability for corporations that violate its norms. . . . *See* Declaration of James Crawford ¶ 10, *Presbyterian Church of Sudan v. Talisman Energy, Inc.*, No. 07-0016 (2d Cir. Jan. 22, 2009) (emphasis added); *see also* Second Declaration of Christopher Greenwood ¶ 13, *Presbyterian Church of Sudan v. Talisman Energy, Inc.*, No. 01 Civ. 9882 (S.D.N.Y. July 10, 2002). . . .

* * *

Together, those authorities demonstrate that imposing liability on corporations for violations of customary international law has not attained a discernible, much less universal, acceptance among nations of the world in their relations *inter se*. Because corporate liability is not recognized as a "specific, universal, and obligatory" norm, *see Sosa*, 542 U.S. at 732 (internal quotation marks omitted), it is not a rule of customary international law that we may apply under the ATS. Accordingly, insofar as plaintiffs in this action seek to hold only corporations liable for their conduct in Nigeria (as opposed to individuals within those corporations), and only under the ATS, their claims must be dismissed for lack of subject matter jurisdiction.

. . . .

Accordingly, the September 29, 2006, order of the District Court is AFFIRMED insofar as it dismissed some of plaintiffs' claims against the corporate defendants and REVERSED insofar as it declined to dismiss plaintiffs' remaining claims against the corporate defendants.

LEVAL, Circuit Judge, concurring only in the judgment:

The majority opinion deals a substantial blow to international law and its undertaking to protect fundamental human rights. According to the rule my colleagues have created, one who earns profits by commercial exploitation of abuse of fundamental human rights can successfully shield those profits from victims' claims for compensation simply by taking the precaution of conducting the heinous operation in the corporate form. Without any support in either the precedents or the scholarship of international law, the majority take the position that corporations, and other juridical entities, are not subject to international law, and for that reason such violators of fundamental human rights are free to retain any profits so earned without liability to their victims.

Adoption of the corporate form has always offered important benefits and protections to business – foremost among them the limitation of liability to the assets of the business, without recourse to the assets of its shareholders. The new rule offers to unscrupulous businesses advantages of incorporation never before dreamed of. So long as they incorporate (or act in the form of a trust), businesses will now be free to trade in or exploit slaves, employ mercenary armies to do dirty work for despots, perform genocides or operate torture prisons for a despot's political opponents, or engage in piracy – all without civil liability to victims. By adopting the corporate form, such an enterprise could have hired itself out to operate Nazi extermination camps or the torture chambers of Argentina's dirty war, immune from civil liability to its victims. By protecting profits earned through abuse of fundamental human rights protected by international law, the rule my colleagues have created operates in opposition to the objective of international law to protect those rights.

. . . In 2004, a substantial minority of the Supreme Court, in *Sosa v. Alvarez-Machain*, 542 U.S. 692, 124 S.Ct. 2739, 159 L.Ed.2d 718, would have essentially nullified the ATS and overturned the *Filartiga* line, by ruling that the ATS did no more than give courts jurisdiction, and that, absent further legislation establishing a legal claim, courts acting under ATS had no authority to grant any substantive relief. The majority of the Supreme Court, however, rejected that argument. The Court ruled that under the ATS, federal courts could award damages for violations of the law of nations. For those who believe the *Filartiga-Sosa* line represents a meaningful advance in the protection of human rights, the majority's decision here marks a very bad day.

To understand this controversy, it is important to understand exactly what is the majority's rule, how it functions, and in what circumstances. To begin, their rule relates to the most abhorrent conduct – those acts that violate norms of the international law of human rights. The ATS gives U.S. courts jurisdiction to award tort damages to aliens who are victims of such atrocities. According to the majority, in cases where the norms of the law of nations were violated by a corporation (or other juridical entity), compensatory damages *may be awarded under the ATS against the corporation's employees*, natural persons who acted in the corporation's behalf, *but not against the corporation* that commanded the atrocities and earned profits by committing them. The corporation, according to my colleagues, has not violated international law, and is indeed incapable of doing so because international law does not apply to the conduct of corporations. Accordingly, a corporation which has earned profits by abuse of fundamental human rights – as by slave trading – is free to retain those profits without liability.

While my colleagues see nothing strange or problematic in this conclusion, their position is that in any event they have no responsibility for it. They invoke the rule simply because, in their contention, it is commanded by the law of nations.

But there is no basis for this contention. No precedent of international law endorses this rule. No court has ever approved it,[5] nor is any international tribunal structured with a jurisdiction that reflects it. (Those courts that have ruled on the question have explicitly rejected it.) No treaty or international convention adopts this principle. And no work of scholarship on international law endorses the majority's rule. Until today, their concept had no existence in international law.

The majority contend, nevertheless, that unambiguous jurisprudence "lead[s] inescapably" to their conclusion. Maj. Op. 17. However, the reasoning that supports the majority's argument is, in my view, illogical, misguided, and based on misunderstandings of precedent.

The argument depends on its observation that international *criminal* tribunals have been established without jurisdiction to impose *criminal punishments* on corporations for their violations of international law. From this fact the majority contend an inescapable inference arises that international law does not govern corporations, which are therefore free to engage in conduct prohibited by the rules of international law with impunity.

There is no logic to the argument. The reasons why international tribunals have been established without jurisdiction to impose *criminal* liability on corporations have to do solely with the theory and the objectives of *criminal punishment*, and have no bearing on civil compensatory liability. The view is widely held among the nations of the world that criminal punishments (under domestic law, as well as international law) are inappropriate for corporations. This view derives from two perceptions: First, that criminal punishment can be theoretically justified only where the defendant has acted with criminal intent – a condition that cannot exist when the defendant is a juridical construct which is incapable of having an intent; and second, that criminal punishments are pointless and counterproductive when imposed on a fictitious juridical entity because they fail to achieve the punitive objectives of criminal punishment. For these reasons many nations in their domestic laws impose criminal punishments only on natural persons, and not on juridical ones. In contrast, the imposition of civil liability on corporations serves perfectly the objective of civil liability to compensate victims for the wrongs inflicted on them and is practiced everywhere in the world. The fact that international tribunals do not impose *criminal punishment* on corporations in no way supports the inference that corporations are outside the scope of international law and therefore can incur no *civil compensatory liability* to victims when they engage in conduct prohibited by the norms of international law.

---

[5] Since the writing of this opinion, in the few days before filing, a California district court dismissed an ATS action in part on the basis of its acceptance of the majority's view that customary international law does not apply to corporations. *Doe v. Nestle, S.A.*, No. CV 05-5133 SVW (JTLx), slip op. at 120 (C.D.Cal. Sept. 8, 2010). To the extent I note in various places throughout this opinion that no court has ever spoken favorably of the majority's proposition that corporations are exempt from the rules of international law, I modify that statement to except the opinion filed last week in California.

The majority next contend that international law does not distinguish between criminal and civil liability. This is simply incorrect. International law distinguishes clearly between them and provides differently for the different objectives of criminal punishment and civil compensatory liability.

The majority then argue that the absence of a universal practice among nations of imposing civil damages on corporations for violations of international law means that under international law corporations are not liable for violations of the law of nations. This argument is as illogical as the first and is based on a misunderstanding of the structure of international law. The position of international law on whether civil liability should be imposed for violations of its norms is that international law takes no position and leaves that question to each nation to resolve. International law, at least as it pertains to human rights, consists primarily of a sparse body of norms, adopting widely agreed principles prohibiting conduct universally agreed to be heinous and inhumane. Having established these norms of prohibited conduct, international law says little or nothing about how those norms should be enforced. It leaves the manner of enforcement, including the question of whether there should be private civil remedies for violations of international law, almost entirely to individual nations. While most nations have not recognized tort liability for violations of international law, the United States, through the ATS, has opted to impose civil compensatory liability on violators and draws no distinction in its laws between violators who are natural persons and corporations. The majority's argument that national courts are at liberty to award civil damages for violations of international law solely against natural persons and not against corporations has no basis in international law and, furthermore, nullifies the intention of international law to leave the question of civil liability to be decided separately by each nation.

The majority's asserted rule is, furthermore, at once internally inconsistent and incompatible with Supreme Court authority and with our prior cases that awarded damages for violations of international law. The absence of a universally accepted rule of international law on tort damages is true as to defendants who are natural persons, as well as to corporations. Because international law generally leaves all aspects of the issue of civil liability to individual nations, there is no rule or custom of international law to award civil damages in any form or context, either as to natural persons or as to juridical ones. If the absence of a universally accepted rule for the award of civil damages against corporations means that U.S. courts may not award damages against a corporation, then the same absence of a universally accepted rule for the award of civil damages against natural persons must mean that U.S. courts may not award damages against a natural person. But the majority opinion concedes (as it must) that U.S. courts may award damages against the corporation's employees when a corporation violates the rule of nations. Furthermore, our circuit and others have for decades awarded damages, and the Supreme Court in *Sosa* made clear that a damage remedy does lie under the ATS. The majority opinion is thus internally inconsistent and is logically incompatible with both Second Circuit and Supreme Court authority.

If past judges had followed the majority's reasoning, we would have had no Nuremberg trials, which for the first time imposed criminal liability on natural persons complicit in war crimes; no subsequent international tribunals to impose criminal liability for violation of international law norms; and no judgments in U.S. courts under the ATS, compensating victims for the violation of fundamental human rights.

The rule in cases under the ATS is quite simple. The law of nations sets worldwide norms of conduct, prohibiting certain universally condemned heinous acts. That body of law, however, takes no position on whether its norms may be enforced by civil actions for compensatory damages. It leaves that decision to be separately decided by each nation. *See infra* Part III.B. The ATS confers on the U.S. courts jurisdiction to entertain civil suits for violations of the law of nations. In the United States, if a plaintiff in a suit under the ATS shows that she is the victim of a tort committed in violation of the norms of the law of nations, the court has jurisdiction to hear the case and to award compensatory damages against the tortfeasor. That is what the Supreme Court explained in *Sosa*. No principle of domestic or international law supports the majority's conclusion that the norms enforceable through the ATS – such as the prohibition by international law of genocide, slavery, war crimes, piracy, etc. – apply only to natural persons and not to corporations, leaving corporations immune from suit and free to retain profits earned through such acts.

I am in full agreement that *this* Complaint must be dismissed. It fails to state a proper legal claim of entitlement to relief. The Complaint alleges that the Appellants – the parent holding companies at the apex of the huge Royal Dutch Shell international, integrated oil enterprise – are liable under the ATS on the theory that their actions aided the government of Nigeria in inflicting human rights abuses on the Ogoni peoples in the jungles of Nigeria. The allegations fall short of mandatory pleading standards. We recently held in *Presbyterian Church of Sudan v. Talisman Energy, Inc.*, 582 F.3d 244 (2d Cir.2009), that liability under the ATS for *aiding and abetting* in a violation of international human rights lies only where the aider and abettor acts *with a purpose* to bring about the abuse of human rights. Furthermore, the Supreme Court ruled in *Ashcroft v. Iqbal*, – U.S. –, 129 S.Ct. 1937, 173 L.Ed.2d 868 (2009), that a complaint is insufficient as a matter of law unless it pleads specific facts supporting a plausible inference that the defendant violated the plaintiff's legal rights. Putting together these two rules, the complaint in this action would need to plead specific facts that support a plausible inference that the appellants aided the government of Nigeria *with a purpose* to bring about the Nigerian government's alleged violations of the human rights of the plaintiffs. As explained in greater detail below, . . . the allegations of the Complaint do not succeed in meeting that test. I therefore agree with the majority that the claims against the Appellants must be dismissed, but not on the basis of the supposed rule of international law the majority has fashioned.

. . . .

The majority's interpretation of international law, which accords to corporations a free pass to act in contravention of international law's norms, conflicts with the humanitarian objectives of that body of law. In order to understand the majority's rule, I explore a handful of concrete examples of how it would operate. Because the liability, if any, of a corporation for violations of international law is likely to arise in two somewhat different contexts – that in which the corporation *itself* inflicts humanitarian abuses, and that in which the corporation *aids and abets* a local government's infliction of the abuses – and because the pertinent considerations in these two circumstances are somewhat different, I discuss them separately.

1) *Direct commission of heinous offenses by corporations*

   a) *Slave trading and exploitation of slaves.* Among the focuses of the Nuremberg trials was the exploitation of slave labor by the I.G. Farbenindustrie Aktiengesellschaft ("Farben") and other German companies. The Farben corporation itself was not on trial, as the proceeding was brought solely against its executives for their complicity in the offenses committed by the corporation. Nevertheless, the tribunal found that Farben's program of exploitation of slave labor violated the standards of international law. Because the Nuremberg tribunal was established with only criminal, and not civil, jurisdiction, it never contemplated imposing civil liability on offenders. No civil proceedings of any kind were brought in that tribunal by the victims of Farben's violations against either natural or juridical persons. The question thus did not arise at Nuremberg whether international law countenances the imposition of civil liability on a corporation or on any other type of actor for exploitation of slave labor. . . .

   b) *Piracy.* Once thought to have faded into a past remembered only in romanticized children's fables and Gilbert & Sullivan whimsy, piracy now reemerges as a threat to international trade. In Somalia, pirates seize vessels in the Indian Ocean and exact large ransom payments from the owners and insurers. In the port of Lagos, Nigeria, armed pirates board anchored vessels waiting for access to the harbor and steal their cargo. My colleagues' new rule offers secure protection for the profits of piracy so long as the perpetrators take the precaution to incorporate the business.

The majority opinion goes still further. Because it claims that juridical entities are not "subjects" of international law and have neither rights nor obligations under it, they can neither sue nor be sued for violations of international law. Accordingly, the seizure by pirates of a vessel *owned by a corporation* (as virtually all commercial vessels are) would not violate international law's prohibition of piracy, and the vessel's corporate owner, from which a ransom had been extorted as the price of freeing its ship, would have no remedy under the ATS or any other comparable provision in any other nation.

c) *Genocide.* A number of the cases brought before our courts under the ATS, including this one, are brought against business corporations engaged in extraction of precious resources from mines, wells, or forests in remote, sparsely populated areas. At times, local tribesmen harass and hinder the corporation's operations, resenting the despoliation of their habitat and the failure to share with them the wealth taken from what they see as their land. The corporation solicits the protection of that nation's police or military forces. Most of the suits we have seen, like this one, have accused the defendant corporations of aiding and abetting the local government in the latter's abuse of the rights of those indigenous persons.

Such a company, however, failing to receive adequate protection from the local authorities, might mount its own protective security force and proceed, either independently or working together with forces of the local government, to exterminate the troublemaking tribes. The complaint under ATS in such a case would charge that the corporation *itself* committed genocide in order to protect its business operations from harassment and increase its profits.

Under the majority's rule, such a corporation would never need to test in court whether it in fact exterminated a tribe, as alleged. It could simply move for the dismissal of the suit, asserting that it is a corporation and therefore by definition could not have violated international law's prohibition of genocide. The plaintiffs could bring a successful ATS suit against the hirelings who carried out the genocide for the corporation (in the unlikely event they could be sued in a court that provided for civil liability). But as for the corporation itself, which committed a genocide to increase its profits, the suit will be dismissed on the ground that the defendant is a corporation.

2) *Aiding and abetting*

As just noted, a number of suits, like this one, charge corporations engaged in the extraction of precious resources in remote places with having *aided and abetted* abuses committed by a foreign government's police or military forces against local populations. In all likelihood, corporations like the defendants in this case, when they ask a relatively impecunious local government to render protection to the corporation's operations, will contribute money and resources to the local government to help it render the protection the corporation needs for its operations. If the government troops then commit atrocities, the victims might sue the corporation on the theory that it aided and abetted the government's brutalities by its contribution of money and resources. Similarly, business corporations engaged in finance or in the sale of food or military supplies might raise funds for, or sell supplies to, a government that is known to violate the law of nations. Victims of that government's abuses might sue the corporation, alleging that the corporation's profit-motivated provision of finance or supplies, done with awareness of the purchasing government's record of atrocities, constitutes aiding and abetting of those atrocities.

Many argue with considerable force that imposition of liability in such circumstances would go too far in impeding legitimate business, by making a business corporation responsible for the illegal conduct of local government authorities that is beyond the corporation's control, and which the corporation may even deplore. ...

... I]n *Talisman*, we ruled on whether a corporation could be held liable for aiding and abetting under the standards of international law merely because it knew that supplies it furnished to a local government would be used in the commission of human rights abuses. Although confronted with evidence of shocking human rights violations committed by the government of Sudan, we found that there is no such aiding and abetting liability.... [W]e concluded that the standards of international law admit of aiding and abetting liability only when the accused aider acts *with a purpose* to bring about the violations of international law. 582 F.3d at 259. In this circuit, supplying financing or military equipment to a local government will not support the imposition of aiding and abetting liability on the corporation for that government's abuses unless the corporation acted *with a purpose* to promote or advance those violations....

                                                    · · ·

... [W]hen one looks to international law to learn whether it imposes civil compensatory liability on those who violate its norms and whether it distinguishes between natural and juridical persons, the answer international law furnishes is that it takes no position on the question. What international law does is it prescribes norms of conduct. It identifies acts (genocide, slavery, war crimes, piracy, etc.) that it prohibits. At times, it calls for the imposition of criminal liability for violation of the law, whether by vesting a tribunal such as the ICC with jurisdiction to prosecute such crimes or by imposing on States a duty to make the crimes punishable under national law. The majority's proposition that one looks to the law of nations to determine whether there is civil liability for violation of its norms thus proves far less than the majority opinion claims. Yes – the question whether acts of any type violate the law of nations and give rise to civil damages is referable to the law of nations. And if the law of nations spoke on the question, providing that acts of corporations are not covered by the law of nations, I would agree that such a limitation would preclude suits under the ATS to impose liability on corporations.

But international law does not provide that juridical entities are exempt. And as for civil liability of both natural and juridical persons, the answer given by the law of nations (as discussed above) is that each State is free to decide that question for itself. While most nations of the world have not empowered their courts to impose civil liability for violations of law of nations, the United States, by enacting the ATS, has authorized civil suits for violation of the law of nations.

In short, the majority's contention that there can be no civil remedy for a violation of the law of nations unless that particular form of civil remedy has been adopted throughout the world misunderstands how the law of nations functions. Civil liability *under the ATS* for violation of the law of nations is not awarded because of a perception that international law commands civil liability throughout the world. It is awarded in U.S. courts because the law of nations has outlawed certain conduct, leaving it to each State to resolve questions of civil liability, and the United States has chosen through the ATS to impose civil liability. The majority's ruling defeats the objective of international law to allow each nation to formulate its own approach to the enforcement of international law.

                                                    · · · ·

VII. The Complaint must be dismissed because its factual allegations fail to plead a violation of the law of nations.

Although I do not share my colleagues' understanding of international law, I am in complete agreement that the claims against Appellants must be dismissed. That is because the pertinent allegations of the Complaint fall short of mandatory standards established by decisions of this court and the Supreme Court. We recently held in *Presbyterian Church of Sudan v. Talisman Energy, Inc.*, 582 F.3d 244 (2d Cir.2009), that liability under the ATS for *aiding and abetting* in a violation of international human rights lies only where the aider and abettor acts *with a purpose* to bring about the abuse of human rights. *Id.* at 259. Furthermore, the Supreme Court ruled in *Ashcroft v. Iqbal*, – U.S. –, 129 S.Ct. 1937, 173 L.Ed.2d 868 (2009), that a complaint is insufficient as a matter of law unless it pleads specific facts that "allow[ ] the court to draw the reasonable inference that the defendant is liable for the misconduct alleged." *Id.* at 1949. When read together, *Talisman* and *Iqbal* establish a requirement that, for a complaint to properly allege a defendant's complicity in human rights abuses perpetrated by officials of a foreign government, it must plead specific facts supporting a reasonable inference that the defendant acted with a purpose of bringing about the abuses. The allegations against Appellants in these appeals do not satisfy this standard. While the Complaint plausibly alleges that Appellants knew of human rights abuses committed by officials of the government of Nigeria and took actions which contributed indirectly to the commission of those offenses, it does not contain allegations supporting a reasonable inference that Appellants acted with a purpose of bringing about the alleged abuses.

. . . . The Complaint pleads in a general manner that Shell

willfully . . . aided and abetted SPDC and the Nigerian military regime in the joint plan to carry out a deliberate campaign of terror and intimidation through the use of extrajudicial killings, torture, arbitrary arrest and detention, military assault against civilians, cruel, inhuman and degrading treatment, crimes against humanity, forced exile, restrictions on assembly and the confiscation and destruction of private and communal property, all for the purpose of protecting Shell property and enhancing SPDC's ability to explore for and extract oil from areas where Plaintiffs and members of the Class resided.

It pleads also in conclusory form that the Nigerian military's campaign of violence against the Ogoni was "instigated, planned, facilitated, conspired and cooperated in" by Shell. Such pleadings are merely a conclusory accusation of violation of a legal standard and do not withstand the test of *Twombly* and *Iqbal*. They fail to "state a claim upon which relief can be granted." . . .

The Complaint goes on to assert (1) that SPDC and Shell met in Europe in February 1993 and "formulate[d] a strategy to suppress MOSOP and to return to Ogoniland," (2) that "[b]ased on past behavior, Shell and SPDC knew that the means to be used [by the Nigerian military] in that endeavor would include military violence against Ogoni civilians," and (3) that "Shell and SPDC" provided direct, physical support to the Nigerian military and police operations conducted against the Ogoni by, for example, providing transportation to the Nigerian forces; utilizing Shell property as a staging area for attacks; and providing food, clothing, gear, and pay for soldiers involved.

These allegations are legally insufficient to plead a valid claim of aiding and abetting because they do not support a reasonable inference that Shell provided substantial assistance to the Nigerian government *with a purpose to advance or facilitate* the Nigerian government's violations of the human rights of the Ogoni people. As outlined in Judge Katzmann's opinion in *Khulumani*, 504 F.3d 254, and adopted as the grounds of our recent decision in *Talisman*, 582 F.3d 244, "a defendant may be held liable under international law for aiding and abetting the violation of that law by another [only if] the defendant (1) provides practical assistance to the principal which has a substantial effect on the perpetration of the crime, and (2) does so with the *purpose* of facilitating the commission of that crime." *Id.* at 258 (emphasis added) (quoting *Khulumani*, 504 F.3d at 277).

The allegation that representatives of Shell and its Nigerian subsidiary met in Europe "to formulate a strategy to suppress MOSOP and to return to Ogoniland" implies neither an intent to violate human rights nor the provision of substantial assistance in human rights abuses. Neither of the alleged goals   to "suppress MOSOP" and "return to Ogoniland" – implies that human rights abuses would be involved in carrying them out. The additional allegation that Shell "knew" the Nigerian military would use "military violence against Ogoni civilians" as part of the effort to suppress MOSOP also does not support an inference that Shell *intended* for such violence to occur. As *Talisman* made clear, proof that a private defendant knew of the local government's intent to violate the law of nations is not sufficient to support aider and abetter liability. *Talisman*, 582 F.3d at 259.

The further allegations of providing physical support to the operations of the Nigerian military and police, including transportation, use of SPDC property for staying, food, clothing, gear, and pay for soldiers fail for the same reasons as those which compelled the award of judgment to the defendant in *Talisman*. In *Talisman*, the evidence showed that Talisman Energy, an oil developer with operations in Sudan, had improved roads and air strips used by the Sudanese military to stage attacks on civilians, paid royalties to the Sudanese government, and provided fuel for military aircraft that participated in bombing missions. *Talisman*, 582 F.3d at 261–62. We ruled that the suit could not be maintained because the evidence failed to show a *purpose* of facilitating the Sudanese government's human rights abuses. The plaintiffs' evidence showed that the oil company provided assistance to the Sudanese government in order to receive security required for the defendant's oil exploration, and was sufficient to show the assistance was provided with *knowledge* that the Sudanese government would use the defendant's assistance in the infliction of human rights abuses. The evidence, however, was insufficient to support the inference of a *purpose* on the defendant's part to facilitate human rights abuses. *Id.*

Similarly, in this case, Shell is alleged to have provided financial support and other assistance to the Nigerian forces with knowledge that they would engage in human rights abuses. But the Complaint fails to allege facts (at least sufficiently to satisfy the *Iqbal* standard) showing a purpose to advance or facilitate human rights abuses. The provision of assistance to the Nigerian military with *knowledge* that the Nigerian military would engage in human rights abuses does not support an inference of a purpose on Shell's part to advance or facilitate human rights abuses. An enterprise engaged in finance may well provide financing to a government, in order to earn profits derived from interest payments, with the knowledge that the government's operations involve infliction of human rights abuses. Possession of such knowledge would not support the inference that the financier acted with a purpose to advance the human rights abuses. Likewise, an entity engaged in petroleum exploration and extraction may well provide financing and assistance to the local government in order to obtain protection needed for the petroleum operations with knowledge that the government acts abusively in providing the protection. Knowledge of the government's repeated pattern of abuses and expectation that they will be repeated, however, is not the same as a purpose to advance or facilitate such abuses, and the difference is significant for this inquiry.

In sum, the pleadings do not assert facts which support a plausible assertion that Shell rendered assistance to the Nigerian military and police for the purpose of facilitating human rights abuses, as opposed to rendering such assistance *for the purpose* of obtaining protection for its petroleum operations with awareness that Nigerian forces would act abusively. In circumstances where an enterprise requires protection in order to be able to carry out its operations, its provision of assistance to the local government in order to obtain the protection, even with knowledge that the local government will go beyond provision of legitimate protection and will act abusively, does not without more support the inference of a purpose to advance or facilitate the human rights abuses and therefore does not justify the imposition of liability for aiding and abetting those abuses.[54]

b) Vicarious liability of shell for the acts of SPDC. In addition to asserting Shell's liability for its own acts of aiding and abetting in human rights violations, the Complaint asserts that Shell is liable for the acts of its subsidiary SPDC, either as an alter ego or as a principal for the acts of its agent because Shell "dominated and controlled SPDC." "It is a general principle of corporate law deeply ingrained in our economic and legal systems that a parent corporation ... is not liable for the acts of its subsidiaries." *United States v. Bestfoods*, 524 U.S. 51, 61, 118 S.Ct. 1876, 141 L.Ed.2d 43 (1998). However, this principle of corporate separateness may be disregarded when a subsidiary acts as an agent of its parent. *See Kingston Dry Dock Co. v. Lake Champlain Transp. Co.*, 31 F.2d 265, 267 (2d Cir.1929) (L. Hand, J.). ... A principal may also be liable for the unauthorized acts of its agent if, for example, the agent's conduct is aided by the existence of the agency relationship, Restatement (Second) of Agency § 216 cmt. a, or the principal ratifies the agent's acts, *Phelan v. Local 305 of United Ass'n of Journeymen*, 973 F.2d 1050, 1062 (2d Cir.1992).

A parent corporation may also be held liable for the acts of its subsidiary when the subsidiary is merely an alter ego of the parent. Alter ego liability exists when a parent or owner uses the corporate form "to achieve fraud, or when the corporation has been so dominated by an individual or another corporation (usually a parent corporation), and its separate identity so disregarded, that it primarily transacted the dominator's business rather than its own." *Gartner v. Snyder,* 607 F.2d 582, 586 (2d Cir.1979) (interpreting New York law). In deciding whether to pierce the corporate veil, "courts look to a variety of factors, including the intermingling of corporate and [shareholder] funds, undercapitalization of the corporation, failure to observe corporate formalities such as the maintenance of separate books and records, failure to pay dividends, insolvency at the time of a transaction, siphoning off of funds by the dominant shareholder, and the inactivity of other officers and directors." *Bridgestone/Firestone, Inc. v. Recovery Credit Servs., Inc.,* 98 F.3d 13, 18 (2d Cir.1996).

The Complaint alleges that, "[s]ince operations began in Nigeria in 1958, Shell has dominated and controlled SPDC." This conclusory allegation does not satisfy the *Iqbal* requirement to plead facts that plausibly support an inference that would justify disregard of the corporate form or a finding of an agency relationship. The further allegations described above – that Shell and SPDC representatives met in Europe after November 1992 to discuss strategies for suppressing MOSOP and that SPDC did certain acts with the approval of Shell – are likewise insufficient.

Ordinarily, subsidiary corporations are not deemed to be the agents of their corporate parents. *See Kingston Dry Dock,* 31 F.2d at 267 ("Control through the ownership of shares does not fuse the corporations, even when the directors are common to each."). The Complaint does not even plead that Shell and SPDC had an agreement establishing an agency relationship. *Cf. Cleveland v. Caplaw Enters.,* 448 F.3d 518, 523 (2d Cir.2006) (finding a pleading of corporate agency adequate where the complaint incorporated by reference an agency agreement). Nor does it plead facts showing that they conducted their operations in an agency relationship. The allegations that Shell approved certain conduct undertaken by SPDC does not show an agency relationship.

. . . The mere allegation that "Shell and SPDC" engaged in certain conduct does not plausibly plead specific facts which would justify treating SPDC as the alter ego of Shell.

Accordingly, on the facts alleged, the Complaint fails to plead a basis for a claim of agency or alter ego liability.

Conclusion

For the foregoing reasons, I agree with the majority that all of the claims pleaded against the Appellants must be dismissed. I cannot, however, join the majority's creation of an unprecedented concept of international law that exempts juridical persons from compliance with its rules. The majority's rule conflicts with two centuries of federal precedent on the ATS, and deals a blow to the efforts of international law to protect human rights.

Flores v. Southern Peru Copper Corp.,
414 F.3d 233 (2nd Cir. 2003) (footnotes omitted)

José A. Cabranes, *Circuit Judge*:

The question presented is whether plaintiffs' claims are actionable under the Alien Tort Claims Act ("ATCA"), 28 U.S.C. § 1350.

Plaintiffs in this case are residents of Ilo, Peru, and the representatives of deceased Ilo residents. They brought personal injury claims under the ATCA against Southern Peru Copper Corporation ("SPCC"), a United States company, alleging that pollution from SPCC's copper mining, refining, and smelting operations in and around Ilo caused plaintiffs' or their decedents' severe lung disease. The ATCA states that "the district courts shall have original jurisdiction of any civil action by an alien for a tort only, committed in violation of the law of nations or a treaty of the United States." 28 U.S.C. § 1350. Plaintiffs claimed that defendant's conduct violates the "law of nations" – commonly referred to as "international law" or, when limited to non-treaty law, as "customary international law." In particular, they asserted that defendant infringed upon their customary international law "right to life," "right to health," and right to "sustainable development."

The United States District Court for the Southern District of New York (Charles S. Haight, Jr., *Judge*), held that plaintiffs . . . had not alleged a violation of customary international law – *i.e.*, that they had not "demonstrated that high levels of environmental pollution within a nation's borders, causing harm to human life, health, and development, violate well-established, universally recognized norms of international law." *Flores v. Southern Peru Copper Corp.*, 253 F. Supp. 2d 510, 525 (S.D.N.Y. 2002) (internal quotation marks omitted). . . .

. . .

The ATCA permits an alien to assert a cause of action in tort for violations of a treaty of the United States and for violations of "the law of nations," which, as used in this statute, refers to the body of law known as customary international law. The determination of what offenses violate customary international law, however, is no simple task. Customary international law is discerned from myriad decisions made in numerous and varied international and domestic arenas. Furthermore, the relevant evidence of customary international law is widely dispersed and generally unfamiliar to lawyers and judges. These difficulties are compounded by the fact that customary international law – as the term itself implies – is created by the general customs and practices of nations and therefore does not stem from any single, definitive, readily-identifiable source. All of these characteristics give the body of customary international law a "soft, indeterminate character," . . . that is subject to creative interpretation. . . . Accordingly, in determining what offenses violate customary international law, courts must proceed with extraordinary care and restraint. . . .

. . .

First, in order for a principle to become part of customary international law, States must universally abide by it. Of course, States need not be universally successful in implementing the principle in order for a rule of customary international law to arise. If that were the case, there would be no need for customary international law. But the principle must be more than merely professed or aspirational.

Furthermore, a principle is only incorporated into customary international law if States accede to it out of a sense of legal obligation. Practices adopted for moral or political reasons, but not out of a sense of legal obligation, do not give rise to rules of customary international law.

Finally, customary international law addresses only those "wrongs" that are "of *mutual*, and not merely *several*, concern" to States. Matters of "mutual" concern between States are those involving States' actions "performed . . . towards or with regard to the other," XV Oxford English Dictionary 154 (2d ed. 1989) – matters that . . . concern the dealings of States "inter se," Matters of "several" concern among States are matters in which States are separately and independently interested. *See* XV Oxford English Dictionary 97 (2d ed. 1989) (defining "several" as having "a position, existence, or status apart[,] separate, [or] distinct" from one another).

Even if certain conduct is universally proscribed by States in their domestic law, that fact is not necessarily significant or relevant for purposes of customary international law. As we explained in *Filartiga* [*v. Pena-Irala*, 630 F.2d 876 (2d Cir. 1980)] and in *IIT v. Vencap, Inc.*, 519 F.2d 1001 (2d Cir. 1975):

> The mere fact that every nation's municipal [*i.e.*, domestic] law may prohibit theft does not incorporate "the Eighth Commandment, "Thou Shalt not steal" . . . [into] the law of nations." It is only where the nations of the world have demonstrated that *the wrong is of mutual, and not merely several, concern, by means of express international accords*, that a wrong generally recognized becomes an international law violation within the meaning of the statute.

Filartiga, 630 F.2d at 888 (quoting *Vencap*, 519 F.2d at 1015) (emphasis added). Therefore, for example, murder of one private party by another, universally proscribed by the domestic law of all countries (subject to varying definitions), is not actionable under the ATCA as a violation of customary international law because the "nations of the world" have not demonstrated that this wrong is "of mutual, and not merely several, concern." *Id.* By contrast, other offenses that may be purely intra-national in their execution, such as official torture, extrajudicial killings, and genocide, do violate customary international law because the "nations of the world" have demonstrated that such wrongs are of "mutual . . . concern," *id*, and capable of impairing international peace and security.

. . .

In determining whether a particular rule is a part of customary international law – *i.e.*, whether States universally abide by, or accede to, that rule out of a sense of legal obligation and mutual concern – courts must look to concrete evidence of the customs and practices of States. As we have recently stated, "we look primarily to the formal lawmaking and official actions of States and only secondarily to the works of scholars as evidence of the established practice of States." *United States v. Yousef*, 327 F.3d 56, 103 (2d Cir. 2003).

In *United States v. Yousef*, we explained why the usage and practice of States – as opposed to judicial decisions or the works of scholars – constitute the primary sources of customary international law. In that case, we looked to the Statute of the International Court of Justice ("ICJ Statute") – to which the United States and all members of the United Nations are parties – as a guide for determining the proper sources of international law. . . .

Article 38 [of the ICJ statute] embodies the understanding of States as to what sources offer competent proof of the content of customary international law. It establishes that the proper *primary* evidence consists only of those "conventions" (that is, treaties) that set forth "rules expressly recognized by the contesting states," *id*. at 1(a) (emphasis added), "international custom" insofar as it provides "evidence of a general practice *accepted as law*," *id*. at 1(b) (emphasis added), and "the general principles of *law* recognized by civilized nations," *id*. at 1(c) (emphasis added). It also establishes that acceptable *secondary* (or "subsidiary") sources summarizing customary international law include "judicial decisions," and the works of "the most highly qualified publicists," as that term would have been understood at the time of the Statute's drafting. . . .

Without taking any view on the merits of different forms of scholarship, and recognizing the potential of theoretical work to advance scholarship, we note that compilations and digests are of greater value in providing "trustworthy evidence of what the law *really is*," whereas expressly theoretical or normative works make their contribution by setting forth the "speculations of . . . authors concerning what the law *ought to be*." *The Paquete Habana*, 175 U.S. 677, 700, 44 L. Ed. 320, 20 S. Ct. 290 (1900) (emphases added).

Notably absent from Article 38's enumeration of the sources of international law are conventions that set forth broad principles without setting forth specific rules – in the words of *Filartiga*, "clear and unambiguous" rules, 630 F.2d at 884. Such a regime makes sense because, as a practical matter, it is impossible for courts to discern or apply in any rigorous, systematic, or legal manner international pronouncements that promote amorphous, general principles. *See Beanal v. Freeport-McMoran, Inc.*, 197 F.3d 161, 167 (5th Cir. 1999) (concluding that customary international law cannot be established by reference to "abstract rights and liberties devoid of articulable or discernable standards and regulations"). Moreover, as noted above, customs or practices based on social and moral norms, rather than international legal obligation, are not appropriate sources of customary international law because they do not evidence any intention on the part of States, much less the community of States, to be legally bound. *See, e.g.*, Clive Parry, *The Sources and Evidences of International Law* 2 (1965) ("The basis of international law as a system and of the rules of which it is composed is the consent of States.").

Our recapitulation of the proper sources of international law is not novel. As one eminent authority has observed, "the records or *evidence* of international law are the documents or acts proving the consent of States to its rules," and "among such records or *evidence*, treaties and *practice* play an essential part." *Id.* at 2. Professor Parry's statement of the proper evidence of customary international law correctly emphasizes that the "acts" and "practices" of States constitute the "essential" evidence of whether States follow a rule as a legal obligation. He also notes that recourse may be had to secondary sources such as "unilateral declarations, instructions to diplomatic agents, laws and ordinances, and *in a lesser degree*, to the writings of authoritative jurists" as evidence of the "acts" and "practices" of States.

In sum, those clear and unambiguous rules by which States universally abide, or to which they accede, out of a sense of legal obligation and mutual concern, constitute the body of customary international law. But where the customs and practices of States demonstrate that they do not universally follow a particular practice out of a sense of legal obligation and mutual concern, that practice cannot give rise to a rule of customary international law. . . .

III. Plaintiffs Have Failed to Allege a Violation of Customary International Law

Having established the proper framework for analyzing ATCA claims, we must now decide whether plaintiffs have alleged a violation of customary international law.

A. The Rights to Life and Health Are Insufficiently Definite to Constitute Rules of Customary International Law

As an initial matter, we hold that the asserted "right to life" and "right to health" are insufficiently definite to constitute rules of customary international law. As noted above, in order to state a claim under the ATCA, we have required that a plaintiff allege a violation of a "clear and unambiguous" rule of customary international law.

Far from being "clear and unambiguous," the statements relied on by plaintiffs to define the rights to life and health are vague and amorphous. For example, the statements that plaintiffs rely on to define the rights to life and health include the following:

Everyone has the right to a standard of living adequate for the health and well-being of himself and of his family. . . .

Universal Declaration of Human Rights, Art. 25, G.A. Res. 217A(III), U.N. GAOR, 3d Sess., U.N. Doc. A/810, at 71 (1948).

The States Parties to the present Covenant recognize the right of everyone to the enjoyment of the highest attainable standard of physical and mental health.

International Covenant on Economic, Social, and Cultural Rights, Art. 12, *opened for signature* Dec. 19, 1966, 993 U.N.T.S. 3, 6 I.L.M. 360.

Human beings are . . . entitled to a healthy and productive life in harmony with nature.

Rio Declaration on Environment and Development ("Rio Declaration"), United Nations Conference on Environment and Development, Rio de Janeiro, Brazil, June 13, 1992, Principle 1, 31 I.L.M. 874.

These principles are boundless and indeterminate. They express virtuous goals understandably expressed at a level of abstraction needed to secure the adherence of States that disagree on many of the particulars regarding how actually to achieve them. But in the words of a sister circuit, they "state abstract rights and liberties devoid of articulable or discernable standards and regulations." *Beanal*, 197 F.3d at 167. The precept that "human beings are . . . entitled to a healthy and productive life in harmony with nature," Rio Declaration, for example, utterly fails to specify what conduct would fall within or outside of the law. Similarly, the exhortation that all people are entitled to the "highest attainable standard of physical and mental health," International Covenant on Economic, Social, and Cultural Rights, proclaims only nebulous notions that are infinitely malleable.

In support of plaintiffs' argument that the statements and instruments discussed above are part of customary international law, plaintiffs attempt to underscore the universality of the principles asserted by pointing out that they "contain *no limitations as to how or by whom these rights may be violated.*" Pls.' Br. at 10 (emphasis added). However, this assertion proves too much; because of the conceded absence of any "limitations" on these "rights," they do not meet the requirement of our law that rules of customary international law be clear, definite, and unambiguous.

For the foregoing reasons, plaintiffs have failed to establish the existence of a customary international law "right to life" or "right to health."

B. Plaintiffs Have Not Submitted Evidence Sufficient to Establish that Customary International Law Prohibits Intranational Pollution

Although customary international law does not protect a right to life or right to health, plaintiffs' complaint may be construed to assert a claim under a more narrowly-defined customary international law rule against *intranational* pollution. However, the voluminous documents and the affidavits of international law scholars submitted by plaintiffs fail to demonstrate the existence of any such norm of customary international law.

1. Treaties, Conventions, and Covenants

Plaintiffs rely on numerous treaties, conventions, and covenants in support of their claims. Although these instruments are proper evidence of customary international law to the extent that they create legal obligations among the States parties to them, plaintiffs have not demonstrated that the particular instruments on which they rely establish a legal rule prohibiting intranational pollution.

Treaties, which sometimes are entitled "conventions" or "covenants," are proper evidence of customary international law because, and insofar as, they create *legal obligations* akin to contractual obligations on the States parties to them. Like contracts, these instruments are legally binding only on States that become parties to them by consenting to be bound. Under general principles of treaty law, a State's *signing* of a treaty serves only to "authenticate" its text; it "does not establish [the signatory's] consent to be bound." A State only becomes bound by – that is, becomes a party to – a treaty when it ratifies the treaty.[9] Accordingly, only States that have ratified a treaty are legally obligated to uphold the principles embodied in that treaty, and the treaty only evidences the customs and practices of those States.

All treaties that have been ratified by at least two States provide *some* evidence of the custom and practice of nations. However, a treaty will only constitute *sufficient proof* of a norm of customary international law if an overwhelming majority of States have ratified the treaty, *and* those States uniformly and consistently act in accordance with its principles. The evidentiary weight to be afforded to a given treaty varies greatly depending on (i) how many, and which, States have ratified the treaty, and (ii) the degree to which those States actually implement and abide by the principles set forth in the treaty. . . .

The treaties on which plaintiffs principally rely include: the International Covenant on Civil and Political Rights; the American Convention on Human Rights; the International Covenant on Economic, Social and Cultural Rights; and the United Nations Convention on the Rights of the Child.

The only treaty relied on by plaintiffs that the United States has ratified is the non-self-executing International Covenant on Civil and Political Rights ("ICCPR"), *opened for signature* Dec. 19,

---

[9] The United States becomes a "party" to a treaty–that is, becomes contractually bound to obey its terms–only when, upon concurrence of "two thirds of the Senators present," U.S. Const. art. II, § 2, cl. 2 the President ratifies the treaty.

1966, 999 U.N.T.S. 171, 6 I.L.M. 368.[10] In addition to the United States, 148 nations have ratified the ICCPR. Plaintiffs rely on Article 6(1) of the ICCPR, which states that "every human being has the inherent right to life" that "shall be protected by law," and that "no one shall be arbitrarily deprived of his life." As noted above, the "right to life" is insufficiently definite to give rise to a rule of customary international law. Because no other provision of the ICCPR so much as suggests an international law norm prohibiting intranational pollution, the ICCPR does not provide a basis for plaintiffs' claim that defendant has violated a rule of customary international law.

Similarly, the American Convention on Human Rights ("American Convention") does not assist plaintiffs because, while it notes the broad and indefinite "right to life," it does not refer to the more specific question of environmental pollution, let alone set parameters of acceptable or unacceptable limits. Moreover, the United States has declined to ratify the American Convention for more than three decades, indicating that this document has not even been universally embraced by all of the prominent States within the region in which it purports to apply.

Plaintiffs also rely on the unratified International Covenant on Economic, Social and Cultural Rights ("ICESCR"). This instrument arguably refers to the topic of pollution in article 12, which "recognizes the right of everyone to the enjoyment of the highest attainable standard of physical and mental health," and instructs the States parties to take the steps necessary for "the improvement of all aspects of environmental and industrial hygiene," *id.* art. 12(2) (b). Although article 12(2) (b) instructs States to take steps to abate environmental pollution within their borders, it does not mandate particular measures or specify what levels of pollution are acceptable. Instead, it is vague and aspirational, and there is no evidence that the States parties have taken significant uniform steps to put it into practice. Finally, even if this provision were sufficient to create a rule of customary international law, the rule would apply only to state actors because the provision addresses only "the steps to be taken *by the States Parties*," ICESCR art. 12(2) (emphasis added), and does not profess to govern the conduct of private actors such as defendant SPCC.

The last treaty on which plaintiffs principally rely is the United Nations Convention on the Rights of the Child, which has not been ratified by the United States. Plaintiffs rely on two sections of the Convention in support of their claims. First, they cite Article 24, section 1, of the Convention, which "recognizes the right of the child to the enjoyment of the highest attainable standard of health." This provision does not address the issue of intranational pollution. Moreover, it is extremely vague, clearly aspirational in nature, and does not even purport to reflect the actual customs and practices of States. Plaintiffs also cite Article 24, section 2(c) of the Convention, which instructs States to "take appropriate measures . . . to combat disease and malnutrition . . . through . . . the provision of adequate nutritious foods and clean drinking water, taking into consideration the dangers and risks of environmental pollution." While Article 24 of the Convention expressly addresses environmental pollution, it does not attempt to set its parameters or regulate it, let alone to proscribe it. . . . Moreover, as with Article 12 of the ICESCR, this provision only addresses concerns as to which "appropriate measures" are to be taken *by States themselves*, and does not profess to govern the conduct of private parties such as defendant SPCC.

For the foregoing reasons, the treaties, conventions or covenants relied on by plaintiffs do not support the existence of a customary international law rule against intranational pollution.

2. Non-Binding General Assembly Declarations

Plaintiffs rely on several resolutions of the United Nations General Assembly in support of their assertion that defendant's conduct violated a rule of customary international law.[11] These

---

[10] The U.S. Senate gave its advice and consent to ratification of the ICCPR on April 2, 1992, and [it] was ratified by the President on June 8, 1992. However, the treaty was ratified with numerous reservations conforming the United States' obligations under the ICCPR to the requirements of the Constitution, and with the declaration that the ICCPR is not self-executing.

[11] General Assembly documents cited by plaintiffs in their briefs include the Universal Declaration of Human Rights, arts. 3 (right to life), 25 (right to health), and the World Charter for Nature.

documents are not proper sources of customary international law because they are merely aspirational and were never intended to be binding on member States of the United Nations.

The General Assembly has been described aptly as "the world's most important political discussion forum," but it is not a law-making body. General Assembly resolutions and declarations do not have the power to bind member States because the member States specifically denied the General Assembly that power after extensively considering the issue [prior to and during the founding of the United Nations]....

In sum, as described in *The Law of Nations*, the classic handbook by Professors Brierly and Waldock of Oxford University:

> All that the General Assembly can do is to discuss and recommend and initiate studies and consider reports from other bodies. It cannot *act* on behalf of all the members, as the Security Council does, and its decisions *are not directions telling the member states what they are or are not to do.*"

J.L. Brierly, *The Law of Nations* 110 (Sir Humphrey Waldock ed., 6th ed. 1963) (second emphasis added). Because General Assembly documents are at best merely advisory, they do not, on their own and without proof of uniform state practice, *see* notes 22 and 26, *ante*, evidence an intent by member States to be legally bound by their principles, and thus cannot give rise to rules of customary international law.

Our position is consistent with the recognition in *Filartiga* that the right to be free from torture embodied in the Universal Declaration of Human Rights has attained the status of customary international law. *Filartiga* cited the Universal Declaration for the proposition that torture is universally condemned, reasoning that "a [United Nations] declaration may *by custom* become recognized as [a] rule[]" of customary international law. The Court explained that non-binding United Nations documents such as the Universal Declaration "create[] an expectation of adherence," but they evidence customary international law only "insofar as the expectation is *gradually justified by State practice.*"

In considering the Universal Declaration's prohibition against torture, the *Filartiga* Court cited extensive evidence that States, in their domestic and international practices, repudiate official torture....

In the instant case, the General Assembly documents relied on by plaintiffs do not describe the actual customs and practices of States. Accordingly, they cannot support plaintiffs' claims.

3. Other Multinational Declarations of Principle

In addition to General Assembly documents, plaintiffs rely on numerous other multinational "declarations" to substantiate their position that defendant's intranational pollution in Peru violated customary international law. A declaration, which may be made by a multinational body, or by one or more States, customarily is a "mere general statement of policy [that] is unlikely to give rise to... obligations in any strict sense." 1 *Oppenheim's International Law* 1189 (Sir Robert Jennings & Sir Arthur Watts, eds., 9th ed. 1996).... Such declarations are almost invariably political statements – expressing the sensibilities and the asserted aspirations and demands of some countries or organizations – rather than statements of universally-recognized legal obligations. Accordingly, such declarations are not proper evidence of customary international law.

Apart from the General Assembly documents addressed above, plaintiffs principally rely on two multinational declarations in support of their claims. First, they draw our attention to the American Declaration of the Rights and Duties of Man, promulgated by the Organization of American States ("OAS"). As one of our sister Circuits has correctly observed, the American Declaration "is an aspirational document which . . . did not on its own create any enforceable obligations on the part of any of the OAS member nations." *Garza v. Lappin*, 253 F.3d 918, 925 (7th Cir. 2001).

Plaintiffs also rely on Principle 1 of the Rio Declaration, which sets forth broad, aspirational principles regarding environmental protection and sustainable development. The Rio Declaration includes no language indicating that the States joining in the Declaration intended to be legally bound by it.

Because neither of these declarations created enforceable legal obligations, they do not provide reliable evidence of customary international law.

4. Decisions of Multinational Tribunals

Plaintiffs also rely on judicial decisions of international tribunals in support of their claims. In particular, they rely on decisions of the International Court of Justice, and on the European Court of Human Rights, a regional institution. But neither of these tribunals is empowered to create binding norms of customary international law....

... Accordingly, the international tribunal decisions cited by plaintiffs are not primary sources of customary international law. And while these decisions may constitute subsidiary or secondary sources insofar as they restate and apply the European Convention, nothing in that regional convention addresses pollution, let alone intranational pollution.

5. Expert Affidavits Submitted by Plaintiffs

Plaintiffs submitted to the District Court several affidavits by international law scholars in support of their argument that strictly *intranational* pollution violates customary international law. After careful consideration, the District Court declined to afford evidentiary weight to these affidavits....

Plaintiffs argue on appeal that the District Court did not accord proper weight to the statements of their experts. They maintain that "the authority of scholars, [and] jurists... has long been recognized by the Supreme Court and this Court as *authoritative sources* for determining the content of international law." Pls.' Br. at 19 (emphasis added). In support of this assertion, they rely upon the Supreme Court's decision in *The Paquete Habana*, 175 U.S. 677 (1900), as well as Article 38 of the ICJ Statute.

In its seminal decision in *Paquete Habana*, the Supreme Court designated "the works of jurists [*i.e.*, scholars] and commentators" as a possible source of customary international law. However, the Court expressly stated that such works "are resorted to by judicial tribunals, *not for the speculations of their authors concerning what the law ought to be*, but for trustworthy evidence of what the law *really is*." *Id.* (emphasis added), *quoted in Filartiga*, 630 F.2d at 881....

Similarly, Article 38 of the ICJ Statute does *not* recognize the writings of scholars as primary or independent sources of customary international law. Section 1(d) of Article 38 provides in pertinent part that courts may consult "the teachings of the most highly qualified publicists [*i.e.*, scholars or "jurists"] of the various nations, *as subsidiary means for the determination of rules of law*." ICJ Statute, June 26, 1945, art. 38(1) (d) (emphasis added).... The other three categories of evidence enumerated in Article 38 constitute primary sources of customary international law, but the works of scholars constitute subsidiary or secondary sources that may only be consulted "for trustworthy evidence" of what customary international law "really *is*."

... The Supreme Court and the drafters of Article 38 recognized the value of the role traditionally played by scholars in identifying and recording the practices of States and thereby revealing the development of customary international law rules. But neither *Paquete Habana* nor Article 38 recognizes as a source of customary international law the policy-driven or theoretical work of advocates that comprises a substantial amount of contemporary international law scholarship. Nor do these authorities permit us to consider personal viewpoints expressed in the affidavits of international law scholars....

Conclusion

For the reasons stated above, we affirm the judgment of the District Court dismissing plaintiffs' complaint for lack of jurisdiction and failure to state a claim under the ATCA.

Questions and Discussion

1. Why is an actionable claim related to environmental destruction rejected by the *Flores* court? Does a norm have to reach the level of *jus cogens* before a corporation can be sued under the ATS? In *Kiobel*, is it correct to import criminal standards of aiding and abetting into civil litigation? Do corporations now get a free ride in U.S. courts?
2. As the following case indicates, common law tort actions may also be brought, without reliance on the Alien Tort Statute. Could the result in *Flores* have influenced the decision on how to characterize this case and where to bring the action?

Provincial Government of Marinduque v. Placer Dome, Inc., Barrick Gold Corp., 582 F.3d 1083 (9th Cir. 2009)

McKEOWN, Circuit Judge:

Under the act of state doctrine, "the acts of foreign sovereigns taken within their own jurisdiction shall be deemed valid." *W.S. Kirkpatrick & Co. v. Environmental Tectonics Corp.*, 493 U.S. 400, 409, 110 S. Ct. 701, 107 L. Ed. 2d 816 (1990). Founded on international law, the doctrine also serves as a basis for federal-question jurisdiction when the plaintiff's complaint challenges the validity of a foreign state's conduct. We consider here whether the district court had subject-matter jurisdiction over this suit, based upon the act of state doctrine, such that removal from state to federal court was proper. Because none of the referenced conduct by the foreign sovereign-in this case, the Philippine government-is essential to any of the plaintiff's causes of action, we reverse the district court's exercise of subject-matter jurisdiction under the act of state doctrine.

BACKGROUND

The Provincial Government of Marinduque ("the Province") sued Placer Dome Corporation in 2005 in Nevada state court for alleged human health, ecological, and economic damages caused by the company's mining operations on Marinduque, an island province of the Republic of the Philippines. According to the complaint, Placer Dome severely polluted the lands and waters of Marinduque for some thirty years, caused two cataclysmic environmental disasters, poisoned the islanders by contaminating their food and water sources, and then left the province without cleaning up the mess-all in violation of Philippine law. The Province further alleges that Placer Dome received certain forms of assistance in its mining endeavors from the Philippine government. More particularly, the Province contends that former Philippine President Ferdinand Marcos, in exchange for a personal stake in the mining operations, eased various environmental protections obstructing Placer Dome's way.

The Province sued in Nevada because, according to the complaint, Placer Dome conducts significant and continuous business in the state.

Immediately after the Province filed suit, Placer Dome removed the case to federal district court for the District of Nevada on the basis of federal-question jurisdiction. Specifically, Placer Dome contended that the case "tender[ed] questions of international law and foreign relations." The Province moved for an order*1086 requiring Placer Dome to show cause why the action should not be remanded to the state court due to a lack of subject-matter jurisdiction. The district court denied the Province's motion, holding that federal-question jurisdiction existed under the act of state doctrine of the federal common law. Placer Dome moved to dismiss the suit for lack of personal jurisdiction and *forum non conveniens*. The district court granted limited discovery on personal jurisdiction.[12] Before discovery was concluded, in March 2007, the United States Supreme Court issued *Sinochem International Co. v. Malaysia International Shipping Corp.*, announcing that district courts have latitude to rule on the threshold issue of *forum non conveniens* before definitively ascertaining subject-matter and personal jurisdiction. 549 U.S. 422, 432, 127 S. Ct. 1184, 167 L. Ed. 2d 15 (2007). The district court stayed jurisdictional discovery, and ordered briefing on the issue of *forum non conveniens*. Invoking *Sinochem*, the district court dismissed the matter on *forum non conveniens* grounds in favor of a Canadian forum. In ruling on the Province's motion for reconsideration, the district court affirmed its earlier conclusion that "subject matter jurisdiction does, in fact, exist in this case, based upon the act of state doctrine."

ANALYSIS

I. Removal to Federal Court

This case was removed from state to federal court under 28 U.S.C. § 1441(a)[13] on Placer Dome's representation that the Province's claims implicated the federal common law of foreign relations. Removal was proper only if the district court would have had original jurisdiction over the claims. Placer Dome asserted jurisdiction pursuant to 28 U.S.C. § 1331, which states that federal courts have jurisdiction over cases presenting questions of federal constitutional, statutory, and common law.

Federal courts may exercise federal-question jurisdiction over an action in two situations. First, and most commonly, a federal court may exercise federal-question jurisdiction if a federal right or immunity is "'an element, and an essential one, of the plaintiff's cause of action.'" *Franchise Tax Bd. v. Constr. Laborers Vacation Trust for S. Cal.*, 463 U.S. 1, 11, 103 S. Ct. 2841, 77 L. Ed. 2d 420 (1983) (quoting *Gully v. First National Bank*, 299 U.S. 109, 112, 57 S. Ct. 96, 81 L. Ed. 70 (1936)). Thus, the federal question on which jurisdiction is premised cannot be supplied via a defense; rather, the federal question must "be disclosed upon the face of the complaint, unaided by the answer." *Phillips Petroleum Co. v. Texaco, Inc.*, 415 U.S. 125, 127–28, 94 S. Ct. 1002, 39 L. Ed. 2d 209 (1974) (*per curiam*). Second, a federal court may have such jurisdiction if a state-law claim "necessarily raise[s] a stated federal issue, actually disputed and substantial, which a federal forum may entertain without disturbing any congressionally-approved balance of federal and state judicial responsibilities." *Grable & Sons Metal Prod., Inc. v. Darue Eng'g & Mfg.*, 545 U.S. 308, 314, 125 S. Ct. 2363, 162 L. Ed. 2d 257 (2005). Such a federal issue must be "a substantial one, indicating a serious federal interest in claiming the advantages thought to be inherent in a federal forum." *Id.* at 313, 125 S. Ct. 2363.

The removal statute is strictly construed against removal jurisdiction. *Syngenta Crop Prot., Inc. v. Henson*, 537 U.S. 28, 32, 123 S. Ct. 366, 154 L. Ed. 2d 368 (2002); *California ex rel. Lockyer v. Dynegy, Inc.*, 375 F.3d 831, 838 (9th Cir.2004). The defendant bears the burden of establishing that removal is proper. *Id.*

II. Determination of Removal Jurisdiction in Light of Sinochem

The question before us, then, is whether the district court had subject-matter jurisdiction under 28 U.S.C. § 1331. We review *de novo* a district court's determination that subject-matter

---

[12] Around this time, Barrick Gold Corporation was joined as a defendant because it had obtained a controlling 81 percent interest in Placer Dome. We refer to both defendants collectively as "Placer Dome."

[13] The removal statute provides that "any civil action brought in a State court of which the district courts of the United States have original jurisdiction, may be removed by the defendant or defendants, to the district court of the United States for the district and division embracing the place where such action is pending." 28 U.S.C. § 1441(a).

jurisdiction exists for a case that has been removed. *Schnabel v. Lui*, 302 F.3d 1023, 1029 (9th Cir. 2002).

Before considering this issue, we first address Placer Dome's assertion that the district court dismissed this case on *forum non conveniens* grounds without resolving the issue of subject-matter jurisdiction. According to Placer Dome, the district court exercised its discretion under the Supreme Court's decision in *Sinochem* "not [to] resolve whether it has authority to adjudicate the cause (subject-matter jurisdiction) or personal jurisdiction over the defendant if it determines that, in any event, a foreign tribunal is plainly the more suitable arbiter of the merits of the case." 549 U.S. at 425, 127 S. Ct. 1184. If the district court did not determine subject-matter jurisdiction, Placer Dome intimates, then we are presented with only the *forum non conveniens* dismissal to review. Placer Dome further argues that, even if the district court concluded that subject-matter jurisdiction existed, that holding was alternative to the *forum non conveniens* determination.

We question whether *Sinochem* restricts our ability to address an issue of subject-matter jurisdiction, even if characterized as an alternative holding. "[W]e have an independent obligation to examine our own and the district court's jurisdiction." *Rivas v. Rail Delivery Serv., Inc.*, 423 F.3d 1079, 1082 (9th Cir.2005). That obligation necessarily carries with it the authority to determine for ourselves, under *Sinochem*, whether the jurisdictional issue should be addressed, regardless of the path the district court chose to take.

In any event, Placer Dome misapprehends the proceedings below. Following removal of this suit, the Province challenged the court's subject-matter jurisdiction. The district court agreed with Placer Dome that removal was proper, holding that the Province's allegations invoked the act of state doctrine and thus triggered federal-question jurisdiction. The district court arguably cast a shadow upon that conclusion when it dismissed the case on *forum non conveniens* grounds. However, in its final order denying the Province's motion for reconsideration, the district court clarified that it had inadvertently placed its subject-matter jurisdiction in doubt and explicitly affirmed its previous conclusion that the complaint presented federal questions under the act of state doctrine. Whether viewed as an alternative holding or not, it is abundantly clear that the district court concluded it had subject-matter jurisdiction over this suit.

In *Sinochem*, the Supreme Court considered whether a district court must first conclusively establish its own jurisdiction before dismissing a suit on the basis of *forum non conveniens*. Answering in the negative, the Court explained that, because jurisdiction is vital only if a court intends to render a determination on the merits of a case, "a federal court has leeway 'to choose among threshold grounds for denying audience to a case on the merits.' " 549 U.S. at 431, 127 S. Ct. 1184 (quoting *Ruhrgas AG v. Marathon Oil Co.*, 526 U.S. 574, 585, 119 S. Ct. 1563, 143 L. Ed. 2d 760 (1999)). And because a *forum non conveniens* dismissal is not a merits determination, the Court held that "[a] district court . . . may dispose of an action by a *forum non conveniens* dismissal, bypassing questions of subject-matter and personal jurisdiction, when considerations of convenience, fairness, and judicial economy so warrant." *Id.* at 432, 127 S. Ct. 1184. The court further observed:

> In the mine run of cases, jurisdiction "will involve no arduous inquiry" and both judicial economy and the consideration ordinarily accorded the plaintiff's choice of forum "should impel the federal court to dispose of [those] issue[s] first." *Ruhrgas*, 526 U.S. at 587–88, 119 S. Ct. 1563. But where subject-matter or personal jurisdiction is difficult to determine, and *forum non conveniens* considerations weigh heavily in favor of dismissal, the court properly takes the less burdensome course.

Id. at 436, 127 S. Ct. 1184 (alterations in original).

In *Sinochem*, the Supreme Court offered the lower courts a practical mechanism for resolving a case that would ultimately be dismissed. For a case originally filed in federal court, the result would be the same, whether dismissed on jurisdictional or *forum non conveniens* grounds-dismissal would be inevitable and conclusive. For a case originating in state court, however, the difference could be significant. If the federal court dismisses on *forum non conveniens* grounds, the case is dismissed. But if removal is improper, the case is remanded to the state court. Thus, in a removal scenario, the sequencing of the decision may have practical consequences.[14] In sum, *Sinochem* presents no bar to our reaching the issue of whether the Province's allegations invoke federal questions. Here, of course, the district court made a threshold determination that it had federal-question jurisdiction under the act of state doctrine, and it is to this question we now turn.

III. The Act of State Doctrine

Ultimately, the question of subject-matter jurisdiction here is not particularly complex. Although the Province's complaint is lengthy, we should not duck the jurisdictional analysis simply because we need to read and benchmark the allegations and claims against the act of state doctrine, a principle that is well established.

Although there is no general federal common law, there are enclaves of federal judge-made law. *Banco Nacional de Cuba v. Sabbatino*, 376 U.S. 398, 426, 84 S. Ct. 923, 11 L. Ed. 2d 804 (1964). One such enclave concerns the law of international relations and foreign affairs. *Id.* at 427, 84 S. Ct. 923. A long-standing common law principle, the act of state doctrine precludes courts from evaluating the validity of actions that a foreign government has taken within its own borders. *See W.S. Kirkpatrick*, 493 U.S. at 409, 110 S. Ct. 701; *Sabbatino*, 376 U.S. at 401, 84 S. Ct. 923; *Underhill v. Hernandez*, 168 U.S. 250, 252, 18 S. Ct. 83, 42 L. Ed. 456 (1897); *see also Timberlane Lumber Co. v. Bank of America*, 549 F.2d 597, 605–07 (9th Cir.1976) (recounting history of the doctrine); Born and Rutledge, *International Civil Litigation in United States Courts* 751–55 (2007) (same). The doctrine reflects the concern that the judiciary, by questioning the validity of sovereign acts taken by foreign states, may interfere with the executive branch's conduct of foreign policy. *W.S. Kirkpatrick*, 493 U.S. at 404, 110 S. Ct. 701.[15] As a result, the doctrine requires that the "official act of a foreign sovereign performed within its own territory" becomes "'a rule of decision for the courts of this country.'" *Id.* at 405, 110 S. Ct. 701 (quoting *Ricaud v. American Metal Co.*, 246 U.S. 304, 310, 38 S. Ct. 312, 62 L. Ed. 733 (1918)).

> [E]ven though the validity of the act of a foreign sovereign within its own territory is called into question, the policies underlying the act of state doctrine may not justify its application." *Id.* at 409, 110 S. Ct. 701 (citing *Sabbatino*, 376 U.S. at 428, 84 S. Ct. 923). The Supreme Court discussed three such policies in *Sabbatino*:

> [T]he greater the degree of codification or consensus concerning a particular area of international law, the more appropriate it is for the judiciary to render decisions regarding it.... [2] [T]he less important the implications of an issue are for our foreign relations, the weaker the justification for exclusivity in the political branches. [3] The balance of relevant considerations may also be shifted if the government which perpetrated the challenged act of state is no longer in existence.

Sabbatino, 376 U.S. at 428, 84 S. Ct. 923; *see also W.S. Kirkpatrick*, 493 U.S. at 409, 110 S. Ct. 701.

---

[14] *Sinochem* did not contemplate the issue of removal, perhaps because the suit under consideration was originally filed in federal court. *See id.* at 427, 127 S. Ct. 1184.

[15] The Supreme Court in *W.S. Kirkpatrick* recognized that "the jurisprudential foundation for the act of state doctrine has undergone some evolution over the years[,]" and explained that the doctrine "is not some vague doctrine of abstention but a *'principle of decision* binding on federal and state courts alike.'" 493 U.S. at 404, 406, 110 S. Ct. 701 (quoting *Sabbatino*, 376 U.S. at 427, 84 S. Ct. 923).

The Supreme Court's leading contemporary act of state decision – *W.S. Kirkpatrick* – encapsulated the doctrine in this way: "Act of state issues only arise when a court *must decide* – that is, when the outcome of the case turns upon – the effect of official action by a foreign sovereign. When that question is not in the case, neither is the act of state doctrine." *Id.* at 406, 110 S. Ct. 701.

We followed this approach to the doctrine in *Patrickson v. Dole Food Co.*, 251 F.3d 795 (9th Cir. 2001), in which we considered a complaint brought by Latin American banana workers who asserted state law claims against multinational fruit and chemical companies alleging exposure to toxic chemicals. Because "nothing in plaintiffs' complaint turns on the validity or invalidity of any act of a foreign state[,]" we rejected application of the act of state doctrine. *Id.* at 800.

The defendants in *Patrickson* argued that, despite there being no act of state issues on the surface of the banana workers' complaint, "the case concerns a vital sector of the economies of foreign countries and so has implications for our nation's relations with those countries." *Id.* We did not embrace that argument, parting ways with other circuits that had more broadly interpreted the doctrine as supplying federal-question jurisdiction over any case that might affect foreign relations regardless of whether federal law is raised in the complaint. *Sabbatino* did not create an exception to the well-pleaded complaint rule. *Id.* at 801–02. "What Congress has not done is to extend federal-question jurisdiction to all suits where the federal common law of foreign relations might arise as an issue. We interpret congressional silence outside these specific grants of jurisdiction as an endorsement of the well-pleaded complaint rule." *Id.* at 803.

With *W.S. Kirkpatrick* and *Patrickson* lighting our way, we reach the heart of the matter.

IV. The Province's Complaint Does Not Implicate the Act of State Doctrine

The Province's complaint weaves together numerous allegations in a chronicle of skullduggery, toxic dumping, a collapsed dam that polluted the surrounding areas, a river flooded with poisonous mine tailings, and a corrupt government that facilitated this conduct. In sum, the Province alleges that Placer significantly harmed Marinduque and its people, including through the contamination and degradation of the environment, which in turn caused blood diseases, skin disorders, and stomach ailments among the islanders. And since Placer Dome left Marinduque in 1997, it has done nothing, according to the Province, to ameliorate the problems it created, and has actively evaded responsibility.

These allegations are the backdrop for thirteen causes of action under Philippine law: (1) violating the public trust; (2) reckless imprudence, in violation of the Philippine penal code; (3) simple imprudence, in violation of the Philippine penal code; (4) violations of the Philippine water code; (5) violations of a Philippine fisheries law; (6) and (7) violations of Philippine pollution control laws; (8) violations of a Philippine mining law; (9) quasi-delict (negligence); (10) quasi-delict (public and/or private nuisance); (11) and (12) breaches of contract; and (13) promissory estoppel. The Province claimed environmental, economic, and human health damages; the cost of medical monitoring and care; and the cost of environmental remediation. It prayed for injunctive relief as well as damages.

In removing this suit to federal court, Placer Dome asserted that the complaint tendered questions of international law and foreign relations that furnished the district court with federal-question jurisdiction. The district court agreed, concluding that "Plaintiff's Complaint is replete with allegations regarding the Philippine Government's activities, which contributed to the environmental harm that Plaintiff has suffered." In particular, the district court identified five allegations that, in its view, invoked the act of state doctrine: (1) President Marcos overturned a presidential proclamation to allow mining in a forest reserve; (2) Marcos, and subsequent to his removal, a presidential commission, owned 49 percent of the shares in Marcopper, a subsidiary of Placer Dome; (3) Marcos ordered a government commission to issue a permit allowing Marcopper to dump toxic tailings into Calancan Bay; (4) Marcos ordered the same pollution commission to remove restraints it had placed on Marcopper's dumping of waste into the bay; and (5) President Aquino ordered a pollution control board not to enforce a cease and desist order against Marcopper. Citing these same allegations, Placer Dome argues that the act of state doctrine bars this suit because the complaint is premised upon conduct that occurred pursuant to governmental permits and other acts or omissions by the Philippine government.

Fatal to the district court's removal jurisdiction, however, is that the act of state doctrine is implicated here only defensively and the complaint does not "necessarily raise a stated federal issue, actually disputed and substantial." *Grable*, 545 U.S. at 314, 125 S. Ct. 2363. As previously explained, "[t]o bring a case within the federal-question removal statute, a right or immunity created by the Constitution or laws of the United States must be an element,[16] and an essential one, of the plaintiff's cause of action." *Rivet v. Regions Bank of Louisiana*, 522 U.S. 470, 475, 118 S. Ct. 921, 139 L. Ed. 2d 912 (1998) (internal quotation marks omitted; alteration omitted). That is, "the presence or absence of federal-question jurisdiction is governed by the 'well-pleaded complaint rule,' which provides that federal jurisdiction exists only when a federal question is presented on the face of the plaintiff's properly pleaded complaint." *Id.* (internal quotation marks omitted). "A defense is not part of a plaintiff's properly pleaded statement of his or her claim." *Id.* (holding removal to federal court may not be predicated upon the defense that a claim is precluded by a prior federal judgment). Alternatively, the complaint must raise a "federal issue[] embedded in state-law claims" that meets the test set forth in *Grable*. 545 U.S. at 314, 125 S. Ct. 2363.

Here, none of the supposed acts of state identified by the district court is essential to the Province's claims. Nor do the other allegations in the complaint invoke an act of state as an essential element of any claim. Nor does the complaint "necessarily raise a stated federal issue, actually disputed and substantial." *Id.* To be sure, the complaint is sprinkled with references to the Philippine government, Philippine law, and the government's complicity in the claimed damage to the Marinduquenos. But the exercise of federal-question removal jurisdiction requires more-it requires the assertion of a federal question on the face of the Province's properly pleaded complaint or a disputed, substantial federal issue that does not disturb any congressionally-approved balances of state or federal judicial responsibilities. Just as raising the specter of political issues cannot sustain dismissal under the political question doctrine, neither does a general invocation of international law or foreign relations mean that an act of state is an essential element of a claim. *Cf. W.S. Kirkpatrick*, 493 U.S. at 409, 110 S. Ct. 701 (holding that federal courts ordinarily have the obligation to exercise their jurisdiction and "[t]he act of state doctrine does not establish an exception for cases and controversies that may embarrass foreign governments"); *Sabbatino*, 376 U.S. at 423, 84 S. Ct. 923 ("[I]t cannot of course be thought that 'every case or controversy which touches foreign relations lies beyond judicial cognizance.'") (quoting *Baker v. Carr*, 369 U.S. 186, 211, 82 S. Ct. 691, 7 L. Ed. 2d 663 (1962)); *Alperin v. Vatican Bank*, 410 F.3d 532, 537 (9th Cir.2005) (observing the justiciability inquiry under the political question doctrine is not applicable to every political case, but is limited to political questions).

Specifically, to prove that Placer Dome violated the various provisions of Philippine law that the Province sued under, such as reckless and simple imprudence, the Province need not prove the validity or invalidity of an act of state. For example, proving that Placer Dome was reckless

---

[16] Therefore, "[a]lthough the act of state doctrine generally serves as a defense, it can also be used affirmatively as the basis of a claim." *Patrickson*, 251 F.3d at 800 n. 2; *see also* Restatement (Third) of Foreign Relations Law § 443 cmt. i (1986) (noting that an act of state may be "necessary to a litigant's claim or defense"); *Republic of Philippines v. Marcos*, 806 F.2d 344, 354 (2d Cir.1986) ("We hold that federal jurisdiction is present in any event because the claim raises, as a necessary element, the question whether to honor the request of a foreign government that the American courts enforce the foreign government's directives to freeze property in the United States subject to future process in the foreign state.").

when it hastily built the Maguila-Guila dam, which allegedly collapsed only two years after being built, does not implicate, let alone require, any act of state. Rather, invocation of the act of state doctrine here would be via Placer Dome's defense to the Province's claims and as such cannot support removal jurisdiction. Nor has the Province "artfully pleaded" its claims to defeat removal by omitting necessary federal questions.[17]

A review of the district court's grounds for finding jurisdiction nicely illustrates the difference between alleging that governmental action led to the defendant's challenged conduct and determining whether that governmental action is a central element of the claim or its validity is actually disputed by the parties. Thus, for example, the claims that former President Marcos opened a forest reserve to mining or owned a high percentage of stock in the mining company or eased pollution restrictions are not elements of the Province's claim that pollution and dumping occurred, that Placer Dome violated Philippine mining, fishing, water and pollution law, or that it breached a contract with the Province. At best, the allegations regarding the Philippine government's involvement in Placer Dome's endeavors, if true, may serve as a defense to the Province's claims, and the validity of these governmental actions is not actually disputed. *See Rivet*, 522 U.S. at 475, 118 S. Ct. 921.

Our conclusion that the complaint does not require an application of the act of state doctrine is buttressed by the observation that some of the key considerations motivating the act of state doctrine carry little weight here. Consideration of how Marcos's corrupt actions facilitated environmental irresponsibility in pursuit of profit is not an inquiry likely to impact current foreign relations, and "the less important the implications of an issue are for our foreign relations, the weaker the justification for exclusivity in the political branches." *Sabbatino*, 376 U.S. at 428, 84 S. Ct. 923. Additionally, criticism of the actions of former Philippine regimes is less treacherous than reviewing the current government's actions, as "[t]he balance of relevant consideration may also be shifted if the government which perpetrated the challenged act of state is no longer in existence . . . for the political interest of the country may, as a result, be measurably altered." *Id.* Finally, as the Province points out, the Philippine government itself has openly condemned the conduct of its past president. *See also Republic of the Philippines v. Marcos*, 862 F.2d 1355, 1360–61 (9th Cir.1988) (*en banc*) ("*A fortiori*, when a ruler's former domain has turned against him and seeks the recovery of what it claims he has stolen, the classification [of Marcos's past acts as 'acts of state'] has little or no applicability."). Most important, the parties' dispute as framed by the complaint does not require us to pass on the validity of the Philippines' governmental actions.

In sum, our review of the complaint does not sustain Placer Dome's claim that the act of state doctrine is in play. Nothing in the complaint would require a court to pass judgment on any official act of the Philippine government. *See W.S. Kirkpatrick*, 493 U.S. at 405, 110 S. Ct. 701.

CONCLUSION

The Province's complaint does not present a federal question based upon the act of state doctrine. The district court therefore lacked subject-matter jurisdiction over this suit and removal from state court was improper. We reverse, vacate the *forum non conveniens* dismissal, and remand with instructions to remand to the state court.

---

[17] In *Rivet v. Regions Bank of Louisiana*, the Supreme Court explained:

> Allied as an "independent corollary" to the well-pleaded complaint rule is the further principle that a plaintiff may not defeat removal by omitting to plead necessary federal questions. If a court concludes that a plaintiff has "artfully pleaded" claims in this fashion, it may uphold removal even though no federal question appears on the face of the plaintiff's complaint. The artful pleading doctrine allows removal where federal law completely preempts a plaintiff's state-law claim. Although federal preemption is ordinarily a defense, once an area of state law has been completely pre-empted, any claim purportedly based on that preempted state-law claim is considered, from its inception, a federal claim, and therefore arises under federal law.

522 U.S. at 475, 118 S. Ct. 921 (internal citations, some quotation marks, and alteration omitted).

VI. International Complaints and Investigations

Promotion and Protection of All Human Rights, Civil, Political, Economic,
Social and Cultural Rights, Including the Right to Development,
Report of the Special Rapporteur on the Right to Food, Addendum
Olivier De Schutter

SUMMARY OF COMMUNICATIONS SENT AND REPLIES RECEIVED FROM GOVERNMENTS AND OTHER ACTORS, A/HRC/13/33/ADD.1, 26 FEBRUARY 2010

1. In the context of his mandate, the Special Rapporteur on the right to food receives a large number of communications alleging violations of the right to food and related rights worldwide.

Such communications are received from national, regional and international non-governmental organizations, as well as intergovernmental organizations and other United Nations procedures concerned with the protection of human rights. This addendum to the report of the Special Rapporteur contains, on a country-by-country basis, summaries of communications, including urgent appeals, allegation letters and follow-up relating to the Special Rapporteur's mandate for the period 5 December 2008 to 5 December 2009 and the responses received until 6 February 2010. The Special Rapporteur urges all Governments and other actors who have not yet done so to respond promptly to his communications and, in appropriate cases, to investigate allegations of the violation of the right to food and related rights and to take all steps necessary to redress the situation.

. . .

3. During the period under review, the Special Rapporteur sent a total of 18 communications concerning the right to food to 16 Member States as well as 13 communications to other actors including corporations. Where appropriate, the Special Rapporteur has sent joint urgent appeals or letters with one or more special procedures of the Human Rights Council where the allegations raised relate to the right to food as well as to rights addressed under other mandates.

3. Since the establishment of his mandate in 2000, the Special Rapporteur has worked continuously, together with the United Nations Office of the High Commissioner for Human Rights, to better publicize his mandate and raise awareness among civil society. It should be emphasized that the communications presented in this document in no way reflect the full extent of the serious obstacles that still remain in the realization of the right to food of all around the world.

. . .

III. SUMMARY OF COMMUNICATIONS SENT TO OTHER ACTORS AND REPLIES RECEIVED
ITM Angola

Follow-up communication

72. On 17 October 2008, the Special Rapporteur sent an allegation letter to ITM Angola, regarding the information received about the activities of ITM-Mining in the Republic of Angola which reportedly involved the confiscation of farmland by Sociedade Mineira do Cuango (in which ITM owns half the shares) in order to carry out diamond mining activities in Cafunfo village in Cuango municipality of Lunda Norte province. On 23 January 2009, the Special Rapporteur sent ITM Angola a follow-up letter reminding to provide him with the information requested in the above-mentioned communication.

Communications Received

73. On 9 February 2009, ITM Mining Limited sent a reply to the Special Rapporteur, explaining that it took note of the allegations made but that the company was not a principal shareholder of the Sociedade Mineira do Cuango, in contrary to what the allegations letter indicated. As all other shareholder, ITM was not in charge of the governing of the mining society, which has its own

managing council. ITM invited the Special Rapporteur to refer his concerns to the said managing council and to the Sociedade Mineira do Calonda.

Newmont Ghana Gold Limited

Communication Sent

74. On 1 July 2009, the Special Rapporteur together with the Independent Expert on the issue of human rights obligations related to access to safe drinking water and sanitation, the Special Rapporteur on adequate housing as a component of the right to an adequate standard of living, and on the right to non-discrimination in this context, the Special Rapporteur on the adverse effects of the movement and dumping of toxic and dangerous products and wastes on the enjoyment of human rights, the Special Rapporteur on the right of everyone to the enjoyment of the highest attainable standard of physical and mental health sent an allegations letter to the Newmont Ghana Gold Limited (NGGL) concerning the reports indicating potential negative impacts that the establishment by NGGL of an open pit gold mine in Akyem, more precisely within the Ajenua-Bepo Forest Reserve in the Birim North District of Ghana's Eastern Region may have on the enjoyment of economic, social and cultural rights of the affected communities.

75. The Special Rapporteurs shared the concerns that they had had raised with the Government of Ghana, which is included in the "Governments" section of this report, and drew the company's attention to the relevant provisions of international human rights law. In addition to comments on the accuracy of the allegations, the Special Rapporteurs informed NGGL about the relevant provisions of international human rights law and requested further information on whether any study on social, environmental and health impact of the open mine project had been realized by NGGL and the conclusions of the studies; on the measures taken by NGGL to ensure that the open mine project does not have disproportionate negative impacts on the environment and on the livelihoods of neighboring communities; on the measures been taken by NGGL to ensure that water resources would be protected from risks of leakages, and to ensure that mining wastes would be disposed of appropriately; if the concerned communities had been allowed to participate from the inception of the plans to construct the mine; if the land subject to expropriation had been duly evaluated; if any ongoing consultation was undertaken with the persons threatened with eviction; on the measures foreseen by NGGL in terms of compensation for the persons threatened with eviction; and on the measures taken by NGGL to ensure that the right to health of neighboring communities was respected.

Communication Received

76. On 8 September 2009, the Special Rapporteur received a reply from Newmont Mining Corporation (NMC). The company stressed its commitment to implement the best possible practices in the areas of social and environmental management and impact mitigation at the Akyem project. Accordingly, Newmont's Akyem project had been studied extensively by international and national environmental experts, members of the communities living in the area, and by agencies and departments of Ghana government, as well as the International Finance Corporation. In addition, Newmont project leaders had engaged with numerous community representatives, government agencies, nongovernmental organizations and international organizations on many occasions. NMC indicated that at three public hearings conducted by Ghana's Environmental Protection Agency (EPA), the Akyem communities had demonstrated overwhelming support for the project. More than 150 Ghanaian community leaders had since issued their own statements in support of the Akyem project. Moreover, the results of the discussions with the local communities had been presented in an environmental impact study that recently reviewed by the Environmental Protection Agency. The latter had granted Newmont an environmental permit to operate at Akyem. Finally, the letter informed that additional enquiry had been made with the Senior Regional Vice President fir Africa at the NMC.

Addax Petroleum Development; Chevron Nigeria Limited; Conoco Phillips; Hardy Oil Nigeria Limited; Mobil Producing Nigeria; Nexen Petroleum Nigeria Offshore; Philips Oil Co. (Nigeria) Limited; Shell Petroleum Development Company of Nigeria Limited; Statoil Hydro, Statoil Nigeria Ltd.; Texaco (Nigeria) Plc; Total E&P Nigeria Limited

Communication Sent

77. On 9 October 2009, the Special Rapporteur together with the Special Rapporteur on the right of everyone to the enjoyment of the highest attainable standard of physical and mental health, Independent Expert on the issue of human rights obligations related to access to safe drinking water and sanitation and the Special Rapporteur on the adverse effects of the movement and dumping of toxic and dangerous products and wastes on the enjoyment of human rights sent an allegation letter to the Addax Petroleum Development, Chevron Nigeria Limited, Conoco Phillips, Hardy Oil Nigeria Limited, Mobil Producing Nigeria, Nexen Petroleum Nigeria Offshore, Philips Oil Co. (Nigeria) Limited, Shell Petroleum Development Company of Nigeria Limited, StatoilHydro, Statoil Nigeria Ltd., Texaco (Nigeria) Plc, and Total E&P Nigeria Limited concerning possible negative impacts that the petroleum industry in the Niger Delta may have had and will likely continue to have on the full enjoyment of economic, social and cultural rights by the affected communities.

The Special Rapporteurs shared the concerns that they had had raised with the Government of Nigeria, which is included in the "Governments" section of this report, and drew the company's attention to the relevant provisions of international human rights law. They mentioned in particular Article 25 of the Universal Declaration of Human Rights, which recognizes that "everyone has the right of living adequate for the health and the well-being of himself and of his family, including food, clothing, housing and medical care and necessary social services." The Universal Declaration of Human Rights proclaims that every organ of society shall strive to promote respect for human rights and fundamental freedoms and to secure their universal and effective recognition and observance. Moreover, in resolution 8/7 (2008), the Human Rights Council affirmed that "transnational corporations and other business enterprises have a responsibility to respect human rights and assist in channelling the benefits of business towards contributing the enjoyment of human rights and fundamental freedoms." The Human Rights Council has also welcomed the policy framework for managing corporate related human rights issues presented by the Special Representative of the Secretary General of the United Nations on human rights and transnational corporate bodies and other business enterprises. The framework identifies differentiated, but complimentary responsibilities of governments and companies with regard to human rights. The framework confirms the State duty to protect against corporate-related human rights abuses but also confirms that the "baseline responsibility is to respect human rights." This responsibility, which applies to all internationally recognized human rights, exists independently of State duties and requires companies to exercise due diligence to become aware, prevent, address and mitigate negative human rights impacts. The due diligence required from the companies entails a responsibility to undertake human rights impact assessment, either in conjunction with or separately, based on recognized international human rights law.

Communications Received
Chevron Nigeria Limited

78. On 4 December 2009, the Special Rapporteur received a reply from Chevron Nigeria Limited (CNL) in which the company acknowledged that the companies can play positive role in contributing to the protection and promotion of human rights. To this end CNL worked actively to conduct its operations in a manner consistent with human rights principles applicable to business. This included recognizing and respecting the relevant ideals expressed in the Universal Declaration of Human Rights. In addition, CNL condemned human rights abuses. In the meantime

CNL pointed out that it was not in a position to comment on the incident concerning release of the crude oil into Bodo creek, as well as in the village of Kira Tai IN Ogoniland, as these incidents had not occur[r]ed in the CNL's area of operations and were not directly linked to company's production activities. CNL further informed the Special Rapporteurs on the actions which the company was taking when oil spills occured, as well as on the relevant regulations contained within Nigerian law. CNL described the process for Environmental, Social and Health Impact Assessments which it observed in its daily practices.

The objective of this process was to identify, assess and mitigate potential operational impacts on the environment and local communities in a formal and structured manner. In addition, CNL commented on its community engagement programs which are an integral part of company's commitment to human rights and which focus on improving access to basic needs supporting education and health care and promoting infrastructure developments and economic livelihoods. As an example of such community engagement it mentioned a community hospital that CNL had built in the Escravos area in order to provide comprehensive health care to the area. Finally, CNL indicated that since 2005 its approach towards community engagement has been based on the Global Memorandum of Understanding signed with communities and governments in 5 states where the company was operating in the Niger Delta.

Nigerian Agip Oil Company Limited

79. On 30 November 2009, the Special Rapporteur received a reply from the Nigerian Agip Oil Company Limited. The company informed the Special Rapporteur that the contents of the allegation letter were currently being reviewed and provided him with its assurances to submit a detailed response soon.

Shell Petroleum Development Company of Nigeria Limited

80. On 6 December 2009, the Special Rapporteur received a reply letter from Shell Petroleum Development Company of Nigeria Limited (SPDC) in which the company recognized its commitment to the principle of sustainable development and determination to always look to improve SPDC's performance in order to reduce environmental impact and footprint as far as possible and to maximize its social contribution. SPDC's operations in Niger Delta were heavily dependent on maintaining good relations with communities. The company found inaccurate the allegation that the petroleum industry, in particular SPDC was responsible for most oil spills, arguing that 85 per cent were the result of criminal activities. It said that SPDC was providing relief materials and carrying out clean up operations whenever spills occurred, and that both government and community representatives monitored these operations. As regards health concerns, SPDC then referred to a 1995 World Bank report that considered oil related pollution a low priority concern, and to an undated WHO report which considered poverty as the main cause of poor health. Waste disposal was said to be carried out by licensed service providers in accordance with regulatory guidelines. As for water discharges, SPDC was committed to gear its operations towards complying to the limits set by the Directorate of Petroleum Resources. As for heavy metals in soils and groundwater, SPDC carried out environmental evaluation reviews for its facilities in old "brown" fields. About impact assessment and community consultations, SPDC replied that for all new projects it conducted environmental social and health impact assessment in line with guidelines of the department of petroleum resources and the federal ministry of environmental. The impact assessment documents were public documents available to all stakeholders in the process, and they were available at local and federal government offices for consultation. SPDC felt that the impact assessment process ensured fair community participation and fair compensation – SPDC compensation rates were negotiated with communities. After oil spills, SPDC complied with all measures required by law, including compensation, relief and clean up operations. Studies on

long term impact had been carried out by UNICAL Consult, World Bank and WHO. For its part, SPDC strongly supported a study undertaken by the World Bank in collaboration with the government on gas flaring, as well as a UNEP-led environmental study on spills in Ogoniland. Finally, SPDC indicated its support to the voluntary guidelines on security and human rights, and to the principle of development, which extended in its case to health, education and microcredit, conflict resolution, and to infrastructure development such as water provision and electrification. SPEC worked alongside with NGOs, UNDP and the World Bank. It also contributed to development commitments through the taxes paid to the federal government.

Total E&P Nigeria Limited

81. On 9 December 2009, the Special Rapporteur received a reply from Total E&P Nigeria Limited (TEPNG) in which the company acknowledged that it was not in a position to provide a response or to comment on the specific allegations contained within the communication received from the Special Rapporteur since the alleged incidents are not related to the TOTAL Group operated activities in Nigeria, but that it wished to clarify its position with regards to the allegations of a general nature. Total and its subsidiaries in Nigeria were responsible operators with stringent environmental and community social responsibility guidelines which place highest importance on the respect for the environment, as well as social and economical development of the local communities. Moreover, spills of a technical nature only amounted to 16% of the incidents, while all others were the result of acts of sabotage. TEPNG's refuted the allegation that operations induced water discharges, it also denied that its operation may induce the presence of heavy metal in soils and groundwater. With regard to emergency water supplies in case of oil spills, this was not a case it had encountered as none of the spills it had suffered reached the extent to which it would be needed. In case of oil spills, TEPNG followed federal guidelines, by informing the department of petroleum resources, negotiating access to affected areas with communities, organising joint inspection visits, negotiating compensations except in cases of sabotage, carrying out repair works, and doing final inspections after the works were completed.

Total was also fully committed to the economic development of communities, and it entered in consultation with them for its operation, notable by signing memorandums of understandings. For all its new projects, it carried out environmental impact assessment as required by the regulations of the oil and gas industry. Total was committed to follow the requirements of these impact assessment processes, including regarding community participation. Finally, TEPNG noted that Total was conscious of its obligations as a good corporate citizen to its environment, its host communities and its host countries, It was also committed to carrying out sustainable development projects in such areas as health, infrastructure, education and capacity building of members and community groups. As it was committed to improving its actions, Total had made efforts to get an independent third party review on the way it implemented corporate social responsibility programmes, of the types of relationships maintained with communities and of necessary improvements.

Promotion and Protection of All Human Rights, Civil, Political, Economic, Social and Cultural Rights, Including the Right to Development, Report of the Special Rapporteur on Adequate Housing as a Component of the right to an Adequate Standard of Living, and on the Right to Non-Discrimination in This Context, Raquel Rolnik, U.N. Doc. A/HRC/13/20/Add.1, at 51–52 (Feb. 22, 2010)

Newman Ghana Gold Limited

Communication Sent

100. On 1 July 2009, the Special Rapporteur together with the Independent Expert on the issue of human rights obligations related to access to safe drinking water and sanitation, the Special

Rapporteur on the adverse effects of the movement and dumping of toxic and dangerous products and wastes on the enjoyment on human rights, the Special Rapporteur on the right of everyone to the enjoyment of the highest attainable standard of physical and mental health and the Special Rapporteur on the right to food sent an allegation letter to Newmont Ghana Gold Limited (NGGL) concerning reports received indicating potential negative impacts that the establishment by Newmont Ghana Gold Limited (NGGL) of an open pit gold mine in Akyem, more precisely within the Ajenua-Bepo Forest Reserve in the Birim North District of Ghana's Eastern Region may have on the enjoyment of economic, social and cultural rights of the affected communities. The Special Rapporteurs shared the concerns that they had had raised with the Government of Ghana, which and drew the company's attention to the relevant provisions of international human rights law. In addition to comments on the accuracy of the allegations, they Special Rapporteurs requested further information on whether any study on social, environmental and health impact of the open mine project had been realized by NGGL and the conclusions of the studies; on the measures taken by NGGL to ensure that the open mine project does not have disproportionate negative impacts on the environment and on the livelihoods of neighboring communities; on the measures been taken by NGGL to ensure that water resources would be protected from risks of leakages, and to ensure that mining wastes would be disposed of appropriately; if the concerned communities had been allowed to participate from the inception of the plans to construct the mine; if the land subject to expropriation had been duly evaluated; if any ongoing consultation was undertaken with the persons threatened with eviction; on the measures foreseen by NGGL in terms of compensation for the persons threatened with eviction; and on the measures taken by NGGL to ensure that the right to health of neighboring communities was respected.

Response Received

101. On 1 July 2009, Newmont Ghana Gold Limited (NGGL) replied to the allegation letter sent on 1 July 2009. NGGL informed their [committment] to implement the best possible practices in the areas of Social and Environmental management and impact mitigation at the Akyem project. Newmont's Akyem project has been studied extensively by international and national environmental experts, members of the communities living in the area, and by Ghana's government, as well as the International Finance Corporation (IFC). It has been the subject of a thorough environmental impact study, public consultation processes, an independent review process, and an overall regulatory review. Newmont project leaders have engaged with numerous community representatives, government agencies, nongovernmental organizations and international organizations on many occasions. 600 meetings and events between 2004 and early 2009 were held with different local and regional stakeholders. The Akyem communities demonstrated overwhelming support for the project at three public hearings. In addition, more than 150 Ghanaian community leaders issued statements in support of the Akyem project. Concerns raised by NGOs during the EIS process were discussed with local communities and the results presented in an environmental impact study that was reviewed by the Ghana EPA. The analyses of the company were also reportedly reviewed by national and international environmental experts. The Ghana EPA was granted Newmont an environmental permit to operate at Akyem

Questions and Discussion

1. As the preceding extract indicates, several U.N. special rapporteurs communicate directly with corporations when they receive communications alleging that corporate conduct is affecting the enjoyment of rights within the rapporteurs' mandates. Is there an advantage to having this direct contact instead of or in addition to raising the issue with the relevant government?

2. Does the rapporteur on the right to food give a legal basis for his attention to corporate accountability? Does he need to?

3. Does the practice of the U.N. special rapporteurs lend weight to arguments for or against the international legal personality of corporations?

4. Do human rights tribunals have any jurisdiction with respect to business enterprises that have a negative impact on the enjoyment of human rights?

Index

For EU product safety concerns, contact us at Calle de José Abascal, 56–1°,
28003 Madrid, Spain or eugpsr@cambridge.org.

www.ingramcontent.com/pod-product-compliance
Ingram Content Group UK Ltd.
Pitfield, Milton Keynes, MK11 3LW, UK
UKHW030658060825
461487UK00010B/930